Higher Learning. Forward Thinking.™  **McGraw-Hill Ryerson**

ning Centre

For the Student

Online Quizzes

Do you understand the material? You'll know after taking an Online Quiz! Try the Multiple Choice and True/False questions for each chapter. They're auto-graded with feedback and the option to send results directly to faculty.

Web Links

This section references various Web sites, including all company Web sites linked from the text.

E-Commerce

Explore the world of E-Commerce using our E-Commerce Modules and chapter-specific E-Learning sessions.

Microsoft® PowerPoint® Presentations

View and download presentations created for each text. Great for pre-class preparation and post-class review.

Internet Application Questions

Go online to learn how companies use the Internet in their day-to-day activities. Answer questions based on current organization Web sites and strategies.

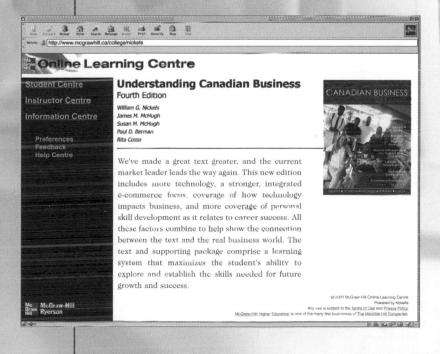

http://www.mcgrawhill.ca/college/nickels

Online Learning Centre

Student Centre
Instructor Centre
Information Centre

Preferences
Feedback
Help Centre

Understanding Canadian Business
Fourth Edition

William G. Nickels
James M. McHugh
Susan M. McHugh
Paul D. Berman
Rita Cossa

We've made a great text greater, and the current market leader leads the way again. This new edition includes more technology, a stronger, integrated e-commerce focus, coverage of how technology impacts business, and more coverage of personal skill development as it relates to career success. All these factors combine to help show the connection between the text and the real business world. The text and supporting package comprise a learning system that maximizes the student's ability to explore and establish the skills needed for future growth and success.

McGraw-Hill Ryerson

© 2001 McGraw-Hill Online Learning Centre
Powered by Novella
Any use is subject to the Terms of Use and Privacy Policy.
McGraw-Hill Higher Education is one of the many fine businesses of The McGraw-Hill Companies.

Your Internet companion to the most exciting educational tools on the Web!

The Online Learning Centre can be found at:

www.mcgrawhill.ca/college/nickels

EDITION 4

UNDERSTANDING CANADIAN BUSINESS

WILLIAM G. NICKELS

University of Maryland

JAMES M. McHUGH

St. Louis Community College at Forest Park

SUSAN M. McHUGH

Applied Learning Systems

PAUL D. BERMAN

Retired Chartered Accountant and Professor of Business

RITA COSSA

McMaster University

McGraw-Hill Ryerson

Toronto Montréal New York Burr Ridge Bangkok Bogatá Caracas Lisbon London Madrid
Mexico City Milan New Delhi Seoul Singapore Sydney Taipei

Dedication

To my thousands of students of varying cultures, ages, interests, and abilities— who taught me so much.

And to all other students who, I hope, will find this text useful in their studies and when thinking about their future careers.

    Paul D. Berman

With love and admiration to my parents Pietro and Rosa Cossa—my first business teachers.

    Rita Cossa

McGraw-Hill
Ryerson Limited

A Subsidiary of The **McGraw·Hill** *Companies*

Understanding Canadian Business,
Fourth Edition

Statistics Canada information is used with the permission of the Minister of Industry, as Minister responsible for Statistics Canada. Information on the availability of the wide range of data from Statistics Canada can be obtained from Statistics Canada's Regional Offices, its World Wide Web site at http://www.stat.can.ca, and its toll-free access number 1-800-263-1136.

ISBN: 0-07-089434-5

2 3 4 5 6 7 8 9 10 TCP 0 9 8 7 6 5 4 3

Printed and bound in Canada

Care has been taken to trace ownership of copyright material contained in this text; however, the publisher will welcome any information that enables them to rectify any reference or credit for subsequent editions.

Vice President and Editorial Director: Pat Ferrier
Sponsoring Editor: Lenore Gray Spence
Managing Editor, Development: Kim Brewster
Director of Marketing: Jeff MacLean
Supervising Editor: Anne Macdonald
Copy Editor: Kelli Howey
Production Coordinator: Paula Brown

Photos and Permissions: Alison Derry, Permissions Plus
Composition: Karen Wolfe/Ruth Nicholson/ArtPlus Ltd.
Cover Design: Sharon Lucas
Cover Image Credits: Stephen Simpson/FPG— Canada Inc.
Printer: Transcontinental Printing

Photo Source p. 362: The HP information, logo, and copyrighted information contained within this textbook is reproduced with the permission of Hewlett-Packard (Canada) Ltd. Hewlett-Packard expressly reserves its copyright interest in all Hewlett-Packard reproduced material in this textbook and is not to be reproduced without the expressed written consent of Hewlett-Packard (Canada) Ltd.

National Library of Canada Cataloguing in Publication Data

Main entry under title:
    Understanding Canadian Business
4th ed.
Includes bibliographical references and index.
ISBN 0-07-089434-5

1. Business. 2. Canada—Commerce. I. Nickels, William G.

HD31.U5135 2002   650   C2001-904210-8

BILL NICKELS is an associate professor of business at The University of Maryland, College Park. With over 30 years of teaching experience, he teaches introduction to business in large sections (250 students) every semester. He teaches smaller sections in the summer. He also teaches the marketing principles course to large sections (500 students). Bill has won the Outstanding Teacher on Campus Award four times. He received his M.B.A. degree from Western Reserve University and his Ph.D. from The Ohio State University. He has written a marketing communications text and two marketing principles texts in addition to many articles in business publications. He believes in living a balanced life and wrote a book called *Win the Happiness Game* to share his secrets with others. Bill gives marketing and general business lectures to a variety of business and nonprofit organizations. Bill and his wife, Marsha, proudly anticipate the impending graduation of their son, Joel, who will become the third Dr. Nickels in the family.

JIM McHUGH is an associate professor of business at St. Louis Community College/Forest Park. He holds an M.B.A. degree from Lindenwood University and has broad experience in education, business, and government. In addition to teaching several sections of introduction to business each semester for 20 years, Jim maintains an adjunct professorship at Lindenwood University, teaching in the marketing and management areas at both the undergraduate and graduate levels. Jim has conducted numerous seminars in business, and maintains several consulting positions with small and large business enterprises. He is also actively involved in the public service sector.

SUSAN McHUGH is a learning specialist with extensive training and experience in adult learning and curriculum development. She holds a M.Ed. degree from the University of Missouri and has completed her course work for a Ph.D. in education administration with a specialty in adult learning theory. As a professional curriculum developer, she has directed numerous curriculum projects and educator training programs. She has worked in the public and private sector as a consultant in training and employee development. While Jim and Susan treasure their participation in the *UB* project, their greatest accomplishment is their collaboration on their three children, Casey, Molly, and Michael, who have all grown up regarding *UB* as a fourth sibling. Casey was a fervent user of the 4th edition, Molly eagerly anticipates using this edition, and Michael will have to wait for the next edition.

PAUL D. BERMAN founded a firm of chartered accountants and was actively engaged in the fields of management consulting, auditing, and taxation for 35 years. These activities involved considerable time overseas. He then went on to John Abbott College near Montreal, where he taught a variety of business courses for more than two decades. After a decade of teaching International Business Policy at McGill University, Paul retired in 1999.

Paul's academic work has also taken him overseas. He has taken students to Denmark and the former East Germany to study these countries' education systems and how they do business. In the late 1980s Paul spent considerable time in China, under a CIDA program, teaching, lecturing, and doing management consulting. This led to a special award from China's highest economic body, the State Economic Commission. Paul has also spent time in Japan, where he engaged in a joint research project with Japanese colleagues, and he has conducted seminars in several countries. Paul has also written a book on small business and entrepreneurship.

RITA COSSA joins this edition as a new co-author. Rita has been teaching at McMaster University since 1999. Currently she teaches both the Introduction to Business and the Introduction to Marketing courses to the Commerce and Engineering Management students. Other courses that she has taught have included M.B.A.-level Marketing and Marketing in the Non-Profit Sector. Upon graduating with an Honours Bachelor of Business Administration degree from Wilfrid Laurier University, Rita began her career working in the banking industry. During these years, Rita obtained her Certified Investment Manager designation and went on to complete her M.B.A., with a Marketing focus. Rita has co-authored a marketing test bank and, more recently, a marketing textbook study guide.

CHAPTER 11:

Using Technology to Manage Information   322

PART 4:

Management of Human Resources: Motivating Employees

CHAPTER 12:

Motivating Employees and Building Self-Managed Teams   352

CHAPTER 13:

Human Resource Management: Managing the Most Important Asset—People   386

CHAPTER 14:

Dealing with Employee–Management Issues and Relations   424

PART 5:

Marketing: Developing and Implementing Customer-Oriented Marketing Plans

CHAPTER 15:

Marketing: Building Customer and Stakeholder Relationships   450

PART 6:
Accounting Information and Financial Activities

CHAPTER 18:
Accounting Fundamentals   562

CHAPTER 19:
Managing Financial Resources 594

In the twenty-first century, we are witnessing a high degree of doubt and uncertainty, as well as many difficult problems, in Canada and around the world. A new and complex world is slowly and painfully taking shape. Change dominates the global economic environment. Rapid and significant political and technological developments are changing the nature of how we live, prepare for careers, and do business with each other. New challenges present new opportunities.

Understanding Canadian Business has been designed to help students understand and cope with the sometimes bewildering array of information they face in learning about business. It also provides insight into career choices and opportunities, as well as a look at the ethical dilemmas businesses and managers face.

This book marks the fourth Canadian edition of one of the most popular introductory business texts in Canada and the United States, where it is in its sixth edition. Hundreds of colleges and universities in both countries have adopted this text. *Understanding Canadian Business* is a complete revision with substantial changes in every chapter to properly reflect the Canadian scene. Most of the examples cited are Canadian companies or transnational companies operating in Canada. The number of chapters, 19, was decided on after careful thought and discussion. This number takes into consideration the limitations of the 13- to 15-week semester or term (commonly found in Canada) and student capacity to absorb information.

Below are a few of the changes and improvements made in response to the recommendations from some dedicated educators (who themselves have now become part of the overall development team).

New Getting Ready For Prime Time

Focus groups communicated that many students do not have the skills they need to succeed in school. The new *Getting Ready for Prime Time* mini-booklet at the front of this text is a fresh and friendly summary of the skills it takes to be a success in school and in business. Coverage includes a unique and popular business etiquette discussion, study skills and time management guidance, a primer to surfing the Internet, and advice about how to get a rewarding job that will lead to a successful career. *Getting Ready for Prime Time* combines the third edition's "Getting the Job You Want" appendix and "Secrets to Your Success" prologue with "Driver's Ed for the Information Superhighway" (from the Study Guide) in one engaging resource.

The Latest in Technology and E-Commerce

Everyone agrees that we are in an era of rapid and constant change. Perhaps the fastest changing and most dynamic element of business today is the use of the Internet. Many new e-businesses have already come and gone, but even in failure they have left in their wake a new way of doing business: clicks and bricks. That is, companies have learned to reach consumers using their traditional stores and the Internet as well. Although the whole business-to-business market is in a state of flux, use of the Internet as a dynamic new business tool has resulted in the rethinking and restructuring of traditional business relationships, redesign of supply chains, and many other new ways of conducting and facilitating customer interaction. We cover them all in this edition.

Reviewers and focus groups communicated that these changes are so important and pervasive that they should be woven into each chapter rather than segregated in a single chapter. In this way, students can see how these new developments are impacting every aspect of business. Therefore, many chapters contain sections that describe e-commerce related issues.

Every chapter also has Taking It to the Net exercises that get students involved in using the Internet to find information and to make decisions.

Beyond integrating technology and use of the Internet in all chapters, we devote all of Chapter 11 to the latest in information technology. In addition, we provide in-depth coverage of how the new economy affects areas such as human resource management, marketing, production, finance, and so on, including problems with privacy and security.

KEEPING UP WITH WHAT'S NEW

Users of *Understanding Canadian Business* have always appreciated the currency of the material and the large number of examples from companies of all sizes and industries (e.g., service, manufacturing, profit, and nonprofit) in Canada and around the world. This edition features the latest developments and practices in business including:

- The rise, and sometimes fall, of B2C and B2B firms
- E-commerce's impact on the role of intermediaries
- E-tailing
- Customer relationship management (CRM)
- Application service providers (ASPS)
- Internet 2
- Knowledge management
- Broadband technology
- Virtual private networks
- Online banking
- Some business impacts as a result of the September 11, 2001 terrorist attacks

KEEPING IN TOUCH VIA THE WEB

We offer several ways to use the Web to gather and use information:

The popular and robust *Understanding Canadian Business* Online Learning Centre is back (www.mcgrawhill.ca/college/nickels)! This interactive site includes such features as links to professional resources and other exciting instructor support tools as well as Web-based projects. All information on the Online Learning Centre is available formatted for use with such standard course management systems as WebCT and Blackboard.

NEW! e-Learning Sessions The e-Learning Sessions put the course content in context for students with a self-quizzing function, a multilingual glossary, Internet exercises, concept checks, and sample PowerPoint slides to help students master the course content in an engaging fashion. These resources are organized into chapter-specific outlines to help students review the material more effectively. Students will have access to the NEW e-Learning Sessions from our Web site www.mcgrawhill.ca/college/nickels.

INTEGRATION OF IMPORTANT CONCEPTS THROUGHOUT TEXT

Based on our research and the preferences expressed by both users and nonusers of our text, we have incorporated the following *key* topics as themes throughout the text:

- E-commerce
- Small business and entrepreneurship
- Global business
- Technology and constant change
- Pleasing customers
- Ethics and social responsibility
- Teams
- Quality
- Cultural diversity

These themes reflect a strong consensus among introduction to business instructors that certain topics deserve and need special emphasis. Among these, they encouraged us to add particular focus in the areas of small business/entrepreneurship, international business, and e-commerce (the positive as well as the negative). In response, we have added even more small business, international, and Internet examples throughout. And we continue to feature boxes titled "Spotlight on Small Business," "Spotlight on Big Business," "Ethical Dilemma," and "Reaching Beyond Our Borders" in every chapter.

Our emphasis on entrepreneurship is maintained with an Entrepreneurship Readiness Questionnaire and a whole chapter on entrepreneurship and the challenge of starting a business. We are confident that no other introduction to business text offers as much coverage of small business and entrepreneurship as does *Understanding Canadian Business*, and since the great majority of students taking this course currently work or will work in small companies, reviewers agree that this emphasis is well placed.

PEDAGOGICAL FEATURES

Here are the major pedagogical devices used in the text:

Learning Goals Tied directly to the summaries and questions at the end of the chapter, these learning goals help students preview what they are supposed to know after reading the chapter, and then test that knowledge by answering the questions in the summary. The study guide is also closely linked to the learning goals as part of the total integrated teaching, learning, and testing system.

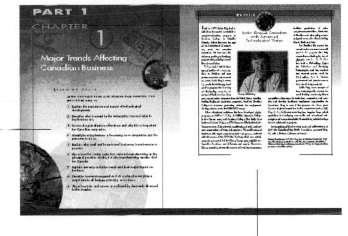

Getting to Know Business Professionals Each chapter begins with a profile of a person and a business that illustrates an important point covered in the chapter. Not all the personalities are famous but they do provide a transition between chapters and a good introduction to the text material.

Progress Checks Throughout the chapters there are progress checks that ask students to assess their understanding of what they have just read. If students are not understanding and retaining the material, the Progress Check will stop them and show them that they need to review before proceeding. We have all experienced times when we were studying and our minds wandered. Progress Check is a great tool to prevent that from happening for more than a few pages.

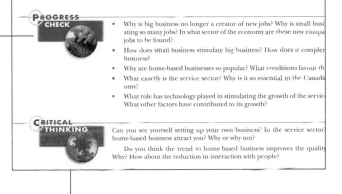

Critical Thinking Questions These unique questions, found throughout each chapter, ask students to pause and think about how the material they are reading applies to their own lives. This device is an excellent tool for linking the text material to the student's past experience to enhance retention. It greatly increases student involvement in the text and the course.

Informative Boxes Each chapter includes boxed inserts that apply the chapter concepts to particular themes, which can include small business, big business, ethical dilemmas, and global business. Although examples of such topics are integrated throughout the text, these boxes highlight the application in a particular chapter.

Cross-Reference System This system, unique to this text, refers students back to the primary discussion and examples of key concepts. A specific page reference appears when a key concept occurs in a chapter subsequent to its original discussion. This feature allows students to quickly

Modern Capitalism

The nineteenth century saw the emergence of the modern industrial-capitalist system. The economic philosophy that underpinned it was first elaborated upon by Adam Smith, whom we met in Chapter 2 ➤P. 37◄. Smith's book *The Wealth of Nations*, published in 1776, gave birth to the concept of **laissez-faire capitalism**. This theory emphasized that, if left alone and unhindered by government, the free market, in pursuit of economic efficiency, would provide an abundance of goods at the lowest prices, improving everyone's life. The workings of this "invisible hand" would reward capitalists for their work and financial risks, thus providing jobs for the population and plentiful goods to satisfy human needs and improve living standards.

laissez-faire capitalism
The theory that, if left alone and unhindered by government, the free market, in pursuit of economic efficiency, would provide an abundance of goods at the lowest prices, improving everyone's life.

review or study that concept (if necessary) in context in order to improve their comprehension of the material. It also eliminates the need to continuously revisit and restate key concepts, thus reducing overall text length.

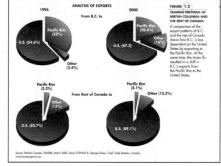

Photo and Illustration Essays We believe that every photo in this edition is pedagogically relevant and we have attempted to treat the illustrative content with as much care as the narrative. As more and more students tell us in our research and classes that they are visually oriented learners, this increased emphasis on the pedagogical value of the illustration program is essential. Each photo and illustration in the text is accompanied by a short paragraph that shows the relevance of the visual to the material in the text. The accompanying descriptions help the student understand what is being shown in the graphic and how it applies to concepts presented in the narrative.

Interactive Summaries The end-of-chapter summaries are directly tied with the learning goals and are written in a unique question and answer format. Answering the questions and getting immediate feedback helps prepare students for quizzes and exams. Students are extremely positive about this format.

Developing Workplace Skills The Developing Workplace Skills section has activities designed to increase student involvement in the learning process. Some of these miniprojects require library or Internet searches, but many of them involve talking with people to obtain their reactions and advice on certain subjects. Students then come to class better prepared to discuss the topics at hand. These assignments can be divided among groups of students so they can learn a great deal from outside sources and about teamwork without any one student having to do too much work.

Taking It to the Net Exercises Optional exercises at the end of every chapter allow students to research topics and issues on the Web.

Practising Management Decisions Each chapter concludes with two short cases to allow students to practise managerial decision-making. They are intentionally brief and meant to be discussion starters rather than take up the entire class period. The answers to the cases are in the instructor's manual. Again these examples of real world problem solving will help students achieve workplace skills.

Video Cases New video cases from the CBC and other sources are provided throughout this edition. These are placed at the end of the chapter and are optional as assignments. They feature companies, processes, practices, and managers that highlight and bring to life the key concepts, and especially the themes of the fourth edition. These videos are provided to Instructors on VHS tapes for classroom viewing, and are also available through password-protected video streaming on our Online Learning Centre (www.mcgrawhill.ca/college/nickels).

SUPPLEMENTS: AN INTEGRATED TEACHING AND TESTING SYSTEM

The following instructor supplements are available on the Instructor's CD-ROM and can also be downloaded from the Online Learning Centre (www.mcgrawhill.ca/college/nickels):

Instructor's Presentation CD-ROM The Computerized Test Bank, the Instructor's Manual, the PowerPoint Presentations, lecture outlines, and more are compiled in electronic format on a CD for your convenience in customizing multimedia lectures.

Instructor's Manual All material in the Instructor's Manual is easy to use and has been widely praised by new instructors, adjunct instructors, and experienced educators alike. Many instructors tell us that the IM is a valuable time-saver. The Instructor's Manual is unique in its thorough integration with both the text and package.

After a short topic outline of the chapter and listing of the learning goals and key terms, you will find a resource checklist with all of the supplements that correspond to each chapter. Consequently, there is no need to flip through half a dozen sources to find which supplementary materials are available for each chapter.

To make the system even easier to use, the detailed lecture outline contains marginal notes recommending where to use supplementary cases, lecture enhancers, and critical thinking exercises.

Computerized Test Bank Available on the Instructor's CD-ROM, the Test Bank comes in a computerized Brownstone version. This enhanced test-generation software allows users to add and edit questions; save and reload multiple test versions; select questions based on type, difficulty, or key word; and utilize password protection. It supports over 250 printers; links graphics, tables, and text to a series of questions; supports numerous graphics including special characters, complex equations, subscripts, superscripts, bolds, underlines, and italics; and can run on a network.

We have provided questions that measure recall and require students to apply the material to real-world situations. A rationale for the correct answer and the corresponding text page add to the uniqueness of our Computerized Test Bank. The Test Bank is designed to test three levels of learning:

1. Knowledge of key terms.
2. Understanding of concepts and principles.
3. Application of principles.

PowerPoint Presentations Available on the Instructor's CD-ROM and download-able from the Online Learning Centre are electronic "slides" that are keyed to the text. These slide shows include many of the figures and tables from the textbook as well as many additional slides that support and expand the text discussion. These slides can be modified with PowerPoint.

Videos for All Chapters A complementary video is available in VHS format to accompany the text. Most segments are 8 to 15 minutes in length and are suitable for classroom, home, or lab viewing. These video segments, selected from the CBC and other sources, are also available on the Online Learning Centre for viewing through password-protected video streaming. Detailed teaching notes are available in the Instructor's Manual and on the Instructor area of the Online Learning Centre.

Online Learning Centre www.mcgrawhill.ca/college/nickels The Online Learning Centre is an interactive site that includes such features as links to professional resources and other exciting instructor support tools.

Media Resource Guide Puzzled about incorporating media in the classroom? Let this guide be your answer by providing helpful instruction on how to use all media components. This supplement is available for downloading from the Instructor area of the Online Learning Centre.

Study Guide The Study Guide contains various forms of open-ended questions that require the student to write out his or her personal summary of the material. The guide gives students the opportunity not only to prepare for tests, but also to develop and practise their business knowledge and skills. The following materials are provided for every chapter: learning goals, key terms and definitions, retention questions, chapter check, and a practice test.

PageOut With PageOut even the most inexperienced computer user can quickly and easily create a professional-looking course Web site. Simply fill in our templates with your information and with the excellent content provided by McGraw-Hill Ryerson, choose a design, and you've got a bang-up Web site specifically designed for your course! Best of all, it's FREE! Visit www.pageout.net to find out more.

WebCT and Blackboard This textbook has course content available in two popular course management delivery platforms, WebCT and Blackboard.

ACKNOWLEDGEMENTS

Many friends, colleagues, academics, entrepreneurs, and managers have made important contributions, in different ways, to *Understanding Canadian Business*. There are too many to be able to thank them all individually. We would like to single out the reviewers from across the country who on several occasions took the time to review different versions of the manuscript for the fourth edition and made invaluable suggestions to improve its quality and coverage. We would like to extend our deepest thanks to all of these people, whose names are listed below:

Laura Allen, Wilfrid Laurier University

Doug Beatty, Lambton College

Chris Gadsby, British Columbia Institute of Technology

Hugh Gunz, University of Toronto

Keith Hebblewhite, Humber College

Chuck Lamantia, Centennial College

Will Thurber, Brock University

Rosemary Venne, University of Saskatchewan

David Wicks, St. Mary's University

We would like to give special thanks to the two executives, Mr. Normand Bédard and Mr. Dennis Reilley, who took time out of their busy schedules to peruse the Ethical Dilemmas posed at the beginning of each chapter and to come up with suggested responses. Their many years of practical experience in the real world of Canadian business, which lend important weight to their opinions, will be greatly appreciated by students.

Many thanks are also due to the following McGraw-Hill Ryerson staff who worked hard to make this book a reality: Pat Ferrier, Vice-President and Editorial Director; Lenore Gray Spence, Sponsoring Editor; Kim Brewster, Managing Editor, Development; Jeff MacLean, Director of Marketing; Anne Macdonald, Supervising Editor; Kelli Howey, Copy Editor; Alison Derry/Permissions Plus, Photos and Permissions; Dianna Little and Sharon Lucas, Designers; and Paula Brown, Production Coordinator.

Paul would like to "extend many thanks to my children, Victor, David, Joanne, Judith, and Rae. I owe them a great deal for their patience and co-operation as I plied them with questions and requests relating to their various fields of expertise. I would also like to thank my three grandsons — Eric, Jamie, and Michel — for their help in giving me incisive comments on the current thinking of undergraduate and graduate students as well as young entrepreneurs. Finally, I would like to express my deep appreciation to my wife, Esther Berman, whose patience, direct and indirect assistance in so many ways, and critical comments over an extended period of time really made this book possible."

Rita would like to "extend my deepest appreciation to my husband, Stephen Solenka, for his constant support during this process. His knowledge and experience was a great source of information and it contributed to some of the many updates and changes in this new edition."

PAUL D. BERMAN
RITA COSSA

PROLOGUE

Getting Ready for Prime Time

TOP 10 REASONS TO READ THIS INTRODUCTION

(EVEN IF IT ISN'T ASSIGNED)

10 You don't want the only time you get a raise to be when the government increases the minimum wage.

9 You already bought the book, so you might as well get your money's worth.

8 You can learn what professional behaviour is all about so you don't suddenly find yourself in a section of the classroom all alone.

7 You need to know that "Point and Click" is not a new music group.

6 You need to know that a time management course is not a class on clock repair.

5 Not many job-producing résumés and interviews start with "Like, you know, this is, like, what I want to, like, do you know."

4 Getting off to a good start in the course can improve your chances of getting a higher grade.

3 It must be important because the authors spent so much time writing it.

2 You want to run with the big dogs someday.

And the number-one reason for reading this introductory section is . . .

1 It could be on a test.

LEARNING THE SKILLS NEEDED TO SUCCEED TODAY AND TOMORROW

Your life is full. You're starting a new semester and you're feeling pulled in many directions. Why take time to read this introductory section? We lightheartedly offer our top 10 reasons to read it on page GR-1, but the real importance of this section to your success is no joking matter. The purpose of this introduction and of the entire text is to help you learn principles, strategies, and skills for success that will help you not only in this course but also in your career and entire life. Whether or not you learn these skills is up to you. Learning them won't guarantee success, but not learning them—well, you get the picture.

We hope you invest the time to read the entire Getting Ready for Prime Time section. However, we realize that some parts of the material may be more relevant to your individual needs than others. To help you focus on the most important information for your needs, we've divided the material into three major categories:

1. **Succeeding in This Course**—an overview of the skills you'll need to succeed in this course and throughout school as well as the skills needed to succeed in your career after you complete your program. READ THIS SECTION BEFORE YOUR FIRST CLASS and make a great first impression!

2. **Surfing the Internet**—a quick and easy overview of how to surf the Internet.

3. **Getting the Job You Want**—guidelines to finding and getting the job you want with emphasis on job search, résumé writing, and interviewing skills.

This is an exciting and challenging time. Never before have there been more opportunities to become successful. And never before have there been more challenges. Success in any venture comes from understanding basic principles and having the skills to apply those principles effectively. What you learn now could help you be a success—for the rest of your life.

Begin applying these skills now to gain an edge on the competition. Good luck. We wish you the best.

SUCCEEDING IN THIS COURSE

Since you've signed up for this course, we're guessing you already know the value of post-secondary education. But just to give you some numerical backup, you should know that the gap between the earnings of high school graduates and post-secondary graduates, which is growing every year, now ranges from 60 to 70 percent. The holders of bachelor's degrees will make an average of $40,478 per year as opposed to just $22,895 for high school graduates.[1] That's an additional $17,583 a year! Thus, what you invest in a college or university education is likely to pay you back many times. That doesn't mean there aren't good careers available to non–college graduates. It just means that those with an education are more likely to have higher earnings over their lifetime.

The value of a higher education is more than just a larger paycheque. Other benefits include increasing your ability to think critically and communicate your ideas to others, improving your ability to use technology, and preparing yourself to live in a diverse world. Knowing you've met your goals and completed your program also gives you the self-confidence to continue to strive to meet your future goals.

Experts say it is likely that today's graduates will hold seven or eight different jobs (often in several different careers) in their lifetime. There are many returning students today who are changing their careers and their plans for life. You too may want to change careers some day. Often that is the path to long-term happiness and success. That means you will have to be flexible and adjust your strengths and talents to new opportunities. Many of the best jobs of the future don't even exist today. Learning has become a lifelong job. You will have to constantly update your skills if you want to become and remain competitive.

If you're typical of many students, you may not have any idea what career you'd like to pursue. That isn't necessarily a big disadvantage in today's fast-changing job market. There are no perfect or certain ways to prepare for the most interesting and challenging jobs of tomorrow. Rather, you should continue your education, develop strong computer skills, improve your verbal and written communication skills, and remain flexible while you explore the job market.

USING THIS COURSE TO PREPARE FOR YOUR CAREER

One of the objectives of this class is to help you choose an area in which you might enjoy working and in which you might succeed. This book and this course together may be one of your most important learning experiences ever. They're meant to help you understand business so that you can use business principles throughout your life. You'll learn about production, marketing, finance, accounting, management, economics, and more. At the end of the course, you should have a much better idea about what careers would be best for you and what careers you would *not* enjoy.

But you don't have to be in business to use business principles. You can use marketing principles to get a job and to sell your ideas to others. You can use your knowledge of investments to make money in the stock market. Similarly, you'll be able to use management skills and general business knowledge wherever you go and in whatever career you pursue—including government agencies, charities, and social causes.

ASSESSING YOUR SKILLS AND PERSONALITY

The earlier you can do a personal assessment of your interests, skills, and values, the better it will be for you in finding some career direction. In recognition of this need, many schools offer self-assessment programs. Many schools use a software exercise called the System for Interactive Guidance and Information (SIGI). A different version, called DISCOVER, is used at many other schools. Both SIGI and DISCOVER feature self-assessment exercises, create personalized lists of occupations based on your interests and skills, and provide information about different careers and the preparation each requires. Visit your school's placement centre, career lab, or library and learn what programs are available for you.

It would be helpful to use one or more self-assessment programs early in this course so you can determine, while you're learning about the different business fields, which ones most closely fit your interests and skills. Self-assessment will help you determine the kind of work environment you'd prefer (e.g., technical, social service, or business); what values you seek to fulfill in a career (e.g., security, variety, or independence); what abilities you have (e.g., creative/artistic, numerical, or sales); and what important job characteristics you stress most (e.g., income, travel, or amount of job pressure).

Armed with the results of your self-assessment, you are more likely to make a career choice that will be personally fulfilling.

Those with post-secondary education make 60 to 70 percent more money in their lifetimes than high school graduates. College or university not only prepares you for the jobs of the future, it also gives you the chance to network with other graduates who may help you find jobs in the future. What can you do while in school to optimize the networking benefits it provides?

LEARNING PROFESSIONAL BUSINESS STRATEGIES

Business professionals have learned the importance of networking and of keeping files on subjects that are important to them. These are two secrets to success that students should begin practising now. One thing that links students is the need to retain what they learn. You need a strategy to help you meet this need. It's also extremely important to keep the names of contact people at various organizations. In addition, you may want to keep facts and figures of all kinds about the economy and business-related subjects. These are all reasons why you should develop resource files.

An effective way to become an expert on almost any business subject is to set up your own information system. Eventually you may want to store data on computer disks for retrieval on your personal computer and to access professional databases as business people do. Meanwhile, it's effective to establish a comprehensive filing system on paper.

If you start now, you'll soon have at your fingertips information that will prove invaluable for use in term papers and throughout your career. Few students do this filing; those who don't lose much of the information they read in school or thereafter. *Developing this habit is one of the most effective ways of educating yourself and having the information available when you need it.* The only space you'll need to start is a small corner of your room to hold a portable file box. The box should hold hanging folders in which you can place a number of tabbed file folders. To start filling these files you might put your course notes in them, with the names of your professors and the books you used. You may need this information later for employment references. Also, be sure to keep all the notes you make when talking with people about careers, including salary information, courses needed, and contacts.

Each time you read a story about a firm that interests you, either cut it out of the publication or photocopy it and then place it in an appropriate file. You might begin with files labelled Careers, Small Business, Economics, Management, and Resource People. You might summarize the article on a Post-it note and stick this summary on the front for later reference. Today, it is possible to find the latest data on almost any subject on the Internet. Good students know, or quickly learn, how to find such information efficiently. The best students know the importance of keeping such information in files so that it is readily accessible. Those files may be in their computers or on their desktops, ready for easy access.

You definitely want to have a personal data file titled Credentials for My Résumé or something similar. In that file, you'll place all reference letters and other information about jobs you may have held. Soon you'll have a tremendous amount of information available to you. You can add to these initial files until you have your own comprehensive information system.

Many people return to school to improve their skills in areas such as computers and writing. Others return because they realize, once they enter the marketplace, how important post-secondary education is. Can you see the advantage of going back to school periodically over your career to keep your skills current?

Business people are constantly seeking ways to increase their knowledge of the business world and to increase their investment returns. One way they do so is by watching television shows such as *CBC News*, *The National*, *Business Report*, *Money Talk*, and *Venture*. Watching such programs is like getting a free graduate education in business. Try viewing some of these shows or listening to similar shows on the radio, and see which ones you like best. Take notes and put them in your files. Another way, one of the best, to increase your business knowledge is to read your local newspaper. Keep up with the business news in your local area so you know what jobs are available and where. You may also want to join local business groups to begin networking with people and learning the secrets of the local business scene. Many business groups and professional societies accept student members.

LEARNING TO BEHAVE LIKE A PROFESSIONAL

Good manners are back, and for a good reason. As the world becomes increasingly competitive, the gold goes to the individuals and the teams that have an extra bit of polish. The person who makes a good impression will be the one who gets the job, wins the promotion, or clinches the deal. Manners and professionalism must become second nature to anyone who wants to achieve and maintain a competitive edge.

Often, students focus on becoming experts in their particular field and neglect other concerns, including proper attire and etiquette. Their résumés look great and they may get through the interview process, but then they get in the workplace and may not succeed. Their behaviour, including their verbal behaviour, is so unacceptable that they are rejected by their peers.

You can begin the habits *now* while you are in school so that you will have the skills needed for success when you start your career. Those habits include the following:

1. **Making a good first impression.** An old saying goes, "You never get a second chance to make a good first impression." You have just a few seconds to make an impression. Therefore, how you dress and look is important.[2] Take a clue as to what is appropriate at any specific company by studying the people there who are most successful. What do they wear? How do they act?

2. **Focusing on good grooming.** Be aware of your appearance and its impact on those around you. Consistency is essential. You can't project a good image by dressing up a few times a week and then show up looking like you're getting ready to mow a lawn. Wear appropriate, clean clothing and accessories. For example, revealing shirts, nose rings, and such may not be appropriate in a work setting. It is not appropriate for men to wear hats inside buildings. It is also not appropriate, usually, to wear wrinkled clothing or to have shirttails hanging out of your pants. More businesses are adopting "business casual" policies, so knowing the proper clothes to buy is critical. What is business casual to some may not be acceptable to others, but there are a few guidelines most organizations accept. First of all, casual doesn't mean sloppy or shabby. For women, casual attire may include simple skirts and slacks (no jeans), cotton shirts, sweaters (not too tight), blazers, low-heeled shoes or boots (always with socks or stockings). For men, acceptable casual attire may include khaki trousers, sport shirts with collars, sweaters or sport jackets, casual loafers or lace-up shoes (no athletic shoes).[3]

3. **Being on time.** When you don't come to class or to work on time, you're sending a message to your teacher or boss. You're saying, "My time is more important than your time. I have more important things to do than be here." In addition to the lack of respect tardiness shows to your teacher or boss, it rudely disrupts the work of your colleagues. Promptness may not be a priority in some circles, but in the workplace promptness is essential. But being punctual doesn't always mean just being on time. You have to pay attention to the corporate culture. Sometimes you have to come earlier than others and leave later to get that promotion you desire. To develop good work habits and get good grades, it is important to get to class on time and not leave early.

A simple file system can provide you with some useful advantages over students who do not keep such files. You will have at your fingertips articles that will be valuable in completing class assignments, the names of people you can use to network, the names of the best professors on campus so you can schedule them, and other resource information you deem worthwhile. What additional benefits do you see from keeping interesting information from newspapers, magazines, and similar sources?

4. **Practising considerate behaviour.** Considerate behaviour includes listening when others are talking—for example, not reading the newspaper or eating in class. Don't interrupt others when they are speaking. Wait for your turn to present your views in classroom or workplace discussions. Of course, eliminate all words of profanity from your vocabulary. Use appropriate body language by sitting up attentively and not slouching. Sitting up has the added bonus of helping you stay awake! Professors and managers get a favourable impression from those who look and act alert. That may help your grades in school and your advancement at work.

5. **Practising good "netiquette."** Computer technology, particularly e-mail, can be a great productivity tool. The basic courtesy rules of face-to-face communication also apply to e-mail exchanges. As in writing a letter, you should introduce yourself at the beginning of your first e-mail message. Next, you should let your recipients know how you got their names and e-mail addresses. Then you can proceed with your clear but succinct message, and finally close the e-mail with a signature.[4] Do not send an attachment (files of text or graphics attached to an e-mail message) with your e-mail unless your correspondent has indicated that he or she will accept it. Ask first!

   You can find much more information about proper Internet etiquette (netiquette) on the Internet. For example, the Web site PlanetClick rates and reviews netiquette Web sites (www.planetclick.com/cgi-bin/category.cgi?T5netiquette).

6. **Practising good cell phone manners.** Cellular phones are a vital part of today's world, but it is important to be polite when using the phone. Turn off the phone when you are in class or a business meeting unless you are expecting a critical call. Your Introduction to Business class is not the place to be arranging a date for tonight. If you are expecting a critical call, turn off the audible phone ring and use the vibrating ring if your phone has that feature. If you do have to have your cellular phone turned on, sit by the aisle and near the door to leave if the phone rings. Leave the room before answering the call. Apologize to the professor after class and explain the nature of the emergency. Most professors are more sympathetic when you explain why you left the room abruptly.

7. **Being prepared.** A business person would never show up for a meeting without reading the materials assigned for that meeting and being prepared to discuss the topics of the day. *To become a professional, you must practise acting like a professional.* For students, that means reading assigned materials before class, asking questions and responding to questions in class, and discussing the material with fellow students.

From the minute you enter your first job interview until the day you retire, people will notice whether you follow the proper business etiquette. Just as traffic laws enable people to drive more safely, business etiquette allows people to conduct business with the appropriate amount of dignity. How you talk, how you eat, and how you dress all create an impression on others. We encourage you to add a course or seminar on etiquette to your academic curriculum. Many businesses today require their employees to complete such a course. Taking the initiative to do so on your own will help sharpen your competitive edge.

Business etiquette may encompass different rules in different countries. It is important, therefore, to learn the proper business etiquette for each country you visit. Areas that require proper etiquette include greeting people (shaking hands is not always appropriate); eating (Europeans, for example, often hold their knives and forks while eating); giving gifts; presenting and receiving business cards; and conducting business in general. Honesty, high ethical standards, and good character (e.g., reliability and trustworthiness) are important ingredients to success in any country. Having a reputation for integrity will enable you to be proud of who you are and will contribute a great deal to your business success. Unethical behaviour can ruin your reputation, so think carefully before you act. When in doubt, don't! Ethics is so important to success that we will include ethics discussions throughout the text.

DOING YOUR BEST IN SCHOOL

The skills you need to succeed in school are the same skills you need to succeed in life after school. Career, family, and hobbies all involve the same organizational and time management skills. Applying these skills during your academic years will ensure that you will have the life skills you need for a successful career. We will try to help you hone your skills by offering hints for improving your study habits, taking tests, and managing your time.

Study Hints

Studying is your business now. When you fill out a form you write "Student" in the occupation box, right? So until you get out of school and into a full-time job, studying is your business. Like any good business person, you aim for success. Let us suggest some strategies for success:

1. **Go to class.** It is often tempting to cut a class on a nice day or when there are other things to do. But nothing is more important to doing well in school than going to class every time. If possible, sit in the front near the instructor. This will help you focus more on what is being said and less on distractions in the room.

2. **Listen well.** It's not enough to show up for class if you use the time for a siesta. Make eye contact with the instructor. In your mind, form a picture of what is discussed. Try to include past experiences in your picture. This ties new knowledge to what you already know.

3. **Take careful notes.** Make two columns in your notebook and use one side to write down the important concepts and the other side to write examples or more detailed explanations. Use abbreviations and symbols whenever possible. Use wide spacing to make the notes easier to read. Rewrite the notes after class, because hastily written notes are often difficult to decipher much later. Rereading and rewriting notes also helps store the information in your long-term memory. You learn the concepts in the course the same way you learn the words to your favourite song: through repetition and review.

4. **Find a good place to study.** Find a place with good lighting and a quiet atmosphere. Some students do well with classical music or other music without lyrics playing in the background. Keep your study place equipped with extra supplies such as pens, pencils, calculator, folders, and paper so that you don't have to interrupt study time to hunt for what you need.

It is crucial that business people learn business etiquette appropriate for the countries in which they do business. Behaviour that we take for granted in Canada can be insulting in other cultures. For example, in some cultures shaking hands when you first meet another person is considered rude. Is there a country in which you might like to do business? What are some of the cultural differences that might affect your business behaviour in that country?

5. **Read the text using a strategy such as "survey, question, read, recite, review."**

    *   *Survey* or scan the chapter first to see what it is all about. This means looking over the table of contents, learning goals, headings, photo captions, and charts so you get a broad idea of the content. Scanning will provide an introduction and help get your mind in a learning mode.
    *   Write *questions,* first by changing the headings into questions. For example, you could change the heading of this section to: "What hints can I use to study better?" Read the questions that appear throughout each chapter in the Progress Check and Critical Thinking sections. The Progress Check questions give you a chance to recall what you've read. The Critical Thinking questions help you relate the material to your own experiences. Research has shown that it is easier to retain information and concepts if you can relate to them personally.
    *   *Read* the chapter to find the answers to your questions. Be sure to read the boxes throughout the text as well. They offer extended examples or discussions of the concepts in the text. You've probably asked, "Will the stuff in the boxes be on the tests?" Even if your instructor chooses not to test over them directly, they are often the most interesting parts and will help you retain the concepts.
    *   *Recite* your answers to yourself or to others in a study group. Make sure you say the answers in your own words so that you clearly understand the concepts. Research has shown that saying things is a more effective way to learn them than seeing, hearing, or reading about them. Used in study groups, recitation is also good practice for working in teams in the work world.
    *   *Review* by rereading and recapping the information. The chapter summaries are written in a question-and-answer form, much like a classroom dialogue. Cover the written answers and see if you can answer the questions yourself first. The summaries are directly tied to the learning goals so you can see whether you've accomplished the chapter's objectives.

6. **Use the study guide.** The Study Guide gives you the chance to practise thinking through answers and writing them down. It also includes practice multiple-choice tests.

Some students prefer to enter class notes directly into their computers during class. Others prefer to write notes by hand, using their own form of abbreviations and codes. What are the advantages of each of these methods? Which method do you use? How effective is it for you? If you take notes by hand, would it help you understand and retain the information if you rewrote your notes or copied them into your computer later? Why?

7. **Use flash cards.** Much of the material in this course consists of terminology. The key terms in the book are highlighted in boldface type, and their definitions appear in the margins. Page references to these terms are provided at the end of each chapter. Write the terms you don't know on index cards and go through them between classes and when you have other free time.

8. **Go over old exams, if possible.** Sometimes a professor will make old exams available so that you can see the style of the exam. If such exams are not available, ask your professor exactly how the exam will be given. That is, ask how many multiple-choice questions and how many true–false and essay questions there will be. It is not unethical to ask your professor's former students what kind of questions are given and what material is usually emphasized. It is unethical, though, to go over illegally obtained exams.

9. **Use as many of your senses in learning as possible.** If you're an auditory learner—that is, if you learn best by hearing—record yourself reading your notes and answering the questions you've written. Listen to the tape while you're dressing in the morning. You can also benefit from reading or studying aloud. If you're a visual learner, you should use pictures, charts, colours, and graphs. Your professor has a set of videotapes that illustrate the concepts in this text. If you're a kinesthetic learner, you remember best by doing, touching, and experiencing. You can benefit from doing some of the Developing Workplace Skills and Taking It to the Net exercises at the end of each chapter.

Test-Taking Hints

Often students will say, "I know this stuff, but I'm just no good at taking multiple-choice (or essay) tests." Other students find test-taking relatively easy. A survey of such students reveals the following test-taking hints:

1. **Get plenty of sleep and a good meal.** It is better to be alert and awake during an exam than to study all night and be groggy. If you keep up with your reading and your reviews, there is no need to pull an all-nighter just before the exam. Proper nutrition plays an important part in your brain's ability to function.

2. **Bring all you need for the exam.** Sometimes you will need HB pencils, erasers, and a calculator. Ask beforehand what you'll need.

3. **Relax.** Begin at home before the test. Take deep, slow breaths. Picture yourself in the testing session, relaxed and confident. Get to class early to settle down. If you start to get nervous during the test, stop and take deep breaths. Turn the test over and write down information you remember. Sometimes this helps you connect the information you know to the questions on the test.

4. **Read the directions on the exam carefully.** You don't want to miss anything or do something you are not supposed to do.

5. **Read all the answers in multiple-choice questions.** Often there is more than one correct-sounding answer to a multiple-choice question, but one is clearly better. Be sure to read them all to be sure that the one you pick is best. A technique that may help you is to cover up the choices while reading the question. If the answer you think of is one of the choices, it is probably the correct answer. If you are still unsure of the answer, start eliminating options you know are wrong. Narrowing the choices to two or three improves your odds.

6. **Answer all the questions.** Unless your instructor takes off more marks for an incorrect answer than no answer at all, you have nothing to lose by guessing. Also, skipping a question can lead to inadvertently misaligning your answers on a scan sheet. You could end up with all of your subsequent answers scored wrong!

7. **Read true–false questions carefully.** All parts of the statement must be true or the entire statement is false. Watch out for absolutes such as never, always, or none. These most likely make a statement false.

8. **Organize your thoughts before answering essay questions.** Think of the sequence you intend to use to present what you want to say. Use complete sentences with correct grammar and punctuation. Explain or defend your answers.

9. **Go over the test at the end.** Make sure you have answered all the questions and that you have put your name on the exam and followed all the other directions.

Time Management Hints

Throughout your life, the most important management skill you will learn is to manage your time. Now is as good a time to learn as any. Here are some hints that other students have learned—often the hard way:

1. **Write weekly goals for yourself.** Make certain your goals are realistic and attainable. Write the steps you will use to achieve each goal. Reward yourself when you reach a goal.

2. **Keep a "to do" list.** It is easy to forget things unless you have them written down. Jot tasks down the first time you think of them so that you don't "rediscover" chores when you think of them again. Writing them down gives you one less thing to do: remembering what you have to do.

3. **Prepare a daily schedule.** Use a commercial daily planner or create your own. Write the days of the week across the top of the page. Write the hours of the day from the time you get up until the time you go to bed down the left side. Draw lines to form columns and rows and fill in all the activities you have planned in each hour. Hopefully, you will be surprised to see how many slots of time you have available for studying.

4. **Prepare for the next day the night before.** Having everything ready to go will help you make a quick, unfrenzied start in the morning.

5. **Prepare weekly and monthly schedules.** Use a calendar to fill in activities and upcoming assignments. Include both academic and social activities so you can balance your work and fun.

Because life really is mostly essay questions, this text includes a couple of critical thinking exercises in every chapter to encourage you to generate your own thoughts about the issues raised in the chapter. Can you see the benefit of pausing to answer such questions as your read? In the first place, it will put the material into your own context. Secondly, it will keep your aware of the issues and force you to think about your own perspectives.

FRANK & ERNEST® by Bob Thaves

6. **Space out your work.** Don't wait until the last week of the course to write all your papers and study for your exams. If you do a few pages a day, you can do a 20-page paper in a couple of weeks with little effort. It is really difficult to push out 20 pages in a day or two.

7. **Defend your study time.** It is important to study a little every day. Use the time between classes to go over your flash cards and read the next day's assignments. Make it a habit to defend your study time so you don't slip.

8. **Take time for fun.** If you have some fun every day, life will be full. But if you don't have fun, life can be a real drag. Schedule your fun times along with your study schedule so that you have balance.

MAKING THE MOST OF THE RESOURCES FOR THIS COURSE

College and university courses are best at teaching you concepts and ways of thinking about business. However, to learn firsthand about real-world applications, you will need to explore and interact with actual businesses. Textbooks are like comprehensive tour guides in that they tell you what to look for and where to look, but they can never replace experience.

This text, then, isn't meant to be the only resource for this class. In fact, it's not even the primary resource. Your professor will be much better than the text at responding to your specific questions and needs. This book is just one of the resources he or she can use with you to satisfy your desire to understand what the business world is all about. There are seven basic resources for the class in addition to the text and study guide:

1. **The professor.** One of the most valuable facets of school is the chance to study with experienced professors. Your instructor is more than a teacher of facts and concepts. As mentioned above, he or she is a resource who's there to answer questions and guide you to the answers for others. It's important for you to develop a friendly relationship with all of your professors. One reason for doing so is that many professors get job leads they can pass on to you. Professors are also excellent references for future jobs. By following the rules of dress and etiquette outlined above, you can create a good impression, which will be valuable should you ask a professor to write a good letter of recommendation for you. Finally, your professor is one more experienced person who can help you find and access resource materials, both at school and in the business world.

2. **The supplements that come with this text, including the Study Guide.** The study guide will help you review and interpret key material and give you practice answering test questions. Even if your professor does not assign the study guide, you may want to use it anyhow. Doing so will improve your test scores and help you compete successfully with the other students.

3. **Outside readings.** We recommend that you review the following magazines during the course and throughout your career: *Canadian Business, Report on Business Magazine* and *National Post Business,* and *Profit.* You may also want to read the business sections in national newspapers such as *The Globe and Mail* and the *National Post* to keep up with current issues. If you're not familiar with these sources, it's time to get to know them. You don't necessarily have to become a regular subscriber, but you should learn what information is available in these sources over time. All of these sources are probably available free of charge in your school's learning resource centre

or the local public library. One secret to success in business is staying current, and these magazines will help you do so.

4. **Your own experience and that of your classmates.** Many students have had experience working in business or nonprofit organizations. Talking together about those experiences exposes you to many real-life examples that are invaluable for understanding business. Don't rely totally on the professor for answers to the cases and other exercises in this book. Often there is no single "right" answer, and your classmates may open up new ways of looking at things for you. Part of being a successful business person is knowing how to work with others. Classrooms are excellent places to practise this skill. Some professors provide opportunities for their students to work together in small groups. Such exercises build teamwork as well as presentation and analytical skills. If you have students from other countries in your class, working with them can help you learn about different cultures and different approaches to handling business problems. There is strength in diversity, so seek out people different from yourself to work with on teams.

5. **Outside contacts.** One of the best ways to learn about different businesses is to visit them in person. Who can tell you more about what it's like to start a career in accounting than someone who's doing it now? The same is true of other jobs. The world can be your classroom if you let it. When you go shopping, for example, think about whether you would enjoy working in and managing a store. Talk with the clerks and the manager to see how they feel about the job. Think about the possibilities of owning or managing a restaurant, an auto body shop, a health club, a print shop, or any other establishment you visit. If something looks interesting, talk to the employees and learn more about their jobs and the industry. Soon you may discover fascinating careers in places such as the zoo or a health club or in industries such as travel or computer sales. In short, be constantly on the alert to find career possibilities, and don't hesitate to talk with people about their careers. Typically, they'll be pleased to give you their time.

6. **The Internet.** Never before have students had access to information as easily as they do today. What makes information gathering so easy now is the Internet. Once you've learned to surf the Internet, you will find more material than you could use in a lifetime. On the Internet you can search through library catalogues all over the world, find articles from leading business journals, view paintings from leading museums, and more—much more. Throughout this text we will present information and exercises that will help you gain experience using the Internet. But don't rely on the text for all your knowledge. Talk with your friends and acquaintances and learn as much as you can about how to use the Internet. This resource will become even more important in the future. Information changes rapidly, and it is up to you to stay current. If you don't already know how to use the Internet, learn to do so now!
Reading the Surfing the Internet skills section will get you started.

7. **The library or learning resource centre.** The library is a great complement to the Internet as a valuable resource. Work with your librarian to learn how to best access the information you need.

SURFING THE INTERNET

Never surfed the World Wide Web? Want to learn some basic tips? The purpose of this section is to help ease novices toward the on-ramp to the information superhighway. If you are an experienced Internet user, you may just want to skim this material for features you haven't used yet. The material is arranged in a question-and-answer format so that you can easily jump to a topic you would like to know more about. Don't worry if you have never so much as pressed an Enter key—we won't get too technical for you. You don't have to understand the technical complexities of the Internet to travel on the information superhighway. But, as in learning to drive, it's usually a good idea to learn where the gas goes.

Technology changes so quickly that writing about how to use the Internet is like washing the CN Tower—as soon as you're finished it's time to start over again. For this reason we've tried to keep the discussion as general as possible and not give too many specific steps that may be out of date by the time you read this.

The important thing to remember is that you can't break anything on the information superhighway, so just jump right in, explore the online world, and have fun!

WHAT IS THE INTERNET?

The **Internet** is a network of networks. It involves tens of thousands of interconnected computer networks that include millions of host computers. The Internet is certainly not new. The U.S. Pentagon began the network in 1969 when the world feared that a nuclear war would paralyze communications. The computer network was developed to reach far-flung terminals even if some connections were broken. The system took on a life of its own, however, and grew as scientists and other academics used it to share data and electronic mail. No one owns the Internet. There is no central computer; each message you send from your computer has an address code that lets any other computer on the Internet forward it to its destination. There is no Internet manager. The closest thing to a governing body is the Internet Society in Reston, Virginia. This is a volunteer organization of individuals and corporate members who promote Internet use and oversee development of new communication software. See Figure G.1 for a description of how the Internet works.

WHAT IS THE WORLD WIDE WEB, AND HOW IS IT DIFFERENT FROM THE INTERNET?

The World Wide Web (WWW, or the Web) is a means of accessing, organizing, and moving through the information in the Internet. Therefore, the Web is part of the Internet. Think of the Internet as a gigantic library and the Web as the Dewey Decimal System. Until the creation of the World Wide Web in 1993, it was as though that gigantic library simply threw all of its books and other materials into mountainous piles. If you wanted to find something on the Internet, you needed to type in a complex code representing the exact address of the site you wanted.

The basic difficulty of navigating the Internet without the Web is twofold: (1) the traffic signs on the Internet are written in Unix, and (2) there is no defined structure for organizing information. Unix is an operating system that was designed long before anyone thought of the term *user-friendly*. And, since the Internet does not

If even the idea of learning how to use the Internet is enough to make your head spin, relax. We'll show you how easy it is to use this powerful business tool. How can the Internet help you simplify many of our everyday tasks, such as communicating with instructors and colleagues, gathering information, and shopping for supplies?

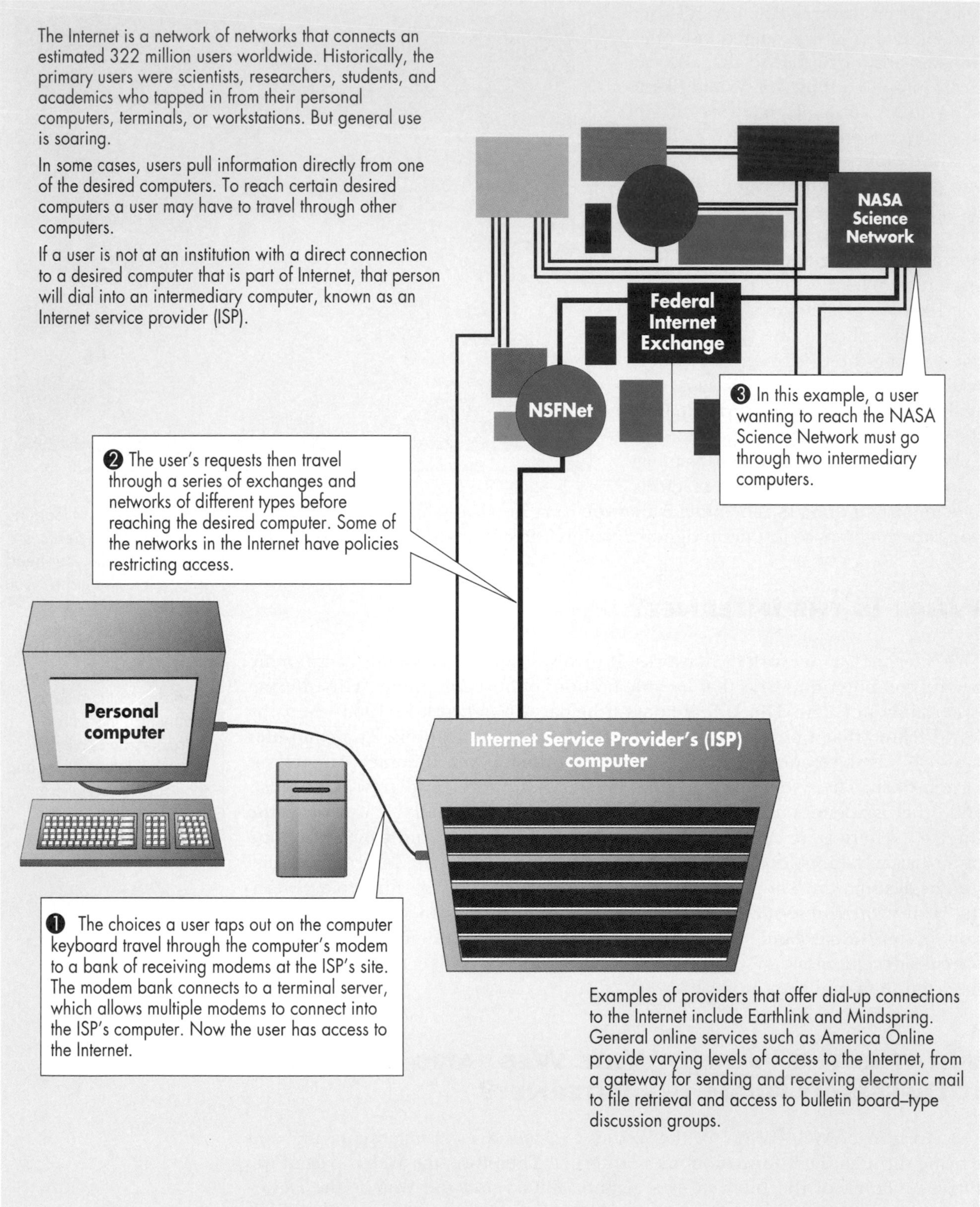

The Internet is a network of networks that connects an estimated 322 million users worldwide. Historically, the primary users were scientists, researchers, students, and academics who tapped in from their personal computers, terminals, or workstations. But general use is soaring.

In some cases, users pull information directly from one of the desired computers. To reach certain desired computers a user may have to travel through other computers.

If a user is not at an institution with a direct connection to a desired computer that is part of Internet, that person will dial into an intermediary computer, known as an Internet service provider (ISP).

NASA Science Network

Federal Internet Exchange

❸ In this example, a user wanting to reach the NASA Science Network must go through two intermediary computers.

NSFNet

❷ The user's requests then travel through a series of exchanges and networks of different types before reaching the desired computer. Some of the networks in the Internet have policies restricting access.

Personal computer

Internet Service Provider's (ISP) computer

❶ The choices a user taps out on the computer keyboard travel through the computer's modem to a bank of receiving modems at the ISP's site. The modem bank connects to a terminal server, which allows multiple modems to connect into the ISP's computer. Now the user has access to the Internet.

Examples of providers that offer dial-up connections to the Internet include Earthlink and Mindspring. General online services such as America Online provide varying levels of access to the Internet, from a gateway for sending and receiving electronic mail to file retrieval and access to bulletin board–type discussion groups.

FIGURE G.1

HOW THE INTERNET WORKS

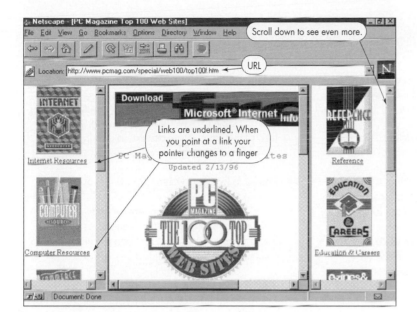

FIGURE G.2

HYPERTEXT LINKS AND A URL

require a prescribed structure for entering information, even experienced users have difficulty retrieving information without a tool like the Web.

When the Web evolved, the game changed. Not only did the Web add graphics and sound, which breathed life into the dreary text-only Internet, but it also made navigating parts of the Internet easy even for beginners. Now Web cruisers don't need to know Unix in order to travel the Net. You can go from place to place on the Web simply by clicking on a word or a picture in a format called hypertext. Hypertext allows any part of any document to be linked to any other document, no matter where it is, allowing you to jump around from place to place with a click of the mouse. Hypertext links are usually shown in a contrasting colour on the computer screen (see Figure G.2). Cruising or surfing means following hypertext links from page to page on the Web.

WHAT DO I NEED TO BE ABLE TO GET ON THE WEB?

The first thing you need in order to cruise the information superhighway is a computer with a modem (a device that connects your computer with other computers via phone lines) and a Web browser. There are other ways to connect to the Internet (through special telephone lines, cable lines, or satellites), but until they become more widely available, many of us will use modems and standard phone lines to access the Net.

If cable Internet or digital subscriber line (DSL) service is available in your area, you may be interested in the comparison of these services that appears in Figure G.3. Keep in mind that your Internet connection is the pipeline used to move data to your computer. The bigger the pipe, the faster the flow. Whether your connection is by cable modem, telephone lines, DSL, satellite, or fixed wireless, the impact is much the same. Data can reach you more than 50 times as fast as with traditional 56k modems and normal phone lines (the kind that came with most computers in the late 1990s and early 2000s).[5]

Many schools offer students Internet service, so check out what is available at your school. You may have already paid computer-service fees that include Internet connection, so get your money's worth and get online now. If you can't connect through your school, you can connect to the Net by signing up with an Internet service provider (ISP). Your ISP will give you the phone number and a set of directions for connecting your computer to the Net. At this time, most ISPs provide unlimited

ADVANTAGES	DISADVANTAGES
Cable • Theoretically, cable has the most bandwidth and therefore the fastest speed—as much as 100Mbps, compared to the mere 56k of traditional phone modems • Uses same cable lines used to deliver TV • Not limited by distance from a central office	• Speed will decrease as more users sign up since all users on the network share the available bandwidth. • Not available in older, high-density areas (like cities), since it is expensive to dig up concrete to bury cables.
Digital subscriber line (DSL) • Downloading speed can be as high as 7Mbps (most of the bandwidth is used for incoming data, with only a small amount used for outgoing). • Uses telephone lines already in place. • Can use the same phone line for voice even while you're online so there's no need for a separate phone line for computer connection.	• Limited to locations within 20,000 feet of telephone central office. • Good for downloading, but not for two-way communication like videoconferencing or Web hosting that requires the same bandwidth for incoming and outgoing data.
Satellite • Download speed can be 400Kbps. Not nearly as fast as cable or DSL, but much better than the traditional 56Kbps.	• Most satellite services can only push data to you. Two-way services may be available by 2002. • Since data are beamed from a satellite in space, you need to place an 18-inch dish in the line of sight to the satellite. Weather conditions can affect reception.

FIGURE G.3

PICK A PIPE

access to the Internet for a flat monthly fee. Some ISPs offer "free" Internet access, but you must be willing to share private information about yourself and to give up a great deal of screen space to advertising messages.

What Is a Web Browser?

A Web browser is a program or application that provides you with a way to access the World Wide Web. The first graphical Web browser that allowed pointing and clicking was Mosaic, developed by Eric Bina and Marc Andreessen at the National Center for Supercomputing Applications. Andreessen, an undergraduate at the time, later went on to fame and fortune as the developer of Netscape Navigator. Mosaic was based on a code written by Tim Berners-Lee of CERN, the European laboratory for particle physics.

Which Is the Best Browser?

Currently, the two most popular Web browsers are Netscape Navigator and Microsoft Internet Explorer. At the time of this writing, the best browser is the one you have access to—in other words, neither one has a clear advantage over the other. The case may be different by the time you read this. If we had to predict the future, we would have to say that both Netscape and Microsoft will continue to improve their browsers to compete with each other and that Web users will benefit from the competition as the browsers become more powerful and easier to use.

WHERE DO I GO WHEN I CLICK ON SOMETHING?

When you're navigating the Net, you can go from a Web page in Paris to one in Peru. What happens? When you click on a link, your computer sends out a request for information to another server. That server, which may be next door or across the planet, interprets your request, finds the information (text, graphics, or entire Web pages), and then breaks it up into packets. The server sends the packets to your computer, where your browser puts them back together and you see the Web page, all in the blink of an eye (or an eternity—they don't call it the World Wide Wait for nothing).

Why Does It Take So Long to Move from One Place to Another on the Web?

The speed with which you reach other Internet sites depends not only on the speed and size of your phone line and computer but also on the speed and size of phone lines and computers at the other site. You won't get to class any faster in a Ferrari than in a bus if you're locked in a traffic jam. The same is true on the information superhighway. Sometimes your computer will seem to take forever to get to a site or to open an image. If this happens, you can click the Stop button on your menu bar and try again later when the Internet may be less busy.

Why Would I Want to Surf the Internet?

You can use the Internet to:

- **Communicate online.** You can communicate with others through the following:

  Newsgroups. These are special-interest groups in which you can get advice or just share thoughts with people.

  Electronic mail (e-mail). E-mail lets you stay in touch with friends, trade files, and do business, all from the comfort of your computer desktop.

  Internet relay chat (IRC). IRCs allow you to chat with other people all over the world in real time (that is, talk with someone else while you are both on the line rather than send messages that are read later). It's live and uncensored, so choose your chats wisely.

  Each of these is discussed in more detail in the pages that follow.

- **Gather information.** Internet users can tap into such diverse sources as Statistics Canada and Strategis (Industry Canada's Web site). Other Web sites offer news headlines, stock market information, access to encyclopedias, and other databases. Search engines can help you find the sites that have the information you need. There are special Web sites that offer push technology that makes gathering information automatic: After you tell it what you are interested in, the program searches the Web periodically and then pushes the information to you without your having to ask for it.

- **Shop.** Forgot your mom's birthday? No problem. Get online and order roses to be delivered to her door before she disinherits you. Or, if things get too bad, book a flight out of town with a few mouse clicks and a credit card number. Note, however, that credit card security is a concern that is getting lots of attention as more and more businesses open their doors to customers on the Internet.

- **Play games (after you finish studying, of course).** You can play games against another person or against the computer while you're online.

Do I Have to Be a Computer Major to Surf the Web?

There are only four simple things you need to know about to navigate the Web: (1) Web addresses, (2) directories and search engines, (3) links, and (4) the Back Page button.

What Are Web Addresses?

Every Web site has an address called a uniform resource locator (URL). Go back to Figure G.2 and look at the top of the browser window. See the line that starts with http://? That's the URL for the page. To get to any Web site, you just type its address in the space for the URL entry in your Web browser. This means, of course, that you know the exact URL. It is important to know that the Web is constantly evolving and therefore URLs often change as new sites are added and old ones dropped. Sometimes a new URL is supplied when you visit an old site, but often it is not, in which case you reach a dead end.

What If I Don't Know Which Site I Need, Much Less Its URL?

To find topics that interest you, you can use one of several Web directories or search engines. Once you are at the search engine's home page, all you have to do is to enter the key words for the topic you want and you will quickly receive a list of links to sites related to your request. Some of the most popular directories and search engines are Yahoo!, Infoseek, Lycos, Alta Vista, Excite, Dogpile, Google, and WebCrawler.

You'll always get better results from a search engine if you define what you're searching for as specifically as possible. The two easiest ways to narrow your search are by adding and subtracting terms from your search string. Let's say you want to buy a new stereo and you aren't sure which brands have the best sound. If you search Yahoo! for "stereo," you may get back 654 (or more) site matches. However, you can focus the search a little more by adding another search word. Just typing in the word itself isn't good enough, though. In order to receive only sites that contain both stereo and the other word, you have to use the word *and* to link them. If you search for "and review" you get eight matches—all sites that review stereo equipment.

If adding search items doesn't narrow the field enough, try subtracting them—tell the search engine what not to look for. Say you're looking for business opportunities. You search for "business and opportunity" and get overwhelmed by more than 2,500 site matches, most of which are Amway-type, multilevel marketing operations (commonly known as MLMs). You can narrow your search by asking for these items to be excluded. For example, use the word *not* instead of *and*. This time you search for "business and opportunity not mlm" and get just seven items back.

A third way to define your search more closely is to put your search term in quotes. That tells the search engine that you're looking for exactly those words in exactly that order.

Don't worry about remembering all these surfing tips. Most search engines have an Advanced Options menu that lists ways to search. Also, many search engines offer specific instructions on how to make the most of your search on their site.

If you try different search engines to look for the same topic, you'll get different results. That's because the search engines are different. Each search engine uses its own program (called a bot or crawler) to search the Web. Not only do these programs use different methods of searching and indexing, but they start from different points on the Web. You probably will also get different results if you search on a directory rather than a search engine, again because of the different approach to indexing sites. You can search on multiple search engines all at once by using a metasearch engine such as WebCrawler or Dogpile. MetaCrawler returns answers to queries from nine popular search engines, 10 search channels, forums, and links to major e-commerce sites. Dogpile returns query results from other Web search engines, Usenet, and file transfer protocol (ftp) sites. It also supplies stock quotes and news from wire services.

What Do I Need to Know about Links?

Once you're at a site, the two main ways to cruise around are by clicking on an icon button link or on a text link. One way to tell if something is a link is to place your cursor over the graphic icon or text. If it changes into a hand, then you know it is a live link. When you click on a link, you will be sent to another Web site or to another page on the current Web site.

What If I Want to Get Back to Someplace I've Been?

If you want to go back to a site you have left recently, you can just click on the Back Page button in your browser. This will lead you back through the exact same page route you travelled before. Or you can enter the desired site's URL. If you are on the same Web site, you can choose the home page link or one of the section icons to take you back to the home page or another section.

HOW CAN I COMMUNICATE WITH OTHERS ONLINE?

You can reach out and touch your fellow Internet surfers via newsgroups, e-mail, or an IRC.

What Are Newsgroups?

The Usenet is a global network of discussion groups known as newsgroups. Newsgroups are collections of messages from people all over the world on any subject you can imagine (and some you'd rather not imagine). Newsgroups are divided into categories indicated by the first letters of their name. There are many different category prefixes, but the main ones you will see are comp (computer), sci (science), rec (recreation), soc (society), and alt (alternative). Under these headings are thousands of subcategories from alt.alien.visitors to za.humour.

How Do I Join a Newsgroup?

Web browsers have built-in newsreading capabilities. You first need to go to the Mail and News options menu and enter your server information, which is usually something like "news.myserver.com" (contact your Internet service provider to find out exactly what it is). There are also options for organizing how you read your messages. Some people like their messages "threaded" (meaning all postings on a particular topic are grouped together), while others prefer to sort their messages by date.

When you find a group you like, don't jump into the conversation right away. Take time to read the frequently asked questions (FAQ) list for that group first. The FAQ list includes the questions that most newcomers ask. After you read the FAQs, you should read at least a week's worth of postings to get a feel for the group and what kinds of discussions its members have. Remember, you may be joining discussions that have been going on for a year

Web browsers, like the one for AOL shown here, offer advice to newsgroup newbies (new users). Notice that AOL suggests that you begin by reading netiquette hints so that you mind your online manners and don't jump into newsgroups on the wrong foot.

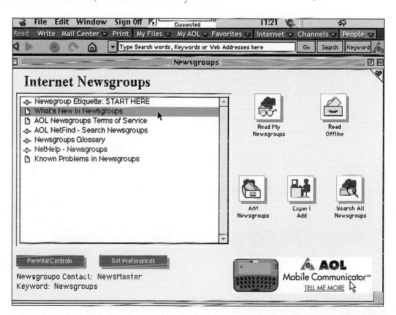

or more, so you may feel like the new kid on the block for a while. But most newsgroups are quite friendly if you use basic netiquette.

How Do I Send E-Mail?

As with "snail mail," or letters delivered by Canada Post, e-mail is delivered to its recipient by an address. An Internet e-mail address has two parts: the user name and the name of the computer on which that user has an account. For example, Professor Ulysses R. Smart's e-mail address at Ignatius Quinius University may be ursmart@iqu.edu. The symbol "@" is pronounced "at." The suffix ".edu" indicates that the address is one of an educational institution.

There are several e-mail software packages available. Netscape and Internet Explorer include e-mail capabilities. To compose a message, click on the Mail button (see Figure G.4). Enter the e-mail address of the person to whom you are writing in the *To:* field. Enter the subject of your message in the *Subject:* field. If you want others to receive the message, enter their e-mail addresses in the *CC:* field and separate each e-mail address with a comma. Next, enter the body of the message in the large space. When you have completed your message, click on the Send button. To check for new messages received, simply click on the Get Mail button. If you have received new mail, the subject and sender will be displayed in a window. Click on a message to display its contents.

You can also send files with your e-mail. To send files from a graphics program or word processor, simply choose *attach file* and navigate your hard drive to find the file you want to send. Before you send an attached file, make sure that the person you are sending it to can receive it. Some people have slow connections that come to a near halt if their system receives a large attachment. Others have mailboxes that fill too quickly if they receive a number of large files. So always ask before the first time you send someone attachments.

One of the more interesting ways to take advantage of e-mail is to join one or more mailing lists (or listservs, to use the technical term).

What Are Listservs?

Listservs, or mailing lists, are similar to Usenet newsgroups. Unlike newsgroups, though, listserv discussions are delivered to your in-box as e-mail, and responding is as easy as punching your Reply button (which sends the message to everyone on the mailing list). To find a mailing list that piques your interest, try the mailing list directory Listz at www.listz.com. Be careful, though; mailing lists can quickly jam your in-box.

FIGURE G.4

E-MAIL FORM

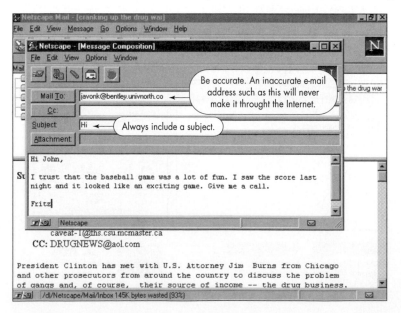

What Is IRC?

Internet relay chat (IRC) is an Internet protocol that allows you to have real-time conversations with other people around the world. As with newsgroups, it's best at first to observe, or "lurk," and see how the others on the IRC channel interact. To use an IRC channel you must have a chat "client" or program. The two most popular freeware chat clients are PIRCH for Windows and Ircle for the Mac. DalNet is one of the largest IRC networks. DalNet offers extensive information on IRC and how to use it.

The first step is to connect to a server. Then choose a nickname, join a room (or "channel"), and start lurking away. All IRC channels start with the number sign (#), and most servers have a channel called #newbie where you can ease into the swing of things.

Not all IRC is idle chat. Many people have discovered ways to use IRC to help one another by developing virtual support groups online. Talk City is one example of an online community that uses IRC as a vehicle for people to draw support in a safe and friendly environment.

Although IRC is one of the most popular uses for the Internet, it could easily be replaced by Internet phones, or more advanced Web chat, like America Online's Virtual Places (VP). VP's attraction is that you create an on-screen avatar, or 3-D representation of yourself. Then you can go to designated Web pages and chat with other people who have VP.

WHERE CAN I GO TO LEARN MORE ABOUT THE WEB?

The best way to learn how to do something is by doing it, so the best place to learn about the Web is on the Web. It's time for you to put the pedal to the metal and get yourself onto the information superhighway. The following Web sites can help you learn more about the Web:

Learn the Net: www.learnthenet.com

Learning to Use the Internet: www.webliminal.com/lrn-net.html

Oprah Goes Online: www.oprahgoesonline.com/learn/index.html

GETTING THE JOB YOU WANT

One of the more important objectives of this text is to help you get the job that you want. First, you have to decide what you want to do. We'll help you explore this decision by explaining what people do in the various business functions: accounting, marketing, human resource management, finance, and so on. There are many good books about finding the job you want, so we can only introduce the subject here to get you thinking about careers as you read the various chapters.

If you are a returning student, you have blessings and handicaps that younger students do not have. First of all, you may have had a full-time job already. You are more likely to know what kind of job you *don't* want. That is a real advantage. By exploring the various business careers in depth, you should be able to choose a career path that will meet your objectives. If you have a full-time job right now, you've already discovered that working while going to school is exhausting. Many older students must juggle family responsibilities in addition to the responsibilities of school and work. But take heart. You have also acquired many skills from these experiences.

Visit our Web site at www.mcgrawhill.ca/college/nickels and look for online help in understanding the concepts you'll be reading about in this text. If you like, send us an e-mail message letting us know what you like about the book and the Web site. If there is something you think we should change, let us know that too!

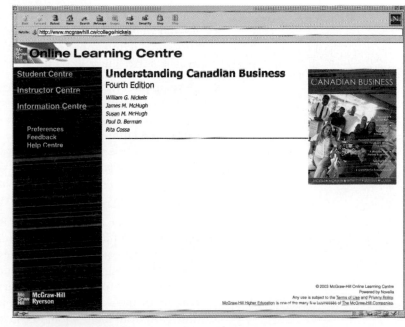

Even if they were acquired in unrelated fields, these skills will be invaluable as you enter your new career. You should have no trouble competing with younger students because you have more focus and experience. We enjoy having both kinds of students in class because of the different perspectives they have.

So, whether you're beginning your first career or your latest career, it's time to develop a strategy for finding and obtaining a personally satisfying job. You can find help with your career search online by clicking to Web sites such as www.monster.ca and www.workopolis.com. Such sites list companies currently looking for workers, offer help in creating a résumé, and provide many additional kinds of advice on conducting a job search.

Job Search Strategy

It is never too early to begin thinking about a future career or careers. The following strategies will give you some guidance in that pursuit:

1. **Begin with self-analysis.** You might begin your career quest by completing a self-analysis inventory. You can refer to Figure G.5 for a sample of a simple assessment.

2. **Search for jobs you would enjoy.** Begin at your school's career planning office or placement office, if your school has one. Keep interviewing people in various careers, even after you've found a job. Career progress demands continuous research.

3. **Begin the networking process.** You can start with your fellow students, family, relatives, neighbours, friends, professors, and local business people. Be sure to keep a file with the names, addresses, and phone numbers of contacts—where they work, the person who recommended them to you, and the relationship between the source person and the contact. A great way to make contacts and a good impression on employers is to do part-time work and summer internships at those firms you find interesting.

4. **Go to the Internet for help.** You will find details about finding jobs on a variety of Web sites. Many of these sites can help you write your résumé as well as help you search for jobs that meet your interests and skills. Later we'll list a number of these sites.

5. **Prepare a good cover letter and résumé.** Once you know what you want to do and where you would like to work, you need to develop a good résumé and cover letter. Your résumé lists your education, work experience, and activities. We'll talk about these key job search tools in more detail.

6. **Develop interviewing skills.** Interviewers will be checking your appearance (clothes, haircut, fingernails, shoes); your attitude (friendliness is desired); your verbal ability (speak loud enough to be heard clearly); and your motivation (be enthusiastic). Note also that interviewers want you to have been active in clubs and activities and to have set goals. Have someone evaluate you on these scales now to see if you have any weak points. You can then work on those points before you have any actual job interviews. We'll give you some clues as to how to do this later.

7. **Follow up.** Write a thank-you note after interviews, even if you think they didn't go well. You have a chance to make a lasting impression with a follow-up note.[6] Keep in touch with companies in which you have an interest. Show your interest by calling periodically or sending e-mail and letting the company know you are still interested. Indicate your willingness to travel to various parts of the country or the world to be interviewed. Get to know people in the company and learn from them whom to contact and what qualifications to emphasize.

Interests

1. How do I like to spend my time?
2. Do I enjoy being with people?
3. Do I like working with mechanical things?
4. Do I enjoy working with numbers?
5. Am I a member of many organizations?
6. Do I enjoy physical activities?
7. Do I like to read?

Abilities

1. Am I adept at working with numbers?
2. Am I adept at working with mechanical things?
3. Do I have good verbal and written communication skills?
4. What special talents do I have?
5. In which abilities do I wish I were more adept?

Education

1. Have I taken certain courses that have prepared me for a particular job?
2. In which subjects did I perform the best? The worst?
3. Which subjects did I enjoy the most? The least?
4. How have my extracurricular activities prepared me for a particular job?
5. Do I want a graduate degree? Do I want to earn it before beginning my job?
6. Why did I choose my major?

Experience

1. What previous jobs have I held? What were my responsibilities in each?
2. Were any of my jobs applicable to positions I may be seeking? How?
3. What did I like the most about my previous jobs? Like the least?
4. Why did I work in the jobs I did?

5. If I had it to do over again, would I work in these jobs? Why?

Personality

1. What are my good and bad traits?
2. Am I competitive?
3. Do I work well with others?
4. Am I outspoken?
5. Am I a leader or a follower?
6. Do I work well under pressure?
7. Do I work quickly, or am I methodical?
8. Do I get along well with others?
9. Am I ambitious?
10. Do I work well independently of others?

Desired job environment

1. Am I willing to relocate? Why?
2. Do I have a geographic preference? Why?
3. Would I mind travelling in my job?
4. Do I have to work for a large, nationally known firm to be satisfied?
5. Must I have a job that initially offers a high salary?
6. Must the job I assume offer rapid promotion opportunities?
7. In what kind of job environment would I feel most comfortable?
8. If I could design my own job, what characteristics would it have?

Personal goals

1. What are my short- and long-term goals? Why?
2. Am I career-oriented, or do I have broader interests?
3. What are my career goals?
4. What jobs are likely to help me achieve my goals?
5. What do I hope to be doing in 5 years? In 10 years?
6. What do I want out of life?

More Hints on the Job Search

FIGURE G.5

A SAMPLE PERSONAL ASSESSMENT

The placement office at your school is a good place to begin reading about potential employers. On-campus interviewing is by far the number-one source of jobs (see Figure G.6). Another good source of jobs involves writing to companies and sending a good cover letter and résumé. You can identify companies to contact in your library or on the Internet. Your library and the Internet may also have annual reports that will give you even more information about your selected companies.

A very important source of jobs is networking, that is, finding someone in a firm to recommend you. As mentioned earlier, you find those people by asking friends, neighbours, family members, and others if they know anyone who knows someone, and then you track those people down, talk with them, and seek their recommendation.

FIGURE G.6

WHERE STUDENTS FIND JOBS

SOURCE OF JOB	PERCENTAGE OF NEW EMPLOYEEES
On-campus interviewing	49.3%
Write-ins	9.8
Current employee referrals	7.2
Job listings with placement office	6.5
Responses for want ads	5.6
Walk-ins	5.5
Co-operative education programs	4.8%
Summer employment	4.7
Faculty/staff referrals	4.5
Internship programs	4.5
High-demand major programs	4.4
Minority career programs	2.9
Part-time employment	2.4
Unsolicited referrals from placement	2.1
Women's career programs	2.1
Job listings with employment agencies	1.9
Referrals from campus organizations	12.8

Workopolis.com is one example of a website that contains information about specific companies for which you would like to work, as well as various articles and resources. How can such information help you land the job you're seeking?

workopolis.com
CANADA'S BIGGEST JOB SITE

Other good sources of jobs include the want ads, job fairs, summer and other internship programs, placement bureaus, and sometimes walking into firms that appeal to you and asking for an interview. The *Occupational Outlook Quarterly* says this about job hunting:

> The skills that make a person employable are not so much the ones needed on the job as the ones needed to get the job, skills like the ability to find a job opening, complete an application, prepare the résumé, and survive an interview.

Here are a few printed sources you can use for finding out about jobs and other career choices:

- *Canada Employment Weekly* (Toronto, ON: Mediacorp Canada Inc.).
- *Canada's Top 100 Employers 2002: Best Places to Work in Canada* (Toronto, ON: Mediacorp Canada Inc., 2001).
- *Canadian Directory of Search Firms 2002: Find All the Canadian Headhunters In Your Field* (Toronto, ON: Mediacorp Canada Inc., 2001).
- *Cover Letter Magic* by Wendy S. Enelow and Louise Kursmark (Indianapolis, IN: JIST Publishing, 2001).
- *E-Job Hunting* by Eric Schlesinger and Susan Musich (Indianapolis: IN: SAMS, 2001).
- *Knock 'Em Dead 2001* by Martin Gate (Holbrook, MA: Adams Media Corporation, 2001).
- *The Career Directory 2002: Make the Most of Your Degree or Diploma* (Toronto, ON: Mediacorp Canada Inc., 2001).
- *The Everything Get-A-Job Book: From Resume Writing to Interviewing to Finding Tons of Job Openings* by Steven Graber and Mark Lipsman (Holbrook, MA: Adams Media Corporation, 2000).

- *What Color Is Your Parachute?* by Richard Nelson Bolles (Berkeley, CA: Ten Speed Press, 2001).
- *Who's Hiring 2002: Discover Canada's Fastest-Growing Employers* (Toronto, ON: Mediacorp Canada Inc., 2001).
- *101 Great Answers to the Toughest Interview Questions* by Ron Fry (Franklin Lakes, N.J.: Career Press, 2000).

The Net is becoming a great place to find jobs. To find information about careers or internships try these sites (though keep in mind that addresses on the Internet are subject to sudden and frequent change):

Canada Career Consortium: www.careerccc.org

Career Edge: www.careeredge.org

Career Experience: www.careerexperience.com

Career Gateway: www.edu.gov.on.ca/eng/career/descrip.html

Career Lab: www.careerlab.com

Job Shark Canada: www.jobshark.ca

Jobs, Workers, Training, and Careers Clusters: www.jobsect.ca

Monster: www.monster.ca

Workopolis: www.workopolis.com

It's never too early in your career to begin designing a résumé and drafting cover letters. Preparing such documents reveals your strengths and weaknesses more clearly than most other techniques. By preparing a résumé now, you may discover that you haven't been involved in enough outside activities to impress an employer. That information may prompt you to join some student groups, to become a volunteer, or to otherwise enhance your social skills.

You may also discover that you're weak on experience, and seek an internship or part-time job to fill in that gap. In any event, it's not too soon to prepare a résumé. It will certainly help you decide what you'd like to see in the area marked Education and, if you haven't already done so, help you choose a major and other coursework. Given that background, let's discuss how to prepare these materials.

Writing Your Résumé

A résumé is a document that lists information an employer would need to evaluate you and your background. It explains your immediate goals and career objectives. This information is followed by an explanation of your educational background, experience, interests, and other relevant data. Be sure to use industry buzzwords in your résumé (see Figure G.7) because companies use key words to scan such résumés. Having experience working in teams, for example, is important to many companies. For online résumé help, go to http://www.members.xoom.com/worksearch/reswri.htm.

If you have exceptional abilities but your résumé doesn't communicate them to the employer, those abilities aren't part of the person he or she will evaluate. You must be comprehensive and clear in your résumé if you are to communicate all your attributes.

Your résumé is an advertisement of yourself. If your ad is better than the other person's ad, you're more likely to get the interview. In this case, "better" means that your ad highlights your attributes attractively. In discussing your education, for example, be sure to highlight your extracurricular activities such as part-time jobs, sports, clubs, and other such activities. If you did well in school, include your grades. The idea is to make yourself look as good on paper as you are in reality.

Managed	Wrote	Budgeted	Improved
Planned	Produced	Designed	Increased
Organized	Scheduled	Directed	Investigated
Coordinated	Operated	Developed	Teamed
Supervised	Conducted	Established	Served
Trained	Administered	Implemented	Handled

The same is true for your job experience. Be sure to describe what you did, any special projects in which you participated, and any responsibilities you had. For the interests section, if you include one, don't just list your interests but also describe how deeply you were involved. If you organized the club, volunteered your time, or participated more often than usual in an organization, make sure to say so in the résumé. See Figure G.8 for a sample résumé. Most companies prefer that you keep your résumé to one page unless you have many years of experience.

PUTTING YOUR RÉSUMÉ ON THE INTERNET

You will probably want to post your résumé on the Internet because many larger firms are seeking candidates on the Net. An Internet résumé is different from a standard one because the elimination process is done by computer. Thus, you must understand what the computer is programmed to look for. It wants nouns, not verbs. Whereas the traditional résumé is built on verbs like *managed* and *supervised*, résumés on the Internet are built around nouns like *program management* and *teams*. They also emphasize software programs you have mastered like Microsoft Word. Listing jobs chronologically is no longer the best thing to do. Instead, emphasize knowledge, skills, and abilities. At the beginning of your résumé or after "Experience," you may write a new section called "Key Skills" or "Functional Expertise" and list all the nouns that fit your experience. For example, a salesperson might put terms that apply to selling such as *prospect, approach, presentations, close sale, follow up, focus groups, service.*

Zalee Harris lost her job just before Christmas but didn't bother going to the company's outplacement service or to the Help Wanted section of the newspaper. Instead, she built her own Web page on the Internet, complete with résumé and statement of purpose. She registered the address in search engines such as Yahoo and WebCrawler. In all, she posted her résumé on some 30 Internet job boards. In just over a month, she received 50 inquiries and found the job she wanted.[7] Harris represents the job candidate of the future, one who is Internet-savvy and knows what she wants. One of the experts in this area says that the best search engine is www.metacrawler.com because it sends queries to a number of search engines simultaneously.

From a company perspective, finding people on the Internet is a lot less expensive than hiring professional recruiters. Because more and more companies are using the Internet to find employees, it would be prudent for you to learn how to use this modern way to find jobs. Here are some hints on preparing your résumé for the Internet:

- Keep it simple. Use text only. Put a summary of your skills and your objective at the top so that the reader can capture as much as possible in the first 30 seconds.

- If you e-mail your résumé, send it in the text of the message: Don't put it as an attachment. It takes too long for the receiver to open an attachment.

- Customize each mailing to that specific company. You may use a standard résumé, but add data to customize it and to introduce it.

Yann Ng

345 Big Bend Boulevard

Antigonish, Nova Scotia, B2G 5V6

902-555-5789

YNG@AOL.COM

Job objectives: Sales representative in business-to-business marketing

Education:

Nova Scotia Community College

B.A.: Marketing major

Earned 100 percent of expenses working 35 hours a week

Member of Student Marketing Association

Vice-President of Student Government Association

Dean's List for two semesters

Work experience:

Schnuck's Supermarket: Worked checkout evenings and weekends for four years while in school. Learned to respond to customer requests quickly, and communicate with customers in a friendly and helpful manner.

Mary Tuttle's Flowers: For two summers, made flower arrangements, managed sales transactions, and acted as assistant to the manager. Also trained and supervised three employees. Often handled customer inquiries and complaints.

Special skills:

Fluent in Vietnamese, French, and English. Proficient at using Word 2000, Excel 2000, and PowerPoint 2000. Developed my own website (www.yan@stilnet.com) and use the Internet often to do research for papers and for personal interests. Sales skills include conducting focus groups, prospecting, making presentations, and customer service.

Other interests:

Cooking: often prepare meals for my family and friends. Reading, especially the classics. Piano playing and aerobics. Travelling: Asia, Europe, and the U.S. Doing research on the Internet.

- Put your cover letter and résumé in one file.
- Use any advertised job title as the subject of your e-mail message, citing any relevant job numbers. (Note that some companies don't want you to e-mail them your résumé and cover letter, preferring letters or faxes instead.)

You can find more details about applying for jobs on the Internet in Margaret Riley Dikel and Frances E. Roehm's 2000–2001 edition of *The Guide to Internet Job Searching* from VGM Career Horizons. See Figure G.9 for a sample Internet résumé.

WRITING A COVER LETTER

A cover letter is used to announce your availability and to introduce the résumé. The cover letter is probably one of the most important advertisements anyone will write in a lifetime—so it should be done right.

First, the cover letter should indicate that you've researched the organization in question and are interested in a job there. Let the organization know what sources you used and what you know about it in the first paragraph to get the attention of the reader and show your interest.

FIGURE G.9

SAMPLE INTERNET
RÉSUMÉ

Yann Ng
345 Big Bend Boulevard
Antigonish, Nova Scotia, B2G 5V6
902-555-5789
YNG@AOL.COM

Job objectives: Sales representative in business-to-business marketing

Education:
Nova Scotia Community College
B.A.: Marketing major
Earned 100 percent of expenses working 35 hours a week
Member of Student Marketing Association
Vice-President of Student Government Association
Dean's List for two semesters

Work experience:

Schnuck's Supermarket: Worked checkout evenings and weekends for four years while in school. Learned to respond to customer requests quickly, and communicate with customers in a friendly and helpful manner.

Mary Tuttle's Flowers: For two summers, made flower arrangements, managed sales transactions, and acted as assistant to the manager. Also trained and supervised three employees. Often handled customer inquiries and complaints.

Special skills: Fluent in Vietnamese, French, and English. Proficient at using Word 2000, Excel 2000, and PowerPoint 2000. Developed my own website (www.yan@stilnet.com) and use the Internet often to do research for papers and for personal interests. Sales skills include conducting focus groups, prospecting, making presentations, and customer service.

Other interests: Cooking: often prepare meals for my family and friends. Reading, especially the classics. Piano playing and aerobics. Travelling: Asia, Europe, and the U.S. Doing research on the Internet.

You may have heard people say, "It's not what you know, but whom you know that counts." This is only partly true, as both knowledge and personal contacts are important. But, if you don't know someone, you can get to know someone. You do this by calling the organization (or better yet, visiting its offices) and talking to people who already have the kind of job you're hoping to get. Ask about training, salary, and other relevant issues. Then, in your cover letter, mention that you've talked with some of the firm's employees and that this discussion increased your interest. You thereby show the letter reader that you "know someone," if only casually, and that you're interested enough to actively pursue the organization. This is all part of networking.

Second, in the description of yourself, be sure to say how your attributes will benefit the organization. For example, don't just say, "I will be graduating with a degree in marketing." Say, "You will find that my college training in marketing and marketing research has prepared me to learn your marketing system quickly and begin making a contribution right away." The sample cover letter in Figure G.10 will give you a better feel for how this looks.

Third, be sure to "ask for the order." That is, say in your final paragraph that you're available for an interview at a time and place convenient for the interviewer. Again, see the sample cover letter in Figure G.10 for guidance. Notice in this letter how Yann subtly showed that she read business publications and drew attention to her résumé.

Principles to follow in writing a cover letter and preparing your résumé include the following:

- Be self-confident. List all your good qualities and attributes.

- Don't be apologetic or negative. Write as one professional to another, not as a humble student begging for a job.

- Describe how your experience and education can add value to the organization.

- Research every prospective employer thoroughly before writing anything. Use a rifle approach rather than a shotgun approach. That is, write effective marketing-oriented letters to a few select companies rather than to a general list.

- Have your materials prepared by an experienced keyboarder if you are not highly skilled yourself. If you have access to a word processing system with a letter-quality laser printer, you can produce individualized letters efficiently.

- Have someone edit your materials for spelling, grammar, and style. Don't be like the student who sent out a second résumé to correct "some mixtakes." Or another who said, "I am acurite with numbers."

- Don't send the names of references until asked.

---

345 Big Bend Blvd.
Antigonish, Nova Scotia, B2G 5V6
October 10, 2002

Mr. Carl Karlinski
Premier Designs
45 Apple Court
Halifax, Nova Scotia, B3J 7C4

Dear Mr. Karlinski: [Note that it's best to know to whom to write by name.]
　　Recent articles in *Canadian Business* and *National Post Business* have praised your company for its innovative products and strong customer orientation. I'm familiar with your creative display materials. In fact, we've used them at Mary Tuttle's Flower Shop—my employer for the last two summers. Christie Bouchard, your local sales representative, told me all about your products and your training program at Premier Designs.
　　Christie mentioned the kind of salespeople you are seeking. Here's what she said and my relevant qualifications.
　　Requirement: Men and women with proven sales ability.
　　Qualifications: Success making and selling flower arrangements at Mary Tuttle's and practising customer relations at Schnuck's Supermarket. As you know, Schnuck's has one of the best customer-oriented training programs in the food industry.
　　Requirement: Self-motivated people with leadership ability.
　　Qualifications: Paid my way through school working nights and summers. Selected to be on the Student Government Association at Nova Scotia Community College. Paid my own way to Asia, Europe, and the Americas.
　　Could you use such a successful salesperson at Premier Design? I will be in Halifax the week of November 4–8. What time and date would be most convenient for us to discuss career opportunities at Premier? I'll phone your secretary to set up an appointment.

Sincerely,

Yann Ng

FIGURE G.10
SAMPLE COVER LETTER

PREPARING FOR JOB INTERVIEWS

Companies usually don't conduct job interviews unless they're somewhat certain that the candidate has the requirements for the job. The interview, therefore, is pretty much a make-or-break situation. If it goes well, you have a greater chance of being hired. That's why you must be prepared for your interviews. There are five stages of interview preparation:

1. **Do research about the prospective employers.** Learn what industry the firm is in, its competitors, the products it produces and their acceptance in the market, and the title of your desired position. You can find such information in the firm's annual reports, and various business publications such as *Canadian Business* and *Report On Business Magazine*. Ask your librarian for help or search the Internet. This important first step shows you have initiative and interest in the firm.

2. **Practise the interview.** Figure G.11 lists some of the more frequently asked questions in an interview. Practise answering these questions and more at the placement office and with your roommate, parents, or friends. Don't memorize your answers, but be prepared—know what you're going to say. Also, develop a series of questions to ask the interviewer. Figure G.12 shows sample questions you might ask. Be sure you know whom to contact, and write down the names of everyone you meet. Review the action words in Figure G.7 and try to fit them into your answers.

3. **Be professional during the interview.** You should look and sound professional throughout the interview. Do your homework and find out how managers dress at the firm. Make sure you wear an appropriate outfit. When you meet the interviewers, greet them by name, smile, and maintain good eye contact. Sit up straight in your chair and be alert and enthusiastic. If you have practised, you should be able to relax and be confident. Other than that, be yourself, answer questions, and be friendly and responsive. When you leave, thank the interviewers and, if you're still interested in the job, tell them so. If they don't tell you, ask them what the next step is. Maintain a positive attitude. Figures G.13 and G.14 outline what the interviewers will be evaluating.

4. **Follow up on the interview.** First, write down what you can remember from the interview: names of the interviewers and their titles, any salary figures mentioned, dates for training, and so on. Put the information in your career file. You can send a follow-up letter thanking each interviewer for his or her time. You can also send a letter of recommendation or some other piece of added information to keep their interest. "The squeaky wheel gets the grease" is the operating slogan. Your enthusiasm for working for the company could be a major factor in hiring you.

FIGURE G.11

FREQUENTLY ASKED QUESTIONS

- How would you describe yourself?
- What are your greatest strengths and weaknesses?
- Why did you choose this company?
- What do you know about the company?
- What are your long-range career goals?
- What courses did you like best? Least?
- What are your hobbies?
- Do you prefer a specific geographic location?

- Are you willing to travel (or move)?
- Which accomplishments have given you the most satisfaction?
- What things are most important to you in a job?
- Why should I hire you?
- What experience have you had in this type of work?
- How much do you expect to earn?

- How long does the training program last, and what is included?
- How soon after school would I be expected to start?
- What are the advantages of working for this firm?
- How much travel is normally expected?
- What managerial style should I expect in my area?
- How would you describe the working environment in my area?
- How would I be evaluated?

- What is the company's promotion policy?
- What is the corporate culture?
- What is the next step in the selection procedure?
- How soon should I expect to hear from you?
- What other information would you like about my background, experience, or education?
- What is your highest priority in the next six months and how could someone like me help?

5. **Be prepared to act.** Know what you want to say if you do get a job offer. You may not want the job once you know all the information. Don't expect to receive a job offer from everyone you meet, but do expect to learn something from every interview. With some practice and persistence, you should find a rewarding and challenging job.

FIGURE G.12

SAMPLE QUESTIONS TO ASK THE INTERVIEWER

1. **Ability to communicate**. Do you have the ability to organize your thoughts and ideas effectively? Can you express them clearly when speaking or writing? Can you present your ideas to others in a persuasive way?
2. **Intelligence.** Do you have the ability to understand the job assignment? Learn the details of operation? Contribute original ideas to your work?
3. **Self-confidence.** Do you demonstrate a sense of maturity that enables you to deal positively and effectively with situations and people?
4. **Willingness to accept responsibility.** Are you someone who recognizes what needs to be done and is willing to do it?
5. **Initiative.** Do you have the ability to identify the purpose for work and to take action?
6. **Leadership.** Can you guide and direct others to obtain the recognized objectives?
7. **Energy level.** Do you demonstrate a forcefulness and capacity to make things move ahead? Can you maintain your work effort at an above-average rate?
8. **Imagination.** Can you confront and deal with problems that may not have standard solutions?
9. **Flexibility.** Are you capable of changing and being receptive to new situations and ideas?
10. **Interpersonal skills.** Can you bring out the best efforts of individuals so they become effective, enthusiastic members of a team?
11. **Self-knowledge.** Can you realistically assess your own capabilities? See yourself as others see you? Clearly recognize your strengths and weaknesses?
12. **Ability to handle conflict.** Can you successfully contend with stressful situations and antagonism?
13. **Competitiveness.** Do you have the capacity to compete with others and the willingness to be measured by your performance in relation to that of others?
14. **Goal achievement.** Do you have the ability to identify and work toward specific goals? Do such goals challenge your abilities?
15. **Vocational skills.** Do you possess the positive combination of education and skills required for the position you are seeking?
16. **Direction.** Have you defined your basic personal needs? Have you determined what type of position will satisfy your knowledge, skills, and goals?

Source: "So You're Looking for a Job?" The College Placement Council.

FIGURE G.13

TRAITS RECRUITERS SEEK IN JOB PROSPECTS

FIGURE G.14

INTERVIEW RATING SHEET

Interviewer: "For each characteristic listed below there is a rating scale of 1 through 7, where '1' is generally the most unfavourable rating of the characteristic and '7' the most favourable. Rate each characteristic by circling just one number to represent the impression the candidate gave in the interview that you have just completed."

Name of Candidate _____

1. **Appearance**
   Sloppy   1   2   3   4   5   6   7   Neat

2. **Attitude**
   Unfriendly   1   2   3   4   5   6   7   Friendly

3. **Assertiveness/Verbal Ability**
   a. Responded completely to questions asked
       Poor   1   2   3   4   5   6   7   Excellent
   b. Clarified personal background and related it to job opening and description
       Poor   1   2   3   4   5   6   7   Excellent
   c. Able to explain and sell job abilities
       Poor   1   2   3   4   5   6   7   Excellent
   d. Initiated questions regarding position and firm
       Poor   1   2   3   4   5   6   7   Excellent
   e. Expressed thorough knowledge of personal goals and abilities
       Poor   1   2   3   4   5   6   7   Excellent

4. **Motivation**
   Poor   1   2   3   4   5   6   7   High

5. **Subject/Academic Knowledge**
   Poor   1   2   3   4   5   6   7   Good

6. **Stability**
   Poor   1   2   3   4   5   6   7   Good

7. **Composure**
   Ill at ease   1   2   3   4   5   6   7   Relaxed

8. **Personal Involvement/Activities, Clubs, Etc.**
   Low   1   2   3   4   5   6   7   Very high

9. **Mental Impression**
   Dull   1   2   3   4   5   6   7   Alert

10. **Adaptability**
    Poor   1   2   3   4   5   6   7   Good

11. **Speech Pronunciation**
    Poor   1   2   3   4   5   6   7   Good

12. **Overall Impression**
    Unsatisfactory   1   2   3   4   5   6   7   Highly satisfactory

13. **Would you hire this individual if you were permitted to make a decision right now?**

        Yes   No

BE PREPARED TO CHANGE CAREERS

If you're like most people, you'll find that you'll follow several different career paths over your lifetime. This is a good thing in that it enables you to try different jobs and stay fresh and enthusiastic. The key to moving forward in your career is a willingness to change jobs, always searching for the career that will bring the most personal satisfaction and growth. This means that you'll have to write many cover letters and résumés and go through many interviews. Each time you change jobs, go through the steps in this prologue to be sure you're fully prepared. Good luck.

PART 1

CHAPTER 1

Major Trends Affecting Canadian Business

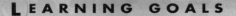

LEARNING GOALS

AFTER YOU HAVE READ AND STUDIED THIS CHAPTER, YOU SHOULD BE ABLE TO

1 Explain the importance and impact of technological developments.

2 Describe what is meant by the *information age* and what its implications are.

3 Discuss the globalization of business and why it is so important for Canadian companies.

4 Identify how big business is becoming more competitive and the pressures to do so.

5 Explain why small and home-based businesses have become so popular.

6 Show how the service sector has replaced manufacturing as the principal provider of jobs, but why manufacturing remains vital for Canada.

7 Explain current population trends and their major impact on business.

8 Describe how environmental and other ethical issues play a major role in all business planning and actions.

9 Show how jobs and careers are affected by the trends discussed in the chapter.

Robin King—A Canadian with Advanced Technological Vision

Back in 1979 Robin King had a wild idea: he wanted to establish a computer-animation program at Sheridan College in Oakville, Ontario. At that time very few people had even heard of computers, much less computer animation. Yet here was this visionary pushing to develop a program that probably seemed like science fiction.

Today, as the former chairman of media and communications at Sheridan and now professor emeritus and research associate, Robin King is receiving accolades for having developed a program that is turning out the leading computer animators in North America. Every

Courtesy of Robin King

year, top animation companies from the United States, including leading Hollywood production companies, head for Sheridan College to interview graduating students for employment. Starting salaries are in the US$45,000 range.

Other educational institutions that have developed similar programs are McKenzie College in Halifax; Algonquin College in the Ottawa area; and Capilano College, The Emily Carr Institute of Art and Design, and The Vancouver Film Institute in the Vancouver area. Today there is a proliferation of public and private organizations offering such programs. This proliferation of institutions with expert computer animation programs, combined with the success of the 1996 film *Toy Story*, which was entirely computer generated, led the Disney Company to establish two Canadian locations, one in Toronto and one in Vancouver. Disney wanted to be near the source of the talent necessary to

facilitate production of other computer-animated films. Graduates of Sheridan and other colleges have animated many other films including *Men in Black* and *Antz*.

For Sheridan this success has caused such an increase in enrollment in the program that King reports they are limiting the size of classes to control quality. Sheridan has built a $35-million Centre for Animation and Emerging Technologies, and has received two research grants, each for $1.5 million, from the Ontario government and private sources for a visual design project.

Robin King is an example of how technologically oriented forward thinking creates significant competitive advantages for institutions, companies, and countries and thereby significant employment opportunities for Canadians. King is one of the pioneers who have given Canada its global reputation in the computer-animation field. King also heads his own consulting firm, Imagina Corp., which specializes in developing new media and educational technologies and is associated with Namzak Labs, which develops Internet collaboration projects.

In recognition of his pioneering work and achievements, in 2001 the Canadian New Media Association presented King, 57, with a Lifetime Achievement Award.

Adapted from: Interview with Robin King, June 25, 2001 and October 26, 1998; Janet McFarland and Gayle MacDonald, "Sheridan's a Draw for Film Makers," *Globe and Mail, Report on Business*, December 4, 1995, p. B6. Reprinted with the permission of the *Globe and Mail*.

ETHICAL DILEMMA
Facing the Issues

As you work your way through the chapter, you will see that, in their ceaseless quest for competitive advantage and growth, companies are constantly searching for the lowest-cost countries to manufacture their products and services. For the same reason, companies are also driven to adopt the latest manufacturing and information technologies. These twin trends often cause hardship for company employees and the communities where operations are located when plants and offices are closed and employees are terminated. At the same time the vast expansion of the economies of many countries has put enormous pressure on our fragile environment, causing problems for the people who inhabit this globe, including Canadians. You will read about these issues in many chapters in this book. The question is, how do we go about solving these difficult problems? Toward the end of the chapter you will see an attempt to come to grips with these difficult issues.

TRENDS

www.sheridanc.on.ca

For more information about Sheridan's computer-animation program, visit its Web site. Click on the icons available to see what Sheridan's program does and discover its impressive achievements. Pay particular attention to its *media releases*.

business
An organization that manufactures or sells goods or services to satisfy some customer's needs in an attempt to generate a profit.

In this chapter we will explore some of the significant trends (many of which nourish each other) that are revolutionizing the nature of the business world. It is this new world in which you will find yourself when you graduate.

Before proceeding, let us define what a *business* is. A **business** is an organization that manufactures or sells goods or services to satisfy some customer's needs in an attempt to generate a profit. A business may be an Internet service provider selling its service to individuals, companies, educational institutions, libraries, hospitals, or governments, or it may be part of a complex chain of providers of goods. An example is a chemical company that sells raw materials to a pharmaceutical company, which manufactures drugs that it sells to wholesalers, which in turn sell to pharmacies, which sell to consumers.

Trends have a profound impact on the kinds of jobs and careers that will be available to you after you graduate from college or university. Specifically, what should you be planning and doing to take advantage of the opportunities that will be there? The last section in this chapter will help to provide answers to this question. These trends also raise significant environmental and other ethical issues. (See the Ethical Dilemma box "Facing the Issues.")

Two Main Trends: Technology and Globalization

The two most important universal trends for business are the extremely rapid developments in technology—the *technological revolution*—and the *globalization* of business, which has become totally international in nature. Computers, robots, lasers, fibre optics, satellites, and many other significant advances in technology have radically altered the way we produce and what we produce, the way we buy and sell things, the way people and businesses communicate, the manner and speed with which goods and information are sent and received, the way funds are obtained, and just about everything else in the business world. The Profile of Robin King and the world of computer animation provides some good examples of such radical changes. Advances in communication and transportation technologies have made the planet into a very small place and have made it possible for business to operate globally. Uptown and downtown may now be, and often are, thousands of kilometres away without causing any great inconvenience. When you phone Air Canada or American Airlines or any large company, you do not know where the person answering you is located. Just try asking an airline what the weather is like and you may find out that the call centre is in Calgary or Denver, Colorado, or Saint John, N.B. The Internet and e-commerce have had an enormous impact.

These two dominant trends have meant a drastic shake-up for business around the globe: giant companies merging into still larger entities; employees and managers laid off by the millions; long-term job security replaced by short-term or temporary jobs; high or persistent unemployment rates, especially among the young, new technologies sprouting weekly; barriers to world trade dropping steadily; fierce competition for consumers' money; the economic awakening of East Asia; companies scouring the world for low cost production areas.

Competition is so intense that many companies and governments have stepped up efforts to find out what competitors and *their* countries' governments are doing. These efforts have led to a sharp increase in what is called *industrial* or *economic espionage*.

These major developments are creating a new economic world order. In the process, tens of millions of people's lives are being turned upside down—some for the better and some for the worse. How these enormous changes are affecting Canada will be the essence of this book, as they are the essence of the world of business today. The rapid rise and fall of the dot-com companies (discussed in more detail in Chapters 7, 11, and 17) is a good example of the effects of the technological revolution on the world of business.

In this chapter we will examine briefly these and other trends that interact with, and are mainly the result of, technological change and the globalization of business. Topics include how companies compete; the drastic reductions in company workforce size; the mushrooming of small-business start-ups, including home-based businesses; the service sector as the main job creator and the continuing importance of the manufacturing sector; changes in demographics; ethical and environmental issues; and higher educational requirements for jobs.

Counter-Trends and Threats

As you will see in Chapter 4, a new phenomenon has appeared on the global scene—widespread protests at meetings of international bodies. Many different religious, environmental, community-based, and other organizations are protesting against the negative impact of globalization in trade and investment on the lives of people and on the freedom of both national and lower levels of government to take actions beneficial for their people. These anti-globalization protests have been growing in strength.

A violent and most unusual threatening development was the terrorist hijacking of four airplanes in the United States on September 11, 2001, two of which were deliberately crashed into the famous World Trade Center towers, resulting in their collapse and causing the deaths of more than 3,000 people. While at the time of publication no organization or group has admitted responsibility or the reason for these violent attacks, suspicion is strongly focused on vocal religious fundamentalist groups in central Asia who praised the attacks and purport to speak in the name of Islam. In addition to voicing strong disapproval of U.S. foreign policies and influence, they also seem to be opposed to many aspects of the modern world, including the globalization of business dominated by the United States and European countries.

The net effect of these terrorist attacks on the global economy has been to sharpen the decline that was already in progress. The damage has been particularly bad in Canada and the United States, and will be discussed in more detail in Chapters 2 and 3.

THE TECHNOLOGICAL REVOLUTION

Human history is characterized by a steady flow of improvements in how work gets done, how products are made, and how life is made easier for people. Every time somebody finds a new way of doing something by using a better or new tool, device, or machine, we have an advance in technology. Sometimes the advance is a revolution.

The "chunnel" train is a technological advance that has made life easier. Developed by Bombardier, the train transports commuters from London to Paris much more rapidly than previously possible. The train uses the tunnel under the English Channel, called the "chunnel."

Canadian Press CP. Photograph by Stephen Ward.

The first animal-drawn plow was such a revolution. Figure 1.1 lists some other important inventions. All these advances made significant changes to how we lived, worked, and produced.

If you look carefully at the list of technological advances in Figure 1.1, which is far from complete, you will note that many inventions took place within the past 200 years. Since then the pace of technological advance has been increasing, especially in the past two decades. Most commentators on technology expect that the rate of change will accelerate even more in the next few decades. See the Reaching Beyond Our Borders box "Small Canadian Firm Has Big International Clout" for an example of how Canada is participating in advancing satellite technology.

The most significant change in our era has been the advent of the computer. The computer and other electronic marvels—CD-ROMs, communication satellites, faxes, modems, cellular phones, the Internet—as well as fibre optics, have had three major effects on business:

1. Operations have been revolutionized.

2. The information age has been ushered in.

3. Our large planet has been made into a small globe.

Throughout this book we examine each of these three phenomena and their spinoffs. These developments have such sweeping ramifications that the operation of modern business cannot be understood unless they are taken into account. Chapters 10 and 11 are devoted to a detailed examination of the impact of technology on production and operations.

THE INFORMATION AGE

Toward the end of the eighteenth century, the invention of steam power in England led to the Industrial Revolution, which started in Europe and quickly spread across the Atlantic Ocean. For the first time in history, it became possible to set up factories employing many people under one roof to produce large quantities of a given product. Prior to that time only limited amounts of consumer and other goods were produced, by hand, at home or in small workshops by craftspeople. Trade was slow and very limited.

FIGURE 1.1

REVOLUTIONARY TECHNOLOGICAL ADVANCES

These inventions radically altered how societies functioned.

Prior to 1700	The wheel, writing, bronze, iron, the arch, printing, gunpowder, clocks
Late 1700s	Steam power
1800s	Railways, telegraphy, photography, telephones, phonographs, steel-making, typewriters, oil and gasoline, rubber, automobiles, electricity, light bulbs, X-rays, a vast array of machinery for agriculture and industry
1900–1970	Motion-picture cameras, radios, refrigeration, airplanes, TV, plastics, atomic energy, rocketry, space exploration, satellites
1970–2000	Photocopiers, telefaxes, computers, modems, portable phones, cable and satellite TV, cell phones, pagers, fibre optics, the Internet

REACHING BEYOND OUR BORDERS   www.telespace.org

Small Canadian Firm Has Big International Clout

Starting from his home office in Toronto, consultant Uriel Domb played a role in more than half the world's satellite projects launched in the 1980s and the early 1990s. Now in a small Toronto office, with field offices in Los Angeles and London, England, Domb, an Israeli-born, U.S.-educated aerospace engineer, first worked at NASA in Washington, DC, from 1967 to 1970. In 1970 he was recruited by Telesat Canada, then establishing its satellite-communications program, to direct ground-control systems. He spent a year at Bell-Northern Research Ltd., Toronto, then left to start Telespace Ltd. He built a team of 25 independent consultants for his company.

The firm has an enviable track record for complicated international communications contracts specializing in satellite-technology consulting. Telespace has helped launch satellites on all continents and for many companies and space agencies. It operates without the sophisticated marketing efforts, office bureaucracy, and centralized operations of large satellite consulting firms.

"My basic philosophy is, it's important to serve our clients where they are," Domb says. And since Canada's satellite-communications market is already mature, Telespace has pursued contracts around the world. Telespace has an international reputation for excellent work, says Keith Rowe, ground-control manager of Inmarsat in London, who has worked with the firm on several projects. "Domb's strength is overall knowledge of satellite operations. But we have used their systems and people in every area."

Most clients learn of Telespace by word of mouth, Domb says. Certainly that was the case with Thailand, which chose Telespace over at least four bigger competitors for a large consulting project in 1991. The first THAICOM satellite was successfully launched only 25 months after contract signature.

Telespace is cost effective, partly because it doesn't spend money on expensive marketing efforts, Domb says. Its resources have instead gone into hiring the right people. Thailand needed a consultant who could provide expertise in all areas of satellite communications, but the Thais wanted to develop their own expertise so they wouldn't remain reliant on consultants. "We found this through our work with Brazil," Domb says. "Developing countries put a high priority on transferring technology and training people."

Domb helped Norway and Israel prepare to launch their own satellites in 1996 and 1997.

Telespace is now concentrating on telecommunications and on direct-broadcasting satellites in Europe, the Middle East, and North America. In Europe Telespace is working with EUTELSAT, which is a consortium of European countries based in Paris. In North America Domb is working with various companies, including Shaw Communications. Telespace is also involved in developing new satellites for mobile telephones as well as the next generation of satellites for Israel.

Sources: Interview with Uriel Domb, February 16, 1996, and October 26, 1998; company publications; Susan Noakes, *Financial Post,* May 1, 1992, p. 1.

Continual inventions expanded production until we reached the almost limitless capabilities we now have. Vast improvements in transportation facilitated trade and increased distribution of the now much greater supply of goods. The nineteenth century into the early twentieth century was the era of production—trying to produce enough of everything from food to cars to meet people's needs. It is obvious that today, at least in Canada and the rest of the developed world, there is no longer a shortage of goods and services. Many individuals may be unable to afford them, but they are certainly available.

Information as a Vital Competitive Tool

information age
An era in which information is a crucial factor in the successful operation of organizations.

Today, producers of goods and services compete fiercely for buyers. Any edge gained by a company gives it a competitive advantage. Information has become a very important edge. That is why our time is called the **information age**, an era in which information is a crucial factor in the successful operation of organizations. (Perhaps inaccurately, we are often said to be living in a postindustrial information society.)

Computers and the whole range of electronic gadgets—laptops, modems, cellular phones, and more—have made the information age possible. One key to competitiveness is access to information about your own operations. You require a similar information flow about your competitors, your markets, government activities, and technological developments that may affect your business. To achieve this, businesses require good communication systems. This area is where computers and information systems play a critical role.

www.fedex.ca

Explore Federal Express's Web site for more information on the company.

Information has become a crucial element for competitiveness, and competition has become fiercer as it has become global. How can the CNR or CPR know exactly where each of their tens of thousands of railcars is located, loaded or empty, anywhere in Canada or the United States? How can a courier service like Federal Express promise next-day delivery to any major city in the world from almost any other city? A computerized information system makes it possible. Every Federal Express unit, truck, and plane has a computer that is tied to the main computer system, so at any given moment the system knows where any parcel is.

None of the large chains of pharmaceutical, department, or supermarket stores would be able to keep track of their vast inventories, which are constantly changing, without a complex computer-controlled information system. Nor could their accounting systems provide the necessary information to managers without highly specialized computer technology. In fact, it is hard to find any size of business in Canada today that can operate without computer technology.

Information technology has revolutionized businesses of all kinds. Farmers now use computers to keep track of all kinds of information, from organizing animal vaccination schedules to figuring out which animal is ready to breed.

This trend has reached a point where new terminology is required to describe the whole range of communication activities. Now we refer to the *information highway* and *electronic data interchange (EDI)*. Attempts are being made to define just what the information highway means or will encompass. (Chapter 11 at the end of Part 3 examines the importance of these technologies in some detail.)

The electronically fed information age also makes possible home-based businesses and home-based employees (discussed later in the chapter). How could they function without the whole battery of modern gadgetry? Information technology also allows companies to operate on a global basis, which is our next topic.

THE GLOBALIZATION OF BUSINESS

From the earliest days, countries have traded with each other. Sailing vessels and other boats crisscrossed many of

Canadian Press MACLEANS. Photograph by Todd Korol.

the oceans, seas, lakes, and rivers of the world. In Canada aboriginal peoples and Europeans travelled by canoe through the Great Lakes and the thousands of rivers and lakes that span North America. What is different about the new globalized world of business, an expression that has become almost a cliché? There is no comparison between doing business today and yesterday.

A Globally Integrated System of Operating

When we refer to the **globalization** of business, we are talking about a globally integrated system of production, marketing, finance, and management. All of these functions are carried out with little regard for borders or distances. Companies that operate globally are often called *transnational companies* (TNCs). Some large Canadian TNCs are Nortel Networks, Nova Corp., Bombardier, Magna International, Inco Limited, and Power Corp. These companies have operations scattered around the world. They may raise funds in Toronto, New York, London, or Tokyo. Some of these funds may be provided by the Royal Bank of Canada, which, like the other major Canadian banks, has agencies and branches around the world to service Canadian and other TNCs.

A telephone or switching equipment, a computer, a plane, or a train may have components from a dozen different countries. Nortel and Bombardier do far more business outside Canada than in their home market, and both have international boards of directors. A so-called Canadian, American, or Japanese car may be designed, engineered, and tested in various countries. It certainly has components made on every continent. That is what globalization means.

Companies scour the world for the most reliable, lowest-cost, highest-quality sources to produce all or part of their products. Management personnel are sought from all over the world. That means that all countries are in a globally competitive market. Tokyo vies with New York to provide financing, Mexico and Brazil with China and Indonesia to provide production, and Canada with the United States or Germany to provide computer software. Toyota and Honda both produce cars in Ontario. This trend toward companies investing and producing in countries outside their home base is a basic aspect of globalization.

As you will see in other chapters in the book, globalization affects all businesses, not only the large ones. Many medium and small businesses rely on foreign companies for supplies or on foreign markets for their products or services. Individuals, as well as companies, are affected by global events: we all see how the price of gas at the pump fluctuates as world oil supplies fluctuate.

Alliances with Competitors A logical extension of this trend includes telecommunication companies worldwide combining to form networks, and General Motors getting together with Toyota to manufacture cars in the United States. GM has a joint venture with Suzuki to produce cars in Ontario and truck engines in California.

globalization
A globally integrated system of production, marketing, finance, and management.

Zim Israel Navigation Company (Canada) Ltd., a subsidiary of Israel-based Zim Israel Navigation Co., is a good example of a global operation. The company's ships and trucks pick up containers of merchandise from cities and ports around the world and deliver them to other global locations. The company's financing and management personnel are sourced from a variety of countries.

Canadian Press CNW.

strategic alliances or joint ventures
Arrangements whereby two or more companies co-operate for a special or limited purpose.

www.pfdf.org/
To learn more about Peter Drucker and his prolific career, visit the Drucker Foundation Web site.

Ford and Volkswagen have also combined their efforts to produce their cars in the same assembly plant in South America. These are **strategic alliances** or **joint ventures**, arrangements whereby two or more companies co-operate for a special or limited purpose.

Peter Drucker, a world-famous management consultant, expects the trend to international investment in manufacturing and financial services to continue to grow in importance.[1] (Chapter 3 is devoted to this global phenomenon.) This means that Canadian, American, Japanese, or Korean firms are losing their clear-cut identities as pure companies of one national origin. As one Harvard economist put it, it is getting increasingly harder to answer the question (in the industrial sense): Who is us?[2]

CRITICAL THINKING

Some people are concerned that technology is "taking over." Do you see technology as a threat or as an opportunity? What about its effect on the job market?

Can you suggest what any particular business should be doing to become more competitive globally? How do you feel about the prospect of working in a global environment?

The Trend Toward the Pacific Rim: B.C. Takes the Lead

Globalization also means that the differences in time zones around the world have been removed. Although half the world is sleeping while the other half is awake, stock exchanges are moving to 24-hour operations and some businesses are operating outside regular hours. The end of the business day in Canada is the start of the next business day in the Pacific Rim countries of the Far East.

The Pacific Rim countries had an erratic economic history during the 1990s. Dynamic and world leader Japan hit an economic slump and has still not been able to show significant growth. While not suffering as badly as Japan, the famous *four tigers*—South Korea, Taiwan, Singapore, and Hong Kong—still lost a lot of their strength. The same happened to the *three mini tigers*—Indonesia, Malaysia, and Thailand. They all went through what was dubbed the "Asian flu" in the late 1990s. The only exception was China, and India is not far behind. These two countries, with 2.5 billion people—40 percent of the world population—represent an enormous market that is growing steadily.

British Columbia leads the country in trade and investment with the Pacific Rim countries. The rest of Canada is mainly dependent on exports to the United States, but British Columbia, while increasing its percentage of exports to our southern neighbour, still has a strong export trade with the Pacific Rim. Figure 1.2 shows the export trends from 1996 to 2000 and the effect of the Asian flu in reducing B.C.'s export percentage from 32.0 to 20.6 while its exports to the United States climbed from 54.6 to 67.2 percent. The figures for the same period for the rest of Canada showed exports to the Pacific Rim dropping from 3.3 to 2.1 percent while exports to the United States rose from 83.7 to 89.1 percent of all exports. These trends also reflect the continuing strength of the United States economy.[3]

***Effect of East-Asian Immigration on B.C. Business*[4]**   Consider what is happening to Vancouver and the lower mainland: "Thousands of newcomers, led by affluent Hong Kong and Taiwanese immigrants, are injecting new vitality and a sharper edge into the city's once parochial business culture." Twenty-five percent of Vancouver's population is of Asian descent, which makes it "the most Asian-flavoured municipality on the continent."

At first, most of the investments were in real estate developments, led by Li Ka-shing, Hong Kong's wealthiest industrialist, who bought one-sixth of downtown Vancouver and is creating a $3-billion minicity on the site of Expo '86. Later, entrepreneurial money began to flow into start-up ventures in electronics, apparel, and other industries. Canada's thriving West Coast jewel was being powered by entre-

ANALYSIS OF EXPORTS

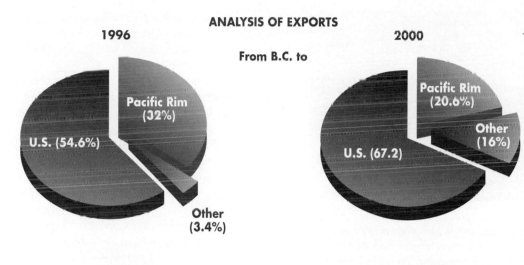

1996   From B.C. to   **2000**

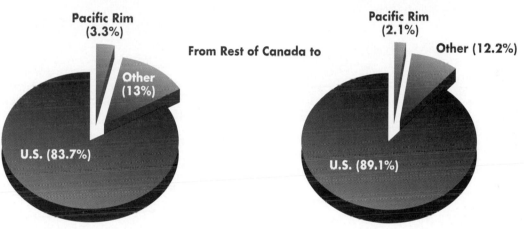

From Rest of Canada to

FIGURE 1.2

TRADING PATTERNS OF BRITISH COLUMBIA AND THE REST OF CANADA

A comparison of the export patterns of B.C. and the rest of Canada shows how B.C. is less dependent on the United States by exporting to the Pacific Rim. At the same time, the Asian flu resulted in a shift in B.C.'s exports from the Pacific Rim to the United States.

Source: Statistics Canada, CANSIM, Matrix 3685, Series D399443-8; George Dufour, Chief, Trade Statistics, Canada, <www.bcstats.gov.bc.ca>

preneurial Asians who were building the economy one small business at a time. Asian investments worth upward of $1.5 billion a year were helping British Columbia set the pace for economic growth in Canada.

The people and investments coming to British Columbia and developing significant trade with the Pacific Rim is a good example of one aspect of the globalization of business. The rest of Canada is well behind B.C. in exporting to Asia. Canada's outlook is still dominated by the free trade agreement with its largest trading partner, the United States. According to Wendy Dobson, director of the Centre for International Business of the University of Toronto and former associate deputy-minister of finance, our trade policy focuses on North America because Asian markets are seen as unprofitable. The large immigrant population in B.C. obviously does not hold those beliefs.

In the late 1990s the Canadian government and important businesses, recognizing this problem, organized some large, high-profile trade missions to East-Asian countries. The prime minister, senior trade officials, and representatives from a variety of businesses met their counterparts in China, Indonesia, and so on. The media gave great prominence to these events. These missions helped to raise Canadian business consciousness about the major opportunities that exist in a region that contains almost half of the world's population and that experienced rapid and major economic growth for three decades. Unfortunately, in mid-1998, this rosy picture changed. Most

Terry Sammon, Air Photo

The Korean coal carrier *Bluebell* comes alongside at Westshore Terminals Berth Two. Korea is the second largest customer for Canadian export coal and has an ownership interest in Greenhills, an Elk Valley Mine in southeastern British Columbia.

of the economies seemed to collapse overnight. Suddenly there were widespread currency- and asset-value declines, followed by inflation, bankruptcies, and unemployment.

In late 1999 there were signs that these Asian countries had begun to recover. Economic, trade, financial, and government experts who were all concerned about the profound effect that this Asian flu and uncertainty were having in Asia, and indeed in the entire world, were expressing cautious optimism. This important change will be examined at greater length in Chapter 3.

We turn next to what Canadian big business is doing to compete in the tough global marketplace.

PROGRESS CHECK

- Why does technology have such an impact on business today? Give some examples. What advance has single-handedly revolutionized how business operates? How?
- What is meant by the *information age*? How is it connected to technology? Why is information so important to business?
- What is meant by the *globalization of business*? How is it different from what came before? Can you give some Canadian examples of globalization?

BIG BUSINESS SHARPENS ITS COMPETITIVE POSITION

A major trend of the last decade involves Canadian companies becoming very cost-conscious, which has led to the severe process of cutting all possible costs of operations. This was part of a greater global trend whereby companies sought to become more competitive by reducing costs. Management, office, and factory personnel all felt the weight of the axe. The recession at the beginning of the 1980s gave strong impetus to this movement. The deepening of the recession into the early 1990s, as global competition heated up, extended the trend into that decade.

Computers Pave the Way

It is not an exaggeration to say that without computers it would have been impossible to engage in such wholesale cutbacks in staffing, usually referred to as *downsizing*. Senior managers use computers instead of middle managers to get information and to keep on top of operations. Factory personnel, secretaries, and assistants have been let go as the ubiquitous computer takes up a lot of the slack. Technology has paved the way for these massive changes, called **restructuring**. This is the process of reorganizing the structure of companies to make them more efficient.

restructuring
The process of reorganizing the structure of companies to make them more efficient.

As a result of these policies, and despite growth in production and sales during the '80s and '90s, there was no increase in the number of people working for large companies from 1980 to 2000. Yet the total number employed in Canada rose by 3.5 million in that period (see Figure 1.3). Who employed them? While governments and nonprofit organizations increased their employment rolls, small business took up the lion's share (see Chapter 7).

Associated Press AP. Photograph by Marty Lederhendler.

In 2001 many companies continued to announce significant layoffs and cutbacks. However, other steps were also taken to improve competitiveness. One of these ties in with the reduction in personnel because it leads to a significantly different managerial style.

Toward More Effective Management

As companies trim the numbers of managers and reduce the size of the workforce, those employees and managers who remain are given more responsibility. This delegation of power downward from the top of the hierarchy is a complex process that simultaneously achieves many desirable effects.

One aid to greater effectiveness is a more rapid response to the demands of the market and to challenges from competitors. The more decision making is **decentralized** (spread downward from the top), the faster the reaction time to these demands and challenges, improving the company's ability to compete.

A second advantage is that employees and lower-level managers feel a greater sense of participation in decision making, which makes their work more meaningful and fulfilling. This, in turn, boosts morale and, therefore, performance. There

Bill Gates is the well-known founder and main driving force of software giant Microsoft. Microsoft's operations reach into every corner of the world and its Windows software dominates many areas of computer functions.

decentralized
Decision making is spread downward from the top of an organization.

YEAR	PEOPLE WORKING (000s)
1950	5,163
1955	5,610
1960	6,411
1965	7,141
1970	8,395
1975	9,974
1980	11,573
1985	12,532
1990	13,681
1995	13,600
2000	14,909

Adapted from: Statistics Canada, *The Daily*, Catalogue No. 11-001, June 15, 2001.

FIGURE 1.3

NUMBER OF PEOPLE WORKING IN CANADA FROM 1950 TO 2000

This figure shows the rise in employment over half a century.

empowerment
The leaders of organizations give their workers the freedom, incentives, and training to be decision makers and creative contributors to the organization.

customer-driven
Customer satisfaction becomes the driving force of the company.

is a growing trend toward the empowerment of employees. **Empowerment** means that the leaders of organizations give their workers the freedom, incentives, and training to be decision makers and creative contributors to the organization.

A third advantage complements this point: employees who are involved in making decisions carry them out more enthusiastically. This *participative management* leads to more suggestions for improvement of procedures and thus to greater efficiency. All of these advantages are illustrated in the Chrysler example in the next section, on quality.

The combined result of these developments is companies that are more customer-focused or **customer-driven**—customer satisfaction becomes the driving force of the company.

Finally, many surveys have shown that a more satisfied workforce means fewer accidents, less absenteeism, and lower turnover of personnel, substantially reducing costs of operations. Parts 3 and 4 of this book present a more detailed discussion of these important issues.

These advantages were normal features of large Japanese companies and were some of the reasons that Japan occupied the top rungs of international competitiveness for so long. Another major feature of Japanese (and German) competitive strength is the high quality of their products.

Quality: A New Interest in an Old Value

An old concept has recently gotten a lot of attention in Canadian (and American) business circles—*quality*. Why is this? Hasn't quality always been a normal way of doing things? Unfortunately, that has not been true since the 1960s. Before that, things were made to last. It didn't matter whether it was a pot, a chair, a car, or a house.

Then a strange new scenario took over. The throwaway philosophy of management gradually became the norm. Perhaps it was meant to boost sales and profits by ensuring a steady flow of replacement purchases. The philosophy was also partly based on the belief that quality work costs more, so no more quality would be provided than was necessary to keep the customers buying.

At about the same time, the Japanese (and the Germans) were going in the opposite direction. Led by an American, Edwards Deming, whose ideas were ignored in his own country, the Japanese proved that quality is not more costly; it provides a wonderful competitive edge, which the Japanese exploited. That edge is the reason their autos and electronic products made such headway in North America and all over the world.

www.deming.org

You can visit the W. Edwards Deming Institute Web site. Find out about Edwards Deming and "the Deming system of profound knowledge."

We finally got the message, almost too late for the electronics industry but not too late for the important auto industry. Deming, who died in 1993 at age 92, and a few others were avidly courted in the United States beginning in the mid-1980s. Their quality message swept through North America, but companies are finding that it is a lot easier to talk about quality than to put it into practice.

Chrysler Sets an Example   Chrysler is one company that has gotten into quality seriously. In June 1992 its then chairman, Lee Iacocca, was in Ontario at the Chrysler plant in Bramalea. Talking about why Canadians are buying so many imported cars, he said to workers and guests at the official launch of production of the new LH models:

> The only question in the mind of the import buyer is quality. Is our quality going to be first class? You bet it is. But we're going to get it right from the start. That's why we've got a slow launch … quality will drive the daily schedule.

Iacocca noted that there is a normal temptation to ease standards and crank up output, but "we've had that in the past and it doesn't work." That statement represented a significant shift of philosophy and showed that the quality message had finally gotten through to Chrysler. The movement to quality production requires that the workforce become more involved in the whole process, which ties in with the trend to greater empowerment and decentralization of management.

Previously, cars were handed over to the plant only 22 weeks before production, but this time workers were involved in assembly nearly a year and a half before start day. At the one-year mark, all preproduction vehicles were being built by the employees. "Decision making at Bramalea has been moved to the lowest levels," said plant manager Jim Franciosi. "So far [workers] have identified many improvements in the product and production processes—and they have been encouraged to continue to do so."[5] These are good examples of decentralization >**P. 13**< and employee empowerment >**P. 14**<.

Chrysler Canada official Walter McCall stated that by 1996 the process had reached the point where this plant became involved 24 months prior to production. He noted that with the LH model in the American auto industry, Chrysler pioneered this process of early input by assembly workers into final product and production.[6] This process has proven so successful that Chrysler invested $500 million to overhaul the Bramalea plant to make it the sole producer of the LH model, which it began to do in 1998.[7]

Now that we have seen what big business is doing, it is time to focus on the important small-business sector.

Canadian Press CP. Photograph by Rene Johnston.

Chrysler is one company that has demonstrated its commitment to quality by having the plant's workforce participate in the decision-making process throughout the production of its vehicles.

PROGRESS CHECK

- Why is there so much pressure on business, especially big business, to be more competitive? Can you name three things business is doing to meet that challenge?

- Why is so much importance attached to quality? What demands are being placed on the new workforce? What opportunities are available?

SMALL BUSINESS: A GROWING IMPACT ON THE CANADIAN ECONOMY[8]

Entrepreneurship—the ability and undertaking to form and operate a business—is flourishing. About 150,000 new businesses are started annually in Canada; most of these new companies are small businesses. There are some 1 million small businesses in Canada (and another million self-employed people). Although 50 percent do not survive the first five years, the number of active small businesses continues to increase and their impact on the economy is very significant.

What exactly is a small business? A *small business*

- is independently operated.
- is not dominant in its field.
- meets certain size limits in terms of number of employees and annual sales. Various organizations, laws, and regulations use different size limits. The number of employees can range from zero to 100, sales up to $10 million, and profits up to $200,000 (or higher) annually.

Statistics Canada reports that such businesses contribute 60 percent of our gross domestic product (GDP) and account for two-thirds of our private-sector employment. Industry Canada's Entrepreneurship and Small Business Office states that some 80,000 small and medium-sized enterprises are exporting.

Small companies frequently provide services such as computer consulting, software development, or auto repairs. Some are restaurants or bars, retail stores such

Small Business's Dynamic Role

Songnian Zhou, president and CEO of Platform Computing Corp., based in Markham, Ontario, offers a simple reason for his company's success: it created a software product needed by businesses around the world. As Babe Ruth said, "It ain't bragging if you can do it."

Since it was founded in 1992 to provide Fortune 500 firms with "workload management" systems—software that essentially manages your computer network's complex functions—Platform has doubled in size each year. In 2000, sales soared to $50.5 million, up from just $273,000 in 1993, with a profit of $10 million.

An associate professor of computer science at the University of Toronto, Zhou pioneered Platform's LSF (load-sharing facility) software while doing his PhD dissertation in 1987. After developing a prototype that was adopted at Northern Telecom, Zhou and two partners launched Platform commercially. Zhou calls LSF "a suite of systems software for managing workload across heterogeneous computers." Translation: LSF acts as "a virtual manager," ensuring computers on a network carry out their duties in a seamless fashion.

"In a human environment, the manager is not there actually doing the work himself. He's there to coordinate the resources, know who all the people are, and know which skill sets are needed," says Zhou, 42. "It's the same principle for computer systems: our software determines which computers and servers are needed, and then manages all the different application resources across the whole network."

Platform's technology is applicable to a variety of industries and runs on any platform, says Zhou. Available customized or off the shelf, the company exports to many countries but its chief market so far is in the U.S. Customers include Boeing, Shell, and Pacific Data Images (PDI), the California-based animation studio that created *Antz*, the computer-animated box-office hit. PDI used Platform's LSF software to track its myriad computers churning out armies of animated ants. "We made sure that no usable machine would stay idle when there was work to do," says Zhou. "If a machine crashed in the middle of the night, we would recover the job" to run on another computer. *Antz* thus enjoyed faster product development and generated higher profits. Still, Zhou is not resting on his laurels.

Platform invests 30 percent of its profit in R&D. It is constantly developing new products as it operates in a very competitive high-tech field. Antz aside, staying on top is no picnic. The company is exploring the desirability of going public.

Adapted from: *Profit*, June 2001, p. 35; David Menzies, *Profit*, June 1999, p. 55; interview with CFO Gordon Booth, June 1, 1999.

as clothing shops, or construction firms. Many are also manufacturing companies. More recently, a growing number of these start-ups are home based. They usually offer a variety of consulting and professional services.

The majority of new small businesses are in the service sector (discussed in more detail later in this chapter). Small business created most of the jobs for the additional 3 million people working in Canada in 2000 (compared to 1980). Industry Canada notes that in recent years small business "has been responsible for almost all net job creation." Many people regard the small-business sector as vital for the continuing success of big business. These entrepreneurs are adventurous and innovative and play "a dynamic role in [our] new [global] economy" by providing essential services to big business. (See the Spotlight on Small Business box "Small Business's Dynamic Role.")

Home-Based Businesses

Already considered the fastest-growing small-business trend in Canada, the home-based business movement is expected to expand even more rapidly in the future. The latest estimates are that 53 percent of all self-employed Canadians are home-based, which accounts for more than 1 million Canadians or about 9 percent of our workforce. Canadian futurists Frank Ogden, Frank Feather, and John Kettle, who operate out of their own home-based offices, predict that telecommuting from home and freelancers working from home will become very common.[9]

Why do people start such businesses? Some disliked their jobs or found them unfulfilling, some had jobs that disappeared or were threatened, others had a dream or strong passion, some want to be their own boss, and still others wanted a change in lifestyle. Many women welcome this opportunity because they find their career path blocked because they *are* women. People who are parents may find that a home-based business is a good way of earning income, being their own boss, and being home to look after their children. The common threads are that:

- Workers are prepared for a major shift from employment to self-employment for reasons noted above.

- The technology of low-cost computers and peripheral equipment along with the Internet makes home-based businesses more feasible.

- Home-based businesses require less capital to start and operate.

- There is a growing market for services to fill big-business needs.

A good example is Judith Aston—who, after completing the professional translation program at McGill University, started a French–English translation service working out of her home. She emphasized high quality and fast service. At first she supplemented her income with a part-time job at a translation service, but as her billings grew she was able to devote all her time to her own business. Working at home kept the overhead low and made it easier for Judith to raise her son, who was 10 when she started. Now, with the help of her husband, John, she runs a very profitable operation, and has moved out of Montreal into a country home in the Laurentians. State-of-the-art equipment enables her to operate from her new home location while enjoying country life.[10]

Here are some other examples from *The Globe and Mail.*[11]

- Terry and Nancy Belgue, aged 53 and 40, "dropped out of the Toronto corporate rat race to move to Victoria and set up an advertising agency in the basement of their home" in the Oak Bay area. They "wanted a slower pace of life and to spend more time with their young boys."

- Louis Garneau, "a former national cycling champion, started his successful sportswear company bearing his name, in St. Augustin, Quebec, by making cycling shorts in his parents' garage."

- Elizabeth and Don Purser transferred the office of their freelance film company, Beulah Films Inc., from a downtown Toronto location to their home in Hamilton. The move cut their costs, gave them more time with their daughters ("I didn't want to see our kids go home with a key"), and allowed for flexible home and business duties, but it also lengthened their work week.

Home Inc.: The Canadian Home-Based Business Guide (McGraw-Hill Ryerson, 1994), the National Home Business Institute, and the Canadian Federation of Independent Business are resources to help home entrepreneurs start and operate their own businesses. The major Canadian banks all provide information and help.

Employees Working at home (Telecommuting)   Working at home is not confined to the self-employed. Many large companies

One of the current trends in business is allowing employees to work from home. They maintain contact with the office and with customers through telephone, e-mail, and fax. This telecommuting frees up office space and eliminates commuting time for employees.

PhotoDisc

are experimenting with having employees in certain departments work out of their homes. The idea is to cut down on expensive office space, employees' time, and the costs of travelling to and from work, without sacrificing efficiency. Tests have shown that employees who arrive at work after a frustrating commute do not function at their best for about an hour, until they settle down. For example, American Express, Digital Equipment, and DuPont all have work-at-home (telework) programs for some Canadian and American personnel and all report excellent results. They also supply varying types and amounts of equipment for home use.[12]

It is clear that the work-at-home trend is well established and growing in importance. Later we will look at the broader question of the rapid growth of the number of small businesses, especially in services, in Canada, and at other developments that are nourishing small business and its home-based aspect. (Also see Chapter 7.)

We now turn to the service sector, where small business plays an important role.

THE SERVICE SECTOR[13]

goods-producing sector
The sector that produces tangible products, things that can be seen or touched.

service sector
The sector that produces services, not goods. Examples are banking, insurance, communications, and transportation.

The service sector of society is distinct from the goods-producing sector. The **goods-producing sector** produces tangible products that can be seen or touched, like clothes, oil, food, machines, or automobiles. The **service sector** produces services rather than goods, like banking; insurance; communications; transportation; tourism; computer servicing, programming, and consulting; and health, recreational, or repair services. In the past 25 years the service sector in Canada and around the world has grown dramatically.

The shift in Canada's employment makeup away from goods-producing industries began slowly, early in the twentieth century, and has accelerated rapidly since the 1950s. The trend is expected to continue, although perhaps at a reduced rate. In 2000, the service sector accounted for 78 percent of all jobs in Canada. This growth is due to a complex series of factors.

First, technological improvements have enabled businesses to reduce their payrolls while increasing their output. This accounts for the fact that despite the huge increase in gross domestic product (GDP) between 1960 and 2000, manufacturing still accounts for 18 percent of GDP (Figure 1.4), while its *percentage* of total workforce has been cut more than half—from 30 to 13 percent—in the same period. At the same time, because staffing has been sharply pruned and business has become more complex and specialized, companies rely more heavily on outside service firms.

In a study of the service sector for the Institute for Research on Public Policy, economist William Empey showed that the service component of Canadian products has been growing steadily since 1971. He argued that "competitiveness in manufacturing depends critically on access to efficient producer services." He mentioned banking, insurance, transportation, and communication as such important services.

Contracting Out

As large manufacturing companies seek to become more efficient, they contract out an increasing number of services, which has led to the proliferation of service specialists. Canada has a large number of high-quality software specialist companies scattered across the country from Halifax, Nova Scotia, to Burnaby, British Columbia, whose products are in demand in Canada as well as in Hollywood, Europe, and Japan. These companies produce everything from computer games to movie special effects. For example, Alias Wavefront software was used by George Lucas's Industrial Light and Magic Company for most of the computer-generated animals in the Robin Williams movie *Jumanji*. Softimage of Montreal created the software that was used to animate the dinosaurs in *Jurassic Park*. Computer animation has played an important role in movie-making from the first *Star Wars* all the way down to *Independence Day*, *Starship Troopers*, *Godzilla*, and *Shrek*. George Lucas's hit in 1999, *Star Wars: Episode I— The Phantom Menace*, uses the most advanced computer-animation techniques. The

	1960	2000
Total employed in Canada	6,400,000	14,909,700
Number employed in manufacturing	1,920,000	2,005,700
Percentage	30%	13%
Manufacturing share of GDP	19%	18%

Adapted from: Statistics Canada, *The Daily*, Catalogue No. 11-001, March 23, 2001.

FIGURE 1.4

ROLE OF MANUFACTURING IN THE ECONOMY

Manufacturing had only a slightly lower percentage of GDP in 2000 than in 1960, despite the fact that it employs only 13 percent of the workforce now compared to 30 percent in 1960, and that GDP has grown enormously. This means a huge increase in manufacturing productivity.

Profile at the beginning of this chapter indicates how Canada's leadership in computer animation led the Disney company to locate branches in Canada to tap into our valuable high-tech animation specialists.

Other service firms have risen or expanded rapidly to provide traditional or personal services that used to be done by women at home. So many women have entered the workforce that there is a greater demand for food preparation, child care, and household maintenance. An additional boost for this type of service was the rise in wages that occurred in the 1950s, 1960s, and 1970s, providing more disposable income for families to pay for such services.

A third area that has contributed to the rise in service-sector jobs is the government or quasi-government area, which includes public administration (federal, provincial, and municipal), health, and education. The postwar baby boom, the installation of medicare in 1970, and the large growth in immigration to Canada all stimulated the demand for such services. This demand has now gone into reverse as governments are cutting back spending, reducing staffing, and privatizing many services.

Given the large growth in service industries, the question that may be asked is, What is happening to manufacturing? We look at this next.

Courtesy of Avid Technology.

Canada is a leader in the production of computer graphics software. Softimage, Inc., a Montreal-based company, provides software used in the motion-picture industry.

CRITICAL THINKING

Can you see yourself setting up your own business? In the service sector? Does a home-based business attract you? Why or why not?

Do you think the trend to home-based business improves the quality of life? Why? How about the reduction in interaction with people?

PROGRESS CHECK

• Why is big business no longer a creator of new jobs? Why is small business creating so many jobs? In what sector of the economy are these new companies and jobs to be found?

• How does small business stimulate big business? How does it complement big business?

• Why are home-based businesses so popular? What conditions favour this trend?

• What exactly is the service sector? Why is it so essential to the Canadian economy?

• What role has technology played in stimulating the growth of the service sector? What other factors have contributed to its growth?

HOW IMPORTANT IS MANUFACTURING TO CANADA?[14]

Given all the changes in the global economy, is manufacturing still important to a modern economy? One person who has strong opinions is Akio Morita, the world-famous founder and retired chief executive of Sony Corp. He spoke in Ottawa in May 1989, warning Canada and the United States about the danger of a shrinking manufacturing sector and reliance on the service sector for growth and stability. According to Morita:

> If Canadians ignore manufacturing, while thinking of themselves as information technicians in a service-based economy, they might find themselves on the sidelines of international business. It is only manufacturing that creates something new, which takes raw materials and fashions them into products which are of more value than the raw materials they are made from.

Sony is a giant transnational corporation with plants, subsidiaries, and operations on all continents, and Morita has been the guiding light in its very successful history. Perhaps we should pay close attention to what he says. He may be biased toward manufacturing, but his views should not be ignored.

Various opinions and data on this important question were examined in a detailed article in *The Globe and Mail*. Michael Walker, director of an ultraconservative think tank, the Fraser Institute, stated that "the service sector could account for 99.9 percent of economic output without damaging the economy."

The opposite opinion was voiced by Jayson Myers, now senior vice-president and chief economist of the Alliance of Manufacturers and Exporters, Canada. He maintained that it was "ridiculous" not to realize the importance of the manufacturing sector. He pointed out that Canada runs an annual deficit of approximately $25 billion in all its dealings with the U.S. If not for the contribution of exports of manufactured goods, this deficit would be a lot greater. A *Globe and Mail* article emphasized the importance of manufacturing to a healthy economy. The headline read: "Manufacturing keeps economy on growth track," and the article noted that manufacturing played an important role in helping the Canadian economy achieve 15 consecutive quarters of growth to March 31, 1999.

Manufacturing and Service Sectors Feed Each Other

Economist Gordon Betcherman suggested that "too much emphasis on one sector at the expense of the other is bad." He pointed out that a study, based on a model of the Canadian economy, determined that

> When you stimulate the goods sector, the whole economy does well. If you stimulate the services sector, there's basically no payoff. Both goods and services are extremely important to a healthy economy.

Echoing Morita's ideas, Betcherman said:

> Japan is the only major industrialized country where employment in manufacturing increased before, during, and after the 1981–82 recession. In both Japan and West Germany manufacturing output and employment is higher as a proportion of the overall economy than in the other industrialized countries. Could there be a link between the size of their manufacturing sector and their economic success?

Finally, Statistics Canada believes that some aspects of what manufacturing companies used to do have shifted to service companies. Tasks such as accounting, payroll, legal work, and advertising are commonly contracted out to service companies specializing in these fields. This accounts for some of the shift in jobs from manufacturing companies, although they were really service jobs all along.

Jayson Myers confirmed this, noting that every dollar of manufacturing output adds three dollars of value to the Canadian economy, so that while directly manufacturing constitutes only 18 percent of the economy, indirectly it creates an additional 37 percent of economic activity.

Another voice downgrading the importance of manufacturing is that of Canadian economist Nuala Beck, who argues:

> A new knowledge economy is rapidly replacing the old mass-manufacturing economy. "Knowledge workers" now make up 30 percent of North America's workforce while only 10 percent are actually involved in production. What's more, knowledge-intensive new industries are creating most of the jobs and driving the economy.[15]

If we look at the significant international competitors (in addition to Japan and Germany) such as South Korea, Taiwan, Singapore, and Hong Kong, we will see that their strength has been and continues to be manufacturing. In these countries that sector directly contributes much more than 13 percent of GDP and employs much more than 15 percent of the workforce, as is the case in Canada (see Figure 1.4).

Are there any lessons here for us? Should we be paying more attention to the importance of manufacturing to our continuing economic health? Or are these the success stories of yesterday, as Nuala Beck and many others claim? The answers to these questions will influence the kind of economy that you will be living in during the decades to come and the kinds of jobs that will be generated.

POPULATION TRENDS[16]

Demographic (population) trends have a significant effect on business planning and activities. For example, in the 20 years following World War II (1946 to 1966), Canada witnessed an unusual phenomenon. Large numbers of war veterans, aided by government grants, got married and acquired housing for their families. In addition, the hundreds of thousands of immigrants who were entering Canada annually also needed housing. Four children per family was the norm. These children were eventually called the *baby boomers*. This explosive growth in population and family formation led to a 20-year boom in many industries.

www.prospeakers.com/speakers/default.asp

This Canadian Web site introduces several well-known personalities who frequently appear as public speakers. It includes biographical information and highlights their achievements, topics they speak on, and examples of comments from audiences. You can visit this Web site to learn more about Nuala Beck.

As the population grows, the construction industry must keep pace to provide accommodation for more people. This, in turn, leads to an expansion in other industries, such as retail.

The Population-Led Postwar Boom

Construction of houses, cottages, apartments, and other dwellings—as well as schools, colleges, CEGEPs, and universities for the hundreds of thousands of children—took off. Home furnishings and appliances, children's clothing, and sports and school supplies industries also flourished. To accommodate this vast growth in retail business, new stores, malls, and shopping centres sprang into being. Companies expanded rapidly and new firms mushroomed, and all required additional space; office towers and factories began appearing everywhere. These offices in turn needed furniture, equipment, and supplies.

The explosion of the construction industries fuelled tremendous growth in all the allied industries and services that feed on new construction: banks, trusts, and insurance companies; lawyers and notaries; lumber, concrete, brick, electrical, paving, plumbing, landscaping, carpentry, painting, and roofing; and telephone, electricity, heating, and air conditioning. All these businesses and many more experienced great expansion in employment, sales, and profits. As suburbs developed to accommodate all this population and business growth, cars and buses were needed for transportation and new roads were built.

Those businesses that analyzed what was happening and prepared for the effect of these demographic trends became very profitable. Today, other important demographic trends have emerged that will have a great impact on the next few decades. Those individuals and companies that correctly analyze these trends and their impact on future business obviously will do very well. What are these current population trends? You may already be familiar with some of them.

The Population Is Aging

The population in Canada has been aging for several decades. More people are living longer due to better medical knowledge and technology; better health habits, proper nutrition, and more exercise; a reduction in number of people smoking; and other reasons. Figure 1.5's data of past and future population trends over a 40-year period show that the two youngest age groups decline steadily from 40 percent to 24 percent, while the two oldest age groups increase steadily from 38 to 56 percent. The middle age group of 20 to 34 shows only a 10-percent drop.

At the same time, the portion of the population that is very young continues to decrease because of declining birthrates since the mid-1960s. Although the rate is low, the actual number of children being born is still large because of the *echo boom.* The echo boom is the result of the large number of baby boomers, born in the 1946–66 period, starting families. The number of annual births hit a peak in 1959 at 480,000 and then declined steadily to 1973 when it fell to 343,000, which was the same as 1946. Then the echo boom kicked in and the number of births started climbing, to hit a peak of 373,000 in 1986. By 1998 the number of births was back to the 1946/1973 level at 342,000. In addition, we have had steady immigration into Canada. In the 1980s more than 1 million immigrants entered Canada. More than half of these were under 30, so many had children. The 1990s saw some 2 million immigrants enter Canada.

What does all this add up to regarding the needs of the population? Businesses that cater to older people should prosper in everything from health care to recreation, from education to travel. Smaller apartments should be in greater demand. More grandparents with more money in their pockets will be buying more gifts for more grandchildren. The continuing large number of births assures prosperity for those businesses supplying children's needs. There should be many opportunities for existing and new businesses to explore.

YEAR	UNDER 4	4–19	20–34	35–64	65 AND OVER
2011	6%	18%	20%	42%	14%
2006	6	19	20	42	13
2001	6	20	21	41	13
1996	7	20	23	38	12
1991	7	21	26	34	12
1981	7	25	27	31	10
1971	9	31	22	30	8

Adapted from: Statistics Canada, *Population Projections for Canada, Provinces and Territories, 1993–2016*, Cat. No. 91-520, 1985 and from the Statistics Canada CANSIM database http://cansim2.statcan.ca.cgi-win/CNSMCGI.EXE, Matrix 6367, May 1999.

FIGURE 1.5

POPULATION DISTRIBUTION BY AGE GROUP

Percentages for 2001, 2006, and 2011 are projected, and the earlier years are actual percentages. If you compare 1971 and 2011 you will note a pronounced shift to a heavier weighting of older persons and a decline in the proportion of the youngest groups.

ENVIRONMENTAL AND OTHER ETHICAL ISSUES

One of the most important ethical and social issues of our times is the serious deterioration of the physical environment of our planet. The unlimited expansion of population and industry has so altered the air, water, forest, insect and plant life, and soil that we face grave threats to our very existence. We are all familiar with the problems of too much waste—much of it highly toxic—and how it pollutes our air, rivers, lakes, oceans, and soil. We have learned about the emission of vast quantities of gases that are heating up the atmosphere and what this greenhouse effect is doing to our climate, agriculture, and ocean levels. We have become aware of the chemicals we put on the food we grow and the indiscriminate destruction of tropical forests leading to soil erosion and silting up of rivers. Many more problems will not be solved unless we begin to live and think in a new, more socially responsible way.

In Canada we are confronted by many of these problems and are seriously affected by acid rain. Thousands of our lakes are completely dead, with no plant or fish life remaining. Our maple trees are dying off, paint is peeling from houses, and bricks are disintegrating. The polluted rain and snow from factory chimneys thousands of kilometres away continue to cause hundreds of millions of dollars in damage in Canada each year. The whole world, from the Arctic to the Antarctic, is affected by this problem. Dr. David Schindler, a biologist at the University of Alberta, reported that a complex interaction between acid precipitation, climate warming, and ultraviolet radiation from the sun is having a serious impact on the deterioration of all life forms in lakes.[17]

Companies can no longer make decisions based only on their immediate economic interests. This new input into the planning and thinking of management involves a major shift and will continue to grow in importance. The Spotlight on Big Business "A Constructive Approach to Environmental Problems" gives some examples of this. Governments have passed many new laws requiring industries to observe ever more stringent environmental standards. This often involves greater costs, which inevitably find their way into the prices consumers have to pay. Are these costs any higher than the damages caused to people and property by unrestricted operations?

New industries and professions are being spawned from the new awareness of environmental issues. Recycling and waste management companies have sprung up, and alternative materials and processes are being explored. This has led to new discoveries, jobs, and investment opportunities. The movement toward conservation has had the same effect. Businesses have discovered ways to reduce costs, making them more competitive.

The concept of **sustainable development** was promoted in 1988 at a major international conference on the environment in Toronto. Sustainable economic

www.climatechange.nrcan.gc.ca

This Natural Resources Canada Web site provides considerable information about the nature and impacts of climate change and how they can be addressed. It also provides feature reports on the topic and links to many other topical items on the World Wide Web.

sustainable development
Economic development that meets the needs of the present without endangering the external environment of future generations.

PhotoDisc

Recycling has resulted from an increasing awareness of the environmental damage caused by waste. This has spawned the development of a new industry dedicated to waste management.

development meets the needs of the present without endangering the external environment of future generations. In the Brundtland report, the prime minister of Norway made it clear that, in her committee's opinion, the only way for the world to survive is to abandon unlimited development for the socially responsible alternative.

Although threats to the environment are obviously an important problem, they are not the only ethical issue that business faces. Doing the *right* thing does not mean only obeying the laws of Canada and the countries in which you do business. A host of issues such as bribery and corruption, price fixing, bid rigging, clear-cutting of forests, product safety, arms sales (especially to dictators), and other ethical questions are occupying an increasingly important position in the corporate agenda. Because of their importance, Chapter 5 is devoted exclusively to a review of ethical and environmental issues. In addition, each chapter makes reference to ethical problems relevant to that chapter.

CAREERS AND JOBS FOR THE FUTURE[18]

What is the effect of all of the trends discussed in this chapter on jobs and careers in this century? To date, the most striking result of these developments is what up to the mid-1990s was called *jobless recovery*. (A good example is the case of Chrysler noted in Chapter 10; Chrysler was investing $600 million in a new plant in Ontario that would not create a single new job.) Perhaps a more accurate description would have been a *slow jobless recovery*.

---

www.canon.ca
www.westport.com

SPOTLIGHT ON BIG BUSINESS

A Constructive Approach to Environmental Problems

Companies around the world have taken major steps to make their operations less harmful to the environment. A typical, and important, case concerns Canada's forest companies, many of which have been on the receiving end of severe criticism for a long time. Major forest companies began marketing "eco-certified wood and paper products" in 1996. These products carry the stamp of the Canadian Standards Association "affirming that they come from sustainable forest operations." This is the Canadian version of a worldwide effort by the International Forest Stewardship Council to accredit independent local auditors.

Canon ran a full-page ad publicizing its toner cartridge recycling program. It thanked "the four biggest participants ... Ontario Lottery Corp., SHL Systemhouse, Commonwealth Insurance Co., and HongKong Bank of Canada," for making possible the recycling of thousands

of cartridges. Canon donates $1 per unit to the World Wildlife Fund and The Nature Conservancy of Canada.

These are but two examples of a heightened awareness by corporations of the need to incorporate environmentally responsible policies in their normal operations. Some critics believe that they are merely responding to societal pressures to behave properly and that these are mere marketing ploys. Nevertheless, regardless of motivation, the result will be a cleaner and safer environment.

Finally, Westport Innovations of Vancouver has produced a clean diesel engine—an elusive goal of engineers for years—based on natural gas. This is another case of a Canadian technology advance that will help to produce a cleaner environment.

Adapted from: Paula Kaihla, "Westport's Green Machine," *Canadian Business*, June 25/July 9, 1999, p. 31; *Globe and Mail, Report on Business*, December 19, 1995, p. B4; Patricia Lush, *Globe and Mail, ROB*, December 28, 1995, p. B4.

The seriousness of this problem was highlighted by the spate of commentaries in all media about the jobless recovery. For example, over a period of four days there were articles in the *Toronto Star* and the *Los Angeles Times*, an editorial in the *Montreal Gazette*, and a long interview with Harvard professor and former U.S. Secretary of Labor Robert Reich on the CBC *National News Magazine* (February 29, 1996). In addition, Prime Minister Jean Chrétien and President Bill Clinton of the United States appealed to businesses to seriously consider ways of providing jobs, especially to young people.[19]

The Bad News[20]

The official unemployment rate in Canada all through the 1990s hovered in the 8- to 10-percent range, finally declining below 8 percent by the end of the decade as the earlier recession moved into a recovery phase. Although the gross domestic product (GDP) continued to rise from 1993 onward, the net increase in the number of people working from 1990 to 1998 was approximately 400,000, or a little below 3 percent. Our country, as well as most European countries, was bedevilled by this problem despite many studies and attempts by governments and experts to *do* something about it. Of all developed countries only the United States was able to decrease its unemployment rate to below 5 percent. In early 2001 the threat of global economic recession, and perhaps worse, was once again a serious concern for governments, for financial and other large business corporations, and for the media and people in all countries. This problem is discussed in greater detail in the next chapter.

Two major effects on the job market of the trends discussed in this chapter are evident, one positive and the other negative. Let's look at the bad news first. The technological and globalization revolutions have been relentlessly reducing the number of jobs in Canada. The United States has been a constant drawing power for our university graduates—well known as the "brain drain." Significant job losses occurred steadily due to many plant closings, record bankruptcy levels, automation, and downsizing by companies and governments. There have also been plant closings and layoffs due to mergers or plants moving to the United States, Mexico, or elsewhere. For most of the 1990s we heard mostly bad news on the job front. The same bad news dominated the first half of 2001.

In the past, as the population increased, the number of people working in Canada had increased every five years despite recessions. But given the very heavy job losses in the early 1990s, the total workforce in Canada remained stuck in the 13,600,000 to 13,700,000 range from 1990 to 1996. The workforce then began to increase, and by the end of 2000 the figure had climbed to almost 15 million (see Figure 1.4). Between April 1998 and April 1999, 371,900 new jobs were created.[21] In addition, an Asian recovery seemed likely. This began to engender some hopeful forecasts for the health of the global economy and added to the signs of good Canadian economic growth. Unfortunately, these positive trends got a bad hit when the high-tech and dot-com companies slid into reverse gear in 2000 causing a major collapse of stock markets in the United States and Canada. Most of these companies announced massive layoffs that continued throughout 2001.

The Good News

Canada has a booming software development industry; some examples were noted earlier in this chapter. There are many large and small software companies scattered across Canada, and they are having great difficulty finding suitable employees. Paul Swinwood, who heads up the Software Human Resources Council in Ottawa, reported that as of February 1996 there were 20,000 job vacancies across Canada in this mushrooming industry. He noted that the software industry is expanding at a 25- to 30-percent annual rate, so it will continue to generate large numbers of jobs. The number of job vacancies was unchanged by 1999.[22]

The problem is that change is so rapid and constant in this field that universities and other educational institutions have difficulty keeping up. Some companies are so desperate for help, said Swinwood, that they have to hire people from Sweden and the United States.

Another bit of good news is that there are more high-paying jobs in the service sector than in the goods-producing sector. Since the mid-1980s the service industry has generated almost all of the increases in employment. Although this growth has slowed, it still remains the largest area of job growth. Chances are very high that you will work in this sector at some point in your career. Do not overlook the retail area; any time a large chain such as Wal-Mart or Loblaw's opens a new store, many managerial jobs are created for college and university graduates. High-paying service-sector jobs can be found in marketing, accounting and auditing, finance, management consulting, telecommunications, transportation, and in many sectors that are related to computers including programming, animation, servicing, and consulting.

Another positive development is in the manufacturing sector, which has been responsible for a continuing boom in exports. This is expected to continue and to prevent further job losses in that sector, which directly employs 2 million people and has a major ripple effect on the service sector. A Canadian Manufacturers' Association survey reported that companies are just about through downsizing and that the emphasis now is on increasing efficiency in other areas.[23]

The Importance of Education

If you examine Figure 1.6 carefully, you will see that one thing is certain: the more education you have, the less likelihood you have of being unemployed. Most of the new jobs being created require a college or university education. A good example is Gallatin Steel Co., which operates a steel mill in the United States in Kentucky, Georgia. This is a joint venture of two Canadian steel companies, Dofasco and Co-Steel. Gallatin is a perfect example of the many-sided effects of the technological revolution.

It used to take 5,000 people to produce as much steel as Gallatin's 300-person workforce can produce. Furthermore, 40 percent of them have college or university degrees, many in mechanical engineering or metallurgy.[24]

These developments require managers and employees who have more advanced education. They must be able to grasp mathematical concepts and reason logically. They need university degrees. This preparation develops a person's confidence to be a modern knowledge worker or manager, to make decisions as authority is decentralized and the entire workforce adapts to the quick response time required in today's fast-moving, highly competitive world.

In the meantime, because we are in the transition period from the old industrial economy to the new information age, finding a job, especially a full-time, permanent job, is a very challenging process.

In today's workplace, higher education is becoming more valuable. Forty percent of Gallatin Steel's employees have degrees, many of them in mechanical engineering or metallurgy.

ETHICAL DILEMMA

Review

At the beginning of the chapter we noted the ethical dilemmas that companies face as they try to be more competitive by moving production to low-cost developing countries, and as they continually update their technology. These changes often mean job cuts, relocations, or plant closings in Canada, causing hardships for employees and for small communities. The issue of negative environmental impacts in loosely regulated developing countries also arises. We present here the responses of two business executives (see Preface) to these issues.

When companies lower their costs, they are more competitive and can expand their businesses. This expansion ultimately creates more jobs. As developing countries raise their standards of living, as we have seen in South Korea, Singapore, Poland, Brazil, and China, they also become consumers of these products, giving the companies a competitive edge there and providing additional jobs at home as the business grows. As for environmental problems, Normand Bédard, vice-president, human resources, of Cambior Inc., believes that "the vast majority of companies are sensitive to the social and environmental impacts that any human activity will entail."

Bédard states that "only naive CEOs think that they can go to countries with less organized environment legislation and carry out activities that they would not carry out in their own country. This practice, if it existed in the past, is no longer acceptable [or] tolerated. Companies must have the same respect for the environment in host countries and they must also consider the impact of their presence on society as a whole."

Dennis Reilley, general manager, Pratt & Whitney Canada International, says that in his experience, "most Canadian high-tech companies operate in this fashion," and that it is possible that "Canadian industrial age or commodity-based companies aren't nearly so concerned about their employees or the environment." These companies have to strike while the iron is hot—commodity market prices are very volatile, so they must take profits quickly.

As for developing countries, Reilley agrees with Prime Minister Chrétien that Canadians need jobs first and cleanup afterwards, "not the other way around." Canadian executives of international firms and host governments need to be educated about the International Monetary Fund and United Nations protocols.

Being ethically and environmentally conscious pays large dividends in the long run.

	PERCENTAGE UNEMPLOYED
Average for total workforce	8.3
Age bracket 25 and over	7.0
Age bracket 15–24	15.0
High-school dropouts	14.7
High-school graduates	8.3
High-school/college graduates	6.6
University graduates	4.3

Adapted from: Statistics Canada, *The Daily*, Catalogue No. 11-001, May 7, 2001.

FIGURE 1.6

UNEMPLOYMENT RATE IN CANADA FOR VARIOUS CATEGORIES OF THE WORKFORCE

Note how the unemployment rate decreases as the years of schooling increase.

YOUR FUTURE IN THE GLOBAL ECONOMY

It's exciting to think about what role you will play in the new global economy. You may be a leader, one of the people who will implement the changes and accept the challenges that the new information-based economy offers. This book will introduce you to some of the concepts that will make such leadership possible. Are you preparing yourself for this challenging new job market? (See the section "Getting the Job You Want" in the Prologue.)

CRITICAL THINKING

Should Canadians strengthen the manufacturing sector? What can they do? Is there a role for government in this effort?

How do you feel about the challenge of a safer environment? Do you see it as an opportunity or a threat to Canadian business?

Do you think we can develop environmental expertise that will create new industries? What, specifically, needs to be done?

Can you think of any type of service or product not currently on the market that would appeal to the growing number of seniors? Would you be interested in trying to develop that item? Why or why not?

Have any of the trends discussed in the chapter given you any ideas for a career? Explain. Are you thinking about whether the rest of your education should be broader or more specialized? Should it be both broader *and* more specialized? Given the globalization of business, should you be acquiring the ability to speak more languages? You will have to think seriously about these options—don't hesitate to consult people whose opinions you respect, both inside and outside your school.

PROGRESS CHECK

- Why are environmental issues so important now? What effect does this have on business plans and actions? What opportunities does it open up for business?

- Why are population trends significant? What are some major current trends that are important to business? Why are they important?

- What is the effect on careers and jobs of current business trends? What should students be doing to meet these requirements?

SUMMARY

1. Explain the importance and impact of technological developments.

1. Technology leads to new products and services being developed and existing methods, products, and services becoming obsolete.
   • *How does this affect business?*
   Technological developments—including more efficient and automated equipment, networks, computers, and robots—lead to a reduction in the number of employees and managers, thus reducing costs. Employees must be trained to cope with the new technology. Companies and individuals that do not keep up with these developments cannot compete in the job and business market.

2. Describe what is meant by the *information age* and what its implications are.

2. The *information age* refers to the fact that rapid, reliable, and relevant information has become a vital component of effective competition.
   • *Why has this development taken place?*
   Computers and ever-improving communication technology have developed information to a high level. They have shrunk the planet into a small world.

Information has become as important a component of operations as finance, materials, and labour. It enables management to plan better and to react more quickly to favourable or unfavourable developments.

3. Big business now operates on a global basis.
   • *What accounts for this development and what are its implications?*
   The technological revolution in transportation and communication has made possible buying, selling, borrowing, staffing, investing, and manufacturing as if the world were one country. Canadian companies search for the lowest costs and markets and opportunities wherever they exist.

3. Discuss the globalization of business and why it is so important for Canadian companies.

4. Canadian companies must participate in the globalized world of business and meet world competitive standards.
   • *How do companies improve their competitiveness?*
   Becoming more competitive means adopting the latest and most efficient means of production, financing, distribution, and management information systems that technology and experience make available. This search is done internationally, as are investment decisions. Alliances and joint ventures are sought on a global basis. The pressures arise from competitors who are engaged in a similar process.

4. Identify how big business is becoming more competitive and the pressures to do so.

5. There has been an explosion in the number of small businesses in Canada. A growing number of these are home based.
   • *What factors led to these developments?*
   Some of the factors are low-cost computers and peripherals; the Internet; the rise in the number of people, particularly parents, in business who find working at home easier and less costly; women finding their career paths blocked due to sexism; the rising number of professionals and managers who find themselves laid off with poor prospects for re-employment; and people opting out of the rat race or seeking more control over their lives.

5. Explain why small and home-based businesses have become so popular.

6. The manufacturing component of the Canadian economy has remained unchanged in the last decade at about 19 percent of GDP.
   • *Despite this, why has the service sector become much more important?*
   The manufacturing sector employs fewer people and its labour force is a much smaller percentage of the total labour force, while the service sector has grown enormously, employing some 75 percent of the workforce. Manufacturers contract out many service aspects of their business and also require new services in the information age. Nevertheless, many people believe that an efficient and competitive manufacturing sector is the motivator of the entire economy.

6. Show how the service sector has replaced manufacturing as the principal provider of jobs, but why manufacturing remains vital for Canada.

7. Shifts in the makeup of the population of Canada have been a constant feature. We have had the baby boom and now the composition of our population is shifting again.
   • *What is the significance of the latest demographic trend for business?*
   Demographic changes create new markets as old markets diminish. They also determine whether there will be an adequate supply of labour. Current trends are for a gradually aging population and a declining percentage of younger people. Businesses must look for opportunities in the new markets being created by the large number of older people.

7. Explain current population trends and their major impact on business.

8. Describe how environmental and other ethical issues play a major role in all business planning and actions.

8. People are increasingly concerned by the actions of business that affect society. This applies to a wide range of activities, including ethical behaviour in general and the environment in particular.
   • *Why have these questions come to the fore recently?*
   A series of scandals in different industries has drawn attention to the need for ethical procedures and ethical behaviour by managers. The serious deterioration of the environment has forced business and government to examine closely every element of operations to ensure that these problems are not being aggravated.

9. Show how jobs and careers are affected by the trends discussed in the chapter.

9. So many trends are changing the way business operates that jobs and careers are being greatly affected.
   • *How is the nature of jobs and careers moving in new directions?*
   Technology now requires better educated, more skilled employees. Decentralization means that managers and employees must be prepared to undertake more responsibility. Everyone has to have wider horizons to encompass global business, which means a broader education. More young people have to think seriously about working for small businesses or starting their own business, perhaps at home.

KEY TERMS

business 4
customer-driven 14
decentralized 13
empowerment 14
globalization 9

goods-producing
   sector 18
information age 8
joint ventures 10
restructuring 12

service sector 18
strategic alliances 10
sustainable
   development 23

DEVELOPING WORKPLACE SKILLS

1. Use a word-processing program to write a one-page report on how technology will change society in the next 10 years. Consider not only computers but the whole range of technological developments discussed in the chapter, and any other developments.

2. The text describes the growth trend in the number of businesses in the service sector. Look through your local Yellow Pages phone book and list five businesses that provide services in your area. The text also describes how certain demographic and social changes affect businesses. Look at your list of local service businesses and consider how these trends affect them—positively or negatively.

3. The stress on quality is having a big impact on business operations. Do you think your education is preparing you to function in a quality-conscious business atmosphere? Where is it succeeding? Where is it failing? How can it be improved?

4. Go to the library and see what small-business magazines you can find. Scan through back issues for some stories of successes and failures. See if you can get a few ideas that might inspire you to consider a small-business venture. Make sure you examine the possibility of a home-based business.

5. Find out which nonprofit organizations in your community might offer you the opportunity to learn the skills that will help you find a job in the field you are interested in. Write a letter inquiring about their programs and the opportunities for volunteering.

TAKING IT TO THE NET

Purpose:

To examine new and emerging trends that are affecting Canadian business today.

Exercises:

1. Using the key term "business trends" (you may have to use quotation marks for the whole phrase) search the Yahoo Canada Web site at <www.ca.yahoo.com> to see what new trends are emerging and affecting business. If your search is not successful try <www.yahoo.com>, which is Yahoo's U.S. site. See if there are any chat groups you can join to discuss this important topic.

2. Try the same sites to answer the question: What are the fastest-growing occupations in Canada and the U.S.? See if you find some that interest you as potential careers.

PRACTISING MANAGEMENT DECISIONS

CASE 1

A REVOLUTION IN A MAJOR CANADIAN COMPANY

In early 1999, one of the oldest, largest, and most prestigious companies in Canada announced a total transformation in what it produces and how it will operate in the future. Northern Telecom had previously changed its name to *Nortel Networks* to better reflect the real nature of the company. In May 1999 Nortel fleshed out the significance of that name change by announcing that it was getting out of manufacturing its traditional lines of telecommunication equipment. It was doing so to better concentrate its resources on high-end software development necessary for modern networking facilities. Nortel's aim is to get rid of most of its manufacturing facilities "as it transforms itself into a so-called systems house with a heavy reliance on outside contractors."

For the next 12 months everything seemed to be working out well for Brampton, Ontario-based Nortel. It had become one of the giant international high-tech firms, with about one-third of its workforce based in Canada. It was one of the darlings of global investors both large and small. Its share price soared to a dizzying CDN$125.00 as the entire high-tech sector in Canada and the United States was enjoying tremendous growth and popularity. Then in mid-2000 the bottom fell out of this sector and all of these companies, including most of the new dot-coms, were suddenly faced with sharp declines in business and rosy profit forecasts suddenly turned into nightmarish forecasts of large losses. The economy in general had entered a recessionary period. The downward economic trend continued well into 2001 and was deepened by the terrorist attacks in New York and Washington on September 11.

Nortel had begun a long, steep decline in 2000 and its share price sank to an incredible low of CDN$7.50

in 2001, when the company was estimating a loss of more than CDN$4 billion for the year. Several times during the year the company announced layoffs from its global workforce, totalling thousands of employees. Company spokespersons, financial commentators, analysts, and media experts were all discussing the near-disaster that had befallen one of the outstanding Canadian companies, one of the main global competitors in its field of high-tech communications equipment and systems. The gloomiest predictions even included the possible bankruptcy of Nortel. As 2001 ended there was still a lot of uncertainty in the air about when an economic turnaround would take place and how and when Nortel would begin an upward movement.

Decision Questions

1. Should companies like Nortel be less aggressive and more cautious in their policies and plans? How can high-tech companies in a very competitive global field do that?

2. Is there any warning in this story of the decline in Nortel's fortunes that raises doubts about the technology trends discussed in the chapter? Or is what happened to Nortel simply a question of a slowdown in the economy hitting all companies?

3. Can you see a connection between any of Nortel's actions and ethical questions raised in the chapter? What are the relevant issues?

4. Does the fact that only one-third of its workforce is in Canada mean that Nortel is no longer a Canadian company? What does the term *Canadian company* mean in the twenty-first century? Does this have any possible significance for your future career?

Adapted from: Michael MacDonald, "Nortel's Changing the Way it Does Business," *Montreal Gazette*, May 15, 1999, C11; many media, print, TV, and radio, 2001.

PRACTISING MANAGEMENT DECISIONS

CASE 2

CANADA'S 100 FASTEST-GROWING COMPANIES

Every year *Profit* magazine publishes a list of Canada's 100 fastest-growing companies. The June 2001 issue reports in detail on the 2000 selection. The importance of many of the major trends discussed in the chapter is quite clear. However, some other interesting facts emerge from the detailed data. For example, the leading 100 are split almost evenly among what the magazine calls *high-tech* and *non-tech* firms. Furthermore, the non-tech companies are growing just as fast as the high-tech ones, and two are in the first ten.

However, even these two use modern technology extensively in their operations. The next 100 leaders include 83 "old economy" companies, so we can conclude that traditional businesses are still flourishing.

The breakdown among manufacturing, service, and other types of companies is as follows:

	TOP 100	NEXT 100
Business services	32	35
Consumer services	8	7
Software development	22	11
Manufacturing	20	33
Other	18	14
Total	100	100

The importance of the service sector is obvious. If software development is included in manufacturing—since the product is manufactured—the manufacturing sector continues to rank just about equally with the service sector.

Other interesting data include the following:

1. The composition of the CEOs of the top 100: 9 completed college, 48 completed university, and 28 had done post-grad work.
2. Regarding small-company data, if we use the under-$10-million revenue (sales) criterion there are 35 in the top 100 and 39 in the next 100.
3. 83 of the top 100 companies exported, and exports accounted for half their sales.
4. Only seven women were CEOs of the top 100.

Finally, what makes them leading companies is that they all grew rapidly, and continue to do so, regardless of what field they are in. Nor did it matter whether they are high-tech or old-economy companies, manufacturing or service companies.

Adapted from: *Profit*, June 2001.

Decision Questions

1. Which of these data support the trends shown in the chapter and which do not? Show the trends in both cases and explain your answers.
2. Can you see how the lines between service and manufacturing companies are getting blurred? Is there a clear distinction between a product and a service?
3. What does all this mean for your career choices? Do you concentrate on high-tech or traditional industries? Is there a clear distinction between the two? Do you look for companies that are globally oriented?
4. What overall conclusions can you draw from these statistics pertaining to the fastest-growing companies in Canada? Is it safe to arrive at any general conclusions based on this information?

GLOBALIZATION AND ITS EFFECT ON CANADIANS

Chapter 1 examined globalization as a major trend affecting Canadian businesses and life in general in Canada. In this video you can see clearly how what happens in far away countries in Asia has a significant effect on Canadian companies and on the Canadian economy. The positive effects meant investment opportunities and profits for many Canadian companies in Asia and elsewhere. Large companies include such transnationals (TNCs) as Nortel, Power Corp., Bombardier, Magna International, Nova Corp., and International Nickel. All the major Canadian banks are also companies whose normal operations now encompass the whole world. Many small companies have also gone global.

The chapter mentions some of these companies and highlights a few in the boxes. As the text notes, this global expansion opened up new job opportunities for Canadians overseas as well as in Canada. Of course local economies also benefited in terms of jobs, new technologies, growth in exports, and economic expansion in general.

Of course a downward turn locally now negatively affects these Canadian and other foreign companies who participated in this global investment and trade. This is the other side of the coin that goes along with the good stuff. As the video shows it was a bumpy ride in 1998 but later developments resulted in continuing ups and downs right into 2002. Later it was not the Asian Flu but other factors that impacted global investment and trade negatively.

The text points out that the combined effects of technological advances in communications and transportation are the main forces that led to the globalization of business. Another important factor was the growth of the service sector, which does not involve the shipment of material objects. Here the development of computers has been the significant driving force. It made possible business-to-business (B2B) and business-to-consumer (B2C) services on a global scale. Also, as will be noted in future chapters, e-commerce is becoming an ever more important factor in the business world as it continues to shrink the globe.

Discussion Questions

1. Given the serious effect in Canada of negative developments in distant countries do you think it would be safer for the TNCs to cut back their foreign operations and concentrate on the home market instead? What effect would that have on the Canadian economy? (Think of expansion, jobs, technological advances, and other effects.)

2. The chapter notes that there is an ongoing series of protests, in various cities around the world, against the negative effect of globalization on the lives of people in many countries. Should this be a factor in company decision-making about globalization issues? Why?

3. The video points out the ease with which huge amounts of money are shifted around the world with the touch of a key on a computer keyboard and the great effect of such actions. Discuss the advantages and disadvantages of this technological development from the point of view of the companies and the countries affected by such transfers.

Source: CBC, *News in Review*, "The Changing World Economy," October, 1998.

CHAPTER 2

How Economic Issues Affect Business

LEARNING GOALS

AFTER YOU HAVE READ AND STUDIED THIS CHAPTER, YOU SHOULD BE ABLE TO

1 Describe how free markets work using the terms *supply*, *demand,* and *prices*.

2 Discuss some limitations of the free market system and what countries are doing to offset these limitations.

3 Understand the mixed economy of Canada.

4 Explain how inflation, recession, and other economic developments affect business.

5 Discuss the issues surrounding the national debt and its effect on business.

John Maynard Keynes

© Betterman/CORBIS/MAGMA

J. M. Keynes (pronounced *canes*), an economist from Cambridge University in England, became famous in the 1930s when Canada, England, the U.S., and most of the world were in the midst of a severe economic depression. His theories became known as *Keynesian economics* and exerted an important global influence for almost 50 years. Keynes suggested ways that governments could get their countries out of the Depression. The basic concepts were that governments should borrow and use the money to stimulate the economy. Complementing that was Keynes's insistence that these loans should be repaid when the economies were flourishing again and governments were collecting enough taxes to make these repayments. Since economic depressions and recoveries have an enormous effect on businesses, employment, and all forms of economic activity, Keynesian ideas attracted a lot of support and were followed by many governments, but there was much disagreement among economists, politicians, business, and labour leaders. The main opposition came from those who continued to support the concepts set forth by Adam Smith, often called the *father of modern economics*, whose ideas will be discussed in this chapter.

Keynes fell into disfavour in the 1980s as various economists and political leaders in the U.S., England, and Canada strongly urged governments to reverse their Keynesian actions and reduce their involvement in the economy as much as possible. These proponents argued that such involvement only disrupted and distorted the free market's ability to function most efficiently, as Adam Smith proposed in 1776. However, in the late 1990s and in 2001, when the world was facing its most serious economic crises in 70 years and the free market seemed unable to solve the grave problems, calls were once again being heard for governments to do something and to come to the rescue. Is Keynes being resuscitated?

To Cut or Not to Cut?

When you study this chapter you will see that an important problem for the Canadian government was how to help keep the Canadian economy in good shape when our national debt had, perhaps, played a big role in dragging the economy down. All our governments embarked on a program of reducing expenditures to avoid incurring annual deficits and adding to the national debt burden. The aim was to start generating annual surpluses to be used to reduce our enormous national debt.

To achieve this goal many civil servants were let go and many programs such as employment insurance, funds for education and health, welfare, and so on were reduced, causing great hardship to many people. Many organizations and individuals were strongly opposed to what governments were doing because of the serious adverse effects on so many people of all ages across Canada. Child poverty levels rose, food banks reported a big jump in the number of people applying for food, and pawn shops, dollar stores, and cheque-cashing services began to appear or expand all across Canada. Supporters of the governments' actions, as well as governments themselves, argued that there was no choice. If cuts were not made, they said, economic and social conditions would deteriorate further and everyone would be worse off.

Think about this difference of opinion as you read the chapter and see how you feel about it. At the end of the chapter we will try to answer these questions: Did the government go too far in cutting expenditures in its deficit battle? Did it have any alternatives that might have produced fewer harsh side effects?

THE ECONOMIC AND POLITICAL BASIS OF BUSINESS OPERATIONS

If you want to understand the underlying situation and conditions in which Canadian business operates, it is essential that you (1) have some grasp of economics, (2) be aware of the impact of the global environment, and (3) understand the role of the federal and provincial governments in Canada. You should pay close attention to these three factors because they strongly influence the kind of careers and jobs that will be available to you. This chapter will deal with the first point and the other two will be reviewed in the next two chapters. See the Ethical Dilemma box "To Cut or Not to Cut?" for some points to keep in mind as you study this chapter.

Economic Flows

The Canadian economy is an integral part of the world economy. Business firms use labour from other countries, export to and import from other countries, buy land in other countries for their facilities, and receive money from foreign investors. To understand events in the Canadian economy, therefore, one has to understand the world economy.

For various reasons, companies find it advantageous to expand outside their home country. Many Canadian assets are cheaper for foreigners to buy because their currency is high in relation to our dollar and because prices for these assets are much higher in their own countries. For example, the famous Chateau Whistler Resort in British Columbia was bought by a Japanese company, Yamanouchi Pharmaceuticals. A French company bought the very successful Connaught Laboratories in Toronto.

Another reason that foreign investors like Canada is because we have a stable economic and political environment. Investing is risky enough without having to worry about unpredictable dictatorial regimes, massive corruption, and a weak rule of law. The country with the largest investment in Canada by far is the United States. British, Dutch, Japanese, and French companies are also significant investors in Canada. At the same time, billions of dollars are invested outside Canada by Canadian companies.

Courtesy Chateau Whistler

WHAT IS ECONOMICS?

Economics is the study of how society chooses to employ resources to produce goods and services and distribute them for consumption among various competing groups and individuals. An important contribution of businesses to an economic system is the constant expansion of available resources. This expansion is achieved by discovering new ways of increasing the variety and production of energy, food, and a wide range of products and services.

A BRIEF HISTORY OF BUSINESS AND ECONOMICS

In 1776 Adam Smith wrote the now-famous book *An Inquiry into the Nature and Causes of the Wealth of Nations*, later considered the foundation of the study and understanding of the newly developing capitalist industrial society. Smith's ideas held sway for about 150 years because many of his ideas and predictions have been proven true. He developed a theory about the (then) new developing industrial economy, **capitalism**, an economic system with free markets and private ownership of companies operated for profit. Smith said that all companies would function best with little government involvement. His most-quoted comment concerns the so-called *invisible hand* that made everything work well in the economy. Individuals take the risk of investing money to build factories to produce what people want, creating profits for the investors and jobs for people. Because more people have jobs and can buy all the new products being produced, their standard of living improves and the factory owners make profits that they can reinvest to build new factories to produce more goods, and so on. In the end, said Smith, individual producers and buyers make for a prosperous and happy society. As the first person to develop a theory about capitalism, Smith is called the *father of economics.*

Unfortunately, the normal operation of our capitalist economy, while producing the benefits noted previously and as envisaged by Adam Smith, also produces many unpleasant side effects. There is much poverty, unemployment, and homelessness. How can rich countries

Adam Smith developed a theory of wealth creation more than 200 years ago. His theory relied on entrepreneurs working to improve their lives. To make money, they would provide goods and services, as well as jobs, for others.

© Bettmann/CORBIS/MAGMA

When Canadians buy Japanese cars, VCRs, and other products, money flows out of the country. It flows back in when Japanese business people buy property such as the Chateau Whistler Resort. Such international flow of money is one example of international economics.

economics
The study of how society chooses to employ resources to produce goods and services and distribute them for consumption among various competing groups and individuals.

capitalism
An economic system with free markets and private ownership of companies operated for profit.

www.adamsmithinstitute.com

This is the Web site of the Adam Smith Institute's International division. The site includes information on Adam Smith himself and on the work of the Institute. Check it out to learn more about this man, whose ideas spawned much of modern thought about how capitalism works.

like Canada allow children to be hungry and homeless? Furthermore, there are up-and-down cycles that are unpredictable and cause a great deal of hardship in and disruption of people's lives. The search for solutions to these and other problems gave rise to attempts to improve or replace capitalism.

DIFFERENT ECONOMIC SYSTEMS

By the twentieth century different countries had developed various forms of capitalism, as well as communist and socialist systems. These systems arose as countries attempted to overcome the weaknesses of the capitalist system. The differences involved greater or lesser degrees of government regulation, control, and ownership of the means of production—the various ways of creating wealth and providing goods and services ➤ **P. 18** ◄ for their people. The United States is the strongest and most important capitalist country. The Soviet Union and China were once the most important communist countries. In between were various countries with a variety of systems, often referred to as **mixed economies**; that is, economies with degrees of state ownership or control of the means of production. At one end of the spectrum, no country, including the United States and Canada, is an example of pure or 100-percent capitalism. Similarly, no country was a pure example of socialism or communism.

Karl Marx and Alternatives to Capitalism

One person who gave a lot of thought to this problem in the middle of the nineteenth century was a German economist called Karl Marx. He eventually wrote a massive multi-volume book called *Das Kapital*, which contained a detailed analysis of capitalism and its contradictions. Marx also laid out a vision for a radically different economic structure, calling it a *socialist* society. He envisioned no private ownership of factories and companies. The state, representing the people, would own all the means of production. Marx believed that this would eventually make it possible for every person to have all their needs provided for, at which time the society would then become a communist system.

This system of Marxian beliefs attracted a lot of support. In the twentieth century Marxism resulted in several revolutions in European countries in the attempt to set up communist states. These revolutions were unsuccessful in Hungary and Germany, but in the huge Russian Empire, a new communist state, the Soviet Union, was established in 1917. By 1949 there were eight communist countries in Eastern Europe and four in east Asia, including China, the most populous country in the world. Finally, North America saw the addition of Cuba in 1960 to the communist family of countries.

All of these countries had repressive, dictatorial governments, but they did achieve some economic growth and avoided the cycles that bedevilled capitalist countries. Everyone was guaranteed a job and free educational and health services; however, the accumulation of a variety of serious problems, both external and internal, led to the collapse of the communist systems in all these states with a few exceptions. By the end of the twentieth century only China, Vietnam, Cuba, and North Korea still made formal claims to espousing Marxian ideology. In reality all these countries, with the exception of North Korea, have adopted important capitalist practices and goals and are moving toward becoming capitalist mixed economies. We will look at mixed economies below.

It is now clear that the capitalist economic system has become the only viable system in the world. That does not mean that there are no problems with it. On the contrary, as we entered the new millennium, there were very serious problems in many countries and in the world's economy. *Time* magazine, for example, referred to "how close the world came to economic meltdown" in 1998.[1] We look at some of these problems in this chapter. In the next chapter we look at how the capitalist system

mixed economies
Economies with degrees of state ownership or control of the means of production.

www.marxists.org

The writings of Karl Marx and his colleague Friedrich Engels are, indeed, diametrically opposed to the capitalist views of writers like Adam Smith and John Maynard Keynes. Visit this Web site to learn more about Marx and his teachings and the work of others who share his views.

works in Canada. In the rest of this chapter we examine how that system works and how it affects Canada and your future, in terms of what career opportunities are likely to be growing or declining. We start by looking at how free markets work.

HOW FREE MARKETS WORK

The free market system is one in which decisions about what goods to produce or services to provide, in what quantities and at what prices, are made by buyers and sellers making free choices. The buyers may be companies or individual consumers. In Canada and all over the world buyers are constantly sending signals to sellers about what they want and at what prices. They send such signals by buying a lot, not very much, or nothing at all. The terms economists use for these activities are *supply* and *demand*. **Supply** is the quantity of particular products or services that suppliers are willing to sell at certain prices and at certain locations. **Demand** is the quantity of those products or services that buyers are willing to buy at those prices and at those locations. Where supply and demand meet or intersect is called the *equilibrium point* and becomes the actual price at which the transaction takes place (see Figure 2.1). That's what the theory says, but let's see how the free market and supply and demand actually play out on a global scale.

Canadian Press CP. Photograph by Jose Goita

World Markets: Supply and Demand

Every day billions of consumers throughout the world are sending signals to millions of producers throughout the world, telling them what they want. The signals are sent through the amount of goods and services being bought. The signals are sent very quickly, so there should be little delay in ending surpluses and shortages. In the real world, however, there are many interferences to the free exchange of goods and services among countries. Consequently, some countries have surpluses (for example, Canada has a surplus of many crops) and others suffer from scarcity (many countries do not have sufficient food). A free market system would seem to be the best system for improving the world's economic condition, yet there are many limitations and impediments to the free market system.

Limitations of the Free Market System

The free market system, with its freedom and incentives, was a major factor in creating the wealth that advanced countries now enjoy. Some experts even speak of the free market system as a true economic miracle. But certain inequities seem to be

Even though people in Cuba are suffering from the lack of goods and services available in many other countries because of the American embargo on trade, loans, and investments, Cuban leader Fidel Castro declared that Cuba would remain communist. Castro has been Cuba's leader since his revolution triumphed in 1959.

supply
The quantity of particular products or services that suppliers are willing to sell at certain prices and at certain locations.

demand
The quantity of particular products or services that buyers are willing to buy at certain prices and at certain locations.

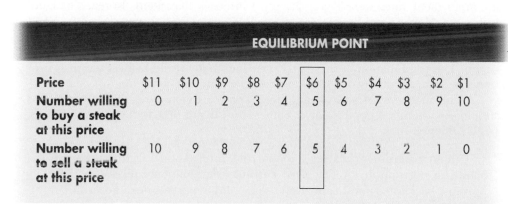

EQUILIBRIUM POINT										
Price	$11	$10	$9	$8	$7	$6	$5	$4	$3	$2	$1
Number willing to buy a steak at this price	0	1	2	3	4	5	6	7	8	9	10
Number willing to sell a steak at this price	10	9	8	7	6	5	4	3	2	1	0

FIGURE 2.1

BUYERS AND SELLERS AT DIFFERENT PRICES

Five people are willing to buy or sell a steak for $6.

inherent in the system. As capitalism developed, business people in England, Europe, the United States, Canada, and other countries began to create wealth. They set up factories and hired people, and the countries began to prosper. Soon these business people became the wealthiest class in each country. Although this new system created jobs and wealth, the benefits did not flow evenly to everybody. Factory owners built large homes, had fancy carriages, and enjoyed luxurious lifestyles. Workers lived in poverty and had no security.

Thus, we have the situation today in which many people cannot afford enough food or adequate housing. The same thing is true of dental care, clothing, and other goods and services: the wealthy seem to get all they need, and the poor get less than they need.

MIXED ECONOMIES

A different and more common path to reduction of the unpleasant side effects of capitalism took the form of government intervention to restrict and regulate the totally free market. Starting in the nineteenth century, governments in the newly industrialized countries in Europe, Japan, and North America began to play a larger role in exerting some control over the rapidly growing capitalist economies. Canada, like the U.S. and other countries, passed laws and regulations and established agencies in the attempt to smooth out the worst features and inequities of the expanding economy mentioned previously in this chapter. These attempts created the category of a *mixed economy* ➤**P. 38**◄. In the next chapter we will examine in detail how and why Canadian governments began to influence the operation of the free market in Canada.

www.time.com/time/
time100/scientist/
profile/keynes.html

Time magazine has chosen John Maynard Keynes as one of the most influential people of the twentieth century. A visit to this Web site will give you the flavour of Keynes's work and the impact that he has had on modern economic thought.

In the 1930s the whole world, except for the Soviet Union, which had a socialist and communist economy, was plunged into a very serious economic decline called the *Great Depression*. This was a terrible period of vast unemployment, hunger, and homelessness. Businesses were going bankrupt and economies were shrinking. For several years nothing governments tried seemed to reverse the conditions. Then economist John Maynard Keynes (profiled at the beginning of the chapter) came up with his proposals to lift the world out of the seemingly endless Depression.

As the Profile notes, Keynesian economics were applied by the U.S., Canada, and many European governments and they seemed to work. A half-century later the world economy was in relatively good shape and a movement developed, led by the English and U.S. governments (which the Canadian government supported), to reduce the role of government. This movement led to a wave of deregulation and privatization (governments selling off companies they owned). The general push was to have freer uncontrolled markets in a back-to-Adam-Smith movement. This movement was led by the giant corporations seeking the ability to operate more freely across borders in the quickly growing globalization of business.

However, as the end of the twentieth century approached, serious cracks in the economies of various countries began to threaten the whole global economy. In country after country that had formerly enjoyed strong growth, currency values were crashing, foreign investors were withdrawing their money, and bankruptcy and unemployment rates were rising sharply. Countries like South Korea, Thailand, Indonesia, Mexico, and Brazil were affected. Russia was a particularly bad case and concern was widespread that it faced the total collapse of its financial institutions and its economy. Mighty Japan had been unable to pull itself out of a decade-long slump. The combination of these problems had many world leaders seriously worried about the possibility of a major global recession and about how to avoid one.

Again, many voices were heard suggesting or demanding that governments should *do something*. A good example comes from an editorial in the prestigious U.S. weekly *Business Week*:

> Without government playing a major role, international capital flows can lead to corruption, overcapacity, currency devaluations, recessions, and even a backlash against capitalism itself.... Free markets need government action to work best.[2]

This editorial also shows how the global economy is quite different from what it was in the 1930s. The entire globe is closely linked and all countries are dependent on each other for investment, employment, technology, and exports. In the next chapter we will look at the global effect of the serious Asian economic problems nicknamed the *Asian flu*. These problems are like a disease that can spread, and in 1998 they started spreading rapidly around the world. Problems such as these affect all Canadians and in particular your job prospects.

The Mixed Economy of Canada

As mentioned earlier, Canada is not a purely capitalist economy. Rather, it has a mixed economy, a combination of free markets and government allocation of resources. As a mixed economy, Canada falls somewhere between a pure capitalist state and a socialist state. This is probably the most common economic system in the world today. The degree of government involvement in the economy is a matter of some debate.

Several features have played a major role in Canada's becoming an independent economic entity with a high percentage of government involvement in the economy.

First, we are one of the largest countries in the world geographically, but we have a small population (31 million in 2001). We have one of the lowest population densities in the world.

Most important, our neighbour to the south has nine times our population and an economy even greater than that proportion, speaks our language, is very aggressive economically, and is the most powerful country in the world. The United States exerts a very powerful influence on Canada. (For an illustration, see the Reaching Beyond Our Borders box "How Two U.S. Companies Affect the Canadian Economy.") To control our destiny, Canadian governments have passed many laws and regulations to make sure significant economic and cultural institutions, such as banks, insurance companies, and radio and TV stations, remain under Canadian control. (Even powerful countries like the United States and Japan have similar regulations.)

All of these factors led to the Canadian capitalist system taking on many characteristics of a mixed economy. Massive government support was necessary to build our first national rail line, the CPR, in the 1880s. When air transport was beginning in the 1930s, no company wanted to risk investing in it in such a large country with only 10 million people spread thinly across the land. So the government set up Air Canada (then called Trans Canada Airlines) to transport mail, people, and freight. There are many such examples of government action to protect the national interest.

In the 1980s many countries, including Canada, began to reduce government involvement in, and regulation of, the economy. This trend toward deregulation was widespread. In Canada, airlines, banks, and the trucking industry have all seen a marked reduction in regulatory control. Even in communist China there have been significant movements in this direction.

The former communist countries of Europe, namely Hungary, Poland, and the Czech Republic, and the republics of the former Soviet Union, are moving rapidly in this direction as well. It may not be an exaggeration to say that communism is disappearing as it moves toward mixed economies, as socialist countries move toward mixed economies, and as mixed economies move toward purer capitalist systems.

ECONOMICS AND BUSINESS

The strength of the economy has a tremendous effect on business. When the economy is strong and growing, most businesses prosper and almost everyone benefits through plentiful jobs, reasonably good wages, and sufficient revenues for the government to provide needed goods and services. When the economy is weak, how-

www.moodys.com
www.standardand
poors.com

Visit these Web sites to
see what services
Moody's and Standard
& Poor's provide.

ever, businesses are weakened as well, employment and wages fall, and government revenues decline as a result.

Because business and the economy are so closely linked, business newspapers and magazines are full of economic terms and concepts. It is virtually impossible to read such business reports with much understanding unless you are familiar with the economic concepts and terms being used. One purpose of this chapter is to help you learn additional economic concepts, terms, and issues—the kinds that you will be seeing daily if you read the business press, as we encourage you to do.

Gross Domestic Product

**gross domestic
product (GDP)**
The total value of a country's
output of goods and services in
a given year.

Almost every discussion about a nation's economy is based on **gross domestic product (GDP)**, the total value of a country's output of goods and services in a given year. It is good for GDP to grow, but not too fast or too slowly. Rapid growth may produce undesirable inflation rate increases; too-slow growth results in not enough new jobs created.

REACHING BEYOND OUR BORDERS
How Two U.S. Companies
Affect the Canadian Economy

www.standardandpoors.com
www.dbrs.com
www.cbrs.com

There are two companies in New York whose decisions have a significant effect on Canadian governments, businesses, and consumers. Both Moody's Investors Service and Standard & Poor's (S&P) are important and famous credit-rating agencies. They evaluate the degree of risk that investors would be exposed to if they bought the bonds of governments or companies around the world. They then give each bond a specific rating, such as AA or B+, and that rating has a major effect on the interest rate that must be set for that bond.

When a Canadian government or company needs to borrow on a long-term basis, which they do regularly, the interest cost for the life of that bond—5, 15, or 25 years—is determined by an American company that has established an excellent international reputation for reliable credit ratings. Each rating level leads to a particular interest rate. The higher the level (meaning lower degree of risk), the lower the interest rate. Conversely, the lower the rating (meaning higher degree of risk), the higher the interest rate investors will demand.

When the Canadian (or a provincial) government issues a 30-year bond and the rating requires a higher interest rate than planned, it could cost that government hundreds of millions of dollars over the 30-year period. That cost could lead to higher taxes and have a ripple effect on the entire economy.

Further, since the level of interest rates for Canadian government bonds affects general interest levels in

Canada, the impact on the economy is very significant, affecting the rates businesses and consumers have to pay when they take loans from banks or other financial institutions. It also affects mortgage rates and the rates financial institutions pay to depositors who invest their money with them. Large businesses that normally borrow by issuing bonds are also directly affected by the ratings of their own bonds by Moody's or S&P. These ratings also determine how much interest they must pay.

There are two Canadian bond-rating companies: the Dominion Bond Rating Service and the Canadian Bond Rating Service. Their ratings are important, but do not carry the international weight that Moody's and S&P do with the international lenders who buy Canadian bonds. In effect, the actions of two foreign companies can have major repercussions in the Canadian economy. Of course, this applies to many countries, not only to Canada.

On March 20, 1996, Premier Bouchard of Quebec, after a three-day meeting with major provincial groups to get consensus on a budget-balancing program, announced he would personally go to New York to convince Moody's and S&P that the plan was sound and that they should maintain their ratings of Quebec bonds.

Adapted from: Interviews with various stockbrokers, March 1999; *Globe and Mail, Report on Business,* March 1996, p. B24ff; CBC news, March 21, 1996.

Here's how Canada's GDP grew, in annual percentage rates, in the last few decades:[3]

1960s	5.2
1970s	4.3
1980s	3.2
1990s	3.7

The indications for 1999 were even better as, based on first-quarter figures, the Bank of Canada says GDP grew at an annual rate of 4.0 percent.[4] One way to increase GDP is to be more productive; to increase productivity. This important subject is discussed in more detail in Chapter 10, but as a brief preview is relevant at this point we will look at productivity shortly.

Distribution of GDP   The money that is earned from producing goods and services goes to the employees who produce them, to the people who own the businesses, and to governments in the form of taxes. The size of the share that goes to governments has a major impact on the economy as a whole. The general trend worldwide is for governments to reduce their share of GDP. A constant debate rages in Canada (and other countries) as to what percentage of the GDP pie should go to governments to most favourably affect the economy.

It is difficult to make comparisons among countries, because the right percentage depends on what services each government provides. For example, in Canada our national health-care system is financed by taxes. In the United States there is no such universal plan, so taxes are lower, but individuals and companies must pay these very substantial costs themselves.

Productivity and Labour Cost

Productivity is measured by dividing the total output of goods and services of a given period by the total hours of labour required to produce them. A similar calculation is done for countries to compare their rates of productivity. An increase in productivity is achieved by (1) producing a *greater* quantity of a certain quality for a *given* amount of work hours or (2) producing the *same* quantity with *fewer* work hours.

Labour cost measures the same equation in dollars. The dollar value of the output is divided by the dollar value of the work hours to arrive at the labour cost per unit. Anything that increases productivity or reduces labour cost makes a business, and a country, more competitive. The great gains in productivity that have occurred during the past century, especially in the past few decades, are due mainly to the introduction of increasingly efficient machinery, equipment, and processes. The past 15 years in particular saw computers and robots play a major role in this development.

You can see how important the issue of productivity is when the prestigious *Report on Business* section of the *Globe and Mail* (on June 20, 2001) has as its main headline "Productivity drops for the first time in 5 years." The headline refers to a Statistics Canada report discussing productivity declines in the first quarter of 2001.

It's a very difficult thing to measure a country's productivity or the rate at which it is improving. In mid-1999 a fierce dispute raged about how much Canada's productivity had improved in the past decade or two. A good example of this argument was an article in the *Montreal Gazette* in which Statistics Canada states that its revised figures show we have been performing as well as, if not better than, the U.S. since at least 1985. However, Industry Canada, another government ministry, maintains that its figures show that Canada is slipping further behind the U.S. Then we have the prestigious Paris-based Organization for Economic Co-operation and Development (OECD) saying it erred in rating Canada too low and it was now in the process of

productivity
The total output of goods and services in a given period divided by the total hours of labour required to provide them.

Workers are becoming more productive as the use of robots, computers, and other machinery increases. It is becoming increasingly important to measure service quality as well as quantity.

revising these figures upward. The OECD blames Statistics Canada for the confusion because the latter revised previously issued statistics.[5]

Further, in the next chapter you will see (from the same *Montreal Gazette* article) that the OECD continues to rate Canada's standard of living as being 10 percent above the average of industrial countries, and the powerful World Economic Forum (see Chapter 10) put Canada fifth in international competitiveness in 1999, only 10 percent behind the U.S. The whole issue of assessing international competitiveness is complex and open to varying opinions, and is discussed in more detail in the next chapter and in Chapter 10.

Any country that does not keep up with the international level of technological improvements falls behind in the fierce global competitive battle. In Canada this is a major problem, because our businesses are spending less on research and development than many advanced countries.

Of course, technological advances usually lead to people being replaced by machines, often contributing to unemployment. We will now examine this important issue.

PROGRESS
CHECK

- What is a mixed economy? What are its advantages over a free market economy?
- What does deregulation mean and how is it affecting the economy of Canada?
- Can you define gross domestic product? Productivity? Labour cost?
- How can productivity be improved and labour cost decreased?
- Why is productivity so important to a country's ability to compete?

THE ISSUE OF UNEMPLOYMENT

For a decade, Canada's official unemployment rate has ranged from 7.5 to 11.3 percent (see Figure 2.2). This means that officially 1 million to 1.5 million people were constantly reported as being out of work. The real rate is much higher because Statistics Canada does not include people who have given up looking for jobs, those who are working at part-time or temporary jobs or who stay in or return to school

FIGURE 2.2

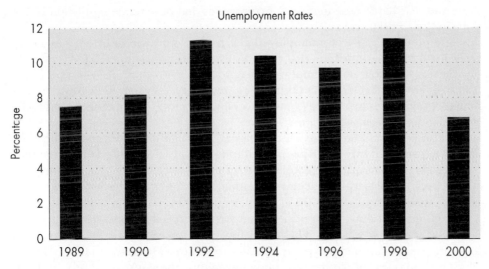

Unemployment Rates

UNEMPLOYMENT RATES

Unemployment rates fluctuated between 7.5 percent and 11.3 percent from 1989 to 1998 and finally fell below 7% in 2000.

Adapted from: Statistics Canada, CANSIM database http://cansim2.statcan.ca.cgi-win/CNSMCGI.EXE, Matrix 3451.

because they cannot find full-time work, and various other categories of people. If you work only one hour per week, you are classified as employed.

People are unemployed in Canada for various reasons. Perhaps their employer goes out of business or their company cuts staff. Young persons enter the job market looking for their first job and other employees quit their jobs but have trouble finding new ones. Companies merge and jobs are consolidated or trimmed. Companies transfer their operations to another country or a branch of a foreign company is closed down.

Of course, in a period of economic recession, such as in the early 1980s or 1990s, or in 2000 and 2001, unemployment increases. Different categories of unemployment are discussed next. However, one of the important causes of unemployment in the past decade has been relentless downsizing by many large companies. Every few weeks a major company announced layoffs of thousands of employees. These layoffs were driven by intense global competition (discussed later in the chapter) and technological advances. The former drove companies to relentlessly reduce costs, while the latter enabled them to operate with fewer employees. In Chapter 8 we will see that some management experts believe that the downsizing trend has been over-

This art student tries to earn tuition fees during a jobless summer by creating street art. Finding innovative ways to earn money can be especially important during difficult economic times.

Michael Poselli

done and may have consequences for companies that have made significant reductions in their workforces.

An important cause of unemployment is technological advances. When a company acquires a new machine that replaces five existing machines, each tended by one person, then four of the employees may no longer be required. When computer terminals are installed at the desks of senior managers, they may need fewer middle managers and secretaries. They can now access and send information directly. This situation creates *technological unemployment*.

Technology can lower costs for companies, making them more competitive and able to expand and hire more people. Although we are now more automated than ever, we also have more people working than ever before. So while people are constantly being displaced by machines, eventually new jobs are created—and somebody has to make and service those new machines.

From the economic point of view, unemployment is a great waste of resources. It means that people who could be producing goods or services are producing nothing—and receiving unemployment benefits or welfare. This reduces GDP. The terrible human cost of continued unemployment—the lack of funds and the demoralization that can destroy individuals and families—must also be considered. Retraining our unemployed citizens to become more skilled and thus help the country become more competitive is a necessity.

Categories of Unemployment

cyclical unemployment
Unemployment caused by a recession or similar downturn in the business cycle.

Cyclical unemployment is caused by a recession or similar downturn in the business cycle. Unemployment fluctuates with the economic cycles of boom and recession that occur regularly in capitalist economies.

seasonal unemployment
Unemployment that occurs when the demand for labour varies with the season.

Seasonal unemployment arises in industries in which the demand for labour varies with the season. For example, ski hills employ very few people in summer. Summer resorts and some children's camps do not employ anyone in winter. The Christmas season sees an increase in retail jobs. Summer is a much bigger tourist season in Canada than winter.

structural unemployment
Unemployment that results from changes in the structure of the economy that phase out certain industries or jobs.

Structural unemployment results from changes in the structure of the economy that phase out certain industries or jobs. Employees of fish plants in the Atlantic provinces are laid off when fish catches are reduced or fishing is banned to rebuild cod stocks. Our shift from a manufacturing-based economy to a service-dominated one is a major structural cause of unemployment. This situation is further aggravated as manufacturers restructure to meet strong international competition. Canada is moving from a resource-based to a knowledge-based economy.

Employees laid off in a tire plant in Ontario do not have the skills to be employed by a forestry company in B.C. that is trying to hire more staff. There is an unfilled demand for knowledge workers in computer software and other aspects of information technology. Retraining programs may help unemployed people to acquire the necessary new skills.

Regional Differences   Finally, since Canada is such a large country with regional economies, there are always major regional differences. For example, when the auto and related businesses were booming in Ontario in the mid-1980s, the Atlantic provinces were enduring unemployment rates in the 15 percent and higher range. When B.C. was booming in the early 1990s, Quebec and Ontario underwent a serious decline and had high unemployment rates. Saskatchewan suffered a decade-long problem of unfair foreign competition in the grain market due to massive government subsidies of competing countries' farmers. The regional unemployment picture is shown in Figure 2.3.

For a discussion of the implications of the Internet on regional employment and in other areas, see the Spotlight on Small Business box "Selling in Cyberspace."

Would Canada be better off today if we had not introduced modern farm machinery? More people would be employed on the farm if we had not. Would the world be better off in the future if we did not introduce new computers, robots, and machinery? They do take away jobs in the short run. What happened to the farmers who were displaced by machines? What will happen to today's workers who are being replaced by machines?

• Can you explain the differences between seasonal, structural, and cyclical unemployment? Which is causing the largest unemployment today?

• What are regional differences in unemployment? Why do they exist?

	1991 (%)	MAY 2001 (%)
Newfoundland	17.4	15.6
Prince Edward Island	14.5	12.0
Nova Scotia	10.4	10.0
New Brunswick	11.5	11.2
Quebec	9.8	9.0
Ontario	6.8	5.9
Manitoba	5.6	4.9
Saskatchewan	6.1	6.3
Alberta	5.9	4.5
British Columbia	8.9	6.8
Canada	**7.9**	**7.0**

FIGURE 2.3

ANNUAL PROVINCIAL UNEMPLOYMENT RATES

You can see how provincial rates of unemployment vary widely.

Source: *Canadian Regional Outlook*, Bank of Montreal, June 2001.

SPOTLIGHT ON SMALL BUSINESS

Selling in Cyberspace

Internet Tax Fairness Coalition
www.salestaxsimplification.org

The impact of the Internet is discussed in several chapters in this book. Every day millions of World Wide Web users are browsing, shopping, ordering, and paying online for all kinds of products and services for individual and commercial usage. Many people also use this medium to search for jobs because they can quickly access a wide range of job possibilities in more than one country. The Internet has totally changed many factors and conditions relating not only to businesses, but also to governments.

Consider this fictional situation: software developer Virinder Assad lives in India and has no office. Assad operates out of his van where he has a fax, laptop, printer, and cellphone. He is an employee of a small software company located in the home of the owner, Tom Lee, in Halifax, Nova Scotia. The company sells software products exclusively via the Internet to buyers all over Canada and the U.S., and is beginning to get nibbles from some European countries. If a customer in Germany downloads software and pays for it by credit card, where was the sale made? Which country is entitled to charge the taxes? In Canada we have the GST and provincial sales taxes (except for Alberta) and Germany has a value-added tax (VAT). What about Mr. Assad? He never comes to Canada, but is he subject to any Canadian employee taxes or benefits? How about Tom Lee's company: can it be deemed to be operating in provinces and U.S. states where buyers are located? If so, will it be subject to taxes and other legislation affecting businesses operating in those jurisdictions?

Because of the explosive growth of Internet developments, the issues of who is entitled to collect taxes or has responsibility for product warranty or employee-related issues are becoming increasingly complex. Determining just where an Internet transaction was made can be difficult. The huge growth in the number of such transactions has significant implications for the economies and tax revenues of countries, provinces, and states.

FIGURE 2.4

CONSUMER PRICE INDEX (CPI)

These figures indicate that a Canadian's income had to rise by 86 percent from 1981 to 1999 just to keep up with the rise in the CPI.

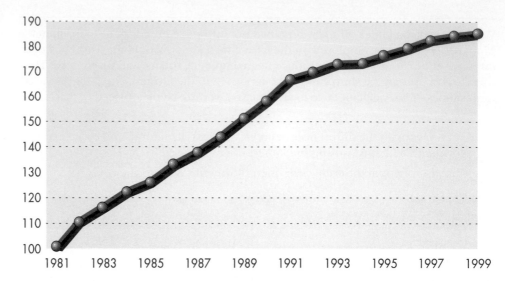

Adapted from: Statistics Canada, CANSIM database http://cansim2.statcan.ca.cgi-win/CNSMCGI.EXE, Matrix 9957.

INFLATION AND THE CONSUMER PRICE INDEX[6]

One of the measures of how an economy is doing is its ability to control inflation. **Inflation** refers to a general rise in the price level of goods and services over time. For 20 years from the early 1970s, Canada's inflation rate was substantially above 3 percent. The rate peaked in 1981 at 12.5 percent, and hovered between 4 and 6 percent until 1992, when it dropped below 2 percent, where it remained until 2001, when it nudged over 3 percent. The question of inflation was a central issue in Canada for almost 20 years. Economists do not agree about the causes of inflation, the specific cures, or whether the cures might be worse than the disease.

Inflation increases the cost of doing business. When a company borrows money, interest costs are higher; employees demand increases to keep up with the rise in cost of living; suppliers raise their prices; and as a result the company is forced to raise its prices. If other countries succeed in keeping their inflation rates down, then Canadian companies will become less competitive on the world market.

One popular measure of price changes over time (inflation indicators) is the **consumer price index (CPI)**. The consumer price index measures monthly changes in the price of a basket of goods and services for an average family. Such an index gives a vivid picture of the effects of inflation on consumer prices. If the cost of the market basket is $1,000 one month and goes up to $1,006 the next, the inflation rate was 0.6 percent for the month, or roughly 7.2 percent annually. At that rate, the cost of consumer goods would double in about 10 years. Figure 2.4 shows the whole CPI picture from 1981 to 1999.

inflation
A general rise in the prices of goods and services over time.

consumer price index (CPI)
Measures monthly changes in the price of a basket of goods and services that an average family would buy.

THE NATIONAL DEBT[7]

Canadian government policies for many years followed only one of Keynes's suggestions. The government borrowed heavily for many years, but it forgot to reduce spending when times were good to pay back these loans. The result is a large **national debt**, the accumulated amount owed by the Canadian government from its past borrowings. This debt totals approximately $600 billion, and the interest alone amounts to approximately $100 million every day. Twenty percent of the total revenues the government receives go to pay interest on the national debt.

national debt
The accumulated amount owed by the Canadian government from its past borrowings.

Governments must borrow when they spend more in a year than they receive from taxes and other sources. An excess of expenditures over revenues is called a **deficit**. In Canada 25 years of annual deficits, starting in the mid-1970s, has resulted in a huge national debt. The United States and many other countries also have serious debt loads that limit efforts by governments to help their economies out of a recession. However, in relation to the size of its economy—its GDP—Canada's debt problem is one of the biggest among developed countries.

deficit
An excess of expenditures over revenues.

A large debt load means that when tough times hit our economy, such as in the early 1990s, our government is unable to follow Keynes's recipe—reduce taxes and borrow to spend more—to help the economy out of a recession. Consequently, taxes remain high just when businesses need to reduce the cost of operations to stay afloat. Individuals also have less take-home pay to put back into the economy through spending. These factors deepen and prolong a recession in Canada.

Wiping Out Annual Deficits: Process and Results

After relentless pressure from business organizations and right-wing political groups, the Canadian government decided in 1996 that the only way out of that recession was to eliminate annual deficits and stop the debt from growing. This plan meant cutting expenses and cash outlays as much as possible, including reducing transfers to provinces to pay for health care, education, and welfare. The government reduced employment insurance (EI) payments by raising eligibility standards, paying for shorter periods, and paying smaller amounts. The government also laid off thousands of people and reduced pension payments to wealthier senior citizens.

These reductions in spending contributed to Canada's slow recovery from the recession. Increased government borrowing and spending stimulates an economy, while cuts in spending have the opposite effect—they slow down the economy.

By 1998 the government was able to announce that, for the first time in 25 years, government operations had resulted in a surplus of $3.5 billion rather than a deficit. Larger surpluses followed in 1999, 2000, and 2001. Minister of Finance Paul Martin announced that these surpluses would be used partially to reduce the national debt and that future surpluses would also be applied to the debt. As the debt comes down, the annual interest costs are reduced. Every billion-dollar reduction in the debt reduces annual interest costs by about $50 million. A cumulative $40-billion reduction leads to a $2.5-billion annual savings in interest. Reducing government spending will allow the government to reduce taxes, which in turn will stimulate the economy as companies and individuals will have more disposable income.

The drastic slashing of government spending was strongly opposed by left-wing political groups and many organizations such as churches, unions, welfare groups, food banks, and many other community-centred groups because of the hardship these cuts inflicted on many people. Reduced EI and welfare payments, a reduction in hospital funding, the closing of hospitals, and so on affected many poor and sick people. Cuts to higher-education funding resulted in fewer staff members and more students per class, higher fees, increased costs of some services, and a reduction of other services. Food banks across Canada reported a jump in the number of people seeking food. When economic problems become severe, attempts to remedy them can be difficult and painful. Part of the surpluses are being used to restore some of the funding cuts to health and education.

Government cutbacks have resulted in reduced payments to better-off seniors. Spending cuts have been implemented to reduce the deficit.

The outlook for the Canadian economy in the next few years affects your future because the economy will determine your prospects for a good job. We look next at how the Canadian economy is likely to perform.

Members of the Poverty Action Network stage a demonstration to demand more welfare money for a longer time.

THE OUTLOOK FOR THE CANADIAN ECONOMY

With the health of the world's economy uncertain at the start of the twenty-first century, the Canadian economy's performance in the next few years is also uncertain. We are living in a very closely connected and interdependent global economy. Economic problems in Asia and South America can quickly spread to Europe and North America. Canada, as a major exporter, immediately feels the impact of economic weakness elsewhere. If the countries that import our products reduce their buying or if world prices of lumber, newsprint, coal, oil, nickel, wheat, canola, or other commodities drop we feel the pinch very quickly.

At the end of the 1990s the state of the global economy was discussed using words like *turmoil, crisis, collapse, depression*. The economy moved from the business pages to the front pages and conflicting analyses were made by economic and business journals, Nobel Laureate economists, financial experts, and governments around the world. By the end of 1999 and into early 2000 our economy had improved considerably but the collapse of technology stocks in the U.S. and Canada had a very negative effect on the economy.

Given this level of confusion, what is reasonable to expect from the Canadian economy in the next few years? Canada emerged from a recession at the beginning of the 1990s and our economy had been expanding, as measured by growth in GDP. Unemployment dropped from more than 11 percent to 7 percent (see Figure 2.2), leaving Canada's unemployment rate in the middle versus other industrialized countries.

In mid-2001 there was an air of uncertainty about the prospects for the Canadian (and American) economy. The sharp decline in profits and stock market values of high-tech companies, and especially the dot-coms, was a major contributing factor to the economic weakness and uncertainty about the future. Economists and business leaders were making cautious and often contradictory predictions about when the economy would improve and how much it would move ahead. Then disaster struck.

On September 11 terrorists hijacked four airplanes in the United States and crashed two of them into the two World Trade Center towers in New York, leading to their collapse and causing the deaths of more than 3,000 innocent people. One plane crashed into the Pentagon and one crashed in a field in Pennsylvania as some passengers fought with the hijackers to prevent them from crashing the plane into another important building in Washington.

These events led to a heightening of uncertainty about the future and caused a further decline in an already weak economy. Particularly hard-hit were the airlines, already in a near-crisis state, and the travel and tourism industries—people were afraid to travel, and many workers in these industries lost their jobs as layoffs became a regular news item. Toward the end of 2001 government officials and economists and analysts in Canada and the United States were forecasting a period of little growth or even the possibility of a decline in economic activity. The most optimistic forecasts said that by the end of 2002 things would be a lot better. In Chapter 4 you will see what the governments and central banks of Canada and the United States did to try to offset the economic reversals. Among the important actions were the substantial reductions in interest rates.

The interest rate cuts were designed to give companies the confidence to continue investing in capital expansion because lower interest rates mean lower costs of borrowing. Lower interest rates also mean lower mortgage rates, encouraging families to buy homes and stimulating the construction industry. Growth in the construction industry then has a spillover effect on many feeder industries. Consumers are also encouraged to spend more as the cost of carrying credit card debt also declines with lower interest rates. Overall, the cuts should stimulate the entire economy, providing more jobs for Canadians.

Review

Remember the question about the huge impact on Canadian life of governments slashing expenditures to reduce and wipe out annual budgetary deficits? Our executives answer that, difficult as it was, with many people losing jobs and government aid, there was no choice. The method used may leave room for argument, but not the need to do it. Reilley notes that "the national debt grew because Canadian governments at all levels kept piling on new and expensive programs without taking stock of either the utility or cost. Also, outdated and inefficient programs remained on the books." He concludes that "the current adjustment in Canada is painful to many. Yet without this adjustment, our standard of living and productivity as a country would erode."

Bédard comments that "what most people demanded of government was not necessarily to slash all social programs; many of these programs are what makes Canada unique. [But] the bureaucracies surrounding many programs are much too heavy and complex. By reducing inefficiencies and waste, many of the objectives could have been attained." He concludes that "Canada can no longer afford to be as generous as it has been, [which is why there was] the need to reduce certain programs to balance the budget."

The arguments about this issue will continue for a while as both sides continue the debate as to the ethical nature of such huge cuts that did so much damage to the social fabric of Canada. The surpluses are making possible the beginnings of restoration of some of the important social funding. As interest costs continue to decline due to national debt reduction more funds should be available to continue this trend.

PROSPECTS FOR CAREERS AND JOBS

What does all this mean as far as your future is concerned? The Canadian and world economic pictures looked clouded in mid-2001, but the long-term outlook is better. The new millennium will offer young people a good choice of jobs and careers, and young people with the most years of education will continue to have a lower unemployment rate. Many jobs will be available in our continually globalizing and technologically driven world. In respect to job prospects, your future looks promising.

- What is a recession? What is inflation?
- What is the size of the national debt? Why is it so important?
- According to Keynes, how should the government use fiscal policy to manage the economy?

PROGRESS CHECK

SUMMARY

1. A free market system is one in which decisions about what to produce and in what quantities are decided by the market.
   - *How do supply and demand affect what kinds of products are produced in a free market system and in what quantity?*

   The price of a product tells producers to make more or less of it. The more money producers make from higher prices, the more product they are likely to produce. Price is determined by supply and demand. The higher the quantity of demand, the higher the price. In turn, the higher the supply, the lower the price.

1. Describe how free markets work using the terms *supply, demand,* and *prices.*

2. Discuss some limitations of the free market system and what countries are doing to offset these limitations.

2. In spite of the wealth that countries with a free market system enjoy, the system suffers from certain inequities.

   • *What are some limitations of the free market system?*

   In countries with free market systems, the rich can buy almost everything, and the poor often cannot buy what they need. There may be a high crime rate and tolerance of negative social behaviour; economic freedoms and social freedoms often go hand in hand.

3. Understand the mixed economy of Canada.

3. Canada does not operate under a pure capitalist system but is a mixed economic system.

   • *What does it mean to say Canada has a mixed economy?*

   Canada falls somewhere between a pure capitalist state and a socialist state. Its economy is a combination of free markets and government allocation of resources.

4. Explain how inflation, recession, and other economic developments affect business.

4. Inflation is the rise in the cost of living and a recession is a decline in the overall economy.

   • *How do these and other economic developments affect business?*

   When the economy is healthy, companies expand, buy new equipment, and hire more employees, which further stimulates the economy. In a recession the reverse happens, deepening the recession. Inflation leads to demands for higher wages as employees try to maintain their standard of living. This raises prices, boosting inflation and making companies less competitive internationally.

5. Discuss the issues surrounding the national debt and its effect on business.

5. When the government is spending more than it is receiving, the national debt increases.

   • *What is the national debt and how did it get so high?*

   The national debt is the sum of money the government has borrowed and has not paid back. It is the accumulation of annual deficits.

   • *How does the large national debt affect Canadian companies?*

   Companies pay higher taxes due to the large annual interest payments, reducing their ability to compete with companies in countries where taxes are lower.

KEY TERMS

capitalism 37
consumer price index (CPI) 48
cyclical unemployment 46
deficit 49
demand 39

economics 37
gross domestic product (GDP) 42
inflation 48
mixed economies 38
national debt 48
productivity 43

seasonal unemployment 46
structural unemployment 46
supply 39

DEVELOPING WORKPLACE SKILLS

1. What are some of the disadvantages of living in a free society? How could such disadvantages be minimized? What are the advantages? How could Canada broaden the base of the free market system? Write a short essay describing why a poor person in India might reject capitalism and prefer a socialist state. You could debate capitalist versus socialist societies with a classmate to further reveal the issues.

2. Identify one of the most widely debated economic issues and discuss the various viewpoints with your classmates and instructor. Choose a position and be ready to defend it by researching facts and figures to support it. Have you set up a filing system yet to maintain such information?

3. The text discusses three major indicators of an economy's health: gross domestic product (GDP), unemployment rate, and consumer price index (CPI). The text also describes the close relationship of productivity to GDP. Each of these indicators rises and falls during periods of recession and periods of growth. Devise two charts to illustrate whether each economic indicator goes up, down, or remains the same during a condition of (1) economic recession and (2) growth.

4. Most of the world's nations are moving toward some variation of a mixed economy that could be labelled welfare capitalism. What do you see as the primary differences between the emergence of welfare capitalism and pure capitalism? Which would you favour and recommend? Why?

TAKING IT TO THE NET

Purpose:

To become familiar with forecasting and analyzing tools.

Exercises:

1. Analyses of the constantly moving economy are made regularly by various experts and government departments. See if you can find some forecasts, using the keywords *Canadian economic forecasts,* of the current outlook for the Canadian economy by searching Web sites such as *The Globe and Mail* <www.theglobeandmail.com>, the *National Post* <www.nationalpost.com>, and *Canadian Business* magazine <www.canbus.com>. Also try a search engine.

2. Can you see, or do any of the articles mention, the possible impact of this information on specific Canadian companies or industries? Perhaps you are considering a career in one of these industries or a job possibility with one of these companies. See if you can find any reports or statements on the Internet from these companies.

PRACTISING MANAGEMENT DECISIONS

CASE 1

A GIANT LABRADOR PROJECT FACES SOME DILEMMAS

Canada is a very large country, rich in minerals and metals. Finding and exploiting these important natural resources have always been important activities that have given a great boost to our economy. Canada is known throughout the world for its natural riches and its ability to develop them into important national assets. Many thousands of enterprising individuals explored Canada searching for deposits of nickel, copper, silver, gold, and other metals. Many companies were created and so were a large number of jobs.

This is a good illustration of the relevance of the theories of Adam Smith mentioned in the chapter. These entrepreneurs were driven by the incentive for profit and wealth. In the process, the economy was developed, jobs were provided, communities were established, and the country as a whole benefited. People usually worked under very difficult conditions

of climate and terrain, and put in long, hard hours, often without success. Eventually some giant companies—Noranda, Inco, Falconbridge—emerged.

In 1995 and 1996, Canadian newspapers were full of stories about a tremendous nickel discovery in a remote area of Labrador. The Voisey's Bay deposit is said to be the largest nickel ore body in the world. Originally, Al Chislett and Chris Verbiski persuaded Diamond Fields Resources to risk almost a half-million dollars to back their search for diamonds and gold. Although no diamonds and no gold were found, they did discover the huge nickel ore body, and both Chislett and Verbiski, as well as Diamond Fields, became very wealthy by later selling the company to Inco. Their discovery will spawn a huge development and provide many jobs in a province that badly needs jobs. In addition, some 285,000 mineral claims have been staked in that area. This story is an excellent example of what entrepreneurial Canada does well.

However, a serious issue was raised by the 6,500 Innu and Innuit aboriginal peoples who inhabit, trap, fish, and hunt in that area. They have been trying unsuccessfully for more than 25 years to get their land claims in that area settled with the federal government. Now they want their share of the new-found riches to be negotiated before work commences. They are also concerned about damage to the environment, which is always a major issue in such developments.

In 1998 a series of developments combined to confuse and delay this giant project. Disputes involving Inco, the Newfoundland and Labrador provincial government, the aboriginal peoples, the federal government, and environmental organizations led to court actions, hearings, and many meetings involving these parties. In addition, the international price of nickel dropped sharply and stayed there.

The provincial government wanted Inco to process all the ore on-site to provide badly needed jobs, thus adding to the local economy and generating revenues for the government. Inco argued that the high price it paid to acquire the location, $3.5 billion, and the low price of nickel meant that the lowest possible cost of production was its prime consideration. The Innu and Innuit wanted jobs, but were concerned about

the possible environmental impact of the operation, as were environmental groups. The Innu and Innuit also wanted settlement by the federal government of their long-outstanding land claims.

By mid-2001 some of these issues appear to have been resolved.

Decision Questions

1. Think carefully about the economic issues in this case. How many such issues can you list? What is the effect of each one on the project?

2. How does this case relate to Adam Smith's theory about capitalism that was reviewed in the chapter? Why is this a good example of his beliefs?

3. Can you see this case as an example of the role of government in the economy? Do you think this case is an example of the positive or negative impact of government? Explain.

4. How much importance do you attach to the environmental issue in this case? What about the ethical issue of aboriginal rights? Do you think that these questions are important enough to delay this giant project?

Practising Management Decisions

CASE 2

OGRE FACES A MARKET ECONOMY

Ogre Mills is a typical factory in Latvia, formerly part of the communist system that existed in the now-defunct Soviet Union. As the world opens to free competition, these factories have to compete with world-class factories in countries such as Canada, the United States, Germany, and Japan. Are they ready for such competition?

Under the previous system, the factory submitted a budget to the government. The government then set quotas for the factory, decided who would supply the factory with raw materials, distributed final goods, and set the price. The government also decided how much workers would be paid. Management's pay was based on whether or not quotas were met and whether the budget was followed.

Now that the mill faces a market economy, things will be very different. The firm must acquire materials in global markets, pay for those goods in hard currency, and price the goods competitively. In most advanced countries, businesses rely on information systems to provide the information needed to set global prices, track inventory and shipping, and track profits. Because the Latvian information systems are not world-class, Ogre Mills will have trouble competing.

The firm has been able to find enough hard currency to buy raw materials overseas. It has also joined the International Wool Society to make sure that its products meet the world's quality standards. Nonetheless, the company still has obsolete production equipment and information systems.

Decision Questions

1. Explain how prices are determined in free markets. How does such a system result in few surpluses or shortages? Contrast that system with the communist economy to which Ogre once belonged.

2. What are some of the advantages and disadvantages that people in Latvia will experience as the country moves toward a free market? How would a mixed economy alleviate some of the problems?

3. What advantages do Latvian firms have over firms in the United States and Germany, if any?

4. If you were a counsellor to the Latvian people, what kind of economic system would you recommend: socialism, capitalism, or a mixed economy? Explain your reasons.

TURMOIL IN THE ECONOMY

When the economies of some Asian countries declined sharply in 1998, an economic sickness dubbed the *Asian Flu*, the bug spread around the world affecting many countries and hit the Canadian economy too. Soon, the entire world was hit with a serious recession. A year or two later, other reasons led to another global crisis. This is one of the negative effects of a globalized world of business. It is the economic equivalent of easier and faster plane travel allowing germs to be spread more easily from country to country.

Then things started to pickup a bit, but in 2000 and 2001 there were several serious reverses. First the hi-tech and dot.com bubble burst and their shares collapsed on the stock markets. The final blow was the terrorist attacks in the U.S. on September 11, 2001 which triggered a chain of negative developments in various sectors of the U.S. and Canadian economies.

As a result, the economy in Canada has been on a roller coaster ride the last few years. In 2001 and early 2002 unemployment started to climb as companies continued to lay off employees due to falling demand. Another effect was the weakening value of the Canadian dollar relative to the U.S. dollar. By 2001/02 our dollar was fluctuating in the record low area of 62-63 cents. Both of these developments, as the chapter noted, resulted in an unprecedented number of interest rate reductions by the Bank of Canada in the attempt to boost the economy. The rate reached levels not seen since the 1960s.

What was strange is that, unlike previous recessions, the new, knowledge-based economy was in trouble while the *old* economy was doing well. Because there was no inflation and interest rates were so low consumers were buying cars and homes, the real estate market was booming, and the 2001 Christmas season saw malls packed with customers.

The experts' disagreements about the exact state of the economy and the varying conditions across Canada make it difficult for businesses and governments to make plans for the future.

Discussion Questions

1. As noted in the textbook, the dominant trend in recent times, in the business world, has been favouring unrestricted, free market operations. The current global economic problems have led to a demand for a greater role for government to limit some of the international free market activities that led to or worsened difficulties in many countries. Discuss the pros and cons of this issue.

2. Imagine your are a CEO of a medium size company in January 2002, located in Alberta and you are aware of the different opinions of business and economic experts about the economy and where it's heading. On January 12 you see a headline in the *Globe and Mail*, "Job losses likely to deepen" followed by a sub-heading, "Calls mounting for federal action to further stimulate flagging economy." Would you support such a *call*? Or would you feel that it's up to each company to solve their own problems? Would you feel differently if your company was in B.C? Explain your position.

Source: *Venture*, show number 773, "The Coming Storm," February 6, 2001, running time 7:53

CHAPTER 3

Competing in Global Environments

LEARNING GOALS

AFTER YOU HAVE READ AND STUDIED THIS CHAPTER, YOU SHOULD BE ABLE TO

1. Discuss the critical importance of the international market and the role of comparative advantage in international trade.

2. Understand the status of Canada in international business.

3. Illustrate the strategies used in reaching global markets.

4. Discuss the hurdles to trading in world markets.

5. Review what trade protectionism is and how and why it is practised.

6. Discuss the future of international trade and investment.

BioChem: From Local Firm to International Success

Francesco Bellini was the founder, chairman, and CEO of BioChem Pharma Inc., a pharmaceutical company based near Montreal that was making a name for itself internationally. Bellini was the driving force in pushing the company from its small beginnings to its international stature. Bellini took the company public to get additional financing to develop two major drugs: 3TC, which is important in the treatment of AIDS, and Zeffix, which was the first oral treatment for hepatitis B. The company was helped in the necessary research by another injection of capital, this time from the giant British pharmaceutical firm Glaxo Wellcome Inc., which received a 12-percent

Courtesy Biochem Pharma Inc.

share in BioChem Pharma. In return for its financing, Glaxo also received the licence to market both of these drugs internationally and the royalties that Glaxo paid for the licence provided BioChem with substantial cash flow.

In 1999 Bellini arranged for BioChem to buy back about half of Glaxo's shares in BioChem for US$160 million, half payable immediately and the balance 18 months later. Bellini believed that this action, combined with the cash flow from the royalties, would enable BioChem to achieve a number of important goals. BioChem would be able "to develop and retain total control of the rights to future drugs and vaccines"

and to set up its own marketing system. The company would also retain a greater share of the profits because it would be paying out less to Glaxo.

These plans were drastically changed in 2001 when BioChem merged with an English firm, Shire Pharmaceuticals Group. Shire has sales and marketing units in the United States, Southern Asia, and all over Europe, and plans to add Japan by 2004. It markets its products in other areas of the world through marketing agencies. This will give a much greater exposure to the products Bellini was developing in BioChem. Francesco Bellini and two other directors of BioChem have joined the board of directors of Shire.

Francesco Bellini is an excellent example of much of the material in this book and in this chapter. A dedicated entrepreneur starts a small company, goes public, then makes connections with a giant firm to further help develop the company. Bellini used licensing as a way to expand internationally, but maintained control of his company. Finally, he merged his company with a larger, international pharmaceutical company, thus becoming part of a company that enabled BioChem to quickly achieve a much greater global reach than it could have by itself.

Adapted from: Sheila McGovern, "BioChem Strikes Out on Own," *Montreal Gazette*, June 12, 1999, C1; http://www.shire.com, 2001.

A Question of Hot Nightgowns

As a top manager of Nightie Nite, a maker of children's sleepwear, you are required to be aware of all the new government regulations that affect your industry. A recently passed safety regulation prohibits the use of the fabric that you have been using for girls' nightgowns for the past 15 years. Apparently the fabric does not have sufficient flame-retardant capabilities to meet government standards. Last week Nightie Nite lost a lawsuit brought against it by the parents of a young child severely burned because the nightgown she was wearing burst into flames when

she ventured too close to a gas stove. Not only did you lose the lawsuit, but you may lose your nightshirt if you don't find another market for the warehouse full of nightgowns you have in inventory. You realize that there are other countries that do not have such restrictive laws concerning products sold within their borders. You are considering exporting your products to these countries. What are your alternatives? What are the consequences of each alternative? What will you do? Ponder these questions as you go through the chapter and we will try to find some answers at the end.

THE GLOBALIZATION OF BUSINESS

If you want to get some idea of how business has become a global affair you need only look at Canada. According to Statistics Canada, *every day* they "process documents containing over twenty million import/export transactions obtained when goods cross the Canadian border, going to or coming from over *200 countries*."[1] [Given such a huge amount of data to store and analyze, you may wonder how reliable Statistics Canada (StatCan) reports are, especially since these transactions are only part of a much larger number of varied economic activities in Canada. The answer is that the internationally prestigious magazine *The Economist* has rated StatCan the number-one statistical agency in the world. [2]

Because of developments in communications and transportation, our planet has become a small place. Products and services are marketed to, and provided from, the whole world. The Reaching Beyond Our Borders box "Canadian Companies Spread Their Wings" is a good example of how closely enmeshed the Canadian economy has become with the rest of the world. All significant business activity involves international aspects. See the Ethical Dilemma box "A Question of Hot Nightgowns" for a problem related to globalization to ponder as you read this chapter.

THE IMPACT OF THE GLOBAL ECONOMY ON CANADA

Why should we in Canada be so concerned about recession in South Korea or Russia or Brazil? We actually export only a small percentage of our products to them and our companies invest relatively little there. So why should we pay careful attention to what's happening to the economies of these distant countries? Will their problems affect your career and job opportunities? To better appreciate the extent to which the economies of all countries are interlocked and interdependent, we turn next to an examination of the globalization ➤**P. 9**◄ of business.

Anyone who reads Canadian newspapers or magazines, uses the Internet, or watches TV business programs can find numerous examples of the ceaseless expansion of Canadian companies into global markets, deals, joint ventures ➤**P. 10**◄, and so forth. World barriers to trade and investment have been dropping steadily.

REACHING BEYOND OUR BORDERS
Canadian Companies Spread Their Wings

The extent of Canadian companies' involvement in the globalization of business can be grasped by looking at news reports. Our mining companies—large and small—are busy exploring in Indonesia, Chile, Kazakhstan, China, Africa, and elsewhere. Bombardier is selling planes and is in joint ventures to supply railcars and set up rail transportation systems around the globe. Roy Thomson and Pierre Peladeau are buying up newspapers and printing companies in Europe and North America. Nortel Networks is heavily involved in major deals in China and has a major contract with AT&T in the United States. Viceroy Homes is supplying Japan with manufactured homes. The architectural firm of Robbie, Young & Wright, which designed the Toronto SkyDome, won the contract for a stadium and sports complex in Frankfurt, Germany.

The Bank of Montreal and the Bank of Nova Scotia acquired stakes in Mexican and Central American banks. Softkey International acquired The Learning Co. to create the world's biggest educational software company. Dreco Energy Services of Edmonton is selling rigs to Siberia. Suncor teamed up with Australian companies for a huge shale oil project there. Vancouver-based QLI Phototherapeutics is selling its new light-activated cancer drug in Europe and the United States. Toronto pharmaceutical firm Biovail Corp. acquired an important Puerto Rican drug company. Hydro-Quebec is part of a joint venture in Japan to manufacture tiny batteries the size of postage stamps. Manulife Insurance beat out 80 major international insurers to win the right to operate in China. Unican Security Systems acquired control of an Italian and a Swiss security system firm. CEO Ross Dembo of the Vancouver company Algorithmics reports that their software models have been sold to 70 banks worldwide.

The list goes on and on. It is almost impossible to find any field of business in which Canadian companies are not involved in significant international investment, trade, or manufacturing.

Adapted from: *Globe and Mail, Report on Business; Montreal Gazette; Financial Post;* the Internet—all 1995, 1996; interview October 18, 1995; *Newsworld Business News,* November 3, 1998.

If we look at some facts about this world market, we will see why this trade is so important:

- There are 31 million customers in Canada but more than *6 billion* potential customers worldwide.
- Every year, the world's population increases by 75–80 million people. That's $2\frac{1}{2}$ times the total Canadian population.
- Combined world trade exceeds *$6 trillion* each year (a trillion is a million million).

Nortel Networks, despite serious difficulties in 2000 and 2001, has become a world player in a big way and so has Bombardier. This type of globalized, or transnational (TNC) company is very different from the old-style multinational (MNC) company that has been engaged in world trade for a long time. Both **TNC** and **MNC** are often used interchangeably to refer to an organization that has investments, plants, and sales in many different countries and has international stock ownership and multinational management.

MNCs did business in various countries and had plants in a number of countries. TNCs have gone from that stage to organizing management, investment, production, and distribution as if the world were one country or even one city. Goods can be designed in one country, their raw material shipped to or from a second country, manufactured partially or completely in a third country, and then shipped to the ultimate customer. The company thus makes maximum use of the competitive advantage (discussed in the next section) of each country to be the most efficient

TNC or MNC
An organization that has investments, plants, and sales in many different countries; it has international stock ownership and multinational management.

Courtesy of Nortel Networks.

Nortel Networks is a world player in the telecommunications field and an example of a Canadian-based company that has transformed itself into a transnational company.

producer. Top management and boards of directors now have an international component to reflect the new nature of operations.

Nortel and Bombardier are good examples of Canadian companies that have been completely transformed by globalization. They have employees and plants all over the world specializing in various aspects of production, and also have international boards of directors. Some of the technological advances that Nortel Networks pioneered helped produce the revolutionary changes in communications that, in turn, facilitated the globalization of business. These activities, combined with the information from the previous chapter, show how interdependent all the economies in the world have become. Thus, we benefit when other countries are booming and we suffer when they turn downward. This is especially true for the effect of such trends in the United States on Canada.

WHY COUNTRIES TRADE WITH EACH OTHER

There are several reasons why a country trades with other countries. First, no country, no matter how advanced, can produce all the products its people need or want. In Canada, we must import those products that our climate does not allow us to grow, including tropical fruits, citrus fruits, and all fruits and vegetables during the winter season. We also cannot grow cotton or rice.

Second, some nations have an abundance of natural resources and lack technological know-how. Others, like Japan, have very few natural resources but may be world leaders in technology.

Third, some countries produce a lot more of certain products than they can consume, so they must export these surpluses. Canada has a small population but produces vast quantities of grains, autos, auto parts, lumber, manufactured goods, newsprint, metals, minerals, and other products. Thus we rank very high among nations that export. In fact, we depend on exports to maintain a substantial segment of our standard of living, around 35 percent. Figure 3.1 shows that in 2000 Canada exported $389 billion, ranking Canada seventh among exporting nations of the world.

	EXPORTS	IMPORTS
Major products or industries, in billions of dollars		
Motor vehicles and parts	85	55
Telecommunications and electronics	33	32
Energy products and systems	52	16
Forest products	32	
Primary metals	13	
Aircraft and parts	12	4
Agriculture and fish products	11	
Machinery and equipment	11	
All other products/industries	140	250
Total	**389**	**357**

Adapted from: Statistics Canada, *The Daily*, Catalogue No. 11-001, June 24, 2001.

FIGURE 3.1

CANADIAN EXPORTS AND IMPORTS

Analysis of Canadian exports and imports of merchandise for 2000.

The Theory of Comparative Advantage

Some countries are better than others at producing certain products in terms of quality or price, so they have what is called a *comparative advantage*. Japan has shown this ability with cars and electronic items. Canada has such an advantage with certain forestry products, aluminum, and various minerals. The guiding principle behind international economic exchanges is supposed to be the economic **comparative advantage theory**. This theory states that a country should produce and sell to other countries those products that it produces most effectively and efficiently and should buy from other countries those products it cannot produce as effectively or efficiently.

In practice, this does not work so neatly. For various reasons, many countries decide to produce certain agricultural, industrial, or consumer products despite a lack of comparative advantage. To facilitate this plan, they restrict imports of competing products from countries that can produce them at lower costs. For example, Japan and South Korea ban all imports of rice. The U.S. makes it difficult to import sugar or cotton and insists that ships carrying cargo between American ports must be U.S.–owned.

Farmers in Europe are subsidized so that their grains can compete with the less expensive ones from countries such as Canada and the U.S. Canada has done the same with cars, textiles, and shoes at different times. The net result of such restraints is that the free movement of goods and services is restricted. We will return to the topic of trade protectionism later in the chapter. It will be useful to examine some of the terminology relating to international trade first.

comparative advantage theory
The theory that a country should produce and sell to other countries those products that it produces most efficiently and effectively and should buy from other countries those products it cannot produce as effectively or efficiently.

PhotoDisc

The theory of comparative advantage dictates that a country should specialize in producing those products it can produce most efficiently and effectively and import those it cannot produce as well or at all. Most Western countries must import rice, as they cannot produce it domestically.

Terminology of International Trade

When you read business periodicals or listen to news reports, you will see and hear terms relating to international business. Some of these terms may be familiar to you, but it will be helpful to review them before we discuss international business in more detail.

balance of trade
The relationship of exports to imports.

trade deficit
Occurs when the value of imports exceeds exports.

trade protectionism
The use of government regulations to limit the import of goods and services, based on the theory that domestic producers should be protected from competition so that they can survive and grow, producing more jobs.

In measuring the effectiveness of global trade, nations carefully follow one key indicator: **balance of trade**. The balance of trade is the relationship of exports to imports. A *favourable balance of trade*, or trade surplus, occurs when the value of exports exceeds imports. An *unfavourable balance of trade*, or **trade deficit**, occurs when the value of imports exceeds exports. It's easy to understand why countries prefer to export more than they import. If I sell you $200 worth of goods and buy only $100 worth, I have an extra $100 available to buy other things. However, I'm in an unfavourable position if I buy $200 worth of goods and sell only $100. For the past two decades, Canada has usually had a favourable balance of trade (see Figure 3.2 for the actual figures for 1996–1999).

Countries often use trade protectionism measures to try to protect their industries. **Trade protectionism** is the use of government regulations to limit the import of goods and services. This is done either to counter what is felt to be unfair trade practices of foreign governments or companies, or to give domestic companies a better chance to grow, produce more jobs, and become better able to compete internationally. We shall discuss trade protectionism in more detail later in the chapter.

FIGURE 3.2

EXPORTS, IMPORTS, AND TRADE BALANCE

These graphs from Statistics Canada show how our exports continue to exceed our imports, resulting in a favourable trade balance. The results are tracked monthly.

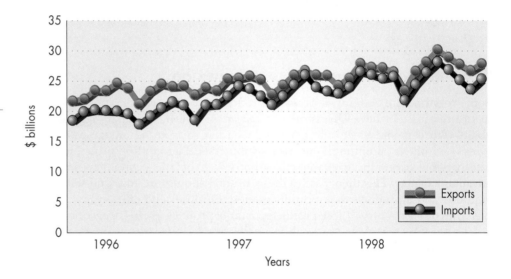

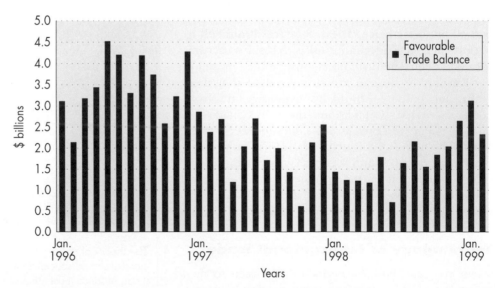

Adapted from: Statistics Canada, CANSIM database http://cansim2.statcan.ca.cgi-win/CNSMCGI.EXE, Matrix 3651, Series D397768, and Matrix 3685, Series D399224, May 1999.

	IMPORTER PAYS	EXPORTER GETS
Import of VCRs from Japan		
72 yen per dollar	$200	¥14,400
90 yen per dollar	160	14,400
Export of potash to Japan		
72 yen per dollar	¥14,400	$200
90 yen per dollar	18,000	200

Note: Prices quoted in the exporter's currency.

FIGURE 3.3

EFFECT OF FLUCTUATIONS IN CURRENCY EXCHANGE RATES ON PRICES OF IMPORTS AND EXPORTS

As the dollar rises in relation to the yen (it takes 90 yen to buy a dollar instead of 72, or one dollar buys 90 yen instead of 72 yen), a Canadian importer now pays less but the Japanese importer pays more.

The **exchange rate** is the value of one currency relative to the currencies of other countries. A *rising value of our dollar* means that a dollar will buy more foreign goods (or will be traded for more foreign currency) than before. A *falling value of our dollar* means that a dollar buys less than it once did, making foreign goods more expensive because it takes more dollars to buy them. It also makes Canadian goods cheaper to foreign buyers because it takes less foreign currency to buy them. The net effect is to export more and buy fewer foreign products, improving the balance of trade but increasing inflation as imported goods now cost more (see Figure 3.3).

For many years the U.S. dollar has played the role of the international currency, so most international transactions are quoted in U.S. dollars. The constant movements in the exchange rate of this dollar relative to other currencies affect nearly all international trade and investments. This is particularly important for Canada, because more than 85 percent of all our imports and exports are with the United States (see Figure 3.4). Since 1980, the value of the U.S. dollar has fluctuated greatly, creating ups and downs for many trading nations. In addition, as the U.S. dollar fluctuates against other currencies it affects Canada's competitiveness with other countries, because it makes our exports more or less expensive.

In mid-1998 the Canadian dollar fell to 63 cents, an all-time low against the U.S. dollar. This record low made it cheaper for American companies to buy Canadian goods and services, while it made it more expensive for Canadian companies and consumers to buy these from Americans. By mid-2001 our dollar was hovering in the 62–63 cent American range, helping us to have a continuing and growing favourable balance of trade in 2001 (see Figure 3.4).

exchange rate
The value of one currency relative to the currencies of other countries.

www.consumersinternational.org/campaigns

This consumers' organization is very concerned about the impact of protectionism on the agricultural industry and on consumers in all parts of the world. Visit this site and click on *food* to learn more about its views.

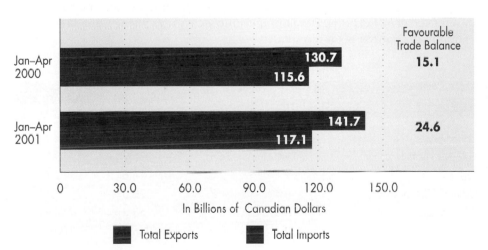

FIGURE 3.4

CANADA'S BALANCE OF TRADE, 2000–2001.

Canada has a growing favourable balance of trade helped by our falling dollar relative to the U.S. dollar.

Adapted from: Statistics Canada, *The Daily*, Catalogue No. 11-001, June 27, 2001.

Now that you understand some terms, we can begin discussing international trade in more depth. The first question to address is how Canada is doing in world trade. First let's check your progress.

PROGRESS CHECK

- Can you cite statistics to show why international trade is so vital for Canadian business (population, size of market, growth of market)?
- What is comparative advantage?
- Can you explain how changes in the value of the dollar affect imports and exports?

TRADING IN WORLD MARKETS: THE CANADIAN EXPERIENCE

Statistics must be examined very closely to make sense of them. This is especially true in the case of Canada's foreign trade statistics. At first glance, they are impressive. For a country with only around 30 million people we usually rank seventh or eighth in volume of world trade.[3] However, if we look carefully at the figures, we see that more than 85 percent of this exporting and importing is with one country, the United States (see Figure 3.5). No other modern industrialized country is so dependent on one country for trade and investments. The controversial Canada–U.S. Free Trade Agreement that came into effect in 1989 was designed to facilitate and further increase trade and investment between the two countries. The 1993 North American Free Trade Agreement (NAFTA) added Mexico to the deal, discussed later in this chapter.

An even closer look at what we export to the United States shows that the largest single category is autos, trucks, and parts and has been so for some time. This is offset by a somewhat smaller amount that we import. All of this stems from the Canada–U.S. Auto Pact signed in the mid-1960s, which was designed to stimulate the auto industry in both countries. This trade is subject to the vagaries of the demand for autos from the Big Three (DaimlerChrysler, Ford, and General Motors) in Canada and the United States. The growing success of Japanese cars severely reduced demand for Big Three cars in 1990 and 1991. The reduced demand had a serious impact on business and employment in Canada, especially in Ontario, which relies heavily on auto parts and auto manufacturing. By 1995, the situation had turned around.

A traditional major area for Canadian exports is natural resources, which are abundant across the country. Pulp and paper products and lumber from our forests and forest industries, combined with agricultural products, fish products, energy (natural gas, coal, and electricity from water power), minerals, and metals, constitute almost half our exports. Developing countries are now giving Canada stiff competition in the natural resource area.

FIGURE 3.5

EXPORTS AND IMPORTS IN 2000

The United States is by far our main trading partner, and we had a $130-billion trade surplus with them in 2000. Overall there was a $55.5-billion surplus.

	EXPORTS $ BILLIONS	%	IMPORTS $ BILLIONS	%
United States	359.2	87.1	229.5	64.4
European Union	19.0	4.5	36.9	10.3
Japan	9.1	2.2	16.6	4.7
Other OECD countries	6.4	1.7	20.3	5.7
All other countries	18.5	4.5	53.4	14.9
Total	412.2	100.0	356.7	100.0

Source: Various Statistics Canada Web sites, June 2001.

Although Canada is still weak in the high-tech "glamour" industries, biogenetics, telecommunications, computers, air and rail transport, and materials technology are some of the areas where high-skilled jobs and exports are expected to be important. There are some Canadian stars that have a strong international posture in some of these areas—for example, Nortel Networks and Bombardier are making substantial gains in exports—but there are not enough of these stars.

A number of smaller but successful firms have made an impact globally: Spar Aerospace, maker of the robotic Canadarm on the U.S. space shuttle; CAE Electronics Ltd., one of the few makers of flight simulators in the world; Rolls Royce (Canada) Ltd., a leader in aircraft and industrial engine repair and maintenance; and Phoenix International Life Sciences Inc., one of the top drug-testing labs in North America, are but a few of dozens of companies with excellent records outside of Canada. We also have some excellent software companies that compete well internationally, such as Softimage and Alias. For an example of a Canadian company that has had international success, see the Spotlight on Small Business box "A Small Cosmetics Firm Hits the Big Time."

You have read that there are 6 billion people in the world, but only a small percentage of Canadian companies engage in world trade. Why is that? What do such figures indicate about the future potential for increasing Canadian exports? What do they say about future careers in international business?

In thinking about other countries, you should be asking yourself: What languages do they speak? What are the trade possibilities? Am I missing out on an opportunity by failing to take other languages in school and courses in international business?

SPOTLIGHT ON SMALL BUSINESS

www.elcompanies.com/

A Small Cosmetics Firm Hits the Big Time

In the mid-1980s, Toronto hairdresser Frank Angelo and photographer Frank Toskan had an idea. They were trying to solve the problem their fashion models encountered with makeup when working constantly under hot lights. Experimenting with homemade lipsticks and eye makeup, they came up with a line of densely pigmented cosmetics that did the trick. Not only did professionals start using this new line of products, but all women were attracted to it. The company, Make-up Art Cosmetics Ltd., better known as MAC, was soon growing rapidly.

Since the two Franks were young and daring and wanted to have a little fun in the process, they broke many of the conventional traditions in the cosmetics industry. First, they selected as a model for their products "RuPaul, a seven-foot-tall African-American drag queen." Second, they did no advertising in an industry that is known for extensive advertising in all media. Neither of these breaks with tradition seemed to hurt MAC as sales continued to leap ahead. Instead of advertising, word-of-mouth was a powerful stimulator of sales with some famous mouths such as Madonna and Princess Diana praising the products.

By the end of 1994 MAC had sales of more than $100 million. They had already expanded into the U.S. and England and now wanted to expand into Europe and Asia. This required large amounts of capital, as did satisfying the mushrooming demand that copycat companies were rushing to meet.

At that point, Toskan and Angelo made a deal with Estée Lauder, who had been pursuing them for three years. They sold half the company and a controlling interest for $38 million. Not bad for a couple of young Canadians who a decade earlier were rank amateurs in business. In 1998 Estée Lauder bought the other half of the company, so our enterprising Canadians ended up with a multimillion-dollar reward for their initiative and efforts.

Sources: Estée Lauder's Web site: www.elcompanies.com/company/timeline/history3.html#1998; various issues of *The Globe and Mail, Report on Business,* 1995; Jennifer Low, "Will Success Spoil MAC?" *Profit,* April–May 1996, pp. 43–44; C. A. Bartlett and S. Ghoshal, *Transnational Management,* 2nd ed. (New York: Times Mirror, 1995), p. 58ff.

STRATEGIES FOR REACHING GLOBAL MARKETS

An organization may participate in international trade in many ways, including exporting, licensing, creating subsidiaries, franchising, joint venturing, foreign direct investment, and countertrading. These topics relate to careers that will be both challenging and rewarding for the future graduate.

Exporting

The simplest way of going international is to export your products. As you will see in the chapters on marketing, many decisions have to be made when a company markets a new product or goes into new markets with existing products. Often the first export sales occur as a result of unsolicited orders received. Regardless of how a company starts exporting, it must develop some goals and strategies for achieving those goals.

www.dfait-maeci.gc.ca

Visit the Department of Foreign Affairs and International Trade Web site. You will learn how DFAIT gets involved in exporting and the services it provides to encourage the export-trade business.

Other decisions include what distribution channels are appropriate: direct sales, sales to wholesalers, or an exporting or importing agency. Each route has its pluses and minuses. Important decisions about pricing policy must also be made. In the next chapter you will see how the Canadian government helps companies that want to export.

Success in exporting often leads to licensing a foreign company to produce the product locally to better serve the local market.

Licensing

licensing
An agreement in which a producer allows a foreign company to manufacture its products or use its trademark in exchange for royalties.

A firm may decide to compete in a growing global market by **licensing** to a foreign company the right to manufacture its product or use its trademark on a fee (royalty) basis. The company generally sends representatives to the foreign producer to help set up the production process and may also assist in such areas as distribution and promotion.

A licensing agreement can be beneficial to a firm in several different ways. Through licensing, an organization can gain additional revenues from a product that it would not have normally generated. In addition, foreign licensees often must purchase start-up supplies, component materials, and consulting services from the licensing firm. Coca-Cola licenses the right to sell merchandise bearing "Coca-Cola" trademarks. Even the Royal Canadian Mounted Police had a licensing agreement with the Walt Disney Company to market products bearing Mounties images, which ended in 1999.[4] One final advantage of licensing worth noting is that licensers spend little or no money to produce and market their products. These costs come from the licensees' pockets. Therefore, licensees generally work very hard to see that the product succeeds in their market.

Millions of times a day, things go better with Coca-Cola. Coca-Cola Ltd. is just one example of a company that licenses the right to sell merchandise bearing its trademarks.

However, as you may suspect, licensing agreements may have some disadvantages for a company. One major problem is that often a firm must grant licensing rights to its product for an extended period, maybe as long as 20 years. If a product experiences remarkable growth in the foreign market, the bulk of the revenues goes to the licensee. Perhaps even more threatening is that a licensing firm is actually selling its expertise in a product area. If a foreign licensee learns that technology, it may break the agreement and begin to produce a similar product on its own. If legal remedies are not readily available in the country the licensing firm may lose its trade secrets, not to mention the agreed-upon royalties.

Courtesy of Coca-Cola ltd.

Creating Subsidiaries

As the size of a foreign market expands, a firm may want to establish a foreign subsidiary or acquire a foreign company. A **foreign subsidiary** is a company that is owned by another company (parent company) in a foreign country. Such a subsidiary would operate much like a domestic firm with production, distribution, promotion, pricing, and other business functions under the control of the foreign subsidiary's management. Of course, the legal requirements of the home and host country would have to be observed. The primary advantage of a subsidiary is that the company maintains complete control over any technology or expertise it may possess.

Canadian subsidiaries of American companies played a major role in developing the Canadian economy. More and more countries are welcoming such investments as a way of developing their economics. The main concern for Canada and these other countries is that decisions made by the parent company are not primarily based on the needs of the country where the subsidiary is located. For example, if an American company decides to reduce its workforce or close a plant, it may more readily do that to a subsidiary in Canada than in its home base in the U.S.

foreign subsidiary
A company owned by another company (parent company) in a foreign country.

Franchising

Franchising >**P. 176**< is popular both domestically and in international markets. Firms such as McDonald's, Ramada Inc, Avis, Hertz, and Dunkin' Donuts have many overseas units operated by franchisees. In Canada there are thousands of franchise units, such as Harvey's, Speedy Muffler, and Delta Hotels, in many categories of business. This topic will be discussed in detail in Chapter 6.

Franchisers have to be careful to adapt to the countries they serve. For example, Kentucky Fried Chicken's first 11 Hong Kong outlets failed within two years. Apparently, the chicken was too greasy and messy to be eaten with fingers by the fastidious people of Hong Kong. McDonald's also made a mistake when entering the Amsterdam market. It originally set up operations in the suburbs, as it does in North America, but soon learned that Europeans mostly live in the cities. McDonald's began to open outlets downtown and thousands of franchises are now operating internationally. McDonald's franchises serve beer in Germany and wine in France.

Courtesy of McDonald's

Franchising is popular in both domestic and international markets. McDonald's operates in many countries around the world. This tray liner is from a McDonald's restaurant in Russia.

International Joint Ventures

An **international joint venture (JV)** is a partnership in which companies from two or more countries join to undertake a major project or to form a new company. This has become a very popular avenue for companies that want to go into business in foreign countries. There are obvious advantages to having a partner that shares in the financial investment and risk, knows the local market, understands local ways of thinking, has good government connections and access to local skilled labour or supplies, and is acquainted with the laws and regulations affecting business in the country. The Canadian or other foreign company brings additional assets to the joint venture. These usually include the technology, management skills, specialized equipment and material, and financing necessary to commence and continue operations.

Sometimes companies, including competitors, form a **consortium**, a temporary association, to submit a joint bid on a very large or complex construction project such as a dam, bridge, tunnel, or large building. This may make it easier for the government or company that asked for bids, since it deals with only one entity instead of many different groups. If the consortium gets the contract, the work is divided up according to the specialties of each member company.

Sometimes two or more competitors make a joint bid. For example, Bombardier teamed up with Alsthom of France to bid successfully for a subway car contract for New York City.

Thousands of joint ventures of different types exist around the world and are constantly being formed. General Motors and Suzuki combined to set up CAMI Automotive in Ingersoll, Ontario. Many such deals are being set up in the former communist countries of eastern Europe and in the independent countries of the former Soviet Union. For example, McDonald's of Canada teamed up with Russian partners to set up the largest franchise unit in the world in Moscow, and Nortel Networks formed a large joint venture with Chinese associates in Shanghai to produce advanced telecommunication products for the Chinese market.

Foreign Direct Investment

Regardless of how a company invests in another country—joint venture, subsidiary, franchise—the total of these *foreign direct investments* has become a significant proportion of any country's economic activity. As Figure 3.6 indicates, the United States is an attractive country for such investments. Canadian companies rank fourth in countries investing in the United States, having invested some US $64 billion there. This includes large companies previously mentioned and others such as Bank of Montreal and Barrick Gold Corp. For another example, see the Spotlight on Big Business box "Bombardier: From Snowmobiles to Airplanes and Trains."

Countertrading

One of the oldest forms of trade is called **bartering**, the exchange of merchandise for merchandise, service for service, or service for merchandise with no money involved. **Countertrading** is more complex than bartering in that several countries may be

FIGURE 3.6

**FOREIGN DIRECT
INVESTMENT**

Countries with the highest
foreign direct investment in
the United States.

	1996	1997
United Kingdom	$121 billion	$130 billion
Japan	115 billion	124 billion
Netherlands	74 billion	84 billion
Canada	55 billion	64 billion

Courtesy of STAT-USA, U.S. Department of Commerce.

Bombardier: From Snowmobiles to Airplanes and Trains

As CEO of Bombardier Inc for more than three decades, 60-year-old chartered accountant Laurent Beaudoin was responsible for the transformation of the company from a local manufacturer of snowmobiles into a giant transnational producing trains, planes, and the famous Ski-Doos and Sea-Doos. From 1985 to 1995 sales increased tenfold to $6 billion. For the year ended January 31, 1999, when Beaudoin stepped down as CEO and was replaced by Robert Brown, gross revenues were almost $12 billion. Revenue for the year ended January 31, 2001 exceeded $16 billion.

Bombardier has a workforce of 79,000 in facilities in 23 countries. The company is a leading contender for aerospace and mass transit contracts all over the world. Bombardier's rail units operate in the Chunnel between France and England, in Disneyland, in Montreal, in New York, and in Asian countries. Its regional jets are everywhere. The company has alliances and joint ventures with dozens of companies around the world. Some are technology-sharing agreements, others are production-sharing agreements, and still others involve operating luxury corporate jet services. Bombardier is a classic example of a true transnational corporation whose domain is the entire world.

J. Armand Bombardier, founder of the company and inventor of the snowmobile, died in 1964. Within 10 years, the company went public, experienced higher gasoline prices due to the energy crisis, and saw sales drop by 70 percent. Beaudoin then led the company through a very imaginative, difficult, and risky but successful transformation. In 1982 the company landed a billion-dollar contract to supply the New York Transit Authority with 825 subway cars. Within the next 10 years Bombardier acquired four aircraft companies—Canadair in Montreal, Learjet in Kansas, Shorts of Northern Ireland, and de Havilland in Toronto. In each case Bombardier bought companies in difficulty and in three cases it got substantial local government aid to expedite the takeover.

Business leaders greatly admired Laurent Beaudoin's brilliant acquisition program and transformation of these money-losing companies into profitable operations. He was no less admired for his ability to create a successful mass transit operation, one of the very few in the world. Hardly a month passes without some reference in the media to Bombardier having landed more orders for its regional jets or its railway and subway cars. At January 31, 2001, the order backlog was a record $32 billion. This track record led Canada's chief executives in 1996 to select Bombardier as the most respected company in Canada. Bombardier exemplifies what this chapter is all about—the globalization of business.

Adapted from: Company reports and documents 1998, 1999, 2000 and 2001; Raymond Boyer, president and COO, Bombardier, speech at McGill University, March 1, 1996; Kenneth Kidd, "The Bombardier Express," *Globe and Mail, Report on Business*, April 1996, p. 48ff.

---

involved, each trading goods or services for other goods or services. It has been estimated that countertrading accounts for 25 percent of all international exchanges.

Examples of countertrade and bartering agreements abound. Chrysler traded its vehicles in Jamaica for bauxite. McDonnell Douglas traded jets in the former Yugoslavia for canned hams. General Motors traded vehicles with China for industrial gloves and cutting tools.

Barter is especially important to poor countries that have little cash available for trade. Such countries may barter with all kinds of raw materials, food, or whatever resources they have. Colombia has traded coffee for buses. Romania traded cement for steam engines. The Sudan pays for Pepsi concentrate with sesame seeds. Tanzania uses sisal and Nicaragua uses sesame seeds and molasses for barter.

With many emerging economies still in a state of flux, countertrading may continue to grow in importance. Trading products for products helps avoid some problems and hurdles experienced in global markets.

PROGRESS
CHECK

- Can you name four ways to enter foreign markets?
- What are the major benefits a firm may gain from licensing its products in foreign markets? What are the primary drawbacks?
- What are the major benefits of a joint venture in global markets?
- How does countertrading work?

HURDLES TO DOING BUSINESS IN WORLD MARKETS

Succeeding in *any* business takes work and effort because of the many hurdles encountered. Unfortunately, the hurdles get higher and more complex in world markets. This is particularly true in dealing with differences in cultural perspectives, societies and economies, laws and regulations, and fluctuations in currencies (see Figure 3.3). Let's take a look at each of these hurdles.

Cultural Differences

Anyone who travels to different countries cannot help noticing peculiarities of life in each country that are different from how we live in Canada. Every company that engages in international trade or investment must take these cultural differences into account if it wants to succeed in these operations.

In Canada and the United States, we like to do things quickly. We tend to call each other by our first names and try to get friendly even on the first encounter. In Japan, China, and other countries these actions would be considered surprising and even rude. Canadian negotiators will say no if they mean no, but Japanese usually say maybe when they mean no. Consumer tastes and preferences also differ from country to country.

Religion is an important part of any society's culture and can have a significant impact on business operations. For example, in Islamic countries, dawn-to-dusk fasting during the month of Ramadan causes workers' output to drop considerably. Also, the requirement to pray five times daily can affect output.

Cultural differences can also have an impact on such important business factors as human resource management. In Latin American countries, managers are looked on by workers as authoritarian figures responsible for their well-being. Consider what happened to one North American manager who neglected this important cultural characteristic. This manager was convinced he could motivate his workers in Peru to higher levels of productivity by instituting a more democratic decision-making style. He brought in trainers from North America to teach his supervisors to solicit suggestions and feedback from workers. Shortly after his new style was put in place, workers began quitting their jobs in droves. When asked why, Peruvian workers said the new production manager and supervisors did not know their jobs and were asking the workers what to do. All stated they wanted to quit and find new jobs, since obviously this company was doomed because of incompetent managers.

Without question, culture presents a significant hurdle for global managers. Learning about important cultural perspectives toward time, change, competition, natural resources, achievement, and even work itself can be of great assistance. Today, firms often provide classes and training for managers and their families on how to adapt to different cultures and avoid culture shock. Your involvement in courses in cultural variations and anthropology can assist you in your career in global business.

Societal and Economic Differences

Certain social and economic realities are often overlooked by North American businesses. General Foods once squandered millions of dollars in a fruitless effort to introduce Japanese consumers to the joys of packaged cake mixes. The company failed to note, among other factors, that only 3 percent of Japanese homes were then equipped with ovens. Similarly, American automakers tried to sell their cars in Japan without providing right-hand-drive vehicles for a country that drives on the left side of the road. Since Japan is such an important trading partner, you would think that business people would have such important information about the Japanese market, but often that is not so.

It's hard for us to imagine buying chewing gum by the stick instead of the package. However, in economically depressed nations like the Philippines, this buying behaviour is commonplace because consumers have only enough money to buy small quantities. Factors such as disposable and discretionary income can be critical in evaluating the potential of a market. What might seem like an opportunity of a lifetime may in fact be unreachable due to economic conditions.

Technological constraints may also make it difficult or impossible to carry on effective trade. For example, some less developed countries have primitive transportation and storage systems. International food exchanges are ineffective because the food is spoiled by the time it reaches those in need.

Exporters must also be aware that certain technological differences affect the nature of exportable products. For example, how would the differences in electricity available (110 versus 220 volts) affect an appliance manufacturer wanting to export?

A good example of how disaster can strike a company that does not fully appreciate that countries have different cultural and social customs is Marks & Spencer. After more than 25 years in Canada, nearly all loss years, the famous British retail clothing chain was forced to cease operations here. The company closed all its stores across Canada in 1999.

Legal and Regulatory Differences

In any economy, the conduct and direction of business are firmly tied to the legal and regulatory environment. Business operations in Canada are heavily affected by various federal, provincial, and local laws and regulations. In global markets, there is naturally a wider variation in such laws and regulations, making the task of conducting world business even tougher.

What business people find in global markets are myriad laws and regulations that are often inconsistent. Important legal questions related to antitrust, labour relations, patents, copyrights, trade practices, taxes, product liability, and other issues are written and interpreted differently country by country. In many countries, bribery is acceptable and perhaps the only way to secure a lucrative contract. How do you think Canadian business and government leaders should handle this ethical dilemma?

To be a successful trader in foreign countries, you might choose to begin by contacting local business people and gaining their co-operation and sponsorship. The problem is that foreign bureaucracies are often stumbling blocks to successful foreign trade; to penetrate those barriers, often you must find a local sponsor who can pay the necessary fees to gain government permission.

TRADE PROTECTIONISM

As noted previously in this chapter, cultural differences, societal and economic factors, legal and regulatory requirements, and currency exchange rate shifts are all hurdles to those wanting to trade globally. What is often a much greater barrier to international trade is the overall political atmosphere between nations.

Business, economics, and politics have always been closely linked. In fact, economics was once referred to as "political economy," indicating the close ties between politics (government) and economics. For centuries, business people have tried to influence economists and government officials. Back in the sixteenth, seventeenth, and

mercantilism
The economic principle advocating the selling of more goods to other nations than were bought from them.

import quota
A limit on the number or value of products in certain categories that can be imported.

eighteenth centuries business people advocated an economic principle called **mercantilism**. Basically, the idea of mercantilism was to sell more goods to other nations than you bought from them; that is, to have a favourable balance of trade. This results in a flow of money to the country that sells the most. Governments assisted in this process by charging a tariff (tax) on imports, making it more expensive to import goods.

Today, there is still much debate about the degree of protectionism a government should practise. For example, when the government was concerned about protecting domestic auto producers and workers from Japanese producers, it convinced Japanese producers to voluntarily limit the number of Japanese cars sold here (see "Protectionism Backfiring," below). The term that describes limiting the number or value of products in certain categories that can be imported is **import quota**.

Nontariff Barriers

James Thwaits, former president of international operations of the 3M Co., said that as much as half of all trade is limited by *nontariff barriers*. In other words, countries have established many strategies that go beyond tariffs to prevent foreign competition. For example, Japan tried to keep out French skis by claiming that Japanese snow was different from French snow; the French retaliated by saying that French rain was different from Japanese rain, which made Japanese motorcycles too dangerous.

France tried to protect its VCR industry by requiring that all imported VCRs be sent through an understaffed customs post that was 160 km from the nearest port. Denmark required that beverages be sold in returnable bottles; this effectively cut off French mineral water producers, who found the cost of returning bottles prohibitive. Margarine must be sold in cubes in Belgium, closing the market to countries that sell margarine only in tubs.

Other nontariff barriers include safety, health, and labelling standards. The United States has stopped some Canadian goods from entering because it said the information on the labels was too small. Canada has stopped American cattle or beef from entering because of hormone and antibiotic injections that violate our health standards. Canadian electrical standards have prevented certain appliances from being imported because they are not safe.

Sometimes, as in the Japanese and French cases, the intent is clearly to put difficulties in the way of imports. Other times it is not so clear whether the barriers are deliberate or are a normal part of a reasonable set of standards. Of course, when a

Farmers demanded millions of dollars in emergency relief when faced with a collapse in pork markets and low wheat prices. Pig farmers have experienced drastic price drops in the past few years.

Canadian Press MACLEANS. Photograph by Ted Korol.

country is in a protectionist mode, it will exploit these standards or use any excuse to try to reduce imports. The 1996 U.S. election triggered a wave of protectionist statements and attitudes.

The same thing seems to have happened before the Congressional election in the fall of 1998. South Dakota and other Midwest states started blocking Canadian exports of wheat and pork, claiming that they didn't meet U.S. health requirements. It was widely believed that farmers in these states were having trouble selling similar products because world prices were depressed and the U.S. dollar was high in value in relation to the Canadian dollar and to other currencies. Feeling this pressure, the farmers used the health excuse to block Canadian exports. As explained previously in the chapter, major currency shifts have an important effect on international trade.

Protectionism Backfiring

Sometimes attempts to keep out foreign goods or restrict their entry into a country lead to strange results. A good example of this occurred in the 1980s with Japanese cars, which had become very popular in Canada and the United States. The cars were of better quality, offered better warranties, used less gas, had better trade-in values, and cost less than the Big Three North American products. Instead of competing on value, the Big Three pressured the Canadian and U.S governments to restrict the entry of Japanese autos. Both governments negotiated deals with the Japanese government and their automakers to "voluntarily" not increase the number of vehicles they would export to Canada and the United States for three years. These quotas were based on the number of units, not total dollar value.

The Big Three, feeling less pressure, raised their prices. The Japanese carmakers proceeded to do the same so that their prices were still competitive. They wound up exporting fewer cars but making more profit. They used this excess profit to build auto plants in Canada and the United States, which ultimately led to Japanese cars capturing an even greater share of the North American market (about 35 percent).

Other Restrictions on International Trade

Sometimes countries restrict trade for purely political or military reasons. For example, for some years Canada and many other countries had an embargo on doing business with South Africa because of its racist laws and policies at that time. An **embargo** is a complete ban on all trade with or investment in a country. The United States has restrictions or embargoes on exporting what it classifies as secret or very high-tech parts or equipment that could be used for military purposes by its enemies. The United States also restricts trade with Cuba because of Cuba's communist government. All these restrictions are of a purely political or military nature and should not be confused with trade protectionism, which is of an economic nature.

embargo
A complete ban on all trade with or investment in a country.

Consequences of Protectionism

Today, nations throughout the world are debating how much protectionism they should use to keep foreign competition from driving their firms out of business. You can read about this trend in current business periodicals. As you do, keep in mind that the severity of the Great Depression of the 1930s was attributed by some people to the passage of the highly protectionist Smoot-Hawley Tariff Act of 1930 in the United States. Economists were almost unanimous in opposing the bill. Nonetheless, believing it would protect American business, the government put tariffs on goods from England, France, and other nations. The result was that other countries raised tariffs in return. This hurt business in all countries badly as world trade dropped sharply.

By 1932 U.S. exports to England were at one-third the 1929 level, exports to France were only one-fourth those of 1929, and exports to Australia were one-fifth.

Wheat exports fell from $200 million to $5 million, and auto exports fell from $541 million to $76 million. In short, some economic theorists contend that protectionist policies of governments (based on old mercantilist thinking) helped create the greatest depression in the history of modern capitalism. Unemployment soared in Canada and most countries, with serious economic consequences.

Having learned a very costly lesson from various attempts at trade protectionism, the major countries began to plan how to avoid such problems in the future. They started thinking about international agreements that would be useful to all countries. We look at this in the next section.

PROGRESS CHECK

- What are the major hurdles to successful international trade?
- Identify at least two cultural and societal differences that can affect global trade efforts.
- What are the advantages and disadvantages of trade protectionism?
- What is an embargo? Can it be applied for noneconomic reasons?

INTERNATIONAL TRADE ORGANIZATIONS

www.wto.org
www.imf.org

The World Trade Organization and International Monetary Fund Web sites provide descriptions of these organizations, their membership, their objectives, and their activities. See, for example, the description "About the IMF" at the IMF Web site.

General Agreement on Tariffs and Trade (GATT)
Agreement among trading countries that provides a forum for negotiating mutual reductions in trade restrictions.

International Monetary Fund (IMF)
An international bank that makes short-term loans to countries experiencing problems with their balance of trade.

World Bank
An autonomous United Nations agency that borrows money from the more prosperous countries and lends it to less-developed countries to develop their infrastructure.

The major trading nations learned an important lesson from the terrible effects of trade protectionism. In 1948 the nations got together and formed the **General Agreement on Tariffs and Trade (GATT)**, an agreement among trading countries that provides a forum for negotiating mutual reductions in trade restrictions. For almost half a century it has succeeded in getting all nations to agree on a gradual reduction in tariffs and nontariff barriers to international trade. The road has not been smooth and there are still serious obstacles, but the trend and goals are clearly established and agreed to by all countries involved. On January 1, 1995, the World Trade Organization (WTO) assumed the task of supervising GATT.

Even before GATT, the **International Monetary Fund (IMF)** was signed into existence by 44 nations at Bretton Woods, New Hampshire, in 1944. The IMF is an international bank supported by its members that usually makes *short-term* loans to countries experiencing problems with their balance of trade. The IMF's basic objectives are to promote exchange stability, maintain orderly exchange arrangements, avoid competitive currency depreciation, establish a multilateral system of payments, eliminate exchange restrictions, and create standby reserves. The IMF makes *long-term* loans at interest rates of just 0.5 percent to the world's most destitute nations to help them strengthen their economies. The function of the IMF is very similar to that of the World Bank.

The **World Bank** (the International Bank for Reconstruction and Development), an autonomous United Nations agency, is concerned with developing the infrastructure (roads, schools, hospitals, power plants) in less-developed countries. The World Bank borrows from the more prosperous countries and lends at favourable rates to less developed countries.

Some countries believed that their economies would be strengthened if they established formal trade agreements with other countries. Some of these agreements involve forming producers' cartels and common markets, to be discussed below.

Opposition and Protests

In the last few years there has been a rising tide of protest whenever a major international body, including those listed in the section above, has one of its regular meetings. Such protests have occurred all over the world—Nice, Geneva, Genoa, Quebec City, and Davos are some examples. A very large protest occurred in Seattle in 1999, preventing the World Trade Organization (WTO) from carrying on its scheduled meeting. To prevent this happening again the WTO scheduled the November 2001 meeting in the tiny Persian Gulf oil-state of Qatar, because Qatar is not a democracy and does not allow protests. However, Qatar did allow a small number of people to enter and carry on a peaceful protest. One of these protesters included well-known Canadian Maude Barlow, the leader of the Council of Canadians.

As mentioned in Chapter 1, the protests are essentially about what has been called *the corporate control of globalization* because it has favoured the large corporations and the wealthier industrialized countries while the poorer and less developed nations have not really felt many benefits. Interestingly, the leaders of the World Economic Forum (WEF) have been warning about this for some years (see Chapter 5). Additional voices have now been heard noting similar complaints. A good example is "The WTO's barriers threaten its survival," as a *Globe and Mail* editorial warned the November 2001 meeting in Qatar. The criticism here is that the trade barriers to imports of agricultural and other commodities by advanced industrialized countries from developing countries have not really been lowered, while the latter have had to lower their barriers to imports from the wealthy countries, making it very difficult for them to benefit from globalization. Therefore, these countries also voiced strong criticisms at the meeting in Qatar.[5]

Producers' Cartels

Producers' cartels are organizations of commodity-producing countries. They are formed to stabilize or increase prices, optimizing overall profits in the long run. The most obvious example today is OPEC (the Organization of Petroleum Exporting Countries). Similar attempts have been made to manage prices for copper, iron ore, bauxite, bananas, tungsten, rubber, and other important commodities. These cartels are all contradictions to unrestricted free trade and letting the market set prices.

producers' cartels
Organizations of commodity-producing countries that are formed to stabilize or increase prices to optimize overall profits in the long run. (An example is OPEC, the Organization of Petroleum Exporting Countries.)

COMMON MARKETS

A **common market** consists of a regional group of countries whose aim is to remove all internal tariff and nontariff barriers to trade, investment, and employment. To achieve this the countries try to harmonize all their laws and regulations so that money, goods, services, and people can move freely among all the members of the group. Some notable examples are the Association of Southeast Asian Nations (ASEAN), the Central American Common Market (CACM), the Caribbean Common Market (CCM), Mercosur in South America, the North American Free Trade Agreement (NAFTA), and the European Union (EU). The last two are particularly important for Canada, so we look at them in the next two sections.

common market
A regional group of countries that aims to remove all internal tariff and nontariff barriers to trade, investment, and employment. (An important example is the European Union.)

The Canada–U.S. Free Trade Agreement[6]

An important common market was established between Canada and the United States when the Free Trade Agreement (FTA) came into effect on January 1, 1989. The agreement affected nearly all goods and services traded between Canada and the United States, as well as intercountry investments. These two countries are each other's largest trading partners. More than 80 percent of Canada's imports and exports are with the United States. The Canada–U.S. trading bloc has the largest two-country trade in the world, about $1.6 billion daily.

The formal purpose of the FTA was to phase out most tariffs and other restrictions to free trade between the two countries over a period of 10 years. The FTA made it easier for cross-country investments and buyouts to take place and guaranteed the United States access to our energy resources. The movement of professionals and certain other categories of people across the border was also eased. For various reasons, each side kept certain items outside the FTA. For example, Canada insisted that beer and cultural industries and products be excluded. The United States insisted that shipping be excluded.

One major goal of the Canadian negotiating team was to provide relief from unilateral U.S. trade restrictions. A binational panel would adjudicate on disputes between the two countries. Unfortunately, this has not stopped the United States from continuing what many Canadians feel is harassment of our exporters (three examples are lumber, wheat, and steel). Some cases were so frivolous (for instance, uranium from Saskatchewan) that they were easily won. But the process involves Canadian exporters in heavy legal costs and draws executives' time away from productive efforts. It also makes foreign companies wary of investing in Canada.

Both Simon Reisman, who was our chief negotiator of the FTA, and his deputy, Gordon Ritchie, were extensively quoted in the media in early 1992, criticizing the United States for continuing actions they deemed not to be in keeping with either the spirit or the letter of the agreement.

One of the most irritating problems in Canadian exports to the United States is the issue of softwood lumber. Every few years the U.S. government finds some excuse to penalize Canadian lumber companies that export this badly needed product to their country, throwing thousands of Canadians out of work. The FTA and its successor (the NAFTA, discussed in the next section) were supposed to solve this problem. Instead the issue seems to never go away, having surfaced once again in 2001. Since softwood lumber is a multibillion-dollar export that affects B.C. particularly, as well as Quebec, Ontario, and N.B., it is of great importance to us.

The softwood lumber debate has spawned hundreds of media reports, editorials, newspaper and online opinion columns, TV and radio commentaries, and a spate of public discussions—most of them critical of U.S. policies and attitudes in this regard. On August 13, 2001 international trade lawyer Barry Appleton, speaking on CBC Radio One, said that the United States has deliberately made trade rules complicated, thus slowing up the process of fighting their trade decisions, even under NAFTA. In a joint article in *The Globe and Mail* on November 7, 2001, former U.S. trade representative Clayton Yeuter and former Canadian finance minister Don Mazankowski say that it is high time that this "destructive conflict" is settled once and for all.

The second aim of the FTA was to expose Canadian companies to greater competition from American companies to force them to become more competitive. This competition was deemed essential for Canada to compete in the tough, globalized business world. The thinking was that, since the world has now become one market, only the best can survive in that fiercely competitive global marketplace. The problem was that the Canadian government gave no aid to help certain industries through what it admitted would be a very difficult transition period, despite promises to do so.

Other countries, such as Japan, Singapore, and Korea, that wanted to raise certain industries to world-class competitiveness followed a different path. They gave their companies three years to shape up while protecting them from foreign competition. The governments aided the companies and monitored them closely to see that they were moving forward, and helped to retrain workers whose jobs were disappearing.

The third aim of the FTA was to give better access to the vast American market for Canadian goods and services. This goal was closely related to forcing Canadian companies to become more competitive, since they would have to compete with American companies.

The North American Free Trade Agreement

On January 1, 1993, the North American Free Trade Agreement (NAFTA) among the United States, Canada, and Mexico came into effect. This replaced the previous FTA between Canada and the United States. Why another free trade agreement? What impact did it have on Canada?

The motivators for NAFTA are basically to be found in the needs of the United States and Mexico. Mexico's population continues to explode, and its economy cannot provide jobs for large numbers of its people. For many years they have been pouring across the long U.S. border, mostly illegally. These uncounted millions of Mexicans are having a major, rapid impact on American society that is disturbing many Americans. The U.S. government seeks to stop this flow by helping the Mexican economy grow fast enough to provide jobs in Mexico. The Mexican government is, of course, interested in developing its economy and sees access to the vast American market as the way to spur growth, provide jobs for its people, and raise the low standard of living in Mexico.

Canadian Press CP. Photography by Richard Sobol Ho.

Canada is really a minor player in this deal. It was concerned that it would be left out or penalized indirectly unless it sat at the table. We do have something to gain by having freer access to the growing Mexican market, but it is still a minor customer for Canada. The United States sought to modify the FTA in its favour as the price for letting Canada be a part of NAFTA. We did not have many bargaining chips and it is unclear if the United States succeeded.

There is a continuing concern in Canada, which is even greater in the United States, that many manufacturing jobs will be lost to Mexico because of NAFTA. Wages and general conditions are much lower in Mexico. This time around (unlike with the FTA), many Canadian business people were opposed because they did not like many of the details. In addition, Mexico has a poor policy on environmental problems, bad working conditions, and a bad record on human rights and political freedom. The country has repeatedly been condemned by many organizations in North America and abroad for serious flaws on all of these counts. Others believe that NAFTA will force Mexico to gradually improve these conditions. This has been happening, but at a very slow pace.

The United States and Canada announced a broad strategy of creating one vast free trade area of the entire western hemisphere. The U.S. sees itself as dominating this bloc, which will give it important leverage in trading with the rest of the world. With Europe moving to a single market and Japan becoming the linch-pin of a huge East Asian bloc, the United States wants to be sure it has the strength to compete with these major trading blocs. However, while protectionist sentiment in the United States is holding back accepting Chile into NAFTA, Canada signed its own free trade deal with Chile. Chile has also become the fifth member of the Mercosur common market, joining Brazil, Argentina, Uruguay, and Paraguay.

Now the United States and Canada have been pushing the idea of a Free Trade Agreement of the Americas (FTAA) to include the countries in Central and South America. At a planning and discussion session in Quebec City in 2000 there were a number of large demonstrations opposing a FTAA that includes the same aspects of NAFTA arousing the dissatisfaction and opposition mentioned in this section. In preparation for the Quebec City meetings authorities made most unusual preparations, turning the city into an armed camp with thousands of police and steel fencing creating a large so-called safety perimeter. Media reports showed many clashes, with lots of tear gas used to quell the demonstrations.

One result of NAFTA is that many manufacturing jobs have been moved to Mexico. It is much cheaper to produce goods in Mexico due to lower wages and lower costs in general.

PROGRESS **CHECK**

- What is the primary purpose of the International Monetary Fund (IMF) and the General Agreement on Tariffs and Trade (GATT)?
- How does a common market work? Why do countries enter into common market agreements?
- What were the objectives that led Canada to sign the FTA and NAFTA?

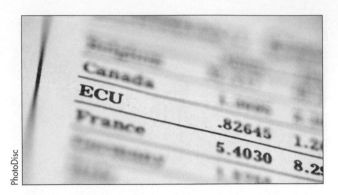

PhotoDisc

The eurodollar came into effect in January 1999. Since that time, prices in the participating countries have been shown in both the national and euro currency.

www.europa.eu.int

See this Web site for more information about the European Union.

The European Union

On December 31, 1992, after 40 years of preparatory organizational structures, 12 nations of Europe organized into a common market called the European Union (EU), effectively dissolving their previous economic borders. In 1994 three more countries were added. (See Figure 3.7 for a detailed list.) Most of the advanced part of Europe is now one vast market of some 370 million inhabitants with the free movement of people, goods, services, and capital. Centuries-old regional characteristics will remain a strong force for many years, but economic, political, and social differences are beginning to narrow. Many EU structures now in place are helping the movement in that direction, including a European parliament.

There were two major goals the EU hoped to achieve by the end of the century: monetary and political union. That means one currency—the euro unit—and an EU government. You can see how having a single currency avoids all the trade problems of currency fluctuations discussed earlier. One government will also make a common trade policy much easier to fashion for the 15 countries. This union is a historic movement toward countries giving up their sovereignty, which is a major reversal of the past few hundred years' evolution toward the modern independent nation-state.

In 1999 it was clear that there were still serious obstacles preventing the achievement of complete monetary and political union. Most of the countries were suffering from economic decline and massive unemployment, possibly the worst crisis since the end of the war in 1945. Other issues were also delaying progress. It is not the first time in the 45-year history of this movement that major problems have arisen. In the past these were overcome, so there is hope that the current difficulties will also be overcome.

Despite all the difficulties, 11 of the 15 members of the European Union agreed to phase out their own currencies and to use the euro as the common currency effective January 1, 2002. This process is complex and is being phased in over a two-year period. Since January 1999 all prices in these 11 countries have been shown in both the euro and the national currency.

The complex and very difficult process of uniting Europe began with six countries in 1957, led by some farsighted politicians in France and Germany. They felt that the only way to avoid even more devastating wars in Europe than the two terrible world wars of the twentieth century was to unite in a common destiny. Gradually, other reasons emerged for strengthening this unity movement. More people began to see such integration as the only way to raise their standard of living while improving their ability to compete with Japan and the United States in European and world markets.

The free movement of people, money, goods, and services; new tax systems; and shared social programs and professional standards are extremely difficult to achieve. This movement is now seen by the rest of Europe as the wave of the future, and many

---

FIGURE 3.7

THE EUROPEAN UNION

The 15 countries that were members of the European Union as of January 2002.

Austria	Germany	The Netherlands
Belgium	Greece	Portugal
Denmark	Ireland	Spain
Finland	Italy	Sweden
France	Luxembourg	United Kingdom

of the countries that are not in the EU are eager to join. The EU will eventually be the largest unified market in the world, packing a powerful economic punch.

One advantage for Canadians is that English is the common business language of the EU. This should help Canadian companies compete in this giant market, as it will be one less barrier to international trade and investment. Figure 3.5 shows that the EU is one of our important trading partners. Some observers fear that a European protectionist superstate, "Fortress Europe," may emerge, but others see no danger of this happening. One of the most significant international developments of the next decade will be the progress of this newly united Europe.

CRITICAL THINKING

Many countries in the world are called less-developed countries. Why are they less developed? Is it the lack of natural resources? Then how do you explain the success of Japan, which has few natural resources?

Does lack of free markets keep countries from developing? Why would a government restrict free trade?

What could happen to the world's standard of living and quality of life if all countries engaged in free trade? What is keeping that from happening? What would it take to eliminate all barriers?

A GLOBAL INDUSTRY RUNS INTO ETHICAL PROBLEMS[7]

Many transnational businesses are constantly searching for countries in which labour costs are low to reduce their manufacturing costs and make them more competitive. Makers of sneakers have practised this international sourcing, particularly in East Asian countries, and as a result ran into substantial criticism in the early 1990s for their weak ethical values. The criticism was mainly directed at the two largest companies in this field, Nike and Reebok. Specifically, the Indonesian Institut Teknology Bandung (ITB) and the Asian-American Free Labor Institute (AAFLI) alleged that "Nike's system of procuring shoes in Indonesia was rife with exploitation." They accused Nike's South Korean contractors of "forcing employees to work overtime, violating child-labor laws, and not respecting special work rules for women," among other violations.

At first Nike said that these factories were owned and operated by independent contractors who produced the running shoes for them. There was similar criticism of Reebok from the International Labor Rights Education and Research Fund (ILRERF) and an initial response from Reebok that aped Nike's. Eventually, both companies issued formal documents specifying principles and procedures that all their subcontractors were required to follow to ensure that human rights and local laws were respected. Reebok's program seemed to have more teeth in it than Nike's. Senior Reebok officials were quoted as saying, "I think corporations are increasingly finding that you need to be more than good business people. You have to be responsible business citizens," and "consumers today hold companies accountable for the way products are made, not just the quality of the product itself."

HOW DOES CANADA SHAPE UP AS AN INTERNATIONAL COMPETITOR?

The 1990s saw a torrent of complaints in Canada that our competitiveness has been sliding steadily. One of the most influential sources assessing Canada's competitiveness is the Porter report, commissioned by the Canadian government. It is called *Canada at the Crossroads: The Reality of a New Competitive Environment.* This year-long study by a team headed by Michael E. Porter, the guru of competition from the

Harvard University Business School, was released in January 1992. It is a very comprehensive analysis; the summary is 101 pages long. The report is based on concepts and techniques elaborated on in Porter's influential book *The Competitive Advantage of Nations.*

What were Porter's conclusions? According to the analysis by Professor Donald N. Thompson of York University, "Drastic and immediate action … [is] required by Canada." He continues:

> It is hard to overstate the urgency of the problem highlighted by Porter. Canada is behind in the technology race, and has shown almost no productivity growth in a decade. Its 30 percent high-school dropout rate is the highest in the western world. In training effectiveness Canada ranks 20th of 24 [developed] countries rated by the OECD (Organization for Economic Cooperation and Development). A government that should be taking the lead in research, technology, and training has spent almost two terms pursuing non-interventionist policies such as deregulation, privatization, and free trade. Reversing that policy and finding initiatives that are affordable is difficult.

Porter "is unrelenting in … [his] criticism of government, business, and labour for Canada's failure to abandon old ways of thinking and to embrace a new economic order of continual productivity growth and innovation."

Porter believes governments should concentrate on education, employee training, developing "closer links between government, universities, and industry research bodies," and specialized regional development policies. Business must "treat labour as a partner and act in a less authoritarian way," be "innovative-driven," spend more on training, "transform foreign subsidiaries into home bases," "rely more on advanced technologies and methods," and "focus on products, markets, and businesses that provide a lasting competitive advantage." Labour's "priorities must become encouragement of technological change and skills upgrading, and more cooperative labour-management relations" as "the best guarantee of good wages" and jobs in the long term.

Porter, an American, notes that "one of Canada's competitive problems is the high concentration of foreign-owned firms that perform little sophisticated production or R&D." Not mentioned by Porter is the fact that these are nearly all subsidiaries of U.S. firms. Nearly half (45 percent) of Canada's manufacturing sector is foreign owned. Thompson points out that "most academics and government officials maintain that the level of foreign ownership is not significant in determining the competitiveness" of Canada. Porter disagrees, arguing:

> It matters a lot where a multinational calls home, because a company's home base is where the best jobs exist, where core R&D is undertaken, and where strategic control rests…. Home bases are important to an economy because they support high productivity and productivity growth.

Thompson notes that in this difference of opinion, Porter takes a position "closer to economic nationalists" than to the more conventional economic wisdom.

Finally, concludes Professor Thompson, the message is "that we must move quickly or risk a real loss in standard of living."[8]

Evidence Contradicting Porter and Conventional Wisdom[9]

Two reports in *The Globe and Mail* seem to be somewhat at odds with all the bad news about Canada's competitive ability. The first, a Statistics Canada study, shows that exports of Canadian manufacturing products accounted for 47 percent of all our merchandise exports in 1990 (compared to only 32 percent in 1980). These exports began increasing in the latter half of the 1980s, despite the rise of the Canadian dollar against the U.S. dollar making our exports more expensive. Later Statistics Canada figures show that the percentage continued to rise between 1991 and 1993, despite the recession. By 1994 manufactured products constituted 68 percent of all exports.

Even when automotive trade with the United States is excluded, manufacturing exports still increased from 20 percent to 37 percent of overall exports in the 1980s. According to Philip Cross, StatsCan's director of current analysis, the big losses in manufacturing appeared to occur in the domestic market. Such industries as textiles, furniture, appliances, food products, printing, and publishing were hit.

Cross's statistics are borne out by the comments of J. Myers, chief economist and senior vice-president of the Canadian Exporters and Manufacturers Association. He says that "the real weakness in manufacturing has not been in exports … but on the domestic side." Myers notes that Canadian manufacturers' share of the domestic market slipped from 73 percent in 1980 to 55 percent in 1991. By 1994 the figure was down to 45 percent, in large extent due to the FTA and NAFTA. This figure had slipped further by 1998. Perhaps even more impressive, Cross says:

> Manufacturing output has declined at a slower pace than has manufacturing employment during the recession as companies have continued to make productivity gains even as output fell, **which is highly unusual** [authors' emphasis]. Productivity is defined as real output per person-hour worked.

These statistics are almost startling in view of all the gloomy statements by Porter and so many others about the poor productivity of Canadian manufacturers.

The second report from *The Globe and Mail* covers a study by a University of Toronto political science professor, Joseph Fletcher, about Canadian attitudes to capitalistic and entrepreneurial ideologies. "Canadians, it turns out, are more American than the Americans." On a long list of questions designed to compare Canadian and American attitudes, we seem to be waving ideological business banners "even more zealously" than our cousins to the south.

While it is rather surprising to discover that we are really so different from the image usually projected of Canadians, there is something even more surprising. This study, entitled *Canadian Attitudes Towards Competitiveness and Entrepreneurship*, was commissioned by the federal government. But it was held up by the Department of Industry, Science, and Technology for nearly a year, until well after the delivery of the Porter report in October 1991. The lengthy delay is understandable, since the study conflicts with a basic premise in Porter's report. The article notes that

> Mr. Porter concluded in his report that the biggest barriers to improving Canada's competitiveness are attitudinal. He said that if his study had only one impact, he hoped it would be the way Canadians think about competitiveness. Although there was not a shred of attitudinal research in the Porter report, big business and government quickly picked up the theme.

In the meantime, various ratings of Canada's international competitiveness position in the early 1990s by the OECD and the World Economic Forum had us fluctuating annually somewhere at the bottom of the top third or quarter of the 24 or 48 countries evaluated.

Nevertheless, the OECD, consisting of the 29 most advanced industrialized countries and whose current secretary-general is Canadian Donald Johnston, continues to rate Canada's standard of living as being 10 percent above the average of industrial countries. The OECD also said that it had erred in evaluating how productive the Canadian economy had been in the 1980s and 1990s.[10] (See additional discussion of the issue of productivity in the previous chapter ➤**P. 43**◄ and in Chapter 10.) The whole issue of assessing international competitiveness is complex and open to varying opinions. For example, as you can see in Figure 3.8, the prestigious World Economic Forum put Canada fifth in international competitiveness in 1998, only 10 percent behind the U.S. Comparing 1996 with 1998, the U.S. has moved from fourth to third place, while Canada moved from eighth to fifth place.

FIGURE 3.8

WORLD ECONOMIC FORUM GLOBAL COMPETITIVENESS REPORT

This report clearly shows that Canada's competitive position is quite strong. In 1999 Canada stayed in fifth place but slipped in 2000 and 2001 to eleventh place. However, Canada was ranked third in growth competitiveness for 2001.

COUNTRY	COMPETITIVENESS INDEX	RANK 1998	RANK 1997	RANK 1996
Singapore	2.16	1	(1)	(1)
Hong Kong	1.91	2	(2)	(2)
United States	1.41	3	(3)	(4)
United Kingdom	1.29	4	(7)	(15)
Canada	**1.27**	**5**	**(4)**	**(8)**

Sources: <www.weforum.org>, May 1999 and November 2001.

As we enter the twenty-first century it is clear that more research is required to explain these contradictions. It seems that no one has the answer to the important question: How productive, and therefore how competitive, is Canada?

PROGRESS CHECK

• What is the EU? What is it trying to achieve?

• What is the Porter report? What are its main conclusions according to Professor Thompson?

• What is the evidence contradicting some of its conclusions?

CAREERS AND JOBS IN THE GLOBAL WORLD OF BUSINESS

Business has become global in nature and this fact should be influencing how you prepare yourself for a promising career or job. Your first thoughts might be about what large company could employ you, and there are many such Canadian companies that are deeply involved in international activities. The major Canadian banks—Royal Bank, CIBC, Bank of Montreal, Scotiabank, and TD Canada Trust—and banks that are subsidiaries of giant international banks like the Hongkong Bank of Canada are good examples. Some major manufacturing and processing companies are Nortel Networks, Magna International, Bombardier, International Nickel, Nova Corp., and the Canadian subsidiaries of the American and Japanese automobile manufacturers. There are also insurance company, forestry and pulp and paper companies, and hundreds of other large companies with major international investments and markets.

Do not overlook the thousands of smaller Canadian companies that are also involved in global business, including software companies. You will see some of the names scattered throughout this book in Profiles or in boxes. Many of them are aided by an extensive federal government program to assist smaller exporters. Or you may even start your own business in Canada or elsewhere as a result of ideas that occur to you while travelling through other countries. A good example is the traveller in Africa who noticed that it was hard to get ice for drinks. He did a little research and found that there was no ice factory in hundreds of kilometres, despite a large market for ice. He found some investors in North America prepared to back him, returned to Africa, and built an ice-making plant. He went on to develop a successful business.

Many small software companies are involved in global business. Even small companies can grow quickly by developing an international presence.

PhotoDisc

ETHICAL DILEMMA

Review

Do you recall the ethical problem about nightgowns at the start of the chapter? Here's what our executives think. Bédard says, "I feel the nightgowns are a write-off. The company has already suffered severely because of this fabric. Unless the nightgowns can be treated with fire-retardant material that would be efficient for the life of the garment, I would suggest that they be destroyed and the company must accept the loss."

Reilley believes that "sales of Nightie Nite (NN) products in less restrictive countries may work in the short term. However, the NN company would become known as being less than ethical and would eventually have to adjust their products to be safe, or lose market share. Emerging-country consumers are becoming more sophisticated all the time and NN's competitors are becoming more ethical on the world market as well." In addition, "world bodies such as the WTO, IMF, and UN are demanding more ethical conduct [in] emerging countries."

To be better equipped for working in the global business atmosphere, you should be thinking about, and doing, the following:

- learning to speak other languages; French, Spanish, and Chinese would all be very useful
- travelling to other countries to observe first-hand how their cultures function
- taking some cross-cultural courses to better understand the attitudes of other peoples
- reading magazines and newspapers that concentrate on business and news from other countries
- forming friendships with students from other countries

All of these actions will help to expand your vision and knowledge of how the world functions, helping you to find a useful niche and to function better in whatever job or career you choose.

SUMMARY

1. The world market for trade is huge. Some 95 percent of the people in the world live outside Canada and the United States.
   - *Why should nations trade with other nations?*
   (1) No country is self-sufficient, (2) countries need products that other countries produce, and (3) there is a world imbalance of natural resources and technological skills.
   - *What is the theory of comparative advantage?*
   The theory of comparative advantage contends that a country should produce and sell those products it produces most efficiently and buy those it cannot produce as effectively.

1. Discuss the critical importance of the international market and the role of comparative advantage in international trade.

2. Understand the status of Canada in international business.

2. Canada has only 31 million people, yet it ranks seventh in the world in volume of international trade. Canadian companies also invest large sums of money in the United States and in other countries.
    *   *What made Canada's success in international trade possible?*
    Canada is an efficient, modern, industrialized country with a well-trained workforce. It has developed high levels of expertise in agricultural, energy, and other natural resource production. Canada produces huge quantities of these products, as well as automotive vehicles and parts, which are exported to the United States under the special Auto Pact. More recently, electronic and telecommunication products and transportation equipment have become major exports.

3. Illustrate the strategies used in reaching global markets.

3. A company can participate in world trade in a number of ways.
    *   *What are some ways a company can get involved in international business?*
    Ways of entering world trade include exporting and importing, joint venturing, licensing, creating subsidiaries, franchising, and countertrading.

4. Discuss the hurdles to trading in world markets.

4. There are many restrictions on foreign trade other than protectionism.
    *   *What are some of the other hurdles that can discourage participation in international business?*
    Potential stumbling blocks to world trade include cultural differences, societal and economic differences, legal and regulatory differences, and fluctuations in values of different currencies.

5. Review what trade protectionism is and how and why it is practised.

5. Political pressures are often the most difficult hurdles to international trade.
    *   *How does trade protectionism reduce international trade?*
    Trade protectionism is the use of government regulations to limit the import of goods and services, based on the theory of favouring domestic producers to help them survive and grow and generate more jobs. Some tools of protectionism are tariffs and quotas.
    *   *What are tariffs?*
    Tariffs are taxes on imports.
    *   *How does a quota differ from a tariff?*
    A quota limits the quantity of particular imports.
    *   *Is trade protectionism good for domestic producers?*
    That is debatable. Trade protectionism hurt all countries badly during the Great Depression of the 1930s because other countries responded to foreign tariffs with tariffs of their own.
    *   *Why do governments continue such practices?*
    Pressure from industries and their associations, unions, and communities affected by imports nurtures the practice of trade protectionism.

6. Discuss the future of international trade and investment.

6. One of the most significant developments for the future of world trade is the formation of 15 European countries into one trading bloc, called the European Union (EU).
    *   *What trading partnership is more important to Canada than the EU?*
    The U.S.–Canada–Mexico North American Free Trade Agreement (NAFTA). It is expected to expand ultimately to include all of South and Central America.
    *   *Will future growth in world trade be with large developed nations?*
    Yes, but there will likely be more growth with the rapidly developing Pacific Rim countries such as China and other countries in Southeast Asia. The former communist countries in eastern Europe and what was the Soviet Union also offer great potential for investment and trade.

balance of trade 62
bartering 68
common market 75
comparative advantage theory 61
consortium 68
countertrading 68
embargo 73
exchange rate 63

foreign subsidiary 67
General Agreement on Tariffs and Trade (GATT) 74
import quota 72
international joint venture (IJV) 68
International Monetary Fund (IMF) 74
licensing 66

mercantilism 72
producers' cartels 75
trade deficit 62
trade protectionism 62
transnational or multinational corporation (TNC or MNC) 59
World Bank 74

DEVELOPING WORKPLACE SKILLS

1. Visit a dealer of Oriental rugs or some other importer of foreign goods. Talk with the owner or manager about the problems and satisfactions involved in international trade. Visit several such organizations and compile a list of advantages and disadvantages. Compare your list with those of other students in your class.

2. Prepare a short essay describing the benefits and drawbacks of trade protectionism. Have your class divide into two sides and debate this issue: "Resolved—that Canada should increase trade protection to save Canadian jobs and Canadian companies."

3. Many firms have made embarrassing mistakes selling overseas. Sometimes the product is not adapted to the needs of the country, sometimes the advertising makes no sense, sometimes the colour is wrong, and so forth. Discuss the steps Canadian businesses should follow to be more responsive to the needs of foreign markets. Discuss your list with others, and together form a plan for improving trade overseas.

4. What aspect of international business interests you most: importing, exporting, investment, production, finance, marketing, or franchising? Why?

5. How seriously have you explored working in a global economy? What courses might you take to better prepare yourself?

TAKING IT TO THE NET

Purpose:

To become proficient at using the Internet to search current news topics, both domestic and international.

Exercises:

1. Trade protectionism is a constant issue in the U.S., especially in periods leading up to elections, which take place in November 2002 and 2004. Because the U.S. is by far our largest customer, this issue is of major importance to us. Search the Web sites of your local newspaper, *The Globe and Mail* and the *National Post* newspapers, and *Canadian Business* or *Maclean's* magazines to see what current news stories there are on this topic, especially reports that affect any Canadian companies or industries.

2. The European Union's plan for a single currency—the *euro*—for its 15 members is unfolding with 11 countries now showing prices in the euro as well as in local currency. This new currency will have a major effect on international business. Use the Yahoo search engine <www.yahoo.com> (or any other such search engine) and the keywords "euro currency" to see what information you can gather about the current situation, such as how many countries are using the euro, how the process is unfolding, what problems have arisen, and any special impact on Canada.

PRACTISING MANAGEMENT DECISIONS

CASE 1

INTERNATIONAL EXPANSION: A CAUTIONARY TALE

Since the collapse of the Soviet Union in 1989 and the splitting up of the country into a dozen independent states, a whole new world of opportunity has opened up for Canadian, and other, companies. These republics are busily engaged in trying to establish capitalist economies and they need a lot of help: capital, technology, and management skills are desperately needed.

This large potential market has attracted hundreds of thousands of companies and individuals who see a great opportunity to get rich quick. Unfortunately, these opportunities are matched by risks of equal size. Because the collapse was so sudden, the attempt to make a complete change has resulted in a very chaotic situation. Laws are weak, confused, nonexistent, or not enforced. Serious corruption and major crimes such as kidnapping and murder are commonplace. Many business people travel only with bodyguards and in bullet-proof cars. Organized crime represents a strong and growing force in these republics.

One of the ongoing problems of doing business in Moscow is the pressure from gangs to pay them to protect you. The gangs provide a "roof" so no other gangs will threaten you. Usually they start with small demands and then gradually increase their price until they take over the whole business and force you to leave the country. Let us examine how one Canadian company coped with this high-risk situation.

Brad Pielsticker operates an airfreight-forwarding company, AES International Ltd., with offices in the Moscow airport and in downtown Moscow. One day he received a call at the airport office from his Russian partner, who told him that the mafia had finally caught up with them. Someone had just entered their downtown office and demanded payment for a roof (protector).

Pielsticker remembered what had happened to his brother, who had had his lucrative software-teaching-skills company taken away from him and given 24 hours to flee the country. Pielsticker decided to bluff. He and his partner told the enforcer that they already had a roof and that he should return in three days if he wanted to meet him.

Pielsticker then hired someone he knew, who had underworld connections and a reputation, to pose as their roof. Fortunately the trick worked, because after one meeting the enforcer did not return. Pielsticker feels very lucky—he had a close call and he knows it.

Decision Questions

1. How would you feel about expanding your business into Moscow? Would the temptation of big bucks overcome your worries?

2. How does a company or individual determine what is an acceptable level of risk? Is it better to always stay away from high-risk situations?

3. Suppose your company sent you to Moscow to manage or work in the local office. Would that be different? Why?

4. Is it better to wait a while, hoping the situation will improve? Suppose your competitors are already there?

Adapted from: John Nadler, "Married (Often Happily) to the Mob," *Canadian Business*, April 1996, p. 30ff.

CASE 2

TO BRIBE OR NOT TO BRIBE? THAT IS THE QUESTION

Condor Manufacturing has a joint venture with a local company in an African country we shall call Lorino. Condor sent you out to be the general manager for three years to train a Lorinese to take over from you. You are facing certain problems that you do not know how to resolve.

Bribery and kickbacks are normal methods of getting things done in Lorino. This applies to dealings with other companies and with the government. Salaries are very low and bribes are expected to make up the shortfall so that people can survive.

The vice-president of international operations for Condor is not very keen about this way of doing business, especially as it violates the company's ethical code. However, he informs you that these are decisions that you will have to make as the general manager. You have tried to pass the buck and it has been passed right back to you.

You have had to bribe people to get certain licences, to get supplies, to have a road repaired, and to get sales contracts signed. You know that other local companies have learned to live with these conditions. Now you are negotiating to buy a piece of land adjacent to the factory because Condor will have to expand in the near future. A substantial bribe is being demanded and you are trying to resist it.

Decision Questions

1. Should you go along with this demand since it is a one-time issue?
2. Should you hold your nose and go along with this "normal" way of doing things?

3. Should you try to get a transfer out of Lorino even if you have to cook up some medical or personal reasons?
4. Do you have any other alternatives? What are the likely results of each of the previous choices?

CBC   VIDEO CASE   www.cbc.ca

GET BIG OR GET LOST

The focus of chapter 3 was on how competition has become global in nature. To compete successfully in today's global world of business, more and more companies are finding that they have to become much larger. Even some of our large banks tried to merge because they believed it necessary to be able to compete against giant banks from other countries.

As the text notes in various chapters, the United States is by far our largest customer — absorbing some 85% of our exports. It is also the country where we get huge amounts of financing in different forms, and where most of our foreign investments are made. So many Canadian companies, especially in the resource sector, find they must grow larger if they want to be strong competitors in the U.S. market. This video shows what this pressure looks like in real life.

Canadian oil and other resource companies that are considered large players by Canadian standards, soon find that they run into difficulties when they turn to the U.S. to obtain the necessary additional financing to support growth. This is because they are looked at as being too small to attract much interest. Because economics and businesses have grown so enormously in the last few decades, financial people now think in billions when they used to think in millions.

More recently, American resource companies have acquired a number of large Canadian resource companies. This is not surprising because, as the video notes, these companies were considered to be undervalued making them a good buy for those who had the necessary financing.

Discussion Questions

1. Do you see any problem with Canadian (and other countries' companies) becoming ever larger giants? Do you see better or worse employment opportunities for yourself and other college/university graduates? Why?
2. Research and development (R&D) in today's world of complex technologies requires expenditures of huge sums of money that only large companies can afford. Isn't this a good argument in support of mergers and the creation of larger business entities?
3. Will the domination of the economy by large transnational companies (TNCs) strengthen it? Some companies now have revenues larger than the GNP of small countries. Is this a threat to government authority? What about the effect on small business, on initiative, and on innovation?

Source: *Venture*, show number 761, "Get Big or Get Lost," October 24, 2000, running time 6:30.

4

The Role of Government in Business

LEARNING GOALS

AFTER YOU HAVE READ AND STUDIED THIS CHAPTER, YOU SHOULD BE ABLE TO

1 Explain the historical role of government in the Canadian economy.

2 List some of the major Crown corporations in Canada and understand their role in the economy.

3 Understand how the start-up and operations of companies take place within a framework of government laws and regulations.

4 Identify major legislation affecting competition in Canada.

5 Discuss the role of government in stimulating or restraining the economy.

6 Understand the role of government in consumer and investor protection.

7 Understand the controversy over a government industrial policy.

Premier Frank McKenna: New Brunswick's Super Salesman

Courtesy of Frank McKenna.

Former Premier of New Brunswick Frank McKenna attracted a lot of attention across Canada, not all of it favourable, for his aggressive campaign to bring new business into his province. McKenna concentrated on making New Brunswick the call-centre capital of Canada.

Most of us are aware that when we call a company today, we never know where the call is being received. Companies used to receive calls at their local offices, but new communication technology has made it more economical to have one centre receive all calls. Modern satellites and fibre optics make it possible for the centre to be anywhere in the world.

Cashing in on this possibility, Frank McKenna was able to attract a wide variety of companies to New Brunswick. The Royal Bank set up its new telebanking centre in Moncton; Hospitality Franchise Systems and ICT Group, a major marketing and information research service, located its centre in Saint John; Sun Life Assurance, IBM Canada, Camco Inc., Pepsi Cola (Atlantic), Xerox, and many others, including important software companies, have also located call centres and related functions in New Brunswick.

The result of these and other recruiting activities was a steady increase in jobs and economic activities in New Brunswick In 1995 alone employment was up by 7,000, reaching an all-time high of 314,000 and bringing unemployment in New Brunswick to 11.5 percent, the lowest level since 1980. Added to two consecutive years of increases in employment participation while the national rate dropped for the sixth consecutive year, this was a very impressive performance. The economic results were quite substantial: inflation below the national rate; GDP, manufacturing shipments, and exports above national rates; retail sales and wages at national rates.

Although there were some protests from other provinces that McKenna was stealing companies from them or engaging in unfair competition, these were not too serious and McKenna continued his campaign of attracting business to New Brunswick.

The efforts of Frank McKenna continued to be felt in New Brunswick into the twenty-first century, long after his departure from the political scene.

ETHICAL DILEMMA
Tackling the Deficit

As you saw in Chapter 2, the federal government was under strong pressure from the business community to reduce and wipe out the annual deficit in the federal budget. Business was convinced that these constant deficits and the resulting accumulated debt were dragging the Canadian economy down and making Canada uncompetitive with other major countries. In this chapter you will see that the government has drastically cut its expenditures, resulting in significant reductions in funding to the provinces for health care, higher education, and other important activities. Combined with other budget-cutting measures that have led to lower and fewer payments to the unemployed, the result has been an increase in poverty levels, especially among children and women. In December 1998 a United Nations committee criticized Canada because of the high percentage of the population in poor circumstances.[1]

These facts lead to some ethical questions: Should such severe budget cuts have been made? Does the business community bear some responsibility for the increase in poverty in Canada? Was there really any other choice given the tough, globally competitive conditions today? We will look for answers at the end of the chapter.

GOVERNMENT INVOLVEMENT IN THE ECONOMY

www.dbic.com
www.cbsc.org

The Doing Business in Canada and Canada Business Service Centres Web sites are federal government services, but include information on services provided by provincial governments, other institutional and private organizations, and federal government agencies.

Crown corporations
Companies owned by the federal or a provincial government.

As discussed in Chapter 2, the Canadian economic system is often described as a mixed economy—that is, a capitalist economy in which government plays an important role ➤**P. 37**◄. If you look at the government of Canada section (and equivalent provincial government sections) in the blue pages of a city telephone directory, you will get some idea of the degree of government involvement in our economy. There are so many services that federal and provincial governments issue publications listing them in detail. For example, the 13th edition of the *Guide to Federal Programs and Services* is a 450-page book. It lists programs and services for 140 government-owned companies, departments, and agencies, with addresses and toll-free phone numbers across the country and other information. Companies owned by the federal or provincial governments are called **Crown corporations**. One aspect of the government's involvement in the economy is explored in the Ethical Dilemma box "Tackling the Deficit."

IMPACT ON CAREERS AND JOBS

As you make your way through the chapter and see the complex activities of governments in Canada, you will not be surprised to learn that they are the largest employers in the country. The federal government and the provinces with the largest populations and levels of economic activity—Ontario, Quebec, B.C., Alberta—head the list of employers. In the past it was quite natural for college and university graduates to find employment with these governments. However, as noted in Chapter 2 and as you will see in this chapter, in the latter half of the 1990s governments cut back many of their activities and reduced their workforces. These measures, combined with continued privatization of government-owned companies, caused a major source of employment to dry up.

HOW GOVERNMENT AFFECTS BUSINESS

Government activities that affect business may be divided into seven categories as shown in Figure 4.1. These include Crown corporations, laws and regulations, taxation and financial policies, financial aid, services, purchasing policies, and other expenditures. As all of these activities are scattered among different levels of government and many departments, agencies, and corporations that do a variety of things, it is not possible to present this information in such neatly divided categories. However, as you make your way through the rest of the chapter you will be able to see elements of these different aspects of government actions affecting business.

All countries' governments are involved in the economy, but the extent of involvement and the specific ways they participate vary a great deal. In Canada there are particular historical reasons why we developed into a nation in which governments play very important roles. Before looking at this history and the many ways that governments affect business, let us look at the current trends of government involvement.

The federal government had a major disposition campaign underway. It sold the Canadian National Railway (CNR), Air Canada, the national system of air traffic control, and the ownership or management of airports. The government also sold the St. Lawrence Seaway, hundreds of ports and ferries, and other maritime installations. The Post Office was also sold. This veritable flood of disposals of government assets and companies signals a minor revolution in Canadian history. The whole process of governments selling publicly owned corporations is called **privatization**.[2] In addition, industries that had been regulated, such as airlines and trucking, were partially or completely deregulated—no longer subject to certain regulations. Similar activities were undertaken by provincial governments.

Some people believed this trend should be reversed to get the economy moving again and to deal with the unprecedented structural changes (discussed in Chapter 1) that occurred in the 1990s. They believed that the lack of a comprehensive, coordinated government plan to guide and revitalize the economy, called an **industrial policy**, would undermine our ability to recover from the very severe recession of the early 1990s. Others were strongly opposed in principle to such government action. We will return to this issue at the end of the chapter.

www.cn.ca/en_about.shtml
www.aircanada.ca/about-us

The CN and Air Canada Web sites provide information about the progress of these two companies since privatization. Visit these sites to learn more.

privatization
The process of governments selling Crown corporations.

industrial policy
A comprehensive coordinated government plan to guide and revitalize the economy.

FIGURE 4.1

GOVERNMENT INVOLVEMENT WITH BUSINESS

Government activities that affect business can be divided into seven categories.

1. **Crown corporations.** There are hundreds of such companies, and they play an important role in the economy. Crown corporations sometimes compete with regular businesses.
2. **Laws and regulations.** These cover a wide range, from taxation and consumer protection to environmental controls, working conditions, and labour–management relations.
3. **Taxation and financial policies.** All levels of government collect taxes—income taxes, the GST, sales taxes, property taxes. Taxation is also fine-tuned by governments to achieve certain goals or to give effect to certain policies. This is called *fiscal policy*.
4. **Financial aid.** All levels of government provide a host of direct and indirect aid packages as incentives to achieve certain goals. These packages consist of tax reductions, tariffs and quotas on imports, grants, loans, and loan guarantees.
5. **Services.** These include a vast array of direct and indirect activities, among them helping specific industries go international, bringing companies to Canada, training and retraining the workforce, and providing a comprehensive statistics service.
6. **Purchasing policies.** Governments are very large purchasers of ordinary supplies, services, and materials for military purposes. Because the federal government is the single largest purchaser in Canada, its policies regarding where to purchase have a major effect on particular businesses and the economy of specific provinces and regions.
7. **Other expenditures.** Governments pay out many billions of dollars to the unemployed, to old-age pensioners, to low-income families, to employees injured at work, and to other categories of people. When these recipients spend this money, business benefits.

Source: The St. Lawrence Seaway Management Corporation.

Many previously government-owned corporations, such as the St. Lawrence Seaway, have been privatized in recent years. Privatization and deregulation have been somewhat controversial because these "new" corporations now operate on the profit principle, not necessarily on what is best for consumers

National Policy
Federal government policy that imposed high tariffs on imports from the United States to protect Canadian manufacturing.

A Historical Review

When Canada was formed as a country in 1867, the federal government was given the power to "regulate trade and commerce." When the western provinces later joined this confederation, it became clear that it would take special efforts to build a united Canada. The very small population was scattered across a huge country and there was no railway connecting them. Trading patterns were in a north to south configuration because, like today, most people lived near the U.S. border. The cross-border shopping phenomenon is not new.

The United States was developing much faster, with a much larger population and a bigger economy that provided products not available in the provinces either because they were not made here or there was no transportation to distribute them.

This led Canadian governments, starting with our first prime minister, Sir John A. Macdonald, to develop what was called the **National Policy**. The Policy placed high tariffs on imports from the United States to protect Canadian manufacturing, which had higher costs. In addition, the government began to grapple with the difficult question of building a costly rail line to the west coast.

These two issues set the tone for the continuing and substantial involvement of Canadian governments in developing and maintaining the Canadian economy. The same type of mixed economy can be found in many countries: advanced countries, like Germany and Japan; newly developed countries, like Taiwan and South Korea; and developing ones, like Brazil and Thailand.

Effect of the 2001 Terrorist Attacks

The September 11, 2001 hijackings and destruction of the World Trade Center Towers in New York City have introduced several new factors in the issue of the role of government in business and the economy. One factor was the significant deterioration in airport security procedures allowing hijackers carrying knives easy access to the planes. Investigations showed that when the U.S. government handed over the job of security checks on passengers to the airline industry the whole system was considerably weakened. The airlines ended up employing the lowest-cost labour, so that security checks were being done by poorly trained employees who were receiving minimum wages. A November 12, 2001 editorial in *The Globe and Mail* noted that managers lied to cover up the fact that they did no background checks when hiring people for such sensitive jobs. This resulted in the airlines hiring people with criminal records and having an abnormally high turnover rate. In addition, there was poor control of who had access to the tarmac. In brief, the whole airport security system was a shambles—so it was not surprising that passenger bookings suffered a large decline.

After the attacks U.S. president George W. Bush completely reversed his policy and that of his Republican Party, which was strongly against government intervention in the economy. He allocated huge sums in the multibillion-dollar range to help New York City recover from the devastating attacks, which hit the economy of the city badly. In addition, the government is helping the airlines, which saw revenues so sharply reduced that some were facing disaster.

In Canada, the government is moving more hesitantly on airport security and is being urged (for example in the same *Globe and Mail* editorial), to move from "talk to action." The government did offer a $25-million loan guarantee with some conditions to the Canada 3000 airline, which was in trouble, but it went bankrupt shortly afterward. Air Canada, which was having difficulty before the attacks, like all airlines was in more serious trouble afterward and was clamouring for government help. The point about the situation in Canada and the United States that is important to our discussion here is that following the terrorist attacks there was almost no opposition to the idea of increased government intervention on a number of fronts in addition to normal disaster relief.

The issue of how much government should be involved in the economy has been the subject of much debate in Canada. In the United States ideology has played a major role in influencing Americans to believe that, in principle, government should "butt out." This thinking ignores the significant role the U.S. government has played and continues to play in its economy. In Canada, we are less negative and perhaps more pragmatic: If it works, let's do it. But where do we go from here? Do we need less or more government involvement? Is it a question of the quality of that involvement? Could it be *smarter* rather than just *less*? What are your thoughts?

CROWN CORPORATIONS

In Canada, an important aspect of the role of government is expressed through Crown corporations. Some major federal ones are Atomic Energy of Canada Ltd., Canada Mortgage and Housing Corporation, the Canadian Broadcasting Corporation (CBC), the Canadian Wheat Board, and the Export Development Corporation. There are many more large and small federally owned Crown corporations.

Each province also owns such corporations. Typically, a Crown corporation owns the province's electric power company. New Brunswick Electric Power, B.C. Hydro, and Hydro-Quebec are some examples. Some of the telephone systems in western Canada are owned by provincial Crown corporations. The provinces also own other specialized corporations. Alberta owns a bank called Alberta Treasury Branches (ATB), originally set up to help farmers in bad times.

Governments set up Crown corporations either to provide services that were not being provided by businesses (which is how Air Canada came into being in the 1930s), to bail out a major industry in trouble (which is how the Canadian National Railway, now privatized, was put together in 1919), or to provide some special services that could not otherwise be made available, as in the case of Atomic Energy of Canada Ltd. or the Bank of Canada. See the Spotlight on Small Business box "Business Development Bank of Canada" for a different type of Crown corporation. Two important examples in Alberta and Quebec are discussed below.

Ogilvy One Worldwide.

The best way to address export risk.

Visit www.edcinfo.com

If your company is currently expanding beyond Canada's borders, visit our website at *www.edcinfo.com*

In 24-hours or less, we can help you significantly reduce your export risk. That's because with our accounts receivable insurance, we can protect you against 90% of your loss, if a foreign buyer doesn't pay. *And you can apply for this insurance on-line.*

Visit our website and you'll also *quickly and easily* find a wide range of financial products that Canadian exporters are using right now to capitalize on global opportunities.

EDC has been working with Canadian exporters to minimize risk and maximize their international presence for more than fifty years. Not surprisingly, our knowledge and expertise of over 200 markets is unparalleled.

It's this *unique knowledge* – as well as the latest industry news, upcoming events, trade links and of course, our insurance and financial products – that make our site an indispensable on-line resource for Canadian exporters.

Visit www.edcinfo.com or call us at 1-800-532-2220

Export Development Corporation   EDC SEE   Minimize risk. Export with confidence.

The Export Development Corporation (EDC) is a Crown corporation that operates as a commercial financial institution. EDC has been helping Canadian businesses grow through exports and international investment since 1944. The trade finance solutions offered by EDC can help exporters compete in more than 200 countries, including higher-risk and emerging markets.

Alison Derry

The federal and provincial governments in Canada are continually reducing their involvement in the economic life of the country. For example, the federal government sold Crown corporations such as Petro-Canada and Air Canada.

Special Financial Role of Two Provincial Crown Corporations The Alberta Heritage Savings Trust Fund was established in the 1970s, when the Alberta economy was prospering as a result of the oil boom and the government set aside part of its oil royalty revenue to start the fund. The Fund's assets total $12.1 billion. It must operate on a sound financial basis, but, as much as possible, it makes investment decisions that will benefit Alberta.

Quebec has the Caisse de dépôt et placement du Québec, a giant fund that was established to handle the funds collected by the Quebec Pension Plan. At $100 billion, it is one of the largest pools of funds in North America. This plan was set up parallel to the Canada Pension Plan in 1966. The fund also handles other Quebec government funds and is a very powerful investment vehicle that is used to guide economic development in Quebec. Although it too must operate on a sound financial basis, it has a lot of scope to make decisions that will benefit the Quebec economy.

A Smaller Role for Government

Elections in Canada in the 1990s saw provincial and federal governments of all parties embark upon a series of measures

---

SPOTLIGHT ON SMALL BUSINESS ——————————————— *www.bdc.ca*

Business Development Bank of Canada

One Crown corporation that is particularly helpful to business is the federal Business Development Bank of Canada (BDC). The bank has been in operation since the mid-1940s and has been invaluable for small and medium-sized businesses. The BDC originally functioned only as a lender—the bank of last resort—but over the years it has developed into a multiservice organization. In the late 1990s the BDC embarked on an aggressive marketing campaign explaining its services to small and medium-sized businesses.

The BDC not only lends money to businesses that cannot get loans from commercial banks, but it also invests in enterprises that are just starting up or expanding. The owners have the right to buy out the BDC holdings in their companies any time in the future at the value then prevailing. When the BDC takes an equity position (buys shares in a company), this often encourages other investors or lenders who might otherwise have been reluctant to participate.

Its emphasis now is on helping businesses that are export-oriented and in the "new economy." That is, businesses that are in high-tech and are thus in areas where

the Canadian and global economies are continuing to evolve. As part of the process of helping such small and medium-sized businesses function and grow, BDC offers counselling services that are focused on the specific needs of these companies.

Another service provided by the BDC is the Automated Information for Management (AIM). This large database contains useful information for small and medium-sized businesses. It lists all assistance programs available from all levels of government in Canada, sources of information, and various business opportunities all over the country.

Among BDC's publications is a bimonthly publication, *Profits*, with useful articles and information for entrepreneurs and small businesses. The autumn issue highlights Small Business Week. This annual event started in British Columbia in 1979, takes place in a different province each year, and includes "business fairs, exhibits, workshops, conferences, luncheons, award ceremonies, and much more."

Adapted from: Business Development Bank of Canada. Sources: BDC, Profit, and annual reports.

designed to continue the reduction of government's role in the economic life of the country. Former large Crown corporations like Teleglobe Canada, Air Canada, Alberta Government Telephone, and Petro-Canada have been sold off. Saskatchewan reduced its interest in giant uranium producer Cameco Corp., Quebec was trying to sell its stake in Domtar Inc., and Alberta is trying to dispose of the Alberta Petroleum Marketing Commission.

PROGRESS CHECK

- What are three of the seven categories of government intervention in the economy?
- What does privatization refer to? Can you cite any examples?
- What are Crown corporations? Why are they set up? Can you name three?

LAWS AND REGULATIONS

Registration

Governments need to know what businesses are in operation to ensure that a wide range of laws and regulations are being followed. Ensuring that names of businesses are not duplicated is important to avoid confusion. Additionally, governments have to be sure that all taxes are being paid. To achieve these and other goals, every company must register at the appropriate provincial authority when it commences business. This is a simple, routine, and inexpensive procedure.

In addition, all corporations must obtain **articles of incorporation**. This is a legal authorization from the federal or a provincial government for a company to use the corporate format. Incorporation is usually done through a legal firm and is discussed in detail in Chapter 6. Governments, and the public at large, thus have a record of the existence of every corporation in Canada.

articles of incorporation
The legal documents, obtained from the federal or provincial governments, authorizing a company to operate as a corporation.

Reporting and Information

Businesses receive many documents from governments during the course of the year. Some are just information about changes in employment insurance, Canada or Quebec Pension Plan, or tax legislation as it affects them and their employees. Then there are various statistics forms that all companies must complete so that governments can compile reports that businesses, individuals, research organizations, and governments need to operate more effectively.

Statistics Canada (StatsCan) maintains vast databases that it creates from these reports and from many other sources, including international databases. StatsCan issues many quarterly, semi-annual, or annual reports on a host of topics. It also publishes a variety of special reports at irregular intervals. Some of them are quoted in this text.

All corporations must also file annual reports containing basic data about themselves: for example, how many shares have been issued, who the officers and directors are, and where the head office is located. Of course, every company must also file annual tax returns containing financial statements and pay the necessary income and other taxes during the year.

TAXATION OF COMPANIES

Each level of government collects some kind of taxes from companies to give it the income it needs to discharge its legal obligations. The main source of income for municipalities is taxes on property, but there are a variety of other taxes and fees as well. Federal and provincial governments rely mostly on income taxes on individuals and corporations. Provincial sales taxes are also an important source of revenue for the provinces (only Alberta has no sales tax), while the goods and services tax (GST) brings very substantial moneys to the federal government. In some provinces, health care is financed by a tax on the total wages and salaries paid by companies.

Taxes on businesses are considered part of the cost of doing business and thus are included in the prices they charge. Small corporations get a tax break; they pay about half the normal income tax rates. Manufacturing corporations also get a reduced rate. Various other fiscal (taxation) devices are discussed in the next section.

Fiscal Measures to Influence the Economy

One purpose of taxation, as we have just seen, is to raise funds for government needs. Governments also use taxation to help the economy move in a desired direction. For example, taxes may be lowered to stimulate the economy when it is weak. Similarly, taxes may be raised when the economy is booming to cool it off and slow down inflation.

fiscal policy
The use of taxation to stimulate or restrain various aspects of the economy or the economy as a whole.

Taxation is often used in more subtle ways to stimulate or restrain various aspects of the economy or the whole economy. This is called **fiscal policy**. For example, to stimulate the economy the government may ease the taxation load of the construction industry, a basic industry that affects many others. When that industry begins to move, the spinoff effect means more equipment, vehicles, and material supplies are purchased. More homes, offices, and factories built and sold lead to more sales of furniture and appliances and new mortgages and insurance, thus stimulating a wide range of industries and services. When government deems the economy to be overheated and inflation is a problem, it implements the opposite policy.

Federal and provincial governments constantly use the lever of fiscal policy to stimulate specific geographic and industrial areas. They offer special tax credits to companies that open plants in areas of chronically high unemployment, such as Cape Breton, the Gaspé, or Newfoundland. All companies that invest in specific activities considered desirable (such activities vary from time to time but usually include manufacturing, processing, or scientific research) receive a tax credit that reduces the income tax they have to pay. Many of these programs have been scaled back or eliminated due to budgetary restraints.

How Governments Spend Tax Dollars to Help Business

Governments in Canada disburse tens of billions of dollars annually in old-age pensions, allowances to low-income families or individuals, employment insurance, welfare, workers' compensation, and various other payments to individuals. These vast sums put a lot of consumer buying power into the hands of Canadians. As they spend these dollars, large numbers of Canadian companies and their employees benefit. Governments, in turn, collect taxes on the profits of these companies and on the salaries and wages of their employees. Increasing or lowering the rates or eligibility for these payments results in further fine-tuning of the economy. Again, lack of money has resulted in the reduction of such payments in recent years.

A Canadian CF-18 hornet fighter pilot takes off from Aviano Air Base in Italy. The military acquisitions program in Canada requires that whatever can be produced or serviced in Canada be acquired from Canadian companies.

Courtesy of Department of National Defense.

Government Purchasing Policies

Most governments are very large purchasers and consumers of goods and services; indeed, in Canada they are the largest buyers. The federal and provincial governments use this enormous purchasing power to favour Canadian companies. The provinces favour those companies in their own territories, and have even set up important trade barriers between provinces (discussed below). When advanced technology items, civilian or military, must be obtained from foreign companies, our governments usually insist that a certain minimum portion must be manufactured in Canada. This enables Canadian companies to acquire advanced technology know-how and to provide employment.

Contracts are awarded most often to help Canadian businesses even if they are sometimes more expensive than bids by non-Canadian companies. This is particularly true in the significant military acquisitions programs. Whatever can be produced or serviced in Canada—ships, electronics, trucks, artillery, ammunition—is acquired from Canadian companies. These federal and provincial policies are being modified as a result of the NAFTA and the GATT as part of the general movement to freer trade. Oddly enough, in many cases it is easier to trade with foreign countries than between provinces. We look at this anomaly next.

No Free Trade between Provinces

The provincial governments have erected walls between the provinces that practically rule out interprovincial government acquisitions. The municipal governments within a province also follow this procedure. These protectionist policies favour the companies in each province, but almost eliminate normal free trade and competition. They also create other distortions by insisting, for example, that a beer company must have a plant in a province if it wants to sell beer there, preventing the normal cost savings that could be achieved with fewer but larger plants. Larger-scale production would result in lower costs, called **economies of scale**, and therefore lower prices to consumers. Lower costs would make many Canadian companies more competitive on the international scene, especially with American firms.

economies of scale
The cost savings that result from large-scale production.

A case that drew a lot of attention a few years ago was a paving job in the town of Aylmer, Quebec, near the Ontario border. The town bought bricks from an Ontario company, but was forced by the provincial government to pull them up and replace them with Quebec bricks. This is an extreme example of a common problem in Canada. "By one estimate there are more than 500 trade barriers between provinces," according to an article in the *Montreal Gazette*.[3]

> For a country that was supposed to have eliminated barriers to trade [within the country] 125 years ago, Canada in some ways behaves more like a collection of warring principalities than a single economic unit. Ontario consumers can't buy milk from Quebec or Manitoba. Quebec wouldn't buy busses from an Ontario plant until the plant moved to Quebec. A phone company in one province won't buy telephone wire from another [province]. Nova Scotia's Moosehead beer is readily available in the U.S., but not in other provinces. [Author's note: American beer is readily available in Canada.]

There is mounting pressure for the provinces to end this uneconomic behaviour, which is estimated to cost the Canadian economy up to $6 billion annually. When we are in a recession and Canada's ability to compete internationally is in doubt, we cannot afford such additional costs.

The question of protectionism comes up regularly at annual meetings of provincial ministers. Everybody agrees that something must be done, but as each year passes no detectable changes take place. The reason is clear: removal of barriers would mean a difficult period of adjustment as each province loses jobs due to the closing of uncompetitive operations. It is strange that provinces that supported the FTA and NAFTA enthusiastically seem to fear provincial competition more than they fear American companies.

PROGRESS
CHECK

- What is Statistics Canada? How is it useful to Canadian businesses?
- What is fiscal policy? What are two purposes of the federal taxation system?
- How do government expenditures affect business? What are three broad categories of such expenditures?
- Are there any barriers to trade among the provinces? What developments will have an effect on this situation?

Other Government Expenditures

Governments spend huge sums of money on education, health, roads, ports, waterways, airports, and various other services required by businesses and individuals. They also provide direct aid to business.

There are many direct and indirect government programs designed to help businesses. Governments also intervene on an ad hoc (special, unplanned) basis in important cases. The Chrysler and de Havilland cases discussed later in the chapter are examples of this. Aid to Saskatchewan farmers and Newfoundland and B.C. fishers when their industries faced severe hardships are other examples.

Direct Intervention   All levels of government offer a variety of direct assistance programs to businesses, including grants, loans, loan guarantees, consulting advice, information, and other aids that are designed to achieve certain purposes. One of the largest special cases occurred early in the 1980s, when a combined Canadian and U.S. government loan guarantee to banks in excess of $1 billion was required to save Chrysler Corp. from collapsing. Had it gone bankrupt, many companies that were creditors of Chrysler would have been dragged down as well and hundreds of thousands of jobs would have been lost in both countries.

Some government aid is designed to help industries or companies that are deemed to be very important—at the cutting edge of technology, providing highly skilled jobs, and oriented toward exports. Thus Ottawa was considering a $150 million aid package for the aerospace industry "to keep this high-tech industry from moving to other countries which offer such inducements."[4]

Similarly, the federal and Ontario governments and Spar Aerospace Ltd. took a "huge gamble" developing an all-weather radar satellite that has the potential "to start a new multibillion-dollar industry in Canada." Both governments combined bore 51 percent of the cost and have the rights to 51 percent of the data. The U.S. government did likewise for a 15-percent stake. The first results made the space scientists at Spar "whoop for joy" as they saw a clear image of Cape Breton Island produced through the rain and in the dark.[5]

Pratt & Whitney Canada Inc., after getting nearly $12 million from the federal and Quebec governments to develop a new aircraft engine—the PW 150 for the de Havilland Dash 8-400 commuter aircraft—was "threatening to move the project outside Canada unless Ottawa [gave] it more." In 1998 the company again warned that it might have to close down. Since this is a $200-million project, both governments agreed to an $11.7-million interest-free loan as part of a $45.7-million program under the Canada-Subsidiary Agreement for Industrial Development.[6]

Major companies often hint or even announce outright that they are planning to close a large plant that they claim is not efficient enough to be competitive. They often suggest they will consolidate operations with other plants in Canada or the United States. These announcements naturally result in a flurry of efforts by all affected parties to prevent the closure. Unions, municipalities, and provincial and federal governments all work to save the jobs and economies of the area. There are many examples of such cases in the last decade.

Auto plants, pulp and paper mills, food processing plants, oil refineries, shipbuilding yards, meat-packing plants, steel mills, and other industries across the

SPOTLIGHT ON BIG BUSINESS
www.bombardier.com

A Rescue Package for an Ailing Giant

In January 1992, in a joint scheme, the Ontario and federal governments announced a $490-million aid package to facilitate a deal whereby Bombardier Inc. of Montreal bought 51 percent and the Ontario government 49 percent of the shares of de Havilland Aircraft in Toronto to save the company from closing. There were many reasons why saving this company was considered vital: it was the largest employer in the Toronto area, with some 4,500 employees still working there after several reductions in workforce, and it had the potential to compete globally since the previous owner, giant Boeing Aircraft Co. of the United States, had spent huge sums acquiring, modernizing, and updating production facilities (with generous grants from both levels of government in Canada). Unfortunately, the deep recession and other factors led Boeing to throw in the towel after several cuts in the workforce.

Bombardier had earned a solid reputation with its successful acquisition of similar troubled companies in the United States and Northern Ireland. As a result Bombardier had become a world leader in the small-aircraft field, which many believe is one of the high-tech industries of the future. In addition, the recession and other factors had seen hundreds of plant closings and hundreds of thousands of jobs lost in Ontario. This combination of social, political, and economic factors led the Ontario and federal governments to ask Bombardier to continue its string of successful takeovers. Bombardier, with its record of sound financial analysis and management, insisted on the substantial aid package from the governments to lay a foundation for the future of de Havilland. Subsequent developments indicate that this deal worked well for all parties.

The continued successes and growth of Bombardier show how a carefully planned government aid package can be a great advantage to all parties: more Canadians got jobs, governments at all levels collected more taxes, Bombardier developed advanced technology and planes and became a leading exporter and transnational corporation, and the company generated more profits for its shareholders. In sum, the Canadian economy received many times over what the government invested.

---

country have faced such closures. In many cases the closures could not have been prevented. But the General Motors plant north of Montreal and the de Havilland plant north of Toronto, among others, were saved by such concerted action. (See the Spotlight on Big Business box "A Rescue Package for an Ailing Giant.")

A newspaper report shows how the Ontario and federal governments combined with the steelworkers' union, banks, and shareholders to prevent the Algoma Steel mill in Sault Ste. Marie, Ontario, from closing. This involved government aid and employee purchase of the plant.[7] A similar rescue of the troubled Sydney Steel complex in Sydney, Nova Scotia in 1981 ended with the Nova Scotia government buying the company. In Alberta, the government had intervened to keep some meat-packing plants alive.

Many of these rescue efforts end in costly failures. For example, the Nova Scotia government announced in February 1992 that it would have to sell or close Sydney Steel, after having spent almost a billion dollars over a decade to modernize it and make it competitive. In January 1999 the federal government announced to a shocked community that it was going to end its long-time financial support of the Cape Breton Development Corp. (Devco), a coal mining operation. After pouring more than a billion dollars into covering deficits, the government decided to close or sell off the mines as there was no hope of profitable operations.[8] Was it

Government, unions, and private business sometimes join forces to save a company from closing. This happened in the case of the Algoma Steel Mill in Sault Ste. Marie, Ontario.

Courtesy of Algoma Steel

worth it to spend such sums to provide hundreds of jobs in chronically depressed Cape Breton? Was it the best way to help the unemployed in this area of high unemployment? These types of questions are constantly being asked in Canada.

www.acoa.ca

A visit to the Web site for the Atlantic Canada Opportunities Agency will introduce you to the range of projects it has engaged in as it seeks to facilitate development in its region. Start by selecting the *About Us* button, and then explore its range of activities. See if you can find other Web sites for parallel agencies.

Equalization Transfer Programs   Canada is a very large country with uneven resources, climate, and geography, which has led to uneven economic development. Ontario and Quebec, with large populations, proximity to the United States, an abundance of all kinds of natural resources, and excellent rail and water transport, were the earliest to develop industrially.

Nova Scotia and New Brunswick began to suffer when wooden ships gave way to metal ships in the last half of the 1800s and their lumber industries declined. The west was sparsely populated until well into the twentieth century. Alberta and British Columbia became strong industrially only in the last 30 years as oil, gas, coal, hydroelectric power, and forestry became significant competitive resources for them. Saskatchewan and Manitoba are essentially tied to the volatile agricultural industry. Newfoundland, which became part of Canada in 1949 and was far behind the average Canadian living standard, has relied mainly on fisheries and pulp and paper. With the collapse of the cod fishery, Newfoundland now looks to the development of the offshore Hibernia and other oilfields to become major factors in its economic growth in the twenty-first century. Nova Scotia is counting on development of the huge gas fields off Sable Island. The Yukon, the Northwest Territories, and Nunavut are very lightly populated and have difficult climates.

A long-standing system of payments (transfers) to poorer provinces, which was financed by the wealthier ones (Ontario, B.C., Alberta), is being gradually reduced by the federal government.

CRITICAL THINKING

Advances in technology are extremely important to keep a country globally competitive. Since governments do not have unlimited amounts of money to spend, they may have to focus on a few areas. Would it be wise for Canadian governments to concentrate on advanced technology? Should they, in conjunction with business, pick some high-tech industries and give them substantial support? Should this include a major effort to get more students to pursue scientific and engineering careers?

THE EFFECT OF OTHER DEPARTMENTS AND REGULATIONS ON BUSINESS

We will now take a closer look at some of the major departments of the federal government that handle these and other activities. There are corresponding departments in many of the provinces, especially the four largest, most developed ones: Ontario, Quebec, B.C., and Alberta.

Department of Industry (Industry Canada)

www.ic.gc.ca

Industry Canada's corporate information Web site provides a wealth of information about the department, its mandate, and the corporate outlook in Canada.

For many years the federal government has had a variety of programs to help small businesses get started. In Chapter 7 you will see a detailed account of how this aid works. The programs are part of a larger one that involves setting up Canada Business Service Centres in every province and territory. These centres are operated jointly with provincial governments and certain local organizations. Industry Canada publishes brochures, booklets, and guides informing business people of the help available and how and where to get it. Industry Canada also participates in the production of publications that promote Canadian businesses internationally: for an example see the Reaching Beyond Our Borders box "Government Aid to High-Technology Companies."

REACHING BEYOND OUR BORDERS

www.dfait-maeci.gc.ca/menu-e.asp
www.ic.gc.ca

Government Aid to High-Technology Companies

The importance of high-technology and global business to a modern economy are repeatedly stressed in this book. Governments in Canada are concerned with the progress of companies in these fields. Two federal departments play important roles in assisting such companies: Foreign Affairs and International Trade, and Industry Canada. Together with Investment Canada and in co-operation with research and technology associations, they publish many informative brochures and listings of Canadian companies active in specific fields. They distribute these to companies overseas and arrange for their representatives to meet with Canadian company representatives.

High-Technology Opportunity: If Software Is Your Business, Canadian Partners Can Make the Difference is a glossy, full-colour brochure with a multilingual introduction. Included in this attractive package is detailed information on all Canadian software companies with good track records. Some of them are already well known to the international business community. The aim is to promote joint ventures and other tie-ins with these companies. This package is of great benefit to the hundreds of smaller high-tech companies that cannot afford such expenditures themselves.

Adapted from: Various publications of Investment Canada and the Departments of Foreign Affairs and International Trade and Industry Canada.

Other programs are designed to encourage businesses to establish themselves or expand in economically depressed areas of the country—populated regions that are industrially underdeveloped, have high unemployment, and lower standards of living. Such regions that were previously mentioned in this chapter include Cape Breton Island of Nova Scotia, the Gaspé area of Quebec, and Newfoundland. The programs include help for the tourist industry and for aboriginal residents of remote areas who want to establish businesses.

Industry Canada also administers a variety of laws affecting consumers and businesses. A later section in this chapter reviews a number of important laws relating to consumer protection. Companies wanting to incorporate federally must apply to this department for articles of incorporation. Industry Canada maintains a complete registry of all companies incorporated under federal law. (Companies may also be incorporated under an equivalent provincial department.) Annual reports are required to keep the register up to date; it is open to public inspection.

The department also administers the Competition Act, which aims to make sure that mergers of large corporations will not restrict competition and that fair competition exists among businesses. The act covers discriminatory pricing, price fixing, misleading advertising, and refusal to deal with certain companies, among other activities.

The federal Bureau of Competition Policy and the Competition Tribunal are busy organizations whose work is constantly in the news. Three recent examples: they challenged the Interac monopoly on electronic payments;[9] they ended a monopoly that ACNielsen had on the "vast data generated by check-out scanners at supermarkets and drugstores across Canada";[10] they investigated a proposed takeover by American food giant Archer-Daniels-Midland of four Maple Leaf flour mills.[11]

In 1998 the Bureau was faced with perhaps one of the most important issues it had ever dealt with. Two proposals involving mergers of the largest banks in Canada, one of the Royal Bank with the Bank of Montreal and the other the CIBC with Toronto Dominion, generated fierce and widespread discussion across the country. The Bureau had the difficult tasks of deciding whether the proposed mergers would reduce competition, and, if so, if it would stop them. The issues were complex, with the banks arguing that they had to merge to stay in the race with the global banking giants, many of which arose out of mergers in the U.S. and Switzerland. Once again we see how the globalization of business has a direct impact on Canada. Opponents argued that competition would decline in Canada and service, especially to seniors, would also decline, as more branches would close and many employees would lose their jobs. The Bureau finally recommended against allowing the mergers and the minister of finance, who has the final say on matters relating to banks, accepted that recommendation.

Department of Communications

The Department of Communications is responsible for the Canadian Radio-television and Telecommunications Commission (CRTC). The CRTC grants licences to radio stations, TV stations, and cable companies for limited periods, usually one to three years. Public hearings are held at licence-granting and renewal times so that anyone can criticize or voice opposition to such renewals. The CRTC also regulates the types of programs and the minimum percentage of Canadian content. It must approve at public hearings all rate and service changes of cable and federally incorporated telephone and telegraph companies.

A typical example of a CRTC activity is its ruling ordering Teleglobe Canada Inc., which has a monopoly on all overseas calls, to reduce its rates by 35 percent over a four-year period.[12] The CRTC has also made many difficult decisions regarding control of satellite dishes and disputes between cable and telephone companies as technology opens up new possibilities for formerly very different companies that now seek to exploit the same technology or markets.

Transport Canada

Transport Canada administers a number of acts, including the Motor Vehicle Transportation Act and the National Transportation Act. These Acts cover all modes of interprovincial transportation in Canada. The National Transportation Agency grants licences, hears complaints, makes sure safety regulations are being followed, and investigates train and plane accidents. The department has inspectors on the road. You can sometimes see their cars beside trailer trucks stopped for inspection.

Department of Finance

www.bank-banque-canada.ca

Visit the Bank of Canada Web site for information about the Bank and a wide range of financial information and data about Canada. See, for example, the discussion of monetary policy at <www.bank-banque-canada.ca/en/monetary.htm>

monetary policy
The Bank of Canada's exercise of control over the supply of money and the level of interest rates in the country.

One of the most influential ministries is the Department of Finance. It has overall responsibility for setting tax (fiscal) and financial policy and thus has a major impact on Canadian business. The annual budget presented to Parliament, usually every spring, by the minister of finance is a major event. The budget is a comprehensive document that reveals government financial policies for the coming year: it shows how much revenue the government expects to collect, any changes in income and other taxes, and whether expenditures will exceed income (resulting in a deficit).

Bank of Canada   A major agency of the Department of Finance is the Bank of Canada, an independent body run by a board of governors appointed by the government. The minister of finance (or his or her deputy minister) attends board meetings but has no vote. The Bank of Canada has two main responsibilities. One is to oversee the operations of all federally chartered banks, which means nearly all the banks in Canada. The banks all report to the Bank of Canada regularly. Some reports are required daily, some weekly, and some monthly.

The second responsibility is to set **monetary policy**, which means to control the supply of money in the country and influence the level of interest rates. Controlling the supply of money in Canada is very complex and involves a variety of methods. You may be most familiar with the determination of the appropriate level of interest rates at any particular time. From time to time the bank announces the rate it will charge commercial banks for borrowing—mostly a symbolic gesture, as these banks do not do much borrowing from the Bank of Canada. The bank rate mainly gives the banks guidelines as to whether they should be raising or lowering their interest rates or leaving them unchanged.

In 2001, when the economy continued the decline that started the previous year, the Bank commenced a series of interest-rate cuts that soon took on historic proportions. With the terrorist attacks of September 11 further weakening an already declining economy the Bank continued its rate cuts; by mid-November there had been a record eight rate reductions for the year totalling an unprecedented 3 percent, and the rate was at its lowest level in 40 years. More cuts were expected by the financial community before the year was out.

As usual we had been influenced by what was happening in the affairs of our largest customer, the United States. There, the Federal Reserve Board had an even more astounding record—it had cut rates an unheard-of 10 times. In both countries these actions pointed to financial authorities attempting to carry out their legal responsibility to help the economy recover.

In 1998 the Canadian dollar dropped to historic lows against the U.S. dollar, falling to 63 cents. Many voices were heard demanding that the Bank of Canada, now under a new governor, Gordon Theissen, raise interest rates to help boost the dollar to a higher exchange value. Many other voices said the Bank should do nothing. By mid-1999 the dollar was up to 68 cents. However, in late 2001 it was hovering in the 62- to 63-cent range, which was a new low. The Bank of Canada keeps a constant eye on the value of the Canadian dollar and other matters to carry out its mandate of setting proper monetary policy.

Photo: W.P. McElligot

The Bank of Canada, located in Ottawa, oversees the operations of all federally chartered banks and sets monetary policy for the country.

PROGRESS **CHECK**

- What are three forms of direct government aid to business? Two forms of indirect aid?

- Name four large companies that owe their existence to such aid. Why was such aid extended?

- How do governments help poorer regions of Canada?

- Why is the Department of Finance so important? What is the annual budget it prepares and why does it attract so much attention?

PROTECTING **C**ONSUMERS

The Department of Industry administers many laws designed to protect consumers. These laws have a great impact on companies, which must make sure their policies and operations conform with legal requirements. Some of the major consumer protection laws are shown in Figure 4.2.

All of these acts, and others under the jurisdiction of other federal or provincial departments, are designed to protect and inform consumers. Every time you buy an agricultural product, you are assured that someone has inspected it or a sample of the batch it came from. The list of ingredients and expiration date are there because of a regulation. The same applies to the clothes you wear, which have a label showing country of origin, size, type of fabric, and washing instructions.

Similarly, you are assured that all the food, drugs, toys, and other products you buy do not contain anything hazardous. Whether you buy a kilogram of grapes or 25 litres of gasoline, you can feel confident that you have gotten a true measure because there is a sticker on the equipment showing when it was last inspected. The provinces have various laws giving consumers the right to cancel contracts or return goods within a certain time of signing or purchase. It is just about impossible to get through

Samples of agricultural products such as fruit and vegetables are inspected before they ever make their way onto store shelves. Such inspection is required to ensure the public consumes only safe and healthy produce.

a day without being helped in some way by legislation or regulation. Similarly, a company cannot get through a day without being affected by various laws.

Canada Deposit Insurance Corporation

www.cdic.ca

Visit the CDIC Web site to find out about its mission statement. The section on *how deposit insurance works* sets out the basic principles of the protection provided.

A body that plays an important role in protecting the consumer is the Canada Deposit Insurance Corporation (CDIC). The CDIC insures individual deposits in banks and trust companies against these institutions' failure or collapse. The CDIC guarantees deposits up to $60,000 and is funded by annual premium payments from all banks and trust companies that want to have their customers' deposits insured, which in practice means just about all such financial institutions. The CDIC reports to the chair of the Treasury Board, who is a minister of state in the government.

FIGURE 4.2

SOME MAJOR FEDERAL CONSUMER PROTECTION LAWS

These laws all provide consumers with information and protection, in various ways. There are also provincial consumer protection laws.

Canadian Agricultural Products Standards Act covers a wide range of farm products, such as meat, poultry, eggs, maple syrup, honey, and dairy products.

Consumer Packaging and Labelling Act applies to all products not specifically included in other acts.

Food and Drug Act covers a whole range of regulations pertaining to quality, testing, approval, packaging, and labelling.

Hazardous Products Act covers all hazardous products.

National Trademark and True Labelling Act includes not only labelling, but also accurate advertising.

Textile Labelling Act includes apparel sizing and many other special areas.

Weights and Measures Act applies to all equipment that measure quantities (scales, gas pumps, and so forth).

Provincial Regulation of Business

The consumer as investor is protected by various laws that lay down the procedures companies must follow to attract investors or lenders through public offerings. Companies seeking public financing must issue a **prospectus**, which provides minimum specified information about the company and its officers and directors to better inform potential investors. This document must be approved by the **securities commission** in the province where public funding is being sought. This is the official body set up by a province to regulate its stock exchange and to approve all new issues of securities in that province.

It is expensive to produce a prospectus, because it requires a lot of input from legal and accounting firms before it can be approved. This cost must be borne by the company that is seeking public financing. There are five stock exchanges in Canada—Toronto, Montreal, Calgary, Vancouver, and Winnipeg—and a securities commission in each of the provinces where these cities are located. One of their aims is to ensure that the small investor is not taken advantage of by powerful or unscrupulous companies or individuals. All companies whose shares are listed on the stock exchanges must issue quarterly reports to their shareholders, as well as annual reports. There are many other provisions in these regulations, which vary somewhat from province to province.

One common regulation makes it illegal for *insiders*—those with inside or private information not yet available to the public—to take advantage of the information. Insiders cannot engage in securities transactions (the sale or purchase of stocks and bonds and related instruments) based on inside information for their personal gain.

For example, suppose your sister told you that her company was about to announce that it had had an unusually profitable period, which would likely send the price of the company's share up sharply. You rushed to buy some shares; when they rose quickly after the announcement, you sold them and made a nice profit in a few days. This is insider trading and is illegal.

All businesses must comply with the consumer protection requirements that affect them. Although this may add to the costs of doing business, everybody is in the same boat, so no company has an edge over any competitor. Furthermore, similar conditions exist in most industrialized countries, so the level playing field extends beyond the borders of Canada. The international competitiveness of Canadian companies is not usually weakened by such regulations.

The Impact of Municipalities on Business

Municipalities also play a role in consumer protection. They all have regulations and laws regarding any establishment that serves food. Inspectors regularly examine the premises of all restaurants for cleanliness. If you look carefully in your local newspaper, you will see lists of restaurants fined for not maintaining required standards.

There are similar laws about noise, smells, signs, and other activities that may affect a neighbourhood. These are called zoning laws because certain zones are restricted to residences only and others permit only certain quiet businesses to operate.

Zoning requirements also limit the height of buildings in certain zones and how far back they must be set from the road. Most Canadian cities require that all high-rise buildings have a certain ratio of garage space so that cars have off-street parking places. Parking problems in residential areas due to overflow of vehicles from adjacent businesses have led to parking being limited to residential permit holders on certain streets, so stores and other places of business must offer commercial parking lots for their customers. Of course, we are all familiar with speed limits set by municipal or provincial authorities.

All businesses must usually obtain a municipal licence to operate so the appropriate department may track them to make sure they are following regulations. Many municipalities also have a business tax and charge for water consumption.

prospectus
A document, which must be prepared by every public company seeking financing through issue of shares or bonds, that gives the public certain information about the company. A prospectus must be approved by the securities commission of the province where these securities will be offered for sale.

securities commission
The official body set up by a province to regulate its stock exchange and to approve all new issues of securities in that province.

www.osc.gov.on.ca

The Ontario Securities Commission Web site provides a full range of information related to the OSC. Look at the section called *about the OSC* to learn how it operates. Skim its rules and regulations to get the flavour of its mandate.

LABOUR STANDARDS AND WORKING CONDITIONS

In later chapters you will learn about the many federal and provincial laws and regulations that affect companies' conditions of employment. We tend to take for granted minimum wages, vacation pay, and a host of other working conditions. Figure 4.3 lists some of the major issues that are affected by legislation.

Figure 4.3 is only a partial list of the legal requirements that employers must meet. The many laws across Canada that protect workers have accumulated over more than 100 years. As the standards of civilized or acceptable behaviour evolved in Canada, laws were passed to reflect these rising expectations. It is a continuing process that sees new developments every few years. One of the most recent issues to evolve is pay equity for women (discussed in Part 4).

ENVIRONMENTAL REGULATIONS

Chapter 5 reviews the importance of concerns with the impact of production activities on our physical environment. These concerns have led to regulatory requirements that are changing how companies operate.

We are all well acquainted with many of the serious consequences to our environment from the uncontrolled operations and growth of industry. We are now faced with the huge problems caused by certain dirty industrial processes and the mountains of waste that are an inevitable result of many business operations.

Some environmental problems are product-related. For example, cars are major contributors to pollution, inefficient users of energy, and increasingly less useful for commuting to and from work due to traffic jams. These kinds of problems are what led governments to create ministries of the environment. Now many companies face heavy expenditures of money and management's energy to become *green*, or environmentally responsible. Some farsighted companies are developing technology for waste management and energy-efficient operations that will give them important competitive advantages.

FIGURE 4.3

SOME ASPECTS OF EMPLOYMENT AFFECTED BY LEGISLATION

This is only a partial list.

Banning of child labour.

Minimum wages.

Overtime pay after a normal workweek.

Specified number of paid holidays.

Paid vacations of not less than two or three weeks (or equivalent pay if employed less than one year).

No firing without cause after a specified period of employment.

No discrimination by sex, nationality, colour, or religion in hiring, remuneration, promotion, or firing.

Unpaid or paid maternity or paternity leave.

No unhealthy or unsafe working conditions.

No sexual or racial harassment.

Employment insurance contributions.

Canada or Quebec Pension Plan contributions.

Workers' compensation for employees injured at work.

Employment and Immigration in Canada

Two departments of the federal government that have a major impact on business are the Department of Citizenship and Immigration and the Department of Human Resources Development, which have a direct impact on the nature, size, and skills of the workforce in Canada. A coherent immigration policy helps to ensure a good inflow of required skills for employers. After all, Canada became a modern industrial country with the aid of the skills and financial capital that immigrants brought here.

One of the anomalies of recent times is that despite the high number of people who are unemployed or working at part-time or temporary jobs, there are still many jobs that cannot be filled because of the lack of applicants with the necessary skills.

Federal and provincial ministries are involved in training and retraining schemes designed to overcome this problem. Such programs encourage unemployed people to enroll in colleges to upgrade their skills and support them financially during their retraining period. Other programs to train or retrain workers are joint efforts of governments, unions, and employers in varying combinations. Some will be discussed in more detail in later chapters.

Education and training are becoming increasingly important as low-skilled jobs disappear due to automation and to companies moving to the United States or Mexico. Rapid changes in technology mean that long-term employment in one job or skill is becoming rare. This issue is forcing increased attention to be paid to the whole question of education, training, and retraining, and is capturing a lot of headlines.

Controlling the flow of immigrants to Canada is another major responsibility of the Department of Citizenship and Immigration. There is much pressure from people in many parts of the world who would like to live in Canada. The department tries to ensure that immigrants have the proper skills or finances to fit into the needs of the Canadian economy. Immigrants have always been a vital factor in the development of Canada and will continue to play an important role. The department must try to find that delicate balance between admitting too many immigrants faster than the economy can absorb, and not admitting enough.

National Research Council[13]

One of the best-kept Canadian secrets concerns the National Research Council (NRC), a federal agency that began in 1916. This organization of some 3,000 scientists, researchers, and technicians is Canada's principal science and technology agency. The NRC plays a significant role in research that helps Canadian industry to remain competitive and innovative. Its Canadian Institute for Scientific and Technical Information (CISTI) has the largest international collection of information on science, technology, and medicine in Canada. CISTI gets about half a million requests for information annually. Subscribers to its online system can access this vast worldwide database directly from their own computer terminals.

The NRC operates the Industrial Research Assistance Program (IRAP) and 16 specialized institutes in some major industries of tomorrow, including biotechnology, industrial materials, environmental science and technology, information technology, automated manufacturing, and microelectronics. Eleven of the institutes are in Ottawa and the other five are spread out from St. John's, Newfoundland, to Vancouver, B.C. Every year thousands of Canadian firms receive technical and financial help through the NRC's industry development programs. Its specialized equipment allows companies to conduct tests and experiments that would otherwise not be possible. This service is especially useful for many smaller high-tech firms. The NRC also operates a Research Press and the Canadian Technology Network (CTN), which provide important information for thousands of Canadian businesses.

During the last few years, the budget and staff of the NRC have been repeatedly cut. It is unfortunate that funding has been reduced for such an important organization in an era when technological know-how is one of the major competitive tools for business. There are constant complaints that the amount of spending on R&D in Canada is lower than that of any other advanced industrial country. The federal government has repeatedly committed itself to raise the level of research and development (R&D) spending, which makes it difficult to understand the reduction in NRC funding. In 1998 the government announced some additional funding to partially offset previous reductions.

GOVERNMENT IMPACT OF FARMING BUSINESS

marketing boards
Organizations that control the supply or pricing of certain agricultural products in Canada.

Marketing boards control the supply or pricing of certain agricultural products. They also promote their products by running advertising campaigns, such as this one from the Canadian Egg Marketing Agency.

In Canada we have a special system of **marketing boards**, which control the supply or pricing of certain agricultural products. This supply management is designed to give some stability to an important area of the economy that is normally very volatile. Farmers are subject to conditions that are rather unique and that have a great effect on their business and on our food supply. Weather and disease are major factors in the operation of farms and are beyond the control of the individual farmer. So are unstable prices and changes in supply resulting from uncoordinated decision making by millions of farmers around the world or the exercise of market power by concentrated business organizations.

In the past, farmers have experienced periods of severe drought, flooding, severe cold, and disease that affect crops, livestock, and poultry. The situation regarding international markets and supply has a serious impact on Canada's grain farmers, since we export much more wheat than we consume domestically. This market fluctuates greatly depending on the supply in other major grain-exporting countries like the United States, Argentina, and Australia. The market also depends on demand from major importers like China and Russia, whose abilities to meet their own requirements are subject to wide variation. Often the Canadian government (like other governments) grants substantial loans with favourable conditions to enable these countries to pay for their imports of our wheat and other agricultural products.

As we export some $25 billion of agricultural products annually, the ability to hold our own in international markets has a major impact on the state of the Canadian economy. When farmers are flourishing, they buy new equipment and consumer goods and their communities feel the effects of ample cash flow. So does the transportation industry. Conversely, when farmers are suffering—which unfortunately was the case for most of the 1980s and well into the 1990s—all these sectors hurt as well.

To smooth out the effect of these unusual conditions on this sector of our economy and to ensure a steady supply of food to consumers at reasonable prices, six government agencies have been set up to control poultry, dairy products, and wheat and barley. The Canadian Wheat Board operates in the three Prairie provinces and is the sole legal exporter of wheat and barley produced in those provinces. The Board is also the sole sales agent domestically for industrial use of these products. The Canadian Dairy Commission controls the output and pricing of milk for processing into other dairy products. (Both of these boards are Crown corporations.)

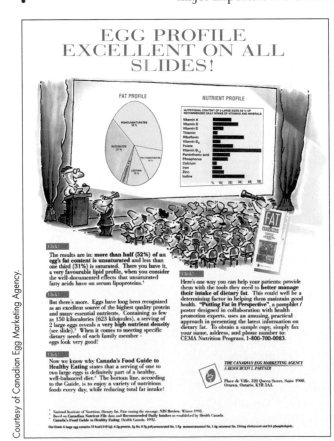

Courtesy of Canadian Egg Marketing Agency.

The Canadian Egg Marketing Agency, Chicken Farmers of Canada, Canadian Turkey Marketing Agency, and Canadian Broiler Hatching Egg Marketing Agency consist of representatives from the provinces that produce these items.

All of these bodies except the Wheat Board control the amount of production for the products under their supervision by allocating quotas to each province that produces them. Provincial agencies administer these quotas and set prices for their province. Each agency controls products that are sold only in its province.

Supply Management in Evolution

A system to manage the supply of agricultural products can be found in many countries, although not necessarily in the same format as in Canada. Various subsidy and indirect support methods can be found almost everywhere. Supply management of farm products is an effective barrier to their entry into Canada, because imports are also subject to the quota system.

The Canadian system of marketing boards has been under attack by various organizations because it does not permit normal competitive conditions to operate in this field. This, they argue, distorts the whole industry and raises prices to Canadian consumers. Defenders of the system argue that other countries, including the United States, have different systems that have the same effect as our marketing boards but are just less visible. The European Union spends many billions of dollars on subsidies for their farmers.

In Chapter 3 we referred to the General Agreement on Tariffs and Trade **>P. 74<**, and to the World Trade Organization that administers it, whose main purpose is to reduce barriers to trade between countries. After lengthy negotiations, Canada agreed in 1994 to a complicated system that replaces the simple restrictive import quota system on these agricultural products. The new system is based on very high tariffs to make it difficult for foreign products to compete with those Canadian agricultural products subject to marketing-board control in Canada. Some people are concerned that this is the thin edge of the wedge leading to the end of our long-standing system of marketing boards.

Meanwhile, the United States claimed that these high tariffs are in violation of NAFTA and filed a formal protest to a binational panel with an outside chair, as provided by NAFTA. The panel ruled in Canada's favour.

Periodically, U.S. farmers have protested the growth of Canadian exports of grains, livestock, pork, and red meat to their country, claiming that Canadian farmers are subsidized. The most recent event occurred in 1998 and made a lot of headlines when farmers in North Dakota physically blocked trucks carrying such Canadian products. The farmers were supported by their own governor as well as governors and farmers in adjacent states. These actions are clearly illegal under NAFTA and other U.S.–Canada agreements. Some subsidization still occurs, and this happens on both sides of the border, such as the contribution of the Quebec government to farm income stabilization programs. However, the growth in Canadian export of grain and livestock to the U.S. in the 1990s is more attributable to other factors, including the combination of a very low Canadian dollar and the cancellation of Canadian grain transportation subsidies under the Western Grain Transportation Act, contributing to lower grain prices and increased livestock production in the Prairie provinces. The tendency for U.S. farmers to protest such growth in Canadian exports to the U.S. and the readiness of U.S. politicians to join the debate increases during an election year, which was the case in 1998, especially when world commodity prices are also low.

The United States, which often complains about other countries' unreasonable trade barriers, as noted above, or about Japanese trade barriers forcing consumers to pay much higher than free market prices for rice, has its own restrictions, such as on peanut and sugar imports. The result is that American consumers pay about 25 percent more than the free market price for sugar.[14]

A spate of articles and reports in the Canadian media in 1995 and 1996 indicated that the whole Canadian agricultural marketing system was undergoing a significant change. The same pressures that led to a freer world market for products and services began to have a serious impact on agriculture. In our country some Alberta wheat farmers are battling the Wheat Board for the right to sell wheat and barley directly and not through the board. The co-op Saskatchewan Wheat Pool has become a public corporation, as has the United Grain Growers of Winnipeg.

Agricultural economists foresee a very different picture emerging worldwide over the next decade: limited protection for domestic markets, reduced tariffs and other restrictions, and the market having a much greater impact on prices and production. The effect on Canadian farmers, and on the whole agricultural industry in general, will be enormous. The next decade will see everyone trying to cope with the necessary adjustments to the new conditions.[15]

We end this chapter with a closer look at national industrial policy.

ROLE OF THE CANADIAN GOVERNMENT DOMESTICALLY AND GLOBALLY

In 1996 most of Canada was still suffering from the very severe recession that had begun in 1990. In the 400 days from the end of 1990 to the beginning of 1992, 1,000 jobs per day were lost, 400,000 in all. Manufacturing was particularly hard-hit. And the carnage continued unabated into 1993.

By the mid-1990s the economy was improving, but it was clear that a new phenomenon had appeared in Canada and in other developed countries: the *jobless recovery*. Our unemployment rate seemed stuck in the 9- to 10-percent range and wasn't expected to improve soon; bankruptcies were at record levels, and plant and office closings and layoffs were still occurring despite many companies reporting record profits.

In early 1996 there were mixed signals about the Canadian economic outlook. Inflation low, interest rates staying down, GDP climbing modestly, exports booming—these were all good signs. British Columbia and Alberta were in better shape and wheat prices had climbed to levels not seen in more than 10 years, giving Prairie farmers a long-awaited boost. New Brunswick was still moving in the right direction, as discussed in the Profile at the start of the chapter. But unemployment and increasing welfare rolls remained serious problems.

By mid-1999 the unemployment situation was better, hovering in the 8- to 8.5-percent range, and forecasts for the economy as measured by GDP growth were more optimistic. The main problem was still the economic weakness and instability in Russia, East and Southeast Asia, and South America. The *Asian flu* ➤**PP. 10, 41**◄ was showing signs of abating. (See Chapter 2 for details on all of these points.)

Many people believe that the best way to protect the Canadian economy is for the federal government to reverse its current direction. Instead of withdrawing from active direction and participation in the economy, as noted in the previous chapter, it should develop a long-term industrial policy of leadership and an active role in shaping the future of the economy. An industrial policy requires close consultation with business and labour to develop a comprehensive program for long-term sustainable industrial development.

Others are opposed in principle to such government involvement. As mentioned previously in this chapter, the 1980s witnessed a movement toward deregulation, privatization, and less government involvement in Canada and in other countries. But the seriousness of the global and economic situation and its impact on Canada are bringing this issue to the forefront once more.

Those who want government to fashion a strategy to lead us back to prosperity and improve Canada's competitive edge point to other countries where this has worked. The best examples are to be found, they say, in Germany, Japan, and the so-called Four Tigers of East Asia: South Korea, Taiwan, Hong Kong, and Singapore. All of these countries are extremely competitive, have trade surpluses, and have developed rapidly economically in the past two decades. These governments continue to play active roles in helping their economies recover from prolonged recessions. In the latter half of the 1990s, financial pages carried many reports of the German and Japanese governments initiating multibillion-dollar projects to give their economies a kick-start and to create jobs. So did the Taiwanese government.[16]

Starting in 1997 and continuing through to early 1999, the East Asian Tigers, as well as Indonesia and Thailand, were having serious economic problems and currency valuation crashes, leading to the Asian flu. Even in Hong Kong, where the government had played a much less interventionist role, it was forced to change tactics. The government intervened strongly when the stock market collapsed and it engaged in substantial buying of shares to shore up the Hong Kong currency and the stock market.

In all of these cases there is no denying that strong government leadership in planning, prioritizing, and direction has contributed to their success. The governments of the European Union (EU) of 15 advanced economies also embarked on an ambitious plan to reduce their serious and pervasive unemployment problems. Faced with some 18 million jobless workers, they decided to consider major expenditures such as transcontinental road and rail links and defence.[17] The question is: Can it work in Canada? We have a different culture; we are a large, dispersed, very diverse, low-density population that rarely unites to pull in the same direction. We have a different history and political structure, with much power dispersed to provincial centres. We are also a democracy, while the Four Tigers have a history of dictatorships (ranging from the brutal to the benign in Singapore).

Germany, however, the country with the greatest exports per capita in the world, is a democracy. Is there anything we can learn from these and other countries about the major role of government in the economy? This question is being increasingly discussed in Canada and even in the United States, where the concept of *laissez-faire* or *leave-it-alone capitalism* is very strong. But even in the U.S. there were important business voices, like the prestigious *Business Weekly* (as noted in Chapter 2), that believed that "free markets need government action to work best."

In the latter half of 1999 and into 2000 the economy was rolling along again, so these discussions were muted or disappeared. Unfortunately, the collapse of the stock market, particularly the high-flying technical and dot-com stocks, in the latter half of 2000 set off a train of poor economic developments in the United States and Canada that continued well into 2001. Major players were hard-hit, including Canada's star performer, Nortel, which began to lay off employees by the thousands. Once again voices were being raised asking governments to *do something*.

The U.S. Federal Reserve Board responded by reducing interest rates an unprecedented six times in the first half of 2001; the Bank of Canada followed the same path, but with fewer and smaller interest-rate cuts. These actions were attempts by independent but government-appointed agencies to stimulate the economies in both countries.

CRITICAL THINKING

You have seen many examples of government initiatives to aid business in Canada. Do we need an overall strategy to plan where our economy should be going? If so, where is the leadership from our major business organizations? Is this a responsibility of government? How relevant are the successful East Asian countries whose governments pursued such a course?

Domestic and Foreign Opinions

A *Financial Post* (now the *National Post*) article disputed that the free market was the best medium for solving society's economic woes. It said, "the only problem with this laissez-faire notion of the world is that it denies history and reality." The article also noted that the management of technology on an international front is long term, large scale, complex, difficult, and risky—and very costly. That is why governments must be involved.

The article gave examples of different countries to show that governments have historically played essential roles in most major developments. The article stressed the role of the American government, as noted in the previous quote, and elaborated on the major contribution of the Japanese government in helping industrial research and development in certain crucial high-tech areas such as superconductivity. In France the government played a critical role in the development of high-speed trains, the supersonic Concorde, and the commercial jet aircraft company Airbus. This company is a joint venture **>P. 10<** of the governments of France, England, Germany, and Spain.

The article concluded that it would be difficult to find a major technology company in the world that did not depend on direct or indirect government support and involvement. Whether it's Boeing or Airbus, the market has hardly been operating in a free and unfettered manner.

The article ended by reminding readers that Canadian history is replete with many successful "examples of government stepping in to produce solutions when the market couldn't," such as the Canadian Pacific Railway, the Trans-Canada Pipeline, Ontario Hydro, Polysar, and our wartime industries during the Second World War.[18]

While many commentators support the continuing shrinkage of governments and their smaller role in the economy, a growing number are taking the opposite tack. Magazines, newspapers, radio, and TV from 1996 to 1999 carried many reports of experts questioning the current trend and worrying about social discontent, as increasing homelessness and poverty, job insecurity, and layoffs took high economic and personal tolls. Many people were also concerned that continuing government cutbacks because of deficit and debt-reduction programs were only aggravating these problems and weakening the education and health-care systems in Canada.[19]

In April 1996 the seven leading industrial countries of the world (Canada is number seven), known as the G7 or Group of Seven, met in France to discuss what could be done about their chronic unemployment problems. Between them the G7 had more than 23 million people unemployed, and that number had been resisting all efforts at reduction. According to *The Economist*, one of the most prestigious magazines in the world, "the Group tried to chart a course between free-marketeers and interventionists."[20]

By the end of 1998 the European unemployment situation was showing no improvement and the Asian flu had heightened fears of the situation worsening. This situation led British Prime Minister Tony Blair to consider calling a meeting of the G7 "to deal with the immediate threat posed by the global financial turmoil."[21]

In June 1999 the Group of Eight (now including Russia) met and decided to aid the recovery of the global economy by reducing the enormous debt to foreign banks and governments of developing poorer countries. These countries would be required to invest the resulting substantial reduction in interest and capital payments, which were a great weight on their economies, into their own infrastructures such as education, health, training, and so on.[22]

We have seen some examples of governments, either directly or through international agencies, intervening in the imperfect functioning of the global free-market system. Other important international voices have been heard questioning whether the time has come for controls of international financial activities by governments through international bodies that represent them. This position reflects the globalized natures of business and economies, which weaken the capacity of national governments to influence events in the direction they deem desirable or necessary.

Two such voices are the Prime Minister of Malaysia, Mahathir Mohamad, and international currency speculator, investor, and philanthropist George Soros. These men have had a running argument since the 1997 collapse of the Malaysian currency and economy that sparked the Asian flu. Mohamad blamed Soros for playing a major role in the Malaysia debacle. In 1999 Mohamad argued that the big powers were controlling the globalization agenda to the detriment of smaller countries like his, and that smaller countries need the freedom to exert some control of their own economies. Soros argued for a change in the roles of the World Bank and the International Monetary Fund so that they could soften the "booms and busts [that] are endemic in financial markets." In effect, Mohamad supports a greater measure of local government involvement, while Soros sees the necessity of government intervention in the global economy via international organizations.[23]

THE INTERTWINING OF ETHICAL AND JOB ISSUES

Government cutbacks in spending not only reduced the number of employees directly working for government in Canada and the number of future job openings, but also had the same effect in the medical and education fields. School and hospital closings occurred nearly everywhere, with similar reductions in employees and job openings. Reduced funding forced colleges and universities to do the same thing. But these cutbacks also raised serious questions about the weakening of the educational system in our country.

With futurists, economists, human resource experts, and others stressing the importance of education in the new information age and the resulting new economy, how can governments justify such cutbacks? How can we train people for tomorrow's jobs and how will Canada remain competitive in this era of tough, globalized business with fewer teachers and professors, larger class sizes, and less funding for education? Administrators are forced to concentrate on budgets instead of on how to improve, update, and modernize the educational process and keep it relevant in a fast-moving world.

So we end the chapter where we started it: looking at the extent of the role that government plays in business. But now we are asking whether it is time to deepen or keep reducing that involvement. What do you think?

ETHICAL DILEMMA

Review

Here's what our two executives have to say about the ways in which Canada tried to reduce its deficit.

Unfortunately, says Bédard, "as the old song would say, when *you owe your soul to the company store* you don't make the decisions or call the shots. Canada was too dependent on the [foreign] banks and their credit rating system to finance current operations." He adds that "again, I feel that Canada did not cut expenses in the proper fashion."

Reilley comments that what was really unethical and irresponsible was to allow our national debt to grow so large. It was unethical not to take steps to reverse the dangerous trend. If any blame is attributable to business it should be "that it didn't, with a loud voice, challenge government's annual deficits much earlier."

PROGRESS
CHECK

- Can you name four laws that are important for consumer protection? What does the CDIC do? How do all of these affect businesses?

- What is a prospectus? What purpose does it serve? How does it affect companies?

- What are two important functions of the Department of Citizenship and Immigration? How do they affect businesses in Canada?

- How does the NRC help technology advancement in Canada? Can you give three specific examples?

- What are marketing boards? What area of business is affected by them?

SUMMARY

1. Explain the historical role of government in the Canadian economy.

1. The Canadian government played a key role from the beginning of the country in 1867 in protecting young manufacturing industries and getting the railroad built to the west coast, helping to bind the country together.
   - *Why did the government have to do what it did?*
   It had the legal power and responsibility. The United States threatened to overwhelm our industry, which was not strong enough by itself to resist or to build the railway.

2. List some of the major Crown corporations in Canada and understand their role in the economy.

2. Crown corporations are one way government did its job.
   - *Why were Crown corporations necessary?*
   Companies were not willing or able to assume certain responsibilities or fill some needs in the marketplace. The CNR, Air Canada, Hydro-Quebec, and Atomic Energy of Canada Ltd. are some important examples. (The CNR and Air Canada are no longer Crown corporations.)

3. Understand how the start-up and operations of companies take place within a framework of government laws and regulations.

3. Companies must be properly registered to have a public record of all business.
   - *Why is registration necessary?*
   Those who do business with a company may want to know who the owners are, when the business started, and other basic information. Governments need to know who is in business to ensure that taxes are paid, statistical data are collected, and information is supplied.

4. Identify major legislation affecting competition in Canada.

4. Many laws and regulations affect competition in Canada.
   - *What is the major piece of federal legislation?*
   The Competition Act is probably the most important act governing competition in Canada.

5. Discuss the role of government in stimulating or restraining the economy.

5. Governments have various methods for stimulating or restraining the economy as they deem necessary.
   - *What are their principal tools?*
   The two main methods are fiscal policy, which adjusts taxation, and monetary policy, which adjusts interest rates and money supply. Monetary policy is the domain of the Bank of Canada.

6. Understand the role of government in consumer and investor protection.

6. Canadian society demands a certain level of consumer and investor protection.
   - *How is this achieved?*
   Each level of government has legislation designed to give such protection. There is a wide range of laws and regulations supervised by consumer protection divisions in government. Investors are protected by provincial security commissions and the CDIC.

7. Many countries have established industrial policies to guide their development.
   • *Why is there controversy in Canada about the desirability of establishing such a policy?*
   Most large businesses lean toward a laissez-faire ideology. They are supported in this thinking by some segments of the population. Other large segments of the country lean toward greater government participation and direction to resolve Canada's economic woes.

7. Understand the controversy over a government industrial policy.

KEY TERMS

articles of
 incorporation 95
Crown
 corporations 90
economies of
 scale 97

fiscal policy 96
industrial policy 91
marketing
 boards 108
monetary policy 102

National Policy 92
privatization 91
prospectus 105
securities
 commission 105

DEVELOPING WORKPLACE SKILLS

1. Scan your local newspapers, *The Globe and Mail*, the *National Post,* or a Canadian magazine like *Canadian Business* for references to government programs of help to Canadian business or a specific company. Bring these articles to class and discuss.

2. Canada is constantly subject to pressure of all kinds from our neighbour to the south. Many American states have strong marketing campaigns to attract Canadian businesses. They also offer many inducements, financial and others, to lure businesses to move there. Should anything be done about this? Most provincial governments have similar programs to attract foreign companies to their jurisdictions. Check out your provincial government's Web site to see what it is doing in this regard. Bring your information to class to discuss this kind of government expenditure.

3. Cross-border shopping continues to be a popular activity. Many Canadians regularly head south to buy gas, cigarettes, clothing, and other consumer goods. This drains billions of dollars from the Canadian economy, hurting businesses, jobs, and government tax revenues. What, if anything, should be done about this problem? What can governments do?

4. Although unemployment remains high, especially among young people, business people complain that they cannot find trained employees to fill existing vacancies. Job candidates lack math and science backgrounds and their written English-language skills are weak. (In Quebec there are similar complaints, but the language problems are in French.) Further, too many are high-school dropouts. What can be done about this serious problem? Should business or government be working on it? What exactly should they be doing?

5. Do some research to see how many points you can find to support each side of the argument concerning a government industrial policy.

TAKING IT TO THE NET

Purpose:
To familiarize students with researching regulations and working within lower level government Web sites.

Exercises:

1. Check out your municipality's Web site to see if you can spot any regulations affecting business that you find surprising. Perhaps the regulation concerns health, parking, necessary permits, or hours of business. Share your findings with your class.

2. Scan the Web site of your local newspaper for any reports of
   a) companies that may have violated any of these municipal regulations
   b) government aid to an existing or new business in your area
   See if you can find some items relating to a) or b) to bring to class for discussion.

PRACTISING MANAGEMENT DECISIONS

CASE 1

GOVERNMENT-OWNED BANKS IN ALBERTA: AN ANOMALY?

Alberta is the only provincial government that owns and operates a bank. Alberta Treasury Branches (ATB) has become a large banking institution in Alberta. ATB serves 239 communities. In 90 of these communities, it is the sole provider of financial services. ATB has 144 branches, 131 agencies, and $11 billion in deposits. The bank generated a record profit of $161 million in the year ended March 31, 2001.

How does it happen that conservative Alberta, with a strong antigovernment, free-enterprise bent, is the only province that owns a bank? The roots of this situation are to be found in the terrible economic depression of the 1930s. Like the rest of Canada, Alberta was flat on its back, so ATB was set up in 1938 to aid Albertans recovering from the Great Depression.

ATB was designed to be of particular use for rural Albertans, who constituted a much larger percentage of the population at that time. ATB was also intended to help small businesses. Originally it was supposed to have a five-year life, just to get the economy going again. ATB has now become a well-established financial institution in Alberta. According to chief operating officer Elmer Leahy, "ATB has been able to provide a measure of stability" through the ups and downs of economic fluctuations.

The only criticisms have been accusations that ATB has moved away from its mandate of concentrating on helping farmers and small businesses by giving loans to big businesses and speculators. ATB has long-range plans to expand into new services at the beginning of the twenty-first century. There has not been any serious movement to privatize the bank at a time when across Canada, including Alberta, many Crown corporations are being sold off.

Decision Questions

1. Should a provincial government be in the banking business? Doesn't this contradict the whole trend toward privatization?
2. Should a Crown corporation be privatized on principle? Even if it is well-run and profitable?
3. What are the main arguments for "getting the government out of business?"
4. How do you feel about this issue? Can you see any situations that justify government owning or operating businesses?

Adapted from: Brent Jang, "Treasury Branches a Special Case," *Globe and Mail, Report on Business,* February 1, 1996, p. B11, reprinted with the permission of the *Globe and Mail*; ATC Web site, <www.atb.com>, September 2001.

CASE 2

GAMBLING: A CASH COW FOR PROVINCIAL GOVERNMENTS

Starting slowly in Quebec in the late 1960s, but catching on quickly across the country, lotteries, casinos, video-lottery terminals (VLTs), and other forms of gambling had become, at the end of the twentieth century, a major source of revenue for many Canadian provincial governments. Quebec went further by heading up a $141-million consortium that built a hotel and casino in Pointe-au-Pic. The hotel is managed by Canadian Pacific Hotels, but the casino is managed by Loto-Quebéc, the government agency that operates all gambling in the province.

You can get some idea of how large the gambling business has become by looking at the revenues and

profits for the Ontario and Quebec governments. For the year ended March 31, 2000 the Ontario Gaming and Lottery Corp. took in $2.2 billion. Loto-Québec has taken in almost $25 billion in its 30 years of operations with its annual revenue now running over $2 billion. In the 30-year period it has yielded the government more than $11 billion in revenue. Both operations allot millions of dollars to help gamblers whose obsession with gambling has proven destructive to themselves or to their families.

Decision Questions

1. Some people and organizations argue that governments should not be in the gambling business, that encouraging gambling is a bad idea. Others

argue that private enterprise should run that kind of business and argue further that companies would generate more profit for governments. Governments reply that they want to keep organized crime from controlling gambling so they must own and run such operations. What do you think? Is it okay for governments to be in business? Should they be in the gambling business?

2. Governments seem to believe that gambling is a great way to raise money because we don't seem to mind creating revenue for them by having some fun, and a chance of big winnings, instead of just paying higher taxes. Besides, they argue, nobody is forced to gamble so it's a kind of voluntary tax. How do you feel about that? Do you buy that argument?

3. Some churches and other institutions concerned with personal and family welfare point to the rising number of family and personal breakdowns caused by people becoming gambling addicts. Also, easy access to VLTs is very bad for young persons. Do you agree with either of these concerns? Why? What can be done to improve the situation?

4. Suppose you agree with those who are totally opposed to governments encouraging gambling. Wouldn't taxes have to be raised to replace these revenues? Would you mind paying more taxes? Do you think your parents or family members would mind? Do you have any other suggestions?

Sources: *Montreal Gazette*, June 17, 1999, p. A3, and June 19, 1999, pp. B3, B4; <www.ontariocasino.ca>; <www.loto-quebec.com>.

CBC | **VIDEO CASE** | **www.cbc.ca**

BANK OF CANADA

This chapter reviewed the role of the government as it affects the economy. You will recall that the Bank of Canada was described as a very important institution created by the federal government. Nevertheless, it operates as an independent body with a board appointed by the government. The current Governor of the Bank of Canada is David Dodge.

The Bank has important responsibilities and the way it carries them out has a huge effect on the Canadian economy and on individual businesses. This video shows David Dodge wrestling with the issue of assessing the condition of the economy so that he can take the proper steps to help keep it in good shape. Normally, the Governor of the Bank would base his decisions on information and statistics from various sources. In the video, the former Minister of Finance comments that it takes too long to get that data. He states that an effective action to counter an economy sliding into a recession requires a quick reaction based on current information and on instinct.

You will see that it is not an easy job but we are fortunate to have David Dodge in charge. He is an economist with many years of experience as Deputy Minister of Finance, and he doesn't lose his cool easily. As the textbook notes, he later took decisive and unprecedented actions. During 2001, he lowered interest rates 8 times, to the lowest levels in 40 years, in the attempt to boost a faltering economy.

Discussion Questions

1. In recent decades a strong movement, led by many business organizations, developed urging privatization of Crown corporations and less government involvement in the economy. However, the chapter notes that when the economy weakened many voices were heard demanding that the government *do* something. What do you think of this apparent contradiction? Should governments limit their role to crisis intervention?

2. The video mentions the unpopularity of the previous Governor of the Bank of Canada; he raised interest rates to unprecedented levels in his lengthy battle against inflation. His unpopularity resulted from the high unemployment his policy produced.

   The textbook notes that the federal government's more recent policy of reducing the large national debt also led to more unemployment and social hardship. This made it unpopular. Do you think that governments should do what they think is right and not worry about being popular? Why?

3. The textbook examines the wide variety of ways in which the laws, regulations, and actions of all levels of government affect businesses and the economy in Canada. Is there any area where you think that this intervention should be reduced? How would you justify your opinion?

Source: *Venture*, show number 776, "David Dodge," February 27, 2001, running time 7:50.

APPENDIX

How Governments Aid Exporters

Because exports are particularly important to the economic well-being of Canada, we have a very large and elaborate government apparatus to assist companies in their exporting and foreign-investment activities. Not only the federal government, but also most provincial and all large municipal governments have various ministries, departments, and agencies that provide a variety of services, including information, marketing, financial aid, insurance and guarantees, publications, and contacts. All major trading countries provide similar support to their exporters.

The federal government agency that has the main responsibility for international business is the Department of Foreign Affairs and International Trade (DFAIT). This ministry has trade commissioners in Canadian embassies abroad and in Canada. DFAIT also maintains "one-stop" international trade centres across Canada. This federal organization engages in a variety of activities that are shown in more detail in the next section. A business that is contemplating going international can get almost any information and help it requires from DFAIT. Further information may be obtained from InfoExport's toll-free line: 1-800-267-8376; and its Web site: <www.infoexport.gc.ca>.

ACCESSING THE GLOBAL MARKET: SERVICES OF THE CANADIAN GOVERNMENT

Because exports have traditionally been such an important issue for Canadians, the federal government has always maintained a high profile in this area. Recently, the government's main efforts have been channelled through DFAIT, which has absorbed previous agencies and developed a comprehensive basket of aid and support for Canadian companies wanting to export, or to engage in investment outside Canada. Advice and aid are administered through some 600 trade commissioners—in a worldwide network of trade commissions in more than 125 cities, in Ottawa, and in more than 13 trade centres across the country. This help is particularly useful for small and medium-sized enterprises that cannot easily get this information. Here is a partial list of some of their important activities.

Trade Counselling and Assistance

- International trade centres in 13 Canadian cities provide one-stop information services. Many of these centres are co-operative efforts of federal, provincial, and local governments, boards of trade, chambers of commerce, and so forth. They are well set up, with extensive facilities for research and helpful staff.
- Geographic trade divisions dividing the world into five regions.
- Sectoral trade divisions dividing marketing, investment, and financing opportunities into 14 product and service sectors.
- Advice about Canadian regulations restricting exports and imports.

Programs That Offer Financial Assistance

- Information and aid on providing military services and supplies to U.S. and European governments under various mutual agreements.
- Export orientation programs to help small and medium-sized companies expand into the United States and overseas.
- Investment development programs to help foreign corporations bring new capital and technology into Canada. Also helps to set up joint ventures with Canadian companies.
- Programs for export market development to facilitate a variety of marketing activities such as attending or setting up booths at trade fairs, setting up permanent sales offices abroad, and arranging visits by foreign buyers to Canada.
- Technology Inflow Program (TIPS) to sponsor group missions or individual companies' visits abroad and visits to Canadian companies by foreign technical experts.

Export Financing and Foreign Sales Procurement

- Industrial Cooperation Program of the Canadian International Development Agency helps Canadian companies seeking investment opportunities and transfer of technology abroad.
- Export Development Corporation provides a full range of financing, insurance, and guarantees to Canadian companies investing or doing business abroad.
- Canadian Commercial Corporation acts as the prime contractor when foreign governments or international agencies want to purchase goods or services from Canada through the government.
- World Information Network for Exports (WINS) lists more than 30,000 Canadian exporters and would-be exporters offering approximately 25,000 products and services. This constantly updated information is used by the trade commissioners mentioned above to find potential buyers for these products. Foreign importers can also access WINS to find products they are seeking.

Trade Data and Publications

- *CanadExport* is a trade newsletter published twice monthly and sent to more than 60,000 readers. It contains a variety of useful information for Canadian companies that export or invest outside of Canada. The newsletter also has a business agenda page that lists seminars, meetings, courses, and conferences across Canada, of interest to those engaged in, or planning to engage in, international business. Many are sponsored by DFAIT or other government agencies. A sample page is shown at the end of this Appendix and above.
- A variety of directories and special studies of use to actual or potential exporters.
- An International Trade Data Bank that stores a wide range of information from the United Nations and various trade blocs about international trade.

Most of this information is available free on the Internet, including the regular issues of *CanadExport*. The main Internet access address is <www.infoexport.gc.ca/canadexport/menu-e.asp>.

BUSINESS AGENDA

International Trade Practices Course

MONTREAL—September 17–December 4—*The Practice of International Trade* is a certified 63-hour evening course on the terms and techniques used in import and export transactions.

Organized by the Quebec Association of Export Trading Houses, it is one of the most comprehensive and complete international trading courses offered in Canada. For information, contact Lilly Nguyen, Tel.: 1-800-465-9615; Fax: (514) 848-9986; e-mail: amceq@amceq.org.

Cross-Canada Seminars on Taiwan

CANADA—A series of information *seminars on business opportunities, challenges and strategies for succeeding in Taiwan* will be held in four Canadian cities beginning in late September.

Hugh Stephens, director of the Canadian Trade Office in Taipei, will give an update on this dynamic market in a series format that includes breakfast, followed by a question period and one-on-one meetings.

Stephens will address such areas as market trends, joint ventures with Taiwan partners, global investment opportunities, trade, tourism, educational services, and other matters relevant to the Canada–Taiwan bilateral relationship. He will also explain the services available through the Canadian Trade Office in Taipei to help Canadian businesses capture some of this market.

Individual appointments with Stephens are on a first-come, first-serve basis. Cities and dates for the information seminars are: Calgary (September 26); Winnipeg (September 27); Toronto (September 30); and Montreal (October 2).

For a complete program outline or for more information on the seminars, contact Elsie Lee, Canada-Taiwan Business Association, Ottawa, Tel.: (613) 238-4000 ext. 240; Fax: (613) 238-7643.

Doing Business With the UN

MONTREAL—October 1—Canadian exporters, especially small and medium-sized firms, are invited to attend a one-day seminar, *How To Do Business With the UN.* Representatives from key United Nations procurement agencies will be present.

In addition to briefings—all speakers are bilingual—there will be afternoon workshops to allow for focused discussions between suppliers and buyers.

The $150 (including lunch and a business guide) event is organized by the United Nations Association in Canada (UNAC), in collaboration with the Department of Foreign Affairs and International Trade, the Canadian Commercial Corporation, the Canadian International Development Agency, and the Quebec Ministry of Industry, Commerce, Science and Technology.

To register, contact Mrs. Sylvie Thibault, World Trade Centre, Montreal, Tel.: (514) 849-1999; Fax: (514) 847-8343.

Cross-Canada Seminars Planned for Canada Expo in Chile

CANADA—A series of seminars across Canada will be held in October to assist exhibitors prepare for the *Canada Expo* trade fair in Santiago, Chile, December 3–6. Following the success of Canada Expo '94 in Mexico City, Expo '96 promises to provide significant potential for new business opportunities, partnerships, and contacts in a variety of sectors. These include industrial, machinery, power and energy, advanced technologies, environmental equipment, health care, construction, infrastructure and building materials, packaging, education, agri-food, consumer products, and professional services.

Canadian companies interested in learning more about Canada Expo and the seminar series should contact the Canada Expo Coordinator, Latin America and Caribbean Trade Division (LGT), Department of Foreign Affairs and International Trade, 125 Sussex Drive, Ottawa K1A 0G2, or facsimile at (613) 944-0479.

FIGURE A.1

SAMPLE PAGE FROM *CANADEXPORT* MAGAZINE. SEE ALSO P.121.

CanadExport

Vol. 20, No. 1 –
January 15, 2002

CANADIAN TRADE REVIEW
(See insert.)

Team Canada

Trade mission to Russia and Germany

Prime Minister Jean Chrétien announced that he will lead the seventh **Team Canada trade mission** from **February 12-22, 2002**, to promote Canada's business ties with Russia and Germany. The Prime Minister will be joined by provincial premiers, territorial leaders and business executives from across the country. They will travel to Moscow, Berlin and Munich.

Team Canada • Équipe Canada
2002

In 2000, Canada's two-way trade with **Russia** reached nearly $870 million. Canadian exports to Russia have grown steadily since 1999, and are up significantly in 2001. Opportunities for Canadian business in Russia reflect our geographic and climatic similarities, with vast natural resource wealth, widely distributed urban settlement, and remote service transportation and communication networks. Emerging opportunities are the result of Russia's evolution toward a more consumer-oriented society, with growing demand for a wider range of products and services. Excellent prospects for Canadian

Continued on page 13 – **Trade**

A successful export "first"

Canadian pig scores big in Russia

The Canadian Swine Exporters Association (CSEA), the Canadian Embassy in Moscow and 535 Canadian pigs play lead roles in the latest Canadian export success story currently unfolding in Russia.

The story begins in April 2001 with a fact-finding "reconnaissance" mission to Russia, the Baltic States, Belorussia and the Ukraine led by Richard Stein,

Continued on page 11 – **Canadian**

Richard Stein (third from left) during one of his recent marketing trips to Russia.

Department of Foreign Affairs and International Trade

Ministère des Affaires étrangères et du Commerce international

Canada

CHAPTER

5

Ethical Behaviour, the Environment, and Social Responsibility

LEARNING GOALS

AFTER YOU HAVE READ AND STUDIED THIS CHAPTER, YOU SHOULD BE ABLE TO

1 Discuss how business in the early capitalist period ignored ethical standards of behaviour.

2 Describe the modern beginnings of business ethics, and understand why ethical issues are so important now.

3 Define management's role in setting ethical standards, and list the six-step approach to ethical decisions.

4 Identify what first led to concern about the environment, and list some of the major environmental problems.

5 Understand why business sees a conflict between a clean environment and competitive ability.

6 Describe the rule of 72, and explain its relationship to growth.

7 Explain how sustainable development has become the major international goal for reconciling growth with environmental constraints.

Rahumathulla Marikkar Charts a Path for Corporate Social Responsibility

Interface Inc. was founded in 1973 by Ray Anderson in Georgia. Through a series of acquisitions the company has become the world's leading commercial carpet and interior fabrics manufacturer. It provides a comprehensive package of interior office environment products and services including replacement and maintenance. It now does business in 110 countries, has 29 global production facilities, 7,500 employees, and sales of US$1.3 billion. One of its important subsidiaries is Interface Flooring Systems (Canada) Inc. located in Belleville, Ontario.

Rahumathulla Marikkar
Courtesy of Interface

Ray Anderson

What is unique about Interface is its total dedication to operating in an environmentally sustainable fashion. The philosophy set out by founder and CEO Ray Anderson, and strongly supported by Rahumathulla Marikkar, Director of Technology and Environment of Interface Canada, can be summed up as follows:

> We are in the process of building the world's first sustainable and eventually restorative enterprise. Our goal—to be the first name in industrial ecology worldwide. It means creating technologies of the future—kinder, gentler, responsible technologies that emulate nature's systems…
> We are creating a company that addresses the needs of society and the environment by developing a system of industrial production that decreases our costs and dramatically reduces the burdens placed upon living systems.

The main components of this sustainability operation include reducing or eliminating waste and harmful emissions, renewable energy sources and closed-loop recycling, using resource-efficient transportation, and engaging stakeholders. The result would make Interface a pioneer in sustainable commerce.

In 1995 Interface began a global initiative to intensify its improvement process with a three-year program known as QUEST—Quality Utilizing Employee Suggestions and Teamwork. The aim was to identify all measurable waste and to reduce it by 50 percent over three years, and this goal was achieved. In 1998 the company's EcoSense environmental guiding principle was combined with QUEST to launch QUEST/EcoSense—2000 as a guide for the next three years.

In 1999 the Belleville plant generated the greatest efficiency improvement of the company's 29 worldwide facilities. It reduced material and energy consumption, achieved zero effluent discharge, and reduced emissions and waste sent to landfills. The parent company rewarded this success by transferring some of its export orders to the Belleville plant, so that exports grew from 15 to 60 percent of its production and profits tripled.

The environmentally sustainable efforts of Interface Canada are guided by the parent company's program and other initiatives:

1. eliminating toxic substances
2. simplifying production processes and lengthening product longevity
3. developing alternatives to the physical movement of people and materials
4. taking thousands of small steps by creating a culture that integrates the principles of sustainability in everyday operations and encouraging others to adopt the same practices
5. pioneering sustainable commerce through education, providing options and market incentives

An important company activity, which resulted in the reduction of greenhouse gases, includes an active program of voluntary initiatives for employees. They take part in a home energy savings program and in alternative transport activities, such as car pooling, walking, biking and in-line skating. Marikkar received a national award from the federal government agency VCR Inc. for extraordinary individual leadership in reducing greenhouse gases. The plant improved its environmental operation while realizing savings through replacing oversized motors; minimizing downtime and reducing startup/shutdown cycles; recovering waste heat to preheat process intake and to warm the building; reformulating the carpet-backing compound to fuse at a lower temperature, bond better, and reduce baking mass; and insulating process equipment to reduce heat loss.

Part of the savings on energy consumption was reinvested in paying a premium to buy certified green energy in an effort to encourage power companies to develop clean power technology. A partnership between Interface Canada and Belleville Utilities to bring windmill power generation to the city should allow Interface to fulfill its goal to use 100 percent sustainable energy by June 2002.

Interface Canada's efforts and achievements have been recognized by the federal Department of Natural Resources with awards and by highlighting its achievements in the Department's publication *Success Stories*. Various media have also reported on the notable environmental success of the company. Articles have appeared in the *Toronto Star*, *Profit magazine*, local Belleville newspapers, and Marikkar has been interviewed by CBC Radio.

Sources: Annual Report 2000, Interface Inc., and other company documents; *Canadian Industry Program, Energy Conservation Success Stories*, Office of Energy Efficiency, Natural Resources Canada.

ETHICAL DILEMMA

Corporate Responsibility: How Does It Measure Up?

In this chapter you will see a review of issues that relate to the principal question of the need and ability of Canadian companies, governments, and all organizations to behave in a responsible way to our society. You will see that some people believe in a limited responsibility for companies, while others believe that corporations, like individuals, cannot duck full responsibility for the level of ethical standards that they have and for the impact of their actions on the environment. Some commentators go so far as to say that business ethics is an oxymoron. That is, it's an absurd contradiction, like saying someone is tall and short or rich and poor. Most people do not take such an extreme position. You can see a good example in the Profile of many things companies do to show their responsibility to society. However, some say this is merely PR—window dressing. What do you think? Is it possible, indeed necessary, that companies adopt, apply, and maintain responsible ethical standards in their policies and practices? As you will see, this is not an easy question in our complex world. We will return to this issue after you have explored the many aspects of the problem in the chapter.

ETHICAL BEHAVIOUR IN BUSINESS AND GOVERNMENT

Throughout this book you will see many comments about the issue of business ethics. Why so much emphasis on ethical behaviour of business people and companies? The reason is that the past decade saw a rising tide of criticism in Canada (and other countries) of various business practices that many Canadians found unacceptable.

Knowing what's right and wrong and behaving accordingly is what ethical behaviour is all about. This goes beyond legal and regulatory requirements or obeying the laws of a country. Social responsibility means that a business shows concern for the welfare of society as a whole. In this chapter we look at ethics from an organizational perspective and how the behaviour of companies and organizations rates on the social responsibility scorecard. For more insight into this question, see the Ethical Dilemma box "Corporate Responsibility: How Does It Measure Up?"

EFFECT ON CAREER CHOICE

How will what you learn in this chapter be likely to affect your choice of career? Most employees are more comfortable working for a company whose policies and practices are solidly based on a responsible approach to their community and country and to the global environment. After all, as an employee you must live by the rules of your company and carry out the orders and wishes of your superiors. Further, some day you will occupy a managerial position and have the responsibility of not only carrying out company policies, but also helping to shape policy and practices. As you work your way through this chapter, you will have plenty of food for thought about these issues.

A BRIEF HISTORY OF ETHICS IN BUSINESS

The recent criticism of business practices in North America can perhaps be traced back to the 1960s in the United States, when a young lawyer named Ralph Nader almost single-handedly took on mighty General Motors. He started challenging GM because of its defective Corvair, which had been responsible for many fatal accidents because of sudden, erratic, and uncontrollable behaviour.

At first, GM regarded Nader as an elephant might regard a pesky mosquito. Gradually, however, his efforts drew more and more support. Despite GM's strenuous opposition, including hiring private detectives to look for dirt on Ralph Nader's personal life to discredit him, GM was forced, for the first time in the history of automobile manufacturing, to recall cars to correct problems. Now, of course, recalls have become standard procedure for all auto manufacturers. This was perhaps the first important signal of a move toward **corporate social responsibility**, the recognition by corporations that their actions must take into account the needs and ethical standards of society.

People have been concerned about business practices for a long time. The advent of the Industrial Revolution **➤P. 6◄** at the end of the 1700s led to serious criticism of its drawbacks (see Chapter 2). Critics of the new capitalist-industrial societies that emerged in the 1800s in western Europe, Canada, and the United States were numerous. Many of them condemned greed and the cruel treatment of workers: harsh and dangerous conditions that caused many deaths and accidents; low pay; long hours; child labour; and so on.

These inhumane practices were the subject of many novels that achieved wide acclaim. Charles Dickens in England and later Sinclair Lewis in the United States are but two novelists who described and condemned these and other business practices of the day. In Chapter 14 you will see how similar harsh conditions in Canada led to the formation of the union movement and eventually laws banning various unacceptable practices.

A Murky Road to Wealth

The accumulation of large fortunes in the 1800s and early 1900s (before the days of income taxes) was usually aided by many shady if not criminal acts, including the alleged killing of competitors and union leaders. In the United States, those early, wealthy capitalists were dubbed **robber barons**, a term that became very popular and is still used today. The classic robber baron was John D. Rockefeller, who established a near-monopoly in the oil business using power tactics. His huge Standard Oil Co. (from which we get the name Esso, S.O.) was finally forced by the U.S. courts at the beginning of the 1900s to split up into a number of companies, each still quite large.

In Canada, one of the most notorious developments occurred during the building of the first railway line to the west coast in the 1870s and 1880s. This vast project, like most railway construction in North America, was accompanied by many scandals and corruption, leading to the resignation in 1873 of the federal government of Canada's first prime minister, John A. Macdonald. The first scandal involved Sir Hugh Allan. His company (which became the CPR) was given contracts, vast sums of money, and huge tracts of land across western Canada, often under questionable circumstances. Many men made fortunes, including Donald A. Smith (later Lord Strathcona) and Sir William Van Horne. Similar scandals in the province of Quebec, on a smaller scale, led to the fall of the government of Honoré Mercier in the 1890s.

Modern Capitalism

The nineteenth century saw the emergence of the modern industrial-capitalist system. The economic philosophy that underpinned it was first elaborated upon by Adam Smith, whom we met in Chapter 2 **➤P. 37◄**. Smith's book *The Wealth of Nations*, published in 1776, gave birth to the concept of **laissez-faire capitalism**. This theory emphasized that, if left alone and unhindered by government, the free market, in pursuit of economic efficiency, would provide an abundance of goods at the lowest prices, improving everyone's life. The workings of this "invisible hand" would reward capitalists for their work and financial risks, thus providing jobs for the population and plentiful goods to satisfy human needs and improve living standards.

corporate social responsibility
The recognition by corporations that their actions must take into account the needs and ethical standards of society.

robber barons
Capitalists of the nineteenth century whose wealth came, in part, through shady if not criminal acts.

laissez-faire capitalism
The theory that, if left alone and unhindered by government, the free market, in pursuit of economic efficiency, would provide an abundance of goods at the lowest prices, improving everyone's life.

For some years this seemed to work as Smith predicted. But (as noted in Chapter 2) there were many booms and busts, the economic cycles we now take for granted. There were also the serious problems of poverty, job-related illnesses, the lack of pensions or compensation to workers for the many industrial accidents, and other such problems. Life for the average person was said to be "short, nasty, and brutish."

The End of Laissez-Faire Capitalism

The twentieth century saw the beginnings of serious attempts to deal with the shortcomings of the capitalist system. In Chapter 4 we saw how Canadian governments were forced to implement a variety of programs to smooth out the rough edges of capitalism and cope with its contradictions of extreme wealth and poverty. Of course, we now take for granted the great productive capacities that capitalism developed, which resulted in greatly improved living standards for the majority of people.

We accept and usually welcome what new technologies make available to us—faster travel, electronic gadgetry and communications, and more—but we also express more concern for human values. In addition, there are many laws banning various practices that Canadians have found unacceptable. Canadian society condemns discrimination in hiring, promotion, or firing; continued high unemployment; poverty; homelessness; and children going to school hungry. We expect solutions. We insist that business managers, company directors, and politicians behave ethically. Activities such as bribery, influence peddling, favouritism, discrimination, and expense padding are denounced. The dumping of wastes and toxic material and many other formerly common practices are now either severely frowned upon or illegal.

These concerns have also found expression on the international scene. For many years, nearly all countries supported the sanctions against South Africa and helped to bring an end to its official racist policy of apartheid, which had kept its black majority in a permanent state of oppression. Canada had laws and policies that banned most dealings with South African government and businesses. Banks and companies that had investments there were severely criticized by shareholders, church leaders, and community groups. Eventually many responded by curtailing or ceasing their activities in that country.

ETHICAL BEHAVIOUR AND THE LAW

We might ask what, exactly, is the difference between ethical behaviour and legal behaviour? It is clear that society has the right to expect corporations and all businesses to obey the laws of Canada. However, when we expect ethical behaviour we are referring to acting in conformity with our values and norms. A society's values, norms, and laws are not fixed but are subject to change. As strong support develops for certain values—for example, discrimination in employment—laws are enacted to incorporate these values.

It should be noted that not all legal behaviour is necessarily ethical. For example, many people question the high level of compensation many top executives get as possibly being unethical, but there is nothing illegal about receiving a large salary.

A company is behaving illegally if it tries to skirt around a law, encourages employees to do so, or tries to cover up such actions. Such behaviour may also be said to be unethical; unethical behaviour consists of activities that violate society's norms or values. Examples of different types of unethical behaviour are shown in this chapter. This whole issue concerns *corporate social responsibility*, which we look at next.

A New Emphasis on Corporate Social Responsibility

Today there seems to be a heightened interest in, and awareness of, the importance of the social responsibility of business, especially for large corporations. An increasing number of comments by Canadian and international business leaders are stressing the obligations that companies have to society. The Spotlight on Big Business "Backlash against Globalization: Corporate Social Responsibility" gives one important example. A brief review of other comments reported in *The Economist, Time* magazine, *The Globe and Mail,* and the *Montreal Gazette* will give some idea of the extent to which this has become a major concern of many business, government, and academic leaders.

Courtesy of Palliser Furniture Ltd.

The Globe and Mail report on the opening addresses at the prestigious World Economic Forum meeting in Davos, Switzerland, in February 1996 is headlined, "Capitalism must develop a heart" and "Davos forum kicks off with a warning that greed is ultimately bad for business." The president of Switzerland, a former U.S. Cabinet member and philosopher and a well-known Harvard professor and business consultant, addressed the gathering of "1,000 [senior] executives and their spouses, 200 government officials and 40 heads of government." All speakers had the same message: unless business demonstrates real commitment to its workforce and to the communities in which it operates, there will be strong, popular reactions, including a resurgent union movement. There is even "a risk globalization [of business] will collapse."[1]

Palliser Furniture is a company that has found success by producing environmentally friendly furniture. The company's A.A. DeFehr Foundation receives 10 percent of the company's income, which is distributed among various charities.

Ethical Behaviour Is Profitable

It is sometimes argued or implied that corporations need only obey the law and not worry about ethical considerations because this might involve extra costs or lower sales, both of which would result in lower profits. However, there is important evidence that this is not necessarily true. At a conference on ethics in business organized by York University and the Canadian Centre for Ethics & Corporate Policy in Toronto in December 1995, Canadian entrepreneur Isadore Sharp, founder of Four Seasons Hotels, pointed out that a Gallup poll showed that the corporation was one of the least trusted institutions in the United States. He also noted the contrast between what corporate leaders and their employees think about their companies. A 1993 poll showed that while 96 percent of the Fortune 500 companies thought their companies behaved ethically, 41 percent of the employees disagreed with their leaders. Another survey, reported Sharp, showed that 70 percent of consumers said they would not buy products from a company they believed to be unethical. A Canadian survey indicated that consumers would overwhelmingly go out of their way, or pay more, to buy ethically produced clothing.[2]

Sharp contrasted the behaviour of two American companies, Johnson & Johnson and Exxon. The former, faced with a major problem when seven people died in Chicago from poisoned Tylenol capsules, made the whole issue public and told retailers to return all their Tylenol stock for full credit. This cost Johnson & Johnson several millions of dollars but restored public confidence in their products quickly. A different story emerged concerning Exxon after the 1989 oil spill catastrophe off Alaska when the giant Exxon *Valdez* tanker went aground. Exxon's delay in assuming responsibility for one of the worst maritime oil disasters ever cost it dearly in public and business ratings and landed it with a $5-billion fine. Sharp concluded by stating that a growing body of evidence indicates that ethical behaviour pays off in higher profits.[3]

www.weforum.org

The World Economic Forum does much more than hold the annual Davos conference to bring world business and political leaders together to exchange views and ideas. Its regular publication, *World Link Magazine,* is circulated to top business leaders around the world. Visit the WEF Web site and find out about *World Link's* editorial policy. What does its content emphasize?

Backlash against Globalization: Corporate Social Responsibility

The World Economic Forum (WEF), based in Geneva, Switzerland, is one of the top global business organizations in the world. Its membership includes many governments and the largest companies in the world, all of which send their leading figures to the annual conference in Davos, Switzerland. Prime ministers and presidents of countries rub shoulders with corporation presidents, chairpeople, and CEOs. So when the founder and president of the Forum makes a public comment, it is a noteworthy event. This is exactly what happened in 1996. Klaus Schwab wrote a joint article with Forum managing director Claude Smadja in the *International Herald Tribune*, one of the great, long-established, truly global newspapers.

The central point of the article is the serious backlash that has developed against the negative effects of the globalization of business and what should be done about it. Schwab and Smadja stated that this backlash has become so serious that it "is threatening to disrupt economic activity and social stability" in the industrial democracies. They used the example of the month-long national strikes and protests that seriously disrupted the French economy in December 1995 (personally witnessed by one of the Canadian authors of this text).

In Canada, Ontario unionists led many major protests and strikes of tens of thousands of people in Toronto, London, and elsewhere in Ontario in 1995 and 1996. In Germany, millions of unionists staged significant protests in June 1996. In the United States, various candidates for the presidential election in 1996 catered to the same widespread sentiments of restrictions against foreign imports. This inward-looking protectionist attitude in the U.S. continues to be a constant problem, according to a 1999 report.

The article noted that it is not surprising that there is so much concern, because rapid globalization of economic activities and technological change have drastically altered life all over the world. Although East Asian countries were benefitting, promised or expected benefits had not been forthcoming in the industrialized democracies. There we have seen downsizing, restructuring, and, despite increased productivity and exports and rapid technological developments, fewer or poorer-quality jobs and lower incomes and benefits. Even in the U.S., where the end of the 1990s saw reduced unemployment, employees' real incomes and benefits were down.

The authors believed that globalization must avoid being seen as a "brakeless rain" caused by an uncontrolled free market. Global corporations have a responsibility to deal with these serious problems by helping governments set national priorities in areas such as training, education, and fiscal policies that provide incentives for entrepreneurs.

This involves going beyond "traditional concept[s] of economic policy." The authors stressed the urgent need for innovative policies to avoid what could become a serious backlash against the effects of the technological revolution and the globalization of business because these trends cannot be reversed.

The backlash they warned of has become a reality. These protests have become stronger and more widespread in the last few years. Meetings of various international bodies and governments have been subjected to large protests in Seattle, Nice, Genoa, Quebec City, and elsewhere as well as in Davos. These protests have received substantial media coverage. A headline accompanying a 2001 story in the *Financial Times* of London read "Power elite at Davos may be eclipsed by protesters." The article referred to the 2,000 government and business leaders gathered at the annual meeting of the WEF in Davos having to compete with an "anti-Davos" protest meeting in Porto Alegre, Brazil. The latter drew some 10,000 international representatives who were opposed to globalization, which they said was having bad effects for many millions of people.

In a later article in the *Financial Times* Smadja warned that in the current period of slower economic growth there was a danger of "selfish interests" becoming more assertive. He was referring to "ever increasing shareholder returns" becoming the major obsession of global corporations. He continued to argue, as he has previously done, that globalization cannot work without "constant corrective action" to eliminate gross inequalities.

Adapted from: Klaus Schwab and Claude Smadja, "Globalization Backlash is Serious," *International Herald Tribune*, February 21, 1996, p. 18; Shawn McCarthy and Heather Scoffield, "Inward-looking U.S. Threatens Canada's Interests, Ministers Fold," *Globe and Mail*, June 30, 1999, p. A4; Guy de Jonquieres, *Financial Times*, January 24, 2001, p. 18; Claude Smadja, "The Dangers of a Divided World," *Financial Times*, January 25, 2001, p. 15.

Proof that ethical behaviour pays off can be found in the profitable existence of companies like The Body Shop International and Ben & Jerry's. Both companies emphasize responsibility to the community and the environment and have successful operations in Canada. Other examples are ethical mutual funds that have good performance records through investing only in companies deemed to be socially responsible. For example, the Clean Environment Equity Fund outperformed the average Canadian mutual fund in 1995 and for the three years ending in 1995.[4] The fund continued its excellent performance for the next three years.

SOME QUESTIONABLE PRACTICES

A growing number of "normal" business activities are coming under increasing scrutiny in Canada (and elsewhere) because of their doubtful ethical practices. As society's values are changing, certain practices are now being deemed controversial or unacceptable. Let us look at some of them.

Weapons Sales

Many people are concerned about the question of selling military equipment, supplies, and sophisticated industrial machinery and products to brutal dictatorships. In 1991 we witnessed a UN-sponsored attack on Iraq, in which Canada participated, because Iraq had invaded its neighbour, Kuwait, in 1990 and refused to withdraw. Saddam Hussein, the dictator who rules Iraq, has an extremely unsavoury record and has often been condemned by Amnesty International and other human rights groups.

Despite this fact many countries, including Canada, had sold him billions of dollars worth of military equipment and supplies—including the capability to produce chemical and nuclear weapons and missiles. There are many media reports that much military equipment continues to be sold to Iraq by various countries, including the United States and Canada. Other countries with odious records send representatives to arms shows in Canada and can pretty well buy whatever they wish from Canadian companies. This problem is not only a Canadian one. The UN Office of Disarmament Affairs and other organizations are concerned about the continuing proliferation of arms sold by the major industrial powers.[5]

Atomic Reactors Sold to Romania

Atomic Energy of Canada Ltd. (AECL), a Crown corporation, was under heavy fire for having sold our nuclear reactors in the 1980s to the late dictator Nicolae Ceaușescu of Romania. These contracts were important to AECL because for years it had been unable to sell any Canadian reactors. It was later learned that the workers who had built the massive reactor housings were practically slave labourers. This was a classic example of the pressures businesses and governments face: a badly needed sales opportunity versus a customer who is ethically very distasteful. The question is made all the more complex when competitors in some countries seem to have no ethical standards at all.

www.depaul.edu/ethics

The DePaul University Institute for Business and Professional Ethics Web site indicates that it is "one of the first ethics-related resources to pioneer a hypertext linked ethics network throughout the Internet." Check it out. Find out about the Institute and its activities. Who are its members? What does membership entail?

Ben & Jerry's is a great example of how ethical behaviour pays off in higher profits. This highly successful company stresses responsibility to the community and to the environment.

Canadian Press CP. Photography by Fred Chartrand.

Jody Williams, Nobel Prize laureate, is a strong advocate for a global ban on land mines.

Land Mines

A notorious issue relates to land mines, which are cheap to buy and are now strewn over many countries in Africa and Asia. Long after fighting has ceased, these mines continue to maim and kill innocent children, women, and men who are working in fields. In countries like Angola, Vietnam, and Cambodia, thousands of people become amputees annually. At a UN-sponsored conference to ban land mines in Geneva in January 1996, it was reported that there are 110 types of mines, in uncounted millions, spread throughout 69 countries, killing 10,000 civilians annually and maiming another 20,000. At this conference, Canada announced "a moratorium on the production, export, and use of antipersonnel mines." Unfortunately, only about 20 countries were in favour of such a ban.

A report on *60 Minutes* in July 1996 said that there were some 100 million land mines threatening people globally. The report also noted that in Cambodia, a small country of 9 million people, there were 60,000 amputees, not to mention all the small children who had been killed. The worst offending nations, according to *60 Minutes*, are China, Pakistan, Russia, and the United States. These countries harbour the main producers and exporters of land mines, some of which sell for as little as two dollars, and have so far refused to support the movement to ban mines. Canada hosted a UN conference in September 1996 to push these and other countries to stop the production of these deadly instruments of destruction.[6]

Canada finally succeeded when 122 countries signed an agreement in Ottawa in December 1997, banning the production, sale, and use of land mines effective when the governments of 40 countries ratified the treaty. Unfortunately three major powers who are all significant manufacturers and exporters of land mines, the U.S., Russia, and China, refused to sign the treaty for various reasons. One year later, there was good news according to the executive director of Mines Action Canada, the coordinating body of 15 Canadian organizations monitoring the implementation of the treaty. He reported that 11 more countries had signed the treaty, bringing the number to 133, and equally if not more important, 55 countries had already ratified the treaty. It came into force March 1, 1999. The U.S. did not sign on by 2000 as expected, but has contributed $100 million toward the important mine-clearing program. Russia has banned the export of mines.[7]

HIV-Infected Blood Supply

One of the big news stories in Canada in 1995 and 1996 concerned the official inquiry by Justice Kever into the serious allegations that the Canadian Red Cross and the federal and seven provincial governments allowed hepatitis-C and HIV-infected blood to be transfused to hemophiliacs. This error resulted in hundreds of hemophiliacs becoming HIV positive and many getting full-blown AIDS and hepatitis-C and subsequently dying. The families and the hemophiliac organizations alleged that, to avoid financial loss, unpurified blood stocks were being used at a time when testing procedures were known and available.

The long and complex hearings, costing many millions of dollars, were coming to an end, and Justice Kever announced that the final report would name individuals and organizations responsible for this tragic incident. The Red Cross and all the governments involved immediately took legal action to prevent Justice Kever from doing that. They claimed that they were not given the opportunity to adequately present their side of the case as required by law.

This set off a round of public statements and editorials condemning them for such action. Many felt that it was ridiculous to spend so many months and millions of dollars to uncover what happened, why it happened, and who was responsible, and then to try to prevent a full report from being issued. It is clear that any person, organization, or government found responsible for this tragedy would face substantial legal claims by the families of the sick and deceased. Some thought it particularly ironic that the federal government that set up the inquiry should now be trying to block its results from becoming known.

Eventually Justice Kever was prevented from naming individuals, government ministries, or organizations who were responsible for this disaster. One of the sad effects of this case was that Canadians lost confidence in the Canadian Red Cross. After more than a half-century of yeoman service getting and storing blood donations and providing hospitals with the blood needed for transfusions, the Red Cross gave up this responsibility.

The Westray Coal Mine Disaster

Another problem that received a lot of attention in Canada from 1992 to 1996 concerned the Westray coal mine explosion that occurred in May 1992 in Plymouth, Nova Scotia, taking the lives of 26 men. Accusations were made by family and friends of the victims and by members of Parliament and the Nova Scotia legislature that both levels of government, acting for political reasons, financed the opening of the mine despite warnings from their mining departments that it was a dangerous mine with a long record of explosions and deaths. After much delay, an official inquiry was launched in 1995 to examine all matters relevant to the disaster.

Company and government officials as well as mine inspectors have testified, often making contradictory statements. Nearly all deny any responsibility for the explosion. Miners have stated that the coal dust hazard was constantly high and that mine officials and government inspectors brushed aside or ignored complaints made to them. Miners claim they were also told not to make complaints if they wanted to keep their jobs.

The Westray disaster is another example of the complex ethical problems that can arise in seemingly ordinary business decisions. Here was a community of miners desperately in need of jobs. The federal and provincial governments were anxious to help provide the jobs as elections were due to take place shortly and a company was prepared to operate the mine. So all parties, including the union, backed the scheme even though there were known risks. The governments helped finance the reopening of the mine.

After the explosion, former federal cabinet minister Tom Hockins, interviewed on the CBC, said that economic considerations rather than safety factors led to the mine opening. The area has a persistently high unemployment rate, so the mine opening was welcome news despite the risks.

Some miners claimed that after operations commenced, they began to worry about the growing risk of an explosion; but it appears that the other parties were too far into the project to want to stop.

According to Nova Scotia reporter Dean Jobb, who wrote a book about the Westray mine disaster, "almost $100 million of public funds" were spent on the mine. He notes that

> In December 1997, an inquiry headed by Justice Peter Richard of the Nova Scotia Supreme Court condemned Westray management as "derelict" in its duty to run a safe mine. Singled out were Curragh [Inc.; the Toronto-based mine owner] chairman Clifford Frame; [on-site managers] Gerald Phillips and Roger Parry. The latter two were charged in 1993 with manslaughter and criminal negligence causing death.

FIGURE 5.1

SOCIALLY RESPONSIBLE BUSINESS ACTIVITIES

A wide variety of activities fall under this heading.

- Community-related activities such as participating in local fundraising campaigns, donating executive time to various nonprofit organizations (including local government), and participating in urban planning and development.
- Employee-related activities such as equal opportunity programs, flextime, improved benefits, job enrichment, job safety, and employee development programs. (You'll learn more about these activities in Chapters 13 and 14.)
- Political activities such as taking a position on issues like nuclear safety, gun control, pollution control, and consumer protection; and working more closely with local, provincial, and federal government officials.
- Support for higher education, the arts, and other nonprofit social agencies.
- Consumer activities such as product safety, honest advertising, prompt complaint handling, honest pricing policies, and extensive consumer education programs.

social audit

A systematic evaluation of an organization's progress toward implementing programs that are socially responsible and responsive.

up the environment, designing more honest advertising, treating women and minorities fairly, and so forth. But is there any indication that organizations are making social responsiveness an integral part of top management's decision making? The answer is yes, and the term that represents that effort is *social auditing*.

A **social audit** is a systematic evaluation of an organization's progress toward implementing programs that are socially responsible and responsive. One of the more difficult problems with social auditing is how to define *socially responsible* and *responsive*. Is it being socially responsible to delay putting in the latest technology (e.g., robots and computers) to save jobs, even if that makes the firm less competitive? Hundreds of such questions make the design of social audits difficult. Another major problem is establishing procedures for measuring a firm's activities and their effects on society. What should be measured? Figure 5.1 outlines business activities that could be considered socially responsible.

There's some question as to whether positive actions should be added and then negative effects (e.g., pollution or layoffs) subtracted to get a net social contribution. Or should just positive actions be recorded? In general, social auditing has become a concern of business. It's becoming one of the aspects of corporate success that business evaluates, measures, and develops.

THE IMPACT OF ENVIRONMENTAL ISSUES ON BUSINESS

The modern concern with environmental issues traces its beginnings to a famous book, *Silent Spring*, written by U.S. government biologist Rachel Carson in the early 1960s. She had noticed that for several years she had not heard many birds singing in spring. That led to the discovery that DDT, a widely used domestic and commercial pesticide, was a deadly poison that was affecting all wildlife and humans as well. That was the beginning of the serious investigation of how modern technology was affecting our environment.

Nearly everyone is now aware that the physical environment of the Earth has been seriously damaged by various activities of human beings. Scientists over a broad range of studies—ecology, genetics, meteorology, botany, chemistry, zoology—warn us about the serious threats that require prompt action if we are to continue living on this planet. Many international conferences have been held on this topic. Perhaps the most important took place in Brazil in 1992. It was called the United Nations Conference on the Environment and Development (UNCED). See the Reaching Beyond Our Borders box "UN Conference on the Environment and

REACHING BEYOND OUR BORDERS
UN Conference on the Environment and Development

www.un.org

After three years of painstaking planning, negotiations, and organizing, the most ambitious conference in history on environmental issues took place in June 1992 in Rio de Janeiro, Brazil. The United Nations brought together 160 nations in a massive effort to achieve a breakthrough on proposals to improve the world's environment. The leaders of more than 100 countries attended. The conference was chaired by Maurice Strong of Canada, who said, "Rio will produce more than any other UN conference in history. If Rio does not succeed, it will be the greatest breakdown of all time for the international community and perhaps the beginning of a rich–poor war."

The conference goal was to "find a way to bridge that divide between wealth and nature, growth and conservation, developed and developing. Summit supporters hoped they would steer the world in a new direction, one in which the rich North would consume less while the poor South will produce more."

Strong noted that UN members approved 98 percent of Agenda 21, a comprehensive 800-page document that outlined how in the next century the world could clean and save its environment. Agenda 21 deals with almost every environmental issue from overpopulation to overfishing.

The problems this conference faced were staggering. Huge sums of money are required if the goals are to be achieved. The rich, developed North says to the poor, underdeveloped South: Stop cutting down your tropical forests, stop burning so much coal. You are adding substantially to the greenhouse effect and reducing the Earth's ability to absorb carbon dioxide. Malaysia answers: we need space for agriculture for our growing population and we need the money from the sale of our timber. And China says: we cannot afford to convert our 750,000 coal-burning industrial boilers to cleaner methods. Furthermore, they all say: you rich Northerners consume too much energy, aggravating the greenhouse effect. You will have to finance us if you want us not to do what we are now doing and what you yourself have done previously.

Strong and others called for a starting fund of US$10 billion of new "green funds" for developing countries. Negotiators for most Northern countries said $3 billion was more likely, but even this amount had not been raised by 1999. Subsequent annual conferences in Geneva (1996), Bonn (1997), and Kyoto (1997–98) showed that progress was very slow. Many Canadian press reports and editorials were critical of governments for moving so slowly on this important question.

The situation remains murky after another conference of 165 nations in Morocco in November 2001 that was supposed to make the Kyoto Protocol a reality. More attempts were made to water the Protocol down further. The United States remains opposed to it—and Canada, as well as other countries, came in for criticism for what some independent observers deemed to be foot-dragging and attempts to weaken the Kyoto proposals further.

Based on: UN press releases, 1996, 1998, 1999; John Stackhouse, "Canadian on Mission to Save This Planet," *Globe and Mail*, May 2, 1992, p. A1; Michel Lalonde, "Cool but...," *Montreal Gazette*, November 11, 2001, p. A7.

Development" for the story. Its chairman was Canadian Maurice Strong, who has been an important international figure for many years.

In 1972 Strong chaired the Stockholm Conference on the Human Environment, the first international conference to put the *green* agenda on the international stage. "We've all lost our innocence," said Strong. "I don't think we can wait another 20 years. The Earth has cancer. In the early stages, the symptoms are minimal, but by the time they become acute it's too late.[15]

Twenty-five years later, in 1997, an important international environmental conference took place in Kyoto, Japan. This meeting resulted in the Kyoto Protocol, whereby many of the nations of the world agreed on a timetable to cut back on the production of greenhouse emissions to the levels of 1990. Unfortunately even that first step is in doubt. Follow-up summits at Buenos Aires and Bonn, aimed at "finding ways to implement the emission-reduction targets" are keeping the treaty signed by 80 nations alive, but no real progress was expected until another meeting in The Hague in 2000. There is still strong opposition from American oil companies, some U.S. senators, and OPEC members. It is really up to the United States, Canada, and other leading industrial countries that produce most of the climate-warming emissions to bite the bullet and start reducing them. Unfortunately, that support from the United States is not likely to develop. On the contrary, shortly after taking office in 2001, President George W. Bush announced that the U.S. will not support the Kyoto agreement because he does not believe it is a workable agreement. This policy statement evoked strong opposition from environmental groups worldwide as well as from the European Union. More muted criticism came from the Canadian government. Our Parliament passed a bill in June 1999 that was supposed to give effect to Canada's commitment at Kyoto, but there were criticisms from many sources that the bill had been so watered-down it would do little to reduce our greenhouse emissions.[16]

www.sierraclub.ca/bc

A visit to the B.C. Sierra Club Web site will tell you more about the issues associated with the environmental impact of harvesting practices in the B.C. forestry industry.

Trade and Environmental Issues

Former U.S. trade representative Carla Hill, who negotiated all trade matters for her country during much of the 1980s, has said, "I do think that [environmental] issues are going to intersect more and more with trade in this decade, and that we're going to have to analyze them and come up with a multilateral way of dealing with them."[17]

The Sierra Club is a major environmental group in the United States and Canada. Its chairman, J. Michael McCloskey, criticized Arthur Dunkel, then director general of GATT ➤**P. 74**◄, as a glaring example of narrow economic thinking. Dunkel said nations can no longer play a role as environmental leaders. He also insisted that agreements concerning ozone depletion, international waste, and endangered species are "possible sources of conflict with the GATT rules." We can see that Dunkel has a different point of view from Hill's. McCloskey went on to state that

The Sierra Club is not opposed to expanded trade but it is opposed to policy that suggests that trade is free of costs to society. Trade agreements can and should become important tools for a more comprehensive form of development, not just narrow economic growth.[18]

The Sierra Club of British Columbia (SCBC) began its work in 1969 in support of efforts to protect the famous West Coast Trail. SCBC's campaign tactics include public education and awareness-raising with the goal of minimizing the destructive effects that logging, mining, and other developments have on the environment.

The Forestry Industry

One of the most serious environmental hazards is created by the giant pulp and paper industry, which may be the largest employer in Canada. From British Columbia to Newfoundland, they spew their deadly wastes into our rivers, lakes, and ocean bays, causing incredible problems: drinking water is contaminated; aboriginals die from eating mercury-poisoned fish; the population at large is warned not to eat fish often; the rare white beluga whales in the St. Lawrence are dying off, so contaminated that their bodies are handled as highly toxic waste.

Unfortunately, according to some reports, mercury pollution has worsened. The *Montreal Gazette* carried a report from the *New York Times*:

Two decades after the government thought that the problem had been put to rest, mercury is accumulating in fish in thousands of lakes across the United States and Canada, poisoning wildlife and threatening human health. Twenty U.S. states have warned people to limit or eliminate from their diets fish they catch in certain lakes because of dangerous levels of mercury.

Canadian scientists have found elevated levels of mercury in fish caught in 95 percent of lakes they tested in Ontario.

(In Ontario and Quebec, the pulp and paper industry is a major contributor to the problem.) Scientists say the principal source of contamination [in the United States] is rain containing traces of mercury from coal-burning power plants, municipal incinerators, and smelters. Other contamination comes from lake and ocean sediments previously polluted by mercury.[19]

Some steps have been taken to improve the situation. Companies have shortened the bleaching process to avoid the use of chlorine. More paper is recycled—we have become familiar with brown envelopes and other recycled paper products. The companies have begun to clean up their operations and waste problems. There are also hopeful signs in new technology emerging to deal with pulp mill sludge.

Good News from the Pulp and Paper Industry   In 1992 the Alberta Newsprint Co. reported that a $2-million pilot project on the use of effluent sludge as a soil conditioner was showing very good results. By 1996 the results were even more encouraging. Technical director Gary Smith reported that, working closely with the Alberta Research Council and Olds College, the project was continuing to show excellent promise. A group of farmers and greenhouses found that the conditioned sludge was very good for the soil and the crops being produced. For example, canola yields had improved considerably. There was now a waiting list for the company's processed effluent.

Smith pointed out that the effluent combined well with peat moss to produce an improved product. He was also pleased to note the whole process provided a useful illustration of conservation, efficiency, and profitability. Wood chips are being recycled into the raw material required to produce newsprint. The effluent is then recycled into agricultural nutrients in combination with peat moss, thus reducing the amount of peat moss used; peat moss is a nonrenewable resource.

Alberta Newsprint is looking at a whole new market for what was formerly a waste product that was costly to dispose of. The company was getting inquiries from potential users who were now importing similar material from Oregon. Furthermore, Alberta Newsprint was even investigating the possibility of a joint venture with a horticultural company to take charge of the entire output.

In Montreal, the chairman of the Canadian Pulp and Paper Association (CPPA) stated that by the end of 1992, 15 mills would be producing recycled newsprint from de-inked paper. In 1998 director of recycling David Church reported that 22 such mills were on-stream. Church indicated that the industry faced many complex problems in its attempts to recycle and to reduce pollution. The cyclical nature of the industry, with sharp ups and downs, and the wide variety of products, which results in a variety of different effluent wastes, compound the difficulties and make solutions slow and costly. Church indicated that despite these problems and the extreme competitive pressures from international markets, the industry continues to develop new technology leading to new methods of reducing pollution.

More good news concerns the multi-pronged effort by the industry on a number of important environment issues. The CPPA (now the Forest Products Association of Canada) reports that the recovery rate of recyclable paper doubled from 1988 to 1997. In addition there has been a steady reduction in toxic wastes; projected levels for 2000 were to be less than one-third of 1993 output. There are similar reductions in water usage in processing, of suspended solids and organochlorides in effluent, in biochemical oxygen demand of effluent, fossil fuel usage, in CO_2 and sulphur emissions, and perhaps even more important, in use of elemental chlorine in bleaching and in the almost complete elimination of deadly dioxins and furans (see Figure 5.2). Achieving these and other beneficial results for our water and air quality has required that the industry invest many billions of dollars.[20]

Another piece of good news is that in 1993, "22 organizations representing virtually all aspects of the Canadian forest products industry" from coast to coast formed the Canadian Sustainable Forestry Certification Coalition. The aim is to develop a national sustainable forest management system under standards developed by the

www.newforestsproject.com

Closely aligned to the pollution issues associated with the pulp and paper business is the deforestation issue on a global scale. For the past two decades there has been a growing level of alarm and concern regarding the rate of forest clearing being carried out. The New Forests Project, based in Washington, DC, is a demonstration of this concern and an attempt to respond positively through encouraging the development of reforestation projects.

Canadian Standards Association (CSA). The CSA is an organization accredited by a government agency, the Standards Council of Canada, which coordinates the national standards system.[21]

There is no doubt that the pressure on the forestry companies to make all of these improvements came from a variety of sources: regulations in U.S. cities and in Canada, environmental groups, competitors' activities, companies' feelings of social responsibility and awareness that some of these changes will ultimately reduce their costs. Regardless of the reasons, the results are good news for all Canadians. You should also remember that this industry is one of the largest in Canada and provides employment for more than one million people directly and indirectly. Their actions have a lot of impact.

Other Problems   The forestry industry, especially in B.C., has run into serious criticism for its rapid depletion of Canada's first-growth forests, which are irreplaceable. A major battle has been fought for some years by aboriginal peoples and environmentalists to save the huge trees that are hundreds of years old in the Carmanah Valley and Clayoquot Sound in B.C.

FIGURE 5.2

SIGNIFICANT IMPROVEMENTS IN PULP AND PAPER PROCESSING AND WASTE

Four examples of areas where the industry is reducing its damage to the environment.

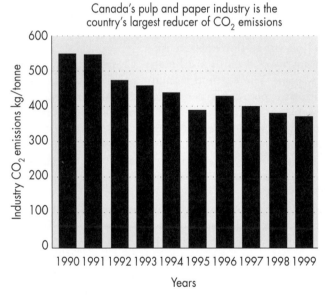

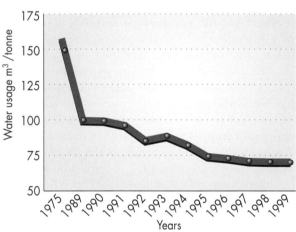

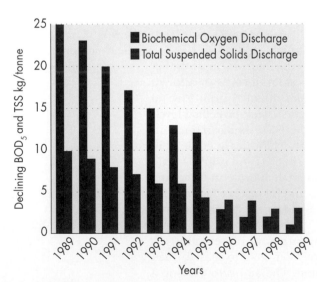

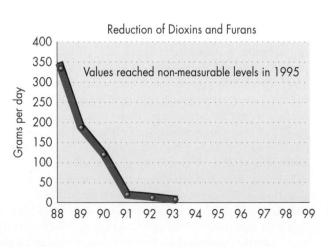

Sources: Canadian Pulp & Paper Association, September 1998; Environmental Progress Report 2000–2001, Forest Products Association of Canada.

This problem does not lend itself to a quick fix. Many large lumber companies, numerous sawmills, and thousands of employees work in this industry. Stopping logging operations completely means disaster for the sawmill operators, many of them carrying on family operations that have run for generations. The same scenario looms over the employees engaged in the various components of this industry. What would they do if logging stopped in certain areas of B.C.? What would it mean for the local economies? These kinds of problems must be solved soon.

Worldwide Deforestation

Vast deforestation has been taking place in Brazil, Borneo, Indonesia, and elsewhere in the world. Deforestation leads to soil erosion, since the treeless soil cannot retain water; silting up of rivers downstream; fewer trees producing less oxygen for a growing world population and absorbing less carbon dioxide; and logs sinking in rivers and lakes, giving off gases as they decay, which adds to the warming of the atmosphere. The solutions are not easy, since many people are trying to survive by clearing forests to farm, raise cattle, or simply earn a living working for logging companies. Tree-planting programs are a partial solution.

Pesticides and Agriculture

A major problem in agriculture is the very extensive, and intensive, use of pesticides and fertilizer as a regular process. David Suzuki, the prominent Canadian geneticist, broadcaster, and writer on environmental issues, pointed out that after almost a half-century of spraying, not a single insect species has been killed off. Instead, new spray-resistant varieties appear, requiring new and more powerful insecticides, in a never-ending vicious circle. Farmers are locked into ever-rising costs just to stand still in their endless battle against insects.

They also face rising personal health hazards from these chemicals. The CBC reported that farmers in Alberta were warned not to wear baseball caps during spraying operations. When they perspire, the chemicals absorbed by the hats leach into their scalps, causing a variety of side effects including vomiting, nausea, and other hazards.[22] Further, the runoff into rivers and lakes causes an accumulation of metals and algae. Fed by fertilizer nutrients, the algae bloom so profusely that they consume all the oxygen, causing fish and all other living matter to die. The algae then produce toxins as they die off.

Every year MacMillan Bloedel plants approximately 7 million seedlings on land it harvests. Ninety percent of its working area of the forest is restocked within three years of harvest, either through replanting or natural regeneration.

Courtesy of MacMillan Bloedel Ltd.

organic farming
Farming that is done without
chemicals.

A significant movement toward chemical-free **organic farming** has developed across Canada, as in other parts of the world. The change is slow, complex, and costly. Organic farming is still a small percentage of total agricultural production. Federal and provincial departments of agriculture have been slow to support this movement, and some people suspect pressure from the giant companies that produce fertilizers and insecticides. An interesting development is occurring at the municipal level. Hudson, a small town just west of Montreal, passed a bylaw banning the spraying of insecticides and pesticides on lawns. Two lawn-maintenance companies contested the legality of that bylaw, arguing that they were using sprays that were approved by the federal government. The case went all the way to the Supreme Court, which ruled in June 2001 that the town had the legal right to ban the use of these substances. According to media reports this decision will lead to other municipalities imposing a similar ban, thus in effect challenging the validity of the federal government's approval of the use of these products. (See the Ethical Dilemma box "The Pesticide Shuffle" for other international ramifications of pesticides.)

ETHICAL DILEMMA   *www.cropro.org*

The Pesticide Shuffle

An article in the respected weekly *Science News* pointed out the complexity, danger, and global ramifications of the global trade in dangerous pesticides. The problems relate to the export of pesticides that are banned in the United States or subject to severe restrictions. Only a small portion of the 250,000 tons of pesticides exported annually from the United States is identifiable. And that portion contains DDT and other dangerous items. It is impossible to get information on the unidentified and much larger portion.

The danger is that users in the countries that receive U.S. products assume that they are safe or the United States would not manufacture or ship them. Labels cannot be read or are ignored, and the results can be disastrous for farmers and other users. Not only that, but after being sprayed, many of these pesticides get into the rivers and lakes or get trapped in trees, soil, and other stable material and then float out into the atmosphere where they may be carried far away, according to chemist Donald Mackay of Trent University in Peterborough, Ontario.

These problems were examined at a Vancouver conference of the Society of Environmental Toxicology and Chemistry in November 1995. It is a complex issue, but according to Mackay, airborne pesticides then find their way into the United States and elsewhere. This may explain pesticides found at nesting sites of albatross in the Midway Islands in the Pacific Ocean and in polar bears and in the breast milk of Arctic Inuit women in northern Canada.

According to Ann McMillan of the Canadian Atmospheric Environment Service in Downsview, Ontario,

the data from exporting industrialized countries like the United States are so incomplete that they are like Swiss cheese—full of holes. The data from importing countries, mostly developing nations, are even worse, so it is extremely difficult for the United Nations to come up with a proper control program to curb "the airborne trek of persistent volatile pollutants across national borders."

A UN commission has been working on the problem of persistent organic pollutants (POPs) since 1979. POPs include very dangerous toxins such as dioxins, PCBs, DDT, toxaphene, and chlordane. Mackay is very anxious to see a treaty signed, compelling "signatory nations to survey which domestic firms [are] making and using the environmentally damaging compounds." Until this is done it will be impossible to control their release. In the meantime, chemical companies continue to produce and export these products.

After years of difficult negotiations, a convention was finally signed on May 23, 2001 at a conference in Sweden. Now begins the task of getting at least 50 countries to ratify it, necessary to make the convention a legal international agreement. Canada has already ratified it. Organizers hope to have the ratifications in place by the next conference, the World Summit on Sustainable Development, to be held in South Africa in September 2002.

Source: Janet Raloff, "The Pesticide Shuffle," *Science News*, March 16, 1996, pp. 174–175; Pesticide Action Network Updates Service.<www.panna.org.>, June 8, 2001.

Sewage Waste and Auto Exhausts

In addition to agricultural runoffs and pulp and paper waste, there is waste from sewage plants; auto exhausts deposits chemicals on the roads and highways. Most of these wastes and runoffs end up in the world's seas and oceans. A 1978 documentary produced by the New Jersey Network, called "Sea under Siege," shows a kilometres-long algae bloom. The documentary cites dolphins, full of heavy metals and dioxins, that get cancer and other illnesses as their immune systems weaken, and warns of the deadly effect on humans of eating fish and shellfish. Numerous reports and studies in the last two decades show that this situation has not improved since 1978.

Effect of Accidents and Bankruptcies

When the huge Lavalin conglomerate went bankrupt in Montreal in 1991, nobody knew who was going to pay for the cost of shutting down and cleaning up the petro-chemical plant it owned in Montreal. It is fortunate that the stranded engineers and employees stayed on without pay to shut down the operation properly to avoid a cat-astrophe. The provincial government, meaning the taxpayers, was stuck with the cost of the cleanup job.

A more important case that attracted a lot of attention in Canada in 1996 con-cerned the raising of an oil barge, the *Irving Whale*, that had gone down during a storm in the Gulf of St. Lawrence in 1970. This barge had been leaking its oil cargo and deadly PCBs from its heating system for many years. Residents from adjacent provinces were constantly worried about damage to the fisheries, sea mammals, and other wildlife. There was endless controversy about how to solve this difficult prob-lem, which was threatening to become even more serious as the leaking continued.

There was also the issue of determining who was responsible for this mess and who should, therefore, pay for the very expensive and complex solution, which involved raising the *Irving Wale*. The Irving Oil Company said its barge had sunk in what were then international waters; besides, the company added, it had paid many millions into an oil industry fund that was supposed to take care of such costs. The

The *Irving Whale* was raised from the bottom of the Gulf of St. Lawrence near Charlottetown. The oil-laden barge was raised to the surface without incident after spending 26 years on the ocean floor.

Canadian Press CP. Photography by Ryan Remiorz

barge was now in Canadian waters, which further complicated matters. The oil industry fund said the sinking occurred before the fund was set up, therefore it could not be responsible for the costs.

Finally, after extensive discussions between environmental experts and federal and provincial governments, it was agreed that despite the dangers of breakup and greater leakage, the *Irving Whale* had to be raised. Under the management of the Canadian Coast Guard, an armada of specialized salvage and environment protection ships, equipment, and personnel were assembled in July 1996. Watched by an army of TV and other media people, the very risky and complex job was successfully accomplished and everybody breathed a collective sigh of relief. Only one question remained to be settled: Is the federal government going to have to pick up the tab for the $30-million salvage job? The courts will have to decide that issue.

Contrast this with a case in Alberta involving a bankrupt oil company. A secured lender, who normally can seize the assets securing a loan, was prevented from doing so in this perhaps historic ruling in Canada. The Alberta Energy Resources Conservation Board ruled that the $200,000 cash that was available to the secured lender must be used to cap the company's oil wells to prevent environmental damage.[23] See the Spotlight on Small Business box "Potential Environmental Legal Nightmares for Small Business" for more on waste-management issues.

Not in My Backyard

NIMBY
"Not in my backyard," meaning that people don't want waste disposal facilities in their towns, though they agree that such facilities are needed somewhere.

One of the major problems with waste—nuclear, ordinary, or toxic—is that nobody wants it. We seem to want the products or processes that produce waste, but everybody says "not in my backyard" (**NIMBY**) when it comes to disposing of it. All across Canada, any time any level of government proposes setting up some waste storage or disposal facility and hearings are held, the overwhelming response is nearly always NIMBY, regardless of the potential economic benefits or jobs that might flow from erecting and operating the facility. We don't mind if our waste is dumped in other provinces or countries if they will accept it.

Obviously, this attitude is neither rational nor practical and offers no long-term solution to waste disposal. Better ways are gradually being adopted. Loblaws, Ontario's largest food retailer, has been putting money into going green. Vice-president Patrick Carson noted that

> If you want to be successful … you have to be realistic, and the reality is that we are living in an environment that is deteriorating. If we make money destroying this planet, we'll have to spend even more money going back to repair [it].[24]

This lesson is slowly being learned by managers, senior officers, and boards of directors. But all the environmental experts are warning us that we will have to move a lot faster if we are to avoid extremely serious problems in the near future. One solution is to do as Bell Canada did—use conservation to reduce the volume of waste—and save substantial dollars in the process.

PROGRESS CHECK

- What are ethical issues relating to arms sales, pharmaceuticals, forestry, and cigarettes?
- How do companies organize to ensure that decisions are made on an ethical basis? What is the six-step approach?
- Explain the difference between the strategic and the pluralist approaches to corporate responsibility.
- What is a social audit? How does social audit help companies improve their ethical behaviour?
- What is NIMBY?

SPOTLIGHT ON SMALL BUSINESS
Potential Environmental Legal Nightmares for Small Business

The potential losses facing business from the mishandling of waste are tremendous. Businesses may require an emissions licence, and a conviction for operating without one can bring heavy fines of up to $100,000 a day. Any company that puffs smoke through a stack on the roof—and that includes restaurants, fast-food or otherwise—may already be breaking regulations without knowing it.

Dry-cleaning firms that flush chemicals directly into the sewer system instead of contracting with bona fide waste-removal firms may be exposing themselves to heavy fines. The owners or officers of businesses might even find themselves hauled off to jail.

A small firm's truck can swerve to miss a rabbit, flip onto its side, and empty its cargo of toxic material, chemicals, or gasoline into a roadside creek, with resulting financial disaster for the truck's owners. The price for the smallest spill—for instance, toxic waste seeping into the soil from defective storage tanks—will include the costs of cleanup, expert assessment of the damage, legal fees, and fines, and can run up to $100,000, said environmental lawyer Roger Cotton. And that does not include the large costs of defending against any legal suits brought by any of the surrounding homeowners.

The pressure is on governments to put teeth into environmental regulations. Unfortunately, insurance is not yet available for this type of problem, which means that all companies, large and small, must consult with waste storage and disposal experts to ensure that they are not breaking any laws.

This issue also affects every purchase of land, buildings, or businesses. Banks will not lend for such purchases unless an environmental audit has been made and a clean bill of health is issued by a reputable company with expertise in environmental problems. Public accounting and management consulting firms also urge their clients to have these audits performed before considering such acquisitions.

Occasional reports in the media indicate that this issue continues to be a problem.

Adapted from: Claire Bernstein, "Problem of Waste Storage and Disposal Has Even Small Companies Worried," *Toronto Star*, April 6, 1992, p. D3; interviews with Ms. Bernstein, February 12, 1999, and chartered accountant L. Wolman, January 10, 1999.

Conservation

One effective way to deal with waste is to *use* less, so less waste is created. The amount of packaging per item in supermarkets and elsewhere is being reduced. Furthermore, containers and other packaging are being made biodegradable. Many fast-food restaurants have followed this trend. These measures do not reduce the volume of waste, but they do make it less threatening to the environment.

Conservation has many more beneficial side effects. More fuel-efficient automotive, marine, and airplane engines reduce demand on the Earth's natural resources, and on the transportation and distribution of fuel oils and gasoline. Fewer marine and truck tankers and storage tanks reduce the risk of accidents and spills. Less fuel burned results in less exhaust gas, reducing the warming of the Earth by the greenhouse effect.

Electricity consumption is being reduced through energy-efficient kitchen appliances, electric motors, and light bulbs, as well as better-insulated buildings and lower room thermostat and hot-water settings. Hydro and power companies are educating themselves and consumers about conservation methods and offering various incentives. These activities avoid the necessity for costly new hydroelectric projects that would flood vast territories, creating various environmental hazards and encroaching on indigenous peoples' lands and rights.

An example of an efficient and environmentally sound operation is the CBC building in Montreal, headquarters of the French network Radio-Canada. According to the chief heating engineer, this 30-year-old building employs heat from

Environment Canada's Green Lane Web site <www.ec.gc.ca> proposes a variety of suggestions to help reduce smog in our communities. One idea is sustainable transportation, which covers many issues such as promoting the use of public transit, car-pooling, and alternative forms of transportation including bicycling and walking.

PhotoDisc

the bodies of its inhabitants and heat generated by the lights in the TV studios to provide almost all the heating required—with very rare supplementation by a conventional heating system.[25]

All new buildings are now better insulated and have special window installations that reduce heat loss, an important factor in energy consumption in our cold northern climate.

The combined energy-efficient operations of equipment, appliances, buildings, and vehicles have an enormous cumulative effect in reducing the emission of gases that contribute to the warming of the planet by the greenhouse effect. They also reduce other environmental damage.

Ozone Problems

For some time, scientists have warned that the ozone layers in the upper atmosphere have developed holes or are thinning, posing greater risks of cancer because increased amounts of ultraviolet radiation are getting through from the sun to us. Yet too much ozone in the lower atmosphere causes deadly smog. An impressive analysis based on 15 years of data compiled by NASA satellites and using "a new, more accurate analytical technique" shows that "the increases [in ultraviolet B radiation] are largest in middle and high latitudes where most people live and where there is the majority of agricultural activity."[26] This region includes Canada.

The Globe and Mail, carrying a news item from the well-respected *Christian Science Monitor* of Boston, noted that California (a forerunner on many environmental issues) has established controls on a wide variety of products that contribute to smog. This includes items like dusting aids, nonstick cooking sprays, charcoal lighter fluid, household adhesives, insecticides, and personal fragrance items. Placing smog controls on these items is expected to cut air pollution in California by the equivalent of one million new cars. Personal fragrance products alone release four tons of volatile organic compounds into the air daily in California.[27]

The California and British Columbia governments have both passed regulations requiring less- or nonpolluting vehicles to be on their roads. These restrictions are being phased in over a 5- to 10-year period to give auto manufacturers the opportunity to gradually reduce exhaust pollutants and to introduce electric vehicles.[28]

Technological Solutions

Some people count on technology as a solution to pollution and other environmental problems. Periodically there are encouraging reports of ingenious ideas that seem to offer some hope. A story in the *Minneapolis–St. Paul Star Tribune* told how engineer Emil Pfender, in his lab at the University of Minnesota, had converted the toxins benzene and acetone into tiny industrial diamonds. He expects to be able to do the same with deadly PCBs as soon as he can solve the problem of handling them safely.[29]

Dale Atkins/AP

Although such advances in science are important, we are a very long way from being able to convert the vast output of waste, toxic or otherwise, into useful substances. It is far more logical to follow the conservation route and start reducing the vast daily outpouring of such products. Conservation has the added advantage of maintaining our resources and natural environment.

The Global Environment

The environmental problems we face in Canada are duplicated all over the world. Typical headlines from Canadian and American newspapers read: "Mexico extends restrictions as capital chokes on smog," "Scientists say people, pollution threaten 'rain forests of the ocean,'" "Alps caught in vise between tourism and trucks," "The Sphinx in danger of collapse," and "Why the environment is the issue of our lives."

This small sample indicates the damage caused to the natural environment by the activities of humans. Most of the problems stem from the explosion of population and industrial activities that we are seeing: the Earth cannot sustain that growth without suffering serious damage.

General Motors Corporation is helping to address the problems of endless growth for the environment through its development of electric cars. An electric motor vehicle doesn't require emissions testing because it doesn't have any emissions. Also, the car does not require gasoline or oil changes, which means cleaner air. The aluminum structure of the car is also 100-percent recyclable.

THE PROBLEM OF ENDLESS GROWTH

All countries, including Canada, believe that growth is a desirable goal. We even worship growth. More plants, more offices, more production, more sales, even more population are all considered positive achievements. In Canada, we worry about our population declining because of our low birthrate. Various countries have programs to encourage larger families to increase population. Only China has undertaken a serious long-term campaign to control population growth.

David Suzuki pointed out that it is only in the last century that growth has become a normal part of our lives. He quoted University of Colorado physicist Albert Bartlett: "The greatest shortcoming of the human race is our inability to understand the **exponential function**." It is simply the mathematical description of anything that changes steadily in one direction over a given period of time. Suzuki gave some interesting examples of where that leads.

The **rule of 72** says that if you divide the rate of increase of any activity into 72, you get the number of years it takes for the result of that activity to double. If the inflation rate is 6 percent, in 12 years prices will double. This holds true whether it is pollution, population, or use of energy that is growing.

The point is that even a small, steady increase can over time have startling effects in one lifetime. A 5-percent annual inflation rate over a 75-year life span would result in gas going from 50¢ to $16 a litre, an $8 movie admission to $256, a $1 soda pop to $32, and a $20,000 car to $640,000! If all of this sounds fantastic, just ask your grandparents if they remember 3¢-per-litre gas, 25¢ movies, 5¢ pop, and $800 new cars.

exponential function
The mathematical description of anything that changes steadily in one direction over a given period.

rule of 72
Divide the rate of increase of any activity into 72 to get the number of years it takes for the result of that activity to double.

Suzuki continued:

> It's the same with exponential increase in our use of energy, forests, or ocean resources.... Yet we continue to demand more. But everything in the universe, including the universe itself, is finite. Nothing in it can grow exponentially indefinitely.... Stanford ecologist Paul Ehrlich is more blunt. Steady, endless growth, he says, is the creed of cancer cells and mainstream economists, and the inevitable result is the same for both.
>
> If you look at the history of mankind on this planet, it is only in [the last] century that growth has become such an obvious part of life. On a graph of our numbers—use of food, air, water, soil—the curves are virtually flat for 99 percent of our history. They begin to turn up perceptibly only in the [nineteenth] century; and then in our lifetime, through exponential growth, they leap off the page.[30]

Suzuki's point is clearly demonstrated if we look at population growth. William K. Stevens, writing in the *New York Times*, pointed out that it took all of human history for the world population to reach 2.5 billion in 1950. But it took only 40 more years for that number to double to 5 billion in 1990. In 2000 we passed 6 billion. While the growth *rate* has gone down, the actual annual increase in population is high, at 75–80 million. At that rate every decade sees the addition of more than three-quarters of a billion people to the world's population.

Stevens quoted from *Beyond the Limits* by Meadows, Meadows, and Raders. Their updated computer simulations indicate that

> If human activity continues as at present, it will "overshoot" the carrying capacity of the biosphere and precipitate a collapse within the next few decades.... The new analysis puts more emphasis on the deterioration of the biosphere, says Dennis Meadows. He notes that "Twenty years ago it seemed to us that there was a period out to 2030 or 2040 in which to fashion a sustainable society." Now, he says, it looks as though if a new set of attitudes and policies is not in place in the next 20 years [2012], it will be too late to avoid an eventual collapse.

This same article carried a report from an important business consulting group that denied that there is anything to worry about for the next 100 to 150 years because the market system has repeatedly stretched the so-called finite limits of the Earth to become "roughly infinite." But researchers in these fields disagree with this optimistic assessment. They see population and emission increases leading to drastic climate and other changes in the biosphere because of overloading.[31]

CRITICAL THINKING

Do you think that environmental concerns are overstated? Even if they are not overstated, technology has always produced ingenious ways of solving many problems. Why not rely on some new process to take care of pollution, the greenhouse effect, the ozone problem, and the rest?

WHAT IS THE ANSWER?

The problem of business and the environment in Canada is quite complicated. An article in the prestigious *Harvard Business Review* by Charles Hampden-Turner, a senior research fellow at the London Business School and at the Centre for International Business Studies in Amsterdam, addressed the issue globally:

Environmental clean-up in the United States has been stalled for a decade by a sterile debate about the "costs" of government regulation to economic competitiveness. In Japan, by contrast, government intervened to encourage the development of antipollution technologies. The result: both cleaner industries and a new generation of companies internationally competitive in the emerging global market for these technologies.[32]

Another decade has passed and the U.S. is still stalling.

The difference in attitudes and action between Japanese and American business and governments is clear. Canada has a better track record than the United States, but environmental and community groups generally accuse governments and business of giving mostly lip service to, rather than being genuinely involved in, a serious effort to improve the situation. We also seem to be held back by concerns about the "costs" question and what it will do to our competitiveness.

Here are some interesting examples of what can be done to cut the use of dirty fuels. The city of Tokyo has 1.5 million buildings with solar hot-water heating. Germany now produces 3,000 megawatts of windpower, while we in Canada produce only 30 megawatts of windpower. In addition Germany created 10,000 new jobs in the windpower industry during the 1990s. Wind is the fastest-growing energy source in the world, with production increasing 25 percent annually during the 1990s, generating some $3 billion in sales in 1998.[33]

The German and Japanese examples are certainly promising ones to follow. In Canada we have also made some technological advances that are helping us export our environmentally friendly expertise.

Global Application of Canadian Technology

Some Canadian companies are already applying their expertise to environmental problems around the world. Some recent examples are:

1. Toronto engineering firm R. V. Anderson Associates Ltd. has an initial $3-million contract to help clean up the sewage system in "one of the world's dirtiest cities," Bombay, India.[34]

2. Spar Aerospace, which built the robotic Canadarm used on American space vehicles, obtained a $22-million contract from the U.S. government to build four robotic backhoes for toxic and other environmental cleanup jobs.[35]

3. Zenon Environmental Inc. of Burlington, Ontario, received a contract from the Egyptian government to provide four membrane-based water purification systems.[36]

4. Scientists at the University of Guelph have developed a genetically engineered pig whose manure contains "very little phosphorus, a water pollutant that promotes the growth of algae" in all waters (thus reducing the amount of oxygen available for fish and other flora). The scientists are also hard at work trying to engineer the reduction of nitrogen, another pollutant in pig waste. Nitrogen is also responsible for the terrible odour in pig manure, which is becoming a serious problem to people living adjacent to pig farms. Going by the trade name *Enviropig,* this is believed to be the first animal engineered to solve an environmental problem.[37]

These are but a few examples of the expertise that can develop when Canadian companies start applying themselves to solving environmental problems.

Sustainable Development

Another useful input into this difficult area is the concept that emerged from the international conference on the environment in Toronto in 1988. The Brundtland

The mission of the International Institute for Sustainable Development (IISD) is to promote sustainable development in decision making internationally and within Canada. IISD was established in 1990 with continuing financial support from Environment Canada, CIDA, and the Province of Manitoba. IISD also receives revenue from foundations and other private-sector sources. The institute is registered as a charitable organization in Canada and a tax-exempt, nonprofit corporation in the United States.

Courtesy of International Institute for Sustainable Development

www.iisd.ca

Visit the International Institute for Sustainable Development's Web site to learn more about the organization and its work. You might find the Institute's definition of *sustainable development* particularly useful.

report (named after the Norwegian prime minister who chaired the commission) suggested that sustainable development is the responsible way of the future. Only economic and industrial development that can be sustained over time without damaging the environment should be pursued. Most governments now support this concept in theory, but its implementation is another story.

In Canada, we have made a good start by establishing the International Institute for Sustainable Development (IISD), set up jointly by the federal and Manitoba governments and headquartered in Winnipeg. The governments appointed the first three members of the board of directors, who then appointed 12 international members from various countries.

> IISD is an independent, non-profit corporation, funded by the governments of Manitoba and Canada. Its mission is to promote the concept and practice of development which integrates the needs of the economy and the environment in decision making. The institute undertakes programs and projects internationally and in Canada. IISD is governed by an independent international board of directors.[38]

Business, governments, and labour, too, are beginning to shift their emphasis from thinking in the short term—profits, jobs, and tax revenues now—to thinking of the long-term effects on the environment. It will take a determined effort from everyone concerned to get decision making moving in the direction of sustainable development, but we have no choice if we want to maintain a habitable world for ourselves and our children.

In past years, steps were taken to improve the environment: catalytic converters on vehicles, reduced gas consumption, banning of spray cans that release ozone-depleting chemicals, elimination of toxins like PCBs, and recycling to reduce waste and tree cutting. However, we have not yet made the really hard decisions that must be made. Further, we sometimes go into reverse, for example the production of vans and SUVs that are notorious gas-guzzlers.

Sustainable Consumption

A concept that complements sustainable development is another UN project called the *United Nations Environment Program (UNEP)*, which works in partnership with the

UN Commission on Sustainable Development. UNEP "goes beyond 'green' consumption and addresses social and equity issues as well." UNEP urges governments and businesses to use procurement and production to "foster demand for cleaner products and services" with the help of advertising agencies. UNEP has worked closely with government agencies in Germany, Japan, Norway, Holland, and Spain, and with the OECD and the European Union in a variety of projects including eco-labelling schemes for developing countries.[39]

ISO 14000 Ratings

In Chapter 10 you will read about how the International Standards Organization (ISO) has developed a widely accepted 9000 series for rating companies all over the world. This rating assures customers of companies with the 9000 rating that quality, delivery, service, and so on will be consistent and reliable. Many companies in Europe and North America will only do business with suppliers who have a 9000 rating. Now the ISO also has a 14000 designation that it issues to companies that operate in an environmentally friendly fashion. If the 14000 rating gains as much support as is the case with the 9000 designation, a significant step will have been taken in the direction of a better global physical environment. The Canadian Standards Association (CSA) is the agent in Canada for issuing the 14000 rating. At the end of the chapter you will see a case of a raspberry-growing operation in Quebec that was the first farm in Canada to receive a 14000 series approval.[40]

A RADICALLY DIFFERENT ANSWER[41]

Paul Hawken is an American entrepreneur, cofounder of Smith and Hawken, catalogue merchandisers, and author of *The Ecology of Commerce* and *Our Future and the Making of Things*. Both books provide some startling answers for the ethical and environmental issues that we face. Hawken believes that a new approach is required if we are to survive on this planet. He claims that if his suggestions were followed they would

- reduce energy and natural resource use in developed nations by 80 percent within a half-century.
- provide secure, stable, and meaningful employment.
- be a "self-actuating" system rather than one that is regulated or moralistic.
- restore degraded habitats and ecosystems rather than merely sustain them at current levels.
- rely on current levels of solar "income."
- be fun, involving, and aesthetic.

This may give the impression of some utopian dream, but Hawken fleshed out his plan in great detail. He has a 12-point program that proposes a radically different system of government taxation and business operation. Ordinary people will also have to change their way of life.

At present, the environmental and social responsibility movements consist of many different initiatives connected primarily by values and beliefs rather than by design. What is needed is a conscious plan to create a sustainable future, including a set of design strategies for people to follow.

The underlying philosophy of his "design strategies" is that the current systems make destructive commercial and industrial behaviour normal and profitable, and it requires high moral principles to act more responsibly. He would change this around so that irresponsible behaviour would be costly and abnormal, whereas socially responsible activities would be cheaper and yield more profits for companies. Hawken says, "we need a system of commerce and production in which each and every act is inherently sustainable and restorative."

Some major aspects of Hawken's 12-point program include:

1. Adjusting prices to reflect all costs. This includes proper waste disposal, damage to environment and to people's health, and so on.

2. Total revision of taxation philosophy so that instead of taxing jobs, payrolls, creativity, and real income, it is degradation, pollution, and depletion that will be taxed.

3. Transformation of the way we design products so that most things will be recyclable or biodegradable. This will involve drastic reduction or elimination of the hundreds of chemicals, metals, plastics, dyes, and pesticides that are part of so many products. This is already being done to a certain extent in Germany and Japan with autos and other items. These are all part of an elaborate scheme that would totally revolutionize how we now function. Hawken insists that we have no choice because even if "every company on the planet were to adopt the environment and social practices of the best companies ... the world would still be moving towards environmental degradation and collapse." He is not alone in this belief.

As with other ethical issues, important changes in thinking and actions by corporate and government management show an acceptance of greater social responsibility. The new generation of managers emerging from business schools has been alerted to these concerns, so the future looks promising. Are we ready for the kind of changes Hawken proposed? Do we have a choice?

IMPACT ON CAREERS

At the beginning of the chapter you were alerted to the possible impact on your career choices of the information provided here. As you have seen, the issues are complex and not open to simple solutions. However, the scope and depth of environmental and ethical problems have resulted in a whole new field of studies in an effort to find workable solutions. New career opportunities have opened up devoted

---

ETHICAL DILEMMA

Review

Our executives believe that the growing interdependency of companies and countries through the globalization of business is leading to international standards of behaviour. Bédard believes that "we are in an era of a more level global playing field because of NGOs [nongovernmental organizations] and other such groups. All companies are under the same watchful eyes and in the long run everyone will learn that ethical standards must be maintained no matter where an operation is carried out."

Reilley emphasizes that "company growth and ethical behaviour are not mutually exclusive. A company won't survive in the long run if it's not proactive on these issues. Also more and more world bodies (WTO, NAFTA, OECD, ASEAN, IMF) are demanding ethical behaviour ... in all countries. Things are changing very quickly, which may not be obvious to those not directly involved. Being at the forefront of this activity positions Canadian companies to gain, not the other way around."

to studying the problems, finding answers, and implementing them. Universities and governments have whole departments grappling with environmental issues and thousands of articles and books are constantly being written exploring problems and solutions. Companies and environmental organizations require employees who are knowledgeable about environmental and ethical problems. You might find a career in this area interesting, challenging, and rewarding.

PROGRESS CHECK

- What is the ozone problem? Why is it so important?
- What is the rule of 72? Why is it useful? Can you give some examples?
- Why is population growth a potential time bomb?

SUMMARY

1. In the 1800s, laissez-faire capitalism was commonly accepted as good and necessary.
    - *Why were ethical standards ignored or so low?*
    It was believed that everyone would benefit from unregulated and unrestricted production and wealth accumulation by capitalists. The evils of this new system were tolerated as being unavoidable.

    1. Discuss how business in the early capitalist period ignored ethical standards of behaviour.

2. Prior to the 1960s, there was little real challenge to the ways companies did business. Then something happened in the United States and a great change occurred in the attitudes of Americans and Canadians.
    - *What was the role of Ralph Nader in changing company attitudes? What are their expectations now?*
    This young lawyer, working almost alone, took on mighty General Motors because of its defective Corvair model. He finally forced GM to recall cars for the first time in automotive history. Greater social responsibility is now demanded from companies, governments, and their officials.

    2. Describe the modern beginnings of business ethics, and understand why ethical issues are so important now.

3. Some managers think ethics are individual issues that have nothing to do with management; others believe ethics have everything to do with management. In practice, it's often difficult to know when a decision is ethical.
    - *What is management's role in setting ethical standards? How can managers determine if their decisions are ethical?*
    Top managers set formal ethical standards and establish company structures to supervise them, but more important are the messages they send through their actions. Tolerance or intolerance of ethical misconduct influences employees more than any written ethics code. (See the six steps that lead to a practical ethical decision-making system.)

    3. Define management's role in setting ethical standards, and list the six-step approach to ethical decisions.

4. The change in attitudes regarding the environment started with a book published in the United States in the 1960s.
    - *What was that book and why did it make such an impact?*
    Silent Spring by Rachel Carson showed how the numbers of birds had declined sharply. The cause was the insecticide DDT, previously used as a cure-all spray. This led to the birth of the modern environmental movement.
    - *What are the most serious, widespread issues now?*
    Global warming, due to an increase in gases trapped in the atmosphere, is causing the greenhouse effect. Ozone depletion at upper levels and an increase at lower levels are other results of certain gas emissions. Pollution of the air, water, and soil is also causing many serious problems.

    4. Identify what first led to concern about the environment, and list some of the major environmental problems.

5. Understand why business sees a conflict between a clean environment and competitive ability.

5. There are heavy costs attached to cleaning up problems from the past and just as great costs in changing how industries operate in the future.
   • *How does this affect competitiveness?*
   This concern is that companies that do a good job will incur heavier costs than those that do not clean up their act. These additional costs will result in higher prices than those of "dirty" competitors.

6. Describe the rule of 72, and explain its relationship to growth.

6. The rule of 72 is a mathematical formula.
   • *What information does it yield and what is the significance of this information?*
   It shows how many years it takes for any steady rate of change to result in a doubling of the results of that change. It is determined by dividing a certain rate of change into 72.

7. Explain how sustainable development has become the major international goal for reconciling growth with environmental constraints.

7. Endless uncontrolled growth has led to many of our environmental problems.
   • *How does sustainable development provide a solution for such problems?*
   Planning only as much growth or expansion as the environment can tolerate without deteriorating is the only way to sustain development over the long term.

KEY TERMS

bid rigging   133
corporate social responsibility   125
exponential function   149

laissez-faire capitalism   125
NIMBY   146
organic farming   144
robber barons   125

rule of 72   149
social audit   138
stakeholders   137
white-collar crimes   132

DEVELOPING WORKPLACE SKILLS

1. Do you believe most businesses today are socially responsible? What is your evidence to back up that position?

2. Discuss the merits of increased legislation versus self-regulation by companies to prevent deceptive business practices. Which is better in the long run? Defend your position.

3. How would you describe the ethical environment in Canada today? How important is the role of business in creating that environment? Do you see leadership emerging to improve ethical standards in Canada? What can you do to support such leadership?

4. You are the purchasing manager of a small, wholesale, giftware company. You have been grooming Catherine, a bright employee, for a managerial position in your department, but the owner of the company springs a surprise on you. He informs you that he would like to bring his son, Josh, into the business and his background makes him suitable for the same managerial position. You are afraid if you tell Cathy the truth she will quit because she will not get a promised promotion. What would you do—tell her some story and hope she will stay and some other opening might take place? Would you try to make Josh's life difficult so he will quit or his father will let him go? Is there any other course of action open to you?

Purpose:

To demonstrate the level of commitment some businesses have to social responsibility, quality, and ethical behaviour.

Exercises:

1. Check out Bombardier's Web site <www.bombardier.com>. Click on *about us*, *social responsibility*, and then on *corporate social commitment* and *corporate environment policy* to see what the company's policy is on these matters. What do you think about these policies? Bring a printout to class for discussion.

2. Examine the Web sites of these two Canadian companies to see what you can learn about the ISO 14000 rating and approval process in Canada:

    MGMT Alliance Inc: <www.mgmt14k.com>.

    Canadian Environmental Auditing Association: <www.ceaa-acve.ca>.

    Print out anything you find interesting and bring it to class.

PRACTISING MANAGEMENT DECISIONS

CASE 1

THE BATTLE BETWEEN THE CORPORATE GIANT AND THE SASKATCHEWAN FARMER

Percy Schmeiser had spent 50 years farming his land near Bruno, Saskatchewan. Suddenly, Schmeiser was fighting what may be the strangest battle in the history of agriculture. "My grandfather and my father homesteaded here," Schmeiser says. "There were no such things as chemical companies, or even seed companies. They were free and independent." Now Schmeiser has been forced to fight the biggest boy on the block; he's battling the world's largest agrochemical company, Monsanto. Monsanto makes the weedkiller called Roundup. Spray it onto a field and it kills everything growing there. Then Monsanto genetically engineered a canola seed so that Roundup doesn't hurt it. That means a farmer can spray Roundup herbicide over an entire field, kill all the weeds growing there, and not hurt the canola crops, as long as it comes from Monsanto's special seed.

In the brave new world of agriculture, it's Monsanto versus the farmer. Farmers buying Monsanto's seed must sign a contract promising to buy fresh seed every year. Then, they must let Monsanto inspect their fields for cheating. Monsanto's regional director in Western Canada is Randy Christenson. He says the company has to be tough. "We've put years of research into developing this technology so we must recoup our investment," Christenson says.

Percy Schmeiser says he's never used Monsanto's seed. He saves the seeds from his own crops, then replants them in the spring. But Monsanto investigators say they've found Monsanto DNA in Schmeiser's crops. Monsanto says Schmeiser never paid for the rights to use its DNA. So they sued Schmeiser. "I've been farming for 50 years, and all of the sudden I have this," Schmeiser says. "It's very upsetting and nerve wracking to have a multi-giant corporation come after you. I don't have the resources to fight this."

Monsanto doesn't apologize for playing hardball. But the Monsanto representatives insist the whole process is very friendly. Monsanto calls its investigations *audits*. "Yes, we do have a group that does audits, they do make farm visits, but they do it in a way that is extremely respectful to the farmers," Christensen says. He insists that farmers who have been through it are very comfortable with what Monsanto is doing because they never go on their property without farmers' permission.

But court documents show Monsanto ordered its investigators to trespass onto Schmeiser's fields and collect samples. Then Monsanto agents paid a secret visit to the company that processes Schmeiser's seeds for planting and were able to get a sample of the seeds. Monsanto says Schmeiser has stolen its DNA. Monsanto has accused dozens of farmers of growing the special seed without paying for it. The problem is, Mother Nature has been moving DNA around for thousands of years. Monsanto's is just the latest. "It will blow in the wind. You can't control it. You can't just, say, put a fence around it and say that's where it stops. It might end up 10 miles, 20 miles away," Schmeiser says.

Schmeiser is backed by scientists from Agriculture Canada who say wind can blow seeds or pollen between fields, meaning the DNA of crops in one field often mixes with another. Seeds or pollen can also be blown off uncovered trucks and farm equipment. But Monsanto seems to be saying it's up to farmers to dig out any crops from seeds they have not bought from

Monsanto. Without a microscope, there's no way to tell regular crops from crops carrying the Monsanto DNA.

This means even the seed that farmers keep from their own crops may contain Monsanto's altered gene. Last year, Edward Zilinski of Micado traded seeds with a farmer from Prince Albert. This is an old farming tradition. But the seeds he got in return had Monsanto's DNA. Now Monsanto says Zilinski and his wife owe them more than $28,000 in penalties. "Farmers should have some rights of their own!" Zilinski says.

Monsanto's heavy hand is sparking the anger of many farmers in Western Canada. The Kram family in Raymore say planes and a helicopter have buzzed their fields. The couple says agents dropped weedkiller on their canola field, to see if the crops had the Monsanto gene. Monsanto says they had absolutely nothing to do with it. The Krams think otherwise: "We are … disgusted with the way things are going," Elizabeth Kram says "Who put the canola in? It was the farmer. It doesn't belong to Monsanto or anybody else and I don't see anybody else's name on the titles of all the land we own. It's my husband and myself. Nobody else. [We're] thoroughly pissed off."

Percy Schmeiser believes Monsanto hopes to force farmers into accepting genetically engineered products. Schmeiser is standing up to Monsanto in court. "I'm going to fight and fight and fight," he says, "because I believe what is happening to farmers is wrong. And I'm fighting this not just for myself, but for my children and my grandchildren. And for my farmer friends."

"As you move to adopt new technology, whether it was from the horse to the car, there was a great deal of controversy, questions being asked, on how to deal with certain issues," Monsanto's Christensen says. But the real question is this, can Monsanto or anybody put a patent on a piece of nature? The answer could determine who controls the future of world farming.

The court gave its opinion in 2001, ruling that Schmeiser had used Monsanto's seeds and must pay the company.

Decision Questions

1. In this case we can see how our technologically driven world creates new ethical dilemmas. Genetic engineering in general has sparked a lot of controversy worldwide because of uncertainty about long-term harmful effects. Here the immediate questions are: should a company have the right to patent new forms of plant or animal life? Can Monsanto carry on its investigations in an acceptable manner? How far should it be allowed to go in enforcing its rights?

2. Assuming that Monsanto discovers its DNA in the fields of a farmer who had not purchased its seeds that year, what should it do? Is it reasonable to expect farmers to dig up crops that may have been affected by wind-blown seeds? Are they supposed to get samples of each stalk and have them examined under a microscope?

3. It is apparent that what we have here is a conflict of rights. Monsanto has been granted certain legal rights by the U.S. Patent Office that are conflicting with the normal rights and freedoms of farmers in Saskatchewan. Whose rights are more important? Can such a distinction really be made?

4. Let's return to the first question about genetic engineering in general. This is a recurring issue in medicine, in biology, and in many other fields. Should we draw a line and not permit technology to go beyond a certain point? How do we determine that point? Who will decide what's ethical?

Source: CBC TV, *The National*, June 8, 1999; CP, "Farmer must pay for Monsanto's canola," *Montreal Gazette*, March 30, 2001, p. A10.

TWO CHEERS FOR RASPBERRIES

Jocelyne Hamelin and her husband Daniel Couture operate a raspberry farm business, La Framboisère, in the Eastern Townships region of Quebec. For many reasons, it is not your ordinary small farm. First, the farm produces 40 tonnes annually, which is a lot of raspberries. The couple have the largest raspberry farm in Quebec. Second, the couple are embarked on a plan to make their operation environmentally friendly. This means reducing pesticide use by 70 percent. The farm also has an underground drip system for irrigation with the result that a pond now irrigates 26 acres instead of 15. This conservation of water is not only good for the environment, but also has increased their production

by 50 percent. Other aspects of an environmentally friendly operation include strict rules on fuel storage, waste management, and recyclable packaging.

As a result of such careful attention to these details of their operations, Hamelin and Couture have achieved an important first—theirs is the first farm in Canada to get the ISO 14001 designation. ISO stands for *International Standards Organization* and it is a very important body. In Chapter 10 you will see how their 9000 series designation has become the major international seal of approval for the ability of companies to consistently and reliably produce, deliver, and service products of good quality. If you observe company signs in your area you may see displays on buildings of companies proudly showing that they have received an ISO 9001 or 9002 rating.

The ISO 14000 series rating is for environmentally friendly operations and is a more recent development. Couture says that it is not yet an important marketing tool, but that "American buyers are catching on" and soon consumers will be looking for that approval on labels. As Couture puts it, "so when you eat a raspberry you will know that you are really eating a raspberry and not pesticide."

Other farmers in the area are catching on because "seven other farms producing milk, pork or Christmas trees are working towards [ISO 14000] certification."

Decision Questions

1. Does the example of La Framboisière mean farmers are not afraid to try something new? Does the fact that other farmers are *catching on* support that belief? Would you be more apt to buy a fruit or vegetable with an ISO 14000 seal of approval?

2. This case demonstrates that being kind to the environment can result in *decreased* and not *extra costs* of operations. Why then do you think that many companies are reluctant to explore more environmentally friendly alternatives? Do you think that consumer products would enjoy greater popularity if they had an ISO 14000 rating?

3. How important do you think it is to move more quickly in the direction of reducing damage to the environment? Do we need stricter laws? Or would stricter enforcement of existing regulations do the job?

4. Some people believe that showing by example is more effective than passing stronger laws. How can we encourage more companies to take the lead so that others will follow? Would you be in favour of tax concessions to aid companies *going green?*

Based on: CBC News Report, CBM Radio, Montreal, June 13, 1999.

CBC   VIDEO CASE   www.cbc.ca

THE WINDS OF CHANGE

Some time in the 1970s, individuals, companies and governments started getting seriously interested in renewable sources of energy. Solar energy had been used by some countries in the global sunshine belt to provide hot water. But now, high oil prices and growing concerns about global pollution – caused by burning coal and oil – led to the development of wind power as an attractive alternate source of energy. It has the additional advantages of being sustainable, non-polluting, and widely available. California and Denmark were among the pioneers in this development. In the late 1970s, one of the authors of this text (Paul Berman) was driving in Southern California and was surprised to see vast numbers of modern-style windmills. He discovered that they were generating large amounts of electricity in this windy desert area. In the early 1980s, while teaching summer courses to Canadian students in Denmark, he found a number of villages whose main source of energy was generated by windmills. By the late 1990s and early 2000s many countries and companies had followed suit.

Wind power has become the fastest growing alternate source of energy. In Canada three companies provide the substantial financing needed for such projects, and one company actually produces the complex finished product and all the necessary installations. While most countries provide tax relief and other incentives to encourage the installation of this clean and renewable energy source, Canada is lagging behind in such measures.

As steady improvement in the technology keeps reducing the price per unit of energy produced, wind power will become increasingly competitive with coal- and oil-based units. Of course, it is only practical in climates where there are steady and strong winds.

Discussion Questions

1. Do you see any contradiction between wind power and the continuing search for, and the development of, new oil and gas sources in various parts of Canada (for instance, offshore Nova Scotia, and Newfoundland and Labrador)? Should they both be ongoing developments or should we be concentrating on the clean source of energy? Why?

2. Do you think the Canadian government should be following the lead of other countries by providing tax relief and other incentives to encourage wind power development? What about the effect on the oil, coal and gas industry in Canada, a major part of our economy? Discuss.

3. The video shows how three Canadian companies are actively seeking projects to finance in Canada, the U.S. and elsewhere. We also see a company that has the technology to produce the units necessary for a wind power installation. What two major trends discussed in chapter one does this highlight? Would this encourage you to seek employment in either the financing or production side? Discuss.

Source: *Venture*, show number 772, "The Winds of Change," January 30, 2001, running time 6:22.

PART 2

CHAPTER

6

Forms of Business Organization

LEARNING GOALS

AFTER YOU HAVE READ AND STUDIED THIS CHAPTER, YOU SHOULD BE ABLE TO

1. List the three basic forms of business ownership and compare the advantages and disadvantages of each.

2. Explain the differences between limited and general partners.

3. Summarize the important clauses of a partnership agreement.

4. Define public and private corporations.

5. Compare the advantages and disadvantages of private and public corporations.

6. Define franchising and examine its advantages and disadvantages.

7. Outline the areas to analyze when evaluating a franchise.

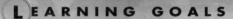

Armand Bombardier, Founder of Bombardier Inc.

Courtesy of Bombardier Inc.

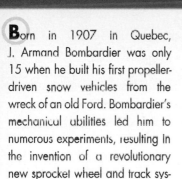**B**orn in 1907 in Quebec, J. Armand Bombardier was only 15 when he built his first propeller-driven snow vehicles from the wreck of an old Ford. Bombardier's mechanical abilities led him to numerous experiments, resulting in the invention of a revolutionary new sprocket wheel and track system in 1935. In 1937 he started a company to mass-produce snow-mobiles based on his invention.

Over the next two decades, Bombardier designed numerous all-terrain vehicles. In 1959 he began marketing the first small Ski-Doo snowmobile. Bombardier thus not only solved the problem of individual transportation on snow, but also created a new sport. Armand Bombardier died in 1964 without an inkling of the market success his invention was to enjoy.

Today Bombardier Inc. is a giant transnational company, and the largest manufacturer of passenger rail cars, with production facilities in Canada, the United States, Mexico, and 20 other countries. It has 44 subsidiaries and 100,000 employees, with activities in all forms of rail transport, aerospace and defence, motorized consumer products, financial services, and real estate development. Its total revenues exceed $16 billion.

Bombardier's company has paid a lot of attention to its social responsibilities by forming the J. Armand Bombardier Foundation. The foundation receives 3 percent of the company's net income before tax and uses these funds to support charitable causes, through student bursaries, donations to educational institutions, and donations to charitable organizations.

Based on: *Annual Report,* January 31, 2001, and other documentation from Bombardier Inc.

ETHICAL DILEMMA
Who Is Liable?

In this chapter you will read about the different legal structures available to individuals who want to operate a business. For example, two people can set up their business as a partnership or as a corporation in which they are the only shareholders. You will learn that each structure has its advantages and disadvantages and that it is possible to go from one format to another one.

Let's look at the partnership Travira Wholesalers, which supplies computer components.

Partners Elvira and Trong have been operating their business for several years. The partners have gotten into a bind and are having difficulty paying their bills. They might have to declare a formal bankruptcy to get out of the mess. However, as they are not a corporation they will still be personally liable for all the unpaid bills of their company, Travira. Trong suggests that they incorporate Travira; that is, form a corporation that takes over all the assets and liabilities of their partnership and continues to operate the business. Then, he explains to Elvira, if the company goes bankrupt they will not be personally liable for the debts of the company because it is now a corporation.

Do you think it is ethical for Elvira and Trong to try to evade their personal liability in this fashion? We will return to this issue at the end of the chapter after you have had time to absorb the material.

FORMS OF BUSINESS OWNERSHIP

Like Armand Bombardier, tens of thousands of people start new businesses in Canada every year. Chances are you have thought of owning your own business or know someone who has. One key to success in a new business is knowing how to get the resources you need to start. You may need to take on partners or find other ways of obtaining money. To stay in business, you may need help from someone with more expertise than you have in certain areas or you may need to raise more money to expand. How you form your business can make a tremendous difference in your long-run success. The three major forms of business ownership are (1) sole proprietorships, (2) partnerships, and (3) corporations. For a perspective on the possible legal ramifications of certain ownership types, see the Ethical Dilemma box "Who Is Liable?" The advantages and disadvantages of each form are shown in Figure 6.1.

It is easy to start your own business. For example, you can begin a word-processing service out of your home, open a car repair centre, start a new restaurant, or go about meeting other wants and needs of the community on your own. An organization that is owned directly, and usually managed, by one person is called a **sole proprietorship**. That is the most common form of business ownership (more than one million firms).

Many people do not have the money, time, or desire to run a business on their own. They prefer to get together with one or more people to form the business. When two or more people legally agree to become co-owners of a business, the organization is called a **partnership**.

Creating a business that is separate and distinct from its owners has its advantages. A legal entity that has an existence separate from the people who own it is called a **corporation**. Owners hold shares in the corporation. There are about 100,000 corporations in Canada, but they have the largest share of business by far (see Figure 6.2 on page 164).

As you will learn in this chapter, each form of business ownership has its advantages and disadvantages. It is important to understand these advantages and disadvantages before starting a business. Keep in mind that just because a business starts in one form of ownership, it doesn't have to stay in that form. Many companies, like Armand Bombardier's, started out as one-person shows, added a partner or two, and

sole proprietorship
A business that is owned directly, and usually managed, by one person.

partnership
A legal form of business with two or more owners.

corporation
A legal entity with an existence separate from its owners.

FORM OF OWNERSHIP	ADVANTAGES	DISADVANTAGES
Sole Proprietorship	Easy to start and end Sole control of company All profits go to owner No restrictions on withdrawal of funds Possible tax advantages	Unlimited (personal) financial liability Ownership not divisible All losses borne by owner No continuity No relief for holidays or sickness Possible tax disadvantages
*Private Corporation	No personal liability Profits are sole property of owner Easy to start and end Owner has sole control Continuity of legal existence Ownership is divisible (up to maximum of 50 shareholders) Possible tax advantages	Funds withdrawal by owner is complex Losses not shared Possible tax disadvantages
Partnership	Not difficult to form but more complex than sole proprietorship Responsibilities shared Complementary skills Partners can help each other Greater financial resources than single owner Losses shared Possible tax advantages	More difficult to dissolve than sole proprietorship Unlimited personal liability of one partner for all partners Conflicts between partners Lack of continuity Profits shared Possible tax disadvantages
†Public corporation	Limited liability of shareholders Greatest possibility of raising finances Unlimited ownership by share issues Large size makes possible specialized management skills	Costly and complex to form Many complex regulations Conflicts between managers Conflicts between managers and shareholders High tax rates

FIGURE 6.1

ADVANTAGES AND DISADVANTAGES OF FORMS OF BUSINESS OWNERSHIP

* One person or partners can form a private corporation. These are usually smaller companies.

† Any business that contemplates large-scale operations requiring large amounts of capital has no choice but to be set up as a public corporation to raise such financing.

eventually became corporations. See the Spotlight on Small Business box "Selecting an Appropriate Form of Ownership" for more on this topic.

ADVANTAGES AND DISADVANTAGES OF DIFFERENT FORMS OF OWNERSHIP

Before examining the possible types of ownership of businesses in Canada, it is important to see how the *size* of a business is related to the choice of ownership form and, therefore, to the advantages and disadvantages it will have. This relationship is often not well understood.

How does an individual decide on the best form of ownership for a new enterprise? It really depends on several factors. If you are starting a service business, say computer software design, you will not be buying and selling raw material or finished goods, and you will not be incurring major debts. Also, if you are starting small, you do not need much capital. Under these circumstances, the advantage of limited liability the corporate form offers is not very important, because proper insurance can avoid major liabilities that could arise from accidents or from product liability. This means that you can start as a sole proprietorship and avoid the disadvantages of incorporating. The same holds true if two partners start a business. If the business expands and conditions change, you can incorporate later.

If you are starting a manufacturing, wholesale, or retail business, it is a different story. Once you start selling goods, you will be buying on credit and, therefore, accumulating debts. At any one time, the business will normally owe at least one or two months' purchases. There may be a long and expensive lease commitment and perhaps a substantial balance owing for equipment and improvements to the premises. Under these circumstances, it would be prudent to incorporate from the start to avoid the possibility of having to assume personal liability for all these debts.

FIGURE 6.2

FORMS OF BUSINESS ORGANIZATIONS

Although corporations make up only 17 percent of the total *number* of businesses, they have 87 percent of the sales volume. Sole proprietorships are the most common form of ownership (74 percent), but they have only 9 percent of sales volume.

WHICH FORM OF BUSINESS ORGANIZATION IS MOST COMMON?

Partnerships (9%)
Corporations (17%)
Sole proprietorships (74%)

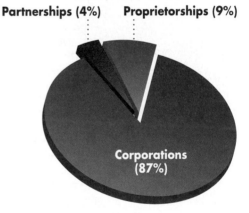

WHICH FORM OF BUSINESS ORGANIZATION HAS THE LARGEST SALES VOLUME?

Partnerships (4%)   Proprietorships (9%)
Corporations (87%)

liability
For a business, it includes the responsibility to pay all normal debts and to pay because of a court order or law, for performance under a contract, or payment of damages to a person or property in an accident.

Another thing that must be looked at before proceeding is the meaning of the term *liability*. Liability is often just another word for *debt*, but it also has a wider and important meaning, as you will see in the following pages. **Liability** for a business includes the responsibility to pay all normal debts and to pay

1. Because of a court order,

2. Because of a law,

3. For performance under a contract, or

4. For damages to a person or property in an accident.

Small Businesses

A small business that is owned by one person may be set up as a sole proprietorship or a corporation. Similarly, a small business that is owned by two or more people may be organized as a partnership or a corporation. In each case, the owners have complete freedom to choose the route they wish to follow. Regardless of the choice, a small business has all the advantages and disadvantages of a small-sized operation and also has the advantages and disadvantages of the corporate or noncorporate form selected.

A sole owner has the advantages of having no boss, making all the decisions, not having to share the profits, and having all the pride and satisfaction of ownership and success. But he or she has the disadvantages of not being able to share responsibility or the heavy workload or losses and financing needs. These conditions exist *whether or not the business is incorporated.*

When two or more persons form a small-business partnership or corporation, the workload, decision making, losses, and financial responsibility are shared. But there may be differences of opinion and conflicts, profits must be shared, and it is complicated if one owner dies or wants to leave. Again, this holds true whether or not the business is incorporated.

Note that in a very small business a sole proprietor cannot usually afford to hire managers, so he or she must carry the full load alone. As a business grows managers may be hired but the owner still bears the heaviest responsibility. An employee may leave to go elsewhere—but not the owner. This holds true whether it is a sole proprietorship or a corporation. This also applies to partners, although here there is a sharing of main responsibility.

A small business, such as this soda shop, may be set up as a sole proprietorship or a corporation. There are advantages and disadvantages to both forms of ownership.

Large Businesses

When it comes to big businesses, the situation is quite different. As you will see later, all large companies must adopt the corporate form of ownership. These companies regularly require substantial investing or borrowing from the public and this can only be done in the corporate form. In addition, the large number of owners (shareholders) means that the limited liability feature of corporations is also necessary. So, while small business owners have a choice of form of ownership, large companies really have no such choice. Some of Canada's largest corporations are shown in Figure 6.3.

Various publications regularly compile lists of Canada's largest 50, 500, or 1,000 companies; all are corporations. Figure 6.4 includes some of the criteria used to measure the largest companies in Canada.

FIGURE 6.3

LARGE CANADIAN CORPORATIONS

These are some of Canada's largest non-financial companies.

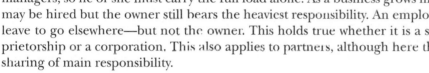

COMPANY	SALES ($ BILLIONS)	ASSETS ($ BILLIONS)	EMPLOYEES (000s)
General Motors of Canada Ltd.	42	n/a	26
BCE Inc.	18	51	75
Ford Motor Co. of Canada Ltd.	25	10	15
Nortel Networks	45	63	95
Seagram Co. Ltd.	23	49	34
DaimlerChrysler Canada Ltd.	22	n/a	17
TransCanada PipeLines Ltd.	21	26	3
George Weston Ltd.	22	11	124
Thomson Corp.	10	24	36
Onex Corp.	25	20	97
Alcan Aluminum Ltd.	14	28	53
Imperial Oil Ltd.	17	11	7
Bombardier Inc.	16	20	58

n/a = not available

Source: *2001 Edition, FP500, Business—National Post,* June 2001, p. 112.

Number of employees: George Weston Ltd.	124,000
Sales: Nortel Networks Corp.	$ 45 billion
Assets: Nonfinancial companies: Nortel Networks Corp.	$ 63 billion
Financial companies: Royal Bank of Canada	$290 billion
Profits: BCE Inc.	$ 4.8 billion

Source: *2001 Edition, FP500, Business—National Post*, June 2001, p. 112.

SOLE PROPRIETORSHIPS

Advantages of Sole Proprietorships

There must be some major advantages to being a sole proprietor. After all, hundreds of thousands of people in Canada have formed this kind of business. Sole proprietorships are the easiest kind of businesses to explore in your quest for an interesting career. Every town has some sole proprietorships that you can visit. There's the local produce stand, the beauty shop, the auto repair garage, and the accountant. If you look closely, you'll find sole proprietors who do income taxes, repair appliances and television sets, and provide all kinds of local services. (Ascertain that they are not corporations.) Talk with them about the joys and frustrations of being on their own. Most people will mention the benefits of being their own boss and setting their own hours. They may also mention the following advantages:

1. **Ease of starting and ending the business**. All you have to do to start a sole proprietorship is buy the needed equipment (for example, a saw, a computer, a tractor, a lawnmower) and put up some announcements saying you are in business. It is just as easy to get out of business; you simply stop. There is no one to consult or to disagree with about such decisions. You may have to get a permit or licence from the government to start, but that is usually no problem. Such businesses can start small and grow rapidly.

2. **Being your own boss**. "Working for others simply does not have the same excitement as working for yourself." That's the way sole proprietors feel. You may make mistakes, but they are *your* mistakes—and so are the many small victories each day.

3. **Pride of ownership**. People who own and manage their own businesses are rightfully proud of their work. They deserve all the credit for taking the risks and providing needed goods or services.

4. **Retention of profit**. Other than the joy of being your own boss, there is nothing like the pleasure of knowing that there is no limit to how much money you can make and you do not have to share that money with anyone else (except the government, in taxes). People are often willing to put in long hours including weekends because the money they earn is theirs to keep.

For these and other reasons, there are more sole proprietorships than any other kind of business in Canada. Tens of thousands of new businesses are formed every year. Most of these are very small companies, so the total amount of business they do is a fraction of the total business done by a much smaller number of very large corporations. And thousands of small businesses fail. Many people dream of owning their own business, but there are also disadvantages to sole proprietorships.

Disadvantages of Sole Proprietorships

Not everyone is cut out to be a sole owner and manager of a business. It is difficult to save enough money to start a business and keep it going. Often the costs of inventory, supplies, insurance, advertising, rent, utilities, and other expenses are simply too much to cover alone. There are other disadvantages:

1. **Unlimited liability—the risk of losses**. When you work for others, it is their problem if the business is not profitable. When you have your own sole proprietorship, you and the business are considered one. The business is not a legal entity distinct from the owner; therefore, you have **unlimited liability**. Any debts or damages incurred by the business are *your* personal debts and *you* must pay them, even if it means selling your home, your car, and so forth. This is the most serious disadvantage of a sole proprietorship. It requires careful thought and discussion with a lawyer and an accountant.

2. **Limited financial resources**. Funds available to the business are limited to the funds that the one (sole) owner can gather. Since there are serious limits to how much one person can do, partnerships and corporations have a greater probability of recruiting the needed financial backing to start a business.

3. **Overwhelming time commitment**. It is hard to own a business, manage it, train people, and have time for anything else in life. The owner must spend long hours working. The owner of a store, for example, may put in 12 hours a day, six or seven days a week. That is almost twice the hours worked by an employee, who may make more money.

4. **Few fringe benefits**. If you are your own boss, you lose many of the fringe benefits that come with working for others. For example, you have no disability insurance, no sick leave, no vacation pay, and so on.

5. **Limited growth**. If the owner becomes incapacitated, the business often comes to a standstill. Since a sole proprietorship relies on its owner for most of its funding, expansion is often slow. This is one reason many individuals seek partners to assist in a business.

6. **Limited life span**. If the sole proprietor dies, the business ceases to exist legally. Practically, unless arrangements have been made to pass the ownership and management on to others, the business ends.

unlimited liability
The responsibility of a business owner for all of the debts of the business, making the personal assets of the owner vulnerable to claims against the business.

Talk with a few small-business owners about the problems they have faced. They know more about the situation in your area than anyone else does. They are likely to have many interesting stories to tell about problems getting loans from the bank, problems with theft, and problems simply keeping up with the business. These problems are the reason that some sole proprietors discourage their children from following in their footsteps, although many would have it no other way. These problems are also the reasons why many sole proprietors choose to find partners to share the load. Remember, though, partnerships have disadvantages, too.

CRITICAL THINKING

Have you ever dreamed of opening your own business? If you did, what would it be? What talent or skills do you have that you could use?

Could you start a business in your home? About how much would it cost to start? Could you begin part-time while you worked elsewhere?

What could you get from owning your own business in the way of satisfaction and profit? What would you lose?

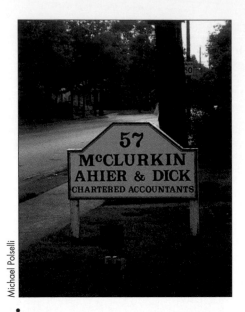

Michael Polselli

PARTNERSHIPS

A partnership is a legal form of business with two or more owners. It is not difficult to form a partnership, but it is wise to get the counsel of a lawyer experienced with such agreements. Lawyers' services are expensive, so would-be partners should reach some basic agreements before calling in a lawyer. It is often easier to *form* a partnership than to operate or end one, and many friendships have led to partnerships.

Advantages of Partnerships

There are many advantages of having one or more partners in a business. Often, it is much easier to own and manage a business with one or more partners. Your partner can cover for you when you are sick or go on vacation. Your partner may be skilled at inventory-keeping, accounting, and finance, whereas you do the selling or servicing. A partner can also provide additional money, support, and expertise.

> **M**any of the disadvantages of owning your own business are taken care of when you find a business partner. When one partner is not there, the other can take over.

Enjoying the advantages of partnerships today, more than ever before, are doctors, lawyers, dentists, and other professionals. They have learned that it is easier to take vacations, stay home when they are sick, or relax a little when there are others available to help take care of clients. With some care, partnerships can have the following advantages:

limited partner
Owner who invests money in the business, but does not have any management responsibility or liability for losses beyond the investment.

1. **More financial resources**. Naturally, when two or more people pool their money and credit, it is easier to have enough cash to start and to pay the rent, utilities, and other bills incurred by a business. A concept called limited partnership is specially designed to help raise capital (money). A **limited partner** invests money in the business, but cannot legally have any management responsibility and has limited liability. **Limited liability** means that limited partners are not responsible for the debts of the business. Their personal property is *not* at risk. The worst that can happen is that they will lose their investment.

limited liability
The responsibility of a business's owners for losses only up to the amount they invest; limited partners have limited liability.

2. **Shared management**. It is simply much easier to manage the day-to-day activities of a business with carefully chosen partners. Partners give each other free time from the business and provide different skills and perspectives. Many people find that the best partner is a spouse. That is why you see so many husband-and-wife teams managing restaurants, service shops, and other businesses.

Disadvantages of Partnerships

Any time two people must agree on anything, there is the possibility of conflict and tension. Partnerships have caused splits among families, friends, and marriages. Other disadvantages are:

general partner
An owner (partner) who has unlimited liability and is active in managing the firm.

1. **Unlimited liability**. Each general partner is liable for all the debts of the firm, no matter who was responsible for causing those debts. Like a sole proprietor, partners can lose their homes, cars, and everything else they own if the business cannot pay its debts. Such a risk is very serious and should be discussed with a lawyer and an insurance expert. A **general partner**, then, is an owner (partner) who has unlimited liability and is active in managing the firm. As with sole proprietorships, this is the most serious disadvantage of partnerships. (As mentioned earlier, a limited partner risks an investment in the firm, but is not liable for the business's losses beyond that investment and cannot legally help to manage the company.)

2. **Division of profits**. Sharing the risk means sharing the profit, and that can cause conflicts. For example, two people form a partnership: one puts in more money and the other puts in more hours. Each may later feel justified in asking for a bigger share of the profits. Imagine the resulting conflicts.

3. **Disagreements among partners**. Disagreements over money are just one example of potential conflict in a partnership. Who has final authority over employees? Who hires and fires them? Who works what hours? What if one partner wants to buy expensive equipment for the firm and the other partner disagrees? Potential conflicts are many. Because of such problems, all terms of partnership should be spelled out in writing to protect all parties and to minimize future misunderstandings.

4. **Difficult to terminate**. Once you have committed yourself to a partnership, it is not easy to get out of it. Questions about who gets what and what happens next are often very difficult to solve when the business is closed. Surprisingly, law firms often have faulty partnership agreements and find that breaking up is hard to do. How do you get rid of a partner you don't like? It is best to decide that up front, in the partnership agreement (discussed in the next section).

Again, the best way to learn about the advantages and disadvantages of partnerships is to interview several people who have experience with such agreements. They will give you additional insights and hints on how to avoid problems.

Categories of Partners

Several types of partners can be involved in a partnership. The most common types are the following:

- *Silent partners* take no active role in managing a partnership, but their identities and involvement are known to the public.

- *Secret partners* take an active role in managing a partnership, but their identities as partners are unknown to the public.

- *Nominal partners* are not actually involved in a partnership, but lend their names to it for public relations purposes.

- *Dormant partners* are neither active in managing a partnership nor known to the public.

- *Senior partners* assume major management roles due to their experience, long tenure, or amount of investment in the partnership. They normally receive large shares of the partnership's profits.

- *Junior partners* generally have less tenure, assume a limited role in the partnership's management, and receive a smaller share of the partnership's profit.

How to Form a Partnership

The first step in forming a partnership is choosing the *right* partner. The importance of this step cannot be overemphasized. Many partnerships dissolve because of disagreements between partners. One should choose a business partner as carefully as a marriage partner. Then, a written **partnership agreement** should be signed. This is a legal document that specifies the rights and responsibilities of each partner. It normally includes the following provisions:

partnership agreement
Legal document that specifies the rights and responsibilities of each partner.

1. The name of the business. All provinces require the firm name to be registered with the province if the firm name is not the name of any partner.

2. The names and addresses of all partners.

3. The purpose and nature of the business and the main location.

4. The date the partnership will start and how long it will last. No mention of termination means that the partnership will continue indefinitely until one of the partners dies or leaves.

5. The amount of cash or other assets each partner will invest.

6. Each partner's management responsibilities and authority.

7. The salaries and drawing accounts of each partner and in what proportion profits and losses will be shared.

8. Provision for the withdrawal of a partner and also for the admission of new partners.

9. Provision for the purchase of a deceased, retiring, or sick partner's share of the business.

10. Provision for how serious disagreements will be resolved.

11. Provision for when and how to dissolve the partnership.

Sole proprietors and partners have to contend with the major disadvantage of unlimited personal liability for company debts. The solution to this problem is to form a corporation. We look at corporations next.

PROGRESS CHECK

www.nova.ca
www.irvingoil.com

Of course, the number of corporations with Web sites describing the corporation and its activities is increasing at a dramatic rate. Soon, virtually all corporations will be on the Net. Check out these two examples of large successful corporations from two different parts of Canada.

public corporation
Corporation that has the right to issue shares to the public, so its shares may be listed on the stock exchanges.

private corporation
Corporation that is not allowed to issue stock to the public, so its shares are not listed on stock exchanges; it is limited to 50 or fewer shareholders.

- Most people who start a business in Canada are sole proprietors, and most of them are no longer in business after 10 years. What are the advantages and disadvantages of this form of business?

- What are some of the advantages of partnerships over sole proprietorships?

- Unlimited liability is one of the biggest drawbacks to sole proprietorships and general partnerships. Can you explain what that means?

- What is the difference between a *limited* partner and a *general* partner?

CORPORATIONS

Although the word *corporation* makes people think of big businesses like Imperial Oil, the Royal Bank, Nova Corp., MacMillan Bloedel, or Irving Oil, it is not necessary to be big to incorporate (start a corporation). Obviously, many corporations are big. However, incorporating may be beneficial for small businesses also.

A corporation is a federally or provincially chartered legal entity with authority to act and have liability separate from its owners. The corporation's owners (shareholders) are not liable for the debts or any other problems of the corporation beyond the money they invest. Corporate shareholders do not have to worry about losing their houses, cars, and other personal property if the business cannot pay its bills—a very significant benefit. A corporation not only limits the liability of owners, it enables many people to share in the ownership (and profits) of a business without working there or having other commitments to it.

In Canada commercial corporations are divided into two classes: public and private. A **public corporation** has the right to issue shares to the public, which means its shares may be listed on a stock exchange. This offers the possibility of raising large amounts of capital and is the reason why all large companies are corporations.

A **private corporation** is not allowed to issue stock to the public, so its shares are not listed on a stock exchange, and it is limited to 50 or fewer shareholders. This greatly reduces the costs of incorporating. Most small corporations are in the private category. This is the vehicle employed by individuals or partners who do not anticipate the need for substantial financing, but want to take advantage of limited liability. Some private corporations are very large.

There is one important advantage Canadian-owned private corporations have over public corporations: the income tax rate on the first $200,000 of annual business profits is half the normal corporate tax rate. It is also about half of what individuals pay when they are not incorporated. This is another feature that leads individuals and partners to incorporate.

Another important advantage for the owner of a private corporation is that he or she can issue shares to a daughter, a son, or a spouse, making them co-owners of the company. This procedure is not available to a sole proprietor. It is a simple and useful way of recognizing the contribution of these or other family members, or employees, to the company. This procedure may also be a good way for the owner to prepare for retirement by gradually transferring ownership and responsibility to those who will be inheriting the business.

There is a formal procedure for forming a corporation that involves applying to the appropriate federal or provincial agency. For small companies this may be done by the founders themselves, thus avoiding the costs of having a legal firm attend to it. The procedure for large or public corporations is much more complex and expensive and definitely requires hiring a legal firm. These costs can easily run into the hundreds of thousands of dollars.

Advantages of Corporations

Most people are prepared to risk what they invest in a business, but are not willing to risk everything to go into business. Yet, for businesses to grow and prosper and create abundance, many people would have to be willing to invest their money in business. The way to solve this problem was to create an artificial being, an entity that exists only in the eyes of the law. That artificial being is called a *corporation*. It has a separate legal identity from the owners—the shareholders—of the company. The corporation files its own tax returns. This entity is a technique for involving people in business without risking their other personal assets.

The first three advantages listed here apply mainly to large public corporations. The last three apply to *all* corporations.

Courtesy NOVA Chemicals Corporation

NOVA Chemicals' Joffre manufacturing facility lies just east of Red Deer, Alberta, and is one of North America's largest petrochemical complexes.

FIGURE 6.5

CORPORATE HIERARCHY

Owners influence how a business is managed by electing a board of directors. The board hires the top managers (or fires them), and sets the pay for top managers. Top managers then select other managers and employees with the help of the human resources department.

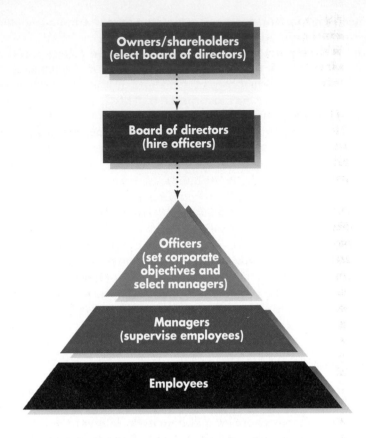

www.incoltd.com

Visit Inco's Web site. What does it produce and sell? How much does it produce? What was its volume of sales last year? How many employees does it have?

1. **More money for investment**. To raise money, a public corporation sells ownership (shares or stock) to anyone who is interested. (We shall discuss shares in Chapter 19.) This means that thousands of people can own part of major companies like Inco, Bombardier, and MacMillan Bloedel. If a company sold one million shares for $50 each, it would have $50 million available to build plants, buy materials, hire people, build products, and so on. Such a large amount of money would be difficult to raise any other way. Laws regulate how corporations can raise this money. The types of shares and the kinds of debt that can be incurred vary from province to province.

2. **Size**. Because they have large amounts of money to work with, corporations can build large, modern factories with the latest equipment. They do long-term research and development (R+D), which requires large investment of funds. They can also hire experts or specialists in all areas of operation. Furthermore, they can buy other corporations in other fields to *diversify their risk*. (When a corporation is involved in many businesses at once, if one fails the corporation will survive.) In short, large corporations have the size and resources to take advantage of opportunities anywhere in the world. However, corporations do not have to be large for their shareholders to enjoy the benefits of limited liability and access to more capital.

3. **Separation of ownership from management**. Public corporations are able to raise money from many different investors without getting them involved in management. The corporate hierarchy is shown in Figure 6.5. The pyramid shows that the owners and shareholders are separate from the managers and employees. The owners elect a board of directors. The directors select the officers, who in turn hire managers and employees. The owners thus have some say in who runs the corporation.

4. **Limited liability**. Corporations in Canada have *Limited*, *Incorporated*, or *Corporation* after their names, as in "Shoppers Drug Mart Ltd." The "Ltd." stands for *limited liability* and is probably the most significant advantage of corporations. Remember, limited liability means that the owners of a business cannot lose more than their investment in that business. The corporation itself is fully liable for all of its debts. Banks and other financial institutions usually require the personal guarantee of the owners of small corporations before making loans to these companies. These owners, therefore, lose the limited-liability protection for those debts.

5. **Perpetual life**. Because corporations are separate legal entities from the people who own them, the death or departure of one or more owners does not terminate the corporation. This makes corporations a better risk to bankers and other lenders, so it is easier to get loans.

6. **Ease of ownership change**. Ownership of public corporations is constantly changing as existing shareholders sell all or part of the shareholdings, and other people or companies buy these shares and become shareholders. This happens very infrequently in private companies, but the procedure has its advantages for private companies, as discussed above.

Disadvantages of Corporations

There are also disadvantages that come with the corporate form of ownership, including:

1. **More paperwork**. There is more documentation involved in setting up and operating a corporation because of government requirements. This leads to more costly legal and accounting fees, as well as more time consuming and, therefore, costly operations.

2. **Less flexibility**. In unincorporated companies, proprietors or partners can withdraw funds as they wish with no impact on tax liabilities. In corporations, such withdrawals are taxed in one way or another. Certain other transactions also involve formal paperwork.

3. **Complex starting and winding-up procedures**. The legal procedures involved in starting and ending a corporation are costly and much more complex than for unincorporated companies.

The National Gallery of Canada is a visual arts museum that holds its collections of art in trust for all Canadians. The mandate of the National Gallery is set out in the 1990 Museums Act. The Gallery is a nonprofit Crown corporation of the federal government.

Other Types of Corporations

When reading about corporations, you may find many confusing terms. A *nonresident corporation* does business in Canada, but has its head office outside Canada. Examples are most foreign airlines. A *personal service corporation* is set up by an athlete, entertainer, or some other high-earning, self-employed person to access some advantages of corporate ownership.

A *nonprofit corporation* is formed for charitable or socially beneficial purposes. It is not run for profit. It has many of the features of business corporations, but it pays no income taxes and does not issue shares. It has no owners or shareholders. The number of nonprofit corporations in Canada runs into the tens of thousands. In some towns, property is tax-exempt if it belongs to nonprofit organizations such as churches, hospitals, colleges, museums, YMCAs, or athletic, artistic, or charitable organizations.

Figure 6.6 compares different types of organizations. This chapter does not discuss another type of corporation, which we reviewed in Chapter 4. You will recall that *Crown corporations* are companies that only the federal or a provincial government can set up and own.

www.ymca.ca

You can learn about various YMCAs in different Canadian cities by visiting this Web site. Check out the one nearest you!

FIGURE 6.6

COMPARISON OF TYPES OF OWNERSHIP

| | | PARTNERSHIPS | | CORPORATIONS | |
	SOLE PROPRIETORSHIP	**GENERAL PARTNERSHIP**	**LIMITED* PARTNERSHIP**	**PUBLIC CORPORATION**	**PRIVATE CORPORATION**
Documents needed to start business	None (may need permit or licence)	Partnership agreement, oral or written	Written agreement; must file certificate of limited partnership	Articles of incorporation, bylaws	Articles of incorporation, bylaws; must meet criteria
Ease of termination	Easy—just pay debts and quit	May be difficult, depending on agreement	Same as general partnership	Difficult and expensive to terminate	Not difficult; pay off debts, sell off assets, withdraw cash, and pay taxes
Life span	Terminates on death, sale, or retirement	Terminates on death or withdrawal of partner[†]	Terminates only on death or withdrawal of general partner[†]	Perpetual life	Perpetual life
Transfer of ownership	Sale terminates sole proprietorship	Requires agreement of partner(s) (per partnership agreement)	Agreement usually allows for such transfers	Easy—just sell shares	Easy—just sell shares[†]
Financial resources	Limited to owner's capital and loans	Limited to partners' capital and loans	Same as general partnership	May issue as many shares and bonds as market will absorb	Owners' capital and loans; no public stock issue allowed
Personal risk of losses	Unlimited liability	Unlimited liability	Limited liability	Limited liability	Limited liability
Income taxes	Taxed as personal income	Taxed as personal income	Taxed as personal income	Corporate income tax plus lower personal tax on dividends	Low corporate rate plus lower personal tax on dividends
Management responsibilities	Owner manages all areas of the business	Partners share management	Cannot participate in management	Management separate from ownership	Owners usually manage all areas

*There must be at least one general partner who manages the partnership and has unlimited liability.
[†]Unless agreement specifies otherwise.

Following the Progress Check and the Critical Thinking exercises, we will look at two topics that do not fit into a narrow definition of forms of business organization, which is the main topic of the chapter. However, because corporate expansion via mergers and acquisitions and franchising are important and special areas of business organization, the discussion of these topics fits best here.

- What are the major advantages and disadvantages of the corporate form of business?
- What is the role of owners (shareholders) in the corporate hierarchy?
- If you buy shares in a corporation and someone gets injured by one of the corporation's products, can you be sued? Why or why not? Could you be sued if you were a general partner in a partnership?

What would Canada be like without major corporations? What products would be hard to get? What would be the benefits?

Now that you've read about the proprietorships, partnerships, and corporations, which sounds like the best place for you to work? Why? Which calls for taking the most risks? Which would be most fun? Most profitable?

What part of your personality most determines where you fit in best?

CORPORATE EXPANSION: MERGERS AND ACQUISITIONS

The last decade saw considerable corporate expansion. Nearly every day a new corporate merger or acquisition was announced. A **merger** occurs when two firms unite to form one company. An **acquisition** occurs when one company buys another company. Acquisitions are much more common than mergers.

There are two major types of corporate mergers or acquisitions: vertical and horizontal. A **vertical merger** is the joining of two firms involved in different stages of related businesses. Pepsi Cola acquired Pizza Hut and KFC to ensure a controlled market for Pepsi beverages. A **horizontal merger** joins two firms in the same or similar industries and allows them to diversify or expand their products. Seagram's acquired the Tropicana fruit juice company when liquor sales were declining. It later acquired control of other companies before merging with another very large company: see item 7 in Figure 6.7, which lists some important mergers and acquisitions of the 1990s involving Canadian companies. Most were horizontal.

The reason for all of this merger and acquisition mania, as some people have called it, is the continuing pressure that companies feel: to compete in the global marketplace, they must be large and powerful. As even old, giant American and European companies continue to merge (witness Daimler and Chrysler in 1999), Canadian companies feel they have no choice but to do likewise. The four huge Canadian banks tried in 1998 to merge into two even larger financial entities to better meet the global competition of similar mergers around the world, but were refused permission to do so. (This is discussed in Chapter 4.)

FRANCHISING[1]

Not everyone wants to start or operate a business as a sole owner. The personality called for is that of a risk taker and innovator. Some people are more cautious or simply want more assurance of success. For them, a very different strategy is available: the opportunity of franchising. Business students often mistakenly identify franchising as

merger
Two firms unite to form one company.

acquisition
One company buys another company.

vertical merger
The joining of two firms involved in different stages of related businesses.

horizontal merger
Joins two firms in the same or similar industries to allow them to diversify or expand their products.

www.pepsico.com

Check out this Web site to learn about the company. If you look at the 1997 press release archive, you will see that PepsiCo announced that it had decided to sell its non-core businesses, including the restaurants. Why do you suppose Pepsi decided to desert its *vertical merger* strategy?

FIGURE 6.7

MERGERS AND ACQUISITIONS

Some major acquisitions and mergers in the 1990s involving Canadian companies.

1. Barrick Gold acquired Lac Minerals, becoming an even larger gold producer.
2. Inco acquired Diamond Resources, whose gigantic mineral discoveries in Labrador made headlines for months.
3. Québecor continued to acquire American and European printing companies to become one of the largest printing companies in the world.
4. Loblaws and Provigo merged to form one of the largest supermarket chains.
5. The giant U.S. chain Wal-Mart entered Canada by acquiring Woolco.
6. Microsoft acquired the innovative SoftImage software company of Montreal, whose Hollywood success attracted mogul Bill Gates's eye.
7. Seagram's, the Canadian liquor and beverage giant, acquired control of the huge U.S. entertainment company MCA and the giant Dutch Company Polygram. In 2000 Seagram itself merged with the giant European entertainment company Vivendi.
8. Two giant American forestry companies each acquired a major Canadian forestry company—MacMillan Bloedel in B.C. and Forex Group in Quebec.

franchising
A method of distributing a product or service, or both, to achieve a maximum market impact with a minimum investment.

franchise agreement
An arrangement whereby someone with a good idea for a business sells the rights to use the business name and sell its products or services in a given territory.

franchisor
A company that develops a product concept and sells others the rights to make and sell the products.

franchisee
A person who buys a franchise.

franchise
The right to use a specific business's name and sell its products or services in a given territory.

an industry. **Franchising** is a *method* of distributing a product or service, or both, to achieve a maximum market impact with a minimum investment.

Some people develop ideas and build a winning product or service that they attempt to exploit through a franchise agreement. A **franchise agreement** is an arrangement whereby someone with a good idea for a business (the **franchisor**) sells to another (the **franchisee**) the rights to use the business name and sell a product or service in a given territory. As you might suspect, both franchisors and franchisees have a stake in the success of the **franchise**.

So what looks like a chain of stores—Canadian Tire, McDonald's, Tim Hortons—is usually a franchise operation with each unit owned by a different person or company; they are all part of a franchise operation, as explained in the previous paragraph. Sometimes one person or group may own and operate more than one franchise unit. In the following pages you will see the advantages and disadvantages of this type of business operation and ownership and learn what to consider before buying a franchise unit.

The franchise structure of ownership has had an important impact on Canadian business. Franchises employ more than one million people directly, provide many more jobs indirectly, and generate annual sales of $100 billion. While the food services industry alone employs half a million people, there are 38 other categories of franchises that have almost 675,000 employees. The greatest growth is expected in the following sectors:

- business aids and services
- construction
- maintenance and cleaning services
- retailing (nonfood)
- automotive products and services
- home improvement
- home inspection services

Figure 6.8 details several interesting facts about franchise operations in Canada.

FIGURE 6.8

FRANCHISING IN CANADA

Here you can see details concerning franchise operations in Canada.

Number of franchisor companies		1,300
Number of franchised units		76,000
Average number of years the franchisor has been in business		21
Average cash outlay by franchisees to acquire a unit		$166,000

The most common categories of franchise units are:

	% of franchisors	% of employees
Hospitality	29.9	36.0
Miscellaneous products	1.8	13.0
Retail	13.8	6.7
All other categories	54.5	44.3
Total	100.0	100.0

FRANCHISOR HEAD OFFICE LOCATIONS

Ontario	56%
B.C.	13
Quebec	12
Alberta	5
Manitoba	3
Nova Scotia	2
Newfoundland	1
Saskatchewan	1
N.B.	1
Foreign	6
Total	100%

www.bison1.com/

Check out this comprehensive Web site devoted to franchises and franchising issues around the world.

The franchise business is even more important in the United States, where some 550,000 franchises generate $800 billion in sales annually. The well known futurist John Naisbitt believes that "franchising is the way of the future" because it "is the most successful marketing concept ever created." In North America alone there are 3,000 franchising companies in 60 different industries.

A very large franchisor in the food industry in Canada is Cara Operations Ltd., which controls Harvey's, Swiss Chalet, and Second Cup franchises. Cara provides food services at all major airports in Canada, as well as to Canadian and international airlines. It has eight subsidiaries and two alliances. Cara has 1,690 outlets, nearly all in Canada. Second Cup itself is concentrating on its 350 units in Canada after having disposed of its 150 U.S. units.[2] We are all familiar with McDonald's, Pizza Hut, Dairy Queen, and so forth, but there are also Shoppers Drug Marts, Tilden Car Rentals, Uniglobe Travel, Beaver Lumber, Jean Coutu drugstores, and many more large nonfood franchises in Canada. See the Reaching Beyond Our Borders box "Canadian Franchisors Make Their Mark" for information on two Canadian franchisors that have successfully expanded into other markets.

Advantages of Franchises

Franchising has penetrated every aspect of Canadian and global business life by offering products and services that are reliable, convenient, and cost effective. Richard Ashman, chairman of the International Franchise Association (headquartered in Washington, DC), probably put it best when he commented, "you name it and there is a good chance that someone out there is franchising it." Obviously, the growth in franchising throughout the world was not accomplished by accident. Franchising clearly has many advantages.[3]

1. **Training and management assistance.** A franchisee (the person who buys a franchise) has a much greater chance of succeeding in business than an independent because he or she has an established product (for example, McDonald's hamburgers), help with choosing a location, training, promotion, and assistance in all phases of operation. It is like having your own business with full-time consultants available when you need them. Furthermore, you have a whole network of peers facing similar problems who can share their experiences with you.

REACHING BEYOND OUR BORDERS
Canadian Franchisors Make Their Mark

www.yogenfruz.com
www.mollymaid.com

Two Canadian franchisors that have successfully moved beyond Canada's borders are Molly Maid Inc. and Yogen Fruz Worldwide Inc. Molly Maid got its start in Toronto in 1979 by setting out to provide domestic cleaning services. As more women were moving into the workforce, the company saw an opportunity to cash in by filling a new need in the marketplace. And fill it it did. Soon the company was expanding outside Canada into countries where similar market niches were opening up. By 1996 it was well established in Japan, Australia, and the United States. The company is highly rated in the United States as one of the "top 10 best low-investment franchises" and various magazines such as *Entrepreneur, Franchise Times, Business Start-Up*, and *Success Magazine*. *Platinum 200* ranked Molly Maid number one among franchisors. The software program the company developed for its franchisees, the Customer Care System, was twice awarded the Microsoft Windows World Open prize. Molly Maid now operates more than 500 franchises in Canada, the United States, England, Japan, and Portugal.

Yogen Fruz, headquartered in Markham, Ontario, has as its mission "to become the world's largest franchisor of frozen yogurt." It is well on the way to achieving that target by acquiring the American franchise I Can't Believe It's Yogurt. Yogen Fruz has acquired about a dozen famous companies in the ice cream and dairy industries, changed its name to Cool Brands International Inc., and has licensing agreements with many well-known brand names such as Betty Crocker and Yoplait. It has franchises in more than 80 countries and had sales of more than $1 billion in 2000. This makes Yogen Fruz the largest franchise outside North America and second largest in the world.

Sources: *Successful Franchising*, April 1996, p. 28; Web sites <www.carlsononline.com>, June 1999, <www.mollymaid.com>, and <www.yogenfruz.com>, November 2001.

This may look like the set of Camelot, but it is actually the Crowne Plaza Hotel in downtown Edinburgh, Scotland. Bass Hotel and Resort franchises try to complement the environment of the areas they serve.

Courtesy of Crown Plaza Hotels and Resorts, Edinburgh

2. **Personal ownership**. A franchise operation is still *your* business and you enjoy most of the freedom, incentives, and profit of any sole proprietor. However, you must follow rules, regulations, and procedures set by the franchisor.

3. **Nationally recognized name**. It is one thing to open a new hamburger outlet or ice cream store. It is quite another to open another Second Cup coffee shop or a Baskin-Robbins ice cream shop. With an established franchise, you get instant recognition and support from a product group with established customers from around the world.

4. **Financial advice and assistance**. Major problems for small business are arranging financing and learning to keep records. Franchisees get valuable assistance in these areas and periodic advice from experts. Some franchisors will even provide financing to potential franchisees they think will be valuable parts of the franchise system.

Disadvantages of Franchises

It may sound as if the potential of franchising is too good to be true. Indeed, there *are* costs associated with joining a franchise. Be sure to check out any such arrangement with present franchisees and discuss the idea with an experienced franchise lawyer. The following are some disadvantages of franchises:

1. **Large start-up costs**. Most franchises demand a fee just to obtain the rights to the franchise. Fees for franchises can vary considerably. The very successful ones demand a fee that will place them out of the reach of a small-business venture. Fees may run well over $250,000 for the well-known franchises, but for newer or unproven ones, it may be anything from zero to $35,000. In addition to this fee are other normal initial cash needs that can easily exceed $100,000. Of course, a home-based franchise will require much less start-up cash.

2. **Shared profit**. The franchisor often demands a large share of the profits, or a percentage commission based on *sales*, not profit. This share is generally referred to as a *royalty*. Often, the share taken by the franchisor is so high that the owner's profit does not match the time and effort involved in owning and managing a business. The royalty demanded by a franchisor is an important factor to consider before going ahead (see Figure 6.9).

3. **Management regulation**. Management assistance has a way of becoming managerial orders, directives, and limitations. Franchisees may feel burdened by the company's rules and regulations and lose the spirit and incentive of being their own boss with their own business.

4. **Coattail effects**. What happens to your franchise if fellow franchisees fail? You might be forced out of business even if your particular franchise was profitable. This is often referred to as a *coattail effect*. The actions of other franchisees have an impact on your future growth and level of profitability. Remember, franchising is a team effort. If you play with a bad team, chances are you will lose.

Buying a Franchise

As we have seen, there are many advantages and disadvantages you need to explore before buying a franchise (see Figure 6.10 on page 181 for a summary). Buying a franchise is an excellent way to enter business as an owner or a manager and make a nice salary and profit.

A good source of information about franchise possibilities is Franchise Watchdog in Burlington, Vermont. It compares what franchisors have to offer, including fees and support services, and also rates franchisors by sampling franchisees.

Be careful of franchises that are just starting, grow too fast, or change ownership often. For example, Mother's Restaurants changed hands three times between 1986 and 1989, and its debt grew substantially as a result. In 1989, the 15-year-old, 90-unit franchise went bankrupt, dragging many franchisees down with it.[4] Be sure to check out the financial strength of a company before you get involved.

There are many things to do before jumping into a franchise. First, get an accountant. Then, have a lawyer review the contract. Remember, you are making a sizable financial investment. Furthermore, you have to analyze yourself, the franchise, and the market. Take some time to go over the checklists in Figures 6.9 and 6.10; they will help you to understand many of the questions franchisees must ask before they invest in a franchise.

CRITICAL THINKING

Is it fair to say that franchisees have the true entrepreneurial spirit? What do you think of the franchise opportunities of the future? Could you see yourself as a franchisee or franchisor? Which one?

THE FRANCHISE	YOU, THE FRANCHISEE
Did your lawyer approve the franchise contract you are considering after he or she studied it paragraph by paragraph?	How much equity capital will you need to purchase the franchise and operate it until your income equals your expenses?
Does the franchise give you an exclusive territory for the length of the franchise?	Does the franchisor offer financing for a portion of the franchising fees? On what terms?
Under what circumstances can you terminate the franchise contract and at what cost to you?	Are you prepared to give up some independence of action to secure the advantages offered by the franchise?
If you sell your franchise, will you be compensated for your goodwill?	Are you ready to spend much or all of the remainder of your business life with this franchisor, offering its product or service to your public?
If the franchisor sells the company, will your investment be protected?	

THE FRANCHISOR	YOUR MARKET
How many years has the firm offering you a franchise been in operation?	Have you made any study to determine whether the product or service that you propose to sell under franchise has a market in your territory at the prices you will have to charge?
Has it a reputation for honesty and fair dealing among the local firms holding its franchise?	Will the population in the territory given to you increase, remain static, or decrease over the next five years?
Has the franchisor shown you any certified figures indicating exact net profits of one or more franchisees that you have personally checked with the franchisee?	Will the product or service you are considering be in greater demand, about the same, or in less demand five years from now?
Will the firm assist you with – a management training program? – an employee training program? – a public relations program? – capital? – credit? – merchandising ideas?	What competition already exists in your territory for the product or service you are contemplating selling?
Will the firm help you find a good location for your new business?	
Has the franchisor investigated you carefully enough to assure itself that you can successfully operate one of its franchises at a profit to both the franchisor and you?	

Based on: *Small Business,* July–August 1990, p. 51.

FIGURE 6.9

CHECKLIST FOR EVALUATING A FRANCHISE

Franchising Opportunities Overseas

If you are contemplating becoming a franchisor, be aware of the ultimate potential of franchise outlets in other countries. We have all seen the attention paid to two of the largest foreign fast-food franchises, McDonald's (Canada) in Moscow and Kentucky Fried Chicken (now KFC) in Beijing. These successful ventures took many years of patient planning, heavy cost, and much frustration. Smaller franchisors have similar opportunities, but will need to build a solid management team, reputation, and strong financial resources before they can move in that direction.

PROGRESS CHECK

- What is a franchise? A franchisor? A franchisee?
- What are the advantages of going into business by acquiring a franchise? What are the disadvantages?

BENEFITS	DRAWBACKS
Nationally recognized name and established reputation.	High initial franchise fee. Monthly fees for advertising.
Help with finding a good location.	A monthly percentage of gross sales to the franchisor.
A proven management system.	
Tested methods for inventory and operations management.	Possible competition from other nearby franchisees.
Financial advice and assistance.	No freedom to select decor or other design features.
Training in all phases of operation.	Little freedom to determine management procedures.
Promotional assistance.	
Periodic management counselling.	Many rules and regulations to follow.
Proven record of success.	Coattail effect.
It's your business!	

FIGURE 6.10

BENEFITS AND DRAWBACKS OF FRANCHISING

The start-up fees and monthly fees can be killers. Ask around. Don't be shy. This is the time to learn about opportunities and risks. (This schedule applies to well-established franchises.)

co-operative
An organization that is owned by members who pay an annual membership fee and share in any profits.

CO-OPERATIVES

Some people dislike the notion of having owners, managers, workers, and buyers as separate individuals with separate goals. They envision a world where people co-operate with one another more fully and share the wealth more evenly. These people have formed a different kind of organization that reflects their social orientation: a co-operative, or co-op.

A **co-operative** is an organization that is owned by members and customers, who pay an annual membership fee and share in any profits (if it is a profit-making organization). Often the members work in the organization a certain number of hours a month as part of their duties. In Canada there is a wide range of co-ops. There are *producer co-ops*. Fishermen on both coasts and farmers on the Prairies, in Ontario, and in Quebec each produce their own product, but part or all of their marketing is done through these jointly owned co-ops. Any *profit* is distributed to the co-op members in proportion to the quantity supplied by each. Profit is regarded as additional payment for produce provided.

Producer co-ops on the Prairies and elsewhere use their combined purchasing power to buy equipment, seeds, and other items at reduced prices. This gives them some bargaining power with the large companies they often deal with.

At *consumer co-ops* in cities, consumers get together and establish a food store in the hope of reducing their food costs. The members work in the store, buy their food there, and share any profits as a reduction of their cost of food.

There are also many *financial co-ops*, called credit unions and *caisses populaires*. These serve the purpose of banks, but they have no shareholders. Instead, they distribute their profits annually to their members in various ways. The caisses populaires in Quebec have become very large and have a significant share of financial business there.

Because co-ops distribute their profits to members as a reduction in members' costs, these profits are not subject to income tax. From

Co-operatives are important in agriculture. They enable farmers to purchase seed and equipment at reasonable prices. They also provide an outlet for farm products. One advantage of co-operatives is that they do not pay taxes as corporations do.

Canadian Press CP Photography by John Ulan.

FIGURE 6.11

CANADIAN CO-OPERATIVES

This is a list of some of Canada's largest financial and nonfinancial co-ops, in order of size.

NONFINANCIAL CO-OPERATIVES	FINANCIAL CO-OPERATIVES
Agricore Cooperative Ltd.*	Mouvement Caisse Desjardins†
Federated Cooperatives	Caisse centrale Desjardins
Agropur Cooperative Agro-Al	Vancouver City Savings Credit Union
United Farmers of Alta. Co-op	Cooperators Group
Calgary Cooperative Assoc.	FCPD de Montreal
Co-op Atlantic	Credit Union Central (Sask.)
Western Co-op Fertilizers	Coast Capital Savings C.U.
Lilydale Cooperative	Credit Union Central (Ont.)
XCAN Grain Pool	Cooperators Life Insurance

Source: "The Top 1000," *Globe and Mail, Report on Business,* July 2001, 111.

*Agricore was created in November 1998 by a merger of the Manitoba and Alberta Wheat Pools.

†The Mouvement Caisse Desjardins operates many bank branches in Manitoba, Ontario, Quebec, and New Brunswick. It is a giant co-op with more than 5.5 million members (mostly depositors) and 33,000 employees. Its assets of $76 billion are double the combined assets of the next nine financial co-ops.

www.desjardins.com

This Web site has a wealth of information about the caisses populaires and their history in *du Mouvement Desjardins*. Visit it to learn about the development of the caisses and their current importance in Quebec. How significant are the caisses populaires today?

time to time various business organizations assert that many co-ops are now more like large businesses and should be taxed. So far this viewpoint has not been successful and does not appear to have much support. Figure 6.11 lists some of the largest co-operatives in Canada. Some co-ops are also becoming corporations.

WHICH FORM IS FOR YOU?

As you have seen, you can participate in the business world in a variety of ways. You can be involved in a sole proprietorship, a partnership, a corporation, a franchise, or a co-operative. There are advantages and disadvantages to each. However, the risks are high no matter which form you choose. The miracle of free enterprise is that the freedom and incentives of capitalism make such risks acceptable to many people, who go on to create the great Canadian businesses.

One of the best known was the (now defunct) giant department store chain, the T. Eaton Co. Ltd. Eaton's was founded 125 years ago by Timothy Eaton in Toronto as a small store. Canadian Tire is another success story. So is Magna International, the large auto parts manufacturer. Bombardier, Canadian Airlines, CAE, and Steinberg's are only a few of the many companies whose success was due to the confidence, hard work, and abilities of the individuals who founded them. (For more details of Bombardier's success, see the Spotlight on Big Business box "How Bombardier Took Off.") They all started small, accumulated capital from profits, grew, and became leaders in their fields. It is still being done today. Could you do the same? (Eaton's went bankrupt in the late 1990s, Steinberg's was sold off in the late 1970s, and Canadian Airlines was acquired by Air Canada in 2000, but their problems were due to descendants of the founders or subsequent purchasers not being able to carry on as successfully as the founders.)

Many students prefer to take the more cautious route of working for a corporation. The advantages are many: a fixed salary, paid vacations, health coverage, limited risk, promotional possibilities, and more.

The disadvantages of working for others are also significant: limited income potential, fixed hours, repetitive work, job insecurity, close supervision, and limited freedom.

SPOTLIGHT ON BIG BUSINESS
How Bombardier Took Off

The Profile at the beginning of this chapter highlighted the career of Armand Bombardier. From his tentative beginnings in 1937 with a vehicle to provide mobility on snow, now known as the *Ski-Doo*, his company, Bombardier, has mushroomed into a giant transnational in the aerospace and rail transportation businesses.

From 1986 to 1992 the company made several major acquisitions in Europe and North America under favourable terms. The best known are Canadair in Montreal, de Havilland in Toronto, Learjet in the U.S., and Short Bros. in Northern Ireland. During this period Bombardier became a technological leader in rail transportation and executive jets. One of the company's major contracts was for 254 train cars and loaders for the English Channel tunnel—the Chunnel—and *Time* magazine said that the cars would be "among the world's most technologically advanced rolling stock when they go into service." The company's jets and railcars and rail systems are sold all over the world.

Bombardier's 2001 annual report indicated that the company had 100,000 employees in 44 subsidiaries, operating in 23 countries. It had assets of $20.4 billion, sales of $16.1 billion, and a record backlog of orders of $31.2 billion. In 1999 Bombardier was selected by business leaders as the most respected company in Canada. Armand Bombardier's little company has come a long way.

Adapted from: *Annual Report*, January 31, 2001; company documents; *Time*, November 12, 1990, p. 27; *Globe and Mail, Report on Business*, April 1999, p. 76.

Sometimes it is exciting to work for others while starting your own business on the side. Apple Computer was started in a garage. Many firms have started in people's basements and attics. Business offers many different opportunities for tomorrow's graduates.

Of course, the option of becoming a franchisee, as discussed before, is also open to you. The problem here is that getting into a successful franchise requires lots of money. The newer or unproven ones require much less cash, but are a lot riskier. However, you might be one of the fortunate few who has a sound idea for franchising that could lead *you* to become the *franchisor*, and you would be collecting fees and royalties from franchisees.

ETHICAL DILEMMA
Review

Remember our couple, Elvira and Trong, who are planning to incorporate their partnership to avoid personal liability for the debts the business has accumulated? Our executives view this dilemma differently.

Bédard has a simple and clear answer: "No way. It is unethical to carry out such practices." Reilley takes a somewhat different tack. By incorporating, he notes, the company's ultimate bankruptcy will leave the owners personally still solvent so that "these two entrepreneurs could (and very likely would) start again, which would eventually create jobs, tax revenue, and so on."

Note that the manoeuvre contemplated by Elvira and Trong will not help them avoid personal liability. If you are in business as a sole proprietorship or partnership, the debts the business incurs remain personal liabilities even after they are taken over by a corporation. According to the law, it is the status existing at the time the debts were incurred that governs, not what happens subsequently. When a supplier sells to an unincorporated business, it knows and expects that, under the law, the owner remains personally responsible for the debt until it is paid.

SUMMARY

1. List the three basic forms of business ownership and compare the advantages and disadvantages of each.

1. A business can be formed in several ways.
   - *What are the three major forms of business ownership?*
   The three major forms of business ownership are sole proprietorships, partnerships, and corporations.
   - *Is there some way to compare the advantages and disadvantages of each form?*
   See Figures 6.1 and 6.6.
   - *Which form of business is the most common and which does most of the business in Canada?*
   Sole proprietorships are most popular, but corporations do most of the business in Canada.

2. Explain the differences between limited and general partners.

2. Not all partners have the same roles and responsibilities.
   - *What are the differences between limited and general partners?*
   General partners are owners (partners) who have unlimited liability and are active in managing the company. Limited partners are owners (partners) who have limited liability and must not be active in the company.
   - *What does unlimited liability mean?*
   Unlimited liability means that sole proprietors and general partners are personally liable for all debts and damages caused by their business. They may lose their houses or other personal possessions if the business is unable to pay its debts.
   - *What does limited liability mean?*
   Limited liability means that corporate owners (shareholders) and limited partners cannot lose more than the amount they invest. Their other personal property is not at risk for business debts.

3. Summarize the important clauses of a partnership agreement.

3. The first and most important step in forming a partnership is choosing the right partner.
   - *How do you form a partnership?*
   The most important step in forming a partnership is choosing a partner wisely. Then, no matter how good of friends you are, put your partnership agreement *in writing*. For major points of such an agreement see pp. 169–170.

4. Define public and private corporations.

4. There are two major categories of corporation: private and public.
   - *What is the major difference between them?*
   Private corporations are limited to a small number of shareholders (usually 50) and cannot sell their shares or bonds (borrowed money) publicly (on the stock exchange). Public corporations have no such limitations and their securities (stocks and bonds) trade on the stock exchange.

5. Compare the advantages and disadvantages of private and public corporations.

5. Private and public corporations each have some advantages and disadvantages.
   - *What are the major ones?*
   The principal disadvantages of private corporations are that shares cannot be sold to the public and the number of shareholders is limited. The advantages are the lower tax rate and much smaller costs of incorporating and ongoing legal and accounting costs. The situation is reversed for public corporations.

6. Define franchising and examine its advantages and disadvantages.

6. A person can participate in the entrepreneurial age by buying the rights to market a new product innovation in his or her area.
   - *What is this arrangement called?*
   A franchise is an arrangement to buy the rights to use the business name and sell its products or services in a given territory.
   - *What is a franchisee?*
   A franchisee is a person who buys a franchise.

• *What are the benefits and drawbacks of being a franchisee?*
The benefits include a nationally recognized name and reputation (for a well-established franchise), a proven management system, promotional assistance, and pride of ownership. Drawbacks include high franchise fees, managerial regulation, shared profits, and the coattail transfer of adverse effects if other franchisees fail.

7. One should not jump blindly into franchise ownership.
   • *What areas should you analyze when evaluating a franchise?*
   Before you buy a franchise, analyze yourself, the franchise, the franchisor, and the market see. See Figure 6.9.

7. Outline the areas to analyze when evaluating a franchise.

KEY TERMS

acquisition 175	**liability** 164	**sole**
co-operative 181	**limited liability** 168	**proprietorship** 162
corporation 162	**limited partner** 168	**unlimited**
franchise 176	**merger** 175	**liability** 167
franchise	**partnership** 162	**vertical merger** 175
agreement 176	**partnership**	
franchisee 176	**agreement** 169	
franchising 176	**private**	
franchisor 176	**corporation** 170	
general partner 168	**public**	
horizontal merger 175	**corporation** 170	

DEVELOPING WORKPLACE SKILLS

1. Find out how much it costs to incorporate a company in your province. Then compare it to the cost of a federal incorporation. Is there a significant difference?

2. Have you ever thought about starting your own business? What kind of business would it be? Think of a friend who you might want for a partner in the business. List the capital and personal skills you need for the business. Then make separate lists of the capital and personal skills you might bring and those your friend might bring. What capital and personal skills do you need that neither of you have?

3. Speak to a lawyer, accountant, or stockbroker to find out how popular limited partnerships are. Inquire under what circumstances limited partnerships are used.

4. Look at a listing of all the Toronto Stock Exchange transactions for a week. You can find this information in the *National Post, The Globe and Mail,* or perhaps your local newspaper. Look at the column called "Volume" for the number of shares of a particular company that were traded that week. Make some reasonable dividing line between very active trading and low-volume trading shares (say, 100,000). Count how many high-volume and low-volume stocks are listed. What does that tell you about large and small Canadian public companies? What useful information does this yield?

5. Get an annual report of a large corporation from the library or on the Internet. What are the firm's annual sales? Net income (profit)? Number of common shares? Dividends paid to shareholders?

TAKING IT TO THE NET

Purpose:

To generate relevant Canadian business data involving business ownership.

Exercise:

1. Find the Web site of the Canadian Federation of Independent Business and do a search using keywords such as *partnerships, corporations,* and *sole proprietorships.* See if you find some interesting data relevant to this chapter to bring to class.

TAKING IT TO THE NET

Purpose:

To explore current franchising opportunities and to evaluate the strengths and weaknesses of a selected franchise.

Exercise:

1. Go to the Web site Be the Boss: The Virtual Franchise Expo Web site at <www.vifexpo.com> and click on About Franchising. Then click on Franchising—An Interactive Self-Test. Complete the test, submit it, and see how you rate as a suitable franchise operator. Remember, it's only a guide and not necessarily foolproof.

    Also check out the Web site of the Canadian Franchise Association at <www.cfa.ca> to see what type of franchises are available and other useful information you can find about franchising.

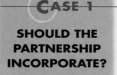

PRACTISING MANAGEMENT DECISIONS

CASE 1

SHOULD THE PARTNERSHIP INCORPORATE?

Helen and Dimitri have worked hard at their business for three years. Their wholesale beauty supplies partnership has come a long way from the early days when they were working in the basement of their home. Last year, sales exceeded $1 million, and this year they are running well ahead of last year. They expect their profit this year to be about $100,000 after deducting their own salaries, which amount to $60,000. They expect sales and profits to rise dramatically in the next three years.

Most of their friends who are in businesses are incorporated and Helen and Dimitri have been wondering if they should go that route too. Their accountant has been urging them to take this step because of the many advantages of the corporate form of ownership.

They are somewhat reluctant to do this because they like the simplicity of their partnership format. They are also concerned about the costs of making the switch, the more complex structure, and the ongoing additional legal and accounting costs of operating as a corporation.

Decision Questions

1. What are the major advantages and disadvantages of each type of ownership?
2. Do you think that in this case the advantages of incorporation outweigh the partnership form? Why?
3. Will it be easier for Helen and Dimitri to obtain funding in the future if they make the switch? Explain.
4. If they incorporate, will they run a greater risk of a hostile takeover? Why?

CASE 2

GOING PUBLIC

George Zegoyan and Amir Gupta face a difficult decision. Their private autoparts manufacturing company has been a great success—too quickly. They cannot keep up with the demand for their product. They must expand their facilities, but have not had the time to accumulate sufficient working capital, nor do they want to acquire long-term debt to finance the expansion. Discussions

with their accountants, lawyers, and stockbrokers have confronted them with the necessity of going public to raise the required capital.

They are concerned about maintaining control if they become a public company. They are also worried about the loss of privacy because of the required reporting to various regulatory bodies and to their shareholders. Naturally, they are also pleased that the process will enable them to sell some of their shareholdings to the public and realize a fair profit from their past and expected future successes. They will be able to sell 40 percent of the shares for $500,000, which is 10 times their total investment in the company. It will also let them raise substantial new capital to meet the needs of their current expansion program.

The proposed new structure will allow them to retain 60 percent of the outstanding voting shares, so they will keep control of the company. Nevertheless, they are somewhat uneasy about taking this step, because it will change the whole nature of the company and the informal method of operating they are used to. They are concerned about having "partners" in their operations and profits. They are wondering whether they should remain as they are and try to grow more slowly even if it means giving up profitable orders.

Decision Questions

1. Are George and Amir justified in their concerns? Why?
2. Do they have any other options besides going public? Is the franchise route a viable option?
3. Do you think they should try to limit their growth to a manageable size to avoid going public, even if it means forgoing profits now? Why?
4. Would you advise them to sell their business now if they can get a good price and then start a new operation? Explain.

VIDEO CASE

YO QUIERO FISH

You have read all about the advantages and disadvantages of the various forms of organization: sole proprietorships, and so forth. It's very exciting to contemplate starting your own business, but there is always the fear of failure. Isn't there some way to start a business that is more likely to have success? Yes, there is. The answer is to buy into an established and growing franchise. You have to look around to find out what is new and exciting. Then you have to do your homework and talk to managers and employees of various franchise organizations to learn all you can. With luck, you will find one that has the excitement and growth potential of Rubio's Baha Grill.

This franchise is based in San Diego. It sells Mexican-style seafood from 128 company-owned restaurants in five western states. Their most popular item is the fish taco. If you are from some other part of the country, a fish taco may not sound too wonderful to you, but in Rubio country, you're talking good-tasting food. People who try them like them. Ralph Rubio is now beginning to offer this successful operation to franchisees. He needed to do that to grow as fast as he would like. He hopes to have a national chain some day.

Rubio's began as a family-owned business. It was a sole proprietorship. A couple of years later, the family decided to incorporate so that ownership could be widely shared and easily transferred. Now that Rubio's is expanding into franchising, it wants to maintain its professional image. Thus it wants franchisees with lots of experience and with the capital and marketing support.

To maintain the same culture in all franchise outlets, training is held in San Diego to capture the Mission Bay feeling. Managers, cooks, and others will travel to the various outlets to see that the processes implemented maintain the same cultural look and feel. It is important, when trying to maintain a quality image, to have only the best workers. To keep workers, Rubio's pays competitive wages and offers flexible scheduling.

Rubio recommends that people have relevant experience before trying to start a franchise of their own. You need to know how to manage the cash register, empty the garbage bins, clean the bathrooms, handle the money, and do everything that a manager has to do. And that means everything! There's risk involved in starting any kind of business. But, with some experience under your belt, and the backing of an established franchisor, your chances of succeeding are much better.

Discussion Questions

1. What do you see as the main impediment to raising money when you start a business using the sole proprietorship or partnership form of business?
2. What disadvantages do you see of buying a franchise rather than starting your own fast-food business? Why do you suppose most people choose franchising?
3. What are some of the bigger franchise organizations in your town? Do they have independent competitors? Which would you rather own and why?
4. As you drive down the road, it seems that there are more and more of the typical fast-food restaurants opening: McDonald's, Burger King, KFC, and the like. What do you see as the advantages and disadvantages of having so many competitors from the same company within such close distances?

CHAPTER 7

Small Business and Entrepreneurship

LEARNING GOALS

AFTER YOU HAVE READ AND STUDIED THIS CHAPTER, YOU SHOULD BE ABLE TO

1 Define small business and discuss its importance to the Canadian economy.

2 Explain why people are willing to take the risks of entrepreneurship.

3 Describe the attributes needed to be a successful entrepreneur, and explain why women have a higher success rate than men.

4 Summarize the major causes of small business failures.

5 Identify ways you can learn about small businesses.

6 Explain what a business plan is, and outline the general areas of information it should include.

7 List the requirements to operate a small business successfully.

Technology: A Vital Element of a Small Business

Jim Carroll, who runs a small business, believes that "technology levels the playing field." Here's part of a column that he wrote in *The Globe and Mail* on October 1, 1998.

I have been an entrepreneur since 1990. I left a public accounting firm after a round of mergers, having determined not to trust my career and my fate to a group of anonymous executives in a boardroom somewhere. Instead of seeking another job, I decided to establish my own consulting firm, and haven't looked back since. As business activities expanded in the early years, I soon found that I needed some help, so my wife quit her job and joined me in the home office. Today, the business consists of a lot of consulting, speaking, and writing. We work out of perhaps the ultimate wired

Courtesy of Jim Carroll.

home—it even has a local area network. I am, I suppose, the only guy in the neighbourhood with a computer-network jack on the patio.

When establishing this small business, one of the first decisions made was that technology would be a key method to ensure its survival. And my experience through the past eight years has left me with a deep appreciation that the effective use of technology by a small business can play an extremely significant role in its success. When it comes right down to it, technology is levelling the playing field for small business in a way that is unprecedented. The combination of laser printers, fax machines, personal computers, the Internet, hand-held organizers, sophisticated telephone technology, cellphones, and countless other innovations have provided small businesses an opportunity to act, think, and look as professional as their larger counterparts.

Not only that, small businesses can work with efficiency and low costs on a global basis in a way that has never been seen before. My own experience is bearing this out. I'm winning new clients through the Internet, and I generate my own colour brochures. I produce my own promotional videos and distribute them on CD-ROM and online. I've saved most of the electronic mail messages sent and received since 1984, thus building a powerful personal knowledge resource. I've mastered the skill of "just-in-time knowledge," meaning I can learn about anything at any time. With the Internet, I've become global in such a way that would have been a dream just a few years ago. Just last weekend, a fellow in Japan bought one of my books from my online store.

Technology has not only been powerful, it has been extremely empowering. No longer do I have to waste hours in a traffic jam early in the morning or late in the day; that time is much better spent being productive in the home office. And the lifestyle implications are enormous—I probably get to spend more time with my two young children than most other fathers. My kids are growing up with me as an integral part of their life, a fact for which I credit technology.

I'm a wired entrepreneur and I'm having a ball. When asked to undertake a column about the use of technology within small business, I jumped at the chance. I am convinced that technology will help to make the twenty-first century the era of small business.

Jim Carroll is the co-author of *Small Business Online—A Strategic Guide for Entrepreneurs*. His e-mail address is <jcarroll@jimcarroll.com>. Or visit his Web site at <www.jimcarroll.ca>.

ETHICAL DILEMMA
Where to Draw the Line?

In this chapter you will see that a common route to starting a business is via a job in a company where young potential entrepreneurs can gain valuable experience and connections. When they deem the time is right, these entrepreneurs start their own ventures. Often, ethical dilemmas arise concerning "stealing" customers or clients or using special technology or processes learned from an employer. Some companies protect themselves by having employment contracts that forbid this happening. However, suppose your venture requires you to compete with your former employer because you are providing similar services and trying to sell them to the same customers. Is it, for example, ethical to take knowledge or customers from your previous employer for your own company? What do you think you would do? Think about it and we'll return to this question at the end of the chapter.

SMALL BUSINESS: A DYNAMIC SOURCE OF CAREERS AND JOBS

Jim Carroll is a good example of the 2.6 million self-employed persons in Canada. Almost half of them are operating businesses employing about 50 percent of the workforce and generating 43 percent of the total economic output, or GDP, of our country. Ninety-seven percent of all businesses are small businesses (see Figure 7.1). Of course, these figures also mean that 3 percent of all businesses are large businesses, but they generate 57 percent of Canadian GDP. During the 1990s small business generated most of the jobs while large companies were laying off employees. Another interesting fact is that women constitute 35 percent of all small-business owners and they generate about half of all new business start-ups.[1]

Carroll is also a good example of what we have discussed in previous chapters. His business is based on modern technology, his market is the entire world, and he operates out of his home. Further, his wife has teamed up with him to operate the business—a common event that will be discussed in this chapter.

This chapter also discusses important factors to consider when starting a small business. One of these is introduced in the Ethical Dilemma box "Where to Draw the Line?"

FIGURE 7.1

ANALYSIS OF CANADIAN BUSINESSES BY NUMBER OF EMPLOYEES

Ninety-seven percent of Canadian companies are small businesses with fewer than 50 employees.

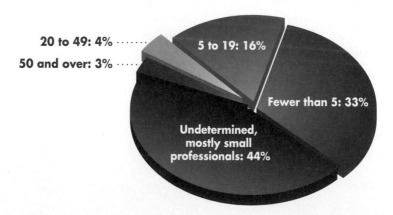

20 to 49: 4%

50 and over: 3%

5 to 19: 16%

Fewer than 5: 33%

Undetermined, mostly small professionals: 44%

Adapted from: The Statistics Canada CANSIM database http://cansim2.statcan.ca.cgi-win/CNSMCGI.EXE, Matrix 3451, Series D986059, D986061, May 1999.

PhotoDisc

Many young people are finding that creating their own job by starting a business is a good career choice. Although some entrepreneurs do not have formal education or training, these master of business administration (MBA) students believe that a degree will provide them with the skills necessary to operate a small business.

An Important Player in the Canadian Economy

Not only do small businesses create many jobs and generate a large segment of the GDP in Canada, but 75,000 small businesses engage in exporting, thus helping to create an international trade surplus for Canada.

Obviously, the small-business sector is a dynamic and vital part of Canadian life. What drives all of these people is often called *entrepreneurship*. **Entrepreneurship** is having the skills and determination to start and operate a business and to accept the calculated risks that are part of such an undertaking. Entrepreneurship helped countries that had little land and few natural resources to prosper. Some excellent examples are Hong Kong, Singapore, Japan, and Taiwan. Canada has both natural resources and entrepreneurs, but its success in the future is more dependent on entrepreneurs than on natural resources. An **entrepreneur** is a person who organizes, manages, and assumes the risks of starting and operating a business to make a profit.

Successful entrepreneurs are usually bold, determined innovators obsessed with an idea that drives them to put up with all sorts of difficulties and discouragement to achieve their goal. Nearly all the modern conveniences and technological advances that we now take for granted were born of the efforts of such entrepreneurs.

The sewing machine, the radio, transistors, TVs, telephones, cars, computers—all were the ideas of various geniuses whose work has been put to practical use by entrepreneurs. Some inventors have also been good entrepreneurs, but that is quite rare. Many entrepreneurs just find better ways to produce or distribute existing products. That's how chain and department stores and supermarkets developed.

Entrepreneurs played a major role in developing the early Canadian economy in fur trading, lumber, shipbuilding, fishing, farming, retail trade, and transportation. Some became giant companies like the Hudson's Bay Co., CPR, MacMillan Bloedel, and Irving Oil.

Since entrepreneurship is still the major driving force in the Canadian economy, we are going to examine its implications for you and your future career. We will be looking at entrepreneurship in large corporations and in small businesses.

entrepreneurship
Having the skills and determination to start and operate a business and to accept the calculated risks that are part of such an undertaking.

entrepreneur
A person who organizes, manages, and assumes the risks of starting and operating a business to make a profit.

THE ENTREPRENEURIAL CHALLENGE

There have been many surveys asking people why they opened their own businesses. Thousands of new businesses are started every month, and most of these are small, owner-managed enterprises. Statistics indicate that the number continues to increase, and that women are playing an ever-increasing role. This occurs despite a very high failure rate. Why do so many men and women, young and old, newly arrived immigrants and long-settled residents, undertake this difficult, risky task? Here are some of the reasons.

www.apple.com/pr/bios/jobs.html

Check out this Web site for a detailed biography of Steve Jobs, one of the most interesting and successful entrepreneurs of his generation. Jobs's achievements include the introduction of the personal computer and the creation of Apple Computer.

- **New idea, process, or product**. Some entrepreneurs are driven by a firm belief, perhaps even an obsession, that they can produce a better widget, or the old widget at a lower cost, than anybody else. Perhaps they have gotten hold of a new widget or have conceived of an improvement that they are convinced has a large potential market. That's how Apple Computer started. Three young engineers led by Steve Jobs left good positions with Digital Equipment to develop the personal computer. Sometimes you just know that you can run that business better than your boss or company.

- **Independence**. Some employees who have imagination and confidence in themselves find their jobs too restrictive. They need breathing space and a little elbow room! Perhaps their company does not encourage innovation in their operations, so they make the break. Some corporate managers are tired of big-business life and are quitting to start their own small businesses. They bring with them their managerial expertise and their enthusiasm. Many people cannot conceive of working for someone else. They like doing things their own way without someone standing over them. This type of person gets a great deal of satisfaction out of what he or she achieves. Do you know anybody who feels that way?

- **Challenge**. Closely related to the previous factors are the excitement and the challenge of doing something new or difficult. Many people thrive on overcoming challenges. These people welcome the opportunity to run their own business.

- **Family pattern**. Some people grow up in an atmosphere in which family members have started their own businesses, perhaps going back several generations. The talk at the dinner table is often about business matters. This background may predispose young men or women to think along the same lines. Sometimes there is a family business, and the next generation grows up expecting to take its place there in due course.

- **Profit**. It's natural for people to benefit monetarily from their ideas and dedication and to be rewarded for the money they risk and their hard work when they run a business. Yet long after a business has produced substantial profits and amassed personal fortunes for its owners, many continue to enjoy the challenge of overcoming the endless problems that every business faces and to enjoy the satisfaction of continued success.

- **Job insecurity or joblessness**. A recent phenomenon is the downsizing policy of many large and medium-sized companies since the serious recessions of the 1980s and 1990s. Companies have been on a long campaign of paring staff to the bone to reduce costs. In combination with the significant inroads made by computers in the same period (the technological unemployment referred to in Chapter 2), many employees, including middle-level and even senior-level managers, have been laid off. This has forced many of them to change their orientation from employee to self-employed. The accelerating movement to home-based operations has made this transition easier.

- **Immigrants**. Many immigrants who come to Canada lack educational skills. This, combined with no Canadian job experience and weak language skills in English or French, makes it difficult for them to find employment. However, they often have the drive and desire to succeed, and if they can obtain the capital, they can start their own business. We see this in the many immigrants who run convenience stores (*dépanneurs* in Quebec), as well as other types of businesses, such as importing and manufacturing. Other immigrants arrive with capital, skills, and strong entrepreneurial backgrounds. Vancouver and B.C. have been major beneficiaries of such immigrants from Hong Kong.

What Does It Take to Be a Successful Entrepreneur?[2]

How do you know if you have the qualities necessary to make a successful business person? There is no foolproof formula. Likely winners have proven to be losers and predicted losers have been big winners. External conditions play a major role in determining the success or failure of a business venture. Wars, recessions, inflation, changes in government policies, competitors' actions, technological developments—all can have a significant effect on businesses, especially new companies.

Nevertheless, certain personal qualities are necessary to start and, more important, to operate a small business. Many skills can be learned through work experience and formal education, but the kind of person you are may be the most important factor. Here are some major qualities that will increase your chances of succeeding as an entrepreneur.

www.yea.ca

See this Web site for more information about the Young Entrepreneurs Association Canada.

1. **Self-direction**. You should be a self-starter, with lots of confidence in yourself. You do not hesitate to step into any situation. Doing your own thing should seem like the only way. Furthermore, you are the boss and everything really rests on your shoulders.

2. **Determination**. Closely related to self-direction is the drive you need to see you through all the obstacles and difficulties that you will encounter. You have to keep going when others would give up. This often accompanies the high degree of self-confidence mentioned above.

3. **High energy level**. You must be able to put in long hours every day, six or seven days a week, for the first few years at least. You must be able to take hard work, physically and mentally.

4. **Risk orientation**. Because there is a high risk of failure, you must be able to live with uncertainty. You must accept the fact that all your hard work and money may go down the drain. On a day-to-day basis, you must make decisions that involve varying degrees of risk.

5. **Vision**. Many successful entrepreneurs have some dream or vision they feel impelled to realize. Perhaps it is to make that product better than anyone else can or to provide a new product or service.

6. **Ability to learn quickly**. Making errors is inevitable. Only those who do nothing make no mistakes. What is important is what you learn from them. Good entrepreneurs are quick to learn such lessons. They adapt and shift gears as required instead of letting pride stand in the way of admitting a mistake.

How do you stack up as a potential entrepreneur? You can take the entrepreneurial readiness questionnaire in Appendix B following this chapter to see how you rate. Remember, these are only guidelines. The only rule about starting a business is that there is no rule. Some people have had an entrepreneurial bent since they were children. They were always promoting something: delivering papers, organizing other kids to collect bottles or plastic containers, selling, or doing other part-time work at an early age. As adults, they don't ask people if they should go into business for themselves—they do it!

A 17-year-old composer once asked Mozart's opinion about the quality of his compositions. After examining the works, Mozart told him they lacked maturity and that he should wait until he was a little older. The visitor, somewhat exasperated, replied that Mozart himself had started composing when he was five! Mozart replied, "That's true, but I didn't ask anybody."

Other entrepreneurs are a little more cautious. They get some education—perhaps a bachelor of commerce (B.Com.) or master of business administration (MBA) degree or a professional designation such as chartered accountant (CA)—as well as some work experience before they decide to venture into business. Some follow this procedure as part of a deliberate plan; others make the decision to go off on their own later, as a result of business experience they have accumulated.

Women Entrepreneurs

www.profitguide.com

A major phenomenon since the late 1970s is the large number of women who have gone into business for themselves. (See *Profit* magazine's October 2001 cover story of five "leading ladies" and the feature in the same issue devoted to successful women entrepreneurs.) Throughout this book, you will see many examples of such enterprises. Between 1975 and 1990, the number of female entrepreneurs grew 172.8 percent. In 1998, as noted previously, 35 percent of all self-employed Canadians were women, up from 19 percent in 1975. Women starting their own businesses have tended to concentrate in the service sector. This is not surprising since more than 75 percent of the workforce is in the service area, which contributes between 75 and 80 percent of GDP.[3] Studies and surveys have revealed a variety of reasons for this significant emergence of female entrepreneurs.

- **Financial need**. The previous decade saw the average real incomes of Canadian employees drop and unemployment remain high. This has forced many women to support the family budget by starting a business, sometimes part-time, sometimes with their husbands.

- **Lack of promotion opportunities**. Most positions in higher management are still dominated by men. Although the situation is improving, the pace is extremely slow. Many women who are frustrated by this pace take the entrepreneurial route.

Nancy Mathis invented the TC Probe used to test properties of solid materials such as wood or plastic. She was encouraged to market her device by the National Research Council and, with her husband, Chris, formed Mathis Instruments, where they have perfected the TC Probe.

- **Women returning to the workforce**. Many women who return to the job market after raising a family find that their skills are outdated. They also encounter subtle age discrimination. These factors encourage many to try self-employment.

- **Feminism**. The feminist movements of the past four decades have given many women the confidence to strike out on their own.

- **Family and personal responsibility**. The high divorce rate in recent years has created a situation in which many divorced women find themselves with children and little or no financial support from their ex-husbands. Some even refuse such support to be more independent. The development of affordable personal computers and other modern technology has made it possible for women to start businesses based at home. There are examples in this book of home-based enterprises run by women.

- **Public awareness of women in business**. As more publicity highlights the fact that growing numbers of women have started their own ventures, the idea catches on and gives others the confidence to try. Often two or more women will team up to form a partnership.

- **Part-time occupations**. Often, married women with some particular talent— for example, publicity, writing, designing, making clothes, cooking, organizing, or human relations—are encouraged to develop their hobby or skills on a part-time basis to see how far they can go with it. This procedure has resulted in many notable success stories, some of which are reported in this book.

- **Couples in partnership**. Some ventures are started by couples who cannot find jobs. Or sometimes one member of a couple joins his or her partner, whose business is growing and who needs more help. (See the Profile at the start of the chapter.)

- **Higher rate of success for women**. Women entrepreneurs seem to have a better success rate than men. Various factors may account for this. Women feel less pressured than men to achieve quick results. They are a little more cautious, so they make fewer mistakes. They also accept advice more readily than men, who may have a macho image of having to know it all. It will be interesting to follow this process to see if women continue to start ventures at the same rate and maintain their remarkable track record.

CRITICAL THINKING

Do you know anyone who seems to have the entrepreneurial spirit? What about him or her makes you say that?

Are there any similarities between the characteristics demanded of an entrepreneur and those of a professional athlete? Would an athlete be a good prospect for entrepreneurship? Why or why not? Could teamwork be important in an entrepreneurial effort?

If you are a woman, are you motivated by women's success rate?

Entrepreneurs of the Future

Many people believe that future entrepreneurs will need better education and preparation than in the past. Business has become much more complex. A complicated mass of governmental laws and regulations, the rapid rate of advances in technology, international competition, and concerns with environmental and ethical issues have all combined to make it far more difficult to start and operate a business now.

International management guru Peter Drucker feels that, in the future, people with college and university training and some corporate experience will do much better as entrepreneurs in the long run. Of course, this should not—and will not—discourage those who are strongly determined to start their own company. Such

www.pfdf.org
The Web site for The Peter F. Drucker Canadian Foundation for Nonprofit Innovation includes information about the foundation and about Drucker himself and his writings in the field of management. Check it out to learn about this *"guru, legend, and business icon."*

Intrapreneurs develop new products for corporations that employ them. The Scotch Pop-up Tape Strips are the latest innovation from 3M, a company the welcomes employee ideas.

determination and self-confidence are major requirements for success in business. It is important to remember that there is no formula that guarantees success.

Entrepreneurial Teams

Large organizations are usually cautious, bureaucratic, and slow to react to changes in the markets they serve. Many companies have set up teams of managers from different areas within the company to overcome such difficulties.

Entrepreneurial teams help the company function efficiently and ensure better co-operation and coordination among different functions of the business.

To encourage the entrepreneurial spirit, employees and managers from different areas of the business who have shown such spirit are organized into special teams. A team can be more effective than an individual because it brings together people with a variety of skills and experience to bounce ideas off each other.

Such teams are said to consist of *intrapreneurs*. An **intrapreneur** is a person with entrepreneurial skills who is employed in a corporation to launch new products. Such people take hands-on responsibility for innovation in an organization.

Some groups become more daring and enterprising and work on what seem like way-out projects. These are known as *skunkworks* (the name comes from the Li'l Abner comic strip) because no one knows what outlandish ideas they may come up with. **Skunkworks** are highly innovative, fast-moving entrepreneurial units operating at the fringes of a corporation.

Many companies have benefited enormously from intrapreneurial teams and from skunkworks. An example is the development of the Avro Arrow military plane by de Havilland in the 1960s, the most advanced plane of its kind. Do some research in your library to see what other examples you can find.

One of the most famous examples of intrapreneurial success is the Post-it gummed note pad, developed at the 3M Company. Despite its many obvious uses, intrapreneurs had to persist for years before it became a major product.

intrapreneur
A person with entrepreneurial skills who is employed in a corporation to launch new products and who takes hands-on responsibility for innovation in an organization.

skunkworks
Highly innovative, fast-moving entrepreneurial units operating at the fringes of a corporation.

www.3m.com

3M has a reputation for an intrapreneurial culture that goes far beyond the example of Post-it Notes. See this Web site for information on other products and the innovative culture at 3M.

- What are the advantages of entrepreneurial teams?
- Can you give five reasons why entrepreneurs go into business themselves?
- Why are so many women becoming entrepreneurs? Why do they have such a high success rate?

WHAT IS A SMALL BUSINESS?

It would be helpful to define what we mean by the term *small business*. Giant companies like Imperial Oil or General Motors may look at most companies as small. Governments have various size guidelines for different aid programs. In the definition we have previously used, a **small business** is independently owned and operated, not dominant in its field, and meets certain standards of size in terms of employees or annual revenue.

By this definition, the vast majority of businesses in Canada are small—fewer than 10 employees and with annual sales under $500,000. This volume of sales, less than $10,000 per week, might be further analyzed as follows (in round numbers):

small business
Business that is independently owned and operated, not dominant in its field, and meets certain standards of size in terms of employees or annual revenue.

NUMBER OF DAYS OPEN EACH WEEK	SALES PER DAY LESS THAN
5	$2,000
6	1,700
7	1,500

Of course, many small businesses have sales in the millions and up to 50 employees (see Figure 7.1).

There is constant movement as far as individual businesses are concerned. Many are closing up while larger numbers are starting. Many are steadily growing larger, and some eventually become very large companies. Some merge with others or are sold as owners retire or die.

It is estimated that there are about 900,000 businesses in Canada. For this purpose, a business is defined as having at least one paid employee plus the owner. Of all these businesses, only a tiny fraction, about 1 percent, have more than 100 employees. The number of businesses that have no employees may reach into the tens of thousands. Statistics Canada states that more than 2,600,000 persons report self-employment income.[4]

This shop is an example of the many small businesses of the "old economy" in Canada. A large number of businesses are started each year by entrepreneurs seeking the challenge of fulfilling a dream.

Michael Polselli

SPOTLIGHT ON BIG BUSINESS

A Small Business Grows to Be a Large Business

In 1961 John Sereny bought a tiny wholesale operation for $1,500. In 1994 he sold it for $25 million to forestry giant MacMillan Bloedel. That year Sereny's Green Forest Lumber Ltd., with sawmills and distribution centres in Ontario and the United States, had sales of $377 million and profits of just under $12 million. At 68, with neither of his two musician sons interested in taking over from dad, Sereny felt that the MacMillan Bloedel offer was one he could not refuse.

There was an additional sweetener to the $25 million that Sereny found enticing. He was asked to run the company for three years so that "big Mac" could train his successor. So once a week the 68-year-old entrepreneur took off in his plane at Toronto's airport and flew to inspect the plants in Windsor and Fort Erie, Ontario, and this after a 10- to 12-hour-a-day workweek. Obviously John Sereny loved his work, and the company left him alone so that he could do the job properly.

MacMillan Bloedel had learned its lesson from previous takeovers in which the companies were incorporated into the company's operations rather than continuing to operate independently, with results that were not entirely satisfactory. Both the company and Sereny had to make adjustments to accommodate to the new situation, but everything worked out well. Is this a story with a happy ending? It certainly is a great success story for John Sereny. The fact that it ceased to be a family-owned business is not unusual. In John Sereny's case, he did what he had to do and his children are doing their thing.

This entire procedure was of an interim or transitional nature. By 1998 Green Forest Lumber had been absorbed directly by its giant parent, MacMillan Bloedel, and ceased to exist as a separate company. John Sereny retired. It's ironic, or perhaps a natural development in the modern world of business, that, in 1999, MacMillan Bloedel itself was acquired by an even larger American forestry firm, Weyerhaeuser.

Based on: Patricia Lush, "Green Forest Pilot Still Flies Solo," *Globe and Mail, Report on Business,* February 28, 1996, p. B10 (reprinted with permission from the *Globe and Mail*); interview with Ruxandra Kovaco, July 2, 1999.

Dynamic Sector

The small-business sector is a very dynamic part of the Canadian economy. It provided nearly all the new jobs created in the 1980s and repeated this process in the 1990s. Small business also is responsible for a big share of innovation and initiative over a wide spectrum of business activities.

Small businesses continue to be feeders for future large businesses. As they prosper and develop new services or products, they are often bought out by large companies, which thus become more competitive. A good example is provided in the Spotlight on Big Business box "A Small Business Grows to Be a Large Business." The founders usually profit handsomely from the transaction while retaining managerial positions and acquiring shares in the larger entity. Alternatively, after small businesses establish a good track record, they convert from private to public companies, enabling them to obtain significant financing and become larger companies.

Nearly all small businesses are Canadian-owned and managed, in contrast to large businesses, many of which are foreign-owned and managed. Small business thus plays a big role in helping to maintain the Canadian identity and Canadian economic independence.

Wide Diversification

Another significant aspect of small business is the wide diversification of its activities. If you look, you will find small businesses in many sectors:

1. **Service businesses.** You are already familiar with the services provided by car mechanics, dry cleaners, travel agencies, lawncare firms, salons, and other

services that cater to you and your family. In your career search, be sure to explore services such as hotels and motels, health clubs, amusement parks, income tax preparation organizations, employment agencies, accounting firms, rental firms of all kinds, management consulting, repair services (for example, computers, VCRs), insurance agencies, real estate firms, stock-brokers, and so on. A major growth area is in computer consulting and the knowledge-based industries generally.

2. **Retail businesses.** You only have to go to a major shopping mall to see the possibilities in retailing. There are stores selling shoes, clothes, hats, skis, gloves, sporting goods, ice cream, groceries, and more. Much more. Watch the trends, and you will see new ideas like fancy popcorn stores and cafés with Internet access areas.

3. **Construction firms.** Drive through any big city and you will see huge cranes towering over major construction sites. Would you enjoy supervising such work? Visit some areas where construction firms are building bridges, roads, homes, schools, buildings, and dams. There is a feeling of power and creativity in such work that excites many observers. How about you? Talk to some of the workers and supervisors and learn about the risks and rewards of small construction firms.

4. **Wholesalers.** Have you ever visited a wholesale food warehouse, jewellery centre, or similar wholesale firm? If not, you are missing an important link in the small-business chain, one with much potential. Wholesale representatives often make more money, have more free time, travel more, and enjoy their work more than similar people in retailing.

5. **Manufacturing.** Of course, manufacturing is still an attractive career for tomorrow's graduates. Surveys show that manufacturers make the most money among small-business owners. There are careers for designers, machinists, mechanics, engineers, supervisors, safety inspectors, and a host of other occupations. Visit some small manufacturers in your area and inquire about such jobs to get some experience before starting your own manufacturing business. The high-tech world of today opens up many opportunities, if you are interested.

There are also thousands of small farmers who enjoy the rural life and the pace of farming. Small farms have been in great trouble for the last few years, but some that specialize in exotic or organic crops do quite well. Similarly, many small mining operations attract college and university students who have a sense of adventure. People who are not sure what career they would like to follow have a busy time ahead. They need to visit service firms, construction firms, farms, mines, retailers, wholesalers, and all other kinds of small and large businesses to see the diversity and excitement available in Canadian business. For some specific examples, see the Spotlight on Small Business box "An Amazing Variety from the Atlantic to the Pacific."

www.digitalocean.ca

The Nautical Data International Web site invites you to "cruise the digital ocean." Try it to learn more about this producer of electronic maps and digital nautical products.

CRITICAL THINKING

Imagine yourself starting a small business. What kind of business would it be? How much local competition is there? What could you do to make your business more attractive than competitors'? Would you be willing to work 60 to 70 hours per week in such a business?

STARTING A SMALL BUSINESS

There are several ways to get into your first business venture.

1.   Start your own company.

2.   Buy an existing business.

3.   Buy a franchise unit.

Franchising was discussed in the previous chapter. Let us first look at some common procedures you should follow regardless of which path you pursue.

Gather Information   The federal Business Development Bank of Canada (BDC) publishes some useful, free material for new entrepreneurs. So do most of the larger banks in Canada and the Canadian Bankers Association. The Canadian Federation of Independent Business (CFIB) is also a useful body for entrepreneurs. It has branches across Canada. Read through some CFIB booklets for important clues as to what you should be doing before starting a business. Other useful federal sources are regional offices of the National Research Council, the Patent Office of the Ministry of Consumer and Corporate Affairs, the Small Business Administration, and the Small Business Data

---

SPOTLIGHT ON SMALL BUSINESS

An Amazing Variety from the Atlantic to the Pacific

www.profitguide.com/hottest
(This Web site has links to the companies listed below)

Extreme TV cameras that peer into active volcanoes. Electromagnetic testing for water pipes. Circuits for the subterranean power grid. Software that helps importers navigate the web of international trade. Mobile-commerce systems for wireless road warriors. Location-tracking systems that bring taxis to your door—and may soon diagnose engine trouble while you drive. Answering services for funeral directors. Graffiti-removal services. Online contests. "White-glove" moving services. Easy financing for MRIs, hair transplants, and dental implants.

These are some of the wide variety of small businesses that were started up in Canada in 1997 or 1998 and grew very rapidly. (All the results shown below compare 1998 with 2000.) They include what *Profit* magazine calls "Canada's Hottest Startups." Number 50, Frantic Films of Winnipeg led by Jamie Brown, which produces a TV series, is still operating at a loss but its sales jumped to $431,000 from $163,000 and its staff went from 4 to 11. Leading the pack is Sigem Inc. of Kanata, Ont., whose CEO is Herb Woods. They make location-tracking systems to help companies keep track of their fleet of vehicles; their sales soared from $68,000 to an unbelievable $13 million although they are still incurring a loss. Employment jumped from 7 to 109 persons.

On the east coast there is Gary Darychuk, founder of Funeral Directors' Choice in Saint John, N.B., an answering service for funeral homes. Sales went from $72,000 to $1.3 million, the company is operating at a profit, and employees increased from 10 to 35. In Vancouver, Ann Kaplan heads up Medicard Finance Inc., which lends consumers money for medical procedures such as dental and cosmetic surgery. Sales jumped from $202,000 to $1,942,000 and the number of employees rose from 7 to 26.

In Markham, Ont., Bahman Koohestani is co-founder of Delano Technology Corp., which develops corporate customer-management software and whose customers include Sprint, Compaq, and Warner Music. Their sales took a giant leap from under a half-million to more than $30 million and employees from 159 to 630, but Delano is still running at a loss. In Calgary, Greg Chudiak runs Pandell Technology Corp., a knowledge-management software company whose clients include Ford, Telus, Syncrude, and the Alberta government. Sales climbed from under $300,000 to more than $1.2 million, and employees from 4 to 20. Kate Bird's Career Essentials Inc., in Toronto, retrains injured workers so that they can return to work. Her company's sales quadrupled from just under $450,000 to more than $1.8 million, and the workforce went from 9 to 55. Both Chudiak and Bird are operating at a profit.

Source: Ian Portsmouth, "Canada's Hottest Startups," *Profit*, September 2001, pp. 37–41.

Base of Statistics Canada. The Statistics Canada database is backed by the federal and provincial governments and provides information on how competitors or potential competitors are performing. Most provincial governments provide a lot of information, assistance, and financing for small business. This is reviewed in some detail in Chapter 4.

There are also many books on starting and operating a small business that can provide a lot of useful information. The *Complete Canadian Small Business Guide* (McGraw-Hill Ryerson) by Douglas and Diana Gray is a big book that is very detailed. It includes a 15-page appendix listing sources of information. A smaller book that includes a disk to help create a business plan is *Small Business and Entrepreneurship* (Prentice Hall Canada) by Paul D. Berman, one of the authors of this text.

Courtesy of Business Development Bank of Canada.

An account manager at BDC Connex®, BDC's virtual branch, examines an online loan application.

Obtain Professional Advice   Find a good accountant, lawyer, or equivalent professional—they will be your most important advisers for starting and running a business. Ask friends, other entrepreneurs, or family to recommend someone. An experienced accountant will give you invaluable advice and help you through all the procedures of getting your company organized and running (see Figure 7.2).

Don't fret about the cost. Remember that you are planning to invest (and borrow) thousands of dollars and invest a long period of hard labour. It is wise to protect that investment by spending a small portion of those dollars at the outset for experienced counsel. Your accountant will also be invaluable on an ongoing basis. He or she will advise you on what computer and software you require, organize your accounting system and your office procedures, produce monthly figures, analyze results, advise on taxation matters, and free you up to concentrate on those functions that only you can and should attend to: buying, selling, servicing customers, collecting payments, and more.

Prepare a Business Plan   It is amazing how many people are eager to start a small business but have only a vague notion of what they want to do. Eventually, they come up with an idea for a business and begin discussing the idea with professors, friends, and other business people. At this stage, the entrepreneur needs a **business plan**, a detailed written statement that describes the nature of the business, the target market, the advantages the business will have over competitors, the resources and qualifications of the owners, and much more.

business plan
A detailed written statement that describes the nature of the business, the target market, the advantages the business will have over competitors, the resources and qualifications of the owners, and much more.

SOURCE	PERCENTAGE USING SOURCE	RANK OF SOURCE
Accountant	78%	1
Other business owners	77	3
Friends/relatives	76	5
Bankers	72	2
Lawyers	63	6
Books/manuals	62	7
Suppliers	59	4
Trade organizations	47	9
Seminars	41	8
Government sources	33	10

FIGURE 7.2

INFORMATION SOURCES

Small-business managers turn to accountants and bankers for important advice. They also question other business owners and friends for ideas.

A business plan forces potential owners of small businesses to be quite specific about the products or services they intend to offer. They must analyze the competition, the money needed to start, and other details of operation. A business plan forces the entrepreneur to translate hopes and dreams into concrete reality: to see how much cash is required, how much sales and profit must be generated to break even, how much profit will be made if all goes well, whether the target market is there, and what the competition is doing. It gives the entrepreneur a good look at what he or she may be walking into.

A business plan also enables investors, bankers, or other lenders to evaluate your proposal properly. You cannot expect to ask for financing without presenting a full picture of what you are all about. A well-prepared business plan provides the vital information these people require to make a decision. It also makes an excellent impression, because it shows that you have gone to a lot of trouble and expense and are very serious about your project.

To prepare a thorough plan, you will most likely need the assistance of a good accountant. In general, a business plan should include the following:

1. A cover letter summarizing the major facets of your proposed business.

2. A brief description of the industry and a detailed explanation of the products or services to be offered.

3. A thorough market analysis that discusses the size and nature of the market, the need for the new product or service, and the nature of the competition.

4. A marketing plan that includes location, signs, advertising, and display.

5. An operating plan that includes a sales and profit forecast and financial projections for at least three years, accounting procedures, and human resources requirements.

6. A comprehensive capitalization plan describing how much money the owner is committing. Few banks or investors will support a new firm unless the owner has made a substantial financial commitment.

7. A description of the experience and expertise of the owner. This may include résumés, letters of recommendation, and financial statements.

Unless you spend adequate time and effort preparing your business plan, it may end up like thousands of others—in a wastebasket, unread! Of 1,200 proposals received in a few months, the Aegis Partners, a Boston venture capital firm, read 600, researched 45, and funded only 14. Why? Because most entrepreneurs don't spend enough time preparing a good business plan, but expect potential lenders to spend several hours reading it.[5]

A proper business plan takes months to prepare, as you and your accountant gather information and organize it into the proper format. Unfortunately, you have to convince your busy readers in just a few minutes that it is worth reading. To do that, the plan has to be a real plan, not something cooked up to justify a decision to go into business made on intuition or some other basis.

Many books and articles have been written on how to prepare and write a good business plan. Many include a software disk. Canadian banks have some useful free material, including software. Most banks and credit unions provide business plan kits. A sample outline of a business plan is provided in Figure 7.3. Your accountant will be well informed on these matters. By working closely with him or her, you will find out what part of the job is yours.

Financing a Small Business

Next, we will discuss some of the many sources of money available to new business ventures. All of them call for a comprehensive business plan. The time and effort invested *before* a business is started pays off many times later. With a small business, the big payoff is survival.

COVER LETTER

Only one thing is certain when you go hunting for money to start a business: You won't be the only hunter out there. You need to make potential funders want to read your business plan instead of the hundreds of others on their desks. Your cover letter should summarize the most attractive points of your project in as few words as possible. Be sure to address the letter to the potential investor by name. "To whom it may concern" or "Dear Sir" is not the best way to win an investor's support.

SECTION 1—INTRODUCTION

Begin with a two- or three-page management overview of the proposed venture. Include a short description of the business, and discuss major goals and objectives.

SECTION 2—COMPANY BACKGROUND

Describe company operations to date (if any), potential legal considerations, and areas of risk and opportunity. Summarize the firm's financial condition. Include past and current balance sheets, income and cash-flow statements, and other relevant financial records. [You will read about these financial statements in Chapter 18.] It is also wise to include a description of insurance coverage. Investors want to be assured that death or mishaps do not pose major threats to the company.

SECTION 3—MANAGEMENT TEAM

Include an organization chart, job descriptions of listed positions, and detailed résumés of the current and proposed executives. A mediocre idea with a proven management team is funded more often than a great idea with an inexperienced team. Managers should have expertise in all disciplines necessary to start and run a business. If they do not, mention outside consultants who will serve in these roles and describe their qualifications.

SECTION 4—FINANCIAL PLAN

Provide five-year projections for income, expenses, and funding sources. Don't assume the business will grow in a straight line. Adjust your planning to allow for funding at various stages of the company's growth. Explain the rationale and assumptions used to determine the estimates. Assumptions should be reasonable and based on industry and historical trends. Make sure all totals add up and are consistent throughout the plan. (It will be necessary to hire a professional accountant or financial analyst to prepare these statements.)

Stay clear of excessively ambitious sales projections; rather, offer best-case, expected, and worst-case scenarios. These not only reveal how sensitive the bottom line is to sales fluctuations but also serve as good management guides.

SECTION 5—CAPITAL REQUIRED

Indicate the amount of capital needed to commence or continue operations and describe how these funds will be used. Make sure the totals are the same as the ones on the cash-flow statement. This area will receive a great deal of review from potential investors, so it must be clear and concise.

SECTION 6—MARKETING PLAN

Don't underestimate the competition. Review industry size, trends, and the target market segment. Discuss strengths and weaknesses of the product or service. The most important things investors want to know are what makes the product more desirable than what's already available and whether it can be patented. Compare pricing to the competition's. Forecast sales in dollars and units. Outline sales, advertising, promotion, and PR programs. Make sure the costs agree with those projected in the financial statements.

SECTION 7—LOCATION ANALYSIS

In retailing and certain other industries, the location of the business is a crucial factor. Provide a comprehensive demographic analysis of consumers in the area of the proposed store as well as a traffic-pattern analysis and vehicular and pedestrian counts.

SECTION 8—MANUFACTURING PLAN

Describe minimum plant size, machinery required, production capacity, inventory and inventory-control methods, quality control, plant personnel requirements, and so on. Estimates of product costs should be based on primary research (see Chapter 15).

SECTION 9—APPENDIX

Include all marketing research on the product or service (off-the-shelf reports, article reprints, etc.) and other information about the product concept or market size. Provide a bibliography of all the reference materials you consulted. This section should demonstrate that the proposed company won't be entering a declining industry or market segment.

Adapted from: Eric Adams, "Growing Your Business Plan," *Home-Computing,* May 1991, pp. 44–48; R. Richard Bruno, "How to Write a Business Plan for a New Venture," *Marketing News,* March 15, 1985, p. 10; Ellyn Spragins, "Venture Capital Express," *Inc.,* November 1990, pp. 159–160.

FIGURE 7.3

OUTLINE OF A COMPREHENSIVE BUSINESS PLAN

- Can you name the five different classes of small businesses?
- What factors are used to classify a firm as a small business?
- What advice would you give a friend who wanted to learn more about starting a small business?
- There are many sections in the business plan. This plan is probably the most important document a small-business person will ever create. Can you describe at least four of the sections?

FUNDING A SMALL BUSINESS

The problem with most new small businesses is that the entrepreneurs have more enthusiasm than managerial skills and capital. Our economic system is called *capitalism* for a reason. It is capital (money) that enables entrepreneurs to get started; buy needed goods, services, labour, and equipment; and keep the business going. Some of the *financial* reasons cited for failure are

- starting with too little capital
- starting with too much capital and being careless in its use
- borrowing money without planning how and when to pay it back
- trying to do too much business with not enough capital
- not allowing for setbacks and unexpected expenses
- extending credit too freely

www.strategis.ic.gc.ca

The marketing research firm mentioned here, Thompson-Lightstone, is listed under the *Business Support and Financing* heading on the Strategis Web site. You can visit this site to learn more about this company. The Strategis Web site itself is a large database provided by Industry Canada as a resource for people who are doing business, or are considering doing business, in Canada. Take some time to explore this site; it has a wealth of very useful information.

Entrepreneurs, like most people, are not necessarily highly skilled at obtaining, managing, and using money. Inadequate capitalization or poor financial management can destroy a business even when the basic idea behind it is good and the products are accepted in the marketplace. One secret of finding the money to start your business is knowing where to look for it.

One of the major problems for new entrepreneurs is misinformation or lack of information about capitalization and financial management. A new entrepreneur has several sources of capital: personal savings, relatives, former employers, banks, finance companies, venture capital organizations, and government agencies.

Small businesses are key clients of Canada's banks. Approximately 95 percent of all bank business-borrowing customers are small and medium-sized enterprises (SMEs). Banks approve 93 percent of all loans from SMEs, according to the 1998 Thompson-Lightstone national SME survey. Banks compete aggressively in the SME market, tailoring loan packages and services to these customers' special needs, and hosting and participating in seminars and workshops designed to ensure an effective partnership between banks and small business. See Figure 7.4 for further information on the importance of bank and other financing.

In Canada the most common sources of commercial financing are the chartered banks. Since small businesses, especially new ventures, are high-risk undertakings, it is not surprising that banks have been very reluctant to make unsecured loans to small-business people. In response to criticism from many quarters about their lack of support of such an important part of the economy, banks have announced a variety of new programs. For example, the Royal Bank announced a joint operation with the federal Business Development Bank of Canada (BDC) in southern Ontario involving expediting loans of $50,000 to $500,000 to export-oriented, high-technology small businesses, the so-called *new economy*.[6] The Royal Bank and the CIBC launched a joint foundation to provide loans of up to $15,000 for unemployed young people who want to start businesses.[7] The Bank of Montreal set up a $200-million financing program for small and medium-sized businesses. It will make traditional loans and also invest in companies.[8] Credit unions, which exist in most provinces, can also be useful source of funding for small businesses.

Entrepreneurs may turn to the federal or provincial governments, which have a variety of agencies and programs to aid new or existing businesses. For example, the Small Business Loans Act authorizes the federal government to guarantee up to 85 percent of loans by authorized lenders, usually banks. As noted in the previous chapter, and in chapter 4, the federal government has a Crown corporation, the Business Development Bank (BDC), which is now focused on helping businesses in the New Economy—those in information technology and hi-tech generally, especially those who export or plan to concentrate on export markets. There are also venture capital companies, whose purpose is to seek out worthwhile new ventures and back them. Investors known as **venture capitalists** may finance your project, for a price. Venture capitalists ask for a hefty stake (frequently 60 percent) in your company in exchange for the cash to start your business. Experts recommend that you talk with at least five investment firms and their clients to find the right one for you.

Michael Paiselli

Venture capital companies are interested only in equity positions—buying shares in the company. The BDC may take an equity position or make a loan. Both will insist on seats on the board of directors to keep an eye on the company's operations. In practice, the venture capitalists play a more active role than the BDC. They also will not usually consider a request for less than $500,000. By contrast, the majority of BDC loans are under $100,000. The BDC plays a crucial role because it will invest in businesses with no track record, making it possible for them to obtain additional financing from other sources.

The financing agreement usually provides that, after a certain period, the entrepreneurs may buy back the shares held by these institutions, at their current value.

As Figure 7.4 indicates, 45 percent of SMEs use personal savings for start-up and operation. Many entrepreneurs also turn to their families for funds. It is important that, when taking loans from family members or friends, there is a clear understanding of the terms of repayment and if any interest is to be charged. Prepare a brief written document covering these and any other pertinent conditions of the loan that all parties will sign. This will prevent misunderstandings and worse from arising in the future.

You may want to consider borrowing from a potential supplier to your future business. Helping you get started may be in the supplier's interest if there is a chance you will be a big customer later. (See Figure 7.4 for more information).

As you may have guessed, technology-minded entrepreneurs have the best shot at attracting start-up capital. Such potential businesses are more attractive to venture capitalists, and the federal and provincial governments have grant programs that provide funds for such ventures.

> **O**ne of the most common mistakes new small-business owners make is waiting too long to talk to bankers. You would be surprised how long it takes to review and process bank loans. Another common mistake is to ask for too little money.

venture capitalists
Individuals or organizations that invest in new businesses in exchange for partial ownership.

- Half of SMEs report that they currently borrow from a financial institution for business financing (50%).
- Supplier credit is the second most used source (48%).
- Credit cards are the third most common source (46%).
- Equipment and vehicle leasing is fourth (28%).

Many companies use multiple sources of financing. In 1998 only 10 percent used a single source. Personal savings were used by 45 percent of SMEs.

FIGURE 7.4

SOURCES OF EXTERNAL FINANCING FOR SMALL AND MEDIUM-SIZED ENTERPRISES (SMEs)

Source: *Small and Medium Sized Businesses in Canada*, Thompson, Lightstone & Co. Ltd., 1998, vol. 1, p. 3 (prepared for Canadian Bankers Association).

There is one more consideration when it comes to financing ongoing operations. If you have a spouse or companion who has a good, steady income and is prepared to finance your combined personal cost of living for a couple of years, that can be very important. If you do not have to draw, say, $30,000 annually for your personal needs, that can be very helpful financially. The business can cut its cash needs by $90,000 in the first three years, which could make all the difference between survival and going under.

Personal Considerations before Going into Business

You have been advised several times that the owner and manager must work long hours and perhaps seven-day weeks, especially for the first couple of years. If you are unattached, then you are free to devote all your time to your business. If you want to sleep on a cot in your office there's nothing to stop you.

But what if you are married and have a child or two? Is your spouse ready to back you by undertaking to play daddy and mommy? Will you be torn between your family and business demands? Suppose you have no kids but you have a spouse or companion. How will she or he react to your constant absence? Have you considered what it may do to your relationship? These questions are often overlooked by entrepreneurs until they crop up and create havoc.

Finally, think about what kind of support system you can draw on when required. You may need some no-cost bodies like family members or friends to pitch in sometimes—to answer the phone, do some bookkeeping, help pack or ship. Do you have a shoulder to cry on when things get rough from time to time, as they certainly will? For some people, it might be advisable to have a Plan B as an alternative or backup plan in case Plan A proves to be a bust. This may include not *burning your bridges* to a past job, if possible. And, of course there is the financial consideration mentioned just before this section.

Once you have passed all these hurdles—business plan, financing, and personal factors—you're ready. So far we have discussed starting a new business. Let us now look at buying a business.

Buying a Business

On the one hand, there are many legitimate reasons for owners of a business to want to sell their company. They may want to retire, they may be ill, or they may have other interests that have become more important. Sometimes partners cannot get along or a company wants to divest itself of a subsidiary that does not fit into its core business.

On the other hand, the main reason for selling might be negative business factors. You must be very careful about this. A business whose profits have been declining for a couple of years may be sick. Or perhaps the business seems to be doing all right, but the owners know of some new factor that threatens its viability. This might be a change in a highway route that would result in a loss of vehicle traffic that is the lifeblood of the business. Perhaps a new competing franchising unit is scheduled to be built nearby. Or maybe the area has become run down and regular customers are turning away.

A new technological advance might threaten to make the company's processes, equipment, or product obsolete. (For example, plastic might replace steel and glass.) Imported competing products might be taking away the company's traditional markets (TVs, autos, jeans, and shoes are good examples). The company may be on the verge of losing a major customer. Or perhaps some new environmental regulations are due to kick in shortly that will involve a substantial outlay for new equipment.

To get the real story, do two things. Engage a professional accountant to examine the books and financial statements for the last three to five years. He or she will assess whether the financial statements give you a reliable picture of the company's operations during this period.

While this audit is being conducted, do some intensive investigation of your own. Check out every possible source of information in the municipality or area. Chambers of commerce, business development bodies, local newspapers, adjacent businesses (especially if you are considering a retail business), real estate agents, and local banks are all good sources of information. Drop in on the company unannounced at different hours to see what the operations look like. You might get a chance to speak to employees and customers. Get information from the trade association and trade publications of the particular industry about problems, trends, and developments.

When the audit and your investigation are both done, it is time to sit down with your accountant and review all the facts. (In effect, you have both been assembling some of the data necessary to prepare a business plan.) If you decide to go ahead, the matter of determining a fair price still remains. A business valuation expert can be very useful at this point. Often your accountant can do the job. If you require financing in addition to your own investment, as is usually the case, it is time to prepare the formal business plan.

Getty Images/FPG International

CAUSES OF SMALL-BUSINESS FAILURE

Statistics show that most new businesses will fail within five years. There are many reasons for this. Most are avoidable weaknesses, what you might call personal or internal mistakes. They are usually lumped together as signs of *poor management*. (Part 3 of this book contains a thorough discussion of management.)

Buying a business requires careful research to determine the owner's reasons for selling and the overall financial stability of the company.

1. *Lack of finances*, due to any one or a combination of the following:

   Insufficient capital at start.

   Extending too much credit.

   Allowing customers to continually pay late.

   Carrying too much inventory.

   Not making sufficient allowance for a slow beginning.

   Inadequate reserve for the unexpected.

   Initial overhead too high.

2. *Lack of experience.*

   Inadequate experience in that line of business.

   No previous work experience at all.

   Poor marketing: pricing, products, or promotion.

3. *Poor allocation of time.*

   Allotting time according to pressure of events.

   Not prioritizing according to importance of activity, such as selling, customer service, and collections.

4. *Weak or no professional guidance.*

   Poor planning.

   Inadequate accounting system and misleading or outdated information.

   Lack of outside objective assessment.

5. *Lack of necessary personal qualities.*

    Strong determination and drive needed to overcome setbacks.

    Ability to live with uncertainty and risk.

    Ability to put in long hours over a long period.

    Completely focused on the immediate tasks.

Often external or objective causes that are not subject to the individual's control play an important role in the collapse of a business. For example, if one or two of your major customers go bankrupt while they owe you substantial sums, as often happens in a recession, you may be dragged down with them. If Chrysler had not been saved by U.S. and Canadian government backing, it would have gone bankrupt in 1980 and would have dragged down many small businesses.

Similarly, changes in government policy sometimes have a major impact on business. The Free Trade Agreement with the U.S. has hit many sectors of business in Canada since 1988—wine producers, fruit growers, furniture manufacturers, and more. Some other external factors are the rate of inflation, recession or boom, high or low interest rates, fluctuation in value of the Canadian dollar, and technological advances. The entrepreneur has no control over any of these. The collapse of the high-tech sector and many dot-com businesses in late 2000 are other examples of external factors that can have a major impact on a fledgling business.

PROGRESS CHECK

-   We gave you seven reasons why small businesses fail financially. Can you name three?
-   Why do so many people continue to start new businesses when the majority of them will be out of business in five years?
-   What are three common causes of business failure?

OPERATING A SMALL BUSINESS

In spite of overwhelming odds against them, entrepreneurs set out to conquer the business world confidently and enthusiastically. How hard do they work? Almost half of the owners work 56 hours a week. Nearly 20 percent of new owners keep up full-time or part-time jobs in addition to the long hours working the new business. Clearly, the job as owner of a new small business calls for considerable stamina. Only 11 percent work fewer than 40 hours; 86 percent put in extra hours on weekends.[9]

Thousands of would-be entrepreneurs of all ages have asked the same question: How do I get started? How can I learn to run my own business? Many of these people had no idea what kind of business they wanted to start; they simply wanted to be in business for themselves. That seems to be a major trend among students today. As you will see shortly, you have to understand business practices or you'll go broke in your own business. Here are some hints for learning about how to run a small business.

Learn from Others

There are courses available that teach small-business management. You might learn by investigating your local schools and colleges for such classes. A great advantage of these courses is that they bring together entrepreneurs, allowing them to exchange experiences and pass on useful information to new small-business owners. The starting place for budding entrepreneurs is talking with small-business owners and managers. Learn from their experience, especially their mistakes.

They will tell you that location is critical for a retail business. They will caution you not to be undercapitalized. They will warn you about the problems of finding and retaining good workers. And, most of all, they will tell you to keep good records and hire a good accountant and lawyer before you start. Small-business owners can give you hundreds of good ideas, ranging from how to get bank loans to how to design creative advertising. This free advice is invaluable.

Figure 7.2 shows where entrepreneurs seek advice and how they rank the importance of those sources. As mentioned previously, accountants are the prime, but not the only, source of useful guidance for small-business owners.

Get Some Experience

There is no better way to learn small-business management than by becoming an apprentice or working for a successful entrepreneur. A high percentage of small-business owners got the idea for their businesses from their prior jobs. The prior jobs of almost half of new business owners were in small businesses. The general rule is this: get three years' experience in a comparable business.

The Key to Successful Operations

By following the procedures discussed above, a new entrepreneur should be able to avoid most of the principal causes of failure indicated previously in this chapter: lack of finances and experience; lack of adequate professional guidance; and poor allocation of time. As for having the necessary personal qualities, these were discussed previously. In addition, the entrepreneurial readiness questionnaire that follows this chapter (Appendix B) will help you make a self-assessment.

PhotoDisc

HOME-BASED BUSINESS

The boom in home-based business operations is one of the major trends in small business. There are estimates that 40 percent of North Americans were working out of their homes in the year 2000. In the U.S. alone this translates into 55 million people working at home, of which some 17.5 million are estimated to be home-based businesses. The U.S. Commerce Department estimates that in 1998 more than half of all small businesses were home-based.[10] Don Dutton, president of the Canadian Home-Based Business Association, noted that the hottest trend is in consulting, with computer management and telecommunications leading the field.[11] It would be a good idea to have another look at Chapter 1, where this important aspect of small business was discussed in detail.

INTERNATIONAL ASPECTS OF ENTREPRENEURSHIP

Our planet has become a small place. We can no longer do business without considering the international market as both an opportunity and a challenge. Foreign companies come to Canada to compete with domestic companies. We, too, have broadened our horizon to think globally.

If you start your own business, be alert to international investment and export possibilities. As shown in Chapter 4, the Canadian and provincial governments offer extensive financial aid, information, and other support for exports. As you grow, you may consider opening branches, sales offices, or even plants in other countries. You might license a patent to, or enter into a joint venture ▸**P. 10**◂ with, a foreign company. See Chapter 3 for more about doing business internationally. The Reaching Beyond Our Borders box "Toys Are Theirs" profiles one Canadian company that has had international success.

Advances in technology are allowing more companies, employees, and entrepreneurs to reconsider the traditional workplace environment. Home-based businesses are growing at record levels.

www.bellzinc.ca

BellZinc.ca is designed to provide information and contacts for owners of small and medium businesses. Can sites like this successfully meet the needs of business people who are cut off from the normal means of interaction with other businesses because they operate out of their homes?

REACHING BEYOND OUR BORDERS
Toys Are Theirs
www.thinkwaytoys.com

In 1995 one of the biggest hit movies was Disney's *Toy Story*. What is perhaps not so well known is that a Canadian company, Thinkway Toys, was the North American licensee for characters based on *Toy Story*. This led to some interesting developments after the movie became a big hit.

Thinkway president Larry Chan got a desperate request from U.S. President Bill Clinton for Buzz Lightyear and Woody. After a frantic effort, the staff came up with 30 playmates ranging from electric toothbrushes to talking money banks, and thus saved the day at the White House Christmas party.

This was just one example of the flood of orders that Larry Chan has had to cope with since October 1995. Eventually he shipped more than $21 million worth of toys around the world. The demand was so heavy that the company could have shipped double that amount, had they been able to produce enough toys.

Larry Chan and his two younger brothers, Michael and Albert, moved to Toronto from Hong Kong in the early 1970s, and they all graduated from the University of Toronto's computer science program. Working with his father-in-law, Chan was importing toys, and eventually Thinkway got its first big break designing and manufacturing the Ninja Turtle Talking Bank.

This success opened the door to a licence from Disney to sell the Little Mermaid Talking Bank in Canada. Chan's proven track record with these products led him to conclude other deals with Disney for characters from the *Lion King* and other Disney features. Subsequently, Chan was able to get other good deals from Lucasfilm and Paramount Pictures.

In 1994 Thinkway was included in *Profit* magazine's annual list of the 100 fastest-growing companies. In every year since then it has won at least one design or retail award because of its imaginative toys or for successful marketing. These toys designed under licence from film studios include characters from *Toy Story 2* and *Star Wars I* and *II*. They have produced award-winning interactive talking banks and figures that speak in eight different languages.

Thinkway Toys has American offices in New York and Dallas, and international offices in Taiwan and Hong Kong and other Chinese cities, but its head office is still in Toronto. It is a good example of a small Canadian company that is making it big on the international scene.

Based on: <www.thinkwaytoys.com>, November 2001. Gayle MacDonald, "Toy Story's Toy Maker Rides a Hit," *Globe and Mail, Report on Business*, December 21, 1995, p. B11. Reprinted with permission from the *Globe and Mail*.

www.edc.ca

Visit the Export Development Canada Web site. What is its function? What dollar volume of business does it support?

Small business plays an important role in Canada's export trade. The Canadian government has long recognized this. Export Development Canada (EDC) helps small and medium-sized businesses in the complex task of exporting to foreign countries. This Crown corporation provides a wide variety of excellent services to such companies. It has offices in major cities and puts out many useful brochures and other material. In 2000 EDC reported that 89 percent of the companies they served, some 5,081 firms, were small and medium-sized (see Figure 7.5). It provided $45.4 billion of financing and insurance in more than 169 markets. EDC has a special business team that helps very small companies, with export sales under $1 million, go international.[12]

Internet computer networks proved to be a mushrooming international phenomenon in early 2001. For small business, they offer an unparalleled opportunity for low-cost, fast, international exposure. An increasing number of small companies are taking advantage of this channel to get free information, to advertise their products and services, and to get expert help and advice. There are many reports in various media about the continuing exploding growth of the Internet.

FIGURE **7.5**

EXPORT DEVELOPMENT CANADA SUPPORT FOR EXPORTERS

You can see how EDC's support for Canadian companies, especially small and medium-sized companies that export, has grown over the period 1996 to 2000.

CUSTOMERS SERVED
(*Number of companies*)

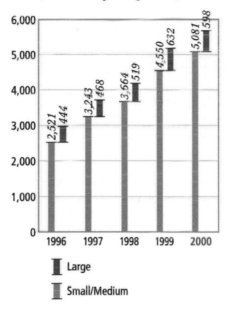

Legend:
- ▮ Large
- ▮ Small/Medium

Source: Export Development Canada, 2000. Reprinted with permission.

ETHICAL DILEMMA

Review

Remember the dilemma posed at the beginning of this chapter? Here's what our executives think. Bédard states that "laws and jurisprudence on the ability of people to use formerly gained information or to contact former customers is fairly well established. Regardless of employee contracts that have been signed, if a person does use information previously gained, it is acceptable as long as it has little or no impact on the former employer. If the impact is important, the former employer is in his rights to have the contract enforced. Unfortunately, such things occur and many of these situations will end up in court."

According to Reilley, "proprietary technology and patents are reasonably easy to protect from theft. However, two issues apply here, assuming that theft is not involved. First, the switcher's new company creates competition, which, in turn, applies pressure on the old firm to sharpen its pencil. (This is good.) Second, often the old larger firm is only too happy, in the fullness of time, to seek more efficient suppliers for niche technologies. The switcher's new firm often fills this need and everyone wins."

Years ago, when one of the Canadian authors of this book decided to leave his last employer to form his own firm of chartered accountants, he was faced with this dilemma. An important client of his employer made him an attractive offer: set up offices on the client's premises with no charge for rent or secretarial services, and take over the auditing and consulting work of the client's group of companies at a reasonable fee. It was a very tempting offer for a fledgling CA with a young family who was seeking clients. What would you have done? It was difficult to refuse, but after careful consideration, the author felt it would be unethical to do this, especially since he had had a very good relationship with his employer. He told this client that, after six months, if they still wanted to make the change it could be done at that time. But the psychological moment had passed and the opportunity was lost.

SUMMARY

1. Define small business and discuss its importance to the Canadian economy.

1. Of all the non-farm businesses in Canada, more than 95 percent are considered small.
   • *Why are small businesses important to the Canadian economy?*
   Small businesses account for a significant portion of the national economy. Perhaps more important to tomorrow's graduates, 90 percent of the nation's new jobs in the private sector are in small business.
   • *What does the "small" in small business mean?*
   A small business is independently owned and operated, is not dominant in its field of operation, and meets certain standards of size in terms of employees (fewer than 100) or sales. (That depends on the size of others in the industry. For example, American Motors was considered small in the auto industry before it merged with Chrysler.)

2. Explain why people are willing to take the risks of entrepreneurship.

2. There are many reasons people are willing to take the risks of entrepreneurship despite the high risks of failure.
   • *What are a few of the reasons why people start their own businesses?*
   Reasons include profit, independence, opportunity, and challenge.

3. Describe the attributes needed to be a successful entrepreneur, and explain why women have a higher success rate than men.

3. Successful entrepreneurship takes a special kind of person.
   • *What does it take to be an entrepreneur?*
   A person must be self-directed, self-nurtured, action-oriented, tolerant of uncertainty, and energetic.
   • *Why are women more successful than men?*
   Generally, women are less pressured to achieve quick success, they are more cautious, and they accept advice more readily.

4. Summarize the major causes of small business failures.

4. More than two-thirds of the small businesses started this year will not survive to celebrate their fifth anniversary.
   • *Why do so many small businesses fail?*
   Many small businesses fail because of managerial incompetence and inadequate financial planning.

5. Identify ways you can learn about small businesses.

5. Most people have no idea how to go about starting a small business. They have some ideas and the motivation; they simply don't have the know-how.
   • *What should you do before starting a small business?*
   First, learn from others. Take courses and talk with some small-business owners. Second, get some experience working for others. Finally, consult with an accountant experienced in small business.

6. Explain what a business plan is, and outline the general areas of information it should include.

6. Begin with a plan. The more effort you put into a business plan, the less grief you'll have later.
   • *What goes into a business plan?*
   See Figure 7.3.
   • *Should you do it all yourself?*
   Most small business owners advise new entrepreneurs to get outside assistance in at least two areas: you need a good lawyer and a good accountant. Also, seek help from government publications and any other sources you can find. The more knowledge you can gain early, the better.

7. List the requirements to operate a small business successfully.

7. The failure rate of new businesses is very high.
   • *What must be done to increase the likelihood of success?*
   You must learn from others, get a few years' experience in the field you are interested in, and get good professional guidance. Make sure you have the necessary personal qualities and conditions for the long haul.

business plan 201   **intrapreneur** 196   **venture capitalists** 205
entrepreneur 191   **skunkworks** 196
entrepreneurship 191   **small business** 197

DEVELOPING WORKPLACE SKILLS

1. Select a type of small business that looks attractive as a career possibility for you. Talk to at least three people who manage and own such businesses. Ask them how they started their businesses. Ask about financing, personnel problems (hiring, firing, training, scheduling), accounting problems, and other managerial matters. Pick their brains. Let them be your instructors. Put together a rough business plan of how you would start such a business. Discuss it in class.

2. Go to the library and review some business magazines for the last couple of years. Look for articles about successful entrepreneurs. Write brief profiles of two of them, focusing on similarities and differences. Make copies for your career file. Share what you found with the class.

3. Put together a list of factors that might mean the difference between success and failure for a new company in the software industry. Can small start-ups realistically hope to compete with biggies such as Lotus or Microsoft? Discuss the list and your conclusions in class.

4. Visit a franchise other than a fast-food restaurant and see what the owners have to say about the benefits and drawbacks of franchising. Would they buy the franchise again if they could start all over? What mistakes did they make, if any? What advice would they give a student interested in franchising? Share your research with your class.

TAKING IT TO THE NET

Purpose:

To assess your potential to succeed as an entrepeneur and practice your search skills in the area of small business research.

Exercises:

1. Using any search engine, such as Yahoo, AltaVista, Google, or Canada.com, see what you can find for *small business*. How many matches did you find on Canada.com? Follow some of the links that interest you. See if you can find anything on home-based businesses. Bring any information to class that you found surprising or that might be useful for students.

2. Check out the Canadian Youth Business Foundation Web site at <www.cybf.ca/> to see what you can find. Is there any help for young persons wanting to start their own business? Is there anything there that stimulates your interest in running your own business?

PRACTISING MANAGEMENT DECISIONS

CASE 1

FIVE ENTREPRENEURS TRY VIDEO GAMES AS A BUSINESS

It's time to herald a new era of airplane travel. Gone are the days of playing solitaire on food-encrusted tray tops. Airlines are introducing seat backs outfitted with digital screens. Soon you'll be able to order video-on-demand, browse the duty-free catalogue, and—thanks to a team of Toronto-based programmers who share a vision for electronic blackjack—zone out playing video games.

The programmers are partners in upstart ISES Corp. The company has finalized a deal with Airtours plc of Manchester, England, and is currently in talks with other major airlines. ISES software will also be used on Air France, which introduced the new seat backs in summer 1999. Steven Johnson, ISES vice-president of marketing, says the company hopes to double its revenue in 1999. But the long-term prospects are the real appeal: as deregulation heightens airline competition, in-flight entertainment (IFE) is expected to explode. ISES hopes to get in on all the action once it has conquered the video-game realm.

ISES was founded when five employees of Toronto-based Gametronics Gaming Equipment Ltd. grasped the potential of the nascent IFE industry and left to form their own company. "OK, we thought," says Dean Davis, one of the founders, "we're going to do this ourselves. We're going to be a games supplier." They set up shop in the solarium of fellow founder Igor Muskatblit's apartment, where they crammed in two picnic tables to serve as computer desks. That was in 1998. Fuelled by the growth of IFE (ISES also works with Motorola on its version of Web TV), it now has moved into a real office. Most impressively, ISES is beating out major game-makers, largely because its 18-strong roster of games is simple, consisting mainly of mind teasers and familiar board games such as hangman and Chinese checkers. "For a short flight, you're not really going to want to learn a new game," says Davis.

Decision Questions

1. The case illustrates a number of themes from this chapter as well as from previous chapters. What issues from previous chapters can you find exemplified in this case?

2. What about trends reviewed in the first chapter? Can you see how this case illustrates one or more of the trends? Which ones?

3. Do you think ISES is likely to succeed? What are the factors that might indicate the likelihood of success? Do you see any obstacles?

4. Can you see a future career for yourself starting a software-related business, alone or with some friends? Do you have anything specific in mind? Would you first get a job in that field to get some experience, as the entrepreneurs in this case did, or would you try to launch your business without doing that?

Source: Cynthia Reynolds, "Daddy, Where's the Flight Simulator?" *Canadian Business,* May 28, 1999, p. 74.

CASE 2

OPPORTUNITIES IN HOME-BASED FRANCHISING

You are toying with the idea of starting your own business but are a little nervous about going it on your own. You like the help you would get with a franchise and that you could still run your own show—almost. The problem is that well-known names demand an investment of $150,000 to $1 million, which is much too rich for your blood.

You have heard recently about home-based franchises that require anywhere from $10,000 to $50,000 to start up. Sheldon Adler, who heads a franchising consulting company, says they are pretty easy to get into. He points out that they have been growing steadily in the United States for the last 15 years and are making headway in Canada. He provides you with a sample listing.

- *Heels on Wheels*, a mobile shoe-repair business operating out of a van. Staff members go directly into offices to fix and polish the shoes of business people. Clients often bring three or four pairs to work for repair.

- *Location Lube*, which provides a similar service for automobile lube jobs. Technicians service the cars in office parking lots, saving car owners the trip to a service station.

- *Colour Your Carpet*, a rug-dyeing business that restores your carpet at a fraction of the price of buying a new one.

As Anne Field discusses in her article, "Franchising," one of the problems with working at home is that there are too many distractions. To avoid this problem, set up a separate work space. Use a spare room or the basement—whatever suits you—and stay there. Make it off-limits to the kids and Fido, too. "When you enter that room, you enter into the realm of work," says Ariel Shlien, president and CEO of Mad Science, a Montreal-based franchise that stages science events for children. (It's also simpler to calculate income tax deductions for use of part of the home for business purposes.)

By running your business from a formally designated space, you may find that you help others take your efforts more seriously as well. That's especially important if you have to hold work-related meetings at home. At Mad Science, for example, franchisees meet weekly with instructors who conduct science workshops in the field; they discuss the week's lineup and exchange equipment. "If you're working at the kitchen table, it's difficult to convey that this isn't a game but your livelihood," says Eric Kimmel, a former franchisee who is now director of franchise support.

It's those midnight faxes that really drive Ian Foster batty. Foster runs his one-year-old Bevinco Bar Systems franchise from his home in San Diego. And often, "in the middle of the night, when the rates are lower, companies fax me all sorts of things," he says. "I'll go running into my office expecting something important, and it's basically just junk mail."

Despite such annoyances, Foster's work-from-home setup is paying off handsomely. He's already so busy that he's had to hire a full-time employee to help conduct his main business—auditing how much of the alcohol sold in bars and restaurants has been paid for by customers. And his operation, which grossed $1,000 a week after functioning for six months, is his second franchise unit (he started the first five years ago in Vancouver). Says Foster, formerly a national sales manager for a major food company, "Running a business from home has its challenges. But it's been great for me."

That could be the sentiment of many a home-based franchisee. Foster is one of a growing brigade of small-business people who run a franchise from their home, car, van—anywhere but an office or storefront. These account for about 15 percent of all franchises, according to Michael Seid of Michael H. Seid & Associates in West Hartford, Conn., up from an estimated 7 percent 10 years ago. They're lured by a host of attractions,

from the flexibility and low start-up (only $26,000 for fees and equipment to get Foster's San Diego unit off the ground) to a commute-free life and the opportunity to hang up the jacket and tie.

Still, there's no free lunch in home-based franchising. As Foster can tell you, running a franchise chez vous presents its own, idiosyncratic array of obstacles. But by learning from the experience of others, you can tackle those problems before they get out of hand. Thus it is possible to have it all: independence, expert guidance, a great income—and a life.

Decision Questions

1. What do you think of the home-based franchise operations discussed above? What questions should you be asking before buying a franchise?

2. Can you find out which franchises seem to be doing well in your area? (Expand your search beyond retail franchises.) Where would you look for such information?

3. Would you be prepared to consider any of the franchises in the case or in the previous question as a possible entry into a small business? What do you find attractive? What is not so attractive?

4. Franchising is increasingly popular, but are the lower risks of franchise organizations worth giving up the freedom of ownership and control? What information do you need to answer this question, and how can you get it?

Source: *Globe and Mail*, Report on Business, September 30, 1991, p. B6. "Franchising," Anne Field, *Success*, Oct. 1998; International Franchise Association, <www.franchise.org>.

CBC   VIDEO CASE   www.cbc.ca

YOUR PAPER DOLL

The chapter makes abundantly clear that it takes a combination of many factors to give your business start-up a fair chance of succeeding. In addition to important personal qualities and conditions, there are financing and marketing needs, and management skills requirements. Some experience in the field of business you are entering is also definitely helpful, if not essential. On top of these, there is the consideration of the actual situation in the market where you are planning to offer your product or services, and the manner in which you propose to reach your market. Finally, there is the state of the economy when you are about to commence business. It takes a combination of all of these factors to give you the best chance of getting off to a good start.

What happens when important aspects of these factors are negative or missing can be seen in this video about the business student who leaves her studies to pursue her dream of an e-commerce business in women's clothing. Nikisha knows from personal experience that proper fit is a key element for women shopping for clothing. She also knows that e-business is hot and believes that it is a great venue for women to ensure proper fit before buying clothes. Unfortunately, things do not work out as she planned or hoped.

Discussion Questions

1. Which of the necessary personal qualities to start and run a business do you think Nikisha demonstrates? Which important personal factors are not mentioned and may be lacking? Do we get to know anything of her background and potential support from family, a partner, or friends? Back up your answers by reference to the text and the video.

2. Nikisha runs into some good luck and some bad luck. List the individual elements of both as demonstrated in the video. Could she have done anything to ensure that these happenings were not a matter of good luck? Could she have done anything to avoid the bad luck? Explain.

3. What about her prior work experience? Could that have made a difference in this case? Explain.

4. Can you point to two weak factors that you think doomed her to failure from the start? Think of one factor that she should have considered and known about, and one factor that was beyond her control.

Source: *Venture*, show number 779, "Your Paper Doll," March 20, 2001, running time 8:41.

APPENDIX B

Entrepreneurial Readiness Questionnaire

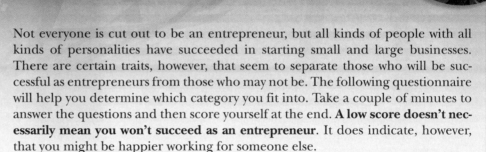

Not everyone is cut out to be an entrepreneur, but all kinds of people with all kinds of personalities have succeeded in starting small and large businesses. There are certain traits, however, that seem to separate those who will be successful as entrepreneurs from those who may not be. The following questionnaire will help you determine which category you fit into. Take a couple of minutes to answer the questions and then score yourself at the end. **A low score doesn't necessarily mean you won't succeed as an entrepreneur**. It does indicate, however, that you might be happier working for someone else.

Each of the following items describes something you may or may not feel represents your personality or other characteristics. Read each item and then put an X in the column that most nearly reflects the extent to which you agree or disagree that the item seems to fit you best.

Scoring: Give yourself one point for each Column 1 or Column 2 response to these questions: 2, 3, 6, 8, 9, 10, 11, 12, 14, 15, 17, 18, 20, 22, 23, 24. Give yourself one point for each Column 4 or Column 5 response to these questions: 1, 4, 5, 7, 13, 16, 19, 21, 25.

Add your points and see how you rate in the categories below:

21–25   Your entrepreneurial potential looks great if you have a suitable opportunity to use it. What are you waiting for?

16–20   This is close to the high entrepreneurial range. You could be quite successful if your other talents and resources are right.

11–15   Your score is in the transitional range. With some serious work, you can probably develop the outlook you need for running your own business.

6–10   Things look pretty doubtful for you as an entrepreneur. It would take considerable rearranging of your life philosophy and behaviour to make it.

0–5   Let's face it. Entrepreneurship is not really for you. Still, learning what it's all about won't hurt anything.

	AGREE			DISAGREE		
	Completely Column 1	Mostly Column 2	Partially Column 3	Completely Column 4	Mostly Column 5	Partially Column 6
1. I am not generally optimistic.	___	___	___	___	___	___
2. I relish competing intensely regardless of the rewards.	___	___	___	___	___	___
3. I do not hesitate to take a calculated risk.	___	___	___	___	___	___
4. When betting I prefer a high-payoff long shot.	___	___	___	___	___	___
5. I like to follow traditional or conventional thinking.	___	___	___	___	___	___
6. I enjoy games like tennis or hardball with someone who is a little better than I am.	___	___	___	___	___	___
7. Making lots of money is largely a matter of getting the right breaks.	___	___	___	___	___	___
8. I am inclined to forge ahead and discuss later.	___	___	___	___	___	___
9. Reward or praise means less to me than satisfaction of a job well done.	___	___	___	___	___	___
10. I usually go my own way regardless of others' opinions.	___	___	___	___	___	___
11. I am not easily discouraged.	___	___	___	___	___	___
12. I am a self-starter needing little urging from others.	___	___	___	___	___	___
13. I do not take criticism easily.	___	___	___	___	___	___
14. I can criticize others without hurting their feelings.	___	___	___	___	___	___
15. I hate being told what to do.	___	___	___	___	___	___
16. I would rather plan than actually carry out plans.	___	___	___	___	___	___
17. I do not acknowledge errors readily.	___	___	___	___	___	___
18. I communicate well with others.	___	___	___	___	___	___
19. I work best with some guidance.	___	___	___	___	___	___
20. I like to know what's going on and take steps to find out.	___	___	___	___	___	___
21. I am generally casual and easy-going.	___	___	___	___	___	___
22. I like solving my problems myself.	___	___	___	___	___	___
23. I do not give up easily.	___	___	___	___	___	___
24. I enjoy impressing others.	___	___	___	___	___	___
25. I do not accept advice easily.	___	___	___	___	___	___

PART 3

CHAPTER 8

Leadership and Management

LEARNING GOALS

AFTER YOU HAVE READ AND STUDIED THIS CHAPTER, YOU SHOULD BE ABLE TO

1. Enumerate the four functions of management and reasons why the role of managers is changing.

2. Relate the planning process to the accomplishment of company goals.

3. Describe the organizing function of management, including staffing and diversity management.

4. Explain the differences between leaders and managers, and describe the various leadership styles.

5. Summarize the five steps of the control function of management.

6. Illustrate the skills needed at each level of management.

Mary Parker Follett: Mother of Modern Management

Joan C. Tonn/Unwich Management Centre

Mary Parker Follett graduated from Thayer College and Radcliffe. While she was in college, Follett taught political science at a nearby secondary school. She was a part of Boston high society and participated on committees that set minimum wages for women and children. The prominent management theorist of that time (the early 1900s) was Frederick Taylor, the "father of scientific management." His writings favoured command-style, hierarchical organizations. Employees were treated much like robots or computers, things to be manipulated and directed. Taylor did not believe in participative management. Managers acted more like dictators.

Mary Parker Follett, in comparison, believed very strongly that the person doing the job was the person most likely to know how to do the job better. She felt that it was human nature to want to be self-managed. Furthermore, Follett believed in the concept of cross-functional rather than vertical authority. Her idea was for people in various departments to share information with one another to the benefit of all.

Follett believed that managers should be leaders rather than dictators. They were to provide a vision and help focus all the resources of the firm on meeting that vision. Follett also felt that knowledge and experience, not titles and seniority, should decide who should lead.

Follett's concepts, written in the 1920s and 1930s, were far ahead of her time. She was relatively ignored while Frederick Taylor grew in importance. But times change and innovative ideas from the past suddenly take on new meaning. That is exactly what has happened to Follett's writings.

A book titled *Mary Parker Follett—Prophet of Management: A Celebration of Writings from the 1920s* was released by the Harvard Business School Press in 1995. In the introduction to the book, guru Peter Drucker stated that it is too bad her works were lost for several decades because she is as pertinent today as she was when she first developed her ideas. In his contribution to this collection of Mary Parker Follett's writings, *Some Fresh Air for Management?* management authority Henry Mintzberg of McGill University wondered what would have happened if "we had spent most of this century heeding Follett instead of Fayol" (see Chapter 9 for a review of Fayol's theories).

London School of Economics chair Sir Peter Parker says that he is not sure who the father of management is, but he is sure who the mother is: Mary Parker Follett. Her ideas about empowerment, self-management, cross-functional co-operation, and conflict resolution are now being implemented in leading firms throughout the world. In this chapter, we shall explore both traditional and new management concepts. Many are based on the fundamentals that Mary Parker Follett established 75 years ago.

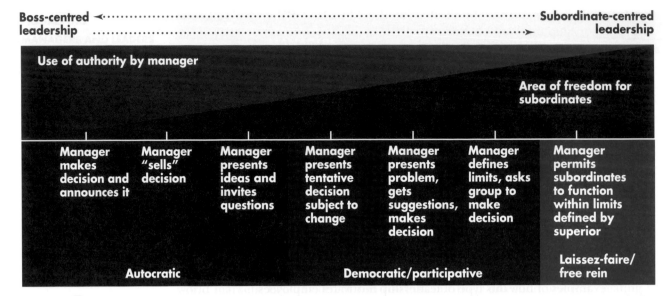

Boss-centred ◄┈┈┈┈┈┈┈┈┈┈┈┈┈┈┈┈┈┈┈┈┈┈┈┈┈┈┈┈┈┈┈┈┈┈┈┈┈┈ Subordinate-centred
leadership   ┈┈┈┈┈┈┈┈┈┈┈┈┈┈┈┈┈┈┈┈┈┈┈┈┈┈┈┈┈┈┈┈┈┈┈┈┈┈┈► leadership

Use of authority by manager

Area of freedom for subordinates

Manager makes decision and announces it	Manager "sells" decision	Manager presents ideas and invites questions	Manager presents tentative decision subject to change	Manager presents problem, gets suggestions, makes decision	Manager defines limits, asks group to make decision	Manager permits subordinates to function within limits defined by superior

Autocratic   Democratic/participative   Laissez-faire/free rein

FIGURE 8.6

VARIOUS LEADERSHIP STYLES

The trend today is toward subordinate-centred leadership.

Source: Reprinted by permission of the *Harvard Business Review*. An exhibit from "How to Choose a Leadership Pattern" by Robert Tannenbaum and Warren Schmidt (May/June 1973). Copyright © 1973 by the President and Fellows of Harvard College, all rights reserved.

SPOTLIGHT ON BIG BUSINESS

www.nspower.ca

New-Style Management at Nova Scotia Power

Corporate Canada, struggling with low morale created by the recession, is facing increasing competition, breakneck change, and overwhelming complexity. The result: increased pressure for results and decreased patience when they are not achieved.

It's not enough anymore to make the strategic decisions from Olympian heights and then point the way ahead. Executives today must understand and respect their employees, create shared values and goals, and march forward right alongside them, creating better customer value in the process. Nova Scotia Power is a good example of a company moving with the times.

L. R. Comeau, president and CEO of Nova Scotia Power Inc., in his 1995 report, his last as head of the company, commented on the many changes during his 13-year stint. Nova Scotia Power made a successful transition from a Crown corporation to a public company. It also transferred much decision-making power down the line.

Our corporate restructuring is itself an exercise in building value into our product. We have successfully created a more effective organization—one that can do "more with less." Most responsibility for decisions and action now rests with people in the field, rather than in Head Office.

This change encourages closer contact between customers and service employees, resulting in "quicker and more personal response to their needs.... Referral to Head Office is the exception rather than the rule." This helps to increase customer value.

From 1995 to 1999 the company continued to develop these policies, and the current director of human resource management feels strongly that the program has achieved company goals. She believes that customers, employees, and managers are all benefitting.

Adapted from: 1995 *Annual Report*, Nova Scotia Power Inc.; documents provided by, and interview with, Elizabeth MacDonald, Nova Scotia Power director, HRM, July 6, 1999.

THE 12 GOLDEN RULES OF LEADERSHIP

1. *Set a good example.* Your subordinates will take their cue from you. If your work habits are good, theirs are likely to be too.

2. *Give your people a set of objectives and a sense of direction.* Good people seldom like to work aimlessly from day to day. They want to know not only what they're doing but why.

3. *Keep your people informed of new developments at the company and how they'll be affected.* Let people know where they stand with you. Let your close assistants in on your plans at an early stage. Let people know as early as possible of any changes that will affect them. Let them know of changes that won't affect them but about which they may be worrying.

4. *Ask your people for advice.* Let them know that they have a say in your decisions whenever possible. Make them feel a problem is their problem too. Encourage individual thinking.

5. *Let your people know that you support them.* There's no greater morale killer than a boss who resents a subordinate's ambition.

6. *Don't give orders.* Suggest, direct, and request.

7. *Emphasize skills, not rules.* Judge results, not methods. Give a person a job to do and let him or her do it. Let an employee improve his or her own job methods.

8. *Give credit where credit is due.* Appreciation for a job well done is the most appreciated of "fringe benefits."

9. *Praise in public.* This is where it will do the most good.

10. *Criticize in private.*

11. *Criticize constructively.* Concentrate on correction, not blame. Allow a person to retain his or her dignity. Suggest specific steps to prevent recurrence of the mistake. Forgive and encourage desired results.

12. *Make it known that you welcome new ideas.* No idea is too small for a hearing or too wild for consideration. Make it easy for them to communicate their ideas to you. Follow through on their ideas.

THE SEVEN SINS OF LEADERSHIP

On the other hand, these items can cancel any constructive image you might try to establish.

1. *Trying to be liked rather than respected.* Don't accept favors from your subordinates. Don't do special favors in trying to be liked. Don't try for popular decisions. Don't be soft about discipline. Have a sense of humor. Don't give up.

2. *Failing to ask subordinates for their advice and help.*

3. *Failing to develop a sense of responsibility in subordinates.* Allow freedom of expression. Give each person a chance to learn his or her superior's job. When you give responsibility, give authority too. Hold subordinates accountable for results.

4. *Emphasizing rules rather than skill.*

5. *Failing to keep criticism constructive.* When something goes wrong, do you tend to assume who's at fault? Do you do your best to get all the facts first? Do you control your temper? Do you praise before you criticize? Do you listen to the other side of the story?

6. *Not paying attention to employee gripes and complaints.* Make it easy for them to come to you. Get rid of red tape. Explain the grievance machinery. Help a person voice his or her complaint. Always grant a hearing. Practice patience. Ask a complainant what he or she wants to do . Don't render a hasty or biased judgment. Get all the facts. Let the complainant know what your decision is. Double-check your results. Be concerned.

7. *Failing to keep people informed.*

Source: "To Become an 'Effective Executive': Develop Leadership and Other Skills," *Marketing News*, April 1984, p. 1; and Brian Biro, Beyond Success, (New York: Berkley, 2001).

FIGURE 8.7

RULES AND SINS OF LEADERSHIP

Empowering Workers

Traditional leaders give explicit instructions to workers, telling them what to do to meet the goals and objectives of the organization. The term for such a process is *directing.* In traditional organizations, directing involves giving assignments, explaining routines, clarifying policies, and providing feedback on performance.

Progressive leaders, such as those in many high-tech firms and Internet companies, are less likely than traditional leaders to give specific instructions to employees. Rather, they're more likely to empower employees to make decisions on their

empowerment
Giving employees the authority
and responsibility to respond
quickly to customer requests.

enabling
Giving workers the education
and tools they need to assume
their new decision-making
powers.

**knowledge
management**
Finding the right information,
keeping the information in a
readily accessible place, and
making the information known
to everyone in the firm.

own. **Empowerment** means giving employees the authority (the right to make a decision without consulting the manager) and responsibility (the requirement to accept the consequences of one's actions) to respond quickly to customer requests. In co-operation with employees, managers will set up teams that will work together to accomplish objectives and goals.[15] The manager's role is becoming less that of a boss and director and more that of a coach, assistant, counsellor, or team member.

The success of empowered workers is based on several factors. The organization must *enable* its employees. **Enabling** is the term used to describe giving workers the education, skills, and tools necessary to make their decisions. Very simply, empowered workers should be able to handle the required *tasks*. As well, the *environment* must be one where workers can react quickly and implement changes. Quick customer response and satisfaction is the goal of a stakeholder-oriented organization.

Managing Knowledge

There's an old saying that still holds true today: "Knowledge is power." Empowering employees means giving them knowledge; that is, getting them the information they need to do the best job they can. Finding the right information, keeping the information in a readily accessible place, and making the information known to everyone in the firm is known as **knowledge management**.[16] The first step to developing a knowledge management system is determining what knowledge is most important. Do you want to know more about your customers? Do you want to know more about your competitors? What kind of information would make the company more effective or more efficient or more responsive to the marketplace? Once you have decided what you need to know, you set out to find answers to those questions.

Knowledge management tries to keep people from "reinventing the wheel"—that is, duplicating the work of gathering information—every time a decision needs to be made. A company really progresses when each person in the firm asks continually, "What do I still not know?" and "Whom should I be asking?" It's as important to know what's not working as what is working. Employees and managers now have e-mail, fax machines, intranets, and other means of keeping in touch with each other, with customers, and with other stakeholders. The key to success is learning how to process that information effectively and turn it into knowledge that everyone can use to improve processes and procedures. That is one way to enable workers to be more effective. We'll discuss information technology and knowledge management in much more detail later in this text.

The Trend toward Self-Managed Teams

One trend today is toward self-managed teams and away from management's emphasis on planning, organizing, leading, and controlling. The trend is toward leadership, with the emphasis on vision and empowerment.

Firms are placing more workers on cross-functional teams composed of people from various departments of the firm, such as marketing, finance, and distribution. Many of these teams are self-managed. Self-managed teams function as independent elements of the firm with an inherent group intelligence of their own. These *smart teams* think and act on their own and seek out any information they need. Such teams need skilled workers who can clearly communicate inside and outside the team. They must co-operate and share ideas, resources, and talents with a focus on the organization's strategic goals.

One purpose of cross-functional teams is to respond quickly to customer needs and market changes. Another purpose is to empower those who know the most about products to do what needs to be done to make the products world-class. To ensure such responsiveness and responsibility, these teams are self-organizing as well as self-managing. This means that more planning, organizing (including hiring and firing members), and controlling functions are being delegated to lower-level managers.[17]

Courtesy of Boeing Company.

This self-managed team at Boeing is an example of employees who are empowered to make decisions. Management is available for backup, training, coaching, or other assistance.

In 1997, Falconbridge Ltd. was involved in a joint union/company initiative to introduce work restructuring using a participative design process. Consultant H. James Harrington responded to queries about the changing supervisory roles by naming the advantages of self-managed teams at Falconbridge. These teams:

- increase employee involvement
- allow employees to become more organization-oriented
- allow employees to gain new skills
- improve employee morale
- allow the elimination of one level of management.[18]

Given this information, you may wonder why it is that not all firms have moved to self-managed teams. A movement to self-managed teams would require an ongoing investment by the organization in terms of training, change management, planning, and coordination. According to Harrington, some additional disadvantages of self-managed teams may include:

- the high cost to train employees
- the fact that not all employees wish to do managerial-type work
- a reduced growth path for some employees
- the fact that present first-level managers are often assigned to lower-level jobs. [19]

What will this trend mean for managers and leaders in the twenty-first century? For one thing, there will be a movement away from autocratic leadership toward laissez-faire leadership. This is a real challenge for traditional managers because it means giving up their traditional command-and-control style of management.

It means developing and training employees to assume greater responsibility in planning, teamwork, and problem-solving. Managers will be empowering teams rather than individual employees. Teamwork usually aids communication, improves co-operation, reduces internal competition, and maximizes the talents of all employees on a project. This team empowerment is an entirely different role for managers and it will take some time to develop. In the end, however, the concept of self-managed teams will enable Canadian companies to compete with anyone in the world.

PROGRESS CHECK

- What are some characteristics of leadership today that make leaders different from traditional managers?
- Explain the differences between autocratic and democratic leadership styles.
- Describe empowerment and explain to which of the four management functions it is related.

CRITICAL THINKING

Do you see any problems with a democratic managerial style? Can you see a manager getting frustrated when he or she can't control others? Can someone who's trained to give orders (e.g., a military sergeant) be retrained to be a democratic manager? What problems may emerge? What kind of manager would you be? Do you have evidence to show that?

CONTROLLING

Often managers get so involved with the firm's planning process and day-to-day crisis management that they shortchange the control function. The control function involves measuring performance relative to objectives and standards and then taking corrective action when necessary. Thus, the control function (Figure 8.8) is the heart of the management system because it provides the feedback that enables managers and workers to adjust to any deviations from plans and to changes in the environment that have affected performance.

Controlling consists of five steps:

1. Establishing clear and specific performance standards.
2. Monitoring and recording actual performance (results).
3. Comparing results against plans and standards.
4. Communicating results and deviations to the employees involved.
5. Taking corrective action when needed.

FIGURE 8.8

THE CONTROL PROCESS

The whole control process is based on clear standards. Without such standards, the other steps are difficult, if not impossible. With clear standards, performance measurement is relatively easy and the proper action can be taken.

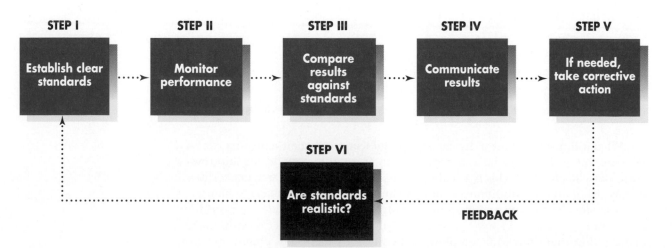

This control process is ongoing *throughout* the year. Continuous monitoring ensures that if corrective action is required, there is enough time to implement required changes. When corrective action is necessary, the decision-making process (discussed near the end of the chapter) is a useful tool to apply. Simply, managers are encouraged to review the situation and, based on collected information, develop alternatives with their staff and implement the best alternative. The focus is to meet the standards that were initially established during the planning stage or the standards that have since been modified. This process is also ongoing. It may take several attempts before standards are successfully met.

The control system's weakest link tends to be the setting of standards. To measure results against standards, the standards must be specific, attainable, and measurable.[20] Vague goals and standards such as "better quality," "more efficiency," and "improved performance" aren't sufficient because they don't describe what you're trying to achieve. For example, let's say you're a runner and you say you want to improve your distance. When you started your improvement plan last year, you ran two kilometres a day. Now you run 2.1 kilometres a day. Did you meet your goal? Well, you did increase your distance, but certainly not by very much. A more appropriate goal statement would be: To increase running distance from two kilometres a day to four kilometres a day by January 1. It's important to have a time period established for when specific goals are to be met. Here are examples of goals and standards that meet these criteria:

- Cut the number of finished-product rejects from 10 per 1,000 to 5 per 1,000 by March 31, 2003.

- Increase the number of times managers praise employees from 3 times per week to 12 times per week by November 1, 2003.

- Increase sales of product X from $10,000 per month to $17,000 per month by July 2001, 2003.

One key to making control systems work is the establishment of clear procedures for monitoring performance. Naturally, management shouldn't be burdened with such control procedures unless the goals are important enough to justify such reporting. Most managers have seen, for example, elaborate accident reports that took hours of management time and that reported, "All is well." To minimize paperwork, such reports could be limited to certain kinds of serious cases. For some suggestions on other ways to reduce the manager's workload, see the Spotlight on Small Business box "How Common Is the Practice of Participative Management?"

New Criteria for Measurement: Customer Satisfaction

The criteria for measuring success in a customer-oriented firm is customer satisfaction of both internal and external customers. **Internal customers** are units within the firm that receive services from other units. For example, the field salespeople are the internal customers of the marketing research people who prepare research reports for them. **External customers** include dealers who buy products to sell to others, and ultimate customers such as you and me who buy products for personal use. One goal today is to go beyond satisfying customers to delighting them with superior goods and services.

Other criteria of organizational effectiveness may include the firm's contribution to society or improvements in the quality of air and water surrounding the plant. The traditional measures of success are usually financial, defined in terms of profits or return on investment. Certainly these measures are still important, but they're not the whole purpose of the firm. The purpose of the firm today is to please employees, customers, and other stakeholders. Thus, measurements of success must take all these groups into account. Firms have to ask questions such as:

internal customers
Units within the firm that receive services from other units.

external customers
Dealers who buy products to sell to others, and ultimate customers who buy products for their own personal use.

SPOTLIGHT ON SMALL BUSINESS

How Common Is the Practice of Participative Management?

Participative management involves employees in setting objectives and making decisions; democratic and laissez-faire leadership are forms of participative management.

Some firms have had difficulty implementing participative management because some managers hesitate to give up what they feel are their rights. That includes, as they perceive it, the right to be bossy, to tell others what to do, and to punish them if they don't. It certainly does not mean working with people as partners. "Why call me a boss if I am just another worker?" is their attitude. Such people must change if the organization is to develop the teamwork necessary to compete in today's changing environment. Many managers in small firms have always practised participative management.

Stephen Levy, who heads up Richter Management Plus, an arm of chartered accounting firm Richter, Usher & Vineberg, is a consultant in the small-business field in the

Montreal area. The 57-year-old Levy has a master's degree in industrial management from prestigious Massachusetts Institute of Technology and 30 years of tough experience in business. This includes running companies and turning around companies in serious difficulties.

He finds that participative management is the norm rather than the exception in small firms. The atmosphere is generally more informal than at large companies, lending itself to greater employee involvement in decision making. Most small-business owners are overloaded with responsibility so they are happy to have their load lightened by employees assuming more responsibility. This tends to change as the company grows and activities become more formal and structured as more managers are added. That is when the battle to retain the open style that empowers employees usually takes place.

Adapted from: "How Common is the Practice of Participative Management?" interview with Stephen Levy, June 13, 1999.

- Do we have good relations with our employees, our suppliers, our dealers, our community leaders, the local media, our shareholders, and our bankers?
- What more could we do to please these groups?
- Are the corporate needs (such as making a profit) being met as well?

TASKS AND SKILLS AT DIFFERENT LEVELS OF MANAGEMENT

Few people are trained to be good managers. Usually a person learns how to be a skilled accountant or sales representative or production-line worker, and then—because of his or her skill—is selected to be a manager. The tendency is for such managers to become deeply involved in showing others how to do things, helping them, supervising them, and generally being very active in the operating task.

The further up the managerial ladder a person moves, the less important his or her original job skills become. At the top of the ladder, the need is for people who are visionaries, planners, organizers, coordinators, communicators, morale builders, and motivators. Figure 8.9 shows that a manager must have three categories of skills:

technical skills
Skills that involve the ability to perform tasks in a specific discipline or department.

1. **Technical skills** involve the ability to perform tasks in a specific discipline (such as selling a product or developing software) or department (such as marketing or information systems).

human relations skills
Skills that involve communication and motivation; they enable managers to work through and with people.

2. **Human relations skills** involve communication and motivation; they enable managers to work through and with people. Such skills also include those associated with leadership, coaching, morale building, delegating, training and development, and help and supportiveness.

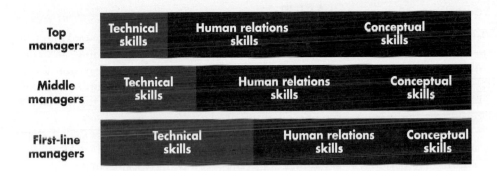

Top managers	Technical skills	Human relations skills	Conceptual skills
Middle managers	Technical skills	Human relations skills	Conceptual skills
First-line managers	Technical skills	Human relations skills	Conceptual skills

FIGURE 8.9

SKILLS NEEDED AT VARIOUS LEVELS OF MANAGEMENT

All managers need human relations skills. At the top, managers need strong conceptual skills and rely less on technical skills. First-line managers need strong technical skills and rely less on conceptual skills. Middle managers need to have a balance between technical and conceptual skills.

3. **Conceptual skills** involve the ability to picture the organization as a whole and the relationships among its various parts. Conceptual skills are needed in planning, organizing, controlling, systems development, problem analysis, decision making, coordinating, and delegating.

conceptual skills
Skills that involve the ability to picture the organization as a whole and the relationship among its various parts.

Looking at Figure 8.9, you'll notice that first-line managers need to be skilled in all three areas. Most of their time is spent on technical and human relations tasks (assisting operating personnel, giving directions, and so forth). First-line managers spend little time on conceptual tasks. Top managers, in contrast, need to use few technical skills. Instead, almost all of their time is devoted to human relations and conceptual tasks. A person who is competent at a low level of management may not be competent at higher levels and vice-versa. The skills needed vary at different levels.

EFFECTIVE MANAGERS

Effective modern managers have three things in common: they are action-oriented, they manage change efficiently, and they are able to build a sense of shared values that will motivate and generate loyalty. Books such as *The One Minute Manager*, by Ken Blanchard and Spencer Johnson, encourage supervisors to actively praise employees. In his speech to the Canadian Club titled "Message to Managers: Get Out of Your Offices," management expert Henry Mintzberg indicated that "...decision makers can't spend their days sitting in offices poring over numbers and flow charts. They have to get out and meet people, be they workers or customers."[21]

Your goal may be to eventually hold a leadership position. Mary Parker Follett had the following view on characteristics of leadership:

> We have heard repeated again and again in the past, "Leaders are born, not made." I read the other day "Leadership is a capacity that cannot be acquired." I believe that leadership can, in part, be learned. I hope you will not let anyone persuade you that it cannot be. The [one] who thinks leadership cannot be learned will probably remain in a subordinate position. The [one] who believes it can be, will go to work and learn it.[22]

The next section will review seven skills that will help develop your managerial potential. These seven skills—decision-making, verbal, writing, computer, human relations, time management, and technical skills—will help you "learn" how to be a good manager and leader. As you build your skills, it helps to think of yourself as a one-person business. Like any business, you must strive for quality and customer service.[23]

Learning Managerial Skills

Decision-Making Skills All management functions involve decision-making. It is the heart of all the management functions: planning, organizing, leading, and controlling. **Decision making** is choosing among two or more alternatives. It sounds easier than it is in practice, as it is estimated that half the decisions in organizations fail. These failures can be traced to managers who impose solutions, limit the search for alternatives, and use power to implement their plans.[24]

As Figure 8.10 shows, the rational decision-making model is a series of steps managers and leaders should follow to make logical, intelligent, and well-founded decisions. These steps can be thought of as the seven Ds of decision making:

1. Define the situation.

2. Describe and collect needed information.

3. Develop alternatives.

4. Develop agreement among those involved.

5. Decide which alternative is best.

6. Do what is indicated (implement the best alternative).

7. Determine whether the decision was a good one and follow up.

The best decisions are based on sound information. Managers often have computer terminals at their desks so they can easily retrieve internal records and look up external data of all kinds. But all the data in the world cannot replace a creative manager who makes brilliant decisions. Decision making is the one skill most needed by managers and leaders. It is the skill that all the other functions depend on for the successful implementation of the organization's strategic goals.

Verbal Skills The bulk of your duties as a manager will involve communicating with others. You'll have to give talks, conduct meetings, make presentations, and generally communicate your ideas to others. To prepare for such tasks, you should take oral communication courses and become active in various student groups. Become an officer of an organization so that you're responsible for conducting meetings and giving speeches. You may want to join a choir or other group to become comfortable performing in front of others.

decision making
Choosing among two or more alternatives.

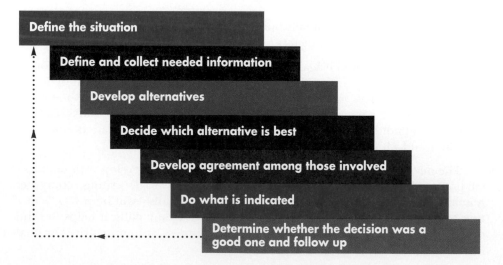

FIGURE 8.10

THE DECISION-MAKING PROCESS

An important step in the decision-making process is to choose the best alternative so that the organization can achieve its goals and objectives. After an evaluation is made of the decision, the process begins again.

At least half of communication is skilled listening. A good manager mixes with other managers, workers, clients, shareholders, and others outside the firm. He or she listens to recommendations and complaints and acts on them. Active listening requires asking questions and feeding back what you've heard to let others know you're truly interested in what they say.

Writing Skills   Managers must also be able to write clearly and precisely. Much of what you want others to do must be communicated through memos, reports, policies, and letters. Organizations everywhere are complaining about many graduates' inability to write clearly. If you develop good writing skills, you'll be ahead of your competition. That means you should take courses in grammar and composition. To learn to write, you must practise writing! It helps to write anything: a diary, letters, notes, and so on. With practice, you'll develop the ability to write easily—just as you speak. With this skill, you'll be better prepared for a career in management.

Computer Skills   Offices today are full of computers and related technology. Memos, charts, letters, and most of your other communication efforts involve the computer. When you're practising writing, practise on a word processor. The truly efficient manager must be able to effectively use and take advantage of the continuing developments in technology.

Human Relations Skills   A manager works with people; good managers know how to get along with people, motivate them, and inspire them. People skills are learned by working with people. Join student groups, volunteer to help at local charities, and get involved in political organizations. Try to assume leadership positions in which you're responsible for contacting others, assigning them work, and motivating them. Good leaders begin early by assuming leadership positions in sports, community groups, and so on.

Be aware of how others react to you. If you cause negative feelings or reactions, learn why. Don't be afraid to make mistakes and upset others. That's how you learn. But do learn how to work with others. Ask your friends what you could do to be a more effective leader.

Time-Management Skills   One of the most important skills for new managers to learn is how to budget their time effectively. There are many demands on managers' time that they need to learn to control: telephone interruptions, visits from colleagues, questions from subordinates, meetings scheduled by higher management, and such. See if your school offers courses in time management. Time-management courses or workshops will help you develop such skills as setting priorities, delegating work, choosing activities that produce the most results, doing your work when you're at your best, and dealing with interruptions. Learning these skills now will help you increase your productivity at school and at home.

Technical Skills   To rise through the ranks of accounting, marketing, finance, production, or any other functional area, you'll have to be proficient in that area. Begin now to choose some area of specialization. To rise to top management, you might supplement your undergraduate studies with an MBA (Master of Business Administration) or some similar degree in government, economics, or hospital administration. More and more students are going on to take advanced degrees. About 60 percent of top managers have taken courses beyond the bachelor's degree. The most common areas of technical expertise among top managers are accounting and finance together. Marketing came in second. Slightly more than half of the top 1,000 chief executive officers in the country have a graduate degree.[25] For more on the skills that will help you further your career as a manager, see the Reaching Beyond Our Borders box "Learning About Managing Business in Volatile Global Markets."

REACHING BEYOND OUR BORDERS

Learning About Managing Businesses in Volatile Global Markets

www.bus.sfu.ca
www.mgmt.utoronto.ca
www.business.queensu.ca

Business schools are seeing a change these days. As students read about countries that make up the former Soviet Union going to a market economy and eastern Europeans opening their doors to western businesses, they're demanding to know more about global business management. Many young people know they'll be involved in international business even if they never leave Canada. They also know that Canadian companies are looking to business schools for managers who know how to work in the new global context.

How are business schools responding to this student demand? Many are revamping their existing curriculums by integrating international examples into basic courses. This reduces the need for specifically international courses. The idea is to bring international dimensions into the mainstream.

Still, some students demand more. They feel that global enterprise is too important to be mixed in with other courses, and they want courses that are entirely international. Many business schools offer semester exchange programs with business schools in other countries. Professors are encouraged to participate in international research to gain teaching experience overseas. Students are encouraged—and in some cases required—to study foreign languages. Students have caught the international fever and have passed the sense of urgency on to their colleges and universities.

Businesses, too, are changing the way they educate employees. Rather than send them for a traditional MBA, firms are teaching their managers how to work in teams, how to use the latest technology, and how to operate in a global economy. It's possible, if not likely, that the entire nature of business education will change over the next decade. Much more information will be available and accessible via computers and computer networks. More courses will be customized to fit the needs of individual firms. Many senior managers are expressing dissatisfaction with the MBA program at most Canadian universities, and apparently newer dynamic companies are not keen on hiring MBAs. Complaints vary, but it would seem that what companies are seeking are more flexible employees who are tuned in to a fast-moving, fast-changing, volatile global market—employees who can "think on their feet." In any case, the future of management promises to be exciting, and so does the future of management education.

Sources: Brian O'Reilly, "How Execs Learn Now," *Business Week*, April 5, 1993, pp. 52–58; Brian O'Reilly, "Reengineering the MBA," *Fortune*, January 24, 1994, pp. 38–47; © 2001 Time Inc. All rights reserved; Harvey Schacter, "Programmed for Obsolescence?" *Canadian Business*, June 25/July 9, 1999, pp. 49–51.

Management Skills Are Transferable

One exciting thing about the study of management and leadership is that it prepares people for careers in all sorts of organizations. Managers and leaders are needed not only in business organizations but also in schools, churches, charities, government organizations, unions, associations, and clubs.

When selecting a career in management, you will have several decisions to make:

- What kind of organization is most desirable? That is, do you want to work for a business, government, or nonprofit organization?

- What type of managerial position seems most interesting? You may become a production manager, a sales manager, a human resource manager, an accounting manager, a traffic (distribution) manager, a credit manager, or some other type of manager. There are dozens of managerial positions from which to choose. In the future, graduates are likely to move among several different functions, so it pays to have a broad education in business.

ETHICAL DILEMMA
Review

You will recall the beginning-of-the-chapter question. Here's what our executives think. Bédard states that "honesty has always been the best policy. Anyone beginning their career with an approach that would be detrimental to a supervisor or a fellow employee, quickly becomes identified as such and would eventually suffer the consequences."

Reilley believes that "you should always keep your superior informed. Perhaps his performance is spotty only in your opinion and by holding back you are harming both the team and yourself. Also, if you aren't a team player, the word soon gets around and it could work against you. Finally, assuming you get the boss's job by this unscrupulous means, how can you engender loyalty from your new team if you suspect others of doing what you have done? If the boss is truly inefficient, his day of reckoning will come. Keep the boss informed. Quick gains by underhanded means will eventually work against you."

Suppose your boss has been very good to you, mentoring and supporting you so that you have made rapid progress. Or, perhaps she has been a rotten boss, always giving you flak and never offering a word of praise or recognition. What if she is in her 50s and her chances of getting another job are very slim? This is, obviously, a tough call and no two individuals will make the same decision. It depends on how ambitious you are, the strength of your personal ethical standards, the nature of your relationship with your boss, and how badly strapped you are for funds. What do you think?

- What type of industry is most appealing to you: sporting goods, computers, automobiles, tourism, aircraft, or what? Would it be more interesting to work for a relatively new firm or an established one? What courses and training are needed to prepare for various managerial careers? Only careful research will help you answer these questions.

Management will be discussed in more detail in the next few chapters. Let's pause now, review, and do some exercises. Management is doing, not just reading.

What kind of management are you best suited for: human resource, marketing, finance, accounting, production, credit? Why do you feel this area is most appropriate? Would you like to work for a large firm or a small business? Private or public? In an office or out in the field? Would you like being a manager? If you aren't sure, read the following chapters and see what's involved.

- How does enabling help empowerment?
- What are the five steps in the control process?
- What's the difference between internal and external customers?
- What kinds of decisions must you make when choosing a career?

SUMMARY

1. Enumerate the four functions of management and reasons why the role of managers is changing.

1. Managers perform a variety of functions.
   - *What are the four primary functions of management?*
   The four primary functions are (1) planning, (2) organizing, (3) leading, and (4) controlling.

2. Relate the planning process to the accomplishment of company goals.

2. The planning function involves the process of setting objectives to meet the organizational goals.
   - *What's the difference between goals and objectives?*
   Goals are broad, long-term achievements that organizations aim to accomplish, whereas objectives are specific, short-term plans made to help reach the goals.
   - *What is a SWOT analysis?*
   Managers look at the strengths, weaknesses, opportunities, and threats facing the firm.
   - *What are the four types of planning, and how are they related to the organization's goals and objectives?*
   Strategic planning is broad, long-range planning that outlines the goals of the organization. *Tactical planning* is specific, short-term planning that lists organizational objectives. *Operational planning* is part of tactical planning and involves setting specific timetables and standards. *Contingency planning* involves developing an alternative set of plans in case the first set doesn't work out.

3. Describe the organizing function of management, including staffing and diversity management.

3. Organizing means allocating resources (such as funds for various departments), assigning tasks, and establishing procedures for accomplishing the organizational objectives.
   - *What are some of the latest trends in organizational management?*
   Many firms are creating self-managed teams. In those firms, managers tend to do more coaching and training than telling people what to do. Another trend is toward stakeholder-oriented management. In those cases, management tries to satisfy the needs of all stakeholders, including employees, customers, suppliers, dealers, environmental groups, and the surrounding communities.
   - *What changes in the marketplace have made staffing more important?*
   E-commerce CEOs must spend a lot of time recruiting because their companies grow so fast and run on the knowledge of mostly young workers. Keeping people is also critical because there are lots of companies seeking new talent and people feel free today to go where the action is fastest (and pays the most in dollars or stock options). Also, the labour force is much more diverse today than in the past and managers must learn to make the most of the talents of each person.

4. Explain the differences between leaders and managers, and describe the various leadership styles.

4. Executives today must be more than just managers; they must be leaders as well.
   - *What's the difference between a manager and a leader?*
   A manager plans, organizes, and controls functions within an organization. A leader has vision and inspires others to grasp that vision, establishes corporate values, emphasizes corporate ethics, and directs change in the organization.
   - *Describe the various leadership styles.*
   Figure 8.6 shows a continuum of leadership styles ranging from boss-centred to subordinate-centred leadership.
   - *Which leadership style is best?*
   The best (most effective) leadership style depends on the people being led and the situation. The challenge of the future will be to empower self-managed teams to manage themselves. This is a move away from autocratic leadership.
   - *What does empowerment mean?*
   Empowerment means giving employees the authority and responsibility to respond quickly to customer requests. *Enabling* is the term used to describe giving workers

the education and tools they need to assume their new decision-making powers. Knowledge management involves finding the right information, keeping the information in a readily accessible place, and making the information known to everyone in the firm. Knowledge management is another way of enabling workers to do the best job they can.

5. The control function of management involves measuring employee performance against objectives and standards, rewarding people for a job well done, and taking corrective action if necessary.

   • *What are the five steps of the control function?*
   Controlling incorporates (1) setting clear standards, (2) monitoring and recording performance, (3) comparing performance with plans and standards, (4) communicating results and deviations to employees, and (5) providing positive feedback for a job well done and taking corrective action if necessary.

   • *What qualities must standards possess to be used to measure performance results?*
   Standards must be specific, attainable, and measurable.

   • *What are the latest performance standards?*
   Modern companies consider customer satisfaction to be a key measure of success. As well, traditional standards of success include profit and return on investment.

5. Summarize the five steps of the control function of management.

6. Managers must be good planners, organizers, coordinators, communicators, morale builders, and motivators.

   • *What skills do managers need to be all of these things?*
   Managers must have three categories of skills: (1) technical skills (ability to perform specific tasks such as selling products or developing software), (2) human relations skills (ability to communicate and motivate), and (3) conceptual skills (ability to see organizations as a whole and how all the parts fit together.

   • *Are these skills equally important at all management levels?*
   Managers at different levels need different skills. Top managers rely heavily on human relations and conceptual skills and rarely use technical skills, while first-line supervisors need strong technical and human relations skills but use conceptual skills less often. Middle managers need to have a balance of all of three skills (see Figure 8.9).

6. Illustrate the skills needed at each level of management.

KEY TERMS

autocratic
  leadership 233
baby boomer 230
conceptual skills 241
contingency
  planning 225
controlling 222
decision making 242
empowerment 236
enabling 236
external
  customers 239
goals 223
human relations
  skills 240
internal
  customers 239

knowledge
  management 236
laissez-faire (free-
  rein) leadership 233
leadership 231
leading 221
management 221
managing
  diversity 230
middle
  management 228
mission
  statement 223
objectives 223
operational
  planning 225
organization
  chart 226

organizing 221
participative
  (democratic)
  leadership 233
planning 221
staffing 229
strategic
  planning 224
supervisory
  management 228
SWOT analysis 223
tactical planning 224
technical skills 240
top management 227
vision 222

DEVELOPING WORKPLACE SKILLS

1. Bring several decks of cards to class and have the class break up into teams of six or so members. Each team should then elect a leader. Each leader should be assigned a leadership style: autocratic, participative, or laissez-faire. Have each team try to build a house of cards by stacking them side by side and on top of each other. Each team member should then report his or her experience under that style of leadership.

2. In small groups, debate the advantages and disadvantages of becoming a manager. Does the size of the business make a difference? What are the advantages of a career in business versus a career in a nonprofit organization?

www.canadianbusiness.com

www.robmagazine.com

www.nationalpostbusiness.com

3. On the Internet or in the library, review several issues of *Canadian Business, Report On Business, National Post Business* and other business journals for information about key executives and managers. How much do they make? (See *Report On Business Magazine*'s annual survey.) Do you believe top managers earn their pay? Be prepared to give a two-minute presentation to the class about your findings and beliefs.

4. Review Figure 8.6 and discuss managers you have known, worked for, or read about who have practised each style. Which did you like best? Why? Which were most effective? Why?

TAKING IT TO THE NET

Purpose:

To test your ability to make appropriate supervisory decisions.

Exercise:

Go to the Leadership Challenge part of the Positive Employee Relations Council Web site <www.perc.net>. This simulation, the site claims, "will involve you in fictional but realistic situations. It is broken down into moves or steps and the objective is to finish with the least number of steps and a high score. You will discover that this simulation is a maze of related decisions and interacting problems. You will find that effective supervisory decisions bring you closer to the end of the challenge, and weaker decisions inhibit your efforts, require additional steps, and get you further involved."

   Print the scorecard to record your results.

1. How did you score?

2. Improve your score by taking the challenge again using what you learned on the first round to make wiser decisions.

3. What did you learn from this exercise?

TAKING IT TO THE NET

Purpose:

To perform a simple SWOT analysis.

Exercise:

Go to <www.marketingteacher.com> and complete the SWOT analysis for Highly Brill Leisure Center.

1. What are Brill's strengths, weaknesses, opportunities, and threats?

2. Analyze Brill's weaknesses. How do you think the company's strengths might be used to overcome some of its weaknesses?

3. Analyze Brill's opportunities and threats. What additional opportunities can you suggest for Brill? What additional threats can you identify?

PRACTISING MANAGEMENT DECISIONS

CASE 1

LEADERSHIP IN A LEADERLESS COMPANY

Business Week magazine devoted a recent issue to the future of business. Writer John Byrne speculated about the future of leadership. He said that the twenty-first century would be unfriendly to leaders who try to run their companies by the sheer force of will. He said that success would come, instead, to companies that are "leaderless"—or companies whose leadership is so widely shared that they resemble ant colonies or beehives. In a world that is becoming more dependent on brainpower, having teams at the top will make more sense than having a single top manager. The Internet enables companies to act more like beehives because information can be shared horizontally rather than sent up to the top manager's office and then back down again. Decisions can be made instantly by the best people equipped to make them.

In the past, uniform thinking from the top could cripple an organization. Today, however, team leadership is ideally suited for the new reality of fast-changing markets. Urgent projects often require the coordinated contribution of many talented people working together. Such thinking does not happen at the top of the organization; it takes place down among the workers.

In the future, therefore, managers are more likely to be chosen for their team experience and their ability to delegate rather than make all key decisions themselves. Companies in the future, it is said, will be "led" by people who understand that in business, as in nature, no one person can be really in control.

Decision Questions

1. What would you look for on a résumé that would indicate that a candidate for work was a self-motivated team player? Are you that type? How do you know?

2. Given your experience with managers in the past, what problems do you see some managers having with letting employees decide for themselves the best way to do things and giving them the power to obtain needed equipment?

3. What would happen if all the businesses in your area had their employees mix with customers to hear their comments and complaints? Would that be a good or bad thing? Why?

4. What are the various ways you can think of for companies to pay bonuses to team members? One way is to divide the money equally. What are other ways? Which would you prefer as a team member?

Sources: John A. Byrne, "The Global Corporation Becomes the Leaderless Corporation," *Business Week*, August 30, 1999, pp. 88–90, and Etienne C. Wenger and William M. Synder, "Communities of Practice: The Organizational Frontier," *Harvard Business Review*, January–February 2000, pp. 139–45.

CASE 2

CHANGING THE PARADIGM

Noel Tichy, a business professor at the University of Michigan, advises you not to try this at home. Consider the two ways to boil a live frog. The first way is to drop little Kermit into boiling water. He'll hop right out, according to those acquainted with the classic physiological phenomenon. But try placing Kermit in a pot of cold water and gradually raising the temperature. He'll sit there and boil to death. This is meant to be a parable for business leadership in the 1990s, not a lesson in animal torture. Kermit failed to adjust to a shifting paradigm. He ignored a critical, though gradual, change in his environment. Before coming to a full boil, he should have remembered the words of American patriot Thomas Paine, "A long habit of not thinking a thing wrong gives it the superficial appearance of being right."

Used in business, the word *paradigm* (pronounced para-dime) simply refers to the accepted view of how things have always been done and should continue to be done. A paradigm shifter is someone who throws out the rules of the game and starts radical change. Tichy, who worked with General Electric's ultimate paradigm shifter, Jack Welch, adds, "It's not just quantum ideas, but the guts to stick with them. In industry after industry, a lot of frogs are waking up and finding it's too late to jump. Banking is there. Auto has had two chances and may not get a third. And now the computer industry is feeling the heat."

Jack Welch's restructuring of GE meant far fewer middle managers and more power to those who remained. John Trani (the Welch lieutenant who overhauled and ran GE Medical Systems) says, "People come to me and ask, 'Why was I good enough yesterday, but not today?' It's simple. In 1954, Roger

Bannister won world acclaim for breaking the four-minute mile. Today many high schoolers can do that. The standard is always changing, but there's always a top 10 and a bottom 10." As a matter of policy, Welch demanded that all GE businesses be number one or number two in their industry.

Decision Questions

1. How is the business environment changing from what it was 10 or 20 years ago? What can managers do to adapt to these changes?
2. Noel Tichy suggests that companies that don't adjust to shifting paradigms face death. As an example, he points to buggy makers who turned up their noses at Henry Ford's smelly exhaust. Can you think of other victims of shifting paradigms?
3. Experts say that for a real paradigm shift to occur within a corporation, top management has to have a strong commitment to change. Says Ram Charan, a consultant to many Fortune 500 companies, "There has to be divine discontent with the status quo at the very top, and courage to do something about it." Explain why top management's commitment to change is crucial to change within a corporation.

CBC **VIDEO CASE** **www.cbc.ca**

THE TROUBLE WITH TEAMS

It's a lovely ideal—democracy in the workplace. In the 1980s business gurus told businesses that they needed to embrace teamwork. The authoritarian structure was no longer effective but with teamwork, businesses would be more successful.

Today, these same gurus are changing their minds. While teams were once actively promoted, individual leaders are now being promoted as the key to success. One of the several companies spotlighted in this video is ESG Canada. Five equal partners produce a sound monitoring system used in underground mines. While the product is a big success, teamwork takes so much time and effort that the partners are considering a change.

The concept of teamwork was first embraced by the auto industry. Automakers were losing market share to the Japanese imports. Many felt that the key to Japanese automakers' success was teamwork. Unlike American workers, Japanese workers did not work in traditional assembly lines. They worked in teams and were given a voice and encouraged to make productivity suggestions.

This concept quickly spread into the auto sector, into other manufacturing sectors, and then into other industries. While many firms have tried to embrace teamwork, it has not led to the success that many expected. Today, while teamwork can provide many benefits, it is still not completely understood what conditions need to be in place for teams to be successful and under what conditions teams can derail.

Discussion Questions

1. What are some of the benefits of teamwork? What are some of the challenges of teamwork?
2. Is there proof that teams improve a company's performance in the long run?
3. Why have automakers not used teams to the extent expected?
4. What impact does our society have on the potential success of teams?

Source: *Venture*, show number 703, "The Trouble with Teams," November 10, 1998, running time 6:16.

CHAPTER

9

Managing the Move toward Customer-Driven Business Organizations

LEARNING GOALS

AFTER YOU HAVE READ AND STUDIED THIS CHAPTER, YOU SHOULD BE ABLE TO

1 Explain the organizational theories of Fayol and Weber.

2 Discuss the various issues involved in structuring and restructuring organizations.

3 Describe traditional organizations and their limitations.

4 Show how matrix-style organizations and cross-functional teams help companies become more customer-oriented.

5 Defend the use of various organizational tools and techniques such as networking, reengineering, and outsourcing.

6 Give examples to show how organizational culture and the informal orgnization can hinder or assist organizational change.

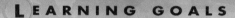

Carly Fiorina of Hewlett-Packard

Corbis Images

Carleton (Carly) Fiorina got her MBA in marketing from the University of Maryland in 1980. She started her career in AT&T's government sales office and then moved into network systems, where she saw more opportunity for her creativity. When Lucent Technologies split off from AT&T to focus on wireless products, Fiorina followed. Using her organizational skills, she was instrumental in making the firm a leading Internet company. She became president of Lucent's global service-provider business in 1998.

When Hewlett-Packard (HP) began searching for a new CEO, it was looking for someone who could restructure the firm to make it a leader in e-commerce. Fiorina was selected from some 300 candidates. One of her competitors for the position was another woman: Ann Livermore, the CEO of Enterprise Computing, one of the four main "product companies" at HP. Livermore had developed HP's e-service strategy and was the top *internal* candidate. She is still at HP, and she and Fiorina together are working to make HP a leading Internet company.

At her first major presentation to Wall Street analysts, Fiorina announced a major reorganization of HP's business structure. Specifically, she planned to merge HP's four product companies into two and put much more focus on customer relations. The idea was to make HP a more flexible, faster-moving, and more customer-oriented firm than it had been. In short, she wanted to "reinvent" the firm. Here is how she described the task: "Reinvention to me is about four things. It's about culture, it's about strategy, it's about what you measure and how you reward those measurements, and it's about business process." In another interview she said, "We're going to preserve the best, and we've got to reinvent the rest—but we've got to get on with it in a hurry . . . We'll startle the world with our speed.

And we'll startle the world delivering on inventions." In the first quarter of Fiorina's leadership, HP saw revenues rise by 14 percent and its stock price by 36 percent.

Fiorina slashed bloated operating costs, reorganized divisions, and changed the sales compensation plan. To increase brand recognition, Fiorina cut the number of different brand names used by the company from 100 to 1. The hiring of Fiorina at HP has been compared to the hiring of Lou Gerstner at IBM. Both companies brought in an outsider to turn a stodgy Fortune 500 technology concern into a more responsive, customer-oriented industry leader.

Many top companies are restructuring their operations in order to focus on pleasing customers. In September 2001, HP and Compaq Computer Corporation announced their intention to merge, creating a global $87-billion company. Fiorina would be chair and CEO of the combined entity, which would retain the HP name. Fiorina described the proposed merger as a more "decisive move that positions us to win by offering even more value to our customers and partners."

This chapter will teach you the foundational principles behind organizational design and then lead you to discover the latest concepts. When Carly Fiorina was selected to be the new CEO at HP, she made a break in the "glass ceiling," the invisible barrier that long seemed to keep women from becoming top managers at leading corporations. Other talented men and women will find such exciting new opportunities in those firms that are dynamic enough to reorganize to meet the demands of the information age.

Adapted from: "Wake-Up Call for HP," *Technology Review,* May–June 2000, pp. 94–100; Quentin Hardy, "Imagine Yourself Differently," *Forbes,* July 24, 2000, p.158; David Hamilton, "Soul Saver," *The Wall Street Journal,* August 22, 2000, pp. A1 & A18. "She Can Turn Anything into Gold," *Success,* December / January 2001, p. 30; and "Are Women Better Leaders," *U.S. News and World Report,* January 29, 2001.

ETHICAL DILEMMA

When Is Learning Unethical?

In this chapter you will see the term *benchmarking*. This refers to trying to discover what the best practices of your competitors are so that you can adopt them and even improve on them. Benchmarking is one of the key strategies for staying competitive in today's rapidly changing marketplace. The ethical questions that arise relate to how far you can go in this research before it becomes unethical. Should you entice some of your competitors' best researchers to work for you? How far can you go in spying on other companies and learning what they are doing? Suppose your boss wants to give you a leave of absence so you can get a job at a competitor to learn their secrets? We will look at these questions again after you have read the chapter.

THE CHANGING ORGANIZATION

Never before in the history of business has so much change been introduced so quickly, sometimes too quickly. As you learned in earlier chapters, much of that change is due to the changing business environment—that is, more global competition and faster technological change, especially new challenges from Internet commerce. Equally important to many businesses is the change in consumer expectations. Consumers today expect high-quality products and fast, friendly service—at a reasonable cost. Managing change, then, has become a critical managerial function.[1] That sometimes includes changing the whole organizational structure, as Carly Fiorina did at Hewlett-Packard. In addition, when managing change organizations must be careful not to compromise their ethics. See the Ethical Dilemma box "When Is Learning Unethical?" for some examples.

Organizations in the past were designed more to facilitate management than to please the customer. Companies designed many rules and regulations to give managers control over employees. To supplement the work of the line managers, who were responsible for making products and distributing them to customers, companies hired specialists in areas such as law and human resource management. We shall explore in some detail the history of organizational design so that you can see what the foundations are. Then we shall explore the newest forms of organization, forms that are being designed to better serve the customer. Though often dramatic and disruptive, the changes keep companies competitive in today's dynamic business environment. One way to introduce such changes is to bring in new managers from *outside* the firm, managers who have experience with the Internet and with flexible ways of organizing. That's what Hewlett-Packard did when it brought in Carly Fiorina.

THE HISTORICAL DEVELOPMENT OF ORGANIZATIONAL DESIGN

To understand what is happening in organizations today, it is best to begin with a firm foundation of organizational principles. Many principles of traditional organizational design are still important today. However, some have lost importance and others may no longer apply at all, and organizational leaders need to understand which principles are still important and which are not. So let's begin by exploring the history of organizations.

Until the twentieth century, most businesses were rather small, the processes for producing goods were rather simple, and organizing workers was fairly easy. Not until the 1900s and the introduction of mass production (efficiently producing large quantities of goods) did businesses become complex in terms of production processes and economics. The bigger the plant, the more efficient production became. Business growth led to what was called **economies of scale**. This term refers to the fact that companies can produce goods more inexpensively if they can purchase raw materials in bulk. Subsequently, the average cost of goods goes down as production levels increase.

During this era of mass production, organization theorists emerged. In France, Henri Fayol published his book *Administration industrielle et générale* in 1919. It was popularized in 1949 under the title *General and Industrial Management*. Sociologist Max Weber (pronounced "Vay-ber") was writing about organization theory in Germany about the same time Fayol was writing his books in France. Note that it was only a little more than 50 years ago that organization theory became popular in North America.

economies of scale
The situation in which companies can produce goods more inexpensively if they can purchase raw materials in bulk. Subsequently, the average cost of goods goes down as production levels increase.

Fayol's Principles of Organization

Fayol introduced such principles as the following:[2]

- **Unity of command**. Each worker is to report to one, and only one, boss. The benefits of this principle are obvious. What happens if two different bosses give you two different assignments? Which one should you follow? To prevent such confusion, each person is to report to only one manager.

- **Hierarchy of authority**. All workers should know to whom they should report. Managers should have the right to give orders and expect others to follow.

- **Division of labour**. Functions are to be divided into areas of specialization such as production, marketing, and finance.

- **Subordination of individual interests to the general interest**. Workers are to think of themselves as a coordinated team. The goals of the team are more important than the goals of individual workers.

- **Authority**. Managers have the right to give orders and the power to exact obedience. Authority and responsibility are related: Whenever authority is exercised, responsibility arises.

- **Degree of centralization**. The amount of decision-making power vested in top management should vary by circumstances. In a small organization, it's possible to centralize all decision-making power in the top manager. In a larger organization, however, some decision-making power should be delegated to lower-level managers and employees on both major and minor issues.

- **Clear communication channels**. All workers should be able to reach others in the firm quickly and easily.

- **Order**. Materials and people should be placed and maintained in the proper location.

- **Equity**. A manager should treat employees and peers with respect and justice.

- **Esprit de corps**. A spirit of pride and loyalty should be created among people in the firm.

Management courses in colleges and universities throughout the world taught these principles for years, and they became synonymous with the concept of management. Organizations were designed so that no person had more than one boss, lines of authority were clear, and everyone knew to whom they were to report. Naturally, these principles tended to be written down as rules, policies, and regulations as organizations grew larger. That process of rule-making often led to rather rigid organizations that didn't respond quickly to consumer requests.

When you go to a store and the clerk says, "I'm sorry I can't do that, it's against company policy," you can blame Max Weber and his theories. At one time, less-educated workers were best managed, it was believed, by having them follow many strict rules and regulations monitored by managers or supervisors. Are there industries or businesses today where you think it would be desirable or necessary to continue to use such controls?

Courtesy of German Information Centre.

Max Weber and Organizational Theory

Max Weber's book *The Theory of Social and Economic Organizations*, like Fayol's, also appeared in North America the late 1940s. It was Weber who promoted the pyramid-shaped organization structure that became so popular in large firms. Weber put great trust in managers and felt that the firm would do well if employees simply did what they were told. The less decision making employees had to do, the better. Clearly, this is a reasonable way to operate if you're dealing with relatively uneducated and untrained workers. Often, such workers were the only ones available at the time Weber was writing; most employees did not have the kind of educational background and technical skills that most of today's workers have.

Weber's principles of organization were similar to Fayol's. In addition, Weber emphasized

- Job descriptions.
- Written rules, decision guidelines, and detailed records.
- Consistent procedures, regulations, and policies.
- Staffing and promotion based on qualifications.

Weber believed that large organizations demanded clearly established rules and guidelines that were to be followed precisely. Although his principles seemed to make a great deal of sense at the time, the practice of establishing rules and procedures became so rigid in some companies that it became counterproductive.

Today, many organizations are attempting to rid themselves of the pyramid structure because it slows the process of change. In the past, when several layers of management had to be included in a decision, that decision could take weeks to make. In today's companies, decisions often have to be made within days or minutes. Thus, many firms are eliminating many managerial and nonmanagerial positions and giving more authority and responsibility to those employees who deal directly with consumers.

downsizing
The process of eliminating managerial and non-managerial positions.

The process of eliminating these positions is called **downsizing**, because it allows the organization to operate with fewer managers and workers. Sometimes the process is called *rightsizing*, because the idea is to make the organization just the right size to adapt quickly to consumer wants and needs. Many managers who have been downsized have started their own businesses, in which they have more control and are able to adapt more quickly to the marketplace than they could in a large corporation.

TURNING MANAGERIAL CONCEPTS INTO ORGANIZATIONAL DESIGN

organizational design
The structuring of workers so that they can best accomplish the firm's goals.

job design
The process of breaking down jobs into specific tasks and assigning these tasks to specific positions.

Following the concepts of theorists like Fayol and Weber, managers in the mid-1900s began designing organizations that could implement those concepts. **Organizational design** is the structuring of workers so that they can best accomplish the firm's goals. Part of this process was the application of job design. **Job design** occurred when jobs were first broken down into specific tasks, and these tasks were assigned to specific positions, and ultimately workers, in the organization.

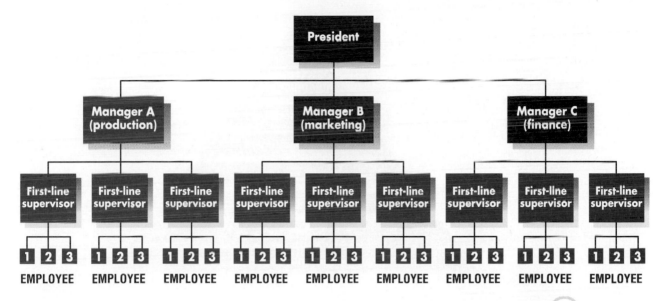

FIGURE 9.1

TYPICAL ORGANIZATION CHART

This is a rather standard chart with managers for major functions and supervisors reporting to the managers. Each supervisor manages three employees.

In the past, many organizations were designed so that managers could control workers, and most organizations are still organized that way, with everything set up in a hierarchy. A **hierarchy** is a system in which one person is at the top of the organization and there is a ranked (in terms of authority or responsibility) or sequential ordering from the top down of managers who are responsible to that person. Since one person can't keep track of thousands of workers, the top manager needs many lower-level managers to help. Figure 9.1 shows a typical hierarchical organization structure, which was introduced in Chapter 8.

Some organizations have had as many as 10 to 14 layers of management between the chief executive officer (CEO) and the lowest-level employees. If employees wanted to introduce work changes, they would ask a supervisor, who would ask a manager, who would ask a manager at the next level up, and so on. Eventually a decision would be made and passed down from manager to manager until it reached the employee. Such decisions could often take weeks or months to be made.

Max Weber used the word *bureaucrat* to describe a middle manager whose function was to implement top management's orders. Thus, **bureaucracy** came to be the term used for an organization with many layers of managers who set rules and regulations and oversee all decisions (see Figure 9.2). It is such bureaucracy that forces employees to say to customers, "I'm sorry, but I can't do what you want. I have to follow the rules." If police officers operated that way, they would *have* to give a ticket to everyone driving over 100 kilometres per hour on a highway where that was the speed limit. Many people would be upset by such a rigid following of the rules. Similarly, many customers are upset by employees who insist on following the rules to the letter and don't go a little out of their way to make customers happy.

When employees have to ask their managers for permission to make a change, the process may take so long that customers become annoyed. This is as true in a small organization such as a flower shop as it is in a major organization like Ford Motor Company. The employee has to find the manager, get permission, come back to the customer, and so on. Since many customers want efficient service—and they want it *now*—slow service due to bureaucracy is not acceptable in today's competitive environment.

To make customers happy, organizations are giving employees more power to make decisions on their own. Rather than having to follow strict rules and regulations, they are encouraged to please the customer no matter what. For example, at Nordstrom, a chain of upscale department stores, an employee can accept a return from a customer without seeking managerial approval, even if the garment was not originally sold at that store. As you read earlier, giving employees such authority and

hierarchy
A system in which one person is at the top of the organization and there is a ranked or sequential ordering from the top down of managers who are responsible to that person.

bureaucracy
An organization with many layers of managers who set rules and regulations and oversee all decisions.

www.nordstrom.com

FIGURE 9.2

**BUREAUCRATIC
ORGANIZATION
STRUCTURE**

responsibility to make decisions and please customers is called *empowerment*. Since an individual employee may not have all the skills and knowledge needed to please customers, employees have been encouraged to form small groups or teams so that someone in the group can be responsive to customer requests. Empowerment can be successful if knowledgeable employees are given limits within which to try to please customers. If the limit is to be exceeded, then another person or group will have the authority to make decisions. After we have explored the major issues involved in organizational design, we will discuss such teams in depth.

Bureaucratic Organizations Emphasize Functional Separation

In a bureaucratic organization, a chain of command goes from the top down. To make the process easier, organizations are set up by function. That is, there are separate departments for design, engineering, production, marketing, finance, human resource management, accounting, legal issues, and so on.

Bureaucracies encourage people to specialize in one function, for which they prepare by specializing in school. Communication among departments in traditional businesses is minimal. Career advancement for the typical employee means moving up within a function. For example, an employee in a traditional company might move up from salesperson to sales trainer to sales manager to regional manager to marketing manager to marketing vice-president.

In the past, a bureaucratic structure worked well because employees could specialize in one area. Today, such a structure would not be as effective for *all* organizations. For the most part, bureaucratic organizations aren't very responsive to specific customer wants and needs, as such a structure tries to ensure impartiality. While this is effective for some organizations—such as fast-food chains, where customers want some level of reliability and predictability in products—not all customers and industries are alike. Therefore, as you shall see later on in the chapter, one answer is to develop cross-functional teams.

Bureaucratic Organizations: Today and Tomorrow The trend today is for companies to shed layers of management (bureaucracy) to speed up their response to customer needs and demands and to cut costs. Technological developments such as automation and computers have hastened the reduction of the workforce and, therefore, the numbers and levels of management. The advent of computers has reduced the layers of middle management, as senior managers can now access information and exercise control directly from their own terminals.

Reprinted with permission from General Motors Corporation.

How we look at every Five Star retailer.

Dodge

Now there's a process that puts dealers under the microscope so you don't have to. Five Star. With audits and customer satisfaction scores determining initial certification as well as annual recertification, it basically redefines the way cars and trucks are sold and serviced. With exacting standards that scrutinize what each retailer does and how they can do it better, only our very best make the grade. Take a closer look at a Five Star Certified Chrysler, Plymouth, Jeep, or Dodge retailer. For the one nearest you, call 1-800-677-5-STAR or visit us on the Web at www.fivestar.com. We're sure you'll really like what you see—but only where you see the Five Star sign.   **Five Star. It's Better. We'll Prove It.**

CHRYSLER
Plymouth
Jeep

Jeep is a registered trademark of DaimlerChrysler.

Casual conversations with people who have bought cars often reveal that the most irritating thing about car dealers, other than pushy salespeople, is poor service. What can an auto manufacturer do to assure customers of the finest service through its dealers? The answer for DaimlerChrysler is to use annual audits and customer satisfaction surveys to establish standards for quality service and to monitor dealer performance and achievement. DaimlerChrysler is convinced that a Five Star Certified dealer will ultimately win the loyalty of customers and generate increased profit. If you were a dealer what would your perspective be on this initiative by DaimlerChrysler?

www.chrysler.com

Hewlett-Packard and many other businesses are adopting other radical ideas, such as doing away with job descriptions and masses of rules, to permit more flexible deployment of the workforce. In other words, they are seeking ways to become more efficient and more competitive.

The HP and Compaq merger briefly discussed in the opening Profile is expected to create substantial cost structure savings. "These anticipated synergies, projected to reach $2.5 billion annually, will come from product rationalization; efficiencies in administration, procurement, manufacturing and marketing; and savings from improved direct distribution of PCs and servers."[3] All of these innovations have become possible because the educated workforce can, and wants to, take on more responsibility and decision making. Flexibility and adaptability are features of many successful companies that are managing in this new mode.

www.compaq.com

That is not to say that there is no room at all for the classic method of bureaucratic operation that Fayol and Weber advocated. (McDonald's functions well under their strict procedures.) What must be understood is that the trend today is away from such structures and management styles. International competitive pressures are forcing all companies to react and adapt much more quickly than they used to and to use all their human resources more effectively. Both of these goals are best achieved by opening up company structures and procedures and breaking down rigid bureaucracies. Here are some Canadian examples of this trend:

- Shell Canada opened a lubricants plant in Brockville, Ontario, where "hierarchical structures and the control-and-command mentality have been

www.shell.ca

swept aside by a dynamic organization driven by commitments rather than reward and punishment. 'I feel more independent. I'm given more responsibility,' says employee Theresa Hetherington."[4]

www.dnd.ca

• The Department of National Defence started a project in its support services whose "aim is to demonstrate that local-level managers can maintain current levels of service more efficiently and economically if given greater authority over assigned resources.[5]

• PanCanadian Petroleum decided to "push decision making down the ranks. It means, for example, giving field operators signing authority for up to $1,000 of purchases; previously, they needed a foreman's approval to buy a broom."[6]

PROGRESS CHECK

• Name and describe four of Fayol's principles.
• What principles did Weber add?
• What is a hierarchy?

ISSUES INVOLVED IN STRUCTURING AND RESTRUCTURING ORGANIZATIONS

restructuring
Redesigning an organization so that it can more effectively and efficiently serve its customers.

Restructuring is redesigning an organization so that it can more effectively and efficiently serve its customers. What decisions are involved in structuring an organization? Since the turn of the century, many business leaders believed that there was one best way to structure an organization. However, this is changing. A starting point is the mission, goals, and objectives of the organization. These directives will impact the firm's structure, as employees must be organized so that they can achieve results. Structuring begins with this stage but must include other criteria.

Henry Mintzberg supports the current view that there is no single structure that will lead to success for all organizations. "Structure should reflect the organization's situation—for example, its age, size, type of production system, and the extent to which its environment is complex and dynamic. As well, a firm's design decisions (such as span of control, centralization versus decentralization, and matrix structures) need to be chosen so they can work within the chosen structure design."[7]

According to Mintzberg, the structure of an organization can be defined simply as the total of the ways in which its labour is divided into distinct tasks and then coordination achieved among those tasks. These coordinating mechanisms can be considered the most basic elements of structure, as they hold the organization together. Four of the six basic coordinating mechanisms are:[8]

1. **Mutual adjustment**, which achieves work coordination by the simple process of informal communication. The people who do the work interact with one another to coordinate activities.

2. **Direct supervision**, in which one person coordinates by giving orders to others. This occurs when many people must work together.

3. **Standardization of outputs**, which focuses on the desired results. In this way, the interface between jobs is predetermined. Examples include when a machinist is told to drill holes in a certain fender so that they will fit the bolts being welded by someone else, or a division manager is told to achieve a sales growth of 10 percent so that the corporation can meet some overall sales target.

4. **Standardization of skills**, as well as knowledge, is another way to achieve coordination. Here, the worker (rather than the work) is taught a body of knowledge and a set of skills (usually outside the organization). Coordination is then achieved by working with others. When an anaesthetist and a surgeon

meet in the operating room to remove an appendix, they need hardly communicate (that is, use mutual adjustment); each knows what the other will do and can coordinate accordingly.

C.K. Prahalad and Gary Hamel believe that organizations need to organize around their core competencies. **Core competency** is defined as "the collective learning in the organization, especially how to coordinate diverse production skills and integrate multiple streams of technology...It is about the organization of work and the delivery of value...and includes communication, involvement, and a deep commitment to working across organizational boundaries."[9]

Organizations need to implement a structure that will allow the organization to focus on those functions that it can do as well as, or better than, any other organization in the world. Nike is strong at designing and marketing athletic shoes. These are its core competencies. It hires other companies to manufacture its shoes, however, as these companies are more efficient at producing these shoes.

By their nature, many organizational structures today are slow and unwieldy. One Canadian management consultant reported that:

> Research shows that 85 to 95 percent of service, quality, or productivity problems stem from the organization's structure and processes.... Ask the question: "For whose convenience are systems designed?" Too often they serve accountants, technocrats, or management. Get the cart behind the horse. Your systems should serve your customers or those producing, delivering, or supporting your products or services.[10]

That is why current trends are toward smaller, more flexible structures that let companies react more quickly to today's fast-changing, technologically competitive business climate. They also unleash employees' initiative and enable them to participate in decision making. In designing or redesigning more responsive organizations, firms have had to deal with the following organizational decisions: (1) tall versus flat organization structures, (2) span of control, (3) departmentalization, and (4) centralization versus decentralization.

Tall versus Flat Organization Structures

As organizations got bigger, some began adding layer after layer of management, sometimes resulting in a dozen or more managerial steps in firms such as Bell Canada. Such organizations have what are called *tall organizational structures*—the organization chart is quite tall because of the various levels of management.

The army is another example of how tall an organization can get. There are many layers of management between a private and a general (e.g., sergeant, lieutenant, captain, major, colonel). You can imagine how a message may be distorted as it moves up through so many layers of management or officers.

Many business organizations took on the same style of organization as the military. The organizations were divided into regions, divisions, centres, and plants. Each plant might have had several layers of management. The net effect was a huge complex of managers, management assistants, secretaries, assistant secretaries, supervisors, trainers, and so on.

core competency
The collective learning in an organization, especially how to coordinate diverse production skills and integrate multiple streams of technology.

One of the most important goals of organizations today is teamwork. Teamwork builds trust, cooperation, and joint commitments to achieve the firm's objectives. Are you working in teams while in school in order to develop the team-building skills that companies will need in the future?

General Motors.

"If the people who make the car don't fit together, the car won't either."

Welcome to the Excel training course. Before it's over, Saturn's Dennis Bowman will take these General Motors employees on a real adventure. They'll scale walls. Walk across high wires. Plunge backwards into the waiting arms of their coworkers. And take away some valuable lessons about trust, cooperation and seeing things from the other person's point of view. Developed by Saturn, Excel is now used throughout General Motors. It's turning out graduates who know the power of teamwork. Who go a little further to build quality automobiles. And who believe that the right way to treat a customer is the way you'd want to be treated yourself.

Office workers were known as *white-collar workers*, as opposed to the *blue-collar workers* who worked on the assembly line. As you can imagine, the cost of keeping all these managers and support people was quite high. The paperwork they generated was unbelievable, and the inefficiencies in communication and decision making became intolerable.

The trend now is toward *flat organization structures*. That is, organizations are continuing to cut layers of management so that lower-level managers do not have to pass through many levels to reach higher managers; they simply report directly to these higher-level managers. This process has been greatly facilitated by the advent of desktop computers, which are now the common method of communication between these levels of managers, who were formerly quite removed from each other.

One benefit of having these managers reporting to a higher-level manager is that the higher-level manager simply does not have time to get involved in the day-to-day work of the managers below. This gives lower-level managers more freedom to make changes as they see fit, makes organizations more responsive, and raises the morale of lower-level managers.

Those organizations that do cut management are often creating teams. People who are considering a career in management, therefore, need to practise working and thinking in teams. You may get a job because of functional expertise (e.g., as a finance major), but your career is likely to take you into many different areas of the firm and demand more general skills. You may have to be a jack-of-all-trades and a master of at least one.

One question that comes up in larger firms trying to become flatter is "How many people can effectively report to one manager?" We'll explore that question next.

Choosing the Appropriate Span of Control

span of control
The optimum number of subordinates a manager supervises or should supervise.

Span of control refers to the optimum number of subordinates a manager supervises or should supervise. There are many factors to consider when determining span of control. At lower levels, where work is standardized, it's possible to implement a wide span of control (15 to 40 workers). For example, one supervisor can be responsible for 20 or more workers who are assembling computers or cleaning up movie theatres. However, the number gradually narrows at higher levels of the organization, because work is less standardized and there's more need for face-to-face communication. Variables in span of control include the following:

1. **Capabilities of the manager**. The more experienced and capable a manager is, the broader the span of control can be. (More workers can report to that manager.)

2. **Capabilities of the subordinates**. The more the subordinates need supervision, the narrower the span of control should be. (Fewer workers report to one manager.)

3. **Complexity of the job**.
   a. *Geographical closeness*. The more concentrated the work area is, the broader the span of control can be.
   b. *Functional similarity*. The more similar the functions are, the broader the span of control can be.
   c. *Need for coordination*. The greater the need for coordination, the narrower the span of control might be.
   d. *Planning demands*. The more involved the plan, the narrower the span of control might be.
   e. *Functional complexity*. The more complex the functions are, the narrower the span of control might be.

Other factors to consider include the professionalism of superiors and subordinates and the number of new problems that occur in a day.

Figure 9.3 ties together span of control and tall and flat organization structures. The tall organization with a narrow span of control might describe a lawncare service with two supervisors who manage four employees each (two of whom are more experienced). The flat structure with a wide span of control may work in a plant where all 10 workers are picking crabmeat. The wider the span of control, the greater the decision-making power of each employee.

In business, the span of control varies widely. The number of people reporting to the president may range from 1 to 80 or more. The trend is to expand the span of control as organizations get rid of middle managers and hire more educated and talented lower-level employees. It's possible to increase the span of control as employees become more professional, as information technology makes it possible for managers to handle more information, and as employees take on more responsibility for self-management.

Departmentalization

Departmentalization is the dividing of organizational functions into separate units. The traditional way to departmentalize organizations is by function. Functional structure is the grouping of workers into departments based on similar skills, expertise, or resource use. There might be, for example, a production department, a transportation department, a finance department, an accounting department, a marketing department, a data processing department, and so on. Departmentalization enables employees to specialize and work together more efficiently. Other advantages include the following:

1. Employees can develop skills in depth and can progress within a department as they master those skills.

departmentalization
The dividing of organizational functions into separate units.

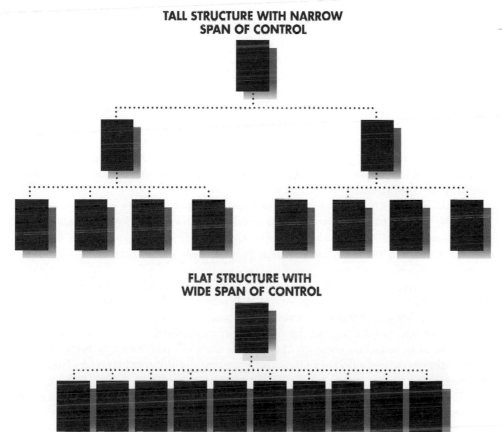

TALL STRUCTURE WITH NARROW SPAN OF CONTROL

FLAT STRUCTURE WITH WIDE SPAN OF CONTROL

FIGURE 9.3

NARROW VERSUS WIDE SPAN OF CONTROL

This figure describes two ways to structure an organization with the same number of employees. The tall structure with a narrow span of control has two managers who supervise four employees each. Changing to a flat surface with a wide span of control, the company could eliminate two managers and perhaps replace them with one or two employees, but the top manager would have to supervise 10 people instead of two.

2.   The company can achieve economies of scale in that it can centralize all the resources it needs and locate various experts in that area.

3.   There's good coordination within the function, and top management can easily direct and control various departments' activities.

As for disadvantages of departmentalization,

1.   There may be a lack of communication among the different departments. For example, production may be isolated from marketing so that the people making the product do not get the proper feedback from customers.

2.   Individual employees may begin to identify with their department and its goals rather than with the goals of the organization as a whole.

3.   The company's response to external changes may be slow.

4.   People may not be trained to take different managerial responsibilities; rather, they tend to become narrow specialists.

5.   People in the same department tend to think alike (engage in groupthink) and may need input from outside the department to become more creative.

Given the limitations of departmentalization, businesses are now trying to redesign their structures to optimize skill development while increasing communication among employees in different departments. The goal, remember, is to better serve customers and to win their loyalty.

Different Ways to Departmentalize Companies have tried various ways to departmentalize to better serve customers. Figure 9.4 shows five ways a firm can departmentalize. One form of departmentalization is by product. A book publisher might have a trade book department (books sold to the general public), a textbook department, and a technical book department. Customers for each type of book are different, so separate development and marketing processes are created for each type.

The most basic way to departmentalize, as we discussed earlier, is by function. This text is divided by business functions because such groupings are most common. Production, marketing, finance, human resource management, and accounting are all distinct functions calling for separate skills. Companies are now discovering, however, that functional separation isn't always the most responsive form of organization.

It makes more sense in some organizations to departmentalize by customer group. A pharmaceutical company, for example, might have one department that focuses on the consumer market, another that calls on hospitals (the institutional market), and another that targets doctors.

Some firms group their units by geographic location because customers vary so greatly by region. Canada may be considered one market area. Japan, Europe, and Korea may involve separate departments. Geographic locations may also be on a smaller scale; for example, by province (e.g., British Columbia) or by city (e.g., Sarnia) southwestern Ontario.

The decision about which way to departmentalize depends greatly on the nature of the product and the customers served. A few firms find that it's more efficient to separate activities by process. For example, a firm that makes leather coats may have one department cut the leather, another dye it, and a third sew the coat together.

Some firms use a combination of departmentalization techniques. For example, they could departmentalize simultaneously among the different layers by function, by geography, and by customers (see Figure 9.5 on page 266).

The development of the Internet has created whole new opportunities for reaching customers. Not only can you sell to customers directly over the Internet,

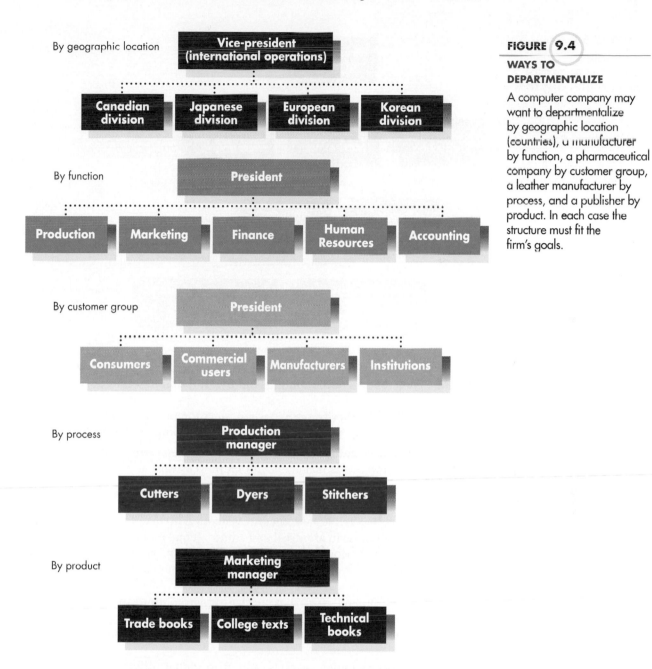

By geographic location

By function

By customer group

By process

By product

FIGURE 9.4

WAYS TO DEPARTMENTALIZE

A computer company may want to departmentalize by geographic location (countries), a manufacturer by function, a pharmaceutical company by customer group, a leather manufacturer by process, and a publisher by product. In each case the structure must fit the firm's goals.

but you can also interact with them, ask them questions, and provide them with any information they may want. Companies must now learn to coordinate the efforts made by their traditional departments and their Internet people to create a friendly, easy-to-use process for accessing information and buying goods and services. Not many firms have implemented such coordinated systems for meeting customer needs, but those that have are winning market share.[11]

Centralization versus Decentralization of Authority

Imagine for a minute that you are a top manager for a large retail chain such as Reitman's. Your temptation may be to maintain control over all your stores to maintain a uniformity of image and merchandise. You have noticed such control works well for McDonald's, why not Reitman's? The degree to which an organization allows

www.reitmans.com

www.mcdonalds.com

FIGURE 9.5

COMBINING DEPARTMENTALIZATION FORMS WITHIN ONE FIRM

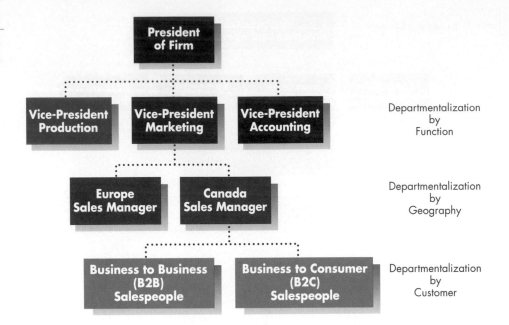

managers at the lower levels of the managerial hierarchy to make decisions determines the degree of decentralization that an organization practises.

centralized authority
Maintaining decision-making authority at the top level of management.

decentralized authority
Delegating decision-making authority to lower-level managers who are more familiar with local conditions.

- **Centralized authority** occurs when decision-making authority is maintained at the top level of management at the company's headquarters.
- **Decentralized authority** occurs when decision-making authority is delegated to lower-level managers and employees who are more familiar with local conditions than headquarters management could be.

At Reitman's, for example, customers in Vancouver are likely to demand clothing styles different from those in Montreal or Toronto. It makes sense, therefore, to give regional managers in various areas the authority to buy, price, and promote merchandise appropriate for each area. Such a *delegation of authority* is an example of decentralized management.

In contrast, McDonald's feels that purchasing, promotion, and other such decisions are best handled centrally. There's little need for each McDonald's restaurant to carry different food products. McDonald's would therefore lean toward centralized authority.

Today's rapidly changing markets, added to global differences in consumer tastes, tend to favour more decentralization and thus more delegation of authority. Even McDonald's has learned that its restaurants in England should offer tea, those in Germany should offer beer, those in Japan should offer rice, and so on. Rosenbluth International is a service organization in the travel industry. It too has decentralized so that its separate units can offer the kinds of services demanded in each region while still getting needed resources from corporate headquarters.

The Reaching Beyond Our Borders box "Ford Decentralizes to Meet the New Competition" describes how Ford Motor Company used the Internet to decentralize decision making.

CRITICAL THINKING

Can you see the connections between flat and tall structures, span of control, and centralization and decentralization? Does a flatter structure mean a wider span of control and thus more decentralization? Does a taller structure mean a narrower span of control and thus more centralized decision making?

REACHING BEYOND OUR BORDERS   www.fordmotorcompany.com
Ford Decentralizes to Meet the New Competition

Nothing has done more to unite organizations throughout the world than the emergence of the Internet. The Internet is a ready-made marketplace that consists of $1 trillion worth of computer power, network connections, and databases stuffed with information about individual consumers and groups. What's more amazing is that it's available free to anyone with a phone line, a personal computer, a modem, and an Internet browser—and it's open 24 hours a day, seven days a week. This may sound wonderful to you, but it is a tremendous challenge to traditional organizations. They simply cannot respond quickly enough to marketplace changes or reach global markets as quickly and efficiently as new companies can—companies designed to take advantage of the Internet. But what are they to do? How do they reorganize to match such competition?

The CEO of Ford Motor Company says that traditional companies have to become more nimble and more closely attuned to consumers. One source at Ford says, "You've got to break down the business into the smallest possible units to give the employees in them authority and accountability." (Throughout this text, we call that *empowerment*.) In the past, Ford centralized worldwide responsibility for functions such as product development, purchasing, design, and manufacturing. The new model decentralizes such decisions so that managers in Europe and South America can more readily adapt to consumers in those markets.

Of course, another way to compete with Internet firms is to start an Internet firm of your own or join one of the established firms. Even smaller firms can reach global markets by joining Amazon.com and selling their products online. Automobile companies can get in touch with consumers throughout the world and learn their preferences. Design and production can be placed anywhere as long as the input of the consumer is readily available. And it is on the Internet.

Sources: Kathleen Kerwin and Jack Ewing, "Nasser: Ford Be Nimble," *Business Week*, September 27, 1999, pp. 42–43; and "Ambitious Ford Aims High as It Sets Targets," *Birmingham Post*, January 12, 2001, p. 22.

PROGRESS CHECK

- What is bureaucracy, and why has it led to the need for restructuring organizations?
- Are businesses moving toward taller or flatter organizational structures? Centralized or decentralized decision making? Why?
- What are some reasons for having a narrow span of control? Is there any advantage to a wide span of control?
- What are the five ways to departmentalize a company?

ORGANIZATION MODELS

Now that we have explored the basic principles of organizational design and learned the benefits of flat versus tall organizations, we can explore in more depth the various ways to structure an organization to accomplish its goals. We will look at (1) line organizations, (2) line-and-staff organizations, (3) matrix organizations, and (4) cross-functional, self-managed teams. Figure 9.6 compares their advantages and disadvantages.

Line Organizations

A **line organization** is one in which there are direct two-way lines of responsibility, authority, and communication running from the top to the bottom and back to the top of the organization, with every employee reporting to only one specific supervisor. Many small businesses are organized this way. For example, a pizza parlour may

line organization
An organization in which there are direct two-way lines of responsibility, authority, and communication running from the top to the bottom and back to the top of the organization, with every employee reporting to only one specific supervisor.

have a general manager and a shift manager. All the general employees report to the shift manager, and the shift manager reports to the general manager.

A line organization has the advantages of having clearly defined responsibility and authority, being easy to understand, and providing one supervisor for each person. (Figure 9.1 is a visual example of a line organization.)

However, a line organization may have the disadvantages of being too inflexible, of having few specialists or experts to advise people along the line, of having long lines of communication, and of being unable to handle the complex decisions involved in an organization with thousands of sometimes unrelated products and tonnes of paperwork.

Line and Staff Organizations

To minimize the disadvantages of simple line organizations, most organizations today have both line and staff personnel.

FIGURE 9.6

TYPES OF ORGANIZATIONS

Each form of organization has its advantages and disadvantages.

	ADVANTAGES	DISADVANTAGES
Line	• Clearly defined responsibility and authority • Easy to understand • One supervisor for each person	• Too inflexible • Few specialists to advise • Long lines of communication • Unable to handle complex questions quickly
Line and staff	• Expert advice from staff to line personnel • Establishes lines of authority • Encourages co-operation and better communication at all levels	• Potential overstaffing • Potential overanalyzing • Lines of communication can get blurred • Staff frustrations because of lack of authority
Matrix	• Flexible • Encourages co-operation among departments • Can produce creative solutions to problems • Allows organization to take on new projects without adding to the organizational structure • Provides for more efficient use of organizational resources	• Costly and complex • Can confuse employees • Requires good interpersonal skills and co-operative managers and employees • Difficult to evaluate employees and to set up reward systems
Cross-functional, self-managed teams	• Greatly increases interdepartmental coordination and co-operation • Quicker response to customers and market conditions • Increased employee motivation and morale	• Some confusion over responsibility and authority • Perceived loss of control by management • Difficult to evaluate employees and to set up reward systems • Requires self-motivated and highly trained workers

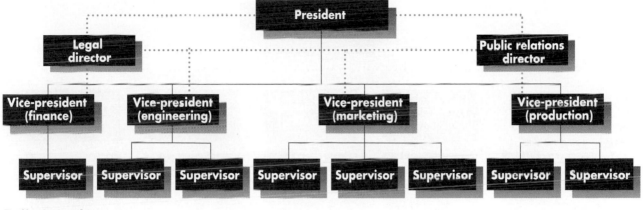

Staff relationships ··············
Line relationships ─────────

- **Line personnel** perform functions that contribute directly to the primary goals of the organization (e.g., making the product, distributing it, and selling it).
- **Staff personnel** perform functions that *advise* and *assist* line personnel in achieving their goals (e.g., marketing research, legal advising, and human resources).

Most organizations have benefited from the expert advice of staff assistants in areas such as safety, quality control, computer technology, human resources, and investing. Staff positions strengthen the line positions and are by no means inferior or lower paid. It is like having well-paid consultants on the organization's payroll.

Figure 9.7 is an example of what a line and staff organization may be like.

Matrix-Style Organizations

Both line and line and staff structures suffer from a certain inflexibility. Both have established lines of authority and communication and both work well in organizations with a relatively stable environment and slow product development (such as firms selling consumer products like toasters and refrigerators). In such firms, clear lines of authority and relatively fixed organizational structures are assets that assure efficient operations.

FIGURE 9.7

SIMPLE LINE AND STAFF ORGANIZATION
Note that the legal and public relations directors are not in the chain of command. They are advisers to the president and vice-presidents.

line personnel
Employees who perform functions that contribute directly to the primary goals of the organization.

staff personnel
Employees who perform functions that advise and assist line personnel in achieving their goals.

Janet Horter

In high-tech industries, technology and competition changes so rapidly that often traditional forms of organization simply won't work. They are being replaced with project management teams and other arrangements that bring together employees from many different areas of the firm. What do you see as the benefits and drawbacks of constant change for employees in high-tech industries?

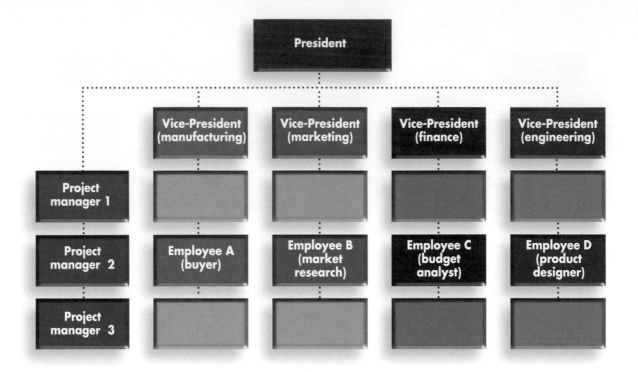

FIGURE 9.8

A MATRIX ORGANIZATION

In a matrix organization, project managers are in charge of teams made up of members of several departments. In this case, project manager 2 supervises employees A, B, C, and D. These employees are accountable not only to project manager 2, but also to the head of their individual departments. For example, employee B, a market researcher, reports to project manager 2 and to the vice-president of marketing.

matrix organization
Organization in which specialists from different parts of the organization are brought together to work on specific projects but still remain part of a line and staff structure.

www.boeing.com

www.lockheedmartin.com

Today's economic scene is dominated by new kinds of organizations in high-growth industries. These include industries such as telecommunications, robotics, biotechnology, and aerospace. In such industries, new projects are developed quickly, competition with similar projects elsewhere is stiff, and the life cycle of new ideas is very short. The economic, technological, and competitive environments are changing rapidly. In such organizations, the emphasis is on new-product development, creativity, special projects, rapid communication, and interdepartmental teamwork.

That environment led to the popularity of the **matrix organization**, in which specialists from different parts of the organization are brought together to work on specific projects, but still remain part of a line and staff structure (see Figure 9.8). In other words, a project manager can borrow from different departments to help design and market new-product ideas or complete complex projects.

Matrix structures were developed in the aerospace industry at firms such as Boeing and Lockheed. The structure is now used in banking, management consulting firms, accounting firms, ad agencies, and school systems. Advantages of a matrix organization structure include the following:

- It gives flexibility to managers when assigning people to projects, as managers have many employees to choose from.
- It encourages intraorganizational co-operation and teamwork.
- It can result in creative solutions to problems such as new-product development.
- It provides for more efficient use of organizational resources.

Although it works well in some organizations, the matrix style doesn't work well in others. Disadvantages are that:

- It is complex and costly.
- It can cause confusion among employees as to where their loyalty belongs— to the project manager or their functional unit. (There is a potential conflict between two bosses.)

- It requires good interpersonal skills and co-operative employees and managers.
- It can only be a temporary solution to a long-term problem.

If it seems to you that matrix organizations violate some traditional managerial principles, you're right. Normally a person can't work effectively for two bosses. (Who has the real authority? Which directive has the first priority: the one from the project manager or the one from the employee's immediate supervisor?) In reality, however, the system functions more effectively than you might imagine. To develop a new product, a project manager may be given temporary authority to "borrow" line personnel from engineering, production, marketing, and other line functions. Together, they work to complete the project and then return to their regular positions. Thus, no one really reports to more than one manager at a time. The effectiveness of matrix organizations in high-tech firms has led to the adoption of similar concepts in many firms, including such traditional firms as Rubbermaid. During most of the 1990s, Rubbermaid turned out an average of one new product every day using the team concept from matrix management.

A potential problem with matrix management, however, is that the project teams are *not permanent*. They are formed to solve a problem or develop a new product, and then they break up. There is little chance for cross-functional learning, because experts from each function are together for such little time.

The newest trend, therefore, is to develop *permanent teams* and to empower them to work closely with suppliers, customers, and others to quickly and efficiently bring out new, high-quality products while giving great service.[12] The teams are often self-managed. That means that the members of the team don't have to ask a manager whether or not they can do what they want to do to please the customer. They automatically have the freedom and authority to do so.

For empowerment and/or self-managed teams to work effectively, the organization has to be changed to support that new orientation. Moving from a manager-driven to an employee-driven or team-driven company isn't easy. Managers often resist giving up their authority over workers, while workers often resist the responsibility that comes with self-management. Nonetheless, many of the world's leading organizations are moving in that direction. They're trying to develop an organizational design that best serves the needs of all stakeholders ➤**P.137**◄—employees, customers, shareholders, and the community.

Cross-Functional, Self-Managed Teams

The matrix style of organization eventually led to cross-functional teams. **Cross-functional teams** are groups of employees from different departments who work together on a semipermanent basis (as opposed to the temporary teams established in matrix-style organizations). Often the teams are empowered to make decisions on their own without seeking the approval of management. That's why the teams are called *self-managed*. The barriers between design, engineering, marketing, distribution, and other functions fall as members of each department work on teams.

Campbell Soup Canada (see the Spotlight on Big Business box "Campbell Soup in Canada: A Success Story of Self-Managed Teams") was very successful in converting to self-managed teams. These cross-functional teams of 10 to 30 people were also able to effectively carry out continual improvement.

cross-functional teams
Groups of employees from different departments who work together on a semipermanent basis (as opposed to the temporary teams established in matrix-style organizations).

Working together in teams is much different from working on your own. You must become multi-skilled, performing your own function, but also be able to understand and relate to people in other activities.

Bruce Ayres/Tony Stone Images

Extranets and Intranets

extranet
An extension of the Internet that connects suppliers, customers, and other organizations via secure Web sites.

intranet
A set of communication links within one company that travel over the Internet but are closed to public access.

www.wellsfargo.com

www.sgi.com

www.hallmark.com

One of the latest organizational trends is to link firms on an extranet. An **extranet** is an extension of the Internet that connects suppliers, customers, and other organizations via secure Web sites. The Spotlight on Small Business box "Networking to Win" gives an example of how small firms combine to form an extranet.

As another example, Wal-Mart is connected to its suppliers via an extranet. It is made up of linked intranets. An **intranet** is a set of communication links within one company that travel over the Internet but are closed to public access.[15] Service organizations like Wells Fargo Bank and manufacturing firms like Silicon Graphics both use intranets.

Although intranets are used mostly at larger firms, smaller firms are using them as well. The idea is to link everyone in the firm electronically so they can communicate freely and work together on projects. For example, workers at Hallmark once pasted creative ideas on a bulletin board for others to comment on. Because of limited space on the physical board, old cards were simply not available for easy comparison. Today, old and new cards are available on the intranet; anyone in the company can make comments about the cards and can adapt them at any time. Any information a Hallmark employee wants others in the firm to see can be placed on the intranet. A company can also make such information available to employees at suppliers and dealers if they are part of an extranet. We shall explore intranets and extranets more fully in Chapter 11.

PROGRESS CHECK

- What are the trends in tall versus flat organizations, narrow versus wide spans of control, departmentalization, and centralization versus decentralization of authority?
- Can you cite the advantages and disadvantages of line, line-and-staff, matrix, and cross-functional organizational forms?
- What is the difference between a matrix form of organization and cross-functional teams?
- What are extranets and intranets?

SPOTLIGHT ON SMALL BUSINESS   www.ibizcenter.com/extranets.htm
Networking to Win

Networking helps large and small organizations to compete in global markets. Beginning in 1989, for example, 3,500 small Danish firms organized into networks (small groups of businesses that work together). In less than two years, they had made a substantial contribution to completely reversing a three-decades-long deficit in the country's trade exports. Networking thus creates jobs. CD (Corporate Design) Line is one of the Danish success stories. A network of 14 textile firms produces part of a complete collection: shirts, suits, skirts, women's knitwear, ties, scarves, and more. Marketing the entire collection together benefits all the firms. Together they hired a quality manager and set up salespeople in their best foreign markets: Sweden and Germany. They jointly contract with famous designers.

They even share an electronic data interchange network on a cost-sharing basis.

Together, this network can now compete with large companies. Smaller organizations use networking to purchase co-operatively, to market jointly, to combine research and development, to establish quality programs, to share in distribution research and costs, and more.

This kind of network is now called an extranet. Some people believe extranets have become essential for small business to compete.

Source: Jessica Lipnack and Jeffrey Stamps, *The TeamNet Factor* (Essex Junction, VT: Oliver Wight Publications, 1993) this material is used with permission of John Wiley & Sons Inc.; Jason Myers, "Rewire Your Business Plan," *Canadian Business*, June 25/July 9, 1999, p. 198.

THE RESTRUCTURING PROCESS AND TOTAL QUALITY

It's not easy to move from an organization dominated by managers to one that relies heavily on self-managed teams. How you restructure an organization depends on the status of the present system. If the system already has a customer focus, but isn't working well, a total quality management approach may work.

Total quality management (TQM) is the practice of striving for maximum customer satisfaction by ensuring quality from all departments. TQM calls for *continual improvement of present processes*. Processes are sets of activities strung together for a reason, such as the process for handling a customer's order. The process may consist of getting the order in the mail, opening it, sending it to someone to fill, putting the order into a package, and sending it out. In Chapter 10 we will review the topic of TQM and its importance in production management.

Continuous improvement (CI) means constantly improving the way the organization does things so that customer needs can be satisfied. Many of the companies spotlighted in this book practise it. Meat-packer Schneider Foods of Kitchener, Ontario, attributes its success in overcoming difficult adjustments to market changes to CI.[16] Another Canadian enthusiast for CI is PanCanadian Petroleum Ltd., which has been applying it in engineering and production:

> Two years into CI, PanCanadian smells a winner. The program has moved in-house, with a squad of company coaches taking over from the TeamPro consultants. Plans are afoot to introduce it into the finance department and to create work teams from different departments.
>
> The early experiments uncapped a vast reserve of creativity. The next step is to give this force some direction without slipping back into the old autocratic style.[17]

It's possible, in an organization with few layers of management and a customer focus, that new computer software and employee training could lead to a team-oriented approach with few problems. In bureaucratic organizations with many layers of management, however, TQM is not useful. Continual improvement doesn't work when the whole process is being done incorrectly. When an organization needs dramatic changes, only reengineering will do. **Reengineering** is the fundamental rethinking and radical redesign of organizational processes to achieve dramatic improvements in critical measures of performance. Note the words *radical redesign* and *dramatic improvements*.

At IBM Credit Corporation, for example, the process for handling a customer's request for credit once went through a five-step process that took an average of six days. By completely reengineering the customer-request process, IBM Credit cut its processing time from six days to four hours! In reengineering, narrow, task-oriented jobs become multidimensional. Employees who once did as they were told now make decisions on their own. Functional departments lose their reason for being. Managers stop acting like supervisors and instead behave like coaches. Workers focus more on the customers' needs and less on their bosses' needs. Attitudes and values change in response to new incentives. Practically every aspect of the organization is transformed, often beyond recognition.

Can you see how reengineering is often necessary to change a firm from a managerial orientation to one based on cross-functional self-managed teams?[18] Reengineering may also be necessary to adapt an organization to fit into a virtual network. Remember, reengineering involves radical redesign and dramatic improvements. Not all organizations need such dramatic change. In fact, because of the complexity of the process, many reengineering efforts fail. In firms where reengineering is not feasible, *restructuring* may do. Restructuring (which we defined earlier in this chapter) involves making relatively minor changes to an organization in response to a changing environment. For example, a firm might add an Internet marketing component to the marketing department. That is a restructuring move, but it is not drastic enough to be called reengineering.

total quality management (TQM)
Striving for maximum customer satisfaction by ensuring quality from all departments.

continuous improvement (CI)
Constantly improving the way the organization does things so that customer needs can be better satisfied.

www.schneiders.ca

www.pcp.ca

reengineering
The rethinking and radical redesign of organizational processes to achieve dramatic improvements in critical measures of performance.

www.ibm.com

Why do some reengineering efforts fail? Given the dramatic changes that occur when companies adopt cross-functional, self-managed teams, what prevents the majority of companies from adopting such an organizational structure?

Given the flexibility and education requirements of empowered employees, what changes must occur in Canadian schools to prepare students for such jobs?

How Restructuring Affects Organizational Design

We have already noted that many firms are discovering that the key to long-term success in a competitive market is to empower front-line people (often in teams) to respond quickly to customer wants and needs. That means restructuring the firm to make front-line workers more important in the organization. For example, doctors have long been treated as the most important people in hospitals, pilots are the focus of airlines, and professors are the central focus of universities—yet front-desk people in hotels, clerks in department stores, and tellers in banks haven't been considered the *key* personnel. Instead, managers have been considered the key people, and they have been responsible for "managing" the front-line people. The organization chart in a typical firm looked something like the organization pyramid shown earlier in Figure 9.2.

inverted organization
An organization that has contact people at the top and the chief executive officer at the bottom of the organization chart.

www.novacare.com

The most advanced service organizations have turned the traditional organization structure upside down. An **inverted organization** has contact people at the top and top management at the bottom. There are few layers of management, and the manager's job is to assist and support front-line people, not boss them around. Figure 9.10 illustrates the difference between an inverted and a traditional organizational structure.

A good example of an inverted organization is NovaCare, a provider of rehabilitation care. At its top are some 5,000 physical, occupational, and speech therapists. The rest of the organization is structured to serve those therapists. Managers consider the therapists to be their bosses, and the manager's job is to support the therapists by arranging contacts with nursing homes, handling accounting and credit activities, and providing training.

Companies based on this organization structure support front-line personnel with internal and external databases, advanced communication systems, and professional assistance. Naturally, this means that front-line people have to be better educated, better trained, and better paid than in the past. It takes a lot of trust for top managers to implement such a system—but when they do, the payoff in customer satisfaction and in profits is often well worth the effort. In the past, managers controlled information—and that gave them power. In more progressive organizations, everyone shares information and that gives everyone power. Figure 9.11 lists some of the dramatic organizational changes that are occurring in the twenty-first century.

Working in an inverted organization is much different from working in a firm with a more traditional structure. Front-line employees are given more training and responsibility, and are expected to do more. These factors make the job more exciting and motivating.

Under what conditions would an inverted organization likely be effective? How must front-line workers be treated, given their greater importance, by support personnel and top management? If top management is now at the bottom, what does this mean to their roles, authority, and compensation?

FIGURE 9.10

COMPARISON OF AN INVERTED ORGANIZATION STRUCTURE AND A TRADITIONAL ORGANIZATION STRUCTURE

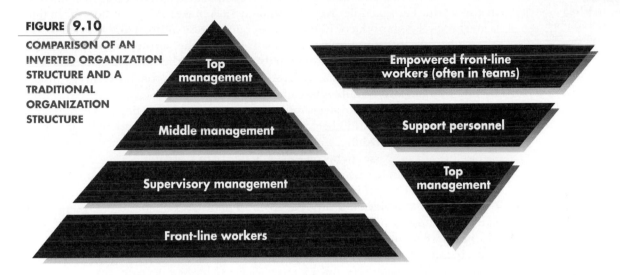

Traditional Organization   Inverted Organization

CHARACTERISTIC	20TH CENTURY	21ST CENTURY
Organization	The Pyramid	The Web or Network
Focus	Internal	External
Style	Structured	Flexible
Source of Strength	Stability	Change
Structure	Self-sufficiency	Interdependencies
Resources	Atom—physical assets	Bits—information
Operations	Vertical integration	Virtual integration
Products	Mass production	Mass customization
Reach	Domestic	Global
Financials	Quarterly	Real-time
Inventories	Months	Hours
Strategy	Top-down	Bottom-up
Leadership	Dogmatic	Inspirational
Workers	Employees	Employees and free agents
Job Expectations	Security	Personal growth
Motivation	To complete	To build
Improvements	Incremental	Revolutionary
Quality	Affordable best	No compromise

FIGURE 9.11

CHANGING ORGANIZATIONAL DESIGN

Source: *Business Week*, August 28, 2000, p.87.

The Movement toward Outsourcing

Traditionally, organizations have tried to complete all functions themselves. That is, each organization had a separate department for accounting, finance, marketing, production, and so on. Today's organizations are looking to other organizations to help them in areas where they are not able to generate world-class quality. Total quality management demands that organizations compare each function against the best in the world. For example, K2 is a company that makes skis, snowboards, in-line skates, and related products. It studied the compact-disc industry and learned to use ultraviolet inks to print graphics on skis. It went to the aerospace industry to get Piezo technology to reduce vibration in its snowboards (the aerospace industry uses the technology for wings on planes). And, finally, it learned from the cable-TV industry how to braid layers of fiberglass and carbon to make skis.[19]

competitive benchmarking
Rating an organization's practices, processes, and products against the world's best.

www.hbc.com/zellers

www.walmart.com

www.ic.gc.ca

www.statcan.ca

outsourcing
Assigning various functions, such as accounting and legal work, to outside organizations.

www.gallo.com

Competitive benchmarking is rating an organization's practices, processes, and products against the world's best.[20] For example, Zellers may compare itself to Wal-Mart to see what, if anything, Wal-Mart does better. Zellers would then try to improve its practices or processes to become even better than Wal-Mart.

Benchmarking has become a significant activity in Canada. Governments and large and small companies are all involved in procedures to discover and apply the best practices available. Industry Canada and Statistics Canada have accumulated extensive statistics on the use of benchmarking in a variety of industries. Some examples are breweries, flour mixing and cereal production, electronic computing, paperboard manufacturing, musical instruments, and the recording industry. The Alliance of Manufacturers and Exporters has established an extensive Promoting Business Excellence (PROBE) program relying largely on the IBM Consulting Group in Canada.[21]

Knowledge is increasing and technology is developing so fast that companies can only maintain a leading edge by benchmarking everything they do against the best in all industries. That's how K2 was able to find the best materials and processes for making its skis. Think of how you could apply this concept in your own life. Whom might you study to learn the best way to prepare for classes and exams? Whom might you talk with to learn how to get at the company best suited to use your skills?

As global competition continues to heat up, the idea of benchmarking is attracting increasing attention. Sometimes managers can become overzealous in their attempts to find out what their strongest competitors are doing, whether in marketing, production, or research. It is important that companies monitor these activities to ensure that managers do not overreach the boundaries of ethical behaviour. (See the Ethical Dilemma box "When Is Learning Unethical?" at the start of the chapter.)

If an organization can't do as well as the best in any particular area, such as shipping, it will try to outsource the function to an organization that is the best (e.g., UPS or FedEx). **Outsourcing** is assigning various functions, such as accounting, production, security, maintenance, and legal work, to outside organizations.[22] Some functions, such as information management and marketing, may be too important to assign to outside firms. In that case, the organization should benchmark on the best firms and restructure their departments to try to be equally good. It is important to monitor benchmarking efforts so that they don't overreach the bounds of ethical behaviour.

As an example, Gallo Winery doesn't grow most of its own grapes. Instead, it sticks to what it does best: producing and marketing (including distributing) wine products. Gallo spends more money on market research than its primary competitors and thus knows more about the market for wines. It also has the most up-to-date information and distribution system. Gallo isn't as skilled in retailing and promotion, so it outsources those functions.

ESTABLISHING A SERVICE-ORIENTED CULTURE

Figure 9.12 summarizes the differences between a bureaucratic and structure customer focused organization. Any organizational change is bound to cause some stress and resistance among members of the firm. Therefore, a shift from bureaucracy to a customer focus should be accompanied by the establishment of an organizational culture that facilitates such change. **Organizational (or corporate) culture** may be defined as widely shared values within an organization that provide coherence and co-operation to achieve common goals. Recall from the chapter opening profile that establishing the right culture was the first of four things that Carly Fiorina focused on at Hewlett-Packard. Usually the culture of an organization is reflected in stories, traditions, and myths.

Cultures are formed in various ways. The vision, mission, goals, and objectives of an organization are critical for conveying the culture to the employees. As noted in Chapter 8, leaders define all these elements in the planning stage of the management process. Their leadership is critical in communicating and sharing this information with others throughout the organization.

It is obvious from visiting any McDonald's restaurant that every effort has been made to maintain a culture that emphasizes quality, service, cleanliness, and value. These values are reflected in each physical location, the goods offered, and the service provided by each employee. This is further reinforced with each newly hired employee who is trained in these beliefs. For a culture to be effective, the values must be supportive of the organization's direction.

According to Steven McShane, organizational stories and legends are effective at communicating cultural values. Stories advise people what or what not to do:[23]

> Research on organizational stories reveals that they tend to answer one or more of the following questions: How does the boss react to mistakes? What events are so important that people get fired? Who, if anyone, can break the rules? How do people rise to the top of this organization? How will the organization deal with crises?[24]

Therefore, depending on what you have heard, seen, or witnessed, these stories and legends communicate the organization's values.

Rituals are "the programmed routines of daily organizational life that dramatize the organization's culture."[25] Rituals may range from how people communicate with each other to whether breaks and full lunchtimes are taken. For example, an organization that believes in face to face communication and where employees regularly take breaks would indicate a culture much different from another organization where most communication is conducted via e-mail and breaks are rarely taken. Each organization would have a different "feel."

organizational (or corporate) culture
Widely shared values within an organization that provide coherence and co-operation to achieve common goals.

rituals
The programmed routines of daily organizational life that dramatize the organization's culture.

BUREAUCRATIC	CUSTOMER-FOCUSED
Coordination from the top	Self-management
Top-down chain of command	Bottom-up power relationships
Many rules and regulations	Employees free to make decisions
Departmentalization by function	Cross-functional teams
Specialization	Integration and co-operation
One firm does it all	Outsourcing
Management controls information	Information goes to all
Largely domestic orientation	Global orientation
Focus on external customers	Focus on both internal and external customers

FIGURE 9.12

BUREAUCRATIC STRUCTURE VERSUS CUSTOMER-FOCUSED ORGANIZATION

4. Divide the class into teams of five. This is the assignment: Imagine that your firm has been asked to join a virtual network. You are a producer of athletic shoes. What might you do to minimize the potential problems of being involved with a virtual corporation? Begin by defining a virtual corporation and listing the potential problems. Also, list the benefits of being part of such a system.

5. Ten years from today, you are operating a successful small business with 35 employees. What kind of organizational structure will you favour, centralized or decentralized? What factors will help you decide? Explain.

TAKING IT TO THE NET

Purpose:

To explore the nature of teams in a business environment.

Exercise:

1. Using a search vehicle like Canada.com, Yahoo, or AltaVista, click on a business, finance, or economics choice and scan some recent business headlines for names of well-known large Canadian companies. Try to contact a company by e-mail and ask human resource management for an *organization chart* or an *organogram*. If you have no success try a major bank, Nortel Networks <www.nortelnetworks.com>, or Bombardier <www.bombardier.com>. When you get a couple of charts, study them and record how many levels of management you can find. Bring the charts to class for discussion about how they meet the modern challenge of less bureaucracy.

PRACTISING MANAGEMENT DECISIONS

CASE 1

RESTRUCTURING HITS MANAGEMENT POSITIONS

Tom Peters, co-author of *In Search of Excellence*, believes the staffs of the Fortune 500 companies are still hopelessly bloated. Peters feels that many of those managers with MBA degrees got to top positions without ever getting real-world experience in designing, making, selling, and servicing products. They tend to rely on technology rather than people for their answers—and ignore the retraining and redeployment of the workforce.

Peters recommends that managers get out of their offices and ask their workers how to make the firm more productive. Then they should visit customers and ask what they would like to see changed. Management is no longer viewed as simply an intellectual position involving planning, organizing, leading, and controlling. It is now a hands-on job, with managers and employees working as a team to make the firm more productive. Those who used to sit and ponder are gone and more cuts will be coming.

Since Peter's comments about U.S. businesses in 1991, Canadian businesses have made drastic reductions in managerial staff. Many smaller companies have let people go. Even top-flight managers with

good work records are not immune to the budget axe. Various studies have indicated that typical 40-year-old white-collar workers will change jobs two or three times during the rest of their careers, at least once voluntarily. This includes a vast group of real estate managers, central purchasing agents, human resource specialists, futurologists, economists, planners, and analysts of all kinds.

Decision Questions

1. What does the reduction in middle-management jobs mean for tomorrow's undergraduate and graduate business students?
2. How would you, as the president of a firm, decide which managers to let go?
3. What are the advantages and disadvantages of cutting staff in areas like human resources, quality control, planning, and auditing? Could there be serious consequences from rapid cutbacks in management?
4. What alternative does a company have when it seems top-heavy with staff other than firing them all and becoming leaner and meaner in one swift action?

Practising Management Decisions

CASE 2

A DRASTIC RESTRUCTURING AT MOHAWK OIL

Every company follows its own path to restructuring. Some close regional offices and plants; others sell off previously acquired companies to concentrate on their core businesses. Still others downsize drastically or adopt massive training and development programs for their managers and employees. But Bill Duncan did something quite different at Mohawk Oil Canada Ltd. of Burnaby, B.C.

When he became CEO in January 1991, the company was in very serious trouble. He had been with Mohawk since 1976 when, at age 24, he was hired as controller. Now he was in charge of a company that had not reacted to changing conditions in its market. From a tiny start in 1961, Mohawk had grown to become a major independent oil distributor in western Canada with 1,260 employees and 250 retail outlets. Price wars and meeting new environmental regulations had hit Mohawk hard, and it was practically bankrupt.

Despite the urgency of the situation, Bill Duncan did not rush into action. After lengthy, careful meetings with outside consultants and a team of Mohawk employees, he led the company through a revolutionary change. The company-owned stations would become franchise dealers and outlets. Many Mohawk employees became franchisees. The plan would see the number of employees drop to 200, and revenue would not include franchise fees and royalties.

Because the employees were involved in the whole process and in the decisions, the suggestions were well received and the transformation was successful. Mohawk emerged from a string of losses to show a profit of $4 million in 1992, and by 1994 it was in good enough shape to go public.

Decision Questions

1. Why do you think Duncan took such a radical step rather than the more common one of cutting staff to reduce costs?
2. The results were good, but does that mean that an alternative course could not have been successful?
3. Do you agree with Duncan's decision? Why?
4. As a general rule, do you think drastic surgery in a serious situation is better than small doses of medicine?

Source: Liz Davis, "Back From the Brink," *Profit*, December–January 1996, p. 28.

CBC VIDEO CASE   www.cbc.ca

REVENGE OF THE MIDDLE MANAGER

The 1990s trend of downsizing, characterized by widespread removal of middle managers, has led to problems and may have backfired in some cases. Many companies are finding it harder to get things done, so productivity drops. Further, there is the example of a shipbuilding company having to spend a lot of money and time on training now that middle management is so thin. In addition, fraud is becoming more common as employees find there is less supervision. Employers usually do not even think about the possibility of opening the door to fraud when they reduce the number of middle managers. Companies do not like to mention the rising problem of fraud but insurance companies that pay for many of these frauds are increasingly concerned.

Discussion Questions

1. Is it possible that the growing problem of fraud and lower productivity as shown in the video arose from the company having eliminated too many managers? Explain.
2. The kind of fraud referred to in the video is called "white-collar crime." Could it be that globalization is a greater contributing factor than the downsizing of middle managers? Explain.
3. Have you ever had a job where there was little supervision and you were expected to solve your problems yourself? If not, would you like such a job because it would give the chance to make your own judgments and decisions? Do you think your productivity would rise in such circumstances? Explain.

Source: *Venture*, show number 724, October 12, 1999, running time 6:17.

CHAPTER 10

Managing Production and Operations

LEARNING GOALS

AFTER YOU HAVE READ AND STUDIED THIS CHAPTER, YOU SHOULD BE ABLE TO

1. Define *operations management*.

2. Describe the operations management functions that are involved in both the manufacturing and service sectors.

3. Discuss the problem of measuring productivity in the service sector, and tell how new technology is leading to productivity gains in service companies.

4. Explain process planning and the various manufacturing processes being used today.

5. Describe the seven new manufacturing techniques that have made companies more productive: just-in-time inventory control, Internet purchasing, flexible manufacturing, lean manufacturing, mass customization, competing in time, and computer-aided design and manufacturing.

6. Explain the use of PERT and Gantt charts.

Erik Brinkman Reinvents the Wheel

Courtesy of Erik Brinkman

Erik Brinkman's design team at Interactive Design Studios, based in Victoria, B.C., came up with a simple, revolutionary invention that eliminates friction wherever things turn, such as with wheels, shafts, and so forth. Scroller rotary motion allows rotation around a shaft, motors, or bicycle wheels by using a continuous band between the shaft and four rollers.

The whole process is now well advanced and the company is discussing financial and organizational progress with investment advisers. Since Brinkman's patenting of the invention, "corporations have beaten a path to the design group's door," reports Brinkman. So have reporters from around the world. He says there are endless applications for this invention. He encourages inquiring companies to play around with the idea a little before coming up with a specific request for a licence to use the patent.

Brinkman and his wife made a crude working model by cutting a broom handle into five pieces, with one serving as a shaft and four as rollers around it. The whole contraption was held together by a strip of paper wound partially around the shaft and then around the four rollers. The strip of paper was made into a continuous piece with Scotch tape.

Modern communication technology made it possible for members of Interactive's design team to be located on three continents—North America, Europe, and Asia (Japan). Six of them worked on the scroller technology. Actually, the original problem facing the team was how to produce a greaseless bicycle for Third World countries where grease is not readily available.

Development has now reached the stage where the bike has actually been designed. Imagine a bicycle without spokes, cables or brakes, requiring no grease, that is foldable, and completely recyclable. Furthermore, it "takes a lot of the load off the rider's knees and makes it look like it wants to jump." Brinkman "designed it to look like an animal on the run."

Brinkman refers to his company as a "cyberspace think tank," with the Internet eliminating borders to research and development (R&D) opportunities. Today, IDS consists of three separate divisions: research, development, and consulting. While IDS works on its own projects, companies and inventors are also encouraged to bring their R&D to IDS for "an infusion." IDS has created a niche by focusing on risky or time-consuming projects as well as reinventing things.

Current projects include Cyclops (an extremely smooth, simple, and inexpensive rotary compressor), an airless tire, a snowmobile that floats (since half of all snowmobile-related deaths are caused by drowning), a robot foot that will maintain balance walking on irregular surfaces, and a fractional fund (an inside-out mutual fund that allows investment in *parts* of a single company instead of a group of similar companies). For more information on these and other projects, visit the company's Web site at www.ids.bc.ca.

This story points to the importance of R&D in developing new products and trying to reinvent current products. R&D is critical to the production and operations functions. This chapter will describe the operations management functions that are involved in both the manufacturing and service sectors, and it will highlight new manufacturing techniques.

One final note: Erik Brinkman is almost totally blind.

Sources: Communications from Erik Brinkman, September 1999; interview with Erik Brinkman, July 11, 1996; "Canadian Reinvents the Wheel," *Globe and Mail, Report on Business*, December 27, 1995, p. B7; www.ids.bc.ca.

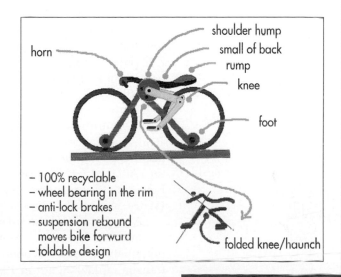

horn
shoulder hump
small of back
rump
knee
foot

folded knee/haunch

- 100% recyclable
- wheel bearing in the rim
- anti-lock brakes
- suspension rebound moves bike forward
- foldable design

ETHICAL DILEMMA

Effect of Relocation on Small Towns

In this chapter you will see that companies engage in a never-ending battle to improve productivity to be more competitive. They automate, integrate newer technologies, use less or better material, modernize, and downsize their workforces, but they also relocate factories and offices and contract out a lot of their work to other companies.

The last two activities often mean that ethical issues are raised. When a company closes down a facility in a small town where it may be the main, or the only, source of jobs, it obviously has a serious impact on the lives of the inhabitants in that town. The same problem, perhaps to a lesser extent, arises when the company outsources work previously done in its town location. This has happened in several Canadian (and American) small towns and is still occurring today. Does the company have an obligation to consider the serious impact of such actions on its employees, their families, and the small retailers who depend on them as customers? Should a company—can it—do anything? Think about these questions as you review the chapter. At the end we will attempt to answer them.

CANADA TODAY

Canada is a large industrial country with many major industries. We are one of the largest producers in the world of forest products, with plants in nearly all provinces turning out a vast array of wood, furniture, and paper products. There are giant aluminum mills in Quebec and B.C.; auto and automotive plants in Ontario and Quebec; aircraft plants in Ontario, Quebec, and Manitoba. Oil, natural gas, and coal are produced in Alberta, Saskatchewan, Newfoundland, Nova Scotia, and B.C. and processed there or in other provinces; a vast array of metals and minerals come from all parts of Canada. These are only some of the thousands of components, products, and natural resources produced or processed in Canada.

Canada is now facing some serious challenges to its ability to remain a modern, competitive, industrial country. For some of the ethical implications of this, see the Ethical Dilemma box "Effect of Relocation on Small Towns." Today's business climate is characterized by constant and restless change and dislocation, as ever newer technologies and increasing global competition force companies to respond quickly to these challenges. Many factors account for our difficulties in the world's competitive race. Among them are inadequate improvement in productivity and unrelenting competition from Japan, Germany, and more recently from China and other Southeast Asian countries; inadequate education and retraining programs for our workforce; our "branch plant economy," whereby many subsidiaries are owned by U.S. parent companies and profits are mostly returned to these foreign-based companies rather then invested in Canada, our constant brain drain to the United States; too little money for research and development; and problems created by the free trade agreement with the United States and Mexico.

Despite these challenges, Canada continues to rank high in competitiveness against other nations. Our exact ranking is difficult to determine, as there is some dispute among the different bodies that conduct the evaluations. Statistics Canada, the Alliance of Exporters and Manufacturers Canada, the Organization for Economic Cooperation and Development (OECD), the World Economic Forum (WEF), and other bodies are trying to come to some agreement.

As an example, the prestigious WEF conducts the yearly Global Competitive Report. This report is a key indicator of competitiveness and it measures a country's potential for future economic growth using per capita gross domestic product. Canada ranked eighth in 1996, fourth in 1997, and fifth in both 1998 and 1999.[1]

In 2000, Canada's ranking fell to seventh place but moved up to third place in 2001.[2] Clearly, the challenges indicated earlier are impacting not only our placement, but also that of other countries.

Research and Development

According to the Canadian Oxford Dictionary, **research and development (R&D)** is defined as "work directed towards the innovation, introduction, and improvement of products and processes." The opening Profile demonstrates how Erik Brinkman, one of many entrepreneurs in Canada, leads his firm to continuously develop its products and those of other inventors. If Canada is to continue to be productive and competitive, it must focus its efforts and resources in the area of R&D.

In the Survey of Innovation conducted in 1999 by Statistics Canada, respondents indicated that the three most important objectives of innovation are to improve product quality, to increase production capacity, and to extend product range. Firms must continuously strive not only to improve the quality of current products, but also to generate new products that will exceed the expectations of their end users. R&D provides the source of this information.

Figure 10.1 outlines Canada's top 10 corporate R&D spenders in 2000. As you may note, five of these organizations are involved in the communications industry. This is not surprising, given the rapid growth and business potential that this industry is reflecting today. In Chapter 11, the importance of technology will be reviewed and this discussion will support the large amount of R&D dollars being spent.

research and development (R&D)
Defined as "work directed towards the innovation, introduction, and improvement of products and processes."

www.researchinfosource.com/top100.html

Research Infosource publishes an in-depth report on Canadian R&D trends. To view the 2001 report, which includes the top 100 R&D spending firms, as well as spending by industry, visit its Web site.

FIGURE 10.1

CANADA'S TOP CORPORATE R&D SPENDERS IN 2000

Rank			R&D Expenditures			Revenue	R&D Ratio	
2000	1999	Company	FY2000 ($million)	FY1999 ($million)	%Change 1999–2000	FY2000 ($million)	R&D as % of Revenue	Industry
1	1	Nortel Networks Corporation*	$5,948.2	$4,548.0	30.8	$44,991.2	13.2	Comm/telcom equipment
2	2	Pratt & Whitney Canada Corp. (fs)	$331.0	$335.0	–1.2	$2,081.0	15.9	Aerospace
3	6	Magna International Inc.*	$246.5	$167.9	46.8	$15,613.9	1.6	Automotive
4	4	Ericsson Canada Inc. (fs)	$237.8	$200.6	18.6	$694.2	34.3	Comm/telcom equipment
5	5	ATI Technologies*	$224.3	$171.1	31.0	$2,037.8	11.0	Computer equipment
6	16	PMC Sierra, Inc. (fs)	$203.0	$70.0	190.0	$635.0	32.0	Electronic parts and components
7	3	Atomic Energy of Canada Limited	$173.4	$203.6	–14.8	$551.9	31.4	Energy
8	30	JDS Uniphase Ltd.*	$168.4	$40.1	319.8	$2,124.4	7.9	Comm/telcom equipment
9	7	Mitel Corporation+	$152.9	$149.8	2.1	$1,396.5	10.9	Comm/telcom equipment
10	9	Bombardier Inc.	$132.2	$127.0	4.1	$13,618.5	1.0	Aerospace
99	83	Genetronics Biomedical Ltd.	$10.4	$12.0	–13.8	$7.5	137.4	Pharmaceutical/biotechnology
100	52	Petro-Canada	$10.0	$22.0	–54.5	$9,372.0	0.1	Oil and gas
100	f.l.	Nexfor Inc.	$10.0	$7.0	42.9	$2,134.0	0.5	Forest and paper products

Expenditures: We have attempted, wherever possible, to provide gross R&D expenditures including investment tax credits or government grants. Some companies are not included due to restrictive disclosure policies. Apparent tied rankings are due to rounding of R&D expenditures. Revenue: We have attempted, wherever possible, to provide revenue figures net of interest and investment income.
* = converted to CDN$ at average 1999 = $1.4858, 2000 = $1.4852 (Bank of Canada)
+ = company's corporate name at fiscal year-end, current name is different.
f.s. = foreign subsidiary
f.l. = first time listed in Fiscal 2000
n.c. = new company   n.d. = not disclosed
**R&D expenditures for Bell Canada do not include subsidiaries.
Numbers do not always add to 100% due to rounding or missing information.

Data used for this table were extracted from the Canadian Corporate R&D Database, a proprietary database available from Re$earch Infosource Inc. Companies wishing to be included in future editions of the Top 100 List and Database, or who wish to adjust their figures should contact us directly. Additional copies of the Top 100 List are available online at www.researchinfosource.com or by calling or faxing us at: Telephone: (416) 481-7070 ext. 22; Fax (416) 481-7120.
Canada's Top 100 Corporate R&D Spenders List 2001 © Re$earch Infosource Inc. 2001.
© Re$earch Infosource Inc. 2001 — Unauthorized reproduction prohibited — Do not copy.

Source: © Re$earch Infosource Inc. 2001, www.researchinfosource.com.

CANADA'S EVOLVING MANUFACTURING AND SERVICES BASE

www.ids.bc.ca

This is the Web site of Interactive Design Studios, Erik Brinkman's company. You will see a lot of imaginative designs here, mostly of a revolutionary nature.

Erik Brinkman's story illustrates what is happening in Canadian industry. The changes are coming fast and furious. Worldwide competition and advances in technology have made these changes necessary. Competition in the workplace means you have to keep up. Some of the ideas are new and complex. Even the terminology is confusing at first. Nonetheless, this chapter is a very important one because it represents the future of Canada and, therefore, your future as well.

What are Canadian manufacturers doing to try to maintain their competitive edge? They are implementing the following:

1. A customer focus.

2. Cost savings through site selection.

3. Total quality management using ISO 9000 and ISO 14000 standards.

4. New manufacturing techniques such as enterprise resource planning, computer-integrated manufacturing, flexible manufacturing, and lean manufacturing.

5. Reliance on the Internet to unite companies.

We'll discuss these developments in detail in this chapter. You'll see that operations management has become a challenging and vital element of Canadian business. The growth of Canada's manufacturing base will likely remain a major business issue in the near future. There will be debates about the merits of moving production facilities to foreign countries. Serious questions will be raised about replacing workers with robots and other machinery. Major political decisions will be made regarding protection of Canadian manufacturers through quotas and other restrictions on free trade. Regardless of how these issues are decided, however, tomorrow's graduates will face tremendous challenges (and career opportunities) in redesigning and rebuilding Canada's manufacturing base.

The service sector of the economy will also be getting more attention as it becomes a larger and larger part of the overall economy. Service productivity is a real issue, as is the blending of service and manufacturing through the Internet. This chapter will devote major attention to operations management in both the service and the manufacturing sectors. Since the majority of tomorrow's graduates will likely find jobs in the service sector, it is important to understand the latest operations management concepts for this sector.

One of the more expensive costs in production processes of the past was labour. But each year companies discover new ways of automating that eliminate the need for human labour. This photo shows a new, automated apparatus known as a Flipper. It can pour a dozen pancakes and flip them when needed on a griddle while, at the same time, flipping burgers on another grill. Are McDonald's or any other restaurants in your area already using equipment like this?

From Production to Operations Management

Production is the creation of goods and services ►P. 18◄ using the factors of production, which are the inputs land, labour, capital, entrepreneurship, and knowledge. Thus, *production management* has been the term used to describe all the activities managers do to help their firms create products. Figure 10.2 outlines the production process.

In Chapter 1, we defined *goods* as tangible products such as food, clothing, cars, and machines. And we defined *services* as intangible products such as banking, health care, and insurance. Services also include those provided by manufacturers, including credit, delivery, and installation.

Production has historically been associated with manufacturing. But the nature of business has changed significantly in the last 20 years or so. The service sector, including Internet services, has grown dramatically, and the manufacturing sector has not grown much at all. More recently, there have been changes of less than half a percentage point in employment in both these areas since 1998. The manufacturing industry employed approximately 16.4 percent of the Canadian workforce (2.01 million) in 2000,[3] compared to approximately 78 percent in the service sector.

Canada now has what is called a *service economy*— that is, one dominated by the service sector. This can be a benefit to future graduates because many of the top-paying jobs are in legal services, medical services, and business services such as accounting, finance, and management consulting.

Carol Higgins is CEO of Binky Computers for Kids. She is an information systems specialist, but recognized that developing the effective Web site she needed and envisioned for her company was too specialized for her to do on her own. She, like many other smaller firms, turned to a professional Web site developer, Vista.com, for help. Using its software, Higgins had an Internet store designed and open for business in just a few hours. Sales tripled!

To reflect the change of importance from manufacturing to services, the term *production* often has been replaced by *operations* to reflect both goods and services production. **Operations management**, then, is a specialized area in management that converts or transforms resources (including human resources) into goods and services. It includes inventory management, quality control, production scheduling, and more.

In an automobile plant, operations management transforms raw materials, human resources, parts, supplies, paints, tools, and other resources into automobiles. It does this through the processes of fabrication and assembly. In a university, operations management takes inputs—such as information, professors, supplies, buildings, offices, computer systems—and creates services that transform students into educated people. It does this through a process called education.

production
The creation of finished goods and services using the factors of production: land, labour, capital, entrepreneurship, and knowledge.

operations management
A specialized area in management that converts or transforms resources (including human resources) into goods and services.

FIGURE 10.2

THE PRODUCTION PROCESS

The production process consists of taking the factors of production (land, etc.) and using those inputs to produce goods, services, and ideas. Planning, routing, scheduling, and the other activities are the means to accomplish the objective—output.

INPUTS	PRODUCTION CONTROL	OUTPUTS
Land Labour Capital Entrepreneurship Knowledge	Planning Routing Scheduling Dispatching Follow-up	Goods Services Ideas

Some organizations—such as factories, farms, and mines—produce mostly goods. Others—such as hospitals, schools, and government agencies—produce mostly services. Still others produce a combination of goods and services. For example, an automobile manufacturer not only makes cars but also provides services such as repairs, financing, and insurance. And at McDonald's you get goods such as hamburgers and fries, but you also get services such as order taking, order filling, and cleanup.

Manufacturers Turn to Services and a Customer Orientation for Profit

www.ibm.com
www.ge.com
www.dell.com

Many traditional large manufacturers have had slow profit growth for the last decade despite spending an enormous amount of money on productivity and quality initiatives. Companies that have prospered and grown—IBM, General Electric, and Dell, to name just a few—have all taken a similar road to success. They've expanded operations management out of the factory and moved it closer to the customer, providing services such as custom manufacturing, fast delivery, credit, installation, and repair.

Take the automobile industry, for example. While new-car sales have been rather flat in recent years, the number of used-car sales has grown. Thus, car companies can potentially increase their revenues by providing parts for and servicing used cars rather than selling new ones.

Another example of the growing importance of services is in the area of corporate computing. The average company spends only one-fifth of its annual personal computer budget on purchasing the hardware. The rest (80 percent) goes to technical support, administration, and other maintenance activities. Because of this, IBM has shifted from its dependence on selling computer hardware to becoming a major supplier of computer services, software, and technology components. General Electric is doing the same; it generates more than $5 billion a year in worldwide revenues from Internet transactions.[4]

www.ford.com

Application service providers (ASPs) are companies that provide software services online so that companies do not have to buy their own software, but can have instant access to the latest programs for a fee. Companies such as Ford Motor Company have outsourced many of their production processes and are focusing more on building customer relationships and building brand images.[5] As you can see, operations management has become much more focused on services, because that's where the growth and profits are.

◉ OPERATIONS MANAGEMENT FUNCTIONS

Operations management in the service sector involves many of the same functions as operations management in the manufacturing sector. Overlapping functions include facility location, facility layout, and quality control. The resources used may be different, but the management functions are similar.

Facility Location

facility location
The process of selecting a geographic location for a company's operations.

www.mcdonalds.com
www.walmart.com

Facility location is the process of selecting a geographic location for a company's operations. One strategy is to make it easy for consumers to access your service. Thus flower shops and banks are putting facilities in supermarkets so that their products are more accessible than they are in freestanding facilities. You can find a McDonald's inside some Wal-Mart stores. The ultimate in convenience is never having to leave home at all to get services. That's why there is so much interest in Internet banking, Internet car shopping, Internet education, and so on. For brick-and-mortar businesses (e.g., retail stores) to beat such competition, they have to choose good locations and offer outstanding service to those who do come. Study the location of service-sector businesses—such as hotels, banks, athletic clubs, and supermarkets—and you will see that the most successful are conveniently located.

Facility Location for Manufacturers A major issue of the recent past has been the shift of manufacturing organizations from one city or province to another or to foreign sites. Such shifts sometimes result in pockets of unemployment in some geographic areas and lead to tremendous economic growth in others.

Why would entrepreneurs spend millions of dollars to move their facilities from one location to another? One major reason some businesses move is the availability of inexpensive labour or the right kind of skilled labour. Even though labour cost is becoming a smaller percentage of total cost in some highly automated industries, the low cost of labour remains a key reason why many less technologically advanced producers move their plants. For example, low-cost labour is one reason why some firms are moving to Malaysia, Mexico, and other countries with low wage rates. Some of these firms have been charged with providing substandard working conditions and/or exploiting children in the countries where they have set up factories. Others, such as Grupo Moraira (Grupo M), a real estate construction and sales company in the Dominican Republic, are being used as role models for global manufacturing. Grupo M provides its employees with higher pay than local businesses, transportation to and from work, day-care centres, discounted food, and health clinics. Its *operations* are so efficient that it can compete in world markets and provide world-class services to its employees.[6]

Inexpensive resources are another major reason for moving production facilities. Companies usually need water, electricity, wood, coal, and other basic resources. By moving to areas where natural resources are inexpensive and plentiful, firms can significantly lower costs—not only the cost of buying such resources but also the cost of shipping finished products. Often the most important resource is people, so companies tend to cluster where smart and talented people are. Witness Silicon Valley North. In the 1970s and 1980s a broad range of emerging firms located in the Ottawa area. Today, the many industry giants include Nortel Networks Corporation, JDS Uniphase Corporation, Mitel Networks, and Cognos Incorporated.

www.nortelnetworks.com

www.jdsuniphase.com

www.mitel.com

www.cognos.com

Reducing time-to-market is another decision-making factor. As manufacturers attempt to compete globally, they need sites that allow products to move through the system quickly, at the lowest costs, so that they can be delivered rapidly to customers. Access to various modes of transportation (i.e., highways, rail lines, airports, and the like) is thus critical. Information technology (IT) is also important to quick response, so many firms are seeking countries with the most advanced information systems.

Locating Close to Markets Many businesses are building factories in foreign countries to get closer to their international customers. That's a major reason why the Japanese automaker Toyota builds cars in Cambridge and General Motors builds cars in Windsor. When firms select foreign sites,

Fresh flowers from a vending machine—anytime, anywhere? Since making goods and services available to consumers when and where they want them is an important key to success, facility location is a critical decision for many companies. The solution for 24-Hour Flower was to place vending machines where people are most likely to buy flowers, such as the exits for commuter trains or in airports and shopping malls. What other kinds of goods or services would you purchase more often if they were more convenient?

Kelly J. Huff

they consider whether they are near airports, waterways, and highways so that raw materials and finished goods can be moved quickly and easily. Businesses also study the quality of life for workers and managers. Quality-of-life questions include: Are there good schools nearby? Is the weather nice? Is the crime rate low? Does the local community welcome new businesses? Do the chief executive and other key managers want to live there? In short, facility location has become a critical issue in operations management.

Facility Location in the Future New developments in information technology (computers, modems, e-mail, voice mail, teleconferencing, etc.) are giving firms and employees more flexibility than ever before in choosing locations while staying in the competitive mainstream.[7] As we noted in Chapter 1, telecommuting (working from home via computer and modem) is a major trend in business. Companies that no longer need to locate near sources of labour will be able to move to areas where land is less expensive and the quality of life may be better.

One big incentive to locate or relocate in a particular city or province is the tax situation and degree of government support. Those with lower taxes, like Alberta, are more attractive to companies. Some provinces and local governments have higher taxes than others, yet many engage in fierce competition by giving tax reductions and other support, such as zoning changes and financial aid, so that businesses will locate there.

Facility Layout

facility layout
The physical arrangement of resources (including people) in the production process.

Facility layout is the physical arrangement of resources (including people) in the production process. The idea is to have offices, machines, storage areas, and other items in the best possible position to enable workers to produce goods and provide services to their customers. Facility layout depends greatly on the processes that are to be performed. For *services*, the layout is usually designed to help the consumer find and buy things. More and more, that means helping consumers to find and buy things on the Internet. Some stores have added kiosks that enable customers to search for goods on the Internet and then place orders in the store. The store also handles returns and other customer-contact functions. In short, businesses are becoming more and more customer-oriented in how they design their stores and their Internet services.[8] Some service providers use layouts that make the production process more efficient, just like other producers. For example, a hospital may be designed that way.

www.delphiautomotive.
com

For manufacturing plants, facilities layout has become critical because the possible cost savings are enormous. The Delphi Automotive Systems plant in Oak Creek, Wisconsin is huge—a walk around the outside would be more than a mile. Delphi makes catalytic converters for 40 different automobile manufacturers. Catalytic converters are those stainless-steel pollution strainers in automobile exhaust systems. Delphi has a history that goes back almost 100 years. Its facility layout was typical of older plants—an assembly line that made all of the converters. The plant floor is now organized around customer-focused work cells that are modular and portable. Delivery once took 21 days, but with today's more modern layout, delivery takes less than a week. The plant was redesigned to reduce cost, to increase productivity, to simplify the process, and to speed things up. Compared to the old plant, the new plant uses only half of the space, 2 percent of its powered conveyor system, and 230 fewer processes. Productivity increased by over 25 percent, and the plant is now more profitable.[9]

Many companies like Delphi are moving from an assembly-line layout, where workers do only a few tasks at a time, to a modular layout, where teams of workers combine to produce more complex units of the final product. For example, where there may have been a dozen or more work stations on an assembly line to complete an automobile engine in the past, all of that work may be done in one module today.

When working on a major project, such as a bridge or an airplane, companies use a fixed-position layout that allows workers to congregate around the product to be completed. Increasingly, however, companies that you would expect to be manufacturing—such as Ford and Cisco—are outsourcing the production function to specialists that can perform the function faster and more efficiently. Figure 10.3 shows an Internet-based layout (process layout example), in which the customer is tied in to the process.

Taking Operations Management to the Internet

Many of today's rapidly growing companies do very little production themselves. Instead, they outsource engineering, design, manufacturing, and other tasks to outside companies, such as Solitron Devices, Flextronics, and SCI Systems, that can perform those functions better.[10] Furthermore, companies are creating whole new relationships with suppliers over the Internet such that operations management is becoming an *interfirm* process where companies work together to design, produce, and ship products to customers. Coordination among companies is nearly as close as coordination among departments in a single firm.

To facilitate such transactions, companies called electronic hubs (e-hubs) have emerged to make the flow of goods among firms faster and smoother. For example, e-hubs Ariba, MRO.com, and BizBuyer.com help companies develop long-term relationships with suppliers. Some e-hubs are industry-specific. For example, Chemdex facilitates exchanges in the chemical industry and PlasticsNet.com does the same in the plastics industry. Much of the attention of investors these days is focused on business-to-business (B2B) transactions and the companies that make them possible.[11] It's no wonder, since the B2B market, which stood at $177 billion in 2000, is expected to reach nearly $2.5 trillion by 2003.[12]

Most of the major manufacturing companies are developing whole new Internet-focused strategies that will enable them to compete more effectively in the future. Such changes are having a dramatic effect on operations managers as they adjust from a one-firm system to an interfirm environment and from a relatively stable environment to one that is constantly changing and evolving.

Quality Control

Quality control is the measurement of goods and services against set standards. Earlier in America, quality control was often done at the end of the production line by a quality control department. Today things have changed. *Quality* now means satisfying customers by building in and ensuring quality from product planning to production, purchasing, sales, and service. Emphasis is placed on customer satisfaction, so quality is everyone's concern, not just the concern of the quality control people at the end of the assembly line. In total quality management (TQM), which we discussed in Chapter 9, everybody is permitted and expected to contribute to the production of a product that meets customer standards every time. Providing such service is expected to lead to more business and more profits.

A major purpose of quality control is to make the consumer happy. Therefore, a TQM program begins by analyzing the market to see what quality standards need to be established. Quality is then designed into products, and every product must meet

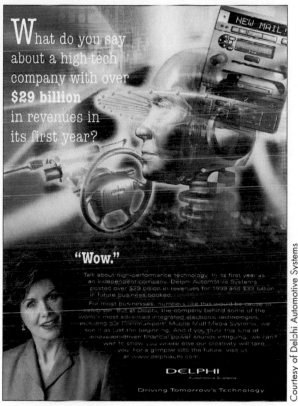

What do you say about a high-tech company with over **$29 billion** in revenues in its first year?

"Wow."

Talk about high-performance technology. In its first year as an independent company, Delphi Automotive Systems posted over $29 billion in revenues for 1999 and $33 billion in future business booked.

For most businesses, numbers like this would be cause to celebrate. But at Delphi, the company behind some of the world's most advanced integrated electronic technologies, including our Communiport Mobile Multi Media Systems, we see it as just the beginning. And if you think this kind of innovation-driven financial power sounds intriguing, we can't wait to show you where else our creativity will take you. For a glimpse into the future, visit us at www.delphiauto.com.

DELPHI
Automotive Systems

Driving Tomorrow's Technology

As this ad communicates, Delphi Automotive Systems is a dynamic company that recognizes constant change and global competition as central factors in today's business environment. It is essential to employ the latest in operations management techniques and to maintain state-of-the-art production facilities that are efficient and more productive. What other implications does the constantly evolving field of technology have for Delphi's managers?

www.cisco.com
www.solitrondevices.com
www.flextronics.com
www.sci.com
www.ariba.com

quality control
The measurement of goods and services against set standards.

FIGURE 10.3

FACILITY LAYOUT

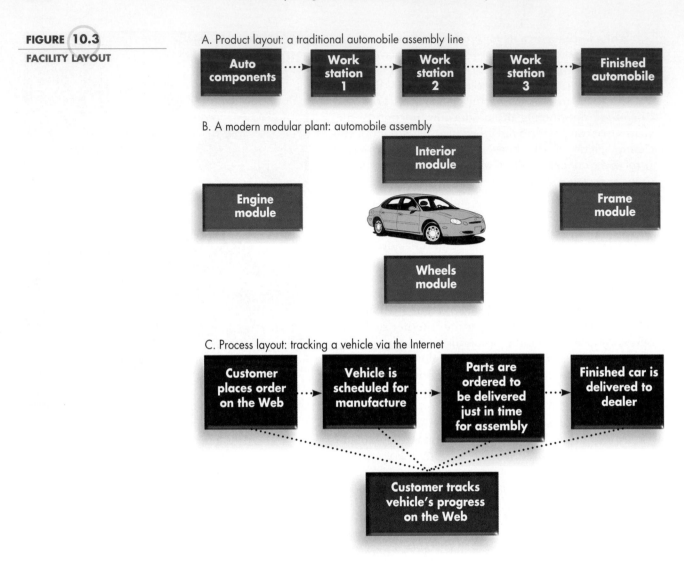

A. Product layout: a traditional automobile assembly line

Auto components ····› Work station 1 ····› Work station 2 ····› Work station 3 ····› Finished automobile

B. A modern modular plant: automobile assembly

Interior module

Engine module   Frame module

Wheels module

C. Process layout: tracking a vehicle via the Internet

Customer places order on the Web ····› Vehicle is scheduled for manufacture ····› Parts are ordered to be delivered just in time for assembly ····› Finished car is delivered to dealer

Customer tracks vehicle's progress on the Web

those standards every step of the way in the production process. The following are examples of how quality is being introduced into service and manufacturing firms:

www.holidayinn.com

- Holiday Inn authorized its hotel staff to do almost anything to satisfy an unhappy customer, from handing out gift certificates to eliminating charges for certain services. Empowered ➤**P. 14**◄ managers and employees were given the authority to waive charges for the night's stay if the customer was still unhappy.

www.motorola.com

- Motorola set a goal of attaining "six sigma" quality—just 3.4 defects per million products. The Spotlight on Small Business box "Meeting the Six Sigma Standard" discusses how small businesses are also using this standard.

- In the past, Xerox found 97 defects for every 100 copiers coming off the assembly line. Now it finds only 12.

Dozens of other manufacturers and service organizations could be discussed here, but you get the idea: The customer is ultimately the one who determines the quality standard. As shown in Figure 10.4 (see page 300), improvements in standards can have an impact on any business. There are many challenges. Service organizations are finding it difficult to provide outstanding service every time because the process is so labour-intensive. Physical goods (e.g., a gold ring)

Meeting the Six Sigma Standard

"Six sigma" is a quality measure that allows only 3.4 defects per million units. It is one thing for Motorola or General Electric to reach for such standards, but what about a small company like Dolan Industries? Dolan is a 41-person manufacturer of fasteners. It spent a few years trying to meet ISO 9000 standards, which are comparable to six sigma.

Once the company was able to achieve six sigma quality itself, it turned to its suppliers and demanded six sigma quality from them as well. It had to do that because its customers were demanding that level of quality. Companies such as General Electric, Allied-Signal, and Motorola are all seeking six sigma quality. The benefits include better-performing products and, more important, happier customers—and higher profits.

Here is how six sigma works: If you can make it to the level of one sigma, two out of three products will meet specifications. If you can reach the two sigma level, then more than 95 percent of products will qualify. But when you meet six sigma quality, as we've said, you have only 3.4 defects in a million products (which means that 99.99966 percent will qualify). The bottom line is that small businesses are being held to a higher standard, one that reaches near perfection.

Sources: Mark Henricks, "Is It Greek to You?" *Entrepreneur*, July 1999, pp. 65–67; John S. Ramberg, "Six Sigma: Fad or Fundamental?" *Quality Digest*, May 2000, pp. 28–32; and Thomas Pyzdek, "Six Sigma: Needs Standardization," *Quality Digest*, March 2001, p. 20.

---

can be designed and manufactured to near perfection. However, it is hard to reach such perfection when designing and providing a service experience such as a dance on a cruise ship or a cab drive.

ISO 9000 and ISO 14000 Standards The International Organization for Standardization (known by the acronym *ISO*) sets the global measures for the quality of individual products. **ISO 9000** is the common name given to quality management and assurance standards. The latest standards, called ISO 9001:2000, were published in November of 2000.[13] They are a revised version of the 1994 standards. The new standards require, for example, that a company must determine what customer needs are, including regulatory and legal requirements. The company must also make communication arrangements to handle issues such as complaints. Other standards involve process control, product testing, storage, and delivery.[14]

Prior to the establishment of the ISO standards, there were no international standards of quality against which to measure companies. Now the ISO, based in Europe, provides a common denominator of business quality accepted around the world.

What makes ISO 9000 so important is that the European Union (EU), the group of European countries that have established free-trade agreements, is demanding that companies that want to do business with the EU be certified by ISO standards. There are several accreditation agencies in Europe and in the United States whose function is to certify that a company meets the standards for all phases of its operations, from product development through production and testing to installation.

ISO 14000 is a collection of the best practices for managing an organization's impact on the environment. It does not prescribe a performance level. ISO 14000 is an environmental management system (EMS). The requirements for certification include having an environmental policy, having specific improvement targets, conducting audits of environmental programs, and maintaining top management review of the processes. Certification in both ISO 9000 and ISO 14000 would show

ISO 9000
The common name given to quality management and assurance standards.

ISO 14000
A collection of the best practices for managing an organization's impact on the environment.

FIGURE 10.4

WHY ZERO DEFECTS?

One aspect of TQM is making the product with zero defects. What happens when you have only 99.9-percent quality rather than 100 percent? Here is a U.S. example.

99.9-percent quality would mean that:

In Medicine

- 50 newborn babies would die daily
- 500 faulty surgical procedures would be performed weekly
- 20,000 drug prescriptions would be improperly filled annually

In the Postal Service

- 16,000 pieces of mail would be lost hourly

Source: M. E. Mengelsdorf, "Why 99.9 Percent Won't Do," *Inc.*, April 1989, p. 26. Used with permission. Copyright Clearance Centre.

that a firm has a world-class management system in both quality and environmental standards. In the past, firms assigned employees separately to meet both standards.

Today, ISO 9000 and 14000 standards have been blended so that an organization can work on both at once.

OPERATIONS MANAGEMENT IN THE SERVICE SECTOR

www.ritzcarlton.com

Operations management in the service industry is all about creating a good experience for those who use the service. As an example, in a Ritz-Carlton hotel, operations management includes restaurants that offer the finest in service, elevators that run smoothly, and a front desk that processes people quickly. It also includes placing fresh-cut flowers in the lobbies and dishes of fruit in every room. More important, it means spending $4,500 for every new employee to provide training in quality management.

Operations management in luxury hotels is changing with today's new executives. As customers in hotels, executives are likely to want in-room Internet access and a help centre with toll-free telephone service. Also, when an executive has to give a speech or presentation, he or she needs video equipment and a whole host of computer hardware and other aids. Foreign visitors would like multilingual customer-support services. Hotel shops need to carry more than souvenirs, newspapers, and some drugstore and food items to serve today's high-tech travellers. The shops may also carry laptop computer supplies, electrical adapters, and the like. Operations management is responsible for locating and providing such amenities to make customers happy.

In short, delighting customers by anticipating their needs has become the quality standard for luxury hotels, as it has for most other service businesses. But knowing customer needs and satisfying them are two different things. That's why operations management is so important: It is the implementation phase of management.[15] Like manufacturers, hotels are turning to the Internet to purchase production inputs inexpensively. Go-Co-Op, Inc., for example, helps hotels reach the 15,000 suppliers who provide them with food, beverages, soap, linens, and other such products.[16]

Measuring Quality in the Service Sector

The greatest productivity problems are reported to be in service organizations. While productivity growth was relatively good for manufacturers during the 1980s and 1990s, it was reported to be next to nothing for service organizations. Figure 10.4 supports the importance of zero defects.

As noted earlier, approximately 78 percent of Canadian jobs are now in the service sector, with more to come. A truly strong country must therefore be progressive in introducing the latest technology to services as well as to manufacturing.

Despite the negative reports mentioned above, there's strong evidence that productivity in the service sector is rising, but the government simply doesn't have the means to measure it.[17] One problem is that productivity measures don't capture improvements in quality. In an example from health care, positron emission tomography (PET) scans are much better than X rays, but that quality improvement is not reported in productivity figures.[18] The traditional way to measure productivity involves tracking inputs (worker-hours) compared to outputs (dollars). Notice that there is no measure for quality improvement. When new information systems are developed to measure the quality improvement of goods and services—including the speed of their delivery and customer satisfaction—productivity in the service sector will go up dramatically.

Using computers is one way the service sector is improving productivity, but not the only way. Think about a labour-intensive business like Burger King, where automation plays a big role in controlling costs and improving service. Today at Burger King, customers fill their own drink cups from soda machines, which allows workers to concentrate on preparing the food. And, because the people working at the drive-up window now wear headsets instead of using stationary mikes, they aren't glued to one spot anymore and can do four or five tasks while taking an order.

www.burgerking.com

Most of us have been exposed to similar productivity gains in banking. For example, people in most places no longer have to wait in long lines for tellers to help them deposit and withdraw money. Instead, they use automated teller machines (ATMs), which usually involve little or no waiting and are available 24/7 (24 hours a day, seven days a week). Internet banking makes certain other processes in banking even easier.

Another service that was once annoyingly slow was grocery store checkout. The system of marking goods with universal product codes enables computerized checkout and allows cashiers to be much more productive than before. Now some stores are enabling customers to go through the checkout process on their own.[19] Some grocery chains and smaller, independent companies are implementing Internet services that allow customers to place orders online and receive home delivery; the potential for productivity gains in this area are enormous.

Airlines are another service industry experiencing tremendous productivity increases through the use of computers for everything from processing reservations, to serving prepackaged meals on board, to standardizing the movements of luggage, passengers, and so on. On the one hand, you may have enjoyed using an automated ticketing machine or ticketless boarding to avoid the congestion at airline ticket counters. On the other hand, you probably have also noticed the need for much more improvement in operations management for the airlines. Long lines, lost bags, and delayed flights annoy customers tremendously.[20]

www.fedex.com
www.att.com

Operations management has added greatly to the productivity of the service sector. This machine dispenses movie tickets to customers who use bank or credit cards.

In short, operations management has led to tremendous productivity increases in the service sector but still has a long way to go. Also, service workers are losing jobs to machines just as manufacturing workers once did. Again, the secret to obtaining and holding a good job is to acquire the appropriate education and training. Such education and training must go on for a lifetime to keep up with the rapid changes that are happening in all areas of business. That message can't be repeated too frequently.

Services Go Interactive

The service industry has always taken advantage of new technology to increase customer satisfaction. Jet travel enabled FedEx to deliver goods overnight. Computer databases enabled AT&T to provide individualized customer service. Cable TV led to pay-per-view services. And now interactive computer networks are revolutionizing services. Interactive services are already available from banks, stockbrokers, travel agents, and information providers of all kinds. Individuals may soon be able to participate directly in community and national decision making via telephone, cable, and computer networks.

You can now buy a greater variety of books and CDs on the Internet than you can in most retail stores. You can also search for and buy new and used automobiles and new and used computers. As computers and modems get faster, the Internet may take over much of traditional retailing. Regardless of what is being sold, however, the success of service organizations in the future will depend greatly on establishing a dialogue with consumers so that the operations managers can help their organizations adapt to consumer demands faster and more efficiently. Such information systems have been developed and should prove highly useful.

PROGRESS CHECK

- Can you name and define three functions that are common to operations management in both the service and manufacturing sectors?
- What are the major criteria for facility location?
- What are ISO 9000 and ISO 14000 standards?

OPERATIONS MANAGEMENT IN THE MANUFACTURING SECTOR

Common sense and some experience have already taught you much of what you need to know about production processes. You know what it takes to write a term paper or prepare a dinner. You need money to buy the materials, you need a place to work, and you need to be organized to get the task done. The same is true of the production process in industry. It uses basic inputs to produce outputs (see Figure 10.2). Production adds value, or utility, to materials or processes.

form utility
The value added by the creation of finished goods and services.

Form utility is the value added by the creation of finished goods and services, such as the value added by taking silicon and making computer chips or putting services together to create a vacation package. Form utility can exist at the retail level as well. For example, a butcher can produce a specific cut of beef from a whole cow or a baker can make a specific type of cake out of basic ingredients.

To be competitive, manufacturers must keep the costs of inputs down. That is, the costs of workers, machinery, and so on must be kept as low as possible. Similarly, the amount of output must be relatively high. The question today is: How does a producer keep costs low and still increase output? This question will dominate thinking in the manufacturing and service sectors for years to come. In the next few sections, we explore process planning and the latest technology being used to cut costs.

Process Planning

process planning
Choosing the best means for turning resources into useful goods and services.

Process planning is choosing the best means for turning resources into useful goods and services. There are several different processes manufacturers use to produce goods. Andrew S. Grove, chairman of computer chip manufacturer Intel, uses a great analogy to explain production:

www.pentium.com

> To understand the principles of production, imagine that you're a chef . . . and that your task is to serve a breakfast consisting of a three-minute soft-boiled egg, buttered toast, and coffee. Your job is to prepare and deliver the three items simultaneously, each of them fresh and hot.

Grove goes on to say that the task here encompasses the three basic requirements of production: (1) to build and deliver products in response to the demands of the customer at a scheduled delivery time, (2) to provide an acceptable quality level, and (3) to provide everything at the lowest possible cost.

Using the breakfast example, it's easy to understand two manufacturing terms: process and assembly. **Process manufacturing** physically or chemically changes materials. For example, boiling physically changes the egg. (Similarly, process manufacturing turns sand into glass or computer chips.) The **assembly process** puts together components (eggs, toast, and coffee) to make a product (breakfast). (Cars are made through an assembly process that puts together the frame, engine, and other parts.)

In addition, production processes are either continuous or intermittent. A **continuous process** is one in which long production runs turn out finished goods over time. As the chef in our diner, for example, you could have a conveyor belt that lowers eggs into boiling water for three minutes and then lifts them out on a continuous basis. A three-minute egg would be available whenever you wanted one. (A chemical plant, for example, is run on a continuous process.)

It usually makes more sense when responding to specific customer orders to use an **intermittent process**. This is an operation where the production run is short (one or two eggs) and the machines are changed frequently to make different products (like the oven in a bakery or the toaster in the diner). (Manufacturers of custom-designed furniture would use an intermittent process.)

Today most new manufacturers use intermittent processes. Computers, robots, and flexible manufacturing processes allow firms to turn out custom-made goods almost as fast as mass-produced goods were once turned out. We'll discuss how they do that in detail later in the chapter. For now, let's look at some of the newer techniques being used to make the production process more efficient.

Materials Requirement Planning

Materials requirement planning (MRP) is a computer-based operations management system that uses sales forecasts to make sure that needed parts and materials are available at the right time and in the right place. In our diner, for example, we could feed the sales forecast into the computer, which would specify how many eggs or how much coffee to order and then print out the proper scheduling and routing sequence. The same can be done with the seats and other parts of an automobile.

MRP is most popular with companies that make products with a lot of different parts. IBM Canada is such a company. "I couldn't deal with the 30,000 to 40,000 parts we have here without an MRP

process manufacturing
That part of the production process that physically or chemically changes materials.

assembly process
That part of the production process that puts together components.

continuous process
A production process in which long production runs turn out finished goods over time.

intermittent process
A production process in which the production run is short and the machines are changed frequently to make different products.

materials requirement planning (MRP)
A computer-based production management system that uses sales forecasts to make sure that needed parts and materials are available at the right time and in the right place.

www.ibm.com

Manufacturing is a complex process involving many steps. The Decorators Supply Corporation, for example, makes detailed replicas of hand carvings. The raw material is called compo (figure on left). It is made of hide glue and molasses. Kneading makes it soft and pliable. Artisans then shape the compo in moulds and do the finishing work by hand (figure on right). This is called process manufacturing.

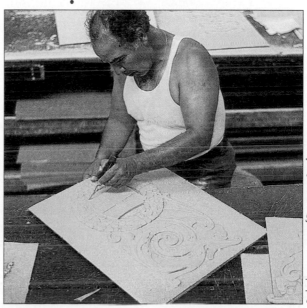

Both photos courtesy of Decorators Supply.

system," said Eugene Polistuk, manager of the IBM plant in Toronto. As better MRP systems developed over the past three decades, efficiency increased. "We had 30 to 40 people in process control," Polistuk said. "There are six today."[21]

MRP is now considered old. MRP quickly led to MRP II, an advanced version of MRP that allowed plants to include all the resources involved in the efficient making of a product, including projected sales, personnel, plant capacity, and distribution limitations. MRP II is called *manufacturing resource* (not *materials requirement*) planning because the planning involved more than just material requirements.

Both systems are being used in modern factories with some success. IBM's computer integration systems have dramatically improved the company's quality and productivity, helping it achieve large sales increases. "Those companies that struggle with MRPs struggle because they really haven't got their arms around the information processing part," said Keith Powell, director of manufacturing at the Nortel Networks Corporation plant in Bramalea, Ontario.[22]

enterprise resource planning (ERP)
Computer-based production and operations system that links multiple firms into one integrated production unit.

The newest version of MRP is **enterprise resource planning (ERP)**. ERP is a computer-based production and operations system that links multiple firms into one integrated production unit. The software enables the monitoring of quality and customer satisfaction as it's happening. ERP is much more sophisticated than either MRP or MRP II because it monitors processes in multiple firms at the same time. For example, it monitors inventory at the supplier as well as at the manufacturing plant. ERP systems are going global now that the Internet is powerful enough to handle the data flows.[23] At the plant level, dynamic performance monitoring (DNP) enables plant operators to monitor the use of power, chemicals, and other resources and to make needed adjustments. In short, flows to, through, and from plants have become automated.

Some firms are providing a service called *sequential delivery*. These firms are suppliers that provide components in an order sequenced to their customers' production process. For example, Ford's seat supplier would load seats onto a truck so that, when off-loaded, the seats would be in perfect sequence for the type of vehicle coming down the assembly line.

www.coorsceramics.com
www.reddevil.com

Eventually, such programs will link more suppliers, manufacturers, and retailers in a completely integrated manufacturing and distribution system that will be constantly monitored for the smooth flow of goods from the time they're ordered to the time they reach the ultimate consumer. Companies now using sequential delivery systems include Coors Ceramics (structural products) and Red Devil (sealants, caulks, and hand tools).

PROGRESS CHECK

- Can you define form utility and process planning?
- Can you explain the differences among the following: process manufacturing, assembly process, continuous process, and intermittent process?
- What is the difference between materials resource planning (MRP) and enterprise resource planning (ERP)?

MODERN PRODUCTION TECHNIQUES

The ultimate goal of manufacturing and process management is to provide high-quality goods and services instantaneously in response to customer demand. As we have stressed throughout this book, traditional organizations were simply not designed to be so responsive to the customer. Rather, they were designed to make goods efficiently. The whole idea of **mass production** was to make a large number of a limited variety of products at very low cost.

mass production
The process of making a large number of a limited variety of products at very low cost.

Over the years, low cost often came at the expense of quality and flexibility. Furthermore, suppliers didn't always deliver when they said they would, so manufacturers had to carry large inventories of raw materials and components. Such inefficiencies made companies subject to foreign competitors who were using more advanced production techniques. The Spotlight on Big Business box "Benchmarking the Best" discusses how companies use benchmarking to compare themselves with the world's leading companies and to find the best practices possible.

Organizations that encourage and measure the efficiency of companies are the International Quality & Productivity Centre, the National Quality Institute in Canada, and the American Productivity & Quality Center. All these organizations have Web sites where companies can go to find companies to benchmark and other useful information that will help them find the best practices and procedures.

As a result of global competition, companies today must make a wide variety of high-quality custom-designed products at very low cost. Clearly, something had to change on the production floor to make that possible. Seven major developments have radically changed the production process: (1) just-in-time inventory control, (2) Internet purchasing, (3) flexible manufacturing, (4) lean manufacturing, (5) mass customization, (6) competing in time, and (7) computer-aided design and manufacturing.

www.iqpc.co.uk

www.nqi.ca

www.apqc.org

Just-in-Time Inventory Control

One major cost of production is holding parts, motors, and other items in storage for later use. Storage not only subjects such items to obsolescence, pilferage, and damage but also requires construction and maintenance of costly warehouses. To cut such costs, the Japanese implemented a concept called **just-in-time (JIT) inventory control**. JIT systems keep a minimum of inventory on the premises; parts, supplies, and other needs are delivered just in time to go on the assembly line. There is a scarcity of land in Japan, so minimizing the area needed for storage is a major issue. There is much more land available Canada. Nonetheless, some Canadian manufacturers have adopted JIT and are quite happy with the results. To work effectively, however, the process requires excellent coordination with carefully selected suppliers. Sometimes the supplier builds new facilities close to the main producer to minimize distribution time.

just-in-time (JIT) inventory control
A production process in which a minimum of inventory is kept on the premises and parts, supplies, and other needs are delivered just in time to go on the assembly line.

Here's how it works: A manufacturer sets a production schedule using ERP or one of the other systems just described, and then determines what parts and supplies will be needed. It informs suppliers electronically of what it will need. The supplier must deliver the goods just in time to go on the assembly line. Naturally, this calls for more effort (and more costs) on the supplier's part. The company maintains efficiency by having the supplier linked electronically to the producer so that the supplier becomes more like another department in the firm than a separate business.

You can imagine how the system would work in Andrew Grove's breakfast example. Rather than ordering enough eggs, butter, bread, and coffee for a whole week and storing them, the chef would have his suppliers deliver a certain amount every morning. That way the food would be fresh and deliveries could be varied depending on customer demand. An employee from the supplier could be on hand at all times to ensure freshness.

At an auto parts factory, a truck pulls up to the shipping dock and loads wheels right off the production line. These wheels were the result of using ERP. Later, the wheels arrive at the auto plant, where they are unloaded and moved a few metres. They reach the assembly line just in time to be bolted on to the next batch of cars coming down the line.

JIT eliminates the need for warehousing and saves hours of materials handling time. Quality improves dramatically; less handling means less damage. The total cost savings can be enormous.

But implementation is far from simple: it requires spending months—or years— preparing and reorganizing your production. Your suppliers also have to be geared into it. Suppliers and customers must be in constant communication. After two years, Ford's Oakville, Ontario, assembly line had only 130 of 1,456 parts on the just-in-time system. At General Motors' massive Oshawa, Ontario, complex, almost all parts are on the system. That means that about 1,200 trucks unload each day.[24]

Today's trend toward globalization means that manufacturers can enter almost any market at almost any time. You can be one of the world's best producers and still lose the bulk of your business if you aren't also one of the most innovative and cost-efficient producers. Mercedes and BMW, for example, had long been known as two of the best car manufacturers in the world. Along came Lexus and Infiniti not only to challenge their technological lead but also to offer similar quality at a much lower price. Consequently, Mercedes was forced to produce less expensive car models. If Mercedes hadn't responded, it would have continued to lose its market share.

Even being an industry leader doesn't ensure world dominance for long. Japan, for example, introduced high-definition television (HDTV) in 1988 at the Olympics in Seoul, Korea. U.S. manufacturers considered this a challenge much like the old challenge to get to the moon. Working together, U.S. manufacturers developed a better technology that leapfrogged Japanese products. European companies are doing the same. Similarly, IBM once led the world in computer technology, but it's now just one of many competitors, no longer the dominant industry leader.

Staying on top means meeting the world's standard (that is, benchmarking on the best companies in the world). A company must compare each one of its processes to that same process as practised by the best. It must then bring its processes up to world-class standard or outsource the process to someone who can. But it can't rest there; it must empower its workers to become the best in the world and to continually improve processes and products to maintain a leadership position. Often that means the company must develop products that will make its own products obsolete. So be it. If it doesn't do so, someone else will. The American Productivity & Quality Center has an International Benchmarking Clearinghouse where companies can learn the best practices of companies throughout the world.

The National Quality Institute awards annual Canada Awards for Excellence to firms that provide outstanding quality products. Among the 2001 award recipients was IBM Solution Delivery Services for its well-managed processes to deliver support services. American Express won the Healthy Workplace Award for its Canadian Regional Operating Centre, which includes a fitness centre, a prayer room, a full health centre, and a bank. Past recipients have included Celestica, Research in Motion Ltd., British Columbia Transplant Society, and Delta Hotels.

Sources: National Quality Institute, <www.nqi.ca>, January 28, 2002; "Two New Benchmarking Studies Released," *Quality Digest*, January 1997, p. 10; Vicki J. Powers, "Selecting a Benchmarking Partner: Five Tips for Success," *Quality Digest*, October 1997, pp. 37–41.

While a lot of planning and logistics effort is focused on ensuring the successful implementation of JIT, it is important to note that such a system is still vulnerable to environmental factors. For example, due to poor weather conditions, airports and roads can be closed, creating delivery delays. Strikes by workers also can delay the prompt delivery of parts and supplies.

As a result of the September 11, 2001 terrorist attacks in the United States, border delays were so long that auto manufacturers had to temporarily stop their assembly lines as parts did not arrive on time. With more than $1.3-billion worth of goods crossing the Canada–U.S. border each day (representing 87 percent of our exports), the efficient flow of products and people is vital to Canada's economy.[25] Companies will need to revisit their JIT schedules given the longer delays at the border to accommodate the increased security measures.

ERP and JIT systems make sure the right materials are at the right place at the right time at the cheapest cost to meet both customer and production needs. That's the first step in modern production innovation: for a real-life illustration, see the Reaching Beyond Our Borders box "How a Quebec Bathtub Company Competes in the United States." Part of that process is rethinking the purchasing process. We shall explore that issue next.

How a Quebec Bathtub Company Competes in the United States

Dagmar Egerer has marketed condos in Spain, peddled Maple Leaf gold coins in Belgium, and worked for a hotel chain in Lebanon and Iran. But Egerer, U.S. sales manager for MAAX Inc., a Quebec bathtub and shower manufacturer, had rarely faced as persnickety a customer as Home Depot Inc.

One of her jobs is to make sure MAAX's bathtubs and showers show up on time at Home Depot's New England outlets. When the giant chain says the period from order to delivery is 18 days, it means 18, not 17 or 19.

The bathtubs weren't shipped to some convenient central warehouse, but to widely scattered stores up to 900 kilometres from MAAX's factory. Egerer and her colleagues performed somersaults to arrange trucking schedules. What's more, Home Depot's obsession with defect-free products meant MAAX had to package each fibreglass shower in a box to avoid mishaps in transit.

The wooing, winning, and servicing of Home Depot was a big coup for little MAAX, located 30 minutes south of Quebec City, with sales of $21 million in 1992. It had secured a toehold with the largest U.S. warehouse retailer of building materials, whose 194 monster outlets did 1992 sales of US$5.4 billion.

After filling in as an emergency supplier of fibreglass showers for two stores, MAAX began shipping to 34 Home Depot outlets in the U.S. northeast, as far away as Maryland. Home Depot became its third largest customer, accounting for 15 percent of sales. MAAX's U.S. sales grew 58 percent in the six months to August 31, 1992, compared with the previous year.

By plugging into Home Depot, MAAX joins the ranks of masochistic suppliers who thrive on being abused by tough customers. In the United States, companies that sell to Wal-Mart stores have to be bent on self-improvement. Softhearted clients are no good for succeeding in the global competitive game, argued Michael Porter, a Harvard University professor and authority on competitive advantage. "A demanding market, rather than a welcoming or easy-to-serve one, is what underpins success," he wrote in a 1991 report for the federal government.

To complicate matters, MAAX fills every truck before it's sent out to minimize transport costs. A typical order might include shipments to two Long Island, New York, outlets and to one in Connecticut. One Long Island store may set a delivery time for midnight, whereas the other, only 20 kilometres away, may insist on 10 hours later. The traffic manager has to juggle to minimize truckers' downtime.

Adaptability was also the rule on the factory floor. Frequent changes in models had so far discouraged much automation (MAAX had only one robot). But Placide Poulin, president and major shareholder, says the just-in-time demands of customers led to flexible manufacturing.

Take thermoforming, the process whereby a sheet of acrylic is heated and then drawn by a vacuum to form the shape of the tub or shower. The existing thermoformers required two to seven hours for a mould change. With 18 models of tubs and showers available, the loss of precious time was immense. So employees ordered a new thermoformer of their own design that could handle two different models at the same time and continue operating while the moulds were being changed.

This eagerness to please paid off. Home Depot agreed to stock MAAX's higher-end acrylic tubs and showers, as well as its lower-end fibreglass lines. It wasn't an easy sell, because acrylic is a luxury for practical do-it-yourselfers. But when a Home Depot buyer requested a "real good price" on a five-foot acrylic whirlpool tub, Egerer came up with a number and the chain ordered a thousand. With this big order, MAAX could bargain harder with its own suppliers. The first tubs carried a retail price of $391, a few hundred dollars cheaper than the competition. Subsequently, Home Depot repeatedly reordered.

By 1996, sales had quadrupled and MAAX was the largest Canadian producer of bathtub fixtures, with a 25-percent market share. It produced 365 different fixtures and had more than 700 employees, nine manufacturing plants, and three distribution centres in North America.

In 2000, sales reached $431.9 million, well ahead of the 1996 goal of $225 million by the year 2000. Today, 2,300 employees work in 20 plants and eight distribution centres across North America. Through intensive R&D and a steady stream of new products, productivity and manufacturing improvements, and acquisitions, MAAX is still Canada's largest bathroom products producer. It is the sixth largest producer in the U.S., which generates 67 percent of its business. With 2001 sales of $477.8 million, MAAX targets sales of $1 billion within five years.

Adapted from: MAAX Inc. <www.maax.com>, January 28, 2002; RBC Dominion Securities report, June 30, 1999; Paul Delean, "MAAX Reports Bright First Quarter," *Montreal Gazette*, June 27, 1996, p. E7; interview with Dagmar Egerer, July 17, 1996; Alan Freeman, "Company Enjoys a 'Shower' of Business," *Globe and Mail*, classroom edition, January 1993, p. 16.

Internet Purchasing

purchasing
The function in a firm that searches for quality material resources, finds the best suppliers, and negotiates the best value deal for goods and services.

Purchasing is the function in a firm that searches for quality material resources, finds the best suppliers, and negotiates the best value deal for quality goods and services. In the past, manufacturers tended to deal with many different suppliers with the idea that, if one supplier or another couldn't deliver, materials would be available from someone. Today, however, manufacturers are relying more heavily on one or two suppliers because the firms share so much information that they don't want to have too many suppliers knowing their business. The relationship between suppliers and manufacturers is thus much closer than ever before.

The Internet has transformed the purchasing function in recent years. For example, a business looking for supplies can contact any one of dozens of Internet-based purchasing services and find the best supplies at the best price (assuming that price is the most important buying criterion). Similarly, a company wishing to sell supplies can use the Internet to find all the companies looking for such supplies.[26] The cost of purchasing items has thus been reduced tremendously.

www.verticalnet.com
www.i2.com
www.e-steel.com
www.buildpoint.com
www.ge.com

Net marketplaces come in three different forms: (1) *trading exchange platforms*, like VerticalNet and i2 Technologies, which assist companies in multiple markets, (2) *industry-sponsored exchanges*, like the one provided by the Big Three automakers, and (3) *Net market makers*, like e-STEEL and BuildPoint, which host electronic marketplaces. You will be reading more and more about these business-to-business (B2B) exchange companies as hundreds emerge to help link companies together efficiently. An example of the savings possible is provided by General Electric, which has estimated that if all of its B2B transactions went to the Web, costs would drop from the current $50–$100 per transaction to just $5 per transaction.[27]

flexible manufacturing
Designing machines to do multiple tasks so that they can produce a variety of products.

Flexible Manufacturing

www.daimlerchrysler.com

Flexible manufacturing involves designing machines to do multiple tasks so that they can produce a variety of products. Ford Motor Company, for example, uses flexible manufacturing at its Romeo, Michigan plant. As many as six variations of V-8 and V-6 engines can be built from the same machinery.

Flexible manufacturing not only leads to improved productivity, but also may result in cost savings. As a result of its new flexible manufacturing, Daimler-Chrysler AG's North American unit was successful in saving $500 million in the fastest product launch in company history. In Windsor, the 2001 minivan models were built, tested, and launched on the same assembly line as the 2000 models. According to Gary Henson, the unit's manufacturing chief, these savings from reducing plant downtime by 80 percent as the company avoided 65 days of lost time during the changeover. It is estimated that the new flexible manufacturing will help save more than $3 billion through 2004 product launches by decreasing plant downtime.[28]

Unsatisfied with what the Internet was providing farmers in the way of products, Ted Farnsworth started farmbid.com, a Web site that allows farmers to buy and sell seed, chemicals, machinery, and other agricultural products. The company has already signed up some 90,000 customers. Farmbid.com, however, is only one of more than a dozen such sites available to farmers, illustrating that the B2B cybermarket is huge, extremely competitive, and growing all the time. Just as many of the B2C Internet companies have failed, not all of the B2B firms will survive either. What are some of the factors that separate the winners from the losers?

Earlier we talked about continuous processes versus intermittent processes. Can you see how flexible manufacturing makes it possible for intermittent processes to become as fast as continuous processes? What are the implications for saving time on the assembly line, saving money, and cutting back on labour?

Lean Manufacturing

Lean manufacturing is the production of goods using less of everything compared to mass production: less human effort, less manufacturing space, less investment in tools, and less engineering time to develop a new product. A company becomes lean by continuously increasing its capacity to produce high-quality goods while decreasing its need for resources.

To make the Saturn automobile, for example, General Motors abandoned its assembly-line production process. The fundamental purpose of restructuring was to dramatically cut the number of worker-hours needed to build a car. GM made numerous changes, the most dramatic of which was to switch to modular construction. GM suppliers preassemble most of the auto parts into a few large components called modules. Workers are no longer positioned along kilometres of assembly line. Instead, they're grouped at various workstations, where they put the modules together. Rather than do a few set tasks, workers perform a whole cluster of tasks. Trolleys carry the partly completed car from station to station. Compared to the assembly line, modular assembly takes up less space and calls for fewer workers— both money-saving steps. (Refer to Figure 10.3 for an example.)

Finally, GM greatly expanded its use of robots in the manufacturing process. A **robot** is a computer-controlled machine capable of performing many tasks requiring the use of materials and tools. Robots, for example, spray-paint cars and do welding. Robots usually are fast, efficient, and accurate. Robots and machinery perform routine, repetitive jobs quickly, efficiently, and accurately. This provides opportunities for workers to be more creative.

Mass Customization

To *customize* means to make a unique good or provide a specific service to an individual. Economies of scale in manufacturing and marketing during the past century made mass-produced goods so affordable that most customers were willing to compromise their individual tastes and settle for standardized products.[29] Although it once may have seemed impossible, **mass customization**, which means tailoring products to meet the needs of a large number of individual customers, is now practised widely. For mass customization to be successful, a firm needs to efficiently produce goods or services to the tastes of individual customers in high volumes and at a relatively low cost.

The National Bicycle Industrial Company in Japan, for example, makes 18 bicycle models in more than 2 million combinations, with each combination designed to fit the needs of a specific customer. The customer chooses the model, size, colour, and design. The retailer takes various measurements from the buyer and faxes the data to the factory, where robots handle the bulk of the assembly. Thus, flexible manufacturing, as described earlier, is one of the factors that makes mass customization possible. Given the exact needs of a customer, flexible machines can produce a customized good as fast as mass-produced goods were once made.

More and more manufacturers are learning to customize their products. For example, some General Nutrition Center (GNC) stores feature machines that enable shoppers to custom-design their own vitamins, shampoo, and lotions. Other companies produce custom-made books with a child's name inserted in key places, and custom-made greeting cards have appeared on the market. The Custom Foot

lean manufacturing
The production of goods using less of everything compared to mass production.

www.saturnbp.com

robot
A computer-controlled machine capable of performing many tasks requiring the use of materials and tools.

mass customization
Tailoring products to meet the needs of a large number of individual customers.

www.gnc.com

www.ic3d.com
www.motorola.com

stores use infrared scanners to precisely measure each foot so shoes can be crafted to fit perfectly. InterActive Custom Clothes offers a wide variety of options in custom-made jeans, including four different rivet colours. Motorola's Pager Division has 30 million possible permutations of pagers.

Mass customization is coming to services as well. Capital Protective Insurance (CPI), for example, sells customized risk-management plans to companies. The latest in computer software and hardware makes it possible for CPI to develop such custom-made policies. Health clubs now offer unique fitness programs for individuals, travel agencies provide vacation packages that vary according to individual choices, and some colleges allow students to design their own majors. Actually, it is much easier to custom-design service programs than it is to custom-make products, because there is no fixed tangible good that has to be adapted. Each customer can specify what he or she wants, within the limits of the service organization—limits that seem to be ever-widening.

Competing in Time

competing in time
Being as fast or faster than competition in responding to consumer wants and needs and getting goods and services to them.

Competing in time means being as fast or faster than competition in responding to consumer wants and needs and getting goods and services to them. Speedy response is essential to competing at all in a global marketplace. Ford Motor Company estimates that, to match the best, it must be 25 percent faster than it is now in creating new products. Using the latest in technology, Ford should have no problem meeting that goal. The following section explores dramatic changes that are making the production process much faster. Such changes as computer-aided design and computer-aided manufacturing enable firms to compete in time and in efficiency.

Computer-Aided Design and Manufacturing

computer-aided design (CAD)
The use of computers in the design of products.

computer-aided manufacturing (CAM)
The use of computers in the manufacturing of products.

The one development in the recent past that appears to have changed production techniques and strategies more than any other has been the integration of computers into the design and manufacturing of products. The first thing computers did was help in the design of products; this is called **computer-aided design (CAD)**. The latest CAD systems allow designers to work in three dimensions. The next step was to involve computers directly in the production process; this is called **computer-aided manufacturing (CAM)**.

CAD/CAM (the use of both computer-aided design and computer-aided manufacturing) makes it possible to custom-design products to meet the needs of small markets with very little increase in cost. A manufacturer programs the computer to make a simple design change, and that change can be incorporated directly into the production line.

Computer-aided design and manufacturing are invading the clothing industry. A computer program establishes a pattern and cuts the cloth automatically. Today, a person's dimensions can be programmed into the machines to create custom-cut clothing at little additional cost. In food service, computer-aided manufacturing is used to make cookies in those fresh-baked-cookie shops. On-site, small-scale, semiautomated, sensor-controlled baking makes consistent quality easy to achieve.

Computer-aided design has doubled productivity in many firms. But it's one thing to design a product and quite another to set the specifications to make a machine do the work. The problem in the past was that computer-aided design machines couldn't talk to computer-aided manufacturing machines directly. Recently, however, software programs have been designed to unite CAD with CAM: the result is

Computer-aided design (CAD) has greatly enhanced manufacturing productivity and has changed the nature of many jobs. This picture shows a car being designed on a CAD system.

Michael Rosenfeld/Tony Stone Images

computer-integrated manufacturing (CIM). The new software is expensive, but it cuts as much as 80 percent of the time needed to program machines to make parts, and it eliminates many errors.

computer-integrated manufacturing (CIM)
The uniting of computer-aided design with computer-aided manufacturing.

Computer-integrated manufacturing (CIM) has begun to revolutionize the production process. Now, everything from cookies to cars can be designed and manufactured much more cheaply than before. Furthermore, customized changes can be made with very little increase in cost. What will such changes mean for the clothing industry, the shoe industry, and other fashion-related industries? What will they mean for other consumer and industrial goods industries? How will you benefit as a consumer?

OUTSOURCING AND SUPPLY CHAIN MANAGEMENT

The previous chapter noted that many companies now try to divide their production between *core competencies*, work *they* do best in-house, and *outsourcing*, letting outside companies service them by doing what *they* are experts at. The result sought is the best-quality products at the lowest possible costs. This process of contract manufacturing has become a hot practice in North America.

Some examples are as follows:

- Nike outsources 100 percent of its apparel production to other companies around the world.

- In November 2001, BMW signed a contract with Magna International Inc. to assemble BMW's X3 sport-utility vehicle, which will hit the roads in 2004. Beginning in 2004, this contract will generate $1 billion (U.S.) in annual revenues for Magna and it will strengthen its growing presence in complete vehicle assembly.[30]

- "With revenues of $9.8 billion in 2000, Celestica Inc. is the third largest EMS (electronics manufacturing services) company in the world. It provides design and manufacturing services to its customers, which include industry-leading original equipment manufacturers (OEMs), primarily in the computer and communications sectors. Celestica's goal is to be the customer's partner of choice in the electronics industry."[31]

www.nike.com
www.bmw.com
www.magnaint.com

Celestica has achieved its worldwide status as a result of its focus on customer service, competitive advantages in technology, quality, and supply chain management. While supply chain management will be discussed in more detail in Chapter 17, it also impacts production and operations.

Supply chain management may involve three parts. First, it is the process of managing the movement of raw materials, parts, works in progress, finished goods, and related information through all the organizations involved in the **supply chain**. Managing the return of such goods, if necessary, may be another function of supply management. Thirdly, recycling materials, when appropriate, can also be another function of supply chain management.

The application of supply chain management is evident in different industries and among many firms. Some examples include:

- "The consulting firm Arthur Andersen helped Sobeys Quebec implement an improved traffic-routing system that has cut 6 percent off its freight costs. The changes also enabled Sobeys to improve the dispatching of trucks to replenish its more than 500 stores in western Quebec from its Montreal warehouse, where stores receive shipments daily."[32]

supply chain management
The process of managing the movement of raw materials, parts, works in process, finished goods, and related information through all the organizations involved in the supply chain; managing the return of such goods, if necessary; and recycling materials when appropriate.

supply chain
The sequence of linked activities that must be performed by various organizations to move goods from the sources of raw materials to ultimate consumers.

www.sobeys.com

- "Canadian National Railway (CN) purchased supply chain management planning software from i2 Technologies to manage its intermodal business. CN has 10,000 freight cars and 7,000 containers that it owns, along with equipment belonging to shippers and other railways. While implementing this software is still a work in progress, CN expects to increase the level of speed and reliability of hauling containers and truck trailers from ports and major cities across North America."[33]

- "Only Canada's Armed Forces surpasses the Cirque du Soleil in terms of the level of supply chain and logistics planning required to deploy large amounts of equipment, supplies, and people all over the world. According to Mr. Migneron, director of international headquarters operations, 'we use computers for a lot of what we do.' The planning and logistics work for each performance begins 12 to 18 months before the first act enters the tent."[34]

The Canadian Association of Supply Chain and Logistics Management (SCL) supports yearly events that highlight issues that are of relevance to firms and suppliers. A recent symposium in Montreal, titled "Grand Prix Logistics: Velocity in the Supply Chain" focused on the importance of getting a company's supply chain operating at top speed.[35] Speakers were chosen to represent every aspect of supply chain and logistics management, including consultants, third-party logistics providers, professors, and transportation companies.

LESS RIGID JOB DESCRIPTIONS AID PRODUCTIVITY

As indicated in an earlier chapter, some companies have been moving away from the traditional, rigid job description as a basis for organizing their operations management. We are seeing a movement toward self-managed teams and shared management responsibilities. Tom Peters pointed out that companies that want to be most productive and react quickly to competitive demands have moved toward flexibility; managers and employees do whatever is required and are not bound by job descriptions. This allows for greater employee initiative and participation, leading to more motivated employees. In today's fast-moving world, reacting quickly gives businesses a competitive edge. In small companies, employees have long functioned as generalists, and are not limited by strict job descriptions. For bigger businesses, this represents a new trend.

The very large companies have been pushing their unions for some time to allow for greater flexibility in moving employees to do what is required. Unions have usually been suspicious of this demand because they worry that it will be used to reduce pay rates. The Big Three auto companies have begun to get important concessions in this regard from the autoworkers' unions in Canada and the United States. They have drastically reduced the number of job descriptions, allowing for more efficient deployment of their workforces. These companies are waging a tough fight to be more competitive with Japanese automakers, and this is one way to improve their productivity.

W. Edwards Deming went much further than that. He stressed the importance of co-operation among workers, saying that "workers in Japan learned how to co-operate because it was the only chance for the country's survival, given its limited resources and land.... People must learn to work together, but it will take time. North American industry must change its philosophy of every man for himself."[36]

CONTROL PROCEDURES: PERT AND GANTT CHARTS

An important function of an operations manager is to be sure that products are manufactured and delivered on time, on budget, and to specifications. The question is, How can one be sure that all of the assembly processes will go smoothly and end up completed by the required time? One popular technique for maintaining some feel for the progress of production was developed in the 1950s for constructing nuclear submarines: the **program evaluation and review technique (PERT)**. PERT users analyze the tasks involved in completing a given project, estimate the time needed to complete each task, and identify the minimum time needed to complete the total project.

Formally, the steps involved in using PERT are (1) analyzing and sequencing tasks that need to be done, (2) estimating the time needed to complete each task, (3) drawing a PERT network illustrating the information from steps 1 and 2, and (4) identifying the critical path. The **critical path** is the sequence of tasks that takes the longest time to complete. The word *critical* is used in this term because a delay in the time needed to complete this path would cause the project or production run to be late.

Figure 10.5 illustrates a PERT chart for producing a music video. Note that the squares on the chart indicate completed tasks and the arrows leading to the squares indicate the time needed to complete each task. The path from one completed task to another illustrates the relationships among tasks. For example, the arrow from "set designed" to "set materials purchased" shows that designing the set must be completed before the materials can be purchased. The critical path (indicated by the bold black arrows) reflects that producing the set takes more time than auditioning dancers and choreographing dances as well as designing and making costumes. The project manager now knows that it's critical that set construction remain on schedule if the project is to be completed on time, but short delays in the dance and costume preparation shouldn't affect completing the total project on time.

A PERT network can be made up of thousands of events over many months. Today, this complex procedure is done by computer. Another, more basic, strategy used by manufacturers for measuring production progress is a Gantt chart. A **Gantt chart** (named for its developer, Henry L. Gantt) is a bar graph that clearly shows what projects are being worked on and how much has been completed at any given time. Figure 10.6 shows a Gantt chart for a doll manufacturer. The chart shows that the dolls' heads and bodies should be completed before the clothing is sewn. It also shows that at the end of week 3, the dolls' bodies are ready, but the heads are about half a week behind. All of this calculation was once done by hand. Now the computer has taken over. Using a Gantt-like computer program, a manager can trace the production process minute by minute to determine which tasks are on time and which are behind so that adjustments can be made to allow the company to stay on schedule.

PREPARING FOR THE FUTURE

Canada remains a major industrial country and is likely to become even stronger. This means that there are tremendous opportunities for careers in operations management. Today relatively few students major in production and operations management, inventory management, and other careers involving manufacturing and operations management in the service sector. That means more opportunities for those students who can see the future trends and have the skills to own or work in tomorrow's highly automated, efficient factories, mines, service facilities, and other production locations.

What does technological innovation mean to you? It means that, as a student of business, you will have marvellous new learning opportunities. It means new career choices and a higher standard of living and quality of life. But it also means preparing for such changes. Clearly, the workplace will be dominated by computers, robots, and other advanced machinery. Even the service sector will require the widespread use of computers, whether desktop, laptop, or handheld.

program evaluation and review technique (PERT)
A method for analyzing the tasks involved in completing a given project, estimating the time needed to complete each task, and identifying the minimum time needed to complete the total project.

critical path
The sequence of tasks that takes the longest time to complete.

www.smartdraw.com

To create great-looking Gantt charts quickly and easily, visit the Gantt Resource Center and download free software, symbols, and templates.

Gantt chart
A bar graph showing what projects are being worked on and what stage they are in at any given time.

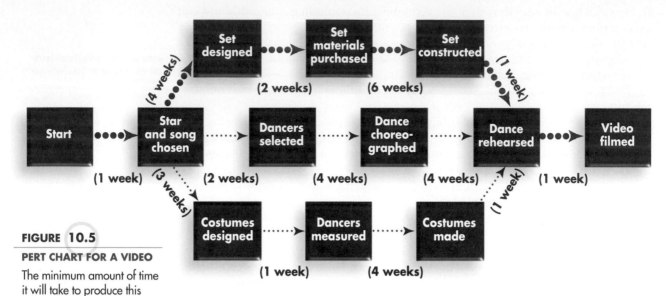

FIGURE 10.5

PERT CHART FOR A VIDEO

The minimum amount of time it will take to produce this video is 15 weeks. To get that number, you add the week it takes to pick a star and a song to the four weeks to design a set, the two weeks to purchase set materials, the six weeks to construct the set, the week before rehearsals, and the final week when the video is made. That's the critical path. Any delay in that process will delay the final video. Delays in other processes (e.g., selecting and choreographing dancers and costume design) wouldn't necessarily delay the video because there are more weeks in the critical path than are needed for those processes.

If all this sounds terribly cold and impersonal, then you recognize one of the needs of the future. People will need much more contact than before with others outside the work environment. There will be new demands for recreation, social clubs, travel, and other diversions. The Canada of the next century will be radically different from the country at the turn of the millennium. It will take both technically trained people and people skilled in human relationships to guide us through the transition.

The trend is toward making production and operations management courses a requisite for graduate degrees in management. Such courses, in combination with those on organizational behaviour, train students to manage the high-tech workers and managers of the new era. Emphasis is on participative management and the design of a work environment suitable to the twenty-first century. A new era is opening up for both manufacturing and the service sector. There will be many exciting, challenging careers in this field.

FIGURE 10.6

A GANTT CHART FOR A DOLL MANUFACTURER

A Gantt chart enables a production manager to see at a glance when projects are scheduled to be completed and what the status now is. For example, the dolls' heads and bodies should be completed before the clothing is sewn, but they could be a little late as long as everything is ready for assembly in week 6. This chart shows that at the end of week 3, the dolls' bodies are ready, but the heads are about half a week behind.

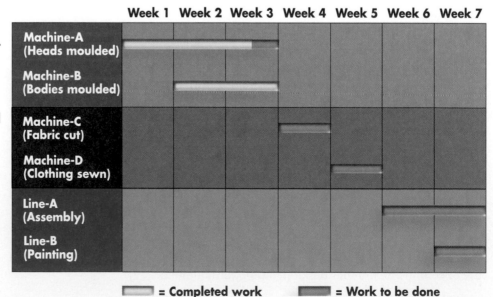

Many educational institutions offer courses in manufacturing management and robotics, as well as other relevant business areas. McMaster University, McGill University, and the University of Toronto, for example, all have substantial research centres.

McMaster University is one of the top-ranked research universities in Canada with research centres in the areas of intelligent machines and manufacturing; health sciences; e-commerce; and management of innovation and new technology, to name just a few. Supporters who understand the importance of research toward developing a more skilled workforce and processes are from a variety of companies including CanWest Global, Dofasco Incorporated, Motorola Canada Limited, and AIC Group of Funds.

What courses are available at your institution that focus on the study of production and operations?

www.mcmaster.ca
www.mcgill.ca
www.utoronto.ca
www.canwestglobal.com
www.dofasco.ca
www.motorola.com
www.aicfunds.ca

PROGRESS CHECK

- What is just-in-time inventory control?
- How does flexible manufacturing differ from lean manufacturing?
- What is meant by the phrase *competing in time*?
- Draw a PERT chart for making a breakfast of three-minute eggs, buttered toast, and coffee. Define the critical path. How could you use a Gantt chart to keep track of production?

ETHICAL DILEMMA

Review

Now let's take another look at the ethical dilemma raised at the beginning of this chapter. Companies in Canada are required by law to give employees sufficient notice of such plant closings, sometimes up to six months. But do companies have obligations beyond those set out by law? Here's what our executives think.

Bédard believes that companies do have responsibilities to their employees and must meet those responsibilities by informing employees of the situation, getting their co-operation, and trying to avoid a closure. If the company opens its books to its employees, they may be able to propose improvements and avoid a plant closure. Further, "companies that think too much in the short term and focus only on the short term will one day pay a price."

Reilley says that companies owe their loyal employees a measure of support when plant closures occur. This support can include relocation to another site, retraining,

or termination packages. The company should also try to attract other firms to the town. Remember, too, outsourcing is not all bad. Redundant employees often form their own enterprises and compete for outsourcing contracts. The company should also try to protect employees through reassignment and early retirement incentives. Reilley notes that "increasing productivity doesn't necessarily mean layoffs and plant closings. Productivity enhancement, if done right, leads to greater market share and thus tends to protect jobs (and even creates new jobs)."

Many companies in Canada and around the world have leap-frogged from country to country chasing lower wages. Some Canadian companies have moved factories first to the northern U.S., then to the southern U.S., and finally to Mexico. Nike and Reebok have followed the same trail from the U.S., outsourcing work to contractors in South Korea and then in Indonesia.

SUMMARY

1. Define *operations management.*

1. Operations management is a specialized area in management that converts or transforms resources (including human resources) into goods and services.
    *   *What kind of firms use operations managers?*
    Firms in both the manufacturing and service sectors use operations managers.

2. Describe the operations management functions that are involved in both the manufacturing and service sectors.

2. Functions involved in both the manufacturing and service sectors include facility location, facility layout, and quality control.
    *   *What is facility location and how does it differ from facility layout?*
    Facility location is the process of selecting a geographic location for a company's operations. *Facility layout* is the physical arrangement of resources (including people) to produce goods and services effectively and efficiently. *Quality control* is the measurement of products and services against set standards.
    *   *Why is facility location so important, and what criteria are used to evaluate different sites?*
    The very survival of manufacturing depends on its ability to remain competitive, and that means either making inputs less costly, (reducing costs of labour and land) or increasing outputs from present inputs (increasing productivity). Labour costs and land costs are two major criteria for selecting the right sites. Other criteria include whether (1) resources are plentiful and inexpensive, (2) skilled workers are available or are trainable, (3) taxes are low and the local government offers support, (4) energy and water are available, (5) transportation costs are low, and (6) the quality of life and quality of education are high.

3. Discuss the problem of measuring productivity in the service sector, and tell how new technology is leading to productivity gains in service companies.

3. There's strong evidence that productivity in the service sector is rising, but the government simply doesn't have the means to measure it.
    *   *Why is productivity so hard to measure?*
    The traditional way to measure productivity involves tracking inputs (worker-hours) compared to outputs (dollars). Quality improvements are not weighed. New information systems must be developed to measure the *quality* of goods and services, the speed of their delivery, and customer satisfaction.
    *   *How is technology creating productivity gains in service organizations?*
    Computers have been a great help to service employees, allowing them to perform their tasks faster and more accurately. ATMs make banking faster and easier, automated chequing machines enable grocery clerks (and customers) to process items faster, and automated ticketing machines make airlines more efficient, although they have a long way to go before they truly delight customers.

4. Explain process planning and the various manufacturing processes being used today.

4. Process planning is choosing the best means for turning resources into useful goods and services.
    *   *What is process manufacturing and how does it differ from assembly processes?*
    Process manufacturing physically or chemically changes materials. Assembly processes put together components.
    *   *Are there other production processes?*
    Production processes are either continuous or intermittent. A continuous process is one in which long production runs turn out finished goods over time. An intermittent process is an operation where the production run is short and the machines are changed frequently to produce different products.
    *   *What relationship does enterprise resource planning (ERP) have with the production process?*
    A manufacturer sets a production schedule. Its suppliers are automatically informed electronically of what will be needed. The supplier must deliver the goods just in time for the production or assembly process, making the supplier part of the process.

5. Companies are using seven new production techniques to become more profitable: (1) just-in-time inventory control, (2) Internet purchasing, (3) flexible manufacturing, (4) lean manufacturing, (5) mass customization, (6) competing in time, and (7) computer-aided design and manufacturing.

    • *What is just-in-time inventory control?*

    JIT involves having suppliers deliver parts and materials just in time to go on the assembly line so they don't have to be stored in warehouses.

    • *How have purchasing agreements changed?*

    Purchasing agreements now involve fewer suppliers who supply quality goods and services at better prices in return for getting the business. Many new Internet companies have emerged to help both buyers and sellers complete the exchange process more efficiently.

    • *What is flexible manufacturing?*

    Flexible manufacturing involves designing machines to produce a variety of products.

    • *What is lean manufacturing?*

    Lean manufacturing is the production of goods using less of everything compared to mass production: less human effort, less manufacturing space, less investment in tools, and less engineering time to develop a new product.

    • *What is mass customization?*

    Mass customization means making custom-designed goods and services for a large number of individual customers. Flexible manufacturing makes mass customization possible. Given the exact needs of a customer, flexible machines can produce a customized good as fast as mass-produced goods were once made. Mass customization is also important in service industries.

    • *How does competing in time fit into the process?*

    Getting your product to market before your competitors is essential today, particularly in the electronics industry. Thus, competing in time is critical. JIT inventory control allows for less inventory and fewer machines to move goods. This allows for more flexibility and faster response times.

    • *How do CAD/CAM systems work?*

    Design changes made in computer-aided design (CAD) are instantly incorporated into the computer-aided manufacturing (CAM) production process. The linking of the two systems—CAD and CAM—is called computer-integrated manufacturing (CIM).

5. Describe the seven new manufacturing techniques that have made companies more productive: just-in-time inventory control, Internet purchasing, flexible manufacturing, lean manufacturing, mass customization, competing in time, and computer-aided design and manufacturing.

6. The program evaluation and review technique (PERT) is a method for analyzing the tasks involved in completing a given project, estimating the time needed to complete each task, and identifying the minimum time needed to complete the total project. A Gantt chart is a bar graph that clearly shows what projects are being worked on and how much has been completed at any given time.

    • *Is there any relationship between a PERT chart and a Gantt chart?*

    Figure 10.5 shows a PERT chart. Figure 10.6 shows a Gantt chart. Whereas PERT is a tool used for planning, a Gantt chart is a tool used to measure progress.

6. Explain the use of PERT and Gantt charts.

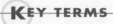

KEY TERMS

assembly
  process 303
competing in
  time 310
computer-aided
  design (CAD) 310
computer-aided
  manufacturing
  (CAM) 310
computer-integrated
  manufacturing
  (CIM) 311
continuous
  process 303
critical path 313
enterprise resource
  planning (ERP) 304
facility layout 296
facility location 294

flexible
  manufacturing 308
form utility 302
Gantt chart 313
intermittent
  process 303
ISO 9000 299
ISO 14000 299
just-in-time (JIT)
  inventory
  control 305
lean
  manufacturing 309
mass
  customization 309
mass production 304
materials requirement
  planning (MRP) 303

operations
  management 293
process
  manufacturing 303
process planning 302
production 293
program evaluation
  and review
  technique
  (PERT) 313
purchasing 308
quality control 297
research and
  development 291
robot 309
supply chain 311
supply chain
  management 311

DEVELOPING WORKPLACE SKILLS

1. Choosing the right location for a manufacturing plant or a service organization is often critical to its success. Have each member of a small group pick one manufacturing plant or one service organization in town and list at least three reasons why its location helps or hinders its success. If its location is not ideal, where would be a better one?

2. In teams of four or five, discuss the need for better operations management at airports and with the airlines in general. Have the team develop a three-page report listing (a) problems students have encountered in travelling by air and (b) suggestions for improving operations so such problems won't occur in the future.

3. Find two resources in the library or on the Internet that discuss some of the advantages and disadvantages of producing goods overseas using inexpensive labour. Summarize the moral and ethical issues of this practice.

4. Find any production facility (e.g., sandwich shop) or service centre at your school (e.g., library) and redesign the layout (make a pencil drawing placing people and materials) so it could more effectively serve its customers and so that the workers would be more effective and efficient.

5. Think about some of the experiences you have had with service organizations recently (e.g., the admissions office at your school), and select one incident where you had to wait for an unreasonable length of time to get what you wanted. Tell what happens when customers are inconvenienced, and explain how management could make the operation more efficient and customer-oriented.

Purpose:

To evaluate the benefits of lean manufacturing.

Exercise:

To see how lean manufacturing improved the production performance of several companies go to Duggan and Associates' Web site at www.dugganinc.com.

1. What is lean manufacturing?

2. What are the five principles of lean manufacturing?

3. Watch the four slide shows that illustrate how lean manufacturing changed the layout and processes in different companies. What were the results of the new lean manufacturing techniques?

Purpose:

To illustrate production processes, using the production of M&Ms as an example.

Exercise:

Take a tour of the M&Ms factory and visit the company store at www.m-ms. com/factory/index.html.

1. Is the production of M&Ms an example of an intermittent or continuous production process? Justify your answer.

2. Is mass customization used in M&M production? If so, how?

3. What location factors might go into the selection of a manufacturing site for M&Ms?

PRACTISING MANAGEMENT DECISIONS

CASE 1

WHY BIG COMPANIES FAIL TO INNOVATE

Matthew Kiernan, based in Unionville, Ontario, is a management consultant whose views command attention. He has a PhD degree in strategic management from the University of London and was a senior partner with an international consulting firm, KPMG Peat Marwick. Subsequently he founded his own firm, Innovest Group International, with a staff operating out of Geneva, London, and Toronto. He was also a director of the Business Council for Sustainable Development based in Geneva.

His book *Get Innovative or Get Dead* took aim at big corporations for their poor record on innovation. Any five-year-old could tell you that companies must innovate to survive, he said, so what's the problem? According to Kiernan, it's one thing to understand something in your head but quite another thing to really feel it in your gut. This is further complicated by the difficulty of getting a big company to shift gears, to turn its culture around so that innovation becomes the norm rather than the special effort.

Kiernan called for a company to develop a style and atmosphere that favours individual risk taking, the intrapreneurial approach discussed in Chapter 7. That means that if a team tries something that doesn't work, you don't shoot them down. Encouraging innovation, which inevitably involves taking risks with the unknown, means accepting the fact that it may take two or three attempts before something useful is developed. Further, it requires "creative thinking to see the potential" in something new or untested.

The 3M company is often used as a great example of a company that encourages creativity. Its policy dictates that 30 percent of annual sales come from products less than four years old. But 3M wasn't always that progressive. When the now legendary Post-it Notes were first developed by an employee, he had a hard time getting the company to see the potential in his idea. This ultimately triggered a major change in the company's policy.

Kiernan pointed out that most companies give lip service to the necessity of innovation but do not act in a credible way as far as their employees are concerned. If you mean business you must take that "bright guy out of the basement, [the one] everybody knows is a genius, but whose last two enterprise efforts came to grief, and visibly promote him."

Decision Questions

1. Do large companies find it difficult to innovate because they resist change? Is it because they are big or because they are afraid of the unknown? Why is that?

2. Do smaller companies do better at innovation because they are not so risk-averse? Is that because most of them are private companies and not accountable to outside shareholders?

3. Can you see any connection between innovation and continuous improvement? Does CI require innovation?

4. If you were a vice-president in charge of production at a big corporation, how would you encourage innovation?

CASE 2

IBM IS BOTH AN OUTSOURCER AND A MAJOR OUTSOURCE FOR OTHERS

Few companies are better known for their manufacturing expertise than IBM. Nonetheless, even IBM has to adapt to the dynamic marketplace of today. In the area of personal computers, for example, IBM was unable to match the prices or speed of delivery of mail-order firms such as Dell Computer. Dell built machines after receiving orders for them and then rushed the computers to customers. IBM, in contrast, made machines ahead of time and hoped that the orders would match its inventory.

To compete against firms like Dell, IBM had to custom-make computers for its business customers, but IBM was not particularly suited to do such work. However, IBM did work with several distributors that were also having problems. The distributors were trying to custom-make IBM machines but were forced to carry a heavy inventory of parts and materials to do so. Distributors were also tearing IBM computers apart and putting them back together with other computer companies' parts to produce custom-made computers.

IBM decided to allow its distributors to store parts and materials and then custom-make computers to satisfy customer demand. In other words, IBM outsourced about 60 percent of its commercial PC business. Distributors such as Inacom Corporation became profitable and IBM was able to offer custom-made PCs competitive in price with those of Dell and other direct-mail companies.

More recently, IBM has begun selling its technology—tiny disc drives, speedy new chips, and more—to its former competitors! For some of these new partners, IBM will design their new products and let them explore its labs. In short, IBM is doing a bit of reverse outsourcing in that it is offering itself as a research and product development company ready to work with others. Thus, IBM will sell networking chips to Cisco Systems and will not compete with that company anymore. And it will likewise sell disk drives to EMC. IBM benchmarked its final products against these companies and saw that it was not winning. The winning strategy, it decided, was to join them and become an even better team.

Decision Questions

1. What does it say about today's competitive environment when leading companies, such as IBM, give up competing and decide to work with competitors instead?

2. What effects will outsourcing have on trade relationships among countries?

3. How much influence will the Internet have on world trade and outsourcing among countries? What does the Internet provide that wasn't available before?

Sources: Daniel Lyons, "IBM's Giant Gamble," *Forbes*, October 4, 1999, pp. 90–95; and Michael Useem and Joseph Harder, "Leading Laterally in Company Outsourcing," *Sloan Management Review*, Winter 2000, pp. 25–36.

VIDEO CASE

THE PRODUCTION PROCESS AT WASHBURN GUITARS

When you think of manufacturing firms, names like GM and IBM come to mind. But there are thousands of smaller manufacturers in the marketplace that provide us with many of the products that make life more enjoyable. Certainly guitars are one of those products. Washburn Guitars in Chicago, Illinois, is a manufacturing company that uses an intermittent process of production called small-batch manufacturing. That is, Washburn makes a few of one model of guitar and then shifts production to a different model.

Even though Washburn makes only a few products each day (about 15 guitars), the company still needs to use the latest in production techniques to stay competitive. For example, it uses flexible manufacturing. The Washburn production facility has a machine that is capable of doing many different tasks: building guitar necks, drilling holes for the fretboard, and so on.

Washburn also follows the total quality concepts that other, larger firms follow. When planning the production process, the company keeps in mind the need for profits. Therefore, the popular, more expensive guitars take precedence over less expensive items. Today, all of Washburn's acoustic guitars are made overseas, but the company is planning to build a new facility for producing acoustic guitars in Nashville, Tennessee. Total quality management and modern production techniques now make it possible to manufacture acoustic guitars in the United States and still stay competitive on price.

When making career plans, you may want to include smaller firms like Washburn Guitars in your thoughts. It is often exciting to work in a small, relatively intimate environment, especially if the firm practices participative management and other modern techniques.

Discussion Questions

1. What small manufacturing facilities are located in or near your city or town? Visit them and see for yourself what it's like to work for a small manufacturer.

2. Do you think that a guitar is the kind of item that lends itself well to continuous process manufacturing? Why?

3. One of the more important aspects of small-batch manufacturing is scheduling. What kinds of scheduling techniques have you learned in this chapter that you could use in a business similar to Washburn?

4. Does a career in production management seem attractive to you? Why or why not?

CHAPTER 11

Using Technology to Manage Information

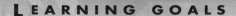

LEARNING GOALS

AFTER YOU HAVE READ AND STUDIED THIS CHAPTER, YOU SHOULD BE ABLE TO

1. Outline the changing role of business technology.

2. Compare the scope of the Internet, intranets, and extranets as tools in managing information.

3. List the steps in managing information, and identify the characteristics of useful information.

4. Review the hardware most frequently used in business, and outline the benefits of the move toward computer networks.

5. Classify the computer software most frequently used in business.

6. Evaluate the human resource, security, privacy, and stability issues in management that are affected by information technology.

7. Identify the careers that are gaining workers due to the growth of information technology.

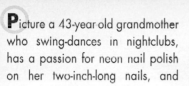 
Rina Delmonico, Ren Consulting, Inc.

Picture a 43-year-old grandmother who swing-dances in nightclubs, has a passion for neon nail polish on her two-inch-long nails, and has recently learned to box. Does that sound like a candidate for the Executive of the Year Award given by the Association of Information Technology Professionals? Well, meet Rina Delmonico, formerly chief information officer (CIO) of Schwinn Bicycle Company. Today, Delmonico owns her own information services consulting firm.

Delmonico has been described as "eccentric" by her colleagues. They also call her brilliant. She makes no excuses for the now famous "Rina style" she sports. As she twirls her long, dark ponytail through her fingers, she seems more like a 20-year-old student than an information technology (IT) expert. Yet despite this youthful appearance and attitude, Delmonico boasts 25 years of experience in IT, during which time she has climbed the ladder at large financial and manufacturing companies such as Citicorp, Johns Manville, and Schwinn. Innovation and a willingness to try new technology applications are the hallmarks of her success. For example, as vice-president of corporate management information systems at First Data Corporation, Delmonico spearheaded the development of the corporate intranet that included a recruitment automation system that slashed hiring costs by 25 percent.

She decided to take on the challenge at Schwinn in 1996, just three years after the company almost fell into bankruptcy. Delmonico became a key player in the attempt to rebuild Schwinn's reputation as a leader in the cycling world. When she started work at Schwinn, the information systems (IS) department was in shambles. Relationships with company vendors were eroding and the firm's enterprise resource planning implementation was so far off the mark that orders could not be shipped.

Ponytail pulled back and two-inch nails clawing, Delmonico jumped headfirst into action and provided the spark needed to rally the 30-person IT staff at Schwinn to help turn the company around. She started first by revamping Schwinn's telecommunications cost structure. By reworking contracts and wiring systems, she immediately saved the firm $500,000. Delmonico also directed the two-month launch of Schwinn's e-commerce Web site and helped install a personal computer and network infrastructure literally from scratch. Delmonico, however, is the first to admit that little could be accomplished without the support of her staff. Therefore, she regularly rewarded her 30 co-workers with small personalized gifts and took them out for pizza or to virtual reality clubs to kick back and relax from the rigours of the job.

Large businesses like Citicorp and relatively smaller firms like Schwinn will succeed or fail in the twenty-first century economy on their ability to manage and make use of information. New technologies enable managers to make more informed decisions and help with vital communications between workers and other stakeholders. Rapid growth of the Internet and technological developments make this one of the most exciting times in history. Rina Delmonico certainly agrees with that statement. And, by the way, she doesn't plan to miss a minute of it.

Sources: Polly Schneider, "Shifting Gears," *CIO*, October 1, 1999, pp. 62–70; and Meridith Levinson, "Zen and the Art of IT Governance," *CIO*, February 15, 2000, pp. 127–32.

ETHICAL DILEMMA

Software: To Copy or Not to Copy

A common practice today is copying software from a friend or company onto disks and then loading it into your computer. Of course, you are then not a registered owner with all the advantages of upgrading and such. When you do this you have stolen a company's product. Is this more acceptable than shoplifting, which is also stealing something without paying for it? We seem to treat software copying like rolling through a stop sign on a deserted street at 2:00 a.m. or exceeding the speed limit by 10 kilometres per hour. The difference is that these driving actions are illegal and may be dangerous but property is not being stolen. It is obviously almost impossible to stop such thefts given the ease and privacy with which it can be done. What would you do if you were operating a small business? Would you encourage your employees to do it or would you do it yourself?

THE ROLE OF INFORMATION TECHNOLOGY

Throughout this text, we have emphasized the need for managing information flows among businesses and their employees, businesses and their suppliers, businesses and their customers, and so on. Since businesses are in a constant state of change, those managers who try to rely on old ways of doing things will simply not be able to compete with those who have the latest in technology and know how to use it.

Business technology has often changed names and roles. In the 1970s, business technology was known as **data processing (DP)**. (Although many people use the words *data* and *information* interchangeably, they are different. *Data* are raw, unanalyzed, and unorganized facts and figures. *Information* is the processed and organized data that can be used for managerial decision making.) DP was used to support an existing business;

data processing (DP)
Name for business technology in the 1970s; included technology that supported an existing business and was primarily used to improve the flow of financial information.

How can retailers learn about the hottest fashion trends in time to get them in their stores before the trends cool? Zara links each of its stores electronically to the company's headquarters, allowing sales information and customer requests to be transmitted daily. Zara designers use this real-time information to quickly create the garments consumers seek. Zara can add new designs twice a week rather than the industry standard of six weeks.

its primary purpose was to improve the flow of financial information. DP employees tended to be hidden in a back room and rarely came in contact with customers.

In the 1980s, business technology became known as **information systems (IS)**. IS moved out of the back room and into the centre of the business. Its role changed from *supporting* the business to *doing* business. Customers began to interact with a wide array of technological tools, from automated teller machines (ATMs) to voice mail. As business increased its use of information systems, it became more dependent on them.

Until the late 1980s, business technology was just an addition to the existing way of doing business. Keeping up-to-date was a matter of using new technology on old methods. But things started to change as the 1990s approached. Businesses shifted to using new technology on new methods. Business technology then became known as **information technology (IT)**, and its role became to *change* business.

How Information Technology Changes Business

Time and place have always been at the centre of business. Customers had to go to the business during certain hours to satisfy their needs. We went to the store to buy clothes. We went to the bank to arrange for a loan. Businesses decided when and where we did business with them. Today, IT allows businesses to deliver products whenever and wherever it is convenient for the customer. Thus, you can order clothes from the Home Shopping Network, arrange a home mortgage loan by phone or computer, or buy a car on the Internet at any time you choose.

Consider how IT has changed the entertainment industry. If you wanted to see a movie 35 years ago, you had to go to a movie theatre. Thirty years ago you could wait for it to be on television. Twenty years ago you could wait for it to be on cable television. Fifteen years ago you could go to a video store and rent it. Now you can order video on demand by satellite or cable.

As IT breaks time and location barriers, it creates organizations and services that are independent of location. For example, the TSE (Toronto Stock Exchange) and the CDNX (Canadian Venture Exchange) are electronic stock exchanges without trading floors. Buyers and sellers make trades by computer.

Being independent of location brings work to people instead of people to work. With IT, data and information can flow more than 12,872 kilometres in a second, allowing firms to conduct work around the globe continuously. We are moving toward **virtualization**, which is accessibility through technology that allows business to be conducted independent of location. For example, you can carry a virtual office in your pocket. Tools such as cellular phones, pagers, laptop computers, and personal digital assistants allow you to access people and information as if you were in an actual office. Likewise, virtual communities are forming as people who would otherwise not have met communicate with each other through the virtual post office created by computer networks.[1]

Doing business drastically changes when companies increase their technological capabilities. For example, electronic communications can provide substantial time savings whether you work in an office, at home, or on the road. E-mail ends the tedious games of telephone tag and decreases the time needed to write and mail traditional paper-based correspondence. Internet and intranet communication using shared documents and other methods allow contributors to work on a common document without the time-consuming meetings. Information technology also impacts a firm's organization, operations, staffing issues, new-product developments, customer relations, and opportunities in new markets. See Figure 11.1 for an elaboration on these areas.

information systems (IS)
Technology that helps companies do business; includes such tools as automated teller machines (ATMs) and voice mail.

information technology (IT)
Technology that helps companies change business by allowing them to use new methods.

www.hsn.com

www.tse.com
www.cdnx.com

virtualization
Accessibility through technology that allows business to be conducted independent of location.

register, it may be automatically fed to a computer, and the day's sales and profits can be calculated as soon as the store closes. The sales and expense data must be accurate, or the rest of the calculations will be wrong. This can be a real problem when, for example, a large number of calculations are based on questionable sales forecasts rather than actual sales.

2. **Completeness**. There must be enough information to allow you to make a decision but not so much as to confuse the issue. Today, as we have noted, the problem is often too much information rather than too little.

3. **Timeliness**. Information must reach managers quickly. If a customer has a complaint, that complaint should be handled instantly if possible and certainly within no more than one day. In the past, a salesperson would make a report to his or her manager; that report would go to a higher-level manager, and the problem would not be resolved for days, weeks, or months. E-mail and other developments make it possible for marketing, engineering, and production to hear about a problem with a product the same day the salesperson hears about it. Product changes can be made on the spot using computer integrated manufacturing, as discussed in Chapter 10.

4. **Relevance**. Different managers have different information needs. Again, the problem today is that information systems often make too much data available. Managers must learn which questions to ask to get the answers they need.

It doesn't matter how interesting your information is if nobody's paying attention. Sorting out useful information and getting it to the right people are the goals in solving information overload. There are Web software programs (e.g., Point Case Network) and services available that do just that—filter information so that users can get the customized information they need.[18] Such a program is known as **push technology** because it pushes relevant information to users so they don't have to find it for themselves and pull it out.

push technology
Web software that delivers information tailored to a previously defined user profile; it pushes the information to users so that they don't have to pull it out.

The major Web browsers—Netscape Navigator and Microsoft Internet Explorer—have incorporated push technology into their browsers in the form of receivers for content channels that can be distributed automatically to the user's desktop.[19] Push technology services may deliver customized news, weather, stock market financial data, dating information, and much more. How does push technology work? Simply:[20]

Filtering is essential to the process. Specify a word, phrase, value range, ticker symbol, or even a complete sentence and the terms are added to a lookup list. When the resulting "list" is matched against information in a newsfeed or other source, the articles where matches occur are routed to the user.

spam
An attempt to deliver a message, over the Internet, to someone who would not otherwise choose to receive it.

What differentiates push technology from spamming? According to the Computer Incident Advisory Center, **spam** (or UCE: Unsolicited Commercial E-mail) is the Internet version of "junk mail." It is an attempt to deliver a message, over the Internet, to someone who would not otherwise choose to receive it and almost all spam is commercial advertising.[21] Very simply, spam is not information that the user has requested. Push technology, on the other hand, permits users to indicate areas of interest and, through their browser, have the information electronically sent to them.

The important thing to remember when facing information overload is to relax. You can never read everything that is available. Set goals for yourself, and do the best you can. Remember, just because there is a public library doesn't mean you should feel guilty about not reading every book in it. And so it is with the information superhighway: you can't make every stop along the route, so plan your trip wisely and bon voyage!

Managing Knowledge

Since knowledge gives a company not only power but also profits, competitive companies must find as many ways as possible to mine the knowledge that is stored in their employees. They certainly can't afford to let that knowledge walk out the door when their employees change jobs or retire. **Knowledge management** means sharing, organizing, and disseminating information in the simplest and most relevant way possible for the users of the information.[22]

Consider this scenario: Hal is a project manager trying to determine the cost of lead pipe in Bangladesh. He's tried searching the Web, calling colleagues, writing e-mails, and sending faxes—with no luck. Sal, the assistant vice-president of logistics in the same company as Hal, has been pricing pipe via an e-mail conversation with a Bangladeshi supplier. How does Hal find Sal? Too often, he doesn't. Now there's a way to make Sal aware of Hal's search. It's called e-mail. Well, actually one company calls it knowledge mail.[23]

Knowledge-mail sorts through the millions of e-mail messages churning throughout a company's system and tracks users' work. It can then alert them that others in the company are doing similar work. This allows people who are working on similar projects (like Hal and Sal) to share information and solve problems. You might be concerned that such monitoring of e-mail is an invasion of privacy. Knowledge-mail systems provide a feature that allow users to mark messages that they think should not be sorted in the system. Another safeguard is a feature that lets the source of the information (Sal) know that someone else (Hal) needs the data. Sal can choose whether or not to make the contact with Hal.

Knowledge management requires organizing information so that it's clean, accurate, and consistent, and communicating it to those who need it in a hot second. Next we will discuss some of the technology that helps this happen.

knowledge management
Sharing, organizing, and disseminating information in the simplest and most relevant way possible for the users of the information.

e-business
The production, advertising, sale, and distribution of products via telecommunications networks.

e-commerce
The process of managing online financial transactions by individuals and companies.

business-to-consumer (B2C)
Market that considers transactions between a business and a consumer for personal use.

ELECTRONIC BUSINESS

A study of several hundred technology companies and their customers showed that Canadian spending on data and Internet services is expected to reach about $6.4 billion in 2002.[24] It is clear that Canadian businesses have embraced technology. While the focus of this chapter is on using technology to manage information, it is important to briefly highlight the importance of electronic business (also known as e-business). Electronic commerce (also known as e-commerce and ecommerce), one element of e-business, will also be reviewed briefly.

The World Trade Organization defines **e-business** as "...the production, advertising, sale, and distribution of products via telecommunications networks." This involves the introduction of new revenue streams through the use of e-commerce, the enhancement of relationships between clients and partners, and improving efficiency from using knowledge management systems. E-business can be conducted over the public Internet, through internal intranets, and over secure private extranets.[25]

E-commerce is the process of managing online financial transactions by individuals and companies. The focus is on the systems and procedures whereby financial documents and information of all types are exchanged, including online credit card transactions, e-billing, electronic invoices, and purchase orders.[26] In 2000, e-commerce transactions generated $7.2 billion in Canadian sales.[27]

In the **business-to-consumer (B2C)** market, it is expected that e-business will account for $177.7 billion in worldwide sales in 2003.[28] The focus in this market is on purchases made by consumers for personal use. Examples include making a bill payment through a financial institution's Web site, purchasing a computer for writing term papers and communicating with friends and family, and purchasing groceries and liquor.

www.grocerygateway.com

Grocery Gateway delivers groceries to homes and offices, at a predetermined time. It is a collection of industry leaders that provide the groceries and the technology.

www.okliquor.ca

OK Liquor Online is Canada's first full online store to offer a complete range of spirits, wine, and beer for next-day delivery. Visit the Web site to review locations, cocktail recipes, awards, and party planner information.

The **business-to-business (B2B)** market considers transactions between businesses. By 2003, it is estimated that worldwide sales will reach approximately $1.1 trillion.[29] Such transactions could include ordering materials and components for auto manufacturers via the Internet through systems such as the Automotive Network eXchange, ensuring the delivery of oil to a firm across the country, and ordering airline tickets for company executives.

E-Business Benefits

What are the benefits of e-business to a firm? According to the E-Business Technology Forecast prepared by PricewaterhouseCoopers Technology Centre:[30]

> E-business affects four broad categories that determine the production and transaction costs of a firm that includes:
>
> - the cost of executing a sale
> - the costs associated with procuring production inputs
> - the costs associated with making and delivering a product
> - the cost associated with logistics
>
> For example, the administrative cost of processing a paper cheque for banks and merchants averages $1.20 and a debit- or credit-card payment averages $0.40 to $0.60. The cost of processing an electronic payment made via the Internet can be as low as $0.01 or less.

What are the benefits to you? Very simply, the technology allows you as a consumer to educate yourself about price and product attributes—at your convenience—24/7. The availability and access to technology makes this possible. Sixty-nine percent of Canadian households owned a personal computer in 2000 and 55 percent had Web access.[31] This number will continue to increase as Canada, with Australia, shares the world's cheapest Internet access—an average $20 per month—as compared to $28 in the United States and $74 in Germany and Mexico.[32]

In Chapter 17 we will see examples of firms that have integrated technology in their marketing activities. For now, let us continue with our focus on using technology to manage information.

THE ENABLING TECHNOLOGY: HARDWARE

We hesitate to discuss the advances that have been made in computer hardware because what is powerful as we write this may be obsolete by the time you read it. In the mid-1970s the chairman of Intel Corporation, Gordon E. Moore, predicted that the capacity of computer chips would double every year or so. This has since been called Moore's law. The million-dollar vacuum-tube computers that awed people in the 1950s couldn't keep up with a pocket calculator today. In fact, a greeting card that plays "Happy Birthday" contains more computing power than existed before 1950.

The speed of evolution in the computer industry has slowed little since Moore's remark, although in 1997 Moore did say that his prediction cannot hold good for much longer because chip makers will sooner or later run into a fundamental law of nature; that is, the finite size of atomic particles will prevent infinite miniaturization. That won't stop computer companies from improving chips in ways other than shrinking them.[33] Rapid advances make products obsolete, helping create demand for newer chips. For example, a three-year-old personal computer is considered out-of-date. So rather than add potentially outdated facts, we offer you a simple overview of the current computer technology.

Hardware includes computers, pagers, cellular phones, printers, scanners, fax machines, personal digital assistants, and so on. The mobile worker can find travel-size versions of computers, printers, and fax machines that are almost as powerful and feature-laden as their big siblings. All-in-one devices that address the entire range of your communications needs are now available. For example, there are handheld units that include a wireless phone, fax and e-mail capabilities, Web browsers, and a personal information manager (PIM). The Spotlight on Small Business box shows how useful these information appliances can be in the life of a home-based worker.

Researchers are working on a human computer interface that combines a video camera and personal computer (PC). When you approach the PC, it recognizes you, asks you how you feel, and determines what tasks you want to complete that day. Instead of hearing a mechanical beep to remind you of your next class, you'll hear a soothing voice say, "Sam, your Introduction to Business final will begin in 30 minutes." Sorry, it won't take the test for you—some things you still have to do for yourself.

Cutting the Cord: Wireless Information Appliances

Some experts think we are entering the post-PC era; that is, that we are moving away from a PC-dominant environment toward an array of Internet appliance options. Internet appliances are designed to connect people to the Internet and to e-mail.[34] They include set-top boxes and gaming devices (such as Sega Dreamcast and Sony PlayStation 2) that provide Web-surfing capabilities on standard TVs, and stand-alone devices such as Netpliance's i-opener.

The biggest move away from PCs, however, is in the direction of wireless handhelds like the Palm, smart-phones, and two-way paging devices. Samsung even offers a watch-phone for wrist-top computing, and GM offers in-dash computers for cars.

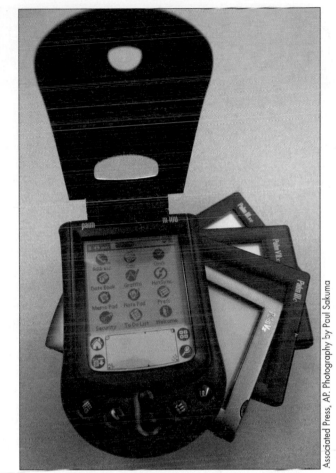

Associated Press, AP. Photography by Paul Sakuma

Personal digital assistants (PDAs), such as these Palm handhelds, allow users to get rid of their paper address books, calendars, memo pads, and all those napkin scribbles. Basic PDAs help keep track of contacts, activities, and to-do lists all with one pocket-sized handheld computer. Higher-end models allow users to add on wireless modems, digital cameras, and more. How could a PDA help you organize your life?

The point is that people are taking the Internet with them, tapping in from time to time to gather information and transact business. This will necessarily change the format in which information is delivered. Because wireless devices are by necessity small, and Web pages have been designed for display on big, high-resolution monitors, it won't work to display Web pages in the same format. Information must be delivered in small bits, using brief lines of text and tiny icons and images. Since mobile users are almost always in a hurry, they will not tolerate irrelevant content.[35] Read the Reaching Beyond Our Borders box "If You Need Me Just Call Me" for a discussion of "narrowband" technology, which holds promise around the world.

www.sega.com
www.sony.com
www.samsung.com
www.gm.com

Computer Networks

Perhaps the most dynamic change in business technology in recent years is the move away from mainframe computers that serve as the centre of information processing and toward network systems that allow many users to access information at the same

A Day in Your Life as a Wired Home-Office Worker

6:30   Get your blood moving with a jog on your Web-enabled treadmill. Log on simultaneously with a friend for a virtual race. On the nearby computer screen, you see your sprint to the finish displayed graphically. You win, of course!

7:30   As you fix your breakfast, you touch the screen of your countertop Internet appliance to see if you received that important e-mail message you are expecting. Yes! You type a quick response and press another on-screen icon for the latest news in your industry. On the way out of the kitchen you press yet another icon to select music downloaded from the Web.

8:00   Time to get to work. You still use a personal computer (PC), but the flat-panel monitor and keyboard are the only hardware parts cluttering your desk. (Of course, there's plenty of paper clutter—the promise of a paperless office has been a dream since the 1950s.) You use the PC for heavy computational tasks and graphics design, but you rely on multiple smaller devices such as your Internet phone for moment-to-moment tasks. Your Internet phone automatically checks for e-mail and alerts you with a blinking light.

11:30   Time to meet a client for lunch at that great new restaurant. Since you don't know the way, your car's in-dash computer with global positioning system (GPS) capabilities guides you with turn-by-turn directions. Speaking to you as you drive, the system warns you to switch lanes and put on your turn signals. You missed a turn; it tells you so and guides you back on track.

12:00   Between the appetizer and the entrée, you realize you forgot to turn off the stove at home. You use your smart phone to call your household computer that monitors all of your appliances and tell it which burner to turn off—and you adjust the house's temperature while you're at it.

2:30   You make it to your next appointment on time because your in-dash computer warns you of an accident and reroutes you.

6:00   Finally back home, you see the Internet phone blinking at you as you walk in the door. You respond and then call it a day. You turn to a good book to relax. You put your electronic book in its cradle and download the newest best-seller from the Web. You turn on your television and play a game of Jeopardy that's been downloaded from your satellite dish. That answer can't be right—you open a picture-in-picture view of the Web and search for more info. But one site leads to another and, before you know it, you've found your answer, downloaded a new album, and bought half your Christmas presents.

10:00   You call it a day and make a mental note to finish that budget spreadsheet tomorrow. You'll use your PC for that, of course. You sleep comfortably, knowing that taking advantage of a wide range of technological options has made both your home and home office life better.

Sources: David Haskin, "A Day in the Post-PC Life," *Home Office Computing*, February 2000, pp. 67–71; and Harold Goldberg, "Gimme That! The Latest Gotta Have Stuff," *Entertainment Weekly*, February 9, 2001.

network computing system (client/server computing)
Computer systems that allow personal computers (clients) to obtain needed information from huge databases in a central computer (the server).

www.synoptics.co.uk

time. In an older system, the mainframe performed all the tasks and sent the results to a "dumb" terminal that could not perform those tasks itself. In a **network computing system** (also called **client/server computing**), the tasks, such as searching sales records, are handled by personal computers called clients. The information needed to complete the tasks is stored in huge databases controlled by the central computer (the server). Networks connect people to people and people to data. The major benefits of networks are the following:

• **Saving time and money.** SynOptics Communications found that electronic delivery of mail and files increased the speed of project development by 25 percent.

REACHING BEYOND OUR BORDERS
If You Need Me
Just Call Me

There's no question that broadband Internet access is the future for PCs, TVs, and other information appliances. In fact, it's hard to pick up a newspaper, watch television, or surf the Net and not be deluged with advertisements promoting superspeed Internet connections via cable modem or digital phone lines. Companies like America Online (AOL) are gearing up their products to include rich audio, video, and interactive media that take advantage of the fatter Net connections. But a challenge looms on the horizon from an unlikely competitor—the telephone.

It seems a number of companies are rolling out Internet-access services that work over both wired and wireless phones. These "**narrowband**" connections use a fraction of frequencies to deliver a tiny trickle of data compared to their broadband counterparts. Users, though, can customize and access useful data just by dialing a toll-free number. For example, recent start-up Tellme Networks provides its users with headlines, sports scores, traffic information, weather reports, and horoscopes. While hardly competition for a colourful Web page, the information is delivered in a pleasant digital voice you can access easily, even as you drive to your next appointment. Besides receiving free customized information, Tellme subscribers can also get movie listings and restaurant reviews—and then be connected directly to the theatres or restaurants. Users navigate the system simply by speaking commands

into the phone instead of having to use cumbersome Touch-Tones.

Since narrowband connections are priced low and available almost everywhere, they could become one of the world's most popular pathways to the Internet. This is particularly important in countries like Japan, where traditional phone lines do not exist as we know them in the United States. The country is so densely populated that it would cost too much to string wire lines today. Therefore, wireless phones may be the most efficient way for many Japanese to surf the Net.

International Data Corporation, an Internet research firm, projects that by 2004 some 600 million people will be hooked up to the Net via PCs. However, the corporation also forecasts that 1.4 billion people will connect through cell phones and another 1.4 billion will get on via wired phones. Such estimates are driving an explosion of new investments in narrowband from Internet heavyweights such as Oracle, IBM, and Amazon.com. It's clear that the global battle for control of information promises to be intense throughout the twenty-first century. Who knows, maybe an old standby from Alexander Graham Bell will become the hot new Web tool.

Sources: Andy Reinhardt, "The Good Old Telephone Becomes a Hot New Web Tool," *Business Week*, April 24, 2000; Irene M. Kunii, "Japan's Cutting Edge," *Business Week*, May 22, 2000; and Nikki Swartz, "Say Hello to Voice Portals," *Wireless Review*, February 1, 2001.

- **Providing easy links across functional boundaries.** With networks, it's easy to find someone who can offer insightful solutions to a problem. The most common questions on computer bulletin boards begin, "Does anyone know . . . ?" Usually someone does.

- **Allowing employees to see complete information.** In traditional organizations, information is summarized so many times that it often loses its meaning. For example, a sales representative's two-page summary may be cut to a paragraph in the district manager's report and then to a few numbers on a chart in the regional manager's report. Networks, on the other hand, catch raw information.

Here's how networks helped software giant Lotus Development. Instead of waiting for the information gained from 4 million annual phone calls to be summarized by technical support people, Lotus Development now sends the information straight into a database, where it's available on demand. Rather than accept someone else's idea of what information is needed, any Lotus development employee can access the

www.lotus.com

data and search according to his or her needs. The result is that many more employees than before have direct access to market information and can act accordingly.

Networks have their drawbacks as well. Maintaining a fleet of finicky desktop PCs can be expensive. Studies show that the cost of maintaining one corporate Windows desktop computer can run up to $10,000 a year.[36] The cost of the computer itself is just the down payment. Computing costs go up with productivity losses as you upgrade and troubleshoot equipment and train employees to use it. By the time you've recouped your costs, it's time for another upgrade. A large part of PC support costs comes from adding software that causes conflicts or disables other software on the system. Doing this upgrading to two or three PCs in a small home office is annoying; doing it to dozens or hundreds of PCs in a corporation is daunting. Using networks requires so many organizational changes and incurs such high support and upgrade costs that some companies that have tried networking PCs are now looking at other options.[37]

www.everdream.com

One option is a new hybrid of mainframe and network computing. In this model, applications and data reside on a server, which handles all of the processing needs for all the client machines on the networks. Called *thin-client networks,* these new networks may resemble the dumb terminals of the 1980s, but the execution is much better. Users can still use the Windows applications that they had been using. In a thin-client network, software changes and upgrades need to be made only on the server, so the cost of ownership can be reduced by 20 percent.

Other options to maintaining the server onsite are to contract with a remote service provider and to lease specific software applications. When you lease software from an applications service provider (ASP), the provider maintains and upgrades the software on its servers.[38] You connect to the ASP's servers via the Internet. You are then using the most current applications without the hassles of upgrading software yourself.[39] A new company called Everdream takes it a step further: Its single-fee service includes a powerful PC, unlimited Internet access, daily data backup, e-mail, popular business software, training, and around-the-clock support that includes remote management. If you have a software or hardware question, you don't have to call a long series of phone numbers until you find someone who can help. All you need is one phone number; Everdream staff members are always there, and they won't hang up until your problem is solved.[40] The greatest benefit of thin-client computing or ASP is that it frees up more time for your business since you'll spend less time tinkering with technological tools.

The Spotlight on Big Business box "It's Only Natural" indicates how scientists have been able to use what they have learned about ants to improve computer network systems.

SPOTLIGHT ON BIG BUSINESS
It's Only Natural

Researchers at British Telecommunications (BT), one of the world's leading telecommunications companies, studied ant colonies, jellyfish, and slime moulds. Why? They hoped that nature could help them solve one of their critical business problems—overloaded or damaged network lines. It could take BT a decade and more than $46 billion to overhaul its phone network the traditional way. So BT asked biologists and entomologists to search the natural world of alternative solutions. "Biological organisms do complex things with very simple software, while man's unbelievably complex systems can only do very simple things," says Peter Cochrane, BT's research director. One of Cochrane's teams modelled a software program on ant colonies. The program sends out "ants," or intelligent agents, to explore alternate routes through overloaded or damaged networks. As each ant returns almost instantaneously with information on how long it takes to travel to different parts of the network, the network can reconfigure itself to bypass the problem in less than a second—much faster than the several minutes it now takes to do the same task.

Where is technology headed? Cochrane envisions people and technology converging to create what he calls "homo cybernetics." For example, we will dress in vests that will use heat from our bodies to power all the technology we will wear. Picture a visor that can project TV-like images or data onto the retina, allowing you to read e-mail or study a map while walking down the street. "People will be walking around online in the early twenty-first century," predicts Cochrane. He also believes that desktop boxes will disappear, replaced by more cuddly interfaces. His favourite example is a computerized robot that "looks like a kitten but doesn't bring in dead mice."

Source: Julia Flynn, "British Telecom: Notes from the Ant Colony," *Business Week*, June 23, 1997, p. 108.

CRITICAL THINKING

What are the implications for world peace and world trade given the ability firms and government organizations now have to communicate with one another across borders? Could the co-operation needed among telecommunications firms worldwide lead to increased co-operation among other organizations on issues such as world health care and worldwide exchanges of technical information?

SOFTWARE

Computer software programs provide the instructions that enable you to tell the computer what to do. Although many people looking to buy a computer think first of the equipment, it is important to find the right software before finding the right hardware. The type of software you want dictates the kind of equipment you need.

Some software programs are easier to use than others. Some are more sophisticated and can perform more functions than others. A business person must decide what functions he or she wants the computer system to perform and then choose the appropriate software. That choice will help determine what brand of computer to buy, how much power it should have, and what other peripherals it needs.

While most software is distributed commercially through suppliers like retail stores or online e-tailers, there is some software, called **shareware**, that is copyrighted but distributed to potential customers free of charge. The users are asked to send a specified fee to the developer if the program meets their needs and they decide to use it. The shareware concept has become very popular and has dramatically reduced the price of software. **Public domain software (freeware)** is software that is free for the taking. The quality of shareware and freeware varies greatly. To help you have an

shareware
Software that is copyrighted but distributed to potential customers free of charge.

public domain software (freeware)
Software that is free for the taking.

idea of the quality of such programs, find a Web site that rates shareware and freeware programs. For example, SoftSeek.com lists the programs downloaded most often, editors' picks, and links to downloadable programs. (See the Ethical Dilemma box at the beginning of the chapter for another factor to consider in choosing software.)

Business people most frequently use software for (1) writing (word processors), (2) manipulating numbers (spreadsheets), (3) filing and retrieving data (databases), (4) presenting information visually (graphics), (5) communicating (e-mail and instant messaging), and (6) accounting. Today's software can perform many functions in one kind of program known as *integrated software* or a *software suite*. Another class of software program, called *groupware*, has emerged for use on networks. Figure 11.2 describes these types of software.

PROGRESS CHECK

- What are the four characteristics of information that make it useful?
- How do computer networks change the way employees gather information?
- Can you list and describe the major types of computer software used in business?

EFFECTS OF INFORMATION TECHNOLOGY ON MANAGEMENT

The increase of information technology has already begun to affect management and will continue to do so. Four major issues arising out of the growing reliance on information technology are human resource changes, security threats, privacy concerns, and stability issues.

Get the right tool for the job. Microsoft did.

Courtesy of Veritas

Human Resource Issues

By now, you may have little doubt that computers are increasingly capable of providing us with the information and knowledge we need to do our daily tasks. The less creative the tasks, the more likely they will be managed by computers. For example, many telemarketing workers today have their work structured by computer-driven scripts. That process can apply to the work lives of customer service representatives, stockbrokers, and even managers. Technology makes the work process more efficient as it replaces many bureaucratic functions. We talked in Chapter 9 about tall versus flat organization structures ➤ **P. 261–262** ◄. Computers often eliminate middle management functions and thus flatten organization structures.

One of the major challenges technology creates for human resource managers is the need to recruit employees who know how to use the new technology

There's the right tool for every job. Bigger isn't always better. The first step in choosing the right information technology tool is to identify what it is you want to accomplish and then go from there. For example, there is no need to invest in a state-of-the-art computer if you plan to use it only for simple word processing.

Word processing programs	With word processors, standardized letters can be personalized quickly, documents can be updated by changing only the outdated text and leaving the rest intact, and contract forms can be revised to meet the stipulations of specific customers. The most popular word processing programs include Corel WordPerfect, Microsoft Word, and Lotus WordPro.
Desktop publishing software (DTP)	DTP combines word processing with graphics capabilities that can produce designs that once could be done only by powerful page-layout design programs. Popular DTP programs include Microsoft Publisher, Adobe PageMaker Plus, and Corel Print Office.
Spreadsheet programs	A spreadsheet program is simply the electronic equivalent of an accountant's worksheet plus such features as mathematical function libraries, statistical data analysis, and charts. Using the computer's speedy calculations, managers have their questions answered almost as fast as they can ask them. Some of the most popular spreadsheet programs are Lotus 1-2-3, Quattro Pro, and Excel.
Database programs	A database program allows users to work with information that is normally kept in lists: names and addresses, schedules, inventories, and so forth. Using database programs, you can create reports that contain exactly the information you want in the form you want it to appear in. Leading database programs include Q&A, Access, Approach, Paradox, PFS: Professional File, PC-File, R base, and FileMaker Pro for Apple computers.
Personal information managers (PIMs)	PIMs or contact managers are specialized database programs that allow users to track communication with their business contacts. Such programs keep track of everything—every person, every phone call, every e-mail message, every appointment. Popular PIMs include Goldmine, Lotus Organizer, ACT, and ECCO Pro.
Graphics and presentation programs	Computer graphics programs can use data from spreadsheets to visually summarize information by drawing bar graphs, pie charts, line charts, and more. Inserting sound clips, video clips, clip art, and animation can turn a dull presentation into an enlightening one. Some popular graphics programs are Illustrator and Freehand for Macintosh computers, Microsoft PowerPoint, Harvard Graphics, Lotus Freelance Graphics, Active Presenter, and Corel Draw.
Communications programs	Communications software enables a computer to exchange files with other computers, retrieve information from databases, and send and receive electronic mail. Such programs include Microsoft Outlook, ProComm Plus, Eudora, and Telik.
Message centre software	Message centre software is more powerful than traditional communications packages. This new generation of programs has teamed up with fax/voice modems to provide an efficient way of making certain that phone calls, e-mail, and faxes are received, sorted, and delivered on time, no matter where you are. Such programs include Communicate, Message Centre, and WinFax Pro.
Accounting and finance programs	Accounting software helps users record financial transactions and generate financial reports. Some programs include online banking features that allow users to pay bills through the computer. Others include "financial advisers" that offer users advice on a variety of financial issues. Popular accounting and finance programs include Peachtree Complete Accounting, Simply Accounting, Quicken, and QuickBooks Pro.
Integrated programs	Integrated software packages (also called suites) offer two or more applications in one package. This allows you to share information across applications easily. Such packages include word processing, database management, spreadsheet, graphics, and communications. Suites include Microsoft Office, Lotus SmartSuite, and Corel WordPerfect Suite.
Groupware	Groupware is software that allows people to work collaboratively and share ideas. It runs on a network and allows people in different areas to work on the same project at the same time. Groupware programs include Lotus Notes, Frontier's Intranet Genie, MetaInfo Sendmail, and Radnet Web Share.

FIGURE 11.2

TYPES OF POPULAR COMPUTER SOFTWARE

or train those who already work in the company. Often they hire consultants instead of internal staff to address these concerns. Outsourcing technical training allows companies to concentrate on their core businesses. Even techno-savvy companies outsource technology training. Employers may post jobs (and you can also view these jobs and post your résumé) on several Web sites including www.monster.ca; www.workopolis.com; and www.hotjobs.ca. Computer companies such as 3Com, Cisco, and Microsoft often hire a technology training company called Information Management Systems to train employees to use their own systems.[41]

Perhaps the most revolutionary effect of computers and the increased use of the Internet and intranets is that of telecommuting ➤ **P. 17** ◂. Mobile employees using computers linked to the company's network can transmit their work to the office, and back, from anywhere. It is estimated that there will be 1.5 million telecommuters in Canada by the end of 2001.[42]

Such work involves less travel time and fewer costs, and often increases productivity. Telecommuting helps firms save money by allowing them to retain valuable employees during long personal leaves or to tempt experienced employees out of retirement. Companies can also enjoy savings in commercial property costs, since having fewer employees in the office means a company can get by with smaller, and therefore less expensive, offices than before. It has also been a boon for disabled workers.[43]

Employees who can work after hours on their home computers rather than at the office report less stress and improved morale. Studies show that telecommuting is most successful among people who are self-starters, who don't have home distractions, and whose work doesn't require face-to-face interaction with co-workers.

Even as telecommuting has grown in popularity, however, some telecommuters report that a consistent diet of long-distance work gives them a dislocated feeling of being left out of the office loop. Some feel a loss of the increased energy people can get through social interaction.[44] In addition to the isolation issue is the intrusion that work brings into what is normally a personal setting. Often people working from home don't know when to turn the work off. Some companies are pulling away from viewing telecommuting as an either–or proposition: either at home or at the office. Such companies are using telecommuting as a part-time alternative. In fact, industry now defines telecommuting as working at home a minimum of two days a week.

Electronic communication can never replace human communication for creating enthusiasm. Efficiency and productivity can become so important to a firm that people are treated like robots. In the long run, such treatment results in less efficiency and productivity. Computers are a tool, not a total replacement for managers or workers, and creativity is still a human trait. Computers should aid creativity by giving people more freedom and more time. Often they do, but unfortunately many take the results of their productivity gains not in leisure (as do the Europeans), but in increased consumption, making them have to work even harder to pay for it all. Information technology allows people to work at home, on vacation, and in the car at any time of the day.

Figure 11.3 illustrates how information technology changes the way managers and workers interact. Both groups use information technology differently, highlighting its importance and flexibility in the workplace.

Security Issues

One current problem with computers that is likely to persist in the future is that they are susceptible to hackers. In 1994, officials were unable to find the hackers who broke into Pentagon computers through the Internet and stole, altered, and erased numerous records. In 2000, hackers tried to blackmail an e-tailer, saying that if the company didn't pay a ransom, they would sell the credit card numbers they had retrieved from its Web site.[45] Cybercrimes cost businesses $266 million in 1999.[46]

Computer security is more complicated today than ever before. When information was processed in a mainframe environment, the single data centre was easier to control

www.3com.com
www.microsoft.com

www.ivc.ca

For more information about telecommuting (also known as telework) in Canada, visit the Canadian Telework Association Web site.

MANAGERS MUST	WORKERS MUST
• Instill commitment in subordinates rather than rule by command and control. • Become coaches, training workers in necessary job skills, making sure they have resources to accomplish goals, and explaining links between a job and what happens elsewhere in the company. • Use new information technologies to measure workers' performance, possibly based on customer satisfaction or the accomplishment of specific goals.	• Become initiators, able to act without management direction. • Become financially literate so they can understand the business implications of what they do and changes they suggest. • Develop new math, technical, and analytical skills to use newly available information on their jobs.

FIGURE 11.3

WHEN INFORMATION TECHNOLOGY ALTERS THE WORKPLACE

since there was limited access to it. Today, however, computers are accessible not only in all areas within the company but also in all areas of other companies with which the firm does business. Many companies have turned to outsource companies to monitor their security needs.[47] "Security is a process, not a product" is the mantra of Counterpane, a computer security company. Software products are created by humans and are therefore flawed. It takes skilled knowledge about how to use them to keep hackers at bay. Oddly enough, the most skilled security consultants are former hackers. Members of what was once known as a "hackers' think tank" formed a company called AtStake that advises the world's largest banks and hospitals about how to keep their data safe.[48]

www.counterpane.com

www.atstake.com

Another security issue involves the spread of computer viruses over the Internet. A **virus** is a piece of programming code inserted into other programming to cause some unexpected and, for the victim, usually undesirable event. Viruses are spread by downloading infected programming over the Internet or by sharing an infected diskette. Often the source of the file you downloaded is unaware of the virus. The virus lies dormant until circumstances cause its code to be executed by the computer. Some viruses are playful ("Kilroy was here!"), but some can be quite harmful, erasing data or causing your hard drive to crash. There are software programs, such as Norton's AntiVirus, that "inoculate" your computer so that it doesn't catch a known virus. But because new viruses are being developed constantly, antivirus programs may have only limited success. Therefore, you should keep your antivirus protection program up-to-date and, more important, practise "safe computing" by not downloading files from unknown sources and by using your antivirus program to scan diskettes before transferring files from them.[49]

virus
A piece of programming code inserted into other programming to cause some unexpected and, for the victim, usually undesirable event.

www.symantec.com

Existing laws do not address the problems of today's direct, real-time communication. As more and more people merge onto the information superhighway, the number of legal issues will likely increase. Already, copyright and pornography laws are crashing into the virtual world. Other legal questions—such as those involving intellectual property and contract disputes, online sexual and racial harassment, and the use of electronic communication to promote crooked sales schemes—are being raised as millions of people log on to the Internet.[50]

Privacy Issues

The increase of technology creates major concerns about privacy. For example, e-mail is no more private than a postcard. You don't need to be the target of a criminal investigation to have your e-mail snooped. More than one-fourth of U.S. companies scan employee e-mail regularly and legally. Just as they can log and listen to your telephone conversations, they can track your e-mail, looking for trade secrets, non-work-related traffic, harassing messages, and conflicts of interest. Also, most e-mail travels over the Internet in unencrypted plain text. Any hacker with a desire to read your thoughts can trap and read your messages. Some e-mail systems, such as Lotus Notes, can encrypt messages so you can keep corporate messages private. If you use browser-based e-mail, you can obtain a certificate that has an encryption key from a company such as VeriSign; the cost is about $10 a year. Of course, users who want to decrypt your mail need to get an unlocking key.[51]

The Internet presents increasing threats to your privacy, as more and more personal information is stored in computers and people are able to access that data, legally or illegally. The Internet allows Web surfers to access all sorts of information about you. For example, some Web sites allow people to search for vehicle ownership from a licence number or to find individuals' real estate property records. One key question in the debate over protecting our privacy is "Isn't this personal information already public anyway?" Civil libertarians have long fought to keep certain kinds of information available to the public. If access to such data is restricted on the Internet, wouldn't we have to reevaluate our policies on public records entirely? The privacy advocates don't think so. After all, the difference is that the Net makes obtaining personal information too easy. Would your neighbours or friends even consider going to the appropriate local agency and sorting through public documents for hours to find your driving records or to see your divorce settlement? Probably not. But they might dig into your background if all it takes is a few clicks of a button.

Average PC users are concerned that Web sites have gotten downright nosy. In fact, many Web servers track users' movements online. Web surfers seem willing to swap personal details for free access to online information. This personal information is shared with others without your permission (regardless of the promises made in the Web sites' privacy policy statements). Web sites often send **cookies** to your computer that stay on your hard drive. These little tidbits often simply contain your name and a password that the Web site recognizes the next time you visit the site so that you don't have to re-enter the same information every time you visit.[52] Other cookies track your movements around the Web and then blend that information with a database so that a company can tailor the ads you receive accordingly.[53] Do you mind someone watching over your shoulder while you're on the Web? Tim Berners-Lee, the researcher who invented the World Wide Web, is working on a way to prevent you from receiving cookies without your permission. His Platform for Privacy Preferences, or P3, would allow a Web site to automatically send information on its privacy policies. You would be able to set up your Web browser to communicate only with those Web sites that meet certain criteria. You need to decide how much information about yourself you are willing to give away. Remember, we are living in an information economy, and information is a commodity—that is, an economic good with a measurable value.[54]

cookies
Pieces of information, such as registration data or user preferences, sent by a Web site over the Internet to a Web browser that the browser software is expected to save and send back to the server whenever the user returns to that Web site.

Stability Issues

While technology can provide significant increases in productivity and efficiency, instability in technology also has a significant impact on business. In fact, some industry experts estimate that computer glitches account for a remarkable $100 billion in lost productivity each year.[55] In 1999, candy maker Hershey discovered the Halloween trick was on it when the company couldn't get its treats to the stores on time. Failure of its new $115 million computer system disrupted shipment, and retailers were forced to order from other companies. Consequently, Hershey suffered a 12-percent decrease in sales that quarter.

www.hersheys.com

What's to blame? Experts say it is a combination of computer error; human error; malfunctioning software; and overly complex marriage of software, hardware, and networking equipment. Some systems are launched too quickly to be bug-proof, and some executives are too naïve to challenge computer specialists. Industry consultant Howard Rubin says, "This stuff is becoming more critical to big business, yet some of it is built like Lego sets and Tinker toys. It's not built for rigorous engineering, and people aren't properly trained to use it. As things get more complex, we'll be prone to more errors."[56]

SOME ISSUES TODAY

While the focus of this chapter has been on using technology to manage information, there are many issues at the time of producing this chapter that are related to managing information. Included is the dot-com crash, ongoing litigations (e.g., record labels versus Napster, the U.S. government versus Microsoft), and broadband battles (e.g., between cable and phone companies). These issues have been debated for some time now and many believe that it will take more time to completely settle them. The following section reviews the dot-com crash and Napster's challenges in more detail.

The Dot-Com Crash

According to Reuters Media, a total of 100,000 jobs have vanished from the Internet economy since December 1999 and a full 50,000 of those jobs have disappeared since February 2000.[57] Many are asking what caused the dot-com crash. Companies such as Nortel, Cisco, and Intel are reporting lower revenues as demand for Internet-based products is decreasing. Major television networks are blaming some of their current revenue declines on the dot-com failures. Who is to blame?

www.nortel.com
www.cisco.com
www.pentium.com

Rob Spiegel wrote an article on businessknowhow.com addressing this question. He believes there were many players and reasons that contributed to this decline:[58]

- Many business models were created to draw audience, rather than profits. Young executives who were hired at large salaries did in fact generate this traffic.

- Venture capitalists provided large amounts of money to fund these new ventures, without making sure the business plans were based on profit objectives. From their perspective, these ventures were risky to begin with and seven out of ten companies were expected to fail.

- The media promoted and built up the New Economy and the dramatic rise of the dot-coms. It is now doing the same for the dot-com crashes.

In Spiegel's summation, no one is really to blame. While others many think otherwise, his view is that we have witnessed both successes and failures. Large businesses are still targeting the Internet and are continuing to invest in IT.

Today, investors are demanding business models that incorporate profit and revenue goals. This is a change from early investors who were expecting great profits and continued to invest millions of dollars in new companies with unproven track records. Companies are restructuring and are providing more sound business plans with specific and measurable targets. Stakeholders demand it.

Napster

With nearly 60 million registered users in early 2001, Napster was one of the most successful applications on the Internet.[59] Founded in 1999, Napster's software application enables users to locate and share media files from one interface. However, Napster has been involved in legal disputes over copyright violations with major record labels, music publishers, and songwriters. Simply, the charges are that Napster users are sharing copyrighted music via the site's MP3 file-sharing software; the free availability of downloadable music has deprived record labels and artists of royalties. As a result of these litigations, Napster's free service was blocked in July 2001. Most of its former fans have gone to rival free services such as MusicCity or Audiogalaxy.[60]

www.napster.com

www.musiccity.com
www.audiogalaxy.com

In late 2001, Napster announced a major deal to pay music publishers and songwriters $26 million to settle its ongoing legal disputes. Record labels are continuing with their own litigation. Napster's impact on music retailers has also been dramatic:[61]

- Record sales dropped in Canada by 7 percent, following a 7-percent drop in 1999.
- Amid mounting pressure from newer rivals and technologies, Sam the Record Man, Canada's last remaining family-owned record store chain, filed for bankruptcy after 53 years in business in 2001.
- Tower Records pulled out of Canada, closing two unprofitable locations.
- British giant HMV, Canada's biggest specialty record seller, admitted the North American market was soft.

www.hmv.com

Napster has announced a new paid subscription service that is to be an authorized version of its file-swapping system. While the company has not yet announced how much it will charge for its subscription service and what proportion of this revenue will go to content owners, it expects to have one to two million subscribers within 18 months of the subscription service launch.[62] Eyes will be on this new service to see if Napster will be an ongoing entity in the years to come.

TECHNOLOGY AND YOU

If you are beginning to think that being computer illiterate may be career-limiting you are getting the point. As Mike Maternaghan, a business development manager for British Telecom, remarked, "It's tempting to say that if you can't use a computer in a couple of years, it will be like not being able to read."[63] Workers in every industry come in contact with computers to some degree. Even fast-food workers read orders on computer screens. It is estimated that by 2006 half of all American workers will be employed in information technology positions or within industries that use information technology, goods, and services extensively.[64]

www.bt.com

Canada is facing an increasing shortage of information technology workers. Such a shortage could have negative implications for Canada's competitiveness, economic growth, and job creation. The increase in demand for skilled IT workers is driving up pay scales. The average annual salary for a chief information officer ranges between $100,000 and $250,000 depending on the location. In fact, a Wall Street CIO with more than four years' experience can command a half-million-dollar salary—and that doesn't include perks such as stock options that can add millions more.[65] Figure 11.4 lists the fastest-growing occupations, according to the U.S. Bureau of Labor Statistics.

If you are still among those considered computer illiterate, do not feel alone. Researchers have found that 55 percent of Americans have some degree of computerphobia (fear of computers). Amazingly, half of all white-collar workers say they are afraid of trying new technologies. Gender, age, and income level don't appear to be linked to computerphobia. The key variable is exposure—that's why Nintendo-era

FIGURE 11.4

FASTEST-GROWING OCCUPATIONS

This figure shows the projected increase from 1996 to 2006. Notice that three of the five fastest-growing occupations are in information technology fields.

Database administrators, computer-support specialists, and all other computer scientists	118%
Computer engineers	109
Systems analysts	103
Personal and home care aides	85
Physical- and corrective-therapy assistants	79

Source: U.S. Bureau of Labor Statistics.

kids take to computers so easily. Computerphobes do not do as well in school as their mouse-clicking classmates. In the workplace, they may get passed up for promotions or lose their jobs. On a psychological level, they often feel inadequate and outdated—sort of like outcasts in a technological, digitized world. Here's the good news: computerphobia is curable, and computer training (the best medicine) is readily available. You may want to start out with low-tech learning aids such as videos and computer books and then gradually move up to training classes or CD-ROMs. As information technology eliminates old jobs while creating new ones, it is up to you to learn and maintain the skills you need to be certain you aren't left behind.[66]

There is so much information available today that it is becoming more and more challenging to find the relevant information for the project at hand. Managing information is critical not only for business people, but also for those studying business and other courses. When conducting Internet searches, one commonly used search technique is **Boolean searching**. Boolean searching is based on a system of symbolic logic developed by George Boole, a nineteenth-century English mathematician. Most keyword-searchable computer databases, as well as search engines, support Boolean searching. Through the use of basic operators (which use the terms AND, OR, and NOT), Boolean searching may be used to perform accurate searches.[67] You are encouraged to visit your library to get more information on this technique as well as other suggestions in helping you use technology to manage information.

In closing, while technological developments are having an enormous effect on people and jobs in business, it is worthwhile considering what Elbert Hubbard (editor, publisher, and author) stated. In his words, "One machine can do the work of 50 men [but] no machine can do the work of one extraordinary man."[68] We can assume that he was also referring to women.

Boolean searching
A search technique that uses keyword operators; it is used to perform accurate searches on computer databases and search engines.

For more information on advanced Web searching techniques, including Boolean searching, visit the following Web sites: www.learnthenet.com/ english/html/ 77advanc.htm; www.lboro.ac.uk/info/ training/finding/sink.htm; www.lscc.cc.fl.us/library/ guides/boolsea.htm.

PROGRESS CHECK

- How has information technology changed the way people work?
- What management issues have been affected by the growth of information technology?
- What career areas are growing as information technology expands?

ETHICAL DILEMMA
Review

Recall the question about illegal software copying from the beginning of the chapter. Here's what our executives have to say. Bédard has this comment: "Unfortunately, small businesses rarely have established policies that employees can refer to. Certain practices are tolerated in smaller businesses that would not be tolerated in more established companies. It is, of course, very difficult to control what employees do when a supervisor or owner is not present. Since it is illegal to copy software, I would recommend having a consistent approach toward honesty. Employees should be informed that this practice is not tolerated by the company. This would send a message that the owner expects his employees to act in a proper fashion in all their dealings."

Reilley has a similar opinion: "No, I would neither do it myself nor encourage my employees to do so. The obvious advantages of not copying software are virus-free and upgradeable software. Copying software is not only an illegal activity, but will contribute to a culture of corporate dishonesty, which can affect a business in many ways.

"For example, an employee might use the same justification ('it's of no consequence') to pilfer company assets, which, of course, would cut into profits. A dishonest mindset could very easily lead to all manner of customer and legal abuses. Dishonest practices will spread across a business and, no matter how seemingly trivial, cannot be tolerated in a serious business venture. Once started they are very, very difficult to stop."

SUMMARY

1. Outline the changing role of business technology.

1. Business technology is continuously changing names and changing roles.
   - *What have been the various names and roles of business technology since 1970?*
   In the 1970s, business technology was called data processing (DP) and its role was to *support* existing business. In the 1980s, its name became information systems (IS) and its role changed to *doing* business. In the 1990s, business technology became information technology (IT) and its role is now to *change* business.
   - *How does information technology change business?*
   Information technology has minimized the importance of time and place to business. Business that is independent of time and location can deliver products and services whenever and wherever it is convenient for the customer. See Figure 11.1 for examples of how information technology changes business.
   - *What is knowledge technology?*
   Knowledge technology adds a layer of intelligence to filter appropriate information and deliver it when it is needed.

2. Compare the scope of the Internet, intranets, and extranets as tools for managing information.

2. To become knowledge-based, businesses must know how to share information and design systems for creating new knowledge.
   - *What information technology is available to help businesses manage information?*
   The heart of information technology involves the Internet, intranets, and extranets. The Internet is a massive network of thousands of smaller networks open to everyone with a computer and a modem. An intranet is a companywide network protected from unauthorized entry by outsiders. An extranet is a semiprivate network that allows more than one company to access the same information.

3. List the steps in managing information, and identify the characteristics of useful information.

3. Information technology multiplies the mountains of information available to business people.
   - *How can you deal with information overload?*
   The most important step in dealing with information overload is to identify your four or five key goals. Eliminate information that will not help you meet your key goals.
   - *What makes information useful?*
   The usefulness of management information depends on four characteristics: quality, completeness, timeliness, and relevance.

4. Review the hardware most frequently used in business, and outline the benefits of the move toward computer networks.

4. Computer hardware changes rapidly.
   - *What was the most dynamic change in computer hardware in the last decade?*
   Perhaps the most dynamic change was the move away from mainframe computers that serve as the centre of information processing toward network systems that allow many users to access information at the same time.
   - *What are the major benefits of networks?*
   Networks' major benefits are (1) saving time and money, (2) providing easy links across functional boundaries, and (3) allowing employees to see complete information.

5. Classify the computer software most frequently used in business.

5. Computer software provides the instructions that enable you to tell the computer what to do.
   - *What types of software programs are used by managers most frequently?*
   Managers most often use word processing, electronic spreadsheet, database, graphics, e-mail and instant messaging, and accounting programs. Another class of software programs, called groupware, allows people to work collaboratively and share ideas.

6. Evaluate the human resource, security, privacy and stability issues in management that are affected by information technology.

6. Information technology has a tremendous effect on the way we do business.
   - *What effect has information technology had on business management?*
   Computers eliminate some middle management functions and thus flatten organization structures. Computers also allow employees to work from their own

homes. On the negative side, computers sometimes allow information to fall into the wrong hands. Managers must find ways to prevent stealing by hackers. Concern for privacy is another issue affected by the vast store of information available on the Internet. Finding the balance between freedom to access private information and individuals' right to privacy will require continued debate.

7. Information technology eliminates old jobs while creating new ones.
   • *Which careers are gaining workers because of the growth of information technology?* Database administrators, computer engineers, and systems analysts are in demand.

7. Identify the careers that are gaining workers because of the growth of information technology.

KEY TERMS

Boolean searching 345	**information systems (IS)** 325	**network computing system (client/server computing)** 334
broadband technology 328	**information technology (IT)** 325	**public domain software (freeware)** 337
business-to-business (B2B) 332	**Internet 2** 329	**push technology** 330
business-to-consumer (B2C) 331	**intranet** 327	**shareware** 337
cookies 342	**knowledge management** 331	**spam** 330
data processing (DP) 324	**knowledge technology (KT)** 326	**virtual private network (VPN)** 328
e-business 331	**narrowband technology** 335	**virtualization** 325
e-commerce 331		**virus** 341

DEVELOPING WORKPLACE SKILLS

1. Interview someone who bought a computer system to use in his or her business. Ask why that person bought that specific computer and how it is used. Ask about any problems that occurred during the purchase process or in installing and using the system. What would the buyer do differently next time? What software does he or she find especially useful?

2. If you have worked with computers, you've probably experienced times when the hard drive crashed or the software wouldn't perform as it should have. Describe one computer glitch you've experienced and what you did to resolve it. Analyze and discuss the consequences of the interruption (e.g., decreased productivity, increased stress). If you haven't had a problem with a personal computer, talk with a friend or classmate who has.

3. Choose a topic that interests you and then, on the Internet, use two search engines to find information about the topic. If the initial result of your search is a list of thousands of sites, narrow your search using the tips offered by the search engine. Did both search engines find the same Web sites? If not, how were the sites different? Which engine found the most appropriate information?

4. Discuss how technology has changed your relationship with specific businesses or organizations such as your bank, your school, and your favourite places to shop. Has it strengthened or weakened your relationship? On a personal level, how has technology affected your relationship with your family, friends, and community? Take a sheet of paper and write down how technology has helped build your business and personal relationships on one side. On the other side of the paper, list how technology has weakened the relationships. What can you and others do to use technology more effectively to reduce any negative impact?

TAKING IT TO THE NET

Purpose:

To examine how information technology changes the way we do business.

Exercises:

1. Let's see how one financial institution, RBC Financial Group, uses information technology to help small businesses simplify their business processes. Go to the site www.royalbank.com. Royal Bank pledges business clients open communication, a credit process with feedback, privacy, professional conduct, and accountability.

    Click on the side buttons including Starting A Business, Managing Your Business, After The Start-Up, and Business Resources. Does Royal Bank deliver on its pledge? What examples can you provide to support your view? Explain how this Web site may help small businesses operate more efficiently and effectively.

2. Check out the Web site of the Information Technology Association of Canada www.itac.ca and follow some of the links to see some current concerns of the association. Is there any progress on some of the problems discussed in the chapter? Are there any new issues being raised? Make a print-out and bring it to class for discussion.

PRACTISING MANAGEMENT DECISIONS

CASE 1

THE SUPER BOWL OF NETWORKS

Couch potatoes may think of the kickoff of the football season as the time to relax and settle in until Super Bowl Sunday, but for the NFL's information technology's networking groups it's the start of a frantic work marathon that won't stop until the championship rings are engraved. Imagine keeping 30 teams connected to the NFL's New York headquarters not only during game time but also at off-site summer training camps, at the annual owners' meeting, and during draft announcements. And, of course, during the event of the year, on Super Bowl Sunday, last-minute venue changes and different networking configurations present ample opportunities to fumble.

The networking team must create quick-turn networks that are used for a limited amount of time and then quickly dismantled. In just one month in 1996, the NFL wired more than 3,000 national and international media people, installed 32 km of telephone cable, set up 800 phone lines and 600 cell phone lines, and created a 140-node network in New Orleans. To make sure that no one drops the ball, the NFL has teamed up with Sprint to create a best-practices playbook for creating quick-turn networks. Having a game plan is definitely worth the effort since the NFL has to do this on a regular basis, according to Craig Johnson, a research analyst at CurrentAnalysis Inc.

Every year since its creation in 1993, the Carolina Panthers team has built a network at the team's training camp at Wofford College in Spartanburg, South Carolina, connecting it to the team's headquarters in Charlotte. The network designers use encryption to ensure security. Coaches and team managers in the field can use the network to reach key databases at headquarters to access information such as player statistics or salary figures. Even though the networking team has a system for the physical setup and breakdown of the network, it must still go through planning exercises each year because of constant changes in software and networking hardware. That means the network's performance must be reevaluated every year.

The most important lesson the NFL/Sprint team has learned is to be prepared. Even the best plans can change unexpectedly. For example, just five days before the NFL's highly publicized annual draft announcements, the location was moved from Detroit to Philadelphia. The networking team put a local telecommunications provider in the new locale on alert for establishing a connection in time for the broadcast. You can't plan for everything, so you have to be prepared to move quickly. It's probably safe to say that the venue for the next Super Bowl won't change. But even if it did, the NFL/Sprint networking team will make certain that couch potatoes all over the world aren't denied.

Decision Questions

1. Most businesses don't normally need to create networks quickly, but occasionally it is necessary. Give some examples of situations in which such quick-turn networks might be used.

2. Of course, the NFL doesn't allow general Internet access to its complete network, but you can check out the NFL's Web site www.nfl.com to get an idea of the kinds of statistics available. What additional kinds of information do you think the NFL manages? As the general manager of an NFL team, how could you use the NFL network in negotiating your players' contracts for the coming year?

3. As the NFL expands its coverage globally, will its quick-turn networks be of value in locations such as London, Tokyo, and Moscow?

Sources: Aileen Crowley, "Playbook Calls for On-the-Fly Networks," *PC Week*, September 15, 1997, p. 99; Bob Wallace, "LAN Blitz Sharpens Panthers' Claws," *Computer World*, September 29, 1997, p. 53.

CASE 2

TAKING IN THE SITES

The World Wide Web is a fast-flowing river of information. Internet surfers have found that navigating the Web takes them to a wide range of sites, from homemade personal sites to multimedia corporate sites. Why are businesses willing to invest $200,000 to $1 million to create an impressive Web site? Some want to bolster their corporate image; others want to sell their products online.

How companies choose to reach out and hold their audiences' attention depends on what they intend their sites to accomplish. Some Web sites function as general promotion and brand identity tools. For example, General Mills doesn't use its Web site to sell Betty Crocker cake mix; rather, it uses the site to present menu plans and household tips. The goal is to link the brand's image with the information the Web site provides.

Another function of some business Web sites is to conduct online business (sometimes called online commerce, e-commerce, or transactional sites). For example, you can book airline tickets, buy a computer on the Gateway 2000, Dell, and Micron sites, or buy stock from many stockbrokers.

Unlike e-commerce sites, some broad-based corporate sites don't sell—they give things away. The aim of these sites is to give surfers easy access to huge banks of free information—particularly information about the companies' products. Microsoft is most likely the largest broad-based corporate site on the Web. The information about Microsoft products is so vast that the site changes about eight times a day as new information is added. Web designers have found that the better the Web site's organization, the more faith visitors have in the site's information and in the company. Corporate Web sites might contain information found in a brochure: description of products, phone numbers, addresses, e-mail address, and so forth. They can also contain information that might be found in an annual report: shareholder information, corporate mission statements, company history, and press releases.

How companies use the Web, then, depends on the type of company and on what the company wants its Web site to accomplish. One thing is certain, though: communication remains the main function of this new medium. People want answers to their questions and the Web can be the most efficient way to get them.

Decision Questions

1. How could your college or university use a Web site to improve its services to students and the community?

2. The purpose of online commerce Web sites is to sell the company's products online. Do you feel comfortable buying online? What are the advantages and disadvantages of online commerce?

3. Suppose you were to design a Web site for our hypothetical product, Fiberiffic. Which of the Web site functions described in this case would you choose (general promotion/brand identity, online business, or broad-based corporate site)? Describe your proposed Web site. What content would you include? Justify using funds to develop this Web site rather than on more traditional promotional and sales tools.

CBC   **VIDEO CASE**   www.cbc.ca

FIRING YOUR CUSTOMER

Companies have some customers who can be said to be bad customers. They are considered bad because they cost more to support than the profit they generate. This may be because they make only small purchases, buy only on sale, miss appointments, take up a lot of time on nuisance calls, or open accounts and then do not buy anything. New technology makes it possible to develop customer profiles that will highlight the unprofitable customers.

The next step is to gently "fire" these customers in a manner that will not offend or create negative word-of-mouth publicity. Usually, no formal notification or procedure is necessary, for example, stop sending catalogues. Sometimes the account can be closed with a polite note to the customer. Great care must be exercised to avoid dumping customers who may become profitable in the future.

Discussion Questions

1. Can you explain why the customer habits discussed in the video make them unprofitable to a company?
2. The video mentions, but does not indicate how to ascertain, that some of these customers may become profitable in the future. How can this be done?
3. Do you know anyone that you think fits the category of an unprofitable customer? Have you ever been an unprofitable customer? Explain.
4. How would you react if you received a polite notice that your account with a store or a credit card company was being temporarily inactivated due to lack of any transactions for the past year but would be reactivated at your next purchase?

Source: *Venture,* show number 710, "Firing Your Customer," January 26, 1999, running time 6:56.

PART 4

CHAPTER 12

Motivating Employees and Building Self-Managed Teams

LEARNING GOALS

AFTER YOU HAVE READ AND STUDIED THIS CHAPTER, YOU SHOULD BE ABLE TO

1. Explain Taylor's scientific management.

2. Describe the Hawthorne studies, and relate their significance to human-based management.

3. Identify the levels of Maslow's hierarchy of needs, and relate their importance to employee motivation.

4. Differentiate among Theory X, Theory Y, and Theory Z.

5. Distinguish between the motivators and hygiene factors identified by Herzberg.

6. Explain how job enrichment affects employee motivation and performance.

7. Identify the steps involved in implementing a management by objectives (MBO) program.

8. Explain the key factors involved in expectancy theory.

9. Examine the key principles of equity theory.

10. Explain how open communication builds teamwork, and describe how managers are likely to motivate teams in the future.

Choice of Motivational Tools: The Carrot or the Stick

Thousands of books and articles have been written about how to motivate a workforce. Not surprisingly, there are many conflicting points of view. In the old days, when you wanted to *encourage* your donkey to move, you could either whack its rear with a stick or dangle a carrot in front of its nose. This was called the *carrot or stick* approach. Something similar holds in the field of motivation theory.

According to Tanja Parsley, vice-president of the consulting firm Outcomes, you cannot use the carrot method (reward system) if your employees work in an atmosphere in which the stick has created fear and victimization attitudes. Change the attitudes, realign the company, and then the carrot will work. Rewards will then lead to attitudinal shifts that will lead to changes in behaviour. That results in a better-motivated workforce.

The precise opposite is argued by Stephen Frey of the United States: If you change the behaviour, you will get a change in attitudes. He is the joint owner of Cin-Made Corporation, a small Cincinnati manufacturer of mailing tubes. After a couple of years of hard struggle with his employees and their union, he finally won them over to a full participatory-style management and a generous profit-sharing scheme. Now they are highly motivated and play a very active role in running the company. Frey said that the employees' attitudes did not change until they tried the new system. That is why he maintains that changed behaviour leads to changes in attitudes and not the other way around.

Author Dr. David Weiss (pictured), a partner in the Toronto-based consulting firm Geller, Shedletsky & Weiss and author of *High-Impact HR*, believes that managers must take a flexible approach to motivating their employees and teams. For Weiss, flexibility has two important aspects. First, select the positive motivators that fit the needs of the particular employee. Second, if your positive motivators do not seem to be working, do not simply do more of the same. Think rather of targeting and removing the negative motivators (or noise as Weiss calls it) in the work environment that are holding back your employees. As you will see in this chapter, people are not all cut from the same cloth and their needs change over time.

Peter Drucker, probably the most respected management theorist in the world, who has been writing books on the subject for 60 years, presents a different twist on the topic of motivation. In his latest book, *Management Challenges for the Twenty-First Century*, he stresses that the majority of workers are now knowledge workers not manual workers and, therefore, a new approach to motivating them is required. In the new economy employees need autonomy and continual innovation and learning, which should be built into the job.

Sources: Harvey Schachter, "Drucker's Take on Management This Century," *Globe and Mail*, May 26, 1999, p. M1; "A Vision of HR as a Business Within a Business," *Globe and Mail*, May 31, 1999, p. C4; interview with David Weiss, August 26, 1999; Dr. David S. Weiss, *High-Impact HR: Transforming Human Resources for Competitive Advantages* (New York: John Wiley & Sons, 1999); Laura Ramsay, "Why Carrot Beats Stick as a Motivational Tool," *Financial Post*, September 18, 1993, p. S30; Robert Frey, "Empowerment or Else," *Harvard Business Review*, September–October 1993, pp. 90–94. Photo source: David S. Weiss. *High-Impact HR: Transforming Human Resources for Competitive Advantage*. John Wiley & Sons, 1999.

As you go through the chapter you will learn how important it is to have a well-motivated workforce. One of the questions that arises is how far you should go as a manager when attempting to improve employees' motivation. Suppose you are a manager of a department in a large retail store and during the Christmas busy season you always hire tempo-

rary help. This year you are having difficulty getting good temp help. Somebody suggests that you should tell the better prospects that the jobs will be permanent, which may entice them to come on board. How ethical is this? Give this some thought as you study motivation in the chapter. We will try to come to grips with this issue at the end of the chapter.

THE IMPORTANCE OF MOTIVATION

www.pfdf.org

Peter Drucker is one of the most prolific and most prestigious contemporary writers on business management. Visit this Web site to see his biography and a list of his publications.

intrinsic reward
The good feeling you have when you have done a job well.

extrinsic reward
Something given to you by someone else as recognition for good work; extrinsic rewards include pay increases, praise, and promotions.

No matter where you end up being a leader—in school, business, sports, the military—the key to your success will be whether you can motivate others to improve their performance. That is no easy job today when so many people feel bored and uninterested in their work. Yet people are willing to work hard *if* they feel that their work is appreciated and makes a difference. As you will see in this chapter, motivation is a complex matter and people are motivated by a variety of things, such as recognition, accomplishment, and status as well as by money. **Intrinsic reward** is the good feeling you have when you have done a job well. An **extrinsic reward** is something given to you by someone else as recognition for good work. Such things as pay increases, praise, and promotions are examples of extrinsic rewards. Although ultimately motivation—the drive to satisfy a need—comes from within an individual, there are ways to stimulate people that bring out the natural drive to do a good job.

An unmotivated employee is often an unhappy one and unhappy workers are likely to leave the company; when this happens, the company usually loses out. Losing an employee could cost more than $100,000 for such things as exit interviews, severance pay, the process of hiring a replacement worker, and lost productivity while the new employee is learning the job. The "soft" costs are even greater: loss of intellectual capital, decreased morale, increased employee stress, and a negative reputation. Motivating the right people to join and remain with the organization is a key function of managers.

One purpose of this chapter is to acquaint you with the concepts, theories, and practice of motivation. By motivation we mean the belief, reason, or feeling that impels or motivates a person or group to do something. The most important person to motivate, of course, is yourself. One way to do that is to find the right job in the right organization, one that will be helpful in your search for the kind of career or work that you are ultimately seeking. A goal of this book is to help you in that search and to teach you how to succeed once you get there. One secret of success is to recognize that everyone else is on a similar search. Naturally, some are more committed than others. The job of a manager is to find that commitment, encourage it, and focus it on some common goal.

Why is motivation so important that we devote a whole chapter to this topic? In addition to the high costs of losing and replacing valuable employees mentioned above, all organizations know that a motivated workforce is much more productive than an unmotivated one. You can easily see this when a baseball, hockey, or football team loses its will to win. The coach will give the players a pep talk to motivate them to win, and the manager will try various other strategies to remotivate them. Same team, same salaries: motivated, they produce; unmotivated, their performance slides. Of course, as the Profile shows, there is some disagreement as to the best way to motivate employees. For some issues to consider regarding motivation, see the Ethical Dilemma box "Tempting—But Is It Ethical?"

Earlier we saw how all companies are striving to increase productivity to be competitive in the tough global environment. Motivation is the key to releasing employee power. You have already seen such key words as *employee empowerment, teamwork, participative management, wide span of control,* and *decentralized decision making.* All these aim to motivate employees to do much more than they have ever done before.

This style of management and leadership is growing rapidly. It is illustrated in this book in many of the profiles, spotlight boxes, and cases about successful companies. You will see such companies in this chapter as well.

Motivation has become even more important as companies have reduced the size of their workforces during the massive restructuring process of the past few years. Fewer employees means more responsibility for each. Every one of them must become a self-starter and use lots of initiative.

Canadian Press CP. Photography by John Lehmann

Even the best athletes sometimes need help getting and staying motivated. Coaches use a variety of techniques to keep athletes in top form. Here, champion figure skater Elvis Stojko is shown receiving the Canadian male athlete of the year award.

This chapter will begin with a look at some of the traditional theories of motivation. You will learn about the Hawthorne studies because they created a whole new interest in worker satisfaction and motivation. Then you will look at some assumptions about employees' motivation. You will read about the traditional theorists. You will see their names repeatedly in business literature: Mayo, Herzberg, Taylor, Maslow, and McGregor. Finally, we will look at the modern applications of these theories and the managerial procedures for implementing them.

EARLY MANAGEMENT STUDIES—TAYLOR

Several books on management in the nineteenth century presented management principles. For example, Charles Babbage (1792–1871) designed a mechanical computer and wrote a book on how to manage a manufacturing firm.[1] However, Frederick Taylor earned the title "father of scientific management" because of his book *Principles of Scientific Management,* which was published in 1911. Taylor's goal was to increase worker productivity so that both the firm and the worker could benefit from higher earnings. The way to improve productivity ➤ **P. 43** ◄, Taylor thought, was to study it scientifically. **Scientific management** thus became the study of workers to find the most efficient ways of doing things and then teaching people those techniques. Three elements were basic to Taylor's approach: time, methods, and rules of work. His most important tools were observation and the stopwatch. It's Taylor's ideas that today determine how many burgers McDonald's expects its flippers to flip and how many callers the phone companies expect operators to assist.[2]

A classic Taylor story involves his study of men shovelling rice, coal, and iron ore with the same shovel. Taylor felt that different materials called for different shovels. He proceeded to invent a wide variety of sizes and shapes of shovels and, with stopwatch in hand, measured output over time in what were called **time–motion studies:** studies of the tasks performed to complete a job and the time needed to do each task. Sure enough, an average person could shovel more (an increase from 25 tonnes to 35 tonnes per day) with the proper shovel and the most efficient motions. This finding

scientific management
The study of workers to find the most efficient way of doing things and then teaching people those techniques.

time–motion studies
Studies of the tasks performed to complete a job and the time needed to do each task.

principle of motion economy
The theory that every job can be broken down into a series of elementary motions.

www.sdsc.edu/
Publications/
ScienceWomen/
gilbreth.html

This Web site provides information about the Gilbreths and their work. It focuses primary attention on Lillian Gilbreth, calling her "*The Mother of Modern Management.*" An amazing achievement; she was also the mother of 12 children!

led to time–motion studies of virtually every factory job. As the most efficient ways of doing things were determined efficiency became the standard for setting goals and measuring efficiency of performance.

Taylor's scientific management became the dominant strategy for improving productivity in the early 1900s. There were hundreds of time–motion specialists in plants everywhere. One follower of Taylor was Henry L. Gantt. He developed charts on which managers plotted the work of employees down to the smallest detail a day in advance (see previous chapter). Frank and Lillian Gilbreth used Taylor's ideas in a three-year study of bricklaying. They developed the **principle of motion economy**, which showed that every job could be broken down into a series of elementary motions called *therbligs*—a slight variation of Gilbreth spelled backward. They then analyzed each motion to make it more efficient.

Scientific management viewed people largely as machines that needed to be properly programmed. There was little concern for the psychological or human aspects of work. Taylor felt simply that workers would perform at a high level of effectiveness (that is, be motivated) if they received high enough pay.

As mentioned earlier, some of Taylor's ideas are still being implemented. Management guru Peter Drucker even calls Taylor's ideas "the most lasting contribution America has made to Western thought. . . ."[3] Some companies still place more emphasis on conformity to work rules than on creativity, flexibility, and responsiveness. For example, United Parcel Service (UPS) tells drivers how fast to walk (three feet per second), how many packages to pick up and deliver a day (average of 400), and how to hold their keys (teeth up, third finger).[4] Nonetheless, the benefits of relying on workers to come up with creative solutions to productivity problems have long been recognized.

CRITICAL
THINKING

We live in a time when human rights are an important part of our legal system and our cultural and social standards. This awareness has had a significant impact on the workplace because employers must pay attention to regulations and attitudes concerning employees' working conditions. In this regard, can you see any ethical question arising out of the rigid application of *Taylorism* as exemplified in the cases of UPS and McDonald's mentioned previously?

THE HAWTHORNE STUDIES—MAYO

One of the studies that grew out of Taylor's research was conducted at the Western Electric Co.'s Hawthorne plant in Cicero, Illinois. The study began in 1927 and ended six years later. The study became famous in management literature as one of the early major studies in productivity.

Elton Mayo and colleagues from Harvard University set out to test the degree of lighting associated with optimum productivity. In this respect, the study was a forerunner of the traditional scientific management study: keep records of productivity performance, varying one factor affecting employees' working conditions.

In this study the idea was to keep records of the workers' productivity under different levels of illumination. But the initial experiments revealed a problem: The productivity of the experimental group compared to that of other workers doing the same job went up regardless of whether the lighting was increased or reduced. This was true even when the lighting was reduced to about the level of moonlight. These results confused and frustrated the researchers, who had expected productivity to fall as the lighting was dimmed.

A second series of experiments was conducted, involving manipulation of temperature, humidity, and other work environment factors; but again, each adjustment resulted in increased productivity. Even when conditions were returned to the original state productivity continued to increase. Because the researchers could not account for these unexpected results the experiment was considered a failure.

Property of AT&T Archives. Reprinted with permission of AT&T

The Hawthorne plant is a classic in the study of motivation. It was at the Hawthorne plant that Elton Mayo and his research team from Harvard University developed human-based motivational theory. Before the studies at Hawthorne, workers were expected to behave like human robots.

In the end, Mayo assumed that some human or psychological factor was involved. He and his colleagues then interviewed the workers, asking them about their feelings and attitudes toward the experiment. The researchers' findings began a profound change in management thinking that continues today. Here is what they concluded:

- The workers in the test room thought of themselves as a social group. The atmosphere was informal, they could talk freely, and they interacted regularly with their supervisors and the experimenters. They felt special and worked hard to stay in the group. This motivated them.

- The workers were involved in the planning of the experiments. For example, they rejected one kind of pay schedule and recommended another, which was used. The workers felt that their ideas were respected and that they were involved in managerial decision making. This, too, motivated them.

- The workers enjoyed the atmosphere of their special room regardless of the physical conditions, and the additional pay they got for more productivity. Job satisfaction increased dramatically.

Now we understand that these employees were motivated because they were being empowered and their social and esteem needs (see Maslow's hierarchy in Figure 12.1) were being met.

Researchers now use the term **Hawthorne effect** to refer to the tendency for people to behave differently when they know they're being studied. The Hawthorne study's results encouraged researchers to begin to study human motivation and the managerial styles that lead to more productivity. The emphasis of research shifted away from Taylor's scientific management to Mayo's new human-based management.

Mayo's findings led to completely new assumptions about employees. One of those assumptions was that pay was not the only motivator. In fact, money was found to be a relatively low motivator. That change in assumptions led to many theories about the human side of motivation. One of the best-known motivation theorists was Abraham Maslow, whose work we discuss next.

Hawthorne effect
The tendency for people to behave differently when they know they are being studied.

MOTIVATION AND MASLOW'S HIERARCHY OF NEEDS

Psychologist Abraham Maslow believed that to understand motivation at work, one must understand human motivation in general. He also believed that motivation arises from need. That is, people are motivated to satisfy *unmet* needs; needs that have been satisfied no longer provide motivation. He thought that needs could be placed on a hierarchy of importance.

Figure 12.1 shows **Maslow's hierarchy of needs**, whose levels are as follows:

- **Physiological needs:** basic survival needs, such as the need for food, water, and shelter.
- **Safety needs:** the need to feel secure at work and at home.
- **Social needs:** the need to feel loved, accepted, and part of the group.
- **Esteem needs:** the need for recognition and acknowledgement from others, as well as self-respect and a sense of status or importance.
- **Self-actualization needs:** the need to develop to your fullest potential.

When one need is satisfied, another, higher-level need emerges and motivates the person to do something to satisfy it. The satisfied need is no longer a motivator.[5] For example, if you just ate a full-course dinner, hunger would no longer be a motivator. Also, lower-level needs (e.g., safety) may emerge at any time they are not met, and take our attention away from higher-level needs such as the need for recognition or status.

Most of the world's workers struggle all day simply to meet the basic physiological and safety needs. In developed countries, such needs no longer dominate, and workers seek to satisfy growth needs (social, esteem, and self-actualization needs).

To compete successfully, firms must create a work environment that motivates the best and the brightest workers. That means establishing a work environment that includes goals such as social contribution, honesty, reliability, service, quality, dependability, unity, and participation in decision making.

Maslow's hierarchy of needs
The theory of motivation that places different types of human needs in order of importance, from basic physiological needs to safety, social, and esteem needs to self-actualization needs.

FIGURE 12.1

MASLOW'S HIERARCHY OF NEEDS

Maslow's hierarchy of needs is based on the idea that motivation comes from need. If a need is met, it's no longer a motivator so a higher-level need becomes the motivator. This chart shows the various levels of need.

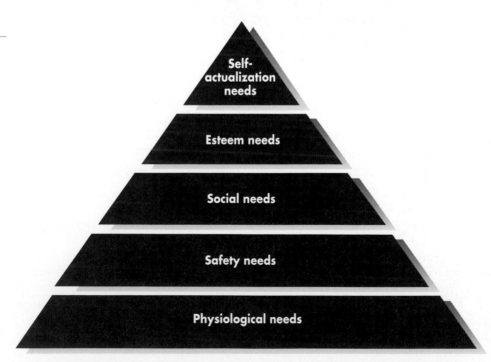

Self-actualization needs
Esteem needs
Social needs
Safety needs
Physiological needs

Your job right now is to finish reading this chapter. How strongly would you be motivated to do that if you were sweating in a 40°C room? Imagine now that your roommate turns on the air-conditioning. Now that you are more comfortable, are you more likely to read? Look at Maslow's hierarchy of needs to see what need would be motivating you each time. Can you see how helpful Maslow's theory is in understanding motivation by applying it to your own life?

Applying Maslow's Theory

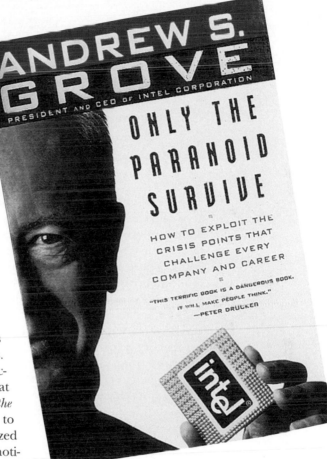

Andrew Grove, chairman and former CEO of Intel, has observed Maslow's concepts in action in his firm. One woman, for example, took a low-paying job that did little for her family's standard of living. Why? Because she needed the companionship her work offered (social/affiliation need). One of Grove's friends had a midlife crisis when he was made a vice-president. This position had been a lifelong goal, and when the man reached it he had to find another way to motivate himself (self-actualization need).

Once you understand the need level of employees, it is easier to design programs that will trigger self-motivation. Grove believes that all motivation comes from within. He believes that self-actualized persons are achievers. Personally, Grove was motivated to earn a doctorate from the University of California at Berkeley and to write a best-selling book, *Only the Paranoid Survive*.[6] He also proceeded at Intel to design a managerial program that emphasized achievement. Now Intel's managers are highly motivated to achieve their objectives because they feel rewarded for doing so.[7]

The contemporary approach to Maslow is to use his model as a framework for needs assessment, recognizing that it provides a relative ranking technique of employee needs. Note that individual need categories can and do shift in either direction when circumstances change.

Andrew Grove, Intel's Board Chairman and former CEO, has long been respected as having one of the best business minds in America. He holds a Ph.D. and is a best-selling author. Grove is also a believer in Maslow's theory and contends that managers can use his concepts to improve workers' job performance. Can you see how managers can apply Maslow's theory in the workplace?

PROGRESS CHECK

- What are the similarities and differences between Taylor's scientific management and Mayo's Hawthorne studies?
- How did Mayo's findings influence scientific management?
- Can you draw Maslow's hierarchy of needs? Label and describe the parts.
- According to Andrew Grove, what is the ultimate source of all motivation?

McGregor's Theory X and Theory Y

The way managers go about motivating people at work depends greatly on their attitudes toward workers. Douglas McGregor observed that managers' attitudes generally fall into one of two entirely different managerial styles, which he called *Theory X* and *Theory Y*.

Theory X

The assumptions of Theory X management are as follows:

- The average person dislikes work and will avoid it if possible.

- Because of this dislike, workers must be forced, controlled, directed, or threatened with punishment to make them put forth the effort to achieve the organization's goals.

- The average worker prefers to be directed, wants to avoid responsibility, has relatively little ambition, and wants security.

- Primary motivators are fear and money.

The natural consequence of such attitudes, beliefs, and assumptions is a manager who is very *busy* and who hangs over people telling them what to do and how to do it. Motivation is more likely to take the form of punishment for bad work rather than rewards for good work. Workers are given little responsibility, authority, or flexibility. Those were the assumptions behind Taylor's scientific management and other theorists who preceded Taylor. That is why management literature focused on time–motion studies that calculated the one *best* way to perform a task and the *optimum* time to be devoted to a task. It was assumed that workers needed to be trained and carefully watched to see that they conformed to the standards.

Theory X management still dominates in some organizations. Many managers and entrepreneurs > **P. 191** < still suspect that employees cannot be fully trusted and need to be closely supervised.[8] No doubt you have seen such managers in action. How did this make you feel? Were these managers' assumptions accurate regarding your attitudes?

Theory Y

Theory Y makes entirely different assumptions about people:

- Most people like work; it is as natural as play or rest.

- Most people naturally work toward goals to which they are committed.

- The depth of a person's commitment to goals depends on the perceived rewards for achieving them.

- Under certain conditions, most people not only accept but also seek responsibility.

- People are capable of using a relatively high degree of imagination, creativity, and cleverness to solve problems.

- The average person's intellectual potential is only partially realized.

- People are motivated by a variety of rewards. Each employee is stimulated by a reward unique to that person (time off, money, recognition, and so on).

Rather than emphasize authority, direction, and close supervision, Theory Y emphasizes a relaxed managerial atmosphere in which workers are free to set objectives, be creative, be flexible, and go beyond the goals set by management.[9] A key technique in meeting these objectives is *empowerment*. Empowerment > **P. 14** < gives employees the ability to make decisions and the tools to implement the decisions they make. (See discussion in Chapter 8.) For empowerment to be a real motivator, management should follow these three steps: (1) find out what people think the problems in the organization are, (2) let them design the solutions, and (3) get out of the way and let them put those solutions into action.

Often employees complain that they're asked to become involved in company decision making, but their managers fail to actually empower them to make decisions. Have you ever worked in such an atmosphere? How did that make you feel?

The trend in many businesses is toward Theory Y management. One reason for this trend is that many service industries are finding Theory Y helpful in dealing with on-the-spot problems. Leona Ackerly of Mini Maid Inc. says, "if our employees look at our managers as partners, a real team effort is built."[10] For more on this, see the Spotlight on Small Business box "Motivating Employees in Small Businesses."

Delta Hotels offers an excellent example of how effective employee empowerment is in increasing morale and motivation. Senior vice-president of people and quality Bill Pallett seeks to empower "more than 9,000 employees across North America to make daily business decisions without having to turn to their managers for approval." This enables front-line employees to offer better service to customers by making on-the-spot decisions such as cancelling a disputed minibar charge or offering a complimentary room when a guest makes a reasonable complaint.[11]

Darren Price

Delta Hotels is known to its employees as a company where they can contribute and grow and also as a great place to work.

SPOTLIGHT ON SMALL BUSINESS   www.richter.ca

Motivating Employees in Small Businesses

Small businesses run into specific problems when it comes to motivating their employees. This is particularly true with companies that have grown from a very small beginning to a point where the owner or founder is having difficulty delegating authority. The owner, feeling that he or she must make every decision, as was done from the start, finds it difficult to let go, and this causes dissatisfaction among the workforce.

Picture a workforce of 35 or 40 people with several managers who feel frustrated because of the limited authority given to them by an anxious employer. Management consultant Stephen Levy commented that this is one of the most common problems he has found in successful small businesses; that is, the founders are actually holding back further progress without being aware that they are the source of the problem.

The notion of teams given authority and responsibility for decision making and results is still foreign to many small-business owners. And Levy finds it difficult to convince them that they could solve many of their problems by empowering employees to play a much greater role in the daily operations of the company.

As the many examples in this and the preceding chapters make clear, the combined energy and resources of a team-based operation yield far superior results to those possible in a boss-centred organization. As a small firm grows it is impossible for one person to continue to be totally aware of every detail of the operations. Teams of employees who are intimately aware of the causes of problems with suppliers, customers, or production are in a much better position to provide solutions or to prevent problems from occurring in the first place. Empowerment of employees and recognition of their achievements lead to a highly motivated staff, as indicated by the theories of Herzberg and Maslow.

Source: Interview with Stephen Levy of Richter Management Plus, June 8, 1999.

 **A**ctivities such as picnics and sports events like this hockey game (played by Hewlett-Packard employees) create an atmosphere in which employees can feel like part of the group. This meets their social needs and they can move on to accomplish things at work to satisfy their self-esteem and self-actualization needs.

Applying Theory X and Theory Y

The trouble with these neat theories is that no company is run in strict accordance with either Theory Y or Theory X, not even the armed forces. There are employees who prefer to be told what to do; they do not want responsibility for making crucial decisions, but, when given precise instructions, perform their assigned tasks with care and diligence. There are also employees who are self-starters and perform best only when they share in the decision-making process; they resent being given orders. Both types can be found in the same company. If you were the chief executive, how would you run that company, by Theory X or Theory Y? Or would you use your common sense and act according to the circumstances at hand? You cannot run a business, or anything else, by blindly following one theory.

Managers must be flexible in applying Theory X or Y to those they supervise. Some people do better with direction; others do better with more freedom. Your natural inclination may be to prefer a Theory Y–type manager as your supervisor, whereas your friend may prefer a Theory X–type supervisor.

The trend in most businesses is toward Theory Y management. As repeatedly noted, participative management, employee empowerment, and team effort all require a democratic style of management. This enables firms to be flexible and to react quickly, putting them in a good position to meet competition from domestic or foreign firms.

This is a good time to have another look at the Profile at the beginning of the chapter. Remember David Weiss's view that flexibility is a key to motivation? Just as important is Peter Drucker's comment about the new information worker being motivated by more autonomy. It is interesting that in the same book review, Schachter notes how Drucker's opinion has changed as the nature of the workforce has changed. Half a century ago, in *The Practice of Management*, he advocated Theory X as the best way to motivate employees.

OUCHI'S THEORY Z

In addition to the reasons given above for the trend toward Theory Y management, another reason for companies to adopt a more flexible managerial style is to meet competition from foreign firms such as those in Japan, China, and the European Union. Back in the 1980s, Japanese companies

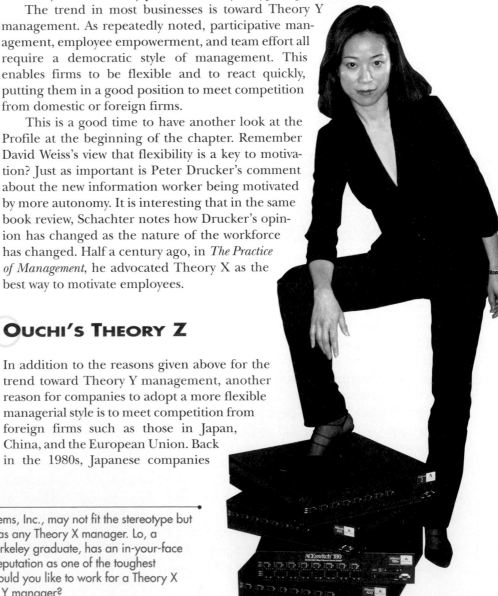

Selina Lo of Alteon Websystems, Inc., may not fit the stereotype but she's as tough and exacting as any Theory X manager. Lo, a University of California at Berkeley graduate, has an in-your-face style that has earned her a reputation as one of the toughest managers in the industry. Would you like to work for a Theory X manager like Lo or a Theory Y manager?

seemed to be outperforming American businesses. William Ouchi, a management professor at UCLA, wondered if the secret to Japanese success was the way Japanese companies managed their workers. The Japanese management approach (what Ouchi called *Type J*) involved lifetime employment, consensual decision making, collective responsibility for the outcomes of decisions, slow evaluation and promotion, implied control mechanisms, nonspecialized career paths, and holistic concern for employees. In contrast, the American management approach (what Ouchi called *Type A*) involved short-term employment, individual decision making, individual responsibility for the outcomes of decisions, rapid evaluation and promotion, explicit control mechanisms, specialized career paths, and segmented concern for employees.

Type J firms are based on the culture of Japan, which includes a focus on trust and intimacy within the group and family. Likewise, Type A firms are based on the culture of America, which includes a focus on individual rights and achievements. Ouchi wanted to help American firms adopt the successful Japanese strategies, but he realized that it wouldn't be practical to expect American managers to accept an approach based on the culture of another country. Judge for yourself. A job for life in a firm may sound good until you think of the implications: no chance to change jobs and no opportunity to move up quickly through the ranks. Therefore, Ouchi recommended a hybrid of the two approaches in what he called Theory Z (see Figure 12.2). Theory Z blends the characteristics of Type J and Type A into an approach that involves long-term employment, collective decision making, individual responsibility, slow evaluation and promotion, implicit, informal control with explicit, formalized control, moderately specialized career path, and holistic concern for employees (including family). The theory views the organization as a family that fosters co-operation and organizational values.

Today, economic decline, demographic and social changes, and fierce global competition are forcing Japanese managers to re-evaluate the way they conduct business. Whereas a decade ago the Japanese system was admired for its focus on building long-term business relationships, today there is a realization that Japanese firms need to become both more dynamic and more efficient in order to compete effectively in today's rapidly changing global economy. Feeling the pain of the worst recession in their country's history, some Japanese managers are changing the way they do business. For example, electronics giant Hitachi is the first major Japanese company to announce it would quit doing corporate calisthenics—exercises done in

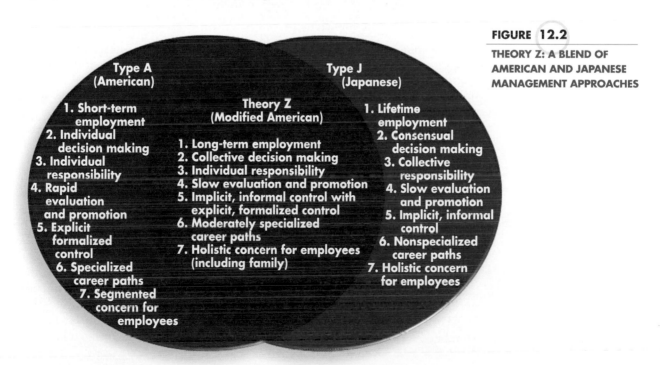

FIGURE 12.2

THEORY Z: A BLEND OF AMERICAN AND JAPANESE MANAGEMENT APPROACHES

Type A (American)
1. Short-term employment
2. Individual decision making
3. Individual responsibility
4. Rapid evaluation and promotion
5. Explicit formalized control
6. Specialized career paths
7. Segmented concern for employees

Theory Z (Modified American)
1. Long-term employment
2. Collective decision making
3. Individual responsibility
4. Slow evaluation and promotion
5. Implicit, informal control with explicit, formalized control
6. Moderately specialized career paths
7. Holistic concern for employees (including family)

Type J (Japanese)
1. Lifetime employment
2. Consensual decision making
3. Collective responsibility
4. Slow evaluation and promotion
5. Implicit, informal control
6. Nonspecialized career paths
7. Holistic concern for employees

THEORY X	THEORY Y	THEORY Z
1. Employees dislike work and will try to avoid it.	1. Employees view work as a natural part of life.	1. Employee involvement is the key to increased productivity.
2. Employees prefer to be controlled and directed.	2. Employees prefer limited control and direction.	2. Employee control is implied and informal.
3. Employees seek security, not responsibility.	3. Employees will seek responsibility under proper work conditions.	3. Employees prefer to share responsibility and decision making.
4. Employees must be intimidated by managers to perform.	4. Employees perform better in work environments that are nonintimidating.	4. Employees perform better in environments that foster trust and co-operation.
5. Employees are motivated by financial rewards.	5. Employees are motivated by many different needs.	5. Employees need guaranteed employment and will accept slow evaluations and promotions.

FIGURE 12.3

A COMPARISON OF THEORIES X, Y, AND Z

Note how Theory X differs from Theories Y and Z, which have some similarities.

groups not only for health but also to foster cohesion among employees. "The idea of getting everyone in one place at the same time to do the same thing is outdated," said a Hitachi spokesperson.[12] Having everyone start the day with group exercises symbolized doing the same thing the same way. It reinforced the cultural belief that employees should not take risks or think for themselves. Many managers think that such conformity is what has hurt Japanese business.[13] Will the Japanese managers move toward the hybrid Theory Z in the future? We'll have to wait and see. The appropriate managerial style is one that matches the culture, the situation, and the specific needs of the organization and its employees. (See Figure 12.3 for a summary of Theories X, Y, and Z.)

Despite these significant cultural differences, Canadian and American companies have adopted some of the features of the Japanese system (Theory Z) listed above. As noted in previous chapters, these include:

- collective decision making (teams)

- expectation of individual responsibility

- few levels of management

The combined effect of such changes is the creation of a sense of involvement, closeness, and co-operation in the organization, which is another of the Theory Z features. In Canada we have also witnessed extensive layoffs as large companies downsize and restructure. This has also eroded the motivation provided by security of employment and promotion.

As these trends evolve, it will be interesting to see how closely the two systems of motivation will resemble each other in the future.

HERZBERG'S MOTIVATING FACTORS

Theories X, Y, and Z are concerned with styles of management. Another direction in managerial theory is to explore what managers can do with the job itself to motivate employees (a modern-day look at Taylor's research). In other words, some theorists are more concerned with the content of work than with style of management. They ask: Of all the factors controllable by managers, which are most effective in generating an enthusiastic work effort?

The most discussed study in this area was conducted by psychologist Frederick Herzberg.[14] He asked workers to rank the following job-related factors in order of importance as motivators. That is, what creates enthusiasm for them and makes them work to full potential? The results were:

1. sense of achievement
2. earned recognition
3. interest in the work itself
4. opportunity for growth
5. opportunity for advancement
6. importance of responsibility
7. peer and group relationships
8. pay
9. supervisor's fairness
10. company policies and rules
11. status
12. job security
13. supervisor's friendliness
14. working conditions

Herzberg noted that the factors receiving the most votes were all clustered around job content. Workers like to feel that they contribute (sense of achievement was number one). They want to earn recognition (number two) and feel their jobs are important. They want responsibility (number six) (which is why learning is so important), but they want that responsibility to be recognized with a chance for growth and advancement. (numbers 4 and 5). Of course, workers also want the job to be interesting (number 3).

Herzberg noted further that factors having to do with the job environment were not considered motivators by workers. It was interesting to find that one of those factors was pay. Workers felt that the absence of good pay, job security, friendly supervisors, and the like could cause dissatisfaction, but the presence of those factors did not motivate them; they just removed the dissatisfaction, thus providing contentment and satisfaction.

Herzberg concluded that certain factors, called **motivators**, gave employees a great deal of satisfaction and made them more productive (see Figure 12.4). These factors mostly had to do with job content and were grouped as follows:

motivators
Factors that provide satisfaction and motivate people to work.

- work itself
- achievement
- recognition
- responsibility
- growth and advancement

Other elements of the job were merely what Herzberg called **hygiene factors**. These had to do mostly with job environment and could cause dissatisfaction but would not necessarily motivate if the source of dissatisfaction were removed. They were:

hygiene factors
Factors that cause dissatisfaction but do not motivate if they are removed.

- company policy and administration
- supervision
- working conditions
- interpersonal relations
- salary, status, job security

Combining McGregor's Theory Y with Herzberg's motivating factors, we can conclude:

- Employees work best when management assumes that they are competent and self-motivated. Theory Y calls for a participative style of management.
- The best way to motivate employees is to make the job interesting, help them to achieve their objectives, and recognize that achievement through advancement and added responsibility.

FIGURE 12.4

HERZBERG'S MOTIVATORS AND HYGIENE FACTORS
There's some controversy over Herzberg's theory. For example, sales managers often use money as a motivator. Recent studies have shown that money can be a motivator if used as part of a recognition program.

MOTIVATORS	HYGIENE (MAINTENANCE) FACTORS
(These factors can be used to motivate workers.)	(These factors can cause dissatisfaction, but changing them will have little motivational effect.)
Work itself	Company policy and administration
Achievement	Supervision
Recognition	Working conditions
Responsibility	Interpersonal relations (co-workers)
Growth and advancement	Salary, status, and job security

Applying Herzberg's Theories

Pat Blake, a Sunnen Products Co. employee, says that what motivates her to work extra hours or to learn new skills is less tangible than money or bonuses—it's a kind word from her boss. "When something good happens, like we have a shipping day with so many thousands of dollars going out the door, they let us know about that." Blake said. "It kind of makes you want to go for the gold."[15] Improved working conditions or better wages are taken for granted after workers get used to them. This is what Herzberg meant by *hygiene factors*: their absence causes dissatisfaction, but their presence doesn't motivate. The best motivator may be a simple and sincere "I really appreciate what you're doing."

Many surveys have been conducted to test Herzberg's theories. They support Herzberg's finding that the number-one motivator isn't money, but a sense of achievement and recognition for a job well done. A 1994 survey by *Industry Week* showed that 80 percent of the employees asked to pick the most important factor in fostering company loyalty chose recognition of good work.[16]

When asked what makes them content with their current jobs, more than half of those surveyed listed open communication with higher-ups, the nature of the work, the quality of management, control over work content, the opportunity to gain new skills, the quality of co-workers, and the opportunity for intellectually stimulating work. Only a third mentioned salary as important.[17]

Similar answers were obtained in more recent surveys.[18] Figure 12.5 (p. 368) shows that there is a strong resemblance between Maslow's and Herzberg's theories.

Ray Dykes, PR Plus Communications

The best motivators in business are achievement, recognition, and a chance for advancement. Westshore Terminals achieved the 400 million tonnes of coal shipped milestone in 1999. The 400 millionth tonne was loaded on board the Greek dry bulk carrier *Aquagrace*. Here Westshore transportaion manager Ron Dion awards a plaque to the ship's master, Captain Dimosthenis Kapetanios.

Courtesy of Harley-Davidson Inc.

Job enrichment motivates workers by appealing to personal values such as achievement, challenge, and recognition. Harley-Davidson is a company committed to the principles of job enrichment. At Harley-Davidson, self-managed teams of workers are trained to perform different tasks and have clear autonomy over how their job is organized.

JOB ENRICHMENT

Both Maslow's and Herzberg's theories were extended by job enrichment theory. **Job enrichment** is a motivational strategy that emphasizes motivating the worker through the job itself. Work is assigned to individuals so that they have the opportunity to complete an identifiable task from beginning to end. They are held responsible for successful completion of the task. The motivational effect of job enrichment can come from the opportunity for personal achievement, challenge, and recognition. Go back and review Maslow's and Herzberg's work to see how job enrichment grew out of those theories (see Figure 12.5). Five characteristics of work are believed to be important in affecting individual motivation and performance:

job enrichment
A motivational strategy that emphasizes motivating the worker through the job itself.

1. **Skill variety**. The extent to which a job demands different skills.

2. **Task identity**. The degree to which the job requires working with a visible outcome from beginning to end.

3. **Task significance**. The degree to which the job has a substantial impact on the lives or work of others in the company.

4. **Autonomy**. The degree of freedom, independence, and discretion in scheduling work and determining procedures.

5. **Feedback**. The amount of direct and clear information that is received about job performance.

The same procedure was employed by many Canadian companies with similar satisfactory results. In previous chapters we have seen how Campbell Soup Canada and other companies have successfully applied the team method to obtain a highly motivated workforce. Later in this chapter, in the Reaching Beyond Our Borders box, you'll see how the same is true for GSW Water Heating Co. In the following pages, the example of Motorola Canada Ltd. also shows successful use of teamwork to motivate employees.

As mentioned previously, job enrichment is based on Herzberg's higher motivators such as responsibility, achievement, and recognition. It stands in contrast to **job simplification**, which produces task efficiency by breaking down the job into simple

job simplification
The process of producing task efficiency by breaking down the job into simple steps and assigning people to each of those steps.

FIGURE 12.5

COMPARISON OF MASLOW'S HIERARCHY OF NEEDS AND HERZBERG'S THEORY OF FACTORS

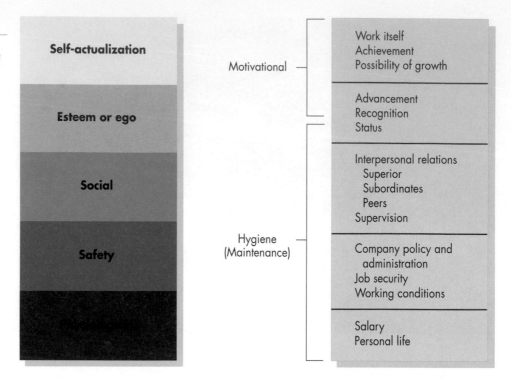

job enlargement
A job enrichment strategy involving combining a series of tasks into one assignment that is more challenging and interesting.

steps and assigning people to each of those steps. There isn't much motivation in doing boring, repetitive work, but some managers who still operate on the Taylor level of motivation use job simplification. Job simplification is sometimes necessary, particularly when people are learning new skills.

Another type of job design used for motivation is **job enlargement**, which combines a series of tasks into one assignment that is more challenging and interesting. For example, Maytag, the home appliance manufacturer, redesigned its work so that employees could assemble an entire water pump instead of just one part. **Job rotation** also makes work more interesting and motivating by moving employees from one job to another. One problem with job rotation, of course, is having to train employees to do several different operations. However, the resulting increase in employee morale and motivation leads to greater productivity; thus, it usually offsets the additional costs.

job rotation
A job enrichment strategy involving moving employees from one job to another.

Job enrichment is one way to ensure that workers enjoy responsibility and a sense of accomplishment. Another way is to get everyone to agree on specific company objectives.

GOAL-SETTING THEORY AND MANAGEMENT BY OBJECTIVES

goal-setting theory
The theory that setting specific ambitious but attainable goals can motivate workers and improve performance if the goals are accepted, accompanied by feedback, and facilitated by organizational conditions.

Goal-setting theory is based on the notion that the setting of specific ambitious but attainable goals is related to high levels of motivation and performance if the goals are accepted, accompanied by feedback, and facilitated by organizational conditions. Nothing makes more sense intuitively than the idea that all members of an organization should have some basic agreement about the overall goals of the organization and the specific objectives to be met by each department and individual. It follows, then, that there should be a system to involve everyone in the organization in goal setting and implementation. Such a system is called *management by objectives (MBO)*.

Peter Drucker developed this system in the 1960s. Drucker asserted that "managers cannot motivate people; they can only thwart people's motivation because people motivate themselves."[19] Thus, he designed his system to help employees motivate themselves. **Management by objectives (MBO)** is a system of goal setting and implementation that involves a cycle of discussion, review, and evaluation of objectives among top and middle-level managers, supervisors, and employees. Large corporations ➤ **P. 162** ◄ such as the Ford Motor Company used MBO and taught the method to the U.S. Defense Department. MBO then spread to other companies and government agencies. When implemented properly, MBO meets the criteria of goalsetting theory and can be quite effective. MBO calls on managers to formulate goals in co-operation with everyone in the organization, to commit employees to those goals, and then to monitor results and reward accomplishment. There are six steps in the MBO process (see Figure 12.6). Can you tell how the model is intended to help workers motivate themselves?

MBO was widely used in the 1960s, and the management literature of the 1970s was packed with articles about MBO, but very little was written about it in the 1980s and 1990s. Some critics of MBO now see it as being out of date and inconsistent with contemporary management thought and practice. Does that mean that MBO isn't used any longer? Not according to one 1995 study, which found that 47 percent of the organizations surveyed used some form of MBO.[20]

MBO is most effective in relatively stable situations where long-range plans can be made and implemented with little need for major changes. It is also important to MBO that managers understand the difference between helping and coaching subordinates. *Helping* means working with the subordinate and doing part of the work if necessary. *Coaching* means acting as a resource—teaching, guiding, and recommending—but not helping (that is, not participating actively or doing the task). The central idea of MBO is that employees need to motivate themselves.

Problems can arise when management uses MBO as a strategy for *forcing* managers and workers to commit to goals that are not really mutually agreed on but are set by top management. Employee involvement and expectations are important.

Victor Vroom identified the importance of employee expectations and developed a process called *expectancy theory*. Let's examine this concept next.

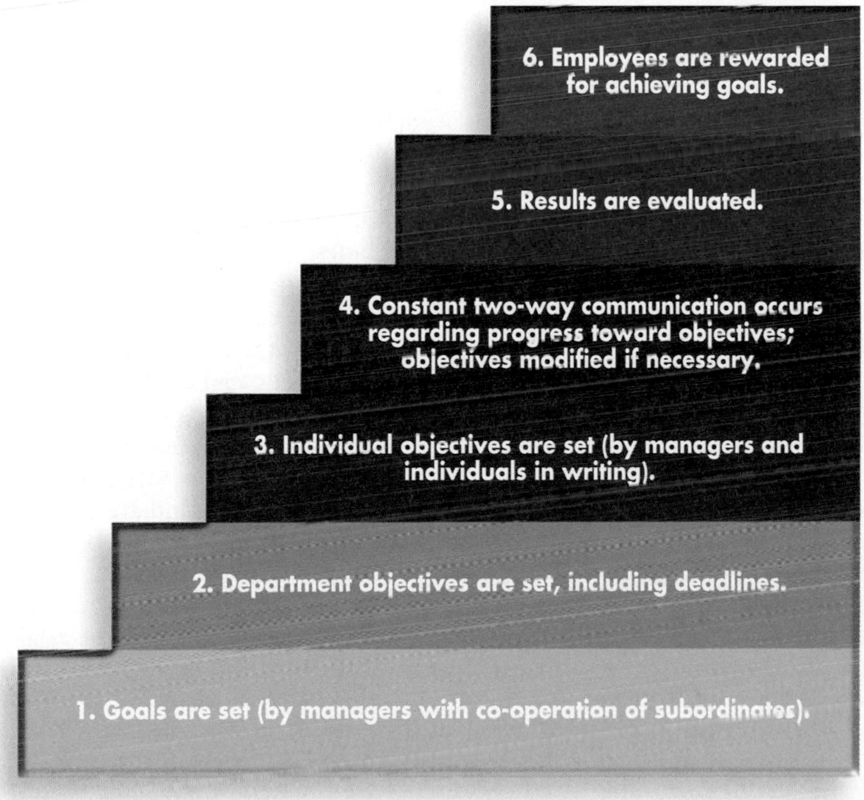

management by objectives (MBO)
A system of goal setting and implementation that involves a cycle of discussion, review, and evaluation of objectives among top and middle-level managers, supervisors, and employees.

FIGURE 12.6

MANAGEMENT BY OBJECTIVES

The critical step in the MBO process is sitting down with workers, discussing the objectives, and getting the workers to commit to those objectives in writing. Commitment is the key!

6. Employees are rewarded for achieving goals.

5. Results are evaluated.

4. Constant two-way communication occurs regarding progress toward objectives; objectives modified if necessary.

3. Individual objectives are set (by managers and individuals in writing).

2. Department objectives are set, including deadlines.

1. Goals are set (by managers with co-operation of subordinates).

Meeting Employee Expectations: Expectancy Theory

expectancy theory
Victor Vroom's theory that the effort employees exert on specific tasks depends on their expectations of the outcomes.

According to Victor Vroom's **expectancy theory**, employee expectations can affect an individual's motivation.[21] Therefore, the effort employees exert on specific tasks depends on their expectations of the outcomes. Vroom contends that employees ask three questions before committing maximum effort to a task: (1) Can I accomplish the task? (2) If I do accomplish it, what's my reward? (3) Is the reward worth the effort?

Think of the effort you might exert in your class under the following conditions: Your instructor says that to earn an A in the course you must achieve an average of 90 percent on coursework plus jump three metres high. Would you exert maximum effort toward earning an A if you knew you could not possibly jump three metres high? Or what if your instructor said students could earn an A in the course but you know that this instructor has not awarded an A in 25 years of teaching? If the reward of an A seems unattainable, would you exert significant effort to try to attain one? Better yet, let's say that you read in the newspaper that businesses actually prefer C-minus students to A-minus students. Does the reward of an A seem worth it? Now think of the same type of situations that may occur on the job.

Expectancy theory does note that expectation varies from individual to individual. Employees establish their own view of task difficulty and the value of the reward. Researchers David Nadler and Edward Lawler modified Vroom's theory and suggested that managers follow five steps to improve employee performance:

1. Determine what rewards are valued by employees.

2. Determine each employee's desired performance standard.

3. Ensure that performance standards are attainable.

4. Guarantee rewards tied to performance.

5. Be certain that rewards are considered adequate.[22]

Treating Employees Fairly: Equity Theory

equity theory
The theory that employees try to maintain equity between inputs and outputs compared to others in similar positions.

Equity theory deals with the question "If I do a good job, will it be worth it?" It has to do with perceptions of fairness and how those perceptions affect employees' willingness to perform. The basic principle is that employees try to maintain equity between inputs and outputs compared to others in similar positions. Equity comparisons are made from the information available through personal relationships, professional organizations, and so on.

When workers do perceive inequity, they will try to re-establish equitable exchanges in a number of ways. For example, suppose you compare the grade you earned on a term paper with your classmates' grades. If you think you received a lower grade compared to the students who put out the same effort as you, you will probably react in one of two ways: (1) by reducing your effort on future class projects or (2) by rationalizing (e.g., by saying "Grades are not that important!"). If you think your paper received a higher grade than comparable papers, you will probably (1) increase your effort to justify the higher reward in the future or (2) rationalize by saying "I'm worth it!" In the workplace, perceived inequity may lead to lower productivity ► **P. 43** ◄ , reduced quality, increased absenteeism, and voluntary resignation.

Remember that equity judgments are based on perceptions and are subject to errors in perception. When workers overestimate their own contributions—as happens often—they are going to feel that any rewards given out for performance are inequitable. Sometimes organizations try to deal with this by keeping salaries secret, but secrecy may make things worse; employees are likely to overestimate the salaries of others in addition to overestimating their own contribution. In general the best remedy is clear and frequent communication. Managers must communicate as clearly as possible the results that are expected and what will follow when those results are achieved and when they are not.

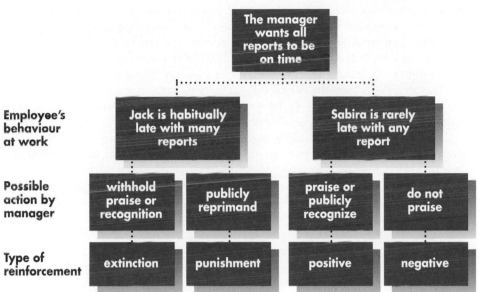

FIGURE 12.7

REINFORCEMENT THEORY

How a manager can use positive and negative reinforcement to motivate employee behaviour.

Reinforcement Theory

Another theory of motivation is based on the work of the famous but controversial psychologist B.F. Skinner, who is considered the father of behaviourism—the notion that people will behave according to their awareness of the consequences of their actions. That means that the carrot-and-stick approach, reward and punishment, would be an effective method of motivating people. Although Skinner's influence has been declining recently, his theories gave rise to the reinforcement theory of motivation.

Reinforcement theory states that positive and negative reinforcers will motivate a desired behaviour. Individuals act to receive rewards and avoid punishment. Positive reinforcements are rewards such as praise, recognition, or a pay raise. Negative reinforcement occurs when a person acts to avoid negative consequences such as reprimands. A manager might also withhold praise (positive reinforcement) and this is called *extinction*. Another way of reducing undesirable behaviour is punishment such as a public reprimand. A detailed example of how reinforcement theory applies to motivating appropriate employee behaviour is shown in Figure 12.7.

www.bfskinner.org

Visit the B.F. Skinner Foundation to read about B.F. Skinner and see what the *"father of behaviourism"* has to say!

reinforcement theory
States that positive and negative reinforcers will motivate a desired behaviour.

- Briefly describe the managerial attitudes behind Theories X, Y, and Z.
- Relate job enrichment to Herzberg's motivating factors.
- What are the six steps in management by objectives?
- What is the difference between helping and coaching? Which motivates workers more?
- Evaluate expectancy theory. Can you think of situations where expectancy theory could apply to your efforts or lack of effort?

PROGRESS
CHECK

BUILDING TEAMWORK THROUGH OPEN COMMUNICATION

Companies with highly motivated workforces usually have several things in common. Among the most important factors are open communication systems and self-managed teams. Open communication helps both top managers and team members understand the objectives and work together to achieve them. Communication must flow freely throughout the organization when teams are empowered to make decisions—they can't make these decisions in a vacuum. It is crucial for people to be able to access the knowledge they need when they need it.

Having teams creates an environment in which learning can happen because most learning happens at the peer level—peers who have an interest in helping each other along. Empowerment **➤ P. 14 ◂** works when people volunteer to share their knowledge with their colleagues. For example, when Flora Zhou, an AES business development manager, was putting together a bid to the Vietnam government, she sent a detailed e-mail about what she was planning to bid and why to about 300 people within AES. She asked for and received lots of advice and comments. Most people thought her proposal was fine, but Sarah Slusser, a group manager in Central America, sent Zhou a three-page response that contained a wealth of information about a similar situation she had with a plant in the Yucatan. Slusser told Zhou what technology issues she needed to pay attention to. A few days later, Zhou made the bid. It was the lowest bid by two-tenths of a percent. Did Slusser tell Zhou the exact dollar to bid? No, but she and many others, including plant leaders and board members, gave her the best information and judgments they had to help her make her decision. They shared everything they knew with her.[23]

Teamwork does not happen by itself. The whole organization must be structured to make it easy for managers and employees to talk to one another. Procedures for encouraging open communication include the following:

- **Create an organizational culture that rewards listening**. Top managers must create places to talk, and they must show employees that talking with superiors counts—by providing feedback, adopting employee suggestions, and rewarding upward communication—even if the discussion is negative. Employees must feel free to say anything they deem appropriate. Jerry Stead, chairman of technology provider Ingram Micro, has his own 24-hour toll-free phone line to take calls from employees. Yes, he really answers it. He says: "If we are doing something right, I love to hear about it. If there's something we should be doing differently, I want to know that too." Stead has also given his home number to all 13,000 Ingram Micro employees.[24]

- **Train supervisors and managers to listen**. Most people receive no such training in school or anywhere else, so organizations must do the training themselves or hire someone to do it.

- **Remove barriers to open communication**. Having separate offices, parking spaces, bathrooms, dining rooms, and so on only places barriers between managers and workers. (For more on effective office design, see the Spotlight on Big Business box "Designing a Motivating Workplace.") Other barriers are different dress codes and different ways of addressing one another (e.g., calling workers by their first names and managers by their last). Removing such barriers may require imagination and willingness on the part of managers to give up their special privileges.

- **Actively undertake efforts to facilitate communication**. Large lunch tables where all organization members eat, conference rooms, organizational picnics, organizational athletic teams, and other such efforts all allow managers to mix with each other and with workers.

Let's see how one organization addresses the challenge of open communication in teams.

Applying Open Communication in Self-Managed Teams

Kenneth Kohrs, vice-president of car product development at Ford Motor Company, says that an inside group known as "Team Mustang" sets the guidelines for how production teams should be formed. Given the challenge to create a car that would make people dust off their old "Mustang Sally" records and dance into the showrooms, the 400-member team was also given the freedom to make decisions without waiting for approval from headquarters or other departments. The team moved everyone from various departments into cramped offices under one roof in an old warehouse. Drafters sat next to accountants, engineers next to stylists. Budgetary walls that divided departments were knocked down as department managers were persuaded to surrender some control over their subordinates.

When the resulting Mustang convertible displayed shaking problems, suppliers were called in and the team worked around the clock to solve the problem. The engineers were so motivated to complete the program on schedule and under budget that they worked late into the night and slept on the floors of the warehouse when

---

SPOTLIGHT ON BIG BUSINESS

www.mckinsey.com

Designing a Motivating Workplace

One of the largest and most prestigious management consulting firms in the world is McKinsey & Co. For more than four years the Toronto office planned the design of their new premises, which they finally occupied at the end of June 1999. The overriding principle governing the design was to have a structure that would take care of all the major needs of their highly skilled, well-paid, and hard-working professional staff of 150. If they succeeded, then they would have a well-motivated workforce that would be very productive. That is why partner Mehrdad Baghai started planning four years before their lease expired. He engaged architect Siamak Hariri, a long-time friend, to draw up plans for the project. Other architects were hired to plan the actual building.

After many meetings and discussions, the decision was reached that three main criteria had to be met: a midtown location, lots of natural light, and fresh air. These criteria were not too difficult to meet. They found a good location, an atrium and open-style work spaces gave lots of light, and windows that opened provided fresh air. Much planning, many meetings, and lots of discussion went into decisions about hundreds of other details.

The open style means that employees can walk down a hall to the central atrium where they can meet other people or have a meal. The work they do requires consulting with each other often. This is made easy by a series of informal meeting rooms off the atrium where staff can brainstorm with each other or with clients. The whole idea is to have an atmosphere that will stimulate employees' creativity in a profession where creativity is a vital component. Workstations, which are located in two

long arms that branch off the central atrium or *hive*, are near large windows that provide lots of light.

One of problems was the fact that employees spend most of their time away from the office at clients' premises, generally returning on Friday. Some companies might take advantage of this to cut office space requirements by having common desk space that anyone could use. McKinsey did not like this solution; they felt that to feel like part of a community, you need to have your own work area where you can place personal objects like pictures of your family.

Another interesting feature is that space is organized so that entry-level employees can easily be mentored by experienced staff. These employees each have a work area, with their own shelves and drawers. On the other side of this area are senior employees whom the juniors can watch at work and from whom they can absorb important lessons like how to talk to clients on the phone. Also unusual is having smaller rooms for senior partners, who normally get large, bright, corner rooms. These prime quarters are now assigned to senior employees who work with the entry-level staff.

Such an approach to workplace design, while still experimental, shows staff that the company is going to great pains to provide the best possible solutions for their employees' physical and perhaps psychological needs as they relate to their job. This effort is bound to be a significant motivator.

Source: Elizabeth Church, "McKinsey Experiments with its Workspace," *Globe and Mail*, June 21, 1999, p. M1. Reprinted with permission from *The Globe and Mail*.

necessary. The senior Ford executives were tempted to overrule the program, but they stuck with their promise not to meddle. The team solved the shaking problem and still came in under budget and a couple of months early. The new car was a big hit in the marketplace, and sales soared.[25] In fact, the automotive pricing and review Web site Edmunds.com named it one of the top American muscle cars of today.

A 1995 survey of U.S. companies showed that two-thirds were using formal teams. For the giant Winnipeg-based Great-West Life, discussed in Chapter 13, open communication is key to motivating employees. This is also a feature at the Rimouski, Quebec, plant of Toronto-based Phillips Cables Ltd., which produces hair-thin fibre-optic cable in a state-of-the-art factory. This is part of a joint venture with Furukawa Electric of Japan called Phillips-Fitel.

Despite the fact that the Furukawa managers speak no French and the plant employees speak almost no English, there is an open communication system that has helped to create a strongly motivated workforce. According to union president Marcel Rouleau, "the only boss we have is the plant manager. We don't have incompetents telling us what to do when we know better. Now they consult us…. We feel a lot more creative and it's rewarding."

CEO Malcolm Stagg noted that there has been a remarkable change in the attitude of the workforce. The whole experiment is being carefully observed to see if it can be duplicated at other Canadian plants.[26]

Open communication and teamwork have helped make Motorola Canada Ltd. very competitive. Teams compete fiercely in devising ways to reduce costs and increase efficiency. There is a formal competition among all 3,700 teams of Motorola's 107,000 employees worldwide.

Nine months of intense preparation have come down to a 12-minute performance to a jury of Motorola Canada Ltd. executives on a Saturday morning in a Toronto hotel. "At 4 o'clock in the morning we were still fine-tuning the presentation," says a nervous Jim Kiriacou, one of the nine men and women in Motorola's Toronto paging operations who make up the team.

Despite the stress, the UltraEagles team performed flawlessly. Garbed in hockey jerseys with [their] team logo, they used charts and statistics to explain how they saved close to $50,000 a year by improving the accuracy of customer accounts…. They managed to narrowly defeat the Montreal Express, becoming Canadian paging champions for the third year in a row.[27]

A poll of 1,000 large companies in the United States showed that "almost 60 percent of workers and 77 percent of managers … would work harder if they knew how their jobs keep the company making money."[28] See the Reaching Beyond Our Borders box "Tapping the Power of Workers' Minds" for a description of how GSW Water Heating Co. applied the team method to build a highly motivated workforce.

To implement such groups or teams, managers at most companies must reinvent work. This means respecting workers, providing interesting work, rewarding good work, developing workers' skills, allowing autonomy, and decentralizing authority. Such principles are particularly important to the many workers who are members of Generation X.[29]

www.gsw-wh.com

You can visit GSW's Web site to learn more about the company, its products, its history, and its approach to doing business.

Highly motivated work teams depend on open communications and self-management. Ford Motor Company provided such an atmosphere for its 400-member "Team Mustang" workgroup.

215-HP 4.6L OHC V-8, 4-WHEEL POWER DISC BRAKES, PASSIVE ANTI-THEFT SYSTEM, AND SPORT-TUNED SUSPENSION ARE ALL STANDARD.   www.ford.com

THIS HORSE IS ROCKING.

MUSTANG GT   HAVE YOU DRIVEN A FORD LATELY?   *Ford*

Courtesy of J. Walter Thompson

REACHING BEYOND OUR BORDERS   www.gsw-wh.com
Tapping the Power of Workers' Minds

By any measure, GSW Water Heating Co. should be struggling just to survive. The hourly labour costs of its unionized workforce are the highest of any water-heater manufacturer in North America and as much as double those of U.S. rivals. The company claims no competitive advantage from unique technology or a state-of-the-art plant. Its factory is a concrete dinosaur, having been on its present site since 1911 with only modest updating. The predecessors built the factory in 1874.

Yet at a time of continuing layoffs, GSW Water Heating is expanding its workforce, doubling the capacity of its assembly lines, and competing aggressively and successfully in the United States. All this springs from a collaboration of management, employees, and the union aimed at improving the plant's products and processes and cutting waste and costs. By passing on cost savings to customers, this unit of Toronto-based GSW Inc. has been able to strengthen its competitive position.

"The company said we had to become a world-class manufacturer to survive, and I want to survive," said Robb Rosso, a three-year assembly-line worker who embodies the spirit in the 296-worker plant. Rosso was part of an employee team sifting through worker suggestions to design a bigger production line. The new line doubled the plant's annual capacity to 700,000 heaters, adding another 20 jobs to the workforce.

GSW's survival strategy is one response to the often-heard argument that high labour costs prevent Canadian manufacturers from competing. Rather than dwell on the wage gap, management has worked to reduce other costs and increase productivity by tapping the brainpower of plant workers, whose wage and benefit packages exceed, on average, $24 an hour.

In 1990 GSW Water Heating seemed an unlikely candidate for change. It did not have a rich history of employee involvement. "Our attitude used to be that employees parked their brains at the door when they reported for work and picked them up when they left," said Roger Lippert, director of human resources and a key player in the new approach.

But with the arrival of Canada–U.S. free trade, management, led by president Terry Parsons, was determined to cut costs. It seized on the idea of world-class manufacturing, a generic term for teamwork, training, and continual improvement. The inspiration came from the ideas of W. Edwards Deming, the American consultant who taught total quality management to the Japanese.

In launching the program in 1991, Parsons assured workers this was not a recipe for downsizing. Specific jobs would be lost, he told them, but employment would not be reduced. Sensitive to competitive pressure, the workers accepted the need for change, volunteering in large numbers for training sessions. "Our biggest problem was explaining to employees why they couldn't all participate at the same time," Lippert said. Teams are continually being formed to tackle assignments; there are now more than 14 in the plant, and the number continues to rise.

One team wondered why water heaters had as many as 14 labels dealing with everything from safety to general instructions. By reducing the number of unnecessary labels, the company saved $1 for each heater, or about $350,000 a year. The apparatus for spraying porcelain enamel on the liners of heater tanks was not leaving a uniform deposit. So the problem was handed to a team, whose proposals saved $250,000 a year.

As costs fell, the company embarked on a sales thrust in the United States, where it soon held 2 percent of the water heater market (compared with a 52-percent share in Canada). The target was the U.S. Northeast, within 1,000 kilometres of Fergus, Ontario, where GSW has a freight-cost advantage over major competitors in the U.S. Southeast and Southwest. By 1996 the company had doubled its U.S. sales. By 2001, the company had developed a wide range of products and was selling its products globally.

Sources: Interview with Roger Lippert, July 15, 1996; Wilfred List, "Tapping the Power of Workers' Minds," *Globe and Mail, Report on Business.* November 10, 1992, p. B26; <www.gsw-wh.com>.

In the process of reinventing work, it is essential that managers behave ethically toward all employees. The Ethical Dilemma box at the beginning of this chapter illustrates the problem managers may face when filling temporary positions.

Reinventing Work

In 1985 John Naisbitt and Patricia Aburdene co-authored a book called *Re-Inventing the Corporation* (Warner Books, 1985). The goal of management, according to Naisbitt and Aburdene, is to adopt "new humanistic values." Such new values enable employees to motivate themselves because they feel more a part of a unified corporate team.

Naisbitt and Aburdene suggested certain steps for creating a better corporate atmosphere. These included calling everyone by his or her first name, eliminating executive parking spots and bathrooms, having everyone answer his or her own phone, eliminating files, doing business only with pleasant people, and throwing out the organization chart.

The authors also suggested that managers reinvent work. This means respecting workers, providing interesting work, rewarding good work, developing workers' skills, allowing some autonomy, and decentralizing authority.

Other points: (1) The manager's role is that of teacher, mentor, and coach; (2) the best people want ownership in the firm; (3) the best managerial style is not top-down, but a networking, people style of management; (4) quality is the key to success; (5) successful large corporations copy the entrepreneurial flavour of small businesses; and (6) the information age enables firms to locate where there is a high quality of life, since they don't have to be concerned exclusively with such industrial considerations as raw materials.

All of these ideas are consistent with what management was thinking in the 1990s and are discussed throughout this book. Clearly, there is a trend toward different management styles. The point of this chapter is that the new management styles are largely motivational tools to bring out the best in more educated, better-trained workers. Those are the workers of the future, and they include you. Look through the points outlined above and see if you don't agree that you would enjoy and be more productive working in such an organization. You would be a more motivated worker and thus do a better job.

Changing Organizations Is Not Easy

We have come a long way from the time–motion studies of Frederick Taylor. Maslow, Mayo, Herzberg, and others have taught us to treat employees as associates and to get them more involved in decision making. This increases motivation and leads to greater productivity.

The problem is that many managers were brought up under a different system. Some were in the military and are used to telling people what to do rather than consulting with them. Others come from the football-coach school of management. They, too, tend to yell and direct rather than consult and discuss.

Furthermore, employees are often not used to participative management. The transition from Theory X to Theory Y management, from Taylor to Herzberg, is still going on. It is important, then, to have examples to follow when trying to implement the new approaches.

www.wal-mart.com

You can visit their Web site to learn more about the company discussed here.

Wal-Mart: A Model for the Future

Perhaps the best example of a company that has achieved enormous success in the last 35 years and became the largest retailer in the world is Wal-Mart. Many of this company's management practices were well ahead of its competitors and of most companies in Canada and the United States. Wal-Mart attributes a good deal of its success to its employee motivation strategies. Because it is such an outstanding example of successful employee motivation and because it is now a major retailer in Canada, Canadians should pay close attention to the Wal-Mart story.

There is much controversy about Wal-Mart in Canada and the United States because it has crushed many small businesses and weakened small U.S. towns. When Wal-Mart entered Canada in 1994 there were dire predictions about the impact on large Canadian retailers. The concern was that they would not be able to compete against this aggressively successful company. However, Canadian Tire and Zellers have successfully countered the Wal-Mart threat, although Eaton's may have been a direct casualty. It remains to be seen how they, and other large retailers, will continue to compete successfully against this American behemoth. In any case, it is incumbent upon Canadian companies to learn from successful companies wherever they may be located and regardless of what business they are in. There are such lessons in motivation to be learned from the Wal-Mart experience.

www.canadiantire.ca
www.hbc.com/zellers

You can visit their Web sites to learn more about the three companies discussed here.

Wal-Mart was founded in 1962 by Sam Walton. Walton, who preferred to be called by his first name, saw the great potential for discount retailing in the United States. However, Wal-Mart sold the same merchandise as its competitors, so how could the company be different and take advantage of this potential boom? Walton felt the key to success in the industry was in the development of a family-type relationship with the firm's employees, whom he preferred to call *associates*. He believed that if you did not involve employees in the organization, you were making a serious mistake, for employees are the only ones who can make an organization work.

In the 1990s Wal-Mart became the world's largest retailer. The firm operates more than 6,000 stores, full-line discount stores, wholesale clubs, Super Centres, and hypermarkets. The company was awarded the Retailer of the Decade award by *Discount Stores News*, and Mr. Sam, who died in 1992, became one of the richest men in the world.

How did all of this happen? Wal-Mart's success can be attributed to many factors. For example, the company was on the cutting edge of technology. It was one of the first firms to implement bar-code scanners in all of its stores. It also developed satellite-based transmissions that moved information rapidly from store to store, store to headquarters, and store to suppliers. Wal-Mart demanded a good deal of effort from suppliers but managed to develop positive and long-lasting relationships with them. This efficiency in distribution helped Wal-Mart fulfill its promise of everyday low prices. Many firms, including Sears, have tried to emulate this successful strategy. However, what Wal-Mart did best overall was develop a successful partnership with its associates. Sam Walton firmly believed that only people can make a business grow. He staked his future and that of the company of this basic principle.

Walton laid the foundation of his partnership with employees on three basic principles:

1. **Treat employees as partners**. Share with them both good news and bad news so they will strive to excel. Also, let employees share in the rewards they help achieve.

2. **Encourage employees to question and challenge the obvious**. Walton believed the path to success included some failures. It was important to use those failures to advantage by learning from them.

3. **Involve associates at all levels in the decision-making process**. Managers should be facilitators, sharing ideas with employees and soliciting ideas from them. Employees should not *ask* to be involved; they should be *required* to be involved.

Although many companies proclaimed such ambitious partnerships, Wal-Mart actually created one. The company regularly provided the good news and bad news just as it promised. Associates were kept informed about costs, freight charges, profit margins, and any other issues considered critical to the firm. Wal-Mart backed up its promise of sharing the wealth by providing a generous bonus plan to deserving employees. Company executives, including Sam Walton, practised participative decision making by visiting Wal-Mart stores throughout the country seeking ideas, advice, and opinions from associates. The company even delegated authority to sales clerks, checkers, and stockpeople to order merchandise they thought they could sell. All employees were encouraged to get involved in operations and make the company better.[30] In Chapter 14 you will see how some companies have handled the issue of unionization attempts at some of its stores.

CRITICAL THINKING

How does Sam Walton's approach to motivation relate to Maslow's theory? Did he try to motivate employees by satisfying their unmet needs? Or do Herzberg's ideas fit better with what Walton did? Is it possible that both Herzberg's and Maslow's theories apply in this case?

MOTIVATION IN THE FUTURE

What can you learn from all the theories and companies discussed in this chapter? You should have learned that people can be motivated to improve productivity and quality of work if managers know which technique to use and when. You should now be aware that

- The growth and competitiveness of industry and business in general depend on a motivated, productive workforce. As mentioned in previous chapters, to sustain competitive advantage in the global marketplace a company's workforce must be engaged in continual improvement and innovation. Only motivated employees can achieve improvement and innovation as normal methods of operations.

- Motivation is largely internal, generated by workers themselves; giving employees the freedom to be creative and rewarding achievement when it occurs will release their energy.

- The first step in any motivational program is to establish open communication among workers and managers so that the feeling generated is one of co-operation and teamwork. A family-type atmosphere should prevail.

Today's customers expect high-quality, customized goods and services **> P. 18 <**. That means employees must provide extensive personal service and pay close attention to details. Employees will have to work smart as well as hard. No amount of supervision can force an employee to smile or to go the extra mile to help a customer. Managers need to know how to motivate their employees to meet customer needs.

Tomorrow's managers will not be able to use any one formula for all employees. Rather, they will have to get to know each worker personally and tailor the motivational effort to the individual. As you learned in this chapter, different employees respond to different managerial and motivational styles. This is further complicated by the increase in global business and the fact that managers now work with employees from a variety of cultural backgrounds. Different cultures experience motivational approaches differently; the manager of the future will have to study and understand these cultural factors when designing a reward system. Here's how Digital Equipment dealt with these cultural issues within global teams.

Even though the concept of teamwork is nothing new, building a harmonious global work team is new and can be complicated. Global companies must recognize differing attitudes and competencies in the team's cultural mix and the technological capabilities among team members. For example, a global work team needs to determine whether the culture of its members is high-context or low-context. In a high-context team culture, members build personal relationships and develop group trust before focusing on tasks. In the low-context culture, members often view relationship building as a waste of time that diverts attention from the task. Koreans, Thais, and Saudis (high-context cultures), for example, often view American team members as insincere due to their need for data and quick decision making.

When Digital Equipment Corporation decided to consolidate its operations at six manufacturing sites, the company recognized the need to form multicultural work teams. Realizing the challenge it faced, Digital hired an internal organization-development specialist to train the team in relationship building, foreign languages, and valuing differences. All team members from outside the United States were assigned American partners and invited to spend time with their families. Digital also flew the flags of each employee's native country at all its manufacturing sites. As communication within the teams increased, the company reduced the time of new-product handoffs from up to three years to just six months.[31]

Cultural differences are not restricted to groups of people from various countries. Such differences also exist between generations raised in the same country. Members of generations such as the baby boomers (born between 1946 and 1966) and Generation X (born between 1967 and 1980) are linked through shared life experiences in their formative years—usually the first 10 years of life. The beliefs you gather as a child affect how you view risk and challenge, authority, technology, relationships, and economics; and, if you are in a management position, they can affect even whom you hire, fire, or promote. While boomers were raised in families that experienced unprecedented economic prosperity, parents with secure jobs, and optimism about the future, "Gen Xers" were raised in dual-career families with parents who focused on work while their children attended day care or became latchkey kids. Their parents' successive layoffs added to their insecurity about a lifelong job.

How do these generational differences affect motivation in the workplace? For the boomer managers, it means that they will need to be flexible with their Gen X employees or they will lose them. For Gen X employees, it means that they will need to use their enthusiasm for change and streamlining to their advantage. Although Gen Xers are unwilling to pay the same price for success that their parents and grandparents did, concern about undue stress and long work hours does not mean they have a lack of ambition. Gen Xers' desire for security equals that of older workers, but there is a big difference in their approach to achieving it. Rather than focusing on job security, Gen Xers focus on career security. As they look for opportunities to expand their skills and grow professionally, they are willing to change jobs to do it.[32]

Many Gen Xers are now or soon will be managers themselves and responsible for motivating other employees. What type of management will this generation provide? In general, Gen X managers will be well equipped to motivate people. They understand that there is more to life than work, and they think a big part of motivating people is letting them know you recognize that fact. As a result, Gen X managers will tend to focus more on results than on hours in the workplace. They will be flexible and good at collaboration and consensus building. They tend to think in broader terms than their predecessors because, through the media, they have been exposed to a lot of problems around the world. They will tend to have a great impact on their team members because they will give the people working for them the goals and the parameters of the project and then leave them alone to do their work.

Radisson Hotels Worldwide recently announced its Employees of the Year at its annual business conference. Three employees from Radisson's 240 North American hotels were chosen from among thousands of employees for the honour. The employees were honoured for their talents, skills, outstanding guest service, and "Yes I can!" attitude.

Darren Price

7. Identify the steps involved in implementing a management by objectives (MBO) program.

7. One procedure for establishing objectives and gaining employee commitment to those objectives is management by objectives.
   - *What are the steps in an MBO program?*
   (1) Managers set goals in co-operation with subordinates, (2) objectives are established for each department, (3) managers and workers together discuss the objectives and commit themselves in writing to meeting them, (4) two-way communication and review show workers how they're doing, (5) feedback is provided and corrections are made if necessary, and (6) employees are rewarded for achieving goals.

8. Explain the key factors involved in expectancy theory.

8. According to Victor Vroom, employee expectations can affect an individual's motivation.
   - *What are the key elements involved in expectancy theory?*
   Expectancy theory centres on three questions employees often ask about performance on the job: (1) Can I accomplish the task? (2) If I do accomplish it, what's my reward? (3) Is the reward worth the effort?

9. Examine the key principles of equity theory.

9. According to equity theory, employees try to maintain equity between inputs and outputs compared to other employees in similar positions.
   - *What happens when employees perceive that their rewards are not equitable?*
   If employees perceive that they are underrewarded, they will either (1) reduce their effort or (2) rationalize that it isn't important. Inequity leads to lower productivity, reduced quality, increased absenteeism, and voluntary resignation.

10. Explain how open communication builds teamwork, and describe how managers are likely to motivate teams in the future.

10. Companies with highly motivated workforces often have open communication systems and self-managed teams.
   - *Why is open communication so important in building effective self-managed teams?*
   Open communication helps both top managers and team members understand the objectives and work together to achieve them. Teams establish an environment in which learning can happen because most learning happens at the peer level.
   - *How are Generation X managers likely to be different from their baby-boomer predecessors?*
   Baby boomers are willing to work long hours to build their careers and often expect their subordinates to do likewise. Gen Xers strive for a more balanced lifestyle and are likely to focus on results rather than on how many hours their teams work. Gen Xers are better than previous generations at working in teams and providing frequent feedback. They are not bound by traditions that may constrain those who have been with an organization for a long time and are willing to try new approaches to solving problems.

KEY TERMS

equity theory 370
expectancy theory 370
extrinsic reward 354
goal-setting theory 368
Hawthorne effect 357
hygiene factors 365
intrinsic reward 354
job enlargement 368
job enrichment 367
job rotation 368

job simplification 367
management by objectives (MBO) 369
Maslow's hierarchy of needs 358
motivators 365
principle of motion economy 356
reinforcement theory 371
scientific management 355
time–motion studies 355

1. Talk with several of your friends about the subject of motivation. What motivates them to work hard or not work hard in school and on the job? How important is self-motivation to them?

2. One of the important managerial practices discussed in the chapter is to organize employees into self-managed teams. Student teams are also often used in colleges and universities when doing cases or other projects. Discuss the benefits and drawbacks of dividing classes into teams.

3. Examine Maslow's hierarchy of needs and try to determine where you fit into the needs structure. Which category of your needs do you feel is not being met now? Can you see how, if those needs were satisfied, you would be better motivated at school or elsewhere, until the next category of needs was unmet?

4. Herzberg found that pay was not a motivator. If you were paid to get better grades, would you be able to get them? Have you ever worked harder at a job as a result of a large raise? Discuss money as a motivator with your friends and class. Do you agree 100 percent with Herzberg?

5. Think of all of the groups with whom you have been associated over the years—sports groups, friends, and so on—and try to recall how the leaders of those groups motivated the group to action. Did the leaders assume a Theory X or Theory Y attitude? How often was money used as a motivator? What other motivational tools were used and to what effect?

Purpose:

To explore how companies are motivating their employees generally, and specifically with money and other means.

Exercises:

1. Scan the search engine Canada.com using the keywords *employee + motivation*. Confine your search to Canada over the past year. You will find many matches. Click on an article that looks interesting to you and see how the report relates to the chapter. Is a company or a manager doing something to improve motivation following any of the theories discussed in the chapter? You might want to bring the article to class for discussion about how this event fits with chapter material.

2. Fast-food chains like McDonald's www.mcdonalds.com, Harvey's www.harveysonline.com and Subway www.subway.com generally pay their employees, mostly young students, minimum wages or only slightly more and they have a high rate of employee turnover. As you saw in the chapter, Frederick Herzberg has shown that money is not generally a good long-term motivator of employees. Do you think this is true for fast-food employees? Would an increase in salary motivate them and perhaps reduce the turnover rate? Check out the Web sites of these companies and see if there is any information relating to this topic. Perhaps you can search for stories relating to attempts by fast-food chains to motivate employees. (See also Developing Workplace Skills #1 above.)

PRACTISING MANAGEMENT DECISIONS

CASE 1

THE WORKPLACE: DOES IT HELP OR HINDER MOTIVATION?

A useful article in the Report on Business section of The Globe and Mail started with the provocative question: "Does the atmosphere inside your company resemble Calcutta in the summer or France's Fontainbleau forest in the spring?" This question was put to prestigious international business executives in luxurious Davos, Switzerland.

The speaker was Sumantra Ghoshal, an internationally recognized author, professor, and authority on management issues. His weighty audience was attending the annual World Economic Forum, which is probably the most important annual meeting of senior government and business leaders in the world. He was obviously trying to alert them to what he feels is a major problem confronting companies in today's highly competitive global economy.

Ghoshal noted that if you want high performance from your employees, look first at the atmosphere in your company before you start thinking about "changing each individual employee." Before you set out to teach old dogs new tricks, you better change the "smell of the place." It is his belief that most firms create a "stifling atmosphere in which employees feel constrained, controlled, and forced to comply with a rigid contract that governs their behaviour."

Ghoshal's equally famous colleague and co-author, Christopher Bartlett of Harvard University, noted that now that "information, knowledge, and

expertise" have become just as important as capital was in the past, emphasis has shifted from the corporation to the individual. This means that whereas earlier managers had to fit into the corporation and become organization people, now the corporation must become flexible and find ways to fit the individual manager.

Decision Questions

1. Do you find it surprising that senior executives have to be reminded of these things? Why are they not already aware of this issue, since it has been actively discussed in business schools and business periodicals for some years?
2. Why are companies so slow to adapt to new conditions? Don't they want a better-motivated workforce?
3. Is it possible that corporations' concentration on downsizing in recent years has blinded them to the changed needs of their remaining employees and managers?
4. What is your own experience in jobs you have had? Did you find the atmosphere conducive to employee motivation?

Source: Madeleine Drohan, "Your Workplace: Hole or Haven?" *Globe and Mail, Report on Business*, February 7, 1996, p. B9. Reprinted with permission from *The Globe and Mail*.

PRACTISING MANAGEMENT DECISIONS

CASE 2

MOTIVATION IN AN ERA OF "DISPOSABLE WORKERS"

News reports from Canada and the United States indicate a new trend in the job market. A decreasing number of people are being given permanent jobs of the kind we used to expect as normal employment. Security of employment with all the usual fringe benefits is being reserved for a privileged few. U.S. data indicate that up to half of all new jobs are temporary, part-time, or some other unconventional type of employment, and this number is expected to grow. What is behind this trend?

Many Canadian companies have adopted a form of workforce management that they believe will enable them to compete better in the world market. They keep

a "core of managers and valued workers whom they favour with good benefits and permanent jobs. They take on and shed other workers as business spurts and slumps." These jobs pay less and have few if any benefits. Many Canadians have lost good jobs and are finding only these unsatisfactory new jobs. Many Canadian students are finding only these poor-quality jobs available upon graduation.

According to Robert Reich, U.S. secretary of labour in the Clinton administration, "the entire system has fragmented." He estimates that about 30 percent of the American workforce is composed of contingent workers, but current statistics suggest this estimate is low.

Current Canadian data are not yet available, but various Statistics Canada reports indicate that many new jobs are of a similarly insecure nature. Apparently Canadian companies that let go hundreds of thousands of employees in the deep recession and restructuring of the 1990s are not rushing to rehire permanent employees if they can avoid it.

Decision Questions

1. What is likely to be the impact of this trend on employee motivation? Will temporary workers be as motivated as permanent employees, especially if they continue to look for a "decent" job?
2. How will this, in turn, affect production and service to customers? Given the growing importance of teamwork and co-operation, is quality production likely to suffer?

3. What are the long-term impacts on the competitiveness of companies? Are companies being too short-sighted in thinking only of current bottom lines?
4. How can companies develop employees' long-term loyalty in such circumstances? Is this still important? Why?

Sources: Peter T. Kilborn, "New Jobs Lack the Old Security in a Time of 'Disposable Workers,'" *New York Times*, March 15, 1993, p. A1; *Globe and Mail*, *Financial Post*, various issues in February and March 1993; Peter Hadekel, "Very Soon the Working World Will Be Divided into Two Types of People," *Montreal Gazette*, March 10, 1993, p. B14; "What's the Big Deal?" *Globe and Mail*, *Report on Business*, December 12, 1995, p. B9; Bruce Little, "Canada Pumps out New Jobs in July," *Globe and Mail*, August 7, 1999, p. B3.

CBC VIDEO CASE   www.cbc.ca

THE COOKWORKS

The importance of teamwork has been mentioned in this and other chapters. It has become increasingly clear that for a company to be efficient and competitive today an important requirement is close collaboration at various levels. There are three such levels: intra-department, inter-department, and inter-company. The first requires teams of managers and employees in specific departments; the second consists of cross-department people; the third involves teams whose members include employees from suppliers or customers.

In our world of highly competitive companies and individuals driven by strong personal ambition, especially at the managerial level, it is not always easy to instill the concept of teamwork. It is often even harder to develop teams with members who enjoy the stimulation of working closely with others of different backgrounds and opinions. Well-functioning, productive teams are

the result when high morale is developed by such motivated team members.

Various methods are employed by companies to achieve such group cohesiveness and harmony. This video shows one unusual example of the kind of training that can produce great teamwork.

Discussion Questions

1. Can you point out specific aspects of the cooking experience that should lead to better co-operation among the team members back at work?
2. Do you think this experience will lead to a better motivated group? What evidence is there in the video to support your opinion?
3. Can you think of any other type of experience that could also produce the same positive results? Could it be the basis for a new small business like the Cookworks idea leading to a new business? Discuss.

Source: *Venture*, show number 778, "The Cookworks," March 13, 2001, running time 3:18.

13

Human Resource Management: Managing the Most Important Asset—People

LEARNING GOALS

AFTER YOU HAVE READ AND STUDIED THIS CHAPTER, YOU SHOULD BE ABLE TO

1 Explain the importance of human resource management, and describe current issues in managing human resources.

2 Describe methods companies use to recruit new employees, and explain some of the issues that make recruitment challenging.

3 Illustrate the various types of employee training and development methods.

4 Summarize the objectives of employee compensation programs, and describe various pay systems and benefits.

5 Explain scheduling plans managers use to adjust to workers' needs.

6 Describe training methods used in management development programs.

7 Illustrate the effects of legislation on human resource management.

Employee Benefits Get a New Look at MacMillan Bloedel

Courtesy of MacMillan Bloedel Ltd.

Dwayne Leskewich, employee benefits administrator at B.C. forestry giant MacMillan Bloedel, has redesigned and modernized the whole program that he administers. For many years the underlying philosophy found in large companies was the basis of the approach at MacBlo. Since January 1995 the employee benefits program has had a totally new look. Choice has been placed in the hands of the employees. The program is called *Partnerships For Success.*

Leskewich points out that the average age of his workforce had edged over 40 and many were asking for the right to choose specific types of benefits rather than having to buy into a fixed package. He knew this was a growing trend in North America and had been thinking about revamping the program to fit modern needs. So Leskewich redesigned it, offering a wide variety of benefits from which employees could select any combination up to a certain maximum dollar amount. Those who opted for a program with a total cost that was less than this figure would have the difference added to their pay.

Prior to decision time, employees were given a wide-ranging introduction to the new program and the choices they would have to make. Brochures, lectures, question periods, videos, and one-on-one sessions prepared the way for the changeover. Some employees cautiously opted for a combination that approximated their existing package. Most adopted variations more suited to their particular needs. By May 1996, some 75 percent of the workforce had switched over to the *cafeteria-*style benefits program and were very satisfied with the change.

In addition to the new benefits program, job sharing and flexible working hours have been available for some time and fit the bill for certain employees. People with young children or elders to care for like such options because they reduce stress and absenteeism. Obviously, this works well for the company, too. It is not easy, or always possible, to institute either of these two arrangements, but for those who really want them, the company tries to find ways to accommodate them.

In August 1999 Leskewich reported that the flexible benefits program was well established and strongly favoured by the workforce—75 percent continue to opt for the choices it gives them. A cafeteria-style program not only gives choices, but employees can also make changes annually. The company also offers flexibility in pension planning. Leskewich notes that he is looking at expanding the benefits package to include flexibility in medical coverage for employees after retirement.

Dwayne Leskewich has joined a growing number of benefits managers who have moved away from rigid programs toward employee participation and empowerment, and less rigidity in the workplace overall.

Sources: Interview with Dwayne Leskewich, May 22, 1996, and August 23, 1999; Deborah Wilson, "Employees Design Benefits Packages," *Globe and Mail, Report on Business,* December 19, 1995, p. B26.

ETHICAL DILEMMA

The Temptation to Get Around the Law

You are a manager in the human resource department and one of your jobs is to do the initial interview with job applicants. As you will see in this chapter it is illegal in Canada for a job application form to ask certain questions, such as age, nationality, or religion. Similarly, as an interviewer, you cannot ask a female applicant if she is planning to have children in the near future as it is illegal not to hire a woman who may become pregnant. You are a bit bothered by these restrictions because of problems with some recent hirees. An older man was often absent because his eyes couldn't stand up to the strain of the job, an orthodox Muslim required much time off for prayer and other religious duties, and a young woman proved to have actually been pregnant when hired. Your superior has hinted that you should find some subtle way to get around the legal restrictions when interviewing applicants. He also has hinted that if your track record improves you might get a nice bonus at year-end. Furthermore, if you do not co-operate, he has hinted you may find it difficult to get a promotion. What would you do? Let's look at this question at the end of the chapter, after you have had a chance to digest its contents.

THE HUMAN RESOURCE FUNCTION

www.onepine.demon.co.uk/pkant.htm

Rosabeth Moss Kanter identified the key skills for managers who see the need to bring about change within their organizations. She has identified a list of things to be avoided, which she calls "Ten rules for stifling change." Visit this Web site to learn these rules and the skills required to bring about successful change.

human resource management (HRM)
The process of evaluating human resource needs, finding people to fill those needs, and motivating employees to get the best work from each one by providing the right incentives and job environment, all with the goal of meeting the organization's objectives.

This chapter will discuss the human resource function, which involves recruiting, hiring, training, evaluating, compensating, and laying off people. **Human resource management (HRM)** is the process of evaluating human resource needs, finding people to fill those needs, and motivating employees to get the best work from each one by providing the right incentives and job environment, all with the goal of meeting the organization's objectives (see Figure 13.1). Let's explore some of the trends in the area of HRM.

Trends and Issues in HRM

Like many other aspects of Canadian business mentioned in other chapters, HRM has been greatly affected by technology and global competition. Both of these factors have led Canadian companies to downsize workforces for both management and employees. While technological developments are having an enormous effect on people and jobs in businesses it is worthwhile considering what one person said: "One machine can do the work of 50 men [but] no machine can do the work of one extraordinary man."[1] (We can assume that the speaker was referring to women as well.) Other employees work at home and only go to company premises occasionally. The nature of work and management has changed enormously. Employees participate more in decision making through teamwork and there is a greater emphasis on quality and customer satisfaction. Better-trained and better-educated employees are now required to work in a more high-tech global business climate. This is only a short list of some of the major issues that are increasing the importance of, and causing a revolution in, HRM operations. Some of the ethical issues are addressed in the Ethical Dilemma box "The Temptation to Get Around the Law."

Importance of HRM

One reason human resource management is receiving increased attention now is the major shift from traditional manufacturing industries to service industries ➤ **P. 18** ◄ and high-tech manufacturing organizations that require more technical job skills. Companies now have fewer employees, but the ones who remain require more education and skills. A major problem today is retraining workers for new, more challenging jobs.

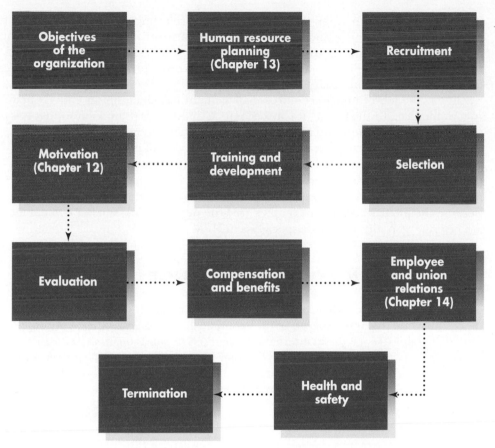

FIGURE 13.1

HUMAN RESOURCE MANAGEMENT

Note that human resource management includes motivation (discussed in Chapter 12) and union relations (discussed in Chapter 14). As you can see from the chart, human resource management involves more than hiring and firing personnel.

BC Telephone has set up an education centre in Burnaby, B.C., to provide proper training for its employees. The National Bank of Canada has set up a banking school by teaming up with the Institute of Canadian Bankers and Université de Québec.[2] These are but two examples of how companies are moving to ensure a properly trained workforce. Here are some other examples:

- Canada Mortgage and Housing Corp., a Crown corporation, has numerous training programs and job exchanges. Temporary vacancies are often filled by people from other departments wanting to enrich their own experience. Each year, CMHC hires 10 university graduates under a two-year training program that exposes them to 10 or 12 departments.

- Allen-Bradley Canada Ltd. manufactures industrial automation equipment. It has more than a thousand employees in three plants in Ontario and emphasizes training. At its Cambridge plant it employs seven full-time and three part-time instructors. The other locations have four full-time instructors. New marketing employees go through a three-month training and orientation program. All new employees attend a two-week business course.[3]

- The Bank of Montreal spent $40 million setting up an Institute for Learning for its employees. The aim of the director of the complex, Dr. James Rush, is to ensure continuing opportunities for the bank's employees to learn and to be creative.[4]

Employees have been called a company's most important resource, and when you think about it, nothing could be more true. People develop the ideas that eventually become the products that satisfy our wants and needs. Take away the creative minds, and organizations such as Bombardier, DuPont, Nortel, and Magna International cease to be leading firms.

www.icb.org/programs

Visit the ICB's Web site to see the broad selection of programs and courses it offers to the financial services industry. It even offers an MBA program in collaboration with UQAM (in French) and Dalhousie University (in English).

Most firms used to assign the job of recruiting, selecting, training, evaluating, compensating, motivating, and firing people to the various functional departments. For years, the personnel department was viewed more or less as a clerical function responsible for screening applications, keeping records, processing payroll, and finding people when necessary.

Today the job of human resource management has taken on an entirely new role in the firm. In the future, it may become *the* most critical function in that it is responsible for the most critical resource—people. The human resource function has become so important that it is no longer the function of just one department; it is a function of all managers. Most human resource functions are shared between the professional human resource manager and the other managers. In smaller companies with no HRM department, one manager or the owner has this responsibility. Because the job has become so complex (see the next section), smaller companies are beginning to turn to outside specialists in HRM.[5]

THE HUMAN RESOURCE CHALLENGE

No changes in the Canadian business system have been more dramatic and had more impact on the future success of the economy than changes in the labour force. Canada's ability to compete in international markets depends on an increase in new ideas, new products, and, as we saw in Chapter 10, increased productivity ➤ **P. 43** ◄. All of these factors critically depend on the ultimate resource—people. Problems being encountered in the human resource area include the following:

- Shortages of young and not so young people trained to work in high-tech growth areas such as telecommunications, computers, biotechnology, robotics, and the sciences.

- A huge population of skilled and unskilled workers (from declining industries such as textiles, apparel manufacturing, and steel and modernizing industries such as automobiles) who are unemployed or underemployed and who need retraining.

- A shift in the age composition in the workforce, including many older workers. (See Chapter 1 for a discussion of demographic trends.)

- A complex set of laws and regulations governing hiring, firing, safety, health, unionization, and equal pay that require organizations to go beyond only profit orientation and become more socially responsible.

- An increasing number of single-parent and two-income families resulting in a demand for day care, job sharing, maternity and paternity leave, flexible schedules, and special career advancement programs for women.

- Relentless downsizing, which is taking its toll on employee morale as well as increasing the demand for temporary workers. Another effect is a decreased sense of employee loyalty resulting in increased employee turnover leading to increasing costs involved in replacing employees.

- A challenge from foreign labour pools available for lower wages and subject to fewer laws and regulations. This results in many jobs being shifted to other countries.

- An increased demand for benefits tailored to the individual including a growing concern over such issues as health, elder, and child care (discussed in Chapter 14), equal opportunities for people with disabilities, and special attention given to employment equity programs.

- A shift in employee attitudes toward work. Leisure time has become a much higher priority, as have concepts such as flextime and a shorter workweek.

Given all these issues, and others that are sure to develop, you can see why human resource management has taken a more central position in management thinking. We will start with a look at planning.

Does human resource management seem like a challenging career to you? Do you see any other issues likely to affect this function? What have your experiences been in dealing with people who work in HRM? Would you enjoy working in such an environment?

DETERMINING HUMAN RESOURCE NEEDS

All management, including HRM, begins with planning. Six steps are involved in the human resource planning process (see Figure 13.2 for a summary).

1. **Preparing forecasts of future human resource needs**.

2. **Preparing a human resource inventory of the organization's employees**. This inventory should include names, education, capabilities, training, specialized skills, and other information pertinent to the specific organization (for example, languages spoken). Such information reveals the status of the labour force.

3. **Preparing a job analysis**. A **job analysis** is a study of what is done by the employees who hold various job titles. Such analyses are necessary to recruit and train employees with the right skills to do the job. The results of a job analysis are two written statements: job descriptions and job specifications. A **job description** specifies the objectives of the job, the type of work to be done, the responsibilities and duties, the working conditions, and the relationship of the job to other functions. **Job specifications** are a summary of the *minimum* qualifications (education, skills, and so on) required of a worker to fill a specific job. In short, job descriptions are statements about the job, whereas job specifications are statements about the person who does the job. See Figure 13.3 for hypothetical examples of a job description and job specifications.

4. **Assessing future demand**. Constantly changing technology means that training programs must be started long before the need is apparent. Human resource managers need to be proactive. In this case that means anticipating the future HR needs of their organization; have the trained human resources available when needed (as identified in step 6).

job analysis
A study of what is done by the employees who hold various job titles.

job description
A summary of the objectives of a job, the type of work to be done, the responsibilities and duties, the working conditions, and the relationship of the job to other functions.

job specifications
A written summary of the minimum qualifications required of a worker to do a particular job.

FIGURE 13.2

STEPS IN HUMAN RESOURCE PLANNING

Human resource planning is a complex process involving six crucial steps.

FIGURE **13.3**

EXAMPLE OF A JOB ANALYSIS

A job analysis yields two important statements: a job description and job specifications. Here you have a job description and job specifications for a cereal sales representative.

Job Analysis

Observe current sales representatives doing the job.

Discuss job with sales managers.

Have current sales reps keep a diary of their activities.

Job Description	Job Specifications
Primary responsibility is to sell cereal to food stores in Territory Z. Other duties include servicing accounts and maintaining positive relationships with clients. Examples of duties required:	Characteristics of the person qualifying for this job include the following:
• Introducing the new cereal to store managers in the area.	• Two years' sales experience.
• Helping the store managers estimate the volume to order.	• Positive attitude.
• Negotiating prime shelf space.	• Well-groomed appearance.
• Explaining sales promotion activities to store managers.	• Good communication skills.
• Stocking and maintaining shelves in stores that want such service.	• High school diploma and two years of college credit.

5. **Assessing future supply**. The labour force is constantly shifting: getting older, becoming more technically oriented, attracting more women, and so forth. There are likely to be continuing shortages of some skills in the future (e.g., software developers) and oversupply of others (e.g., assembly line workers).

6. **Preparing a comprehensive or strategic plan**. The plan must address recruiting, selecting, training and developing, appraising, compensating, and scheduling the labour force. Because the previous five steps lead up to this one, this chapter will focus on these elements of the strategic human resource plan.

www.monster.ca
www.canadajobs.com
www.cooljobscanada.com
www.workopolis.com

Visit the Web sites of these services to get more information about the services and jobs they offer. See if you can find a job posting that interests you.

Internet job site services are useful tools for external recruiting of employees (some major ones are listed in the Taking It to the Net exercises at the end of the chapter). The Spotlight on Small Business box "Small Businesses Must Compete to Attract Qualified Workers" outlines some of the affordable ways businesses can address their recruiting needs. Although recruiting from most external sources seems straightforward, sometimes this may involve difficult ethical decisions. At the beginning and end of Chapter 9 the question of enticing desirable employees from other companies was reviewed. It might be a good idea to take another look at those pages now.

RECRUITING EMPLOYEES

recruitment
The set of activities used to obtain a sufficient number of the right people at the right time and to select those who best meet the needs of the organization.

Recruitment is the set of activities used to obtain a sufficient number of the right people at the right time and to select those who best meet the needs of the organization. One would think that, with a continual flow of new people into the workforce, recruiting would be easy. But the truth is that recruiting has become very difficult for several reasons.

SPOTLIGHT ON SMALL BUSINESS

Small Businesses Must Compete to Attract Qualified Workers

It's harder now than ever before for businesses to find qualified employees, and it is becoming more expensive. Small-business owners across the country agree that competition for qualified employees is intensifying. Small businesses want top talent but often can't afford corporate-level benefits or expensive recruiters to hunt them down. Despite the hurdles, small-business management consultants say there are many ways to lure desirable workers:

- *Transform ads into promotional tools.* For example, Ecoprint, a small print shop in Maryland, brags about the benefits of working for this collegial company in its advertisements.

- *Post job openings on the Internet.* Running a 20-line ad on an online service like Monster.ca costs $100 to $150 for 30 days. A comparable ad in a major newspaper can cost 20 times that amount.

- *Let your staff help select hires.* The more people involved in the interview process, the better chance you have to find out if the person has the personality and skills to fit in.

- *Create a dynamic workplace to attract local, energetic applicants.* Sometimes word of mouth is the most effective recruiting tool.

- *Test-drive an employee.* Hiring temporary workers can allow you to test candidates for a few months before deciding whether to make an offer or not.

- *Hire your customer.* Loyal customers sometimes make the smartest employees.

- *Check community groups and local government agencies.* Don't forget to check out province-run employment agencies. The new welfare-to-work programs may turn up excellent candidates you can train.

- *Lure candidates with a policy of promotions and raises.* Most employees want to know that they can move up in the company. Give employees an incentive for learning the business.

Sources: "Hire.com Helps Level the Recruiting Playing Field for Emerging Businesses," *Business Wire*, May 16, 2000; and "Some Employers Can't Afford the Minimum Wage," *Business Week*, August 7, 2000, p. 15

- Legal restrictions, such as the Charter of Rights and Freedoms, make it necessary to consider the proper mix of women, minorities, people with disabilities, and other qualified individuals.

- Sometimes the people with the necessary skills are not available. Then promising employees must be hired and trained internally.

- The emphasis on corporate cultures, teamwork, and participative management makes it important to hire skilled people who also fit in with the culture and leadership style of the organization.

- Firing unsatisfactory employees is getting harder to justify legally. This is especially true of discharges involving possible discrimination by factors such as age, sex, or ethnicity. Therefore, it's necessary to screen and evaluate applicants carefully to select those most likely to be effective long-term members of the organization.

- Some organizations have unattractive workplaces or offer low wages, which makes recruiting and keeping employees difficult.

Because recruiting is a difficult chore that involves finding, hiring, and training people who are an appropriate technical and social fit, human resource managers turn to many sources for assistance (see Figure 13.4 on page 395). These sources are classified as either internal or external. *Internal sources* include hiring from within the firm (transfers, promotions, and so forth) and employee recommendations. Internal sources are less expensive than recruiting outside the company. The greatest advantage of hiring from within is that it helps maintain employee morale. However, it isn't always possible to find qualified workers within the company, so human resource managers must use *external recruitment sources* such as ads, public and private employment agencies, college and university placement bureaus, management consultants, professional organizations, referrals, and applicants who simply show up at the office (walk-ins). Internet job sites have become increasingly important. (See the illustration of Jobs Canada below and the Taking It to the Net exercises at the end of this chapter.)

SELECTING EMPLOYEES

selection
The process of gathering information to decide who should be hired, under legal guidelines, for the best interests of the organization and the individual.

Selection is the process of gathering information to decide who should be hired, under legal guidelines, for the best interests of the organization and the individual. The cost of selecting and training employees is prohibitively high in large firms. Think of the costs involved: interview time, medical exams, training costs, unproductive time spent learning the job, moving expenses, and so on. It's easy to see how such expenses can run more than \$50,000 for a manager. Even entry-level workers can cost $1\frac{1}{2}$ times their annual salary to recruit, process, and train. Companies try to avoid the substantial costs of a high turnover rate. Thus, the selection process becomes an important element in any human resource program. A typical selection process involves six steps (see Figure 13.5 on page 396). The whole process must not only conform to legal requirements but also must be ethically acceptable. These requirements can be better understood as we examine each step in the process.

1. **Completion of an application form**. Once this was a simple procedure. Today, legal guidelines limit the kinds of questions you can ask. (Sex, ethnicity, religion, age, or nationality are taboo). Nonetheless, such forms help managers discover educational background, past work experience, career objectives, and other information directly related to the requirements of the job.

2. **Initial and follow-up interviews**. Applicants are often screened in a first interview by a member of the HRM staff. If the interviewer considers the applicant a potential employee, the manager who will supervise the new employee interviews the applicant as well. It's important that managers prepare adequately for the interview process to improve the likelihood of making the best selections. They must avoid asking the wrong question such as asking a

Jobs Canada lists the 1,000 best job opportunities in Canada weekly.

Courtesy of Jobs Canada

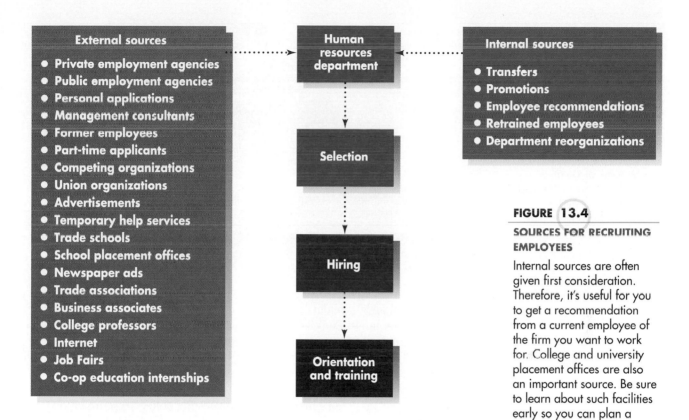

External sources

- Private employment agencies
- Public employment agencies
- Personal applications
- Management consultants
- Former employees
- Part-time applicants
- Competing organizations
- Union organizations
- Advertisements
- Temporary help services
- Trade schools
- School placement offices
- Newspaper ads
- Trade associations
- Business associates
- College professors
- Internet
- Job Fairs
- Co-op education internships

Human resources department

Selection

Hiring

Orientation and training

Internal sources

- Transfers
- Promotions
- Employee recommendations
- Retrained employees
- Department reorganizations

FIGURE 13.4

SOURCES FOR RECRUITING EMPLOYEES

Internal sources are often given first consideration. Therefore, it's useful for you to get a recommendation from a current employee of the firm you want to work for. College and university placement offices are also an important source. Be sure to learn about such facilities early so you can plan a strategy throughout your post-secondary career.

female about her family plans. No matter how innocent the intention, that could be used as evidence if the applicant files discrimination charges.

3. **Employment tests**. Employment tests have been severely criticized on charges of discrimination. Nonetheless, organizations continue to use them to measure basic competencies, test specific job skills (for example, welding or word processing), and help evaluate applicants' personalities and interests. It's important that the employment test be directly job-related. This will make the selection process more efficient, will usually satisfy legal requirements, and will also be ethically valid.

4. **Background investigations.** Most organizations are now more careful than they had been in the past about investigating a candidate's work record, school record, and recommendations. It is simply too costly to hire, train, and motivate people only to lose them and then have to start the process over. Background checks help weed out candidates least likely to succeed and identify those most likely to succeed in a specific position. It is not always easy to obtain this information, however. Many companies no longer provide references for fear of liability suits if they give negative reports.

5. **Physical exams**. A complete medical background and checkup can help screen candidates. There are obvious benefits in hiring physically and mentally healthy people. However, medical tests cannot be given just to screen out specific applicants—that could lead to a charge of discrimination. If such tests are given, they must be given to everyone at the same point in the selection process. A major controversy erupted in the late 1980s related to pre-employment testing to detect drug or alcohol abuse or AIDS.

jobswithoutborders.com

By combining immigration and employment services, Jobs Without Borders provides highly trained individuals for companies in Canada and the U.S. Companies may post job openings, browse through the database, and interview online.

FIGURE 13.5

STEPS IN THE SELECTION PROCESS

There are several steps you must take to obtain a job. First, you fill out an application form. Then you must go through an interviewing process and all or some of the other steps shown here. The goal is to find a job that is satisfying to you and that you will do well.

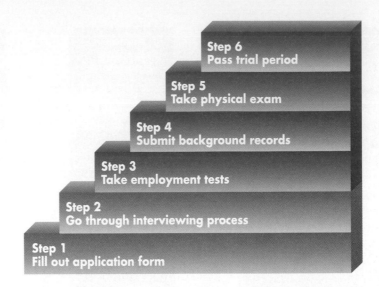

Step 6
Pass trial period

Step 5
Take physical exam

Step 4
Submit background records

Step 3
Take employment tests

Step 2
Go through interviewing process

Step 1
Fill out application form

More than 70 percent of CEOs endorse drug testing in some instances. The Toronto Dominion Bank asked 250 top executives to undergo drug tests and made testing mandatory for all new employees. The Canadian Civil Liberties Association asked the Canadian Human Rights Commission to quash this program as discriminating on the basis of disability but lost the case. However, in 1998 the Federal Court of Appeal ruled that the bank's "mandatory random and universal pre-employment urinary drug-testing policy is discriminatory." In a similar case in Ontario involving the Imperial Oil Co.'s drug-testing policy, both the Human Rights Tribunal and a lower court ruled that the policy was discriminatory and the case has now gone to the Ontario Appeal Court. David Korn, president of The Donwood Institute, a public hospital in Toronto, said company funds should not be used in the search for a quick fix to a very complex issue. Levi Strauss & Co. (Canada) Inc. does not test prospective employees for AIDS but has a thorough educational program for them. By contrast, the Canadian AIDS Society, in a survey of 500 businesses, discovered that only 4 percent are developing policies and programs to deal with AIDS; 22 percent said it was not their job to inform employees about AIDS.[6] Some of these issues are still unresolved as cases work their way slowly through the courts.

6. **Probationary periods.** Often an organization will hire an employee conditionally. This enables the person to prove his or her worth on the job. After a period of perhaps six months or a year, the firm has the right to discharge that employee based on evaluations from supervisors. Such systems make it easier to fire inefficient or problem employees but do not eliminate the high cost of turnover.

The selection process is often long and difficult, but it's worth the effort because of the high costs of replacing workers. The high costs consist of all that's involved in recruiting, selecting, hiring, orienting, and training new employees, as discussed in the preceding and following pages. The process helps ensure that the people an organization hires are competent in all relevant areas, including communications skills, education, technical skills, experience, social fit, and health. Finally, where a company has a collective labour agreement—a union contract with its employees—the selection process must also follow the provisions of that agreement. This is discussed in more detail in the next chapter.

Hiring Contingent Workers

When more workers are needed in a company, human resource managers may want to consider creative staffing alternatives rather than simply hiring new permanent employees. A company with a varying need for employees, from hour to hour, day to day, week to week, and season to season may find it cost-effective to hire contingent workers. **Contingent workers** are defined as workers who are not regular, full-time employees. Such workers include part-time workers, seasonal workers, temporary workers, independent contractors, interns, and co-op students.

A varying need for employees is the most common reason for hiring contingent workers. Companies may also look to hire contingent workers when full-time employees experience downtimes, there is a peak demand for labour, or quick service to customers is a priority. Companies in which the jobs require minimum training or that are located in areas where qualified contingent workers are available are most likely to consider alternative staffing options.

Temporary staffing has evolved into a major industry. Contingent workers receive few benefits; they are rarely offered insurance or private pensions. They may also earn less than permanent workers. On the positive side, many of those on temporary assignments are eventually offered full-time positions. Managers see using temporary workers as a way of weeding out poor workers and finding good hires. Furthermore, in an era of downsizing and rapid change, some contingent workers have even found that temping can be more secure than full-time employment.

Many people like the idea of working part-time or for short periods because their personal needs fit into such situations. They may be single parents or part of a couple where one wants only part-time work. Or an individual short of funds wants extra income for a short period. Sometimes a person is working on some project not yet producing income, or they may have a hobby and need some income to supplement the budget. People who have lost a job may want a temporary job while looking for regular employment in their field.

contingent workers
Workers who are not regular, full-time employees.

PROGRESS CHECK

- What is human resource management?
- What are the six steps in human resource planning?
- What factors make it difficult to recruit qualified employees?
- What are the six steps in the selection process?
- What are contingent workers and why do companies and individuals need this category?

TRAINING AND DEVELOPING EMPLOYEES FOR OPTIMUM PERFORMANCE

Because employees need to learn how to work with new equipment and software, companies are finding that they must offer training programs that often are quite sophisticated. **Training and development** include all attempts to improve productivity by increasing an employee's ability to perform. Training is short-term-skills oriented, whereas development is long-term-career oriented. But both training and development programs include three steps: (1) assessing the needs of the organization and the skills of the employees to determine training needs, (2) designing training activities to meet the identified needs, and (3) evaluating the effectiveness of the training. Some common training and development activities are employee orientation, on-the-job training, apprentice programs, off-the-job training, vestibule training, job simulation, and management training.

- **Employee orientation** is the activity that introduces new employees to the organization; to fellow employees; to their immediate supervisors; and to the policies, practices, and objectives of the firm. Orientation programs include everything from informal talks to formal activities that last a day or more and include scheduled visits to various departments and required

training and development
All attempts to improve productivity by increasing an employee's ability to perform.

employee orientation
The activity that introduces new employees to the organization; to fellow employees; to their immediate supervisors; and to the policies, practices, and objectives of the firm.

This UBC finance student is able to gain valuable hands-on work experience through her internship at CIBC Wood Gundy headquarters in Toronto.

on-the-job training
A training program in which the employee immediately begins his or her tasks and learns by doing, or watches others for a while and then imitates them, right at the workplace.

apprentice programs
Training programs involving a period during which a learner works alongside an experienced employee to master the skills and procedures of a craft.

FedEx, the overnight delivery giant, spends 3 percent of its total expenses on training, six times the average spent by most companies. Here employees play blindfolded basketball, a bonding exercise intended to build trust among workers and managers. The company enjoys a remarkably low 4-percent employee turnover rate. How do you think its training program helps FedEx retain employees?

reading of lengthy handouts. All firms try to recruit people who have the potential to be productive employees. They realize that potential involves effective training programs and proper managerial incentives. Carefully orienting individuals to their new environment can be an important step for the human resource manager. For employees to feel they *fit in* they must be aware of the company's culture. The proper integration or socialization of new employees will give them a base from which they will have a good shot at delivering their best efforts.

- **On-the-job training** is the most fundamental type of training. The employee being trained on the job immediately begins his or her tasks and learns by doing, or watches others for a while and then imitates them, right at the workplace. Salespeople, for example, are often trained by watching experienced salespeople perform. Naturally, this can be either quite effective or disastrous, depending on the skills and habits of the person being watched. On-the-job training is obviously the easiest kind of training to implement and can be effective when the job is relatively simple, such as clerking in a store, or repetitive, such as collecting refuse, cleaning carpets, or mowing lawns. Most jobs are more demanding or intricate so they require a more intense training effort. Intranets and other new forms of technology are leading to cost-effective on-the-job training programs available 24 hours a day, all year long. Computer systems can monitor workers' input and give them instructions if they become confused about what to do next. MCI WorldCom's intranet training system saved the company nearly $3 million by reducing the training cost per employee by 22 percent.[7]

- **Apprentice programs** involve a period during which a learner works alongside an experienced employee to master the skills and procedures of a craft. Some apprentice programs also involve classroom training. Many skilled crafts, such as bricklaying and plumbing, require a new worker to serve as an apprentice for several years. Trade unions often require new workers to serve apprenticeships to ensure excellence among their members as well as

to limit entry to the union. Workers who successfully complete a formal provincial apprentice program earn the classification of *journeyman* and get a licence to practise their trade. In the future, there are likely to be more but shorter apprentice programs to prepare people for skilled jobs in changing industries. For example, auto repair will require more intense training as new automobile models include more advanced computers and other electronic devices.

- **Off-the-job training** occurs away from the workplace and consists of internal or external programs to develop any of a variety of skills or to foster personal development. Training is becoming more sophisticated as jobs become more sophisticated. Furthermore, training is expanding to include education (through the Ph.D. level) and personal development—subjects may include time management, stress management, health and wellness, physical education, nutrition, and even art and languages.

- **Online training** offers an example of how technology is improving the efficiency of many off-the-job training programs. In such training, employees "attend" classes via the Internet.[8] For example, The Business Channel (TBC) offers business education programs over the Internet. Such programs are sometimes called *distance learning* because the students are separated by distance from the instructor or content source.[9]

off-the-job training
Training that occurs away from the workplace and consists of internal or external programs to develop any of a variety of skills or to foster personal development.

online training
Training programs in which employees "attend" classes via the Internet.

www.pbstbc.com

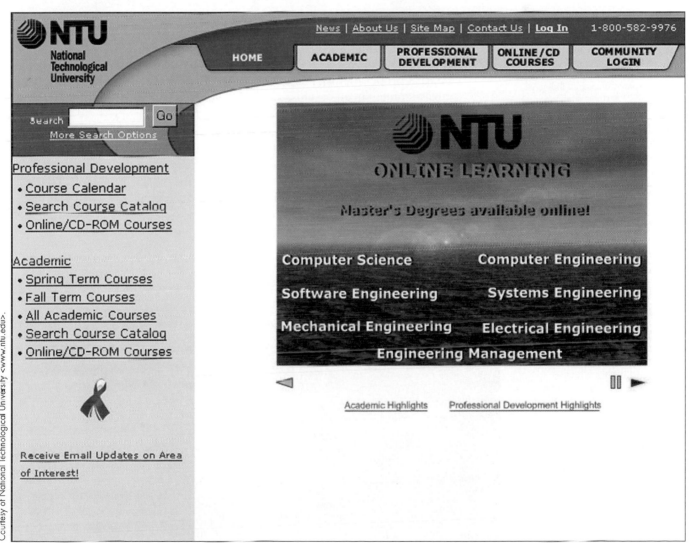

Courtesy of National Technological University <www.ntu.edu>.

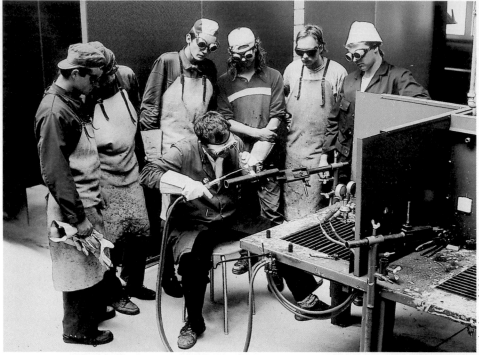

These apprentice welders learn their craft from a skilled professional. Practical hands-on experience is usually combined with classroom training.

Michael Rosenfeld/Tony Stone Images

vestibule training
Training done in schools where employees are taught on equipment similar to that used on the job.

job simulation
The use of equipment that duplicates job conditions and tasks so that trainees can learn skills before attempting them on the job.

- **Vestibule training** is done in classrooms where employees are taught on equipment similar to that used on the job. Such schools enable employees to learn proper methods and safety procedures before assuming a specific job assignment in an organization. Computer and robotics training is often completed in a vestibule school.

- **Job simulation** is the use of equipment that duplicates job conditions and tasks so that trainees can learn skills before attempting them on the job. Job simulation differs from vestibule training in that the simulation attempts to duplicate the *exact* combination of conditions that occur on the job. This is the kind of training given to astronauts, airline pilots, army tank operators, ship captains, and others who must learn highly skilled procedures off the job.

John Cleese, the Monty Python comic, co-founded Video Arts, a company that develops multimedia business training programs. The innovative CD-ROMs provide witty and highly effective training. The program also monitors what workers input and is ready to give them instructions if they become confused about what to do next.

Courtesy of Video Arts

For example, imagine that a very large crude carrier (VLCC) takes 9.6 kilometres to stop when running at 15 knots. By reversing the engines, you can cut the stopping distance to 3.2 kilometres. At any of the half-dozen training institutions in Canada, trainees learn how to pilot such ships on a simulator that resembles a giant video game. You can imagine piloting a ship that is as long as the C.N. Tower is high through a narrow passage with boats all around you. Any accident can cause serious environmental damage. You don't want to learn such skills on the job in a trial-and-error fashion!

Management Development

Managers need special training. They need to be good communicators and especially need to learn listening skills and empathy. They also need time-management, planning, and human relations skills.

Management development is the process of training and educating employees to become good managers and then developing managerial skills over time. Management development programs have sprung up everywhere, especially at colleges, universities, and private management development firms. Managers participate in role-playing exercises, solve various management cases, and are exposed to films, lectures, and all kinds of management development processes.

In some organizations, managers are paid to take university courses through the doctoral level. Most management training programs also include several of the following features. (Refer to the discussion of the Bank of Montreal Institute for Learning earlier in the chapter.)

- **On-the-job-coaching**. A senior manager assists a lower-level manager by teaching him or her needed skills and generally providing direction, advice, and helpful criticism. On-the-job coaching is effective only when the senior managers are skilled themselves and have the ability to educate others. This is not always the case.

- **Understudy positions**. Job titles such as "undersecretary of" and "assistant to" reveal a relatively successful way of developing managers. They work as assistants to higher-level managers and participate in planning and other managerial functions until they are ready to assume such positions themselves. Such assistants may take over when higher-level managers are on vacation or on business trips.

- **Job rotation**. To expose managers to different functions of the organization, they are often given assignments in a variety of departments. Top managers, and potential top managers, must have a broad picture of the organization; such rotation gives them that exposure.

- **Off-the-job courses and training**. Managers periodically go to schools or seminars for a week or more to hone their technical and human relations skills. Such courses expose them to the latest concepts and create a sense of camaraderie as the managers live, eat, and work together in a college-type atmosphere. This is often where case studies and simulation exercises of all kinds are employed.

Networking **Networking** is the process of establishing and maintaining contacts with key managers in your own organization and in other organizations and using those contacts to weave strong relationships that serve as an informal development system. Of equal or greater importance to potential managers are **mentors**, corporate managers who supervise, coach, and guide selected lower-level employees by introducing them to the right people and generally being their organizational sponsors. In reality, an informal type of mentoring goes on in most organizations on a

management development
The process of training and educating employees to become good managers and then developing managerial skills over time.

www.ml.ca

You may be considering a career in the financial services sector. If so, be sure to visit the Merrill Lynch Canada Web site. Of particular interest are its comments regarding careers offered and its corporate culture.

networking
The process of establishing and maintaining contacts with key managers in your own organization and other organizations and using those contacts to weave strong relationships that serve as an informal development system.

mentor
An experienced employee who supervises, coaches, and guides lower-level employees by introducing them to the right people and generally being their organizational sponsor.

PhotoDisc

Networking and mentoring are particularly important for women and minorities. It has been difficult for them to attract mentors but progressive companies now actively take the initiative to develop these employees.

regular basis as older employees assist younger workers. However, many organizations, such as Merrill Lynch and Federal Express, use a formal system of assigning mentors to employees considered to have strong potential.[10]

It's also important to remember that networking and mentoring can go beyond the business environment. For example, college is a perfect place to begin networking. Associations you nurture with professors, with local business people, and especially with your classmates might provide you with a valuable network you can turn to for the rest of your career.

Diversity in Management Development As women moved into management, they also learned the importance and value of networking and having mentors. But since (even now) most older managers are male, women often have more difficulty attracting mentors and entering the network, because those males are not used to working with female managers. A series of court rulings has made men-only clubs illegal in Canada, so women are now entering these formerly male preserves and making all the usual business contacts. More and more, women are entering the system or, in some instances, creating their own networking systems. According to Dr. Nina Colwill, consultant on HRM in Brandon, Manitoba, "men, seeing networks as utilitarian, are more likely to receive utilitarian benefits. Women, seeing them as social, may reap mainly social rewards." She believes that it is easy for each side to feel that their approach is superior, whereas it would be much better if each were to learn from the other.[11]

Companies that take the initiative to develop female and minority managers understand three crucial principles: (1) grooming women and minorities for management positions isn't only about legality, morality, or even morale; it is also about bringing more talent in the door—the key to long-term profitability; (2) as opportunities expand the best women and minorities will become harder to attract and retain; and (3) having more women and minorities at all levels means that businesses may be able to serve their increasingly female and minority customers better. If you don't have a diversity of people working in the back room, how are you going to satisfy the diversity of people coming in the front door?

APPRAISING EMPLOYEE PERFORMANCE TO GET OPTIMUM RESULTS

performance appraisal
An evaluation in which the performance level of employees is measured against established standards to make decisions about promotions, compensation, additional training, or firing.

Managers must be able to determine whether or not their workers are doing an effective and efficient job, with a minimum of errors and disruptions. They do so by using performance appraisals. A **performance appraisal** is an evaluation in which the performance level of employees is measured against established standards to make decisions about promotions, compensation, additional training, or firing. Performance appraisals consist of six steps.

1. **Establishing performance standards**. This is a crucial step. Standards must be understandable, subject to measurement, and reasonable. They must be accepted by both manager and employee.

2. **Communicating those standards**. Often managers assume that employees know what is expected of them, but such assumptions are dangerous at best. Employees must be told clearly and precisely what the standards and expectations are and how they are to be met.

3. **Evaluating performance**. If the first two steps are done correctly, performance evaluation is relatively easy. It is a matter of evaluating the employee's output to see if it matches standards.

4. **Discussing results with employees**. Most people may make mistakes and fail to meet expectations at first. It takes time to learn a new job or process and do it well. Discussing an employee's successes and areas that need improvement can provide managers with an opportunity to be understanding and helpful and to guide the employee to better motivation and performance. Additionally, the performance appraisal can be a good source of employee suggestions on how a particular task could be better performed.

5. **Taking corrective action**. As an appropriate part of the performance appraisal, a manager can take corrective action or provide corrective feedback to help the employee perform his or her job better. Remember, the key word is *performance*. The primary purpose of conducting this type of appraisal is to improve employee performance, if possible.

6. **Using the results to make decisions**. Decisions about promotions, compensation, additional training, or firing are all based on performance evaluations. An effective performance appraisal system is also a way of satisfying certain legal conditions concerning such decisions.

Effective management means getting results through top performance by employees. That is what performance appraisals are for—at all levels of the organization. Even top-level managers benefit from performance reviews made by their subordinates. The latest form of performance appraisal is called the 360-degree review because it calls for feedback from all directions in the organization: up, down, and all around. Figure 13.6 illustrates how managers can make performance appraisals more meaningful.

This requires a Theory Y management style, not Theory X (see Chapter 12). Technology is introducing a whole new approach to performance appraisal, according to one well-known Harvard authority. Rosabeth Moss Kanter has stated that, "in the wired workplace of the future, people will be able to keep track of their own performance on their computers." She believes that they will even be able to calculate their own rewards in the same fashion.[12]

1. **DON'T** attack the employee personally. Critically evaluate his or her work.
2. **DO** allow sufficient time, without distractions, for appraisal. (Take no phone calls and close the office door.)
3. **DON'T** make the employee feel uncomfortable or uneasy. *Never* conduct an appraisal where other employees are present.
4. **DO** include the employee in the process as much as possible.
5. **DON'T** wait until the appraisal to address problems with the employee's work that have been apparent for some time.
6. **DO** end the appraisal with positive suggestions for employee improvement. (Let the employee prepare a self-improvement program.)

FIGURE 13.6

MAKING EMPLOYEE APPRAISALS AND REVIEWS MORE EFFECTIVE

- Can you name and describe four training techniques?
- What is the primary purpose of a performance appraisal?
- What are the six steps in a performance appraisal?

COMPENSATING EMPLOYEES TO ATTRACT AND KEEP THE BEST

Employee compensation is one of the largest operating costs for many organizations. The long-term success of a firm—perhaps even its survival—may depend on how well it can control employee costs and optimize employee efficiency. For example, service organizations such as hospitals, airlines, railways, and banks have recently struggled with managing high employee costs. This is not unusual since these operations are considered *labour intensive*; that is, their primary cost of operations is the cost of labour. In the 1990s firms in the airline, auto, and steel industries asked employees to take reductions in wages to make the organizations more competitive. The alternative was to risk going out of business and losing jobs forever. In other words, the competitive environment is such that compensation and benefit packages are being given special attention and are likely to remain of major concern in the near future. (See Figure 13.7 for some common compensation methods.)

A carefully managed compensation and benefit program may accomplish several objectives. They include the following:

- Attracting the kind of people needed by the organization and in sufficient numbers.
- Providing employees with the proper rewards for working efficiently and productively.
- Keeping valued employees from leaving and going to competitors or starting competing firms.
- Maintaining a competitive position in the marketplace by keeping costs low through high productivity by a satisfied workforce.
- Providing some financial security for employees when unexpected problems araise, such as layoffs, sickness, and disability.

Compensation for Women

For many years statistics have shown that Canadian women earn less than men do. As more women obtain university degrees, the salary differential in professional and executive categories is decreasing. However, for the past decade there has been little progress in the huge gap between the earnings of the average woman and the average man. Women have remained stuck at about 65 percent of men's earnings.

In July 1993 the *Toronto Star* carried a report from an annual United Nations study that showed that "Canadian women make 63 percent of the wages of Canadian men." Later statistics show little change. Reporter Debra Black quoted Ms. Menon, the policy analyst in the human development report office of the UN: "In Japan it's 51 percent. In no industrial country is it 90 percent or above. Sweden has the best record with 89 percent." The report's conclusion was that "Canadian women are still get-

Service industries, such as the airline industry, are heavily labour intensive. It is imperative in such industries to control employee costs.

PhotoDisc

ting short shrift when it comes to politics and wages. Women in Canada just aren't treated the same as men." Menon noted, "Canada has done a lot in terms of literacy and education, but not enough has been done in terms of employment wages."[13] There are many historical reasons for this large wage gap. The traditional *women's* jobs—teacher, nurse, secretary—have always paid poorly. But there is much evidence of outright salary discrimination in other types of jobs. By 1998 women's earnings had made some progress but were still way behind men's. Statistics Canada figures[14] showed that the average weekly salary for women in all occupations and industries was $473.00, compared to $683.00 for men. That means that the average woman earned 69 percent of what the average man earned. The highest and lowest percentage of men's earnings that women achieved in 1998 (the most recent figures available) were as follows:

	BEST %	WORST %
By industry categories		
Management and administration	83	
Health care and social assistance	81	
Construction		61
Trade and other services		61
By occupations		
Natural and applied sciences and related occupations	84	
Recreation, sports, travel, and accommodation	82	
Teachers and professors	81	
Retail clerks, cashiers, and supervisors		57
Occupations unique to primary industries		53

As noted in Chapter 1, there are now laws banning such discrimination. Pay equity legislation is beginning to make its way through the provinces and has passed federal hurdles. Unfortunately the governments of Canada, Ontario, and Quebec are setting bad examples by delaying or whittling down the implementation of their laws as they affect their own employees. Officials cite budget cutbacks and the huge costs of making up for past inequitable compensation to female employees as the reasons. Pay equity requires equal pay for work of comparable value, which requires defining *comparable*. For example, which job has more value, nurse or trash collector? This is a difficult and controversial issue because it involves a complex system of job evaluation. HRM departments are alert to this problem.

Pay Systems

Like other aspects of HRM, pay systems have undergone an evolutionary development. When work was done at home or in small factories, individuals were paid by piecework—so much for each unit produced. When production became more complex and large numbers of employees worked in big factories where the processes involved joint efforts, piecework was replaced by hourly or daily wages.

Today piecework is prevalent only in low-wage countries or industries. Remnants of piecework can be found in some homeworker situations. (See the Working at Home section later in this chapter.) In Canada and all modern industrial countries, this method of compensation has been replaced by a whole range of methods in conformity with a better understanding of employee motivation (as discussed in Chapter 12), the realities of modern production, union contracts, competitive standards, and modern social attitudes. With the overwhelming number of Canadians employed in the service sector, hourly and salary remuneration has become the norm. Commissions are the only payment method that are in effect piecework (see Figure 13.7).

Employee Benefits

Employee benefits include sick leave pay, vacation pay, pension plans, health plans, and other benefits that provide additional compensation to employees. They may be divided into three categories. One group derives from federal or provincial legislation (which varies somewhat from province to province) and requires compulsory deductions from employees' paycheques, employer contributions, or both. These include the Canada/Quebec Pension Plan, employment insurance, health care, and workers' compensation. You have probably seen some of these deductions from your pay. The second group consists of legally required benefits, including vacation pay, holiday pay, time and a half or double time for overtime, and unpaid maternity leave with job protection.

The third category includes all other benefits and stems from voluntary employer programs or from employer–union contracts. Some are paid by the employer alone and others are jointly paid by employer and employee. Among the most common are bonuses, company pension plans, group insurance, sick leave, termination pay, and paid rest periods.

The list of benefits is long and has become quite significant—around 35 percent of regular pay. Often, labour negotiations are more likely to concern employee benefits than wage rates. They are no longer at the fringe of negotiations.

For executives and more highly paid managers, the benefits package is more important than additional remuneration. They are already in a high tax bracket and any additional direct income might be taxed at 50 percent, so increases in such nontaxable benefits as dental and health insurance, company contributions to pension plans, and stock options are very attractive.

FIGURE 13.7

COMMON COMPENSATION METHODS

Talk to someone who gets paid in each of the ways described. You will learn how quickly the money can accumulate when you receive overtime. Ask about the pressure of piecework versus the added potential for earnings. Each compensation plan has its benefits and drawbacks. See if you can learn what they are.

PAYMENT METHOD	DESCRIPTION
Straight salary	Weekly, monthly, or annual amount
Hourly wages	Number of hours worked times agreed-on hourly wage
Commission system	Sales times some fixed percentage
Salary plus commission	Base salary (weekly, monthly, or annual) plus sales times some fixed percentage
Piecework	Number of items produced times some agreed-on rate per unit

ADDED COMPENSATION	
Overtime	Number of hours worked beyond standard (for example, 40 hours a week) times hourly wages at time and a half or at double time for weekends, after hours, and holidays
Bonuses	Extra pay for meeting or exceeding objectives
Profit sharing	Additional compensation based on company profits
Cost-of-living allowances (COLAs)	Annual increases in wages based on increases in consumer price index (in union contracts).

www.gwl.ca

Why Are These Employees So Pleased?

The employees of Great-West Life Assurance Co. work for a major player in the insurance and mutual fund business in North America. The head office is in Winnipeg, and there are offices in all Canadian provinces and American states. They're pleased because the company has an unusual array of employee benefits. The Canadian Mental Health Association honoured the company with a Work and Well-Being Award for its impressive integrated programs, services, and policies designed to look after employees' health and other needs as well as for providing satisfying work and workplaces. A poll conducted by outside consultants found that the employees gave Great-West a higher than 90-percent approval rating.

That is no surprise considering the extensive array of benefits. Besides the typical ones, the company offers such things as insulin supply coverage for diabetics up to $700 annually and a onetime $350 allowance for equipment. It offers mortgages at 80 percent of current rates and contributes $1 for each $3 a worker saves in an employee savings plan. Workers can also buy life insurance free of commission charges.

Employees can take time for work-related courses, and the company pays the cost of tuition and up to $500 for successful graduates. There is a 20,000-volume library and a beautiful art collection, as well as large comfortable lounges, a fitness club, a 240-seat theatre, and a bank on the premises. Postage stamps and bus passes are also available. If an employee is concerned about his or her health, a staff nurse will check his or her blood pressure or give an eye examination. Employees can also get free financial and personal counselling.

Great-West also has a job-sharing program and other flexible work arrangements that are proving attractive to some employees with young children. In addition to all of this, the company has good pay levels, promotion opportunities, and job security. Wouldn't you smile if you worked for such a company? Of course the company is also smiling, because it believes it is benefiting from a satisfied workforce. In late 2001 employee benefits manager J. Domenico reports that all the programs are functioning well and achieving the desired results. Furthermore, he notes that the programs have also been adopted by the London Life Insurance Company that Great-West acquired in 1998 and are achieving similar beneficial results there.

Sources: Interview with J. Domenico, manager of employee benefits at Great-West, November 27, 2001; E. Innes, J. Lyons, and J. Harris, *The Financial Post 100 Best Companies to Work for in Canada* (Toronto: HarperCollins, 1996), pp. 57–60.

Employee benefits can also include everything from paid vacations to group insurance plans, recreation facilities, company cars, country club memberships, daycare services, and executive dining rooms. Managing the benefits package is a major HRM issue. Employees want packages to include dental care, legal counselling, maternity leave, and more. (Some types of benefits are recognized as taxable by the Canada Customs and Revenue Agency.) For examples of some less-typical benefits, see the Spotlight on Big Business box "Why Are These Employees So Pleased?"

To counter these growing demands, many firms are offering **cafeteria-style benefits**, from which employees can choose the type of benefits they want up to a certain dollar amount, such as in the example in the chapter-opening Profile. *Choice* is the key to flexible cafeteria-style benefit plans. Employees' needs are more and more varied. Managers can equitably and cost-effectively meet these individual needs by providing benefit choices. For example, older employees might be more interested in good pension plans and holidays, whereas younger employees might concentrate on child care, maternity or paternity leave, or an education package. Employers on *Fortune* magazine's list of the 100 best companies to work for offer so-called soft benefits. Soft benefits help workers maintain the balance between work and family life that is as important to hard-working employees as the nature of the job itself. These perks include things such as on-site haircuts and shoe repair, concierge services, and free breakfasts. Freeing employees from spending time on errands and chores gives them more time for family—and work.[15]

cafeteria-style benefits
Benefit plans that allow employees to choose which benefits they want up to a certain dollar amount.

Managing the benefit package will continue to be a major human resource issue in the future. The cost of administering benefits programs has become so great that a number of companies are outsourcing ➤ **P. 278** ◂ this function—that is, they are hiring outside companies to run their employee benefits plans. IBM, for example, decided to spin off its human resources and benefits operation into a separate company, Workforce Solutions, which provides customized services to each of IBM's independent units. The new company saves IBM $45 million each year. Workforce Solutions now handles benefits for other organizations, such as the National Geographic Society. In addition to saving them money, outsourcing fringe benefits administration helps companies avoid the growing complexity and technical requirements of the plans.

Compensating Teams

Thus far we've talked about compensating individuals. What about teams? Since you want your teams to be more than simply a group of individuals, would you compensate them as you would individuals? If you can't answer that question immediately, you are not alone. A 1996 team-based pay survey found that managers continue to be more positive about the use of teams (87 percent) than about how to pay them (41 percent). This suggests that team-based pay programs are not as effective or as fully developed as managers would like. Measuring and rewarding individual performance on teams while at the same time rewarding team performance can be tricky. Nonetheless, it can be done. Football players are rewarded as a team when they go to the play-offs and to the Super Bowl, but they are paid individually as well. Companies are now experimenting with and developing similar incentive systems.

Jay Schuster, co-author of an ongoing study of team pay, found that when pay is based strictly on individual performance it erodes team cohesiveness and makes it less likely that the team will meet its goals as a collaborative effort. Schuster recommends basing pay on team performance.[16] Skill-based pay and profit-sharing are the two most common compensation methods for teams.

Skill-based pay is related to the growth of both the individual and the team. Base pay is raised when team members learn and apply new skills. The drawbacks of the skill-based pay system are twofold: the system is complex, and it is difficult to correlate skill acquisition and bottom-line gains.

In most gain-sharing systems, bonuses are based on improvements over a previous performance baseline. For example, Behlen Manufacturing, a diversified maker of agricultural and industrial products, calculates its bonuses by dividing quality pounds of product by worker-hours. *Quality* means no defects; any defects are subtracted from the total. Workers can receive a monthly gain-sharing bonus of up to $1 an hour when their teams meet productivity goals.

It is important to reward individual team players also. Outstanding team players—those who go beyond what is required and make an outstanding individual contribution to the firm—should be separately recognized for their additional contribution. Recognition can include cashless as well as cash rewards.

A good way to avoid alienating recipients who feel team participation was uneven is to let the team decide which members get what type of individual award. After all, if you really support the team process, you need to give teams freedom to make these decisions.

ADOPTING FLEXIBLE WORK SCHEDULES

By now, you are quite familiar with some of the trends occurring in the workforce. (For some insights into international trends, see the Reaching Beyond Our Borders box "Social Benefits, Motivation, and the Free Trade Agreements.") You also know that managers and workers are demanding more from jobs in the way of flexibility and responsiveness. From these trends have emerged several new or renewed ideas such as job sharing, flextime, compressed workweeks, and in-home employment. Let's see how these innovations affect human resources management.

REACHING BEYOND OUR BORDERS
Social Benefits, Motivation, and the Free Trade Agreements
www.bcni.com
www.cfib.ca

Ever since the Free Trade Agreement between Canada and the United States was signed in 1988, various business leaders have suggested that the costs of Canada's social benefits are hindering the ability of our companies to compete with American companies. The Business Council on National Issues (BCNI), which represents the very largest companies in Canada, the Canadian Manufacturers Association (CMA), the Canadian Federation of Independent Business (CFIB), and individual business people have made such comments. They have pointed out that such costs are lower in the United States, which weakens the competitiveness of Canadian companies.

When the FTA was being fiercely debated before the 1988 election, these same organizations and other groups who supported the FTA (including former Prime Minister Brian Mulroney) repeatedly assured Canadians that the agreement would pose no threat to our social safety net and our social programs. Now we see them claiming that Canada cannot afford such programs and still remain competitive.

In early 1992 the federal government announced that it was not going ahead with its oft-promised national child-care scheme. The program has been a major demand of a large number of working parents who cannot afford the high cost of private arrangements. Ottawa also abolished family allowances in 1993 and employment insurance benefits were reduced. Our health-care system is also under considerable attack as being too expensive. So once again the question of social benefits is on the agenda, especially as Mexico was brought into the North American Free Trade Agreement.

We have seen how important a highly motivated workforce is in boosting productivity, thus reducing costs and making businesses more competitive. Successful companies consider expenditures on employee benefits a very good investment. Far-seeing, progressive companies realize that well-motivated employees more than pay for the costs of keeping them motivated. The evidence is very clear on this point. (See this chapter's Profile and the Spotlight on Big Business box "Why Are These Employees So Pleased?")

A working parent who has no anxiety about whether his or her children are being well looked after in affordable child-care facilities is a better-functioning employee. Similarly, knowing that the health of your family is looked after by our national health-care system boosts morale and therefore productivity. It seems very short-sighted to think only about immediate dollar outlay rather than about the long-term benefits to companies of having a less worried workforce.

North American executives are often faulted for having a short-term outlook. This is in contrast to companies and governments from the Pacific Rim and Europe that are top international competitors because they have a long-term focus.

We have quoted various commentators who say we have to learn to work smart, not cheap, and point out that Germany, one of the most competitive countries in the world, has better social benefits than we have. That also applies to Scandinavian countries. In Japan, large companies provide a very extensive network of benefits to their employees. All of these countries are now cutting back on these programs, but still remain well above Canadian standards. Which path will we follow?

Job Sharing

Job sharing is an arrangement whereby two part-time employees share one full-time job. The concept has received great attention in the past 15 years as more and more women with small children entered the labour force. Job sharing enables mothers or fathers to work part-time while the children are in school and to be home when the children come home. Job sharing has also proved beneficial to students, older people who want to work part-time before fully retiring, and others who prefer to work only part-time. The advantages are that:

job sharing
An arrangement whereby two part-time employees share one full-time job.

- There are increased employment opportunities for people who cannot or prefer not to work full-time.

- An employee is more likely to maintain a high level of enthusiasm and productivity for four hours than for eight hours.

- Problems such as absenteeism and tardiness are greatly reduced as part-timers have the free time to attend to personal matters.

- Employers are better able to schedule people into peak demand periods when part-time people are available.

However, as you might suspect, disadvantages include having to hire, train, motivate, and supervise twice as many people and to prorate some employee benefits. Nonetheless, most firms that were at first reluctant to try job sharing are finding the benefits outweigh the disadvantages.

Flextime Plans

flextime plans
Work schedules that give employees some freedom to adjust when they work, within limits, as long as they work the required number of hours.

core time
The period when all employees must be present in a flextime system.

Flextime plans give employees some freedom to select starting and quitting time, as long as they work the required number of hours. The most popular plans allow employees to come to work at 7, 8, or 9 a.m. and leave between 3:30 and 6:30 p.m. (see Figure 13.8). Usually flextime plans incorporate **core time**, particular hours of the day when all employees are expected to be at their job stations. For example, an organization may designate core-time hours between 9:30 and 11:00 a.m., and 2:00 and 3:30 p.m. During these hours, *all* employees are required to be there. Flextime plans, like job-sharing plans, are designed to allow employees to adjust to the new demands of the times, especially the trend toward two-income families. Flextime has been found to boost employee productivity ➤ **P. 43** ◄ and morale. Specific advantages of flextime are that:

- Working parents can schedule their days so that one partner can be home to see the children off to school and the other partner can be home to greet them after school.

- Employees can schedule doctor's appointments and other personal tasks during the day by coming in early and leaving early or by coming in late and leaving late.

- Traffic congestion is greatly reduced as employees arrive and leave over several hours instead of all at once.

- Employees can work when they are most productive; some people are most alert in the morning, whereas others can't get going until 10 a.m.

- Having some choice about sleeping late once in a while or taking off early on Friday afternoon in the summer gives a person a big psychological boost.

FIGURE 13.8

A FLEXTIME CHART

Employees can start any time between 6:30 and 9:30 a.m. They then take half an hour for lunch and can quit from 3:30 to 6:30 p.m. Everyone works an eight-hour day. The blue arrows show a typical flextime day.

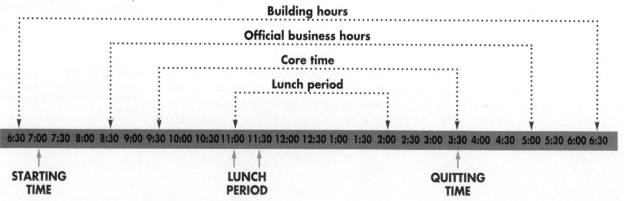

- It has obvious advantages for creative people who are most productive at certain times of the day. But it's also helpful for anyone who must work longer hours when a proposal is due.

- It helps companies keep employees who might leave otherwise.

There are some real disadvantages to flextime as well. It does not work in assembly-line processes where everyone must be at work at the same time. Nor is it effective for shift work.

Another disadvantage to flextime is that managers often have to work longer days to be there to assist and supervise employees. Some organizations operate from 6 a.m. to 6 p.m. under flextime, a potentially long day for supervisors. Flextime also makes communication more difficult; certain employees may not be there when others need to talk to them. Furthermore, some employees could abuse the system if not carefully supervised, causing resentment among others.

Compressed Workweeks

Another option in some organizations is a **compressed workweek**. That means that an employee works four 10-hour days and then enjoys a three-day weekend, instead of working five eight-hour days with a traditional weekend. There are obvious advantages of working only four days and having three days off, but some employees get tired working such long hours, and productivity could decline. Some employees find such a system of great benefit, however, and are quite enthusiastic about it.

An Example of a Modern HRM Department

The Royal Bank is a good example of a large organization whose HRM department has adopted a very progressive and modern approach. For some years the bank had been experimenting with a wide array of options to make the workplace as flexible as possible to meet the changing needs of its workforce. Manager Norma Tombari says that paying careful attention to employees' needs is the only way to go. The work and family program consists of an elaborate series of services covering a wide range of issues.

Each service is explained in an attractive brochure and includes information on elder care and child care and how to access the employee and family assistance program. Employees can access magazines, articles, books, and videotapes. There are also three detailed brochures concerning flexible work arrangements: part-time/job sharing, flextime and compressed workweek, and flexiplace.

Tombari says flexible working arrangements are becoming increasingly popular. She notes, however, that compressed workweeks do not lend themselves to branches that are open evenings and weekends. As of 1999, some 30 percent of Royal Bank employees (about 14,000) were on some form of nontraditional workweek arrangement, and the number was growing steadily. The most popular are job sharing and flexible hours. Tombari reported that a survey by independent consultants showed a 30-percent productivity improvement among employees opting for flexible arrangements.

A 1998 report by the same consultants, Canadian Work/Family Directions, Co., showed that the flexible work arrangements (FWA) program was yielding important positive results for the Royal Bank. Employees and managers, even nonusers of FWA, agreed that it reduced stress and absenteeism, gave greater employee satisfaction and motivation, and enhanced customer services and workforce development while reducing expenses. The report noted that such a program will not work unless managers give it strong support. A notable effect was that employees interpreted the bank's introduction and support of FWA as a sign of a "desirable employer." Finally,

Canadian Press CP

Phoebe Wright, a CIBC vice-president, has found that part-time work hasn't hurt her career. Her part-time job also allows her to spend more time with her children.

compressed workweek
A work schedule made up of four 10-hour days.

www.royalbank.com/
careers/workressurv/
hr_pandp.html

Check out this Web site for current data on the Royal Bank's comprehensive flexible work arrangements plan.

the study found no evidence to support concerns that activities like job sharing or flexible hours resulted in less efficiency, disruptions of customer service, or higher costs. As noted above, the results were all positive.[17]

Recently, Workplace 2000 was developed to further communicate the new world of work with employees. Workplace 2000 positioned change as being driven externally by our customers, communities and shareholders and driven internally by the changing needs and expectations of our employees. Workplace 2000 represents a partnership in employability rather than a paternalistic relationship, and as a philosophy is reflected in most human resource practices. These include pay for performance rather than time on the job, employee and employer focus on building skills and competencies relevant to Royal Bank Financial Group (RBFG) as well as employability skills.

Workplace 2000 also removed Human Resources as a go between [between] employees and the manager. Frontline managers are positioned with responsibility for people management. Human Resources supports that through the development of policies and practices as well as centralized resources. This empowers the manager and the employee to do what's right and results in a stronger employee–manager relationship.

Since 1980, Royal Bank staff have followed the Code of Conduct: Principles of Ethical Behaviour. The Code, augmented by detailed Employee Rules, was updated in 1993. Both the Principles and Rules are signed-off annually by each employee during performance reviews.[18]

The Royal Bank provides an abundance of information to its employees outlining such services as child care, elder care, and the employee and family assistance program. Royal Bank is a good example of a large organization whose HRM department has adopted a very progressive and modern approach.

Courtesy of the Royal Bank

Working at Home

Until the late eighteenth century, there were no factories or plants as we know them today. People who sewed, knitted, wove, or did a variety of other jobs did them at home. This practice still survives in many countries, including Canada. Go into any large city and you will find contractors or subcontractors who farm out work. Usually the workers are women, recent immigrants who have no other skills, people who do not speak English or French, or people who have small children. They are paid by piecework.

In the last decade a new phenomenon has arisen—a modern homeworker of a totally different type. Typically he or she has a computer and other electronic communication equipment and may be self-employed or employed by a large company. When these workers are employees, they are paid like other employees, but they can perform their duties at home, thus reducing their costs as well as avoiding travelling time. They save on eating out, clothing, commuting costs, and so on. Employers also cut costs by needing less office space and furniture and having more motivated employees. Working at home is especially attractive for single parents and dual-career families.

The old term for working at home is *telecommuting*.[19] The new term is *virtual office*, to reflect the practice of carrying office technology in your briefcase or car so you're ready to work anywhere.[20] Peter Firestone, a senior manager in Ernst & Young's information technology consulting division, has no permanent office. His clients provide him with a desk for the duration of each project and he stays linked to his employers by computer and voice mail. The flexibility is a plus, but the downside is not having the camaraderie of fellow workers.[21]

Telecommuting can be a cost-saver for employers. For example, IBM used to have a surplus of office space, maintaining more offices than there were employees. Now the company has more mobile workers, with employees telecommuting, "hotelling" (being assigned to a desk through a reservations system), and "hot-desking" (sharing a desk with other employees at different times). About 10,000 IBM employees now share offices, typically with four people to an office.

As mentioned in the first chapter, working at home is expected to become a major aspect of life in this decade. How does this affect the responsibility of HRM? The solutions are now being discussed as HRM strives to cope with this new factor. Figure 13.9 lists the benefits and challenges of telecommuting.

Mobile workers create virtual offices that allow them to work from places other than the traditional office. They can use laptops, cellphones, pagers, fax machines, and network services to conduct business wherever it is convenient.

PhotoDisc

What effect have dual-career families had on the human resource function? Have you noticed any changes in nepotism rules with so many marriages involving two professionals? (*Nepotism* means favouring relatives when hiring.)

What problems can arise when family members work together in the same firm? What is your reaction to employees who date one another?

- Can you name and describe five alternative compensation techniques?
- Can you list five important employee benefits?
- Why is flextime useful?
- What are three major benefits and three major challenges of working at home?

MOVING EMPLOYEES UP, OVER, AND OUT

FIGURE 13.9

BENEFITS AND CHALLENGES OF HOME-BASED WORK

Home-based work (also known as telecommuting) offers many benefits and challenges to organizations, to individuals, and to society as a whole.

Employees don't always stay in the position they were initially hired to fill. They may excel and move up the corporate ladder or fail and move out the front door. In addition to promotion and termination, employees can be moved by reassignment and retirement.

Employment is normally terminated in one of three ways: layoff or dismissal, voluntary departure, or retirement. In all cases HRM is involved, as it is responsible for employees during their entire period of employment. Each of these issues is discussed below.

	BENEFITS	CHALLENGES
To Organization	• Increases productivity due to fewer sick days, fewer absences, higher job satisfaction, and higher work performance ratings • Broadens available talent pool • Reduces costs of providing on-site office space	• Makes it more difficult to appraise job performance • Can negatively affect the social network of the workplace and can make it difficult to promote team cohesiveness • Complicates distribution of tasks (Should important documents be allowed to leave the office?)
To Individual	• Makes more time available for work and family by reducing or eliminating commute time • Reduces expenses of buying and maintaining office clothes. • Avoids office politics • Helps balance work and family • Expands employment opportunities for disabled individuals	• Can cause feelings of isolation from social network • Can raise concerns regarding promotions and other rewards due to being "out of sight, out of mind" • May diminish individual's influence within company due to limited opportunity to learn the corporate culture
To Society	• Decreases traffic congestion • Discourages community crime that might otherwise occur in bedroom communities • Increases time available to build community ties	• Increases need to resolve zoning regulations forbidding business deliveries in residential neighbourhoods • May reduce ability to interact with other people in a personal, intimate manner

Promoting and Reassigning Employees

Many companies find that promotion improves employee morale. Promotions are also cost-effective in that the promoted employees are already familiar with the corporate culture and procedures, and managers do not need to spend valuable time on basic orientation.

Because of the prevalence of flatter corporate structures, there are fewer levels for employees to reach now as compared to the past. Therefore, it is more common today for workers to move *over* to a new position than to move *up* to one. Such lateral transfers allow employees to develop and display new skills and to learn more about the company overall. This is one way of motivating experienced employees to remain in a company with few advancement opportunities.

Terminating Employees

As we discussed in previous chapters, downsizing and restructuring ➤ **P. 12** ◄ increasing customer demands for greater value, the relentless pressure of global competition, and shifts in technology have human resource managers struggling to manage layoffs.

The issue of layoffs has become very important because of the large number of people let go in the early 1990s and in 2000 and 2001. Often, older employees are offered early retirement packages. Many companies counsel these employees to enable them to better cope with their loss of job and to help them find new jobs. Some set up in-house outplacement facilities so that employees can get counselling on obtaining a new job. For senior managers, the company usually pays for private-agency career counselling.

The threat of job loss has introduced a strong feeling of insecurity into the Canadian workforce. Insecurity undermines motivation, so HRM must deal with this new issue. Keeping employees fully informed and having a clear policy on termination pay helps to remove some uncertainty. It is important to note that most Canadian jurisdictions require that larger companies give three to six months' notice before large layoffs.

Termination usually involves special costs such as terminal pay or penalties, which may be determined by contract for executives, or by union contracts or government regulations. When large companies announce a substantial downsizing you will usually see reference to a special cost charge for the current year that can easily run into many tens of millions of dollars. This is another attraction for companies to employ temporary help, which avoids such costs. Outsourcing ➤ **P. 278** ◄ is another way around this problem.

Voluntary Departure

When an employee leaves as a normal departure, there is no problem. However, if someone leaves because of perceived discrimination—whether because of age, nationality, sex, religion, or ethnicity—then it is a different story. Similarly, if a woman leaves because she feels sexually harassed, the situation is quite different from a person quitting to get a better job or to go back to school. HRM must be alert to any signs or complaints of discrimination or sexual harassment. Not only are these undesirable practices, indicating some potentially serious problems, they are also illegal.

Unfortunately, sexual harassment and discrimination cases continue to crop up regularly across the country. A female engineer working for a subcontractor on the refurbishing of the Peace Tower in Ottawa charged that the main contractor's project manager constantly abused her because she was a woman.[22] The female coordinator of a company in Strathroy, Ontario, filed a complaint with the Ontario Labour Relations Board because she had to go on "stress-induced medical leave." She claimed that she was exposed to "nude calendars, pornographic pictures, and lewd comments." Furthermore, she was told she was "overly sensitive" for complaining.[23]

Retiring Employees

In addition to laying off employees, another tool used to downsize companies is to offer early retirement benefits to entice older (and more expensive) workers to resign. Such benefits usually involve such financial incentives as one-time cash payments (golden handshakes). The advantage of offering early retirement benefits over laying off employees is that early retirement offers increase the morale of the remaining employees. Retiring senior workers also increases promotion opportunities for younger employees. The better companies help employees prepare for retirement in various ways. They range from seminars on how to plan your financial affairs as income drops to advice on how to develop activities to keep you busy.

Losing Employees

In spite of a company's efforts to retain talented workers by offering flexible schedules, competitive salaries, and attractive fringe benefits, some employees will choose to pursue opportunities elsewhere. Learning about their reasons for leaving can be invaluable in preventing the loss of other good people in the future.[24] One way to learn the real reasons employees leave is to have a third party (not the employee's direct manager) conduct an exit interview. Harvard Pilgrim Health Care goes a step further—it offers a "knowledge bounty" of up to $5,000 for departing information left behind in a document or in a conversation with senior-level managers.[25]

LAWS AFFECTING HUMAN RESOURCE MANAGEMENT

Canada has many laws affecting nearly all aspects of human resource management. We have referred to these laws earlier in this chapter, but now we'll take a closer look.

Because Canada is a confederation of provinces, jurisdiction over many aspects of our lives is divided between the federal and provincial governments. The federal government legislates on national issues, such as employment insurance and pensions; however, the provinces have jurisdiction over most matters, including minimum wages, hours of work, workers' compensation, and discrimination in the workplace.

But it's a little more complicated than that. The federal government also has jurisdiction over certain types of businesses that are deemed to be of a national nature. Banks, insurance companies, airlines, railways, shipping companies, telephone, radio, TV, cable companies, and others are subject to federal law, as are all federal employees. Fewer than 10 percent of all Canadian employees are subject to federal legislation. However, the national Charter of Rights and Freedoms, which is part of the Canadian constitution, overrides all other laws. The federal government had to amend the Unemployment Insurance Act because the Supreme Court had ruled that the act went against the Charter in denying coverage to employees over age 64.

What all this means is that there are literally hundreds of laws and regulations, federal and provincial, that apply to all aspects of human resource management. Furthermore, they are constantly being revised because of social pressure or rulings by human rights commissions or courts. One of the most regulated areas involves discrimination.

Laws in all jurisdictions in Canada make it illegal to discriminate against employees because of age, sex, nationality, ethnicity, religion, or marital status. Only Yukon fails to ban discrimination due to physical disability; Saskatchewan, Alberta, and Yukon do not ban discrimination in the case of mental disability. Only Quebec, Ontario, and federal law forbid discrimination based on sexual orientation. Some other forms of discrimination are banned in some provinces or under federal law.

When an employer selects, hires, trains, pays, promotes, transfers, retires, lays off, or fires an employee, HRM must ensure that what is being done and how it is being done do not break any laws. (See Case 1 at the end of this chapter.) HRM must also make sure health and safety laws are obeyed. You can see how important the job of HRM is. Managers working in this area must be very sensitive not only to legal requirements but also to union contracts and social standards and expectations, which may be even more demanding.

Employment Equity and Affirmative Action

A well-known 1980s case of discrimination highlights a major problem and how it was solved. A group of women accused the CNR of not hiring them because they were women. The CNR, like many other companies, did not hire women for jobs that were thought to be traditional men's jobs, those for which heavy physical labour was required. In this case the jobs involved maintenance and repairs of the tracks. The Canadian Human Rights Commission ruled in favour of the women. The CNR appealed and the courts ruled against it all the way to the Supreme Court of Canada.

ETHICAL DILEMMA
Review

Remember the dilemma introduced at the beginning of the chapter? Your boss wants you to find a way, that is not too obvious, of bypassing legal restrictions when interviewing job applicants. He is dangling some monetary bait to tempt you to go along with his plan and threatening not to promote you if you don't. Let's take a look at the opinions of our executives.

Bédard believes that "there are, of course, many subtle questions that are legal and tend to be used to obtain certain information. I have found that when being very honest with candidates, they will often advance information on their own. Employees are usually looking for long-term relationships with an employer and will not want to start off on the wrong foot. Many times accommodations can be made with little disruption."

Reilley has a somewhat different approach. He says that "the law is clear: discrimination of any sort is illegal and unethical. I would communicate my misgivings in writing to my superior. If our working relationship deteriorated, I would seek an interview with my boss's boss and probably start seeking another job if matters didn't improve."

This is what happened in one case, as reported to one of the Canadian authors of this text. At first the employee started thinking up ways to achieve what his boss wanted, perhaps by developing a little secret code for comments about likely age, nationality, and so on, which he would determine by indirect questioning and by making notes on an official-looking sheet. After the interview he would copy the codes to a sticky-note memo, stick it on the application, and then shred the original sheet. The boss could destroy the memo after he had read it. For a while he felt quite satisfied with himself because he thought he had devised a neat system that would satisfy his boss and for which there would be no evidence of anything illegal.

A few days later the employee began to have second thoughts about the scheme. While dining at his mother's, she told him how she was discriminated against when she was first in the job market, and how his Sikh uncle suspects that he had suffered similar discrimination. By the time he reached his apartment he was troubled about his plan. He was in a tough spot because he liked his job and the company he worked for, and believed that he had a good shot at early promotion.

He decided to try what Bédard suggests instead. For example, he thought of asking if the applicant was available for weekends, shift work, and holidays, or for travel assignments, if any of these became necessary. This is a perfectly legal question and the answer might indicate if the applicant is married or has a partner. It might also indicate if the person has religious beliefs that do not permit Sunday or religious-holiday work. Direct questions about these matters are illegal and discriminatory.

affirmative action
Employment activities designed to right past wrongs endured by females and minorities by giving them preference in employment.

reverse discrimination
The unfairness unprotected groups may perceive when protected groups receive preference in hiring and promoting.

There the CNR was told that it had to adopt an affirmative action plan to ensure that women would gradually form a significant part of the maintenance crews.

Affirmative action refers to employment activities designed to right past wrongs endured by females and minorities by giving them preference in employment. This means that CNR had to develop a plan that would result in more women than men being hired for such jobs until the balance was more even. The result is that when a man and a woman are equally qualified the woman must be given preference for a number of years to allow the balance to be adjusted.

Some people argue that affirmative action is really a form of reverse discrimination. **Reverse discrimination** refers to the unfairness unprotected groups (say, white men) may perceive when protected groups receive preference in hiring and promoting. The Canadian Charter of Rights specifically allows for affirmative action as a method to overcome long-standing discrimination against groups. Therefore, the courts accept it as being nondiscriminatory in the legal sense. In the United States, and to a lesser extent in Canada, there has been a growing movement against affirmative action because of the reverse discrimination aspect. This has now become a controversial issue.

PROGRESS CHECK

- Can you name five areas of HRM responsibility affected by government legislation?
- Explain what affirmative action is and give one example.
- Why should HRM be concerned about legislation or court rulings when terminating employment?

SUMMARY

1. Explain the importance of human resource management, and describe current issues in managing human resources.

1. Human resource management is the process of evaluating human resource needs, finding people to fill those needs, and optimizing this important resource by providing the right incentives and job environment, all with the goal of meeting organizational objectives.

   • *What are some of the current problems in the human resource area?*
   Many current problems revolve around the changing demographics of workers: more women, minorities, immigrants, and older workers. Other problems concern a shortage of trained workers and an abundance of unskilled ones; skilled workers in declining industries requiring retraining; changing employee work attitudes; and complex laws and regulations.

2. Describe methods companies use to recruit new employees, and explain some of the issues that make recruitment challenging.

2. Recruitment is the set of activities used to obtain enough of the right people at the right time and to select those that best meet the needs of the organization.

   • *What methods do human resource managers use to recruit new employees?*
   Recruiting sources are classified as either internal or external. Internal sources include hiring from within the firm (transfers, promotions, etc.) and employees who recommend others to hire. External recruitment sources include advertisements, public and private employment agencies, college and university placement bureaus, management consultants, professional organizations, referrals, walk-in applications, and the Internet.

   • *Why has recruitment become more difficult?*
   Legal restrictions complicate hiring and firing practices. Finding suitable employees can also be difficult if companies are considered unattractive workplaces. Also, it is difficult to find candidates with the higher educational levels and technical skills needed now.

3. Employee training and development include all attempts to increase an employee's ability to perform through learning.
   • *What are some of the procedures used for training?*
   They include employee orientation, on- and off-the-job training, apprentice programs, online training, vestibule training, and job simulation.

   3. Illustrate the various types of employee training and development methods.

4. Employee compensation is one of the largest operating costs for many organizations.
   • *What compensation systems are used?*
   They include salary systems, hourly wages, piecework, commission plans, bonus plans, and profit-sharing plans.
   • *What types of compensation systems are appropriate for teams?*
   The most common are gains-sharing and skill-based compensation programs. It is also important to reward outstanding individual performance within teams.
   • *What are employee benefits?*
   Benefits include sick leave, vacation pay, pension plans, health plans, and other services that provide additional compensation to employees.

   4. Summarize the objectives of employee compensation programs, and describe various pay systems and benefits.

5. Workers' increasing need for flexibility has generated innovations in scheduling.
   • *What scheduling plans can be used to adjust to employees' needs for flexibility?*
   Such plans include job sharing, flextime, compressed workweeks, and working at home.

   5. Explain scheduling plans managers use to adjust to workers' needs.

6. Management development is the process of developing managerial skills over time.
   • *What methods are used to develop managerial skills?*
   Management development methods include on-the-job coaching, understudy positions, job rotation, and off-the-job courses and training.
   • *How does networking fit into this process?*
   Networking is establishing contacts with key managers within and outside the organization to get additional development assistance.
   • *What are mentors?*
   Mentors are experienced staff members who coach and guide selected lower-level people and act as their organizational sponsors.

   6. Describe training methods used in management development programs.

7. There are many laws that affect human resource planning.
   • *What areas do these laws cover?*
   All areas are affected because of laws prohibiting discriminatory practices, setting standards such as minimum wages, and regulating health and safety conditions, hours of work, holiday and vacation pay, retirement and firing, pensions, and employment insurance.

   7. Illustrate the effects of legislation on human resource management.

KEY TERMS

affirmative action 418
apprentice programs 398
cafeteria-style benefits 407
compressed workweek 411
contingent workers 397
core time 410
employee orientation 397
flextime plans 410
human resource management (HRM) 388
job analysis 391
job description 391
job sharing 409
job simulation 400

job specifications 391
management development 401
mentor 401
networking 401
off-the-job training 399
on-the-job training 398
online training 399
performance appraisal 402
recruitment 392
reverse discrimination 418
selection 394
training and development 397
vestibule training 400

DEVELOPING WORKPLACE SKILLS

1. If you experience a typical career you are likely to have about eight different jobs in your lifetime. Therefore, you will have to prepare several résumés and cover letters. Write a cover letter and résumé seeking employment for an entry-level position in your local area using the formats suggested in the Getting the Job You Want section in the Prologue or the additional resources section on the Web site for this book. Keep it in your file for use when you are job hunting. Don't forget to update it.

2. Read the current business periodicals to find the latest court rulings on issues such as pay equity, affirmative action, unjustified firing, discrimination, and other HRM issues. What seems to be the trend? What will this mean for tomorrow's graduates?

3. Recall the various training programs you have experienced including both on-the-job and off-the-job training. What is your evaluation of such programs? How would you improve them? Share your ideas with the class.

4. Look up the unemployment figures for individual provinces. Notice there are pockets of very high unemployment. What causes such uneven employment? What can be done to retrain workers who are obsolete because of a restructured economy? Is that the role of government or of business? Discuss. Could government and business co-operate in this function?

5. Find several people who work under flextime or part-time systems and interview them regarding their experiences and preferences. Using this information, draft a proposal to your company's management advocating an option for a four-day workweek. Debate this proposal with your class.

TAKING IT TO THE NET

Purpose:

To determine the usefulness and thoroughness of Web resources for job searching.

Exercises:

1. Access some of the following job info sites and examine what they contain. Do you find any important differences? List their strengths and weaknesses, from your point of view. Which do you think would be most useful to you if you were job-hunting now? Why?

    1. CanadaCareers.com lists major Canadian job boards, including some that are listed below.

    2. As of August 2001 this site claims that it is "Canada's Biggest Job Site" with more than 25,000 jobs listed: workopolis.com

    3. The Human Resources Development Canada site gives access to job banks at all federal job centres: hrdc-drhc.gc.ca

    4. This site offers a diverse range of job search tools: campusworklink.com

    5. To browse by fields or regions in Canada, try: canadajobs.com

    6. The Monster Boards are very popular sites: Canadian jobs: monster.ca
        American jobs: monster.com

    7. For Canadian tourism and hospitality jobs, try: cooljobscanada.com

    8. Jobs in higher education, faculty and administrative, in major English-speaking countries can be found by discipline and by country at academic360.com.

2. Can you see yourself searching those sites when you graduate? Do you see any positions now available that interest you? Do you see any category that lists many job openings? Are you tempted to plan the rest of your courses so that, on graduation, you would qualify for that type of job?

PRACTISING MANAGEMENT DECISIONS

CASE 1

THE DANGERS OF FIRING AN EMPLOYEE

If someone is fired, HRM must be certain the employee's legal and union (if there is one) rights are not abrogated and relevant federal and provincial laws are followed. The history of employer–employee relations has been one of movement from the absolute right of the employer to do as it wishes to important protections for employee rights. One area of protection relates to termination of employment.

Claire Bernstein, a Montreal lawyer and syndicated columnist, has written many columns about this issue. She cited a case of an Alberta employer who fired an employee for refusing to work on Easter Monday. Mondays were the busiest day in his company and all employees knew they had to work that day. The employee took the owner to court and the case went all the way to the Supreme Court, which ruled in the employee's favour. The court agreed with his contention that his religious rights had been violated since his religion forbade him from working on Easter Monday.

Other cases concern workers fired without notice, with no or inadequate compensation, and without cause. For a long-time employee, even a year's pay has been held insufficient. Courts have awarded increased amounts as well as punitive damages for "brutal and callous firing," meaning without notice or cause.

Decision Questions

1. What are the implications for the HRM department of legal rulings against firing for unjust cause?

2. If you were an employer, would you put more effort into screening and training employees, given these rulings? How would this help? Who might benefit from or be hurt by such changes?

3. In some cases, an arbitrator has been brought in to settle wrongful discharge cases. What are the benefits of arbitration rather than legal action? Who benefits?

Source: Claire D. Bernstein, *That's Business, But Is It Legal?* (Toronto: Methuen, 1995).

CASE 2

EMPLOYERS' LIABILITY TAKES SOME SURPRISING TWISTS

The potential liability that an employer may have concerning the actions of employees has recently been extended by a decision of the Supreme Court of Canada. The case concerned an employee, Donald Curry, of The Children's Foundation of Vancouver, who was found guilty of 19 pedophilic attacks on children in the Foundation's care. The Foundation is a nonprofit institution that cares for emotionally disturbed children aged 6 to 12. It fired Mr. Curry when it became aware that he had abused another child.

One of the victims, Patrick Bazley, now a 41-year-old resident of Alberta, sued the Foundation claiming that it was responsible for its employees' criminal actions and should be held legally liable for damages. In a unanimous decision, 7 to 0, the Supreme Court ruled that The Children's Foundation was liable despite the fact that it was not negligent and had honourable motives. It was supposed to care for "innocent, helpless, and vulnerable" children, so it had a legal responsibility to see that they came to no harm.

In a different event, a university department trying to address the problem of a persistently low percent-

age of female faculty ran into a possible legal challenge when it tried to correct this imbalance. When professor Angelo Santi became chairperson of the psychology department July 1, 1999, he found that only 3 of 21, or 14 percent, of full-time department faculty were females. The department had been having difficulty attracting women, and three who had been offered positions had accepted offers at other universities. The vice-president, academic, and the university's lawyer were concerned that the university could be found in violation of federal and Ontario employment-equity legislation. So Santi took a bold and unusual step: he placed an ad for a psychology professor specifying that only women should apply. The ad noted that this was an attempt to correct a gender imbalance and that such a procedure was allowed by the Ontario Human Rights Commission.

This ad caused an explosion of opposition in the academic community led by the Society for Academic Freedom and Scholarship (SAFS). Its president, Dr. Doreen Kimura, "internationally acclaimed [retired] scientist ... at Simon Fraser University was 'appalled.'" A fierce dialogue broke out between various camps across Canada. Dr. Kimura pointed to statistics that only 20.5 percent of applicants across all disciplines at universities in Canada were women, but that 34 percent of all hirees were women. This showed that women were twice as likely as men to be hired and that the problem was that not enough females applied for positions. Female PhD and graduate students interviewed thought the ad was a great idea. The SAFS is planning a legal challenge.

Decision Questions

1. If you were a senior manager at The Children's Foundation what would you suggest as a procedure that would ensure that employees are not harming children? Do you see any way that companies can make sure that employees are not being sexually harassed? What can be done other than issuing clear policy statements that such behaviour is illegal and will not be tolerated?
2. Have you personally witnessed any such behaviour at any job you had? Was anything done about it? Do you feel the situation was properly handled by your employer? If you were in charge what would you have done?

3. What do you think of this attempt by the psychology department of the university to remedy its problem? Do you think it was too extreme or was it necessary under the circumstances? Can you think of any other way that the department could correct the gender imbalance?
4. The United States has long had many affirmative action laws and regulations to help correct the lack of minority, primarily African-American, representation in many aspects of U.S. life. The opponents of affirmative action have long argued that such laws are unfair and undemocratic. In various states affirmative action has been declared a violation of the U.S. constitution. Are you familiar with the specific arguments opponents used? Would any of them apply in the university case?

Sources: "Employer Found Liable for Sexual Abuse," *Globe and Mail*, June 16, 1999, p. A9; Jenefer Curtis, "All's Fair for the Fair Sex," *Globe and Mail*, August 14, 1999, p. D6.

CBC   **VIDEO CASE**   **www.cbc.ca**

LOYALTY IN THE WORKPLACE

This chapter explores the difficulties and challenges for HRM in finding and keeping good employees. The video looks at the problem of *keeping* employees in whom employers have invested large sums of money recruiting, hiring, orienting, training, and developing. Gone are the days when a person could expect to spend his or her entire working life at General Motors, at IBM, or at any of a thousand other companies. Today's workforce includes a large number of temporary workers, outsourcers, part-timers, and so on.

The challenges that HRM has faced in previous years have been compounded by the relentless downsizing that has occurred over the past two decades. How can companies expect employees to be loyal to them when companies' past behaviour has indicated how easily expendable employees are? Endless headlines stating that major companies have laid off thousands of employees have left their mark on the workforce's psyche.

In an era of fierce global competition and high expectations from both businesses and consumers regarding quality and service, a dedicated workforce is required that will go all out for a company. The video reveals this dilemma between employer and employee.

The former seeks loyalty while the latter looks for the best opportunities for his or her personal advancement.

Discussion Questions

1. How do you think companies can solve the problem of weak, or no, company loyalty? Would a guaranteed long-term employment contract do the trick? Can companies really offer such guarantees given the unstable global economy?
2. In a world where working at home (or telecommuting), the virtual office, or setting up your own consulting company is so common, does it still make sense to speak of loyalty to a company? Can you see a new company structure emerging consisting of a core of loyal, permanent, well-treated employees and the rest being labelled others?
3. Do you think that today's young men and women graduates welcome the likelihood of working for different employers in the course of their careers? Do you think they would prefer to spend many years with one company that treated them right? Would you? What about the appeal of self-employment?

Source: *Venture,* show number 777, "Loyalty in the Workplace," March 6, 2001, running time 7:20.

Dealing with Employee–Management Issues and Relations

LEARNING GOALS

AFTER YOU HAVE READ AND STUDIED THIS CHAPTER, YOU SHOULD BE ABLE TO

1 Understand that the most difficult issues facing labour and management today are retraining, job security, and job flexibility.

2 Trace the history and role of labour unions in Canada.

3 Discuss the major legislation affecting labour and management.

4 Outline the collective bargaining process.

5 Describe union and management pressure tactics during negotiations.

6 Explain a strike and a lockout and who uses these procedures.

7 Explain the difference between mediation and arbitration.

Chief Justice Alan Gold, A Star Labour Mediator

Courtesy of Alan B. Gold

For almost a quarter of a century, some of the toughest and most stubborn characters in Canada have succumbed to the charms of Alan Gold. From grizzled longshoremen to armed Mohawk warriors, he has succeeded in winning their trust and reaching agreements where few people expected any progress.

Gold, former chief justice of Quebec Superior Court, gained fame in 1968 when he headed off a strike by longshoremen at the port of Montreal. He mediated a strike by 56,000 rail workers in 1973, ended a bitter postal strike in 1981, and has played a key role in resolving many other labour disputes in construction and airlines as well as at the Royal Mint and the Department of External Affairs.

He was chief arbitrator under the collective agreements between the Quebec government and its employees from 1966 to 1983, when he was appointed chief justice of the Superior Court. He is an honorary life member of the National Academy of Arbitrators (USA), a founding member of the Society of Professionals in Dispute Resolution (USA) and an honorary member of the Corporation professionelle des conseilliers en relations industrielles du Québec.

In the summer of 1990, Gold astonished many observers by negotiating an agreement on human-rights issues in the Oka crisis in Quebec. It was a complex three-way negotiation among the federal government, the Quebec government, and Mohawk warriors at Oka. Before his arrival on the scene, the Oka standoff had seemed virtually impossible to resolve. But his mediation led to the only significant breakthrough in the entire 78-day crisis.

"Whether people are carrying guns or they have economic guns to your head, there are all kinds of pressures ... in these situations," said Gold's son, Marc Gold, who is a law professor at Osgoode Hall Law School (Toronto). He said his father always enjoys a tough job, even if it is regarded as hopeless. He likes to be challenged.

Stewart Sax, a labour lawyer who has worked with former chief justice Gold in labour negotiations, noted that Gold has a history of handling the most intractable disputes "where nobody has the slightest idea of how anyone is ever going to solve the mess."

The key to his father's success, said Marc, is that "he's known to be fair and people trust him to do the fair thing. He's also a very good listener. Most important, he understands that all these issues are human issues. He deals with them on a very human level. He's wonderfully good with people—he likes people." At crucial moments in negotiations, former chief justice Gold is not afraid to use humour to defuse a tense situation.

The long and distinguished career of former chief justice Gold as a jurist, conciliator, arbitrator, and mediator has led to many honours and degrees being showered on him. He has sat on or chaired the boards of many major educational and cultural institutions in Quebec. In retirement he is still active in his specialized field of mediation and arbitration.

Based on: Geoffrey York, "Peacemaker Has Fine Record," *Globe and Mail*, September 7, 1991, p. A8, Thursday Report, Concordia University, September 12, 1991; interviews with Alan Gold, May 14, 1996, and December 28, 1998.

ETHICAL DILEMMA
A Conflict of Values

The main thrust of this chapter concerns labour–management or company–union relations. Sometimes ethical issues arise in these often difficult relations. Suppose you are a chemist working for a small paint company and you are aspiring to a management position. You are a member of the union in your plant, but you are not very pleased with Mike, who is president of your union local. You find him a bit too argumentative and aggressive for your taste, but the majority of employees keep electing him because they are pleased with the contracts he has been able to work out with the owners of the company.

Negotiations have commenced for renewal of the union agreement, which expires shortly. You are on the negotiating team. Both sides are expecting the negotiations to be tough and drawn out. You are friendly with your supervisor, Norman, and he knows you are not enamoured of your union local president. Norman also knows that you would like to be promoted to a junior management position. One evening, when you are having a beer with him after work, he asks you how you would feel about keeping him posted about what is discussed at the negotiating team meetings. You are a little taken aback by this request. Norman explains that the company is in a weak financial position and Mike seems to have convinced the team to take a firm stand on their demands, which will raise labour costs considerably.

All Norman really wants to know is if the union is bluffing so that the company will know how to play its negotiating hand. Norman hints that if you do him this favour he will recommend your promotion to a managerial job. You tell him that you want to think about his request and you will let him know in a couple of days. What would you do? Think about this as you peruse the chapter and we'll come back to the question at the end of the chapter.

THE MAJOR ISSUES FACING LABOUR–MANAGEMENT RELATIONS

Throughout this book we have highlighted the importance of technological change and its impact on the economies of modern industrial societies. You have also seen how maintaining the ability to compete in a globalized trading system is essential if companies want to survive. The North American Free Trade Agreement has added competitive pressures as well as opportunities.

The relationship between management (representing owners or shareholders) and unions (representing employees) has a built-in adversarial basis. Management has the responsibility of operating as profitably as possible and generating growth, with maximum productivity (➤ **P. 43** ◄ see also Chapter 10) being one of the important tools in achieving those goals. Unions' primary responsibility is the welfare of their members. This includes such factors as decent working conditions, respect and dignity for workers, a reasonable share of the wealth their labour produces for the employer, and assurance the conditions of the contract and government labour laws will not be abrogated. As you will see shortly, with so many employees having lost their jobs in the last decade, the issues of job security and retraining for the new information-age jobs have become key concerns for unions and the people they represent. For a discussion of some ethical implications, see the Ethical Dilemma box "A Conflict of Values."

As Canadian companies try to compete more effectively under the demands of technology and world competitiveness, while coping with a roller-coaster economy, management has been laying off employees, automating operations, and demanding more flexibility in how it uses its remaining workforce. Management must do what its strongest competitors everywhere are doing: adopt the most advanced technological methods, simplify and thin out the organizational structure, and increase productivity.

Plant Closings and Layoffs

These pressures on companies led to numerous layoffs of employees, plant closings, and the loss of more than 300,000 manufacturing jobs in Canada in the early 1990s. Skilled employees with 15, 20, or 25 years of experience at their companies found themselves without jobs and wondering what had hit them.

Hardly a week went by without announcements of companies closing, laying off people, or moving all or part of their operations to the southern United States, to Mexico, or even to Asia. These changes were the reason unions in Canada (and in the U.S.) were so opposed to the North American Free Trade Agreement (NAFTA) as discussed in Chapter 2. In both countries there was concern about a wholesale movement of companies' operations to low-wage Mexico. This trend had abated somewhat by the late 1990s, but most Canadian employees had begun to worry about the security of their jobs. Everybody knew somebody, even long-term employees, who had lost their job. Thus, job security, as well as job retraining, became major demands of unions in contract negotiations with companies.

The stage was set for sharp conflicts between unions and management. Unions try desperately to hold on to jobs for their members while management fights determinedly to stay alive in the fiercely competitive world in which they find themselves. Unions say: our members need job security, training, and retraining to qualify for the new jobs that require more education and different skills. Management says: we need more flexibility in how we deploy our workforce. We must be free to have employees perform multiple tasks and not be bound by rigid job descriptions spelled out in union contracts.

As more traditional labour-intensive jobs are lost due to technology and competition from lower-wage countries, training and retraining become high priorities to prepare the Canadian labour force for the jobs of today and tomorrow. Demands for job security must be tied to job flexibility. To secure a job today, an employee must be able to do a variety of tasks and work well in teams. These problems are a continuing issue as many layoffs were announced in 2000 and 2001.

The Canadian Auto Workers (CAW) has negotiated with companies such as General Motors to ensure that clauses related to job security and job retraining are included in their contract.

Photographer: David Hartman, Toronto. CAW GM negotiating team meeting, Toronto, October 1996.

SPOTLIGHT ON BIG BUSINESS
Labour, Management, and Government Co-operate in Retraining

When put to the test, labour and management *can* work together. It happened at Algoma Steel Corporation Ltd., where former NDP premier Bob Rae of Ontario appointed some union heads to a special task force. The steel industry's co-operation with labour at Algoma and other sites, well before the special Ontario committee was formed, is seen as one of the few bright lights of labour relations. The Canadian Steel Trade and Employment Congress, a union–management initiative with federal funding, arranged for retraining for 5,000 steelworkers over a three-year period. In some cases, that has meant entirely new careers, such as teaching and nursing. In 1993 the Congress was working with 1,300 labourers at Algoma and with 6,000 workers by 1996.

The forest sector is organizing similar retraining initiatives, while high-tech electronics manufacturing and communications companies have even more innovative programs. The powerful Canadian Auto Workers (CAW) (formerly led by Bob White, probably the most important union leader in Canada and a former leader of the Canadian Congress of Labour) is moving along the same lines. In the 1990 contract with the Big Three auto companies, the union negotiated an income-security clause to assist workers laid off due to technological changes. The CAW also insisted on a three-year program to certify 10,000 workers as having trained on specific types of technical equipment. This retraining program will increase their job mobility.

The recession of the 1990s saw hundreds of thousands of workers lose their jobs without finding new ones, making the question of retraining a pressing economic, social, and political issue.

---

www.caw.ca

The Canadian Auto Workers union has a section on its Web site in which it formally states its policy on significant current workplace issues. One of these, titled "Work Reorganization: Responding to Lean Production," details the union's position regarding the impact of work reorganization and downsizing. The CAW points out that their goal is to develop "an effective working relationship with management based not on any superficial partnership, but on a negotiated compromise that addresses both worker and corporate concerns." Be sure to visit this site to learn how the CAW views these issues.

How management and labour adapt to these issues will determine our economic and political well-being in the years ahead, and will require substantial co-operation and new attitudes on both sides. In addition, significant funding and close co-operation among government, management, and unions will be necessary to launch and maintain useful training and retraining programs. There are some promising signs of labour–management co-operation that augur well for the future (see the Spotlight on Big Business box "Labour, Management, and Government Co-operate in Retraining"), but the process is proving difficult; it will take years to become a significant factor in Canada.

The Impact of Old Attitudes

The problems are greatly complicated by old attitudes that each side brings to the bargaining table. You will recall from Chapter 12 that some managers believe in Theory X for managing people: Work is unpleasant and workers have to be treated by the carrot-and-stick method. Most managers follow the Herzberg/Maslow/Theory Y approach: Workers must be treated as humans. They have different needs and like to participate in decision making.

Similarly, many union representatives are suspicious of management's intentions. They believe that management's goals are to cut wages, reduce the number of jobs, and weaken the union. More far-seeing union leaders realize that there are major, long-term problems that require co-operative efforts to solve.

The result is that specific negotiations succeed or fail depending to a large extent on which of these attitudes the negotiators bring to the table. These issues are not going to disappear. So you can see why there is a continuing need for skilled conciliators like Alan Gold.

Transformation of the Canadian Economy: Part of a Universal Process

We are in the midst of a historic transformation of modern industrial society from labour-intensive manufacturing to an automated manufacturing and service economy in which machinery does most of the hard, dirty, dangerous, boring, repetitive jobs, and human beings use their brains rather than their muscles on the job. This process has been developing slowly over the past 200 years, but it picked up speed in the early 1950s and is now rolling along in high gear. Its impact on jobs and relations between management and labour has been, and continues to be, significant and considerable, requiring endless adjustments. Let's start by looking at the role played by trade unions in attempting to cope with these critical developments.

HISTORY AND ROLE OF TRADE UNIONS IN CANADA

A long, rocky road has been travelled in Canada to arrive at the current stage of relatively civilized relationships between owners and managers of businesses and their employees. A complex and often bitter series of events over the last century and a half has involved workers, owners and managers, and government in a long process of evolution that has transformed the rights and obligations of all the parties. This evolution was occurring not only in Canada but also in England, the United States, and other countries experiencing the Industrial Revolution.

The Rise of Industrial Capitalism

The nineteenth century witnessed the emergence of modern industrial capitalism. The system of producing the necessities of society in small, home-based workplaces gave way to production in large factories driven by steam and later electricity, both new inventions. Large numbers of people left their homes (or homelike workplaces) to work in large, noisy, dark, dangerous, cold or hot, impersonal places. Accidents were frequent and injured workers were just thrown out and replaced by others. Many writers described these depressing conditions in dramatic terms; the phrase "dark, satanic mills" (coined 200 years ago by famous British artist and poet William Blake) became well known.

This period of almost total disregard of the human needs of workers—especially marked by a dawn-to-dusk work day for miserable wages—was infamous for the brutal exploitation of very young children. Charles Dickens became world-famous in the mid-1800s because of his novels about the maltreatment of children in England. The situation was not very different in Canada. A century ago, eight-year-old Canadian children still worked in textile mills on a 12-hour shift for less than $100 a year. Small boys worked long hours in mines, in areas that were inaccessible to adults, for a few cents an hour. A workweek of 80 hours was not uncommon. In addition, the Chinese immigrants who built the rail lines in western Canada in the late 1800s were badly discriminated against, and many groups, including women and minorities, suffered lesser discrimination because of their race, religion, or colour right up to the late twentieth century. While the early trade-union movement participated in this discrimination, the unions gradually shifted to their current position of fighting against all discrimination.

Beginnings of Trade Unionism

These conditions gave impetus to the fledgling union movement, started earlier in the new railway and printing industries. Unions set out to establish more humane working conditions and to provide workers with a living wage. The struggle was not

Photo courtesy of Rockwell

Retraining is a critical issue facing labour–management relations today. This photo shows a Rockwell training instructor explaining a new linking system.

www.cpp-rpc.gc.ca

The Canada Pension Plan has come under considerable attack in recent years. CPP was introduced in the late 1960s to ensure that all working Canadians and their dependants would have a pension income after retirement. Rapid changes in the demographic landscape and cost structures have resulted in a rise in required contributions from employees and employers.

The CPP Web site features "An Information Paper for Consultations on the Canada Pension Plan." Visit the site to learn more about the history and future of the Canada Pension Plan.

Labour Relations Board (LRB)
A quasi-judicial body consisting of representatives of government, labour, and business. It functions more informally than a court but has the full force of law. Different boards administer labour codes in each jurisdiction, federal or provincial.

an easy one because, before 1872, it was illegal to attempt to form unions in Canada. The pioneers in the early struggles were treated as common criminals—arrested, beaten, and often shot.

Long after it was no longer illegal, the idea of workers forming unions to protect their interests was still regarded with suspicion by employers and governments in Canada. Democratic rights for all was still a weak concept and the idea of people getting together to fight for their rights was not accepted as it is today. The union movement was greatly influenced by immigrants from Britain and Europe, who brought with them the ideas and experiences of a more advanced and often more radical background. The growing union movement in the United States also influenced Canada. Many Canadian unions started as locals of American unions, and this relationship persists today (as shown later in Figures 14.5 and 14.6). As democracy gradually gained strength, the union movement grew with it. Its participation, in turn, helped democracy sink deeper, wider roots in Canada.

Workers' Rights Entrenched in Law

As with other movements for greater fairness and equality in our society—women's right to vote, equal rights for minorities and women, protection of children, and so on—when support for employees' rights became widespread in Canada, laws were passed to enforce them. Today we have laws establishing minimum wages, paid minimum holidays and vacation, maximum hours, overtime pay, health and safety conditions, workers' compensation for accidents, Employment Insurance, the Canada/Quebec Pension Plan, and a host of other rights. It is strange to realize that at one time or another these were all on the agenda of unions and were opposed by employers and governments for many years. They often denounced these demands as radical notions.

The effect of unions goes far beyond their numbers. Companies that want to keep unions out often provide compensation, benefits, and working conditions that match or exceed those found in union plants or offices. Thus, the levels established by unions spill over to nonunion companies. Michelin Tire plants in Nova Scotia are good examples.

LEGISLATION AFFECTING LABOUR–MANAGEMENT RELATIONS

Due to the nature of confederation in Canada under the Constitution Act of 1867, power and authority are divided among the provinces and the federal government. The federal government has control over specified fields of activity that are national in nature—that is, they operate in more than one province—for example, banks, railways, airlines, telephone companies, broadcasting, and pipelines. So federal legislation applies to unions and labour–management relations in these businesses, as well as to all federal Crown corporations and federal civil servants. All other companies are subject to provincial laws, covering perhaps 90 percent of all employees.

Over the years the federal government has passed various laws affecting labour–management relations for those areas under its jurisdiction. These were all consolidated in 1971 into the Canada Labour Code, which is administered by the Department of Labour of the federal government through the Canada Labour Relations Board. The **Labour Relations Board (LRB)** is a quasi-judicial body consisting of representatives of government, labour, and business. It functions more informally than a court but has the full force of law. Similar provincial codes and labour relations boards operate in each province for those areas under their jurisdiction. The laws, regulations, and procedures vary from province to province.

- What are the major issues facing labour–management relations?
- What is being done to solve these problems?
- Can you name the legal body that regulates these relations?

THE COLLECTIVE BARGAINING PROCESS

The Labour Relations Boards (LRBs) oversee **collective bargaining**, the process by which a union represents employees in relations with their employer. Collective bargaining includes how unions are selected, the period prior to a vote, certification, ongoing contract negotiations, and behaviour while a contract is in force and during a breakdown in negotiations for a renewal of a contract. The whole bargaining process and the important certification procedure are shown in detail in Figure 14.1. It is now illegal for employers to fire employees for union activities.

As you can see, the process is quite regulated and controlled, so that employers and employees, as well as unions, have to follow a strict procedure to ensure that everybody is playing by the rules. The procedure is democratic, and, as in any election, the minority has to accept the majority's decisions. The actual contract is quite complex, covering a wide range of topics as shown in Figure 14.2 on page 433. We look at some of the major ones next.

Hiring Conditions

One of the important clauses in a union contract concerns the conditions attached to hiring employees. There are basically four types of conditions.

1. The one favoured by unions is called a **closed shop**, which means that all new hires must be union members. In effect, hiring is done through the union. Unemployed members of the union register for employment or show up daily at a union hiring hall.

2. One step down is a union shop. In a **union shop**, the employer is free to hire anybody but the recruit must then join the union within a short period, perhaps a month.

3. One of the most common conditions is an **agency shop**, which is based on the **Rand formula**. The new employee is not required to join the union but must pay union dues. This historic formula was devised by Supreme Court Justice Rand in 1946 when he arbitrated a major case involving Ford of Canada Ltd. The argument for this requirement is that all employees who benefit from a contract signed by the union should help to pay for the costs of maintaining that union—its officers, union expenses, negotiating committee, shop stewards, and so forth.

4. The hiring condition least popular with unions and the one favoured by employers is the **open shop**, where employees are free to join or not join the union and to pay or not pay union dues.

collective bargaining
The process by which a union represents employees in relations with their employer.

Most of Canada's Labour Relations Boards can be found on the Internet. Do a bit of surfing to learn more about what they do. For example, the Manitoba Labour Board has descriptions of its role and objectives at <www.gov.mb.ca/labour /labbrd>. The Nova Scotia Labour Relations Board appears at <www.gov.ns.ca/enla/lrb>. There are a number of centres for research and study in the labour relations area and regarding Labour Relations Boards.

closed shop
A workplace in which all new hires must already be union members.

union shop
A workplace in which the employer is free to hire anybody, but the recruit must then join the union within a short period, perhaps a month.

agency shop (Rand formula)
A workplace in which a new employee is not required to join the union but must pay union dues. This historic formula was devised by Justice Rand.

open shop
A workplace in which employees are free to join or not join the union and to pay or not pay union dues.

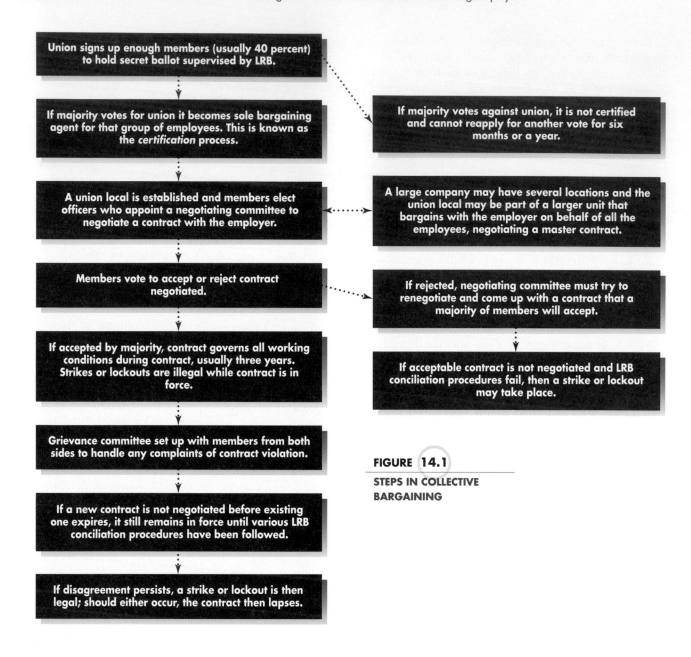

FIGURE 14.1

STEPS IN COLLECTIVE BARGAINING

check-off clause
A contract clause requiring the employer to deduct union dues from employees' pay and remit them to the union.

Regardless of which hiring condition prevails, the contract usually contains a **check-off clause** requiring the employer to deduct union dues from employees' pay and remit them to the union (except for nonmembers in case 4). It would obviously be a lot harder to collect union dues individually.

You have seen how the nature of work is changing. Companies are downsizing and modernizing, so fewer workers are to be found in large workplaces. More and more people are working out of their homes. What adjustments do you think unions will have to make to accommodate these developments? What signs are there that they are making such changes? Will the nature of unions change?

Grievance Procedure

No matter how carefully union contracts are drafted, it is impossible to avoid disagreements. There are always differences of opinion on the exact meaning or interpretation of certain words or clauses. Every day management takes action on

1. Wages, salaries, and other forms of compensation, including the important cost-of-living adjustment clause (COLA).
2. Working hours and time off—regular; overtime; mealtimes; paid holidays, vacations, rest periods, and sick leave; leaves of absence; flextime.
3. Seniority rights—promotions; transfers; layoffs and recalls.
4. Benefit programs—group insurance: medical, dental, and life insurance, pensions; child and elder care; supplementary employment insurance; termination pay; maternity and paternity leave.
5. Grievances—composition of committee; processing of grievances.
6. Health and safety—provision of special clothes or equipment and safe working conditions.
7. Union activities—collection of union dues by the employer (check-off); shop stewards on the floor; union notices.
8. Hiring conditions—closed shop, union shop, agency shop, or open shop.
9. Discipline—rights of management regarding suspension, fines, and termination; hearing process.

FIGURE 14.2

WHAT IS IN A UNION CONTRACT

In general, the contract defines the rights of each party, union and management. There is a long list of topics included in such contracts. The major points are listed here.

transfers, promotions, layoffs, discipline, change in work procedures, and more. Sometimes these actions cause individual workers or the union local to perceive that the contract has been violated. So they file a **grievance**, a formal protest by an individual employee or a union when they believe a particular management decision breaches the contract.

Companies in which relations between management and union are poor or deteriorating usually have a big backlog of unresolved grievances. This is not good for the morale of the employees and, if allowed to continue for any length of time, will ultimately result in lower productivity. Where relations are good, there are few grievances and those that arise are quickly settled.

Figure 14.3 indicates all the steps, specified by the contract, in the processing of a grievance. Typically there are five or six levels in this procedure. If the grievance cannot be settled at one level, it moves up to the next level. The final step is an outside arbitrator or arbitration board, but in practice this is quite rare. Many complaints are settled informally and never put in writing.

grievance
A formal protest by an individual employee or a union when they believe a particular management decision breaches the union contract.

Arbitration

Arbitration is the process of resolving all disputes, not only grievances, through an outside, impartial third party. The arbitrator renders a decision that is binding on both disputing parties. The arbitrator may be a single person or a three-person board that is acceptable to both sides. The arbitrator decides in favour of one of the parties.

Arbitration may be *voluntary*: both sides decide to submit their case to an arbitrator. Or it may be *compulsory*: imposed by the government or by Parliament or a provincial legislature. Compulsory arbitration usually occurs in a major or prolonged strike with serious consequences for the public. Usually, nongrievance arbitration (say, for contract disputes) is voluntary and grievance arbitration is compulsory.

arbitration
The process of resolving all disputes, not only grievances, through an outside, impartial third party.

Mediation

Sometimes, in bitter disputes between management and labour, arbitration may not be acceptable to both sides. When the differences between the two are extreme or there is much distrust or neither side wants to risk an all-or-nothing decision by an arbitrator, they may opt for mediation. **Mediation** is the use of a third party to

mediation
The use of a third party to attempt to bring disputing parties to a resolution by modifying their positions.

FIGURE 14.3

STAGES IN PROCESSING GRIEVANCES

The representatives from each side are listed with the stages.

	MANAGEMENT	UNION
Stage 1	First-level supervisor	Shop steward
Stage 2	Second-level supervisor	Chief steward
Stage 3	Plant manager	Chief grievance officer
Stage 4	Director of industrial relations	National or international union official
Stage 5	CEO or president	President of union or central labour body
Stage 6	Dispute goes to arbitration (quite rare)	

attempt to bring the parties to a resolution of their dispute. The mediator tries to get both parties to modify their positions.

Mediators must possess certain important qualities to undertake such a difficult task. After all, they are attempting to bring together parties that are far apart or that may hardly be talking to each other. They obviously must be well respected, have excellent negotiating skills, and be patient and determined. It is a high-pressure job involving long sessions and sometimes around-the-clock meetings.

We are fortunate in Canada to have a number of excellent people who possess such qualities and who have resolved some very bitter disputes. One of them is William Kelly, who is now retired after many years of outstanding service. Kelly was a railway man, an officer in one of the rail unions, who was appointed to head up the conciliation branch of the Federal Department of Labour. He settled many notable disputes, thus avoiding strikes in the rail and telephone industries, the postal service, and grain shipping. He was awarded the Order of Canada for his successful mediation efforts.

Former chief justice Alan Gold, of Quebec Superior Court, is another outstanding individual with a notable record of achievement in mediation. Gold has also settled many bitter labour–management conflicts involving longshoremen in Quebec, the postal service, and others. He is profiled at the beginning of this chapter.

It should be noted that both arbitration and mediation can be difficult, long, and costly procedures, especially when both sides are locked into rigid positions. That is why negotiators from both sides usually try to settle their differences before resorting to these steps.

WHEN UNIONS AND MANAGEMENT DISAGREE

Because the media give a lot of attention to strikes, you might get the impression that this is the usual pattern of negotiations. But in reality, only a small fraction of contract negotiations between unions and management end in such bitter altercations. Let us examine what happens when an agreement is not reached. What tactics and strategies are available to each side?

Usually, the union is demanding some improvement in benefits, working conditions, job security, or pay increases. The employer usually offers less or very little or sometimes nothing. The union must take actions to try to force the employer to meet its demands. These actions may include such tactics as work-to-rule (working to the exact letter of the agreement), slowdowns, refusal to work overtime, and booking off sick. A favourite negotiating tactic of the police is to refuse to hand out tickets, thus reducing the flow of income to provincial or municipal governments that are unwilling to budge from their bargaining position.

Strikes and Lockouts

If union leaders feel there is strong support among the members, they will call for a strike vote, which is a secret ballot authorizing the union leadership to call a strike when they see fit. If they get a strong mandate, say more than 80 percent in favour, they use this as a lever to convince management to accept their demands without actually going on strike. If management does not give in, the union will have to strike. Of course, if there is a slim majority, say 55 percent, for a strike, union leaders will be very hesitant to call a strike.

Before a strike can be called, all legal requirements must be met. In most jurisdictions in Canada the union must first ask the government to appoint a conciliator, who has a certain time limit to try to bring the parties together. If he or she fails, the union is then legally able to go on strike. The employer is then also free to declare a lockout.

In a **lockout** the employer locks the premises against the employees. In either a strike or a lockout, employees are no longer paid their wages or salaries. Clearly, a strike is a weapon of last resort, used only when all else fails. Similarly, management is reluctant to lock out its employees and call a halt to operations. No product, no profits.

lockout
A negotiating strategy in which the employer locks the premises against the employees.

Some disputes that received a lot of publicity in 1994 were the acrimonious strike of the major league baseball players, the lockout by baseball owners of the umpires, and the lockout by the NHL owners of the hockey players. Two 1996 disagreements that drew much attention in British Columbia were the lockouts by Safeway and Overwaitea Foods. Both companies were adamant that they would not negotiate with their employees until the unions lowered their demands. Other strikes that were important and drew a lot of attention were transit strikes in Calgary and in Vancouver in 2001. The Vancouver strike was bitter and protracted and thus inconvenienced many people for a long time.

A lockout that was a major news item in the latter half of 1998 concerned another sport, basketball. The main issues were a salary cap on the multimillion-dollar salaries of many veterans, minimum wages levels, and the percentage of total team revenue that would go to the players. The team owners of the NBA locked out the players by refusing to start the 1998–99 season in June 1998. After six months of on-and-off negotiations, there was still no settlement of this bitter dispute. In December the board of governors and the commissioner of basketball threatened to cancel the remaining season if no settlement was in place by the seventh of January 1999.[1]

The dispute was finally resolved in February 1999 with everybody agreeing to a shortened season so that the playoffs could commence on time. We can see how important the public's attitude is in such conflicts by looking at the slogans the league used. Prior to the lockout the well-known NBA slogan was "I love the game." To win back public support after the lockout the slogan became "I STILL love this game."

Bell Canada employees demonstrate in front of the Yellow Pages offices to further their contract demands. During a strike action, employees do not receive wages or a salary.

Battles for Public Support

In major cases where the public is affected—the postal service, nurses, doctors, teachers, transportation, telecommunication, civil servants at all levels—each side plays a propaganda game to win the public to its side. It can be difficult for those not directly involved to really sort out the issues. Sometimes management, if it thinks the public is on its side and the union is perhaps not well organized or lacks strong support, will provoke the union into an unsuccessful strike, weakening the union's bargaining position.

boycott
The practice of urging union members and the public at large not to buy a particular company's products or services.

Unions sometimes ask the public and other union members to **boycott**, or not buy the employer's products or services. One of the most famous and lengthy boycotts in recent history was led by Cesar Chavez of the United Farm Workers, centred in California. The workers were low-paid Mexican immigrants who waged a multi-year battle to improve miserable conditions. In the 1970s they asked people to boycott California grapes to force the growers to negotiate with them.

Their cause was taken up by many organizations in Canada and the United States. At supermarkets in both countries, people picketed and paraded with signs asking shoppers not to buy California grapes. After several years, the growers finally relented and negotiated more reasonable conditions. Most boycotts, in contrast, tend to fizzle out without achieving their goal.

Other Tactics

Union tactics include rotating strikes—on and off or alternating among different plants or cities—rather than a full-fledged strike in which all employees are off the job for the duration. With rotating strikes, employees still get some pay, which would not be the case in an all-out strike. Many unions build up a strike fund from union dues and use it to give their members strike pay, but that's usually a fraction of their normal wages. Sometimes, in important or long-lasting strikes, other unions will give moral or financial aid.

Management may announce layoffs or a shortened workweek and blame it on declining business. It may say the company is having trouble competing due to high labour costs. It may even adopt the lockout tactic when it seems less costly to close down and cease paying wages than to put up with slowdowns, rotating strikes, or work-to-rule union tactics, all of which can be very disruptive. This tactic may force the union to reduce its demands if individual members cannot do without an income for very long or if there is a weak strike-vote majority.

Remember that arbitration and mediation are always available to the parties in dispute. They may take advantage of these procedures before, during, or after a strike or lockout.

PROGRESS
CHECK

•   Can you list the eight steps in the collective bargaining process?

•   What are the major areas included in a union contract?

•   What is the difference between arbitration and mediation?

picketing
The process whereby strikers carrying picket signs walk back and forth across entrances to their places of employment to publicize the strike and discourage or prevent people, vehicles, materials, and products from going in or out.

replacement workers
Management's name for strikebreakers.

scabs
Unions' name for strikebreakers.

injunction
An order from a judge requiring strikers to limit or cease picketing or stop some threatening activity.

STRIKES, LOCKOUTS, AND THE LAW

When a strike is in progress, striking workers usually picket the place (or places) of employment. **Picketing** is the process whereby strikers carrying picket signs walk back and forth across entrances to their places of employment. The aim of these picketers is to publicize the strike and to discourage or prevent people, vehicles, materials, and products from going in or out. They usually allow management personnel through, since they are not union members.

Sometimes, when a company tries to bring in strikebreakers (called **replacement workers** by management and **scabs** by the union) to carry on normal activities, bitter feelings are engendered. This often leads to violence. Picketers mass in large numbers to block buses carrying these strikebreakers. Shouts are uttered, articles are thrown, vehicles are attacked, and so on.

If management's tactics are not successful, it may ask for police protection for the vehicles or ask the courts for an injunction to limit the number of picketers. An **injunction** is an order from a judge requiring strikers to limit or cease picketing or to stop some threatening activity. Injunctions are not as commonly granted now as they used to be.

In Quebec and British Columbia it is illegal for companies to hire replacement workers when a legal strike is in progress. Quite often management employees may continue to work and try to do some of the tasks formerly done by the striking workforce.

Restrictions on Right to Strike

There are restrictions on the right to strike of various levels of civil servants and quasi-government employees such as hospital workers and electric and telephone utility workers. The provinces and the federal government forbid some employees under their jurisdiction from striking. In other cases, certain minimum levels of service must be provided. For example, when the federal civil service went out on strike in the fall of 1991, employees of the customs service, prison guards, meat inspectors, airport firefighters, and certain other employees were not allowed to strike. When employees of the public bus system in Montreal went on strike in 1990, the provincial Essential Services Council decided what minimum level of services had to be provided during the strike. The same thing happened when Quebec nurses went on strike in 1999. In nearly all provinces, firefighters and police officers are not allowed to strike.

Legislating Strikers Back to Work

Governments have the power to end a particular strike by passing specific legislation to that effect. Provincial and federal governments have done this from time to time to end strikes by teachers, nurses, postal workers, bus drivers, and others. Governments pass back-to-work legislation when they believe they have enough support among the population for such action because of serious hardship to businesses or individuals. For example, the government in British Columbia ordered teachers back to work during the spring of 1993, and health and public transit workers in 2001; so did the Quebec and Saskatchewan governments when the nurses went on strike in 1999. This also occurred in Nova Scotia in 2001.

Back-to-work legislation is a denial of the legal right to strike, so it is to a certain extent a restriction of the democratic rights of individuals. Consequently, there is often much controversy about such legislation. It is rarely used to deal with strikes against private businesses. If union members remain on strike after they have been legislated back to work they are engaging in an illegal strike and are subject to punishment, as are all lawbreakers. In the case of the Quebec nurses the union had to pay substantial fines.

Striking union locals often turn to affiliated unions for help. Let us now look at the structure of unions in Canada so we can better understand these relationships.

Government sometimes implement back-to-work legislation that forces striking workers back to their jobs. This 15-year-veteran postal worker went back to his route after back-to-work legislation ended a two-week postal strike.

Canadian Press CP. Photograph by Ryan Remiorz

STRUCTURE AND SIZE OF TRADE UNIONS IN CANADA[2]

The organization structure of unions in Canada is quite complex. The most basic unit is the union local. One local usually represents one school, government office, or a specific factory or office of a company. However, that local can also cover several small companies or other work units. A local is part of a larger structure that may be a national or an international body. For example, a local of the Ford plant in Windsor is part of the Canadian Auto Workers (CAW) union, which is a national body. A local of the Stelco plant in Hamilton is part of the United Steel Workers (USW) union, which is an international (Canadian and American) body based in the United States.

www.clc-ctc.ca/policy

The Canadian Labour Congress plays the role of being the political voice of its member unions. For example, 1998 saw a major controversy regarding the attempt by large Canadian banks to merge. The CLC made a submission to the House of Commons Standing Committee on Finance. In it, the CLC argued very strongly against permitting these bank mergers, taking the position that the public interest requires that they be carefully regulated by government. Visit this Web site to see the CLC submission.

www.psac.com

Most unions act as advocates for the political interests of their members, or workers in general. PSAC, for example, has taken a very strong position in favour of pay equity for women. When the Federal Court of Appeal rendered its decision in the *Muldoon case*, PSAC immediately circulated bulletins, press releases, and letters to government officials urging the immediate implementation of pay equity. Visit this Web site to see PSAC's summary of the government's actions and its responses.

In turn, both the CAW and USW are part of a central labour organization called the Canadian Labour Congress (CLC). But the USW is also affiliated with another central body, the AFL-CIO, based in the United States. Other union locals are part of a union that is affiliated with a different central body called the Canadian Federation of Labour (CFL). Some of these are also affiliated with the AFL-CIO and some are not. In addition, some Canadian locals are part of international unions that are only affiliated with the AFL-CIO central body. There are also provincial and some regional bodies to which various unions belong. These are usually unions that are part of the CLC, the AFL-CIO, or both.

The Canadian Union of Public Employees (CUPE) and the Public Service Alliance of Canada (PSAC) are two of the largest unions in Canada. Together, they represent about 435,000 government employees and are affiliated with the CLC.

To make matters even more complex, while all of the unions referred to above exist in Quebec, there are additional unions in that province that are not connected to any of the central bodies previously mentioned. The Confederation of National Trade Unions (CNTU, or CSN in French) is a federation of mostly Quebec-based unions, as is the Centrale des Enseignants de Québec (CEQ), which is a federation of some Quebec teachers' unions. There are also some smaller organizations.

As indicated in Figure 14.4, the total number of union members was under 4 million in 1998. There has been a small gradual decline in union membership since 1989. About 59 percent of union members are male and 41 percent female. Fifty-six percent are in national unions, 30 percent in international, and 14 percent are government employees. About 35 percent of all Canadian employees are union members.

Figure 14.5 shows the breakdown by different central organizations. The CLC is by far the largest group with some 67 percent of all union membership, including those who are also affiliated with the AFL-CIO. The next largest group at 16 percent are unaffiliated national unions. The general trend over the last few decades has been to more independent Canadian unions. Figure 14.5 shows that just under 28 percent have any affiliation with American-based AFL-CIO.

Unionization rates are highest in the public service and the educational sector. On a provincial basis, Newfoundland has the highest rate of unionization. Although it is difficult to pin down these figures precisely, it has been estimated that if the agricultural sector were omitted and nonunion members in shops with union contracts were included, nearly half the workforce would be covered by union contracts.

FUTURE OF LABOUR–MANAGEMENT RELATIONS

What about the future of labour–management relations? Obviously we have come a long way in working conditions, hours of work, and wage levels. Many of these gains are now protected by law. Are unions still necessary? We are fortunate to be living in a democratic country where free and private enterprise is the vital feature of our capitalist economic system ➤ **P. 37** ◄. We believe that all citizens have the right to do what they can, within legal and ethical limits, to better themselves. Improving your financial situation is an admired goal, and those who do so are usually seen as good examples.

In this book you have seen many profiles and other examples of such successful men and women. You are probably thinking about what skills and education you need to achieve financial success and security. We have given you many suggestions of paths you might follow as either an employee or an entrepreneur.

If you select the entrepreneurial route, you will try to build a successful company by providing a necessary service or product in a manner that your customers appreciate ➤**P. 192**◄. If you are successful, you will ultimately accumulate profits and personal wealth. Perhaps you will be very successful and accumulate great wealth and financial security for yourself and your family. One of the costs of doing business that you will be

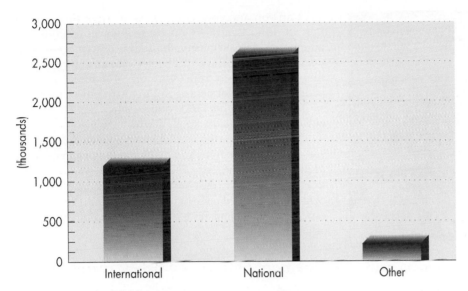

Source: *Directory of Labour Organizations in Canada*, Human Resources and Development Canada, 1998.

FIGURE 14.4

TOTAL NUMBER OF UNION MEMBERS IN CANADA, 1998

The chart shows the breakdown by affiliation as follows:

National	2,556,000
International	1,177,000
Other	204,000
Total	3,937,000

keeping an eye on is wages, salaries, and benefits paid to employees. Will you want a well-trained, smart workforce capable of keeping up with the rapid pace of technological advances, or will you want your employees to work "cheap"? Will you consider unions nothing but a hindrance?

Suppose you do not see yourself as an entrepreneur and instead go the employee route. Imagine yourself 10 years down the road: You have a mate and two children and are now a computer software specialist working for a large company in a nonmanagerial role. Will you seek the best salary you can possibly get? Will you want to be part of a group insurance plan to protect your family? How about working hours? Your spouse also works and you need flexible arrangements to be able to spend time with your children and deliver them to school and various other activities. How about overtime demands on the job that cut into time with your children? Will you have adequate, affordable child care?

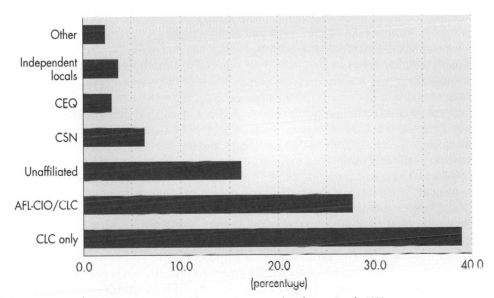

Source: *Directory of Labour Organizations in Canada*, Human Resources and Development Canada, 1998.

FIGURE 14.5

UNION MEMBERSHIP BY CONGRESS AFFILIATION

This figure shows how union membership is distributed by type of affiliation to central labour federations. The chart indicates that about 72 percent of Canadian unionists have no affiliation with U.S. federations. (See text for explanations of the different organization symbols.)

Canadian Press CP. Photography by Steve McKinley.

Can you and your co-workers arrange these and a host of other issues—bonuses, sick leave, termination pay, pensions, retraining, holidays, and more—on a personal basis? Or are you better off with an organization—a union—to represent all of you in making proper contractual arrangements with your employer so that your rights and obligations as well as the employer's are clearly spelled out?

What about all the workers who are less skilled than you are? Some are illiterate; many did not graduate from high school. Hundreds of thousands of employees have lost their jobs in the past decade through no fault of their own. Do they need a strong union to protect their interests? These questions have to be addressed by the people affected.

The Canadian Labour Congress (CLC) is the largest and most important labour organization in Canada. Here, outgoing CLC president Bob White celebrates with president-elect Ken Georgetti.

Can Unions and Management Still Afford Adversarial Roles?

Obviously there are conflicting interests between employers and employees. But every firm seeks to have a highly motivated workforce, which requires good labour–management relations. That means that each side has to appreciate the needs of the other. A progressive union with modern attitudes can co-operate with a progressive, modern management to arrive at workable compromises. Unfortunately, there are as yet very few examples of such co-operation. One good illustration is discussed in the Spotlight on Big Business in this chapter, which shows how steel giant Algoma Steel, the Ontario and federal governments, and the United Steel Workers Union worked out a retraining program for redundant Algoma employees. Another good example is the GSW Water Heating Co., discussed in the Reaching Beyond Our Borders box "The Future of Labour–Management Relations."

In recent years these relations have been greatly strained because of the massive layoffs and plant closings that have dominated the industrial and commercial landscape of Canada. The most important concern of the average worker has become job security. How can any worker be sure that a job will continue to exist next week, next month, or six months from now? This is a period of great stress in the lives of tens of thousands of Canadian families.

At the same time, businesses are desperately trying to hang on in the face of the many problems that are hurting their ability to compete in the marketplace. These issues have been discussed in various chapters of the book. Bankruptcies have been occurring at record levels, so business owners and managers also wonder if they will still be around next year, or even next month.

Even giant companies like Nortel Networks and JDS Uniphase were reporting multibillion-dollar losses in 2001, saw their shares shrink to a small fraction of their previous values, and had their credit ratings reduced. This even led to some questioning of their ability to survive. As mentioned in previous chapters, the economic situation was given a further nasty knock after terrorists destroyed the twin towers of the World Trade Center in New York on September 11, 2001. More layoffs and office and plant closings followed. While both the economy and the stock markets had rebounded somewhat by the end of the year, there were no announcements of rehirings.

These serious economic problems have made labour–management relations very difficult as each side struggles for existence in the highly competitive, technological, globalized business world that now exists. The 1990s saw many tough battles such as those at Air Canada and Canadian Airlines, and those at the Big Three auto companies and many other companies where unions and management went through long and bitter negotiations that often ended in strikes or just narrowly adverted them. From 1999 to 2001 nurses and other health workers went on strike in most provinces. By August 1999 Quebec looked as if it would hit record levels of lost-work days due to strikes and lockouts.[3] These issues are made more complicated

www.gsw-wh.com

REACHING BEYOND OUR BORDERS

The Future of
Labour–Management Relations

Canada faces a choice of the road that labour management relations will travel. We can either stay on the embattled road we have travelled so far or look to other countries—like Germany, the Scandinavian countries, Austria, and Japan—where a different ideology is at work. All of these countries are making or have made the transition to modern high-tech competitive economies where workers are well educated and trained for the new skilled jobs so they can enjoy high incomes and social benefits. There they are learning to work smart, not cheap.

A good Canadian example is the GSW Water Heating Co. of Fergus, Ontario. As shown in Chapter 12 in the Reaching Beyond Our Borders box "Tapping the Power of Workers' Minds," GSW is successfully expanding its sales internationally despite the high wages of its workforce. The secret is a close and trusting relationship with its union, the United Steel Workers. This (unusually for

Canada) close relationship has led to increasing productivity based on excellent and flexible teamwork. The high degree of active employee participation has also led to many cost-saving suggestions. The result has been a Canadian company able to successfully compete with U.S. firms that pay lower wages. Instead of downsizing, GSW continues to hire more employees.

This path requires significant changes in the attitude of workers, unions, managements, and governments. All of us have to change our ways. What is required is a massive, long-term co-operative program involving better education, on-the-job training and retraining programs, substantial investments in new equipment, and government-led incentives to help make it all happen. Nothing less than such an all-out effort will make us more competitive, develop new job opportunities, and keep those opportunities expanding. Are we prepared for such a great challenge? Do we have a choice?

by the lingering suspicions that each party is trying to take advantage of the other. Until these barriers are replaced by co-operation, it will be impossible to move into the new era demanded by the competitive conditions of today and tomorrow. Both sides will have to take a good hard look at themselves if progress is to be made.

Some Important Issues Unions are Currently Championing

Recent newspaper reports indicate some of the interesting things that unions are doing. For example, the Public Service Alliance of Canada (PSAC) has been fighting a long battle for settlement of wage discrimination by the federal government in female-dominated jobs. The union figures that as much as $1.5 billion in retroactive pay is due to female employees, going back to 1984. The employees involved were clerks, secretaries, typists, data processors, librarians, hospital service staff, and educational support staff. There are tens of thousands of people involved, and the union argues that the federal government's pay equity legislation has not been adhered to.[4]

As mentioned in Chapter 4, in 1999 the Canadian Human Rights Council finally ruled on the case going back to 1984. It ordered the federal government to obey its own laws by compensating employees (mostly women) who had suffered pay discrimination for 14 years. A fierce public debate developed in Canada on this issue because very large sums of money were involved. Various estimates placed the amount that the federal government would have to pay out in the range of $4 to $6 billion. If it had been a smaller amount, there likely would have been far less disagreement about the principle involved—pay equity. The federal government launched an appeal of this ruling but a settlement was finally agreed upon in 2000.

It is somewhat ironic that *The Globe and Mail* of March 9, 1999, carried a reprint of its front page of March 9, 1951, 48 years earlier, with these headlines:

Canadian Press CP. Photography by Paul Chaisson.

This nurse is taking a break as her colleagues walk the picket line during an illegal strike staged in 1999 by Quebec nurses.

Sex Discrimination Barred
Equal Pay for Men, Women on Same Job,
New Bill Rules

The report goes on to note that the then Premier Frost said that the bill was prepared after careful study of similar laws in the U.S. and after a study by a British Royal Commission of the "equal pay problem" in England. Frost further stated that the law was in conformity with the United Nations Universal Declaration of Women's Rights (of which Canada is a signatory). A half-century later we are still struggling with pay equity.

In another case, the Canadian Union of Public Employees (CUPE) was attempting to provide pensions for same-sex spouses of two of its staff. It was prevented from doing so by certain regulations in the federal Income Tax Act. It was fighting this case not only for its own staff, but also to set a precedent that governments and companies would have to follow.[5] The laws were finally amended to remove discrimination against same-sex couples.

In a third case, Air Canada Pilots' Union and CUPE complained that Air Canada was overworking its staff because of workforce reductions. This caused some dangerous situations, and the company was pressured to increase its staff. Air Canada finally agreed to do so.[6]

Many other issues involve labour–management relations, some of which were discussed in the previous chapter: testing for drugs and AIDS, working with employees who have AIDS, pay equity for women, affirmative action, and so on. These issues are often difficult to address because of differences of opinion among union members, among managers, and among Canadians in general.

HOW ETHICAL ARE UNIONS?

An oft-heard opinion is that unions are too powerful in Canada. This opinion is demonstrated by the inconvenience caused by strikes that disrupt public services from time to time. We also hear charges that some union leaders are more interested in building and protecting their little empires than in protecting their members' interests. Added to this list of criticisms is the charge of a lack of democracy in union operations and even some cases of corruption. It is important to maintain a proper perspective when considering these and other charges against unions. An overall assessment is difficult in this complex situation.

We should remember that occasionally businesses are accused of illegally trying to fix prices. They are also charged with polluting the environment or breaking environmental laws. Companies that provide food or pharmaceutical products are sometimes accused of playing with people's health. Some of these companies are found guilty of the charges. Obviously this does not mean that all managements should be condemned. Similarly, we should exercise caution when evaluating corruption or careerism in unions. We should not forget unions' significant achievements of improving the living standards and working conditions of millions of Canadians.

EXECUTIVES AS EMPLOYEES OF COMPANIES

We normally think of senior and middle managers as people who run companies. While they are not labour and are not eligible to join unions, they are also employees and are subject to company policies. Some important issues concerning executives are discussed below.

Executive Compensation

Most senior executives are well paid and have generous benefits such as stock options, pensions, and bonuses. They carry heavy responsibility, and their compensation should be proportional to that responsibility. In the United States compensation information relating to public companies must be published, but it is not required under Canadian law, except in Ontario. The Ontario Securities Commission requires most publicly listed companies to divulge the compensation of their top executives.

Ironically, we also get a peek into compensation for some Canadian executives if their companies operate in the United States because they are subject to American disclosure regulations. As a result, there has been much criticism in Canada about the high levels of such compensation and some generous settlements when CEOs are terminated. These are called *golden parachutes* because they provide a gentle landing.

Critics have directed their fire at companies that were being particularly generous with their top people despite doing poorly or incurring substantial losses as a corporation. An article in *Canadian Business* showed that many Canadian CEOs were getting multimillion-dollar annual salaries and bonuses; but the author called the whole system a "crapshoot" because often compensation bears no relationship to performance.[7] The whole issue of rising executive compensation is becoming more contentious in Canada. In 2001 much criticism was directed at CEO John Roth of Nortel for the multimillion-dollar salary, bonus, and stock options profits that he made at a time when his company was reporting record losses into the billions and making regular announcements of layoffs by the ten of thousands. As the gap between executive and employee compensation continues to widen, union leaders and other Canadians are concerned that this issue is symptomatic of the general divergence in income between the upper 20 percent of the population and everyone else. The gulf is not yet as wide as in the U.S., where this issue is also attracting a lot of attention.

One of the most prestigious management consultants in the world, Peter Drucker, has been critical of executive pay levels since the mid-1980s, when he suggested that CEOs should not earn much more than 20 times the salary of the lowest-paid employee. Some companies have followed Drucker's advice. For example, at Herman Miller Inc., a Michigan producer of office furniture, the chief executive is limited to 20 times the average worker's pay. The company has a long record of being at the forefront of the movement to make employees feel that they are an integral part of the company, resulting in excellent labour–management relations. Unfortunately, many companies have ignored Drucker's suggestion. If you were a hot-dog vendor making minimum wage at any of the Walt Disney theme parks, it would take you 17,852 years to make as much as CEO Michael Eisner earned in 1996. Today the average chief executive of a major corporation makes 209 times the pay of a typical factory worker.

An editorial in *The Globe and Mail (G&M)* on June 6, 1999, strongly supports a chorus of shareholder complaints criticizing the incredible remuneration of the chairman of Repap Enterprises Inc., which *The G&M* calculates at $38 million for a company that has posted losses for three years. The editorial notes a string of well-known Canadian companies—and it cites examples such MacMillan Bloedel, the Loewen Group, and Spar Aerospace—where shareholders have been expressing disapproval of high compensation for company chiefs. These are signs, says *The G&M*, that the days of the "old boys' network," which never embarrassed members of the club openly, are over.

Executive Responsibility and Risk

In many companies, senior executives are also on the board of directors that has the final legal and managerial responsibility for the company on behalf of the shareholders. Some people argue that given this heavy burden executives are entitled to adequate compensation. Several recent cases highlight this issue.

The Ontario Court of Appeal ordered three directors, two of whom were executives, to personally pay almost half a million dollars to 100 former employees for wages and termination pay because they were laid off when the plant was closed. In another case, the Canada Labour Relations Board ordered four directors who were executives of STN Inc. to pay $567,000 in vacation, severance, and termination pay to 316 former employees of bankrupt STN.[8]

In a different case, General Motors filed a suit against a former top executive and Volkswagen in Europe accusing him of stealing thousands of company documents and turning them over to Volkswagen when he left GM to become a senior executive at VW. He denied the charges and says he merely took his expertise to his new job.[9] Eventually VW agreed to pay a multimillion-dollar settlement.

Problems of Middle Managers

The main problem facing middle managers today is the reduction in their ranks. Computers, recessions, employee empowerment, and fiercer global competition have all combined to play havoc with the role of these managers. Entire levels of management have been removed, and bureaucracies have become flatter as companies become decentralized. This reduces costs while enabling greater participation in decision making by all employees and faster responses to market conditions. Thus a major problem for this group of managers is insecurity of employment.

The high-tech world of business has given rise to a new phenomenon concerning angry or disgruntled managers and employees who have been laid off. For example, a 56-year-old fired systems administrator, annual salary US$186,000, caused $20 million in damages to his former New Jersey chemical company employer: using another executive's password, he accessed the company's system from his home using the Internet and erased important inventory and personnel files. A survey of companies in the U.S. shows that an estimated US$378 million in damages of this sort occurred in 2000.[10]

CARING FOR CHILDREN AND ELDERS

One of the growing problems in employee–manager issues arises as a result of the entry of large numbers of women into the workforce. One of the issues has to do with caring for children and the elderly. Although men are increasingly shouldering responsibility in these areas, most of the responsibility still falls on women, which has resulted in very heavy burdens being placed on them. These burdens lead to greater stress and absenteeism.

In general, employers have been slow to respond to this situation. "What often puts elder care on the agenda," according to Anne Martin-Matthews, a professor of family studies at the University of Guelph, who did a survey on this issue, "is when a (senior) executive ... has a mother who breaks her hip." That's when the company's traditional evaluation of what a good employee is begins to be questioned.[11]

Whereas managers might have said the first in in the morning and the last to leave at night is the best employee, they are now being encouraged to focus on output rather than time spent in the office. So an employee (often women) who works fewer hours because of elder-care or child-care responsibilities is not automatically rated below best. What is accomplished rather than when it is done becomes more important in progressive companies. As noted in previous chapters, companies like the Royal Bank, Bank

Many companies recognize the need to adjust to the changing demands of the workforce by offering employees day-care centres such as this one. Child care and elder care are two issues gaining the attention of employers.

of Montreal, MacMillan Bloedel, Great-West Life, and others have become sensitive to these needs of their employees. Flexible hours and job sharing go a long way to reducing employee stress and absenteeism.

Top executives' high pay creates tremendous incentives for lower-level executives to work hard to get those jobs. Their high pay also creates resentment among workers, some shareholders, and some members of the general public. What's your position on the proper level of top-executive compensation? Is there a way to make the pay more equitable?

How do you justify the fact that many sports and entertainment stars make millions of dollars? Should top executives take a cut in pay when these people don't? What's the difference between the two groups?

- What is the relationship between injunctions and picketing?
- When is back-to-work legislation used?
- How do labour and management have to co-operate to solve current problems?

ETHICAL DILEMMA
Review

Remember the dilemma about a supervisor's request that you keep him posted about discussions at the union negotiating committee's meetings? Our executives have similar outlooks on this one. Bédard believes that "the situation is delicate because of the relationship with Mike, the union's president. A person in a position of trust must not betray that trust. Information tends to eventually leak out and once credibility is lost, it is lost forever. Whether within the union or in a management position, honesty is the best policy."

Reilley believes employees must respect social norms and suggests some specific behaviour. "I would not provide Norman [with] any inside union information. Nor would I inform the union president of Norman's intervention as this could be very damaging to the negotiations and labour–management relations. I would at least remain entirely neutral. I would also consider resigning from the contract negotiating team."

It is definitely unethical to reveal information concerning confidential negotiating team meetings. The proof is in how you would feel if what you had done leaked to your co-workers. You should also be aware that Norman's request is probably an infringement of the particular labour code governing these negotiations. Furthermore, the bait Norman is dangling might even be interpreted as a bribe, which could be a criminal offence. This situation is more than one of ethics.

SUMMARY

1. Understand that the most difficult issues facing labour and management today are retraining, job security, and job flexibility.

1. There are many difficult issues facing labour and management.
   • *What are the most difficult?*
   Tough recessions and competitive and technological pressures force management to push for job flexibility and to pare labour costs to the bone. This results in large job losses at a time when new jobs are hardest to find, so systematic retraining on a large scale has emerged as a key issue. Retraining requires substantial funding and close co-operation among government, management, and unions.

2. Trace the history and role of labour unions in Canada.

2. Unions have a long history in Canada.
   • *What was their main objective and was it achieved?*
   Their main purpose was to improve workers' poor conditions and wages by forming unions that would fight for workers' rights. All this has been largely achieved and many early demands are now entrenched in law.

3. Discuss the major legislation affecting labour and management.

3. Much labour legislation has been passed by federal and provincial governments.
   • *What is the major piece of legislation?*
   The Canada Labour Code of 1971 consolidated all the federal laws into one. It set up the Canada Labour Relations Board to administer the code. There are equivalent provincial laws and boards.

4. Outline the collective bargaining process.

4. The whole process of employees bargaining with their employers through a union is called collective bargaining.
   • *What are the steps in this process?*
   See Figure 14.1 for the steps in collective bargaining.

5. Describe union and management pressure tactics during negotiations.

5. During negotiations, each side employs various tactics to further its strategy.
   • *What tactics are commonly used?*
   Labour may engage in slowdowns, booking off sick, refusing to work overtime, work-to-rule, or it may take a strike vote. Management may announce layoffs or shorter work weeks, claiming lack of orders due to uncompetitiveness because of high labour costs.

6. Explain a strike and a lockout and who uses these procedures.

6. When negotiations break down, management and labour can employ their ultimate weapons.
   • *What are these?*
   Employees can go on strike, withdrawing their services. Management can lock out its employees—literally shutting the doors and preventing them from coming to work.

7. Explain the difference between mediation and arbitration.

7. There are methods of settling differences when the parties are at a stalemate.
   • *What are these methods?*
   Arbitration is one option. This means a third party is asked to settle the points of disagreement by ruling in favour of one side or the other. Mediation is another option. This involves asking a third party to try to reconcile the parties. This means asking both to modify their demands.

DEVELOPING WORKPLACE SKILLS

1. Debate the following in class: Unions are necessary because the only way employees can protect their interests is by having their own organization to represent them and fight for their rights.

2. Develop a list of three issues of importance to employees that are not mentioned in this chapter. Talk to a union official or a human resource manager of a large company about these issues.

3. Your union is divided on the question of employment equity to correct the inferior position of women in your industry. Some men say that it is unfair to them to allow preferential hiring for women. What do you think? Is this reverse discrimination? Is it justifiable?

4. Debate the following in class: Business executives receive a total compensation package that is far beyond their value. Take the opposite side of the issue from your normal stance to get a better feel for the other point of view.

5. Child care, parental leave, and flexible working hours are important issues for many fathers and mothers. Should businesses and government agencies be required to provide these? Do you think that legislation is necessary to meet these requirements? Is there any other way to achieve these?

TAKING IT TO THE NET

Purpose:

To research union coverage on the Internet and interpret that coverage in relation to today's union–management environments.

Exercises:

1. Search through the Web sites of your local newspapers for reports on union–management controversies or agreements in your area. If you cannot find anything, search www.newswire.ca for news about Ford and the CAW (Canadian Auto Workers), who were involved in important negotiations in September 1999. Search under CAW and Ford. Do these reports indicate any interesting new developments in the relations between these two parties? Do you see any signs of conciliation or compromise so that together they can face the difficult adjustments of competing globally in the new millennium, as discussed in this chapter?

2. Do some surfing through the major search engines by inputting the keywords *labour (or labor)* unions. Try also *union management.* Confine your search to the last two years. Can you find any references to speeches by union or management leaders about the need to be less adversarial? If you can't find much, try *Canadian Labour Congress* as the keywords.

PRACTISING MANAGEMENT DECISIONS

CASE 1

PLANT CLOSINGS, UNIONS, AND CONCESSIONS

The last decade was disastrous for hundreds of thousands of Canadian employees, especially in the manufacturing area. Hundreds of plants and offices laid off tens of thousands of people, or closed because of bankruptcy, consolidation, or transfer of operations to the United States or Mexico. In some cases, management advised unions that the only way they could avoid closing would be substantial concessions in wages and other changes in existing contracts.

Union leaders and their members are in a quandary when faced with such decisions. Sometimes they think management is bluffing. Sometimes they are reluctant to give up contract conditions they fought long and hard for. Accepting wage cuts or benefit reductions when the cost of living continues to rise is not easy. Agreeing to staff reductions to save other jobs is also a tough decision. Unions worry about where these concessions will end. Will there be another round of layoffs or even worse in a few months?

A good example is Phillips Cable Ltd. in Brockville, Ontario, where 350 workers lost their jobs when the plant was closed. This occurred despite drastic worker concessions in 1991 that were supposed to be "the miracle cure to keep the operations afloat." Brian McDougall, president of Local 510 of the Communications, Energy, and Paperworks Union, Canada, said that everyone was devastated and in shock and disbelief.

This example highlights the dilemma facing unions. Many reports indicate that the new millennium will see tough bargaining, with labour–management peace imperilled.

Decision Questions

1. What would you recommend to union workers whose employer is threatening to close down unless they agree to wage or other concessions?
2. Is there some alternative to cutting wages or closing down? What is it?
3. Union workers often feel that the company is bluffing when it threatens to close. How can such doubts be settled so that more open negotiations can take place?
4. Laws have been passed that require plants with more than a certain number of employees to give up to six months' notice of intention to close. Do you think that such legislation helps businesses to show employees that they are serious about closing a plant and thus get concessions from labour? Are such tactics ethical? Do these laws have any effect on investment decisions?

Sources: Susan Bourette, "Labour Peace May Be in Peril," *Globe and Mail, Report on Business,* February 5, 1996, p. B1; Margot Gibb-Clark, "Unions Predict Bargaining 'Tension' in 1996," *Globe and Mail, ROB,* January 3, 1996, p. B15; Gayle MacDonald, "Workplace Experiment Fails to Save Plant," *Globe and Mail, ROB,* February 21, 1996, p. B6. Reprinted with permission from *The Globe and Mail.*

CASE 2

MOMMY AND DADDY TRACKS

In 1989, an article by Felice N. Schwartz called "Management Women and the New Facts of Life" appeared in the *Harvard Business Review.* The article dealt with the increase of women in the workplace and the career challenges they would face in the highly competitive work environment of the 1990s. Schwartz said that the problem in the past has been that women had to choose between the fast track at work or staying home to care for their children. What she proposed was called a "mommy track" in business.

Fundamentally, a woman could opt for one of two choices in her work career. She could choose not to have children and to get on the fast track, thus competing equally with men. Then she would have a shot at making partner in the law firm or chief executive officer in her business career. Or she could choose the mommy track, where options for taking extended leave or working part-time would allow for balancing work and family. The second choice would pretty much preclude a woman from making partner or becoming the top executive. Many women cheered the article because they felt it brought attention to a major issue in employee relations. The National Association of Female Executives membership endorsed the idea with more than a 60-percent majority.

The mommy-track controversy was not overlooked by business. Extended parental leaves, flexible work schedules, and job sharing were just a few of the creative ways business sought to deal with the problem of balancing work and home. Today the controversy has taken a new turn. Daddy tracking is a key employee issue that emerged in the 1990s. The daddy track appears to be reserved mostly for professionals, such as Mark Janosky of Eastman Kodak, who took off four months from the company (with benefits but no pay) to be a full-time father. Janosky is typical of many men trying to balance the questions of career and family. James A. Levine, director of the New York-based Fatherhood Project, suggested that if legal trends continue, firms that offer maternity leaves for women may have to provide paternity leaves for men.

How far will men go toward pursuing the daddy track? It's hard to tell. Men do earn on the average almost 40 percent more than women, so the family budget could suffer a big setback. Also, many men feel the hint of a daddy track could be detrimental to their career and provoke negative reactions from family and work peers.

Even the thought of such a tracking system causes much controversy. The debate is healthy and productive because it is an important question. Canada can only benefit from getting this issue out into the open and trying to develop practical, ethical solutions.

Decision Questions

1. Divide the class into two groups: those who like the idea of mommy and daddy tracks and those who do not. Each group should defend the position it is normally against so you have a chance to view the controversy from the other side. Debate the issue and see if you can come to some consensus.

2. In some European countries companies pay full salaries for up to 15 months to men and women who take family leave. Is such a benefit possible or acceptable in the Canadian system?

3. Is the issue of family responsibility the same for men and women or do you see some real differences? What specific differences, if any, do you note? Should companies put equal emphasis on both mommy tracks and daddy tracks?

4. Do you think it's possible for a man or woman to be on the mommy or daddy track at one stage in life and then move to the career fast track when the children get older?

Sources: "The Mommy Track Debate," *The Wall Street Journal*, May 23, 1989, p. A1; Keith H. Hammonds, "Taking Baby Steps Toward a Daddy Track," *Business Week*, April 15, 1991, pp. 90–92; interviews with LC Consultants, Montreal, June 1996; a variety of newspaper, magazine, and TV news reports, 1999 and 2000.

CBC   VIDEO CASE   www.cbc.ca

RÉSUMÉ LIES This chapter and the previous two chapters have been concerned with the issues relating to employees and their employers. While this chapter concentrates on union–management issues, it also discusses the issues of executives and managers as employees of their companies. Let us expand this category to include the large number of what used to be called *white-collar workers* but are now more accurately known as *knowledge workers*. These are the people who dominate our information age due to the accumulation and flow of information that has become a major component of successful global competitiveness.

Companies today are constantly on the alert to hire these new-age, well-educated, computer-savvy individuals and many graduates are competing for these jobs. As a result, candidates are tempted to dress up their résumés to improve their chances of getting the job. Companies have become more aware of this manipulation and exaggeration of the facts and they have taken measures to cope with the problem.

This video profiles new companies that have sprung up whose job it is to verify the information on applicants' résumés. The fact that they are constantly busy shows that businesses obviously consider the service worth the cost. It is a new specialty because most companies find they do not have the resources or skills to do the job as effectively in-house.

Discussion Questions

1. Are you surprised that companies are so concerned with checking résumés? Why do you think they are concerned? Wouldn't important holes in a new employee's background show up soon enough?

2. Why exaggerate or lie on your résumé when the shortcomings in your background will affect your ability to do the job and lead to your dismissal? If you were hired through an employment agency, wouldn't they give you a black mark when you are fired?

3. What about the issue of trust or confidence when the employer discovers a serious exaggeration or lie? Suppose you are performing well on the job. Do you think that will offset the negative impact of your résumé? What about possible promotions being denied or delayed?

Source: *Venture*, show number 773, "Résumé Lies," February 6, 2001, running time 7:30.

Marketing: Building Customer and Stakeholder Relationships

LEARNING GOALS

AFTER YOU HAVE READ AND STUDIED THIS CHAPTER, YOU SHOULD BE ABLE TO

1. Explain the marketing concept.

2. Give an example of how to use the four Ps of marketing.

3. Describe the marketing research process, and tell how marketers use environmental scanning to learn about the changing marketing environment.

4. Explain various ways of segmenting the consumer market.

5. List several ways in which the business-to-business market differs from the consumer market.

6. Show how the marketing concept has been adapted to fit today's modern markets.

7. Describe the latest marketing strategies, such as stakeholder marketing and customer relationship management.

Robert L. Johnson: BET Holdings Inc.

Courtesy of Black Entertainment Television/Holdings (BET)

Robert L. Johnson is a dreamer, but one who works tirelessly to make his dreams come true. As the ninth of ten children of factory workers, Johnson dreamed of a better life and he knew he needed a good education to get it. He realized his dream when he earned a degree in international affairs from Princeton University. In 1979, when he was vice-president of the U.S. National Cable TV Association, he had a dream of a cable channel targeted to an African American audience. Johnson developed a plan for such a channel, got funding, and bought two hours of weekly satellite time. At 11 p.m. on January 8, 1980, Johnson's dream reached 3.8 million subscribers. The first Black Entertainment Television (BET) signal carried the 1974 African safari movie *Visit to a Chief's Son*. BET now airs 24 hours a day and reaches about 67 million homes, including almost 100 percent of the 6.8 million African American households with cable.

BET Holdings has expanded into a billion-dollar enterprise with two movie channels, a jazz channel, BET Weekend (a weekend newspaper insert), a health and fitness magazine called *Heart and Soul*, a financial services company, a clothing line, an airline called DC Air, and more, including a planned chain of music-themed restaurants. Also in the plans are 10 TV movies, a late-night talk show, and a Las Vegas restaurant.

All of this success is due to an entrepreneur with a vision. Johnson noted that African Americans watched more TV than many groups, and that advertisers wanted to reach them. The market potential was so great that Johnson was able to get funding easily. That's the power of market segmentation—breaking the total market into smaller segments based on age or sex or income or some other category (such as ethnicity)—and then designing products and services to meet the specific needs of those segments.

Once you have found such a market niche, the next step is to develop a close relationship with those customers and develop a loyal following among them. Most of BET's nearly 600 employees are African American. Many of them are young and knowledgeable about their peers. They are able to talk with BET's customers and work with them to develop new goods and services that they want. The African American market segment is made up of some 35 million people, and their incomes are rising fast. Johnson recognizes the fact that there are other market segments that may prove equally profitable. He says, "We're moving toward more market fragmentation, so markets can become sustainable with smaller and smaller numbers, customized down to even one person. . . You can combine strong brand identification with niche marketing if you're nimble."

Media giant Viacom bought BET Holdings for $3 billion in 2000. Viacom has the money, TV movies, feature films, and other resources to greatly improve BET's offerings. Viacom already owned CBS, UPN, MTV, VH1, Nickelodeon, TNN, Showtime, Country Music Television, and TV Land—and some of these shows may soon be shown on BET.

There are marketing opportunities available in other market segments, including people over the age of 60, Asian Americans, and teens. You could be the next entrepreneur who develops TV shows, restaurants, and other products to meet the needs of these specialized market segments. In this chapter, we explore marketing in general and then look at marketing strategies, including market segmentation, targeting, and relationship building.

Sources: Scott S. Smith, "BETting on Success," *Entrepreneur*, August 1999, pp. 112–16; Peter Binzen, "Indian Food Maker Hopes to Fly Like Its Cuisine," *Philadelphia Inquirer*, March 13, 2000, pp. F1, F3; Brian Sharp, "BET Executive Robert Johnson, an Icon in the Making," *Gannett News Service*, June 16, 2000; and Neil Irwin, "Deal Means Potential Change for BET.com," *The Washington Post*, November 4, 2000, pp. E1, E2.

ETHICAL DILEMMA

Wired for Action

Roy, Maria, and Hector are three aging baby boomers, all having crossed the 50-year line this year. They've known each other for several years, through work and recreational contact. At different times each has expressed a desire to start his or her own business. After lengthy discussions they decide to set up shop together, providing recreational products to their contemporaries. Since demographic data points to a surge in the baby boomer population bubble, they believe they can develop a profitable business using their considerable work experience in this area.

Their first hurdle is doing some market research to get specific reliable information about what unfulfilled niches there are in the market. Since all three friends mix extensively with their contemporaries at work, at play, and when socializing, they came up with the idea of wearing concealed tape recorders that will pick up what the people around them are saying. They can throw innocent questions at friends, associates, and so on about products they would like to have but cannot seem to get. They expect everyone to speak freely, without concerns about being recorded. Their plan is to tape conversations for a month, then sit down and screen the tapes carefully to see what useful ideas emerge. They could then compare these ideas with information from business magazines, newspapers, the Internet, and TV programs.

What do you think about the idea of secretly taping people's conversations and comments? Is there anything unethical about this procedure? Would you undertake such a procedure for market research? Would you feel upset about someone taping you secretly? Think about these questions as you go through the chapter and we'll have a look at possible answers at the end.

WHAT IS MARKETING?

marketing
The process of determining customer needs and wants and then developing goods and services that meet or exceed these expectations.

Marketing is the process of determining customer needs and wants and then developing goods and services ➤P. 18◄ that meet or exceed these expectations. Needs are not created by marketers but in fact are basic to all humans and exist at some level. For example, all humans need water, food, and security. If you are hungry, you *need* food; however, do you *want* pasta, a hamburger and fries, or a plate of vegetables to sustain your body? If you choose a hamburger, do you want a McDonald's burger, a Burger King burger, or a Lick's burger? The successful marketer will be able to influence this want by producing a burger that you recognize and believe will meet your need, available at a reasonable price and in a location near you.

market
A group of people with unsatisfied wants and needs, who have the resources, willingness, and authority to buy products.

The main term in marketing is **market**. A market is defined as a group of people with unsatisfied wants and needs, who have the resources, willingness, and authority to buy products. A market is, therefore, created as a result of this demand for goods and services. Thus, if there are people who want a high-fibre, low-sugar cereal—like Fiberrific—and if these people are willing to buy this cereal, can afford the price, and make the final decision to buy the cereal, then there is a market for this product. Later in this chapter we will review the marketing research process that will outline a process to help marketers answer questions such as "Is there a demand for my product?"

Knowing what customers want is much easier today than ever before, because purchases can be recorded in a database.[1] For example, a grocery store that uses such a database knows what each customer has purchased over the last few months. Such purchases may include cereal, milk, baby food, and dog food. From that information, the store knows that the customer likely has small children and a dog. Using that information, the store can send out coupons and advertisements specifically designed to be useful to families with small children and pets. You can see, then, how a store can establish a close relationship with its customers and provide them with a group of goods and services made specifically for their needs.[2] For some issues to consider concerning the ethics of obtaining this type of information, see the Ethical Dilemma box "Wired for Action."

Nonprofit Organizations Use Marketing Too

Even though the marketing concept emphasizes a profit orientation, marketing is a critical part of almost all organizations, whether profit or nonprofit.[3] Charities use marketing to raise funds or to obtain other resources. For example, Canadian Blood Services might run a promotion to encourage people to donate blood when local or national supplies run low. Churches use marketing to attract new members and to raise funds. Politicians use marketing to get votes. Provinces use marketing to attract new businesses and tourists. Schools use marketing to attract new students. Other organizations, such as unions and social groups, also use marketing. The Advertising Council, for example, uses marketing to create awareness and change attitudes on such issues as drunk driving and fire prevention.[4]

www.bloodservices.ca

www.adcouncil.org

A BRIEF HISTORY OF MARKETING

When asked what marketing is, many students initially say "selling" or "advertising." There was a time when the emphasis in marketing was on selling and advertising, but today many organizations have moved beyond this focus. Let us briefly review the evolution of the marketing concept.

Production Era

From the time the first European settlers arrived in Canada until the start of the 1900s, the general philosophy of business was to produce as much as possible. Given the limited production capabilities and the vast demand for products in those days, such a *production orientation* was both logical and profitable as demand exceeded supply. Manufacturers focused on production, as most goods were bought as soon as they became available. The important marketing needs were for distribution and storage.

Sales Era

In the early twentieth century, competition was increasing and businesses developed mass-production techniques. Automobile assembly lines are a prime example of this development. Production capacity and supply often exceeded the immediate market demand and the business philosophy turned to a *sales orientation*. To delete this overcapacity, businesses used selling, advertising, publicity, and sales promotion techniques to sell their products. The philosophy was that consumers would buy due to these techniques.

Marketing Concept Era

After the Second World War (1945), there was tremendous demand for products among the returning veterans, who were starting a new life—many with new families. Competition increased and businesses recognized that they needed to be more responsive to consumers. For the first time, consumers were asked what they wanted at the beginning of the marketing process, rather than having the firm produce first, and then sell later.

marketing concept
A three-part business philosophy:
(1) a customer orientation,
(2) a service orientation,
(3) a profit orientation

The **marketing concept** has three parts:

1. *A customer orientation.* Find out what consumers want and provide it for them. (Note the emphasis on consumers rather than promotion.)

2. *A service orientation.* Make sure everyone in the organization has the same objective—*customer satisfaction.* This should be a total and integrated organizational effort.

3. *A profit orientation.* Market those goods and services that will earn the firm a profit and enable it to survive and expand to serve more consumer wants and needs.

It took a while for businesses to implement the marketing concept. During the 1980s, businesses began to apply the marketing concept more aggressively than they had done over the preceding 30 years.

Market Orientation Era

customer relationship management (CRM)
Learning as much as possible about customers and doing everything you can to satisfy them or even delight them with goods and services over time.

In the 1990s, managers extended the marketing concept by adopting the concept of customer relationship management. **Customer relationship management (CRM)** is learning as much as possible about customers and doing everything you can to satisfy them or even delight them with goods and services over time.[5] The idea is to get very close to your present customers and to spend more time with them rather than to constantly seek new customers. We shall explore this concept in more depth later in the chapter.

A firm that practises a *market orientation* focuses its efforts on (1) continuously collecting information about customers' needs and competitors' capabilities, (2) sharing this information across departments, and (3) using the information to create customer value.[6] As discussed in Chapter 8, a SWOT analysis ➤**P. 223**◄ is a technique that can provide internal company information (specifically its strengths and weaknesses) and external company information (specifically opportunities and threats). The marketing environment that will be discussed later in this chapter highlights the five main factors that will impact a firm. By continuously collecting this information and monitoring the environment, a firm will be in a stronger position to create customer value through its offerings.

www.crm-forum.com

This site is for CRM Forum Academy. It features academic papers on the topic of customer relationship management and conferencing facilities for its members to discuss these issues.

The Importance of Ethics

Marketers today recognize that their behaviour and products impact not only their consumers, but also society in general. By focusing on all three elements—the needs of consumers, the firm's goals, and the interests of society—an organization is adopting a broader *societal marketing orientation.* There is much pressure on businesses to become involved in programs designed to train the disadvantaged, improve the community, reduce the use of energy and pollution emissions, involve employees in community projects, and generally respond to the broader needs of society.

www.jnj.com

An example is the Johnson & Johnson (J&J) recall of its Tylenol product in 1982. Eleven people died from swallowing cyanide-laced capsules, and although the firm believed that the pills had been altered in only a few stores, not in the factory, J&J quickly recalled its entire product. The recall cost the company $240 million in earnings, but in the long run the company's swift recall of Tylenol strengthened consumer confidence and loyalty.[7]

There was more. J&J immediately stopped advertising the product and made television announcements advising the public of the problem, it established a hotline, and it offered a refund to those who had purchased capsules. Finally, J&J quickly redesigned the package to make it more tamper-resistant.[8]

www.bridgestone.com

The Ford Explorer (rollovers) and Firestone (tread separation) situation highlights a different approach. The Bridgestone/Firestone Inc. recall of 6.5 million defective tires in August 2000 was implemented only after months of vague and inconsistent communication.[9] The firm has alleged that the Explorer's design was partly to blame for the rollovers, while Ford Motor Company points to the tires.

In October 2001, the U.S. National Highway Traffic Safety Administration ordered the tire maker to replace 3.5 million more tires after a $1\frac{1}{2}$-year investigation.[10] While John Lampe, CEO, does not agree with these findings, "we have decided that it is in the best interests of our company, our employees, our dealers and our customers if we replace the tires in question and close this chapter in the company's history."[11]

As a result of this situation, Ford Motor Company ended its long-time relationship with the company and victims have initiated lawsuits claiming criminal negligence.

CRITICAL THINKING

Using the concept of "Find a need and fill it," which of your needs are not being met by businesses in your area? Are there enough people with similar needs to attract a business that would meet those needs? How would you find out?

MARKETING MANAGEMENT AND THE MARKETING MIX

Implementing the marketing concept has led to more emphasis on marketing management and pleasing the customer — now the priority. **Marketing management** is the process of planning and executing the conception, pricing, promotion, and distribution (place) of products to create mutually beneficial exchanges. The idea is to please customers *and* make a profit doing so.

marketing management
The process of planning and executing the conception, pricing, promotion, and distribution (place) of products to create mutually beneficial exchanges.

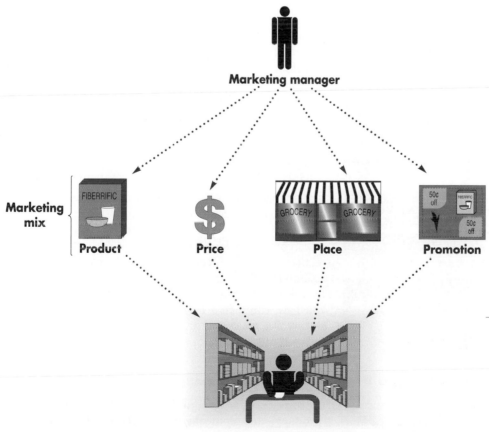

Cohesive marketing program aimed at satisfying customers

FIGURE 15.1

THE MARKETING MIX AND THE MARKETING MANAGER'S ROLE

The marketing manager chooses the proper product, price, promotion, and place to develop a comprehensive marketing program. This figure shows the mix for a new cereal.

Find a need

Conduct research

Design a product to meet the need based on research

Conduct product testing

Determine a brand name and design a package

Set an appropriate price

Select a distribution system

Design a promotional program

Build a relationship with customers

marketing mix
The ingredients that go into a marketing program: product, price, place, and promotion.

Much of what marketing managers do has been conveniently divided into four factors, called the *four Ps*, to make them easy to remember and implement. They are:

1. Product (to be discussed more fully in Chapter 16)
2. Price (to be discussed more fully in Chapter 16)
3. Place (to be discussed more fully in Chapter 17)
4. Promotion (to be discussed more fully in Chapter 17)

Managing the controllable parts of the marketing process, then, involves: (1) designing a want-satisfying *product*, (2) setting a *price* for the product, (3) distributing the product to a *place* where people will buy it, and (4) *promoting* the product. These four factors are sometimes called the **marketing mix** because they're the ingredients that go into a marketing program. A marketing manager designs a marketing program that effectively combines the ingredients of the marketing mix (see Figure 15.1).

Applying the Marketing Process

One of the best ways for you to understand the marketing process is to take a product and follow the process that led to the development and sale of that product (see Figure 15.2). Remember that the basis of marketing is finding a need and filling it. So your first step is to find a need. Imagine that you and your friends don't have time to eat big breakfasts. You want something for breakfast that's fast, nutritious, and good tasting. Some of your friends eat a cereal made with 100-percent natural oats and honey, but you and others are not happy with this product. In fact, you know that the Centre for the Public Interest named this cereal number one on its list of "10 Foods You Should Never Eat!" because of its high sugar content. Furthermore, you've read in a magazine that the cereal industry has been slow to innovate.[12] You sense opportunity.

You ask around among your acquaintances and find that a huge demand exists for a good-tasting breakfast cereal that's nutritious, high in fibre, and low in sugar. This fact leads you to conduct a more extensive marketing research study to determine whether there's a large enough market for such a cereal. Your research supports your assumption: there *is* a large market for a high-fibre cereal. By now it's becoming obvious that you have found a need. You have completed one of the first steps in marketing: researching consumer wants and needs and finding a need for a product that's not yet available.

Designing a Product to Meet Needs

product
Any physical good, service, or idea that satisfies a want or need.

Once you have researched consumer needs, the four Ps of marketing begin. You start by developing a product. A **product** is any physical good, service, or idea that satisfies a want or need. In this case, your proposed product is a multigrain cereal made with an artificial sweetener. It's a good idea at this point to conduct *concept testing*. That is, you develop an accurate description of your product and ask people, in person or online, whether the concept (the idea of the cereal) appeals to them.[13] If it does, you might go to a manufacturer that has the equipment and skills to design such a cereal, and begin making prototypes. *Prototypes* are samples of the product that you take to consumers to test their reactions. The process of testing products among potential users, for a limited time and in a specific area or areas, is called **test marketing**.

For our cereal, while the whole market may be considered Canada, test marketing may occur in a limited number of cities across the country, instead of every single province and territory. The costs would be too high to completely test the product everywhere, and these experimental markets can provide a reliable estimate of product demand at a more reasonable cost.

If consumers like the product and agree they would buy it, you may turn the production process over to an existing manufacturer or you may decide to produce the cereal yourself. *Outsourcing,* **▶P. 278◀** remember, is the term used to describe the allocation of production and other functions to outside firms. The idea is to retain only those functions that you can do most efficiently and outsource the rest.

Once the product meets taste and quality expectations, you have to design a package and think of an appropriate brand name.[14] A **brand name** is a word, letter, or group of words or letters that differentiates one seller's goods and services from those of competitors. Cereal brand names, for example, include Cheerios, Frosted Flakes, and Raisin Bran. Let's say that you name your cereal Fiberrific to emphasize the high fibre content and terrific taste. We'll discuss the product development process, including packaging, branding, and pricing, in detail in Chapter 16. In other chapters, we will follow the Fiberrific case to show you how the concepts apply to one particular product. For now, we're simply sketching the whole process to give you an idea of what the overall marketing picture is all about. So far, we've only covered the first P of the marketing mix: product. Next comes price.

Setting an Appropriate Price

After you've developed the good or designed the service you want to offer consumers, you have to set an appropriate *price*. That price depends on a number of factors. For example, the price could be similar to what other cereal makers charge since most cereals are priced competitively. You also have to consider the costs involved in producing, distributing, and promoting the product. We shall discuss all of these issues in more detail in Chapter 16.

Getting the Product to the Right Place

Once the product is manufactured, you have to decide how to get it to the consumer.[15] Remember, *place* is the third P in the marketing mix. You may want to sell the cereal directly to supermarkets or health food stores, or you may want to sell it through organizations that specialize in distributing food products. Such organizations, called *intermediaries*, are in the middle of a series of organizations that distribute goods from producers to consumers. (The more traditional word for such companies is *middlemen.*) Getting the product to consumers when and where they want it is critical to market success. We'll discuss the importance of marketing intermediaries and distribution in detail in Chapter 17.

Developing an Effective Promotional Strategy

The last of the four Ps of marketing is promotion. **Promotion** consists of all the techniques sellers use to motivate people to buy products. They include advertising; personal selling; public relations; word-of-mouth; and various sales promotion efforts, such as coupons, rebates, samples, and cents-off deals.[16] Promotion is discussed in detail in Chapter 17.

This last step in the marketing process often includes relationship building with customers. That includes responding to suggestions consumers may make to

test marketing
The process of testing products among potential users, for a limited time and in a specfic area.

brand name
A word, letter, or group of words or letters that differentiates one seller's goods and services from those of competitors.

promotion
All the techniques sellers use to motivate people to buy goods or services.

improve the product or its marketing. Postpurchase, or after-sale, service may include exchanging goods that weren't satisfactory and making other adjustments to ensure consumer satisfaction, including recycling. Marketing is an ongoing process. To remain competitive, companies must continually adapt to changes in the market and to changes in consumer wants and needs.

PROGRESS CHECK

- What are the three parts of the marketing concept?
- What are the four Ps of the marketing mix?

PROVIDING MARKETERS WITH INFORMATION

marketing research
The analysis of markets to determine opportunities and challenges, and to find the information needed to make good decisions.

Every step in the marketing process depends on information that is used to make the right decisions. **Marketing research** is the analysis of markets to determine opportunities and challenges and to find the information needed to make good decisions. If you were to major in marketing, marketing research would be one of the courses you would likely take.

Marketing research helps determine what customers have purchased in the past, and what situational changes have occurred to alter not only what consumers want now but also what they're likely to want in the future. In addition, marketers conduct research on business trends, the ecological impact of their decisions, international trends, and more. Businesses need information to compete effectively, and marketing research is the activity that gathers that information. Note, too, that in addition to listening to customers, marketing researchers should pay attention to what employees, shareholders, dealers, consumer advocates, media representatives, and other stakeholders have to say.

The Marketing Research Process

The marketing research process consists of four key steps:

1. Defining the problem (or opportunity) and determining the present situation.

2. Collecting data.

3. Analyzing the research data.

4. Choosing the best solutions.

The following sections look at each of these steps.

Defining the Problem (or Opportunity) and Determining the Present Situation It's important to know what an organization does well; it's also critical to know what it doesn't do so well. Marketing researchers should be given the freedom to help discover what the present situation is, what the problems or opportunities are, what the alternatives are, what information is needed, and how to go about gathering and analyzing data.

Collecting Data Obtaining usable information is vital to the marketing research process. You must first determine the scope and estimated costs of doing research. Research can become quite expensive, so some trade-off must often be made between the need for information and the cost of obtaining that information.

secondary data
Information that has already been collected by other sources, for their own purposes.

Normally, it is quicker and less expensive to gather information that has already been compiled by others. These existing data, called **secondary data**, can be found within an organization (e.g., the accounting department has a copy of last month's balance sheet), in published newspapers, magazines, and textbooks, and online. Figure 15.3 lists some sources of secondary marketing research information. You are encouraged to visit your library to see what sources are available to you.

Often, secondary data does not provide all the information necessary. This data was collected for other purposes and it may be out of date, incomplete, or not applicable to your specific problem or opportunity. When additional in-depth data is needed, marketers must do their own research. The collection of this new information is called **primary data**. Primary data are facts and figures that you have gathered on your own.

primary data
Information collected for specific purposes.

FIGURE 15.3

SOURCES OF PRIMARY AND SECONDARY INFORMATION

PRIMARY INFORMATION

Observation	Personal interview
Survey/questionnaire	Focus group

SECONDARY INFORMATION

Government Publications

Annual Retail Trade
Canadian Economic Observer
Family Expenditure Guide
Market Research Handbook
Statistics Canada Catalogue

Newspapers

The Globe and Mail
The National Post
The Wall Street Journal
Local newspapers

Internal Sources

Company records
Financial statements
prior research reports

Indexes and Directories

Business Periodical Index
Canadian Business Index
Canadian Statistics Index
Scott's Directories
Standards Periodical Directory

Trade Sources

A.C. Nielsen
Conference Board of Canada
Compusearch
Dun & Bradstreet

General Internet Sites

Strategis: Industry Canada's Web site—
www.strategis.ic.gc.ca

Statistics Canada's Web site — www.statcan.ca

To find a business or person —
canada411.sympatico.ca

Track market news, industries,
annual reports, etc. — ca.finance.yahoo.com

Periodicals

Advertising Age
Adweek
Journal of Marketing
Marketing Magazine

Databases

ABI Inform
CANSIM (Statistics Canada)
CPI.Q

One primary research technique is *observation*. This occurs when trained people observe and record the actions of potential buyers. For example, companies have followed customers into supermarkets to record their purchasing behaviours for products such as meat, bread, and laundry detergent. These marketers may observe that consumers do not bend to look at products, that they compare prices, and that they touch the product to see how heavy it is. This method may provide insight into behaviours that consumers do not even know they exhibit when shopping. Do you think that the observation method would be helpful in gathering the information you need to promote Fiberrific?

A more formal way to gather primary data is to develop a list of questions and to conduct a *survey* (also known as a questionnaire). Telephone surveys, mail surveys, and online surveys are the most common forms. Often confidential, you can use the information to understand behaviours, perceptions, preferences, and opinions. While the information gathered is useful, there are some disadvantages to this method. Not everyone who is approached may be willing to answer your questions, respondents may not be truthful, and, for written surveys, not everyone can read and write. To increase the response and accuracy rate, marketers use personal interviews.

Personal interviews are a face-to-face opportunity to ask consumers prepared questions. While it is easy for consumers to throw out a mail survey or ignore an online survey, marketers may be more successful with this method. While this research method can be more expensive than surveys, the interviewer has the opportunity to observe reactions and to dig a little deeper with the questions if the respondent wishes to add more information. As with surveys and interviews, this method is useful to understand behaviours, perceptions, preferences, and opinions.

Focus groups are another method of gathering primary data. A *focus group* is a small group of people (usually 8 to 14 individuals) who meet under the direction of a discussion leader. These respondents are asked to communicate their opinions about an organization, its products, or other issues. Have you ever been approached to answer questions at school, in a mall, or in a grocery store?

focus group
A small group of people who meet under the direction of a discussion leader to communicate their opinions about an organization, its products, or other issues.

One-way glass walls enable managers and employees to watch consumers as they discuss various aspects of a company and its products. From those discussions, companies learn exactly what consumers like and dislike about products and what they would like to see developed in the future. Can you imagine professors using such techniques to learn about various lectures and how they might be improved?

Analyzing the Research Data The data collected in the research process must be turned into useful information. Careful and unbiased interpretation of the data collected can help a company find useful alternatives to specific marketing challenges. For example, Fresh Italy, a small Italian pizzeria, found in its research that its pizza's taste was rated superior compared to the larger pizza chains. However, the company's sales lagged behind the competition. Research pointed out that free delivery (which Fresh Italy did not offer) was more important to customers than taste. Fresh Italy now delivers and has increased its market share.

Choosing the Best Solutions After collecting and analyzing data, market researchers determine alternative strategies and make recommendations as to which strategy may be best and why. Once a strategy is chosen, it is to be implemented and the results reviewed periodically to see if results meet expectations.

If not successful, the company can take corrective action and conduct new studies in the ongoing attempt to provide consumer satisfaction at the lowest cost. You can see, then, that marketing research is a continuous process of responding to changes in the marketplace and changes in consumer preferences.

Company Web sites have vastly improved the marketing research process in both domestic and global markets. Businesses can now continuously interact with their customers as they strive to improve goods and services.[17] The information exchanged can be very useful in determining what customers want. Keeping customer information in a database enables a company to improve its product offerings over time and to design promotions that are geared exactly to meet the needs of specific groups of consumers. That is the idea behind continuous improvement ➤**P. 275**◂.

In today's customer-driven market, ethics is also important in every aspect of marketing. Companies should therefore do what's right as well as what's profitable. This step could add greatly to the social benefits of marketing decisions.

The Marketing Environment

A market orientation requires that managers are aware of the surrounding environment when making marketing-mix decisions. **Environmental scanning** is the process of identifying the factors that can affect marketing success. When developing a SWOT analysis, (as discussed in Chapter 8 ➤**P. 223**◂) environmental scanning highlights the opportunities and threats that may impact the firm. As you can see in Figure 15.4, these five factors include global, technological, social, competitive, and economic influences. Firms cannot control these factors, but through their own strengths and weaknesses (controllable factors) firms can try to take advantage of opportunities and can try to minimize the negative impact of threats.

Global Factors A dramatic global change is the elimination of borders and the growth of the Internet. Now businesses can reach many of the consumers in the world relatively easily and carry on a dialogue with them about the products they want. This globalization ➤**P. 9**◂ puts more pressure on domestic firms as they need to be able to compete with international firms. This global trend is creating opportunities for increased revenues for companies such as FedEx and Purolator, which have a strong reputation for delivering goods quickly. The Reaching Beyond Our Borders box "Canadian Cancer Drug Hits the World Market" describes how one Canadian company has seen global success.

environmental scanning
The process of identifying the factors that can affect marketing success.

FIGURE 15.4

THE MARKETING ENVIRONMENT

Technological Factors The most important technological changes also involve the Internet and the growth of consumer databases. Using databases, companies can develop products that closely match the needs of consumers. As you read in Chapter 10, it is now possible to produce customized goods and services for about the same price as mass-produced goods. Thus, flexible manufacturing and mass customization are also major influences on marketers. Consequently, if an organization does not integrate these technological changes (while its competitors are doing so), this may create a threat to its revenues and profits, potentially impacting its ability to attract investors and retain its workforce.

Social Factors Changing demographics, for example, are social trends that can affect sales. The fastest-growing segment of the Canadian population is the baby boomers. By 2031, one in every four Canadians will be 65 years or older.[18] As this segment ages, there will be growing demand for recreation, travel, continuing education, health care, and nursing homes. As well, opportunities exist for firms that target Canada's 2.4 million "tweens" (ages 9 to 14).[19] According to a study conducted by YTV, these children of the baby boomers control $1.8 billion in spending with most of their money spent on candy, clothes, shoes, and music.[20]

Competitive Factors Many brick-and-mortar companies must be aware of new competition from the Internet, including those that sell automobiles, insurance, music, videos, clothes, groceries, and more.[21] In the book business, Chapters Online competes with Amazon.com's huge selection of books; while Chapters Online stocks almost 50,000 of the best-selling titles, Amazon stocks hundreds of thousands of titles.[22] Now that consumers can search the world for the best buys through the Internet, marketers must adjust their pricing policies accordingly. The following scenario will give you some insight into what is happening between these two players:[23]

> Amazon.com is preparing to slash prices for books, music and videos as the crucial Christmas season approaches. In an interview, Chapters Online president Peter Cooper responded "To bring customers online because prices are cheaper is a recipe for financial disaster. Retailers can't survive on the thin margins that result from this discounting… Select items will continue to be discounted but we are not going to be participating in a price war…We have to be absolutely rigorous in countering with service, availability, and value."

Continuous environmental scanning discovers trends, and successful firms react quickly to both opportunities and threats in their environment.

Economic Factors Marketers must pay close attention to both upturns and downturns in the economy. The unemployment rate and the level of disposable income (income that is left after taxes) are indicators of the financial potential of consumers. During recessions, consumers put off buying luxury goods such as expensive automobiles, and vacations. The opposite tends to be true during periods of economic prosperity. Marketers have to adapt by offering products that are less expensive or more tailored to consumers with modest incomes.[24] As an example, when the economy slows down, consumers are more likely to do more of their own repairs and projects in the home versus hiring out these services. This has created opportunities for retailers such as Home Depot, which has responded to this trend by offering free sessions, such as how to build a deck or how to lay patio stones. The company's intention is that once this relationship is established, these consumers will purchase their supplies at Home Depot locations instead of going to a competitor.

Calgary-based Liquidation World, Canada's largest liquidator, has been successful when the economy has been strong or weak. How is this possible? Dale Gillespie, CEO, responds "when times are good, customers have more to spend, and manufacturers get rid of excess inventory more willingly. When times are tough, cash-

www.homedepot.com

www.liquidationworld.com

strapped shoppers beat down the door in search of low prices. As more and more businesses are boarded up, Liquidation World is there to snatch up their inventories at rock-bottom prices."[25]

CRITICAL THINKING

What environmental changes are occurring in your community? What environmental changes in marketing are most likely to change your career prospects in the future? How can you learn more about those changes? What might you do to prepare for them?

REACHING BEYOND OUR BORDERS
Canadian Cancer Drug Hits the World Market

QLT Phototherapeutics Inc., formerly Quadra Logic Technologies Inc., of Vancouver, is hitting the headlines with an unusual new cancer drug. Photofrin is a light-activated drug that treats patients who have esophageal cancer. The drug has been many years in development and has been slowly gaining approval from governments around the world. As of December 1995, Japan, Canada, and the Netherlands had approved Photofrin for treating several types of cancer.

The big battle had been to get into the U.S. market, which required approval from the U.S. Food and Drug Administration (FDA). As the FDA receives many requests for drug approval and is naturally very cautious before giving the go-ahead, it takes some time before products are approved. In the summer of 1995, QLT was finally given the green light to market Photofrin in the United States. By early 1999 a few more European countries had approved usage of Photophrin.

People who have esophageal cancer suffer from a slowly constricting throat until eventually they cannot even swallow their own saliva, let alone eat or drink. Some 13,000 Canadians and Americans die annually of this disease.

Photofrin is the first of a new type of drug that makes possible what is called *photodynamic therapy*. What happens is that the drug makes the tumour sensitive to light, and the light then kills the cancer cells. The way Photofrin works in the esophagus is quite extraordinary. First, Photofrin is injected into the patient. Some hours later, fibre-optic cables are inserted into the esophagus and a bright light is directed at the tumour. The light activates the Photofrin, which leads to the production of free radicals that kill the cancer cells. This enables patients to once again swallow on their own.

According to FDA drug chief Dr. Robert Temple, "it only makes you sick where the light hits it," which is an obvious advantage for treating cancer patients. He indicates that photodynamic therapy is also being tested for treatment against other tumours affecting the bladder and the bronchial tubes.

In 1999 QLT announced it had concluded arrangements with the Ciba Vision Corp., a subsidiary of the giant international pharmaceutical company Novartis, for the marketing of a new drug. This drug, vertoporfin, to be sold as Visudyne, was developed for the treatment of macular degeneration, a serious eye problem that is a common cause of blindness for people under 50.

This Canadian company, founded by University of British Columbia (UBC) researcher Dr. Julia Levy in the late 1980s, is aided in its research by Dr. David Dolphin, also of UBC. The company employs well over 100 researchers; many are graduates from UBC. QLT has been the recipient of important financial aid from the Natural Sciences and Engineering Research Council (NSERC). The close co-operation between NSERC, UBC, and QIT is a good example of what is required today to generate successful companies in the high-tech world. QLT is a company on the cutting edge of biotechnology, which is expected to play a very important role in the twenty-first century. QLT is developing products for global use and is organizing a marketing system that will enable it to reach well beyond Canadian borders.

Sources: Natural Sciences and Engineering Research Council Web site, <www.nserc.ca>; Canada NewsWire Web site, <www.newswire.ca>, August 18, 1999. "QLT Given Green Light to Market Cancer Drug," *Globe and Mail, Report on Business*, December 28, 1995, p. B2.

RECOGNIZING DIFFERENT MARKETS: CONSUMER AND BUSINESS-TO-BUSINESS

Marketers must know as much as possible about the market they wish to serve. A market consists of people with similar unsatisfied wants and needs who have both the resources and the willingness to buy. Thus, if there are people who want a high-fibre, low-sugar cereal, like Fiberrific, and if those people have the resources and willingness to buy it, then it is said that there's a market for Fiberrific.

There are two major markets in business: the consumer market and the business-to-business market. The **consumer market** consists of all the individuals or households that want goods and services for personal use. The **business-to-business (B2B) market** consists of all the individuals and organizations that want products to use in producing other products or to sell, rent, or supply products to others for business purposes. Oil drilling bits, cash registers, display cases, office desks, public accounting audits, and corporate legal advice are examples of B2B goods and services. Traditionally, they have been known as *industrial goods and services* because they were used in industry.

The important thing to remember is that the buyer's reason for buying—that is, the end use of the product—determines whether a product is considered a consumer product or a B2B product. For example, a box of Fiberrific cereal bought for a family's breakfast is considered a consumer product. However, if the same box of Fiberrific were purchased by Dinnie's Diner to sell to its breakfast customers, it would be considered a B2B product. The following sections will outline in more detail consumer and B2B markets.

consumer market
All the individuals or households that want goods and services for personal consumption or use.

business-to-business (B2B) market
All the individuals and organizations that want products to use in producing other products or to sell, rent, or supply products to others for business purposes.

PROGRESS CHECK

- What are the four parts of the marketing research process?
- What is environmental scanning?
- Can you define the terms *consumer market* and *business-to-business market*?

THE CONSUMER MARKET AND MARKET SEGMENTATION

mass marketing
Developing products and promotions to please large groups of people.

In the world of mass production following the Industrial Revolution ►P. 6◄, marketers responded by practising mass marketing. **Mass marketing** means developing products and promotions to please large groups of people. The mass marketer tries to sell the same product to as many people as possible using mass media such as TV, radio, and newspapers. Although mass marketing initially led to success for many firms (as demand exceeded supply and there were fewer competitors), marketers often got so caught up in their products and competition that they became less responsive to the market. This created an opportunity: for other, more responsive, firms to enter the industry and meet these unfulfilled needs. Levi Strauss, for example, lost a good deal of its market share because it didn't respond quickly enough to new consumer tastes.

In his famous article titled "Marketing Myopia," Theodore Levitt speaks of the pitfalls that some industries have encountered because they defined themselves too narrowly. In his opinion, the railroads were in trouble because they let others take customers away from them because they assumed themselves to be in the railroad business rather than in the transportation business. At the onset of television, had Hollywood been customer-oriented (providing entertainment) rather than product-oriented (making movies), it too would not have gone through such a drastic reorganization.[26]

With a Canadian population of over 31 million people, Canadian marketers can look beyond our borders and view the total potential consumer market as consisting of more than 6 billion people in global markets. The movement toward a more global economy and the increasing use of the Internet makes these international markets accessible for our products. Because consumer groups differ greatly in age, education, income level, and tastes, a business cannot fill the needs of every individual. So, for the most part, a mass marketing strategy will not be successful today.

The process of dividing the total market into several groups whose members have similar characteristics is called **market segmentation**. Marketing directed toward those groups (market segments) that an organization decides it can serve profitably is called **target marketing**.

Take Campbell soups, for example. Campbell is known for its traditional soups, such as chicken noodle, tomato, and cream of mushroom. Campbell has also expanded it product lines to appeal to a number of different tastes. Campbell noticed the population growth in the American South and in the Latino community in cities across the United States, so it introduced a Creole soup for the southern market and a red bean soup for the Latino market. In Texas and California, where people like spicy food, Campbell makes its nacho cheese soup spicier than in other parts of the country. Campbell is just one company that has had some success studying the consumer market, breaking it down into categories, and then developing products for separate groups of consumers.

The following sections will highlight the different levels of market segmentation and the bases that marketers can use to try to segment a market. The best segmentation strategy is to try to use *all* the bases to come up with a target market that is sizeable, reachable, and profitable for the organization.

Levels of Market Segmentation

The first level of market segmentation is mass marketing. As implied earlier, this is the simplest method, as a marketer treats consumers as one market. The advantages of this approach are that organizations can take advantage of economies of scale (as they are producing one or several products) and lower promotional costs due to bulk purchases of promotional tools (e.g. TV). Unfortunately, this approach does not consider the differences among consumers. Oftentimes, one product cannot meet all the needs and wants of all consumers.

market segmentation
The process of dividing the total market into several groups whose members have similar characteristics.

target marketing
Marketing directed toward those groups (market segments) that an organization decides it can serve profitably.

www.campbellsoup.com

One to one marketing means designing a separate product for each individual customer. An example is Kool Calendars. Using Xerox technology, the company can take pictures that you give it and make a customized calendar from those pictures. It is easier to customize services because you only have to find what a customer wants and then adapt the service accordingly. For example, it is relatively easy to customize a workout schedule at a health club. What other services could be customized to each individual?

William Steinmetz/Philia Inquirer

niche marketing
The process of finding small but profitable market segments and designing products for them.

one-to-one (individual) marketing
Developing a unique mix of goods and services for each individual customer.

relationship marketing
Marketing with the goal to keep individual customers over time by offering them products that exactly meet their requirements.

www.cibc.com

www.levi.com/original_ spin
Find out how to own a pair of Levi's jeans that are customized to fit specific preferences: Levi's Original Spin lets customers create their own pants.

Niche marketing is the process of finding small but profitable market segments and designing products for them. Just how small such a segment can be is illustrated by Fridgedoor.com. This company sells refrigerator magnets on the Internet. It keeps some 1,500 different magnets in stock and sells as many as 400 a week.[27]

One-to-one (also known as individual) marketing means developing a unique mix of goods and services for each individual customer. Travel agencies often develop such packages—including airline reservations, hotel reservations, rental cars, restaurants, and admission to museums and other attractions—for individual customers, based on their own tastes and requirements.

Moving toward Relationship Marketing The goal of **relationship marketing** is to keep individual customers over time by offering them products that exactly meet their requirements. The latest in technology enables sellers to work with individual buyers to determine their wants and needs and to develop goods and services specifically designed for them (e.g., hand-tailored shirts and unique vacations). One-way messages in mass media give way to a personal dialogue among participants. The following are just a couple examples of relationship marketing:

• Computer companies such as Dell and Gateway, which sell only via the Internet directly to consumers, have had phenomenal success. They package a computer, printer, and other peripherals to the exact requirements of each customer. The product is delivered directly to the customer with detailed instructions for assembly, backed up by seven-day, 24-hour service by phone or the Internet.

• Airlines, rental car companies, and hotels have frequent user programs through which loyal customers can earn special services and awards. For example, a traveller can earn bonus points good for free flights on an airline. 1,400 CIBC Visa Aerogold members fly free every day.[28] Customers can also earn benefits at a car rental agency (including no stopping at the rental desk—just pick up a car and go), and special services at a hotel including faster check-in and check-out procedures, flowers in the room, free breakfasts, and free use of exercise rooms.

Relationship marketing is more concerned with retaining old customers than with creating new ones. Special deals, fantastic service, and loyalty programs are just the beginning. By maintaining current databases, companies can custom-make products for individuals. Levi Strauss tried to recapture lost market share by permitting some stores to sell custom-made Levi's for about $10 more than mass-produced Levi's. Through an agreement with Levi's, once the store has your measurements you can be assured of a perfect fit every time (as long as you don't gain or lose weight) at a reasonable price. The Spotlight on Small Business box "Relationship Marketing

Relationship marketing is especially important for lifetime services such as financial planning and insurance. The idea is to establish a relationship with the customer to learn all of his or her needs and then to develop a product that will serve those needs over a long period of time. Can you see how relationship marketing would help someone trying to sell computer consulting services?

of Bicycles" shows how a small business can compete with larger firms by using relationship marketing.

Forming Communities of Buyers Relationship marketing eventually leads to a dialogue with customers, often on the Internet (e.g., consumer chat rooms).[29] Fly & Field, for example, is a small store that sells fly-fishing equipment. Fly fishers are a relatively small market locally, but a nice-sized market nationally. To reach the national audience, Fly & Field has established an interactive Web site (www.fly-field.com) where customers and prospects can chat with each other. Naturally, visitors to the site can also access fly-fishing materials and an online catalogue where they can buy what they want.

Many companies are using interactive Web sites as part of the move from relationship marketing to forming communities of buyers. Others are using a wide variety of activities. Harley-Davidson has a 220,000-member club that has its own newsletter, meetings, and rallies. The Wally Byam Caravan Club is made up of owners of Airstream trailers and motor homes; they have events for which the manufacturer sends merchandise, information, giveaway items, and more. Community bonding leads to a strong commitment to the products and the company. Such loyalty is hard to match.

SPOTLIGHT ON SMALL BUSINESS

www.zanescycles.com

Relationship Marketing of Bicycles

Putting into practice old marketing techniques has enabled small retailers to compete with the giants such as Wal-Mart and Sears. Zane's Cycles in Branford, Connecticut, is a good example. Chris Zane, the owner, began the shop when he was still a teenager. Early on, he learned that to keep customers a store has to offer outstanding service and more. The principle behind such service is a concept now called *customer relationship management*. Long before such a concept emerged, however, small stores knew that the secret to long-term success against giant competitors is to give superior service.

Most large stores focus on making a sale, and give follow-up service little thought. The goal is to make the transaction, and that is the end of it; thus, such an approach is called *transactional marketing*.

With relationship marketing, on the other hand, the goal is to keep a customer for life. Zane's Cycles attracts customers by setting competitive prices (and providing free coffee). Zane keeps customers by giving them free lifetime service on their bicycles. He also sells helmets to young people at cost to encourage safety.

Zane keeps a database on customers so he knows what they need and when they will need it. For example, if he sells a bicycle with a child's seat, he knows that soon that customer may be buying a regular bicycle for the child and he can send out an appropriate brochure at just the right time. Zane encourages people to give him their names, addresses, and other such information by offering to make exchanges without receipts for those people whose transaction information is in the database.

Zane also establishes close community relationships by providing scholarships for local students. Because of Zane's competitive prices, great service, and community involvement, his customers recommend his shop to others. No large store can compete with Zane's in the areas of friendly service and personal attention to each customer. That is what the new style of marketing is all about.

Sources: Rekha Balu, "Listen Up," *Fast Company*, May 2000, pp. 304–14; Ross Atkin, "Getting Past the Schwinn Mentality," *The Christian Science Monitor*, August 8, 2000, p. 16, and Donna Fenn, "A Bigger Wheel," *Inc.*, November 2000, pp. 78–88.

geographic segmentation
Dividing a large market by geographic area.

census metropolitan area (CMA)
A geographic area that has a population of 100,000 or more inhabitants.

www.statcan.ca

The Statistics Canada Web site provides useful segmentation information that is collected periodically. Results from the 2001 Census will be released in increments from Spring 2002 to May 2003.

www.lexus.com

demographic segmentation
Dividing the market by age, income, and education level.

psychographic segmentation
Dividing the market according to personality or lifestyle.

www.pepsi.com

behavioural segmentation
Dividing the market based on behaviour with or toward a product.

Bases for Segmenting the Consumer Market

There are several bases that an organization can use to segment, or divide, the consumer market. Figure 15.5 summarizes some of the main dimensions of geographic, demographic, psychographic, and behavioural segmentation.

Geographic segmentation is the oldest and easiest method to segment a market, as a manager could divide a large market (e.g., the whole of Canada) by geographic area. For example, rather than trying to sell Fiberrific throughout Canada, one might try to focus on just one or two regions, or even cities.

A **census metropolitan area (CMA)** is a geographic area that has a population of 100,000 or more inhabitants. The following approximations outline Canada's largest CMAs: Toronto (4.75 million); Montreal (3.48 million); and Vancouver (2.05 million).[30] As a marketer, if you wished to target Fiberrific to only one city, you might decide to target one of these CMAs due to the large consumer base.

Alternatively, you could aim Fiberrific's promotions toward people aged 25 to 45 who have a college or university education and have above-average incomes. Automobiles such as Lexus are often targeted to this audience. This segment is interested in health and fitness and might respond to a new, healthy cereal. Segmentation by age, income, and education level are examples of **demographic segmentation**.

You may want Fiberrific ads to portray a group's lifestyle. To do that, you could study the group's values, attitudes, and interests. This segmentation strategy is called **psychographic segmentation**. Psychographic segmentation divides the market according to personality or lifestyle. For example, if you decide to target Generation Y (teenagers), you would do an in-depth study of their values and interests. Such research reveals which TV shows they watch and which celebrities they like the best. That information could then be used to develop advertisements for those TV shows using those stars. Pepsi Cola did such a segmentation study for its Mountain Dew brand. The resulting promotion dealt with Generation Y's living life to the limit.

What Fiberrific benefits might you talk about? Should you emphasize high fibre, low sugar, price, nutritional benefits, or what? **Behavioural segmentation** divides the market based on behaviour with or toward a product.[31] You can determine which benefits are preferred by consumers and promote the product based on these benefits. You may choose to separate the market by product usage. For example, you could determine who big cereal eaters are. Children certainly eat a good deal of cereal, but so do adults. Most cereal companies seem to target children. Why not go for the adult segment, a less competitive area?

In summary, the best segmentation strategy is to use all these bases to come up with a target market (or more) that is sizeable, reachable, and profitable.

The Consumer Decision-Making Process

Relationship marketing depends greatly on understanding consumers and responding quickly to their wants and needs. Therefore, knowing how consumers make decisions is important to marketers. An understanding of the consumer decision-making process helps marketers adapt their strategies in reaching customers and developing lasting relationships.

A major part of the marketing discipline is called *consumer behaviour*. Figure 15.6 (on page 471) shows the consumer decision-making process and some of the outside factors that influence it. Marketing researchers investigate consumer thought processes and behaviour at each of the five steps to determine the best way to facilitate marketing exchanges.

MAIN DIMENSION	SAMPLE VARIABLES	POTENTIAL SEGMENTS
Geographic Segmentation	Region	British Columbia, Prairies, Nunavut, Eastern Quebec, Sydney, St. John's
	City or Census Metropolitan Area (CMA) Size	under 5,000; 5,000–20,000; 20,001–50,000; 50,001–100,000; 100,001–250,000, 250,001–500,000; 500,001–1,000,000; 1,000,001–5,000,000; 5,000,000+
	Density	urban; suburban; rural
Demographic Segmentation		
	Gender	male; female
	Marital Status	single; married; widowed; divorced
	Age	infant; under 6; 6-11; 12–17; 18–24; 25–34; 35–49; 50–64; 65+
	Education	0–8 years; some high school; high school graduate; some post-secondary; post-secondary certificate or diploma; university degree; some postgraduate; graduate or professional degree
	Ethnic Origin	British, French, Native Canadian, Chinese, Italian, German, African, South American, Middle Eastern, other
	Occupation	professional; technical; clerical; sales supervisor; farmer; homemaker; self-employed; student; unemployed; retired; other
	Religion	Catholic, Protestant, Islam, Hindu, Eastern Orthodox, other, none
Psychographic Segmentation		
	Personality	gregarious; compulsive; extroverted; aggressive; ambitious
	Social Class	lower lowers; upper lowers; working class; middle class; upper middles; lower uppers; upper uppers
Behavioural Segmentation		
	Benefits Sought	quality; service; low price
	Usage Rate	light user; medium user; heavy user
	User Status	non-user; ex-user; prospect; first-time user; regular user
	Loyalty Status	none; medium; strong

FIGURE 15.5

MARKET SEGMENTATION
This table shows some of the methods marketers use to divide the market. The aim of segmentation is to break the market into smaller units.

The first step—problem recognition—may occur, say, when your washing machine breaks down. This leads to an information search. You look for ads about washing machines and read brochures about them. You may even consult a secondary data source like *Consumer Reports* or other information sources. And, most likely, you will seek advice from other people who have purchased washing machines. After compiling all this information, you evaluate alternatives and make a purchase decision. But the process does not end here. After the purchase, you evaluate your level of satisfaction.

www.consumerreports.com

Sports Illustrated recognizes that it appeals to different market segments. Thus, they have issues called *Sports Illustrated for Kids, Sports Illustrated for Women,* and so forth. Do you think there's a sufficient market for a college and university edition of *Sports Illustrated*?

Cognitive dissonance is a type of psychological conflict that can occur after a purchase. If you have ever purchased something and then asked, "Why did I buy this? Did I choose the wrong one? Maybe I should have…," then you have experienced cognitive dissonance. Marketers must therefore reassure consumers after the sale that they made a good decision. An auto dealer, for example, may send positive press articles about the particular car that the consumer purchased. The dealer may also offer product guarantees and provide certain free services to the customer. Remember, the primary objective of the marketer is to establish a long-term relationship and to positively reinforce the purchase. This is all part of CRM.

Marketers also study the various influences that impact on consumer behaviour. Figure 15.6 shows several such influences that affect consumer buying: *marketing mix variables* (the four Ps); *psychological influences*, such as perception and attitudes; *situational influences*, such as the type of purchase and the physical surroundings; and *sociocultural influences*, such as reference groups and culture. Other factors important in the consumer decision process whose technical definitions may be unfamiliar to you include the following:

- *Learning* involves changes in an individual's behaviour resulting from previous experiences and information. For example, if you've tried a particular brand of shampoo and you don't like it, you may never buy it again.

- *Culture* is the set of values, attitudes, and ways of doing things that are transmitted from one generation to another in a given society. "National identity is a very important issue for Canadians, and we look endlessly for qualities that make us distinct [from Americans]… If they're brash risk-takers, then we're solid, reliable, and decent. Canadians are more class-aware, law-abiding, and group-oriented."[32]

- *Subculture* is the set of values, attitudes, and ways of doing things that result from belonging to a certain ethnic group, religious group, racial group, or other group with which one closely identifies (e.g., teenagers). This group is one small part of the larger culture. Your subculture may prefer rap and hip-hop music, while your parents' subculture may prefer light jazz.

Consumer behaviour courses are a long-standing part of a marketing curriculum. Today, schools are expanding their offerings in marketing to include courses in business-to-business marketing. The following section will give you some insight into that growing and important area.

THE BUSINESS-TO-BUSINESS MARKET

B2B marketers include manufacturers; intermediaries such as retailers; institutions (e.g., hospitals, schools, and charities); and government purchasers. The basic principle of B2B marketing is still "Find a need and fill it," but the strategies differ from consumer marketing because the nature of the buyers is different. Several factors make B2B marketing different. Some of the more important differences are as follows:

1. The *number* of customers in the B2B market is relatively few; that is, there are just a few construction firms or mining operations compared to the more than 31 million potential customers in the Canadian consumer market.

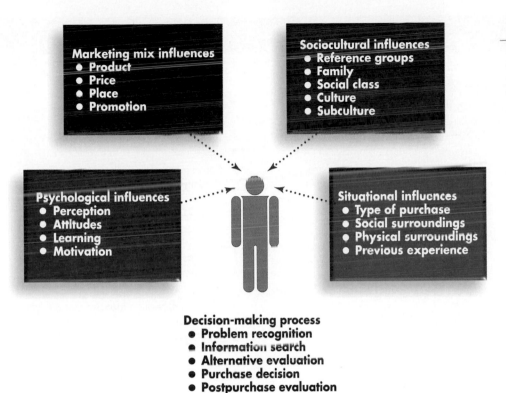

Marketing mix influences
- Product
- Price
- Place
- Promotion

Sociocultural influences
- Reference groups
- Family
- Social class
- Culture
- Subculture

Psychological influences
- Perception
- Attitudes
- Learning
- Motivation

Situational influences
- Type of purchase
- Social surroundings
- Physical surroundings
- Previous experience

Decision-making process
- Problem recognition
- Information search
- Alternative evaluation
- Purchase decision
- Postpurchase evaluation (cognitive dissonance)

FIGURE 15.6

THE CONSUMER DECISION-MAKING PROCESS AND OUTSIDE INFLUENCES

There are many influences on consumers as they decide which goods and services to buy. Marketers have some influence, but it's not usually as strong as sociocultural influences. Helping consumers in their information search and their evaluation of alternatives is a major function of marketing.

2. The *size* of business customers is relatively large; that is, a few large organizations account for most of the employment and production of various goods and services. Nonetheless, there are many small to medium-sized firms in Canada that together make an attractive market.

3. B2B markets tend to be *geographically concentrated.* For example, oil and gas firms tend to be concentrated in Alberta. Consequently, marketing efforts may be concentrated on a particular geographic area, and distribution problems can be minimized by locating warehouses near industrial centres.

4. Business purchases tend to be *larger* than consumer purchases (e.g., several hundred computers for an entire organization versus one computer for the home); therefore, business buyers are more *rational* (as opposed to emotional) than ultimate consumers in their selection of products. Since the costs and risk (e.g., impact on profits and meeting client needs and deadlines) associated with these purchases is higher, buyers use specifications and often more carefully weigh the "total product offer" including quality, price, and service.

5. Most B2B sales tend to be *direct.* Manufacturers sell products, such as tires, directly to auto manufacturers but tend to use intermediaries, such as wholesalers and retailers, to sell to ultimate consumers. One technology research firm estimates that the worldwide B2B market will grow from $145 billion in 1999 to $7.29 *trillion* in 2004.[33]

6. There is much more emphasis on *personal selling* (the use of a salesforce) in B2B markets than in consumer markets. Whereas consumer promotions are based more on advertising, B2B sales are based on personal selling because there are fewer customers who demand more personal service, and the quantities being purchased justify the expense of a salesforce.

	BUSINESS-TO-BUSINESS MARKET	CONSUMER MARKET
Market Structure	• Relatively few potential customers • Larger purchases • Geographically concentrated	• Many potential customers • Smaller purchases • Geographically dispersed
Products	• Require technical, complex products • Frequently require customization • Frequently require technical advice, delivery, and after-sale service	• Require less technical products • Sometimes require customization • Sometimes require technical advice, delivery, and after-sale service
Buying Procedures	• Buyers are trained • Negotiate details of most purchases • Follow objective standards • Formal process involving specific employees • Closer relationships between marketers and buyers • Often buy from multiple sources	• No special training • Accept standard terms for most purchases • Use personal judgment • Informal process involving household members • Impersonal relationships between marketers and consumers • Rarely buy from multiple sources

FIGURE 15.7

COMPARING BUSINESS-TO-BUSINESS AND CONSUMER BUYING BEHAVIOUR

Figure 15.7 shows some of the differences between buying behaviour in the B2B market compared to the consumer market. You will learn all about the business-to-business market if you take advanced marketing courses.

UPDATING THE MARKETING CONCEPT

As we noted earlier in the chapter, the marketing concept was developed in the 1950s to meet the consumer needs of the time. Now that we're in the twenty-first century, marketers have to readjust their strategies to meet the needs of modern consumers. That means each of the elements of the marketing concept: a consumer orientation, a service orientation, and a profit orientation all have to be updated. Let's explore each of those changes next.

From a Consumer Orientation to Delighting Customers and Other Stakeholders

Marketing's goal in the past was to provide customer satisfaction. Today, the goal of some total quality firms is to delight customers by providing products that exactly meet their requirements or exceed their expectations. One objective of a company's marketing effort, therefore, is to make sure that the response to customers is so fast and courteous that customers are truly surprised and pleased by the experience.

You don't have to look far to see that most organizations haven't yet reached the goal of delighting customers. Retail stores, government agencies, and other organizations may still irritate customers as often as they please them. Nonetheless, global competition is forcing organizations to adopt total quality concepts, which means, above all, adapting organizations to customers.

Businesses have learned that employees won't provide first-class products to customers unless they receive first-class treatment themselves. Marketers must therefore work with others in the firm, such as human resource personnel, to help make sure that employees are pleased. In some firms, such as IBM, employees are called *internal customers* to show the need to treat them well—like customers.

From an Organizational Service Orientation to Uniting Organizations

As we explained in Chapter 9, determining whether organizations are providing first-class service and quality is done through *competitive benchmarking* ▶**P. 278◀**. That means that companies compare their processes and products with those of the best companies in the world to learn how to improve them. Xerox Corporation, for example, has benchmarked its functions against corporate leaders such as American Express (for billing), Ford (for manufacturing floor layout), and Mary Kay Cosmetics (for warehousing and distribution).

www.xerox.com

www.americanexpress.com

www.ford.com

www.marykay.com

Manufacturers, unfortunately, cannot delight consumers on their own. They have to have the co-operation of suppliers to assure customers that they are getting the finest parts. They have to have close relationships with dealers to make sure that the dealers are providing fast, friendly service. We shall discuss the close relationships among marketing intermediaries in Chapter 17.

ESTABLISHING RELATIONSHIPS WITH ALL STAKEHOLDERS

Marketing managers must make sure that everyone in the organization understands that the purpose behind pleasing customers and uniting organizations is to ensure a profit for the firm. Using that profit, the organization can then satisfy other stakeholders of the firm such as shareholders, environmentalists, and the local community.

The traditional marketing concept emphasized giving *customers* what they want. Modern marketing goes further by recognizing the need to please other stakeholders as well. If you go too far in giving customers what they want, the organization may lose money and hurt other stakeholders. Likewise, you could please customers but harm the environment, thus harming relationships with the larger community. Balancing the wants and needs of all the firm's stakeholders—employees, customers, suppliers, dealers, shareholders, media representatives, and the community—is a much bigger challenge than marketing has attempted in the past.

Stakeholder marketing, then, is establishing and maintaining mutually beneficial exchange relationships over time with all the stakeholders of the organization. (Here we see the application of the societal marketing orientation, discussed near the beginning of this chapter.) Organizations that adopt stakeholder marketing take the community's needs into mind when designing and marketing products. For example, many companies have responded to the environmental movement by introducing "green products" into the marketplace. A **green product** is one whose production, use, and disposal is not harmful to the environment. For example, Ventura, California–based Patagonia sells outdoor clothing that exclusively uses organically grown cotton; that means less use of fertilizers to pollute the soil. Patagonia also pledges 1 percent of sales or 10 percent of pretax profit, whichever is greater, to local preservation efforts.

stakeholder marketing
Establishing and maintaining mutually beneficial exchange relationships over time with all the stakeholders of the organization.

green product
A product whose production, use, and disposal don't damage the environment.

www.patagonia.com

Marketing tries to please all stakeholders, including those concerned with the environment. This ad for Patagonia's outdoor clothing emphasizes the use of organic cotton. Growing such cotton protects people's health and at the same time preserves the air, water, and land.

Courtesy of Patagonia

www.relationship
mktg.com

Relationship Marketing Resources is an example of a company that provides consultative services to businesses that want to enhance their customer relationships. This Web site will give you some insight into what this field is about

www.the-cma.org

The Canadian Marketing Association is a professional association for people in marketing. It has established a code of ethics and standards of practice. If you are thinking of a career in marketing, be sure to check this out!

Customer Relationship Management

In marketing, the 80/20 rule says that 80 percent of your business is likely to come from just 20 percent of your customers. That's why some companies, like banks, have found it more profitable to discourage some unprofitable customers and put more focus on profitable ones—giving them better, more personal service. It is far more expensive to get a new customer than to strengthen a relationship with an existing one.

Robert Reichheld of Bain & Company estimates that retaining 2 percent more customers has the same effect on profit as cutting costs by 10 percent.[34] Relationship marketing means establishing *and maintaining* long-term relationships with customers. Personalized service helps to ensure this. That is what CRM is all about.

What makes CRM so popular today is the number of companies competing to provide computer software to make the process more effective. These companies have made CRM an all-encompassing business strategy, and a "customer-centric" philosophy of doing business. Top-selling software includes ACT! and Goldmine for small businesses and SalesLogix and Pivotal for mid-range companies.[35] Siebel.com, for example, is a leading provider of e-business applications software, including CRM technology for larger companies. Nexgenix.com offers an integrated CRM program with database management, relationship marketing, and brand-loyalty programs. Epiphany.com and peoplesoft.com are other CRM vendors. We mention these companies because you will be hearing more and more about them as customer relationship management becomes the most profitable way of doing business.[36]

Your Prospects in Marketing

There is a wider variety of careers in marketing than in most business disciplines. Therefore, if you were to major in marketing, a wide variety of career options would be available to you. You could become a manager in a retail store, like Sears. You could do marketing research or get involved in product management. You could go into selling, advertising, sales promotion, or public relations. You could get involved in transportation, storage, or international distribution. You could design interactive Web sites to implement customer relationship management. These are just a few of the possibilities. As you read through the following marketing chapters, consider whether a marketing career would interest you. We'll discuss marketing careers again later, after you have reviewed all the marketing chapters.

When businesses buy goods and services from other businesses, they usually buy in very large volume. Salespeople in the business-to-business area usually are paid on a commission basis; that is, they earn a certain percentage of each sale they make. Can you see why B2B sales may be a more financially rewarding career area than consumer sales? Industrial companies sell goods such as steel, lumber, computers, engines, parts, and supplies. Where would you find the names of such companies?

- Can you name and describe four ways to segment the consumer market?
- What are four key factors that make industrial markets different from consumer markets?
- What is niche marketing, and how does it differ from one-to-one marketing?
- What is stakeholder marketing?

ETHICAL DILEMMA

Review

Remember our three friends who want to do market research by secretly taping conversations? Here's what our executives have to say. Bédard is very clear in his response. "Recording a conversation without someone's knowledge is against the law" and "offensive to many people" because they "will say things that they would never say if they knew they were being taped. Other methods can be found that would produce the same data."

Reilley has an equally clear and strong opinion on this dilemma. "This procedure is unethical (and illegal in some jurisdictions). I would state this openly to Roy, Hector, and Maria. I would be very upset if anyone taped me in this manner. I might even consider legal action."

Let's look at a different scenario. Suppose the three friends went ahead with their taping, and noted who was being taped and when. After listening to the mater-

ial and determining what recreational products these people need, they invite the friends and associates they had taped to dinner and drinks and explain what they did and why. They explain that no names were recorded or mentioned in the final conclusions and any personal or confidential information they had inadvertently recorded had been erased. They say that anyone can request a private session to listen to the tapes of their own comments. After that, the tapes would be erased, since they had served their purpose. Finally, they ask everyone to sign a release that they have no claims against Roy, Maria, and Hector as a result of the tapings. As a sweetener, everyone could be offered a token number of shares in the new company if the trio go ahead with their plan to start a company. What do you think of this alternative?

SUMMARY

1. Explain the marketing concept.

1. Marketing is the process of determining customer needs and wants and then providing customers with goods and services that meet or exceed their expectations.
   - *What are the three parts of the marketing concept?*
   The three parts of the marketing concept are (1) a customer orientation, (2) a service orientation, and (3) a profit orientation (that is, market those goods and services that will earn the firm a profit and enable it to survive and expand to serve more customer wants and needs).
   - *What is the basic goal of marketing?*
   To find a need and fill it.
   - *What kinds of organizations are involved in marketing?*
   All kinds of organizations use marketing, both profit and nonprofit organizations (including charities, churches, and schools).

2. Give an example of how to use the four Ps of marketing.

2. The marketing mix consists of the four Ps of marketing: product, price, place, and promotion.
   - *How do marketers implement the four Ps?*
   The idea is to design a product that people want, price it competitively, place it in a location where consumers can find it easily, and promote it so that consumers know it exists.

3. Describe the marketing research process, and tell how marketers use environmental scanning to learn about the changing marketing environment.

3. Marketing research is the analysis of markets to determine opportunities and challenges and to find the information needed to make good decisions.
   - *What are the steps to follow when conducting research?*
   (1) Define the problem or opportunity and determine the present situation, (2) collect data, (3) analyze the research data, and (4) choose the best solution.
   - *What is environmental scanning?*
   Environmental scanning is the process of identifying the factors that can affect marketing success. Marketers pay attention to all the environmental factors that create opportunities and threats.
   - *What are some of the more important environmental trends in marketing?*
   The most important global and technological change is probably the growth of the Internet. An important technological change is the growth of consumer databases. Using consumer databases, companies can develop products that closely match the needs of consumers. There are a number of social trends that marketers must monitor to maintain their close relationship with customers—population growth and shifts, for example. Of course, marketers must also monitor the dynamic competitive environment and pay attention to the economic environment.

4. Explain various ways of segmenting the consumer market.

4. The process of dividing the total market into several groups whose members have similar characteristics is called market segmentation.
   - *What are some of the ways marketers segment the consumer market?*
   Geographic segmentation means dividing the market into different regions. For example, you could choose Saskatoon as a market segment of the province of Saskatchewan (or even Canada). Segmentation by age, income, and education level are ways of demographic segmentation. We could study a group's values, attitudes, and interests; this segmentation strategy is called psychographic segmentation. Determining which benefits customers prefer and using those benefits to promote a product is called behavioural segmentation. This also includes studying consumers' usage rate, user status, and their level of loyalty. The best segmentation strategy is to use all the variables to come up with a consumer profile (a target market) that's sizable, reachable, and profitable.

5. The B2B market consists of manufacturers, intermediaries such as retailers, institutions (e.g., hospitals, schools, and charities), and the government.

• *What makes the business-to-business market different from the consumer market?*

The number of customers in the B2B market is relatively small and the size of business customers is relatively large. B2B markets tend to be geographically concentrated, and industrial buyers generally are more rational than ultimate consumers in their selection of goods and services. B2B sales tend to be direct, and there is much more emphasis on personal selling in B2B markets than in consumer markets. In the automobile industry, for example, there are only a few manufacturers; these few companies tend to buy directly from suppliers with no intermediaries. Companies that sell tires and other parts and supplies tend to use salespeople and little advertising.

5. List several ways in which the business-to-business market differs from the consumer market.

6. Now that we're in the twenty-first century, marketers have to readjust their strategies to meet the needs of modern consumers. That means each of the elements of the marketing concept—a consumer orientation, a service orientation, and a profit orientation—all have to be updated.

• *How has the marketing concept been adapted to today's environment?*

Marketing is becoming more customer-oriented than ever before. Originally, marketing's goal was simply to satisfy customers. Now marketing tries to please or "delight" customers. Rather than rely on their own resources to provide quality service, companies are counting on their suppliers, dealers, and others to help provide world-class service to customers. And profit is being maintained by focusing on current customers rather than finding new customers all the time.

6. Show how the marketing concept has been adapted to fit today's modern markets.

7. Stakeholder marketing is establishing and maintaining mutually beneficial exchange relationships over time with all the stakeholders of the organization. Organizations that adopt stakeholder marketing consider the community's needs when designing and marketing products.

• *What is customer relationship management?*

Customer relationship management (CRM) is learning as much as possible about customers and doing everything you can to satisfy them or even delight them with goods and services over time. The objective is to build a long-term, profitable relationship with your customers.

7. Describe the latest marketing strategies, such as stakeholder marketing and customer relationship management.

KEY TERMS

behavioural segmentation 468
brand name 457
business-to-business (B2B) market 464
census metropolitan area (CMA) 468
consumer market 464
customer relationship management (CRM) 454
demographic segmentation 468
environmental scanning 461
focus group 460

geographic segmentation 468
green product 473
market 452
market segmentation 465
marketing 452
marketing concept 454
marketing management 455
marketing mix 456
marketing research 458
mass marketing 464
niche marketing 466

one-to-one (individual) marketing 466
primary data 459
product 456
promotion 457
psychographic segmentation 468
relationship marketing 466
secondary data 458
stakeholder marketing 473
target marketing 465
test marketing 457

DEVELOPING WORKPLACE SKILLS

1. Develop what you would consider an effective marketing mix for one of the following goods and services: a new electric car, an easy-to-use digital camera, or a car wash for your neighbourhood. Write a one-page description of that strategy.

2. Working in teams of five (or on your own), think of a good or service that your friends want but cannot get on or near campus. You might ask your friends at other schools what's available there. Find a good or service to fill that need. Develop a promotional scheme and design a system to distribute it to students.

3. Relationship marketing efforts include frequent-flyer deals at airlines, special discounts for members at certain supermarkets (e.g., A&P Food Stores), and Web sites that remember your name and what you've purchased in the past and recommend new products that you may like (e.g., Amazon.com). Evaluate any one of these programs (look up such programs on the Internet). What might they do to increase your satisfaction and loyalty?

4. How would you segment the market for a new, nutritious cereal that contains no sugar and has all the vitamins required for a day? Describe a target market that you feel would be the most profitable.

TAKING IT TO THE NET

Purpose:

To demonstrate how the Internet can be used to enhance relationship marketing.

Exercises:

1. Nike wants to help its customers add soul to their soles and express their individuality by customizing their own shoes. See for yourself at www.nike.com. Click on NIKEID and build a shoe that fits your style.

   a. What if you're in the middle of your shoe design and have questions about what to do next? Where can you go for help?

   b. How does Nike's Web site help the company strengthen its relationships with its stakeholders? Give examples to support your answer.

   c. How do the elements of the Web site reflect Nike's target market?

   d. Does Nike invite comments from visitors to its Web site? If so, how does this affect its attempt to build positive relationships with its customers?

2. Imagine that you are working in the marketing department of a computer company and your manager asks you to do some research into the possible consumer demand for a better type of mouse. Many users have complained of various pains and aches arising from heavy usage of the ordinary type of mouse. Your first step should be to see what research others have done, so you would commence by seeking these secondary data. How would you begin? Where would you look? You could start with searching Yahoo with the key words *computer mouse*. You may be surprised at how much you can find there.

3. Suppose your search for secondary data is not very fruitful. That is, you cannot find much information because there has been little research done or not much has been written on this topic. You then decide to do your own research and collect some primary data. Do you think you can get a focus group organized and working satisfactorily by using a real-time chat room? Can you explain exactly how that could work? Is there any other way you can use the Internet to collect primary data? Get some information on focus groups and prepare a list of questions you should ask participants. Then try to organize a couple of focus groups with 10 people in each group. Summarize your findings in a report to your class.

PRACTISING MANAGEMENT DECISIONS

CASE 1

IMPACT OF BABY BOOMERS ON MARKETING RESEARCH

In 1996 Dr. David Foot, economist and demographer at the University of Toronto, came out with a book that became one of the all-time bestsellers in Canada. On the bestseller list for two years, it sold more than 250,000 hardcover copies. There was also a French translation. The book was called *Boom Bust & Echo* and it talked about the major impacts that the special demographic trends of the postwar years were having on Canadian business and would continue to have for years to come. He divided Canadians born in the last half of the twentieth century into three main groups. The oldest are the large number of *boomers* born between 1947 and 1966 when the birth rate was high, about 400,000 births annually.

The 10 million boomers constitute one-third of the Canadian population and, in Dr. Foot's opinion, have the largest impact of any group on the demand for various products. For Dr. Foot the *generation Xers* is that segment of the baby boomers born at the tail end—from 1960 to 1966. Next comes the relatively small *bust generation*, born between 1967 and 1980. The last group, the large number of children of the boomers that Foot calls the *echo generation*, are those born between 1980 and 1995. In 1999 Dr. Foot produced an updated paperback version of his book in which he continued to predict the likely significant effect on Canadian business of these two groups, the baby boomers and their children, the echo boomers. He believes that the baby boomer bulge, as it moves through the population, is the most significant factor in understanding business trends. In 1992 the nine million boomers aged between 26 and 45 were the largest segment of the Canadian adult market. In 2002 they will be ages 36 to 55. The needs and lifestyles of this large segment have ruled the marketplace for many years and will continue to do so for many more years.

Foot gives examples of the economic impact of the boomers' changing demands as they move through their life cycle. When they were children, toys, schools, housing, and baby clothes were in great demand. When they became adults and had their own children, that cycle was repeated. Their lifestyle led to a boom in recreational-related products —sportswear and athletic equipment, health clubs, moving from cities to suburban areas.

In 1994 the baby boom peak reached age 34. "That's the average age at which Canadians buy homes," says Foot. So he predicted that demand for housing would begin to fall off after 1995. This prediction was partially confirmed by a decline in the housing market. Other changes he foresaw include "the beer and beef industries are in trouble; young people drink beer and eat beef and that market's getting older…Per capita, chicken has been rising as the baby boomers are getting older. Madonna, hockey, football, and skiing will all see declining markets for the same reason."

David Foot ends by urging businesses to look at the demographic profile, by age, of the consumers who buy their products or services. By relating this information to the baby boom bulge, they should have a good picture of what is likely to happen to their market. In 2004 the baby boom peak will be age 44.

Decision Questions

1. Can you think of what marketing research you should do to test the validity of Foot's predictions? Would you try to set up some focus groups of baby boomers? What else would you do? How about the other groups he refers to?

2. Assume that Foot is correct in his predictions. What business opportunities do you see that you might take advantage of? What additional market research would you undertake to support that business idea?

3. Suppose you own a small supermarket. Do you think that you will have to make any changes in the type of products you carry if you accept Foot's analysis? If so, what changes should you make? Would you do some market research before deciding? What exactly would you do?

4. If Foot is correct, will businesses have to continually shift the nature of their products to adapt to the market changes as the boomers age? Would that involve continual market research?

Some products, like corn flakes, never seem to lose their popularity. How is this explained?

Sources: Radio interview series of David Foot with Peter Gzowski, host of CBC "Morningside," May 1996. *Boom Bust & Echo: How to Profit from the Coming Demographic Shift*, David K. Foot, with Daniel Stoffman (MacFarlane Walter and Ross, 1996); *Boom Bust & Echo 2000: Profiting from the Demographic Shift*, David K. Foot, with Daniel Stoffman (MacFarlane Walter and Ross, 1999); Interview of David Foot by Layth Matthews of Canadian-Investor.com, May 11, 1999, as reported on Web site <www.davidfoot.com/interview.html>.

PRACTISING MANAGEMENT DECISIONS

CASE 2

APPLYING CUSTOMER-ORIENTED MARKETING CONCEPTS AT THERMOS

Thermos is the company made famous by its Thermos bottles and lunch boxes. Thermos also manufactures cookout grills. Its competitors include Sunbeam and Weber. To become a world-class competitor, Thermos completely reinvented the way it conducted its marketing operations. By reviewing what Thermos did, you can see how new marketing concepts affect organizations.

First, Thermos modified its corporate culture. It had become a bureaucratic firm organized by function: design, engineering, manufacturing, marketing, and so on. That organizational structure was replaced by flexible, cross-functional, self-managed teams. The idea was to focus on a customer group—for example, buyers of outdoor grills—and build a product development team to create a product for that market.

The product development team for grills consisted of six middle managers from various disciplines, including engineering, manufacturing, finance, and marketing. They called themselves the Lifestyle Team because their job was to study grill users to see how they lived and what they were looking for in an outdoor grill. To get a fresh perspective, the company hired Fitch, Inc., an outside consulting firm, to help with design and marketing research. Team leadership was rotated based on needs of the moment. For example, the marketing person took the lead in doing field research, but the R&D person took over when technical developments became the issue.

The team's first step was to analyze the market. Together, they spent about a month on the road talking with people, videotaping barbecues, conducting focus groups, and learning what people wanted in an outdoor grill. The company found that people wanted a nice-looking grill that didn't pollute the air and was easy to use. It also had to be safe enough for apartment dwellers, which meant it had to be electric.

As the research results came in, engineering began playing with ways to improve electric grills.

Manufacturing kept in touch to make sure that any new ideas could be produced economically. Design people were already building models of the new product. R&D people relied heavily on Thermos's strengths. Thermos's core strength was the vacuum technology it had developed to keep hot things hot and cold things cold in Thermos bottles. Drawing on that strength, the engineers developed a domed lid that contained the heat inside the grill.

Once a prototype was developed, the company showed the model to potential customers, who suggested several changes. Employees also took sample grills home and tried to find weaknesses. Using the input from potential customers and employees, the company used continuous improvement to manufacture what became a world-class outdoor grill.

No product can become a success without communicating with the market. The team took the grill on the road, showing it at trade shows and in retail stores. The product was such a success that Thermos is now using self-managed, customer-oriented teams to develop all its product lines.

Decision Questions

1. How could the growth of self-managed cross-functional teams affect marketing departments in other companies? Do you believe that would be a good change or not? Why?

2. How can Thermos now build a closer relationship with its customers using the Internet?

3. What other products might Thermos develop that would appeal to the same market segment that uses outdoor grills?

4. What do you think the Thermos team would have found if it had asked customers what they thought about having consumers put the grills together rather than buying them assembled? What other questions might Thermos place on its Web site to learn more about customer wants and needs?

INSIDE INFORMATION

Marketers obsessively survey and track consumers to find out information about their opinions and to understand their buying behaviour. While marketers pay for personal information, consumers do not (or may not) disclose all their personal motivators or reasons for why products are purchased. Today, some marketers are venturing beyond traditional focus groups and questionnaires and into the heads of consumers through a variety of techniques, including measuring impulses and hypnosis, in their quest for more information.

Some experts today are measuring subconscious processes. This is not scientific research, this is market research. By getting into people's brains, marketers can find out what messages cut through the clutter of advertisements. From peaks and valleys displayed on monitors, consultants can understand what grabs the attention of the receivers and what turns them off regarding the ads that they are being exposed to during experiments. Follow-up discussions with the participants help marketers understand the source of these reactions and hopefully will provide insight for future campaigns.

Brain waves, emotions, subconscious feelings … are marketers getting too close to the inner consumer? Hypnosis is being used to allow respondents to honestly share their opinions and emotions, and to allow them to express information that is not accessible when one is awake.

With the results of this experimentation, new ideas can be developed. In an ideal advertising world, there would not be any secrets that could not be accessed. If marketers can access this information, this would give them an advantage over their competitors. What do you think? Is this the future for all marketing research?

Discussion Questions

1. What is the incentive for respondents to participate in these types of focus groups?
2. Do you think that putting consumers under hypnosis to get information is ethical? Explain.
3. What are the benefits to marketers in getting subconscious information from respondents?
4. How can this information benefit firms? How can this information benefit consumers?

Source: *Undercurrents*, show number 190, "Inside Information, "January 22, 2001, running time 8:27.

CHAPTER 16

Developing and Pricing Quality Products

LEARNING GOALS

AFTER YOU HAVE READ AND STUDIED THIS CHAPTER, YOU SHOULD BE ABLE TO

1 Explain the concept of a value package.

2 Describe the various kinds of consumer and industrial products.

3 Give examples of a brand, a brand name, and a trademark, and explain the concept of brand loyalty.

4 List and describe the five functions of packaging.

5 Explain the role of brand managers and the six steps of the new-product development process.

6 Identify and describe the stages of the product life cycle, and describe marketing strategies at each stage.

7 Give examples of various pricing objectives and strategies.

8 Explain why nonpricing strategies are growing in importance.

Christine Magee: Service within Sleep Country Canada Inc.

"Sleep Country Canada! Why Buy A Mattress Anywhere Else?" is the jingle for Sleep Country Canada, repeated in all of its television and radio commercials across Canada. Its spokesperson—Christine Magee—has become synonymous with mattresses. As Magee explains, "The goal was to create a brand name and associate the name Christine Magee with it." This has been reinforced in each of the company's stores, with Magee's image being featured along with stories about her and the business.

Highly specialized in sleep products, Sleep Country Canada was started in 1994 by three partners: Christine Magee (President), Stephen Gunn, and Gordon Lownds. Today, there are 72 stores in three provinces: British Columbia (16), Alberta (12), and Ontario (44). The company is also considering expansion into the United States.

A graduate from the University of Western Ontario with an honours degree in business, Magee spent 12 years in commercial and corporate banking. During that time, she was involved in the areas of commercial, corporate, and merchant lending, including leverage and management buyouts. Previous to that, she worked in the retail sector, managing a women's apparel store, where she gained valuable merchandising and retail experience.

While employed in the banking industry, Magee decided to enter the mattress business, despite its negative image. "Opportunity often exists where you least expect it, and I recognized that. We came to the conclusion that the retail business for mattresses and box springs wasn't being done well and could be done better. It had always been dominated by department stores that really didn't specialize." Magee validated the idea for Sleep Country Canada by visiting a company based in Seattle that was providing the level of service Sleep Country Canada was designed to provide. Along with her two partners, she bought the trademark name and infamous jingle, and borrowed a few marketing tools from the U.S. store. In 1994, the partners moved to Vancouver and opened their first store. At this time, the Sleep Country TV and radio ads were produced. Today, the company has three regional offices and seven warehouses, and new company commercials appear every six months or so. Part of the company's advertising power is repetition: the ads are everywhere and they are played over and over again.

Courtesy of Sleep Country Canada

Sleep Country Canada has received many awards in recognition of its success. It has been named one of the top 50 best-managed privately held companies in Canada in 1997 and 1998. In the July 2000 issue of *BC Business*, it is ranked number 26, with 1999 revenues of $90 million. Other awards and achievements include B.C. Furniture Association Retailer of the Year (1996); The *Financial Post* Ontario Entrepreneur of the Year—Retail/Wholesale (1998); Canada's Top 40 Under 40 (1997); and member of AVCO's Dealer Advisory Council.

While the marketing program has contributed to its success, it is the firm's mission of complete dedication to customer service that has given it a competitive edge. The mission is to exceed customer expectations when they purchase a new sleep set. This is the firm's opportunity to earn the trust of their customers. Customer assurances of value and service are provided by offering a comprehensive assortment of quality sleep products, guarantees, and free services—in attractive, convenient retail stores staffed by a knowledgeable, helpful, and friendly salesforce. A dedicated team of customer-service and delivery associates support all these efforts. Company ads feature testimonials from satisfied customers. They are talking about the service, not the product. They say such things as, "They came to deliver my mattress just when they said they would" and "I was so impressed when I saw the men putting on those little booties before they walked into my house."

As part of the commitment that Sleep Country Canada has to its customers, there is also a commitment to the community. Part of its service is the Donated Bed Program, where Sleep Country Canada provides free removal of old mattresses. These old mattresses are then made available to charitable organizations to assist those in need. Sleep Country Canada is also a supporter of many community charities including Children's Aid Society, Easter Seals, Salvation Army, YMCA, YWCA, Covenant House, Renascent Centre, George Hull Centre, Massey Centre, Starlight Children foundation...and many more.

Sources: www.ryerson.ca/CESAR/NightViews/May%20June%202001.htm; www.ryerson.ca/baar/news/past/winter99_presidents_note.htm; sbinfocanada.about.com/library/weekly/aa120200a.htm, www.sleepcountry.ca; www.uwo.ca/alumni/gazette/winter99/magee.htm.

A "Small" Problem of Radiation

This chapter introduces you to new-product development. Let's take a look at an ethical issue that can arise in the area of new-product development. Suppose you are an importer of toys and games for children and that you have been having severe financial problems for the past year. You have been seeking some new products that will give your sales and profits a much-needed boost. You meet Adam, an exporter whom you know well, having dealt with him for some years. He invites you out for dinner one evening and you talk about business.

During the conversation, Adam says that he has a terrific deal for you. He has a big lot of new games and toys that he can let you have at a great price. You are all ears because it's exactly the transfusion your business needs. You are a little suspicious because the price is so low, so you ask Adam why it's such a bargain. He reluctantly tells you, because you are a valued customer, that there is a *small* problem. The material the toys and games are made of has been accidentally exposed to some radiation near a nuclear power plant. Because of that exposure, Adam was able to buy the whole lot at a ridiculous price and he is prepared to pass on these savings to you.

Adam tells you that the radiation level is very low and will not hurt children. As a matter of fact, Adam tells you, he lets his own children play with these products. He takes you up to his hotel room and shows you some of the merchandise. You are very impressed with their novelty and quality—they are just what you need to improve your business's financial health. What would you do?

INTRODUCTION

In the last chapter we introduced the four Ps framework (product, price, place, and promotion) that marketers review when developing goods and services to meet the needs of their target audience. In this chapter, we will focus on the first two elements: product and price. Chapter 17 will discuss place and promotion.

THE UTILITIES CREATED BY MARKETERS

When developing products, marketers are concerned with utility. **Utility** is the value or want-satisfying ability that is added to goods or services when the products are made more useful and accessible to consumers. Six utilities are added: Form, time, place, information, possession, and service utility.

Form utility is performed mostly by producers that take raw materials and change their form so that they become more useful products ➤P. 456◄. Thus, a Tim Hortons staff member who makes coffee just the way you want it is creating form utility. **Time utility** is created when products are available *when* they are needed (e.g., coffee was ready) and **place utility** looks after having these products available *where* people want them (e.g., a Tim Hortons around the corner). Another retailer, Canadian convenience store leader Alimentation Couche-Tarde, offers more than 2,500 products in each of its outlets.[1] These outlets also provide place utility.

Information utility opens two-way flows of information between marketing participants. For example, Joseph can't decide what personal computer to buy. He speaks with several retailers about the benefits and features of several models. He also reviews several ads, as well as some brochures that he brought home. (This is not considered a two-way flow of information, yet still provides information utility.)

Possession utility is doing whatever is necessary to transfer ownership from one party to another, including providing credit, delivery, installation, guarantees, and follow-up service. Possession utility also makes it possible for consumers to use goods

utility
An economic term that refers to the value or want-satisfying ability that's added to goods or services by organizations when the products are made more useful or accessible to consumers than before.

form utility
Taking raw materials and changing their form so that they become useful products.

time utility
Adding value to products by making them available when they're needed.

place utility
Adding value to products by having them where people want them.

information utility
Adding value to products by opening two-way flows of information between marketing participants.

possession utility
Doing whatever is necessary to transfer ownership from one party to another, including providing credit, delivery, installation, guarantees, and follow-up service.

through renting or leasing. In his discussion with the salespeople, Joseph discovers that there is a special loan promotion and he would not have to make a payment for one year.

Lastly, marketers add **service utility** by providing fast, friendly service during and after the sale and by teaching consumers how to best use products over time. Both the computer manufacturer and the retailer where Joseph bought his computer continue to offer help whenever he needs it. He also gets software updates for a small fee to keep his computer up-to-date. Service utility is rapidly becoming the most important utility for many retailers because without it they could lose business to direct marketing (e.g., the Internet).

PRODUCT DEVELOPMENT AND VALUE

To remain competitive, Canadian firms must design and promote better products—meaning products that are perceived to have the best **value**. For all customers, choice is influenced by perceptions of value, which are formed primarily by perceptions of quality, price, and convenience.[2] Another way to interpret value is good quality at a fair price. When consumers calculate the value of a product, they look at the benefits (such as quality, convenience, and utility) and then subtract the cost (such as price) to see if the benefits exceed the costs. As we'll see in this chapter, whether a consumer perceives a product as the best value depends on many factors, including the benefits they seek and the package or bundle of services they receive.[3] To satisfy consumers, marketers must learn to listen better than they do now and to adapt constantly to changing market demands. Managers must also constantly adapt to price challenges from competitors.

Fast-food organizations, for example, must constantly monitor all sources of information for new-product ideas. KFC put in a new line of chicken sandwiches.[4] Wendy's was able to greatly increase its product sales when it added stuffed pitas to its product mix. Offerings differ in various locations, based on the wants of the local community. At Bob's Big Boy in Thailand, for example, you can get Tropical Shrimp.[5]

www.couchetard.com/overview_en.html

Alimentation Couche-Tard Inc. operates a network of stores in Canada. You may recognize some of its banners: Mike's Mart, Becker's, Daisy Mart, Winks, Red Rooster, and Couche-Tard.

www.consumerreports.org

Consumer Reports Online is published by an independent, non-profit organization. Its mission is to test, inform, and protect consumers. If you are thinking of purchasing a product and want more information, visit this Web site.

service utility
Providing fast, friendly service during and after the sale and by teaching customers how to best use products over time.

value
Good quality at a fair price; when consumers calculate the value of a product, they look at the benefits and then subtract the cost to see if the benefits exceed the costs.

www.kfc.com
www.wendys.com
www.bobs.net

Does *your* McDonald's deliver? This one in central London does! Of all the marketing utilities, possession utility is the least understood. It is a catch-all utility that means adding value by doing whatever the customer needs to complete the sale, including providing credit, delivery, or whatever. What other products might benefit by offering free delivery?

Producers are constantly adapting products to meet the changing needs of consumers. For example, this photo shows a product that reads your fingerprint and then starts the engine of your car, adjusts the steering wheel and mirrors to your specifications, and tunes the radio to your favourite station. Soon such products will be used to open the car doors, give you access to buildings, and more. Do you sometimes feel that technology has gone too far?

Courtesy of Siemens Corp.

value package
Everything that consumers evaluate when deciding whether to buy something; also called the *total product offer*.

Developing a Value Package

From a strategic marketing viewpoint, a value package is more than just the physical good or service. A **value package** (also called the *total product offer*) consists of everything that consumers evaluate when deciding whether to buy something. Thus, the basic product may be a good (e.g., a washing machine) or a service (e.g., an insurance policy). The *core* of the product is the benefit that the product provides the end user, whether it is clean clothes or peace of mind. In addition to this core benefit, the value package may contain the following:

Price.	Guarantee.
Package.	Brand name.
Reputation of the producer.	Service.
Buyer's past experience.	Delivery speed.
Marketer accessibility (e.g., on the Internet).	Store surroundings.

When people buy a product >**P. 456**<, they may evaluate and compare value packages on all these dimensions. Note that some of the attributes are tangible (the good itself and its package) and others are intangible (the reputation of the producer and the image created by advertising). A successful marketer must begin to think like a consumer and evaluate the value package as a total collection of impressions created by all the factors listed above. It is wise to talk with consumers to see which features and benefits are most important to *them*.

Let's go back and look at the highly nutritious, high-fibre, low-sugar breakfast cereal Fiberrific. The value package as perceived by the consumer is much more than the cereal itself. Anything that affects a consumer's perceptions about the cereal's benefits and value may determine whether he or she purchases the cereal.

A high price may indicate exceptional quality. The store surroundings also are important. If the cereal is being sold in an exclusive health food store, it takes on many characteristics of the store (e.g., healthy and upscale). A guarantee of satisfaction can increase the product's value in the mind of consumers, as can a well-known brand name.[6] Advertising can create an attractive image, and word of mouth can enhance the reputation.[7] Thus, the Fiberrific value package is more than a cereal; it's an entire bundle of impressions.

As you learned earlier one way to keep customers happy is by establishing a dialogue with them and keeping the information they provide in a database. The easiest way to do this is to establish a Web site where consumers can ask questions, get information, and chat with others. Having a close personal relationship with customers adds to the perceived benefits of products because most people would prefer to buy from someone they know and like.

The Spotlight on Small Business box "Stay Close to Your Customers and Make Sure You Are Providing What They Need" discusses this issue in more depth.

Product Lines and the Product Mix

Companies usually don't sell just one product. Rather, they sell several different but complementary products. Figure 16.1 shows product lines for Procter & Gamble (P&G). A **product line**, as the figure shows, is a group of products that are physically similar or are intended for a similar market. P&G's product lines include bar soaps and dishwashing detergents. In one product line, there may be several competing brands. Thus, P&G has many brands in its laundry detergent product line, including Bold, Cheer, Tide, and Ivory Snow. All of P&G's product lines make up its **product mix**, which is the combination of product lines offered by a manufacturer.

Service providers have product lines and product mixes as well. For example, financial services institutions—such as banks, trust companies, and life insurance firms—may offer a variety of services, from savings accounts to insurance to mutual funds. A bank's product mix may include savings products (such as chequing accounts, term deposits, RRSPs, and mutual funds), credit products (including loans, mortgages, overdraft protection, and credit cards), and a variety of other services (such as safety deposit boxes and traveller's cheques).

Companies must decide what mix is best. The mix may include both goods and services to ensure that all of the customer's needs are being met. As well, a diversified mix would minimize the risks associated with focusing all of a firm's resources on only one target market.

product line
A group of products that are physically similar or are intended for a similar market.

product mix
The combination of product lines offered by a manufacturer.

SPOTLIGHT ON SMALL BUSINESS
Stay Close to Your Customers and Make Sure You Are Providing What They Need

One major advantage small businesses have over large ones is their ability to get closer to the customer and provide more personal and friendly service. But don't assume that a small business provides better service. Small-business managers must constantly improve their goods and services. To facilitate this objective they should frequently poll their customers and employees to see what they think, using this feedback as the catalyst for change.

Small businesses shouldn't react negatively to the demands that customers place on them. Rather, they must encourage employees to give customers friendly, responsive service. Failing to do so means competitors that emphasize service will take away business.

Another good idea for small businesses is to analyze two major competitors to find weaknesses in their products, then exploit those weak links, using them as a competitive edge. Smaller airlines, for example, are competing with major carriers by offering service to more areas at lower prices. Smaller retailers are taking slices of the market by specializing in one or two products. You can now find stores selling just sunglasses or just kites.

Small businesses must constantly review their product mix and eliminate those products that no longer appeal to the market niche being served. That means constantly monitoring consumer trends and quickly adapting the product mix to meet current demands. Today, many of the greatest marketing opportunities are beyond our borders. Adapting products to successfully penetrate such markets is now and will continue to be the challenge.

PRODUCT LINES	BRANDS
Bar soaps	Camay, Coast, Ivory, Kirk's, Lava, Monchel, Safeguard, Zest
Laundry detergents	Bold, Cheer, Dash, Dreft, Era, Gain, Ivory Snow, Liquid Bold-3, Liquid Cheer, Liquid Tide, Oxydol, Solo, Tide
Dishwashing detergents	Cascade, Dawn, Ivory Liquid, Joy, Liquid Cascade
Shampoos	Head & Shoulders, Ivory, Lilt, Pert-Plus, Prell
Toothpastes	Crest, Denquel, Gleem
Disposable diapers	Luvs, Pampers

CRITICAL THINKING

When Armand Bombardier started his small company more than half a century ago, it manufactured his new invention, a Ski-Doo snowmobile. Three decades later, Bombardier Inc. was producing railway and subway cars for Canadian and American needs. Fifteen years later the company was making aircraft on an international scale with companies in Canada, the United States, and Ireland. What do you think prompted such major changes in its product lines? Why was Bombardier looking for other lines? Why was it expanding in these directions?

PRODUCT DIFFERENTIATION

**product
differentiation**
The creation of real or
perceived product differences.

Product differentiation is the creation of real or perceived product differences. Actual product differences are sometimes quite small, so marketers must use a clever mix of pricing, advertising, and packaging to create a unique, attractive image. Evian, for example, which sells bottled water, successfully attempted product differentiation. The company made its water so attractive through pricing and promotion that now restaurant customers often order it by brand name instead of ordering tap water or even other products such as pop.

There's no reason why you couldn't create an attractive image for your product, Fiberrific. With a high price and creative advertising, it could become the Evian of cereals. But different products call for different marketing strategies, as we'll see next.

Small businesses can often win market share with creative product differentiation. For example, yearbook photographer Charlie Clark competes with other yearbook photographers by offering multiple clothing changes, backgrounds, and poses along with special discounts and guarantees. He has been so successful that companies use him as a speaker at photography conventions. This is just one more example of how small businesses may have the advantage of being more flexible than big businesses in adapting to customer wants and needs and giving them attractive product differences.

Each time a customer comes in contact with an employee, there is another chance to handle that customer's needs better, faster, or in a friendlier manner than competitors do. That is what differentiation is all about.

Marketing Consumer Products

Several attempts have been made to classify consumer goods and services. One classification, based on consumer purchasing behaviour, has four general categories—*convenience*, *shopping*, *specialty*, and *unsought*.

1. **Convenience products** are goods and services that the consumer purchases frequently and with a minimum of effort (e.g., candy, gum, milk, snacks, gas, banking services). Grocery stores, convenience stores (e.g., 7-Eleven) and gas stations (e.g., Petro-Canada) carry a wide assortment of convenience goods. Location, brand awareness, and image are important for marketers of convenience products. The Internet has taken convenience to a whole new level, especially for banks and other service companies. Companies that don't offer such services are likely to lose market share to those who do unless they offer *outstanding* service to customers who visit in person.

2. **Shopping products** are those goods and services that the consumer buys only after comparing value, quality, style, and price from a variety of sellers. Consequently, there is more effort expended on the part of consumers than for convenience products. Shopping products are sold largely through shopping centres, where consumers can shop around and receive feedback from the salespeople. Sears is one store that sells mostly shopping goods. Because many consumers carefully compare such products, marketers can emphasize price differences, quality differences, or some combination of the two. Examples include clothes, shoes, appliances, and auto repair services. It is so easy to make price comparisons on the Internet today that companies will instead have to compete on service.

3. **Specialty products** are goods and services that appeal to a relatively small market segment, but have a special attraction to consumers who are willing to go out of their way to obtain them due to their features and attributes. Examples are bee-keeping equipment, fur coats, jewellery, fine chocolates, and expensive imported cigars. Services include those provided by medical specialists or business consultants. A Porsche automobile dealer is an example of a specialty good retailer. These products are often supported by a specialized workforce in traditional brick-and-morter locations. They can also be marketed through specialty magazines. For example, specialty skis may be sold through sports magazines and specialty foods through gourmet magazines. By establishing interactive Web sites where customers can place orders, companies that sell specialty products can make buying their products as easy as or easier than shopping at a local mall.

4. **Unsought products** are goods and services that consumers are unaware of, haven't necessarily thought of buying, or find that they need to solve an unexpected problem. Some examples of unsought products are car-towing services, burial services, and insurance. Oftentimes, these products are supported by aggressive promotional campaigns to increase awareness and remind consumers of their existence.

The marketing task varies depending on the category of product; that is, convenience goods are marketed differently from specialty goods, and so forth. The best way to promote convenience goods is to make them readily available and to create the proper image. Price, quality, and service are the best appeals for shopping goods. Specialty goods rely on reaching special market segments through advertising. Unsought goods such as life insurance rely on personal selling; car towing relies on Yellow Pages advertising.

The advent in the 1990s of shopping via the Internet has had an almost revolutionary impact on specialty and shopping categories. Since their involvement is higher than for convenience products, consumers do more shopping and evaluating before the purchase. Most companies now have interactive Web sites where consumers can browse, do comparison shopping, communicate with companies, and, finally, order and pay by credit card without ever leaving their chairs. Think of the convenience (saved time, cost, and frustration by not having to drive in traffic and to look for parking) provided by this additional shopping tool.

convenience products
Goods and services that the consumer wants to purchase frequently and with a minimum of effort.

www.7-eleven.com

www.petro-canada.ca

shopping products
Goods and services that the consumer buys only after comparing value, quality, and price from a variety of sellers.

specialty products
Goods and services that have a special attraction to consumers who are willing to go out of their way to obtain them.

unsought products
Goods and services that consumers are unaware of, haven't necessarily thought of buying, or find that they need to solve an unexpected problem.

Whether a product falls into a particular class depends on the individual consumer. A shopping good for one consumer (e.g., coffee) could be a specialty good for another consumer (e.g., flavoured gourmet coffee). Some people shop around to compare different dry cleaners, so dry cleaning is a shopping service for them. Others go to the closest store, making it a convenience service. Therefore, marketers must carefully monitor their customer base to determine how consumers perceive their products. Can you see how Fiberrific could be either a convenience good or a shopping good?

Furthermore, the Internet has made it possible for consumers to purchase shopping goods from home. That puts much greater pressure on traditional retailers to offer such outstanding service that consumers will be willing to leave their homes to get it.

Industrial Products

industrial products
Goods and services used in the production of other products.

Industrial products are goods and services used in the production of other products. They are sold in the B2B market, which also means that they are used for organizational (non-personal) purposes. This is quite different from consumer products, which are purchased for personal use. As an example, while some products, such as

FIGURE 16.2

VARIOUS CLASSES OF CONSUMER AND INDUSTRIAL PRODUCTS

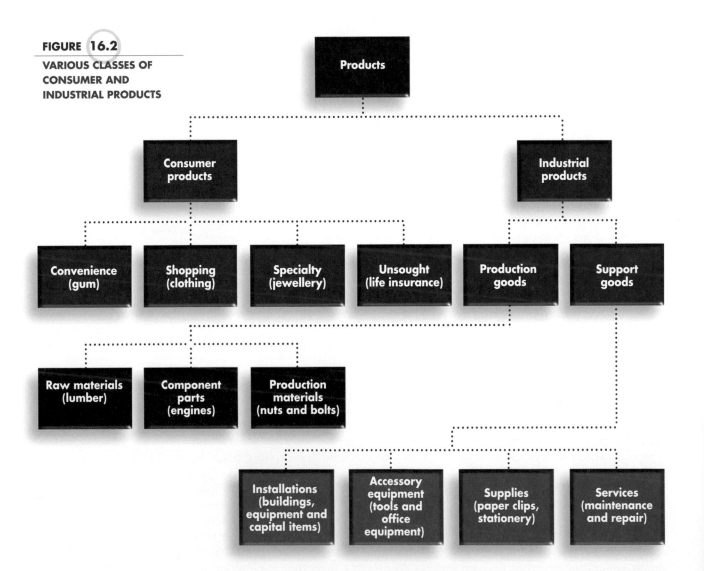

a computer, can be sold to both types of markets, the purchase purpose determines whether it was a consumer market purchase (e.g., to write reports for school) or an industrial market purchase (e.g., to create payroll reports). Figure 16.2 outlines the categories of both consumer and industrial products.

Items used in the manufacturing process that become part of the final product are **production goods**.[8] *Raw materials* (e.g., steel and lumber) can be used in the production of other products such as generators and doors. *Component parts* are required for a product to be complete. When we consider cars, component parts include the engine, the steering wheel, tires, and windshield wipers. Each of these parts is produced separately, yet must be assembled to create the end product. *Production materials*, which can include nuts and bolts, are necessary for component parts to be built. The marketing of production goods is based on factors such as price, quality, delivery, and service, and marketers of these products tend to sell directly to industrial users.[9]

> **production goods**
> Items used in the manufacturing process that become part of the final product.

Support goods are the second classification of industrial goods and services. These are items that are used when producing industrial products or in the running of the business. They include installations, accessory equipment, supplies, and services.

> **support goods**
> Products used in the operation of the business, including installations, accessory equipment, supplies, and services.

1. **Installations** consist of major capital equipment such as buildings (e.g., factories and offices) and heavy machinery (e.g., furnaces and elevators). Installations are products that last a long time and cost a lot of money. A new factory building where Fiberrific would be produced would be considered an installation. Due to the high capital cost associated with such purchases, a supplier needs to have a knowledgeable salesforce that is able to adapt the products to the buyers' needs. Given the investment and long-term use, such purchases are usually made over a long period of time.

> **installations**
> Major capital equipment such as buildings and heavy machinery.

2. **Accessory equipment** consists of capital items that are not quite as long-lasting or as expensive as installations. Examples include computers, photocopy machines, and various tools (e.g., hand tools). These products are usually purchased more often than installations and are usually less expensive than installations. Firms usually deal with their list of in-suppliers when making such purchases.

> **accessory equipment**
> Capital items that are not quite as long-lasting or as expensive as installations.

3. **Supplies** (e.g., paper clips, stationery) are considered the convenience goods of industrial products as they are purchased frequently and with a minimum of effort. Price and delivery are key factors considered when purchasing supplies.[10]

> **supplies**
> Goods that are purchased frequently and with a minimum of effort.

4. **Services** are intangible activities used in the running of the business. Examples include maintenance and repair, and legal, accounting, and tax services. These services may be provided internally (e.g., finance department) or outsourced to another organization. If the service is outsourced, the firm must consider the reputation and the quality of the service provider when a supplier is chosen.

> **services**
> Intangible activities that may be provided internally or outsourced to another organization.

- What attributes are included in a value package?
- What's the difference between a product line and a product mix?
- Name the four classes of consumer products, and give examples of each.
- Describe two different types of industrial products and give examples of each.

PROGRESS CHECK

BRANDING

One element to consider when preparing products for the marketplace is branding. A **brand** is a name, symbol, or design (or combination thereof) that identifies the

> **brand**
> A name, symbol, or design (or combination thereof) that identifies the goods or services of one seller or group of sellers and distinguishes them from the goods and services of competitors.

The Quebec Winter Carnival is the world's biggest snow carnival. For 17 days, the Bonhomme Carnaval greets visitors and plays a central role in the events. Generating more than $36 million a year in economic spin-offs for Quebec City, this event attracts more than 1 million participants a year.

trademark
A brand that has been given exclusive legal protection for both the brand name and the pictorial design.

www.sears.com

www.sony.com

www.pg.com

www.daimlerchrysler.com

www.mazda.com

www.suzuki.com

www.royalbank.com

www.volkswagen.com

products of one seller or group of sellers and distinguishes them from the products of competitors. The term *brand* is sufficiently comprehensive to include practically all means of identification of a product. A *brand name* is that part of the brand consisting of a word, letter, or group of words or letters comprising a name that differentiates a seller's goods or services from those of competitors. Brand names you may be familiar with include Air Canada, Roots, and the Bank of Montreal. Such brand names give products a distinction that tends to make them attractive to consumers.

A **trademark** is a brand that has been given exclusive legal protection for both the brand name and the pictorial design. The McDonald's Golden Arches, widely recognized around the world, are one example. Another example is the Bonhomme Carnaval, Quebec's winter carnival mascot. In 2001, Pierre de Nos wrote a police thriller and his cover featured a murderous Bonhomme Carnaval pointing a pistol. A character in the novel smuggled drugs across the Canada – U.S. border inside the Bonhomme's snowman costume.[11] The cover was withdrawn after Carnaval organizers threatened a court injunction. They felt that this family-oriented event could be tainted by any suggestion of a giant snowman attacking visitors.

Choosing a Brand Name

When choosing a brand name, marketers use some guidelines. The brand name should:

1. **Reflect some of the benefits of the product** so consumers can easily relate to the purpose of the product. Examples include Craftsman tools, Sony PlayStation consoles, and Beautyrest pillows.

2. **Be easy to say, recognize, and remember.** This is well applied when we consider some of the Procter & Gamble laundry detergent brands such as Bold, Cheer, and Tide.

3. **Be distinctive** so that it stands out and catches the attention and imagination of the consumer. Examples include the Chrysler PT Cruiser, the Mazda Protegé, and the Suzuki Swift.

4. **Translate well in international markets**, as we are a global economy. RBC Financial Group (formerly Royal Bank of Canada) and KFC (formerly Kentucky Fried Chicken) are just two examples of firms that have changed their names to work in international markets. As an illustration, KFC sells fish (not just chicken) in Asia.

5. **Be legal and protected through registration.** Specifically, users of a brand name must ensure that another person or entity has not already registered it. As well, you have an obligation to protect your registered name and prohibit someone else from using it or you may lose the sole rights to this name. This applies to new brand names and current brand names, as Volkswagen AG (VW) discovered. As described by *Vintage Cars* journalist Teri Olcott, the following occurred:[12]

In 1998, VW paid $790 million to Vickers PLC to purchase Rolls-Royce Motor Cars Ltd., which was known for its Rolls-Royce and Bentley cars. Soon after, BMW (VW's earlier bidding competitor) announced that it had purchased the Rolls-Royce brand name and the emblem that is on the hoods of all Rolls-Royce cars from Rolls-Royce PLC for $65 million. VW had overlooked that Vickers did not own the rights to the Rolls-Royce name; the name belonged to another company, Rolls-Royce PLC (an aerospace company). Amid threats of lawsuits, it was settled that VW would own the Rolls-Royce name until the end of 2002. In 2003, BMW would manufacture a new line of Rolls-Royce cars under the BMW name. Did VW get what it paid for? Bentleys account for approximately 60 percent of Rolls-Royce Motor Cars' sales, but the Rolls-Royce name is more well-known than the Bentley name. What do you think?

www.bmw.com

Brand Equity

Why do marketers spend millions of dollars building a brand? Marketers do so to build brand equity. **Brand equity** is the combination of factors (such as awareness, loyalty, perceived quality, images, and emotions) that people associate with a given brand name.

The core of brand equity is brand loyalty. **Brand loyalty** is the degree to which customers are satisfied, like the brand, and are committed to further purchases. A loyal group of customers (defined as those who buy the product regularly without the need for incentives) represents substantial value to a firm. As an example, based on future expected earnings the Coca-Cola brand today is considered the world's most valuable brand, with a brand-equity value of US$68.95 billion.[13]

In the past, due to increased competition, companies tried to boost their short-term revenues by offering promotions (such as coupons) to move goods quickly.[14] These actions eroded consumers' loyalty toward these brand names and many consumers would associate value with reduced prices. Today companies realize the value of brand equity and are trying to measure the earning power of strong brand names without these incentives.[15]

Perceived quality is an important part of brand equity. A product that's perceived as being of better quality than its competitors can be priced higher and thus improve profits. The key to creating a quality image is to identify what the consumer looks for in a quality product and then communicate a quality message in every message the company sends out. Factors influencing the perception of quality include price, appearance, features, and reputation.

Another element of brand equity is brand awareness. **Brand awareness** refers to how quickly (or easily) a given brand name comes to mind when a product category is mentioned. As a test, what brand do you think of first when you consider computers, or music, or cars? The names you come up with reflect your brand awareness and brand recall. Promotional efforts—such as advertising and publicity—help build strong brand awareness. Older brands, such as IBM and General Electric, are usually the highest in brand awareness because they have had the years to build brand equity. Event sponsorship (e.g., the Molson Indy auto race and the Rogers AT&T Cup tennis tournament) also helps to improve brand awareness.

brand equity
The combination of factors (such as awareness, loyalty, perceived quality, images, and emotions) that people associate with a given brand name.

brand loyalty
The degree to which customers are satified, like the brand, and are committed to further purchases.

brand awareness
How quickly or easily a given brand name comes to mind when a product category is mentioned.

www.ibm.com

www.ge.com

Generating Brand Equity In generating brand equity, there are advantages for both the buyer and the seller. For the buyer (that is, the consumer), a brand conveys information and value. It gives products distinction and differentiates them from competitors' products. If you have tried a product and were satisfied with it, familiar brands reduce search time as you will consciously seek out this brand, minimizing the possibility of a negative experience with an unknown brand. People are often

www.bayer.com

impressed by certain brand names, even though they say they know there's no difference between brands in a given product category. For example, when people say that all headache medicine is alike, put two bottles in front of them—one with the Bayer label and one labelled with an unknown brand. See which they choose. Most people choose the brand name, even when they say there's no difference. This is the value of brand equity.

As the seller, marketers can build on the strength of the brand when promoting the product. A brand that has existed over time may have a personality attached to it (e.g., the Green Giant) and branding helps promotional efforts, contributing to repeat purchases. For some products, a strong brand translates into higher prices.

A strong brand name also lends strength to new-product introductions. If a consumer has confidence in the brand and the quality of the current products, these positive feelings can be transferred to new-product introductions, increasing the new-product adoption rate.

Brand Categories

manufacturer's brand names
The brand names of manufacturers that distribute products nationally.

www.roots.com

www.ford.com

knockoff brands
Illegal copies of national brand-name goods.

dealer (private) brands
Products that don't carry the manufacturer's name but carry a distributor or retailer's name instead.

generic brands
Nonbranded products that usually sell at a sizeable discount compared to national or private brands.

Several categories of brands are familiar to you. **Manufacturer's brand names**, also called **national brands**, are the brand names of manufacturers that distribute products nationally. Examples include Roots and Ford. Since these products have such high brand recognition (because they are so familiar to consumers), manufacturers are often able to gain better shelf spaces in stores.

Knockoff brands are illegal copies of national brand-name goods. If you see an expensive brand name item such as a Polo shirt or a Rolex watch for sale at a ridiculously low price, you can be pretty sure that it is a knockoff.[16]

Dealer (private) brands are products that don't carry the manufacturer's name but carry a distributor or retailer's name instead. This is why they are also known as *house brands* or *distributor brands*. Canadian Tire sells the Motomaster brand.

In Canada, the grocery retailing industry averages between $59 and $60 billion in sales. Private labels (e.g., Our Compliments and President's Choice) account for almost one-third of all sales in some stores, with Loblaw leading the industry in private-label sales.[17] Private brands are most prevalent in the categories of paper and wrapping, frozen and refrigerated food, and dessert and snacks. They are becoming more popular as these retailers can net a larger margin (typically 1 to 2 percent) on the sales of their own products. They can control the quality, promotion, and placement of their own products instead of always having to negotiate for manufacturers' brands.

Generic brands are nonbranded products that usually sell at a sizeable discount compared to national or private brands. Characteristics include basic packaging

President's Choice is a private brand of products developed by Loblaw Companies Limited. These products have been extremely successful in Canada and are now being sold in other countries.

Darren Price

with a description of the contents, and they are supported by little or no advertising. For example, a label on a generic can of peaches will simply say "Peaches," with no brand name. In the past, the quality has varied considerably among generic goods. Consumers today are buying more generic products because their overall quality has improved so greatly in recent years that it approximates or equals that of the more expensive brand names.

The Battle of the Brands Since the 1980s there has been a dramatic surge in the popularity of private labels in supermarkets. As a result of 1998 consolidations, Canada's two largest players (Loblaw and Sobeys) control approximately 58 percent of the Canadian industry.[18] Supermarkets will keep growing their private labels as a way to differentiate their products and to gain greater pricing flexibility.[19] The increasing competition for market share and store shelf space between national brands and private brands is termed the "battle of the brands."

This "battle" poses a problem for major manufacturers like Ault Foods Ltd., which makes the national milk brands Sealtest and Lactantia. The production of its own brands does not require the use of all the manufacturing capacity Ault has. Since it is costly to have idle, unused plant capacity, it has been drawn into—guess what?—producing private-label products for supermarkets. Ault produces about half the country's private-label ice-cream products, including the very popular President's Choice product line for Loblaws stores.

Doesn't it seem strange that companies produce products that compete with their own brands? Yet the economics of the situation dictate that they are better off, at least in the short run, to profit from the use of their idle capacity. There is also the pressure from supermarkets like Loblaws to produce their private labels because they also carry the national brands.

National brands do compete with private labels. If the former could increase their market share, the companies would have less idle capacity, resulting in less pressure to produce private labels. Private labels' share has been increasing because they often sell for lower prices. As the supermarkets sell more of their own labels, they reduce shelf space for national brands, resulting in still lower sales for them.

Generic Names Many manufacturers fear having their brands become generic names, as they would lose the sole rights to the brand name. A **generic name** is the name for a product category. For example, *linoleum, nylon, escalator,* and *zipper* were once brand names. They all became so popular and many so identified with the product that these brands lost their branded status and became generic. A brand name becomes generic if its patent expires or if the court decides that the branded name has become part of everyday society and, thereby, no one has claims to it.

What can producers do if this occurs? They need to develop new names. Aspirin, for example, was renamed Bayer Aspirin. Here, the firm put its name before the product so consumers could differentiate between this firm's product and that of other competitors, building on the strength of the Bayer name. Companies that are working hard to protect their brand names today include Xerox (one ad reads, "Don't say 'Xerox it'; say 'Copy it'") and Rollerblade (in-line skates). When one thinks of in-line skates, one should think of *Rollerblade* in-line skates (putting the brand name before the product) instead of calling all in-line skates Rollerblades (where the brand replaces the product category).

www.cdngrocer.com

Canadian Grocer is an online industry trade magazine. What other developments of significance to this industry can you find reported? If you were in the industry, would you visit the site regularly and frequently? Why?

generic name
The name for a product category.

Creating Brand Associations

brand association
The linking of a brand to other favourable images.

www.mercedes-benz.com

www.buick.com

The name, symbol, and slogan a company uses can assist greatly in brand recognition for that company's products. **Brand association** is the linking of a brand to other favourable images. For example, you can link a brand to other product users, to a popular celebrity, to a particular geographic area, or to competitors. Note, for example, how ads for Mercedes-Benz and Buick associate those companies' cars with rich people who may spend their leisure time playing or watching golf or polo. What person might we associate with Fiberrific to give the cereal more appeal?

The person responsible for building brands is known as a brand manager or product manager. We'll explore that position later in this chapter.

PROGRESS CHECK

- What's the difference between a brand name and a trademark?
- Can you explain the difference between a manufacturer's brand, a private brand, and a generic brand?
- What are the key components of brand equity?

PACKAGING

Consumers evaluate many aspects of the value package, including the brand. Companies have used packaging to change and improve their basic product. Thus, we've had squeezable ketchup bottles; plastic bottles for motor oil that eliminate the need for funnels, and toothpaste pumps. In each case, the package changed the product in the minds of consumers and opened large markets. Packaging can also be changed to refresh an older product: see the Spotlight on Big Business box "Students Design a Face-Lift for Kraft Dinner."

Packaging can also help make a product more attractive to retailers. For example, the Universal Product Codes (UPCs) on many packages make it easier to control inventory; the UPC is the combination of a bar code (those familiar black and white lines) and a preset number that gives the retailer information about the product (price, size, colour, etc.). In short, packaging changes the product by changing its visibility, usefulness, or attractiveness.

Packaging Functions

Packaging has always been an important aspect of the product offer, but today it's carrying more of the promotional burden than in the past. Many products that were

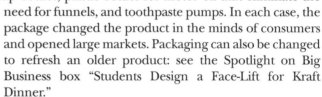

No figure in golf is more instantly recognizable than Tiger Woods. By using Tiger in its ads, Buick hopes to attract readers' attention and to have them associate Buick with a quality winner. Buick is trying to build its image among golfers because Tiger brings to mind many positive traits Buick hopes consumers will associate with its brand. What other products might benefit from having Tiger Woods as a spokesperson?

SPOTLIGHT ON BIG BUSINESS

www.kraftfoods.com

Students Design a Face-Lift for Kraft Dinner

Kraft Canada Inc. decided it was time to design a new package for its popular Kraft Dinner product. One way of giving a lift to an old product is to give it a "face-lift." What makes this particular situation interesting is that Kraft chose a unique method for solving the problem. In 1994, together with the Packaging Association of Canada, The Thomas Pigeon Design Group, and Shikatani Lacroix Design Inc., Kraft sponsored a competition for Toronto students to come up with a winning design.

Ultimately, 81 students from the Ontario College of Art, George Brown College, Humber College, and Mohawk College submitted entries to their schools. The conditions they had to meet were quite demanding. The cheese had to be separated from the macaroni; the package had to be so attractive that it would "block out" other items on the shelf; students had to understand printing processes so that they didn't come up with something that could not be produced; and, finally, it had to be a low-cost item to manufacture since Kraft Dinner is a low-priced product.

The schools selected 17 of the 81 designs for preliminary judging by a seven-person panel. The panel chose two from each school for final judging. From this group, they selected a design by Tina Crosby, of the Ontario College of Art. She got a $1,500 bursary for winning the competition.

One of the seven judges, J.P. Lacroix, president of Shikatani Lacroix Design, commended Crosby for her excellent design. She met all the requirements with an eye-catching format that consisted of two separate boxes, one each for the cheese and macaroni, both held together by a transparent seal with the Kraft logo on it. The two boxes were illustrated with tumbling macaroni and cheese. Lacroix noted that Crosby showed excellent understanding of the printing process required. She also provided "good written documentation to back up her ideas."

Source: Paula Kulig, "Old Fave Gets a Facelift," *Globe and Mail, Report on Business*, August 29, 1995, p. B22.

---

once sold by salespersons are now being sold in self-service outlets, and the package has been given more sales responsibility. The package must perform the following functions:

1. Protect the goods inside, stand up under handling and storage, be tamperproof, deter theft, and yet be easy to open and use.

2. Attract the buyer's attention. The average package gets one-tenth of a second's consideration from consumers; therefore, as the silent salesperson, it must communicate "buy me and here's why."[20]

3. Describe the contents and give content information on the label.

Recently there has been a glut of tuna on the market, making it difficult for tuna sellers to make much money. The price of a can of tuna was simply too low for much profit. Therefore, Sunkist turned to packaging to generate more profit. It developed resealable pouches that made sandwich-making easier. There is no need to drain the tuna, the package is sandwich sized, and there is a firmer texture to the product. Are there other packaging innovations that you have found helpful or convenient?

AP Photo/Keit Srakocic

4.   Provide information on warranties, warnings, and other consumer matters.

5.   Give some indication of price, value, and uses.

Clearly, packaging has become a critical part of product design. An interesting example is the problem Ault Foods faced when it sought a design for its purified, premium Lactantia milk containers. Because Ault developed this product through a patented filtering process, the company wanted a special look. At first its advertising agency, Trudhope Associates, designed a high-tech silver package. However, survey groups overwhelmingly opted for a simple farm look: cows, greenery, and a country home. You can see this design today on Ault's cartons and plastic containers.[21]

Packaging Services

Packaging of services has been getting more attention recently. For example, Virgin Airlines includes door-to-door limousine service and in-flight massages in its total package. When combining goods or services into one package, it's important not to include so much that the price gets too high. It's best to work with customers to develop offers that meet their individual needs.

Extended warranties are another service often offered when products are sold. The warranty covers the cost of certain repairs after the manufacturer's warranty (usually one year) has expired. These warranties can range anywhere from 10 percent to 30 percent of the product's retail price. Is it worth it to get an extended warranty? An estimated 80 percent of consumers who purchase this insurance never make a claim against it.[22] Consumers Union estimates that profit margins range from 40 percent to 77 percent for the retailer, and it notes that most product defects are typically revealed in the first 90 days, when the manufacturer's warranty is still in effect.[23]

Packaging and the Environment

On a worldwide scale, $540 billion is spent yearly on packaging.[24] With increased interest in the environment consumers are demanding that marketers reduce the amount of packaging and produce more products that are environmentally friendly. The introduction of *green products* has been a response to these demands. Firms today are continuously trying to develop packages that can be easily recycled, including refillable bottles and boxes that use recycled cardboard. Such attempts are evident in the Canadian aluminum industry, which recycles nearly two-thirds of all aluminum cans for reuse.[25]

www.pac.ca

There are industry associations and government regulations that speak to the importance of packaging. For example, the Packaging Association of Canada represents both users and suppliers of packaging and works with industry, consumers, and government to promote the production of packaging that has the least possible impact on the environment. The Consumer Packaging and Labelling Act is in place to protect consumers against product misrepresentation in packaging and labelling. While we are seeing industry and government moving to protect the environment and Canadians, more work still needs to be done.

Nearly three-quarters of Canadians feel that protecting the environment is more important than promoting economic growth.[26] However, many consumers are still not prepared to pay higher prices. Given this, what incentive will there be, then, for businesses to produce such products?

Labelling

Labelling is another element marketers must address when developing products. Labels should be attractive and informative. They are used to communicate important information to the consumer including the contents and ingredients. From the marketing point of view, a good label helps to identify the product and differentiate it from competing products.

There are many Canadian government resources available to companies and consumers alike that outline label requirements. One example is the Consumer Packaging and Labelling Act and Regulations. It requires that the label contain three mandatory statements, which must be present on the principal display panel. Each label must include:[27]

1. The **Product Identity Declaration,** which communicates the product's common name in both English and French.

2. The **Net Quantity Declaration,** which must indicate a unit of measurement that is appropriate to the product; for example, by volume (liquid or gas) or by weight (solids).

3. The **Dealer Identification,** which must indicate the dealer's name and place of business. The address should be sufficient to ensure postal delivery.

An area that is receiving more scrutiny is the labelling of genetically modified (GM) foods. While most Canadians have indicated that they want the right to choose whether they buy GM foods (as indicated on food labels), this information is not readily available. The Canadian Food Inspection Agency has both a mandatory and a voluntary labelling policy. All foods that have been changed nutritionally or compositionally, or that contain possible allergens, require a label.[28] If tests show that the nutrition or composition of GM foods remains unchanged, no special label is required.

The Canadian Health Food Association (CHFA) is lobbying the government for a national, mandatory labelling standard for all GM foods. The Canadian Biotechnology Advisory Committee (created by the government) advocates a gradual and voluntary approach to the labelling of GM foods.[29] The debate continues over both labelling requirements and the unknown long-term effects of eating GM foods.

If you are concerned about GM foods, then you may consider purchasing goods from health-food stores. President and CEO of CHFA Donna Herringer has indicated that "many health food stores have moved to meet consumer concerns by stocking organic and non–GM labelled products in their stores."[30]

When producing goods internationally, marketers must also review the packaging and label regulations that are in place in these foreign markets. Languages, government regulations, and national and local traditions and practices vary. It is always a good idea for Canadian producers to include the "Made In Canada" endorsement so consumers know the place of origin.

What kind of package and label would you design for Fiberrific?

www.strategis.ic.gc.ca

Visit the government's Strategis Web site for more information on government acts and other business-related topics.

BRAND MANAGEMENT

A **brand manager** (known as a *product manager* in some firms) has direct responsibility for one brand or one product line. This responsibility includes all the elements of the marketing mix: product, price, place, and promotion. Thus, the brand manager might be thought of as a president of a one-product firm. Imagine being the brand manager for Fiberrific. You'd be responsible for everything having to do with that one brand. One reason many large consumer-product companies created the position of brand manager is to have greater control over new-product development and product promotion.

brand manager
A manager who has direct responsibility for one brand or one product line.

New-Product Success

What is considered a new product? This depends on your perspective. According to Consumer and Corporate Affairs Canada, a product can be called new for up to 12 months. From other perspectives, one can consider newness compared to existing products; newness from the firm's perspective; or newness from the consumer's perspective.[31]

All marketers wish to introduce successful new products into the market. They are critical to long-term success and can provide a firm with a long-term and sustainable competitive advantage.[32] Many studies have been conducted on establishing the key factors for successful products. The following are the top three success factors:[33]

1. **A unique superior product** that is differentiated from its competitors.

2. **A strong market orientation** where there is a market-driven and customer-focused new-product process.

3. **A product that has an international orientation** in design, development, and target marketing.

Despite all their efforts to produce products that we like, companies fail more often than not. The New Products Showcase and Learning Center in Ithaca, New York, has thousands of such failed products on display. What products have you noticed disappearing from the grocery shelves?

Why Do New Products Fail?

New-product failure rates are high; success depends not only on the industry but also on how one defines a new product and a failure. While the true failure rate is about 35 percent, this figure does not include the majority of new-product projects that are discontinued before launch yet still involve considerable time and money from a company.[34]

Not delivering what is promised is a leading cause of new-product failure. Other reasons for failure include poor marketing research, technical problems, insufficient marketing effort, and bad timing.[35] Smaller firms may experience a lower success rate unless they conduct proper product planning.

Examples of some new-product failures include Kleenex Avert Virucidal Tissues; Gillette's For Oily Hair Only Shampoo; Nullo, the edible deodorant; and Crystal Pepsi (a clear drink with a cola taste).[36] Why do you think that these products failed?

The New-Product Development Process

The implementation of a new-product development process (see Figure 16.3) consists of six stages. New products continue to pour into the market every year, and the profit potential looks tremendous. Think, for example, of the potential of interactive TV, virtual reality games and products, Internet-connected phones, and other innovations. Where do these ideas come from? How are they tested? What's the life span for an innovation? The following sections look at these issues.

Generating New-Product Ideas Figure 16.4 gives you a good idea of where new-product ideas come from. Note that 38 percent of the new-product ideas for consumer products come from analyzing competitors. Such copying of competitors slows the introduction of original ideas. Consumer and supplier suggestions are also key sources of new ideas.

product screening
A process designed to reduce the number of new-product ideas being worked on at any one time.

Product Screening **Product screening** is designed to reduce the number of new-product ideas being worked on at any one time. Criteria needed for screening include whether the product fits in well with present products, profit potential, marketability, and personnel requirements. Each of these factors may be assigned a weight, and total scores are then computed. A software package called Quick Insight now helps companies analyze the potential of new goods and services. By answering about 60 questions and then reviewing the answers, the user can gain an understanding of the likely problems and potential strengths of the new offering. Nonetheless, it still takes about seven ideas to generate one commercial product.

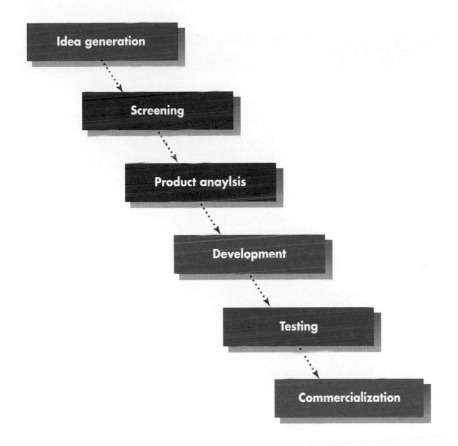

FIGURE 16.3

THE NEW-PRODUCT DEVELOPMENT PROCESS

Product development is a six-stage process. Which stage do you believe to be the most important?

Product Analysis **Product analysis** is done after product screening. It's largely a matter of making cost estimates and sales forecasts to get a feeling for profitability. Products that don't meet the established criteria are withdrawn from consideration.

Product Development and Testing If a product passes the screening and analysis phases, the firm begins to develop it further. A product idea can be developed into many different *product concepts,* which are alternative product offerings based on the same product idea that have different meanings and values to consumers.[37] For example, a firm that makes packaged meat products may develop the concept of a chicken dog—a hot dog made of chicken that tastes like an all-beef hot dog. A *prototype,* or sample, may be developed so that consumers can actually try the taste.

 Concept testing involves taking a product *idea* to consumers to test their reactions (see Figure 16.5). Do they see the benefits of this new product? How frequently would they buy it? At what price? What features do they like and dislike? What changes would they make? Different ideas are tested using different packaging,

product analysis
Making cost estimates and sales forecasts to get a feeling for profitability of new-product ideas.

concept testing
Taking a product idea to consumers to test their reactions.

CONSUMER PRODUCTS (based on a survey of 79 new products)	
Analysis of the competition	38.0%
Company sources other than research and development	31.6
Consumer research	17.7
Research and development	13.9
Consumer suggestions	12.7
Published information	11.4
Supplier suggestions	3.8

FIGURE 16.4

SOURCES OF NEW-PRODUCT IDEAS

This survey shows where ideas for new products originate. As you know, research plays an important role in the development of new products. Have you ever tried to sell a new product idea to a company?

FIGURE 16.5

STEPS TO TAKE BEFORE
TEST MARKETING A
PRODUCT

Product development,
communication development,
and strategy development
all are used as a company
develops a new product.
Extensive testing is used to
guarantee the new product's
success. Have you ever
participated in such testing?

PRODUCT DEVELOPMENT	COMMUNICATION DEVELOPMENT	STRATEGY DEVELOPMENT
Identify unfilled need	Select a name	Set marketing goals
Preliminary profit/payout plan for each concept	Design a package and test	Develop marketing mix (after communication developed)
Concept test	Create a copy theme and test	
Determine whether the product can be made	Develop complete ads and test	Estimate cost of marketing plan (after product development)
Test the concept and product (and revise as indicated)		
Develop the product		
Run extended product use tests		

branding, ingredients, and so forth until a product emerges that's desirable from both production and marketing perspectives. A good example is the testing of the package design for Ault Lactantia milk described earlier. Can you see the importance of concept testing for Fiberrific?

Commercialization Even if a product tests well, it may take quite a while before the product achieves success in the market. Take the zipper, for example. It took more than 15 years to perfect the product—and even then consumers weren't interested. Finally, the U.S. Navy started using zippers during the First World War. Today, Talon Inc. is the leading U.S. maker of zippers, producing some 500 million of them a year.

commercialization
Promoting a product to
distributors and retailers to get
wide distribution and
developing strong advertising
and sales campaigns to
generate and maintain interest
in the product among
distributors and consumers.

This example shows that the marketing effort must include **commercialization**. This includes (1) promoting the product to distributors and retailers to get wide distribution and (2) developing strong advertising and sales campaigns to generate and maintain interest in the product among distributors and consumers. New products are now getting rapid exposure to global markets by being promoted on the Internet.[38] Interactive Web sites enable consumers to view new products, ask questions, and make purchases easily and quickly.

The International Challenge

Marketers have learned through experience that the secret to success in today's rapidly changing environment is to bring out new products that are high in quality, and to bring them out quickly. This is especially true in light of the rapid development process occurring in other countries.

Xerox executives were surprised by Japanese competitors who were developing new copier models twice as fast as Xerox and at half the cost. Xerox had to slash its traditional four-to-five-year product development cycle. After millions of dollars of investment, Xerox can now produce a new model in less than two years. To keep products competitive requires continuous incremental improvements in function, cost, and quality. Cost-sensitive design and new process technologies are critical.

More attention must be given to the product development process; that is, developing products in co-operation with their users. To implement the new-product development process, managers must go out into the market and interact closely with their dealers and their ultimate customers. Successful new-product development is an interactive process whereby customers present their needs and new-product designs are prepared to meet those needs. Changes are made over time to make sure that the total product offer exactly meets the customer's needs. The focus shifts from internal product development processes to external customer responsiveness.

Fast-food patrons will have noticed that recently McDonald's has added new products to its franchises and changed the way it prepared them. But don't forget that McDonald's sells about half of its burgers in foreign markets, and it is rapidly gobbling up market share. In fact, 95 percent of all new McDonald's stores will be overseas, at least for the next several years. Since 1993, McDonald's has opened 415 stores in France alone. There are some 700 stores in Brazil. Therefore, McDonald's has to use product development to keep its customer base in foreign markets as well.

Why is McDonald's so successful in global markets? Because it adapts its products to local tastes. In Taiwan and Singapore, the stores sell a bone-in chicken dish called Chicken McCrispy. In the United Kingdom, people love Indian food, so McDonald's offers a McChicken Tikka Naan dish to satisfy that desire. In Australia, there is the McOz burger, and in Japan the Chicken Tatsuta. In India, you can buy a Maharajah Mac.

McDonald's is also patient. It doesn't mind taking years to become established in a new foreign market. When McDonald's opened a store in Rome near the Spanish Steps, the outcry from Italian citizens was so loud that zoning laws were passed to keep the stores out of city centres. But McDonald's was able to buy an Italian burger chain called Burghy's and now has 220 stores in Italy and some 98 percent of the burger market there.

McDonald's is now in 117 countries and has some 40 million customers served daily, up from 30 million just five years ago. Some 11,300 new stores will go up outside of the United States by 2004.

Sources: Bruce Upbin, "Beyond Burgers," Forbes, November 1, 1999, pp. 218–23, Louise Kramer, "Fast-Feeders Play Game of Chicken," Advertising Age, November 8, 1999, p. 44; and Robert Frank, "Big Boy's Big Adventure in Thailand," The Wall Street Journal, April 12, 2000, pp. B1, B4.

The Reaching Beyond Our Borders box "The Globalization of McDonald's" explores how McDonald's has been so successful in global markets. The answer has been to adapt the product offering to the wants and need of consumers in each country.

THE PRODUCT LIFE CYCLE

Once a product has been developed and tested, it is placed in the market. Products often go through a life cycle consisting of four stages: introduction, growth, maturity, and decline. This is called the **product life cycle**. The traditional product life cycle illustrated in Figure 16.6 is a theoretical model of what happens to sales and profits for an individual product or for a product class (e.g., all dishwasher soaps) over time. Today we are seeing shortening product life cycles due to environmental factors such as increasing global competition, the rapid introduction of new products, changing consumer tastes, and technological improvements. It is for these reasons that marketers find it so important to manage products at each stage of their product life cycles and to generate as much revenue as possible in each stage.

Not *all* products and product classes follow this traditional shape, for the following reasons:

product life cycle
A theoretical model of what happens to sales and profits for a product class over time.

1. Each one progresses through the four stages at a different rate, as we will see with fashions and fads.

2. The magnitude between sales and profits may vary at each stage, depending on demand, price, and costs

3. Product strategy decisions made by managers (as a result of their SWOT analysis) impact the product life cycles.

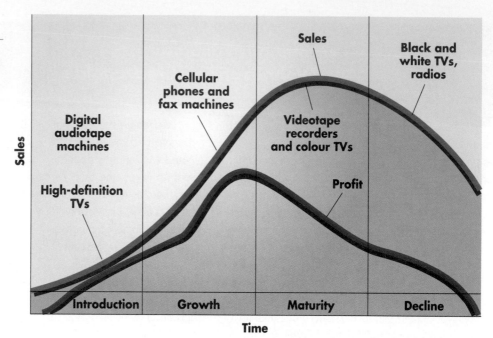

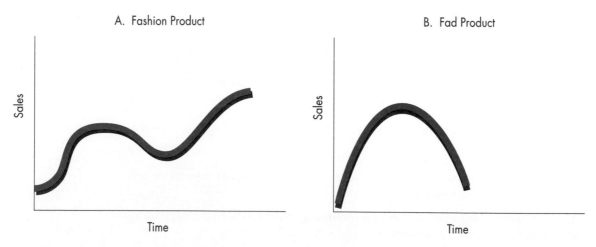

FIGURE 16.6

SALES AND PROFITS DURING THE PRODUCT LIFE CYCLE

Note that profit levels start to fall *before* sales reach their peak. When profits and sales start to decline, it's time to come out with a new product or to remodel the old one to maintain interest and profits.

FIGURE 16.7

SALES AND PROFITS OVER TIME DURING THE FASHION AND FAD PRODUCTS LIFE CYCLES

Fashion products—such as hemline lengths on skirts or bottom widths on pants—go through the complete product life cycle and then return again as they come into fashion. Given its return popularity, clothing often falls within this category. The length of the cycles may be years or decades.[39] Figure 16.7a shows what a typical fashion product life cycle looks like.

Fad products, which typically include novelties (such as Beanie Babies, Furby, mood rings, Pet Rocks, and Pogs), experience rapid sales on introduction and then an equally rapid decline.[40] Fads are short-lived, as they are popular to a limited number of consumers and when this group's interest fades so do product sales. Figure 16.7b shows the rapid rise and fall of fad product life cycles.

When comparing Figure 16.6 and Figure 16.7, remember that, while all products do not follow the same product life cycle, all products do in fact go through the four stages. They just progress at different rates. For example, while frozen foods as a generic class may go through the entire cycle, one brand may never get beyond the introduction stage. Nonetheless, the product life cycle may provide some basis for

A. Fashion Product

B. Fad Product

anticipating future market developments and for planning marketing strategies. Some products, such as microwave ovens, stay in the introductory stage for years and are then adopted by many consumers. Other products, such as fad clothing, may go through the entire cycle within a few months.

Example of the Product Life Cycle

You can see how the theory works by looking at the product life cycle of instant coffee. When it was introduced, most people didn't like it as well as "regular" coffee, and it took several years for instant coffee to gain general acceptance (introduction stage). At one point, though, instant coffee grew rapidly in popularity, and many brands were introduced (growth stage). After a while, people became attached to one brand and sales levelled off (maturity stage). Sales then went into a slight decline when freeze-dried coffees were introduced (decline stage). At present, freeze-dried coffee is, in turn, at the maturity stage. It's extremely important to recognize what stage a product is in, because such an analysis must precede intelligent and efficient marketing decisions.

The Importance of the Product Life Cycle

The importance of the product life cycle to marketers is this: Different stages in the product life cycle call for different marketing strategies. Figure 16.8 outlines the marketing-mix decisions that might be made. As you go through the table, you'll see that each stage calls for multiple marketing mix changes. Remember, these concepts are largely theoretical and should be used only as guidelines.

Figure 16.9 shows in table form the theory of what happens to sales volume, profits, and competition during the product life cycle. You can compare this table to the graph in Figure 16.6. For instance, both figures show that a product at the mature stage may reach the top in sales growth while profit is decreasing. This occurs for several reasons. In the maturity phase, many competitors are in the market (having been attracted by the profit potential in the growth stage) and prices are decreasing. As well, firms are increasing their promotional efforts to attract and retain consumers. While sales are increasing, these actions are impacting profits

FIGURE 16.8

SAMPLE STRATEGIES FOLLOWED DURING THE PRODUCT LIFE CYCLE

	MARKETING-MIX ELEMENTS			
LIFE CYCLE STAGE	PRODUCT	PRICE	PLACE	PROMOTION
Introduction	Offer market-tested product; keep mix small	Go after innovators with high introductory price (skimming strategy) or use penetration pricing	Use wholesalers, selective distribution	Dealer promotion and heavy investment in primary demand advertising and sales promotion to get stores to carry the product and consumers to try it
Growth	Improve product; keep product mix limited	Adjust price to meet competition	Increase distribution	Heavy competitive advertising
Maturity	Differentiate your product to satisfy different market segments	Further reduce price	Take over wholesaling function and intensify distribution	Emphasize brand name as well as product benefits and differences
Decline	Cut product mix; develop new-product ideas	Consider price increase	Consolidate distribution; drop some outlets	Reduce advertising to target only loyal customers

FIGURE 16.9

HOW SALES, PROFITS, AND COMPETITION VARY OVER THE PRODUCT LIFE CYCLE

All products go through these stages at various times in their life cycle. What happens to sales as a product matures?

LIFE CYCLE STAGE	SALES	PROFITS	COMPETITORS
Introduction	Low sales	Losses may occur	Few
Growth	Rapidly rising sales	Very high profits	Growing number
Maturity	Peak sales	Declining profits	Stable number, then declining
Decline	Falling sales	Profits may fall to become losses	Declining number

(due to lower prices and more costly promotions). Finally, new products entering the market may be superior, with more features and of more interest to consumers. Consequently, demand may be shifting to other products, also ultimately affecting revenues and profits.

www.churchdwight.com

At the maturity stage, a marketing manager may use market research to find a new use for its product. Church and Dwight, maker of Arm & Hammer baking soda, has mastered the art of finding new uses for this product. It has been promoted as a refrigerator deodorant, a cat litterbox additive, a carpet cleaner, and as a replacement for harsh chemicals in swimming pools. By listening to market research, Church and Dwight managers have been able to introduce new growth cycles into the product life cycle of this product.

CRITICAL THINKING

In what stage of the product life cycle are laptop computers? What does Figure 16.8 indicate firms should do at that stage? What will the next stage be? What might you do at that stage to optimize profits?

Peanut butter is in the maturity or decline stage of the product life cycle. Does that explain why Skippy recently introduced a reduced-fat version of its peanut butter? What other variations on older products have been introduced in the last few years?

PROGRESS CHECK

- What are the six steps in the new-product development process?
- Can you draw a traditional product life cycle and label its parts? Do the same for a fashion and a fad product life cycle.

COMPETITIVE PRICING

Price is only element of the four Ps mix that generates revenues. Like product, place, and promotion, price is also a critical ingredient in consumer evaluations. In this section, we'll explore price both as an ingredient of the value package and as a strategic marketing tool.

Pricing Objectives

A firm may have several objectives in mind when setting a pricing strategy. When pricing Fiberrific, we may want to promote the product's image. If we price it high and use the right promotion, maybe we can make it the Evian of cereals. We also might price it high to achieve a certain profit objective or return on investment. We could price Fiberrific lower than its competitors because we want disadvantaged people to be able to afford this nutritious cereal. That is, we could have some social or ethical goal in mind. Low pricing may also discourage competition because the profit potential is less in this case. A low price may also help us capture a larger share of the market. The point is that a firm may have several pricing objectives over time, and it must formulate these objectives clearly before developing an overall pricing strategy. Popular objectives include the following:

1. **Achieving a target return on investment or profit**. Ultimately, the goal of marketing is to make a profit by providing goods and services to others. Naturally, one long-run pricing objective of almost all firms is to optimize profit.[41]

2. **Building traffic**. Supermarkets often advertise certain products at or below cost to attract people to the store. These products are called *loss leaders*. The long-run objective is to make profits by following the short-run objective of building a customer base. Yahoo is providing an auction service for free in competition with eBay. Why give such a service away free? Because it generates more advertising revenue on its site and it attracts more people to its other services.[42]

   www.yahoo.com

   www.ebay.com

3. **Achieving greater market share**. The Canadian auto industry is in a fierce international battle to capture and hold market share. It has lost market share to foreign producers, and has used price incentives (and quality) to try to win it back.

4. **Increasing sales**. Sometimes a firm will lower prices to increase sales. Such a move could hurt profit margins in the short run but could enable the company to become more financially secure in the long run. Then prices could again be raised.

5. **Creating an image**. Certain watches, perfumes, and other socially visible products are priced high to give them an image of exclusivity and status. Examples include Rolex watches and Ralph Lauren fashions.

   www.polo.com

6. **Furthering social objectives**. A firm may want to price a product low so that people with less money can afford the product. The government often gets involved in pricing farm products so that everyone can get basic needs such as milk and bread at a reasonable price.

Let us illustrate a target profit scenario. A target profit is usually set for a particular period of time. For example, for Fiberrific we might aim for a $3-million profit over 18 months. This might be broken down into three-month (quarterly) goals:

1st quarter	$ –400,000 (loss)
2nd quarter	–100,000 (loss)
3rd quarter	200,000
4th quarter	500,000
5th quarter	1,000,000
6th quarter	1,800,000
Total	$3,000,000 profit

Note that a firm may have short-run objectives that differ greatly from its long-run objectives. Both should be understood at the beginning and put into the strategic marketing plan. Pricing objectives should be influenced by other marketing decisions regarding product design, packaging, branding, distribution, and promotion. All of these marketing decisions are interrelated.

People believe intuitively that the price charged for a product must bear some relation to the cost of producing the product. In fact, we'd generally agree that prices are usually set somewhere above cost. But as we'll see, prices and cost aren't always related.

Cost-Based Pricing

Producers often use cost as a primary basis for setting price. Costs establish a price floor below which you cannot sell your products. They develop elaborate cost accounting systems to measure production costs (including materials, labour, and overhead), add in some margin of profit, and come up with a price. The question is whether the price will be satisfactory to the market as well. In the long run, the market (that is, you and I as consumers that want the product—not the producer) determines what the price will be. Pricing should take into account costs, but it should also include the expected costs of product updates, the objectives for each product, and competitor prices.

An opposing strategy to cost-based pricing is one called target costing. **Target costing** is designing a product so that it satisfies customers and meets the profit margins desired by the firm. Target costing makes cost an input to the product development process, not an outcome of it. You estimate the selling price people would be willing to pay for a product and subtract the desired profit margin. The result is the target cost of production. Japanese companies such as Isuzu Motors, Komatsu Limited, and Sony all use target costing.

target costing
Designing a product so that it satisfies customers and meets the profit margins desired by the firm.

Value Pricing

Value pricing is determined with the input of consumers. As we discussed near the beginning of this chapter, value is person-specific and it is evaluated on the criteria of price, quality, and convenience. In value pricing, marketers set brand-name product prices at a fair price. This price reflects the importance of quality and convenience to the consumer at a price that is perceived by consumers to be fair.

Manufacturers and service organizations, as you might expect, are finding it hard to maintain profits while offering value pricing to consumers. The best way to offer value prices and not go broke is to redesign products from the bottom up and to cut costs wherever possible. Taco Bell, for example, cut its kitchen space to provide more seating and specifically designed its menu to increase the number of items that took little kitchen space to prepare. Now 70 percent of each Taco Bell restaurant is seating, compared with 30 percent in the past. Some companies are refurbishing old equipment and selling it at attractive prices.

Small businesses can often capture a healthy share of the market by offering a great price right from the start. Emachines, for example, sold computers at prices between $399 and $599. The only lower prices are those computers that companies are offering for free! The catch is that you either have to pay for several years of high-priced Internet services or put up with lots of ads on your computer screen. Today it is getting easier and easier for consumers to find the best values in goods and services.[43] All they have to do is use a shopping site like my Simon.com to find good values.

value pricing
When marketers provide consumers with brand-name goods and services at fair prices.

www.tacobell.com

Value Pricing in the Service Sector

Value pricing isn't just for fast-food restaurants and grocery stores. It's rapidly expanding to other parts of the service sector as well. Airlines such as Air Canada, for example, are struggling to meet the pricing challenge of low-cost carriers such as Calgary-based WestJet Airlines Ltd. and Dallas-based Southwest Airlines.

Service industries are adopting many of the same pricing tactics as goods-producing firms. They begin by cutting costs as much as possible. Then they determine what services are most important to customers; those that aren't important are

www.aircanada.ca

www.westjet.com

cut. For example, some airlines have eliminated meals on their flights. Southwest does not incur the administrative costs of assigned seats. In return, customers get good value. Some of the bigger airlines are trying to cut costs but are stuck with high fixed costs (e.g., higher staff wages). To compete with discounters such as WestJet, Air Canada introduced Tango, its no-frills brand. Airlines must still offer good service, despite low seat fares, if they wish to remain competitive. This is how consumers calculate the full value package.

With both goods and services, the idea is to give the consumer value. But trying to give the consumer value while maintaining profits is a challenge. Break-even analysis helps an organization relate sales, profit, and price.

Break-Even Analysis

Before you go into the business of producing Fiberrific cereal, it may be wise to determine how many boxes of cereal you'd have to sell before making a profit. You'd then determine whether you could reach such a sales goal. **Break-even analysis** is the process used to determine profitability at various levels of sales. The break-even point is the point where revenues from sales equal all costs. The formula for calculating the break-even point is as follows:

$$\text{Break-even point (BEP)} = \frac{\text{Total fixed cost (FC)}}{\text{Price of one unit (P)} - \text{Variable cost (VC) of one unit}}$$

break-even analysis
The process used to determine profitability at various levels of sales.

Total fixed costs are costs that do not change in relation to how many products are made or sold. Among the expenses that make up fixed costs are the amount paid to own or rent a factory or warehouse and the amount paid for business insurance. **Variable costs** change according to the level of production. Included are the expenses for the materials used in making products and the direct costs of labour used in making those products.

For example, imagine that you are a manufacturer selling a sweater for $20 and have a fixed cost of $200,000 (for mortgage interest, real estate taxes, equipment, and so on). Your variable cost (e.g., labour and materials) per sweater is $10. The break-even point would be 20,000 sweaters. In other words, you wouldn't make any money selling sweaters unless you sold more than 20,000 of them:

total fixed costs
Costs that do not change in relation to how many products are made or sold.

variable costs
Costs that change according to the level of production.

$$\text{BEP} = \frac{\text{FC}}{\text{P} - \text{VC}} = \frac{\$200,000}{\$20 - \$10} = \frac{\$200,000}{\$10} = 20,000 \text{ sweaters}$$

PRICING STRATEGIES

There are several pricing strategies used by retailers. One is called **everyday low pricing (EDLP)**. That's the pricing strategy used by Home Depot and Wal-Mart. Such stores set prices lower than competitors and do not have any special sales. The idea is to have consumers come to those stores whenever they want a bargain, rather than wait until there is a sale, as they do for most department stores.

Department stores and other retailers most often use a **high–low pricing strategy**. The idea is to have regular prices that are higher than those at stores using everyday low pricing but also to have many special sales where the prices are lower than those of competitors. The problem with such pricing is that it teaches consumers to wait for sales, thus cutting into profits. As the Internet grows in popularity, you may see fewer stores with a high–low strategy because consumers will be able to find

everyday low pricing (EDLP)
Setting prices lower than competitors and then not having any special sales.

www.homedepot.com

www.walmart.com

high–low pricing strategy
Setting prices that are higher than EDLP stores, but having many special sales where the prices are lower than those of competitors.

better prices on the Internet and begin buying more and more from online retailers.

Some retailers use price as a major determinant of the goods they carry. For example, there are stores that promote goods that sell for only $1 (e.g., dollar stores) or only $10. Outlet stores sell brand-name goods at discount prices. Other stores, sometimes called discount stores, sell "seconds," or damaged goods. Consumers must take care to examine such goods to be sure the flaws are not too major. Some additional pricing strategies used by marketers can be found in Figure 16.10.

Pricing Strategies for New Products

Imagine a firm has just developed a new line of products, such as high-definition television (HDTV) sets. The firm has to decide how to price these sets at the introductory stage of the product life cycle. Two strategies are a skimming price strategy and a penetration price strategy.

A **skimming price strategy** is one in which a new product is priced high to make optimum profit while there's little competition. With such a strategy, marketers can try to quickly recover R&D costs. A skimming price strategy also sends a message that the product is a quality product and, therefore, a high price is warranted. Such a strategy would be successful when there are few competitors, there is prestige attached to product ownership, and there are enough consumers who are willing and able to pay the high price to justify production and profit goals. When marketers have exhausted the market demand at this initial price, then they will lower the price to make the product price more attractive to new consumers.

As time goes on (and as more competitors enter the market as a result of the profit potential), marketers will continue to decrease the price. This is what happened

One way producers are able to keep prices low is to downsize the product. Usually customers can't tell the difference, and the producer is able to keep prices low and still make a good profit. What are the ethical implications of such practices?

skimming price strategy
A strategy in which a new product is priced high to make optimum profit while there's little competition.

FIGURE 16.10

ADDITIONAL PRICING STRATEGIES

1. *Adaptive pricing* allows an organization to vary its prices based on factors such as competition, market conditions, and resource costs. Rather than relying on one set price, the firm adjusts the price to fit different situations.

2. *Cost-oriented pricing* is the strategy of setting prices primarily on the basis of cost. For example, retailers often use cost plus a certain markup, while producers use a system of cost-plus pricing.

3. *Customary pricing* means that most sellers will adapt the product to some established, universally accepted price, such as the price for gum or candy bars. Notice that when the price goes up, almost all producers adjust their price upward.

4. *Product-line pricing* is the procedure used to set prices for a group of products that are similar but aimed at different market segments. For example, a beer producer might have a low-priced beer, a popular-priced beer, and a premium-priced beer.

5. *Target pricing* means that an organization will set some goal such as a certain share of the market or a certain return on investment as a basis for setting a price. Usually, market conditions prevent a firm from establishing prices this way, but such goals do give some direction to pricing policies.

6. *Uniform pricing, also known as single-price policy,* means that all customers buying the product (given similar circumstances) pay the same price. Although it's the most common policy, uniform pricing is unusual in many foreign markets, especially among private sellers.

7. *Odd pricing or psychological pricing* means pricing an item a few cents under a round price ($9.99 instead of $10) to make the product appear less expensive.

8. *Price lining* is the practice of offering products at a few set prices such as $30, $40, and $50. Such a tactic makes both pricing and checkout easier, and it appeals to a market segment interested in that level of pricing.

when high-priced HDTVs were introduced in the 1990s. We have also seen prices decrease for microwave ovens, computers, and DVD players.

A **penetration price strategy** is one in which the product is priced low to attract many customers and discourage competitors. A low initial price would attract more customers and would enable the firm to penetrate or capture a large market share quickly. It would also be a barrier to competitors that couldn't match the low price, as there would be little incentive for customers to switch. Such a strategy would be successful if consumers are price-sensitive and enough people purchase the product for the firm to 1) get a large market share and 2) take advantage of economies of scale. Finally, the low price must deter competitors from entering the market with their own product versions.

The Japanese successfully used a penetration strategy with videocassette recorders. No American firms could compete with the low prices offered by the Japanese manufacturers and they quickly gained a large share of the market. One strong drawback of a penetration strategy is that it is difficult for manufacturers to raise prices once consumers have become used to the low price. Therefore, it is critical that production and pricing work well together.

How Market Forces Affect Pricing

Ultimately, price is determined by supply and demand **>P. 39<** in the marketplace, as described in Chapter 2. For example, if you charge $3 for Fiberrific and nobody buys your cereal at that price, you'll have to lower the price until you reach a point that's acceptable to customers and to you. The price that results from the interaction of buyers and sellers in the marketplace is called the *market price.*

Recognizing the fact that different consumers may be willing to pay different prices, marketers sometimes price on the basis of consumer demand rather than cost or some other calculation. That's called *demand-oriented pricing* and is reflected by movie theatres with low rates for children and by drugstores with discounts for senior citizens. You may have noticed that Halloween candy is cheapest the day after Halloween. Prices tend to be lower when demand is lower.

Besides supply and demand forces, another factor in the marketplace is competition. **Price leadership** is the procedure by which one or more dominant firms set the pricing practices that all competitors in an industry follow. You may have noticed that practice among oil and cigarette companies. Competition-oriented pricing is a strategy based on what all the other competitors are doing. The price can be at, above, or below competitors' prices. Pricing depends on customer loyalty, perceived differences, and the competitive climate.

Marketers will face a new pricing problem in the next few years. Customers can now compare prices of many goods and services on the Internet. For example, you may want to check out deals on sites such as DealTime.com, BrandsForLess.com, or ICanBuy.com. Priceline.com introduced us to a "demand collection system," where buyers post the prices they are willing to pay and invite sellers to either accept or decline the price. Consumers can get great prices on airlines, hotels, and other products by naming the price they are willing to pay. Furthermore, Mercata introduced us to group buying. Individuals can gather into buying blocs to leverage their combined purchasing power to get prices lower.[44] You can also buy used goods online. Have you or any of your friends bought or sold anything on eBay or Amazon.com?[45] Clearly, price

penetration price strategy
A strategy in which the product is priced low to attract many customers and discourage competitors.

price leadership
The procedure by which one or more dominant firms set the pricing practices that all competitors in an industry follow.

This is DealTime's Web site. Such companies enable consumers to compare prices across a broad range of items. You can also search for gift ideas and more. Do you know people who hesitate to use such online companies? What is holding them back?

Courtesy of DealTime.com

competition is going to heat up as consumers have more access to price information from all around the world. In that case, nonprice competition is likely to increase.

NONPRICE COMPETITION

In spite of the emphasis placed on price in microeconomic theory, marketers often compete on product attributes other than price.[46] You may have noted that price differences are small with products such as gasoline, candy bars, and even major products such as compact cars. Typically, you will not see price used as a major promotional appeal on television. Instead, marketers tend to stress product image and consumer benefits such as comfort, style, convenience, and durability.

Many smaller organizations promote the services that accompany basic products rather than price in order to compete with bigger firms. The idea is to make a relatively homogeneous product "better" by offering more service. Danny O'Neill, for example, is a small wholesaler who sells gourmet coffee to upscale restaurants. He has to watch competitor prices and see what services they offer so that he can charge the premium prices he wants. To charge high prices, he has to offer superior service.

Larger companies often do the same thing. For example, some airlines stress friendliness, promptness, better meals, and other such services. High-priced hotels stress "no surprises," business services, health clubs, and other extras.

Nonprice Strategies

Often marketers emphasize nonprice differences because prices are so easy to match. However, few competitors can match the image of a friendly, responsive, consumer-oriented company. The following are some other strategies for avoiding price wars:

www.toro.com

1. **Add value**. Some drugstores add value by offering home delivery. Lawnmower manufacturer Toro gives "lawn parties" during which it teaches customers lawn care strategies. United Parcel Service drivers wear ring scanners, an electronic device on their index finger wired to a small computer on their wrist that shoots a pattern of photons at a barcode on a package to let a customer know exactly where his or her package is at any given moment.[47]

2. **Educate consumers**. Home Depot teaches its customers how to use the equipment it sells and how to build decks and other do-it-yourself projects. Training videos show consumers how to use newly purchased products.

3. **Establish relationships**. Customers will pay more for products when they have a friendly relationship with the seller. Today auto dealers, like Saturn, may send out cards reminding people when service is needed. They also have picnics and other special events for customers. Airlines, supermarkets, hotels, and car rental agencies have frequent-buyer clubs that offer all kinds of fringe benefits to frequent users. The services aren't less expensive, but they offer more value.

As you can see, this chapter begins and ends with one theme: Give customers value and they'll give you their loyalty. We have reviewed product and price. Chapter 17 discusses the last two Ps, promotion and place.

PROGRESS CHECK

- Can you list two short-term and two long-term pricing objectives? Are the two compatible?
- What's wrong with using a cost-based pricing strategy?
- What's the purpose of break-even analysis?
- Can you calculate a product's break-even point if producing it costs $10,000 and revenue from the sale of one unit is $20?

ETHICAL DILEMMA
Review

Do you remember the dilemma about the toys that have been exposed to radiation? Here are the answers from our executives on this one. Bédard has a detailed and clear-cut reply. "Intentionally marketing products, especially to children, that present health hazards, though minor, is highly unethical. Children are much more susceptible to developing problems when exposed to certain contaminants that would not normally affect adults. This proposition is unacceptable and the games or toys should not be bought. A company's reputation could be destroyed with such a decision."

Reilley says, "I would turn him down. Not only would it be illegal but it would [start] me on a slippery slope that could end who knows where."

It's easy to say no, but if this purchase might save your business shouldn't you, perhaps, give it a little thought? Suppose you took the sample items from Adam and had them checked out by Emiko, a scientist you know, who can verify the radiation count at her lab. You do that, and she confirms Adam's contention that there is

a very low level of harmful radiation. When you discuss this further with Emiko she tells you that most kids are exposed to just as much radiation from the atmosphere and various activities our civilization generates. However, when you ask her if she would let *her* kids play with these products she is not so sure she would.

So now what do you do? You decide to consult a medical radiation expert whom Emiko suggests you see, for another opinion. After his tests, he confirms that the risk for children is small and it probably will not have any really harmful long-term effects. He has no children but, if he did, he also is not sure if he would let them play with these toys or games. What to do? Suppose the articles Adam gave you are not really representative of the radiation levels in the whole lot. Their level could be higher or lower. You believe that you could make about $50,000 profit from the whole shipment, which would pull you out of the financial hole you are in. Adam is back in Asia and is asking you for an answer. He needs an answer so he can sell them to somebody else if you refuse. What would *you* do?

SUMMARY

1. A value package consists of everything that consumers evaluate when deciding whether to buy a product.
   - *What's included in a value package?*
   A value package includes price, brand name, satisfaction in use, and more.
   - *What's the difference between a product line and a product mix?*
   A product line is a group of physically similar products. (A product line of gum may include bubble gum, sugarless gum, etc.) A product mix is a company's combination of product lines. (A manufacturer may offer lines of gum, candy bars, chewing tobacco, etc.)
   - *How do marketers create product differentiation for their goods and services?*
   Marketers use a mix of pricing, advertising, and packaging to make their products seem unique and attractive.

1. Explain the concept of a value package.

2. Consumer goods and services are sold to ultimate consumers like you and me and not to businesses.
   - *What are the four classifications of consumer products, and how are they marketed?*
   There are convenience products (requiring minimum shopping effort), shopping products (for which people compare price and quality), specialty products (which consumers go out of their way to get), and unsought products (which

2. Describe the various kinds of consumer and industrial products.

consumers did not intend to buy when they entered the store). Convenience products are best promoted by location, shopping products by some price/quality appeal, and specialty products by word of mouth. Unsought goods (impulse items) are often displayed at the checkout counter, where consumers see them while waiting in line and are motivated to buy them.

• *What are industrial products and how are they marketed differently from consumer products?*

Industrial products are products sold in the business-to-business market (B2B), and are used in the production of other products. They're sold largely through salespeople and rely less on advertising. Installations are major capital equipment such as new factories and heavy machinery. Accessory equipment is capital items that are not quite as long-lasting or as expensive as installations. Examples include computers, photocopy machines, and various tools.

3. Give examples of a brand, a brand name, and a trademark, and explain the concept of brand loyalty.

3. Branding is part of the product decision.

• *Can you give examples of a brand, a brand name, and a trademark?*

One example of a brand name of crackers is Triscuit by Nabisco. The brand consists of the name Triscuit as well as the symbol (a red triangle in the corner with Christie circled in white). The brand name and the symbol are also trademarks, since Nabisco has obtained legal protection for this brand.

• *What is brand loyalty, and how do managers create brand awareness?*

Brand loyalty is the degree to which customers are satisfied, like the brand, and are committed to further purchases. Customer relationship management is designed to create brand loyalty. Advertising helps build strong brand awareness. Event sponsorship (e.g., the Molson auto race and Bell Canada golf tournament) helps improve brand awareness. Brand association is the linking of a brand to other favourable images. For example, you can link a brand to other product users, to a popular celebrity, to a particular geographic area, or to competitors.

4. List and describe the five functions of packaging.

4. Packaging is part of the product and is becoming increasingly important, taking over much of the sales function for consumer goods.

• *What are the five functions of packaging?*

The five functions are (1) to attract the buyer's attention; (2) to describe the contents; (3) to provide information on warranties, warnings, and other consumer matters; (4) to indicate price, value, and uses; and (5) to protect the goods inside, stand up under handling and storage, be tamperproof, deter theft, and yet be easy to open and use.

5. Explain the role of brand managers and the six steps of the new-product development process.

5. Brand managers coordinate new product, price, place, and promotion decisions for a particular product.

• *What are the six steps of the new-product development process?*

The steps are (1) generation of new-product ideas, (2) screening, (3) product analysis, (4) development, (5) testing, and (6) commercialization.

6. Identify and describe the stages of the product life cycle, and describe marketing strategies at each stage.

6. Once a product is placed on the market, marketing strategy varies as the product goes through various stages of acceptance, called the product life cycle.

• *How do marketing strategies theoretically change at the various stages?*

See Figures 16.6, 16.8, and 16.9.

• *What are the stages of the product life cycle?*

They are introduction, growth, maturity, and decline.

7. Give examples of various pricing objectives and strategies.

7. Pricing is one of the four Ps of marketing.

• *What are pricing objectives?*

Objectives include achieving a target profit, building traffic, increasing market share, increasing sales, creating an image, and meeting social goals.

• *What's the break-even point?*
At the break-even point, total cost equals total revenue. Sales beyond that point are profitable.

• *What strategies can marketers use to determine a product's price?*
A skimming price strategy is one in which the product is priced high to make optimum profit while there's little competition, whereas a penetration strategy is one in which a product is priced low to attract more customers and discourage competitors. Demand-oriented pricing is based on consumer demand rather than cost. Competition-oriented pricing is based on all competitors' prices. Price leadership occurs when all competitors follow the pricing practice of one or more dominant companies. Review Figure 16.10 to be sure you understand all the terms used for other pricing strategies.

8. In spite of the emphasis placed on price in microeconomic theory, marketers often compete on product attributes other than price.

    8. Explain why nonpricing strategies are growing in importance.

• *Why do companies use nonprice strategies?*
Pricing is one of the easiest marketing strategies to copy. Therefore, often it is not a good long-run competitive tool. Instead, marketers may compete using nonprice strategies that are less easy to copy, including offering great service, educating consumers, and establishing long-term relationships with customers.

KEY TERMS

DEVELOPING WORKPLACE SKILLS

1. Look around your classroom and notice the different types of shoes that students are wearing. What product qualities were they looking for when they chose those shoes? What was the importance of price, style, brand name, and colour? Describe the product offerings you would feature in a new shoe store designed to appeal to students in your class.

2. A value package consists of everything that consumers evaluate when choosing among products, including price, package, service, and reputation. Working in teams, compose a list of factors that consumers might consider when evaluating the following products: a vacation resort, a lawyer, and a new car.

3. Take some time when you are at your local grocery store and compare prices from different manufacturers on items such as cereal, peanut butter, and soup. What is the relationship of brand name to price, if any? Develop what you would consider the best-value package of goods based on your research. Write a brief analysis of your findings.

4. Go to your medicine cabinet and take an inventory of all the branded and non-branded items. Then discuss with your classmates the brand names they buy for the same goods. Do most students buy brand-name goods or generic goods? Why?

5. Determine where in the product life cycle you would place each of the following products and then prepare a marketing strategy for each product based on the recommendations in this chapter:
    a. Alka-Seltzer.
    b. Cellular phones.
    c. Electric automobiles.
    d. Campbell's chicken noodle soup.

Purpose:

To assess how various sites on the Internet can be used to shop for any number of products or services.

Exercise:

Shopbots are Internet sites that you can use to find the best prices on goods you need. No shopbot searches the entire Internet, so it's a good idea to use more than one to get the best deals. Furthermore, not all shopbots figure in shipping and handling. Here are some to try:

mySimon.com
Bottomdollar.com
ShopFind.com
PriceSCAN.com

Questions:

1. Which of the shopbots seem most comprehensive—offering the most goods or the most information?
2. Which shopbot is the easiest to use? The hardest?
3. Write down some of the prices you find on the Internet and then go to a local discount store, such as Wal-Mart, and compare prices. Which are lowest, or does it depend on the product?
4. Evaluate shopping on the Internet versus shopping in stores. What are the advantages and disadvantages of each?

Purpose:

To determine appropriate pricing strategies for specific products.

Exercise:

Go to www.marketingteacher.com and review the various types of pricing strategies.
1. Click on the exercise button and place the products listed in the appropriate cells of the grid provided.
2. Click on the answer button to check your work. If you do not agree with the answers, scroll down the screen for an explanation.

PRACTISING MANAGEMENT DECISIONS

CASE 1

EVERYDAY LOW PRICING (EDLP)

Wal-Mart, Zellers, and wholesale clubs such as Costco have had great success with a concept they call everyday low pricing (EDLP). Rather than have relatively high prices and then barrage consumers with coupons and price discounts (a high–low pricing strategy), such stores promote the fact that they offer lower prices every day. Similarly, some manufacturers are offering everyday low purchase prices. Instead of having a relatively high price for products sold to retailers, manufacturers such as Procter & Gamble have everyday low purchase prices. It's the same concept as EDLP applied to industrial goods instead of consumer goods.

Many retailers have decided to follow the lead of Wal-Mart and others by cutting prices on all their goods. But recent research shows that this approach isn't always wise. For example, consumers say location is usually their most important factor in choosing a supermarket. Thus, supermarkets shouldn't have to have the lowest prices to keep market share.

Usually sales volume falls after the introduction of everyday low prices, but it picks up later. That is true in Europe as well.

In spite of the potential drawbacks of everyday low pricing, 7-Eleven implemented it in 250 stores in the Dallas–Fort Worth area. This pricing policy was just one part of an overall revamping of 7-Eleven's image, including updated interiors, fresh produce, and gourmet items. In fact, 7-Eleven no longer wants its former image of a high-priced convenience store, and is seeking to appear as a small yet viable alternative to supermarkets.

Decision Questions

1. As a consumer, would you prefer that your local supermarket offer everyday low prices, offer some products at major discounts (half off) periodically, or offer some combination of the two?
2. What could your local supermarket do other than offer low prices or price discounts to win your business (delight you) and still maintain a high profit margin?
3. What advantages and disadvantages do you see for manufacturers to offer everyday low purchase prices to retailers?
4. Are manufacturers and retailers pushing price so much that they're in danger of lowering profits? Is this especially true on the Internet? Why is price competition so common?

CASE 2

GENETICALLY MODIFIED FOOD: A FRANKENSTEIN HARVEST?

In this chapter you learned about the importance and the process of developing new products. We live in an era when the food we eat has undergone enormous changes as a result of scientific research. One of the most important changes is the introduction of genetically modified (GM) food. This process involves inserting foreign genes into plant and animal structures so that new strains are developed that are resistant to pests or disease and harsh climates, or that give higher yields. An estimated 60 percent of the food offered for sale in Canada contains GM components. Canadian and American farmers are heavily involved in producing genetically altered food. Farmers like GM food because it makes farming more profitable. The whole process is complex, involving strong control exercised by major chemical companies like Monsanto. There are currently several legal battles being waged

between Canadian farmers and Monsanto. If we look at one crop, we can see how important this issue is to Canada. The production of canola by Canadian Prairie farmers constitutes 80 percent of world trade in canola, and half of these farmers are growing GM canola.

The European Union does not allow the import of GM foods, because it is concerned that there may be long-term dangers to human health. Many Americans and Canadians have similar objections. In the late fall of 1999 a major campaign was launched by Greenpeace, the Sierra Club, the Council of Canadians, and other organizations to alert consumers to the possible dangers of GM food. Similar concerns are being raised in many other countries in South America and Asia. At the very least, they argue, food containing GM should be labelled so that consumers have the choice of buying these or non-GM foods. Organizations in the U.S. have announced plans to launch suits in 30 countries against major GM seed companies, complaining that they have too much control over seed supplies.

Concerns are raised because this decade has seen some important health issues arise from what we do to animals and plants. Europe had a serious scare with mad cow disease, and the bovine growth hormone (BGH), which is injected into American cattle to increase milk production, is banned in the European Union. The EU will not allow dairy products from such cattle to be imported into the Union. Canadian health authorities have so far also not allowed the use of BGH in Canadian cattle, despite enormous pressure from pharmaceutical companies. Companies in North America, such as Gerber and HJ Heinz Co., have begun phasing out GM foods from their baby-food lines. Other major companies will not accept farm products or ingredients that are not acceptable to the European Union.

Decision Questions

1. It often happens that certain products, old or new, generate a lot of controversy. Selling toy guns to children has sometimes sparked arguments. Do you think this food issue is different? Why?

2. The problem with genetically modified foods or adding hormones is that it takes a long time to find out what the long-term effects may be. For example, some researchers believe that the addition of substantial amounts of antibiotics to cattle feed is responsible for the generation of highly resistant super-bugs that are becoming a serious problem for humans now. What do you think is a good approach to solving this type of problem?

3. Farmers and their organizations point out that using genetically modified strains means that agriculture requires less pesticide and insecticide use, which is beneficial to our environment. Is it possible to evaluate whether the benefits exceed the risks? How can that be done? Who should do it?

4. Some people maintain that technology has gone too far. They contend that just because we *can* make something doesn't necessarily mean that we *must* make it. How do you feel about that? Should science and technology have limitations placed on them? Why? By whom?

Sources: Cynthia Reynolds, "Frankenstein's Harvest," *Canadian Business*, October 8, 1999, p. 65; CBC newscasts September 1999.

CBC   VIDEO CASE   www.cbc.ca

FOOD FIGHTS The grocery store industry in Canada is highly competitive, with increasingly fewer players and more demand being placed on food suppliers. The pressure on food manufacturers began through two consolidations. The giant Loblaws purchased Quebec-based Provigo, and Sobeys purchased the Oshawa Group. Almost overnight, more than half of the grocery industry was in the hands of two firms: Loblaws (36 percent) and Sobeys (22 percent). The mergers gave both grocery giants huge leverage and gave them bargaining power over their suppliers.

Many suppliers, especially the small ones, are not willing to discuss on camera about how they feel that they are being mistreated. They are concerned about being de-listed by the retailers. Not only are they facing pressures to hold their prices, but they are also being strongly encouraged to lower them.

Today, the grocery store chains are dropping number-three or number-four products and replacing them with their own private labels. Suppliers are finding it hard to get shelf space in the big chains—and they are most at risk, as larger suppliers (such as Heinz and Kraft) have more leverage than smaller suppliers.

Grocery store chains believe that suppliers are treated fairly. The $60-billion grocery retailing industry has net margins of between 1 and 2 percent. While these margins are now rising as a result of the mergers and the growing power of retailers, retailers continue to demand concessions from their suppliers. There are rumours that retail giant Wal-Mart may be entering the Canadian grocery industry and this has the industry worried.

Discussion Questions

1. What are some private-label brands in Canada? What grocery store chains carry them?
2. Why do some manufacturers produce private-label products for the grocery store chains in addition to their own national brands? What are the benefits to these manufacturers? What are some of the challenges?
3. Why is the potential entry of Wal-Mart a threat to this industry?
4. What do suppliers need to do to become more powerful?

Source: *Venture*, show number 742, March 7, 2000, running time 7:09.

CHAPTER 17

Promoting and Distributing Products Efficiently and Interactively

LEARNING GOALS

AFTER YOU HAVE READ AND STUDIED THIS CHAPTER, YOU SHOULD BE ABLE TO

1. Define promotion and list the four traditional tools that make up the promotion mix.

2. Define advertising and describe the advantages and disadvantages of various advertising media, including the Internet.

3. Illustrate the seven steps of the selling process and discuss the role of a consultative salesperson.

4. Describe integrated marketing communication and the role of interactive communications within it.

5. Explain the concept of marketing channels and the value of marketing intermediaries.

6. Describe the various wholesale organizations in the distribution system.

7. Explain the ways in which retailers compete and the distribution strategies they use.

8. Explain the various kinds of nonstore retailing.

9. Discuss how a manufacturer can get wholesalers and retailers in a channel system to co-operate by the formation of systems.

Guy Laliberté of Cirque du Soleil

Photo: Francesco Bellorno © Cirque du Soleil Inc.

Having performed for more than 30 million people worldwide, Montreal-based Cirque du Soleil started as a small group of travelling performers and has become a unique entertainment organization. Each show is a theatrical blend of circus arts and street performance, wrapped up in spectacular costumes and fairyland sets and staged to spellbinding music and magical lighting. There are no animals in the show, so all concentration is on the human performers.

Guy Laliberté is the driving force behind the Cirque du Soleil. Born in Quebec City in 1959, Laliberté was an accordion player, stiltwalker, and fire-eater. He recognized and groomed the talents of street entertainers, and in 1982 he organized a street performers' festival in the St. Lawrence Valley town of Baie St. Paul. It was such a success that in 1984 Laliberté and Daniel Gauthier created the Cirque du Soleil.

Initially, bankers declined to financially support the company. As a last resort, they appealed to the Quebec government, which gave the troupe $1.5 million to buy equipment in 1997. They spent all this money on one performance at an arts festival in California, and the critics and fans loved the show.

Today, the mission of the Cirque du Soleil is to *invoke* the imagination, *provoke* the senses, and *evoke* the emotions of people around the world. Creativity is the cornerstone of the organization's identity. Every concept and scenic element is created at the Studio, a training facility established in 1997 in Montreal. Here, more than 500 of the 2,100 employees work together to create new shows and costumes.

An important element to the success of the Cirque is its global appeal. At the beginning, the life of the show was limited to only summer months. Since it takes 18 months to develop a new show, a much larger audience than Montreal was required to make it a viable operation. The marketers looked to Japan as a potential market, and with careful research they were soon able to achieve a similar success there. The first part of the tour is spent touring North America, the second touring Europe, and the third touring the Asia-Pacific region and Japan. To extend the show's life even further, attention turned to Europe—today, their European headquarters are in Amsterdam.

The staff carefully plan a marketing campaign for each country. In general, their target market is the middle-income and high-income 25- to 45-year-old age groups, but each country is treated differently. In Berlin, they concentrated on an extensive outdoor billboard campaign, and for the six-city German tour they spent $250,000 on a two-week TV, radio, and newspaper campaign offering free trips to Las Vegas, Nissan cars, and personal computers.

The entire carefully thought-out marketing plan has paid off handsomely, extending the life of the shows. From the start, the Cirque du Soleil was selling out most performances. While the organization draws approximately 85 percent of its revenues from box-office sales, it also reaps substantial revenues from merchandising, food, and beverage sales. The organization manages the production of its audiovisual works and oversees the marketing of various show soundtracks with BMG Music. Licensing agreements and corporate alliances are formed on a regular basis. The first retail outlet was opened in Walt Disney World in Florida in 1998.

The Cirque du Soleil's mission includes social responsibility to communities all over the world, wherever it operates. As well, it donates money to other parts of the world such as Brazil, Chile, Mexico, Senegal, Ivory Coast, Cameroon, South Africa, and Mongolia. Its focus is on youth at risk, especially street kids. One percent of potential revenues from ticket sales is devoted each year to outreach programs in support of youth in difficulty.

When asked if corporate growth would stifle the risks that have propelled the Cirque du Soleil to such heights, Laliberté has replied no. He says that he keeps the company in private hands, sharing profits with the employees, precisely so they can continue to be creative and take risks. Laliberté approaches business with an entertainment aspect, which is with pleasure and fun. Recognized for his great contribution to Quebec culture, he received the Ordre National du Quebec in 1997, the highest distinction awarded by the Government of Quebec.

So what does the future hold? In 16 years this small organization has become a global success. There are separate shows in Asia, Europe, and North America, with permanent shows in Disney World and Biloxi, Mississippi. As well, there are two permanent shows in Las Vegas, including a water circus called "O," which sells out 10 shows a week at the 1,600-seat ($100 a ticket) theatre. Guy has indicated that expansion plans call for developing up to a half-dozen entertainment complexes around the world in the next 15 years. Likely starting with London or Las Vegas, each complex could cost from $324 million to $1.3 billion.

Sources: Brian Dunn, "How Quebec's Cirque du Soleil Conquered Europe," *Marketing*, March 4, 1996, p. 5; www.cirquedusoleil.com, August 28, 2001; communications with the marketing department of Cirque du Soleil, August 1999; www.chebucto.ns.ca/Culture/BluenoseJugglers/soleil.html, August 28, 2001.

ETHICAL DILEMMA
Is the Ad as Honest as the Product?

You are producing a high-fibre, nutritious cereal called Fiberrific and are having a modest degree of success. Research shows that your number of customers, or market segment, is growing but is still a relatively small percentage of breakfast cereal buyers. Generally, Fiberrific appeals mostly to health-conscious people in age groups from 25 to 60. You are trying to broaden the appeal of your cereal to the under-25 and over-60 age groups. You know that Fiberrific is a tasty and healthy product that is good for customers' health. Joan, one of your managers, suggests that you should stretch the truth a bit in your advertising and publicity material so that it will attract more consumers in the age groups you are targeting. After all, your product can't hurt anybody and is actually good for them.

Joan's idea is to develop two ads, each with two segments. The first segment of one ad would show a young woman on a tennis court holding a racquet and talking across the net to a young man. She is complaining that she seems to tire easily. The next segment would show the same two people, with the woman looking lively and saying that she tried this new breakfast cereal, Fiberrific, for two weeks and feels so energized, like a new person. A similar ad would be used to show two senior citizens walking uphill and talking. The first segment would have the man wondering why he tires so easily and the second one would show the same scene, with one man now a little ahead of the other, looking lively and stating that he is amazed at the improvement in his energy and endurance after eating Fiberrific for only two weeks. Would you go along with Joan's suggestion? We'll get back to this question at the end of the chapter.

INTRODUCTION

In Chapter 15 we introduced you to the four Ps of the marketing mix: product, price, promotion, and place. Marketers review all four elements when they sell their products and ideas. In the previous chapter we reviewed the first two elements—product and price. In this chapter, we will discuss the third and fourth elements, namely promotion and place. As you read through this chapter, you may wish to apply this information to Fiberrific. What are suggestions that you would make to promote and distribute this product efficiently and interactively?

THE PROMOTION MIX

promotion
An attempt by marketers to inform people about products and to persuade them to participate in an exchange.

promotion mix
The combination of promotional tools an organization uses.

integrated marketing communication (IMC)
A technique that combines all the promotional tools into one comprehensive and unified promotional strategy.

Promotion is an attempt by marketers to inform people about products and to persuade them to participate in an exchange. Marketers use many different tools to promote their goods and services. Traditionally, as shown in Figure 17.1, those tools included advertising, personal selling, public relations, and sales promotion. The combination of promotional tools an organization uses is called its **promotion mix**. The value package is shown in the middle of the figure to illustrate the fact that the product itself must meet the target audience's needs and that the promotion mix supports the product.

Integrated marketing communication (IMC) combines all the promotional tools into one comprehensive and unified promotional strategy. The idea is to use the promotional tools and company resources to create a positive brand image.[1] Lately, companies have been including Internet promotions in that mix. Later, we'll take a special look at both promotion on the Internet and the process for creating an integrated marketing communication system, because they are two of the fastest-growing parts of promotion.

How Constant Change Is Affecting Promotion

The rapidly changing business environment has affected promotion as much as any other area in business. Technology has changed the role and activities of salespeople. Similar changes have occurred in all the promotional areas. For example, the dramatic increase in the number of television channels available has lessened the number of viewers for any given program. This means that advertisers must be more creative in trying to reach large audiences, and competition for advertising on popular shows has risen rapidly.

The Internet is changing the whole approach to working with customers. Note that we said "working with" rather than "promoting to."[2] The latest trend is to build relationships with customers over time. That means carefully listening to what consumers want, tracking their purchases, providing them with better service, and giving them access to more information.

Interactive promotion changes the promotion process from a *monologue*, where sellers tried to persuade buyers to buy things, to a *dialogue*, in which buyers and sellers can work together to create mutually beneficial exchange relationships.[3] For example, Garden.com is an online retailer of garden products. Dionn Schaffner, vice-president of marketing, says, "Gardening is an information-intensive activity. Customers obviously want to learn about gardening, but they also seek inspiration by communicating with fellow gardeners and experts."

Garden.com's answer is an interactive Web site through which customers can chat with each other and ask gardening questions. When customers come to the site, the company knows who they are and what they have asked in the past because it keeps track of them using cookies (little bits of data about customers that are kept on a database). Schaffner says, "By knowing about our customers, we can personalize the information content, as well as our product, for specific areas of the country."[4]

© 2000 Tommy Hilfiger Licensing, Inc./Liz Collins

The latest trend in advertising is "hybrid" campaigns that integrate traditional media with the Web, making consumers active participants. One of these campaigns is for Tommy Hilfiger. The ads feature finalists from an online talent search. Consumers are encouraged to go to Tommy.com to hear the various competitors and elect a winner, who will then record a demo. Have you become involved with such interactive ads? Do you like the idea?

interactive promotion
Changing the promotion process from a monologue, where sellers tried to persuade buyers to buy things, to a dialogue, in which buyers and sellers can work together to create mutually beneficial exchange relationships.

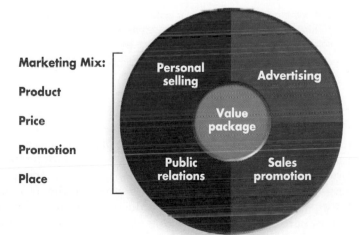

Marketing Mix:

Product

Price

Promotion

Place

Personal selling

Advertising

Value package

Public relations

Sales promotion

FIGURE 17.1

THE TRADITIONAL PROMOTION MIX

A good promotion campaign involves all the elements shown here.

As we discuss each of the promotional tools, we shall explore the changes that are occurring in those areas. Then, at the end of this section, we shall examine the latest promotional strategies and how they can be combined to build better relationships with customers and other stakeholders.

ADVERTISING: PERSUASIVE COMMUNICATION

Advertising is paid, nonpersonal communication through various media by organizations and individuals who are in some way identified in the advertising message. Figure 17.2 lists various categories of advertising.

Often government and nonprofit organizations use advertising to get their message out to the public. This message, for example, is part of an anti-smoking campaign. How effective do you think such ads are in stopping smoking among teens and others?

advertising
Paid, nonpersonal communication through various media by organizations and individuals who are in some way identified in the advertising message.

FIGURE 17.2

MAJOR CATEGORIES OF ADVERTISING

Different kinds of advertising are used by various organizations to reach different market targets. Major categories include the following:

• *Retail advertising*—advertising to consumers by various retail stores such as supermarkets and shoe stores.

• *Trade advertising*—advertising to wholesalers and retailers by manufacturers to encourage them to carry their products.

• *Business-to-business advertising*—advertising from manufacturers to other manufacturers. A firm selling motors to auto companies would use business-to-business advertising.

• *Institutional advertising*—advertising designed to create an attractive image for an organization rather than for a product. "Beautiful British Columbia" and "Ontario—Yours To Discover" are examples of provincial government campaigns that create an attractive image.

• *Product advertising*—advertising for a good or service to create interest among consumer and industrial buyers.

• *Advocacy advertising*—advertising that supports a particular view of an issue (e.g., an ad supporting responsible drinking or protecting the environment). Such advertising is also known as cause advertising.

• *Comparison advertising*—advertising that compares competitive products. For example, an ad that compares two different cold care products' speed and benefits is a comparative ad.

• *Interactive advertising*—customer-oriented communication that enables customers to choose the information they receive, such as interactive video catalogues that let customers select which items to view.

• *Online advertising*—advertising messages that appear on computers as people visit different Web sites.

The public benefits greatly from advertising expenditures. First, ads are informative. Newspaper advertising is full of information about products, prices, features, and more. So is direct-mail advertising. Advertising not only informs us about products but also provides us with free TV, community newspapers, and radio programs; the money advertisers spend for commercial time pays for the production costs. Advertising also covers the major costs of producing newspapers and magazines. Some companies have recently offered free goods—such as phone service or personal computers—to anyone who agrees to listen to or watch enough ads. When we buy a magazine, we pay mostly for mailing or promotional costs. Figure 17.3 discusses

MEDIUM	ADVANTAGES	DISADVANTAGES
Newspapers	Good coverage of local markets; ads can be placed quickly; high consumer acceptance; ads can be clipped and saved.	Ads compete with other features in paper; poor colour; ads get thrown away with paper (short life span).
Television	Uses sight, sound, and motion; reaches all audiences; high attention with no competition from other material	High cost; short exposure time; takes time to prepare ads.
Radio	Low cost; can target specific audiences; very flexible; good for local marketing.	People may not listen to ad; depends on one sense (hearing); short exposure time; audience can't keep ad.
Magazines	Can target specific audiences; good use of colour; long life of ad; ads can be clipped and saved.	Inflexible; ads often must be placed weeks before publication; cost is relatively high.
Outdoor	High visibility and repeat exposures; low cost; local market focus.	Limited message; low selectivity of audience.
Direct mail	Best for targeting specific markets; very flexible; ad can be saved.	High cost; consumers may reject ad as "junk mail"; must conform to post office regulations.
Yellow Pages advertising	Great coverage of local markets; widely used by consumers; available at point of purchase.	Competition with other ads; cost may be too high for very small businesses.
Internet	Inexpensive global coverage; available at any time; interactive.	Relatively low readership.

FIGURE 17.3

ADVANTAGES AND DISADVANTAGES OF VARIOUS ADVERTISING MEDIA

The most effective media are often very expensive. The inexpensive media may not reach your market. The goal is to use the most efficient medium that can reach your desired market.

the advantages and disadvantages of various advertising media to the advertiser. Newspapers, radio, and the Yellow Pages are especially attractive to local advertisers. Advertising in international markets is a little more difficult. Marketers must learn to adjust to the practices and culture of each country.

You may see ads just about anywhere these days, including on the car next to you on the freeway. Thanks to a practice known as "car wrapping," companies are turning ordinary cars into mobile billboards. People who are willing to have their cars wrapped get $400 a month. What is your reaction to having such mobile ads?

www.cma.ca

The Canadian Marketing Association (CMA) is the largest marketing association in Canada. It promotes industry growth, development, and education and it is involved in responding to public policy issues. Visit its Web site for more information.

Marketers must also adjust their practices to changes in the environment. Continuous scanning is not only part of the management process (as discussed in Chapter 8) and SWOT analysis ➤ **P. 223** ◄: it is also critical when marketers are choosing their promotional tools, and environment conditions will impact the effectiveness of their campaigns. For example, amid growing fears about anthrax, the multibillion-dollar direct marketing industry was forced to change its methods radically; the plain white "teaser" envelopes and unusual packages were pulled to minimize consumer worries.[5] According to John Gustavson, president and CEO of the Canadian Marketing Association, "marketers still sending things out in plain, unmarked envelopes are going to pay a penalty as consumers will not open them." The anthrax scare has created more opportunities for the use of e-mail as a marketing tool and may lead to tamper-proof envelopes and other measures.

Television offers many advantages to national advertisers, but it's expensive. For example, the cost of 30 seconds of advertising during the Super Bowl telecast has risen to over $2 million (U.S.).[6] Many Internet advertisers were so eager to get advertising time that they were willing to buy the time from others; some companies paid as much as $3 million (U.S.) for 30 seconds of advertising![7] How many bottles of beer or bags of dog food must a company sell to pay for such commercials? The answer may seem to be a lot, but, in the past, few other media besides television allowed advertisers to reach so many people with such impact. Marketers must now choose which media can best be used to reach the audience they desire.

Radio advertising, for example, is less expensive than TV advertising given that radio reaches people as they are driving; using this medium is effective for selling services that people don't usually read about in print media—services such as banking, mortgages, continuing education, brokerage services, and the like.

The Growing Use of Infomercials

infomercial
A TV program devoted exclusively to promoting goods and services.

One growing form of advertising is the infomercial. An **infomercial** is a TV program devoted exclusively to promoting goods and services. Infomercials have been so successful because they show the product in great detail. A great product can often sell itself if there's some means to show the public how it works. Infomercials provide that opportunity. People have said that a half-hour infomercial is the equivalent of sending your very best salespeople to a person's home where they can use everything in their power to make the sale: drama, demonstration, testimonials, graphics, and more. You may have seen infomercials for such products as the Thighmaster, car wax, silver cleaner, golf clubs, and more. RotoZip Tool Company thought that consumers would never buy its Spiral Saw line unless they saw the saws being used, so RotoZip spent $250,000 for an infomercial. Sales zoomed by 300 percent.[8]

www.rotozip.com

Some products, such as personal development seminars or workout tapes, are hard to sell without showing people a sample of their contents (possible using infomercials) and using testimonials. The Spotlight on Small Business box "Using Testimonials to Build Business" discusses in more detail the benefit of testimonials in advertising.

Advertising and Promotion on the Internet

www.adstandards.com

Advertising Standards Canada (ASC) is a national industry association committed to creating and maintaining community confidence in advertising. Visit the Web site to review the responsibilities of the ASC.

Advertising on the Internet is a relatively new phenomenon in marketing.[9] *Red Herring* magazine reports, "Most ads on the Internet today are like handbills stapled on telephone poles: you walk by them, but don't pay too much attention to them."[10] Despite the fact that most people tend to ignore Internet ads, companies continue to use them because they hope to tap into the huge potential that online marketing offers. Ultimately, the goal is to send customers and potential customers over to a Web site where they can learn more about the company and vice versa. The benefits of the Internet become apparent once a customer visits the Web. Then the company has the opportunity to provide information and interact with the customer (that is,

www.redherring.com

communicate with the customer). Internet advertising thus becomes a means to bring customers and companies together.

Because online promotion is so new, companies like Wal-Mart have turned to outside professionals to help them create world-class systems. Wal-Mart had been selling online since 1997, but rapid changes in the environment forced the retailer to upgrade in 2000. It wanted to integrate its existing system for order fulfillment, credit card processing, and inventory keeping with BroadVision's One-to-One Retail Commerce software for customer relationship management. Wal-Mart also wanted its Web site to have the look and feel of its stores. Thus, you can click on tabs for the various departments—home, apparel, electronics—and the system takes you where you want to go.[11]

www.walmart.com

www.broadvision.com

Customer relationship management software, along with software such as Silknet Software Inc.'s Trusted Advisor, makes it possible to track customers' purchases and answer their questions online. Often the system can be so smooth and effective that people don't realize they are talking with a computer. One subscriber to *Inc.* magazine, for example, wrote a letter to "Jill," *Inc.*'s online electronic help function, thanking her for her personal advice.[12]

www.silknet.com

Another example of a site that tracks traffic is www.thehungersite.com. When you click on the "Give Free Food" tab, your click will provide the hungry with the value of 1.3 cups of staple food. This site also tracks your giving history so you know how many cups of food the Web site sponors have provided based on your visits (and clicks). Visit the site and see for yourself how your click is tracked!

New technology will greatly improve the speed and potential of Internet dialogues. Companies will be able to provide better online videos, online chat rooms, and other services that will take customers from a banner ad to a virtual store where

SPOTLIGHT ON SMALL BUSINESS
www.jwrobel.com/test.html
Using Testimonials to Build Business

Carol Boucher has a small company called Bridal Event that gives bridal shows. There is a lot of competition for such shows and Boucher wanted to stand out from the others. She went to an advertising consultant, who recommended the following:

1. Top your ads with an attention-capturing headline like "I DO."
2. Put in a series of testimonials from attendees at previous shows (e.g., "I DO prefer the Bridal Event because . . ." and list the positive things people have said).
3. Remember that satisfied customers provide your best ad copy.

Some small companies pay their previous customers to recommend new customers. For example, they may give a previous customer $5 for every new customer who comes to the show because of their recommendation.

An important part of promotion for small businesses is getting stories printed about them in the local papers.

The way to get such free publicity is to take a picture of several brides and grooms and write an interesting story about how they met and why they went to a bridal show. Other stories could feature new wedding gowns, fun things to do at wedding receptions, or unusual flower arrangements. The latest thing is to fax the stories to the various papers or to make a short video and mail it to them. If the stories are interesting enough, they will get published free in the local paper.

According to *American Demographics*, "Eighty-three percent of consumers ask for information from those they know already own the product." Gathering testimonials makes the whole process easier because people can see what others are saying without having to search them out themselves.

Source: Jerry Fisher, "Says Who?" *Entrepreneur*, October 1999, p. 134; and Rebecca Gardyn, "I'll Have What He's Having," *American Demographics*, July 2000, p. 22; and Anthony Tjan, "Challenge No. 9: Generating Buzz and Building a Brand," *Red Herring*, March 2000, pp. 82–83.

they will be able to talk to other customers, talk to salespeople, examine goods and services (including watching a video), and buy products. To create relationships, Internet advertising will be combined with Internet promotions (e.g., incentives to buy in volume) to give customers points for buying things that can be used to buy more products in the future.

The fact that much of this information is available on palm-sized computers makes prospects for the future even more interesting. Consumers are able to *cyber-shop* at the same time they are shopping in a mall. They can get information, compare prices, and more. Thus, constant change will be affecting brick-and-mortar and online retailers for a long time to come. For one thing, more stores will have computer kiosks where customers can search for products and information and then pay in the store. In short, brick-and-mortar marketers will also be cybermarketers, and there will be complete integration between them. One term for this is *click-and-mortar* retailing; Wal-Mart calls it *surf and turf*.

www.coors.com

www.clairol.com

www.kellogs.com

Many advertisers think it is a good idea to develop special ads for each country rather than use one campaign for all countries. This ad for Visa is in Italian. Could you see using the same visual for other countries, including Canada? What kind of appeal could Visa use to gain your business?

Global Advertising

Harvard professor Theodore Levitt supports global marketing. His idea is to develop a product and promotional strategy that can be implemented worldwide through the application of technology. Not only can technology increase worldwide product awareness, but it can also standardize production, marketing (including product, distribution, and promotion), and other processes. Certainly standardized products would be a more efficient use of resources. In fact, this is the strategy being used by major companies such as Compaq, IBM, and Intel.

Other experts think that promotions targeted at specific countries or regions may be more successful than global promotions. Each country has its own culture, language, and buying habits that a standard advertising campaign may not capture.

While not as efficient in resource allocation, evidence does support the theory that promotional efforts specifically designed for individual countries may be more effective. For example, commercials for Camay soap that showed men complimenting women on their appearance were jarring in cultures where men don't express themselves that way. A different campaign is needed in such countries.

In Chapter 3, we listed some problems that well-known companies encountered in global marketing. Others include the following: When a Japanese company tried to use English words to name a popular drink, it called the product Pocari Sweat, not a good image for most English-speaking people. People in Canada may have difficulty with Krapp toilet paper from Sweden, but perhaps it's not as bad as the translation of Coors' slogan "Turn it loose" where it became "Suffer from diarrhea." Clairol introduced its curling iron, the Mist Stick, to the German market: the problem is that mist in German can mean "manure." As you can see, getting the words right in international advertising is tricky and critical. So is understanding the culture.

People in Brazil rarely eat breakfast, but they treat Kellogg's Corn Flakes as a dry snack like potato chips. Kellogg is trying a promo-

CON VISA MI SONO GIÀ PRESO UNA FETTA D'ESTATE.

GODITI LA VISA. PER I PICCOLI E I GRANDI ACQUISTI. VISA HA UN MODO UNICO DI AUGURARTI BUONA ESTATE. A LEI BASTA ESSERCI. QUALUNQUE ACQUISTO TU ABBIA IN MENTE, INFATTI, VISA SARÀ SEMPRE LA BENVENUTA. USALA. ANCHE PER UN'ANGURIA.

NEL FUTURO C'È VISA.

tional strategy that shows people in Brazil how to eat cereal with cold milk in the morning. Many more situations could be cited to show that international advertising calls for researching the wants and needs of people in each specific country and then designing appropriate ads and testing them.

Even in Canada we have regional differences that are important enough to constitute separate market segments. Each province has its own history and culture. The large metropolitan areas like Toronto, Montreal, Vancouver, and Edmonton are different from the rest of the provinces in which they are located. All require their own promotions and advertising.

In short, much advertising today is moving from globalism (one ad for everyone in the world) to regionalism (specific ads for each country or for specific groups within a country). In the future, marketers will prepare more custom-designed promotions to reach smaller audiences—audiences as small as one person.

Now that there is a greater possibility of interactive communications between companies and potential customers, do you see the importance of traditional advertising growing or declining? What will be the effect on the price we consumers must pay for TV programs, newspapers, and magazines, if any?

Personal Selling: Providing Personal Attention

Personal selling is the face-to-face presentation and promotion of products. It also involves the search for new prospects and follow-up service after the sale. Effective selling isn't simply a matter of persuading others to buy. In fact, it's more accurately described today as helping others to satisfy their wants and needs.

Given that perspective, you can see why salespeople are starting to use the Internet, portable computers, paging devices, fax machines, and other technology. They can use this technology to help customers search the Net, design custom-made products, look over prices, and generally do everything it takes to complete the order. The benefit of personal selling is that there is a person there to help you complete a transaction. The salesperson is there to listen to your needs, help reach a solution, and do all that is possible to make accomplishing that solution smoother and easier.

It is costly to provide customers with personal attention, especially since some companies are replacing salespeople with Internet services and information. Therefore, those companies that retain salespeople must train them to be especially effective, efficient, and helpful.

The average cost of a single sales call to a potential B2B buyer is about $400. Surely no firm would pay that much to send out anyone but a highly skilled, professional marketer and consultant. But how does one get to be that kind of sales representative? What are the steps along the way? Let's take a closer look at the process of selling.

Steps in the Selling Process

The best way to understand personal selling is to go through the selling process with a product and see what's involved. As we noted in Chapter 15, one product that is in high demand, and one that is becoming critically important to establishing long-term relationships with customers, is customer relationship management (CRM) software. Imagine that you are a software salesperson whose job is to show business users the advantages of using a particular program. Let's go through the selling process to see what you can do to make the sale. Although this is a business-to-business (B2B) example, the process is very much the same in consumer selling.

personal selling
The face-to-face presentation and promotion of products and services.

prospecting
Researching potential buyers and choosing those most likely to buy.

qualify
In the selling process, to make sure that people have a need for the product, the authority to buy, and the willingness to listen to a sales message.

prospects
People with the means to buy a product, the authority to buy, and the willingness to listen to a sales message.

1. **Prospect and Qualify** The first step in the selling process is prospecting. **Prospecting** involves researching potential buyers and choosing those most likely to buy. That selection process is called *qualifying*. To **qualify** people means to make sure that they have a need for the product, the authority to buy, and the willingness to listen to a sales message. People who meet these criteria are called **prospects**. You often meet prospects at trade shows, where they come up to booths sponsored by manufacturers and ask questions. Other prospects may visit your Web site seeking information. But often the best prospects are people at companies who were recommended to you by others who use your product or know all about it.

2. **Preapproach** Before making a sales call, you must do further research. Robert E. Keller, author of *Negotiating Skills That Sell*, says that 50 percent of a sales negotiation's outcome is determined before you meet the customer face-to-face.[13] You must learn as much as possible about customers and their wants and needs. Before you try to sell the CRM software, you would want to know which people in the company are most likely to buy or use it. What kind of customers do they deal with? What kind of relationship strategies are they now using? All that information should be in a database, so that your company can carry information about customers from salesperson to salesperson, in case one representative leaves the firm. Note that the selling process may take a long time and that gathering information before the sale takes place is critical.

3. **Approach** An old saying goes, "You don't have a second chance to make a good first impression." That's why the approach is so important. When you call on a customer for the first time, your opening comments are important. The idea is to give an impression of friendly professionalism, to create rapport, to build credibility, and to start a relationship. Often the decision of whether or not to use a software package depends on reliable service from the salesperson. You can help the prospect company train its employees to use the software and to upgrade the package when necessary, and it's important to make this known from the start.

4. **Make Presentation** In the actual presentation of the CRM software, the idea is to match the benefits of your value package to the client's needs. The presentation may involve audiovisual aids. Since you've done your homework and know the prospect's wants and needs, you can tailor the presentation accordingly. Using a portable computer, you can access the Internet to find any and all additional information you need. This is a great time to use testimonials to show potential buyers that they are joining leaders in other firms in trying this new software.

5. **Answer Objections** You should anticipate any objections the prospect may raise and determine proper responses. Think of questions as opportunities for creating better relationships, not as a challenge to what you're saying. Customers have legitimate doubts, and you are there to resolve those doubts. Relationships are based on trust, and trust comes from successfully and honestly working with others. Often you can introduce the customer to others in the firm who can answer their questions and provide them with anything they need. Using a laptop computer, you may set up a virtual meeting where the customer can chat with other members of the firm and begin building a relationship.

closing techniques
Ways of concluding a sale including getting a series of small commitments and then asking for the order and showing the client where to sign.

6. **Close Sale** You have to "ask for the sale" to finalize the sales process. As a salesperson, you have limited time and can't spend all of it with one potential customer answering questions and objections. **Closing techniques** include getting a series of small commitments and then asking for the order

and showing the client where to sign. For example, the goal of the first close may be to get the client to agree to watch a demonstration. At the demonstration, the goal of the close may be to get the customer to try the product for a month to see its usefulness. Once a relationship is established, the goal of the sales call may be to get a testimonial from the company. As you can see, salespeople must learn to close many times before a long-term relationship is established.

7. **Follow Up** The selling process isn't over until the order is approved and the customer is happy. The sales relationship may continue for years as you respond to new requests for information. You can see why selling is often described as a process of establishing relationships, not just a matter of selling goods or services. The follow-up step includes handling customer complaints, making sure that the customer's questions are answered, and quickly supplying what the customer wants. *Often, customer service is as important to the sale as the product itself.* Most manufacturers have therefore established Web sites where information may be obtained and discussions may take place.

The selling process varies somewhat among different goods and services, but the general idea is the same. Your goals as a salesperson are to help the buyer buy and to make sure that the buyer is satisfied after the sale.

Using Technology to Practise Consultative Selling

Salespeople now have at their fingertips data about the customer, about competitors, about where products are in the supply chain, about pricing and special promotions, and more. You also are aware that B2B customers are buying more goods over the Internet. That means that B2B salespeople will have new roles to play in the future. Here is how Marc Miller, president and CEO of Change Master (a sales-productivity improvement firm) puts it: "If you're a salesperson who only communicates product value—'This is what we make, let me give you a presentation'—you're gone. But if you know how to *add value*, you're going to have a nice business as a consultative salesperson."[14]

What's a consultative salesperson? A **consultative salesperson** begins by analyzing customer needs and then comes up with solutions to those needs. At Dell Computer, for example, it's the sales team, not tech support, that builds and manages customers' extranet sites. They help determine what information should be available on such sites and they generally act as consultants on all matters having to do with computers, software, purchasing issues, and more.

Will selling to the consumer market change as dramatically as selling to the B2B market has? Probably so. Salespeople in retail stores will also see dramatic changes in the way they do things. Imagine an automobile salesperson, for example. A customer can go to a dealer and sit down with a salesperson at a computer and design a car custom-made to his or her specifications. Any product information the customer wants is available online, and the salesperson assists customers in finding that information. Often, customers will have searched the Internet to determine what car they want and will have explored most of the options. So what is the role of the salesperson? As in B2B selling, the role of the salesperson is to be a *consultant*; that is, to provide such helpful assistance that the customer feels it is worthwhile to go to the dealership to get help. That means that the salesperson will have to be computer proficient and be able to walk the customer through the whole exchange process quickly and easily, including not only getting financing, licence plates, and insurance but also ensuring prompt delivery at the customer's convenience.

There will always be a need for the kind of salesperson who directs people to the proper place to find things, discusses product features, and helps buyers complete the sales process. But such salespeople will be fewer and will get paid much less than

www.dell.com

consultative salesperson
A salesperson who analyzes customer needs and then comes up with solutions to those needs.

consultative salespeople who can use computers and other technology to help customers find and buy things quickly.

What kind of products do you think you would enjoy selling? Think of the customers for that product. Can you imagine yourself going through the seven-step selling process with them? Which steps would be hardest? Which would be easiest? Which step could you avoid by selling the product in a retail store? Can you picture yourself going through most of the sales process on the phone (telemarketing)?

Now apply these steps to your job search. Which steps would be the hardest? Which steps would be the easiest?

PROGRESS
CHECK

- What are the four traditional elements of the promotion mix?
- Outline the advantages and disadvantages of four different advertising media.
- What are the seven steps in the selling process?

PUBLIC RELATIONS:
BUILDING RELATIONSHIPS WITH ALL PUBLICS

public relations (PR)
The management function that evaluates stakeholder attitudes, changes policies and procedures in response to stakeholder requests, and executes a program of action and information to earn public understanding and acceptance.

Public relations (PR) is defined as the function that evaluates stakeholder attitudes, changes policies and procedures in response to stakeholder requests, and executes a program of action and information to earn understanding and acceptance. In other words, a good public relations program has three steps:

1. **Listen to the stakeholders.** Public relations starts with good marketing research ("evaluates stakeholder attitudes"). Stakeholders include existing and potential customers, employees, shareholders, governments, the local community, and the whole country.

Companies today have to be really careful to treat their customers well. If not, unhappy customers can turn to Web sites like AngryConsumer.com to get even, and get even they do. They can tell their story on the site and reach thousands of people with their tale of woe. Are you so upset with the service you've received somewhere that you would write something to AngryConsumer.com?

2. **Change policies and procedures**. Businesses don't earn understanding by bombarding the public with propaganda; they earn understanding by having programs and practices in the public interest. The best way to learn what the public wants is to listen to them often—in different forums, including on the Internet.

3. **Inform people that you're being responsive to their needs**. It's not enough to simply have programs in the public interest. You have to tell the public about those programs so that they know you're being responsive.

PR departments aim to give their company the best public image possible. When there is good news, like a major contract, the job of the PR department is to give that news the widest possible distribution. On the other hand, when there is bad news—like massive losses—the PR people do their best to limit the damage to the company's reputation.

Public relations demands a dialogue with stakeholders so that information can be exchanged over time and trust can be developed through responsiveness. Customers today often complain that it is hard to find someone to talk to in a firm. They may spend literally hours on the phone going through choices, waiting, and not being satisfied. In desperation, they often call the PR department. In the past, the PR department sent them off to someone else in a long and futile chase for someone to handle the problem. Today, however, PR is taking a much more active role in listening to consumers and working with them to handle problems. That means that PR must establish good relationships with production and service people so they can find answers to customer questions quickly.[15]

PR is becoming so critical to a firm's success that many smaller companies cannot find a PR firm with which to work—they are too busy with larger firms. One firm that has had huge success because of PR is Yahoo. It began its PR campaign when the "new" Internet (one that was not just for academics) was just getting started in the early 1990s. The idea was to get stories in the media about the growing importance of the Internet. The second phase of the PR campaign came before the company sold any stock. The idea was to use the media to promote the head of the company, Tom Koogle, and his professionalism. If investors were not assured that the company had a good business model, it would not be able to sell much stock to first-time buyers. Once the company got started, the goal of PR was to show the company as a major Internet company, the equivalent of America Online. Then the goal was to show that Yahoo was as important to Internet commerce as it was to Internet communications. The success of Yahoo, then, is directly attributable to its long-term PR strategy.[16]

Publicity: The Talking Arms of PR

Publicity is the talking arm of public relations. Here's how it works: Suppose that you want to introduce your new Fiberrific cereal to consumers but you have very little money to promote it. You need to get some initial sales to generate funds. One effective way to reach the public is through publicity. **Publicity** is any information about an individual, product, or organization that's distributed to the public through the media and that's not paid for, or controlled by, the seller. You might prepare a publicity release describing Fiberrific and the research findings supporting its benefits and send it to the various media. Much skill is involved in writing the story so that the media will want to publish it. Generally speaking, PR is controlled and paid for by the seller. While publicity is one element of PR, it is not controlled by the seller. The media decide what to communicate, when, where, and how often.

You may need to write different stories for different media. If the stories are published, release of the news about Fiberrific will reach many potential consumers (and investors, distributors, and dealers), and you may be on your way to becoming a successful marketer.

publicity
Any information about an individual, product, or organization that's distributed to the public through the media and that's not paid for or controlled by the seller.

The best thing about publicity is that the various media will publish stories for *no fee* if the material seems interesting or newsworthy. The idea, then, is to write publicity that meets those criteria. Consequently, today we see publicists being hired to promote anything from companies and events to politicians and celebrities:

> Hotellier Ian Schrager, who presides over the planet's hottest designer hotels in New York, Los Angeles, Miami, and London, told a magazine that he refuses to advertise, adding, "you can get a million dollars of free publicity by underwriting a party for $10,000, thereby confirming in many minds, the value of the publicist over the marketing manager and advertising agency."[17]

Besides being free, publicity has several further advantages over other promotional tools, such as advertising. For example, publicity may reach people who wouldn't read an ad. Publicity may be placed on the front page of a newspaper or in some other prominent position, or given air time on a television news show. Perhaps the greatest advantage of publicity is its believability. When a newspaper or magazine publishes a story as news, the reader treats that story as news—and news is more believable than advertising.

There are several disadvantages to publicity as well. For example, you have no control over how, when, or if the media will use the story. The media aren't obligated to use a publicity release, and most are thrown away. Furthermore, the story may be altered so that it's not so positive. There's good publicity ("Roots introduces Olympic team uniform") and bad publicity ("Firestone tires allegedly cause accidents"). Also, once a story has run, it's not likely to be repeated. Advertising, on the other hand, can be repeated as often as needed. One way to see that publicity is handled well by the media is to establish a friendly relationship with media representatives, co-operating with them when they seek information. Then, when you want their support, they're more likely to co-operate.

PROGRESS CHECK

- What are the three steps involved in setting up a public relations program?
- What are the advantages and disadvantages of publicity over advertising?

SALES PROMOTION: GETTING A GOOD DEAL

sales promotion
The promotional tool that stimulates consumer purchasing and dealer interest by means of short-term activities.

www.pg.com

Sales promotion is the promotional tool that stimulates consumer purchasing and dealer interest by means of short-term activities (such things as displays, trade shows and exhibitions, and contests). Figure 17.4 lists some *B2B* sales promotion techniques. Those free samples of products that you get in the mail, the cents-off coupons that you clip from newspapers (or download from a Web site), the contests that various retail stores sponsor, and the prizes that can be won entering contests (e.g., Tim Hortons' Roll Up the Rim to Win), are examples of *consumer* sales promotion activities (see Figure 17.5). Sales promotion programs are designed to supplement personal selling, advertising, and public relations efforts by creating enthusiasm for the overall promotional program. There was a big increase in such promotions as the twenty-first century began. Procter & Gamble, for example, successfully used coupons and other promotions to sell laundry detergent, paper towels, and diapers.[18]

Sales promotion can take place both internally (within the company) and externally (outside the company). It's just as important to generate employee enthusiasm about a product as it is to attract potential customers. The most important internal sales promotion efforts are directed at salespeople and other customer-contact people, such as complaint handlers and clerks. Internal sales promotion efforts include (1) sales training; (2) the development of sales aids such as flip charts, portable audiovisual displays, and videotapes; and (3) participation in trade shows where salespeople can get leads. Other employees who deal with the public may also be given special training to make them more aware of the company's offerings and a more integral part of the total promotional effort.

After generating enthusiasm internally, it's important to get distributors and dealers involved so that they too are eager to help promote the product. Trade shows are an important sales promotion tool because marketing intermediaries are able to see products from many different sellers and make comparisons among them. Today, virtual trade shows—trade shows on the Internet—enable buyers to see many products without leaving the office. Furthermore, the information is available 24 hours a day, seven days a week.

After the company's employees and intermediaries have been motivated with sales promotion efforts, the next step is to promote to final consumers using samples, coupons, cents-off deals, displays, store demonstrations, premiums, contests, rebates, and so on. Sales promotion is an ongoing effort to maintain enthusiasm, so different strategies must be used over time to keep the ideas fresh.

Coupons	Bonuses (buy one, get one free)
Cents-off promotions	Catalogues
Sampling	Demonstrations
Premiums	Special events
Sweepstakes	Lotteries
Contests	In-store displays

Sampling Is a Powerful Sales Promotion Tool

One popular sales promotion tool is **sampling**—letting consumers have a small sample of the product for no charge. Because many consumers won't buy a new product unless they've had a chance to see it or try it, grocery stores often have people standing in the aisles handing out small portions of food and beverage products. Sampling is a quick, effective way of demonstrating a product's superiority at the time when consumers are making a purchase decision.[19]

Recently, Pepsi introduced its Fruit Works product line with a combination of sampling, event marketing, and a new Web site. *Event marketing* means sponsoring events such as rock concerts or being at various events to promote your products. In the case of Fruit Works, Pepsi first sent samples to Panama City, Florida, and South Padre Island, Texas, for spring break. Students got free rides on the trucks and samples of the drinks. Similar sampling and event marketing efforts had been successful for SoBe (herbal-fortified drinks) and Snapple (fruit drinks and iced teas).[20]

The idea of couponing is to get customers to try the product. If customers don't come back, it is not the fault of coupons; it probably means that there is something wrong with your product. But if you have a great product, couponing and sampling are wonderful ways to get people to try it sooner than they might have as a result of any other kinds of promotion. What products do you now use regularly that you first bought because of a sample or a coupon?

Other Ways That New Technologies Are Affecting Promotion

As we have explained in earlier chapters, as people purchase goods and services on the Internet, companies keep track of those purchases and gather other facts and figures about those consumers. Over time, companies learn who buys what, when, and how often. They can then use that information to design catalogues and brochures specifically to meet the wants and needs of individual consumers as demonstrated by their actual purchasing behaviour. So, for example, a flower company may send you a postcard first reminding you that your spouse's birthday is coming up soon and that you bought a particular flower arrangement last time, and then recommending a new arrangement this time. Because so much information about consumers is now available, companies are tending to use the traditional promotional tools (e.g., advertising) less than before and are putting more money into direct mail and other forms of direct marketing, including catalogues and the Internet. Consumers are reacting favourably to such promotions, so you can expect the trend toward direct sales and Internet sales to accelerate. Promotional programs will change accordingly.

Technology offers consumers a continuous connection to the Internet and enables marketers to send video files and other data to them faster than ever before. Using such connections, marketers can interact with consumers in real time. As you have read in this chapter, that means that you can talk with a salesperson online and chat with other consumers about their experiences with products. You can also search the Net for the best price and find any product information you may want in almost any form you want—copy, sound, video, or whatever.

Such technology gives much more power to consumers like you. You no longer have to rely on advertising or other promotions to learn about products. You can search the Net on your own and find that information when you want it. If you cannot find the information you want, you can request it and get it immediately. Thus, promotion has become much more *interactive*. That is, you and the seller are able to participate in a dialogue over the Internet.

MANAGING THE PROMOTION MIX: PUTTING IT ALL TOGETHER

Each target group calls for a separate promotion mix. For example, large, homogeneous groups of consumers (that is, groups whose members share specific similar traits) are usually most efficiently reached through advertising.

Large organizations are best reached through personal selling. To motivate people to buy now rather than later, sales promotion efforts such as sampling, coupons, discounts, special displays, premiums, and so on may be used. Publicity adds support to the other efforts and can create a good impression among all consumers.

Promotional Strategies

push strategy
Promotional stategy in which the producer uses advertising, personal selling, sales promotion, and all other promotional tools to convince wholesalers and retailers to stock and sell merchandise.

pull strategy
Promotional strategy in which heavy advertising and sales promotion efforts are directed toward consumers so that they'll request the products from retailers.

There are two key ways to facilitate the movement of products from producers to consumers. The first is called a push strategy. In a **push strategy**, the producer uses advertising, personal selling, sales promotion, and all other promotional tools to convince wholesalers and retailers to stock and sell their merchandise. Therefore, when consumers walk into a store, the product is available and ready for purchase. One example of a push strategy is to offer dealers one free case for every dozen cases purchased. The idea is to push the product through the distribution system to the stores (see Figure 17.6).

A second strategy is called a pull strategy. In a **pull strategy**, heavy advertising and sales promotion efforts are directed toward consumers so that they'll request the products from retailers. Such a strategy may be implemented if manufacturers face resistance from channel members who do not want to order a new product or increase inventory levels of an existing brand.[21] Seeing the demand for the products, the store owner will then order them from the wholesaler. The wholesaler, in turn, will order them from the producer. Products are thus pulled through the distribution system (see Figure 17.7).

Of course, a company could use both push and pull strategies at the same time in a major promotional effort. For example, an auto manufacturer may promote discounted rates to potential consumers for its cars on television (pull strategy) and also run a campaign where the dealership that sells the most cars will receive a cash prize (push strategy).

It is important to make promotion part of a total systems approach to marketing. That is, promotion should be part of supply-chain management. In such cases, retailers would work with producers and distributors to make the supply chain as efficient as possible. Then a promotional plan would be developed for the whole system. The idea is to develop a value package that would appeal to everyone: manufacturers, distributors, retailers, and consumers.

Creating an Integrated Marketing Communication (IMC) System

An integrated marketing communication (IMC) system is a formal mechanism for uniting all the promotional efforts in an organization to make them more consistent with each other and more responsive to that organization's customers and other stakeholders. In an IMC system, all elements of the promotion mix—advertising, personal selling, public relations, and sales promotion—emphasize the same information and reinforce the product's strengths. The result is a unified image of the product in the public's mind.

In the past, advertising was created by ad agencies, public relations was created by PR firms, and selling was done in-house. There was little coordination across promotional efforts. As a result, consumers often received conflicting messages about a

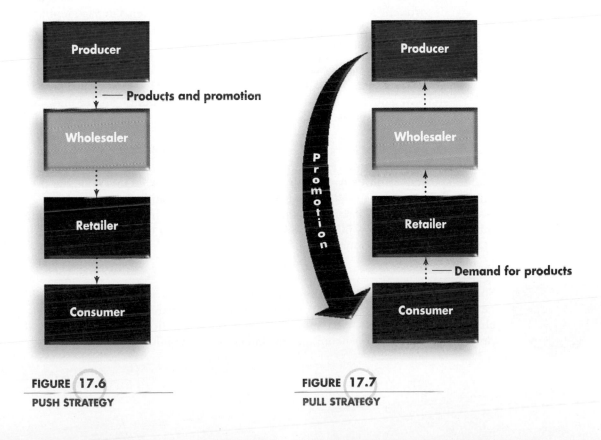

FIGURE 17.6

PUSH STRATEGY

FIGURE 17.7

PULL STRATEGY

company and its products. For example, TV advertising may have emphasized quality while the sales promotion people were pushing couponing and discounting. Such conflicting images aren't as effective as a unified image created by all promotional means.

Today, more and more companies are trying to create an integrated approach to promotion.[22] Ad agencies are buying direct marketing companies so that they can offer an integrated approach. To implement an IMC system, you start by gathering data about customers and stakeholders and their information needs. Gathering such data and making that information available to everyone in the value chain is a key to future marketing success. All messages reaching customers, potential customers, and other stakeholders would be consistent and coordinated.

Building Interactive Marketing Programs

interactive marketing program
A system in which consumers can access company information on their own and supply information about themselves in an ongoing dialogue.

Earlier in this chapter, we described interactive promotion as an *exchange* between buyers and sellers. Thus, an **interactive marketing program** is one where consumers can access company information on their own and supply information about themselves in an ongoing dialogue. Here are the basic steps for implementing such a program:

1. *Constantly gather data about the groups affected by the organization (including customers, potential customers, and other stakeholders) and keep that information in a database.* Make the data available to everyone in the value chain. An up-to-date, easily accessible database is critical to any successful program. Today, a company can gather data from sales transactions, letters, e-mail, and faxes. It may also turn to a company that specializes in gathering such data.

2. *Respond quickly to customer and other stakeholder information by adjusting company policies and practices and by designing wanted products for target markets.* A responsive firm adapts to changing wants and needs quickly and captures the market from other, less responsive firms. That's why information is so vital to organizations today and why so much money is spent on computers and information systems. You can also see how important it is for the marketing department to work closely with the information systems department and other departments in the firm to make the process of ordering and delivering products fast and smooth.

3. *Make it possible for customers and potential customers to obtain the information they need to make a purchase.* Then make it easy for people to buy your products in stores or from the company directly by placing an order through e-mail, fax, phone, or other means.

The advantages of interactive marketing on the Internet include the fact that information is available 24 hours a day, seven days a week (24/7); that ads and catalogues can be updated continually; that buyers and sellers can engage in a dialogue over time; and that it can be used by small as well as large companies.

This completes our discussion of promotion, the third P in the four Ps marketing mix. Next, we will review place (also known as distribution) to complete our review of the main elements of marketing.

CRITICAL THINKING

Soon there may be as many Internet malls as there are regional malls. Shoppers will be able to request information from multiple firms, compare prices, and make purchases from their homes. What effect will this have on traditional retailers? What will promoters have to do to encourage customers to keep coming into their stores?

539

- How many sales promotion techniques for reaching consumers can you remember? How many for reaching businesses?
- Could you describe how to implement a push strategy? A pull strategy?
- What are the three steps used in setting up an interactive marketing communication system?

THE IMPORTANCE OF CHANNELS OF DISTRIBUTION

Thus far, we've looked at three of the four Ps of the marketing mix: product, price, and promotion. We'll now look at the fourth element: place. Products have to be physically moved from where they're produced to a convenient place where consumer and industrial buyers can see and purchase them.

Look around at your fellow students. Some of them may be wearing shoes made by Timberland. Now, try to imagine the challenge of getting the raw materials together, making 12 million pairs of shoes, as Timberland does, and then distributing those shoes to stores throughout the world. That's what thousands of manufacturing firms—making everything from automobiles to toys—have to deal with every day. It is an important task and creates a vast number of career opportunities. There are hundreds of thousands of marketing intermediaries whose job it is to help move goods from the raw-material state to producers and then on to consumers. All of them need educated workers to manage their operations.

Marketing intermediaries are organizations that assist in moving goods and services from producers to business and consumer users. They're called intermediaries because they're organizations in the middle of a whole series of organizations that join together to help distribute goods from producers to consumers. (Traditionally, such firms were called *middlemen* because they were in the middle of the distribution network, but that term has been rejected by many as being sexist.) A **channel of distribution** consists of a whole set of marketing intermediaries, such as wholesalers and retailers, who join together to transport and store goods in their path (or channel) from producers to consumers. A **wholesaler** is a marketing intermediary that sells to other organizations, such as retailers, manufacturers, and hospitals. They are part of the B2B system. A **retailer** is an organization that sells to ultimate consumers (that is, people like you and me). Figure 17.8 shows channels of distribution for both consumer and industrial products.

Channels of distribution ensure communication flows and the flow of money and title to goods. They also help ensure that the right quantity and assortment of goods will be available when and where needed. The latest trend in distribution channels is to try to eliminate wholesalers and the need for retail stores by selling over the Internet and shipping directly to customers. The Spotlight on Big Business box "E-Commerce Calls for New Distribution Systems" discusses the problems that such efforts have caused and the remedies that are needed.

Why Marketing Needs Intermediaries

Manufacturers don't always need marketing intermediaries to sell their goods to consumer and business buyers. Figure 17.8 shows that some manufacturers sell directly to buyers. You can sell directly to buyers on the Internet as well. So why have marketing intermediaries at all?

The answer is that intermediaries perform certain marketing tasks such as transporting, storing, selling, advertising, and relationship building more effectively and efficiently than most manufacturers could. A simple analogy is this: You could

marketing intermediaries
Organizations that assist in moving goods and services from producers to industrial and consumer users.

channel of distribution
A whole set of marketing intermediaries, such as wholesalers and retailers, who join together to transport and store goods in their path (or channel) from producers to consumers.

wholesaler
A marketing intermediary that sells to other organizations.

retailer
An organization that sells to ultimate consumers.

Channels for industrial goods

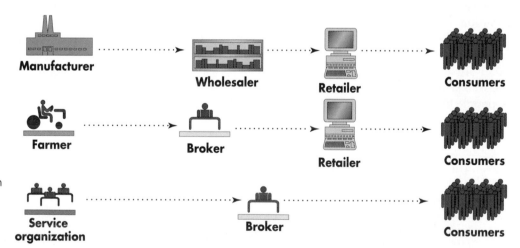

This is the common channel for industrial products such as glass, tires, and paint for automobiles.

This is the way that lower-cost items such as supplies are distributed. The wholesaler is called an industrial distributor.

This channel is used by craftspeople and small farmers. Many manufacturers are also selling on the Internet.

This channel is used for door-to-door distribution by companies like Avon (cosmetics) and Electrolux (vacuum cleaners).

This channel is used for cars, furniture, and clothing.

Channels for consumer goods

This channel is the most common channel for consumer goods such as groceries, drugs, and cosmetics.

This is a common channel for food items such as produce.

This is a common channel for consumer services such as real estate, stocks and bonds, insurance, and nonprofit theatre groups.

FIGURE 17.8

CHANNELS OF DISTRIBUTION FOR INDUSTRIAL AND CONSUMER PRODUCTS

www.fedex.com

www.ups.com

deliver packages in person to people anywhere in the world, but usually you don't. Why not? Because it's usually cheaper and faster to have them delivered by Canada Post or some private agency such as FedEx. Universal Parcel Shipping Software Systems provides software that helps larger companies compare prices and shipping methods (ground, next-day air, and so forth) to locations in and throughout Canada and the world. Small companies can get similar help through SmartShip.com. So companies, like you do, often outsource distribution to others.

Similarly, you could sell your home by yourself or buy stock directly from other people, but most people don't. Why? Again, because there are specialists (brokers)

www.grocerygateway.com
www.amazon.com

SPOTLIGHT ON BIG BUSINESS
E-Commerce Calls for New Distribution Systems

E-businesses like Amazon.com and online grocers Webvan and Grocery Gateway thought that they could sell products online and then have producers ship the goods directly to the consumer. By eliminating the wholesaler, the whole process would be more efficient. Such e-tailers learned quickly that it wouldn't be as easy as they thought. Manufacturers ran out of inventory and delivered late; also, multiple items from one order—shipped from multiple firms—arrived at different times, making product returns costly.

Amazon.com responded by spending $300 million to build 3 million square feet of warehouse space to store its books, CDs, and other products. Webvan spent $1 billion to build a warehouse system including a fleet of delivery vans. Privately held Grocery Gateway bought Direct Home Delivery, giving it a national distribution system. In short, e-commerce companies cannot get rid of the wholesale function, although they may shun traditional wholesalers and do the job themselves. More often than not, however, traditional wholesalers remain in business because they have learned to perform their functions (storage and delivery and information processing) more

efficiently than others. Will such changes lead to success in the long term? Time will tell. Webvan filed for bankruptcy in July 2001, due to slower deliveries and the collapse of the capital market for dot-com firms. Regardless of how strong a distribution system is, customers are still critical for success.

Traditional retailers like Sears have also learned that selling on the Internet calls for a new kind of distribution system. Sears' warehouses are accustomed to delivering truckloads of goods to their retail outlets. But they are not prepared to make deliveries to individual consumers—except for large orders like furniture and appliances. It turns out, therefore, that both traditional retailers and new e-tailers have to develop new distribution systems to meet the demands of today's Internet-wise shoppers.

Sources: Robert D. Hof, "What's with All the Warehouses?" *Business Week e.biz*, November 1, 1999, p. EB88; and Bill Fahrenwald and Dean Wise, "E-Commerce Meets the Material World," *Business Week*, June 26, 2000, pp. 109ff; Jerry Weber, "Grocery Gateway snags national distribution network," *The Globe and Mail*, July 16, 2001 via the World Wide Web: www.globeandmail.com.

---

who make the process more efficient and easier. **Brokers** are marketing intermediaries who bring buyers and sellers together and assist in negotiating an exchange, but don't take title to the goods—that is, at no point do they own the goods. Usually, they don't carry inventory, provide credit, or assume risk. Examples include insurance brokers, real estate brokers, and stockbrokers. In the airline industry brokers consolidate airline seats and sell them for a discount. Many students are finding challenging and lucrative jobs as stock, insurance, or real estate brokers.

brokers
Marketing intermediaries who bring buyers and sellers together and assist in negotiating an exchange but don't take title to the goods.

How Intermediaries Create Exchange Efficiency

The benefits of using marketing intermediaries can be illustrated rather easily. Suppose that five manufacturers of various food products each tried to sell directly to five retailers. The number of exchange relationships that would have to be established is 5 or 25. But picture what happens when a wholesaler enters the system. The five manufacturers would contact one wholesaler to establish five exchange relationships. The wholesaler would have to establish contact with the five retailers. That would mean another five exchange relationships. Note that the number of exchanges is reduced from 25 to only 10 by the addition of a wholesaler. Figure 17.9 shows this process.

In the past, intermediaries conducted exchanges not only more efficiently than manufacturers but also more effectively. This meant that intermediaries were often better at performing their functions than a manufacturer could be. Recently, how-

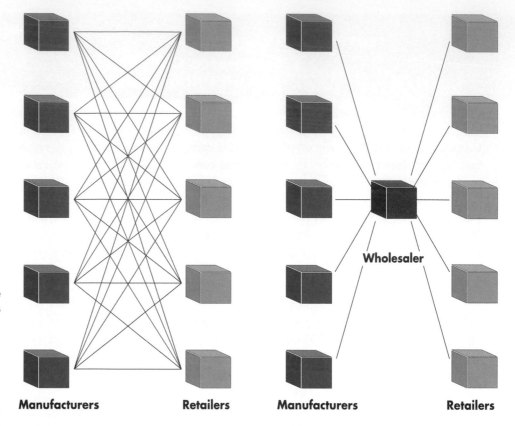

FIGURE 17.9

HOW INTERMEDIARIES CREATE EXCHANGE EFFICIENCY

This figure shows that adding a wholesaler to the channel of distribution cuts the number of contracts from 25 to 10. This makes distribution more efficient.

Manufacturers   **Retailers**   **Manufacturers**   **Retailers**   **Wholesaler**

You can buy and sell items online at eBay and other sites, but where do businesses go to buy, sell, and barter items? One site is iSolve.com. If a business gets stuck with too much inventory, it can go online and sell to other businesses. Outlet stores can find discount items at the same site. How will such sites affect traditional outlet stores and intermediaries?

ever, technology has made it possible for manufacturers to reach consumers much more efficiently than in the past. For example, some manufacturers reach consumers directly on the Internet. Companies such as Dell Computer are famous for their direct-selling capability. They then outsource their delivery function to a distribution firm. See the Reaching Beyond Our Borders box "What Intermediaries to Use" for more on the importance of carefully choosing distribution systems.

The Value versus the Cost of Intermediaries

Marketing intermediaries have always been viewed by the public with some suspicion. Some surveys have shown that about half the cost of the things we buy are marketing costs that go largely to pay for the work of intermediaries. People reason that if we could only get rid of intermediaries, we could greatly reduce the cost of everything we buy. Sounds good, but is the solution really that simple?

Let's take as an example a box of Fiberrific cereal that sells for $4. How could we, as consumers, get the cereal for less? Well, we could all drive to Winnipeg where some of the cereal is produced and save some shipping costs. But would that be practical? Can you imagine millions of people getting in their cars and driving to Winnipeg just to buy some

REACHING BEYOND OUR BORDERS
What Intermediaries to Use

It's one thing to decide to sell a product internationally; it's something else again to try to implement such a program. How are you going to reach the consumer? You could, of course, send sales representatives to contact people directly, but that would be costly and risky. How can you get your product into foreign markets at a minimum cost and still have wide distribution?

- *Use brokers.* As explained in the chapter text, a broker is an intermediary who keeps no inventory and takes no risk. A broker can find distributors for you. Brokers sell for you and make a commission on the sale. This is the least expensive way to enter foreign markets, but you still assume the risks of transportation.

- *Use importers and exporters.* Importers and exporters take all the risks of business and sell your products to international markets. Their commission is much higher than that of brokers, but they do much more for you. They may find you distributors or do the selling to ultimate consumers themselves.

- *Call on distributors directly.* You can bypass exporters and brokers and call on distributors yourself. In that case, you actually become your own exporter and deliver directly to distributors, but again you assume the risks of transportation.

- *Sell direct.* The most costly and risky way to sell internationally is to set up your own distribution system of wholesalers and retailers. On the other hand, this maximizes potential profits in the long run. Many firms start out selling through importers and exporters and end up setting up their own distribution system as sales increase.

- *Use third-party logistics (3PL) providers.* This new kind of company will distribute goods worldwide for you. Ryder Integrated Logistics is one firm that provides this service. It designs, implements, and manages the whole system for delivering goods nationally and internationally.

International distribution will be a major growth area in marketing, with many challenges and opportunities for tomorrow's graduates. Does a career in this area sound interesting to you?

Sources: Jerry Bowles, "Building the Enterprise Supply Chains Ecosystem," *Fortune*, May 10, 1999, pp. S1-S12; Scott Thrum, "Winning and Losing Suppliers," *The Wall Street Journal*, March 26, 1999, pp. A1, A12; Christopher A. Bartlett and Sumantra Ghoshal, "Going Global," *Harvard Business Review*, March–April 2000, pp. 133–42; Amy Feldman, "Investing Coke: The Real Thing Coke Stock Finally Has Some Fizz Again," *Money*, October 1, 2000, p. 33; and Courtney Fingar, "Are You World Ready?" *Global Business*, January 2001, pp. 28–30.

cereal? No, it doesn't make sense. It's much cheaper to have intermediaries bring the cereal to major cities. That might involve transportation and warehousing by wholesalers. These steps add cost, don't they? Yes, but they add value as well: the value of not having to drive to Winnipeg.

The cereal is now in a warehouse somewhere on the outskirts of the city. We could all drive down to the wholesaler and pick it up. But that still isn't the most economical way to buy cereal. If we figure in the cost of gas and time, the cereal would be too expensive. Instead, we prefer to have someone move the cereal from the warehouse to a truck, drive it to the corner supermarket, unload it, unpack it, stamp it with a price, put it on the shelf, and wait for us to come in to buy it. To make it even more convenient, the supermarket may stay open for 24 hours a day, seven days a week. Think of the costs. But think also of the value! For $4, we can get a box of cereal when we want it, with little effort on our part.

If we were to get rid of the retailer, we could buy a box of cereal for a little less, but we'd have to drive farther and spend time in the warehouse looking through rows of cereals. If we got rid of the wholesaler, we could save a little more money, not counting our drive to Winnipeg. But a few cents here and a few cents there add up—to the point where marketing may add up to 75 cents for every 25 cents in manufacturing costs.

Here are three basic points about intermediaries:

- Marketing intermediaries can be eliminated, but their activities can't; that is, you can eliminate some wholesalers and retailers, but then consumers or someone else would have to perform the retailer's tasks, including transporting and storing goods, finding suppliers, and establishing communication with suppliers. Today, many of those functions are being performed on the Internet, and intermediaries are being eliminated.

- Intermediary organizations have survived in the past because they have performed marketing functions more effectively and efficiently than others could. To maintain their competitive position in the channel, intermediaries must adopt the latest in technology.[23]

- Intermediaries add costs to products, but these costs are usually more than offset by the values they create. Value includes time, place, possession, information, and service utility.

WHOLESALE INTERMEDIARIES

There's often some confusion about the difference between wholesalers and retailers. It's helpful to distinguish wholesaling from retailing and to clearly define the functions performed so that more effective systems of distribution can be designed. Some producers won't sell directly to retailers but will deal only with wholesalers. Some producers give wholesalers a bigger discount than retailers. What confuses the issue is that some organizations sell much of their merchandise to other intermediaries (a wholesale sale) but also sell to ultimate consumers (a retail sale). The office superstore Staples is a good example. It sells office supplies to small businesses and to consumers as well. Warehouse clubs, such as Price Club and Costco, are also examples.

The issue is really rather simple: A **retail sale** is the sale of goods and services to consumers for their own use. A **wholesale sale** is the sale of goods and services to businesses and institutions (e.g., hospitals) for use in the business or to wholesalers or retailers for resale. Wholesalers sell in the business to business market.

Merchant Wholesalers

Merchant wholesalers are independently owned firms that take title to the goods they handle. About 80 percent of wholesalers fall in this category. There are two types of merchant wholesalers: full-service wholesalers and limited-function wholesalers. *Full-service wholesalers* perform all of the distribution functions: transportation, storage, risk bearing, credit, market information, standardization and grading, buying, and selling (see Figure 17.10). *Limited-function wholesalers* perform only selected functions, but try to do them especially well.

Rack jobbers furnish racks or shelves full of merchandise to retailers, display products, and sell on consignment. This means that they keep title to the goods until they're sold, and then they share the profits with the retailer. Merchandise such as toys, hosiery, and health and beauty aids are sold by rack jobbers. (A rack jobber that doesn't supply credit to customers is classified as a limited-function wholesaler.)

Cash-and-carry wholesalers serve mostly smaller retailers with a limited assortment of products. Traditionally, retailers went to such wholesalers, paid cash, and carried the goods back to their stores—thus the term *cash-and-carry*. Today, stores such as Office Depot and Staples allow retailers and others to use credit cards for wholesale purchases.

Drop shippers solicit orders from retailers and other wholesalers and have the merchandise shipped directly from a producer to a buyer. They own the merchandise but don't handle, stock, or deliver it. That's done by the producer. Drop shippers tend to handle bulky products such as coal, lumber, and chemicals.

www.staples.com

www.costco.com

retail sale
The sale of products to consumers for their own use.

wholesale sale
The sale of goods and services to businesses and institutions for use in the business or to wholesalers or retailers for resale.

merchant wholesalers
Independently owned firms that take title to (own) the goods they handle.

rack jobbers
Wholesalers that furnish racks or shelves full of merchandise to retailers, display products, and sell on consignment.

cash-and-carry wholesalers
Wholesalers that serve mostly smaller retailers with a limited assortment of products.

drop shippers
Wholesalers that solicit orders from retailers and other wholesalers and have the merchandise shipped directly from a producer to a buyer.

FIGURE 17.10

A FULL-SERVICE WHOLESALER

A full-service wholesaler will:

1. Provide a salesforce to sell the goods to retailers and other buyers.
2. Communicate manufacturers' advertising deals and plans.
3. Maintain inventory, thus reducing the level of the inventory suppliers have to carry.
4. Arrange or undertake transportation.
5. Provide capital by paying cash or quick payments for goods.
6. Provide suppliers with market information they can't afford or can't obtain themselves.
7. Undertake credit risk by granting credit to customers and absorbing any bad debts, thus relieving the supplier of this burden.
8. Assume the risk for the product by taking title.

The wholesaler may perform the following services for customers:

1. Buy goods the end market will desire and make them available to customers.
2. Maintain inventory, thus reducing customers' cost.
3. Transport goods to customers quickly.
4. Provide market information and business consulting services.
5. Provide financing through granting credit, which is especially critical to small retailers.
6. Order goods in the types and quantities customers desire.

Source: Thomas C. Kinnear and Kenneth L. Bernhardt, *Principles of Marketing, 2nd ed.* (Glenview, IL: Scott, Foresman, 1986).

Smaller manufacturers or marketers that don't ship enough products to fill a railcar or truck can get good rates and service by using a freight forwarder. A **freight forwarder** puts many small shipments together to create a single large shipment that can be transported cost-effectively to the final destination. Some freight forwarders also offer warehousing, customs assistance, and other services along with pickup and delivery. You can see the benefits of such a company to a smaller shipper.

freight forwarder
An organization that puts many small shipments together to create a single large shipment that can be transported cost-effectively to the final destination.

RETAIL INTERMEDIARIES

Perhaps the most useful marketing intermediaries, as far as you're concerned, are retailers. They're the ones who bring goods and services to your neighbourhood and make them available day and night. A supermarket is a retail store. A retailer, remember, is a marketing intermediary that sells to consumers. Next time you go to the supermarket to buy groceries, stop for a minute and look at the tremendous variety of products in the store. Think of how many marketing exchanges were involved to bring you the 18,000 or so items that you see. Some products (e.g., spices) may have been imported from halfway around the world. Other products have been processed and frozen so that you can eat them out of season (e.g., corn and green beans).

Retailing is important to the Canadian economy. This industry generated more than $277 billion in 2000.[24] There are approximately 242,850 retail trade establishments,[25] and this number does not include the retail Web sites on the Internet. Retail organizations employ more than 1.8 million people[26] and are one of the major employers of marketing graduates. There are many careers available in retailing in all kinds of firms.

The number of categories of stores is truly astounding. Supermarkets, discounters, factory outlets, giant warehouse stores, department stores, specialty stores, hypermarkets, convenience stores, chain stores—the list goes on and on. Not only are Canadian retailers facing competition from each other, but also there is increasing competition from American retail chains. This competition is from new entrants, current players, and from buyers of Canadian retailers. Many—such as

Warehouse clubs and wholesalers such as Costco operate in many Canadian cities. They provide a special type of cash-and-carry service to members.

American Eagle Outfitters, Old Navy, Pottery Barn, and Williams-Sonoma—have announced plans to expand into Canada. Other retailers, such as Wal-Mart, already have a presence. Buyouts, such as Best Buy Co. Ltd.'s purchase of Future Shop Ltd., guarantee U.S. retailers a presence—in this case, nearly 16 percent of the home entertainment market.[27]

American retailers continue to have an impact on the Canadian retail industry in numbers, as well as in size. In 1992 there were 21 American retailers in Canada; in 2001 there were 101, and it is forecast that by 2015 50 percent of retail space will be foreign-controlled.[28] American retailers will continue to expand into Canada as our economy is stable and growing and they need to also expand as their own market is becoming saturated. If Canadian retailers fail to provide service, selection, and reasonable prices to their customers, they risk losing market share to these larger competitors.

The traditional brick-and-mortar retailers are also facing increasing competition from the nonstore retailing sector. We will discuss this shortly.

How Retailers Compete

There are five major ways for retailers to compete for the consumer's dollar: price, service, location, selection, and entertainment. Since consumers are constantly comparing retailers on price, service, and variety, it is important for retailers to use benchmarking to compare themselves against the best in the field to make sure that their practices and procedures are the most advanced. The following sections describe the five major ways to compete.

www.hbc.com/zellers

www.sears.com

www.walmart.com

www.homedepot.co

www.ikea.com

www.westjet.com

www.hrblock.com

www.motel6.com

www.botspot.com

Price Competition Competing on the basis of price is not new. Honest Ed's in Toronto and similar stores across Canada became famous for their ads loudly proclaiming the lowest prices in town. Today, however, most stores have taken up this cry and giant stores (pharmacy and other chains, supermarkets, discounters, department stores, warehouse clubs, and more) are all competing fiercely based on price. Established companies like Zellers and Sears are now fighting it out with the new or revitalized kids on the block: Wal-Mart, Home Depot, and Ikea. Endless ads in all media—newspaper inserts, junk mail, door-to-door weekly handouts, and so on—stress sales and special prices for every conceivable type of product. Retailers who do not adapt to this changing environment run into trouble, evidenced by the disappearance of such stalwarts as Woodward's in the west, the Robert Simpson department stores, and the collapse of the once-prestigious national department store giant, the T. Eaton Co. Ltd.

Service organizations also compete on price. Note, for example, WestJet Airlines' success with its low-price strategy. The same is true of H&R Block in income-tax-preparation services, and Motel 6 for motel-room rentals.

Price competition is getting fiercer as Internet firms like mySimon.com help consumers find the best prices on a wide range of items. Look up BotSpot for other companies that do price searches. As you learned earlier, prices are easy to match, so most retailers have to turn to other strategies—like service—to win and keep customers.

Service Competition A second competitive strategy for retailers is service.[29] Retail service involves putting the customer first. This requires all frontline people to be courteous and accommodating to customers. Retail service also means follow-up service such as on-time delivery, guarantees, and fast installation. Consumers are frequently willing to pay a little more for products if the retailer offers outstanding service.

Smaller stores have a chance to star in this category because they can give personal service. Department stores, having trimmed personnel to stay in the black, have been criticized for the lack of staff when customers need service. Keeping customers waiting on the telephone or at cash counters is a sign of inadequate service. For companies that provide services, such as banks, couriers, and Internet service providers, excellent service is obviously a key competitive strategy.

Location Competition Many services, especially convenience services like banks and dry cleaners, compete effectively by having good locations. That's why you find automated teller machines in convenient places such as supermarkets and train stations. Many fast-food stores, such as Burger King and Pizza Hut, now have on-campus locations so that students can reach them quickly. Some dry cleaners pick up and deliver laundry at your home or business.

Often, nothing is more convenient than shopping online: You don't have to go outside at all and fight crowds or traffic. But online retailers have to learn to deliver goods faster and more reliably and handle returns better, or they will lose the advantage of convenience. Also, many consumers are nervous about giving their credit card numbers to online retailers for fear of having them stolen. Each of these problems will be solved someday, but meanwhile competition between brick-and-mortar retailers and online retailers will intensify.[30]

Selection Competition A fourth competitive strategy for retailers is selection. Selection is the offering of a wide variety of items in the same product category. **Category killer stores** offer wide selection at competitive prices. Toys "R" Us stores carry some 18,000 toys, and the company has more than 500 stores around the world. Many small, independent toy stores went out of business because they simply couldn't compete with the low prices and selection found at Toys "R" Us. Borders Books carries some 150,000 different titles. PetsMart and other pet food superstores have some 10,000 items each. Service organizations that compete successfully on selection include Blockbuster (wide selection of rental videos) and Schwab Mutual Funds (hundreds of funds).

category killer stores
Large stores that offer wide selection at competitive prices.

www.toysrus.com

www.schwab.com

Despite their initial success, many category killer stores are in turn being "killed" by discount department stores like Wal-Mart.[31] Wal-Mart has become a huge challenge to Toys "R" Us. Consumers are finding it more convenient to shop for multiple items at stores like Costco rather than go out of their way to find stores selling only sports equipment or only pet supplies. Thus, location may be more important than selection for consumer items.

Internet stores can offer products from dozens of suppliers and offer almost unlimited selection (e.g., Amazon.com). There may come a day when category killer online retailers drive brick-and-mortar category killers out of the market.

Small retailers sometimes compete with category killers by offering wide selection within one or a few categories of items. Thus, you have successful small stores that sell nothing but coffee beans or party products. Small retailers also compete with category killers by offering personalized service.

Entertainment Competition The Internet may be a convenient place to shop, but it can't possibly be as much fun as a brick-and-mortar store designed to provide entertainment as well as a place to buy things. One example is the West Edmonton Mall, the largest mall in the world. It offers more than 800 stores and services and more than 110 eating establishments (including two McDonald's restaurants). There are 19 movie theatres, a miniature gold course, an indoor water park with 20 water slides, an indoor amusement park with 28 rides, a lake with submarines, and a skating rink. Considered the largest tourist attraction in Alberta, it attracts millions of shoppers a year.

Retail Distribution Strategy

A major decision marketers must make is selecting the right retailers to sell their products. Different products call for different retail distribution strategies. There are three categories of retail distribution: intensive distribution, selective distribution, and exclusive distribution.

intensive distribution
Distribution that puts products into as many retail outlets as possible.

Intensive distribution puts products into as many retail outlets as possible, including convenience stores, schools, hospitals, and vending machines. Products that need intensive distribution include convenience goods such as candy, cigarettes, gum, and popular magazines. The objective is to saturate the market and gain a large market share.

selective distribution
Distribution that sends products to only a preferred group of retailers in an area.

Selective distribution is the use of only a preferred group of the available retailers in an area. Such selection helps to assure producers of quality sales and service. Manufacturers of appliances, furniture, and clothing (shopping goods) usually use selective distribution. Employees are better trained and can provide more assistance with these higher-involvement products.

exclusive distribution
Distribution that sends products to only one retail outlet in a given geographic area.

Exclusive distribution is the use of only one retail outlet in a given geographic area. Because the retailer has exclusive rights to sell the product, it is more likely to carry more inventory, give better service, and pay more attention to this brand than to others. Examples include Harley-Davidson dealerships, auto manufacturers (e.g., BMW), and producers of specialty goods such as skydiving equipment or fly-fishing products. And a final example is Peachtree Network Inc. of Montreal. It is a builder of Internet stores for traditional grocers such as AM Foodfare, which represents a group of 15 independent grocers in Manitoba, Saskatchewan, and Ontario.[32]

NONSTORE RETAILING

Nothing in retailing has received more attention recently than e-tailing. This may be one more step in the evolution of retailing away from traditional stores to nonstore retailing. Other categories of nonstore retailing include telemarketing; vending machines, kiosks, and carts; direct selling; and direct marketing.

E-tailing

www.forrester.com

e-tailing
Selling goods and services to ultimate customers over the Internet.

E-tailing means selling goods and services to ultimate consumers (e.g., you and me) over the Internet. Many smaller companies think that selling over the Internet is a simple, low-overhead way to build a business. Often it isn't. According to a recent study by Forrester Research, 47 percent of U.S. companies spend up to $5 million developing a Web site and 17 percent spend more than $20 million.[33] But getting customers is only half the battle, as we have been telling you throughout this chapter. The other half is delivering the goods, providing helpful service, and keeping your customers. When e-tailers fail to have sufficient inventory or fail to deliver goods on time (especially at Christmas time and other busy periods), customers give up and go back to brick-and-mortar stores.

Most e-tailers now offer e-mail confirmation. But sometimes e-tailers are not so good at handling complaints, taking back goods that customers don't like, and providing online personal help. Some sites are trying to improve customer service by adding help buttons that you can click on to get almost instant assistance from a real person. Rightstart.com, for example, is a seller of children's toys and products. It has a live chat function to its online retailing. If you have a problem, you click the live help icon and a customer-service representative answers within minutes.[34]

The latest trend in e-commerce is for the traditional retailers like Wal-Mart and Zellers to go online. They know that competition is only a click away and thus need to offer low prices and good service to keep customers coming.[35]

What is happening rapidly is that old brick-and-mortar stores are going online. The result, sometimes called a click-and-mortar store, allows customers to choose which shopping technique suits them best. They may shop online and then go to a store to get the merchandise, or go to a store to learn all they can about product choices and then go to the Internet to find the best deal. In any case, most companies that want to compete in the future will probably need both a real store presence and an online presence to provide consumers with all the options they want. Part of that strategy is to include the company's phone number in any promotions so that consumers can call in an order as well.

Telemarketing

Telemarketing is the sale of goods and services by telephone. Some 80,000 companies use telemarketing today to supplement or replace in-store selling and to complement online selling. Many send a catalogue to consumers and let them order by calling a toll-free number. As we noted, others provide a help feature online that serves the same function.

telemarketing
The sale of goods and services by telephone.

Vending Machines, Kiosks, and Carts

A vending machine dispenses convenience goods when consumers deposit sufficient money in the machine. The benefit of vending machines is their location in airports, office buildings, schools, service stations, and other areas where people want convenience items. Vending machines in Japan sell everything from bandages and face cloths to salads and spiced seafood. Vending by machine will be an interesting area to watch as such innovations are introduced in Canada.

Carts and kiosks have lower overhead costs than stores do; therefore, they can offer lower prices on items such as T-shirts and umbrellas. You often see vending carts outside stores on the sidewalk or along walkways in malls; mall owners often love them because they're colourful and create a marketplace atmosphere. Kiosk workers dispense coupons and provide all kinds of helpful information to consumers, who tend to enjoy the interaction. Hot items in kiosks today include miniature aquariums, candles, diet supplements, aromatherapy, and calendars.

www.avon.com

www.electrolux.com

There are literally thousands of vending machines all over Japan selling almost anything you need. In this photo, a woman is using a vending machine that provides photos of men as part of a dating service. Would you like to see such a machine on campus?

Direct Selling

Direct selling involves selling to consumers in their homes or where they work. Major users of this category include cosmetics producers (Avon) and vacuum cleaner manufacturers (Electrolux). Trying to emulate the success of those products, other businesses are now using direct selling for lingerie, artwork, plants, and many other goods. Many of these sales are made at "house parties" sponsored by sellers.

Because so many women work now and aren't at home during the day, companies based on direct selling are sponsoring parties at workplaces or in the evenings and on weekends. Some companies, such as those selling encyclopedias, have dropped direct selling in favour of Internet selling.

Direct Marketing

One of the fastest-growing aspects of retailing is direct marketing. Direct marketing includes any activity that directly

links manufacturers or intermediaries with the ultimate consumer. Thus, direct retail marketing includes direct mail, catalogue sales, and telemarketing as well as online marketing. Popular consumer catalogue companies that use direct marketing include L. L. Bean and Lands' End. Direct marketing has created tremendous competition in some high-tech areas as well. For example, direct sales by Dell Computers, Gateway 2000, and other computer manufacturers has led IBM and Compaq to use price-cutting tactics to meet the competition. Compaq also decided to go online to compete more directly and to offer its own custom-designed computers.

www.llbean.com

www.landsend.com

www.gateway.com

Direct marketing has become popular because shopping from home or work is more convenient for consumers than going to stores. Instead of driving to a mall, people can "shop" using catalogues and free-standing advertising supplements in the newspaper and then buy by phone, by mail, or by computer. Interactive online selling is expected to provide even greater competition for retail stores in the near future.

Direct marketing took on a new dimension when consumers became involved with interactive video. Producers now provide all kinds of information on CD-ROMs or on Web sites that consumers access with their computers. The potential of such systems seems almost limitless. Consumers can ask questions, seek the best price, and order goods and services—all by computer. Companies that use interactive video and interactive Web sites have become major competitors for those who market by catalogue.

CRITICAL THINKING

How important are intermediaries such as wholesalers, retailers, trucking firms, and warehouse operators to the progress of less developed countries? Is there a lack of intermediaries in less developed countries? How do intermediaries contribute to the development of a less developed country? How will the Internet provide third-world consumers with access to worldwide markets? What intermediaries will be needed most to serve those customers?

BUILDING CO-OPERATION IN CHANNEL SYSTEMS

One way that traditional retailers can stay competitive with online retailers is to make the whole system so efficient that online retailers can't beat them out on cost—given the need to pay for delivery. That means that manufacturers and wholesalers and retailers (members of the channel of distribution) must work closely together to form a unified system. How can manufacturers get wholesalers and retailers to co-operate to form such an efficient distribution system? One way is to somehow link the firms together in a formal relationship. Four systems have emerged to tie firms together: corporate systems, contractual systems, administered systems, and supply chains.

Corporate Distribution Systems

corporate distribution system
A distribution system in which all of the organizations in the channel of distribution are owned by one firm.

A **corporate distribution system** is one in which all of the organizations in the channel of distribution are owned by one firm. If the manufacturer owns the retail firm, clearly it can influence much greater control over its operations. Au Coton, for example, owns its own retail stores and thus coordinates everything: display, pricing, promotion, inventory control, and so on.

Contractual Distribution Systems

contractual distribution system
A distribution system in which members are bound to co-operate through contractual agreements.

If a manufacturer can't buy retail stores, it can try to get retailers to sign a contract to co-operate. A **contractual distribution system** is one in which members are bound to co-operate through contractual agreements. There are three forms of contractual systems:

www.baskinrobbins.com

1. Franchise systems include Sports Experts and Baskin-Robbins. The franchisee agrees to all of the rules, regulations, and procedures established by the franchisor. This results in the consistent quality and level of service you find in most franchised organizations.

2. Wholesaler-sponsored chains include Ace Hardware and IGA food stores. Each store signs an agreement to use the same name, participate in chain promotions, and co-operate as a unified system of stores, even though each store is independently owned and managed.

3. Retail co-operatives include Associated Grocers. This arrangement is much like a wholesaler-sponsored chain except that it is initiated by the retailers. The same co-operation is agreed to, however, and the stores remain independent. The normal way such a system is formed is for retailers to agree to focus their purchases on one wholesaler, but co-operative retailers could also purchase a wholesale organization to ensure better service.

www.acehardware.com

www.igainc.com

www.agbr.com

Administered Distribution Systems

If you were a producer, what would you do if you couldn't get retailers to sign an agreement to co-operate? One thing you could do is to manage all the marketing functions yourself, including display, inventory control, pricing, and promotion. A system in which producers manage all of the marketing functions at the retail level is called an **administered distribution system**. Kraft does that for its cheeses; Scott does it for its seed and other lawn-care products. Retailers co-operate with producers in such systems because they get so much free help. All the retailer has to do is ring up the sale.

administered distribution system
A distribution system in which producers manage all of the marketing functions at the retail level.

Supply Chains

The latest in systems coordination involves the supply chain. The **supply chain** consists of all the organizations that move goods and services from the source of raw materials to the final customer. The supply chain is longer than a channel of distribution because it includes suppliers to manufacturers, whereas the channel of distribution begins with manufacturers. Channels of distribution are part of the overall supply chain (see Figure 17.11). Included in the supply chain, therefore, are farmers, miners, suppliers of all kinds (e.g., parts, equipment, supplies), manufacturers, wholesalers, and retailers.

Companies such as SAP and Manugistics have developed software that makes it possible to coordinate the movement of goods and information so that consumer wants can be translated into products with the least amount of materials, inventory, and time. **Electronic data interchange (EDI)** is an example of such software. It enables the computers of producers, wholesalers, and retailers to communicate with each other.[36] EDI makes it possible for a retailer to be directly linked with a supplier electronically. As a result, the supplier can ship new goods as soon as the retail sale is made. With the application of such software, the flows among firms are almost seamless. Naturally, the systems are quite complex and quite expensive, but they pay for themselves in the long run because of inventory savings, customer service improvement, and responsiveness to market changes.[37]

supply chain
The sequence of linked activities that must be performed by various organizations to move goods from the sources of raw materials to ultimate consumers.

www.sap.com

www.manugistics.com

electronic data interchange (EDI)
Software that enables the computers of producers, wholesalers, and retailers to communicate with each other.

FIGURE 17.11

THE SUPPLY CHAIN

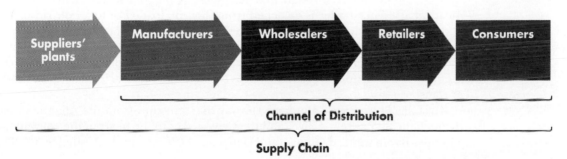

Suppliers' plants → Manufacturers → Wholesalers → Retailers → Consumers

Channel of Distribution

Supply Chain

- Can you briefly describe the activities of rack jobbers, drop shippers, and freight forwarders?

- Can you describe and give examples of the six ways that retailers compete?

- What kind of products would call for each of the different distribution strategies: intensive, selective, exclusive?

- Can you explain each of the four systems that have evolved to tie together members of the channel of distribution?

CHOOSING THE RIGHT DISTRIBUTION MODE AND STORAGE UNITS

A primary concern of supply-chain managers is selecting a transportation mode that will minimize costs and ensure a certain level of service. (*Modes*, in the language of distribution, are the various means used to transport goods, such as by truck, train, plane, ship, and pipeline.) Generally speaking, the faster the mode of transportation, the higher the cost. Today supply chains involve more than simply moving products from place to place; they involve all kinds of activities such as processing orders and taking inventory of products. In other words, logistics systems involve whatever it takes to see that the right products are sent to the right place quickly and efficiently.

Transportation Modes

In Canada we have always had a particular economic problem regarding the transportation component of operating costs. Canada is a very large country with a very low population density. Competitors in the United States and Japan have high population densities and relatively short distances in their domestic markets. This transportation factor makes unit costs in Canada higher, which makes us less competitive.

This Canadian situation makes the job of supply chain managers particularly important. They select transportation modes that minimize costs while maintaining the required level of service speed and reliability. When railroads were first built, they carried the overwhelming bulk of goods in Canada where water transport was not available. With the establishment of a wide network of paved highways in the middle of the twentieth century, trucking became an important mode of transportation. By the beginning of the 1990s, truck tonnage exceeded rail tonnage by some 30 percent.[38]

There are distinct advantages of using one mode over the other. Trucks reach more locations than trains and they can deliver almost any commodity door-to-door. However, trains are quicker if you are looking at crossing great distances (e.g., from the east coast to the west coast) and, with increasing fuel prices, railroad shipment is a relatively energy-efficient way to move goods.

Today, the progress of modern technology is making it increasingly difficult to make clear distinctions between these and other modes. Railroads are attempting to transport more goods through practices such as piggyback shipments. *Piggyback* means that a truck trailer is detached from the cab; loaded onto a railroad flatcar; and taken to a destination where it will be offloaded, attached to a truck, and driven to customers' plants. There are also new, 6-metre-high railroad cars, called double-stacks, which can carry tow truck trailers, one on top of each other. These piggyback methods make the total trip as efficient as possible and blur the lines between modes of transport.

In Canada we have a unique waterway that stretches from the Atlantic Ocean through the St. Lawrence River and the Great Lakes to the heart of the continent—Thunder Bay in western Ontario and Detroit and Chicago in the United States. This major transportation artery carries a huge volume of tonnage through the St. Lawrence Seaway channel (which is closed for the three winter months). The locks at Sault Ste. Marie and the Welland Canal are among the busiest in the world. This system has made Quebec City, Montreal, and Toronto into significant ports. Our ports on the Atlantic and Pacific oceans are busy all year long receiving and shipping vast amounts of cargo.

Whereas trucks and railway cars carry similar products, ships are most useful for very large bulky objects. Airplanes, which have the obvious advantage of speed, have the disadvantage of size limitations and high costs. Airplanes are an economic mode for high-cost, small items like jewellery or replacement parts for downed equipment that is delaying huge projects or important manufacturing processes. They are also ideal for the daily transport of parcels and envelopes that form the bulk of the rapid delivery required by business. Thus, we have companies like Canada Post, Purolator, and Air Canada guaranteeing overnight delivery to any part of Canada. (It takes a little longer for delivery to other parts of the world.) When truck trailers are placed on ships to travel long distances at lower rates, the process is called *fishyback* (see the explanation of piggyback). When they are placed in airplanes, the process is called *birdyback*.

Pipelines are a form of transportation used mostly for oil and natural gas. They crisscross the North American continent carrying these natural resources long distances, 24 hours a day, 365 days a year, immune from weather and other hazards. They also carry coal and other products, in small pieces, in water, or *slurry*. The water is removed at the end of the journey.

The job of the supply chain manager is to find the most efficient combination of these forms of transportation. Figure 17.12 shows the advantages and disadvantages of each mode.

Intermodal Shipping

Intermodal shipping uses multiple modes of transportation—highway, air, water, rail—to complete a single long-distance movement of freight. Services that specialize in intermodal shipping are known as intermodal marketing companies. Today railroads are merging with each other and with other transportation companies to offer intermodal distribution.

You can imagine such a system in action. Picture an automobile made in Japan for sale in Canada. It would be shipped by truck to a loading dock where it would be moved by ship to a port in Canada (e.g., Halifax). It may be placed on another truck and taken to a railroad station for loading on a train that will take it across country to again be loaded on a truck for delivery to a local dealer. No doubt you have seen automobiles being hauled across country by train and by truck. Now imagine that all of that movement was handled by one integrated shipping firm. That's what intermodal shipping is all about.

intermodal shipping
The use of multiple modes of transportation to complete a single long-distance movement of freight.

FIGURE 17.12

COMPARING TRANSPORTATION MODES

Combining trucks with railroads lowers costs and increases the number of locations reached. The same is true when combining trucks with ships. Combining trucks with airlines speeds goods long distances and gets them to almost any location.

Mode	Cost	Speed	On-time Dependability	Flexibility Handling Products	Frequency of Shipments	Reach
Railroad	Medium	Slow	Medium	High	Low	High
Truck	High	Fast	High	Medium	High	Most
Pipeline	Low	Medium	Highest	Lowest	Highest	Lowest
Ship (water)	Lowest	Slowest	Lowest	Highest	Lowest	Low
Airplane	Highest	Fastest	Low	Low	Medium	Medium

The Storage Function

About 25 to 30 percent of the total cost of physical distribution is for storage. This includes the cost of the warehouse and its operation plus movement of goods within the warehouse. There are two major kinds of warehouses: storage and distribution.

A *storage warehouse* stores products for a relatively long time. Seasonal goods such as lawn mowers would be kept in such a warehouse. *Distribution warehouses* are facilities used to gather and redistribute products. You can picture a distribution warehouse for Canada Post handling thousands of packages for a very short time.

Don't underestimate the importance of materials handling to the whole supply-chain process. As you can see from this photo of Harry and David's packing facility, it is important to have a smooth flow of goods going to each packing module. Without a carefully designed system, goods can pile up and get lost and get ruined. Can you imagine the materials handling system necessary to bring all the parts together to assemble a car or an airplane?

materials handling
The movement of goods within a warehouse, factory, or store.

Materials Handling

Materials handling is the movement of goods within a warehouse, factory, or store. The increased use of just-in-time inventory control (discussed in Chapter 10) is cutting back on the significant costs associated with such movement. Many manufacturers have also installed robots and automated equipment to move goods efficiently within the firm. Nonetheless, materials handling can still be quite costly to some firms.

What All This Means to You

This is an exciting time to study marketing. The four elements of marketing—product, price, promotion, and place—all have an impact on the success of a firm. You now know that place (also known as distribution) often depends on the firm's ability to take orders, process them, keep the customer informed as to the progress of the order, get the goods out to customers quickly, handle returns, and manage any recycling issues. While distribution is critical, promotion is also essential to communicate the features of these products, in addition to their availability and location. Soon you may read ads on your cellular phone or portable computer and order products immediately with just a push of a button.[39]

What all this means to you is that there are many new jobs becoming available in the exciting area of marketing. In addition to marketing managerial and sales positions, there are jobs that look after handling information flows between and among companies (e.g., Web site development), that process orders, that keep track of inventory, and much more.

PROGRESS CHECK

- How does supply chain management differ from managing the channel of distribution?
- Which transportation mode is fastest, which is cheapest, and which is most flexible?
- Which transportation modes can be combined?
- What percentage of the distribution cost comes from storage?

ETHICAL DILEMMA

Review

Now that you have worked your way through the chapter, how do you feel about the ethical question posed at the beginning of the chapter? Here's the response of our two business people.

Bérdard says that "False advertising is illegal." Reilley is of the opinion that "stretching the truth can lead to questions being raised by Health Canada and other agencies. Also, your competitors might publicly attack your claims, which could harm your business. My answer would be no. Rather, I would attempt to make our ads more attractive, increase our marketing efforts, and overhaul production and distribution to increase business."

Some of you might say, "What's the big deal? Lots of ads exaggerate." Others might be concerned about how ethical it is to use such an ad. Does the answer depend on what your personal values are and how

strongly you feel about them? We are often confronted with decisions that are more or less ethical, and sometimes it may seem as if a particular issue is not too important. Is it okay to cheat when writing exams? If a cashier omitted punching in an item would you tell him?

We may tell little white lies to make life more convenient. For example, if you want to avoid going out with someone, you might say you are too busy or that you have a bad headache. How often have you used a phony alibi when you didn't do your homework, you came home late, or didn't do some household chore? Is there any significant difference between any of these scenarios and the ad problem? The decision about using or not using that ad will finally depend upon your own set of ethical standards.

SUMMARY

1. Promotion is an attempt by marketers to inform people about products and to persuade them to participate in an exchange.
   • *What are the four traditional promotional tools that make up the promotion mix?*
   The four traditional promotional tools are advertising, personal selling, public relations, and sales promotion.

1. Define promotion and list the four traditional tools that make up the promotion mix.

2. Advertising is limited to paid, nonpersonal (not face-to-face) communication through various media by organizations and individuals who are in some way identified in the advertising message.
   • *What are the advantages of using the various media?*
   You can review the advantages and disadvantages of the various advertising media in Figure 17.3.
   • *Why the growing use of infomercials?*
   Infomercials are growing in importance because they show products in use and present testimonials to help sell goods and services.

2. Define advertising and describe the advantages and disadvantages of various advertising media, including the Internet.

3. Personal selling is the face-to-face presentation and promotion of products and services. It also involves the search for new prospects and follow-up service after the sale.
   • *What are the seven steps of the selling process?*
   The steps of the selling process are (1) prospect and qualify, (2) preapproach, (3) approach, (4) make presentation, (5) answer objections, (6) close sale, and (7) follow up.
   • *What does a consultative salesperson do?*
   A consultative salesperson begins by analyzing customer needs and then comes up with solutions to those needs. He or she does much more than make sales presentations. Such salespeople are truly business consultants who do things like develop intranets for clients.

3. Illustrate the seven steps of the selling process and discuss the role of a consultative salesperson.

4. Describe integrated marketing communication and the role of interactive communications within it.

4. Marketers use various promotional strategies to move goods from producers to consumers.
    - *What are the various promotional strategies?*
    In a push strategy, the producer uses advertising, personal selling, sales promotion, and all other promotional tools to convince wholesalers and retailers to stock and sell merchandise. In a pull strategy, heavy advertising and sales promotion efforts are directed toward consumers so that they'll request the products from retailers.
    - *How do you set up an integrated marketing communication system?*
    An integrated marketing communication system consists of three ongoing parts: (1) listen constantly to all groups affected by the organization, keep that information in a database, and make that information available to everyone in the organization; (2) respond quickly to customer and other stakeholder information by adjusting company policies and practices and by designing wanted products for target markets; and (3) use integrated marketing communication to let all customers and other stakeholders know that the firm is listening and responding to their needs.
    - *How do you set up interactive marketing programs?*
    There are three steps in setting up an interactive marketing program: (1) gather data constantly about the groups affected by the organization, (2) respond quickly to customer and other stakeholder information by adjusting company policies and practices and by designing wanted products for target markets, and (3) make it possible for customers and potential customers to obtain the information they need to make a purchase. Then make it easy for people to buy your products in stores or from the company directly by placing an order through e-mail, fax, phone, or other means.

5. Explain the concept of marketing channels and the value of marketing intermediaries.

5. A channel of distribution consists of marketing intermediaries, such as wholesalers and retailers, who join together to transport and store goods in their path (or channel) from producers to consumers.
    - *What are marketing intermediaries?*
    Marketing intermediaries are organizations that assist in moving goods and services from producers to industrial and consumer users.
    - *Why do we need marketing intermediaries?*
    We need intermediaries when they perform marketing functions more effectively and efficiently than others can. Marketing intermediaries can be eliminated, but their activities can't. Intermediaries add costs to products, but these costs are usually more than offset by the values they create.

6. Describe the various wholesale organizations in the distribution system.

6. A wholesaler is a marketing intermediary that sells to organizations and individuals, but not to final consumers.
    - *What are some wholesale organizations that assist in the movement of goods from manufacturers to consumers?*
    Merchant wholesalers are independently owned firms that take title to (own) goods that they handle. Rack jobbers furnish racks or shelves full of merchandise to retailers, display products, and sell on consignment. Cash-and-carry wholesalers serve mostly small retailers with a limited assortment of products. Drop shippers solicit orders from retailers and other wholesalers and have the merchandise shipped directly from a producer to a buyer. Freight forwarders consolidate small shipments into larger ones that can be shipped less expensively.

7. Explain the ways in which retailers compete and the distribution strategies they use.

7. A retailer is an organization that sells to ultimate consumers.
    - *How do retailers compete in today's market?*
    There are five major ways of competing for the consumer's dollar today: price, service, location, selection, and entertainment.

• *What are three distribution strategies retailers use?*

Retailers use three basic distribution strategies: Intensive (putting products in as many places as possible, selective (choosing only a few stores in a chosen market), and exclusive (using only one store in each market area).

8. Retailing is evolving away from traditional stores to nonstore retailing.

   • *What is included in nonstore retailing?*

   Nonstore retailing includes e-tailing (online marketing); telemarketing (marketing by phone); vending machines, kiosks, and carts (marketing by putting products in convenient locations, such as in the halls of shopping centres); direct selling (marketing by approaching consumers in their homes or places of work); and direct marketing (direct mail and catalogue sales). Telemarketing and online marketing are also forms of direct marketing.

   • *What's the difference between direct selling and direct marketing?*

   Direct selling means that a salesperson will come to your home or office to make the sale. Direct marketing uses catalogues, the Internet, phone marketing, and other means to sell directly to customers without being physically present.

8. Explain the various kinds of nonstore retailing.

9. One way of getting manufacturers, wholesalers, and retailers to co-operate in distributing products is to form efficient distribution systems.

   • *What are the four types of distribution systems?*

   The four distribution systems that tie firms together are (1) corporate systems, in which all organizations in the channel are owned by one firm; (2) contractual systems, in which members are bound to co-operate through contractual agreements; (3) administered systems, in which all marketing functions at the retail level are managed by manufacturers; and (4) supply chains, in which the various firms in the supply chain are linked electronically to provide the most efficient movement of information and goods possible. Note that the supply chain system is longer because it includes organizations selling to manufacturers, while the other systems merge firms in the channel of distribution only after a product is made.

9. Discuss how a manufacturer can get wholesalers and retailers in a channel system to co-operate by the formation of systems.

KEY TERMS

administered distribution system 551
advertising 524
brokers 541
cash-and-carry wholesaler 544
category killer store 547
channel of distribution 539
closing techniques 530
consultative salesperson 531
contractual distribution system 550
corporate distribution system 550
drop shipper 544
e-tailing 548
electronic data interchange (EDI) 551

exclusive distribution 548
freight forwarder 545
infomercial 526
integrated marketing communication (IMC) 522
intensive distribution 548
interactive marketing program 538
interactive promotion 523
intermodel shipping 553
marketing intermediaries 539
materials handling 554
merchant wholesaler 544
personal selling 529
promotion 522

promotion mix 522
prospects 530
prospecting 530
public relations (PR) 532
publicity 533
pull strategy 536
push strategy 536
qualify 530
rack jobbers 544
retail sale 544
retailer 539
sales promotion 534
sampling 535
selective distribution 548
supply chain 551
telemarketing 549
wholesale sale 544
wholesaler 539

DEVELOPING WORKPLACE SKILLS

1. Choose four ads from a newspaper, magazine, or any other medium—two that you consider good and two that you don't consider good. Be prepared to discuss why you feel as you do about each ad. Select ads from at least two different media.

2. In small groups, discuss whether or not you are purchasing more goods using catalogues and/or the Internet and why. Do you look up information on the Internet before buying goods and services? How helpful are such searches? Present your findings to the class.

3. In small groups or individually, make a list of six products (goods and services) that most students own or use and then discuss which promotional techniques prompt you to buy these goods and services: advertising, personal selling, publicity or sales promotion. Which tool seems to be most effective for your group? Why do you suppose that is?

4. This text describes five kinds of retail competition: price, service, location, selection, and entertainment. Using local stores as examples, give a three-minute report on your experience as a consumer with at least two types of competition. Do you prefer one type of store over the others? Why?

5. Visit the stores in your community or use your experience having done so. Compare their prices, goods, and services with companies on the Internet selling the same products (e.g., books, VCRs, insurance). Write a one-page paper discussing the differences in price (be sure to add shipping costs).

6. Recall some of the experiences you have had with telemarketers (those people who tend to call at dinnertime trying to sell you things). How could they change their approach so you would be more responsive and positive about their calls?

TAKING IT TO THE NET

Purpose:

To learn about online sales promotion efforts and save some money.

Exercise:

Many marketers put coupons in magazines and newspapers. Others have coupons in supermarkets and other stores where you can tear them off from displays. The latest in couponing is to place them on the Internet. To find such sites, go to www.freestuffcenter.com and click on the Coupon Links button. Go to various sites and explore what is available. Sometimes the best deal is to pay nothing at all. To check out free offers on the Internet, go to www.yesfree.com and explore what is available there.

1. Are you willing to register at these various sites to get free coupons faxed to you? Why or why not?

2. What could these Web sites do to become more user friendly for you and your friends?

3. Have you become more price conscious now that Web sites give so much competitive information about price and coupons for so many products that are readily available? Is that a good thing or not for marketers?

4. Integrated marketing communication efforts are designed to create a good image for a firm, one that is consistent. Do sites like these fit into such a scheme? Why or why not?

Purpose:

To examine how small businesses can learn to use the Internet to distribute their products directly to customers.

Exercise:

Many small businesses have no idea how to begin selling goods over the Internet. Several free Web sites have been developed to help small businesses get started. Some have links to other sites that provide all kinds of help, from setting up the site to doing marketing, handling credit purchases, and more. Many businesses will need help setting up Web sites of their own. You may be able to help if you learn now all that is involved. Begin by going to www.bigstep.com to learn the steps involved. Take the eight-step tour and learn as much as you can. Then go to www.workz.com and check out all the sites that are available to provide help.

1. What kind of information were you able to gather about starting a Web site?

2. What additional information would you like before getting started? Where might you turn for such help?

3. What other advice would you give a small company about trying to sell on the Internet? What would you say about credit cards, answering consumer questions, distribution, and returns?

4. What other issues may come up for foreign visitors to the site?

PRACTISING MANAGEMENT DECISIONS

CASE 1

AIRWALK FOOTWEAR

Airwalk Footwear recently turned to Lambesis, a full-service promotional firm, to design a promotional strategy for its shoes. The goal was to create a brand image that would appeal to young people, which meant listening to that group more closely than most companies had done before. There was very little research available, so the company had to do its own. Lambesis went where teenagers ate, shopped, and hung out. Marketers observed, asked questions, and learned as much as possible about teens' lifestyle, especially among the trendsetters. At first the idea was to target the U.S. market, but Lambesis decided that a global appeal would be more effective. The company's research showed that a 17-year-old in Mexico City or Moscow had the same wants and needs as a 17-year-old in the United States. That may not be true of a different age group, but it was true of this one. Based on that research, Lambesis tried to design a universal message, perhaps one including romance, that would have appeal to teenagers in all countries.

Lambesis took an integrated marketing communication approach. To this company, that meant having all departments working together as a team to develop one unified message in all media and in all communications. Team members from product development, research, broadcast, and Web site development worked together to develop an overall strategy for Airwalk.

The strategy had three themes: (1) entertainment, (2) sports, and (3) style. Every message would try to combine these three elements—even the shoebox was designed in keeping with the themes. The integrated marketing communication effort included advertising, public relations, sales promotion, word of mouth, direct selling, and the Internet. Advertising vehicles included television programs, T-shirts, and posters all over town. A pull strategy was used for advertising. That is, advertising for leading-edge products was directed at teenagers, who then went into shoe stores and requested specific Airwalk shoes. The magazines chosen were mostly underground magazines, and the TV shows were ones that appealed to this group but few others. Sales promotion efforts included contests where the winners won trips to various places. Gifts were also sent to people who responded to direct-marketing appeals.

Much effort also went into public relations and event sponsorship. That included events such as snowboard contests where the participants wore Airwalk snowboarding boots. Rock bands were given free shoes, and special promotions were built around those bands. Every communication tool conveyed the same clear message: these shoes are designed for you and your friends—and they are exciting. Word of mouth spread naturally among the targeted teens. The Web site was constantly updated to attract people back. It takes all the elements of entertainment, sports, and style to attract people to a Web site and have them spend some time there.

In short, the campaign was targeted precisely to the Airwalk teenage market. As a result of the integrated marketing communication effort, Airwalk sales doubled and then doubled again. Sales globally went from $20 million to $300 million in 14 different countries.

Decision Questions

1. What are some of the challenges you would face if you were trying to develop a Web site for Airwalk Footwear that would have global appeal (multiple languages) and would allow teens to order by phone, fax, or mail?
2. Could Airwalk expand its market to other market segments? Which segments would offer the greatest opportunities?
3. Would you expand the Airwalk product mix to include clothing for skateboarders and snowboarders? Give reasons why or why not.
4. If you were in charge of developing a promotional strategy for the coming year, what would you do differently to maintain interest among this target audience? Would you emphasize advertising, public relations, sales promotion, word of mouth, direct marketing, or some combination? Justify your strategy.

PRACTISING MANAGEMENT DECISIONS

CASE 2

MULTILEVEL MARKETING

Multilevel marketing often doesn't get the respect it deserves in marketing literature. When multilevel marketing companies succeed, their growth is often unbelievable. At least six multilevel marketing companies have reached the $500-million level in sales.

Multilevel marketing companies work like this: The founders begin by recruiting a few good people to go out and find managers to sell their products and to recruit other supervisors. These supervisors then recruit additional salespeople. That is, 20 people recruit 6 people each. That means 120 salespeople. Those people then recruit 6 people each, and you have 720 salespeople. If in turn those people all recruit 6 people, you then have almost 5,000 salespeople. All supervisors earn commissions on what they sell as well as on what everyone under them sells. When you get thousands of salespeople selling for you, commissions can be quite large. One company promotes the fact that 1 percent from 100 salespeople is as good as 100 percent from one successful salesperson. Companies often add new products or expand to other countries to keep a continuous growth pattern.

Distribution under multilevel marketing is relatively easy. Often the salespeople will carry inventory in their own homes and deliver products as ordered.

Many companies also offer direct shipping to customers using UPS or other delivery firms.

Marketers cannot ignore the success of this sales and distribution strategy. Nu Skin (a seller of health and beauty products) alone will soon have $1 billion in sales. Looking for more growth, the company started a new division, Interior Design Nutrition, to make and sell vitamins and weight-control products. Amway, perhaps one of the most well-known multilevel marketers, has chosen the international route for growth; recently, its sales of home and personal care products increased by over $1 billion in one year.

Decision Questions

1. Amway and others have been successful in Japan. To what other countries could you lead such companies so that you could become a top earner?
2. What will happen as multilevel marketing distributors begin recruiting and selling using the latest in technology such as the Internet?
3. Why do you suppose multilevel marketing hasn't received the same acceptance as other retail innovations such as catalogue sales? What could the companies do to improve their image?
4. If multilevel marketing works so well for beauty and health-care products, why not use the same concept to sell other products?

CREATING A CRAZE

The marketing pressure on teens is intense. Getting the attention of tweens—those between the ages of 8 and 14—is of much interest to record companies, as these consumers spend a lot of their money on music. The Internet is one direct tool that is being used today to attract and retain this media-savvy group.

The Internet was successfully used to create buzz for the B4-4 boy band. Within weeks of being signed, Sony Music Canada's New Media team meticulously manufactured and executed interest in this group. To increase the profile of the band, from Thornhill, Ontario (made up of Dan Kowarsky, Ryan Kowarsky, and Ohad Einbinder), New Media created the snappy Web site www.b4-4.com.

The Internet is an ideal tool to attract tween fans, as they use the Internet 24 hours a day. They can ICQ (find other fans on the Net), do homework and research, hang out online—very simply, they spend more time online than offline. By visiting the Web site, fans could create a fansite and visit other fansite links. Step by step instructions to create a fansite were provided along with pictures of the guys. Once this personal Web site was created, it was then linked up to the corporate Web site. At the official Web site, fans could read fan mail, share likes, dislikes and B4-4 stories, sign up to have B4-4 news sent directly to them, join a chat room, or e-mail the group.

While not always successful, this strategy has contributed to the band's popularity. Their first CD went gold in just six weeks. It worked because the fans were there due to the buzz created. This was supported by the regular contact between the band members and their fans in chat rooms. Fans can also leave phone messages and send e-mail to the members.

Discussion Questions:

1. Have you heard of B4-4? If yes, how? If not, how else could Sony successfully target people—via personal selling, advertising, public relations, and sales promotion—who have never heard of B4-4?

2. How important is a Web site to the success of a new band? How likely would you be to visit a new band's official Web site for information and to chat online about the band?

3. Do you think that New Media acted ethically in creating buzz about a group that had not even recorded a CD? How about hiring a fan and having her visit competitors' sites trying to lure fans to the B4-4 site? Explain.

4. In your opinion, is word of mouth critical for band success?

5. Now that B4-4 has released a CD, what are some ways that continued interest and support can be generated via the Internet?

Source: *Undercurrents*, show number 182, "Creating A Craze," November 5, 2000, running time 8:39.

PART 6

CHAPTER 18

Accounting Fundamentals

LEARNING GOALS

AFTER YOU HAVE READ AND STUDIED THIS CHAPTER, YOU SHOULD BE ABLE TO

1. Define accounting and explain the differences between (a) managerial accounting and financial accounting and (b) private and public accountants.

2. Compare accounting and bookkeeping.

3. Identify and describe the major accounts used to prepare financial statements.

4. Understand simple income statements and balance sheets, and explain their functions.

5. Describe the role of computers in accounting.

6. Explain the concept of cash flow.

7. Explain how a business can be making profits and still be short of cash.

8. Understand the new concerns of accounting.

Richter, Usher & Vineberg after 75 Years

In 1926, two young McGill graduates, chartered accountants Bill Richter and Cecil Usher, established their accounting and auditing firm, Richter, Usher & Co. Seventy years later, Richter, Usher & Vineberg threw a big party to celebrate the achievements and foresight of both founders, now deceased. As senior partners Howard Gilmour and Marvin Corber noted, the firm now has more than 500 employees, with offices in Montreal, Toronto, Halifax, and New York, encompassing a wide variety of activities.

The firm has continued to evolve with changing market demands and has expanded beyond the traditional audit and

Courtesy of Richter and Usher.

tax practice. Richter now offers professional services in the areas of corporate finance, financial reorganization, business valuations, forensic accounting, management consulting, government assistance, research and development, estates and trusts, and wealth management.

Longtime practitioners Gilmour and Corber have witnessed the transition to a computer-dominated method of practising, which has revolutionized operations. They have participated in the development of the other services indicated above, which were a natural outgrowth of their clients'

needs. They have also had to cope with a host of major new issues that all accounting firms must contend with.

For example, they now counsel clients not to undertake any mergers or acquisitions or any purchase of land or buildings without an environmental audit. Such an audit would reveal any potential environmental liabilities stemming from previous activities. Similarly, the real value of many companies cannot be determined simply by examining their financial statements and accounting records. A highly skilled workforce or valuable know-how and patents might be a company's most important asset. These assets may yield high profits in the future without showing up at all or at true value on a company's current balance sheet.

Senior partners Gilmour and Corber see accounting and the profession as being in a constant state of evolution. As society, the economy, and business continue evolving, so must practitioners modify their thinking and practices to meet the new challenges constantly being generated. For more information, see www.richter.ca.

Sources: Interviews with Howard Gilmour and Marvin Corber, September 9, 1999, and June 25, 1996; and company documents.

INPUTS: ACCOUNTING DOCUMENTS	PROCESSING:	OUTPUTS: FINANCIAL STATEMENTS
Sales documents Purchasing documents Shipping documents Payroll records Bank records Expense records	1. Entries are made into accounts for each type of transaction. 2. The entries in each account are added and the balance arrived at. 3. All accounts are summarized.	Income statement Balance sheet Reports (for example, annual reports)

FIGURE 18.1

THE ACCOUNTING SYSTEM

The inputs to an accounting system include documents arising from sales, cash, purchases, and other transactions. The data are recorded, classified, and summarized. They are then put into summary financial statements such as an income statement and a balance sheet.

managerial accounting
Providing information and analysis to managers within the organization to assist them in decision making.

but it is also the language used to report financial information about nonprofit organizations such as religious and community organizations, schools, hospitals, and governmental units. Accounting can be divided into two major categories: managerial accounting and financial accounting.

Managerial accounting is used to provide information and analysis to managers within the organization to assist them in decision making. Managerial accounting is concerned with measuring and reporting costs of production, marketing ➤**P. 452**◄, and other functions (cost accounting); preparing budgets (planning); checking whether or not departments are staying within their budgets or meeting sales and other targets (controlling); and designing strategies to minimize taxes (tax accounting).

Simple analysis of corporate figures can disclose important information. For example, a slight month-to-month increase in payroll costs may not appear significant. But multiply that increase by 12 months and the increase in costs can be important. Monitoring profit margins, unit sales, travel expenses, cash flow, inventory turnover, and other such data is critical to the success of a firm. Management decision making is based on such data.

Some of the questions that managerial accounting reports are designed to answer include:

- What goods and services are selling the most and what promotional tools are working best?
- How quickly is the firm selling what it buys?
- How much profit is the firm making?
- What are the firm's major expenses? What are the total costs?
- How much money does the firm make on the owners' investment in the business?
- How much tax is the firm paying, and how can it minimize that amount?
- Will the firm have enough cash to pay its bills? If not, has it made arrangements to borrow that money?

FIGURE 18.2

USERS OF ACCOUNTING INFORMATION AND THE REQUIRED REPORTS

Many different types of organizations use accounting information to make decisions. The kinds of reports these users need vary according to the information they require. An accountant, then, needs to prepare the appropriate reports.

USERS	TYPE OF REPORT
Government taxing authorities	Tax returns
Government regulatory agencies	Required reports
People interested in the income and financial position of the organization: shareholders, creditors, financial analysts, suppliers, others	Financial statements found in annual reports (e.g., income statement, balance sheet)
Managers of the firm	Financial statements and other financial reports distributed internally

In all cases, results are compared with budgets to see if the results are achieving the targets set for the month, for the quarter, and for the year. When they do not, management must figure out how performance can be improved. Results are also compared with those of the particular industry to see that they are in line with, or better than, the results in competing firms. Finally, trends that the results may reveal are carefully examined to ensure that good trends are continued and unfavourable ones reversed. This prevents negative activities from continuing unnoticed until they create serious problems. You can see how important such information is. That is why accounting is a good subject to learn.

Financial accounting includes the preparation of financial statements for people inside and outside the firm (for example, investors). Financial accounting differs from managerial accounting in that the information and analyses it provides are also needed by people outside of the organization. This information goes to owners and prospective owners (new shareholders), creditors and lenders, employee unions, customers, government units, and the general public. The external users are interested in the organization's profits, its ability to pay its bills, and other financial information. Much of the information is contained in the annual report, a yearly statement of the financial condition and progress of the firm. Various quarterly (every three months) reports keep the users more current. These reports are required by law for the shareholders of all public companies (those whose shares trade on a stock exchange).

Financial accounting reports answer such questions as

- Has the company's income been satisfactory? Should we invest in this company?
- Should we lend money to this company? Will it be able to pay it back?
- Are our costs getting out of control?
- Is the company financially strong enough to stay in business to honour product warranties?
- Should we sell to this company? Will it be able to pay its bills?

We hope you are getting the idea that accounting is critical to business and to anyone who wants to understand business. You may want to know more about accounting firms, the people who prepare these reports, and how you can be sure that they know what they are doing. Accounting data can be compiled by accountants who work for the firm or by independent accounting firms.

Private and Public Accountants

Private accountants are employees who carry out managerial and financial accounting functions for their employer. Many have degrees in accounting and are qualified professionals. Very small companies often cannot afford, or do not require, accounting employees, so they hire independent public accounting firms.

Public accountants are independent firms that provide accounting, auditing, and other professional services for different clients on a fee basis. These firms employ qualified accountants and auditors, apprentices, and other types of personnel. The most prestigious professional accounting degree in Canada is that of chartered accountant (CA). This degree is granted by a provincial Institute of Chartered Accountants (L'Ordre des comptables agréés in Quebec) that supervises the training, education, and practice of chartered accountants in that province. The final examinations are very rigorous, to ensure that only qualified candidates will earn the designation of CA.

All provincial institutes together have organized the Canadian Institute of Chartered Accountants, which sets accounting and auditing standards across the

financial accounting
The preparation of financial statements for people inside and outside of the firm (for example, investors).

www.cica.ca

The Canadian Institute of Chartered Accountants (CICA) is organized provincially, but admission to the profession requires passing a standard set of national tests. Prior to taking the tests, candidates must hold a university degree and successfully complete a period of indentureship and courses while working for a firm of chartered accountants. The CICA Web site provides more information about the organization and its program. The site also provides a number of other services to CAs and others who are interested in issues associated with the accounting profession.

private accountants
Employees who carry out managerial and financial accounting functions for their employers.

public accountants
Independent firms that provide accounting, auditing, and other professional services for clients on a fee basis.

www.cga-canada.org

Members of the Certified General Accountants' Association of Canada who have successfully completed its program of studies hold the designation of CGA. The CGA Canada Web site provides a history of the organization, as well as useful information for its members, prospective students, and others interested in the profession's activities.

independent audit
Examination of a company's books by public accountants to give the public, governments, and shareholders an outside opinion of the fairness of financial statements.

country. The CICA also prepares the Uniform Final Examination (UFE), which is given every September over a four-day period in many cities across Canada.

There are chartered accountants or their equivalents in all industrialized countries. All the national organizations coordinate their work and theories by membership in international accounting associations.

There are two other important associations of professional accountants in Canada. Certified General Accountants (CGA) and the Society of Management Accountants (CMA) also train and certify accountants. Large companies, governments, and nonprofit bodies employ many accountants; some do financial accounting, others managerial accounting. Many financial accountants have a CA degree, whereas managerial accountants generally opt for a CMA degree. Many CGAs are employed by governments; others are in public practice.

Public accounting firms have other important functions. Their most important activity for businesses and other organizations—and their largest income producer—is performing independent audits (examinations) of the books and financial statements of companies. An **independent audit** gives the public, governments, and shareholders (owners) an outside opinion of the fairness of financial statements. This audit is required by law for all public corporations in Canada.

Public accounting firms also provide consulting services to management, give tax advice to companies and individuals, and prepare income tax returns for smaller companies. Large accounting and auditing firms operate internationally to serve large transnational companies.

As you can see, a variety of interesting challenges are part of the daily fare of professional accountants. Many successful executives in senior management positions started their careers as public accountants. Think carefully about a career for yourself in this field. Accounting is a continually expanding area with many specialties. Yes, it is difficult (to get a degree), but what worthwhile professional career is not?

ACCOUNTING AND BOOKKEEPING

bookkeeping
The recording of transactions.

www.cma-ontario.org
www.cma-canada.org

The Society of Management Accountants of Canada (CMA-Canada), which awards the designation of chartered management accountant (CMA) is, like the CICA, an amalgam of provincial organizations with uniform national standards and examinations. CMA-Canada, too, requires a university degree. The CMA-Canada Web site includes a summary of the distinctions among the three professional accounting bodies and their members.

Bookkeeping involves the recording of transactions. It is a rather mechanical process that does not demand much creativity. Bookkeeping is part of accounting, but accounting goes far beyond the mere recording of data. Accountants *classify* and *summarize* the data. They *analyze* and *interpret* the data and *report* them to management. They also *suggest strategies* for improving the financial condition and progress of the firm. Accountants are especially valuable for providing income tax advice and preparing tax returns.

Now that you understand what accountants do and whom they do it for, we can get down to the fundamental aspects of bookkeeping and accounting.

At the end of this chapter, you should have a better idea of what accountants do and how they do it. You should also be able to read and understand financial statements and discuss accounting intelligently with an accountant and others in the world of business. The goal is not to learn how to be an accountant, but to learn some terms and concepts. So let's start at the beginning.

Bookkeepers record all the transactions of a company, which usually include

- sales documents (sales slips, cash register receipts, and invoices)
- purchasing documents
- shipping documents
- payroll records
- bank documents (cheques, deposit slips)
- various expense documents.

- Can you explain the difference between managerial and financial accounting?
- Could you define accounting to a friend so that he or she would clearly understand what is involved?
- What is the difference between a private and a public accountant? What professional degrees do accountants have?
- What is the difference between accounting and bookkeeping?
- Can you name five original transaction documents that bookkeepers use to keep records?

PROGRESS CHECK

In business, hundreds of documents are received or created every day, so you can appreciate the valuable role a bookkeeper plays. Can you see why most businesses have to hire people to do this work? Would it be worth the owners' time to do all the paperwork? Can you understand why most bookeepers find it easier to do this work on a computer?

CRITICAL THINKING

THE ACCOUNTS OF ACCOUNTING

When bookkeepers record transactions they use six major categories of accounts to accumulate useful information. These accounts are a basic part of the accounting system. These categories are:

1. **Assets:** things of value owned by the firm (cash, inventory, buildings)
2. **Liabilities:** debts owed by the firm to others
3. **Owners' (or Shareholders') Equity:** the amount owners (or shareholders) invest in the business plus accumulated profits less dividends or other withdrawals of profits
4. **Revenues:** sales of goods or services rendered
5. **Cost of Goods Sold:** cost of goods sold and recorded as revenues
6. **Expenses:** costs incurred in operating the business (rent, wages, insurance, taxes)

The next few sections will fill in the details concerning these categories of accounts.

assets
Things of value owned by a business.

liquidity
How quickly an asset can be turned into cash.

A bookkeeper gathers accounting documents such as sales slips, bills, cheques, payroll, and travel records, and records them in journals and ledgers. These are the first steps in the accounting system, which provides managers and interested parties with the information they need regarding the financial progress and condition of the firm.

Asset Accounts

Assets are things of value owned by the business. Assets include the following: cash on hand or in the bank, accounts receivable (money owed by customers), inventory, investments, buildings, trucks and cars, patents, and copyrights.

Assets are listed according to how liquid they are. **Liquidity** refers to how quickly an asset can be turned into cash. A business is said to have a high degree of *liquidity* if it has enough liquid assets to easily pay its bills and other debts as they come due. When inventory is sold and the customer pays, this asset becomes cash. Because this normally happens in a few months, inventory and accounts receivable are said to be liquid assets.

PhotoDisc

Assets are divided into three main categories, listed in order of liquidity (see Figures 18.3 and 18.4).

1. **Current assets.** Cash and assets that are normally converted into cash within one year.

2. **Fixed or capital assets.** Assets that are acquired to produce services or products for a business. They are not bought to be sold. These assets include equipment, buildings, trucks, and the like.

3. **Other assets.** Assets that are not included in the first two categories. This catchall group includes items such as copyrights and patents, which have no physical form, and long-term deposits.

You can see why one of the key words in accounting is *assets*. Take a few minutes to go through the list, visualizing the assets. Notice that they are things of value.

The valuation of assets can be a complex matter beyond the scope of this book. All assets are normally recorded at the cost of acquisition. When you look at a balance sheet (see Figure 18.6 later in this chapter), you see assets listed at their original cost. The real values are often different from their *book values*. In other words, the market value—what would be realized if the asset were sold—is normally different from the value as shown on the books.

The long, steady period of inflation we have witnessed since the 1960s has resulted in most book values being substantially below market value. For example, a building purchased in 1960 for $1 million could have a market value of perhaps 30 times that amount today. Nevertheless, it remains on the books at original cost. This asset, and therefore total assets, are grossly understated.

Obviously, this is not a satisfactory state of affairs. The accounting profession and other interested parties have been struggling with alternatives for many years. It's a problem awaiting a creative solution that will not cause more problems than it solves. Perhaps one of you will take up the challenge and come up with the answer.

Liability Accounts

Another important term in accounting is *liabilities*. **Liabilities** are what the business owes to others. As with assets, you will more easily understand what liabilities are when you review a list of some examples (see Figure 18.4):

- **Accounts payable.** Money owed to others for merchandise and services purchased on credit but not yet paid. If you have such an unpaid bill, you have an account payable.

- **Accrued expenses payable.** Expenses the firm owes but that have not been billed by the end of the month, when financial statements are prepared (e.g., utilities bills, credit card statements).

  - **Bonds payable.** Long-term loans to the business.

  - **Notes payable.** Usually shorter-term loans from banks.

  - **Taxes payable.** Sales taxes and GST collected, and income tax payable.

All liabilities that are due within one year from the balance sheet date are classified as *current liabilities*. Those amounts due later are called *long-term liabilities*. You can see these categories later in Figure 18.6.

---

current assets
Cash and assets that are normally converted into cash within one year.

fixed or capital assets
Assets that are acquired to produce services or products for a business. They are not bought to be sold.

other assets
Assets that are not current or fixed. Includes items such as copyrights and patents, which have no physical form, and long-term deposits.

liabilities
Amounts owed by the organization to others.

FIGURE 18.3

CLASSIFICATIONS OF ASSETS

Assets are classified by what normally happens to them. Cash and those assets that usually turn into cash (inventory and accounts receivable) are considered to be liquid. They are called *current assets*. Those assets that are bought to run the business (e.g., equipment, trucks) are not bought to be sold, so they are called *fixed or capital assets*. Patents and copyrights are listed in a third class called *other assets*.

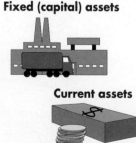

Fixed (capital) assets

Other assets

Copyright

Current assets

FOR THE BALANCE SHEET			FOR THE INCOME STATEMENT		
ASSETS	**LIABILITIES**	**SHAREHOLDERS' EQUITY**	**REVENUES**	**EXPENSES AND COSTS**	
Cash	Accounts payable	Capital stock	Sales	Wages	Interest
Accounts receivable	Notes payable	Retained earnings (accumulated profits not paid out)	Rentals	Rent	Donations
Inventory	Bonds payable		Commissions	Repairs	Licences
Investments	Taxes payable		Royalties	Travel	Professional fees
Equipment	Accrued expenses payable			Insurance	Supplies
Land				Utilities	Advertising
Buildings				Entertainment	Taxes
Motor vehicles				Storage	Purchases
Goodwill					

FIGURE 18.4

SAMPLE OF SPECIFIC ACCOUNT TITLES

Each account accumulates data relating to a specific activity.

owners' equity
Owners' investments in the company plus all net accumulated profits.

Owners' Equity Accounts

The **owners' equity** in a company consists of all that the owners have invested in the company *plus* all the profits that have accumulated since the business commenced but that have not yet been paid out to them. This figure *always* equals the book value of the assets minus the liabilities of the company, as you will see later on. Why this is so will be discussed shortly.

In a partnership, owners' equity is called *partners' equity* or *capital*. In a sole proprietorship, it is called owner's or *proprietor's equity* or capital. In a corporation, it is called *shareholders' equity* and is shown in two separate accounts. The amount the owners (shareholders) invest is shown in one account, called *common stock*; the accumulated profit that remains after dividends have been paid to shareholders is shown in an account called *retained earnings*. You can see this later in Figure 18.6.

Revenue Accounts

Revenue accounts are where income from all sources is recorded. That includes sales, rentals, commissions, royalties, and other sources of income. These amounts are shown in the income statement. (A sample income statement is shown in Figure 18.5 later in the chapter. See also Figure 18.4.)

Cost of Goods Sold Accounts

Cost of goods sold accounts are used when a company sells products. The account shows all the costs of selling products that were recorded in the sales (revenues) account. These costs include transportation, storage, packaging and purchases of goods for resale, as well as the cost of manufacturing these goods sold. These amounts appear on the income statement. The cost of goods sold will be discussed further in the section on financial statements.

Expense Accounts

Expense accounts are where the expenses of running a business are recorded. These are costs such as rent, insurance, salaries, utilities, and advertising. They are also shown on the income statement. Figure 18.4 lists many of the usual expense accounts.

Double-Entry Accounting System

The method of recording transactions that is practised throughout the world is called the *double-entry* accounting system. As the name implies, two entries are made for each transaction: a debit and a credit. For example, when a noncash sale is made on credit for $100, the accounts receivable account is debited for $100 and the sales account is credited with $100. When the customer pays for this sale, the cash account is debited and the accounts receivable account is credited.

This ingenious method, reputed to have been invented in Northern Italy about 600 years ago, has several important features. When you make a monthly summary, listing all balances in the accounts (a *trial balance*), the sum of all the debits must equal the sum of all the credits. If it doesn't, you know you have made some errors. You must find them and redo your trial balance to see if the debits now equal the credits. Computers eliminate the need for a trial balance because they do not make the kind of arithmetic errors that humans can and do make.

So, while computerized accounting has made this feature somewhat redundant, other aspects of the double-entry system continue to be useful and important. These include the easy accumulation of specific and accurate information (sales, purchases, expense details by category), ensuring that all transactions have been recorded, and other features the details of which are beyond the scope of this book.

PROGRESS CHECK

- Name the six classes of accounts that are used in accounting, and give two examples of items that go into each of those classes.
- Can you list various assets by degree of liquidity?
- What goes into the category called liabilities?
- What is the formula for owners' equity?

FINANCIAL STATEMENTS

financial statements
Report the operations and position (condition) of a firm; they include the income statement and the balance sheet.

income statement
Reports revenues, expenses, and profit or loss during a specific period of time.

balance sheet
Reports the financial position of a firm at the end of a specific period of time. Balance sheets show assets, liabilities, and owners' equity.

The accounting process consists of two major functions: (1) recording data from transactions and (2) preparing financial statements from that data. **Financial statements** report the operations and position (condition) of a firm. The two most important financial statements are the income statement and the balance sheet.

1. The **income statement** shows revenues, expenses, and profit or loss resulting from operations *during* a specific period of time.

2. The **balance sheet**, which consists of assets, liabilities, and owners' equity, shows the financial position of a firm at the *end* of that period.

Think of a balance sheet as a snapshot or freeze-frame of a company *at* a certain point in time. The income statement shows the company in action and the results of activities for a period *ending* on the same date as the balance sheet.

Financial statements are an important indication of the health of a firm. That is why they are of interest to the managers, owners (shareholders), banks, suppliers, and future investors. (There is another important financial statement, *statement of cash flow*, but it is more complex and beyond the scope of this introductory text.)

To understand accounting, you must be able to read and understand both income statements and balance sheets as well as understand cash flow. In the following sections, we shall explore financial statements and cash flow. Once you learn the concepts, you will know more about accounting than many small-business managers.

The Income Statement

The financial statement that shows the bottom line (that is, profit after expenses and taxes) is the *income statement* or *profit and loss statement* (see Figure 18.5). The income statement summarizes all the resources that come into the firm from operating activities (called *revenue*), resources that are used up (*cost of goods sold* and *expenses*), and what resources are left after all costs and expenses are incurred (*net income* or *net loss*). The income statement reports the results of operations over a period of time. The income statement may be summarized by the following formulas.

$$\text{Beginning inventory} + \text{Purchases} - \text{Ending inventory} = \text{Cost of goods sold}$$

$$\text{Revenue} - \text{Cost of goods sold} = \text{Gross margin (Profit)}$$

$$\text{Gross margin} - \text{Operating expenses} = \text{Net income before taxes}$$

$$\text{Net income before taxes} - \text{Income taxes} = \text{Net income}$$

Revenues For a company selling products, sometimes revenues come only from sales of its products. In that case revenues and sales are equal and refer to the same thing. However, in many cases, there are additional sources of revenue such as rent, interest, fees, and royalties. In those instances total revenue is greater than sales and the two terms are *not* synonymous. It is also important not to confuse *revenue* with *income*. In accounting terminology *income* or *net income* refers to what's left after costs and expenses are deducted from revenue. Net income is sometimes called the *bottom line* because it is the last line at the bottom of an income statement (see Figure 18.5).

Be careful not to confuse the terms *revenue* and *income*. Revenues are at the top of the income statement and income is at the bottom; net income is revenue *minus* costs and expenses.

Cost of Goods Sold To calculate how much a business earned by selling merchandise, subtract how much it cost to buy that merchandise. That cost includes the purchase price plus any freight charges paid to bring in the goods plus the costs associated with storing the goods. In other words, all the costs of buying and keeping merchandise for sale, including packaging, are included in the **cost of goods sold**. You must also take into account how much stock or inventory you had at the beginning and end of the period (see the first equation above).

When you subtract the cost of goods sold from net sales, you get what is called gross margin or *gross profit*. **Gross margin**, then, is how much the firm earned by buying and selling merchandise before the expenses of operations are deducted.

In a service firm, there may be no cost of goods sold because the firm is not buying and selling goods and therefore has no gross margin. However, the gross margin or gross profit figure doesn't tell you enough. What you are really interested in is net profit or net income. To get that, you must subtract expenses.

Operating Expenses Every business incurs expenses in the course of its operations. **Operating expenses** are the various expenses a business has, such as taxes, utilities, communication, travel, salaries, and so on, incurred in the course of earning its revenue. After cost of goods sold and operating expenses are deducted from revenue, we arrive at net profit or net income. Pause here and review the income statement in Figure 18.5 until you feel you understand it. Also, have a look at the formulas below.

cost of goods sold
A particular type of expense measured by the total cost of merchandise sold, including costs associated with the acquisition, storage, transportation, and packaging of goods.

gross margin (profit)
Net sales minus cost of goods sold before expenses are deducted.

operating expenses
Various expenses of a business incurred in the course of earning revenue.

Gross margin is calculated by subtracting the cost of goods sold from net sales (revenue). The revenue from the sale of products can be quite high. But so can the cost of all the materials needed to make the products. You will know how much gross profit (margin) you make by subtracting the cost of goods sold from the sales revenue. When you subtract other expenses, you get the net profit (income) from operations.

PhotoDisc

FIGURE 18.5

CLASSIC CEREALS INCOME STATEMENT

Note that revenues are at the top of the income statement and income is at the bottom. A simple formula for the income statement is revenue minus costs and expenses equals income.

CLASSIC CEREALS, INC.
Income Statement
For the Year Ended October 31, 2003

Revenues:			
Gross sales		$720,000	
Less: Sales returns and allowances	$ 12,000		
Sales discounts	8,000	20,000	
Net sales			$700,000
Cost of goods sold:			
Beginning inventory, Jan. 1		$100,000	
Merchandise purchases	400,000		
Freight	40,000	440,000	
Cost of goods available for sale		540,000	
Less: Ending inventory, Oct. 31		130,000	
Cost of goods sold			$410,000
Gross profit (gross margin)			$290,000
Operating expenses:			
Selling expenses:			
Salaries for salespeople	$ 85,000		
Advertising	12,000		
Amortization (Depreciation)	8,000		
Supplies	2,000		
Other sales expenses	3,000		
Total selling expenses		$110,000	
General expenses:			
Office salaries	60,000		
Amortization (Depreciation)	8,500		
Insurance	1,500		
Rent	28,000		
Light, heat, power	12,000		
Miscellaneous expenses	2,000		
Total general expenses		$112,000	
Total operating expenses			$222,000
Net profit (Income) from operations			68,000
Less: Interest expense			10,000
Net income before taxes			58,000
Less: Income tax expense			13,500
Net income (profit)			$ 44,500

net income
Revenue minus costs and expenses.

retained earnings
Accumulated profits less dividends to shareholders.

Remember that the *bottom line*, the **net income** for a particular year, is the revenue minus the costs and expenses of that year. The net income is then added to the accumulated profits from previous years (recorded in an account called *retained earnings*). When the company decides it wants to pay out some of the retained earnings to shareholders in the form of dividends, this amount is deducted from the **retained earnings** account. So we see that retained earnings consist of accumulated profits less dividends to shareholders.

The Balance Sheet

A balance sheet is the financial statement that reports the financial position of a firm at a *specific date*. The balance sheet is composed of assets, liabilities, and owners' equity. Note that the income statement reports on changes *over a period* and the balance sheet reports conditions *at the end of that period*.

The term *balance sheet* implies that the statement shows a balance, an equality between two figures: assets equal liabilities plus owners' equity. If you look at Figure 18.6, you will see this.

The Fundamental Accounting Equation Suppose a company doesn't owe anybody any money. That is, it has no liabilities. Then the assets it has (cash and so forth) are equal to what it owns (equity). The **fundamental accounting equation** is rather obvious. If a firm has no debts, then

Assets = Owners' equity

This means that the owners of a firm own everything. If a firm has debts, the owners own everything except the amount due others, or

Assets – Liabilities = Owners' equity

Another way of stating this is:

Assets = Liabilities + Owners' equity

> **fundamental accounting equation**
> *Assets = liabilities + owners' equity;* it is the basis for the balance sheet.

If you look at the balance sheet in Figure 18.6, you will note that total assets (in the middle of the page) equal the combined total of liabilities and shareholders' equity, in this case $801,000. This basic accounting equation derives from the double-entry accounting system mentioned earlier. You will recall that because transactions are entered in this way, the numbers on both sides—debits and credits—have to be in balance.

Let us analyze this equation in a little more depth. Where does a firm get its assets? If you think about it for a moment, you will see that there are only three sources:

1. The money the owners invested → shares issued to shareholders (common stock)

plus   plus

2. Profits the company generates → $\dfrac{\text{retained earnings}}{\text{= shareholders' equity}}$

plus   plus

3. Creditors who have not been paid → $\dfrac{\text{liabilities}}{\text{= Total assets}}$

= Total sources of assets →

The balance sheet shows that assets are divided into three categories: (1) current assets such as cash or accounts receivable, (2) fixed or capital assets, and (3) other assets, such as patents and copyrights.

Liabilities are divided into two categories: (1) current liabilities such as accounts payable and (2) long-term liabilities such as bonds. Shareholders' equity consists of common stock (investment in the company) and retained earnings (earnings not distributed to owners). For businesses that are not corporations, these terms are different. The retained earnings account is the link between the income statement and the balance sheet. The net income (profit) shown at the bottom of the income statement is transferred to the retained earning account each year.

FIGURE 18.6

**CLASSIC CEREALS
BALANCE SHEET**

Assets = Liabilities +
Shareholders' Equity. In
this case, each side totals
$801,000.

CLASSIC CEREALS, INC.
Balance Sheet
Dec. 31, 2003

Assets

Current assets		
Cash	$115,000	
Accounts receivable	200,000	
Notes receivable	50,000	
Inventory	130,000	
Total current assets		$495,000
Fixed assets		
Land	$ 40,000	
Buildings and improvements	200,000	
Equipment and vehicles	120,000	
Furniture and fixtures	26,000	
Less: Accumulated depreciation	(180,000)	
Total fixed assets		$206,000
Other assets		
Goodwill	$ 20,000	
Patents and copyrights	80,000	
Total other assets		$100,000
Total assets		**$801,000**

Liabilities and Shareholders' Equity

Current liabilities		
Accounts payable	$ 40,000	
Notes payable	8,000	
Accrued taxes	150,000	
Accrued salaries	15,000	
Employees' Pension fund	75,000	
Total current liabilities		$288,000
Long-term liabilities		
Notes payable	$ 30,000	
Bonds	190,000	
Total long-term liabilities		$220,000
Total liabilities		$508,000
Shareholders' equity		
Common stock *	$ 100,000	
Retained earnings **	193,000	
Total shareholders' equity		$293,000
Total liabilities and shareholders' equity		**$801,000**

* Invested by owners/shareholders
** Accumulated profits after paying dividends

If you go back to the beginning of this chapter and reread the sections on the accounts of accounting (asset accounts, liability accounts, and so on), you will see that the asset, liability, and owners' equity accounts are all part of the preparation of the balance sheet. Review the lists of items in these accounts (see Figure 18.4) to learn more about what is behind the figures on the balance sheet.

Ratio Analysis

Now that we have the financial statements, how do we interpret these results? One of the most common and useful methods of analyzing financial statements is by calculating a series of ratios, called **ratio analysis**. These figures are then compared to those of the previous year, the budget or plan for the year, and competing firms.

Many ratios are used to better understand a company's operations and position. Some of the important ones are reviewed in Appendix C, which follows this chapter. See also the Spotlight on Small Business box "Keep Your Banker Happy with a Steady Flow of Information."

Courtesy of Home Depot

ACCOUNTING COMPLEXITY

If accounting were nothing more than the repetitive function of gathering and recording transactions and preparing financial statements, the major functions could be assigned to computers. In fact, most firms have done just that. The truth is that there is much more involved.

Take depreciation, for example. **Amortization (depreciation)** is based on the fact that assets such as machinery have a certain life span. Therefore, part of the cost of the machinery is calculated as an expense each year over its useful life. Subject to certain technical rules that are beyond the scope of this chapter, a firm may use one of several techniques for calculating depreciation. However, once a method is chosen, it is difficult to change. Each technique results in a different bottom line, a different net income. Net incomes can change dramatically based on the specific amortization procedure that is used. Accountants can recommend ways of handling this problem as well as other issues such as insurance, valuing inventory and investments, and other accounts that will also affect the bottom line.

Accountants have to make many judgments and decisions regarding the recording of certain types of transactions. Say, for example, that when you started your business your sister gave you a computer and printer as a gift to help you on your way. You know that all assets are supposed to be recorded at cost, but how do you record something that has no cost because it was a gift? Or suppose you bought two machines for your factory; one proved useless and ended up quietly gathering dust in a corner. You normally amortize the cost of a machine (apportioned over its useful life) by charging a portion annually as an expense (depreciation). What do you do about the unused machine that contributes nothing to the annual profit but still has a cost?

Generally Accepted Accounting Principles

These and many more complicated transactions require certain guidelines that help accountants to make proper and consistent decisions. These guidelines are called *generally accepted accounting principles (GAAP)*. They are published in the handbook of the Canadian Institute of Chartered Accountants, along with many other important guidelines. This handbook is the ultimate authority of the accounting profession. Bankers, financial analysts, and others also refer to it. From time to time (and after much discussion) it is updated or modified.

There are about a dozen important accounting principles. Every audited set of financial statements includes a series of notes explaining how these principles have been applied, as well as a report by the auditors that GAAP have been used. (To appreciate how important these notes are, we have only to look at the financial

---

Home Depot maintains an enormous inventory. That's why it depends heavily on ratio analysis to make certain it is effectively managing its resources compared to the competition.

ratio analysis
A way to analyze financial statements by calculating a series of ratios.

amortization (depreciation)
Since assets such as machinery lose value over time, part of their cost is calculated as an expense each year over their useful life.

www.cica.ca

The CICA Handbook is the primary authority on accounting principles and practices in Canada. The Handbook is on the Internet, but is available only to members and others who have arranged for access. In addition to the Handbook itself, the CICA Web site also provides related information and articles on current issues regarding the application of these principles.

SPOTLIGHT ON SMALL BUSINESS

Keep Your Banker Happy with a Steady Flow of Information

As you learned in Chapter 7, positive or negative relations with your banker can often be predictors of success or failure for a small business. Entrepreneurs learn fast that keeping their banker happy can pay off, particularly if the company finds itself in a financial crunch. How do you keep your bank happy? That question occupies a good deal of the entrepreneur's time. One answer is accounting information. Few entrepreneurs realize that financial ratios (see Appendix C after this chapter) are important numbers to bankers and often form the basis of the decisions bankers make concerning financing requests.

Financial ratios not only can help the entrepreneur manage his or her business more efficiently, but they also can make your banker a more reliable business partner. Bankers see ratios as useful measurements for comparing a company's financial position to that of competing companies. Also, bankers see ratios as an effective guide for evaluating the firm's performance compared to industry standards or trends that are occurring in the market. What are some of the more important ratios at which the banker looks closely?

Bankers believe that a firm's ability to repay bank loans and make timely interest payments is important for evaluating financial requests. Liquidity ratios such as the current ratio (current assets divided by current liabilities) are important in determining the firm's short-term financial strength. Is it best for a firm to always maintain a high current ratio? Not necessarily! If a company has too high a current ratio, bankers may feel it is making poor use of resources. If your current ratio is falling, you must be prepared to explain why this is happening. Staying on top of the situation may mean receiving continued financial support from your bank. Keeping track of inventory and the debt position of the firm will also impress your banker. Low turnover of inventory could suggest to bankers that trouble is ahead. Excess inventory can boost interest rates and possibly lower profits. Ratios such as inventory turnover can offer valuable insights into how to prevent these problems and keep the bank on your side. Debt is a potential source of worry for both the business person and the bank. Therefore, debt to equity and total debt to total assets are ratios of major concern.

What should small-business managers do to build a working relationship with their bankers? Working closely with their accountant, they should prepare and regularly update a report binder that contains key financial ratios as well as cash-flow forecasts and projections. The entrepreneurs should discuss with the banker what ratios are most relevant to their businesses and then keep track of them on a regular basis. With such diligence, you not only build a good working relationship with your banker, but you also build a partnership with an informed partner.

---

statements of large companies—for example, Bombardier's 2001 statements contain 29 pages of notes from the company and the auditors.) This makes it possible for financial statements to be compared from one year to the next as well as from one company to another. Accountants all over the world are working to harmonize GAAP (see the Reaching Beyond our Borders box "Accounting Problems When Going International").

CRITICAL THINKING

Take a look at the table of contents in this book and think about how many of the chapters involve calculation, measurement, recording, and analysis of data. Do you think there are any chapters in which the material discussed does not involve accounting? Does this make accounting a critical skill for effective business operations? How about nonprofit organizations? Is accounting of equal importance in hospitals, school systems, universities, museums, and government?

As you have made your way through this book, you have seen many examples of Canadian companies that have developed important ties beyond our borders. As part of the globalization of business, Canadian companies look to joint ventures and alliances with other companies in the Pacific Rim, Europe, Mexico, and elsewhere. For example, McDonald's Canada Ltd. formed a joint venture with a Russian agency to operate the largest McDonald's unit in the world, in Moscow. Sometimes Canadian businesses buy out other companies. Bombardier bought the national Mexican railway car construction company in 1992 and several large companies since then. Smaller companies are also getting involved in this process.

One problem that often arises is how to determine the real value of the foreign company. The starting point is an examination of its financial statements. Have they been prepared on the basis of the same generally accepted accounting principles (GAAP) that are applied in Canada and the United States? (The two are very similar.) Often there are major differences that make it difficult to determine the real value of the company. Obviously, this is very important, especially if you are trying to establish how much you should offer to buy the company or you want to be sure that the assets being contributed to a joint venture have the value your partner claims.

Accounting bodies all over the world have been working for many years toward establishing a common set of GAAP through organizations like the International Federation of Accountants. It is a major task that is slowly being achieved.

CASH-FLOW PROBLEMS

Cash flow is the difference between cash receipts and cash disbursements. One of the greatest problems confronting business is ensuring that there will always be enough cash to meet payments as they fall due. This is a constant challenge for businesses of all sizes. Sometimes very large companies are forced to sell off one or more of their good subsidiaries to raise cash because of recession or other unexpected developments. This is the problem that caused the huge Olympia & York Developments to go bankrupt in 1992. Sometimes, as in the case of Campeau Corp. in the early 1990s, a company is practically destroyed by cash-flow problems.

The problem is most severe with small companies because they often have very few resources to fall back on. We can all understand a company having a cash shortage when it is suffering losses, but what about companies that are doing well? Why should they run short of cash?

cash flow
The difference between cash receipts and cash disbursements.

If you ask small business owners for a wish list of items that would make their lives easier, one request that's sure to be close to the top is a simple way to handle the firm's financial information. Peachtree Software is one of several companies that offer software packages that address the specific accounting needs of small businesses.

There are several reasons profitable companies have this problem. If they are growing very rapidly, their profits may not be sufficient to finance the greater inventories and accounts receivable they are forced to carry because of increased sales. Or they may be buying a lot of new equipment to increase production to keep up with the increased demand. Growing slowly gives companies the chance to avoid this problem.

The two companies mentioned above expanded very rapidly, using extensive borrowed capital, and then ran into trouble, leading to a collapse of their empires. In O&Y's case, the cash flow it was getting from its other holdings dropped sharply. In addition, the British government kept stalling on a promise to sign a lease for a big chunk of space in the new buildings—so O&Y could not get a mortgage, which would have enabled it to pay off some enormous bank loans. In Campeau's case, the cash flow from the new U.S. acquisitions was much smaller than expected so the company could not meet the payments on its loans as they fell due. In both cases, the serious recession of the 1990s was the underlying cause of their downfall. It's as though you had a well-paying job and bought a big home with a large mortgage and a luxury car that also required big monthly payments. What if you suddenly lost your job, the only job you could get quickly was at a much lower salary, and you had no savings to help you out? You would soon lose your home and your car—unless you had a rich friend or family member who was prepared to bail you out!

Sometimes a company that is not well managed will tie up too much cash in inventory or let customers delay payments for too long. This obviously will put pressure on the cash balance. If you hire an accounting firm before you start a business, it will prepare (with your help) a cash-flow forecast. This is a schedule for one year that shows clearly what the cash situation will be every month, based on your estimate of monthly sales, expenses, terms of credit, and other data. The cash flow can be prepared in three versions: optimistic, pessimistic, and most likely. This equips you to anticipate any scenario, so you can act in accordance with whichever one unfolds and avoid crises. Cash flow will be discussed in more detail in the next chapter.

The Canadian Institute of Chartered Accountants represents a membership of more than 65,000 professional accountants and 8,500 students. The CICA conducts research into current business issues and sets accounting and auditing standards for business, nonprofit organizations, and governments.

Sharon and Brian Rowan's Surprise

The Rowans (remember them from the beginning of the chapter?) had a different problem. They had no cash-flow problems, so they were surprised when their accountants told them they were incurring losses. How could they feel no cash pressure, a rare occurrence in a new business, while they were losing money? There are several possibilities. Since they started with their large inheritance, they may simply have been eating into their original investment. Their bank balance was declining and eventually they would have run into trouble.

Another possibility is that as a retail store they did not extend any credit, so they were getting paid cash for their sales. At the same time they were getting credit from their suppliers. That gave them a cushion of a month or two of cash income before they had to start paying creditors. This would have caught up with them in a short while.

Finally, they may have stocked up heavily at the start and were now depleting their inventory. This was providing them the cash to pay their bills. Again, they soon would have had to start building up stock and that would have created additional cash pressures.

So we see how business people may be deceived by either cash shortages or surpluses into thinking

SPOTLIGHT ON BIG BUSINESS

Accounting for New Kinds of Assets and Liabilities

Technology is not the only thing that is changing today. A host of new issues in accounting are causing the profession some giant headaches. One area of problems relates to environmental issues.

There are four aspects to this area. One is the production process that harms the environment. Smoke emission containing harmful gases and liquid emission into rivers and lakes into the ground are two common problems. Then there are solid wastes that are accumulated or dumped into rivers and lakes. Third, there is the problem of acquiring a site that a previous user or owner has polluted, unbeknown to the new owner. Finally, there is the issue of accidents—nuclear, oil spills, PCB and tire dump fires, and many others. All of these have occurred in Canada and elsewhere in the world.

In all of these cases, liability for past damage or cost of future cleanup arises. The difficulty lies in assessing the dollar amount and determining who is liable. The issue is further complicated by the fact that different environmental laws came into force at different times in different provinces and countries. It is a nightmare scenario from the accounting point of view, because the amounts involved can be extremely large.

A different topic relates to the fact that in today's high-tech world, knowledge is a major asset. Indeed, some people argue that it may be more important than all the physical assets of companies. How does a company evaluate the education, skills, and experience of its workforce? These assets are called *off-balance sheet assets* because they do not show up there and yet they may be the crucial assets for many important companies. In Canada we have hundreds of software companies whose real assets are the brains of their owners and employees.

These problems are obviously not easy to solve, but they must be dealt with if financial statements are to reflect reality. These challenges and many more await the next generation of accountants and auditors. They make this profession a lot more interesting than the image that is commonly portrayed.

Sources: Nelson Luscombe, "A Learning Experience," *CA Magazine,* February 1993, p. 3: "Sustainable Decision Making," ibid., p. 19; Robert Walker, "In Search of Relevance," ibid., p. 26; Michael Stanleigh, "Accounting for Quality," *CA Magazine,* October 1992, p. 40; interviews with three CAs, May 1999.

---

that their businesses are doing well or not doing well. A proper accounting system and an understanding of the information it yields are essential for a reliable assessment of how a business is performing.

SOME CONCERNS OF THE ACCOUNTING PROFESSION

The Spotlight on Big Business box "Accounting for New Kinds of Assets and Liabilities" and the Profile at the beginning of the chapter highlight a growing concern of accountants about some difficult issues. The new knowledge-based industries and environmental problems have created whole new sets of issues that must be considered if financial statements are to truly reflect the financial position of companies. The troubling questions relate to how to evaluate certain significant, intangible (nonphysical) assets and some potentially huge liabilities.

As the Spotlight notes, how can brainpower, skills, and abilities be valued in dollars? Yet these assets are becoming increasingly important in today's high-tech world. Similarly, the problem with buying or selling polluted or toxic materials, land, buildings, or other assets, or hazards arising from production processes, is that potential buyers, consumers, affected persons, or governments may launch major damage suits. How are such potential liabilities to be evaluated?

A balance sheet is supposed to show all the assets and liabilities of a company at a given date. If important assets and liabilities are omitted, does the balance sheet reflect reality? These are the current concerns of the accounting profession.

CAREERS IN ACCOUNTING

Would accounting be a good career for you? Certain aptitudes are important for anyone who wants to be an accountant: an appreciation of accuracy, a feel for figures, an analytical mind, an ability to handle masses of detail without losing perspective, and a sense of order

If you have not done well in math in school and don't particularly enjoy working with figures, you probably would not enjoy accounting. A good accountant must also be able to spot inaccuracies and work creatively with numbers, because he or she often works with figures prepared by others. If that sounds interesting to you, you might find accounting a rewarding career.

You should also be aware that obtaining an accounting degree is often the first step to wider opportunities in business consulting or in senior management positions. Many accountants, after extensive experience in the business world, have gone on to lead companies as chief executive officers (CEOs). To give one well-known example, the former CEO of Bombardier, Laurent Beaudoin, is a highly regarded chartered accountant (CA) who successfully led his company for many years. One of the Canadian authors of this book, who is a CA, has had an interesting career in different fields that have taken him to many countries around the world.

PROGRESS CHECK

- What four formulas make up the income statement? What is the difference between revenue and income on that statement?
- What is the fundamental accounting equation used to make up the balance sheet? What is balanced on the balance sheet?
- What is the connection or link between the income statement and the balance sheet?
- What is cash flow? How can a small business protect itself against cash-flow problems before they occur?

ETHICAL DILEMMA

Review

Do you recall the ethical question at the start of the chapter that involved "cooking" the books? Our executives agree on the answer to this one. Bédard is very clear in his response. "You must respect the law. As chief financial officer you have an obligation to disclose all important information in the financial statements. This information appears to be material and should be disclosed."

Reilley is equally clear. "I would take no part in fudging the books. Rather, the company should present the situation openly to the bank, complete with sound business and restructuring plans for improving the situation."

You should be aware that there are two serious risks involved if you go along with the suggestion made by your boss: losing your professional licence and being found guilty of fraud. You don't want to threaten your career and perhaps your whole life. Difficult as the situation may be, you really have no choice. If your boss does not agree with the suggestions of our two executives, you will have to refuse your employer's request and find a new job.

SUMMARY

1. Accounting is the recording, classifying, summarizing, and interpreting of financial transactions that affect the organization. The methods used to record and summarize accounting data into reports are called an accounting system.
    *   *How does managerial accounting differ from financial accounting?*
    Managerial accounting provides information and analyses to managers within the firm to assist them in decision making. Financial accounting provides information and analyses to managers and to external users of data such as creditors and lenders.
    *   *What is the difference between a private and a public accountant?*
    Public accountants are independent firms that provide services for a fee to a variety of companies; private accountants are employees of a company. Only public accountants perform independent audits.

2. Many people confuse bookkeeping and accounting.
    *   *What is the difference between bookkeeping and accounting?*
    Bookkeeping is part of accounting, but only the mechanical part of recording data. Accounting also includes classifying, summarizing, interpreting, and reporting data to management.

3. There are six major classes of accounts in accounting: assets, liabilities, owners' equity, revenues, cost of goods sold, and expenses.
    *   *What are assets?*
    Assets are economic resources owned by the firm, such as cash, inventory, buildings, and machinery. Current assets are converted to cash within a year; fixed assets are relatively permanent and are used to operate the business. Liquidity refers to how fast an asset normally becomes cash. Current assets are thus more liquid than fixed assets.
    *   *What are liabilities?*
    Liabilities are debts owed by the organization to others (for example, suppliers, bond holders).
    *   *What is owners' equity?*
    It is the sum of owners' investments plus profits to date not yet paid out to owners.
    *   *What are revenues?*
    Revenues are what are received from the sale of goods or services rendered.
    *   *What are cost of goods sold?*
    They are a particular type of cost consisting of the total cost of merchandise sold.
    *   *What are expenses?*
    Expenses are incurred in operating the business to earn the revenues. They include salaries, rent, and utilities.

4. The primary financial statements provided by accountants are income statements and balance sheets.
    *   *What is an income statement?*
    An income statement reports revenues, costs, and expenses for a specific period of time. The basic formula is revenue minus costs and expenses equals income. (Note that income and profit mean the same thing.)
    *   *What is a balance sheet?*
    A balance sheet reports the financial position of a firm at a specific date. The fundamental accounting equation used to prepare the balance sheet is assets = liabilities + owners' equity.

1. Define accounting and explain the differences between (a) managerial accounting and financial accounting and (b) private and public accountants.

2. Compare accounting and bookkeeping.

3. Identify and describe the major accounts used to prepare financial statements.

4. Understand simple income statements and balance sheets, and explain their functions.

5. Describe the role of computers in accounting.

5. Most business people realize the value of using computers to help them with their accounting activities.
   - *How can computers help accountants?*
   Computers can easily record and analyze data and quickly provide financial reports. Software is available that can continually analyze and test accounting systems to be sure they are functioning correctly. This software makes regular reporting very easy. Computers can help in decision making by providing appropriate information, but they cannot make good financial decisions independently. Management judgment and creativity are still human traits.

6. Explain the concept of cash flow.

6. Cash flow is the difference between cash in and cash out.
   - *Why is cash flow so important?*
   Having enough cash at all times to be able to pay bills, salaries, loans, and the like is the first requirement for a business if it is to stay alive. Making a profit is not enough. Many small businesses do not estimate cash flow in advance, and it is one of the main reasons why they fail.

7. Explain how a business can be making profits and still be short of cash.

7. Profits and cash are not the same thing.
   - *What happens to profits?*
   Cash and profits are not the same thing (except for street vendors who have no inventory and no expenses and sell for cash only). Usually when companies sell goods, profits get tied up in additional inventory, accounts receivable, or equipment and are not available to pay bills. This usually happens when companies are growing rapidly. Slow, steady growth allows profits to show up in stronger cash positions.

8. Understand the new concerns of accounting.

8. Important assets and liabilities are not being accounted for in financial statements.
   - *What are these assets and liabilities, and why are they not stated on balance sheets?*
   Major assets are the skills and education of the employees. Another one is the combined technological knowledge of a company. All these intangible assets may be more important than a company's tangible assets. Similarly, liability for environmental damage has emerged as a major potential liability for many companies. The problem is that there is no recognized method for evaluating these assets and liabilities.

KEY TERMS

accounting 565
accounting system 565
amortization (depreciation) 577
assets 569
balance sheet 572
bookkeeping 568
cash flow 579
cost of goods sold 573
current assets 570
financial accounting 567

financial statements 572
fixed or capital assets 570
fundamental accounting equation 575
gross margin (profit) 573
income statement 572
independent audit 568
liabilities 570
liquidity 569

managerial accounting 566
net income 574
operating expenses 573
other assets 570
owners' equity 571
private accountants 567
public accountants 567
ratio analysis 577
retained earnings 574

1. Why are college and university students, even students of business, so hesitant to take accounting courses? Would a different approach by colleges and universities be more successful? What should that be?

2. Take a sheet of paper. On every fourth line, write one of the following headings: assets, liabilities, owners' equity, expenses, and revenues. Then list as many items as you can under each heading. When you are finished, look up the lists in the text and add to your own. Keep the lists for your notes. As you complete the lists, create a mental picture of each account so that you can understand the concepts behind accounts and accounting.

3. Prepare an income statement for your own imaginary company. See how far you can get without looking back to Figure 18.5. Then check the text to see what you have forgotten, if anything.

4. Now prepare the balance sheet. Remember the simple formula: Assets = Liabilities + Owners' equity. Go back and check your balance sheet against Figure 18.6.

5. Write your own explanation of how small businesses get into trouble with cash flow by expanding too rapidly. Think of several ways a business could expand rapidly and still avoid such problems. Discuss your thoughts with the class.

Purpose:

To research careers in accounting and other information related to the field of accounting, specifically the income statements and balance sheets of Canadian companies.

Exercises:

1. Check out the Web sites of the three large professional accounting organizations in Canada:
   a. Canadian Institute of Chartered Accountants (CA), www.cica.ca
   b. Chartered Management Accountants of Canada (CMA Canada), www.cma-canada.org
   c. Certified General Accountants' Association of Canada (CGA), www.cga-canada.org
   and follow the links to careers and other information that might interest you. Note that there are links to specific provinces so that you can click on your province to get relevant information.

2. Using your favourite search engine, find the Web sites for some large public Canadian companies. From their most recent annual report, examine their financial statements. Scrutinize the income statement and the balance sheet. Do they look like the ones shown in Figures 18.5 and 18.6? If not, what are the differences? What are the similarities? Discuss in class.

PRACTISING MANAGEMENT DECISIONS

CASE 1

CONSTRUCTING AN INCOME STATEMENT AND A BALANCE SHEET

Stuart Jenkins started Neighbourhood Landscaping Service when he was in high school. As the business grew, Stu hired several of his friends. He is doing well and is now in a position to begin keeping better records. After six months, Stu has written down some of his figures, but he doesn't know how to interpret them. He wants to take out a loan and needs to prepare a balance sheet to calculate his financial position. These are his figures:

ASSETS	
Cash	$ 5,350
Truck	13,500
Accounts receivable	2,400
Equipment	6,300
Office furniture	945
Supplies	550
Total assets	$29,045

LIABILITIES	
Money owed bank	$7,500
Money owed supplier	545
Money owed for equipment	500
Total liabilities	$8,545

Some other figures Stu hastily put together in no particular order are:

Income from work done	$64,000
Costs incurred for trees, shrubs, etc.	15,000
Salaries of helpers (2)	16,000
Advertising	1,350
Insurance	2,000
Office costs (phone, heat, rent, etc.)	8,400
Depreciation on truck and equipment	4,000

Stu paid $1,250 for other supplies such as gravel, sand, and slate used for walkways.

Decision Questions

1. How much did Stu earn? Prepare an income statement to show Stu how you calculated his profit for six months.
2. Make a balance sheet. What is Stu's equity? Can you figure out his initial investment?
3. Use the balance sheet to determine if Stu is in a good financial position. Can he pay his debts?

CASE 2

WHERE DID KATHERINE GO WRONG?

Katherine Potter knew a good thing when she saw it. At least, it seemed so at first. She was travelling in Italy when she spotted pottery shops that made beautiful products ranging from ashtrays to lamps. Some of the pottery design was stunning.

Katherine began importing the products to Canada, and sales took off. Customers immediately realized the quality of the items and were willing to pay top price. Katherine decided to keep prices moderate to

expand rapidly, and she did. Sales in the second three months were double those of the first few months. Sales continued to grow during the rest of the first year.

Every few months, Katherine had to run to the bank to borrow more money. She had no problems getting larger loans, because she always paid promptly. To save on the cost of buying goods, Katherine always took cash discounts. That is, she paid all bills within 10 days to save the 2 percent offered by her suppliers for paying so quickly.

More customers bought Katherine's products on credit. They would buy a couple of lamps and a pot and Katherine would allow them to pay over time. Some were very slow in paying her, taking three months or more.

Toward the end of the year, Katherine noticed a small drop in her business. The local economy was not doing well because many people were being laid off from their jobs. Nonetheless, Katherine's business stayed level. One day the bank called Katherine and told her she was late in her payments. She had been so busy that she hadn't noticed that. The problem was that Katherine had no cash available to pay the bank. She frantically called several customers for payment, but that raised very little cash as only one person was able to pay immediately. Katherine was in a classic cash-flow bind.

She decided to raise prices and refused to make any sales on credit. She started delaying payment on her bills, thus losing the discounts. Then she engaged an accounting firm to review her financial condition.

Their examination showed that she had made nice profits and her overall position was good. Her cash problems were due to the fact she had allowed customers to run behind in payments and she had built up a lot of inventory that she had paid in full. They prepared financial statements and a cash-flow projection, which showed a good picture.

Based on this information, the bank increased her loan. But it urged her to get after her late-paying customers and reduce her inventory, both actions that would considerably improve her cash flow. Her accountants had told her the same thing.

Decision Questions

1. Do you see how it was possible to have high sales and profits and still run out of cash? How could Katherine have avoided the problem?
2. Do you think it was wise of Katherine to raise prices and refuse to sell on credit? Will it hurt future business?
3. Was she right to get an accountant at this point? Should she have done so earlier? How would that have prevented her from having a cash squeeze?

CBC **VIDEO CASE** **www.cbc.ca**

Part 1
CREDIT CRUNCH

For most people, accounting and accountants are a bit of a mystery. We know about marketing and sales because of the constant barrage of ads and giveaways and promotions wherever we are. We also have some contact with human resource management when we are interviewed for a job or when we are employed. Everyone has some knowledge of, and experience with, money and financing problems. But what exactly do professional accountants do?

It is important to distinguish among the services required by large and small companies. The video does not address the professional accounting firm's very different relationship to large companies, where the role is that of external auditor. In this video we see a much closer relationship of auditor/accountant to client. In addition to normal auditing and taxation services, we see the accountant trying to help his clients through a difficult time.

One of the authors of this book, Paul Berman, notes that during his years of experience as a practising CA he has gone through this experience many times with new and not so new entrepreneurs. One of his jobs as a CA was helping to prepare a proper business plan (reviewed in detail in Chapter 7) that shows the entre-preneur what the company would look like over the next few years if all the estimates became a reality. The next step is to convince the bank of credibility, so that the bank will maintain the financing required and reverse the business plan's decision to call in the loan.

Discussion Questions

1. An important component of the business plan is the financial statements. One of these is the *balance sheet*. What information does the balance sheet yield? Can you list some of its major categories? Why would this information be helpful to a lender such as a bank?
2. Another important financial statement is the *income statement*. What are some of its major categories? Of what use is this information to a bank reviewing your loan status?
3. Can you see how an experienced and reputable professional accountant can be helpful at a meeting with a banker when seeking financing? Aren't the figures and the business plan clear enough? What does the accountant add by being present?

Source: *Venture*, show number 811, "Credit Crunch," January 20, 2002, running time 7:06.

Financial Ratios: Evaluating a Company's Operations and Financial Health

Everyone interested in finance needs to understand basic accounting. What is especially helpful to financial analysis is the use of ratios to measure a company's health. You are familiar with ratios. They are used all the time to measure the success of sports teams. For example, in basketball, the ratio of shots made from the foul line versus attempts is measured. TV announcers say, "Alou is shooting 85 percent from the foul line, so he is not the one to foul in the final minutes." We judge basketball players by such ratios: 80 percent is good for foul shots, 65 percent is not good. We calculate similar ratios for baseball ("He's batting .300," or 30 percent), football ("He's completed 50 percent of his passes"), and so on. Note that each percentage for a particular game cannot usefully be compared to other percentages for that game or with those of other games. Batting percentage cannot be compared with ERA, RBI, and certainly not with pass percentage completion in football or number of goals scored in hockey. Likewise, in business, apples can be compared only with apples and oranges only with oranges. Meaningful, comparative information is obtained when comparisons are made with the company's previous year, its budget or projection for the current year, and the performance of competitors. So ratios are not hard to understand or compute, and they give a lot of information about the relative performance of athletes or of business. Now let's look at some key ratios that business people use. All the data are obtained from the balance sheet or the income statement.

HANDLING CASH-FLOW PROBLEMS: AVERAGE COLLECTION PERIOD OF RECEIVABLES

We have already noted that a major financial problem of small business is poor liquidity or cash flow. In many cases, poor cash flow is caused by not collecting accounts receivable fast enough. Many customers do not pay their bills until they are reminded or pressured to pay. Incentives such as discounts for paying early are often helpful for minimizing collection time. To determine whether or not a business is collecting its receivables as it is supposed to or in a reasonable period of time, an analyst calculates the average collection period. Unlike the other financial analysis calculations, this one takes two steps. The first step is to divide the annual credit sales by 365 to obtain the average daily credit sales. The second step is to divide accounts receivable (the amount customers owe) by the average daily credit sales (the first step) to get the average collection period in days. For example:

1. Average daily credit sales $= \dfrac{\text{Total annual credit sales}}{365 \text{ days}}$

2. Collection period in days $= \dfrac{\text{Accounts receivable}}{\text{Average daily credit sales}}$

If total annual credit sales were $365,000, then the average daily credit sales would be $1,000:

Average daily credit sales $= \dfrac{\$365,000}{365} = \$1,000$

If the accounts receivable today were $60,000, then the collection period would be 60 days:

Average collection period of receivables $= \dfrac{\$60,000}{\$1,000} = 60 \text{ days}$

If your terms of sale were 30 days, then this would show that, on average, your customers are taking twice as long as they should to pay their bills.

INVENTORY TURNOVER

A business supply store once asked a consultant why its inventory turnover ratio was so low. The consultant walked through the warehouse and found box after box filled with computer software. These obsolete items were being carried on the books as inventory and lowering the turnover ratio. What signalled the problem was that the owner compared his turnover ratio to the average industry ratio and to what the store's ratio was in previous years.

A lower than average ratio indicates obsolete merchandise or poor buying practices. A higher than average ratio may indicate an understocked condition, where sales are lost because of inadequate stock, or a very good buyer of merchandise. The faster merchandise moves out, the greater the inventory turnover. The result is greater profit without investing more money in increased inventory. The aim is to have the smallest inventory that can produce the greatest amount of sales.

Calculate the ratio to determine inventory turnover by dividing the cost of goods sold by the average inventory for the period. For example, if the cost of goods sold were $160,000 and the average inventory were $20,000, the turnover ratio would be 8. That means 8 times during one year or every 1.5 months. This figure by itself is rather meaningless. It has to be compared to industry figures to tell a company how it is doing in relation to competitors. It must also be analyzed to see if it makes sense for that particular type of business. The calculation looks like this:

$$\text{Turnover} = \dfrac{\text{Cost of goods sold}}{\text{Average inventory}} = \dfrac{\text{Cost of goods sold}}{(\text{Beginning} + \text{Ending inventories}/2}$$

$$= \dfrac{\$160,000}{(\$23,000 + \$17,000/2} = \dfrac{\$160,000}{\$20,000} = 8 \text{ times annually}$$

If you are operating a high-fashion women's clothing store, your inventory changes with every season. If you carry clothes for four seasons, then you try to sell everything by the end of each season, which is why you always see end-of-season sales. For example, you don't want to carry this fall's line over to next fall because styles will change and very few women will want to buy the previous year's styles. So, if you have four seasons' merchandise and clear them out each season, your inventory turnover ratio should be four. If it is more than four, it means you are not selling out each season's stock and are carrying more inventory than you should, and one that's losing value. If your ratio is less than four, it means that you are an excellent buyer and able to generate sales with minimal inventory, replacing fast-moving items often.

In general, with just-in-time (JIT) inventory systems and electronic data interchange (EDI) among all members of the supply chain (mentioned in previous chapters) becoming more and more common, many companies are able to operate with minimal inventories, thus tying up less money. This ability should be reflected in inventory turns going up in companies that are following these procedures.

Gross Margin (or Profit)

A major concern for all retail merchandising companies is the rate of profit earned on the merchandise sold. If you buy sweaters for $50 and sell them for $120, your markup is $70. That means you have added $70 to your cost to arrive at your selling price. This markup, or gross margin (or gross profit), is usually expressed as a percentage of the selling price.

$$\text{Gross margin rate} = \frac{\text{Gross margin}}{\text{Sales}} = \frac{\$70}{\$120} = .58, \text{ or } 58\%$$

You know the average gross margin rate of your sales from prior years, so you can apply that to the sales in any period, say one month, and get a rough approximation of your total gross profit for that period. Then, subtracting your estimated monthly expenses from monthly gross margin immediately tells you what profit or loss you have made that month.

Similarly, it is easy to calculate your break-even point—how much in sales you must do just to cover your expenses. The procedure is a little more complicated for a manufacturing company.

Return on Sales (ROS)

Each industry has a different rate of return on sales; that is, the percentage of profit your sales generate. Such figures are well known in the industry. Therefore, a firm can determine whether or not it is doing as well as other businesses by calculating the return-on-sales ratio. This involves dividing net income by net sales. If net income were $10,000 and net sales were $200,000, the return-on-sales ratio would be 5 percent:

$$\text{Return on sales} = \frac{\text{Net income}}{\text{Net sales}} = \frac{\$10,000}{\$200,000} = .05, \text{ or } 5\%$$

Investors pay attention to the return-on-sales ratio. One way to increase the ratio is to increase prices, but a competitive market usually keeps prices low. Another way is to reduce costs. Shareholders compute return on sales when evaluating a firm (or look up the ratio in business reports). Another ratio they look for is return on investment.

Return on Investment (ROI)

Shareholders invest in a business expecting to make a greater return on their money than if they made a low-risk investment, like depositing it in a bank or buying government bonds. You can calculate the return on equity (current book value of your investment) in a firm by dividing net income by the owners' equity. You are more likely to hear this formula referred to as *ROI*, or *return on investment*. If net income were $10,000 and shareholders' equity (investment) were $100,000, the return on investment would be 10 percent:

$$\text{ROI} = \frac{\text{Net income}}{\text{Owners' equity}} = \frac{\$10,000}{\$100,000} = 10\%$$

EARNINGS PER SHARE (EPS)

Earnings per share (EPS) measures the profit a company earns for each share of common stock it has outstanding. As you probably guessed, this is a crucial ratio for corporations since earnings stimulate growth in the company and pay for shareholders' dividends. Earnings per share is calculated as follows:

$$\text{Earnings per share} = \frac{\text{Net income}}{\text{Number of common shares outstanding}} = \frac{\$120,000}{100,000} = \$1.20 \text{ earnings per share}$$

Earnings per share is an excellent indicator of a firm's current performance and growth on a year-by-year basis. Continued earnings growth is well received by both investors and lenders.

DEBT/EQUITY RATIO

The debt/equity ratio tells you how much money the company has borrowed compared to the shareholders' (owners') equity. A high ratio triggers caution among investors. But high or low is meaningful only as compared to the average of the same industry.

If total liabilities were $150,000 and owners' equity were $150,000, the debt/equity ratio would be 1:

$$\text{Debt/equity ratio} = \frac{\text{Total liabilities}}{\text{Owners' equity}} = \frac{\$150,000}{\$150,000} = 1$$

Most consultants feel a ratio greater than 1 is not good, but again that varies by industry. Sometimes more debt is a good sign if it means the company is trying to optimize the return to shareholders by assuming more risk. Industry Canada reported that the primary reason for banks turning down loan applications is an unsatisfactory debt/equity ratio.*

LIQUIDITY: CAN PAYMENT COMMITMENTS BE MET?

Analysts are also interested in certain other ratios. One important calculation analysts make is the current ratio:

$$\text{Current ratio} = \frac{\text{Current assets}}{\text{Current liabilities}}$$

This ratio measures a company's ability to pay its short-term debts. A ratio of 1.5 or higher is usually desired. Anything more than 1 indicates the firm is able to pay its debts. Less than 1 means that its current liabilities exceed its current assets, so the company cannot pay its bills as they come due.

---

*George Haines and Alan Riding, Carleton University, *Access to Credit. Lending Priorities and SMEs*, submitted to Industry Canada, August 17, 1994.

If we leave inventories out of the above equation, we get a more accurate feel for whether or not a business could quickly pay its current liabilities. Thus, another test is called the *quick ratio* or *acid-test ratio*. This is the supposed acid test of whether a firm is on solid ground, short term or not. The formula is:

$$\text{Quick ratio} = \frac{\text{Current assets} - \text{Inventory}}{\text{Liabilities}}$$

If the result is 1 or more, it means that the company can very easily pay its bills, which indicates a sound current financial condition. These two ratios measure a company's liquidity; the more liquid a company is, the more easily it can pay its bills.

Who Is Interested in Ratios?

There are three groups that pay close attention to ratios: managers, shareholders, and outside parties. The latter include lenders (like banks), creditors, and potential investors. Managers want to watch out for problem areas and to improve performance. Shareholders are interested in seeing if the company is being well run. This is particularly true of major shareholders like mutual funds. If they feel there are long-standing problems, they may ask for a change in management. Everybody pays attention to the trend over a period of years. Are the ratios improving, getting worse, or remaining unchanged? These are the important questions.

Professionals use several other ratios to learn more about the condition and performance of a business, but this appendix gives you an idea of what ratios are and how they are used. The point is that financial analysis begins where accounting reports end. Ratios represent the link between accounting and finance.

Managing Financial Resources

LEARNING GOALS

AFTER YOU HAVE READ AND STUDIED THIS CHAPTER, YOU SHOULD BE ABLE TO

1 Explain the role and importance of finance and the responsibilities of financial managers.

2 Outline the steps in financial planning by explaining how to forecast financial needs, develop budgets, and establish financial controls.

3 Recognize the financial needs that must be met with available funds.

4 Distinguish between short-term and long-term financing and between debt capital and equity capital.

5 Identify and describe several sources of short-term capital.

6 Identify and describe several sources of long-term capital.

7 Compare the advantages and disadvantages of issuing bonds, and identify the classes and features of bonds.

8 Compare the advantages and disadvantages of issuing stock, and outline the differences between common and preferred stock.

Coping with and Surviving Cash Crises

Greig Clark is an entrepreneur and a veteran in the struggles to overcome cash squeezes. On a rafting trip with three others in British Columbia, the rugged camp owner tells Clark that what they're facing is not Class 1 or Class 2 rapids, which are for "Eastern wimps." Ahead are Class 3, which are dangerous. "Class 4 could kill you and Class 5 probably will." Similarly, Clark believes that you are not a real entrepreneur unless you have faced and overcome "the top three classes of cash crunches." He knows what he is talking about after 20 years of experience running companies.

Courtesy of Greig Clark

Clark quotes the well-known American Harold Geneen, former CEO of ITT, who has written extensively on managing companies. Geneen said, "Keep your eyes on your cash, because if you run out of cash they take you out of the game." For 18 years Clark owned and ran College Pro with a unique financing system peculiar to that type of business. Every spring Clark would pledge all his personal assets to the bank to support a $1 to $2 million line of credit, which he needed to meet his weekly payrolls. It wasn't until late summer that the business was generating enough cash to operate without a bank loan.

In subsequent businesses Clark continued to learn the hard lesson that cash is king. Once, while on a ski trip in Whistler with his brothers, he got a call from his chief financial officer advising him that the bank had called in their loan (demanded payment in full). Clark had to drop everything, get on the phone and round up the necessary funds. Clark has been through the fire many times. He has weathered his Class 3, 4, and 5 cash crises. Now he operates the Horatio Enterprise Fund out of Toronto.

Source: Greig Clark, "Show Me the Money," *Profit*, October 1999, p. 31

ETHICAL DILEMMA

To Tell or Not to Tell?

You are the chief financial officer of Proto Corp. and have just completed all the preparations for a $60-million bond issue. The president of Proto has had extensive discussions with the president of Petra Trust Co., which manages some large pension funds, and Petra has agreed to buy the entire issue. You are not confident about the future of Proto because of some deep-rooted problems that are not yet public knowledge. These problems could have a serious impact on Proto's financial position and even threaten its existence.

A few days later you are having lunch with Karina, a good friend of yours, who is a manager of one of the pension funds overseen by Petra Trust. She tells you that her fund will be buying $20 million of the bond issue, and she seems quite pleased with this investment decision. You are somewhat uneasy because of your concerns about the long-term viability of Proto.

You are torn between your responsibility to your company and your friendship with Karina and the possible risk to her pension fund. You know that if it were your own money, or that of a pension fund you were managing, you would not make this investment. What should you do? What would be the result of your decision? Let's return to this question at the end of the chapter.

FINDING FINANCING: A CRUCIAL ISSUE

The story of Greig Clark's efforts to obtain financing illustrates how vital financing is both to a new and an existing business. Because this is one of the toughest problems facing small, medium, and large businesses, this chapter explores the different avenues available for obtaining finances.

THE ROLE OF FINANCE

An accountant in a company may be compared to a skilled laboratory technician who takes blood samples and other measures of a person's health and writes the findings on a health report (financial statements). A financial manager in a business is the doctor who interprets those reports and makes recommendations to the patient regarding changes that would improve health. Financial managers use the data prepared by the accountants and make recommendations to top management regarding strategies for improving the health (financial strength) of the firm. Financial managers also face important ethical responsibilities: see the Ethical Dilemma box "To Tell or Not to Tell?" for an example.

A manager cannot be optimally effective at finance without understanding accounting. Similarly, a good accountant needs to understand finance. There is some overlap between the work of an experienced professional accountant and an experienced financial manager. The former, as mentioned in the previous chapter, will often go beyond the preparation and analysis of reports and financial statements and make suggestions for improving the financial health of a business. This is particularly true for smaller businesses that do not employ financial managers.

Where there is a financial manager, he or she starts with these reports and concentrates exclusively on improving the company's financial strength and preventing financial problems from arising in the future. This is the financial manager's *main* area of expertise, whereas it is only the *peripheral* area for the accountant.

Venture magazine ran an article citing the mistakes companies make in this area: "Sources for this story couldn't emphasize enough that many companies' financial and money-raising woes come down to inaccurate financial reporting. Young, growing companies need to live and die by the numbers, they say."[1] The message could not be clearer—good finance begins with good accounting.

As you may remember from Chapter 7, and as you can see from the Profile of Greig Clark, financing a *small* business is a difficult but critical function if a firm expects to survive, especially during the first two years. The simple reality is that the need for careful financial management is an essential, ongoing challenge for a business of any size throughout its entire life. Financial problems can arise in any organization.

Causes and Effects of Financial Problems

The most common causes of financial problems are:

1. *Undercapitalization.* This means not enough funds to start or to continue operations. Many small businesses fall into this trap. Starting on a shoestring and a prayer is a good formula for failure.

2. *Inadequate expense control.* This leads to constant unpleasant surprises.

3. *Credit terms.* Consistently giving your customers more time (long terms) to pay their accounts than you get from your suppliers will reduce your cash flow and squeeze you financially.

In addition, events occur over which firms have no control. An important customer may go bankrupt, creating a large, uncollectible amount (a bad debt). A major customer may stop carrying your products or may be acquired by another company that has a different supplier of your products. A new local or foreign competitor may make serious inroads with some important customers. These, and other business factors, will all impact negatively, some seriously, on your sales, profits, and financial health.

There are also generally changes in the macroenvironment, the world outside the company, that are beyond normal business relationships. New government policies on taxes, interest rates, or imports; fluctuations in Canadian-dollar exchange rates with the U.S. dollar; inflation or deflation; recession; cross-border shopping; technological developments; and new competitors can all play havoc with the best-laid plans. In Part 1 these issues were discussed in more detail.

Three very large Canadian companies ran into serious trouble in the past decade because of a big drop in their cash flows ➤ **P. 579** ◄. Robert Campeau of Campeau Corp. and the Reichman brothers of Olympia & York were both mentioned in the previous chapter as examples of when extreme cash-flow problems caused the collapse of an empire.

A third member of this triumvirate was the giant Edper conglomerate of hundreds of companies, reputed at the time to be the largest such grouping in Canada, controlled by Peter and Edward Bronfman. Severe cash-flow problems had them selling off companies and adopting other drastic measures to survive.

In all three cases, the companies were in trouble because they had huge debts acquired in various expansions and they were counting on continual inflation and prosperity to provide enough cash to meet their crushing interest and capital repayment requirements. The recession in the United States, Canada, and England and the collapse of the real estate market upset their plans.

One does not have to pursue finance as a career to be interested in finance. Financial understanding is important to anyone who wants to invest in stocks and bonds or plan a retirement fund. In short, finance is something everyone should be concerned with. Let us take a look at what finance is all about.

FIGURE 19.1

**WHAT FINANCIAL
MANAGERS DO**

Many of these functions
depend on the information
provided by the accounting
statements discussed in
Chapter 18.

- Planning
- Budgeting
- Obtaining funds
- Controlling funds (funds management)

- Collecting funds (credit management)
- Internal auditing
- Managing taxes
- Advising top management on
  financial matters

finance
The business function that is
responsible for the acquisition
and disbursement of funds.

What Is Finance?

Finance is the business function that is responsible for the acquisition and disbursement of funds. Figure 19.1 outlines the responsibilities of financial managers. The
major preoccupation of finance managers is developing a financial plan for the
amount of funds required and how to obtain them. Without a carefully calculated
financial plan, a firm has little chance for survival regardless of its product or marketing effectiveness. Managing finances is the crucial link that makes both production and marketing effective.

You are probably somewhat familiar with several finance functions—for example, the idea of buying merchandise on credit and collecting payment from companies that buy the firm's merchandise or services. Both *credit* and *collections* are
important responsibilities of financial managers. The finance manager must be sure
that the company does not lose too much money because of bad debts (people or
firms that don't pay). Naturally, this means that the finance department is further
responsible for collecting overdue payments. These functions are critical to all types
of businesses but particularly important to small and medium-sized businesses,
which typically have smaller cash or credit cushions than large corporations.

Tax payments represent an outflow of cash from the business. Therefore, they
too fall under finance. As tax laws and tax liabilities have changed, finance people
have taken on the increasingly important responsibility of tax management. Tax
management is the analysis of the tax implications of various managerial decisions
in an attempt to minimize taxes paid by the business. Businesses of all sizes must concern themselves with managing taxes.

Relationships with banks
are invaluable to
businesses. Bankers can
assist with financial
planning, financial
management, and, of
course, obtaining
needed funds.

Canadian Press CP. Photography by Phill Snel

Finally, the finance department has an internal audit division. The internal auditor makes sure company assets are properly controlled and secured, company accounting and financial procedures are carried out, and all transactions are properly recorded. In smaller companies, the internal auditing role is divided between the owners and the external auditors.

Without internal audits, accounting statements would be much less reliable. Regular internal audits offer the firm assurance that financial planning will be effective. We turn next to how financial planning is carried out.

FINANCIAL PLANNING

Planning has been a continual theme throughout this book. We have emphasized the importance of planning as a managerial function and offered insights into planning your career. Financial planning involves analyzing the short- and long-term money flows to and from the firm. The overall objective of financial planning is to optimize profits by making the best use of money. It's probably safe to assume that we all could use better financial planning in our lives.

Financial planning involves three steps: (1) forecasting financial needs, both short- and long-term, (2) developing budgets to meet those needs, and (3) establishing financial control to ensure the company is following the financial plans. Let's look at the important role each step plays in the financial health of an organization.

Forecasting Financial Needs

Forecasting is an important component of financial planning (see Figure 19.2). A **short-term forecast** is a prediction of revenues, costs, and expenses usually for one year. This forecast is the foundation for most other annual financial plans, so its accuracy is critical. Part of the short-term forecast may be a **cash-flow forecast**, which projects the expected cash inflows and outflows. Naturally, the inflows and outflows recorded in the cash-flow forecast are based on expected sales revenues and on various costs and expenses incurred and when they'll come due. A firm uses past financial statements as a basis for these forecasts.

A **long-term forecast** is a prediction of revenues, costs, and expenses for more than 1 year, sometimes as far as 5 or 10 years into the future. This forecast plays a crucial part in the company's long-term strategic plan. The strategic plan asks questions such as What business are we in, and should we be in it five years from now? How much money should we invest in automation and new equipment over the next decade? Will there be cash available to meet long-term obligations? If not, what is the best way to obtain these funds?

The long-term financial forecast gives top management and operations managers some sense of the income or profit potential of different strategic plans. Additionally, long-term projections assist financial managers with the preparation of company budgets.

short-term forecast
A prediction of revenues, costs, and expenses for one year.

cash-flow forecast
A projection of expected cash inflows and outflows in the coming year.

long-term forecast
A prediction of revenues, costs, and expenses for more than 1 year, sometimes extending 5 or 10 years into the future.

FIGURE 19.2

FINANCIAL PLANNING
Note the close link between financial planning and budgeting.

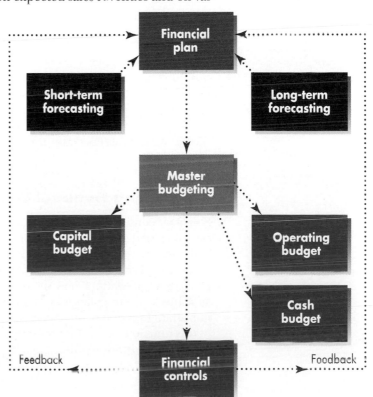

Developing Budgets

A budget is itself a financial plan. Specifically, a budget sets forth management's expectations for revenues and, based on those financial expectations, allocates the use of specific resources throughout the firm. You may live on a carefully constructed budget of your own. A business operates in the same way. A budget becomes the primary basis and justification for financial operations in the firm.

Most firms compile yearly budgets from short- and long-term financial forecasts. This leads to a master budget that has three components (see Figure 19.2):

- an operating budget
- a capital budget
- a cash budget

operating budget
The plan of the various costs and expenses needed to operate the business, based on the short-term forecast.

An **operating budget** is the plan of the various costs and expenses needed to operate the business, based on the short-term forecast. How much the firm will spend on supplies, travel, rent, advertising, salaries, and so on is planned in the operating budget.

capital budget
The spending plan for the acquisition of capital assets that involve large sums of money.

A **capital budget** highlights the firm's spending plans for the acquisition of capital assets. The capital budget primarily concerns itself with the purchase of such capital or fixed assets as land, buildings, and equipment that involve large sums of money.

cash budget
The projected use of cash during a given period (e.g., monthly, quarterly, or annually).

A **cash budget** is based on the cash-flow forecast and projects the use of cash over a given period (e.g., monthly, quarterly, or annually). Cash budgets are important guidelines that assist managers in anticipating borrowing, debt repayment, operating expenditures, and short-term investment expectations.

At this point, it should be obvious to you that financial managers play an important role in the operations of the firm. These managers often determine what long-term investments to make, when specific funds will be needed, and how the funds will be generated. Once a company has projected its short- and long-term financial needs and established budgets to show how funds will be allocated, the final step in financial planning is to establish financial controls.

CRITICAL THINKING

Budgets are designed to keep strict controls on spending. An important theme of this book is the need for managers to be flexible so that they can adapt quickly to rapidly changing conditions. This often means modifying previous plans. Do you see any conflict between budgets and such flexibility? How do managers stay within the confines of budgets when they must shift gears to accommodate a rapidly changing world? Which forecasts are more affected by these problems, short-term or long-term? Why?

Establishing Financial Control

Financial control means that the actual revenues, costs, and expenses are periodically reviewed and compared with projections. Deviations can thus be determined and corrective action taken. Such controls provide feedback to help reveal which accounts, which departments, and which people are varying from the financial plans. Such deviations may or may not be justified. In either case, some financial adjustments to the plan may be made. You will recall reading in Chapter 8 that an important function of managers is controlling. Financial control is one major aspect of this function. After the Progress Check we will explore specific reasons why firms need to have funds readily available.

- Name three finance functions that are important to the firm's overall operations and performance.
- In what ways do short-term and long-term financial forecasts differ?
- What is the organization's purpose in preparing budgets? Can you identify at least three different types of budgets?

THE NEED TO HAVE FUNDS AVAILABLE

Sound financial management is essential to businesses because the need for operating funds never seems to cease. Also, like our personal financial needs, the capital needs of a business change over time. For example, as a small business grows, its financial requirements shift considerably. The same is true with large corporations such as Bell Canada and Canadian Tire. As they venture into new product areas or markets, their capital needs intensify. It's safe to say that different firms need available funds for a variety of reasons. However, in virtually all organizations, funds must be available to finance specific operational needs. Let's take a look at the financial needs that affect the operations of both the smallest and the largest business enterprises.

Financing Daily Operations

If employees are scheduled to be paid on Friday, they don't expect to have to wait until Monday for their paycheques. If tax payments are due on the 15th of the month, the government anticipates the money will be there on time. If the interest payment on a business loan is due on the 30th, the lender doesn't mean the 1st of next month. If you habitually pay late, you may be subject to interest and penalties or refusal of future loans. As you can see, funds have to be available to meet the daily operational costs of the business. The challenge of sound financial management is to see that funds are available to meet these daily cash expenditures without compromising the investment potential of the firm's money.

David Berch, the president of Cognetics, Inc., has this to say about cash flow:

> Cash flow is a constant issue if you don't go for large outside financing, which we've chosen not to do. You've got a fixed payroll. Everything on the expense side is fixed, and everything on the revenue side is variable. Somebody gets sick and doesn't pay on his receivable, or a salesperson gets lazy and doesn't sell for a couple of months. All of a sudden your cash flow goes to [pot]. You find yourself constantly managing cash flow. It's a major issue.[2]

As you may know, money has a time value. In other words, if someone offered to give you $200 today or $200 one year from today, you should take the $200 today. Why? A very simple reason. You can invest the money now and receive dividends or interest, or your investment can grow in value so that by the end of a year your $200 would be worth more than $200. In business, the income gained on the firm's investments is important in maximizing its profit. For this reason, financial managers often try to have receipts at a maximum and keep cash expenditures at a minimum to free funds for investment. It's not unusual for financial managers to suggest that the firm pay bills as late as possible (unless a cash discount is available) and set up collection procedures to ensure that the firm

Credit cards serve multiple purposes for business. Like you and me, however, businesses must be careful about spending too freely. Financial budgeting helps managers control spending.

Photo Disc

gets what's owed to it as fast as possible. This way financial managers maximize the investment potential of the firm's funds. As you might expect, efficient cash management is particularly important to small firms in conducting their daily operations.

Financing Accounts Receivable

All companies that sell or provide services to other companies give their customers credit. These sales are called *credit sales.* They send an invoice to the customer who is expected to pay it when due, according to normal company credit terms, or at another date if special arrangements were made. As we saw in Chapter 18, the debts owed by customers are called *accounts receivable.* Because accounts receivable are usually a significant part of the total assets, financial managers have to pay close attention to ensure that payments are on time—and they must go after those who are delinquent. If you pay suppliers faster than your customers are paying you, it means that you are financing your accounts receivable. In addition, your accounts that are usually slow in paying their bills could be in financial difficulty and you could end up not getting paid at all if they go bankrupt.

The whole problem is compounded if you are trying to break into a new market or to attract new customers. Under these circumstances you will be tempted to give credit to accounts that do not have a high credit rating and thus increase the risk of not being paid at all. You can see that financial managers have to keep their eye on the ball when dealing with accounts receivable.

Financing the Purchase of Inventory

As we noted earlier, the marketing concept implies a clear consumer orientation. One implication of this concept is that service and availability of goods are vital if a firm expects to prosper in today's markets. To satisfy customers, businesses are forced to maintain inventories that involve a sizeable expenditure of funds. Most companies that sell products—whether retailers, wholesalers, or manufacturers—have to carry a wide variety of merchandise or raw materials, and in sufficient quantities, to be able to satisfy the demands of their customers. Think of an auto manufacturer, a hardware store, or a department store. Although it's true the firm expects to recapture its investment in inventory through sales to customers, a carefully constructed inventory policy assists in managing the use of the firm's available funds and maximizing profitability. As you may recall from Chapter 10, innovations such as just-in-time inventory ➤ **P. 305** ◄ reduce the funds the firm has tied up in inventory. Ratio analysis ➤ **P. 577** ◄ of inventory turnover (see Chapter 18, Appendix C) also helps to prevent inventory from getting too high or having too many slow-moving or unsaleable goods.

Financing Major Capital Expenditures

In many organizations, it is essential to purchase major assets such as land for future expansion, plants to increase production capabilities, new research facilities, and equipment to maintain or exceed current levels of output or to reduce costs by modernizing. As you might imagine, these purchases require a large expenditure of the organization's funds. It's critical that the firm weigh all of the possible options before it commits what may be a large portion of its available resources. (As you may remember, these purchases are referred to as capital or fixed assets ➤ **P. 570** ◄.) Financial managers and analysts are called in to provide important insights into the appropriateness of such purchases.

In recent years numerous airlines have struggled with severe financial difficulties. Onex Corporation of Toronto announced in August 1999 a comprehensive plan to revitalize Canada's troubled airline industry by creating a new air carrier through the acquisition and merger of Air Canada and Canadian Airlines. The Onex plan was rejected and Air Canada absorbed Canadian Airlines, but it continues to have severe financial problems.

Canadian Press CP. Photography by Nick Procaylo

Let's look at an example. Suppose a firm needs to expand its production capabilities because of increases in demand. One option is to buy land and build a new plant from scratch. Other options are to purchase an existing plant, rent a building, or contract out some part of the work. Can you think of financial and accounting considerations that would come into play in this decision?

It's evident the firm's need for available funds raises several questions that need to be considered. How does the firm obtain funds to finance operations and other business necessities? How long will specific funds be needed? Will funds have to be repaid at a later date? What will the needed funds cost? How much profit will the expansion yield? These questions will be addressed in the next section.

- Money is said to have a time value. What exactly does this mean?
- Why are accounts receivable a financial concern to the firm?
- Is an efficient account collection plan more important to a small firm or a large corporation? Why?
- What is the major reason organizations spend a good deal of their available funds on inventory?

ALTERNATIVE SOURCES OF FUNDS

Earlier in the chapter, you learned that finance is the function in a business that is responsible for acquiring funds for the firm. The amount of money needed for various periods and the most appropriate sources of these funds are fundamental questions in sound financial management. We will look at the different methods and sources of acquiring funds next, but first let's highlight some key distinctions involved in funding the firm's operations.

Large corporations regularly encounter short- and long-term financing needs. *Short-term financing* refers to the need for capital that will be repaid within one year and that helps finance current operations. *Long-term financing* refers to capital needs for major purchases that will be repaid over a specific period longer than one year. We will explore sources of both short- and long-term financing in the next section. See the Spotlight on Big Business box "Canada's Airlines: A Case of Financial Crash" for more on the importance of financing.

A firm can seek to raise capital through debt or equity sources. **Debt capital** refers to funds raised through various forms of borrowing that must be repaid (debt). **Equity capital** is money raised through the sale of shares (equity) in the firm. Again, we will discuss these two financing alternatives in depth later.

debt capital
Funds raised by borrowing that must be repaid.

equity capital
Funds raised from selling shares in the firm.

SHORT-TERM FINANCING

The bulk of a finance manager's time is not spent obtaining long-term funds. The nitty-gritty, day-to-day operation of the firm takes up most of the manager's time and calls for the careful management of short-term financial needs. Cash may be needed for additional inventory or some emergency that may arise unexpectedly. As with your personal finances, a business sometimes needs to obtain short-term funds when other funds run out. This is particularly true of small businesses. It's rare that small businesses even attempt to find funding for long-term needs. They are more concerned with just staying afloat until they are able to build capital and creditworthiness. Short-term financing can be obtained in a variety of ways, and we look at some of these next.

SPOTLIGHT ON BIG BUSINESS

Canada's Airlines: A Case of Financial Crash

One of the major stories that dominated Canadian headlines in the 1990s was the financial mess of Canada's two largest airlines. Both Air Canada and Canadian Airlines International suffered enormous losses in 1991, 1992, and into 1993. The airlines' very existences were in question, and each sought deliverance through alliances with U.S. airlines. How did they get into such a terrible state?

There were many problems, but the basic cause was the deep, long recession: revenues slid steeply, resulting in huge losses. Both of these companies had large debts from airplane acquisitions and big operating expenses, so when cash flow dried up because revenues collapsed they found themselves in serious trouble. It's the classic problem that hits most businesses from time to time: shortage of cash to pay their bills.

How did they cope? Well, they could not get funds by loans or bond issues because nobody would lend them money then. It was too risky. They were unable to raise equity capital because nobody would buy their shares. So they resorted to the only methods left: they reduced operational expenses by laying off employees and cutting other costs. They also delayed paying their creditors or didn't pay them at all, as Canadian Airlines did for a few months in late 1992 and early 1993.

Canadian airlines were not the only ones hurting. Airline companies all over the world were having problems. Some well-known American companies, like Eastern Airlines and PanAmerican Airlines, went under or were taken over by other airlines.

By 1999 Air Canada was in good shape again but Canadian Airlines was still in serious financial trouble. The following year Canadian was taken over by Air Canada. In 2001 Air Canada was again in financial difficulty, and after the September 11 terrorist attacks in the U.S. the situation worsened considerably as passenger traffic fell off and security costs rose. The past decade has been a financial yo-yo for Air Canada.

Trade Credit

trade credit
The practice of buying goods now and paying for them in the future.

The most widely used source of short-term funding is called **trade credit**. This means that a business is able to buy goods > **P. 18** < today and pay for them sometime in the future. When a firm buys merchandise, it receives an invoice (bill).

Every purchase is made under certain credit terms. The invoice will indicate that payment is due in 30 or 60 days or whatever arrangements have been made. Sometimes terms may read "2/10, net 30," which means that if payment is made within 10 days, a 2-percent discount will be deducted. Otherwise, payment is due in full in 30 days. Figure 19.3 shows when it pays to take discounts.

Sometimes companies that are strapped for cash offer larger discounts, 5 or 10 percent for immediate payment. These discounts clearly mean a big reduction in cost to the purchaser who has the cash to take advantage of such offers.

The decision to take or not to take discounts is often not based on financial considerations alone. If a firm deals with certain suppliers on a regular basis and has a reputation for paying bills promptly, it will be a favoured customer. This status could be very useful whenever it needs a special order, a rush delivery, or merchandise that is in short supply. Of course, if it is short of cash, it may not be able to take advantage of discounts.

Family and Friends

A second source of short-term funds for most smaller firms is money lent by family and friends. Because short-term funds are needed for periods of less than a year, often friends are willing to help. Such loans can be dangerous if the firm does not understand cash flow > **P. 579** < and cannot repay them when promised. As we dis-

FIGURE **19.3**

CREDIT TERMS

Discounts can yield major savings on the cost of merchandise purchases.

Where terms of payment are 2/10, N30, 60, or 90, there can be quite a difference between taking the 2 percent discount versus paying in full in 30 or 60 or 90 days.

Approximate gain

2% for 20 days (10 instead of 30) = 36% per annum

2% for 50 days (10 instead of 60) = 15%

2% for 80 days (10 instead of 90) = 9%

If a company is borrowing from the bank at 15 percent per annum, there is no advantage in earning 15 percent, a loss in earning 9 percent, and a big gain in earning 36 percent. If a company is borrowing at 8 percent, it pays to take the discount in all cases.

cussed earlier, the firm may suddenly need funds and have no other sources. It is better not to borrow from friends, but instead go to a commercial bank that understands the risks and can help analyze future financial needs.

If the firm does borrow from family or friends, it is best to be very professional about the deal and (1) agree on terms at the beginning, (2) write an agreement, and (3) pay them back the same way it would a bank loan. If the firm is lucky, the family members or friends who lend the money might say, "Pay me back whenever you can."

Commercial Banks

Banks are in the business of loaning but they are often reluctant to loan money to small businesses. Nonetheless, the most promising and best-organized ventures can usually get bank loans. If they're able to get such a loan, small to medium-sized businesses should have the person in charge of the finance function keep in close contact with the bank. It's wise to see your banker periodically (as often as once a month) and send the banker all financial statements so that the bank continues to supply funds when needed.

Try to imagine different kinds of business people going to the bank for a loan, and you'll get a better feel for the role of the financial manager. Picture, for example, a farmer going to the bank to borrow funds for seed, fertilizer, equipment, and other needs. Such supplies may be bought in the spring and paid for when the fall harvest comes in. Now picture a local toy store buying merchandise for Christmas. The money for such purchases might be borrowed in October and November and paid back after Christmas. A restaurant may borrow funds at the beginning of the month and pay by the end of the month. Can you see that how much a business borrows and for how long depends on the kind of business it is and how quickly the merchandise purchased with a bank loan can be resold or used to generate funds?

Obviously, if the firm has carefully prepared a cash-flow forecast, there will be fewer surprises. No cash-flow forecast can prevent a drop in sales or the sudden bankruptcy of a major customer. But it does help to alert the firm to the size of the problem immediately. Sometimes a business gets so far into debt, so far behind in its payments, that the bank refuses to lend it more. Suddenly the business can't pay its bills. More often than not, this results in bankruptcy or business failure, and you can chalk up another business failure to cash-flow problems.

Can you see why it's important for a business person to keep friendly and close relations with his or her banker? The banker may spot cash-flow problems early and point out the danger. Or the banker may be more willing to lend money in a crisis if the business person has established a strong, friendly relationship built on openness and trust. It's always important to remember that the banker wants the firm to succeed almost as much as the firm does. Bankers can be an invaluable support—especially to small, growing businesses.

www.cba.ca/eng/index.cfm

The Canadian Bankers Association's Web site provides a wealth of information about the activities of Canada's banks. The site includes a breakdown of the number of branches by province, interest rates on mortgages, the number of credit cards in circulation, the number of bank accounts, the dollar volume of activities, the number of automated banking machines and transactions they are used for, the level of small-business lending, and much more. The site even includes information on the status of the GDP and the national debt. Be sure to visit this Web site to get the latest information!

In the past, there has been much criticism of Canadian banks for their apparent reluctance to make loans to small companies. Many small-business owners voiced their complaints about the banks. The banks have reacted to the criticism with a whole range of measures to improve the situation (see Chapter 7). Data from the seven largest banks show that 754,000 business customers had loans of less than $1 million each, totalling $70 billion. Of this group 556,000 customers had loans of less than $100,000 each, totalling $15 billion. There were also 36,000 business customers with authorized loans of more than $1 million each, totalling $467 billion.[3]

Banks have initiated a wide variety of direct and indirect ways and many policies to help small business. These are outlined in publications such as *Serving the Needs of Small Business* and *Small Business Annual Reports.*[4]

Because the six largest banks (see Figure 19.4) are responsible for an estimated 80 percent of all loans to small firms, these policies have a major impact on the ability of small businesses to obtain financing. The banks point out that research has shown that venture capital angels refuse 97 percent of requests for funding and venture capital firms reject 95 percent of them.[5] They also note that Statistics Canada has determined that friends and relatives refuse only 12 percent, banks 19 percent, and other financial institutions 16 percent of all applicants for funding.[6]

Different Forms of Bank Loans The most difficult kind of loan to get from a bank or other financial institution is an unsecured loan, a loan not backed by any collateral. Normally, only highly regarded customers of the bank receive unsecured loans. A **secured loan** is one backed by collateral, something valuable such as property. If the borrower fails to pay the loan, the lender may take possession of the collateral. That takes some of the risk out of lending money. **Pledging** is the term for using accounts receivable, inventory, or other assets as security. Other property can also be used as collateral, including buildings, machinery, and other things of value, for example company-owned stocks and bonds.

If your business is sound and you develop a good relationship with a bank, it will open a **line of credit** for you, meaning it will agree to lend the business up to a given amount. The purpose of a line of credit is to speed the borrowing process so that a firm does not have to go through the hassle of applying for a new loan every time it needs funds. The funds are available as long as the credit ceiling is not exceeded. As businesses mature and become more financially secure, the amount of credit is often increased. A line of credit is a particularly good way to obtain funds for future or unexpected cash needs.

secured loan
A loan backed by something valuable, such as property.

pledging
Using accounts receivable, inventory, or other assets as security for a loan.

line of credit
The maximum amount a bank will agree to lend a borrower.

FIGURE 19.4

DATA OF CANADA'S SIX LARGEST BANKS

These data are for banks at October 31, 2000. These banks account for 98 percent of all banking assets and loans in Canada.

	ASSETS	LOANS	NET INCOME FOR YEAR
	(IN BILLIONS OF DOLLARS)		
Royal Bank	291	173	11.3
CIBC	268	146	10.9
Toronto Dominion Bank	265	135	9.5
Bank of Nova Scotia	253	134	8.1
Bank of Montreal	233	134	8.2
National Bank	76	47	2.9
Total	1,386	801	50.9

Source: Data of Canada's Six Largest Banks. www.cba.ca

The Prime Rate Periodically you will read that the prime rate has been raised or lowered. For most people, that report has little meaning. But for a financial manager, the level of the prime rate is very important. The *prime rate* is the short-term interest rate that banks charge their preferred (creditworthy) customers. Most firms pay more than the prime rate for a loan, but some very good credit risks can negotiate loans at prime. In either case, the prime rate is the base from which many loan rates are calculated.

Government Programs

Elaborate programs of government financing for specific purposes are available. These programs were discussed in detail in Chapter 4 and Appendix A.

Factoring

One relatively expensive source of short-term funds for a firm is called *factoring*. It works like this: as we know, a firm sells many of its products on credit to other businesses. Some of these buyers are slow in paying their bills. The company may thus have a large amount of money due in accounts receivable. A *factor* buys the accounts receivable from the firm at a discount (usually advancing 50 to 70 percent of the value of the accounts receivable) for cash. The factor then collects and deducts the amount that was advanced plus its charges and remits the balance to the company.

Factoring, then, is the process of selling accounts receivable for cash. How much this costs the firm depends on the age and the quality of accounts receivable, the nature of the business, the general interest rate level, and the conditions of the economy. Factoring is the most expensive form of financing. It is more common in industries where businesses are undercapitalized and have no other source of funds.

factoring
Selling accounts receivable for cash.

Commercial Paper

Sometimes a large corporation needs funds for a few months and wants to get lower rates than those charged by banks. One strategy is to sell **commercial paper**, which consists of promissory notes, in amounts starting at $25,000, that mature in 270 days or fewer. A promissory note shows the fixed amount of money the business agrees to repay the lender on a specific date. The interest rate is identified on the face of the promissory note, and the accumulated interest is payable on the date the note matures. Commercial paper is unsecured, so only large and financially stable firms can sell it. Since most commercial paper comes due in 30 to 90 days, it is also an investment opportunity. Buyers, often companies with surplus funds, can put cash into commercial paper for short periods to earn some interest.

commercial paper
A short-term corporate equivalent of an IOU that is sold in the marketplace by a firm. It matures in 270 days or fewer.

- If you received terms of 3/10, net 25, what would this mean?
- What is the difference between trade credit and a line of credit at a bank?
- What is meant by factoring? What are some of the considerations for establishing a discount rate in factoring?
- How does commercial paper work? What is the main advantage of issuing commercial paper?

PROGRESS CHECK

LONG-TERM FINANCING

Financial planning and forecasting help the firm develop a financial plan. This plan specifies the amount of funding that the firm will need over various periods and the most appropriate sources of those funds. In setting long-term financing objectives, the firm generally asks itself three major questions:

- What are the long-term goals and objectives of the organization?
- What are the financial requirements needed to achieve these long-term goals and objectives?
- What sources of long-term capital are available and which will best fit our needs?

In business, long-term capital is used to buy fixed (capital) assets such as a plant or equipment and to finance any expansion of the organization. The revenue generated from these assets is expected to continue over many years, so it will finance the repayment of the cost of these assets. In major corporations, decisions concerning long-term financing normally involve the board of directors and top management, as well as finance and accounting managers. Sometimes an expert investment banker is included in the decision-making group. In smaller businesses, the owners are always actively involved in seeking all forms of financing.

Initial long-term financing usually comes from three sources: surplus funds, debt capital, and equity capital, shown in detail in Figure 19.5. The role of government in financing, especially for small business, is highlighted in the Spotlight on Small Business box "The Vital Role of the Business Development Bank of Canada" (see also Chapter 4). The important role of venture capitalists in small business is discussed in Chapter 7.

Surplus Cash Funds

Successful businesses often generate surplus cash over and above their normal operating requirements. All or part of these funds may be available for investment in fixed (capital) assets that the company requires. The financial managers will compare how much interest these funds are earning to how much interest will have to be paid for loans. Usually the loan costs will exceed the revenue from the investments made with the surplus funds, so the decision is not too difficult. If you are

www.bdc.ca

This is the Web site of the Business Development Bank of Canada. The site is well designed and has a lot of useful information and links explaining what the Bank does and how to contact it in every province.

FIGURE 19.5

SOURCES OF LONG-TERM FUNDS

The three major sources are surplus internal cash funds, debt capital, and equity capital.

SURPLUS INTERNAL CASH FUNDS:

- Generated from profits and sale of assets and not required for current use

DEBT CAPITAL (FROM):

- Sale of bonds
- Long-term loans from banks and other financial institutions
- Mortgage on buildings
- Dealer financing of equipment

EQUITY CAPITAL (SHARES SOLD TO):

- Current shareholders
- New investors
- Venture capital companies
- Business Development Bank of Canada (BDC)

The Vital Role of the Business Development Bank of Canada

Since 1945, the federal Business Development Bank of Canada (BDC) has been an important source of financing for small- and medium-sized businesses in Canada. The BDC has gradually widened its activities to embrace a whole range of financing and management aids to new and existing businesses. A good example is the Orchid company.

In 1988, Grant Bibby, president of Orchid Automation Group Inc. of Cambridge, got a $900,000 loan from the BDC. He actually asked for $400,000, but the BDC's examination showed that the company really needed more than that to function satisfactorily. It isn't every 29-year-old who can command enough confidence to secure a $900,000 loan, of course. But Bibby had a hot product.

Orchid had devised computerized equipment that could change the dies on big metal-stamping machines, used by titans like Chrysler, in three minutes flat instead of the traditional seven days. In 1990, two years after its launch, Orchid boasted sales of $1.1 million. By 1992 the figure was $5.2 million, and Bibby was predicting that would rise to $30 million within five years. (In fact, the company did much better.)

In planning for expansion, Bibby tried to avoid the cash shortages that traditionally plagued and sometimes killed fast-growing small firms. It wasn't easy. Like many businesses, Orchid was started on a shoestring.

In 1991 Bibby recognized that further help from traditional lenders was a nonstarter, since they liked their loans to be secured by tangibles such as buildings or machinery. Orchid was leasing its factory space and had already put its existing machines on the line to secure a modest term loan.

Bibby heard he might qualify for a new pilot project called the Venture Loan program, which had been launched by the federal government's BDC in 1991 and was aimed at businesses three to five years old that were profitable and ripe for expansion. Venture loans mix elements of a bank loan with techniques used by venture capitalists and, most crucial to Bibby, don't require any collateral. Instead, the BDC bets on the future earnings of the borrower. "They came in, analyzed our operations, did a 100-page report, and concluded that we would hit our sales and profit goals," said Bibby.

He was even more pleased when the BDC didn't demand an ownership stake in Orchid, something most venture capitalists would insist upon. "Entrepreneurs hate to give up ownership of their companies," said Francois Beaudoin, former president and CEO of BDC. "They've slaved for years to build what they've got and they don't want to dilute the ownership." Under the deal he struck with BDC, Bibby agreed to repay the Venture Loan over five years, with a 20-percent annual return on the investment for the bank. The payback is a combination of an interest payment and a royalty that's based on the company's revenues.

The BDC justifies its return on the grounds that its government mandate requires it to be self-financing. And although 20 percent is much higher than a standard bank loan (typically the prime rate plus 1 or 2 percent), it's far lower than the 35 to 45 percent expected by traditional venture capitalists. What's more, with the BDC's $900,000 in its coffers, Orchid was able to obtain an additional $600,000 from banks at just over the prime rate.

Recently the BDC has become a lot more aggressive in publicizing its existence and funding capabilities. The Bank has sharply increased the number of its ads on TV and in print media and has changed the tone of these ads. The BDC has more funding and a wider scope, and its successful Venture Loan program has had a steady increase in funding.

In 2001, 71 Venture loans were made totalling $114 million, with a total of $296 million outstanding from 131 companies at March 31, 2001. The total amount of all loans owing to the BDC at that date was a record $6.1 billion. It had also increased its customer base to a record 20,000. That makes BDC one of the biggest venture-financing operations for Canadian small businesses.

Because BDC operates at a profit and most of the money goes to high-tech firms with growing workforces and significant exports, the federal government continues to increase its funding to this Crown corporation.

Sources. BDC Web site, <www.bdc.ca>, November 2001 and July 1998; *Together We Make It Happen*, annual report 1995, Federal Business Development Bank; Jerry Zeidenberg, "Shaking the Money Tree," *Globe and Mail, Report on Business*, June 1993, pp. 73–74.

earning 6 percent and have to pay 9 percent to borrow, you save money by using your own funds for new equipment rather than borrowed monies. Sometimes there are other considerations that will lead a company to borrow despite the extra cost.

Debt Financing

A business can meet long-term financing needs through debt capital. Debt capital is funds the firm borrows from lending institutions or acquires from selling bonds (explained later in the chapter). With debt financing, the company has a legal obligation to repay the amount borrowed plus regular interest at fixed or variable rates.

Once a firm is established and has developed a rapport with a bank, it can often secure a long-term loan. (For small businesses, the Business Development Bank of Canada [BDC], a Crown corporation, is often a good source of such loans—see the Spotlight on Small Business box.) Long-term loans are usually repaid within three to seven years but may go even longer. For such loans, a business must sign a term-loan agreement, which is a promissory note that requires the borrower to repay the loan plus interest in specified installments, usually monthly. For a real-life situation involving debt financing, see the Reaching Beyond Our Borders box "Hands Across the Border."

A mortgage on land and buildings is a long-term loan that is secured by the property. If the firm does not pay installments as they come due the property may be seized by the mortgagor and sold to repay the amount owing. Any excess amount is returned to the borrower. Most long-term loans require some form of collateral, perhaps real estate, machinery, or inventory. The interest rate for such loans is based on factors such as whether there is adequate collateral, the firm's credit rating, and the general level of market interest rates. The rates are usually higher than for short-term loans because of the longer period.

If an organization cannot meet its long-term financing needs from a lending institution, it may decide to issue bonds. Businesses compete with governments to sell bonds. Bonds sold by the federal or provincial governments are risk free because they are backed by the taxing power of governments, which makes them attractive. Bonds may be issued for 5, 10, or even 20 or 30 years. If a firm cannot secure a long-term loan from a lender or issue bonds, it often turns to equity capital. Sometimes there are good reasons to turn to equity capital first.

The Business Development Bank of Canada (BDC) is a small-business bank that helps create and develop Canadian small and medium-sized businesses. The BDC plays an important role in delivering financial and management services, with a particular focus on the high-tech and exporting sectors of the economy.

Courtesy of Business Development Bank of Canada

Equity Financing

Basically, equity financing refers to issuing (selling) shares or stock of the company. The new owners of shares in the company acquire a piece of the ownership or equity. The firm may offer shares to

1. Existing owners by asking them to buy additional stock. If the company is doing well, existing owners may be pleased to do so.

2. The public in general through stockbrokers who handle such transactions. This arrangement will be necessary if more shares have to be sold than existing shareholders are willing to buy. (This option is not available to private companies; see next section.)

3. Venture capital companies. (These were discussed in Chapter 7.)

4. The Business Development Bank of Canada (discussed previously).

Bonds and shares are discussed in detail in the rest of the chapter.

PROGRESS CHECK

- What is the difference between long-term and short-term capital? Do firms actually need both types of funding?
- What are the two major forms of debt financing available to a firm?
- How does debt financing differ from equity financing?
- What are four sources of equity financing?
- How are private companies restricted?

REACHING BEYOND OUR BORDERS

www.sleeman.com

Hands Across the Border

John Sleeman's family had been in the brewery business for three generations before they closed down in the 1930s. In 1984 Sleeman decided to rebuild the family brewery, armed with the family recipe book and a 20-percent U.S. partner, Stroh Brewing Co. But in August 1988, a month away from bottling the cream ale aging in its casks, Sleeman hit a $3-million snag.

After agreeing to finance the brewery with a $3-million loan, Sleeman's bank abruptly decided it wanted its money back—within 30 days. The bank had second thoughts, doubting that the venture could succeed. They couldn't see how Sleeman hoped to compete against Molson and Labatt, "when Molson was spending more just to advertise the launch of Molson Dry in Ontario" than Sleeman was spending for his entire operation.

But John Sleeman isn't the kind of man who will allow his business to fail. His attitude is, "if you want it bad enough, you find a way to fund it and keep it going." So he spent the first 15 days soliciting other Canadian banks, which, he says, treated him "like a

leper." Then Sleeman looked south—and the first U.S. bank he approached, The National Bank of Detroit, agreed to finance the company. Sleeman's U.S. partner Stroh's 20-percent interest in the company helped swing the deal.

Sleeman is now Canada's third-largest brewer and John Sleeman holds no grudges. In 1996, when he felt that the company had outgrown its Detroit bankers, Sleeman turned to Canadian banks again and this time, not surprisingly, he had no problems. Sleeman is very satisfied with the support his bank gives him now. Still, he says, "if I had given up when the Canadian bank said 'game's over,' I wouldn't be having this conversation." Sleeman's sells $150 million in beer annually and employs 600 people. His advice is that if you "have a good idea and you've done your homework, don't give up on it."

Sources: Rick Kang, "Banks for Nothing," *Profit*, October 1999, p. 9; <www.ale-sleeman.com>, July 2001.

SECURITIES MARKETS

The importance of obtaining long-term funding cannot be overemphasized, because the most common problem facing new companies is starting without sufficient capital. Adequate long-term funding allows a firm to concentrate on operations instead of always looking for funds. It gives company managers a stable base from which to operate.

You will remember from Chapter 6 that only public companies can obtain financing by selling bonds and shares (securities) to the public at large. This selling is made possible by the existence of markets—*stock exchanges*—through which stockbrokers buy and sell these securities on behalf of clients. **Stock exchanges** are markets where the securities of public companies are traded and they are efficient places for carrying out these transactions. Pension funds, mutual funds, insurance companies, banks and other companies, and individuals with funds to invest (domestic or foreign) constitute a market with a huge appetite for quality securities.

Companies that issue securities to raise funds obtain them only when the securities are first sold. All subsequent trading is between buyers and sellers and has nothing to do with the issuing company. This trading constitutes the bulk of trading on stock exchanges and is called *secondary trading*.

stock exchanges
Markets where the securities of public companies are traded.

DEBT FINANCING THROUGH SELLING BONDS

To put it simply, a bond is a certificate (see Figure 19.6) indicating that the owner has lent money to the issuer of the bond. The company (or government) has a legal obligation to make regular (annual or semi-annual) interest payments and to repay the principal, all on the dates indicated on the certificate. Bonds come in a wide variety, with a terminology to match.

The Terminology of Bonds

A **bond** is a contract of indebtedness issued by a corporation or government unit that promises payment of a principal amount at a specific future time plus annual or semi-annual interest at a specified or variable rate. As you may suspect, the interest rate paid varies depending on many factors, such as the general level of interest rates, the reputation of the company, and the rate being paid for government bonds. Generally, once an interest rate is set for specific bonds, it cannot be changed. **Principal** refers to the *face value* of the bond (common bonds are almost always issued in multiples of $1,000).

The borrower is legally bound to repay the bond principal in full to the bondholder on the bond's **maturity date**. For example, if you purchase a $1,000 bond with an interest rate of 9 percent and a maturity date of July 1, 2010, the firm undertakes to pay you $90 interest annually. This is done in two semi-annual installments on January 1 and July 1 each year until July 1, 2010, when it must repay the full $1,000.

bond
A contract of indebtedness issued by a corporation or government unit that promises payment of a principal amount at a specified future time plus annual or semi-annual interest at a specified or variable rate.

principal
The face value of a bond.

maturity date
The date on which a borrower must legally repay the bond principal to the bondholder.

Advantages and Disadvantages of Issuing Bonds

As a source of long-term capital, bonds offer advantages to an organization. The decision to issue bonds is often based on careful evaluation of all of the following advantages and disadvantages:

- Bondholders have no vote on corporate affairs, so management maintains control over the firm's operations. Remember, bondholders are creditors of the firm, not owners as shareholders are.

- The interest paid on bonds is a deductible expense to the firm's operations, which reduces income taxes.

- Bonds are a temporary source of funding for a firm. They are eventually repaid and the debt obligation eliminated.

However, bonds also have some significant drawbacks.

- Bonds are an increase in *debt* (liabilities) and may adversely affect the market's valuation of the firm.

- Interest on bonds is a legal obligation. It must be paid even when the company is incurring losses or is short of cash. If interest is not paid when due, bondholders can take legal action to force payment and seize any assets securing the bond.

- The face value of the bonds must be repaid on the maturity date. This could cause a possible cash shortage for the firm on that date. In practice another bond is often issued to raise the necessary funds to repay the bond.

unsecured bonds
Bonds that are not backed by any collateral.

Different Classes of Bonds

An organization can choose between two different classes of corporate bonds. The first class is **unsecured bonds**, sometimes called *debentures* or *debenture bonds*. These bonds are not supported by any special type of collateral on the part of the issuing firm. In other words, the primary security the bondholder has is the reputation and credit rating of the company. Unsecured bonds are issued only by well-respected firms with excellent credit ratings. Such bonds do have the backing of all corporate assets not otherwise pledged, but other creditors have an equal claim on those assets.

FIGURE 19.6

A SAMPLE BOND CERTIFICATE FROM IBM

This is an unsecured and convertible bond (debenture) paying 7 7/8 percent interest. The bond matures November 21, 2004, when the principal amount (or face value) of the bond must be repaid.

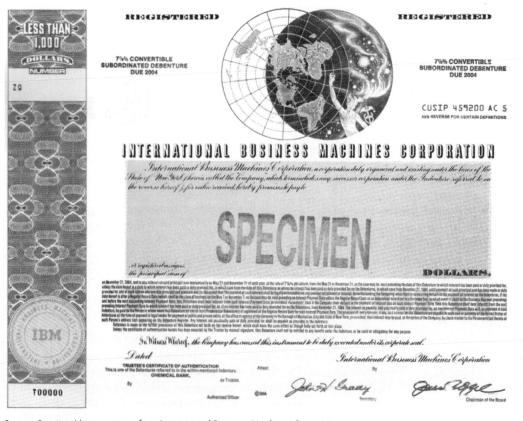

Source: Reprinted by permission from International Business Machines Corporation.

secured bonds
Bonds backed by some tangible asset that is pledged to the bondholder to guarantee payment of principal and interest.

The second kind of bonds is **secured bonds**. These are bonds backed by some tangible asset that is pledged to the bondholder. If interest or principal is not paid when due, the assets may be seized. There are several kinds of secured bonds:

- *First mortgage bonds* are backed by the company's real assets such as land and buildings. They are the most common of secured bonds and among the most desirable.

- *Collateral trust bonds* are backed by the stock that the company owns and that is held in trust by a financial institution (thus the word trust in the title).

- *Equipment trust bonds* are backed by the equipment the company owns. This may include trucks, aircraft, and other equipment that is widely used in industry. A trustee often holds title to the equipment pledged until the bondholders are paid.

Secured bonds are obviously quite a safe investment, while unsecured bonds are less safe but still less risky than investment in shares. Bond interest rates are closely related to the degree of risk—the higher the risk the higher the interest rate. Some bonds have a variable interest rate. The market price of bonds is usually quite stable with none of the wide price swings often seen with shares. Bonds have a wide range of other features that we look at next.

CRITICAL THINKING

Considering the disadvantages and advantages of different forms of raising funds, which method would you adopt if you had to make that decision in your company? How would your decision be affected in a high-interest year? If your company did well? What would you do for short-term financing? For long-term financing? How would you justify your choices?

Special Bond Features

One special feature of a bond issue is a call provision, which lets the issuer pay off a bond prior to its maturity date by *calling in* the bond. Call provisions must be clearly indicated in the original bond issue so that investors are aware of this clause.

This feature is useful for the issuer; if interest rates fall, the issuer can recall the bonds and pay them off with a new issue at a lower interest rate. Normally this right cannot be exercised until several years after the original issue date, as shown on the bond certificate.

There is often a *redemption* feature that gives the bondholder the right to redeem the bond. That means the right to be repaid prior to date of maturity. The bondholder would exercise this right if interest rates had risen and higher interest could be obtained elsewhere.

convertible bond
A bond that can be converted into shares of common stock.

A last feature that can be included in bonds is convertibility. A **convertible bond** is one that can be converted into a fixed number of shares of common stock in the issuing company. This feature can be an inducement for an investor to buy the bond because common stock has the potential to grow in value over time. When we discuss common stock this advantage will become evident to you.

Bonds as Investments

As investments, bonds are safer than shares. But two questions often bother first-time investors in corporate bonds. One question is: "If I purchase a corporate bond, do I have to hold it to the maturity date?" No! You do not have to hold a bond until maturity, because bonds are bought and sold daily on securities markets. However, if you sell your bond to another investor, it's unlikely you will get the face value (usually $1,000), since prices fluctuate, usually in a narrow range. You would get a higher or lower amount.

The second question on investors' minds is, "How do I know how risky an investment a *particular* bond issue is?" Fortunately, four companies, Dominion Bond Rating Service, Canadian Bond Rating Service, Standard & Poor's, and Moody's Investors Service (the first two are Canadian, the last two are American), rate various corporate and government bonds' degree of risk to investors. Naturally, the higher the risk associated with the bond issue, the higher the interest rate the organization must offer investors. Investors will not assume high levels of risk if they don't feel the potential return is worth it.

Bonds provide an excellent source of long-term financing for firms and good investment vehicles for investors. They are a form of debt financing as opposed to equity financing. Let's explore the most common form of equity financing, the issuing of corporate stock (shares).

PROGRESS CHECK

- Why are bonds considered a form of debt financing?
- What is meant if a firm states it is issuing a 7-percent debenture bond due October 1, 2010?
- Explain the difference between an unsecured and a secured bond.
- Why do issuing companies typically like to include call provisions in their bonds?
- What role do the bond rating services play in the bond market?

EQUITY FINANCING THROUGH ISSUING STOCK

As noted earlier, equity financing is another form of long-term funding. *Equity financing* is the obtaining of funds through the sale of shares of ownership in the corporation. There are two different classes of equity instruments: preferred and common stock. We will discuss each after a brief look at the terminology of stock and the advantages and disadvantages of issuing stock as a financing alternative.

The Terminology of Stock

Stocks are shares of ownership in a company. A **stock certificate** is tangible evidence of stock ownership. It is usually a piece of paper that specifies the name of the company, the number of shares it represents, and the type of stock it is. **Dividends** are the part of a firm's profits that are distributed to shareholders. Dividends can be distributed in the form of cash or more shares of stock.

stock certificate
Tangible evidence of stock ownership.

dividends
The part of the firm's profits that are distributed to shareholders.

Advantages and Disadvantages of Issuing Stock

There are some advantages to raising long-term funds via equity financing.

- Because shareholders are owners of the business, their investment never has to be repaid. These funds are therefore available for acquisition of fixed (capital) and other assets.
- There is no legal obligation to pay dividends to shareholders. Note that dividends are payable only when the board of directors declares a dividend out of accumulated profits. In practice, most stable firms declare dividends regularly to keep their shares attractive for investors. New companies normally retain the profits for additional investment and growth for a few years before they begin to pay dividends.

Dominion Bond Rating Service (DBRS) is one of four companies that rates various corporate and government bonds' degrees of risk to investors.

Courtesy of Dominion Bond Rating Service

- Selling shares rather than bonds can actually improve the company's financial position because it does not increase the company's debt.

Nevertheless, as the saying goes, there's no such thing as a free lunch. As you might suspect, there are disadvantages to equity financing as well.

- As owners of the firm, shareholders have the right to vote for the board of directors. As you remember from Chapter 6, the board of directors decides who will manage the firm and what its policies will be. Hence the direction of the firm can be altered through a significant sale of shares. In reality this rarely happens, because most issues add only a small percentage of shares to the total amount outstanding.

- Dividends are not a deduction for tax purposes, but interest on bonds is.

- Management decision making is often tempered by the need to keep shareholders happy. This often forces managers to use short-term tactics to keep earnings up rather than strategies to keep the firm profitable in the long run. Thus, the true cost of equity financing may be much higher than is shown on the books of the company.

Figure 19.7 summarizes some important features of equity and debt financing. Let's see how bonds, preferred stock, and common stock differ. See Figures 19.8 and 19.9 for further information on these differences.

Issuing Preferred Stock

preferred stock
Stock that gives owners preference over common shareholders in the payment of dividends and in a claim on assets if the business is liquidated; it does not include voting rights.

Preferred stock gives its owners preference over common shareholders in the payment of dividends and in a claim on assets if the company is liquidated. However, it normally does not include voting rights in the firm. Preferred stock is frequently referred to as a *hybrid investment* in that it has characteristics of both bonds and stock. (This can be seen in Figure 19.7.) To illustrate, consider the treatment of preferred stock dividends.

Preferred stock dividends differ from common stock dividends in several ways. Preferred stock is generally issued with a par value, which becomes the basis for the dividend the firm is willing to pay. For example, if a par value of $100 is attached to a share of preferred stock and a dividend rate of 8 percent is attached to the same issue, the firm is committing to an $8 annual dividend for each share of preferred stock the investor owns (8 percent of $100 = $8). If you own 100 shares of this preferred stock, your yearly dividend should be $800. Furthermore, this dividend is *fixed*, meaning it does not change each year. Also, if any dividends are paid, the dividends on preferred stock *must* be paid in full before any common stock dividends can be distributed. The common dividend may then be whatever rate the board of directors wants to pay out. Preferred shareholders normally lose their voting rights in the firm in exchange for this preferred dividend treatment.

As you can see, a similarity exists between preferred stock and bonds in that both have a face (or par) value and both have a fixed rate of return. Why not just refer to preferred stock as a form of bond? Remember, bondholders must receive interest and be *repaid* the face value of the bond on a maturity date. Preferred stock dividends do not legally *have* to be paid unless the stock is redeemed or called. Nor are the shares usually repurchased. Both bonds and preferred stock can fluctuate in market price.

cumulative preferred stock
Preferred stock that accumulates unpaid dividends.

One of the more important features of preferred stock is that it is often cumulative. **Cumulative preferred stock** guarantees an investor that if one or more dividends are not paid or only partially paid, the missed dividends will be accumulated. All the dividends, including the back dividends, must be paid in full before any common stock dividends can be paid. For example, as producers of Fiberrific, we may decide not to pay our preferred shareholders the full 8 percent dividend this period to retain funds for further research and development. The preferred shareholders must be paid the missing amount the following period before we can pay any dividends to common shareholders. If preferred stock is noncumulative, any dividends missed are lost to the shareholder. Figure 19.9 illustrates how this process works.

Figures 19.7 and 19.8 show some of the features available with preferred stock. If preferred stock does not meet the objectives of the firm or an individual investor, the firm can issue, or the individual can invest in, common stock. Let's look at this interesting alternative.

Issuing Common Stock

Common stock represents ownership of a firm and gives shareholders the rights to vote and to receive all of the firm's profits after preferred shareholders are paid. As long as the company exists, these profits can be received only in the form of dividends declared by the board of directors. Shareholders influence corporate policy by electing the board of directors, which selects the management and makes major policy decisions.

common stock
Represents ownership of a firm and the rights to vote and to receive all of the firm's profits (after preferred shareholders are paid), in the form of dividends declared by the board of directors.

	BONDS	PREFERRED STOCK	COMMON STOCK
Interest or Dividends			
Must be paid	Yes	No	No
Pays a fixed rate	Yes	Yes	No
Deductible from payor's income tax	Yes	No	No
Canadian payee is taxed at reduced rate	No	(if payor company is Canadian) Yes	Yes
Stock or bond			
Has voting rights	No	Not normally	Yes
May be traded on the stock exchange	Yes	Yes	Yes
Can be held indefinitely	No	Usually	Yes
Is convertible to common stock	Maybe	Maybe	Not applicable

FIGURE 19.7

COMPARISON OF BONDS, PREFERRED STOCK, AND COMMON STOCK OF PUBLIC COMPANIES

The different features help both the issuer and the investor decide which vehicle is right for each of them at a particular time.

PREFERRED STOCK FEATURE	DESCRIPTION
Convertible	The shares may be exchanged after a stated number of years for common shares at a preset rate, at the option of the shareholder.
Cumulative	If the dividend is not paid in full in any year, the balance is carried forward (accumulates). The cumulative unpaid balance must be paid before any dividends are paid to common shareholders.
Callable	The company that issued the shares has the right after a stated number of years to call them back by repaying the shareholders their original investment.*
Redeemable	After a stated number of years, the investor may return the stock and ask for repayment of his or her investment.*

FIGURE 19.8

OPTIONAL FEATURES AVAILABLE WITH PREFERRED STOCK

Each feature holds some attraction for the potential investor.

*If the shares are also cumulative, all dividend arrears must be paid as well.

Common stock is considered more risky and speculative than either bonds or preferred stock. Remember, common shareholders receive dividends only after both bondholders and preferred shareholders receive their interest and dividends. Also, if a company is forced to cease operations and money remains after creditors are paid, common shareholders share the funds only *after* bondholders and preferred shareholders recover their loans and investments.

Why, then, would investors select common stock as an investment alternative? Because the risk is balanced by the expectations of higher returns. Several investment opportunities are available. For example, an investor may select a growth stock, a stock of a corporation whose earnings are expected to grow faster than other stocks or the overall economy. High-technology companies fall into this category. Rapid-growth stocks are often quite speculative and pay rather low dividends, but the potential for growth is strong. Income stocks offer investors a rather high dividend yield on their investment. Care must be taken to ensure that these are good stocks, referred to as *blue chip*. **Blue-chip stocks** are those of high-quality companies. Canadian banks, Bell Canada, and Microsoft are some examples.

Investors can even invest in a type of stock called a *penny stock*, which sells for less than $1 per share. Such stocks frequently represent ownership in mining companies and are usually highly speculative. The Vancouver Stock Exchange has many such offerings.

It's important to remember that the value of common stock is very dependent on the performance of the corporation. Common stock is often referred to as *participating stock* because shareholders participate in the success or failure of the firm.

blue-chip stocks
Stocks of high-quality companies.

FIGURE 19.9

A COMPARISON OF DIVIDENDS FOR VARIOUS TYPES OF SHARES

This figure shows what happens to different stock when dividends are missed or paid later. Note that if a dividend is not paid or only partially paid for noncumulative stock, it is never made up. Common stock cannot be paid anything if preferred is not first paid, and cumulative must be paid in full for all arrears. The schedule shows the year by year situation for cumulative preferred stock.

8% CUMULATIVE PREFERRED

Year	Due	Paid	Owing
2000	8%	4%	4%
2001	12%	5%	7%
2002	15%	15%	0%

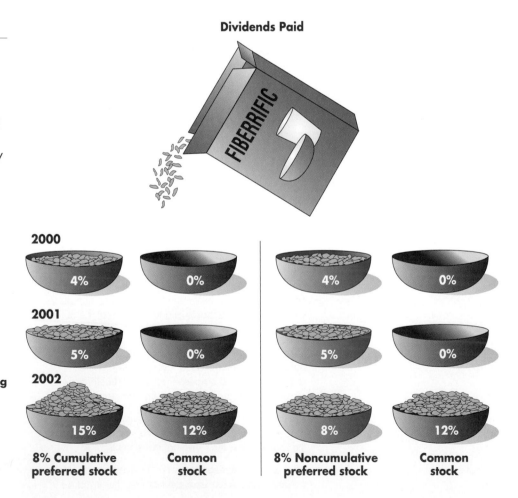

Dividends Paid

Common stock offers great opportunities but is subject to a high degree of risk, as was evidenced by the major stock market crash of 1987 and the great volatility in share prices in the last five years.

PROGRESS CHECK

- Name at least two advantages and two disadvantages of issuing stock (equity financing).
- What are the major differences between preferred stock and common stock?
- In what ways are preferred stock and bonds similar? In what ways are they different?
- How does an investor benefit by owning cumulative preferred stock as opposed to noncumulative preferred?
- What is the difference between blue-chip stocks and penny stocks?

TRADING IN BONDS AND STOCKS

Bonds and shares of public companies are bought and sold by investors through stockbrokers, who charge a commission on all sales and purchases. These brokers have representatives on the floor of the stock exchanges, where actual trading occurs. That is where a broker's agent with a security for sale on behalf of a client who has given the broker a sell order finds a broker's agent with a similar order to buy.

If you look at the financial pages, where the shares traded are listed daily, you will see that a vast number of shares of many different securities are traded regularly. For example, the Toronto Stock Exchange was trading about 145 million shares daily in July 2001. See Figure 19.10 for an excerpt from a daily listing.

Several major stock exchanges around the world dominate securities trading. New York, Tokyo, Frankfurt, and London are such major markets where billions of shares are traded daily. Five Canadian cities have local stock exchanges: Toronto, Montreal, Vancouver, Calgary, and Winnipeg. There are specialized exchanges in major financial centres where trading in commodities, futures, and other activities is carried on. These are complex fields where expert knowledge is required.

In the late 1990s a new phenomenon in security trading emerged, called e-trading. The Internet, whose impact we have seen throughout this book, has also made its presence known in this area. Many financial institutions and brokerage firms offer discount rates for trading via the Internet. Using your computer and a connection to one of these companies, you can easily buy and sell securities at very low cost. A good example is TDWaterhouse (see margin Web address).

Buying Securities on Margin

Buying on margin means you purchase securities by borrowing some of the cost from your broker, who holds them as collateral security until you pay the balance due. In effect the broker lends you the money and charges you interest. Provincial regulatory agencies, such as the Ontario Securities Commission, control all aspects of this industry, including what minimum percentage of the purchase price must be paid in cash. For example, if the current rate is 50 percent for shares and 10 percent for bonds, you would have to invest a minimum of $4 to buy an $8 share (plus commissions to the broker), and $97 to buy a bond selling for $970.

If the stock or bond drops in price, you will get a *margin call* from your broker. This means that you will have to make a payment to your broker to maintain the margin of collateral protection that the broker is obligated to observe. In this case, the loan cannot exceed 50 percent of the stock value or 90 percent of the bond value.

www.tse.com

The Toronto Stock Exchange (TSE) Web site provides information on stock market conditions in general, as well as specific information of interest to investors. The site includes a useful glossary of terms used by the industry. Check it out and learn the jargon of this exciting business.

www.tdwaterhouse.ca

This is the online trading system used by Green Line, the discount brokerage arm of the Toronto-Dominion Bank (TD). Although TD is one of the smaller banks in Canada, and very small by global standards, its acquisition of the U.S. discount giant Waterhouse resulted in TDWaterhouse ranking among the largest discount brokerage firms in the world. Investors who want to trade directly online can do so via the Internet.

buying on margin
Purchasing securities by borrowing some of the cost from the broker.

Personal Situations of Investors

Any type of investing carries some amount of *risk* with it. Some investments are riskier than others. The personal situation and temperament of an investor dictates the type of investment he or she will choose. Important considerations are the age, income,

FIGURE 19.10

DAILY STOCK TRANSACTIONS

This is a small segment of the list of stocks traded on the Toronto Stock Exchange (TSE), October 21, 1999, as reported the following day in *The Globe and Mail.*

Here is an explanation of what the column headings mean:

A & B: highest and lowest price in the last year

C: abbreviated name of the company

D: the symbol used to identify the company for trading purposes

E: annual dividend per share

F, G, & H: highest, lowest, and closing price for *that* day

I: change in closing price from the previous day

J: number of shares traded that day in hundreds (e.g., first line is 3,000 shares)

K: *yield* refers to estimated percent income your investment would yield if you bought at closing price and kept the stock for a year. It is the ratio of annual dividend to closing price. There is no yield for those companies that show no dividend paid.

L: *P/E ratio* refers to ratio of closing price to estimated earnings per share (which is not shown but is known). Where no ratio is shown it means either that the company is not making any profits or that no estimate of earnings is available.

A	B	C	D	E	F	G	H	I	J	K	L
365-day									**Vol.**		**P/E**
high	**low**	**Stock**	**Sym**	**Div**	**High**	**Low**	**Close**	**Chg**	**(100s)**	**Yield**	**ratio**
1.00	0.33	ABL Cda	ABL		0.45	0.45	0.45		30		
9.20	**7.70**	**ADF Group**	**DRX**		**8.95**	**8.95**	**8.95**	**+0.50**	**10**		**10.2**
28.10	15.55	AGF Ma	AGF.B	0.32	21.00	20.00	20.55	−0.75	263	1.6	14.3
25.50	**18.95**	**AJC Divers**	**ADC**		**19.25**	**19.25**	**19.25**	**−1.25**	**6**		
25.00	23.25	AIC	ADC.PR.A	1.50	23.85	23.40	23.40	−0.45	61	6.4	
1.75	0.30	AIT Advanc	AIV		0.70	0.65	0.65		23		
16.50	3.40	♣ ALI Tech	ALT		3.70	3.60	3.65	+0.05	358		14.6
3.15	1.75	AMR Tech	AMR		2.00	2.00	2.00	−0.30	13		
11.05	4.50	AT Plastics	ATP	0.18	4.90	4.65	4.75	+0.10	177	3.8	13.6
49.00	41.87	AT&T Cd	TEL.B		49.00	48.25	48.60	+0.20	183		37.4
27.90	11.20	♣ ATI Tech	ATY		17.10	16.10	16.90	−0.60	28208		18.4
23.50	9.50	ATS Autom	ATA		13.50	13.25	13.35	−0.30	123		20.2
6.50	**4.80**	**Aastra Tec**	**AAH**		**6.00**	**5.45**	**5.90**	**+0.40**	**1307**		
0.88	0.19	Abacan	ABC		0.23	0.20	0.21	+.005	2692		
16.10	6.80	Aber Res	ABZ		8.25	7.90	8.25	+0.30	871		
20.55	11.65	Abitibi Cons	A	0.40	18.00	17.00	17.90	+0.65	11245	2.2	
6.50	5.25	Acanthus	ACR	0.48	6.00	6.00	6.00		50	8.0	9.7
6.60	1.90	Acetex	ATX		6.00	6.00	6.00	+0.25	21		
14.25	**11.15**	**Acktion**	**ACK**		**12.00**	**12.00**	**12.00**	**−0.70**	**10**		**12.5**
5.50	4.80	Ad Opt Tec	AOP		5.00	5.00	5.00	+0.10	1		
0.55	0.22	Adrian Res	ADL		0.26	0.25	0.25	−0.01	204		
0.59	0.15	Advantex	ADX		0.52	0.44	0.50	−0.02	545		
14.25	5.60	Agnico-Ea	AGE	0.03	12.35	11.40	11.80	−0.55	2529	0.2	
11.75	7.95	♣ Agra	AGR	0.16	11.00	10.35	11.00	−0.15	109	1.4	14.3
17.25	11.85	Agrium	AGU	.163	14.20	13.95	14.15	−0.15	708	1.1	12.4
15.00	**7.00**	**Armglobal**	**AGT**		**9.40**	**8.55**	**8.60**	**−9.65**	**18**		
12.85	2.60	Ainsworth L	ANS		6.90	6.45	6.45	−0.05	253		5.9
11.20	5.70	Air Canada	AC		10.15	9.65	10.15	+0.40	7729		
10.50	4.60	Air Canad	AC.A		9.70	9.10	9.70	+0.45	2589		
5.50	2.45	AirBoss	BOS		4.47	4.45	4.45	+0.05	48		14.3
11.45	6.10	Akita	AKT.A	0.28	9.40	9.25	9.25	−0.15	25	3.0	14.7
1.18	0.70	Alarmforce	AF		1.00	1.00	1.00		10		14.3
48.90	30.75	♣ Alta Ener	AEC	0.40	43.40	42.70	43.20	+0.30	2936	0.9	
26.00	24.55	AltaE	AEC.PR.A	2.125	25.40	25.30	25.40	+0.10	155	8.4	
54.90	34.15	♣ Alcan	AL	.892	49.70	48.80	49.40	+0.20	6016	1.8	21.0
26.10	25.00	♣ Alcan	AL.PR.E	1.681	25.55	25.50	25.50	+0.05	31	6.6	
24.10	22.40	♣ Alcan	AL.PR.F	1.172	23.00	23.00	23.00		2	5.1	
1.73	0.22	Alexa Vent	AXA		1.35	1.30	1.35	−0.01	255		
3.48	1.63	Altoma Stl	ALG		2.15	2.08	2.10	+0.02	867		
5.45	3.00	Algonquin	AM	0.40	4.60	4.60	4.60	−0.10	1	8.7	
25.75	21.50	Aliant	AIT	0.90	22.70	22.15	22.50		431	4.0	18.0
38.40	21.50	Allbanc	ABK		26.75	25.75	26.50	+0.25	96		21.9
26.25	24.50	Allba	ABK.PR.A	1.385	25.00	24.50	24.55	−0.45	203	5.6	
6.35	**2.00**	**♣ Allelix**	**AXB**		**2.45**	**2.45**	**2.45**	**+0.20**	**8**		
29.50	17.25	AlincAti	AAC.A		20.00	20.00	20.00		10		
29.50	12.50	AincAt	AAC.B		14.00	14.00	14.00	+0.25	120		14.6
20.75	13.85	♣ AllianceFo	ALP		17.50	17.00	17.25	+0.20	6337		

wealth, and philosophy of the investor. A young person with a good income and a daring outlook will be likely to take a higher risk when investing. A retired person will be less interested in risk and more concerned about the security of the investment and a reliable, steady flow of income, particularly if he or she has limited funds.

The existence of such a widely diversified market of potential investors lets public companies create varying kinds of securities to raise the funds they need by satisfying a wide spectrum of investor needs. However, the largest buyers of securities are not individuals. They are pension funds, mutual funds (discussed below), banks, insurance and trust companies, stock brokerage firms, and large corporations with surplus funds not immediately required for operations.

Diversifying Investments

A prudent policy for investors is to avoid having all their eggs in one basket. If you place all your money in one stock you have a great deal of confidence in, you are exposing yourself to high risk should you be wrong. Diversify your investment by buying a variety of stocks and bonds that give you a mix of income, security, and growth.

One way to achieve this goal when your money is limited is to invest in mutual funds. A **mutual fund** buys a variety of securities and then sells units of ownership in the fund to the public. It has expert analysts who constantly watch the market. Mutual funds let even the smallest investor diversify a portfolio. A wide assortment of mutual funds specialize in acquiring certain types of domestic and foreign securities. This can satisfy the needs of all investors. Every day the units of some 1,000 mutual funds are traded in Canada; the total number of Canadian mutual funds exceeds 2,000. There are thousands in the U.S.

At the same time, by enlarging the market for securities, mutual funds make it easier for public companies to obtain financing for their operations and expansion.

mutual fund
A fund that buys a variety of securities and then sells units of ownership in the fund to the public.

CRITICAL THINKING

What form of investment seems most appropriate to your needs now? Do you suspect your objectives and needs will change over time?

Would investing other people's money be an interesting career to pursue? What are some of the problems stockbrokers or mutual fund managers might face in the course of their jobs?

Does it make sense for investors to diversify their investments or would it be more logical to put all of their eggs in one basket?

STOCK INDEXES

Stock indexes measure the trend of different stock and commodity exchanges. Every country with stock exchanges has such indexes. In Canada there are several thousand companies listed on various exchanges, and the prices of their shares fluctuate constantly. Some may be rising over a certain period and others may be falling. Some may see-saw up and down. Various indexes have been developed to give interested parties useful information about significant trends.

In Canada a commonly used index is the TSE 300, which consists of the weighted average of 300 of the most important stocks listed on the Toronto Stock Exchange. In the United States, the major (and oldest) index is the Dow Jones Industrial Average: the *Dow*, as it is commonly called. The Dow measures the movements of the shares of 30 of the largest companies in the United States that are listed on the New York Stock Exchange. It is an important index that receives worldwide attention.

Both of these averages have been carefully designed to give a realistic picture of the results of all trading in their respective stock exchanges each day. They do not work perfectly, but usually give a fair picture. You can find these and other indexes in the financial pages of your daily newspaper, in the financial papers, and on the Internet.

CYCLES IN THE STOCK MARKET AND INTEREST RATES

There are many reasons why the prices of shares listed on stock exchanges fluctuate. A popular stock in strong demand will rise because of that demand. A company that is doing well or that is rumoured to be on the verge of being taken over will usually see its stock go up. Certain industries are favoured or out of favour at certain times because they are expected to do well or poorly.

On the other hand, rumours of financial troubles or scandals will drive a stock down. Some industries, like pulp and paper, are said to be cyclical. That is, they have a few good years followed by some poorer years. Naturally, their stock prices fluctuate in such periods.

Another major cause of stock price fluctuation is that the capitalist economic system undergoes periodic cycles of recession and recovery. These ups and downs are reflected in the general movement of price levels of stocks. The stock market does not move in tandem with the level of economic activity; it does not exactly parallel but rather is thought to predict the cyclical movement of the economy in a particular country.

With the globalization of business, volatility in international economies now has a marked effect on every domestic economy, including Canada's. When the Russian economy and many Asian economies took a big tumble in 1998, their stock exchanges and currencies practically collapsed, and the effect was felt globally. Of course, our exchanges and currency were not immune from the "Asian flu," ➤**P. 11◄** so we suffered too.

In 2001, North American and foreign markets took a major tumble when the high-flying technology stocks crashed and took most other stocks down with them. A recession was again occurring and it contributed to the sharp drop. One of the most talked-about Canadian stocks was Nortel Networks, hitherto a star high-tech performer and a major global player. The collapse of its share price from a high of $140 in 2000 to a low of $8 in 2001 sent shock waves through Canada and globally.

The level of interest rates in a country also fluctuates, and this has a marked effect on the stock market. In Canada in the 1980s, interest rates climbed to historic highs. Banks were charging ordinary businesses 22 percent for commercial loans in 1980. In mid-2001, this rate was down to 7.5 percent. The rate continued to drop, as the Bank of Canada took the unprecedented step of lowering interest rates nine times in 2001 by the end of November. This was done to help stimulate the declining economy, which, as mentioned previously, suffered further shocks after the terrorist attacks in the U.S. on September 11. The reasons for such fluctuations are complex. If you are interested in following up on this important topic, consider taking courses in economics.

These fluctuations have a major impact on bond prices and on the interest rates of new bond issues. Preferred share prices are also affected, as are the dividend rates on new issues. If a business is going into the market for funding, it must plan carefully to avoid getting caught in a long-term commitment to high dividends and interest costs. That is one reason there is such a variety of vehicles that enable businesses to make flexible financing arrangements.

CAREER OPPORTUNITIES

As you can see, the financial world offers a choice of careers. You can work in the finance division of any company or in a financial institution like a bank, insurance, trust, or brokerage company, any one of which has a large number of positions. You can also, as many of the authors' students do, get one of the many jobs available with investment bankers or business consulting firms. Concentrating on the areas of finance and international business would be a good way to find an interesting, global career in finance.

- What does buying on margin mean? How does it work?
- What exactly are mutual funds? How do they benefit small investors?
- What is a stock index? What is its purpose? Can you name a Canadian index? A U.S. index?

PROGRESS CHECK

ETHICAL DILEMMA

Review

It's time now to try to cope with the dilemma discussed at the beginning of the chapter. Our two executives have somewhat different answers to this question. Bédard has this response: "A chief financial officer of a company has an obligation to make public all material information on the viability of the company. I believe that it should be disclosed."

Reilley feels that "this is a hard question because Proto's problems could be overcome with no one being the wiser and with everyone winning. I would suggest to Karina, in a neutral fashion, that, in spite of our friendship and as good business practice, I would expect her to undertake extensive due-diligence before she acted."

Since you have some serious concerns about the financial health of the company, you have probably been thinking about looking for another position in a stronger company where security and the chances of promotion are much better. Since you may be leaving Proto in the near future, why not drop a hint to Karina that she should reconsider her pension fund's plan to buy Proto's ordinary debenture bonds. However you should tell her that you will only share information if she agrees not to ask for explanations or discussions and to keep your suggestion confidential. Remember that if you are licensed by a professional organization, it most likely requires that you do not divulge confidential information that you have obtained through your work.

You have another option and that is to get the message to her via a third party she trusts and who would keep your name out of it, preferably someone Karina does not know is your acquaintance. As far as Proto Corp. is concerned, it may very well sell the bond issue to other buyers so no harm would have been done to the company and you would have protected Karina from recommending a risky investment for her pension fund.

SUMMARY

1. Sound financial management is critical to the well-being of any business.
   - *What are the most common financial problems?*
   The most common financial problems are (1) undercapitalization, (2) poor cash flow, and (3) planning and control weaknesses. Finance is that function in a business responsible for acquiring funds for the firm and managing funds within the firm by, for example, preparing budgets, analyzing cash flow, and planning for the expenditure of funds on various assets.
   - *What do financial managers do?*
   Financial managers plan, budget, control funds, obtain funds, collect funds, audit, manage taxes, and advise top management on financial matters.

1. Explain the role and importance of finance and the responsibilities of financial managers.

2. Financial planning involves short- and long-term forecasting, budgeting, and financial controls.
   - *What are the three budgets of finance?*
   The *operating budget* is the projection of dollar allocations to various costs and expenses, given various revenues. The *capital budget* is the spending plan for capital or fixed assets. The *cash budget* is the detailed cash-flow forecast for the period.

2. Outline the steps in financial planning by explaining how to forecast financial needs, develop budgets, and establish financial controls.

3. Recognize the financial needs that must be met with available funds.

3. During the course of a business's life, its financial needs shift considerably.
   • *What are the areas of financial needs?*
   Businesses have financial needs in four major areas: (1) daily operations, (2) credit to customers, (3) inventory purchases, and (4) major assets purchases.

4. Distinguish between short-term and long-term financing and between debt capital and equity capital.

4. Businesses often have needs for short- and long-term financing and for debt capital and equity capital.
   • *What is the difference between short- and long-term financing?*
   Short-term financing refers to funds that will be repaid in less than one year; long-term financing is money that will be repaid over a longer period.
   • *What is the difference between debt capital and equity capital?*
   Debt capital refers to funds raised by borrowing (going into debt). Equity capital is raised by selling ownership (stock) in the company.

5. Identify and describe several sources of short-term capital.

5. There are many sources for short-term financing, including trade credit, family and friends, commercial banks, government programs, factoring, and commercial paper.
   • *Why should businesses use trade credit?*
   Because it is financing without cost.
   • *What is a line of credit?*
   It is an advance agreement by a bank to loan, up to a specified amount, money to the business whenever the business requires it.
   • *What is the difference between a secured loan and an unsecured loan?*
   An unsecured loan has no collateral backing it. A secured loan is backed by accounts receivable, inventory, or other property of value (called pledging).
   • *Is factoring a form of secured loan?*
   No, factoring means selling accounts receivable for a fee.
   • *What is commercial paper?*
   Commercial paper is a promissory note maturing in 270 days or fewer.

6. Identify and describe several sources of long-term capital.

6. An important function of a finance manager is to obtain long-term capital.
   • *What are the three major sources of long-term capital?*
   Major sources of long-term capital are surplus cash funds, debt capital (including dealer financing), and equity capital. See Figure 19.5 for full details.

7. Compare the advantages and disadvantages of issuing bonds, and identify the classes and features of bonds.

7. Companies can raise capital by debt financing, which involves issuing bonds.
   • *What are the advantages and disadvantages of issuing bonds?*
   The advantages of issuing bonds include (1) management retains control since bondholders cannot vote, (2) interest paid on bonds is tax deductible, and (3) bonds are only a temporary source of finance. The disadvantages of bonds include (1) because bonds are an increased debt, they may adversely affect the market's valuation of the company; (2) interest must be paid on bonds; and (3) the face value must be repaid on the maturity date.
   • *Are there different types of bonds?*
   Yes. There are unsecured (debenture) and secured bonds. Unsecured bonds are not supported by collateral. Secured bonds are backed by tangible assets such as buildings and equipment. They all have different features.

8. Compare the advantages and disadvantages of issuing stock, and outline the differences between common and preferred stock.

8. Companies can also raise capital by equity financing, which involves selling stock.
   • *What are the advantages and disadvantages of issuing stock?*
   The advantages of issuing stock include (1) the stock never has to be repaid since shareholders are owners in the company, (2) there is no legal obligation to pay dividends, and (3) no debt is incurred, so the company is financially stronger. The disadvantages include (1) shareholders are owners of the firm and can affect its management through election of the board of directors, (2) it is

more costly to pay dividends since they are paid after taxes, and (3) managers may be tempted to make shareholders happy in the short term rather than plan for long-term needs.

• *What are the differences between common and preferred stock?*

Holders of common stock have voting rights in the company. Holders of preferred stock have no voting rights. In exchange for the loss of voting privileges, preferred stocks offer a fixed dividend that must be paid in full before holders of common stock receive a dividend. Preferred stock has various other features.

KEY TERMS

blue-chip stocks 618
bond 612
buying on margin 619
capital budget 600
cash budget 600
cash-flow forecast 599
commercial paper 607
common stock 617
convertible bond 614

cumulative preferred stock 616
debt capital 603
dividends 615
equity capital 603
factoring 607
finance 598
line of credit 606
long-term forecast 599
maturity date 612
mutual fund 621

operating budget 600
pledging 606
preferred stock 616
principal 612
secured bonds 614
secured loan 606
short-term forecast 599
stock certificate 615
stock exchanges 612
trade credit 604
unsecured bonds 613

DEVELOPING WORKPLACE SKILLS

1. Obtain annual reports from three major corporations. Study the balance sheets. Which assets are fixed and what is their value? How much have the companies borrowed? (Look under liabilities.) Which one is in the best financial condition? Why?

2. Visit a local bank lending officer. Ask what the current interest rate is and what rate small businesses pay for short- and long-term loans. Ask for blank forms that borrowers use to apply for loans. Share these forms with your class, and explain the types of information they ask for.

3. Use information from the Canadian and Dominion Bond Rating Services to find their evaluation of the bonds of three large Canadian companies. Ask the librarian what similar references are available. Report what you find to the class.

4. The banking crisis of the early 1990s made banks even more reluctant to lend money to small businesses. Assume you are a small-business consultant. Draft a memo to your clients advising them regarding the best sources for financing.

5. Analyze the risks and opportunities of investing today in stocks, bonds, and mutual funds. Assume your great-aunt Hildi just left you $10,000. Since you and your parents already saved enough money to cover your education bills, you decide to invest the money so that you can start your own business after you graduate. How will you invest your money? Why? Name specific investments.

TAKING IT TO THE NET

Purpose:

To research the current lending practices between banks and small businesses.

Exercises:

1. Check out the Web site of the Canadian Bankers Association www.cba.ca to see if you can find information on the trend in lending to small business. Are more companies receiving loans? What was the rate of refusal of loans to small businesses during the last few years? Is the refusal rate rising, declining, or unchanged?

2. Look through the Web site of the Business Development Bank of Canada (BDC) at www.bdc.ca to see how helpful it is. If you were starting a small business, would the information lead you to apply for a loan with the BDC? Is there anything you were looking for that you cannot find? Is there much information for those wanting to start an Internet-based company?

PRACTISING MANAGEMENT DECISIONS

CASE 1

VANCITY ENTERS SMALL-BUSINESS VENTURE CAPITAL MARKET

Vancouver City Savings Credit Union is a well-known credit union that has expanded into various banking activities in the Vancouver area. VanCity decided to add providing venture capital loans to small businesses to its activities by setting up VanCity Capital Corp. in January 1999. President and CEO Dave Mowat, who had 20 years of experience with the Business Development Bank of Canada, says that they are not going after any "elephants" and that they will settle for loans of less than $1 million. There won't be much glamour but neither will there be massive write-offs of bad loans. By October 1999 VanCity had invested in 18 companies and the average loan was $270,000. By the end of 2000, total loans exceeded $6 billion.

VanCity co-operates with other local organizations in helping to finance local companies. It has joined Working Opportunity Fund in a $1.75-million venture capital loan to Soft Tracks Enterprises Inc., "a Vancouver company that makes software for wireless point-of-sale transactions." VanCity has a reputation for stressing ethical investments, and this venture appears to be in line with this policy. Included in the 18 companies are Co-operative Auto Network, a co-op that runs a fleet of cars for its members, and the Victorian Order of Nurses, a well-known nonprofit agency "that will use its loan to expand its contract nursing services."

Mowat plans invest about $25 million over the next three to five years. The company will also consider investments beyond the Vancouver area once the company is well established. VanCity is Canada's largest credit union and "makes a good profit for its

members," but it likes to give back to the community because "the healthier the community, the healthier the service providers in the community."

Decision Questions

1. Do you think that this new venture shows that the market for small business financing is continuing to expand? Or does it indicate that current sources of financing are not doing enough for small business? Look at the chapter carefully and see if its possible that both of these statements are correct.

2. Do you think VanCity's policy of financing co-ops and nonprofit organizations is a good idea? Do you think they are riskier than loans made to new small businesses? Why?

3. Have you seen any reports in the media or on the Net mentioning difficulties that small businesses are having getting financing? Have you seen any referring to companies in your city or region? Do you think there is a need for a VanCity in your area? Explain.

4. VanCity Savings Credit Union has been operating profitably for its members for several years. It has been able to do so despite the limitation of investing in only what it deems are ethical companies. Do you find it encouraging that this is the case? Would you like to work for such a company? Even if the salary structure or promotion possibilities are not as good as elsewhere? Discuss.

Sources: Wendy Stueck, "VanCity Capital Settles on Boring But Profitable," *Globe and Mail, Report on Business,* October 11, 1999. p. B5, reprinted with permission from *The Globe and Mail;* <www.vancity.com> July 2001.

PRACTISING MANAGEMENT DECISIONS

CASE 2

BONDS OR STOCK? THAT IS THE QUESTION

In 1963, Carlos Galendez had dreams but very little money. He spent the past 10 years working as a dishwasher and then a cook for a major restaurant. His dream was to save enough money to start his own Mexican restaurant. In 1965 his dream finally came true. With a small business bank loan, he opened his first Casa de Carlos restaurant. His old family recipes and appealing decor helped the business gain immediate success. Galendez repaid his loan within 14 months and immediately opened a second, then a third, location. By 1975 Casa de Carlos was the largest Mexican restaurant chain in the nation.

In 1976 the company decided to go public. Galendez believed continued growth was beneficial to the company, and he felt offering ownership was the way to bring in loyal investors. Nevertheless, he made certain his family maintained controlling interest in the firm's stock: in its initial public offering, Casa de Carlos offered to sell only 40 percent of the available shares in the company to investors. The Galendez family kept control of 60 percent of the stock.

As the public's craving for Mexican food grew, so did the fortunes of Casa de Carlos Inc. Heading into the 1980s, the company enjoyed the position of being light on debt and heavy on cash. But in 1983, the firm's debt position changed when it bought out Captain Al's Seafood Restaurants. Three years later, it expanded into full-service wholesale distribution of seafood products with the purchase of Mariner Wholesalers. The firm's debt increased, but the price of its stock was up and demand at all three operations was booming.

In 1995 Galendez died. His oldest child, Maria, was selected to take control as chief executive officer. Maria had learned the business from her father. He taught her to keep an eye out for opportunities that seemed fiscally responsible. Unfortunately, in 1999 the fortunes of the firm began to shift. Two major competitors were taking market share from Casa de Carlos, and the seafood venture began to flounder. The recession in 2001 didn't help either. Consumers spent less, causing some severe cash problems. Maria Galendez had to decide how to get the funds the firm needed for improvements and other expenses. Banks wouldn't extend the firm's credit line. She considered a bond or stock offering to raise capital.

Decision Questions

1. What advantages and disadvantages of offering bonds to investors should Maria consider?
2. What would be the advantages and disadvantages to the company of offering new stock to investors?
3. Are any other options available to Maria Galendez?
4. If you were Maria, what choice would you make? Why?

CBC   VIDEO CASE   www.cbc.ca

Part 2
CREDIT CRUNCH

This chapter stresses the importance of financing when starting and operating a business. You learn that while this applies to all businesses, large and small, they have different ways of solving their financing problems. Larger companies are set up as public companies, allowing them to sell shares and bonds to the public. We can invest in these companies by buying their shares, or we can lend them money by buying their bonds. Of course, they also borrow from banks, which are in the business of lending money, usually for shorter terms.

Because they are not usually public corporations, small businesses cannot issue shares or bonds to the public. As discussed in Chapter 7, the most common source of financing for them are the commercial banks, although there are other sources as well. Most loans made by banks have strict conditions that must be met for the duration of the loan. In addition, the banks usually make these *call* loans, meaning the lender bank can demand payment in full whenever it wishes. Banks justify this policy because, in effect, they are using depositors' money to make these loans so they have to be prudent and cautious to protect their depositors.

In this video we see three existing businesses suddenly have their banks call the loans—the entrepreneurs are naturally very upset. They have met all payments on their loans and their businesses are not in difficulty, so the bank demand comes as a big shock. The bank justified calling in the loans because of the declining economy and their concern that the industries these businesses are in would be hard-hit.

Discussion Questions

1. Do you agree that, because the banks are in effect lending other people's money, they must be extremely cautious? Should this include the right to do what they did in this video? Explain your opinion.

2. How can small businesses be assured of continued financing from their banks, especially when their businesses are doing well and they have met all their payments when due? Should there be any legal or other restriction preventing banks from pulling financing? What would you suggest? Wouldn't this be a major interference with commercial activity?

3. Suppose you started a business and had enough financing to carry on at the level of sales you were projecting. However, your business does very well and you find you need to go to your bank to finance the larger inventories and more equipment you will need, as well as to carry the larger accounts receivable you will have. Would your concern with bank loans suddenly being called lead you to refuse to expand your business and stay small? If all small businesses did that how would the economy grow and new jobs be created?

Source: *Venture*, show number 811, "Credit Crunch," January 20, 2002, running time 7:06.

CHAPTER ENDNOTES

Prologue

1. Joshua Mills, "Computer Science and Engineering Majors Earn Top Dollars," *University Wire*, January 9, 2001; "The Old College Try," *The Wall Street Journal*, March 4, 1999, p. A14; and Sergio Bustos, "Hispanics in America: Education and the Work Force," *Gannett News Service*, December 20, 2000.

2. Sally Johnston, "Casualties of Relaxed Dressing/Wardrobe Can Spell Success or Failure," *Edmonton Sun*, February 1, 2000 and Patricia Kitchen, "The Proper Attire Will Suit You Well," *Newsday*, January 6, 2001.

3. Marjorie Brody, "Wardrobe Wisdom: Dress for Success," Special to CNBC.com, May 25, 2000 and Lesley Kennedy, "Putting 'Casual' in Black and White Terms," *Denver Rocky Mountain News*, January 7, 2001.

4. Zatni Arbi, "Some Small Things to Remember about E-Mail," *Jakarta Post*, May 8, 2000 and Karla Dougherty, *The Rules to be Cool: Etiquette and Netiquette* (Berkeley Heights, New Jersey: Enslow Publishers, 2001).

5. "Broadband Bulletin," *Cablefax Daily*, January 3, 2001; "Internet Fuels Demand for Faster Access," *Nation*, January 3, 2001; and Ephraim Schwartz, "Broadband Wireless is Getting Closer," *InfoWorld*, January 8, 2001.

6. Margaret Littman, "Good Economy, Bad Candidates," *Marketing News*, April 10, 2000, pp. 12–13; "Planning Helps Students Get Good Recommendations," *The Dallas Morning News*, January 4, 2001, p. 6C; and Maria Mallory, "In Hiring Personality Still Counts," *The Atlanta Journal and Constitution*, January 7, 2001, p. R1.

7. Bill Breen, "Full House," *Fast Company*, January 1, 2001; Jerry Useem, "For Sale Online: You," *Fortune*, July 5, 1999, pp. 67–78; and Bob Edwards, "War Over Classified Ads," *Morning Edition*, January 1, 2001.

Chapter 1

1. "From World Trade to World Investment," *The Wall Street Journal*, May 26, 1987.

2. Robert Reich, "Who Is Us?" *Harvard Business Review*, January–February 1990, p. 53.

3. Statistics Canada, CANSIM Matrix 3685, Series D399443-8; George Dufour, Chief, Trade Statistics Canada, <www.bcstats.gov.bc.ca>.

4. Sources for the entire section are Wendy Dobson, "Canada Missing Business Opportunities in East Asia," *Financial Post*, September 23, 1995, p. 25; *Globe and Mail* series, "The Changing West," January 1996.

5. Timothy Pritchard, "Chrysler Changes Tone to Woo Customers," *Globe and Mail, Report on Business,* July 1, 1992, p. B1.

6. Interview with Walter McCall, February 20, 1996.

7. Greg Keenan, "$500-million Overhaul Slated for Bramalea Plant," *Globe and Mail, ROB,* February 16, 1996, p. B1; interview with Walter McCall, November 17, 1999.

8. Compiled from a variety of sources including reports and Internet sites of Industry Canada, Business Development Bank of Canada, Statistics Canada, Export Development Corp., Royal Bank, and articles in *Profit* and *Canadian Business* magazines, *Globe and Mail, ROB,* and the *Montreal Gazette.*

9. Bill Taylor, "The Next Millennium," *Montreal Gazette,* January 10, 1966, p. C1.

10. Interview with Judith Aston, February 15, 1996.

11. Shirley Won, "Homing in on New Careers," *Globe and Mail, ROB,* April 25, 1992, p. B1.

12. Cleta Moyer, "Sending Your Employees Home," *Profit,* October–November 1995, p. 9.

13. Some of the data in this section are from *Manufacturing Our Future,* Canadian Manufacturers Association (CMA), 1995, and four articles by Susan Noakes in the *Financial Post,* December 17–21, 1990.

14. Bruce Little, "Manufacturing Keeps Economy on Growth Target," *Globe and Mail, ROB,* June 1, 1999, C1. Michael Valpy, "Fate of Manufacturing, a Make-or-Break Crisis," *Globe and Mail,* May 8,

1989, p. A8; Madeleine Drohan, "Service Becoming Canada's New Backbone," *Globe and Mail, ROB,* April 16, 1990, p. B1; *Manufacturing Our Future,* CMA.

15. Nuala Beck, *Shifting Gears: Thriving in the New Economy* (Toronto: Harper & Collins, 1992), as reported by Crawford Kilian, *The Province* (Vancouver), reprinted in the *Montreal Gazette,* December 19, 1992, p. B6.

16. All the data in this section come from Ronald Logan, "Immigration During the 1980s," and Gordon Priest, "The Demographic Future," *Canadian Social Trends,* Spring 1991, Statistics Canada, Cat. No. 11-008E. Also Statistics Canada, 1996 data, the Internet.

17. David Schindler, interviewed on "Quirks and Quarks," CBC, February 24, 1996.

18. Daily Archives, Statistics Canada, <www.statcan.ca>, February 29, 1996.

19. *Montreal Gazette,* March 2, 1996, pp. B4–5; "Cross-Country Checkup," CBC, March 3, 1996.

20. Statistics Canada, <www.statcan.ca>, May 1999.

21. Daily Archives, Statistics Canada, <www.statcan.ca>, May 1999.

22. Interview with Paul Swinwood, "Daybreak," CBM Montreal, CBC, February 23, 1996; interview with Paul Swinwood, April 16, 1999.

23. *Manufacturing Our Future,* CMA.

24. John Holusha, "First College, then the Mill," *New York Times,* as reported in *Globe and Mail, ROB,* August 29, 1995, p. B10.

Chapter 2

1. *Time,* February 15, 1999, 36.

2. "Lessons from the Brink," *Business Week,* September 21, 1998, p. 146.

3. Daily Archives, Statistics Canada, <www.statcan.ca>, May 1999.

4. Bruce Little, "Manufacturing Keeps Economy on Growth Track," *Globe and Mail, ROB,* June 1, 1999, B1.

5. Eric Beauchesne, "OECD Admits Error," *Montreal Gazette*, May 21, 1999, C1.

6. Compiled from various reports: Bank of Canada, Statistics Canada, and 1999 federal budget documents.

7. Sandra Cordon, "Strong Growth Forecast," *Montreal Gazette*, May 20, 1999, A1; "Sheltered from the Global Storm," *Scotia Plus*, Spring/Summer 1999, p. 5.

Chapter 3

1. Daily Archives, Statistics Canada, <www.statcan.ca>, May 1999.

2. Ibid.

3. Madelaine Drohan, *Globe and Mail, ROB,* March 28, 1996, p. B3.

4. "A Musical Ride to the Cash Register," *Maclean's,* March 11, 1996, p. 10.

5. "The WTO's barriers threaten its survival," *Globe and Mail,* November 8, 2001, p. A22.

6. "Free Trade Closer for Canada and Chile," *Financial Post,* March 23, 1996, p. 10.

7. Bartlett & Ghoshall, *Transnational Management* (Irwin, 1995), p. 176–182.

8. Donald N. Thompson, "Porter on Canadian Competitiveness," *Business Quarterly,* Winter 1992, p. 55.

9. This section is based on three sources: Alan Freeman, "Manufacturing Exports on a Roll," *Globe and Mail,* April 25, 1992, p. G1; Harvey Enchin, "Competitiveness Not New to Canadians," *Globe and Mail, ROB,* May 7, 1992, p. B1; *Manufacturing Our Future,* 1995.

10. Eric Beauchesne, "OECD Admits Error," *Montreal Gazette,* May 21, 1999, C1.

Chapter 4

1. CBC News, December 4, 1998.

2. Various titles of *Globe and Mail, ROB,* December 1995 and January and February 1996.

3. Joe Bryan, "Delegates Will Week Way to Untangle Barriers to Interprovincial Trade," *Montreal Gazette,* February 1, 1992, p. B1.

4. "Ottawa Mulls $150 Million Aid for Aerospace Industry," *Financial Post,* January 25, 1996, p. 4.

5. Oliver Bertin, "Spar's Radarstat Succeeds in Sending Clear Image," *Globe and Mail, ROB,* December 15, 1995, p. B9.

6. Barrie McKenna, "$200-Million Aerospace Project Threatened," *Globe and Mail, ROB,* January 19, 1996, p. B1.

7. Anne-Marie Tobin, "Algoma Steel Rescued by Employee Takeover," *Montreal Gazette,* February 29, 1992, p. D3.

8. CBC News, January 27, 1999.

9. John Partridge, "Bank Machine Revolution Near," *Globe and Mail, ROB,* September 11, 1995, p. B1.

10. Barrie McKenna, "Nielsen Data Monopoly Cancelled," *Globe and Mail, ROB,* August 31, 1995, p. B1.

11. Rod Macdonell, "Proposed Takeover of Maple Leaf Mills Raises Fears of Concentration of Flour Power," *Montreal Gazette,* April 6, 1996, p. D1.

12. Lawrence Surtees, "CRTC Orders Cut in Overseas Phone Rates," *Globe and Mail, ROB,* February 3, 1996, p. B1.

13. Annual Reports, National Research Council; other NRC publications, 1991–1998.

14. "U.S. Agricultural Policy Facing Radical Changes," *Globe and Mail, ROB,* September 11, 1995, p. B10.

15. Interview with agricultural economist Dr. Garth Coffin, Associate Dean, MacDonald College, McGill University, April 6, 1996, and October 10, 1998.

16. For example, see *Globe and Mail, ROB,* September 21, 1995, p. B14 and February 13, 1996, p. B9.

17. *Montreal Gazette,* October 25, 1998, D7.

18. John Godfrey, "Big League Trade," *Report on the Nation, Financial Post,* Winter 1989, p. 26.

19. Headlines such as "Slash-and-Burn Equals Civil Strife," "Rethinking Employment," "Budget Cutters Thinking Twice," and "Watching Government Shrink," can be found throughout many media in January, February, and March 1996; these articles express varying degrees of concern about or disagreement with current policies. Important radio and TV business programs in Canada and the United States expressed similar opinions.

20. "Politics This Week," *The Economist,* April 6, 1996, p. 4.

21. *Montreal Gazette,* October 25, 1998, D7.

22. CBC News, June 18, 1999.

23. *Civilization,* June/July 1999, pp. 86 and 87.

Chapter 5

1. Madelaine Drohan, "Capitalism Must Develop a Heart, Executives Told," *Globe and Mail, ROB,* February 2, 1996, p. B7.

2. John Neinzel, "Ethics Sell, Consumers Say," *Globe and Mail, ROB,* December 1, 1995, p. B15.

3. Douglas Goold, "Sharp Words on Corporate Ethics," *Globe and Mail, ROB,* December 1, 1995, p. B15.

4. Shirley Won, "Clean Environment Turns in Polished Performance," *Globe and Mail, ROB,* February 8, 1996, p. B18.

5. Linda Hossie, "UN Stymied on Stopping Weapons Sales," *Globe and Mail, ROB,* May 29, 1993, p. A7.

6. "Canada Praised for Land-Mine Stand but Efforts at Moratorium Fall Short," *Montreal Gazette,* January 20, 1996, p. H10; "60 Minutes," CBS, August 4, 1996; Hossie, "UN Stymied on Stopping Weapons Sales."

7. Interview on CBC Radio, CBM Montreal, with Paul Hannon December 2, 1998;<www.minesactioncanada.com/home/country.cfm?ID=2&lang=e>, accessed December 3, 2001.

8. Dean Jobb, "A Legal Minefield," *Elm Street,* November 1998, p. 71.

9. *Globe and Mail,* March 7, 1992, p. A3.

10. *Financial Times,* March 16, 1992, p. 2.

11. Ibid.

12. "Gas-Cartel Fines Should be a Lesson to Others," *Financial Times,* September 23, 1991, p. 34.

13. *Canadian Business.*

14. Michael Lane, "Improving American Business Ethics in Three Steps," *CPA Journal,* February 1, 1991; Susan Sonnesyn, "A Question of Ethics," *Training and Development Journal,* March 1, 1991.

15. John Stackhouse, "Canadian on Mission to Save the Planet," *Globe and Mail,* May 2, 1992, p. A1.

16. Keith Bradsher, "Trade Official Assails Europe over Ecology," *New York Times,* October 31, 1991, p. D2.

17. "Kyoto Planners Pessimistic about Pact," *Globe and Mail,* June 17, 1999, A11.

18. "Trade and the Environment," *New York Times,* March 11, 1992, p. D1.

19. *Montreal Gazette,* September 21, 1991, p. K6.

21. Interview with David Church, October 29, 1998; Canadian Pulp and Paper Association charts and publications, 1998; *Globe and Mail, ROB,* May 4, 1992, B2.

22. Report prepared by Kathy Abusow, Abusow International Ltd., 1997.

22. "Morningside," CBC, March 8, 1992.

23. Claire Bernstein, "Heavy Legal Artillery Now Turned against Environment Offenders," *Toronto Star*, December 16, 1991, p. B3.

24. Douglas Goold, "Laidlaw Is a 'Green Jungle' Risk," *Globe and Mail*, ROB, March 14, 1992, p. B25.

25. Interview with A. Delisle, Radio Canada's chief heating engineer, June 8, 1993.

26. Kathy Sawyer, "Satellite Findings Show Harmful Radiation Has Increased while Ozone Layer Thinned," *Washington Post*, as reported in *Montreal Gazette*, August 2, 1996, p. B1.

27. *Globe and Mail*, ROB, March 16, 1992, p. B18.

28. Robert Williamson, "B.C. Passes Regulations for Less Polluting Vehicles," *Globe and Mail*, ROB, December 8, 1995, p. B4.

29. Jim Dawson, "A Gem of an Idea," *Montreal Gazette*, March 7, 1992, p. J8.

30. David Suzuki, "Only in This Century Has Growth Become Part of Life," *Montreal Gazette*, July 20, 1991, p. J8.

31. "Living on Borrowed Time," *Montreal Gazette*, May 9, 1992, p. K6.

32. Charles Hampden-Turner, "The Boundaries of Business: The Cross-Cultural Quagmire," *Harvard Business Review*, September–October 1991, p. 94.

33. John Stackhouse, "Toronto Engineering Firm Sees Profit in Bombay Sewage," *Globe and Mail*, ROB, January 4, 1996, p. B9.

34. Newsletter, David Suzuki Foundation, June 7, 1999.

35. Oliver Bertin, "Spar to Build Canadarm for Toxic, Nuclear Waste Cleanup," *Globe and Mail*, ROB, December 5, 1995, p. B5.

36. "Zenon Wins Pact with Egypt," *Globe and Mail*, ROB, December 7, 1995, p. B12.

37. Kim Honey, "These Little Piggies Are a Scientific Marvel," *Globe and Mail*, June 23, 1999, p. A1.

38. Annual Report, 1998–1999, Institute for Sustainable Development.

39. *Sustainable Consumption*, Brochure UNEP, Division of United Nations, 1999.

40. CBC News Report, CBM Radio Montreal, June 13, 1999.

41. Paul Hawken, "A Declaration of Sustainability," *Utne Reader*, September/October 1993, 54–61.

Chapter 6

1. D. Gray and N. Friend, *So You Want To Buy a Franchise*, (Toronto: McGraw-Hill Ryerson, 1998), <www.francom.com/franchise_facts.htm>. Interview with Sue McSherry, Canadian Franchisors' Association, May 2, 1996.

2. Annual Report, 1998, Cara Ltd.; interview with Ms. Jennifer Quinn, June 30, 1999.

3. Meg Whitmore, "Franchising Options for Opportunity," *Forbes*, August 24, 1987, pp. 83–87.

4. Allan Freeman, "Trade Surplus Biggest Since 1991," *Globe and Mail*, ROB, March 19, 1999, p. B9.

Chapter 7

1. Statistics Canada, CANSIM, Matrix 3451, Series D986059, 986061, May 1999.

2. *Starting a New Business in Canada: A Guide for New Canadians*, Federal Business Development Bank, 1990.

3. *Business Report*, Royal Bank, Fall 1995; *Financing a Small Business: A Guide for Women Entrepreneurs*, Federal Business Development Bank, 1992; Statistics Canada, <www.statcan.com>, August 1995 and May 1999.

4. Statistics Canada, ibid.

5. Douglas R. Sease, "Entrepreneurship 101," *The Wall Street Journal*, May 15, 1987, pp. D32–35.

6. "Royal Bank, Ottawa, Offering Shortcut for Small Business," *Globe and Mail*, ROB, March 3, 1996, p. B2.

7. *Globe and Mail*, <www.globeandmail.com>, accessed April 5, 1996.

8. "B of M Offers Small-Business Incentive," *Globe and Mail*, ROB, January 13, 1996, p. B5.

9. *Small Business*, October 1990, p. 9.

10. Web site of National Association of Home-Based Businesses (NAHBB), <usahomebusiness.com>, accessed July 2, 1999.

11. Diane Luckow, "The Hottest Home-Based Businesses," *Globe and Mail*, ROB, January 6, 1996, p. B19.

12. Annual Report, 2000, Export Development Corp. (now Export Development Canada).

Chapter 8

1. Michael H. Jordan, "The Role of Top Management," *Harvard Business Review*, January–February 1995, pp. 142–144.

2. Edward Iwata, "Despite the Hype, B2B Marketplaces Struggle," *USA Today*, May 10, 2000, pp. 1–2.

3. Nicholas G. Carr, "On the Edge," *Harvard Business Review*, May–June 2000, pp. 118–25.

4. "Molson Breweries Decentralizes," *Globe and Mail*, ROB, December 20, 1995, p. B13.

5. Claire Ansberry, "Let's Build an Online Supply Network!" *The Wall Street Journal*, April 17, 2000, pp. B1, B10.

6. John A. Byrne, "Borderless Management," *Business Week*, May 23, 1994, pp. 24–26.

7. Kevin Werbach, "Syndication," *Harvard Business Review*, May–June 2000, pp. 85–93.

8. *Montreal Gazette*, February 19, 1991, p. D3.

9. Tyler Hamilton, "Nortel cuts 10,000 jobs, projects record losses." *The Toronto Star*, June 16 2001, pp. A1, A34.

10. David K. Foot and Daniel Stoffman, *Boom Bust & Echo 2000* (Toronto: Macfarlane Walter & Ross, 1998).

11. Jane Southworth, "Beware of looming manager shortage," *Globe and Mail*, June 25, 2001, p. M1.

12. Ibid.

13. <http://www.spst.edu/Leadership/winter94.htm>.

14. Michael Elliot, "Take Me to Your Leader," *Newsweek*, April 25, 1994, p.6.

15. Suzy Wetlaufer, "Organizing for Empowerment: An Interview with AES's Roger Sant and Dennis Bakke," *Harvard Business Review*, January–February 1999, pp. 111–23.

16. Alan M. Webber, "Why Can't We Get Anything Done?" *Fast Company*, June 2000, pp. 168–80.

17. Charles Fishman, "Team-Work," *Fast Company*, April 2000, pp. 156–61.

18. Association for Quality and Participation, "Ask the Consultant," October 1997. Accessed at <http://www.jhpin.com/HJH%20articles/aqp.htm>, June 21, 2001.

19. Ibid.

20. Joy Riggs, "Empowering Workers by Setting Goals," *Nation's Business*, January 1995, p. 6.

21. "Message to Managers: Get Out of Your Offices," *Montreal Gazette*, February 19, 1991, p. D3.

22. <http://www.spst.edu/Leadership/winter94.htm>

23. Walter Kiechell III, "A Manager's Career in the New Economy," *Fortune*, April 4, 1994, pp. 68–72.

24. Paul C. Nutt. "Surprising But True: Half the Decisions in Organizations Fail." *The Academy of Management Executive*, November 1999, pp. 75–90.

25. Sunita Wadekar Bhargava and Fred F. Jespersen, "Portrait of a CEO," *Business Week*, October 11, 1993, pp. 64–65.

Chapter 9

1. Robert D. Hof, "Remember the Tortoise," *Business Week E.BIZ*, January 22, 2001, p. 66.

2. J. Stewart Black and Lyman W. Porter, *Management: Meeting New Challenges* (Upper Saddle River, NJ: Prentice-Hall, 2000), pp. 44–45.

3. "HP and Compaq: A Compelling Combination," n.d. Palo Alto: Hewlett-Packard Company. Retrieved November 1, 2001, <www.hp.com/hpinfo/newsroom/hp-compaq/index.htm>.

4. Bruce Little, "How to Make a Small Smart Factory," *Globe and Mail, ROB*, February 2, 1993, p. B24.

5. Major Rick Charlebois, "A Trial in Decentralized Decision-Making," *CMA Magazine*, June 1992, p. 8.

6. Cathryn Motherwell, "From the Oilfield to the Boardroom," *Globe and Mail*, classroom edition, December 1992, p. 14.

7. Henry Mintzberg and James Brian Quinn. *The Strategy Process: Concepts and Contexts* (New Jersey: Prentice-Hall, Inc., 1992).

8. Ibid.

9. C.K. Prahalad and Gary Hamel. "The Core Competence of the Corporation." *Harvard Business Review* 90, no. 3, May–June 1990, pp. 79–91.

10. Jim Clemmer, "How to Make Empowerment Work," *Globe and Mail*, classroom edition, April 1993, p. 17.

11. Chris Nolan, "Attention KMART Shoppers," *Smart Business*, February 2001, pp. 113–119.

12. Scott Kirsner, "Faster Company," *Fast Company*, May 2000, pp. 163–72.

13. Bruce Little, "How to Make a Small Smart Factory," *Globe and Mail, ROB*, February 2, 1993, p. B24.

14. Cheryl D. Krivda, "E-Supply Chain," a special advertising section in *Fortune*, June 26, 2000, pp. 341ff.

15. Suzy Girard, "Extranet: If You Build One, Will They Come?" *Success*, December/January 2001, p. 42.

16. D.B. Scott, "Lean Machine," *Globe and Mail, ROB*, November 1992, p. 90.

17. Cathryn Motherwell, "From the Oilfield to the Boardroom," *Globe and Mail*, classroom edition, December 1992, p. 14.

18. Jeffrey E. Christian, "Leading in a Team-Based Culture," *Beyond Computing*, May 2000, p. 10.

19. Almar Latour, "Ericsson Plan to Outsource Handsets," *The Wall Street Journal*, January 29, 2001, p. B8.

20. Erika Morphy, "Best Practices Made Perfect," *Global Business*, May 2000, pp. 60–63.

21. Canadian Industry Statistics (CIS), Classic 1, 2, and 3: SIC-E 1052, 1131, 2713, 3361, 3511, 3994; Bob Besaari, Alliance of Manufacturers and Exporters Canada, <besaari@the-alliance.com>.

22. Gary McWilliams, "Motorola Joins Technology-Outsourcing Wave," *The Wall Street Journal*, June 1, 2000, p. B6. Sheridan Prasso, "Boeing Jettisons a Plant," *Business Week*, February 5, 2001, p. 14.

23. Steven McShane, *Canadian Organizational Behaviour*, 4th ed. (Toronto: McGraw-Hill Ryerson, 2001), p. 510. Citing R. Zemke, "Storytelling: Back to a Basic," *Training*, 27 (March 1990), pp. 44–50; A.L. Wilkins, "Organizational Stories as Symbols Which Control the Organization," in L.R. Pondy, P.J. Frost, G. Morgan, and T.C. Dandridge (eds.), *Organizational Symbolism* (Greenwich, CT: JAI Press, 1984), pp. 81–92; J. Martin and M.E. Powers, "Truth or Corporate Propaganda: The Value of a Good War Story," in Pondy et al. (eds), *Organizational Symbolism*, pp. 93–107.

24. Ibid. Citing J. Martin et al., "The Uniqueness Paradox in Organizational Stories," *Administrative Science Quarterly*, 28 (1983), pp. 438–53.

25. Ibid.

26. Ibid. Citing J.M. Beyer and H.M. Trice, "How an Organization's Rites Reveal Its Culture," *Organizational Dynamics*, 15(4)(1987), pp. 5–24; L. Smirchich, "Organizations as Shared Meanings," in Pondy et al. (eds), *Organizational Symbolism*, pp. 55–65.

27. Henry Mintzberg and James Brian Quinn. *The Strategy Process: Concepts and Contexts*. New Jersey: Prentice-Hall, Inc., 1992.

28. McShane, p. 513. Citing J. Kotter, "Cultures and Coalitions," *Executive Excellence*, 15 (March 1998), pp. 14–15; Kotter and Heskett, *Corporate Culture and Performance*.

29. Ibid. Citing the features of adaptive cultures described in W.F. Joyce, *MegaChange: How Today's Leading Companies Have Transformed Their Workforces* (New York: Free Press, 1999), pp. 44–47.

Chapter 10

1. World Economic Forum Web site: <weforum.org/Publications/GCR/99rankings.asp>, accessed July 31, 1999.

2. David Crane, "Canada's competitiveness rating falls again," *Toronto Star*, September 7, 2000, p. D1.

3. Statistics Canada, "Employment in the finance and other service industries," <http://www.statcan.ca/english/Pgdb/Economy/Finance/fin11.htm>, accessed July 16, 2001; Statistics Canada, "Employment (manufacturing and construction),"<http://www.statcan.ca/english/Pgdb/Economy/Manufacturing/manuf06.htm>, accessed July 16, 2001.

4. Howard Rudnitsky, "Changing the Corporate DNA," *Forbes*, July 17, 2000, pp. 38–40.

5. Sheridan Prasso, "Slimming Down," *Business Week*, February 5, 2001, p. 14.

6. Mary Ellen Mark, "The New Fabric of Success," *Fast Company*, June 2000, pp. 252–70.

7. Kevin Voigt, "For Extreme Telecommuters, Remote Work Means Really Remote," *The Wall Street Journal*, January 31, 2001, pp. B1 & B7.

8. William M. Bulkeley, "Clicks and Mortar," *The Wall Street Journal*, July 17, 2000, p. R4.

9. David Dorsey, "Change Factory," *Fast Company*, June 2000, pp. 209–24.

10. Scott Thurm, "Is a Call That Will Bolster Flextronics," *The Wall Street Journal*, January 29, 2001, p. B8.

11. Steven Kaplan and Mohanbir Sawhney, "E-Hubs: The New B2B Marketplaces," *Harvard Business Review*, May–June 2000, pp. 97–103.

12. Ahmad Diba, "The B2B Boom: What's What," *Fortune*, May 15, 2000, pp. 142–43.

13. Scott Madison Paton, "Transitioning to ISO 9001:2000," *Quality Digest*, March 2001, p. 4.

14. Jeanne Ketola and Kathy Roberts, "Product Realization," *Quality Digest*, May 2000, pp. 39–43.

15. Judith Evans, "Executive with a First-Class Vision," *Washington Business*, August 23, 1999, pp. 13–14; and Salina Khan, "Hotels Target Generation X," *USA Today*, February 10, 2000, pp. B1, B2.

16. Doug Tsuruoka, "Marriott, Hyatt Plan Own E-Room Service," *Investor's Business Daily*, May 9, 2000, p. A8.

17. J. Bradford Delong, "Estimating Growth Is a True Odyssey," *Fortune*, June 26, 2000, pp. 62–64.

18. Curt Suplee, "Scientists Claim to Pinpoint Cerebral Source of Human IQ," *The Washington Post*, July 21, 2000, pp. A14, A15.

19. Kathleen Seiders, Leonard Berry and Larry G. Gresham, "Attention, Retailers! Is Your Convenience Strategy?" *Sloan Management Review*, Spring 2000, pp. 79–89.

20. "Air-Traveler Abuse," *The Washington Post*, July 25, 2000, p. A22.

21. Geoffrey Colvin, "Capitalist Century: Managing in the Info Era," *Fortune*, March 6, 2000.

22. John A. Byrne, "The 21st Century Corporation: Back to the Future: Visionary vs. Visionary," *Business Week*, August 28, 2000, p. 210.

23. Barbara McNurlin, "Will Users of ERP Stay Satisfied?," *MIT Sloan Management Review*, Winter 2001, p. 13.

24. Patricia Lush, "Just-in-Time Pays Off for the Auto Sector," *Globe and Mail*, ROB, February 21, 1990, pp. B1 and B4.

25. Isabel Teotonio, "Keep borders open for trade, industry warns," *The Toronto Star*, October 27, 2001, p. A13.

26. Jerry Bowles, "How Digital Marketplaces Are Shaping the Future of B2B Commerce," *Forbes*, July 24, 2000, pp. 215ff.

27. Howard Rudnitsky, "Changing the Corporate DNA," *Forbes*, July 17, 2000, pp. 38–40.

28. "Chrysler hails record retooling," *Toronto Star*, August 26, 2000.

29. Eric N. Berkowitz, et al., *Marketing*, 4th Canadian ed. (New York: McGraw-Hill Limited, 2000), 258.

30. Greg Keenan, "Magna sees $1-billion boost in BMW contract," *Globe and Mail*, November 1, 2001, p. B1.

31. "Celestica Investor Relations," n.d., Toronto: Celestica Incorporated. <www.celestica.com/cfm/investor/index.cfm?Act=Investor>, November 1, 2001.

32. "Grocery chain in drive to improve," *National Post*, October 31, 2001, p. JV2.

33. "New thinking puts CN on track," *National Post*, October 31, 2001, p. JV3.

34. "The juggling act behind the Cirque," *National Post*, October 31, 2001, p. JV4.

35. "Increased security versus flow of goods and sevices," *National Post*, October 31, 2001, p. JV1.

36. "The Big Payoff from Computers," *Fortune*, March 7, 1994, p. 28.

Chapter 11

1. Reg Gale, "There's a Community Spirit on the Net," *Newsday*, February 6, 2001.

2. James Coates, "Classroom in a Box," *Chicago Tribune*, January 5, 1998, section 4, p. 1.

3. Don Tapscott, "Minds over Matter," *Business 2.0*, March 2000; and Rache Boddy, "Farmers Slow on the IT Uptake," *Waikato Times*, January 27, 2001, p. 18.

4. Craig K. Dillon, "Be Nimble," *CIO*, April 15, 2000, p. 190; and Allan E. Alter, "Knowledge Management's 'Theory–Doing Gap,'" *Computerworld*, April 10, 2000, p. 33.

5. John Storck and Patricia A. Hill, "Knowledge Diffusion through 'Strategic Communities,'" *Sloan Management Review*, Winter 2000, pp. 63–74; and Mike Heck, "K-Station Portal Brings New Life to Business Information," *Info World*, February 5, 2001.

6. Steve Mott, "Winning One Customer at a Time," *Business 2.0*, March 2000; and Ann Orubeondo and Mario Apicella, *InfoWorld TestCenter*, February 5, 2001.

7. Simon Tuck, "Canada No. 1 in federal e-service," *Globe and Mail*, April 4, 2001, p. B7.

8. Richard Mackie and Wallace Immen, "Canada third in world for use of Net," *Globe and Mail*, July 2, 2001, p. A1.

9. Ann Harrison, "Corporate Security Begins at Home," *Computerworld*, March 6, 2000, p. 14; and Bill Husted, "Firewalls Still Your Best Bet For Security," *The Palm Beach Post*, February 11, 2001.

10. Mark Hall, "Intranet Developers Say Systems, Security Top Priorities," *Computerworld*, March 6, 2000, p. 28; and Ian Howell, "Doing Projects Online Boosts Your Bottom Line," *Electrical Construction and Maintenance*, January 1, 2001.

11. Frank J. Derfler Jr., "Virtual Private Networks," *PC Magazine*, January 4, 2000, pp. 146–48; and Eric Greenberg, "VPNs and Windows 2000," *PC Magazine*, January 18, 2000, p. 139; Frank J. Derfler Jr. and Cary Gunnerson, "Ready, Set, Retool," *PC Magazine*, March 7, 2000, pp. 142–52; Steve Ulfelder, "Virtual Private Networks Made Easy," *Computerworld*, March 6, 2000, p. 80; Frank Derfler Jr., "Internet Infrastructure," *PC Magazine*, February 22, 2000, p. 124; and Jim Barthold, "Networking the Internet," *Telephony*, February 5, 2001.

12. Dana James, "Broadband Horizons," *Marketing News*, March 13, 2000, pp. 1, 9; Dave Johnson, "The Fastest Towns in America," *Home Office Computing*, April 2000, pp. 46–50; Alan Cohen, "High-Speed Browsing," *PC Magazine*, January 18, 2000, p. 32; David A. Harvey, "Broadband—Anywhere and Everywhere," *Home Office Computing*, January 2000, p. 22; David Haskin, "The Need for Speed," *Home Office Computing*, January 2000, p. 40; and "Broadband Bulletin," *Cablefax Daily*, January 3, 2001, and Jennifer Jones, "Cable Cuts Out a Slice of the Broadband Pie," *Info World*, January 29, 2001.

13. Yael Li-Ron, "This Will Change Everything," *Newsweek*, September 18, 2000, and Bob Low, "Twelve Months That Shook Cyberspace," *Daily Record*, January 6, 2001, pp. 38–39.

14. Josh Bozarth, "Companies Showcase Internet 2 Technologies at Oklahoma State U," *University Wire*, March 8, 2000.

15. Sue Zeidler, "Napster Changes Tune to Overcome Network Overload," *Reuters Business Report*, March 23, 2000, and Alison Shapiro, "Life in the Fast Lane," *Jerusalem Post*, February 9, 2001, p. 4.

16. Thomas E. Weber, "Instant Messages Aren't Just for Chat," *The Wall Street Journal Interactive Edition*, April 11, 2000, and Chad Hammond, "The Intelligent Enterprise," *Info World*, February 5, 2001.

17. Jesse Berst, "B2B? That's Like, So Last Month," *ZDNet AnchorDesk*, April 13, 2000, and Michael Vizard, "Top Ten Technology Trends for 2001," *Info World*, January 8, 2001.

18. Jane Linder and Drew Phelps, "Call to Act," *CIO*, April 1, 2000, pp. 166–74; Lester C. Thurow, "The Wealth of Knowledge," *CIO*, January 1, 2000, pp. 81–86; and Michelle Bearden, "Casting the Net," *The Tampa Tribune*, January 6, 2001, p. 4.

19. *Technology Forecast 2000* (Menlo Park: PricewaterhouseCoopers Technology Centre, 2000), p. 487.

20. Stephen E. Arnold and Erik S. Arnold, "Push Technology—Driving Traditional Online into a Corner,"

<http://www.onlineinc.com/database/AugDB97/arnold8.html>, accessed July 23, 2001.

21. "I-005c: E-mail Spamming Countermeasures,"<http://ciac.llnl.gov/ciac/bulletins/j-005c.shtml>, accessed July 23, 2001.

22. Meg Mitchell, "Law in Order," *CIO*, April 1, 2000, pp. 158–62; Carol Hildebrand, "Case Files: United Technologies," *CIO*, February 1, 2000, pp. 134–36; Carol Hildebrand, "It's a Jungle in There," *CIO*, April 15, 2000, p. 42; Rosemary Faya Prola, "Knowledge Management Nets Big Rewards," *Smith Business,* Winter 2000, pp. 6–13, and Tim Fielden, "A Knowledge Management State of Mind," *InfoWorld TestCenter,* February 5, 2001.

23. John Webster, "Getting to Know You," *CIO*, February 15, 2000, pp. 150-56; Fraser Rolff, "Down-time Vital for Sharing Knowledge," *New Zealand Infotech Weekly,* January 29, 2001, p. 5; and Victoria Murphy, "You've Got Expertise," *Forbes Magazine,* February 5, 2001, p. 132.

24. Keith Damsell, "Tech spending seen climbing," *Globe and Mail,* February 26, 2001, p. B1.

25. "E-Business and E-Commerce: An Introduction," <http://www.k-solutions.com/library/white.../e-commerceEbusinesswhitepaper31May2000.htm>, accessed July 24, 2001.

26. "e-Definitions," <http://www.highlatitude.com/e-definitions>, accessed July 24, 2001.

27. Statistics Canada, "Electronic Commerce and Technology 2000," *Innovation Analysis Bulletin,* 3, no. 2, May 2001, p. 8.

28. *E-business Technology Forecast* (Menlo Park: PricewaterhouseCoopers Technology Centre, 2000), p. 13.

29. Ibid.

30. Ibid, pp. 2–3.

31. Patrick Brethour, "Canadian love affair with Net has PC ownership booming," *Globe and Mail,* April 13, 2001, p. B1.

32. "Canadian Telework Scene," (n.d.), Canada: Canadian Telework Association,<http://www.ivc.ca/part12.html>, accessed July 23, 2001.

33. Peter Cochrane, "Hard Drive Powering Down to Quantum Level," *Daily Telegraph,* March 2, 2000, p. 12, and "The Intel Economy?" *Newsweek International,* January 29, 2001, p. 22.

34. Harold Goldberg, "Gimme That! The Latest Gotta Have Stuff," *Entertainment Weekly,* February 9, 2001; Brice Scheschuk, "My Pipe Dream,"

Maclean's, February 12, 2001; and Ernest Holsendolph, "Internet Growing Without PC Use," *The Atlanta Constitution,* February 21, 2001.

35. Rhonda L. Wickman, "The Always Onslaught," *Wireless Review,* January 31, 2001; Christopher Dickey, "The Cold Facts," *Newsweek International,* January 15, 2001; Tim Larimer, "Internet A La I-Mode," *Time,* March 5, 2001; and "Wireless Web History in the Making," *Wireless Today,* March 1, 2001.

36. Bill Howard, "Thin Is Back," *PC Magazine,* April 4, 2000, pp. 168–82, and Barry Kipnis, "Technology 2001: A Glimpse to the Future," *National Real Estate Investor,* January 1, 2001.

37. Peter Burrows, "Technology on Tap," *Business Week,* June 19, 2000, pp. 74–84; and Barry Nance, "Down on the (Server) Farm," *Computerworld,* April 3, 2000, pp. 68–70.

38. Robert Lau, "Flexible Infrastructure: The Key for ASPs," *Business Times,* August 16, 2000, and Ben W. Johnson, "Outsourcing: Bigger and Getting Better," *National Real Estate Investor,* January 1, 2001.

39. Wayne Walley, "Making the Right Move," *Global Telephony,* February 1, 2001 and Tyler Hamilton, "Workplace Revolution," *The Toronto Star,* February 26, 2001.

40. Jennifer Hagendorf, "Everdream Touts SMB Subscription Service," *Computer Reseller News,* February 24, 2000; Alfred Poor, "Why Own When You Can Rent?" *PC Magazine,* March 7, 2000; Jonathan Burton, "Putting Their Money Where the Future Is," *New York Times,* March 29, 2000; Bronwyn Fryer, "PC Subscription Services," *Upside Today,* March 31, 2000; and "Bulletproof PCs," *Business 2.0,* January 2000.

41. Sakina Spruell, "Training an IT Nation," *Black Enterprise,* February 2000, pp. 69–70 and Sheila Poole, "Innovator Cites Education's Value," *The Atlanta Journal and Constitution,* January 28, 2001.

42. Natalie Southworth, "Informality governs most telecommuters," *Globe and Mail,* April 4, 2001, p. B11.

43. "Adaptive Technology: Seeing It Their Way," *CIO,* February 1, 2000, p. 50; Joanne Cleaver, "Homeward Bound," *Home Office Computing,* March 2000, pp. 68–71; and Deborah K. Dietsch, "Universal Design is No Barrier to Style," *The Washngton Post,* February 22, 2001, p. H1.

44. Jonathan Coleman, "Is Technology Making Us Intimate Strangers?" *Newsweek,* March 27, 2000, p. 12, and

Anne Meyers, "Telework Requires Extensive Preparation," *The Atlanta Journal and Constitution,* January 4, 2001, p. 3.

45. Jeffrey Kluger, "Extortion on the Internet," *Time,* January 24, 2000.

46. Ann Harrison, "Survey: Cybercrime Cost Firms $266M in '99," *Computerworld,* March 27, 2000, p. 28, and "Commission Unveils Legislative Proposal to Fight Cybercrime," *Tech Europe,* February 2, 2001.

47. Elinor Abreu, "Leave It to the Experts," *Industry Standard,* April 10, 2000, p. 120, and Jeff Smith, "Onesecure Launches New System Platform Making Protecting Computers Easier, Cheaper," *Denver Rocky Mountain News,* January 29, 2001, p. 11B.

48. Ted Bridis, "Hackers Become Security Consultants," *AP Online,* January 6, 2000.

49. Robin Marshall, "Update for VirusBuster," *The Press,* January 11, 2001, p. 15; Doug Stanley, "Worm Digging Its Way Through E-mail," *The Tampa Tribune,* January 22, 2001, p. 3; and Robin Marshall, "Hunting for the Snow White Virus," *The Press,* February 1, 2001, p. 17.

50. Bill Machrone, "Law and Technology Collide," *PC Magazine,* April 18, 2000, p. 93; "EU Seeks to Clamp Down on Drug Trafficking on the Internet," *European Report,* February 14, 2001; "Analysts Worry Over Internet Regulations," *The St. Petersburg Times,* February 13, 2001; and "Gulf Countries Urged to Adopt E-Commerce Regulations," *Xinhug,* February 27, 2001.

51. David Crowe, "Cutting Edge Security," *Wireless Review,* January 1, 2001.

52. "Watch Your Cookies," *International Herald Tribune,* February 12, 2001.

53. Sebastian Rupley, "You, Under the Microscope," *PC Magazine,* January 18, 2000, p. 30; Elizabeth Weise, "A New Wrinkle in Surfing the Net," *USA Today,* March 21, 2000, p. 3D; Daintry Duffy, "You Know What They Did Last Night," *CIO,* April 1, 2000, p. 188; and Cass Rains, "Cookies Leave Bad Taste Behind," *University Wire,* January 16, 2001.

54. Patricia Keefe, "Privacy: Fight for It," *Computerworld,* March 27, 2000, p. 36; John Buskin, "Our Data, Ourselves," *The Wall Street Journal,* April 17, 2000, pp. R34, R36; "The Privacy Debate," *The Wall Street Journal Interactive Edition,* April 11, 2000; Mindy Blodgett, "E-Business and Privacy for All?" *CIO,* April 15, 2000, pp. 101–4; and "How to Keep Electronic 'Big Brother' At Bay," *The Toronto Star,* January 8, 2001.

55. Gary Strauss, "When Computers Fail,"

USA Today, December 7, 1999, P. A2; "Local Power Bill Doubled by Computer Glitch," *The Edmonton Sun,* February 8, 2001, p. 14.

56. Strauss, "When Computers Fail."

57. Rob Spiegel, "Dot Com Crash: Whose Fault Is it Anyway?" n.d. Business Know-How, <www.businessknowhow.com/managed /dotcomcrash.htm>, November 2, 2001.

58. Ibid.

59. Matt Gallaway, "Napster Case Reveals the Flaws in Copyright Law," *Business 2.0,* February 20, 2001, <http://www.business2.com/articles/web/0,16 53,9475,00.htm>, accessed November 2, 2001.

60. John Borland, "Napster reaches settlement with publishers," (September 24, 2001).CnetNews,<http://news.cnet.com /news/0-1005-202-7283716.htm>, accessed November 2, 2001.

61. Hollie Shaw, "Napster, soft market spell end for outlets," *National Post,* October 31, 2001, p. A3.

62. John Borland, "Napster reaches settlement with publishers."

63. Meg Mitchell, "Children of the Revolution," *CIO,* January 1, 2000, pp. 159–68.

64. U.S. Department of Commerce, "The Emerging Digital Economy II," June 1999, and "Fed Survey Shows Slow Growth But No Recession," *Minneapolis Star Tribune,* January 18, 2001, p. 4D.

65. Bronwyn Fryer, "Payroll Busters," *Computerworld,* March 6, 2000, p. 82, and Kenneth Bredemeier, "What Slump? Forecast Still Bright for Tech," *The Washington Post,* February 5, 2001, p. E3.

66. Sharon Watson, "The Best Jobs," *Computerworld,* April 3, 2000, pp. 46–48, and Daniel McGinn and Keith Naughton, "How Safe is Your Job?" *Newsweek,* February 5, 2001, p. 36.

67. Denise English, "Boolean Search Tips," (March 19, 2001). Leesburg: Lake Sumter Community College, <http://lscc.cc.fl.us/library/guides/bo olsea.htm>, accessed November 3, 2001.

68. M. Kesterson, "Social Studies," *Globe and Mail,* August 2, 2001, p. A14.

Chapter 12

1. Richard L. Daft, *Management* (Hinsdale, IL: Dryden Press, 1988), p. 39.

2. Alan Farnham, "The Man who Changed Work Forever," *Fortune,* July 21, 1997, p. 114.

3. Ibid.

4. Douglas A. Blackmon, "Shippers Pitch Power of Gizmos and Gadgets," *The Wall Street Journal,* June 2, 1997, p. B1.

5. Abraham H. Maslow, *Motivation and Personality* (New York: Harper & Brothers, 1954).

6. David Kirkpatrick, "Intel's Amazing Profit Machine," *Fortune,* February 17, 1997, pp. 60–72.

7. Andrea Gabor, "Hard Work and Common Sense," *Los Angeles Times,* February 8, 1998, p. 5.

8. Jim Collins, "The Human Side of Enterprise," *Inc.,* December 1996, p. 55.

9. "First Discipline Then Empowerment," *The Wall Street Journal,* February 20, 1998, p. A19.

10. Robert Maynard, "How to Motivate Low-Wage Workers," *Nation's Business,* May 1997, pp. 35–39.

11. *Globe and Mail,* "Delta Promotes Empowerment," May 31, 1999, p. C5.

12. Michael A. Lev, "Recession Forcing Japanese to Rethink Business Methods," *Arizona Republic,* May 5, 1999, p. E5.

13. Demelza Baer, "Speaker Visits Northwestern U., Criticizes Japanese Business Structure," news release, University Wire, May 19, 2000, and Cait Murphy, "What's Up in Japan," *Fortune,* January 8, 2001, p. 46.

14. Frederick Herzberg, *Work and the Nature of Man* (New York: World Publishers, 1966).

15. Virginia Baldwin Hick, "What Works at Work: Kind Word from Boss," *St. Louis Post-Dispatch,* January 3, 1994, p. 1C.

16. "Loyalty Surprise," *Boardroom Reports,* April 15, 1994, p. 15.

17. Jim Barlow, "Company Loyalty: The Feeling Is Mutual," *Washington Times,* April 18, 1994, p. E13.

18. Meg Carter, "What to Ask the Workers," *Financial Times,* February 18, 1998, p. 23; Bob Nelson, "Dump the Cash, Load on the Praise," *Personnel Journal,* July 1996; p. 65; Sherwood Ross, "Employees Prize Career Development When Deciding to Change Jobs," *St. Louis Post-Dispatch,* February 2, 1998, p. BP4.

19. Herman Cain, "Leadership Is Common Sense," *Success,* February 1997, pp. 41–48.

20. Theodore H. Poister and Gregory Streib, "MBO in Municipal Government: Variations on a Traditional Management Tool," *Public Administration Review,* January-February 1995, pp. 48–56.

21. Victor H. Vroom, *Work and Motivation*

(New York: John Wiley & Sons, 1967).

22. David Nadler and Edward Lawler, "Motivation—a Diagnostic Approach," in *Perspectives on Behavior in Organizations,* ed. Richard Hackman, Edward Lawler, and Lyman Porter (New York: McGraw-Hill, 1977).

23. "Organizing for Empowerment: An Interview with AES's Roger Sant and Dennis Bakke," *Harvard Business Review,* January 1, 1999, p. 110.

24. Ibid.

25. "Mustang Muscle Car Makes a Comeback," *Sunday Star Times* (New Zealand), April 4, 2000, p. 10, and Dave Moore, "Mustang Gets the Bullitt, *The Press,* January 13, 2001, p. 65.

26. Barrie McKenna, "Reborn in Rimouski," *Globe and Mail,* ROB, July 20, 1993, p. B20.

27. High McBride, "A Corporate Obsession Pays Off," *Globe and Mail,* ROB, July 13, 1993, p. B22.

28. "Open the Books," *Globe and Mail,* ROB, December 19, 1995, p. B9.

29. Diane Summers, "Generation X Comes of Age," *Financial Times,* February 16, 1998, p. 16

30. Sam Walton, "In His Own Words," *Fortune,* June 29, 1992, pp. 98–106.

31. Sylvia Odenwald, "Global Work Teams," *Training and Development,* February 1996, pp. 54–60; Vijay Govindarajan and Anil Gupta, "Success is All in the Mindset," *Financial Times,* February 27, 1998, p. 2.

32. Sharon Williams, "Generation Xers Dedicated but Know How to Have Fun," *Evening Post* (Wellington, New Zealand), April 12, 2000, p. 3; Ann Dickerson, "Couple Probes What Makes the Generations Tick," *Atlanta Journal and Constitution,* January 27, 2000, p. J5; John Eckberg, "Weighing Future of Work Force," *Gannett News Service,* May 31, 2000; Mark Memmott, "Reich Knows High Cost of Success," *USAToday,* January 8, 2001, and Jim Miller, "Motivation, Flexibility Key to Retaining GenX Workers," *The Arlington Morning News,* January 25, 2001.

33. Maria Mallory, "Platinum Rule Rules How to Meet Challenge of Generational Conflict," *Atlanta Journal and Constitution,* March 5, 2000, p. R1; Carla D'Nan Bass, "Seeking Insight into Work Force, Sonic Study Finds Kids Are All Right," *Dallas Morning News,* June 18, 2000, p. 12L; and Vicky Uhland, "Generations at Crossroads Boomers and Xers Butt Heads over Values in the Workplace," *Denver Rocky Mountain News,* February 6, 2000, p. 1J.

Chapter 13

1. M. Kesterson (quoting Elbert Hubbard), "Social Studies," *Globe and Mail*, August 2, 2001, p. A14.

2. Campbell Clark, "National Sets Up Banking School," *Montreal Gazette*, February 7, 1996, p. D8.

3. E. Innes, J. Lyons, and J. Harris, *The Financial Post 100 Best Companies to Work for in Canada* (Toronto: HarperCollins, 1990).

4. Salem Alaton, "The Learning Organization," *Globe and Mail, ROB*, December 19, 1995, p. B26.

5. David Shoalts, "HR Adopts Virtual Concept," *Globe and Mail, ROB*, December 19, 1995, p. B24.

6. Interview with Toronto-Dominion HRM manager S. Churchin, May 17, 1996; *Canadian Business*, August 1989, p. 9; Hewitt Associates, "Benefits by the Year 2000," *Benefits Canada*, February 1991, p. 11; *Financial Post*, January 8, 1990, p. 3.

7. "MCI World Com Honored by CIO Magazine as Top 50 Internet/Intranet Site," *PR Newswire*, July 13, 1999; and Margie Semilof, "MCI WorldCom Mantra: We Do More Than Just Sell Pipes," *Computer Reseller News*, April 17, 2000, p. 7.

8. Teresa L. Ebert and Mas'ud Zavarzadeh, "E-Education Is Really Job Training," *Newsday*, March 26, 2000, p. A27, and Arlene Levinson, "Online Classes Serve Millions," *AP Online*, January 22, 2001.

9. Thomas E. Weber, "The New Dress Code for Corporate Training," *The Wall Street Journal Interactive Edition*, January 31, 2000.

10. Christopher Caggiano, "How You Gonna Keep 'em Down on the Firm," *Inc. Online*, January 7, 1998.

11. Nina Colwill, "Understanding the Aspects of Networking," Women in Management, National Centre for Management Research and Developments' Women in Management Program, Western Business School, August-September 1994, p. 6.

12. Rosabeth Moss Canter, "Wired Rewards," *A World of Networks*, a Northern Telecom publication, as reported in *Globe and Mail, ROB*, December 19, 1995, p. B9.

13. Debra Black, "Canadian Women Get Short Shrift, UN Says," *Montreal Gazette*, July 5, 1993, p. C1.

14. Labour Force Survey, Statistics Canada, Cat. No. 71F0004XCB, 1999.

15. "Taking Care of Fuzzy Friends," *CFO*, June 2000, p. 27; and Edward Iwata, "Staff-Hungry Tech Firms Cast Exotic Lures," *USA Today*, February 1, 2000, p. B1; Robert Levering and Milton Moskowitz, "The 100 Best Companies to Work For," *Fortune*, January 8, 2001, p. 148.

16. Perry Pascarella, "Compensating Teams," *Across the Board*, February 1997, p. 16–23.

17. Interviews with Norma Tombari, May 19, 1996 and December 15, 1998; various publications of Royal Bank.

18. <http://royalbank.com/careers/workressurv/hr_pandp.html>, accessed January 9, 2002.

19. Robert Maynard, "The Growing Appeal of Telecommuting," *Nation's Business*, August 1994, pp. 61–62.

20. Virginia Baldwin Hick, "Virtual Office Means More Home Work," *St. Louis Post-Dispatch*, March 21, 1994, pp. B1 and 2.

21. Bob Weinstein, "New Frontiers," *Entrepreneur*, May 1995, pp. 158–65.

22. "Sunday Morning," *CBC Radio*, May 19, 1996.

23. Margot Gibb-Clark, "Sex Harassment Case Sent to Labour Board," *Globe and Mail, ROB*, February 26, 1996, p. B10.

24. Steve Ulfelder, "Signs of Defection," *ComputerWorld*, April 3, 2000, pp. 42–43; and "Keeping Your Star Performers," *ComputerWorld*, April 3, 2000, p. 44.

25. Dave D. Buss, "Be Ready When Employees Walk out the Door," <startup.wsj.com>, June 30, 1999.

Chapter 14

1. Yahoo Internet site, <www.dailynews.yahoo.com>, December 31, 1998.

2. Directory of Labour Organizations in Canada, Human Resources and Development Canada, 1998.

3. Mike King, "Lost Work-Days Could Hit Record Level in '99," *Montreal Gazette*, August 16, 1999, p. A5.

4. Sheila McGovern, "Wage-Discrimination Settlement Could Cost $1.5 Billion," *Montreal Gazette*, February 17, 1996, p. G2.

5. Margot Gibb-Clark, "CUPE to Appeal Same-Sex Spouse Ruling," *Globe and Mail, ROB*, September 20, 1995, p. B4.

6. Oliver Bertin, "Air Canada Beefs Up Staff," *Globe and Mail, ROB*, March 1, 1996, p. B4.

7. Ian McGugan, "A Crapshoot Called Compensation," *Canadian Business*, July 1995, p. 67.

8. Margot Gibb-Clark, "Court Restores Award to Lark Employees." *Globe and Mail, ROB*, December 12, 1995, p. B4; Alan Freeman, "Ex-STN Directors Ordered to Pay $567,000 to Workers," *Globe and Mail, ROB*, September 20, 1995, p. B1.

9. Mike Brennan, "GM Suing VW Executives for Espionage," Knight-Ridder Newspapers, as reported in *Montreal Gazette*, March 9, 1996, p. E2.

10. Garth Alexander, *London Sunday Times*, as reported in *Montreal Gazette*, August 5, 2001, p. C6.

11. Gayle MacDonald, "Who's Minding the Parents?" *Globe and Mail, ROB*, January 30, 1996, p. B12.

Chapter 15

1. Thomas H. Davenport, Jeanne G. Harris, and Ajay K. Kohli, "How Do They Know Their Customers So Well," *Sloan Management Review*, Winter 2001, pp. 63–73.

2. Michael Krauss, "Filter Out Archaic, One-Size-Fits-All Strategies," *Marketing News*, March 27, 2000, p. 9.

3. Greg Jaffe, "Target Market," *The Wall Street Journal*, February 14, 2001, pp. A1 & A10.

4. Alan R. Andreasen, Rob Gould, and Karen Gutierrez, "Social Marketing Has a New Champion," *Advertising Age*, February 7, 2000, p. 38.

5. Kristina Blachere, "Satisfaction Guaranteed," *Smart Business*, March 2001, pp. 126-131.

6. Eric N. Berkowitz, et al. *Marketing*, 4th Canadian ed. (Toronto: McGraw-Hill Ryerson, 2000), p. 20.

7. Philip Kotler, et al. *Principles of Marketing*, 4th Canadian ed. (Scarborough: Prentice Hall Canada Inc., 1999), p. 20.

8. Rich Kish & Mary Ann Platt, "Product Recall and Crisis Management," p.4, <http://www.foodquality.com/prorcal.html>, accessed August 14, 2001.

9. Ibid.

10. Nedra Pickler, "Total Recall at Firestone Grows to 10 Million Tires," *Toronto Star*, October 5, 2001, p. C3.

11. Ibid.

12. Amy Kover, "Why the Cereal Business Is Soggy," *Fortune*, March 6, 2000, p. 74.

13. Charles Newman, "Online Testing Rated," *Advertising Age*, May 8, 2000, p. 64.

14. Mary Jo Hatch and Majken Schultz, "Are the Strategic Stars Aligned for Your Corporate Brand?" *Harvard Business Review*, February 2001, pp. 129–34.

15. Courtney Fingar, "Supply Chain," *Global Business*, January 2001, pp. 28–32.

16. Jonathan Kaufman, "The Omnipresent Persuaders," *The Wall Street Journal*, January 1, 2000, p. R26.

17. Ruth L. Williams, "Four Smart Ways to Run Online Communities," *Sloan Management Review*, Summer 2000, pp. 81–91.

18. Lynda Hurst, "How the boomers will go bust," *Toronto Star*, September 23, 2000, p. A29.

19. Shawna Steinberg, "Have Allowance Will Transform Economy," *Canadian Business*, May 13, 1998, p. 60.

20. Paul Brent, "2.5 million 'tweens' pack financial power in their pockets," *Financial Post*, November 17, 2000.

21. William M. Bulkeley, "Clicks and Mortar," *Wall Street Journal*, July 17, 2000, p. R4.

22. Marina Strauss, "Chapters Online to shun price war," *Globe and Mail*, July 31, 2001, p. B4.

23. Ibid.

24. E.S. Browning, "Stocks Rise, Then Fall on Greenspan Talk," *Wall Street Journal*, February 14, 2001, p. C1.

25. Raizel Robin, "Your pain his gain," *Canadian Business*, March 19, 2001, p. 38.

26. Theodore Levitt, "Marketing Myopia (With Retrospective Commentary)," *Harvard Business Review*, September–October 1975, p. 29.

27. Elcena De Lisser, "Online Retailers Slice and Dice Niches Thinner Than Julienne Fries," *Wall Street Journal*, November 29, 1999, pp. B1 and B5.

28. Dana Flavelle, "Loyalty cards muscle in," *Toronto Star*, July 28, 2001, p. C8.

29. Frederick F. Reichheld and Phil Shefter, "E-Loyalty," *Harvard Business Review*, July–August 2000, pp. 105–13.

30. Statistics Canada, "Population of major census metropolitan areas," <http://www.statcan.ca/english/Pgdb/People/Population/demo05.htm>, accessed August 17, 2001.

31. Eric N. Berkowitz et al., *Marketing*, 4th Canadian Edition. (Toronto: McGraw-Hill Ryerson, 2000), p. 261.

32. Stanley J. Shapiro, et al., *Basic Marketing: A Global-Managerial Approach*, 10th Canadian ed. (Toronto: McGraw-Hill Ryerson, 2002), p. 86. Citing Seymour Lipset, *Continental Divide: The Values and Institu-

tions of the United States and Canada* (New York: Routledge, 1990).

33. Jerry Bowles, "How Digital Marketplaces Are Shaping the Future of B2B Commerce," *Forbes* (advertisement), July 24, 2000, pp. 215ff.

34. William H. Davidow and Michael S. Malone, *The Virtual Corporation* (New York: HarperBusiness, 1992), p. 153.

35. Mark Henricks, "More Than a Fling," *Entrepreneur*, September 2000, pp. 124–27.

36. Laurie Freeman, "Top 10 Trends for 2001 Rooted in B-to-B Reality," *B to B*, January 8, 2001, pp. 22, 24.

Chapter 16

1. Couche-Tard, "About Us," <http://www.couchetard.com/overview_en.html>, accessed August 23, 2001.

2. Roland T. Rust, Valarie A. Zeithaml, and Katherine N. Lemon, *Driving Customer Equity: How Customer Lifetime Value Is Reshaping Corporate Strategy* (New York: The Free Press, 2000).

3. Keith Naughton, "Tired of Smile-Free Service?" *Newsweek*, March 5, 2000, pp. 44–45.

4. Aixa M. Pascual, "The Whopper Plays Catch-Up," *Business Week*, May 25, 2000, pp. 98–100.

5. Robert Frank, "Big Boy's Adventures in Thailand," *The Wall Street Journal*, April 12, 2000, pp. B1, B4.

6. "Building the New Basics of Branding," *Advertising Age*, May 15, 2000, pp. 40, 42.

7. Rebecca Gardyn, "I'll Have What He's Having," *American Demographics*, July 2000, p. 22.

8. Eric N. Berkowitz, et al., *Marketing*, 4th Canadian ed. (Toronto: McGraw-Hill Ryerson, 2000), p. 290.

9. Ibid.

10. Ibid.

11. Ingrid Peritz, "Publisher ices Bonhomme 'murderer' book cover," *Globe and Mail*, July 11, 2001, p. A2.

12. Teri Olcott, "The latest news on the last British luxury car," *Vintage Cars*, August 15 1998, pp. 1–2. <http://www.vintage-cars.about.com/library/weekly/aa081598.htm>, accessed August 22, 2001.

13. John Heinzl, "Coca-Cola brand gets top ranking," *Globe and Mail*, July 28, 2001, p. B5.

14. Jack Neff, "New Dial CEO Baum Will Stress Marketing," *Advertising Age*, August 14, 2000, p. 8.

15. "Brands In Trouble—In Demand," *Advertising Age*, January 8, 2001, p. 4.

16. Mercedes M. Cordona, "Trendsetting Brands Combat Knock-Offs," *Advertising Age*, August 21, 2000, pp. 20, 24.

17. *Current Affairs*, Show Number 742, "Food Fights," aired March 7, 2000.

18. Ibid.

19. Canadian Grocer Web site <www.cdngrocer.com>, August 1999.

20. *Venture*, Show Number 674, "Global Packaging," aired January 13, 1998.

21. Salem Alaton, "Design Solutions from Candies to Countries," *Globe and Mail*, ROB, August 29, 1995, p. B22.

22. David Menzies, "Guaranteed rip-off," *Canadian Business*, April 16, 2001, 66.

23. Ibid.

24. Ibid.

25. Berkowitz et al., *Marketing*, p. 107.

26. "Economic Issues Take A Back Seat, New Global Survey Reveals," *Health, Safety and Environment Newsletter*, 5, No. 8 (August 1997), <http://www.caw.ca/whatwedo/health&safety/newsletter/5.8.cfm>, accessed August 25, 2001.

27. Fair Business Practices Branch, "Consumer Packaging and Labelling General Worksheet" (August 25, 1997), <http://strategis.ic.gc.ca/SSG/cp01055e.html>, accessed August 24, 2001.

28. Leanne Hachey, "The fuss over genetically modified food," CBC News, <http://cbc.ca/news/indepth/foodfight/hachey.html>, accessed August 25, 2001.

29. Daniel Leblanc, "Monitor GM food safety, Ottawa told," *The Globe and Mail*, August 24, 2001, p. A9.

30. "Natural Health Food Sector Says Canadians Need Freedom Of Choice On GMO Issue," *Canada Newswire*, June 13, 2001, <www.newswire.ca/releases/June2001/13/c3802.html>, accessed August 25, 2001.

31. Berkowitz et al., *Marketing*, pp. 291–293.

32. Robert G. Cooper, *Winning at New Products: Accelerating the Process from Idea to Launch*, Third ed. (Cambridge: Perseus Publishing, 2001), p. 10.

33. Ibid, pp. 83–89.

34. Ibid, p. 11

35. Ibid, pp. 23–24.

36. Ellen Roseman, "Product graveyard can teach lessons," *Toronto Star*, August 16, 1999, p. E1.

37. David J. Lipke, "Product by Design," *American Demographics,* February 2001, pp. 38–41.

38. Dana Blankenhorn, "How to Manage Your Online Campaign," *BtoB,* April 24, 2000, pp. 17–20.

39. Berkowitz, et al., *Marketing,* Canadian 4th ed., p. 320.

40. Ibid.

41. "The Power of Smart Pricing," *Business Week,* April 10, 2000, pp. 160–64.

42. Mark Henricks, "On the House," *Entrepreneur,* June 2000, pp. 114–17.

43. Indrajit Sinha, "Cost Transparency: The Net's Real Threat to Prices and Brands," *Harvard Business Review,* March–April 2000, pp. 43–50.

44. Paul Nunes, Diane Wilson, and Ajit Kambil, "The All-in-One Market," *Harvard Business Review,* May–June 2000, pp. 19–20.

45. Walter Baker, Mike Marn and Craig Zawada, "Price Smarter on the Net," *Harvard Business Review,* February 2001, pp. 122–27.

46. Akshay R. Rao, Mark E. Bergen, and Scott Davis, "How to Fight a Price War," *Harvard Business Review,* March–April 2000, pp. 107–16.

47. Douglas A. Blackmon, "Shippers Pitch Power of Gizmos and Gadgets," *Wall Street Journal,* June 2, 1997, p. B1.

Chapter 17

1. Luc Hatlestad, "Branding," *Red Herring,* January 2000, pp. 172–73.

2. Kate Fitzgerald, "All Eyes Zero On Emerging T-Commerce," *Advertising Age,* January 15, 2001, p. 512.

3. Tobi Elkin, "Interacting with ITV: Marketers Are Tuning In," *Advertising Age,* January 15, 2001, pp. S2-S4.

4. Pamela Houghtaling, "Mobilizing Your Sales Force," *Beyond Computing,* April 2000, pp. 31–35.

5. John Heinzl, "Junk mail industry scrambles to change," *Toronto Star,* October 24, 2001, p. A1.

6. Eric Fisher, "Just 3 Dot-Coms on Super Bowl," *The Washington Times,* January 24, 2001, pp. B7 & B9.

7. Jon Fine, "Cross-media Catches Fire," *Advertising Age,* October 25, 2000, pp. S2 & S4.

8. "RotoZip: You Have to See It to Believe It," *Marketing News,* March 27, 2000, p. 17.

9. Paul C. Judge, "Will Online Ads Ever Click?" *Fast Company,* March 2001, pp. 182-191.

10. Peter Schwartz, "Internet Advertising Is Going to Change. But How?" *Red Herring,* February 2000, pp. 76–78.

11. Jacqueline Emigh, "Many Hands Make Site Work," *Sm@rt Reseller,* February 16, 2000.

12. Lisa Vaas, "Earn Customers' Love," *PC Week,* February 13, 2000.

13. Kristin Dunlap Godsey, "Critical Steps in the Sales Process," *Success,* May 1997, pp. 24–25.

14. Dana James, "Hit the Bricks," *Marketing News,* September 13, 1999, pp. 1, 15.

15. Kelly Shermach, "As PR Changes, the More it Stays the Same," *Marketing News,* March 12, 2001, p. 4.

16. Kenneth Neil Cukier, "Crisis in PR," *Red Herring,* May 2000, pp. 207–18.

17. Serena French, "Getting the Celebrity to Show Up," *National Post,* August 2, 2001, p. B3

18. Roger O. Crockett, "Penny Pinchers' Paradise," *Business Week E.BIZ,* January 22, 2001, p. EB12.

19. "Boosting Sales Through In-Store Sampling Programs," *Incentive,* August 2000, p. 85.

20. Stephanie Thompson, "Pepsi Favors Sampling over Ads for Fruit Drinks," *Advertising Age,* January 24, 2000, p. 8.

21. Eric N. Berkowitz, et al., *Marketing,* 4th Canadian ed. (Toronto: McGraw-Hill Ryerson, 2000), p. 492.

22. Don E. Schultz, "ARF's New Model Rooted in Old Ideas," *Marketing News,* September 25, 2000, p. 8.

23. Courtney Fingar, "Are You World Ready?" *Global Business,* January 2001, pp. 28-30.

24. Statistics Canada, "Retail Trade," (n.d.),<www.statcan.ca/english/Pgdb/Economy/Communications/trade15.htm>,accessed August 27, 2001.

25. Statistics Canada, "Establishments by industry," (n.d.), <www.statcan.ca/english/Pgdb/Economy/Economic/econ18.htm>, accessed August 27, 2001.

26. Berkowitz et al., *Marketing,* 459.

27. Steven Theobold, "U.S. retailer seals its Future with $580 million purchase," *Toronto Star,* August 15, 2001, p. E1.

28. *Venture,* Show Number 780, "Retail Wars II," aired March 27, 2001.

29. Charles Fishman, "But Wait, You Promised...," *Fast Company,* April 2001, pp. 114–118.

30. Amy Borrus, "The Broad Backlash Against E-Tailers," *Business Week,* February 5, 2001, p. 102.

31. William M. Bulkeley, "Cut Down to Size," *Wall Street Journal,* March 9, 2000, pp. A1, A8.

32. Sandra Keeley, "Setting Up an E-Commerce Site Isn't So Cheap—Or So Easy," *The Philadelphia Inquirer,* November 7, 1999, p. E3.

33. Ellen Neuborne, "It's the Service, Stupid," *Business Week e.biz,* April 3, 2000, p. EB 18.

34. Tobi Elkin, "Best Buy Takes Cue from Retail Shops," *Advertising Age,* March 6, 2000, p. S8.

35. Showwei Chu, "More than 100 North American chains are on Net, and many outperform pure plays," *Globe and Mail,* May 24, 2001, p. B17.

36. "EDI in Action," *Business Week,* March 30, 1992, pp. 85–92.

37. Bill Fahrenwald, Dean Wise, and Diane Glynn, "Supply Chain Collaboration," *Business Week,* March 26, 2000, pp. 265ff.

38. Statistics Canada, "Rail in Canada," Cat. No. 52-216, 1990, p. 174.

39. John Ellis, "The Wireless Technology Gap," *Fast Company,* July 2000, pp. 302–6.

Chapter 19

1. Eileen Davis, "The Root of All Evil," *Venture,* December 1988, pp. 77–78.

2. "David L. Berch," *Inc.,* April 1989, pp. 38–39.

3. Canadian Bankers Association, <www.cba.ca/eng/statistics_results.cfm>, accessed May 1999.

4. *Serving the Needs of Small Business,* Canadian Bankers Association, May 28, 1996; *Small Business Annual Report 1995,* Canadian Bankers Association, p. 21.

5. Ibid.

6. Ibid.

GLOSSARY

accessory equipment Capital items that are not quite as long-lasting or as expensive as installations. (p. 491)

accounting The recording, classifying, summarizing, and interpreting of financial transactions to provide management and other interested parties with the information they need. (p. 565)

accounting system The methods used to record and summarize accounting data. (p. 565)

acquisition One company buys another company. (p. 175)

adaptive culture An organizational culture in which "employees focus on the changing needs of customers and other stakeholders, and support initiatives to keep pace with these changes." (p. 280)

administered distribution system A distribution system in which producers manage all of the marketing functions at the retail level. (p. 551)

advertising Paid, nonpersonal communication through various media by organizations and individuals who are in some way identified in the advertising message. (p. 524)

affirmative action (employment equity) Employment activities designed to right past wrongs endured by females and minorities by giving them preference in employment. (p. 418)

agency shop (Rand formula) A workplace in which a new employee is not required to join the union but must pay union dues. This historic formula was devised by Justice Rand. (p. 431)

amortization (depreciation) Since assets such as machinery lose value over time, part of their cost is calculated as an expense each year over their useful life. (p. 577)

apprentice programs Training programs involving a period during which a learner works alongside an experienced employee to master the skills and procedures of a craft. (p. 398)

arbitration The process of resolving all disputes, not only grievances, through an outside, impartial third party. (p. 433)

articles of incorporation The legal documents, obtained from the federal or provincial governments, authorizing a company to operate as a corporation. (p. 95)

assembly process That part of the production process that puts together components. (p. 303)

assets Things of value owned by a business. (p. 569)

autocratic leadership Leadership style that involves making managerial decisions, based on information available to the manager, without consulting others; it implies power over others. (p. 233)

baby boomer Represents the group of people who were born between 1947 and 1966 and are now living in Canada. (p. 230)

balance of trade The relationship of exports to imports. (p. 62)

balance sheet Reports the financial position of a firm at the end of a specific period of time. Balance sheets show assets, liabilities, and owners' equity. (p. 572)

bartering The exchange of goods or services for other goods or services. (p. 68)

behavioural segmentation Dividing the market based on behaviour with or toward a product. (p. 468)

bid rigging Secret agreement among competitors to make artificially high bids.

blue chip stocks Stocks of high-quality companies. (p. 133, 618)

bond A contract of indebtedness issued by a corporation or government unit that promises payment of a principal amount at a specified future time plus annual or semi-annual interest at a specified or variable rate. (p. 612)

bookkeeping The recording of transactions. (p. 568)

Boolean searching A search technique that uses keyword operators; it is used to perform accurate searches on computer databases and search engines. (p. 345)

boycott The practice of urging union members and the public at large not to buy a particular company's products or services. (p. 436)

brand A name, symbol, or design (or combination thereof) that identifies the goods or services of one seller or group of sellers and distinguishes them from the goods and services of competitors. (p. 491)

brand association The linking of a brand to other favourable images. (p. 496)

brand awareness How quickly or easily a given brand name comes to mind when a product category is mentioned. (p. 493)

brand equity The combination of factors (such as awareness, loyalty, perceived quality, images, and emotion) that people associate with a given brand name. (p. 493)

brand loyalty The degree to which customers are satisfied, like the brand, and are committed to further purchases. (p. 493)

brand manager A manager who has direct responsibility for one brand or one product line. (p. 499)

brand name A word, letter, or group of words or letters that differentiates one seller's goods and services from those of competitors. (p. 457)

break-even analysis The process used to determine profitability at various levels of sales. (p. 509)

broadband technology Technology that delivers voice, video, and data through the Internet. (p. 328)

brokers Marketing intermediaries who bring buyers and sellers together and assist in negotiating an exchange but don't take title to the goods. (p. 541)

bureaucracy An organization with many layers of managers who set rules and regulations and oversee all decisions. (p. 257)

business An organization that manufactures or sells goods or services to satisfy some customer's needs in an attempt to generate a profit. (p. 4)

business plan A detailed written statement that describes the nature of the business, the target market, the advantages the business will have over competitors, the resources and qualifications of the owners, and much more. (p. 201)

business-to-business (B2B) Market that considers transactions between businesses. (p. 332, 464)

business-to-consumer (B2C) Market that considers transactions between a business and a consumer for personal use. (p. 331)

buying on margin Purchasing securities by borrowing some of the cost from the broker. (p. 619)

cafeteria-style benefits Benefit plans that allow employees to choose which benefits they want up to a certain dollar amount. (p. 407)

capital budget The spending plan for the acquisition of capital assets that involve large sums of money. (p. 600)

capitalism An economic system with free markets and private ownership of companies operated for profit. (p. 37)

cash-and-carry wholesalers Wholesalers that serve mostly smaller retailers with a limited assortment of products. (p. 544)

cash budget The projected use of cash during a given period (e.g., monthly, quarterly, or annually). (p. 600)

cash flow The difference between cash receipts and cash disbursements. (p. 579)

cash-flow forecast A projection of expected cash inflows and outflows in the coming year. **(p. 599)**

category killer stores Large stores that offer wide selection at competitive prices. **(p. 547)**

census metropolitan area A geographic area that has a population of 100,000 or more inhabitants. **(p. 468)**

centralized authority Maintaining decision-making authority at the top level of management. **(p. 266)**

ceremonies Planned activities conducted specifically for the benefit of an audience. **(p. 280)**

channel of distribution A whole set of marketing intermediaries, such as wholesalers and retailers, who join together to transport and store goods in their path (or channel) from producers to consumers. **(p. 539)**

check-off clause A contract clause requiring the employer to deduct union dues from employees' pay and remit them to the union. **(p. 432)**

closed shop A workplace in which all new hires must already be union members. **(p. 431)**

closing techniques Ways of concluding a sale including getting a series of small commitments and then asking for the order and showing the client where to sign. **(p. 530)**

collective bargaining The process by which a union represents employees in relations with their employer. **(p. 431)**

commercial paper A short-term corporate equivalent of an IOU that is sold in the marketplace by a firm. It matures in 270 days or fewer. **(p. 607)**

commercialization Promoting a product to distributors and retailers to get wide distribution and developing strong advertising and sales campaigns to generate and maintain interest in the product among distributors and consumers. **(p. 502)**

common market A regional group of countries that aims to remove all internal tariffs and nontariff barriers to trade, investment, and employment. (An important example is the European Union.) **(p. 75)**

common stock Represents ownership of a firm and the rights to vote and to receive all of the firm's profits (after preferred shareholders are paid), in the form of dividends declared by the board of directors. **(p. 617)**

comparative advantage theory The theory that a country should produce and sell to other countries those products that it produces most efficiently and effectively and should buy from other countries those products it cannot produce as effectively or efficiently. **(p. 61)**

competing in time Being as fast or faster than competition in responding to consumer wants and needs and getting goods and services to them. **(p. 310)**

competitive benchmarking Rating an organization's practices, processes, and products against the world's best. **(p. 278)**

compressed workweek A work schedule made up of four 10-hour days. **(p. 411)**

computer-aided design (CAD) The use of computers in the design of products. **(p. 310)**

computer-aided manufacturing (CAM) The use of computers in the manufacturing of products. **(p. 310)**

computer-integrated manufacturing (CIM) The uniting of computer-aided design with computer-aided manufacturing. **(p. 311)**

concept testing Taking a product idea to consumers to test their reactions. **(p. 501)**

conceptual skills Skills that involve the ability to picture the organization as a whole and the relationship among its various parts. **(p. 241)**

consortium A temporary association of two or more companies to bid jointly on a large project. **(p. 68)**

consultative salesperson A salesperson who analyzes customer needs and then comes up with solutions to those needs. **(p. 531)**

consumer market All the individuals or households that want goods and services for personal consumption or use. **(p. 464)**

consumer price index (CPI) Measures monthly changes in the price of a basket of goods and services that an average family would buy. **(p. 48)**

contingent workers Workers who are not regular, full-time employees. **(p. 397)**

contingency planning The process of preparing alternative courses of action that may be used if the primary plans do not achieve the objectives of the organization. **(p. 225)**

continuous improvement (CI) Constantly improving the way the organization does things so that customer needs can be better satisfied. **(p. 275)**

continuous process A production process in which long production runs turn out finished goods over time. **(p. 303)**

contractual distribution system A distribution system in which members are bound to co-operate through contractual agreements. **(p. 550)**

controlling A management function determining whether or not an organization is progressing toward its goals and objectives, and taking corrective action if it is not. **(p. 222)**

convenience products Goods and services that the consumer wants to purchase frequently and with a minimum of effort. **(p. 489)**

convertible bond A bond that can be converted into shares of common stock. **(p. 614)**

cookies Pieces of information, such as registration data or user preferences, sent by a Web site over the Internet to a Web browser that the browser software is expected to save and send back to the server whenever the user returns to that Web site. **(p. 342)**

co-operative An organization that is owned by members who pay an annual membership fee and share in any profits. **(p. 181)**

core competency The collective learning in an organization, especially how to coordinate diverse production skills and integrate multiple streams of technology. **(p. 261)**

core time The period when all employees must be present in a flextime system. **(p. 410)**

corporate distribution system A distribution system in which all of the organizations in the channel of distribution are owned by one firm. **(p. 550)**

corporate social responsibility The recognition by corporations that their actions must take into account the needs and ethical standards of society. **(p. 125)**

corporation A legal entity with an existence separate from its owners. **(p. 162)**

cost of goods sold A particular type of expense measured by the total cost of merchandise sold, including costs associated with the acquisition, storage, transportation, and packaging of goods. **(p. 573)**

countertrading Bartering involving several countries. **(page 68)**

critical path The sequence of tasks that takes the longest time to complete. **(p. 313)**

cross-functional teams Groups of employees from different departments who work together on a semipermanent basis (as opposed to the temporary teams established in matrix-style organizations). **(p. 271)**

Crown corporations Companies owned by the federal or a provincial government. **(p. 90)**

cumulative preferred stock Preferred stock that accumulates unpaid dividends. **(p. 616)**

current assets Cash and assets that are normally converted into cash within one year. **(p. 570)**

customer-driven Customer satisfaction becomes the driving force of the company. **(p. 14)**

customer relationship management (CRM) Learning as much as possible about customers and doing everything you can to satisfy them or even delight them with goods and services over time. **(p. 454)**

cyclical unemployment Unemployment caused by a recession or similar downturn in the business cycle. **(p. 46)**

data processing (DP) Name for business technology in the 1970s; included technology that supported an existing business and was primarily used to improve the flow of financial information. **(p. 324)**

dealer (private) brands Products that don't carry the manufacturer's name but carry a distributor or retailer's name instead. **(p. 494)**

debt capital Funds raised by borrowing that must be repaid. **(p. 603)**

decentralized Decision making is spread downward from the top of an organization. **(p. 13)**

decentralized authority Delegating decision-making authority to lower-level managers who are more familiar with local conditions. **(p. 266)**

decision making Choosing among two or more alternatives. **(p. 242)**

deficit An excess of expenditures over revenues. **(p. 49)**

demand The quantity of particular products or services that buyers are willing to buy at certain prices and at certain locations. **(p. 39)**

democratic (participative) leadership Leadership style that involves managers and employees working together to make decisions. **(p. 233)**

demographic segmentation Dividing the market by age, income, and education level. **(p. 468)**

departmentalization The dividing of organizational functions into separate units. **(p. 263)**

dividends The part of the firm's profits that are distributed to shareholders. **(p. 615)**

downsizing The process of eliminating managerial and non-managerial positions. **(p. 256)**

drop shippers Wholesalers that solicit orders from retailers and other wholesalers and have the merchandise shipped directly from a producer to a buyer. **(p. 544)**

e-business The production, advertising, sale, and distribution of products via telecommunications networks. **(p. 331)**

e-commerce The process of managing online financial transactions by individuals and companies. **(p. 331)**

economics The study of how society chooses to employ resources to produce goods and services and distribute them for consumption among various competing groups and individuals. **(p. 37)**

economies of scale The cost savings that result from large-scale production; the situation in which companies can produce goods more inexpensively if they can purchase raw materials in bulk. Subsequently, the average cost of goods goes down as production levels increase. **(p. 97, 255)**

electronic data interchange (EDI) Software that enables the computers of producers, wholesalers, and retailers to communicate with each other. **(p. 551)**

embargo A complete ban on all trade with or investment in a country. **(p. 73)**

employee orientation The activity that introduces new employees to the organization; to fellow employees; to their immediate supervisors; and to the policies, practices, and objectives of the firm. **(p. 397)**

empowerment The leaders of organizations give their workers the freedom, incentives, and training to be decision makers and creative contributors to the organization; giving employees the authority and responsibility to respond quickly to customer requests. **(p. 14, 236)**

enabling Giving workers the education and tools they need to assume their new decision-making powers. **(p. 236)**

enterprise resource planning (ERP) Computer-based production and operations system that links multiple firms into one integrated production unit. **(p. 303)**

entrepreneur A person who organizes, manages, and assumes the risks of starting and operating a business to make a profit. **(p. 191)**

entrepreneurship Having the skills and determination to start and operate a business and to accept the calculated risks that are part of such an undertaking. **(p. 191)**

environmental scanning The process of identifying the factors that can affect marketing success. **(p. 461)**

equity capital Funds raised from selling shares in the firm. **(p. 603)**

equity theory The theory that employees try to maintain equity between inputs and outputs compared to others in similar positions. **(p. 370)**

e-tailing Selling goods and services to ultimate customers over the Internet. **(p. 548)**

everyday low pricing (EDLP) Setting prices lower than competitors and then not having any special sales. **(p. 509)**

exchange rate The value of one currency relative to the currencies of other countries. **(p. 63)**

exclusive distribution Distribution that sends products to only one retail outlet in a given geographic area. **(p. 548)**

expectancy theory Victor Vroom's theory that the effort employees exert on specific tasks depends on their expectations of the outcomes. **(p. 370)**

exponential function The mathematical description of anything that changes steadily in one direction over a given period. **(p. 149)**

external customers Dealers who buy products to sell to others, and ultimate customers who buy products for their own personal use. **(p. 239)**

extranet An extension of the Internet that connects suppliers, customers, and other organizations via secure Web sites; a semiprivate network that uses Internet technology and allows more than one company to access the same information or allows people on different servers to collaborate. **(p. 274)**

extrinsic reward Something given to you by someone else as recognition for good work; extrinsic rewards include pay increases, praise, and promotions. **(p. 354)**

facility layout The physical arrangement of resources (including people) in the production process. **(p. 296)**

facility location The process of selecting a geographic location for a company's operations. **(p. 294)**

factoring Selling accounts receivable for cash. **(p. 607)**

finance The business function that is responsible for the acquisition and disbursement of funds. **(p. 598)**

financial accounting The preparation of financial statements for people inside and outside of the firm (for example, investors). **(p. 567)**

financial statements Report the operations and position (condition) of a firm; they include the income statement and the balance sheet. **(p. 572)**

fiscal policy The use of taxation to stimulate or restrain various aspects of the economy or the economy as a whole. **(p. 96)**

fixed or capital assets Assets that are acquired to produce services or products for a business. They are not bought to be sold. **(p. 570)**

flexible manufacturing Designing machines to do multiple tasks so that they can produce a variety of products. **(p. 307)**

flextime plans Work schedules that give employees some freedom to adjust when they work, within limits, as long as they work the required number of hours. **(p. 410)**

focus group A small group of people who meet under the direction of a discussion leader to communicate their opinions about an organization, its products, or other given issues. **(p. 460)**

foreign subsidiary A company owned by another company (parent company) in a foreign country. **(p. 67)**

formal organization The structure that details lines of responsibility, authority, and position; that is, the structure shown on organization charts. **(p. 281)**

form utility The value added by the creation of finished goods and services; taking raw materials and changing their form so that they become useful products. **(p. 302, 484)**

franchise The right to use a specific business's name and sell its products or services in a given territory. **(p. 176)**

franchise agreement An arrangement whereby someone with a good idea for a business sells the rights to use the business name and sell its products or services in a given territory. **(p. 176)**

franchisee A person who buys a franchise. **(p. 176)**

franchising A method of distributing a product or service, or both, to achieve a maximum market impact with a minimum investment. **(p. 176)**

franchisor A company that develops a product concept and sells others the rights to make and sell the products. **(p. 176)**

freight forwarder An organization that puts many small shipments together to create a single large shipment that can be transported cost-effectively to the final destination. **(p. 545)**

fundamental accounting equation Assets = liabilities + owners' equity; it is the basis for the balance sheet. **(p. 575)**

Gantt chart A bar graph showing what projects are being worked on and what stage they are in at any given time. **(p. 313)**

General Agreement on Tariffs and Trade (GATT) Agreement among trading countries that provides a forum for negotiating mutual reductions in trade restrictions. **(p. 74)**

general partner An owner (partner) who has unlimited liability and is active in managing the firm. **(p. 168)**

generic brands Nonbranded products that usually sell at a sizeable discount compared to national or private brands. **(p. 494)**

generic names The name for a product category. **(p. 495)**

geographic segmentation Divide a large market by geographic area. **(p. 468)**

globalization A globally integrated system of production, marketing, finance, and management. **(p. 9)**

goals The broad, long-term accomplishments an organization wishes to attain. **(p. 223)**

goal-setting theory The theory that setting specific ambitious but attainable goals can motivate workers and improve performance if the goals are accepted, accompanied by feedback, and facilitated by organizational conditions. **(p. 368)**

goods-producing sector The sector that produces tangible products, things that can be seen or touched. **(p. 18)**

grapevine The system through which unofficial information flows between and among managers and employees. **(p. 281)**

green product A product whose production, use, and disposal don't damage the environment. **(p. 473)**

grievance A formal protest by an individual employee or a union when they believe a particular management decision breaches the union contract. **(p. 433)**

gross domestic product (GDP) The total value of a country's output of goods and services in a given year. **(p. 42)**

gross margin (profit) Net sales minus cost of goods sold before expenses are deducted. **(p. 573)**

Hawthorne effect The tendency for people to behave differently when they know they are being studied. **(p. 357)**

hierarchy A system in which one person is at the top of the organization and there is a ranked or sequential ordering from the top down of managers who are responsible to that person. **(p. 257)**

high-low pricing strategy Setting prices that are higher than EDLP stores, but having many special sales where the prices are lower than competitors. **(p. 509)**

horizontal merger Joins two firms in the same or similar industries to allow them to diversify or expand their products. **(p. 175)**

human relations skills Skills that involve communication and motivation; they enable managers to work through and with people. **(p. 240)**

human resource management (HRM) The process of evaluating human resource needs, finding people to fill those needs, and motivating employees to get the best work from each one by providing the right incentives and job environment, all with the goal of meeting the organization's objectives. **(p. 388)**

hygiene factors Factors that cause dissatisfaction but do not motivate if they are removed. **(p. 365)**

import quota A limit on the number or value of products in certain categories that can be imported. **(p. 72)**

income statement Reports revenues, expenses, and profit or loss during a specific period of time. **(p. 572)**

independent audit Examination of a company's books by public accountants to give the public, governments, and shareholders an outside opinion of the fairness of financial statements. **(p. 568)**

industrial policy A comprehensive coordinated government plan to guide and revitalize the economy. **(p. 91)**

industrial products Goods and services used in the production of other products. **(p. 490)**

inflation A general rise in the prices of goods and services over time. **(p. 48)**

infomercial A TV program devoted exclusively to promoting goods and services. **(p. 526)**

informal organization The system of relationships and lines of authority that develops spontaneously as employees meet and form power centres; that is, the human side of the organization that does not appear on any organization chart. **(p. 281)**

information age An era in which information is a crucial factor in the operation of organizations. **(p. 8)**

information systems (IS) Technology that helps companies do business; includes such tools as automated teller machines (ATMs) and voice mail. **(p. 325)**

information technology (IT) Technology that helps companies change business by allowing them to use new methods. **(p. 325)**

information utility Adding value to products by opening two-way flows of information between marketing participants. **(p. 484)**

injunction An order from a judge requiring strikers to limit or cease picketing or stop some threatening activity. **(p. 436)**

installations Major capital equipment such as buildings and heavy machinery. **(p. 491)**

integrated marketing communication (IMC) A technique that combines all the promotional tools into one comprehensive and unified promotional strategy. **(p. 522)**

intensive distribution Distribution that puts products into as many retail outlets as possible. **(p. 548)**

interactive marketing program A system in which consumers can access company information on their own and supply information about themselves in an ongoing dialogue. **(p. 538)**

interactive promotion Changing the promotion process from a monologue, where sellers tried to persuade buyers to buy things, to a dialogue, in which buyers and sellers can work together to create mutually beneficial exchange relationships. **(p. 523)**

intermittent process A production process in which the production run is short and the machines are changed frequently to make different products. **(p. 303)**

intermodal shipping The use of multiple modes of transportation to complete a single long-distance movement of freight. **(p. 553)**

internal customers Units within the firm that receive services from other units. **(p. 239)**

international joint venture (JV) A partnership in which companies from two or more countries join to undertake a major project or to form a new company. **(p. 68)**

International Monetary Fund (IMF) An international bank that makes short-term loans to countries experiencing problems with their balance of trade. **(p. 74)**

Internet 2 The new Internet system that links government supercomputer centres and a select group of universities; it will run more than 22,000 times faster than today's public infrastructure and will support heavy-duty applications. **(p. 329)**

intranet A set of communication links within one company that travel over the Internet but are closed to public access; a companywide network, closed to public access, that uses Internet-type technology. **(p. 274, 327)**

intrapreneur A person with entrepreneurial skills who is employed in a corporation to launch new products and who takes hands-on responsibility for innovation in an organization. **(p. 196)**

intrinsic reward The good feeling you have when you have done a job well. **(p. 354)**

inverted organization An organization that has contact people at the top and the chief executive officer at the bottom of the organization chart. **(p. 276)**

ISO 14000 A collection of the best practices for managing an organization's impact on the environment. **(p. 299)**

ISO 9000 The common name given to quality management and assurance standards. **(p. 299)**

job analysis A study of what is done by the employees who hold various job titles. **(p. 391)**

job description A summary of the objectives of a job, the type of work to be done, the responsibilities and duties, the working conditions, and the relationship of the job to other functions. **(p. 391)**

job design The process of breaking down jobs into specific tasks and assigning these tasks to specific positions. **(p. 256)**

job enlargement A job enrichment strategy involving combining a series of tasks into one assignment that is more challenging and interesting. **(p. 368)**

job enrichment A motivational strategy that emphasizes motivating the worker through the job itself. **(p. 367)**

job rotation A job enrichment strategy involving moving employees from one job to another. **(p. 368)**

job sharing An arrangement whereby two part-time employees share one full-time job. **(p. 409)**

job simplification The process of producing task efficiency by breaking down the job into simple steps and assigning people to each of those steps. **(p. 367)**

job simulation: The use of equipment that duplicates job conditions and tasks so that trainees can learn skills before attempting them on the job. **(p. 400)**

job specifications A written summary of the minimum qualifications required of a worker to do a particular job. **(p. 391)**

just-in-time (JIT) inventory control A production process in which a minimum of inventory is kept on the premises and parts, supplies, and other needs are delivered just in time to go on the assembly line. **(p. 305)**

knockoff brands Illegal copies of national brand-name goods. **(p. 494)**

knowledge management Finding the right information, keeping the information in a readily accessible place, and making the information known to everyone in the firm; sharing, organizing, and disseminating information in the simplest way and most relevant way possible for the users of the information. **(p. 236, 331)**

knowledge technology (KT) Technology that adds a layer of intelligence to information technology, to filter appropriate information and deliver it when it is needed. **(p. 326)**

Labour Relations Board (LRB) A quasi-judicial body consisting of representatives of government, labour, and business. It functions more informally than a court but has the full force of law. Different boards administer labour codes in each jurisdiction, federal or provincial. **(p. 430)**

laissez-faire capitalism The theory that, if left alone and unhindered by government, the free market, in pursuit of economic efficiency, would provide an abundance of goods at the lowest prices, improving everyone's life. **(p. 125)**

laissez-faire (free-rein) leadership Leadership style that involves managers setting objectives and employees being relatively free to do whatever it takes to accomplish those objectives. **(p. 233)**

leadership Creating a vision for others to follow, establishing corporate values and ethics, and transforming the way the organization does business so it is more effective and efficient. **(p. 231)**

leading A management function that involves creating a vision for the organization and guiding, training, coaching, and motivating others to work effectively to achieve the organization's goals and objectives. **(p. 221)**

lean manufacturing The production of goods using less of everything compared to mass production. **(p. 309)**

liabilities Amounts owed by the organization to others. **(p. 570)**

liability For a business, it includes the responsibility to pay all normal debts and to pay because of a court order or law, for performance under a contract, or payment of damages to a person or property in an accident. **(p. 164)**

licensing An agreement in which a producer allows a foreign company to manufacture its product or use its trademark in exchange for royalties. **(p. 66)**

limited liability The responsibility of a business's owners for losses only up to the amount they invest; limited partners have limited liability. **(p. 168)**

limited partner Owner who invests money in the business, but does not have any management responsibility or liability for losses beyond the investment. **(p. 168)**

line of credit The maximum amount a bank will agree to lend a borrower. **(p. 606)**

line organization An organization in which there are direct two-way lines of responsibility, authority, and communication running from the top to the bottom and back to the top of the organization, with every employee reporting to only one specific supervisor. **(p. 267)**

line personnel Employees who perform functions that contribute directly to the primary goals of the organization. **(p. 269)**

liquidity How quickly an asset can be turned into cash. **(p. 569)**

lockout A negotiating strategy in which the employer locks the premises against the employees. **(p. 435)**

long-term forecast A prediction of revenues, costs, and expenses for more than 1 year, sometimes extending 5 or 10 years into the future. **(p. 599)**

management The process used to accomplish organizational goals through planning, organizing, leading, and controlling people and other organizational resources. **(p. 221)**

management by objectives (MBO) A system of goal setting and implementation that involves a cycle of discussion, review, and evaluation of objectives among top and middle-level managers, supervisors, and employees. **(p. 369)**

management development The process of training and educating employees to become good managers and then developing managerial skills over time. **(p. 401)**

managerial accounting Providing information and analysis to managers within the organization to assist them in decision making. **(p. 566)**

managing diversity Building systems and a climate that unite different people in a common pursuit without undermining their individual strengths. **(p. 230)**

manufacturer's brand names The brand names of manufacturers that distribute products nationally. **(p. 494)**

market A group of people with unsatisfied wants and needs, who have the resources, willingness, and authority to buy products. **(p. 452)**

marketing The process of determining customer needs and wants and then developing goods and services that meet or exceed these expectations. **(p. 452)**

marketing boards Organizations that control the supply or pricing of certain agricultural products in Canada. **(p. 108)**

marketing concept A three-part business philosophy: (1) a customer orientation, (2) a service orientation, and (3) a profit orientation. **(p. 454)**

marketing intermediaries Organizations that assist in moving goods and services from producers to industrial and consumer users. **(p. 539)**

marketing management The process of planning and executing the conception, pricing, promotion, and distribution (place) of products to create mutually beneficial exchanges. **(p. 455)**

marketing mix The ingredients that go into a marketing program: product, price, place, and promotion. **(p. 456)**

marketing research The analysis of markets to determine opportunities and challenges, and to find the information needed to make good decisions. **(p. 458)**

market segmentation The process of dividing the total market into several groups whose members have similar characteristics. **(p. 465)**

Maslow's hierarchy of needs The theory of motivation that places different types of human needs in order of importance, from basic physiological needs to safety, social, and esteem needs to self-actualization needs. **(p. 358)**

mass customization Tailoring products to meet the needs of a large number of individual customers. **(p. 309)**

mass marketing Developing products and promotions to please large groups of people. **(p. 464)**

mass production The process of making a large number of a limited variety of products at very low cost. **(p. 304)**

materials handling The movement of goods within a warehouse, factory, or store. **(p. 554)**

materials requirement planning (MRP) A computer-based production management system that uses sales forecasts to make sure that needed parts and materials are available at the right time and in the right place. **(p. 303)**

matrix organization Organization in which specialists from different parts of the organization are brought together to work on specific projects but still remain part of a line and staff structure. **(p. 270)**

maturity date The date on which a borrower must legally repay the bond principal to the bondholder. **(p. 612)**

mediation The use of a third party to attempt to bring disputing parties to a resolution by modifying their positions. **(p. 433)**

mentor An experienced employee who supervises, coaches, and guides lower-level employees by introducing them to the right people and generally being their organizational sponsor. **(p. 401)**

mercantilism The economic principle advocating the selling of more goods to other nations than were bought from them. **(p. 72)**

merchant wholesalers Independently owned firms that take title to (own) the goods they handle. **(p. 544)**

merger Two firms unite to form one company. **(p. 175)**

middle management The level of management that includes general managers, division managers, and branch and plant managers who are responsible for tactical planning and controlling. **(p. 228)**

mission statement An outline of the fundamental purposes of an organization. **(p. 223)**

mixed economies Economies with degrees of state ownership or control of the means of production. **(p. 38)**

monetary policy The Bank of Canada's exercise of control over the supply of money and the level of interest rates in the country. **(p. 102)**

motivators Factors that provide satisfaction and motivate people to work. **(p. 365)**

mutual fund A fund that buys a variety of securities and then sells units of ownership in the fund to the public. **(p. 621)**

national debt The accumulated amount owed by the Canadian government from its past borrowings. **(p. 48)**

National Policy Federal government policy that imposed high tariffs on imports from the United States to protect Canadian manufacturing. **(p. 92)**

net income Revenue minus costs and expenses. **(p. 574)**

networking Using communications technology and other means to link organizations and allow them to work together on common objectives; the process of establishing and maintaining contacts with key managers in your own organization and other organizations and using those contacts to weave strong relationships that serve as an informal development system. **(p. 273, 401)**

network computing system (client/server computing) Computer systems that allow personal computers (clients) to obtain needed information from huge databases in a central computer (the server). **(p. 334)**

niche marketing The process of finding small but profitable market segments and designing for them. **(p. 466)**

NIMBY "Not in my backyard," meaning that people don't want waste disposal facilities in their towns, though they agree that such facilities are needed somewhere. **(p. 146)**

objectives Specific, short-term statements detailing how to achieve the goals. **(p. 223)**

off-the-job training Training that occurs away from the workplace and consists of internal or external programs to develop any of a variety of skills or to foster personal development. **(p. 399)**

one-to-one (individual) marketing Developing a unique mix of goods and services for each individual customer. **(p. 466)**

online training Training programs in which employees "attend" classes via the Internet. **(p. 399)**

on-the-job training A training program in which the employee immediately begins his or her tasks and learns by doing, or watches others for a while and then imitates them, right at the workplace. **(p. 398)**

open shop A workplace in which employees are free to join or not join the union and to pay or not pay union dues. **(p. 431)**

operating budget The plan of the various costs and expenses needed to operate the business, based on the short-term forecast. **(p. 600)**

operating expenses Various expenses of a business incurred in the course of earning revenue. **(p. 573)**

operational planning The process of setting work standards and schedules necessary to implement the tactical objectives. **(p. 225)**

operations management A specialized area in management that converts or transforms resources (including human resources) into goods and services. **(p. 293)**

organic farming Farming that is done without chemicals. **(p. 144)**

organizational (or corporate) culture Widely shared values within an organization that provide coherence and co-operation to achieve common goals. **(p. 279)**

organizational design The structuring of workers so that they can best accomplish the firm's goals. **(p. 256)**

organization chart A visual device that indicates who is accountable for the completion of specific work and who reports to whom. **(p. 226)**

organizing A management function that includes designing the structure of the organization and creating conditions and systems in which everyone and everything work together to achieve the organization's goals and objectives. **(p. 221)**

other assets Assets that are not current or fixed. Includes items such as copyrights and patents, which have no physical form and long-term deposits. **(p. 570)**

outsourcing Assigning various functions, such as accounting and legal work, to outside organizations. **(p. 278)**

owners' equity Owners' investments in the company plus all net accumulated profits. **(p. 571)**

partnership A legal form of business with two or more owners. **(p. 162)**

partnership agreement Legal document that specifies the rights and responsibilities of each partner. **(p. 169)**

penetration price strategy A strategy in which the product is priced low to attract many customers and discourage competitors. **(p. 511)**

performance appraisal An evaluation in which the performance level of employees is measured against established standards to make decisions about promotions, compensation, additional training, or firing. **(p. 402)**

personal selling The face-to-face presentation and promotion of products and services. **(p. 529)**

picketing The process whereby strikers carrying picket signs walk back and forth across entrances to their places of employment to publicize the strike and discourage or prevent people, vehicles, materials, and products from going in or out. **(p. 436)**

place utility Adding value to products by having them where people want them. **(p. 484)**

planning A management function that involves anticipating trends and determining the best strategies and tactics to achieve organizational goals and objectives. **(p. 221)**

pledging Using accounts receivable, inventory, or other assets as security for a loan. **(p. 606)**

possession utility Doing whatever is necessary to transfer ownership from one party to another, including providing credit, delivery, installation, guarantees, and follow-up service. **(p. 484)**

preferred stock Stock that gives owners preference over common shareholders in the payment of dividends and in a claim on assets if the business is liquidated; it does not include voting rights. **(p. 616)**

price leadership The procedure by which one or more dominant firms set the pricing practices that all competitors in an industry follow. **(p. 511)**

primary data Information collected for specific purposes. **(p. 459)**

principal The face value of a bond. **(p. 612)**

principle of motion economy The theory that every job can be broken down into a series of elementary motions. **(p. 356)**

private accountants Employees who carry out managerial and financial accounting functions for their employers. **(p. 567)**

private corporation Corporation that is not allowed to issue stock to the public, so its shares are not listed on stock exchanges; it is limited to 50 or fewer shareholders. **(p. 170)**

privatization The process of governments selling Crown corporations. **(p. 91)**

process manufacturing That part of the production process that physically or chemically changes materials. **(p. 303)**

process planning Choosing the best means for turning resources into useful goods and services. **(p. 302)**

producers' cartels Organizations of commodity-producing countries that are formed to stabilize or increase prices to optimize overall profits in the long run. (An example is OPEC, the Organization of Petroleum Exporting Countries.) **(p. 75)**

product Any physical good, service, or idea that satisfies a want or need. **(p. 456)**

product analysis Making cost estimates and sales forecasts to get a feeling for profitability of new-product ideas. **(p. 501)**

product differentiation The creation of real or perceived product differences. **(p. 488)**

production The creation of finished goods and services using the factors of production: land, labour, capital, entrepreneurship, and knowledge. **(p. 293)**

production goods Items used in the manufacturing process that become part of the final product. **(p. 491)**

productivity The total output of goods and services in a given period divided by the total hours of labour required to provide them. **(p. 43)**

product life cycle A theoretical model of what happens to sales and profits for a product class over time. **(p. 503)**

product line A group of products that are physically similar or are intended for a similar market. **(p. 487)**

product mix The combination of product lines offered by a manufacturer. **(p. 487)**

product screening A process designed to reduce the number of new product ideas being worked on at any one time. **(p. 500)**

program evaluation and review technique (PERT) A method for analyzing the tasks involved in completing a given project, estimating the time needed to complete each task, and identifying the minimum time needed to complete the total project. **(p. 313)**

promotion All the techniques sellers use to motivate people to buy products or services; an attempt by marketers to inform people about products and to persuade them to participate in an exchange. **(p. 457, 522)**

promotion mix The combination of promotional tools an organization uses. **(p. 522)**

prospecting Researching potential buyers and choosing those most likely to buy. **(p. 530)**

prospects People with the means to buy a product, the authority to buy, and the willingness to listen to a sales message. **(p. 530)**

prospectus A document, which must be prepared by every public company seeking financing through issue of shares or bonds, that gives the public certain information about the company. A prospectus must be approved by the securities commission of the province where these securities will be offered for sale. **(p. 105)**

psychographic segmentation Dividing the market according to personality or lifestyle. **(p. 468)**

public accountants Independent firms that provide accounting, auditing, and other professional services for clients on a fee basis. **(p. 567)**

public corporation Corporation that has the right to issue shares to the public, so its shares may be listed on the stock exchanges. **(p. 170)**

public domain software (freeware) Software that is free for the taking. **(p. 337)**

publicity Any information about an individual, product, or organization that's distributed to the public through the media and that's not paid for or controlled by the seller. **(p. 533)**

public relations (PR) The management function that evaluates stakeholder attitudes, changes policies and procedures in response to stakeholder requests, and executes a program of action and information to earn public understanding and acceptance. **(p. 532)**

pull strategy Promotional strategy in which heavy advertising and sales promotion efforts are directed toward consumers so that they'll request the products from retailers. **(p.536)**

purchasing The function in a firm that searches for quality material resources, finds the best suppliers, and negotiates the best value deal for goods and services. **(p. 307)**

push strategy Promotional strategy in which the producer uses advertising, personal selling, sales promotion, and all other promotional tools to convince wholesalers and retailers to stock and sell merchandise. **(p. 536)**

push technology Web software that delivers information tailored to a previously defined user profile; it pushes the information to users so that they don't have to pull it out. **(p. 330)**

qualify In the selling process, to make sure that people have a need for the product, the authority to buy, and the willingness to listen to a sales message. **(p. 530)**

quality control The measurement of goods and services against set standards. **(p. 297)**

rack jobbers Wholesalers that furnish racks or shelves full of merchandise to retailers, display products, and sell on consignment. **(p. 544)**

ratio analysis A way to analyze financial statements by comparing a series of ratios. **(p. 577)**

real time The present moment or the actual time in which something takes place; data sent over the Internet to various organizational partners as they are developed or collected are said to be available in real time. **(p. 273)**

recruitment The set of activities used to obtain a sufficient number of the right people at the right time and to select those who best meet the needs of the organization. **(p. 392)**

reinforcement theory States that positive and negative reinforcers will motivate a desired behaviour. **(p. 371)**

relationship marketing Marketing with the goal to keep individual customers over time by offering them products that exactly meet their requirements. **(p. 466)**

replacement workers Management's name for strikebreakers. **(p. 436)**

research and development (R&D) Defined as "work directed towards the innovation, introduction, and improvement of products and processes." **(p. 291)**

restructuring Redesigning an organization so that it can more effectively and efficiently serve its customers. **(p. 12, 260)**

retailer An organization that sells to ultimate consumers. **(p. 539)**

retail sale The sale of products to consumers for their own use. **(p. 544)**

retained earnings Accumulated profits less dividends to shareholders. **(p. 574)**

reverse discrimination The unfairness unprotected groups may perceive when protected groups receive preference in hiring and promoting. **(p. 418)**

rituals The programmed routines of daily organizational life that dramatize the organization's culture. **(p. 279)**

robber barons Capitalists of the nineteenth century whose wealth came, in part, through shady if not criminal acts. **(p. 125)**

robot A computer-controlled machine capable of performing many tasks requiring the use of materials and tools. **(p. 309)**

rule of 72 Divide the rate of increase of any activity into 72 to get the number of years it takes for the result of that activity to double. **(p. 149)**

sales promotion The promotional tool that stimulates consumer purchasing and dealer interest by means of short-term activities. **(p. 534)**

sampling A promotional tool in which a company lets consumers have a small sample of a product for no charge. **(p. 535)**

scabs Unions' name for strikebreakers. **(p. 436)**

scientific management The study of workers to find the most efficient way of doing things and then teaching people those techniques. **(p. 355)**

seasonal unemployment Unemployment that occurs when the demand for labour varies with the season. **(p. 46)**

secondary data Information that has already been collected, by other sources, for their own purposes. **(p. 458)**

secured bonds Bonds backed by some tangible asset that is pledged to the bondholder to guarantee payment of principal and interest. **(p. 614)**

secured loan A loan backed by something valuable, such as property. **(p. 606)**

securities commission The official body set up by a province to regulate its stock exchange and to approve all new issues of securities in that province. **(p. 105)**

segment marketing Decide which groups to serve and then develop products specially tailored to their needs. **(p. 466)**

selection The process of gathering information to decide who should be hired, under legal guidelines, for the best interests of the organization and the individual. **(p. 394)**

selective distribution Distribution that sends products to only one retail outlet in a given geographic area. **(p. 548)**

services Intangible activities that may be provided internally or outsourced to another organization. **(p. 491)**

service sector The sector that produces services, not goods. Examples are banking, insurance, communications, and transportation. **(p. 18)**

service utility Providing fast, friendly service during and after the sale and by teaching customers how to best use products over time. **(p. 485)**

shareware Software that is copyrighted but distributed to potential customers free of charge. **(p. 337)**

shopping products Goods and services that the consumer buys only after comparing value, quality, and price from a variety of sellers. **(p. 489)**

short-term forecast A prediction of revenues, costs, and expenses for one year. **(p. 599)**

skimming price strategy A strategy in which a new product is priced high to make optimum profit while there's little competition. **(p. 510)**

skunkworks Highly innovative, fast-moving entrepreneurial units operating at the fringes of a corporation. **(p. 196)**

small business Business that is independently owned and operated, not dominant in its field, and meets certain standards of size in terms of employees or annual revenue. **(p. 197)**

social audit A systematic evaluation of an organization's progress toward implementing programs that are socially responsible and responsive. **(p. 138)**

sole proprietorship A business that is owned directly, and usually managed, by one person. **(p. 162)**

spam An attempt to deliver a message, over the Internet, to someone who would not otherwise choose to receive it. **(p. 330)**

span of control The optimum number of subordinates a manager supervises or should supervise. **(p. 262)**

specialty products Goods and services that have a special attraction to consumers who are willing to go out of their way to obtain them. **(p. 489)**

staffing A management function that includes hiring, motivating, and retaining the best people available to accomplish the company's objectives. **(p. 229)**

staff personnel Employees who perform functions that advise and assist line personnel in achieving their goals. **(p. 269)**

stakeholder marketing Establishing and maintaining mutually beneficial exchange relationships over time with all the stakeholders of the organization. **(p. 473)**

stakeholders Those people who can affect or are affected by the achievement of an organization's objectives; they include shareholders, employees, customers, suppliers, distributors, competitors, and the general public. **(p. 137)**

stock certificate Tangible evidence of stock ownership. **(p. 615)**

stock exchanges Markets where the securities of public companies are traded. **(p. 612)**

strategic alliances or joint ventures Arrangements whereby two or more companies co-operate for a special or limited purpose. **(p. 10)**

strategic planning The process of determining the major goals of the organization and the policies and strategies for obtaining and using resources to achieve those goals. **(p. 224)**

structural unemployment Unemployment that results from changes in the structure of the economy that phase out certain industries or jobs. **(p. 46)**

supervisory management Managers who are directly responsible for supervising workers and evaluating their daily performance. **(p. 228)**

supplies Goods that are purchased frequently and with a minimum of effort. **(p. 491)**

supply The quantity of particular products or services that suppliers are willing to sell at certain prices and at certain locations. **(p. 39)**

supply chain The sequence of linked activities that must be performed by various organizations to move goods from the sources of raw materials to ultimate consumers. **(p. 311, 551)**

supply chain management The process of managing the movement of raw materials, parts, works in process, finished goods, and related information through all the organizations involved in the supply chain; managing the return of such goods, if necessary; and recycling materials when appropriate. **(p. 311)**

support goods Products used in the operation of the business, including installations, accessory equipment, supplies, and services. **(p. 491)**

sustainable development Economic development that meets the needs of the present without endangering the external environment of future generations. **(p. 23)**

SWOT analysis An analysis of an organization's strengths, weaknesses, opportunities, and threats. **(p. 223)**

tactical planning The process of developing detailed, short-term decisions about what is to be done, who is to do it, and how it is to be done. **(p. 224)**

target costing Designing a product so that it satisfies customers and meets the profit margins desired by the firm. **(p. 508)**

target marketing Marketing directed toward those groups (market segments) that an organization decides it can serve profitably. **(p. 465)**

technical skills Skills that involve the ability to perform tasks in a specific discipline or department. **(p. 240)**

telemarketing The sale of goods and services by telephone. **(p. 549)**

test marketing The process of testing products among potential users, for a limited time and in a specific area. **(p. 457)**

time–motion studies Studies of the tasks performed to complete a job and the time needed to do each task. **(p. 355)**

time utility Adding value to products by making them available when they're needed. **(p. 484)**

top management Highest level of management, consisting of the president and other key company executives who develop strategic plans. **(p. 227)**

total fixed costs Costs that do not change in relation to how many products are made or sold. **(p. 509)**

total quality management (TQM) Striving for maximum customer satisfaction by ensuring quality from all departments. **(p. 275)**

trade credit The practice of buying goods now and paying for them in the future. **(p. 604)**

trade deficit Occurs when the value of imports exceeds exports. **(p. 62)**

trademark A brand that has been given exclusive legal protection for both the brand name and the pictorial design. **(p. 492)**

trade protectionism The use of government regulations to limit the import of goods and services, based on the theory that domestic producers should be protected from competition so that they can survive and grow, producing more jobs. **(p. 62)**

training and development All attempts to improve productivity by increasing an employee's ability to perform. **(p. 397)**

TNC or MNC (multinational or transnational corporation) An organization that has investments, plants, and sales in many different countries; it has international stock ownership and multinational management. **(p. 59)**

transparency A concept that describes a company being so open to other companies working with it that the once-solid barriers between them become "see-through" and electronic information is shared (often on extranets) as if the companies were one. **(p. 273)**

union shop A workplace in which the employer is free to hire anybody, but the recruit must then join the union within a short period, perhaps a month. **(p. 431)**

unlimited liability The responsibility of a business owner for all of the debts of the business, making the personal assets of the owner vulnerable to claims against the business. **(p. 167)**

unsecured bonds Bonds that are not backed by any collateral. **(p. 613)**

unsought products Goods and services that consumers are unaware of, haven't necessarily thought of buying, or find that they need to solve an unexpected problem. **(p. 489)**

value Good quality at a fair price; when consumers calculate the value of a product, they look at the benefits and then subtract the cost to see if the benefits exceed the costs. **(p. 485)**

value package Everything that consumers evaluate when deciding whether to buy something; also called the *total product offer*. **(p. 486)**

value pricing When marketers provide consumers with brand-name goods and services at fair prices. **(p. 508)**

variable costs Costs that change according to the level of production. **(p. 509)**

venture capitalists Individuals or organizations that invest in new businesses in exchange for partial ownership. **(p. 205)**

vertical merger The joining of two firms involved in different stages of related businesses. **(p. 175)**

vestibule training Training done in schools where employees are taught on equipment similar to that used on the job. **(p. 400)**

virtual corporation A temporary, networked organization made up of replaceable firms that join the network and leave it as needed. **(p. 273)**

virtualization Accessibility through technology that allows business to be conducted independent of location. **(p. 325)**

virtual private network (VPN) A private data network that creates secure connections, or "tunnels," over regular Internet lines. **(p. 328)**

virus A piece of programming code inserted into other programming to cause some unexpected and, for the victim, usually undesirable event. **(p. 341)**

vision A sense of why the organization exists and where it's heading. **(p. 222)**

white-collar crimes Crimes, usually theft, committed by executives or other white-collar office workers. **(p. 132)**

wholesaler A marketing intermediary that sells to other organizations. **(p. 539)**

wholesale sale The sale of goods and services to businesses and institutions for use in the business or to wholesalers or retailers for resale. **(p. 544)**

World Bank An autonomous United Nations agency that borrows money from the more prosperous countries and lends it to less-developed countries to develop their infrastructure. **(p. 74)**